King of the Peds

P. S. Marshall

authorHOUSE®

AuthorHouse™ UK Ltd.
500 Avebury Boulevard
Central Milton Keynes, MK9 2BE
www.authorhouse.co.uk
Phone: 08001974150

©2008 P. S. Marshall. All rights reserved.

This book is a work of non-fiction. Unless otherwise noted, the author and the publisher make
no explicit guarantees as to the accuracy of the information contained in this book and in
some cases, names of people and places have been altered to protect their privacy.
No part of this book may be reproduced, stored in a retrieval system, or transmitted
by any means without the written permission of the author.

First published by AuthorHouse 5/29/2008

ISBN: 978-1-4343-3467-1 (sc)

Library of Congress Control Number: 2007909917

Printed in the United States of America
Bloomington, Indiana

This book is printed on acid-free paper.

CONTENTS

ILLUSTRATIONS		vii
ACKNOWLEDGEMENTS		ix
Chapter 1	The Wily Wobbler!	1
Chapter 2	500 Miles in Six Days?	35
Chapter 3	What Else Happened in 1875	55
Chapter 4	The Plucky Pedestrian!	56
Chapter 5	Weston Walks in Britain	82
Chapter 6	What Else Happened in 1876	101
Chapter 7	O'Leary v Weston	106
Chapter 8	What Else Happened in 1877	119
Chapter 9	"Go-As-You-Please"	123
Chapter 10	Brawn v Brains	141
Chapter 11	Pussy Footing	151
Chapter 12	Questionable "Sport?"	160
Chapter 13	What Else Happened in 1878	174
Chapter 14	2,000 Miles in 1,000 Hours	177
Chapter 15	Rise and Fall	191
Chapter 16	Flags, Flowers and Femininity	223
Chapter 17	American Championship Belt	226
Chapter 18	2nd Long Distance Astley Belt	232
Chapter 19	4th International Astley Belt	238
Chapter 20	5th International Astley Belt	249
Chapter 21	1st O'Leary Belt	305
Chapter 22	Rose Belt	328
Chapter 23	What Else Happened in 1879	334
Chapter 24	3rd Long Distance Astley Belt	347
Chapter 25	2nd O'Leary Belt	351
Chapter 26	A New Kid on the Block!	362
Chapter 27	The Master v The Apprentices	375
Chapter 28	What Else Happened in 1880	388
Chapter 29	1st O'Leary International Belt	404
Chapter 30	3rd O'Leary Belt Race & a "Four-Cornered Event"	412
Chapter 31	2nd O'Leary International Belt	426

Chapter 32	7th International Astley Belt	434
Chapter 33	Ennis International Belt	438
Chapter 34	What Else Happened in 1881	443
Chapter 35	There once was an Ugly Duckling…..	446
Chapter 36	Walking on Top of the World!.	474
Chapter 37	1st Astley Challenge Belt	483
Chapter 38	2nd Astley Challenge Belt	489
Chapter 39	Did he Fall or was he Pushed?	494
Chapter 40	3rd Astley Challenge Belt	506
Chapter 41	What Else Happened in 1882	512
Chapter 42	Murder and Suicide!	514
Chapter 43	4th Astley Challenge Belt	517
Chapter 44	What Else Happened in 1883	523
Chapter 45	$1,400 Go-As-You-Please Sweepstakes	525
Chapter 46	Man v Horse	559
Chapter 47	5th Astley Challenge Belt	561
Chapter 48	What Else Happened in 1884	571
Chapter 49	International Pedestrian Tournament	573
Chapter 50	What Else Happened in 1885	584
Chapter 51	What Else Happened in 1886	590
Chapter 52	International Pedestrian Go-As-You-Please Tournament	593
Chapter 53	"Championship of the World" Sweepstakes	602
Chapter 54	Riot!	607
Chapter 55	What Else Happened in 1887	612
Chapter 56	Hall's Tournament	616
Chapter 57	O'Brien's Tournament	636
Chapter 58	Joe Scott	657
Chapter 59	What Else Happened in 1888	679
Chapter 60	Fox's Tournament	680
SUMMING UP		700
PEDESTRIAN INDEX		709
NAMES INDEX		720

ILLUSTRATIONS

(Chapter 1) 1; Photo of Edward Payson Weston: *Reproduced with kind permission from John Weiss:* **2; Weston's signature:** *Reproduced with kind permission from John Weiss:* **3; Weston's photograph which he sold on his walk:** *Reproduced with kind permission from John Weiss:* **(Chapter 3) 4; Daniel O'Leary:** *The National Police Gazette:* **5; George Parry and Peter Crossland:** *The National Police Gazette:* **6; William Howes:** © *The British Library; All Rights reserved; The Penny Illustrated:* **7; Peter Crossland:** © *The British Library; All Rights reserved; The Penny Illustrated:* **(Chapter 5) 8; The Agricultural Hall, Islington:** *With the permission of Islington Local History Centre:* **9; Illustration of the two different styles of Perkins and Weston:** © *The British Library; All Rights reserved; The Penny Illustrated:* **10; "500 Mile Walk in 6 Days!" Weston poster March 6th – 11th 1876:** *With the permission of Islington Local History Centre:* **11; Weston "Against the World" poster, December 18th – 23rd 1876:** *With the permission of Islington Local History Centre:* **(Chapter 6) 12; Henry Vaughan:** © *The British Library; All Rights reserved; The Penny Illustrated:* **(Chapter 7) 13; Memorandum of Agreement Poster:** *With the permission of Islington Local History Centre:* **14; O'Leary v Weston poster, Agricultural Hall, Islington, 1877:** *With the permission of Islington Local History Centre:* **15; O'Leary v Weston, April, 1877:** © *The British Library; All Rights reserved; The Penny Illustrated:* **(Chapter 8) 16; Gale on the move:** © *The British Library; All Rights reserved; The Penny Illustrated:* **17; Gale walks his last mile and a half:** © *The British Library; All Rights reserved; The Penny Illustrated:* **(Chapter 9) 18; Sir John Astley:** © *The British Library; All Rights reserved; The Penny Illustrated:* **19; The Astley Belt:** *With special thanks to Miriam Payne:* **20; W. Corkey of London:** © *The British Library; All Rights reserved; The Penny Illustrated:* **21; George Ide of North Woolwich:** © *The British Library; All Rights reserved; The Penny Illustrated:* **22; Walter Lewis:** © *The British Library; All Rights reserved; The Penny Illustrated:* **23; James McLeavy:** © *The British Library; All Rights reserved; The Penny Illustrated:* **24; Daniel O'Leary:** © *The British Library; All Rights reserved; The Penny Illustrated:* **25; W. Smith of Paisley:** © *The British Library; All Rights reserved; The Penny Illustrated:* **26; W. H. Smythe of Dublin and America:** © *The British Library; All Rights reserved; The Penny Illustrated:* **(Chapter 10) 27; O'Leary is on the outer path and Hughes on the inner:** *Frank Leslies Illustrated Newspaper:* **(Chapter 11) 28; Scenes after the race:** © *The British Library; All Rights reserved; The Penny Illustrated:* **(Chapter 12) 29; Daniel O'Leary and Peter Napoleon Campana:** *The National Police Gazette:* **30; "GO!"** *The National Police Gazette:* **31; Campana and O'Leary running:** *The National Police Gazette:* **(Chapter 13) 32; Great 26 Hours Walking Match poster:** *With the permission of Islington Local History Centre:* **(Chapter 14) 33; Uphill work for the judges:** © *The British Library; All Rights reserved; The Penny Illustrated:* **(Chapter 15) 34; Daniel O'Leary, Charles Rowell, John Ennis and Charles Harriman:** *The National Police Gazette:* **35; A cartoon showing O'Leary, Rowell, Harriman and Ennis:** *Library of Congress, Prints & Photographs Division, (reproduction number: - LC-USZC2-2537):* **36; Rowell leads Harriman with O'Leary on the inside of Ennis:** *Harpers Weekly:* **37; Mayhem!:** *The National Police Gazette:* **38; Scenes from the race: Ennis leads Rowell with Harriman following. As portrayed in** *Frank Leslies Illustrated Newspaper* **on the 29th of March 1879:** *Library of Congress, Prints & Photographs Division, (reproduction number: - LC-USZ62-88335):* **39; Rowell carries a bunch of flowers round the track. As portrayed in** *Frank Leslies Illustrated Newspaper* **on the 29th of March 1879:** *Library of Congress, Prints & Photographs Division (reproduction number: - LC-USZ62-88335):* **40; Ennis shakes hands with Rowell. As portrayed in** *Frank Leslies Illustrated Newspaper* **on the 29th of March 1879:** *Library of Congress, Prints & Photographs Division, (reproduction number: - LC-USZ62-88335):* **41; A cartoon showing Ennis, Harriman and Rowell:** *Library of Congress, Prints & Photographs Division, (reproduction number: - LC-USZC2-2536):* **42; The winner and runner-up:** *Library of Congress, Prints & Photographs Division (reproduction numbers: - LC-USZ62-8835 and LC-USZC2-2710):* **(Chapter 17) 43; Stephen Brodie: 44; Peter Panchot:** *Frank Leslies Illustrated Newspaper:* **(Chapter 18) 45; Great International Contest April 21st to 26th 1879:** *With the permission of Islington Local History Centre:* **(Chapter 19) 46; The 4th Astley Belt Contest poster:** *With the permission of Islington Local History Centre:* **47; The Winner!:** © *The British Library; All Rights reserved; The Penny Illustrated:* **48; Weston in a white sash:** *The National Police Gazette:* **(Chapter 20) 49; George**

Hazael: *The National Police Gazette:* **50; Scenes before the start:** *The National Police Gazette:* **51; Lining up for the start of the 5th Astley Belt race:** *The National Police Gazette:* **52; They're off!** *Frank Leslie's Illustrated Newspaper:* **53; Weston sheds his coat and gets down to business:** *The National Police Gazette:* **54; Dutcher faints for the second time:** *The National Police Gazette:* **55; Hart "dogs" Rowell:** *The National Police Gazette:* **56; The view from the Madison Avenue side, the "Star of Africa in the Ascendant:"** *The National Police Gazette:* **57; Race scenes; George Hazael in the lead:** *Frank Leslie's Illustrated Newspaper:* **58: Attendant and ped: (Chapter 21) 59; The O'Leary Belt:** *The National Police Gazette:* **60; The start of the "1st O'Leary Belt:"** *The National Police Gazette:* **61; Nick Murphy:** *The National Police Gazette:* **(Chapter 22) 62; Frank Hart: 63; Fred Krohne:** *The National Police Gazette:* **64; Christian Faber:** *The National Police Gazette:* **(Chapter 23) 65; George Guyon:** *The National Police Gazette:* **66; Patrick Fitzgerald:** *The National Police Gazette:* **67; John Peter Colston:** *The National Police Gazette:* **(Chapter 24) 68; Championship of England poster Feb 16th – Feb 21st 1879:** *With the permission of Islington Local History Centre:* **(Chapter 25) 69; Scenes from the race:** *The National Police Gazette:* **70; Frank Hart:** *The National Police Gazette:* **(Chapter 26) 71; The Agricultural Hall, Wolverhampton:** *From the collections of Wolverhampton Archives and Local Studies;* **72; Sam Day:** *The National Police Gazette:* **73; George Cartwright:** *The National Police Gazette:* **74; Poster "Six days championship of the world:"** *With the permission of Islington Local History Centre:* **(Chapter 27) 75; George Littlewood: 76; Dobler is just ahead of Brown and Littlewood:** © *The British Library; All Rights reserved; The Penny Illustrated:* **77; Rowell, Littlewood and Dobler:** © *The British Library; All Rights reserved; The Penny Illustrated:* **(Chapter 28) 78; "26 Hours Walking Match" poster:** *With the permission of Islington Local History Centre:* **(Chapter 29) 79; John Hughes being attended to by his wife:** *The National Police Gazette:* **80; Hughes leads Albert:** *The National Police Gazette:* **81; John Hughes: (Chapter 30) 82; Charles Rowell:** *Frank Leslies Illustrated Newspaper:: Library of Congress, Prints & Photographs Division, (reproduction number: - LC-USZ62-88335):* **(Chapter 31) 83; Madison Square Garden: 84; Robert Vint:** *The National Police Gazette:* **(Chapter 32) 85; Charlie Rowell in suit:** *Reproduced with kind permission from John Weiss:* **86; Charlie Rowell bare-chested:** *Reproduced with kind permission from John Weiss:* **(Chapter 34) 87; Charles A. Harriman:** *The National Police Gazette:* **88; William Gale, the worlds "Endurance Pedestrian:"** *The National Police Gazette:* **(Chapter 35) 89; Rowell:** *The National Police Gazette:* **90; George Hazael:** *Frank Leslies Illustrated Newspaper:* **(Chapter 36) 91; The Drill Hall Sheffield:** *By permission of Sheffield City Libraries:* **(Chapter 39) 92; Peter Duryea:** *The National Police Gazette:* **93; Frank Hart: (Chapter 41) 94; The start of the race at the Casino in Boston:** *The National Police Gazette:* **(Chapter 42) 95; Beattie shoots Mrs. Cameron:** *The National Police Gazette:* **(Chapter 45) 96; Nit-Aw-E-Go-Bow: 97; "Come back here!"** *The National Police Gazette:* **98; Mr. Vanderbilt, owner of the Garden, watches proceedings with his friends:** *The National Police Gazette:* **99; The Doctors Box during the night…** *The National Police Gazette:* **100; "Wake up! Wake up!"** *The National Police Gazette:* **101; Rowell gets a bath!** *The National Police Gazette:* **102; Patrick Fitzgerald: (Chapter 46) 103; George Littlewood running:** *By permission of Sheffield City Libraries:* **(Chapter 48) 104; Weston's Flyers:** *Reproduced with kind permission from John Weiss:* **(Chapter 51) 105; George D. Noremac: (Chapter 54) 106; The rioting at Lillie Bridge:** © *The British Library; All Rights reserved; The Penny Illustrated:* **107; The aftermath!:** © *The British Library; All Rights reserved; The Penny Illustrated:* **(Chapter 55) 108; Cox, Faber, Golden, Hart, Hegelman, Herty, Krohne, Noremac, Strokel and Vint:** *The National Police Gazette:* **(Chapter 56) 109; The Racers and the Track:** *The Boston Globe:* **110; Connor, Hegelman, Herty, Hughes and Moore: 111; The start!** *The National Police Gazette:* **112; Jimmy Albert: 113; The first five:** *The Boston Globe:* **(Chapter 57) 114; Alf Prater: 115; William O'Brien:** *The National Police Gazette:* **116; Gus Guerrero: 117; George Littlewood: (Chapter 58) 118; Joe Scott:** *Photograph with permission of the NZ Sports Hall of Fame:* **(Chapter 60) 119; Richard K. Fox:** *The National Police Gazette:* **120; The Fox Belt:** *The National Police Gazette:* **121; Dan Herty: 122; George Littlewood, Dan Herty, Edward C. Moore and George Mason's soles: 123; Edward C. Moore:** *The National Police Gazette:* **124; Passing the scorers……Cartwright leading the way:** *The National Police Gazette:* **125; Spurt! Cartwright goes for it!:** *The National Police Gazette:* **126; "Littlewood the Lionheart:"** *Photograph kindly donated by Sue Crowther:*

ACKNOWLEDGEMENTS

"50 Years of my Life" by Sir John Astley.

"The Pedestrians Adventures" by Edward Payson Weston.

Newspaper sources:

Atlanta Constitution; Atlas in the World; Bell's Life; Birmingham Daily Gazette; Birmingham Daily Post; Boston Globe; Boston Journal; Brooklyn Daily Eagle; Buffalo Commercial Advertiser; Buffalo Courier and Republic; Buffalo Evening Republic; Cambridge Chronicle; Chester Daily Times; Chester Times; Chicago Field; Chicago Journal; Chicago News; Chicago Tribune; Christchurch Star; Cleveland Courier; Cleveland Herald; Cleveland Plain Dealer; Commercial Advertiser; Daily Kennebec Journal; Daily Miner; Davenport Daily Gazette; Decatur Daily Republican; Defiance Democrat; Dubuque Daily Herald; Evening Auburnian; Fitchburg Daily Sentinel; Fitchburg Sentinel; Fort Wayne Daily Sentinel; Franklin Gazette; Freeborn County Standard; Fresno Weekly Republican; Fulton Times; Glen Cove Gazette; Harpers Weekly; Hobart Mercury; Indiana Progress; Isle of Ely and Huntingdonshire Gazette; Islington Gazette; Kansas City Star; Kansas City Times; Liverpool Post; Mail and Express; Manitoba Daily Free Press; Marion Weekly Star; Massillon Independent; Melbourne Sportsman; National Police Gazette; New York Evening Post; New York Evening World; New York Herald; New York Sportsman; New York Sun; New York Times; New York World; Newark Daily Advocate; Newcastle Daily Chronicle; Oakland Tribune; Ohio Democrat; Olean Democrat; Otago Witness; Penny Illustrated; Philadelphia Inquirer; Philadelphia Times; Port Jervis Evening Gazette; Portland Argus; Providence Evening Press; Providence Journal; Reno Evening Gazette; Rochester Journal; Sheboygan County Herald; Sheffield and Rotherham Independent; Sheffield Independent; Sheffield Telegraph; Sioux Valley News; Spirit of the Times; Sporting Life; St. Joseph's Herald; St. Louis Dispatch; Sydney Morning Herald; The Daily Era; The Globe; The Lancet; The Mercury; The News of the World; The Scotsman; The Sportsman; The Sun; The Times; Titusville Morning Herald; Turf, Field and Farm; Washington Patriot; Washington Post; Waukesha Freeman; Wellington Evening Post:

I would like to thank to all the library staff that have been so helpful in making this book possible, particularly Martin Banham and Geraldine Thornton.

Finally I want to say a big thank you to John Weiss of California. Although we have never met, John has gone out of his way to help in providing much information. John has also allowed me to use some of the material in his collection to be displayed in this book.

NB: The international version of the Astley Belt can be viewed at the Cambridge & County Folk Museum, Castle Street, Cambridge CB3 0AQ, England, which is well worth a visit. I would also like to thank their staff for their help too.

You, the reader, are a member of a worldwide jury. After sifting through the evidence contained in the pages of this book, you will have hopefully come to your own conclusion as to who is the.........

KING OF THE PEDS

"PEDESTRIAN"

A person travelling on foot; a walker.

"PEDESTRIANISM"

The act, art, or practice of a pedestrian; walking or running; travelling or racing on foot.

The *"Adonis," "Black Dan," "Blower Brown,"* the *"Brooklyn Cobbler,"* the *"Cambridge Wonder," "Corkey,"* the *"Flying Collier," "Harlequin," "Honest John,"* the *"Lepper," "Old Sport,"* the *"Pie Eater,"* the *"Sharp Sheffield Blade,"* the *"Steamboat,"* and the *"Wily Wobbler,"* were affectionate nicknames used to refer to a few of the many professional pedestrians that graced the brutal sport of the "go-as-you-please" races, or *"walking matches,"* as they were often referred to.

The contests, which were prevalent during the mid to late 1870's, and throughout the 1880's, lasted anything up to 142 hours. The popular 72-hour races, which were 12 hours a day, six days a week events, would usually start on a Monday at around midday and end the following Saturday before midnight. The 142 hours races which would inevitably begin again on a Monday at just after midnight, so as to avoid the Sabbath, would end the following Saturday at around 10 p.m.

Whilst some of the longer pedestrian races lasted just 24 hours, others were timed over periods of 26, 30, 36, and occasionally, 84 hours. Some athletes would match themselves "against time," where they would set out to cover distances of up to 500 miles in a pre-determined time. Shorter distances of say 120 yards, half a mile and two to five miles, were also popular, but it was the longer *"go-as-you-please"* and *"straight heel-and-toe"* events that attracted the really big prizes. These contests attracted many prospective competitors to the huge arenas that catered for such events; predominantly in Britain, North America, Australia and New Zealand.

Betting was a popular pastime during the 1800's, and huge sums of money were wagered on the participants. Some races, particularly the longer ones, sometimes attracted scores of entries, all paying an entrance fee to even be considered to take part. These would be whittled down by the promoters of the "matches" who would attempt to eliminate the men they felt would have little chance against the more hardened pros or *"cracks"* as they were called.

The races themselves would attract thousands of people, many of whom who would queue for hours on end to make sure they could gain entry. Apart from the racing, many of the attending spectators were attracted to the side-shows which the promoters would include to boost their profits. These could be in the guise of circus acts, shooting galleries and the like. The Victorians used to refer to ales and spirits as *"stimulants,"* and bars would operate throughout the duration of the races, the lure of alcohol being another big attraction for some spectators.

Once inside, and amid the foul stench of lingering tobacco smoke, the crowd would shout themselves hoarse whilst the pedestrians, wearing an array of colourful costumes, competed against each other on the track. In the go-as-you-please races, a man would convey himself around the track (which could be from anything from 7 to 38 laps to the mile) literally as he saw fit, as long as he did it fairly and to the rules. Popular and more conventional used methods were jogging, trotting and straight heel-and-toe. At the start of a race, the competitors would invariably run hell for leather for the first five miles or so, and then settle down to what was known as a *"jog-trot."* Some of the peds preferred to make their miles using their favoured heel-and-toe method of locomotion and would rarely run. They were known as the *"pure walkers"* and depended on stamina to see them through the race. Others, who had come from sprinting backgrounds, relied upon opening up wide gaps at the start of races and maintaining the distance achieved much like a "front runner" in a horse race. *"Mixers,"* were men who could walk and run with equal effect, whilst any man indulging in a *"spurt"* would be sure to get a positive response from the crowd. This in modern language was a sprint whilst running, or when walking, a quicker version of that type of gait. Bands, and even orchestras, would be employed by the promoters to entertain, not only the crowd, but also the men on the track. Many would respond positively to the music they played and negatively when they didn't.

Competitors would often seek a *"backer,"* not only to finance their participation in a race, but to also to administer and pay for the costs of his training and management before and during it. For their outlay, backers would take an agreed percentage of winnings as well as giving a cut to other interested parties like trainers and *"attendants"* which were employed to achieve the goal. Apart from preparing a pedestrian for a race, trainers would devise their athlete's strategy during it, and advise them accordingly. They would also be in charge of the attendants whose job it was to prepare food and drinks for the competitors, prepare baths, and rub the *peds* down.

Successful athletes could make a lot of money if they won, but placed prize money was also highly revered. To make money however, the ped had to be good. Many miles on the tracks and roads at the time would be covered on a daily basis in preparation for a race. Not only were the men's legs trained for the arduous journey ahead, but the organ that fed the muscles in the legs would be given a lot of attention too. The stomach, what was put inside it, and how it reacted during a race, was perceived to be paramount to the success or demise of an individual's chances of winning. But what could really make or break a man, especially in a six-day race, was whether he could cope with the little bit of sleep he was allowed to indulge in by his trainers……………………

The *Fort Wayne Sentinel* of Indiana, USA, once printed the following interesting article. It was a variation of another article which was reproduced by several American newspapers in 1879, 1880 and 1881. It refers in part to Daniel O'Leary of Chicago, USA, and Henry Vaughan of Chester, England, who competed against one another in the "1st Astley International Belt" race which was held at the Agricultural Hall in Islington, a suburb of London, between Monday, the 18th and Saturday, the 23rd of March 1878. The text in **bold** was added later and refers to the "5th Astley International Belt" race which took place at Madison Square Garden in New York between the 22nd and 27th of September 1879. Both races are extensively covered in this book.

WHAT SLEEP BRINGS.

Nine cots, with, excelsior mattresses, are standing beneath the tents at the side, of the track. Weston and Rowell sleep in rooms at the eastern end of the garden. Guyon rests in the Putnam House, near the Fourth Avenue entrance. All the other walkers sleep in their tents. The hours of unconsciousness are few. They can hardly be called hours of rest. The weary pedestrian is sponged or has a bath. He pitches in his cot. He is wrapped in his blankets. The lights in his tent are extinguished. He closes his eyes and enters a world of phantoms.

The cheers of the crowd, the music of the band, the clapping of hands, the murmur of a vast hive of bees, and the tread of many feet flit through his sleep. His body is racked with pain. There is appalling heat in his feet. His temples throb. The blood is stagnant, and frequently nightmare follows. The dreamer is still on the track. He sees his competitors passing him one by one, and is unable to increase his own speed. O'Leary said that during his walk for the belt in London he never went to sleep without the shadow of Vaughan before him. It would follow him around a phantom track with looks of exultation in its eyes. At times it would bar his way. It would stand facing him at the curves, making grimaces and contortions. Up to the moment of his waking, Vaughan's shade never left his sleep.

Guyon has a similar experience. On Wednesday night he slept the sleep of the damned. The pain in his feet was so intense that it turned his stomach. Weston was ever before him. When he turned in Merritt had passed him and taken second place. Weston was doing splendid work, and rapidly over hauling him. A ghostly Weston was pursuing him in his dreams. Whichever way he turned Weston was at his heels. Nor was Weston the only phantom. The dials assumed the faces of other contestants and taunted him as he passed - a spirit of Krohne fifty feet high was walking after him. Although he was in the Putnam House, far removed from sight or sound of the garden, he heard the murmur of the crowd the roar of brass instruments, the tread of a thousand feet, and peals of laughter. When he awoke toward morning he found a tumbler beneath his pillow. The pillow was drenched. He was unable to account for it until he remembered that in his dreams he had a spirited contest with Weston. Every nerve had been strained to hold his own, but the champion gained upon him. At the critical moment the dreamer recuperated and was able to prevent the spectral champion from passing him and taking third place. Then he was seized with a terrible thirst. He turned into a phantom tent and saw the apparition of Jim Smith, the trainer. Seizing the glass of water, he tried to swallow the liquid. To his horror it would not go down his throat, but ran out of his mouth over his chin, and drenched his nightshirt. Rushing from the phantom tent, he saw Weston's ghost sweeping around the track with a look of joy. The ghost had taken third place. While thus dreaming Guyon had really arisen and got a glass of water, spilling its contents upon his pillow. This is not strange, for Guyon's trainer, Smith, who has had even less sleep than Guyon, says that he has thrice administered to the wants of

his principal while asleep. He has rubbed him down, given him water, and answered questions without being aware of it until told of it the next day.

The dreams of the pedestrian are based on the condition of his stomach. When the stomach refuses nourishment, threatening apparitions frequently appear. In one case a pedestrian fancied that he was rolling among old logs covered with a thousand leg worms. In another case the pedestrian thought himself on the track, but unable to walk. Upon glancing at his feet he was shocked to see that they had turned into hickory saplings, and the saplings grew with such rapidity that they raised him in the air.

The agony of those hours of unrest is increased when the hapless walker awakes. His blood is still stagnant. There is a prickly heat upon his skin. He feels as though he was being pricked by a million of needles. His joints are stiff. His eyelids seem paralyzed. Worst of all, his feet and shin bones are numbed. Every movement sends a thrill of pain through the body. He is oiled and rubbed. A swallow of warm beef tea or some other concoction puts him into a glow and infuses him with a painful energy. He wobbles upon the track, and the noise, the lights and the dark shadows strikes him unpleasantly. He makes one lap, and the impulse to re-enter his cot is frequently too great that he finds it irresistible.

Before coming on the track he lies upon his cot in a semi - unconscious state, while he is rubbed and clad. He hardly appreciates the situation before he finds himself on the track. If his shoes have been changed during the rest, his feet feel like lumps of lead. The sore spots smart more than ever, and it is with the greatest difficulty that he can lift his feet from the track. He occasionally feels a nausea about the stomach, and his nerves are strung up to the utmost tension. The cracking of a whip, a deformed face, a wide-brimmed hat or a peculiarly shaped bouquet excites his mind, and he becomes in a measure insane.

Pedestrianism wasn't just confined to racing on tracks or against other men, or indeed women against women. Some would prefer to walk alone, covering huge distances. Edward Payson Weston was one such man, and it is with him that this remarkable story starts. Our journey begins in the year 1860.

CHAPTER 1

The Wily Wobbler!

Edward Payson Weston has been described as the *"purest walker of all time."* He was born in *Providence, Rhode Island, on the 15th of March 1839, weighing only 4 pounds 6 ounces, to parents who were said to be *"...of the highest respectability, his father being a man of wealth and his mother a woman of rare accomplishments."* During his early years, he was said to show no promise of athletic ability and was described as being *"weak and sickly."*

*The London *Sporting Life* on the 12th of February 1876 reported that he was born in Litchfield, Connecticut.

The *Decatur Daily Republican*, of Illinois, on the 28th of June 1879 gave its readers a little bit of insight into the man's formative years: The Rev. J. C. Fletcher, of Indianapolis gives an interesting account of the successful pedestrian, E. P. Weston. He says that when a child Weston was the leanest, sweetest little blonde boy that he ever knew. He always had his Sunday-school lesson perfectly, and was well trained at home, in Providence, by his small, slender mother. "But," added Mr. Fletcher, "Edward Payson Weston was the most uneasy bright boy I ever saw. There was no keeping him still."

When young Eddy was ten years of age, his father, then a merchant, left his wife and four children and travelled west to California during the gold rush. During that winter, and whilst being visited by the Hutchinson family who were travelling musicians, the boy asked his mother if she would give him permission to let him tour with them. After much pestering, his mother gave her consent and off he went. Weston made himself useful on his year long journey by selling candy and song books during their concerts. When he returned, he kept up his ties with the family by living with Jesse Hutchinson, at High Rock, Lynn, Massachusetts.

In 1851, he was educated for six months at the old Adam's School in Boston where the proprietor, Mr. John P. Ordway allowed him to sell candy at Ordway Hall during each secular evening to help pay for his board.

In the summer the year after, his father returned home. The young boy listened intently as he told him many tales about his travels. The teenager was clearly so impressed with his father's exploits that in 1853 he published a pamphlet describing his dad's adventures. He then went on to successfully sell many of them, as he worked as a newsboy in the big cities on the New York, Providence and Boston Railroads.

As a 15-year-old he found employment in a similar job on the *Empire State*, a steamship which cruised between Fall River in Massachusetts and New York. His father, who wasn't keen on him doing that, advised him to return home to Providence, where he was found a more appropriate job as a clerk in a merchant's office. The lad obviously wasn't too keen in pursuing the same career as Weston Senior, and as a consequence only remained in the post for six months, after which he was found another job yet again by his father, as a jeweller's apprentice in Providence. The youth apparently put a lot of effort into his new vocation but alas with little remuneration for his efforts, he left that venture too. In the winter of 1855, he published another pamphlet about his father's travels in the "*Western Islands*." Its failure to sell left Weston disheartened. However, in the spring of the year after, and working under an assumed name, he joined a travelling circus, a job which he stuck to till June when he was nearly killed by a stroke of lightning whilst riding on a wagon near Tyngsboro, Massachusetts. When he refused to appear in the ring a few days later, he was fired. Again, down on his luck, he headed over the border into Canada where he found a job as a drummer at Spalding & Rogers Circus in Quebec. The only problem was that Weston had never played the drums in his life! Nonetheless he was given lessons by a bugler called Edward Kendall, who, along with his son George, put some positive rhythm back in his life. Caring for him like a son, Kendall accompanied him as the circus toured throughout Canada and the western states till it disbanded in Cincinnati, Ohio, in the winter of 1856, after which Weston returned to New York where he resumed his career selling books.

Edward Payson Weston

Reproduced with kind permission from John Weiss (Illustration no: 1)

In February of 1859, the then 19-year-old attaché for the *New York Herald* had been given the task of unloading a box of hot house flowers, which was a gift from the wife of Mr. Bennett, the editor of the newspaper he was employed at, to the wife of the Postmaster General in Washington. The box was due to be loaded on to the six o'clock train for the capital that very same evening. Due to Weston making an error, the flowers had somehow found their way back into the wagon, which at two o'clock in the afternoon, promptly left the office to return to the same place it had left earlier. At three o'clock and as Weston was going about his duties, a man called at the office to collect the box destined for the train station. Quickly realising his mistake, Weston had to think of a solution to redress the situation. He knew that at that time of day, and with the streets being crowded, the wagon couldn't have got very far in the time elapsed, so, amid catcalls and jeering from his work colleagues who thought there was no way he could catch it up, Weston, starting from the corner of Fulton and Nassau Street, ran after the wagon at a tremendous pace. He was right. The traffic *was* heavy and the wagon *had* made slow progress. As a consequence he was able to catch it up on the corner of Seventieth Street and Broadway. On achieving his objective Weston would later recall how exhausted he was after the chase, and how for some time, he was unable stand up thereafter. However, after he had rested, and now with the box in his arms, he ran back as far as Fifty Ninth Street, boarded a streetcar, and returned to the *Herald* office a few minutes after five o'clock. For his devotion to duty, he would later be rewarded by his boss, who being very impressed with his actions, apparently doubled his wages to $6 a week.

The Reverend Fletcher went on to say: **His father was a man restless in his brain, and finally died insane. The mother of E. P. W. was a woman of intellectual parts, and at her husband's death, in order to support the family she wrote a number of interesting *books for children. Those were printed, and then, instead of being published, were hawked about Providence and elsewhere in the state of Rhode Island by Edward Payson, who walked from house to house all over the state and thus the early habit of walking.**

*One of the books written by his mother entitled, "Kate Felton; or, "A Peep at Realities," actually sold well in 1859.

Later reports about his physical prowess suggested that he won prizes for *"wrestling, running, walking and leaping competitions."*

In 1860, Weston, who at the time was residing in Hartford, Connecticut, made a bet with George B. Eddy of Worcester, Massachusetts, that if Abraham Lincoln won the presidency, he would walk the 478 miles from the State House in Boston to the Capitol building in Washington D.C. in 10 days, timing it to be there to witness the inauguration. On his part, Mr. Eddy agreed to do the same if Mr. Lincoln wasn't elected; but in reality, neither thought that either would have to carry out the task. Weston lost, and after contemplating the task in hand, asked his friend Mr. Foster on Christmas Day that, if he would follow him behind in a carriage, he *would* attempt the feat. Weston by that time, apart from showing some locomotive skills in his "office run," hadn't shown any promise at all as a walker and the idea of tramping all that way was causing him some worry.

Weston, needing to know how he would cope, walked the 36 miles from Hartford to New Haven, Connecticut, on the 1st of January 1861, setting off from the City Hall at 07:30. During the journey which took him 10h.40m, he dropped off 150 circulars promoting a book at the doors of as many houses and stopped for an hour to eat. Having arrived at New Haven at 18:30, he spent that night at the Tontine Hotel. The day after, Weston, who had left New Haven at 09:30, stopped at 125 of the houses he had left a circular at, and managed to sell several copies of the book before arriving back at Hartford eleven and a half hours later.

Later that month, and as a further test of his powers of endurance, Weston set off at 17:30 on Friday, the 25th from New Haven Post Office to Hartford, carrying the 350 circulars he intended to drop off at as many houses on the way. On his return journey, he added four miles to his trip by passing through the village of Wallingford which made a total distance for the hike of 76 miles. Mission accomplished, he got back to New Haven at 17:05 making the distance, including stops, in a time of 23h.35m. The only real costs for Weston on the venture were the condition of his boots, which were by then noticeably devoid of their soles, due to the state of the roads he had to encounter on his walk. Of what happened next, Weston would later write:

After partaking of a hearty supper, I retired at eight o'clock, p. m., and did not awake until eight o'clock the next morning. I felt as well as usual, and attended church during the day.

The proposed feat was now being advertised through reports in the press. The *New York Times* on the 31st of January 1861 wrote: **Mr. E. P. Weston walked from New Haven to Hartford and back on Friday and Saturday in less than twenty-four hours. The road was covered with ice and slush. He left a pamphlet at each house on the road. He starts from Boston on the 22d of February to walk to Washington in ten days.**

Happy with how he had performed, Weston now had another problem to solve. How could he afford to finance the trip? After all, he had to have proof that he had performed it fairly and that consideration would mean taking people with him to testify he had. That also meant that he would have to stump up the cost of providing a carriage for his witnesses to travel with him. The solution was quickly found and George K. Whiting of New Haven,

Connecticut, agreed that he would provide not only a horse and carriage, but a driver as well, for $80. Weston agreed that he would further pay all acquired expenses, from the time the party left Boston until twenty-four hours after they arrived in Washington. The idea then was that the owner would sell the horse and carriage in the capital. Time was now running short before the great feat started, and in his quest to find more funding for his trip, Weston headed for New York to persuade businesses to use his journey as an advertising medium.

He was helped by C. C. Yeaton of the Grover & Baker Sewing Machine Co, who, for a payment of $100, asked him to distribute 5,000 copies of a small book called *"A Home Scene"* which explained the virtues of their product, along with a 100,000 cards which also advertised the machines. Weston also succeeded in getting contracts to distribute 5,000 circulars on behalf of Frederick Y. Rushton, druggist, of Astor House, 477 Broadway; Messrs. J. Gurney & Son, photograph artists, 707 Broadway; Joseph Burnett's of Boston, and F. M. Shepard of the Rubber Clothing Co, 201 Broadway, who gave the pedestrian a *"best quality"* rubber suit to protect him from the rain. The deal was that Weston would deliver the bundled circulars which would be enclosed in a wrapper, and that he would leave a set at every house he passed on the road between Boston and Washington, with the exception of those he passed on Sundays.

With that settled, the *"worn out"* Weston, made his way from New Haven to Boston arriving in the city on the morning of the 22nd of February having spent four sleepless nights beforehand, due to the *"continued exertion and anxiety."* There he would meet Charles H. Foster who would take care of him during the journey, and Abner A. Smith, the driver. Having eaten a light lunch and changed his clothes at the Tremont House Hotel, Weston, riding in the carriage that would later follow him, made his own way to the State House, to prepare himself for the start of his journey at 11:40.

When he arrived ten minutes later, he was greeted by Constable A. G. Dawes, who, one would have thought, was there to oversee the crowds that had amassed to bid him a safe journey. However, the lawman informed him that there was a claim against him, in favour of *"Bean & Clayton."* Weston told the constable that he wasn't in a position to settle it until he returned from Washington. That been said, he was then informed that he was under arrest. With admirable calm, Weston invited the officer into the carriage to take him where he thought fit, and while they were getting in, another man confronted the walker with a similar claim in favour of a man called D. F. Draper. Weston thereafter told both men about his financial circumstances, informing them that he would entertain the claims on his return to Boston. When the men wouldn't listen to his pleas for reason, it was reported that Weston became quite upset. He said the only option that was available to him was to give them orders on the businesses that had hired him to deliver their advertisements, and as he was penniless, if they didn't accept his offer, he would have to take the poor debtor's oath. That offer was put to Draper, who, agreeing, had an order prepared on the Grover & Baker's Company for $25, which Weston then signed. Officer Dawes then went to find the lawyer who had instigated Weston's arrest on behalf of Bean and Clayton. When he arrived, and after Weston had explained his financial situation, the lawyer conferred with his clients. Returning shortly after, he informed Weston that subject to paying $10 for *"charges"* he would be released. Weston reiterated that he couldn't pay, and after further consultation with his clients, the lawyer gave the officers permission to release him, provided that on his return to Boston, he settled the claim.

The time was 12:45 when Weston arrived back to the State House, where he was the recipient of continual calls to make a speech. Standing on the steps, he apologised for keeping everybody waiting. He said he regretted what had happened, blaming his creditors for seizing the perfect opportunity to get their money; the crowd responding with requests for their names and shouts of "Shame on them!" The young man then informed them that although he had not wagered any cash on his hopeful success, he had bet half a dozen half pints of peanuts that he would be victorious. Then, to loud cheers, the 21-year-old, who stood 5 feet 7½ inches, weighed 130 pounds, measured 34 inches around his chest and 26½ inches around the waist, began his journey at 12:48. The noisy assemblage, comprising several hundred people, which followed him down Beacon Street, gradually diminished in size when the party arrived at the toll-gate on the mill dam. The remaining hangers-on then gave him three cheers, and the light carriage that followed him was accompanied by a few friends who said their goodbyes at Newton. Weston walked his first five miles in 47 minutes, settling down thereafter to a steady three and a quarter mile an hour pace.

Seventeen miles down the road from Boston, Weston was greeted at Natick by a company of parading soldiers who *"presented arms"* and gave him three cheers. Bowing in acknowledgment, he continued on to Framingham, where; and when he was within a mile of entering the town he was greeted by a group of drummers, who informed him that they would escort him into town. So on to the Framingham Hotel he marched, and amid the resounding beat, he arrived there at 17:45, having covered a distance of 21 miles from the start.

After thanking his noisy companions, Weston and party were fed by the hotel proprietors, Mr. and Mrs. Bolles. After their meal, he was encouraged to go into the parlour where some ladies were anxious to meet him. One of them asked, with his permission of course, if he would deliver a kiss to the President. Informing her he couldn't guarantee delivery, he nevertheless said he had no objections to the request and was accordingly kissed not only by her, but the rest of the ladies too!

After thanking his hosts and making a short speech to the gathered crowd outside, Weston left the hotel, and accompanied by many of the villagers and the drummers, headed towards Worcester. After walking three miles, a carriage drew up to him, containing a man and two women, who told him they had ridden ten miles, with an intention to shake his hand. Having acceded to their request he continued on his way at a rapid gait, and after passing the town of Westborough, 16 miles from Natick, he was heard laughing, after a young man had told him that he had bet $20 that Weston would arrive in Washington "on time."

Being most anxious to reach Worcester, which was 10 miles from Westborough, within the time set out in his schedule, he pressed on. Trouble however lay ahead when he was met by a Mr. Balcom, another man to whom he owed money to. Occupying an open carriage, along with the town's sheriff, Balcom informed the walker that as soon as he entered the city limits he would be under arrest. Weston insisted that he would like to sort the problem out at the Lincoln House Hotel. It was reported that when he arrived there he was said to get quite upset about the predicament he had found himself in, so much so that others had to intervene on his behalf and endorse his promise to pay the amount owed to Mr. Balcom in two months.

Shortly after 2 a.m., he left the hotel and went to a friend's house where a spread had been put on for him. The ravenous appetite that Weston normally had was all of a sudden gone as *"when he went to the table he could not eat, and behaved more like a madman than anything else."* Despite being urged to have a lie down, Weston insisted that he wanted to continue on his journey and make the six miles to Leicester. Thus at 03:15 he set off in the 12-inch deep snow on the morning of Saturday, the 23rd of February.

After walking about a mile he complained of feeling strange, stating he couldn't keep his eyes open. After finding it difficult to stand, he fell down several times. He soon gave the order to turn back but almost immediately changed his mind saying he would rather die on the road than give up. After slowly struggling through the 2-feet deep snow, he got within two miles of the village. It was here that he experienced a heavy nose bleed. The incident however appeared to have a positive effect upon him, in that it appeared to wake him up, after which he went along with more purpose in his step. He arrived at his destination at dawn, had a bath in the local hotel, and continued on his trek towards East Brookfield, a distance of eight miles from Leicester, with a bagful of freshly fried doughnuts to sustain him along the way.

Now refreshed and feeling much better, he bounded on to his next port of call, arriving at the Wawaconnuck Hotel at 08:40. After being served with a most delicious breakfast by the proprietor, Peter Perntean, he slept for a couple of hours; and after being given a vigorous rub down, headed on to South Brookfield at midday.

The villagers of South Brookfield, which was three miles away, welcomed him with a twelve-piece brass band. From there he moved on to West Brookfield where he was given a rousing reception and three cheers. His next stop was West Warren, and when he turned up there at 15:00, not only was he presented with a small American flag by a lady, but he was also given a seven gun salute from *"small cannon."* As he tramped on towards Palmer, an old man asked if he could walk with him for a few miles. The young ped agreed to the request and slowed down his pace to accommodate that of his slower companion.

The flag given to him earlier nearly caused an accident later. As it fluttered in the whip-socket on the following carriage, it frightened the horse which started to run and there was some concern that the conveyance might capsize. The driver managed to avert tragedy by pulling up the horse, after which the flag was removed. The old man left them after a while and the pedestrian continued on his way, at a pace of 3¾ mph. Some people on the way gave him drinks like milk and water, but when offered cider, he refused.

His last mile into Palmer, which was nine miles from West Warren, was made in extra quick time and he arrived at the Antique House Hotel at 18:20. Here he was given a splendid welcome, not only by the townsfolk, but also by the proprietor E. B. Shaw, who, refusing payment for food and lodgings provided Weston with *"an excellent apartment."* After receiving another welcome rub down, he slept in from 20:30 till 02:30 on the morning of Sunday, the 24th of February.

The youth was ready in 15 minutes to recommence his walk, and with the *"bountiful lunch"* Mr. Shaw had prepared for their journey, the group set off for Hartford, Connecticut. Weston, who was experiencing problems with his left knee, walked lame for some miles, but after a short stop at the house near Butlerville belonging to S. M. Bliss, he arrived at Wilbraham eight miles away at 6 a.m. It then began to rain, which gave Weston an excuse to try out the rubber suit he had been supplied with. The weather was later to take a turn for the worse; the cold wind and the muddy slippery conditions on the road causing him to become irritable. His timetable had dictated that he should have reached his destination by 12 o'clock, but as it was he entered Hartford, a distance of 45 miles from Palmer, at 16:45. It was here that he went straight to the residence of Mrs. Lambe, who cared for the men till they left at midnight, after Weston had slept for a good three hours.

It was now Monday, the 25th February, and Weston was accompanied out of Hartford by a man called Mr. Clapp, who stayed with him for several miles before waving him goodbye. Seven miles out of the town Weston sprained his left ankle after trying to keep a dog at bay, but despite his injury he walked a further 10 miles to Meriden, where he rested for an hour after arriving there at 06:00. From there he passed through Yalesville where he stopped off to apologise to Mr. G. I. Mix who he should have stayed with the night before. From there he walked to Wallingford, where after he breakfasted at the house of D. S. Stephens, he reached Ben Bryan's house at 135 Crown Street, New Haven, which was 21 miles from Meriden at 2 p.m. After being cheered by a large crowd which he made a speech to, he left the town at 17:15.

Now re-supplied with a fresh horse and bundles of advertisements, he walked from New Haven towards Bridgeport, a trek of 19 miles. Before he got there at 11 p.m. he was the recipient of another enthusiastic reception at Milford, where the ladies came out waving handkerchiefs, amid the light of blazing bonfires. The night was spent at the Sterling House Hotel, from which he headed on to Fairfield, a distance of four miles away, the next day Tuesday, at 05:30. After passing through there he walked on to Westport five miles further on, and at 11 a.m., arrived at Norwalk where he had been earlier been invited to stop at the house of Mr. T. O. Kelly, the proprietor of the Connecticut Hotel. Unable to find his house, the pedestrian was treated to a hearty breakfast at the hotel before leaving for Stamford nine miles or so further down the road at a *"brisk pace"* at midday. After passing through Darien at 13:45, he arrived at the Stamford Hotel at 14:45, where, and after he had been cared for by the proprietor, Mr. W. G. Nichols, a man mounted a platform and proposed *"three cheers for the predestrinarian!"*

After leaving Stamford an hour after he arrived, he headed on to *Greenwich. It was here that he was presented with a medal which bore the portraits of Lincoln and Hamlin by a six-year-old boy called "Little Freddie." From there he moved on to Port Chester, a journey of three miles during which time he was given a present by a man driving a bakers wagon. The gift of a loaf of bread nourished him till he crossed the state line between Connecticut and New York at 18:19. The crowd that followed him on that last mile into the village must have been amazed at the sight of the fastest walking man they had ever seen, for by the time he arrived at Port Chester at 18:30, he had walked his last two miles on the *"rough and muddy"* road in a surprisingly good time of just 19 minutes. Amid much enthusiasm and noisy cheering, Weston stayed for a short time before recommencing the hike of nine miles towards New Rochelle, where he turned up at Sibery's Hotel at 10 p.m. It was here that he was introduced to several young ladies, who were said to *"feel sorry for him."*

*Where during the American Revolution, General Israel Putnam made a daring escape from the British on the 26th of February 1779.

Wednesday, February the 27th was the day Weston would walk to New York, which was a distance of 22 miles from New Rochelle, which he left at 5 a.m. He arrived at the Harlem Bridge at 09:45, and playing to the audience which watched his progress with interest, conveyed himself along at sizzling speed before arriving at the city's

Metropolitan Hotel at 11:30. After breakfast, Weston was driven to the studio of J. Gurney and Son of 707 Broadway, where, not only did he have his photograph taken, but was also presented with three dozen *"cartes de visite"* of himself by the proprietors. He was later reunited with George Eddy, the man he had the original bet with. Eddy then accompanied him to a host of engagements before they departed on the ferry to Jersey City at 5 o'clock. Thereafter, they both briskly walked along the plank-road toward the city of Newark where he was met by a large crowd, which pestered him so much that the services of several policemen were required to keep them from mobbing him. After arriving at the City Hotel at 19:00, the by now exhausted pedestrian went to bed at 20:30.

The day after, the *Brooklyn Daily Eagle*, under the heading **FAST WALKING,** wrote: Mr. Edward P. Weston, of Boston, who having lost a wager on the Presidential election, considers himself under high moral obligations to walk all the way from his city to Washington in ten days, reached the metropolis yesterday morning about 1 ½ o'clock, having accomplished the distance from Boston (285 miles) since 1 ¾ P. M. on the 22d inst., or 47 miles per day. Mr. Weston is now about half through his journey, and, although very much fatigued, expects to perform his allotted task, and be present at the Inauguration. After resting and refreshing himself at the Metropolitan Hotel, he resumed his walk at 4 P. M. yesterday.

On Thursday, the 28th of February, Weston, Eddy and company set off from Newark, at 15 minutes past midnight. Along with a large crowd of well wishers, they headed towards Elizabethtown which they arrived at a couple of hours later. From there, and with Mr. Eddy now gone, he trudged his way on to Rahway through deep mud, the going being very difficult for Weston, who appeared quite fatigued. Having passed through Rahway, he complained of having a severe chest pain—which he blamed on the mustard in the sandwiches he had eaten previously. Stopping every quarter of a mile to sit and sleep, he became very irritable, his mood having a demoralising affect on the team following him. The jaded and dejected pedestrian then suggested they return to Rahway so that he could sleep at the village's public house. After heading back just a few steps, he had a dramatic change of heart. Throwing off the blanket around his shoulders he shouted, "No, I won't go back!" turned around, and recommenced his walk towards New Brunswick.

After a couple of miles they all stopped at the house of Samuel Forbes, who supplied them with some breakfast. That sustained them till they reached the Williams's Hotel, at 11:15. It was here that, after he had slept for a couple of hours, he met a party of Lloyds Minstrels, one of whom was called *"Cool White,"* and although he then permitted a lady to cut a lock of hair from his head as a souvenir, *"the walkist"* refused to have his photograph taken.

After leaving New Brunswick at 14:15, again accompanied by the now usual large crowd, he found the road conditions advantageous. Making good headway he arrived at the residence of Charles Shaun at South Brunswick at 18:30, who offered him the chance to stay overnight. Weston however declined the offer, making it clear that he wanted to get to Trenton that night. After supper he set off on roads that had again became difficult to walk on, and about nine p.m., complained of ankle trouble. Refusing to entertain any idea of being driven to Trenton, Weston gritted his teeth and made it to Clarksville, arriving at a tavern owned by Mr. Fairbrothers at 11 o'clock. It was here that the pedestrian had the longest sleep of the walk up to that point; six and a half glorious hours, from 23:30 till 06:00 the next day, Friday, March 1st.

Much refreshed by his rest, the seven-mile journey to Trenton, which he commenced at 06:45, was completed on a straight road in a couple of hours, despite spraining his big toe. When he arrived at the American Hotel, he was informed by the proprietor, Mr. J. V. D. Joline, that there had been much disappointment expressed by the citizens as a grand reception had awaited him. Weston, as ever apologetic said, "Being detained at Worcester, Massachusetts, had caused the deviation from my time-table, and came very near preventing my arrival here at all." Before he left Trenton at 10:15, he was presented with a sheet of music, entitled, *"Liberty's Reveille,"* which was dedicated to the Hon. John J. Crittenden of Kentucky. He was then congratulated by a number of prominent citizens before making a short speech from the balcony of the hotel.

"Crossing the bridge into the state of Pennsylvania, he soon passed William Penn's manor and enjoyed his walk there," along the banks of the Delaware River. Finding the dusty roads to his liking, Weston kept up a brisk pace towards Bristol, where another large crowd escorted him to the Railroad House Hotel. It was here he was met by the proprietor William Early, who told him the *"Bristol Brass Band"* had waited a couple of hours to escort him into town. Weston again explained why he had been delayed, before setting off for Philadelphia at 14:00, followed by a large crowd.

King of the Peds

Although the road was hilly and he found it *"uncomfortable walking on the flag-stones and brick sidewalks,"* Weston managed to arrive at the Continental Hotel at 20:15, where he refused to ride on the new steam elevator to his upstairs room, exclaiming, "As I commenced to walk, I will not alter my mode of travel until I arrive in Washington!"

Having renewed his stock of advertisements, Weston left Philadelphia on Saturday, the 2nd of March at 03:15, and after crossing Market Street Bridge, headed towards Baltimore on what he thought was the old stage-road. However, and after going a distance of 12 miles, he realised he was walking on the wrong road and that fact made him quite angry. For some reason he reacted to the mistake by drinking copious amounts of water which was said to make him *"feel quite sick and weak."* Mr. D. R. Hawkins, the proprietor of the Charter House Hotel in Media would have been quite shocked, when, the by now famous pedestrian, quite unexpectedly turned up at his establishment. After a sleep of an hour, and for the first time on the trip indulging in an alcoholic beverage, a glass of sherry wine, Weston, who rid himself of his coat and changed into lighter shoes, responded positively to three more cheers, and possibly one for the road, as he headed back out onto the hilly tracks on a warm and sunny day.

At 18:30, he crossed the Brandywine River at Chadd's Ford and shortly after arrived at the Washington Hotel, Hamorton, Chester County, where, after being entertained by the proprietor Mr. Conlin, he retired and slept until midnight.

On Sunday, March the 3rd at 00:30, the group set off towards Port Deposit, Maryland. The *"long and tedious walk"* of 40 miles which took 12h.45m ended up with Weston arriving at his destination at the Washington House Hotel in his *"undress uniform"* having earlier taken the wrong road. It was here that the proprietor, William Crompton, went out of his way to find the owners of the boat that would ferry the contingent across the Susquehanna River. At the steam-boat landing, Weston demonstrated to the watching crowd that, apart from walking, he was also good at jumping. Finding a suitable fence, and reportedly in a jovial mood, he leapt over one nearly as high as himself! When the party crossed the water, they were given three cheers by the watching crowd. After walking for some miles at a good clip, and after passing the village of Belair, the party stopped at the house of Mr. Rogers, who let the tired young man sleep beside his stove for an hour before proceeding on his way.

It was now Monday, the 4th of March. The next leg of the journey, which was made beneath dark menacing clouds, would take Weston through numerous toll-gates, all of which had to be opened by the gate-keepers who operated them. Even though a lot of their time was wasted having to wait around for them to get out of bed, the party eventually reached the Eutaw House Hotel in Baltimore at 04:30. Anxious to make sure that the young man got to Washington on time, the well-known proprietor, Robert B. Coleman, who also owned the International Hotel at Niagara Falls, hurried up proceedings so that the young athlete could make a hasty departure, and after a quick breakfast, Weston hit the road again at 6 a.m.

After making a distance of seven miles an unfortunate incident happened. The horse pulling the carriage all of a sudden stopped walking and it was evident that it was in such distress, that a replacement would be needed. Weston promptly went a couple of miles out of his way to try and secure a new horse at the Relay House Hotel at Washington Junction, which was 30 miles from the Capitol. However, with no horse available there, he instructed his companions to get to Washington by train, where, after walking the rest of the journey alone, he would meet them later.

"His lips were very much parched" as he walked along at a thunderous pace, but the brave ped finally *arrived in America's first city, followed by another large crowd. Rescued from the attentions of the intrigued public, an officer of the law took him to a house, and after giving him a glass of ale, accompanied him to where he was staying. After being welcomed by friends who lived in the city, he attended the Inauguration Ball, but too sleepy to enjoy it, left after a short time and returned to his quarters where he indulged in a marathon 13 hours of blissful shut-eye from 10 p.m.

*At 17:00 exactly, having walked a distance including deviations estimated at 510 miles in ten days, four hours and twelve minutes.

Now refreshed and declaring that he "never felt better in my life," Weston met the Hon. Christopher Robinson, of Rhode Island, who introduced him to a number of the members of Congress, which included the Hon. Stephen A. Douglas who, at a later date introduced Weston to the President and Mrs. Lincoln at the couple's first levee. Mrs.

Lincoln was said to be surprised at the extraordinary feat he had performed. The *President offered to pay the pedestrian's fare back to Boston but Weston declined the offer telling him, "As I have failed in my first attempt I feel obliged to try it again, but this time walking from Washington to Boston."

*Lincoln who it was said, got to know Weston very well, compared Weston to an Indian wagon wheel, *"as he was never tired."*

Weston originally planned to start his return journey of ten consecutive days on the 23rd of April, but the Southern Rebellion which broke out at the time changed his mind. Due to the riot in Baltimore on the 19th of April which caused communication problems between that city and Washington, he decided to help the government by taking 117 letters addressed to the Massachusetts and New York regiments stationed in Annapolis, Maryland and Washington, from Boston and New York –– in disguise! He set off from New York for Philadelphia on the 26th of April, and during the next four days, embarked on a series of adventures which eventually saw him captured by the very troops he was serving, arrested, and held in custody, until he proved who he was.

In the year after on Monday, the 19th of May 1862, he set off on his proposed journey of 478 miles in eight days, from Washington to Boston. However, he had a serious accident during a storm on Tuesday evening on the banks of the Susquehanna River, injuring both his legs, meaning the subsequent delay *"caused him to be one day behind his timetable."* It is thought that Weston, as a consequence of the accident gave up his attempt, as there were no further reports of the walk in the newspapers.

After getting married, *"he settled in a villa overlooking the Hudson River, about eight miles from the city, and walked to and from the office every day, beating the time of the tramways from ten to twenty five minutes."*

1867

In the late summer of 1867, Weston made a bet that he could walk 1,226 miles in 30 days. The amount wagered was $10,000 and the route would be from Portland, Maine, to Chicago, Illinois, using the *"Post road."* It was stipulated, and as can be seen in the agreement below, that during the walk he would have to make a distance of 100 miles in any 24-hour period. He would be allowed five attempts at making the 100 miles and should he fail he would forfeit $6,000 or six tenths of his stake.

THE ARTICLES OF AGREEMENT

Witnesses - In behalf of George K. Goodwin, John Grindell, trainer; Edward Ingalls, confidential agent, driver of each conveyance. In behalf of T. F. Wilcox, Benjamin M. Curtis, John T. Laphen, strangers appointed by postmasters.

I, George K. Goodwin, of New York city do wager and bet the sum of $10,000 in United States currency with T. F. Wilcox, of New York city, that Edward Payson Weston, late a resident of Boston, Mass, and aged but twenty eight years, can and will walk from Portland, Me, to Chicago, Ill, and make a fair and honest walk, to the distance of twelve hundred statute miles, of seventeen hundred and twenty eight yards each in length, in thirty consecutive days, and without walking between the hours of twelve p.m. on Saturday and twelve p.m. on Sunday, making a deduction of four entire days, and leaving but twenty six secular days in which to walk the distance, the said T. F. Wilcox wagering the said Weston cannot perform the feat, subject to the following.

Conditions—**It is agreed and understood by the said Weston and the parties to this wager that the said Weston is to walk on what is known as the Post Road; and it is further agreed that the said Weston is to walk 100 consecutive miles inside of twenty-four consecutive hours as part and portion of this journey, the said Weston being privileged to make five trials of this feat on such days included in the "thirty" as he may elect, should he fail in the first attempt. And if, after making the trial five times, he fails the said one hundred miles inside of the said 24 consecutive hours, even though he makes the distance from Portland, Me., to Chicago, Ill., in the specified time (thirty consecutive days), then it is agreed that the said Weston forfeit six tenths of his wager; and should the said Weston fail to make the distance on foot, and does not arrive at the at Chicago, Ill., in accordance to the time fixed for the route and timetable hereunto annexed, then the said Weston and his backer, the said Goodwin, do lose and forfeit the entire $20,000 – the amount wagered. It is hereby further agreed by the said Weston and the parties to this wager, that the said Weston is to be accompanied by two sworn witnesses for each side - who are to follow the said Weston in a conveyance provided, and who are** each in turn to witness the said Weston and to make each and every statement under oath as to the progress on foot of the said Weston. If at any time, or under any circumstances, the said Weston enters any vehicle, or mounts any animal or conveyance, for the purpose of riding, or does ride one foot of the distance to be walked, then this wager is forfeited against the said Weston and his backer. This will in no way interfere with his continuance on the Sabbath, as it is understood he starts after 12 p.m. on Sunday from the precise place as at which he stops 12 p.m. on Saturday. If the said Weston walks to make to time on his route between the hours of twelve p.m. on Saturday and twelve p.m. on Sunday then he forfeits the wager against himself and his backer. It is agreed that the witnesses to this walk shall be trustworthy and reliable men, and are responsible for each and every statement made after the said Weston makes the start until he arrives at Chicago, Ill., or forfeits this wager. If the said Weston successfully accomplishes this walk entire, in accordance with this agreement, and it be sworn to by the four witnesses, the backer of the said Weston shall have paid over to him, the said Goodwin immediately on the arrival of the said Weston in Chicago, Ill., the sum of $20,000 previously deposited in the stakeholders hands. In pursuance of, and as surety of this wager, I, George K. Goodwin, and I, T. F. Wilcox, have deposited in the hands of Mr. E. H. Elias, stakeholder, the sum of $600 as forfeit; the balance being $9,400 each, we do agree to deposit with the stakeholder on Monday, September 30, 1867, at 3 o'clock, p.m., or the part failing to appear forfeits. It is agreed that the said Weston is to make the start from Portland, Me., on a stated day between the 1st and 15th of October, 1867, and failing to make the start in the specified time, then the said Goodwin pays forfeit.

Signed the seventh day of August, in the city of New York.   GEORGE K. GOODWIN   T. F. WILCOX

SEPTEMBER 30.—At the final deposit of stakes made this day it was further agreed between the parties to this wager and the said Weston (who made the request for an extension of two weeks time to change the date of start to October 29) that such request be granted and that the said Weston be required to make the distance of 1,226 miles according to his revised timetable instead of 1,200 miles, and to leave Portland, Me., at 12m., October 29, 1867. This is to be considered an equivalent for the $600 to have been forfeited if he failed to start between October 1 and 15.

THE ROUTE

Day	Date	From/To	Miles	Day	Date	From/To	Miles
	OCT						
Tue	29th	Portland, MA	35	Wed	13th	Buffalo, NY	45
Wed	30th	North Berwick, MA	55	Thur	14th	Brocton, NY	54
Thur	31st	North Attleboro, MA	48	Fri	15th	Erie, PA	46
	NOV			Sat	16th	Geneva, OH	54
Fri	1st		72	Mon	18th	Cleveland, OH	48
Sat	2nd	Hartford, CT	40	Tue	19th	Wakeman, OH	49
Mon	4th	Cornwall Bridge, CT	57	Wed	20th	Fremont, OH	41
Tue	5th	Chatham F C, NY	52	Thur	21st	Springfield, OH	45
Wed	6th	Schenectady	46	Fri	22nd	Bryan, OH	41
Thur	7th	St. Johnsville, NY	47	Sat	23rd	Ligonier, OH	62
Fri	8th	Rome, NY	47	Mon	25th	Mishawaka, IN	38
Sat	9th	Weedsport, NY	61	Tue	26th	Laporte, IN	32
Mon	11th	Palmyra, NY	32	Wed	27th	Calumet, IN	22
Tue	12th	Byron, NY	45	Thur	28th	Chicago Junc, IL	12
						TOTAL	1,226

Of the forthcoming walk, Weston wrote:

"The calculation for each day's travel is made on the supposition that I do not fail to make 100 miles in the walk from North Attleboro to East Hartford. Failing in this however, I have four other trials, which I shall make at intervals of five days. In 1861 I made an average of 51 miles per day for ten consecutive days, in the worst season of that year for walking—February and March. On this trip my average will be but 47 miles, and the feat is to be performed during the pleasantest part of the year. I have tried nine different times to walk 100 miles in 21 consecutive hours, but have never succeeded. On one trial I came within two miles of it. I think I can accomplish the feat after a week's practice, and if I am successful on the fourth day of the trip I would not give ten cents to be insured the victory."

As he prepared himself, he wrote a letter to his local newspaper, the *Providence Journal* of which some paragraphs appear below:

"In the winter of 1866 I became somewhat involved in debt by entrusting money to other parties. Eventually I lost all I had, and some thousands of dollars which kind friends had loaned me. When I informed them of my situation, and that I was totally unable to make them any payment for an indefinite time, instead of upbraiding me for the loss of their money (though they were not in circumstances to afford such a loss) they kindly told me to give myself no uneasiness on their account. For months I toiled to try and gain even a small amount to pay on account, but could barely gain a living for my family. I am naturally ambitious, and happening to meet Mr. Goodwin at a time when I was very low spirited, he asked me if I could walk yet. Subsequently the wager was made.

I need only say that should I win, I receive an amount sufficient to pay my indebtedness and to reinstate myself in business. Some people condemn me for this undertaking and look upon it the same way as they would upon a prize fight. They think because my Maker has endowed me with perhaps greater walking abilities than most of my fellow men, and because I walk for a wager, no matter to what laudable purpose my winnings will be applied, if I am successful, that I must be classed with prize fighters. Now this is a slander of an honest man who is willing to do anything under the sun that will legitimately enable him to liquidate his debts.

I never witnessed a prize fight in my life as it is a species of brutality that has ever excited my utter abhorrence. I am not a sporting man in any sense; but a plain business man, and I fail to see wherein I am doing wrong. If base ball or boat racing is a crime, then I am wrong; otherwise I am right.

I am daily asked as to my chances of winning this race, I can only answer, that after I arrive at Hartford. Conn., I can tell better. Be assured that I will do my best to win, and I may say without egotism that over many weeks I will convince the good people of my native city and State that I will reflect no disgrace on my birthplace.

I leave Portland, Maine, at 12m., Tuesday October 29. I shall be in Providence during the Saturday and Sunday previous, at the residence of my sister, in South Providence, where I will be happy to meet any friends and old schoolmates who may be pleased to call.

In conclusion, I would add that, though I lay no pretensions to piety, common sense teaches me there is a God in everything, and that, understanding my motive for this race, and the just principle which actuated the motive, he will guide me to my journey's end."

Before Weston left on his epic journey he wrote the following letter to his witnesses:

GENTLEMEN:

You have been selected to be my companions and witness to my coming walk from Portland, Me., to Chicago, Ill., it is necessary that I should make a few suggestions, which shall govern your actions on this race.

On the 29th instant you will meet me at the Prebble House, Portland, Me., at eleven (11) a.m. there to take the prescribed oath. At 12m. Mr. John Grindell will assume entire charge of my person in this race, and the others will please confer with and be governed by his advice thereafter, and under no circumstances will either of you interfere, or allow others to interfere with, with his treatment of me, as I rely most implicitly on his kindness of heart, experience, judgment, and the interest he has in the successful accomplishment in this race.

Neither of you are expected to show me any favor incompatible with your oath. I need not remind you that you will be narrowly watched by the public, and that your actions should in every way be guarded that none, however, fastidious, may take exception to your characters as gentlemen.

You may expect to come into contact with all classes, and some may use offensive language to you. I hope, however that you will bear with such, that we may proceed quietly on our journey, remembering that anything that you do will reflect on the general character of this race.

You will please extend every courtesy to the various Postmasters who have kindly assisted me in obtaining the correct distance, and who may be pleased to accompany you a portion of the journey (their names will be found in the "Route Book"), and impart any information in regard to the race that might prove of interest in regard to them.

You will please observe that no particle of food or drop of beverage is to be given to me unless prepared under the immediate supervision of Mr. Grindell. This is of the utmost importance, and I trust it will not be construed into any act of disrespect to the proprietors of any hotels at which we stop, as it is in accordance with the

King of the Peds

earnestly expressed desire of my backer, Mr. George K. Goodwin. And now all I ask of you is to do your duty like just men, having faith in Him who doeth all things well and upon whom I rely entirely on complete success.

Yours truly,

Edward Payson Weston *(Illustration no: 2)*

The, *"five foot seven and a half inches tall"* 28-year-old, weighed 125 pounds when he eventually left Portland at the time planned on Tuesday, the 29th of October. He was a canvasser by occupation and carried with him 30,000 copies of his little paper *"The Time Table"* which probably contained a copy of his photograph, which he would sell for 25 cents each. As he strode resplendently up Federal Street in Portland minutes into his long arduous journey, he was cheered with much enthusiasm by the gathered crowds.

Weston's photograph which he sold on his walk

Reproduced with kind permission from John Weiss (Illustration no: 3)

He reached Saco via Oak Hill and Dunstan Corner's at 15:25, thirty-five minutes ahead of schedule. After an hours break, he got as far as Berwick, a distance of 35 miles, by midnight, having passed through Biddeford and Kennebunk. During that time he went three miles out of his way having *"missed the road twice."* Despite that mishap however, he was said to be *"bright and lively."* At New Berwick, he stayed at John Hamilton's residence for the night.

On Wednesday he started his journey at 06:30 passing through eight towns on his way to Ipswich, where he slept on Wednesday night. These included South Berwick (7 miles) at 08:00, Elliott (8 miles) at 09:10, Portsmouth, New Hampshire, (7 miles) at 11:15, where he had lunch and departed at 13:27, Hampton (11 miles) at 15:45, Seabrook (4 miles) at 16:45, Newburyport, Massachusetts, (5 miles) at 18:20, where he had supper departing there at 21:20, and eventually reaching Ipswich 12 miles away, at 00:25.

He set off from Ipswich at 08:10 and after travelling through Beverly, ten miles away at 10:35, arrived in Salem at 11:00, where he had a snack at the Essex House Hotel, leaving that town at 14:25. He then passed through Wenham and Lynn before pushing on westward through Chelsea and Charlestown over the Warren Bridge, eventually arriving at the Parker House Hotel in Boston on Thursday, the 31st of October at 16:00, fifteen minutes ahead of time, having made the 105-mile journey in 52 hours. His tramp through the streets was watched by thousands, and as he was cheered, he repeatedly raised his hat to the crowds. The *Boston Journal* described what he wore: **Mr. Weston was dressed in a dark blue cloth jacket, with pants to match, coming to the knee where they were met by red woollen stockings; his feet being encased in a heavy pair of boots, laced to the ankles. His hat was of white marselles, gathered at the top with a small button. He carried in his hand a small switch, which he occasionally was obliged to use vigorously over the heads and shoulders of some too enthusiastic admirers who impeded his progress.**

He left the hotel at 21:00 after making a brief appearance on a balcony for the waiting crowd. He then resumed his tramp towards Jamaica Plains and Dedham, where he arrived at the Phoenix House Hotel at 12:20 a.m. on Friday, the 1st of November.

Weston decided to begin his first trial of making 100 miles in 24 hours from Dedham to Andover, Connecticut. He left Dedham at 12:19 and headed towards Providence via Walpole, which was 8 miles away, at 15:18. There he stayed for lunch till 15:50 before recommencing his walk to Wrentham, North Attleboro (18:00) and Pawtucket, Rhode Island. It was here that he was *"thrown to the ground and trampled on"* just before eight o'clock due to the actions of the surging crowd. *"The crowd at this place was very great, and Mr. Ingalls and his trainer who were walking with Weston were both badly injured by being run over in their efforts to keep the people from crushing the pedestrian; while Weston himself nearly had his left hip dislocated."*

He arrived at Providence at 20:45 where he was escorted by a *"strong, active, and efficient posse of police under Captain Gross,"* due to the large crowds waiting for him. At this stage, he was 18 minutes ahead of time having made 32 miles of his proposed 24-hour "century." He used 15 of those gained minutes resting for a short while at the City Hotel before heading out of town towards Cranston, Rhode Island, at 21:16. As he passed up Claverick Street, *"a young lady made her way through the crowd and bestowed upon him a kiss and a God-speed in the same breath."* He then passed through Cranston and Natick before stopping at the house of Mr. Ferdinand Richmond in Washington, where he was presented with a handsome wreath by two young ladies, in return giving them a couple of his photographs.

He left that town in the very early morning of Saturday, the 2nd of November at 01:15 accompanied by a large delegation of townsfolk, who with three cheers, left him on its outskirts, to navigate the sandy and rough roads during the rest of the dark hours. At a remarkable pace, and still feeling the effects of the mishap in Pawtucket, the horses which were following him had to be cajoled into a trot every so often to keep up with the speedy young fellow. He went on to reach the village of Oneco at 05:55 and Sterling Hill 20 minutes later. Here a consultation was held with his trainer, Mr. Grindell, and it was decided that Weston would give up the idea of making the 100 miles by 13:00, believing at the time that he would not be able to make the 37 miles necessary in the six hours remaining. Thus Weston stayed at the residence of Jerry Young in Sterling Hill until 12:30, before commencing his marathon towards Plainfield five miles away, where he was met by the Postmaster Waldo Tillinghast and invited by him to have a substantial rest in the village over the Sabbath at his home.

On Sunday, the 3rd of November, Weston was said to have *"respected the Sabbatarian prejudices of New England"* by attending church that morning. It was there that he was entertained at the Postmasters house and where the church choir sang for him. After that he walked about town all day. He was led out of town by the lights of the villagers' lanterns the next day at 00:30 and strode towards Hartford, Connecticut. A lonely journey was ahead in the dark cold night, and as it began to rain heavily, he donned his rubber coat and walked as fast as he could *"on one of the worst roads he had traveled since leaving Portland,"* through the mud till he reached Willimantic at 06:10, a journey of about 18 miles. It was here that he had a leisurely breakfast whilst resting for just over three hours during which time some locals apparently *"besieged his windows endeavoring to get a glimpse of the wonderful fellow."*

He left Willimantic at half past nine and made for Andover. The *Providence Journal* then describes what happened when Weston got five miles into his journey: **He came across a poor family consisting of a one armed man, his wife and two children. The woman was cooking some dinner in a pot on a little fire of a few sticks picked up by the roadside, and on an old rag spread on the ground, were a few cold potatoes. This formed there scanty meal. Ned's (Weston) heart was touched, and stopping in his walk, he came to the carriage, and taking a large paper of sandwiches, which had been put up for his own use, gave them to the woman, accompanying the gift** by a small donation of money. He then passed on while the woman invoked blessing and good luck on him throughout his journey.

He kept going at a steady pace by racing a couple of men who thought they could keep up with him on the way to Andover (9 miles) which he reached at 11:30 and Vernon (10 miles) at 13:40. On his arrival at East Hartford at 15:35, he was met with an enthusiastic crowd who had to run along to keep up with the pedestrian near the bridge. On he went into Hartford through Morgan, Main and Asylum Streets to the Allyn House Hotel where he stayed and was sketched by Mr. Fox, the artist of *Harpers Weekly*. He was later presented with a memento of his journey: a fine Malacca cane by Mr. Whittlesey and friends of that city.

He left Hartford amongst many people and carriages, which followed him as he departed at 17:00 on Tuesday, the 5th of November, to start his second 100-mile trial. His route would take him to a point 2 miles beyond West Stockbridge, Massachusetts, via the Albany turnpike. He then walked over Talcott Mountain, passed through Avon at 19:20, passed by Igley's tavern at 20:40 and New Hartford (21 miles from Hartford) at 21:38. He then made his way through Winsted, Connecticut, before arriving at Hitchcockville at 12:15 a.m. on Wednesday, the 6th. New Boston, Massachusetts, was his next point of arrival at 02:15 before tramping through Great Barrington and finally East Lee, 19 miles from New Boston, at 08:00, where he gave up the 100-mile attempt. Due to a snow storm halting his progress, he stayed there till 16:45 before heading on, reaching West Stockbridge at 19:25 where he took supper. Emerging from there at 21:00, he continued on his epic journey.

From West Stockbridge he planned to pass through Sand Lake, New York state, on his way to Troy. He arrived at East Chatham, Columbia County, just after midnight on Thursday the 7th where he rested at the Sheridan House Hotel until 07:15 the next morning. He then recommenced his journey towards Troy via the Greenbush highway, 28 miles away, and arrived there at 14:30, thirteen hours ahead of schedule. *"He wore a conspicuous white hat, a short close fitting black coat, a ruffled shirt bosom, a pair of black pants, made after the English fashion, and a pair of army shoes, very wide at the bottom, and fixed so as to preserve his ankles. He also wore a leather belt, bearing the initials – "E. P. W." in the front."* As he headed for his quarters at the American House Hotel at a rapid pace, Captain Northrop and Sergeants English and Allen, were finding it not only difficult to keep the gathered crowds back, but his fast pace compelled them to run alongside him in order to protect the speedy fellow from his admirers who repeatedly cheered him on.

After retiring to his room for a while, he took off his shoes which he then showed to the gathered crowd, telling them and Mayor Flagg that he *"had walked thirty miles since 07:30 without stopping"* and that he *"wasn't as much fatigued as hungry."* He said he was grateful to Captain Northrop for the efficiency of the police arrangements and for keeping the people off his heels. Weston then impressed all present with his witty charm and remarks about his trip. He left the town at 18:10 after eating a hearty meal which he was charged $15 for, and sleeping for an hour. As he left, the police again found it difficult to keep up with him as they escorted him to the outskirts of town. The cheers of the immense crowd rang in his ears as he headed for Amsterdam, Montgomery County, where he would stay overnight. Weston however had failed to deliver on his second attempt at the coveted century, the excuse being due to the *"almost impassable condition of the roads."*

The enigmatic ped arrived at the Carley House Hotel in Schenectady at 22:30, where an immense crowd of people were assembled to meet him. He was now in full control of his destiny as his trainer had left him at Troy, the reasons for his departure being unclear. He left that city at 07:30 the next morning, Friday, the 8th, expecting to reach Herkimer, which was 60 miles away, by that evening. On his way there, he lunched at the Union Hotel in Amsterdam, about 17 miles from the point of his departure, before leaving at midday. He then pushed on for Fonda 10 miles distant, which he reached at 14:30. Getting away from Fonda at 16:25, he arrived at St. Johnsville, 21 miles further on, at 20:13, where he had supper at the Franklin House Hotel. Leaving there at 21:15, he reached Little Falls at 00:45 on Saturday, November the 9th where he stayed in that town's like-named hotel before departing for Utica about eight o'clock in the morning. He reached Herkimer at eleven, and by 2:30 p. m., was approaching the Mohawk River bridge accompanied by hundreds of delighted local citizens.

The *Utica Daily Observer* wrote: He was clad in a white hat, ruffled shirt, blue jacket and tight pants, with red stockings and heavy walking shoes. He is as slim and sinewy as a man can well be made, one of the best specimens of a Yankee under thirty. His hair was well brushed, and his appearance indicated preparation for a gala occasion rather than hard work. A smile lighted his face while he talked, and he spoke with a right good humor in answer to all the questions asked.

WESTON'S party were in a barouche following him, except that one walked beside or behind him. The latter and WESTON carried little riding whips, and occasionally scourge the legs of the pedestrian, to assist the circulation of the blood in his extremities.

As he was hurtling along at six miles an hour, the dapper young man went on to remark to a spectator that if it wasn't for the fact that he was suffering from a "severe attack of stomach ache for the last five miles, I would like to show the people some fast walking." The poor policemen who were escorting him must have wished they were carrying out other duties, for, try as they might, they couldn't keep up with the man of the moment, despite breaking out into a canter as the mob chased behind them into town.

Weston arrived at his hotel in Utica at 14:45, where he was welcomed by Mayor Wilson and Common Council. The *Utica Daily Observer* in it's coverage of his arrival continued: **He was then taken in charge by Mr. SOUTHWORTH, of Bagg's Hotel and conducted to a room where his shoe were taken off by one of his attendants and his limbs wrapped in a warm woolen shawl. Here the great pedestrian exhibited no signs of fatigue, but quietly seating himself at a desk proceeded to open and read the letters, papers, and dispatches which he found awaiting his arrival.**

He dined at the Bagg's House Hotel and left at 16:30 for Oneida, reaching Rome, 15 miles from there where he had supper at Stanwix Hall. Having left Rome at 20:10, he headed on into Oneida, where after arriving there at midnight, he stayed at the National Hotel during Sunday having accomplished 513 miles in eleven walking days—an average of 46 ½ miles per day.

Of his journey, the *Boston Journal* was telling its readers that: **The idea is very commonly entertained in this city and vicinity that there is something loose about the great pedestrian trip from Portland to Chicago. It has been noticed that Weston's friends have been very active in betting against his hundred miles a day performance.**

The *Providence Evening Press* meanwhile wrote: **It is generally believed Weston is in league with one or more parties who have staked large sums of money against his accomplishing the one hundred mile feat, and he will receive more money in by failing in it than he would otherwise. One rumor is that John Morrissey has made a bet of $100,000 that Weston would not do it, and that he is to give Weston $20,000 in order that he may win. There are strong evidences that he might have made the one hundred miles either in the first or second trial if he had been so disposed.**

Other unsubstantiated rumours suggested that he might be getting rides from those travelling with him. However, one man had offered to bet that Weston would perform every condition of his walk, to which the *Portland Argus* retorted: **Of course he will. Some people this way have understood that from the start.**

On Monday, the 11th of November, he turned up in Syracuse at 09:05 having arrived from Oneida 28 miles away via Fayetteville. After his stop there, which had lasted just under four hours, and where he rested at the Globe Hotel, he had intended on walking to Lyons, a trip of about 50 plus miles. However, due to a bad storm, he was compelled to spend the night in the village of Weedsport, 21 miles further up the road, which he entered at 20:05, staying the night at the Mansion House Hotel.

He set off from Weedsport on Tuesday morning at 05:30, and pushing himself along at high speed, leaving those who "*dared*" to race with him, puffing away in his wake. The weather was cold that day and the 126 steps to the minute he used to propel himself forward meant that he reached Port Byron at 06:45, and Lyons under a combination of rain and snow at 11:45, having made 24 miles despite the heavy going. Cheered at a respectful distance along the way, he made his way to the Graham House Hotel where he sat down for lunch. Of his diet en route, he was reported to eat only eggs, chicken, beef-steak and stale bread. That day at the Graham House he indulged in a rare beef-steak, fried potatoes and *"whatever else was on the table was partaken with relish."* After a 20-minute snooze the hero of the hour was back on the road at 14:00 towards Palmyra, accompanied by would-be pedestrians, who tried to keep up with him as the party headed for the next village of Newark. No chance! One by one, they fell away and headed back to Lyons to tell their family and friends, "I raced against Weston!"

He passed through Newark at 15:25 and when he reached Palmyra at 17:15 he had great difficulty reaching the Palmyra House Hotel, where he was staying due to the large group of people that crowded around him. A throng of the prettiest girls in the village applauded, smiled and fluttered their eyelashes at him from the halls and landings in the building, all no doubt mightily impressed by Weston's physique, charm and good manners, as he responded to their attentions with a bow. After a very short sleep he bounded out of his room and made a few of the fair fillies blush as he chatted to some of them before hitting the cold night air at 18:00, and the prospect of the 23-mile jaunt to Rochester. On his tramp there he passed through Macedon at 19:20, and later succeeded in passing the halfway mark of his mammoth 1,226-mile trip at Fairport when he arrived there at 22:00, a day ahead of time. Half an hour later he entered Pittsford, by which time he had marched 62 miles since the start of his day. Here he ate supper after which he set off for Rochester eight miles away, arriving there at 1:20 a.m. on Wednesday, the 13th of November.

The streets were unusually deserted when "Ned" hit town, the reason being that earlier in the evening a rumour had been spread that the ped would arrive 19:30. The story goes that a young man named Whyland dressed himself up to look like Weston. Setting off from the New England House Hotel in a carriage, the impostor drove up East Avenue, got off it, and with the carriage following behind, heeled-and-toed it into town and through the streets whilst thousands looked on. Whyland, eventually seeing the error of his ways, made his escape from State Street into Allen Street where he sought refuge in the Waverley House Hotel. What happened to him after that is anybody's guess, but it was stated he required protection from his *"deluded followers."*

According to reports, when Weston spent the night at the Congress Hall in that town, with his trainer allowing him to rest about ten hours, *"he sat in an armchair reading a paper, drinking tea, and receiving the few visitors who were admitted to his room with the greatest politeness and answering the questions put to him with the utmost readiness and courtesy."*

It was here that quite a lot of information was gleaned about the journey from Portland by the *Rochester Journal*: In an interview with Mr. Weston, we learned from him some facts which may be of interest to our readers. He considers himself thirty one hours ahead of time, exactly why we couldn't understand, as Pittsford is just half way from Portland to Chicago, and this time will be half up at noon today, making him fourteen hours ahead of time in Pittsford. His timetable, however, sets down his arrival at Batavia as to occur this morning, so he is behind that reckoning. Large numbers of telegrams await him in every place, and he answered one here declining to visit the Buffalo Opera House tonight. One of his companions stated that his strength was fully as great now as when he started from Portland. The only difficulty which he has experienced in walking was in Connecticut, where the ground was frozen in ruts, and where he sprained both ankles, though, even then, he walked five miles in two hours. Six persons accompanied him - Edward Ingalls and John T. Laphen of New York, George L. Gower of the Providence Journal, Charles Van Ornen of Albany, and D. E. Priest and E. K. Randall of Utica. The first four are judges and, the fifth an umpire to decide disputed points, and the sixth is the driver, who drove the carriage from Utica. At some places the Postmaster appointed another person to go to the next town, though no such person reached here. Mr. Weston desired us to return his thanks to the tavern keeper at Pittsford, who declined to get him a cup of tea, because, as he expressed it, "All the women were gone to bed." This was in great contrast to the treatment which he had uniformly received before that, everybody bestowing all possible attention upon him and doing everything that could be done for his comfort.

The *Davenport Daily* Gazette of Iowa on the 25th of November 1867 described in the following first paragraph, the daily procedure Weston put himself through after opening his eyes after a sleep: The moment Mr. Weston rises, he is seized by his trainers, one of whom scrapes him vigorously with a chip until he is of a bright magneta color, while another feeds him from a bottle. He is then wrapped in blankets, while his feet are carefully washed and shaved, after which they are delicately touched up with rouge to a beautiful life like tint, when he is declared ready. His clothes are then put on, the door opened, and the word given him to go. Two men follow him in a wagon, carrying spare shoes. These shoes are of the regular army pattern, plack bottomed, and made to shed rain. They were made expressly for Mr. Weston who, to prevent any foul play, sawed the wood and cut the pegs himself, and passed them out separately to the manufacturer. The leather was cut from the outside skin of a favorite ox belonging to Mr. Weston's father - this also was done to prevent foul play.

In height, Mr. Weston is somewhat spare, with well developed eyes and teeth; and has a look of general intelligence all over him. His clothes indicate that be knows his "biz." His ears are luxuriant, and the manner in which his hair is arranged shows that he has a true appreciation of the value of time. He carries his shirt in his satchel, and makes conundrums as he goes along, which he sells to the newspapers to pay his way. Some of these are very good, but bear evident, marks of haste. As the questions are sometimes got up in one town and the answers in another, they don't always hang together as well as could be desired, but that makes little difference.

P. S. Marshall

Weston left a windy Rochester at 11:20 for Buffalo after indulging in a seven-hour sleep from 02:00 till 09:00. He had previously told reporters that he denied that he was in league with those who were betting against him. Setting out on his way under a darkening sky, the athlete slightly wrenched his knee after catching his foot in the street railroad track. The road out of Rochester was muddy due to the snow that had been falling earlier, but this didn't deter his progress and his party popped into Bergen, 16 miles west of Rochester, reaching there 4h.30m after the day's start. It was here where Weston's knee was rubbed and the group had a meal. From Bergen, Weston headed towards Batavia and when he was ten miles from there, he was met a couple of miles east of Byron at about six in the evening by his friend Charles Tunicliffe of Chicago and Superintendent Reynolds of the "*Frontier Police*." Both men were anxious to make sure that the travelling group would not be met with problems on their way to Buffalo.

The party was accompanied to the Byron Centre Hotel where a short break was indulged in and where a reporter from the *Buffalo Commercial Advertiser* started to interview the walker. The interview continued as Weston walked along and the reporter later wrote of his encounter: We found him a modest, well-spoken, really polite individual– with nothing about him in the remotest degree resembling the "sporting man," or gambler; no slang, no profanity; his language and manner being that of a respectable, well bred gentleman. He remarked to us with evident pride, that there was "not a sportsman in his party." He was exceedingly cheerful, and appeared confident of winning the wager. He told us that he had never felt weary since he started, though on one occasion he had become quite sleepy. He remarked to us that he had undertaken the seemingly impossible task solely with the view of benefiting his family, consisting of a wife and one child, of whom he spoke in the most affectionate terms, and whom he was to meet in Chicago.

Besides his little riding whip, Mr. Weston carries suspended to his coat a small metal whistle, with which to signal those who accompany him - who follow in a carriage some three or four rods behind, and which is in no event to go in front of him. Mr. Weston explained the signals given by him on his whistle as follows.

One short whistle signified - "Which road?"

One long whistle - "What time is it?"

Two short whistles - Call for Mr. Gower.

Three short whistles - For the person with the bottle containing water or cold coffee for him to drink.

Four short whistles - Call for Mr. Ingalls. *

In his walk from Portland to Chicago Weston must take 2,589,312 steps. To do this in twenty-seven days he must take 95,000 steps per day. He has gained one pound in weight since he set forth on his long tramp. His walk is quick, even motion, a straight to the front step, striking heel-and-toe. His body is well set upon his legs, the action of which is principally from the knees, he swings his arms but little and carries a small whip, which he occasionally uses on himself, and on the boys that crowd in his way. He wears a suit of blue flannel jacket and knee breeches, red woollen stockings, and high laced boots, with heavy soles, (he has used up one pair already,) ruffled shirt and hat of white corded silk lined with cork. Around his waist he wears a broad canvas belt and when passing through a city he wears white cotton gloves.

We were somewhat surprised on comparing Weston's walking boots with the shoes he wears ordinarily. The later are three sizes smaller than the former, which have low heels, broad soles, and are quite heavy.

Although Weston is of strictly temperate habits, the same can not be said of his walking-shoes, as a dram of whisky is frequently given them, being poured into them by means of a small funnel inserted at the side. This is done to keep his feet from chaffing or swelling, and is said to be an excellent preventive.

All seem to be anxious that Weston shall succeed and win his wager, and we shall be pleased to chronicle that fact when his task shall have been accomplished.

*More signals found in other reports: Four blasts – "Whiskey for my shoes." Several rattling blasts - "Dogs" or a general alarm.

Reynolds had doubtless been informed that the town was expecting his arrival and large groups of people had been gathering on the way in anticipation of it. As it transpired the forces of law and order had done their job well, for when the young man hoofed it towards Main Street in the town which was lit with a huge bonfire, order was preserved by the sheriff of the county and his posse of officers. *"On entering the easterly end of the village the street was fairly alive. Not only this, but the doors, windows and balconies of the dwellings were crowded with ladies and children, all anxious to get a glimpse of the remarkable individual as he passed."* Anxious onlookers lining the streets were wondering where the great man was. *"A quarter of a mile. It is getting exciting. "He is just back of us," shouts a party who dash up the street and dismount at the hotel amidst various conjectures as to whether Superintendent Reynolds, who is of the number, is the trainer of the now famous youth. A moment more and Weston's white hat gleams in the moonlight along Bank Street, and amid the cheers of the multitude he turns into Main Street and faces for the hotel. The crowd close in behind him."*

At 20:45, the man of the moment clambered up the stairs leading into the lobby of the Eagle Hotel, went upstairs to a room previously reserved for him and stood at the window, to be greeted by the cheers from outside. (Weston by the way, according to his custom, had changed his dress before entering the village and appeared in a double-breasted frock coat and ruffled shirt.) Thereafter he took a comfortable position on an inviting sofa and had his shoes taken off. These at once became an object of curiosity to those in the room and he began laughing and joking with all; *"Indeed he did not appear at all fatigued, and went through the operation of standing on his hands, to see, as he said, if his arms were in as good condition as his lower limbs."* Some ladies were invited in and allowed to chat with him for a while, but when asked to leave by his trainer, Weston protested saying, "Well, you see I'm in better humour than last night." The disappointed fillies withdrew with one making the comment, "Why, what a little hand he has," as she left the room.

Weston settled down to a dinner of beefsteak and chicken and glanced over jealously as his fellow diners seasoned their meals with accompaniments, of which cranberry sauce caught Weston's eye. He turned to his trainer who said to him, "If you don't eat it, it can't hurt you," and with that Superintendent Reynolds ate the sauce instead, much to Weston's disgust.

Young Eddy retired to bed at 22:00. As he slept, the horses, which had been pulling the coach behind him for 205 miles since Utica, munched away at their meal in the warmth of the hotel's stables. His sleep didn't last for long for he was soon hard at it again, after leaving Batavia just after two o'clock on the morning of Thursday the 14th, after which he passed Corfu at 05:59, Aldan at 06:40 and arrived in Millgrove at 08:45 where breakfast was taken at the *"Traveler's Home."*

The following paragraph from the *Davenport Daily Gazette* of the 25th of November describes Weston's approach to the outskirts of his next port of call: **Buffalo is a great place, and the man who was born there needn't do anything else but be proud of it all the rest of his life. Everybody there was on the lookout for Weston. All the standing places on the Rochester road for three miles out had been taken up two days previous by the Buffalonians. It was beautiful sight to see them standing in two rows, all with telescopes pointed down the road, like two ranks of the militia aiming by right and left oblique. A native informed us that telegrams had been received from Weston, engaging beds at the Tift, Courtier, Bonney's, and the National; private boxes at the different theaters, and a cell at each station house. The man said it was policy. Weston wanted to please the Buffalonians. Shrewd Weston!**

Weston made his entrance into Buffalo via the Bowmansville Road into Genesee Street at a point a mile and a half beyond the first toll-gate where the crowds started to gather. Reynolds had instructed Captain Nicholson of Precinct No. 1 to ready his detail of 24 patrolmen to wait at that point to escort the pedestrian into the city. At midday and to shouts of "He is coming!" the roving pedestrian appeared, accompanied by a crowd of people and numerous vehicles. Amongst the chaos of the traffic, he moved along the crowded Main Street and zoomed up Eagle Street at a pace that left everybody behind him running along to keep up. He eventually passed the town clock at 12:48 and entered the Mansion House Hotel, where he quickly took of his shoes, leaving masses of people outside with their memory of the day they saw Weston coming into town.

Initially it was stated that he planned to leave at five o'clock in the evening, but other reports suggested he would leave at midnight on his proposed 100-mile hike to Erie, Pennsylvania, after visiting the theatre.

On the 22nd of November, the *Ohio Democrat* gave some insight on what happened after Weston *left* Buffalo (the report was in **bold**):

BUFFALO, Nov. 15: Weston, after remaining here part of yesterday and last night and visiting the theater, left early this morning for his walk west. By calculation here he has to make 53 ¼ miles daily to get to Chicago in the next eleven days.

Weston's visit to the theatre that evening produced cheering and applause as he sat in one of the boxes. He left his hotel at 06:35 stating he was 74 miles ahead of time and that he never felt better. On his way out of the city, and after passing the swing bridge across the creek, he strode along the road known as the "Tift farm," which, for a couple of miles, proved difficult to walk on due to the amount of sand blown across it from the beach. The police force that had initially escorted him out of Buffalo turned back beyond the toll-gate and left him with but four of the *"harbor police"* and a few stragglers. When he arrived at Crandall's tavern eight miles out of the city, he said goodbye to Reynolds whom he thanked for his help. He later arrived at Evan's Center, 20 miles from his departure point at 11:05, had lunch and left at midday for…………

SILVER CREEK, N. Y. Nov. 15: Everything promises gaily for the hundred mile tramp of Weston. He dined here in the best of spirits at 3:05 P.M., having walked from Buffalo, 36 miles eight hours and thirty-five minutes. He ate a hearty meal, and after receiving some calls, went to bed. He rose at 9:15, ate heartily, and left with a rush at 10:15. The weather is cloudy, the wind southwest and against him. He says he will reach Ashtabula tomorrow night, or lose his legs. He is nervous and apprehensive of foul play by some one opposed to his success, but is otherwise in perfect health and spirits. He is a wonder; he walks with a splendid sweeping stride that carries him over the road like the wind. Four miles and a half per hour is an easy gait for him; and, barring accidents, the next 24 hours will see the great hundred mile walk an accomplished fact. The Sheriff of Chataqua County and his deputy accompany him as an escort, and a carriage with lamps goes before as a guide. Dan Rice and P. T. Barnum are at Erie; the former is making arrangements for an escort for Weston through Erie county. The interest and enthusiasm of the people increase with every mile.

ERIE, Midnight: The weather is cloudy, and the wind is blowing half a gale from the southwest, and almost directly in his teeth, but the roads are good and he shows the greatest pluck, talking little but cheerily, declaring that unless his feet come off they should land him in Ashtabula at 10:50 P. M., Nov. 16.

He evinces some little nervous apprehension of the danger of untoward accidents. I do not think that he fears, as has been intimated, anything like foul play on the part of his opponents in the large wager which is depending upon the result of this unprecedented effort. But, this nervousness is due, rather, to the unfortunate experiences he has already had, having been seriously bruised in Connecticut by falling under the press of a curious crowd which rushed on and trampled over him, and also again, this side of Rochester, when his foot caught in the rails on the track and threw him down. It is only misfortunes of this sort that he seems to dread.

He expresses great confidence in his ability to dine at Erie tomorrow, and to take tea, by invitation, with Dan Rice at Girard, and that confidence is generally shared by the people here and elsewhere along the route.

The excitement here over the matter is really extraordinary. Everybody is discussing it and all eager for the latest rumor concerning the pedestrian hero. It is needless to add that the sympathies and good wishes of all are with him.

Weston arrived at North East, Pennsylvania at 08:55, in a journey time of 10h.5m from Silver Creek. That trek included a break of 55m for breakfast at Ripley, having earlier passed through Westfield at 05:17. He walked the distance of six miles from the State Line to North East in a time of 55 minutes. At North East, he took a light lunch and proceeded on his way at 09:00, *"Erieward nearly sixteen miles distant, at a five mile gait."* Again he was followed by the usual misfits who thought they had better legs than his, but he saw them all off. Indeed, it was only the horses that could keep up with him as they went along at a *"Methodist preacher's trot."* At 10:52, he passed the *"brick yard,"* six miles west of Erie, having made ten miles in less than two hours. The wind from the west blew dust in his face as he showed some sign of fatigue in his relentless pursuit of his prize.

King of the Peds

The pedestrian was morbidly sensitive about being approached closely whilst at work, evidently fearful that someone with a pecuniary interest in the result of his task would tread on his feet and therefore handicap him. He always walked in a clear space of some 10 feet in diameter, preceded and followed by one of his attendants, whose duty it was to see that the *"charmed circle was not intruded upon."* On this part of the road, those attendants were having some difficulty in keeping anyone who wanted to intrude into that personal space, away from him. He slowed his pace down somewhat four miles out of town as he inspected a bundle of letters that was thrust into his hand. After this the crowds really began to build up. All of a sudden there were several thousand souls rushing behind him eager to keep up with him, whilst an equal amount stood behind fences offering him encouragement. It took the best efforts of Chief Crowley and his men to keep the mob away from getting in his way, but his posse did a splendid job. Weston was able to gain entrance through a side door of the National Hotel at Erie, after which he responded to the appreciative crowd, who waited to see him go by, waving and doffing his hat in acknowledgement to the *"three times three"* which he received from them. As was predicted, some in the crowd made the usual rush to the door, with some lucky ones getting in. However, Crowley and his men beat them back, thus allowing the nervous pedestrian time to relax.

Inside, Weston, appearing tense and irritable, was having strong words with his advisor Mr. Ingalls. He was asked whether he could make the hundred miles and replied, "Yes, sometime next week if they time me like they are doing now," and later, when he was about to leave to recommence his journey and referring to the timekeepers he said, "I am well, but very much annoyed." He was reported to be finding fault with everything, especially those hired to *look after him and was reported to have *"cried like a child."* His tantrum didn't last long however as he was observed tucking into beef-steak, potatoes, toast, bread, butter and coffee. His appetite was immense, but the energy he used in walking at such a rapid rate in such a short distance of time needed replenishing; those watching him devour his meal were in awe of how much the man could consume.

*There was considerable sympathy for Weston by the reporters who travelled with him. Many felt that he wasn't getting the service he deserved from those who were employed to support him on his journey. One wrote: "With probably two exceptions, he has not a man with him that is any benefit to him. There seems to be a peculiar lack of judgment in all their movements. Nobody seems willing to do anything for his principal unless he is requested to do it." Another later wrote: "He likened them to six pine sticks, and intimated that the number of pieces of timber would do him as much good as the six blood and flesh objects who accompany him as a body guard."

Having gone through his usual procedure of pouring whiskey into his shoes to prevent his feet from getting sore, Weston left South Erie and started *"on the line of his march"* at 12:55. Outside, it was both windy and raining on the Ridge Road where he continued his hike. He thereafter made good progress towards Girard, which was 16 miles away and reached there at 15:20, going at a rate of a mile every 9m.4s. *"The walk of the pedestrian is in itself a novelty. He is a little man, but has an immense stride. He steps out fully three and a half feet, with a light springing bound, planting down his foot firmly, and withdrawing it as cleanly as a horse, and almost as rapidly."*

It was on the road side at Girard where he met Colonel Dan Rice (the showman and Presidential candidate) and his family. There he indulged in conversation, and unusually for Weston, drank a glass of wine. He was also presented with a bouquet by Rice's daughter.

After that, the party headed on towards Conneaut, via Springfield, with Weston walking in the middle of two attendants, who later carried lanterns to light the way. These two men it is thought were supplied by Mr. Rice, as there were fears that Weston might be attacked on the way. Weston was said to have consumed a couple of spoonfuls of brandy, and continued to pour whisky into his shoes to soothe his sore feet.

CONNEAUT, OH., NOV. 16: Weston arrived here at 8:12 p.m. His feet were so badly swollen that he could proceed no further tonight, thus failing to make the hundred miles.

Weston ended up staying at the Tremont House Hotel, which was 9 miles short of the proposed 100 miles he had tried for. *"His shoes were pulled off and his feet were sore and discolored."* The footsore youth then stated that although he was very tired, he thought he could make the required distance. However, he was advised not to by Ingalls who cautioned against the notion, saying that if he tried, he would probably be laid up for the rest of the week. Time was running short and Weston had to make up his mind quickly. Ultimately he decided not to try to make up what was required.

This third failed attempt on his journey to make the required "ton" provoked strong suspicion that, for some reason, Weston didn't want to go the distance. The distance from Silver Creek to Conneaut was 91 miles and that left a further nine miles to make in the time available, which was, more or less, 3 mph. As he appeared in good spirits on his arrival and had been moving himself along at speeds of up to 5 mph, his failure to continue the "trial" couldn't be accounted for.

Under the heading: **Why Weston Failed,** the correspondent covering the story for the *Cleveland Herald* wrote: The Weston "hundred mile" farce was played out here tonight, or rather it stopped short, with nine miles lacking of its being played out. I have no personal grudge against Weston, not having been, as some have, "done out" of a few stamps by his failure - nor ability - to come to time, but I have a strong feeling those who "backed their opinion" that he would do the hundred miles have been victimized by - somebody. Just look at it.

Weston sets out on his one hundred mile journey, does half of it with perfect ease, gaining time all the way, and with no signs of fatigue; makes three fourths of the journey, still ahead of time and not suffering in the least, swings along the last part of the stretch at the rate of five miles and a half an hour, as fresh as a lark, and has but nine miles more to go with three hours and seven minutes to do it in, when he - no, not he, but the men who have him in charge - declare that he can go no farther, that his feet are badly swollen, and that to accomplish the nine miles might peril the chance of performing the walk to Chicago within the stipulated time. Swelled feet indeed! Who ever heard of a man with badly swelled feet hopping along hour after hour at the rate of from five to five and a half miles per hour? His friends (?) say he will do the hundred miles yet, beginning near Cleveland. Perhaps he will, in fact. I feel assured if he can and will, if he is permitted, but I have no desire to bet on the fact of his doing so.

It is said - perhaps it may not be true - that the whole thing is a "put up," that Weston is hired by his backer and "opponent" for $4,000 to walk from Portland to Chicago in 30 days; that between the two points he is to be wholly under the control of the "ring" who tell him when to go and when to stop; that the hundred miles attempts and failures are made according to direction, and are manoeuvred so as to rope in the green ones, and that Weston, having sold himself under those conditions considers the whole affair a legitimate transaction so far as he is concerned, and will live up to his bargain, although he bitterly feels the degrading fact of his being made a stool pigeon by the men who have him under control.

In confirmation of the story that the backer and opponent of Weston are in "cahoots," is the fact at Erie, the man who, east of that place, pretended to represent the interest of his opponent, was the one who poured whisky into his shoes and gave all his wants close personal attention.

Weston has had no trainer; never had a trainer; does not require a trainer. I have not the slightest doubt that he can make the hundred miles in twenty four hours whenever he chooses to do so or whenever his owners choose that he shall do it. The story of Morrissey winning from eighty to a hundred thousand dollars on the failure was probably started to induce others to bet that Weston would fail to make the next 100 miles.

The apprehension of danger so plainly manifested by Weston, in all of his movements arises from the fact that persons who are not in the "ring," may attempt private personal injury - perhaps death - in order to win large sums of money against him.

Weston himself, in addition to the sum which he is to receive from his walk, is realising a handsome amount of from the sale of photographs along the route.

My advice to every one disposed to "arbitrate something" for or against Weston, is to "go lightly." What he can do, there is no knowing - it is evident he can do more than he has done. What he will do, is altogether another affair. The best and most reliable horses in a race have their speed regulated by their jockeys, and the action of the jockeys regulated by their bets, "A word to the wise is sufficient."

However, a very different perspective was shed on Weston's effort by Dan Rice who was later to write a letter to the *Cleveland Herald*:

The night he started from Silver Creek, and after he had commenced his long tramp, I drove with my family from Erie to my home, through a storm almost as violent as any I have ever, in my long experience, encountered on the road. The wind – which it should be borne in mind, was almost directly in the pedestrians face – blew so tremendously that the ladies were greatly alarmed and apprehensive that the carriage would be overturned. Clouds of dust and gravel were flying in our faces, compelling the driver to stop a number of times, as both he and the horses were completely blinded. Nor was it a temporary commotion of the elements, for almost a

hurricane kept full possession of the night, and even until the next evening the wind was so high as to very seriously retard fast walking, and spiteful snow squalls contributed their cold and wet quota of elementary opposition. Both nights too were very dark, and the lanterns carried by Weston's attendant walkers scarcely dispelled the gloom sufficiently to insure safe footing.

Everyone the least experienced in such matters concluded that Mr. Weston would abandon his third trial on Friday night, but they underrated both his pluck and his wonderful powers of endurance.

Whilst out in the storm, my mind reverted to him with considerable apprehension, and I did not deem it possible for him to proceed. Judge, then, of my astonishment when I learned the next morning that he had successfully battled through that long tempestuous night and was untiringly striding on to apparent victory.

Every four miles he accomplished then was equivalent to five miles under ordinary circumstances, and cost him a much greater effort to make the ninety miles he did than it would have done to have walked one hundred in pleasant weather, over the same roads.

The distance covered in this part of the walk proved to be most controversial and was dealt with later in an article in the *Cleveland Plain Dealer* entitled: **Weston's One Hundred Miles:**

Although it has gone out to the world that Weston failed in his, five several attempts to walk 100 miles in 21 hours, the *Plain Dealer* claims that he did make it in his third effort from Silver Creek to Conneaut. But more than this, we assert that he has already accomplished the hundred mile feat. Let us examine the distance from Silver Creek to Conneaut, and we leave it to any fair and candid reader if he has not achieved the Herculean undertaking. From Buffalo to Brockton, according to Weston's published time table, is exactly 54 miles, and Silver Creek, his starting point, is 30 miles from Buffalo, leaving, therefore, 24 miles to Brockton. From Brockton to Erie is 46 1/2 miles, 16 from Erie to Girard, and 14 miles from Girard to Conneaut, making in the aggregate 100 miles, and not nine miles short of the one hundred as at first so persistently asserted. Let our reader's judge for themselves; we have taken some pains to ascertain the actual distance from Silver Creek to Conneaut, and find that we are correct. A gentleman who is now acting as ticket agent on the C. & K. road, and who was long connected with the Stage Company as agent on that route, stated that the distance from Silver Creek to Conneaut by the stage road, was always called 101 miles.

NB: Weston was later to complain bitterly on his arrival in Chicago about the anomaly in distance. It was later mentioned by the press that that part of the route would be surveyed and accurately measured to determine the truth of the matter.

Whilst Weston was in or around Conneaut, the journalists at the *Titusville Morning Herald* were getting themselves in a right old lather about their meeting with the famous fellow. In the edition of the 19th of November, they wrote: We met the great pedestrian Saturday, and upon mentioning that we once walked to *Hydetown and back were shown every attention. In our opinion Mr. Weston is the greatest man that the world ever saw. George Washington and Grant will be forgotten, but "Westy" never, he kindly allowed us to pull off his boots (which are "No. nine's" and copper-toed) and gauze upon his pedal extremities. - We have never seen finer looking hoofs, he is slightly web-footed, which is an immense assistance to him in walking against the wind. He has only one corn, about the size of a hen's egg, and says that he shall not raise his own corn any longer than after this trip.

Weston would have accomplished his one hundred miles if he had not "stubbed" his toe against an empty whisky bottle near Conneaut. He says he will not run for president against Grant but will if nominated, walk against him. His personal appearance is very prepossessing, but since his march commenced, his calves (which he takes along with him,) have increased in size until they resemble young cows. So afraid is he of getting injured by those who are betting against him that Saturday, as a citizen of Erie thrust a piece of Bologna towards him, he cried out, "I'm stabbed!" and keeled over. He is very nervous. He spans six feet with his two feet with every step he takes. - ** He is realizing quite a handsome profit from the sale of his pictures.

*Hydetown is three and a half miles from Titusville.

**Weston was said to have sold tens of thousands of pictures of himself on his journey. It was said that he sold 60,000 of these before he reached Buffalo, thus making for himself $15,000. It is reasonable to suppose that he made that amount after Buffalo.

In the same edition, a further small report regarding his photographs was found. It read: "If Weston arrives at Titusville between nine o'clock tonight, he will stop at the Pendleton, where our citizens can buy photographs of his "great feet" at a dollar each."

After his stay in Conneaut, Weston set off for Painsville, which was 42 miles away, on Monday, the 18th at 02:00, reaching that destination at 13:23 via Ashtabula, which he stopped at for half an hour or so between the hours of five and six o'clock. It was at Painsville that he had a meal and at 15:20 set off from for Cleveland 29 miles away. He was expected to reach there at 21:00, but in fact got there 3h.18m later, having stopped at Willoughby for supper between six and seven o'clock earlier. It was in Cleveland that he slept at the Kennard House Hotel.

His Arrival in Cleveland:

Weston glided into Cleveland from Conneaut, on Monday night at 12 o'clock under flying colours and as gay as a lark. The citizens were out in mass to greet him, men, women and children.

On Tuesday morning he continued his western tramp, in the best of spirits.

He has yet to walk from Cleveland to Chicago, 343 miles, and has till the close of the 28th inst. to do it - a fraction over 38 miles a day, which he can accomplish like atop, baring accidents. He has yet two trials for the one hundred miles in 24 hours, if he wishes to try it again.

Despite the above report, Weston actually left Cleveland at 14:45 on the afternoon of the 19th and headed for Fremont. There were reports that a 14-year-old boy who worked for the *Cleveland Leader*, and who was described as the *"devil of that office,"* walked with him from Cleveland to Berea 17 miles away, arriving there at 18:42, and on time too. The boy's name was Weston! It is not known whether the ped bought his namesake his supper at Berea, but what is known is that the party left that place at 20:40 for Grafton, 12½ miles further on, at 23:30 where they spent the night.

On Wednesday, the 20th of November, no time was lost in hitting the trail again at 09:25, destination: Lagrange, which was five miles away. Here he had a 40-minute rest before heading for Wakeman and then Norwalk, where the *"Walkist"* was reportedly thrown down and hurt by the boisterous crowd, and where he was said to become very *"nervous and excited."* Having failed to sleep, he listened to some music in the parlour before recommencing his journey at 22:40 to walk firstly to Clyde, and then to Bellevue, which he left at 10:37 the next day Thursday, having stayed all night at the town's Exchange Hotel.

On entering the city of Fremont, where he arrived at 14:35, *"The crowd pressed upon him so closely that it was feared he would sustain serious injury but the police succeeded in keeping them off. Whether they intended personal injury or the rush was merely the result of the excitement which prevailed is a mooted question."*

Having had a meal at Kessler's Hotel, he left Fremont at 16:37. Considering he was hiking on a rough road, he made good time as he made his way towards Elmore at a rate of 5 mph, arriving at the town's name hotel at 20:20. He then headed off for Toledo at 21:25, and on his way passed through the Black Swamp before arriving at his intended destination at 02:11 on Friday, the 22nd. It was here where he stayed overnight at the Olive House Hotel for 12 hours before starting off for Bryan via Stryker at 14:15. From there he would make his fourth attempt to accomplish the task of making 100 miles in 24 hours, the distance ending one mile short of Rome, Indiana.

The reporter for the *Chicago Tribune*, who was travelling with the party, took up the next part of the journey: Leaving Toledo, we passed over a good level road, quite elastic and hard, and in every way favorable for walking. He accomplished the first five miles out in one hour and five minutes. At a distance of seven miles from Toledo, Weston made his first halt, when he drank a big swig of what looked very much like old rye, but which I am informed, was molasses and water. I presume he drank half a pint of the liquor. About a gill of whiskey was emptied into his shoes at this point. The crowd continued with us as far as Springfield, eleven miles distant, which point we passed at twenty four minutes passed four o'clock. Along the route, crowds were gathered at various distances apart, who cheered the pedestrian on with pleasant remarks, such as, "How are your poor feet Weston?" "Have you sold the race?"

Weston does not think much of the people on the way. He is particularly down on Toledo, the people of which town he does not think bid the fair thing by him. He had to wait two hours after reaching the Olive House this morning at two o'clock, before he could obtain a cup of tea, and this afternoon, as we quit the city, the police escort demanded ten dollars which was paid to them.

King of the Peds

The party ate supper in Delta where they stayed for 1h.20m and after that headed towards Wauseon, six miles further on at 21:00. Whilst on his journey there, his attendants failed to light the lanterns until after Weston had tripped over roots and stones in the road, causing him to fall to the ground on a couple of occasions, an event which reinforced Weston's and the reporters opinion of the *so-called* support, his *so-called* "team" were giving him.

The timetable that Weston judged his distances by gave the distance between Toledo and Delta as 26 miles, when in fact it was 28. The timetable had been written before he left Portland upon information given to him by postmasters, as to distances between towns on the journey. However, many of them had misunderstood the situation, giving the distance as travelled by railroad, and *not* turnpike, which meant that the bends on the roads were not taken into consideration. This meant that Weston suffered as a result of some significant discrepancies in the calculated distances. To illustrate the point, the six miles to Wauseon turned out to be eight, and when he headed off towards Archibold thinking that would be six too, it actually turned out to be ten.

It was at Archibold which he reached at 01:10 on Saturday morning, where he talked of abandoning his 100-mile attempt. However, a meal of oatmeal gruel seemed to perk him up and he continued on the six-mile journey to Stryker which he reached at 02:45, and where he subsequently held a *"council of war"* at the Eagle Hotel.

Whilst Weston sat in a rocking chair and studied his timetable with his crew and some principal men in the town, the commotion caused by his visit had woken up the slumbering citizens, who, when they heard who had arrived in town, rushed down to the building he occupied to see him for themselves. A huge crowd gathered outside the kerosene lit room he sat in, and because the shades were raised, they had an inhibited view of the man all America was talking about. As they gazed at him, Weston made the decision to abandon the trail there and then. A number of straw mattresses were found for him and the rest of the troop, the blinds were lowered and everybody slept for five hours till daybreak. Breakfast for Weston consisted of fried eggs, the mandatory raw beef-steak, stale bread, crackers and several cups of *"good tea."*

The *Defiance Democrat*, of Defiance, Ohio, provided a most interesting little story of what happened when a local lady tried to get a little too close to the pedestrian: The ladies of Stryker, Williams County, surmount all obstacles in pursuing their anatomical and physiological studies, us the following sketch shows: This morning whilst Mr. Weston was performing his toilet at Stryker, he having been assigned a sleeping apartment in the ladies parlor, a good looking female, probably not more than thirty years of age, made several applications to see the pedestrian, but was told that she must wait until he was ready to receive company. Knowing where he was located, the undaunted female stationed herself near the door of his apartment, and after making several valiant efforts to force a passage, finally seemed willing to abide the issue. She remained quiet a few seconds, when someone of the attendants on the pedestrian having occasion to enter his room, the sly female managed to crush in behind him, and before Weston, who was almost entirely "en dishabille," could seize upon a convenient garment to cover himself, she was in the centre of the room. A scene seldom witnessed pursued. The woman was instantly ejected from the apartment, but then her curiosity to see the pedestrian was gratified and she went among her friends triumphant. Weston remarked; "The woman beats the devil."

From Stryker, he headed off towards Bryan at 11:25 on a beautiful sunny day *"through broken country, well cleared of timber, but presenting a parched and desolate appearance, the late drought telling terribly upon the grass,"* with the *"fall wheat looking sickly and yellow."* On reaching Bryan at 14:00 he felt a bit peckish and so popped into the town's hotel where he ordered some tea and crackers. After the light meal he asked the waitress for a napkin. Not being able to understand the request, she asked a fellow waitress to address it, and it was she who promptly informed Weston that all the napkins had been eaten earlier at the other table, but, if he wanted to wait, she would bake some for him. "Ned" declined the offer, paid his bill and left.

He was then met by the Deputy Sheriff W. E. Callender of Edgerton who had arrived with a group of men to make sure he got to that town safely. Leaving Bryan at 15:00, they reached Edgerton without problems at 17:58 and rested a short while before heading off to Waterloo via Butler in Indiana 17 miles away at 19:35. Hurtling along at 6 mph, and grateful to the citizens who held up lanterns and *"transparencies"* to light his way, he reached the village of Butler, eight miles up the road, at 21:35. Here he was met with a real treat because not only had the whole population turned out to see him, but they had lit numerous bonfires to greet him. Although he was doubtless humbled by his reception, he sped through the little place. Then, walking on an unsuitable track, he pushed himself along, covering the nine miles to his next stop at Waterloo in a little less than two hours, reaching the Lent's Hotel at 23:32, where another magnificent bonfire lit up his path. Waterloo was where he would put his feet up during Sunday, after which he would make his fifth and final attempt to make the required century of miles in a day.

Weston slept in the bridal suite of the hotel after having his head bathed in lukewarm water. The day after, he was doubtless woken by the throngs gathered outside. Dressed up in his finery of *"an elegant suit of broadcloth, patent leather boots, and green kids to match,"* he was whisked off to the United Brethren Meeting House in a carriage for the Sunday service, the normally used Presbyterian Church being closed for repairs. However, the quiet service that he expected turned out to be a bit of a disaster in that it was ruined by the behaviour of some mischievous young boys, one of whom tried to steal his handkerchief. Whilst he was away, the young *"darkey,"* employed to clean his walking shoes, put them on and walked up and down the main street exclaiming to the amused hoards who followed him, "I golly, how deeze ere shoes does make a feller lite out!" After lunch at 13:00 Weston went to bed where he slept till ten o'clock in the evening, just as the rain started to fall.

The party started from Waterloo at 00:26 on Monday, the 25th towards Corunna and Kendallville, reporters being informed that the pedestrian was in *"capital health and spirits and full of confidence."* The man himself was attired in a light coloured rubber coat which reached to his knees, a pair of black rubber leggings which went up to his waist, a cape and a waterproof cap. He reached Corunna, seven miles away, at 02:00 precisely, and Kendalville, 14 miles from Waterloo at 03:50, having stopped at Edding's Corners to have the *"stickiest kind of yellow mud"* scraped off his costume. Weston's language towards one of his guides–– who took him a mile out of his way due to misdirecting him towards Rome City rather than Rome Station (now Brimfield?) on the way to Wawaka–– was of course unprintable in the newspapers, but he did reach Wawaka at 07:05 and from there Ligonier at 09:17, where he took breakfast at the Crosby House Hotel. Now attired in a pair of sky blue tights and a chequered flannel undershirt, having shed his *"duds"* at the hotel, he left Ligonier amongst the usual hangers on at 10:00. His plan was to walk to Elkhart where he would have dinner and finish his task six and a half miles east of Laporte, Indiana, at Rolling Prarie, or as he put it in his own words, "die in the effort."

About two miles east of Goshen, as he made his approach to the town, he was met by *"a large number of able bodied *Hoosiers headed by the Goshen Brass Band in full uniform,"* who, as soon as he came into view, played "Hail to the Chief." The citizens were mightily disappointed that the famous pedestrian didn't honour their town by spending a few minutes, as he made his way past the Violette House Hotel at 14:20. He, unfortunately for them, was in too much of a hurry to get to Elkhart, and paid no attention to a giant of a man named called **John Casey who was a shoemaker in Goshen. The grand sum of $600 had been wagered by Casey's friends that he couldn't beat Weston into Elkhart. Casey, who had $10 on himself to succeed, won his bet arriving 28 minutes ahead of Weston, who sauntered along at 4½ mph, apparently oblivious of his unknown competitor's aspirations. Casey, *"the winner,"* was escorted into town by the Elkhart Brass Band where they left him at the Clifton House Hotel to turn back down the road to greet and escort into town the real hero of the hour.

At the Clifton House, and whilst eating supper, Weston stated that he had walked 70 of his 100 miles and that meant he only needed to reach New Carlisle to accomplish his feat. He also told reporters that if the 100 miles was disputed, he would personally go back and measure the distance with an odometer after reaching Chicago. However, there were many in the town who said that he would not make the distance and that he would pretend to break down east of New Carlisle.

*Hoosier (native or resident of Indiana) is a term in Indiana that apparently has been used for 150 years.

On the 4th of December 1867, the *Sheboygan County Herald*, Sheboygan Falls, Wisconsin, reported that: **Casey, a man who walked from Goshen to Elkhart ten miles, and beat Weston twenty eight minutes on Monday, on a bet of $40, is dead. The *Davenport Daily Gazette* however, brought him back to life when they reported: FORT WAYNE: Dec. 9.–John Casey, C. Barnhart and T. A. Gilmore, started at 2:20 yesterday, to walk from Goshen to this place, a distance of 57 miles, the match being on the quickest possible time. Casey entered this place alone, having accomplished the distance in 13 hours, an extremely fast rate speed considering the condition of the roads. Barnhart gave out after walking 20 miles, and Gilmore, after having accomplished 40 miles. About $3,000 changed hands upon the result. Casey is the man who beat Weston from Goshen to Elkhart.

King of the Peds

The weather was dark and rain threatened when Weston left Elkhart at 17:05, accompanied by several hundred citizens in carriages. The road thereafter was sandy and wet, and in many places, entirely covered in water. He reached Mishawaka at 19:45 having accomplished 11 miles in 2h.40m. It was near here he was met by a group of amateur pedestrians who carried lanterns and torches to illuminate the way for the plucky young athlete. All of them tried to keep up with the fast fellow, but all had to resort to either running, or adopting a slow trot as they splashed along in the mud and slush. *"One big raw boned Hoosier woman overtook the pedestrian as he was just entering the village and kept up with him until he had reached a point two miles west of the town. She felt very proud of her achievement, and was heard to exclaim, "I'll bet forty cents that that I could keep up with him to Chicago."* After Mishawaka, the rain caused problems for Weston and his progress was curtailed somewhat due to streams running across the road. At one point, a log had to be thrown over one in order to continue.

Weston arrived at South Bend at 21:00. He was immediately surrounded by one of the wildest and noisiest crowds of men, women and children. *"They were perfectly crazy evincing an entire disregard for their personal safety, by rushing madly forward, stumbling over one another in their desire to see the pedestrian. Weston was pushed and crushed and trampled upon at every step of his progress as the band played in the background."* He eventually managed to scramble into the Dwight House Hotel, which was stormed by some of the mob whilst others amused themselves by breaking the building's windows with stones.

In his room, he informed the press that he had given up the 100-mile attempt, blaming the conditions of the roads and claiming that there were discrepancies in the distances. He said that he had actually made 86 miles instead of the 76 that he had been credited with. He informed reporters that it was utterly impossible to reach New Carlisle, which was 14 miles away, in the 2¾ hours remaining of the allocated 24. "I cant' do it and I'll be damned if I am going to kill myself in the effort!" he said, going on to complain of a sore ankle which he mentioned had been trampled on by the crowd.

By the time he left South Bend, he had been joined by a deputation of Chicago police, consisting of Superintendent Nelson, Capt. Hickey and Sergeants Garbing and Moore, who would follow his party from there to the end of his race. The men had been hired some time before his travels because of the belief that there were some people who were determined to either, poison, abduct, or even assassinate him as he made his final bid for glory. Weston was also joined by two old friends, Will Tunnicliffe and Mr. C. C. Chase, who had met him at the Dwight House.

At 09:55, on the 26th of November, Weston began his march from his hotel in South Bend to his next destination: the village of New Carlisle. Drama was to follow seven miles into this stage of the journey when a Mr. Dalton, who was some way ahead of the party, fell from his seat whilst steering his carriage up a hill, causing him to get his coat trapped in the wheel. His frantic attempts to release himself caused him to shatter the bones in his arm, the unfortunate accident holding up Weston for a considerable length of time. Further on, one of the reporters tagging along decided to try his hand at speed walking, but he came a cropper when he landed on his back in a mud hole after his attempt to jump over it failed, much to the amusement of those who watched. Weston's two friends wanting a piece of the action joined him on the road and kept up with him for 1h.20m until they reached Terre Coupe at 11:45. Here the entire population of the village turned out to see him before he toddled on to Plainfield, a mile and a half west of there, before arriving at New Carlisle which he left at 3 p.m.

After initially travelling along at 6 mph, he slowed himself down and this might have been because of an incident which emotionally affected him, causing him to shed a few tears. Apparently as he was walking past a house on his way to Laporte, he came across an old lady who led a *"beautiful young woman"* out on to the road to meet him. As the woman's hand was placed in his, he was told that she had lost her sight as a child and that she took a great interest in his personal welfare. It was said that nothing had touched him more than his meeting with the blind girl.

He reached the Teagarden House Hotel in Laporte at 18:17 where he remained for the night, due to a change of plan. Originally, he was to spend just a couple of hours resting at the hotel before starting out for Calumet 17 miles to the west. However, the arrival of Mr. Van Orden changed all that because of Orden's suggestion that it would be better to enter Chicago on Thanksgiving Day, as there would be more people around to greet the "ped."

The next day, the 27th, the newspapers of Chicago were telling their readers that the pedestrian would not arrive in the city that day as expected. The reason offered by the journalist for not proceeding to Calumet as planned, was the *"lack of trusty guidance"* and Weston's mistrust of strangers for fear of being misled.

Many *"sporting men"* who had apparently put bets on Weston accomplishing the last of his 100-mile trials were calling the affair a *"cheat and a dodge."* However, his failure did not stop any interest in his overall achievement and much chaos was expected as the victorious pedestrian made his way into the city. Plans were already being made to control the thousands of people that were expected to watch the enigmatic character arrive.

Weston and friends left Laporte at 05:10 on the 27th of November. The route taken was initially through unbroken swampy country covered in many places with dense undergrowth of young pines and burr oaks. The first four miles were covered before sunrise and he reached the village of Pinhook, or New Durham, which was 17½ miles from Laporte. All the villagers, which consisted of the postmaster, the grocer, the blacksmith and their families, had been waiting in the cold for him since 9 o'clock the previous evening. Weston was deeply touched by the villagers' attentions and what happened next was reported by the *Chicago Tribune*: In order to show his appreciation of the kindly feelings of the villagers, Mr. Weston prevailed upon Sergeant Tom Moore to review the "body guard," this was done in magnificent style, and the masterly manner in which the "boys in blue" went through the military evolutions elicited the approbation of the entire population of Pinhook otherwise New Durham, situated in Laporte County, Indiana.

ENCOUNTER WITH AN INTELLIGENT NATIVE

While this performance was going on, one of the natives, a long legged, raw-boned, big fisted individual, who presided at the "corner grocery," stepped up to the carriage containing Superintendent Nelson, and in the peculiar dialect of the backwoodsmen of his region said;

"Be you the General, boss?"

Nelson - "Yes, sir,"

Hoosier - "To what branch of the service do you fellows belong?"

Nelson - "The cavalry."

Hoosier - "Gwine to fight the Injuns, het?"

Nelson - "Yes."

Hoosier - "How is the Injuns now; be they troublesome near Chicago?"

Before Jack could reply to this last interrogatory, the teams were started ahead, and the searcher after knowledge was left ignorant of the condition of the Aboriginees about Chicago.

The roads thereafter were in a terrible condition. The wheels of the carriages turned ever so slowly in the soft spongy soil that was so deep that it went up to the wheel hubs. Weston expended so much energy struggling through it all that he had to put a halt to his progress on many occasions to rest on the side of the road. To make matters worse, the horses had to be led on a two-mile detour because of a fallen tree which blocked their path. "Westy" was not in a good mood and went about his business in silence for the next two miles, until that is, when an out of breath woman came up to him carrying a baby boy wrapped in a shawl. She told the pedestrian that she was going to call her son Edward Payson Weston Thompson. Weston was said to be so pleased at having a namesake, that he gave the woman a photograph of himself, and the boy one of his riding whips.

He arrived in Calumet, 42 miles from Chicago, at 11:05 where he stayed at the Northern Indiana Hotel. The owner had put on a magnificent spread for him and his troops. Again, the *Chicago Tribune* told its readers what happened next: After a short rest Weston went for the grub and the way he hid away "*vittles" fully corroborated all that has been written of his appetite. A man who had obtained a position near the dining room door observed to the landlady, who was standing near, "That little cuss can make grub sicker than any man of his size I ever see. Why, darned if he aint et a whole chicken and nigh onto a peck of mashed taters, and he's going for more."

King of the Peds

*Vittles – wild game recipes.

Whilst Weston digested his meal reading the newspapers, a man asked permission to see him. With permission granted, the heavily perspiring individual stood before the cool ped and told him that he heard that someone was going to try and assassinate him on the last stage of his journey. He informed him that he had brought along with him a 15-month-old bull terrier pup which was as savage as a wild cat. He then produced the animal, which was quite a fearsome creature, and, after a long silence, Weston told him that he would accept it if the owner came along with him and looked after it. Needless to say, Weston left the hotel depending solely on the protection of the boys dressed in blue.

He reached Miller's Station, Indiana, 26 miles from Chicago at 17:35, having walked 40 miles from Laporte, but wouldn't have stopped there had it not been for the horses being fatigued. His route from Calumet had been quite difficult as it had been negotiated over and through sandy hills and valleys. It was at Millers Station that he had supper and set off again for Gibson's Station an hour later, arriving there at 21:30.

On November the 28th it was reported that he had been staying the night at Hyde Park, Illinois, six miles south of Chicago. It was thought he would reach there by 10 p.m., but the condition of the roads made his progress slow. The Hyde Park Hotel was brilliantly illuminated upon his arrival at 03:50, and the sight must have elated Weston as he stepped inside, prompting a journalist to write, *"When he reached Hyde Park after a walk, in twenty-one hours and a half; on terribly muddy roads, of between sixty and seventy miles, he manifested the highest exultation over the fact of the near completion of his feat. He laughed with the loudest; cracked jokes by scores and in a hundred ways set forth the joy which filled his heart. His frequent boast is that more than 1,200 miles of track have been demonstrated by him to be of but little practical use, except for transportation of freight."*

It was at the hotel where he was joined by his wife and child who had made the journey there by train. While there it was reported that, *"A true-born Yankee, and a prospective showman offered Weston the sum of $12,000 to go to Europe and travel on exhibition for only two months. The walker did not, however, entertain the idea."* The above was probably a reference to Dan Rice.

Weston left the hotel at 08:30 with every intention of reaching the winning line at 10:40, where it was supposed he would stand on the post office steps and publicly announce the accomplishment of the feat. His route would bring him up Cottage Grove Avenue, 22nd Street, Wabash Avenue, Monroe Street and west to the post office. The plan was that he would then attend a concert at the Opera House in the afternoon, and later deliver a lecture on *"Athletic Sports"* in the evening. There was also a suggestion that he would perform a walk 100 miles in 24 hours at the Dexter Park course during the two weeks he proposed to stay in Chicago, following the end of his task. He was then supposed to go home by rail thereafter.

As he walked along towards the city, *"Weston was dressed in a natty costume, consisting of a blue jacket with no vest, ruffled shirt, tight blue pants, a fancy waist-belt, red leggings, immensely large and heavy, and a white canvas round hat. He exhibited but small evidences of fatigue, and moved along during the latter part of his journey at a very quick pace, necessitating an occasional run on the part of those desirous of keeping up with him."*

Nothing of note happened between the hotel and the southern line of the city, but as he neared Oakland on the outskirts of Chicago, he was met by F. Munson who was President of the National Fire Insurance Company, who accompanied him to the city limits, where he arrived at 09:07. It was here where he was met by a platoon of police and where he was officially welcomed by Munson, who congratulated him on his success. Weston thanked him and said he looked forward to his reception in the city, and declaring his ability to repeat the feat said, "I can walk just as long at this rate as I have a mind to, and I can walk one hundred miles in twenty-four hours. I like the looks of Chicago, and I am going to have a good time with her people while I stay."

From early in the morning, the trickles of people heading into the city to see the boy wonder became streams. The streams became rivers, and the rivers converged into a wave of humanity that later crashed into Chicago's main streets. Thirty First Street became a sea of men, women and children, many attempting to find unobstructed views of the pedestrian's progress by perching themselves on top of trees, or finding a spot on a balcony, in a window or on a door step. It was estimated that there were 50,000 people standing along the line of the march. The *Chicago Journal* reported: **Make your own estimates of the numbers upon this basis, a solid mass of humanity,** one hundred feet wide three miles long, and you can guess the number as well as we. The streets were crowded with vehicles of all descriptions, laden to their utmost capacity with human freight, and as he walked along, he was *"hailed almost continuously with vociferous cheering."*

Weston's police escort consisted of a company of horsemen (the advanced guard) whose job it was to clear the street. Whilst Captain Hickey and Sergeant Garbing sat in an open barouche, riding either side of them were Captain Jack Nelson and Mr. W. Pinkerton. They were followed by a company of 80 policemen who formed a hollow square and in the middle of them walked Weston.

At Twenty Second Street, he was met by the 30-piece Great Western Light Guard Band, which enlivened the march with such appropriate music as, "See the Conquering Hero Comes," "Jordan am a Hard Road to Travel" and "The Arkansas Traveller." At 10:00, the sound from the band which preceded him in the distance told the accumulated throngs that the man was on his way, and it was easy to see by the wave of fluttering white handkerchiefs from windows overlooking Wabash Avenue, that indeed, that was the case.

"Weston walked briskly along in the center of the hollow square, smiling graciously as he proceeded and occasionally waving with a graceful action his elegant white hat."

"All along the route it was a scene of the wildest enthusiasm. Cheer after cheer went into the air, while waving hats, fluttering handkerchiefs and floating, banners met the eye in every direction."

Turning down Monroe Street, he reached the post office at 10:36. From Monroe and Madison Streets, he made his way up Dearborn Street to Lake Street, from Lake Street to Clark Street and then on to Sherman Street. The original idea was to take the procession round by the Court House and move on to the Crosby's Opera House where the pedestrian would be *"exhibited to the multitude."*

"In the vicinity of the Sherman House the scene was an extraordinary one, the streets in all directions being completely blocked with people on foot, on horseback and in vehicles, all manifesting the greatest excitement. The throng was so great that for a considerable period the street cars were unable to make their trips."

It was here that the decision was made to get him into the Sherman House Hotel, and as he entered, and in response to loud calls, he soon made his appearance on the balcony, where he was introduced to the crowd by Mr. H. H. Hamlin of that establishment. Kissing his flaxen curly haired little girl of about two years old in his arms, he waved his hat at the crowd, who he addressed after repeated calls of "Speech, speech!" saying, "Gentlemen, I have a short speech to make, but it is for the little one here. I have now won the pony for this baby!" There followed cheers from the crowds as held her up and kissed her on the forehead. He then waved and went back inside. The *Chicago Tribune* commented: **Not Grant nor Sherman, nor any of our country's heroes, where ever made the subject of more ardent curiosity on the part of our citizens than the hero of a thousand mile walk. The excitement at times reached almost to the point of frenzy and in their eagerness to gain a standing point right in front of the window at which the beaming countenance of the great man was seen, the crowd came in sharp collision with the police. Wrights restaurant was crowded to the door with by a genteel mob of Weston hunters of the gentler sex, who manifested a surprising eagerness to get a look at the dear man.**

He then descended to the street, and again escorted by the police, he was followed by an immense number of people to the Opera House where a private room had been furnished for him. The carriage, which had accompanied him from Portland carrying his witnesses, remained in the street during the afternoon and attracted great numbers of curious spectators whilst Weston remained inside the building. Of the people inside who were desperate to get a glimpse of him, the *Chicago Tribune* reported: **They surged up the Opera House stairs. They flattened their fair noses against the glass doors of Mr. Crosby's room, they reconnoitred the interior from the stairs above, they looked with envy upon the few favored individuals who were permitted to shake the distinguished hand, and, in short, they were "dying" for an introduction.**

It was here that Weston announced that he wouldn't be walking at Dexter Park as previously thought. "But tell the people," he said, "that if any Englishman undertakes to beat what I have done, then I will go over to England and lick hell out of them!"

King of the Peds

During the afternoon and in the evening he made addresses in the intervals of the concert at the Opera House, the price of admission to which was a dollar and fifty cents. The auditorium was crowded on each occasion, and the street in front of the house was filled with persons anxious to catch a glimpse of the pedestrian.

AFTERNOON SPEECH

"I hardly know as I can say anything here this afternoon that will be at all acceptable. I cannot say that that I can talk as well as some people think I can walk - especially some of the respectable Chicago editorial corps, who have followed me during the past week, and they know whether Indiana mud is a good test.

I am not well prepared to make any extended remark this afternoon. Yesterday I was obliged to do more than I had made calculations for, and today, since I have been in town, I have done considerably more than I calculated to do. However, I will do the best I can.

It has been announced that I would state the reasons why I undertook the journey from Portland, Maine, to Chicago, Illinois. Last winter the wager was made between a friend of mine and a banker in New York, in one of the hotels of that city. The gentleman asked me what I could do. I told him I thought I could walk from Portland, Maine, to Chicago, Illinois, and make twelve hundred miles in thirty consecutive days. Nothing was then said about the exclusion of the Sabbath. I am not a religious man, I am sorry to say, but at the same time I don't approve of horse racing on the Sabbath any more than anything else, and pedestrianism, in the eyes of some would be the same as that. At the same time I excluded the Sundays from the walk, and made it twenty six secular days; it was with the understanding that the hundred miles in one day was not to be performed or attempted. I may say here, and I think I am justified in doing so, that it was cruel to put a task of that kind into a walk of twenty six days, for no rest which could be obtained in twenty four hours would fit any man on earth to continue a journey over such roads as I have been obliged to travel within the past month.

My private reasons for undertaking this walk were, of course to relieve my family from pecuniary embarrassment. It is possible that, if I had been wholly successful in it as I had tried, most earnestly tried, (applause), it might have been better for me. There is a time when every man must experience complete exhaustion, to liken it to an animal or if I may be permitted to use a vulgar expression, "fag out." He will go as far as he can, and go no further. You can test a man's power of endurance and he will go as far as nature permitted him, and he can go no farther. A man may walk until he drops, and then he remains there. But when he recovers from exhaustion, he is not injured at all, but he can get up and do the same thing the following day.

People argue that because I failed in my hundred mile walk and yet walked seventy two miles the next day that I might have walked that if I liked. I should have been very happy to have "liked" to have done it if I could. (Applause)

Walking as an exercise, is something I wish to see encouraged - something that I think will benefit the youth of America – will benefit the youth of any land. It is an exercise, not only healthy, but it is a pleasure, at times, and as good an exercise as a man can take.

I will make this apology frankly for my remarks this afternoon: During the past forty eight hours, I have been compelled to travel over 100 miles through the roughest country there is lying between here and Portland, and have had but three hours sleep in that time. Of course, mentally, I am not in the best condition. (In a sub tone.) At no time am I in the best.

One thing I can say is, I have my race. I arrived here as I agreed to, before twelve o'clock at noon, the 28th of November. I agreed to walk twelve hundred and twenty six miles. Instead I have walked thirteen hundred and sixteen miles. I have encountered many difficulties. For instance, I started from Calumet yesterday afternoon at one o'clock. We had a pilot. I asked him if he knew the distance from Calumet to Chicago. He said, it is forty one miles by rail, and it is forty one miles by road-wagon road. He said surely forty four miles. I went on. After I had travelled the road, and after I had reached Millers Station, some seventeen miles from Calumet, I asked another man how far it was from there to Chicago, and he said, "Well, I don't know, but we always call it round here forty five miles." I thought then I had been very "backward" in getting "forward," and that I had been some time in doing it. That is the way I have miles "tacked" on to me ever since the time I started. It seemed at times as though Chicago was moving off. I know Chicago is a "moving" city, and I do not know but it at it is well it should move off as far as possible from some places almost neighbours to it. I don't know but it that it might move off with advantage from Toledo, for instance. That is a good to move away from if you want to get anything to eat.

I do not mean this as flattery. I return my most sincere thanks to your Superintendent of Police, Mr. Rehm, for the courtesy he has shown me, and the protection he afforded, and also to Mr. Charles Tunnicliffe for the courtesies he extended to me while on the road.

I had received numerous anonymous letters – letters, written, no doubt, by parties who had wagered against me, in which I was threatened and it was stated that I would not come into this city alive. I did not propose to come in here a dead man. They came out and accompanied me on my walk. They also sent four men, strong, healthy and able bodied officers, who escorted me to this place. I assure you the police force of Chicago possesses some very excellent pedestrians. They accompanied me admirably yesterday, and certainly they had "try" enough in the Indiana mud and sand. At times it was knee deep.

As to Chicago, I must say I never saw a more orderly crowd, than I saw here today, since I left Portland. I wish to say this, and I assure you I do not say it in the spirit of egotism, as I have shown I can beat any other man in America as a pedestrian, I shall stand ready to prove that no man in England, so long as I stand on my two feet, can beat any man in America at pedestrianism. (Applause) I do not propose to enter the arena as a sporting man in pedestrianism. As I told my friends this morning, I have accomplished this feat, and it shall be my duty to do just what I have intimated I can do.

Again, I say, I hope you will excuse these disconnected remarks, as this evening I will recount in detail the particulars of the race I have just concluded. I need some little rest before that time. Besides the matter of rest, I was "invited out to dine," and "I have just come from dinner" and "I don't feel like talking." I assure you I would rather walk fifty or sixty miles than talk.

I now conclude, assuring you that you that I feel one hundred percent better than the day I left Portland."

EVENING SPEECH

"LADIES ANDS GENTLEMEN. I feel very thankful to you for the kind manner I have been received in Chicago today. I am not quite so vain as to take it all as complimentary to myself alone, or to my action during the past thirty days; but as a compliment to an American citizen, who, I think, has shown that in the art, if I may so term it, of walking, he has eclipsed any act of a similar nature across the water. The fatigue and trouble through which I have passed during the last month is entirely forgotten when I think of the kind manner in which my exertions have been rewarded.

I have received a great deal of censure from various parties for not accomplishing one portion of this feat – that of walking one hundred miles inside of twenty four consecutive hours, during this walk, which was originally intended as 1,226 miles. I can only say that the assertion of this fact amounts to nothing, for in my own heart, I know I speak candidly and honestly when I say that I need every exertion to accomplish that feat. "I tried but in vain." I had every obstacle to contend with. I agreed to walk one hundred miles inside of twenty four consecutive hours, but I agreed that those miles should be at a measurement of 1,728 yards; and when I say that, I don't contend I can do more than any other American citizen, but I think it will puzzle an Englishman (applause) – but the miles, or many of them, that I have been obliged to travel, have been Indiana miles (laughter). They were all the way from two yards up to two thousand. (Laughter)

I merely state one anecdote which, though I was sleepy this afternoon, I tried to tell as well as I could: I started from Calumet, Indiana, to come to Illinois, and we engaged a pilot there. I asked the pilot before we started, said I, "Pilot, how far do you call it now to get to Chicago?"

"Well," says he, "by the road that we take, – now let me see – nine and two are twelve and three is eighteen," says he, "it is just forty four miles from here to Chicago by road, and forty one by railroad. The road is very good," says he "there is some sand."

I found "some sand." (Laughter.) I started, and I had a glorious company, and we pulled over that road at the rate of 4 mph for four hours, and we stopped for tea, and we were just seventeen miles from Calumet to Chicago. I stopped there and partook of refreshments and coming out met another Indiana Hoosier. (Laughter.) I asked him; "My good friend, will you please be so kind enough to tell me how far it is from here to Chicago?" "Well," says he, "it's just forty five miles by wagon road." (Great applause and laughter.)

So I had been four hours getting one mile backward? I thought I had done well, but that was not Chicago and if Chicago had been one hundred miles off, I felt bound to get there before 12 o'clock today, because I had no invitation to dine here, and I have a peculiar faculty for keeping my appointments, especially on Thanksgiving Day. That is Yankee fashion.

In this manner I have been thwarted when I have tried to perform this feat of walking one hundred miles inside of twenty four hours. I have had no opportunity to look over my route and timetable to make my estimate in regard to that, but now I contemplate having an opportunity of doing so tomorrow evening.

I want to state here that I have been for the past week under a fearful state of excitement from the fact that I have received an innumerable number of letters, a great many of them anonymous, threatening me with the use of a coffin to get into Chicago with, from the limits that is. I was promised to just outside of Chicago; but I feel that I don't look quite dead yet.

I want to take this opportunity to thank once more your able Superintendent, Mr. Rehm, of the Chicago police, and his assistant, Mr. Nelson, and one or two sergeants and a Captain who were sent out to New Carlisle at the suggestion of Mr. Charles Tunnicliffe, whom I regard as a sincere friend, and I feel assured that I need not tell the citizens of Chicago what he is, for all know him very well, but I thank him for giving me giving me such protection today, as to relieve me from anxiety, and I felt perfectly free when I struck Chicago. And though I have been unfortunate in a portion of this race, I had some friends and came in with that feeling – one of gratitude – which relieved me of every feeling of weariness or anything of the kind, and when we arrived at the limits of this city at a quarter past nine, knowing that I had won the race, I could not but feel that I had accomplished that which more than in the sanguine expectations of my friends. (Applause.)

I have been requested to make some few remarks tonight on athletic sports. I don't profess to be a lecturer, and I do not know until today that I have ever made a speech before in my life, except once when I said "Not Guilty," I believe (Laughter.) But I will do the best I can.

During the past forty eight hours I have had a great deal of road to travel over; nice road; Indiana road. I have a peculiar love for that kind of road, and I have not had any opportunity to prepare any other remarks. What remarks I make I must offer an apology for, because they may be somewhat disconnected.

There are many sports termed athletic sports; such as gymnastics, rowing, yachting, base ball playing, horse racing, and pedestrianism. I do not think that prize-fighting comes under the same head. There are other sports termed brutal sports, such as dog fighting, cock fighting, and prize fighting. I have been associated – or rather people have tried to associate me with that class of people – prize-fighters. I say it here, as I have always said it, if it were for no other reason, if I had no principal to guide me than the respect that I have for my mother, I would not allow myself to be associated with men who stand up and hammer each others faces to pieces for a few thousand dollars. (Applause.) Why pedestrianism should be classed as a crime, or why a person, because he walk a few miles, more or less, should be called a prize-fighter, or because he bets on that race should be called a gambler, I "can't see it."

You can get your life insured, or an accident policy is issued to you for $5,000, for one day, a week or a month. If for a month, the company which insures your life against accident for $5,000 bets you $5,000 against $5 that you will not be killed inside of the month. If a man starts to walk on a joke, or anything of a kind, from his office to his house, and his friends know it, and they say to one another, "I will bet you the oyster supper that so-and-so can't walk to his house inside of the time," is the man that does the walking obliged to answer for the sins, if sins you may call them, of these betting the oyster supper? I can't see it. (Laughter and applause.)

As I told a clergyman who said to me before I started, said he, "Weston, I think that you can walk some, and the only bad feature about this is that you are walking on water. If you win the race you win quite an amount of money, and you are encouraging gambling." I said to him, "With due respect to the clergymen of America, I think, if you should offer any clergymen $5,000 to walk from Portland, Maine, to Chicago, Illinois, in thirty consecutive days, and he could do it, I think that he would be very apt to do it, and he would not contribute twenty five hundred of it to the American Tract Society." He didn't say that he would. (Laughter and applause.)

Athletic sports tend to strengthen the youth of any country, not only their bodies but their minds. A sound mind will be all the sounder for dwelling in a sound body, and that is a combination we all want. Such sports – if you can term them such – as prize-fighting, not only tend to ruin the morals but to make men depraved, to forget that they are men; to forget that they are images of the Great creator.

I do not contend, and I don't wish to, that performing this feat of walking, which my friends, the reporters, have been to term a great feat and unequalled pedestrian performance, I have done anything more than any American citizen can do. In walking 1,316 miles in 26 days, while it is a very fair walk for this season of the year, when you come through Indiana, (laughter) yet at the same time I don't contend that I have done anything more than any American young man can do. But I must contend that it is with pride I do say, that I think it would puzzle an Englishman to do it. He might find some fault with the miles, but then they call them "English miles."

As I remarked this afternoon, I don't propose to join the sporting fraternity, but I do propose, so long as I can stand on two feet, if any Englishman gets up and walks from Portland, Maine, to Chicago, Illinois, the distance I have walked, better than I have, I shall think it is my bounden duty, out of respect to the plaudits that I have received from the American people, to get up and beat him. (Applause.) I will have to do it, and I think I can. (Renewed applause.)

I have often seen, while on the route, boys and men, and not only that but little children, running beside me, which, I assure you, was a great pleasure to me, to see the little people running and exercising themselves, and saying, and saying "this is fun" for a mile or two, "but I guess I will go home now." (Laughter.) This exercise of walking puts a glow upon their cheeks and makes them look healthy, and I think that if the American people, in the young men of America, were to walk more – and I hope the Superintendent of the horse railroads will pardon me – and patronize the horse railroads less, that they would be more healthy; that they would eat heartier meals, and they would feel better when they retire at night and arise much better in the morning, I state from this the fact: Before I started up on this race, I never ate any breakfast of any account in the morning. I simply drank a cup of coffee and ate a piece of bread and butter, whereas, since I have started on this race, I have eaten – well, I say moderately – five or six meals a day (laughter and applause), and hearty ones, as my good friend, the proprietor of the Kinnard House, in Cleveland, had occasion to remark. He said that he would like to board me, but if I was going to take pedestrian trips all my life time, he would rather board me a week than a month. (Laughter)

And if you will bear with me I will relate here an anecdote which may have some bearing on this question of eating: I once boarded with a lady in New York, who is one of those landladies that kept a boarding house and retired with a large fortune in a short time, and her boarders retired with her, but they were a very bad looking set of boarders when they left. She used to come to me every morning – I was naturally a plain blunt sort of man – and she came to me one morning, and says she, "Mr. Weston, I take a motherly interest in you." "Well," says I, "I am very glad of it; I like to have anyone to take a motherly interest in me. "Says she, "I have been thinking some time that you are injuring yourself." And I asked her why. "Well, "says she, "you eat too much!" (Laughter) Now this landlady used to have, if you will excuse the expression, fried eggs for breakfast, and there were twelve boarders of us, and she used to cook thirteen eggs, and they would go around one apiece. I would manage to be the last young man at the table and I would generally call for an extra egg. The good lady stood that as long as she could, for about a week or more, and one morning we (she and I) sat at the breakfast table alone, and I called for an extra egg as usual. Said she, "Mr. Weston, you know that I told you the other day that I took a motherly interest in you, and you won't misconstrue my motives, but," says she, "you will excuse my remarking that you are eating too much, and I don't think that you had better have another egg. I should just as leave you would have it, but two eggs will make you bilious!" I told her I should like to be bilious, and, therefore would take two eggs." (Laughter)

You can hardly expect to much of me tonight, because I do not profess to be to be any speaker at all, and I do not profess to be much of a walker, but I am proud to say, though I am not much of a walker, I did walk from Portland, Maine, to Chicago, and arrived here in this good city on time, and won my wager, which is very pleasant to me and to many friends of mine.

There are many of you, probably, who have some curiosity to know in what manner this race has affected me bodily. As you have probably seen, as I have – for my friends, the reporters here have given me right and left through the press, Biblical allusions, etc. – I have been under a great state of excitement during the whole time. One reason is, it has been a bad season of the year for walking, although my Creator has been exceedingly kind to me in giving me as little bad weather as one could possibly expect at this season of the year. Still, I have been obliged to strain my nervous system to the utmost in order to accomplish this task, and have hardly known what I have been about some of the time. I was labouring under great disadvantages throughout the entire journey, and, as I remarked before, I don't wish to take any flattering receptions I have received in the cities through which I have passed as a compliment to myself entirely (I hope I am not so vain as that) but as a compliment to the energy of an American citizen; and I think any one will say the same, that any young American man that will try it will do as well as I have. I hope he will do better, and, be assured, I would not be jealous, and would not try to walk further or do better than he has; but I would simply suggest, if anyone is ambitious to do anything of the kind, that he should avoid Indiana (applause) unless they take the Michigan Central Railroad. The bed of the road is splendid, and I propose to take it on my way home, but I propose to take a car along with me. As I told my guide last night, – I would keep asking him how far we were – "when I win this race I am going out in Indiana and buy land by the mile, and I will make a fortune in a few days, for if I buy five miles I have got the whole state. (Laughter)

I made calculation to walk from Laporte to the Hyde Park House, which was given to me as fifty seven miles only, and this is a very moderate day's work. I could have arrived here at 8 o'clock in the evening without any extra exertion, but when I came to walk it, the Hyde Park House kept moving off, and I walked 73 miles before I reached it, and before I reached it I came near going swimming in Lake Michigan, before I got there. I had guides, too, and I think they were all right, but they nearly gave me a swim; but the officers that were with me preferred not to go into swim at that early hour in the morning. But finally I arrived.

In conclusion, let me once more ask you to pardon the manner in which I have made these few remarks tonight. I have no opportunity to prepare remarks; I am not a public speaker, and never made a speech before until this afternoon, and then, I confess, I was sleepy and, to use a vulgar expression, I didn't know whether I was afoot or horseback. I hope before I leave Chicago to have a chance to meet with many of your citizens, and let me take this opportunity to thank you most sincerely for your cordial and hearty welcome. (Great applause)"

King of the Peds

"His arrival assumed the shape of a sudden tornado which swept over the city for a few hours and then subsided into as sudden a calm leaving the majority of the people in a kind of mystified wonderment as to what it really meant after all."

Weston was said to have earned about $4,000 from his jaunt, and *"It is, however, probable that he has made a "nice thing" out of the journey by the sale of photographs, with which he was liberally provided and for which there was a constant demand by the women along the route. It would seem that the main attraction of the man is in his legs, which were encased in a pair of tight fitting blue pants, and whose actions are described by one enthusiastic Western reporter, to be the "same of aesthetics in motion.""*

A "benefit" took place for him on Wednesday night, the 4th of December at the Farwell Hall where he was said to tell his captivated audience of incidents en route and why he failed in his mission to walk the 100 miles in 24 hours. He was also said to have given an exhibition of walking in the hall, delighting those attending with samples of his four, five and six-mile gaits as he circumnavigated the place.

Soon after the completion of his walk, Weston was reported to have received an offer of $1,000 to go to St. Louis and lecture there, but was said to have refused it as it would have meant cancelling previous engagements. However, it appears that the money was too tempting for him, because on the 9th of April, he apparently lectured to an audience in the Mercantile Library in that city, *"after which he showed off his various paces, and walked nineteen times around the hall in nine minutes and forty seconds."*

CHAPTER 2

500 Miles in Six Days?

1868

On Thursday, February the 20th, Weston was due to appear in Titusville, Pennsylvania, for a *"Walk and Talk"* in the Corthinian Hall, but following a cancellation due to the train being delayed by snow, he didn't appear until the Saturday night. All hotels in the town were said to be full of people from surrounding counties, and as a consequence, the exhibition was reported to be a sell-out.

In Buffalo on March 27th, Weston was *reported* to have made an appearance at a *"grand entertainment for the benefit of the poor"* at the St. James Hall. He later won a bet when he accomplished the task of walking 103 miles in 23h.58m, or inside the allotted time of 24 hours, on the 4th of April from near Erie, Pennsylvania, to Buffalo. An immense crowd was in attendance in the afternoon to witness his arrival at the post office at 17:14, having tramped through a heavy snow storm and muddy roads. On his arrival he was said to be *"looking as fresh a lark."*

On May 9th, a story was being circulated in the press that Weston was being backed to complete a 5,000-mile walk from Bangor, Maine, to St. Paul, Minnesota, and then return to Buffalo. The wager was for $25,000 a side and the walk would have to be completed in 100 days. One of the stipulations was that he wasn't to travel on any Sunday and all such days would be included in the hundred. He would have to be accompanied by six sworn judges and the date for the start would be August 18th. A purse of $2,500 was to be raised which would be presented to him if he should accomplish the feat. The other stipulations were that he would also have to walk 100 miles inside of 23 consecutive hours five times during the walk, and should he fail in doing this once, he would forfeit all claims to the $2,500 purse and also forfeit $2,000 for each event to the backers. He would also be expected to walk 50 miles in 10 consecutive hours and once in each 1,000 miles. In both of these feats he would be allowed two trials at each event.

Weston then attempted to walk 100 miles in 23 hours, starting off at Riverside Park, Boston, on the 4th of June at 16:30 for a wager of $2,500. A large number of spectators were present and there was a lot of cheering during the first mile which was made in 15m, half a mile of which was walked backwards. His quickest mile during the afternoon was 10m.16s. In front of a large crowd of about 5,000, and despite being urged on by a brass band, he managed to make only 90½ miles in 22h.52m before giving up, thus losing $4,000 on the outcome of the effort.

The newspapers reported that Weston was to be matched against George Topley, the *"English champion pedestrian,"* who he would walk 100 miles for $3,000 at Boston, between the 15th and 18th of June, under a forfeiture of $1,500. The race actually started on the afternoon of Friday, the 19th June at Mystic Park, with Topley completing his first 25 miles a mile ahead of Weston, in a time of 5h.23m.46s, *"thus winning the first thousand dollars."*

The *"walking match"* finished on Saturday with Weston, having walked 24 hours, refusing to put another step forward in the race. Topley kept on the course to complete his 74th mile and then stopped to rest. *"Soon afterwards Mr. Goodwin, Weston's backer, came out and announced that Topley had been drawn, and the judges declared Weston the winner."* Weston's time for 75 miles was 23h.57m.45s. Topley's time for his 74 miles was 24h.57m.30s.

The *New York Times* reported to its readership on July 21st under the headline, **Another Failure by Weston, the Pedestrian,** that in Portland on Monday July 10th: WESTON, the pedestrian, failed to accomplish fifty miles in eleven hours at the Forest City Park, on Saturday. His time was eleven hours six and a half minutes.

King of the Peds

Weston then engaged Cornelius Payn of Albany in a 100-mile walking contest on the half mile circular track at Rensselaer Park, Troy, on the 22nd of August. Weston withdrew from the race when he had made 81 miles and Payn quit after walking 84 miles, the match ending at 5 o'clock in the afternoon. Earlier in the morning at seven o'clock, Weston, who was 1h.18m ahead of his opponent, and reportedly going really well having scored 61 miles in the 14 hours since the start, then drank a glass of wine which apparently had a terrible effect on him and his efforts to win the race thereafter. He was said be in pitiable condition, suffering from fever, excruciating pains and staggering about the track all afternoon. The match was watched by 2,000 people who collectively paid $300 for the privilege.

Payn then beat Weston in a similar contest at the venue on the 8th and 9th of September, the 100 miles being made in 23h.23m.8s. Weston claimed that he was unable walk on a circular track effectively giving that reason as the cause of both his failures at Troy.

However, it wasn't all doom and gloom for the "Walkist," as he was now being dubbed, when it was announced that he had secured a new world record when walking 100 miles in 22h.19m.8s on the 8th of October 1868. The best previous time had been made by Laycock at Troy in September of the same year in a time of 22h.59m.54s. Weston left Rye Station a little before noon, having only about 6½ miles to walk with two hours to spare to accomplish the required distance in. He arrived at the Orawarhum Hotel, White Plains, Westchester County, New York, 11 minutes ahead of time. He was received by a large gathering to which he made a short speech. *"The walk was made with little difficulty with no apparent ill effects afterward."*

The newspapers were now readying their readers for Weston's greatest challenge to date:

"Commencing the 1st of December he is to walk five thousand miles in one hundred consecutive days, when snow rain and cold, blustering winds impede every step; not for a wager, but for a purse of twenty thousand dollars proposed by DAN RICE, and subscribed by a number of gentlemen. WESTON is selected for the trial because he is an American, is young and enthusiastic, and, for the additional reason that he has never descended to the number one vulgarity and low trickery of the track professionals."

The following is Dan Rice's proposition to Weston, which was published in the *Turf, Field and Farm*:

CONTINENTAL HOTEL, PHILADELPHIA, Oct. 20, 1868.

EDWARD PAYSON WESTON, ESQ.: — In accordance with the promises I voluntarily gave you, based upon the condition precedent of your successfully performing the feat at White Plains, of walking 100 miles' in less than twenty two and one-half hours, I now make you a formal proposition as follows:

If you will walk 5,000 miles, as you propose, in one hundred consecutive days, subject to the subjoined regulations and instructions, I hereby bind myself to secure to you by general contribution, a purse of not less than $20,000.

You are neither to lay any wager yourself upon the result of your effort to walk 5,000 miles, as aforesaid, nor to permit any other person or persons to do so in your behalf or for your interest.

In accomplishing said 5,000 miles, you are to start from the city of Bangor, Me., on or before the 1st day of December next, between the hours of 2 and 4 o'clock P. M., and proceeding via the city of St. Paul, Minn., by such intermediate points as you may select, conclude your journey at the city of New York, on or before March 11th 1869 between the hours of 2 and 4 P. M. of that day.

You are to accomplish the said distance of 5,000 miles within 100 days from the time of starting from Bangor, including Sundays, but in no event will you be permitted to walk between the hours of midnight on Saturday and midnight on Sunday, at any time during the prosecution of said journey. You are to be accompanied by not less than eight responsible persons, none of whom are to be directly or indirectly interested in the success or failure of your journey; all of whom shall be duly sworn to diligently, faithfully and impartially discharge the duties of judges, time-keepers and protectors, and not three of whom shall be designated by me.

You shall be accompanied by at least one carriage during the whole of said distance of 5,000 miles, to which shall be attached a Prescott & Gage odometer, by which the distance walked by you from day to day and the total number of miles accomplished by you shall be determined. Such odometer shall be in the exclusive charge of the judges aforesaid, whose duty it shall be to detach it from the carriage at the end of each day's route, in the presence of some disinterested and responsible citizen of the town, whose attention shall be

specially called to the index, and in whose presence the distance as noted by it shall be entered in a diary of distance to be regularly kept by the judges for that purpose. Said odometer to be again attached to the carriage in the presence of said citizen just previous to again to starting on your journey, and his attention to be then called to the index, that he may be able to determine whether the same has been changed or not.

Whenever it shall be deemed necessary for you to cross any ferry or ferries, immediately previous to so doing, you will walk double the distance to be ferried. Such distance to be determined by the ferryman in charge of the ferry, subject to the approval of the judges accompanying you – it will be understood that such distance or distances shall not be included or allowed for in computing the said distance of 5,000 miles.

During said journey you are not, at any time or under any circumstances, on any secular day, to enter any vehicle used for transportation, but are to walk invariably, whether prosecuting such journey or not.

You are to invariably walk not more than 100 feet in advance of the principle vehicle containing the judges accompanying you.

You are not to avail yourself of the assistance of any means of transportation or of that of any person or persons, directly or indirectly, to aid you in the act of walking.

No delay or detention shall be allowed for except where it shall be clearly proved that the same was the result of malicious injury to your person, but in event of such injury, if of a character to permanently disable you or prevent or prevent you from successfully prosecuting your journey, I am to fulfil my obligation as if the said journey had been accomplished as herein before agreed.

All questions with reference to said journey arising during the prosecution thereof, to be decided by a majority of the judges accompanying you.

The Postmaster of each city or village through which you can pass shall be entitled to a seat in the judges' carriage, either for himself or such friend as he may designate, and every reasonable facility shall be extended to him for the purpose of enabling him to satisfactorily determine the manner which yourself and your judges prosecute said journey, provided, however, that, no such person shall be privileged to occupy a seat as aforesaid for a greater distance than nine miles.

All expenses incident to said journey or the preparations therefore, to be borne by you.

In making the above proposition I am governed by two motives - first, to be the humble instrumentality of rewarding you for a display of physical and moral courage in the face of almost insurmountable obstacles and most cruel and undeserved suspicions and criticism, secondly to foster and encourage a taste for pedestrianism, made requisite by the fashionable and enervating indolence of the times.

I am pleased to able to say that I regard you, in every respect, as a gentleman fit to be a pioneer in this sadly neglected branch of physical culture. I am not prepared to predict success in so Herculean a task as the one proposed, but I believe that you can and will accomplish it if fortune favors your efforts.

Awaiting an early answer, I remain your admirer and well wisher.

DAN RICE

Weston announced that he would start his marathon hike on December the 1st starting from Bangor, where he would head due west, to Buffalo, then through Michigan to Chicago and on to Prescott where he would cross the Mississippi. From there he would head up the river bank to St. Paul where he should have reached by the 29th of January. On the way back, his route would take him through Minnesota, Iowa, St. Louis, Terro Haute, Indianapolis, Cincinnati, Columbus, Wheeling, Steubenville, Pittsburgh, Hollidaysburg, Harrisonburg, Baltimore, Philadelphia and New York. His route would mean that if successfully completing it, he would pass through 17 states, 188 counties, 728 cities and towns, and take 9,794,996 steps averaging $58\,{}^{1}/_{7}$ miles or 113,895 steps a day.

1869

He was originally set to start on his 100-day trip, on the afternoon of the 4th of December. However, on account of lameness, he postponed the start until the 5th. He subsequently further postponed it until Tuesday, January the 19th 1869 when he finally took his first steps: The *Ohio Democrat* takes up the story: Weston, the great pedestrian, started from here on his 5,000 mile walk to-day. He is to do the 5,000 miles in one hundred days, resting on

King of the Peds

Sundays. He started from the steps of the Court House at exactly 4 P. M. An immense crowd lined the streets, and vigorously cheered him on his way. He was dressed in a semi-military costume, and flourished a tiny whip in his gloved hand. This whip has a gold handle, and was presented to Weston by Warren Leland, of the Metropolitan Hotel. He started off with a light, springy step, in good humor, and merrily laughing at the quizzing endearments of the ladies, who waved their handkerchiefs at him from the windows of their residences. At 4 o'clock precisely he was kissed by an enthusiastic female admirer. In nine more minutes he had accomplished his first mile, and within an hour he was six miles west of the city, walking as swift and as light as a rabbit.

Two close covered carriages accompanied him, containing your correspondent and Weston's backers, with several of his personal friends. The horses are kept at a brisk trot by Weston's feet. At 7 P. M. Weston ate a light lunch without stopping, and as I write, the cheering fragrance of his prime cigar is floating on the chill breeze behind him. He feels confident of reaching St. Paul on time, and says that if he succeeds in this, his journey thence to New York will be comparatively easy. He said before he started, "I have invited my newspaper friends to dine with me at Warren Leland's Hotel on the 29th of April next, and you may rest assured I am too much of a gentleman to disappoint them." If Weston succeeds in his undertaking he is to receive $20,000.

That same day Weston reached Belfast, 38 miles away, after trudging through much snow. The next that is heard of him is when he stayed at Hallowell, Maine, having arrived at that place at half past six on the morning of the 21st showing signs of tiredness. It was reported that he would stay there for a few hours before resuming his tramp.

He reached Bellows Falls, Vermont, on the Friday the 29th some hours behind schedule owing to the bad conditions on the roads and was said to have been making 50 miles a day. He reached Danby, Vermont, the next day, and walked through Manchester at the foot of the Green Mountains early in the morning. During that period of his trek, he had encountered numerous obstacles and huge snow drifts, reporting that he had to stop at a farm house near the summit to rest the horses and find horseshoes.

The *St. Joseph's Herald* of Michigan then reported a most amusing story entitled **The Two Westons:** A Burlington, Vt, dispatch of Feb. 1, says: On Saturday evening a fictitious Weston passed through this city, clad in military uniform, and followed by three horse sleighs. A multitude of persons walked with him through the city, and he left us amid the light of bonfires, asserting that be would rest over Sunday in Swanton Falls, 32 miles distant. This morning the genuine Weston came into the city, having walked from New Haven Center, Addison County, to this place, a distance of 32 miles, before breakfast. The whole city was astonished. Mayor Ballon, who had paid his respects to the sham Weston, called on the real pedestrian at his hotel, and after a short conversation became satisfied that he had hold of the genuine article. The affair has created much indignation. It is said that the walkist was personated by two students of the Burlington college, who took turns in walking through the various towns and villages, and rode through the country in a sleigh. The real Weston is now nearly two days behind time, and is much annoyed by the sham affair ahead of him. It is reported the people of St. Albans have been humbugged in the same manner. Weston left here at 1:20, and will walk hence to Rouses Point, N. Y., 535 miles from Bangor, before stopping. He is still confident of making up lost time. The young lady who followed the sham Weston 22 miles in a cutter for the purpose of presenting him with a pair of woollen gloves of her own manufacture, is greatly mortified. Her brother threatens vengeance on the mischievous students.

Having passed through St. Albans, and after reaching Rouses Point, he headed for Mooers, Clinton County, which was 546 miles from Bangor. He was then said to have been mobbed at Swanton Falls, where he ran into the woods in terror, whilst his comrades in the sleigh drove fiercely in the direction of Alburgh, New York. Weston said he was confident of making up the lost time and had lost 6 pounds in weight since leaving Bangor.

On Friday, Feb 12th at 15:30, he walked into Oswego, New York, where he was greeted by an immense crowd, leaving there later via Syracuse. The next day, the 13th, a congregation of churchgoers rushed out of a prayer meeting in Ellenborough, New York, to gaze at the pedestrian, *"leaving the pious parson alone."*

He left Buffalo on the morning of the 24th, planning to arrive in Cleveland on Thursday. The *Cleveland Courier* wrote: The party accompanying Weston consists of seven persons; himself; Mr. Busby of Turf, Field and Farm, his advance agent, Mr. Salmon, reporter of the Turf, Field and Farm, Mr. Morey, reporter of the New York Tribune, Mr. Palmer, general manager; Mr. Totten who looks after his personal welfare; and the driver, whoever he may chance to be. On the road, a buggy drawn by one horse precedes Weston, and a two horse vehicle follows him, in which conveyances the party travel who accompany the pedestrian. He wears a gorgeous suit, a naval suit, similar to those worn by marine corps officers, with shoulder knots, and a forage cap of beaver richly ornamented with bullion, and surmounted by a white cockade. For night tramps he has had a light lantern constructed, which takes the place of the well known riding whip. In stormy weather, and such has been the rule with him since he commenced his ramble, he dons the old suit in which Buffalo has seen him several times.

Judging from surface indications, the prospects of his success are gloomy. According to his timetable published in the Turf, Field and Farm, he should have reached Buffalo on the 10th inst., hence he is ten days behind. He has walked to that point eleven hundred and fifty three miles in thirty two days, an average of about thirty three miles a day, including Sundays. This leaves him sixty-eight days in which to accomplish the remaining thirty eight hundred and forty seven miles, an average of about fifty six miles a day again including Sundays, certainly not a flattering prospect. Still, Mr. Weston is entirely confident. In his private calculation he allowed for ten day's loss of time between Bangor and St. Paul, as compared with the published table. He has lost this already, but thinks, and with good show of reason, that he can gain on what he intended to do from this point, on account of the improvement in roads. It requires no little credulity to believe that he has thus far walked in mid winter through Maine and New Hampshire, over the Green Mountains and through the northern wilds of this state, contending against most discouraging obstacles. He has waded for miles in snow up to his waist. One day he walked fifty miles without meeting a team, his party breaking the road. Another day, the most strenuous exertions only availed to accomplish twelve miles in nine hours. He feels that he has gone over by far the worst part of the road, and thinks that he can do eighty miles a day on the remainder of the route more easily than thirty miles a day have been made to Buffalo. It remains to be seen whether he deludes himself as to his powers and whether the Western roads will prove as good as he hopes. He is in splendid condition, and full of confidence. The fact that failure in this attempt would put a stop to his career in the future will spur him on, and we are sure that he will do everything that indomitable pluck and extraordinary endurance can. His route lies through Conneaut, Ashtabula, Geneva, Madison, Painesville, Willoughby, Euclid, Cleveland, Rockport, Olmsted, Ridgeville, Elyrin, Amherst, Brownhelm, Vermillion, Berlin, Huron and Sandusky.

Weston abandoned his attempt to walk the 5,000 miles, at Buffalo. He was unusually sanguine of accomplishing it at first, but later found that he didn't possess enough money to pay his travelling expenses along the entire route. He was also disappointed that he didn't receive much assistance from the public. He started on his walk with several hundred dollars, but the cost of living en route meant he could only pay his way for so far. During the 36 days of his journey he walked 1,153 miles, averaging out at slightly over 32 miles per day. That average increased to just over 36 miles a day, when taking the four Sundays when he didn't walk into consideration.

Weston then went on to organise a walking match of 100 miles from Walnut Creek, 10 miles north of Erie, Pennsylvania, to Buffalo with the 22-year-old from Albany, Cornelius N. Payn for a purse of $500 between the 30th and 31st of March. The **articles of agreement** stated:

This agreement, made and executed this sixth day of March, A. D., 1869, by and between Edward Payson Weston and Cornelius N. Payn—witnesseth that the said parties agree to walk a square heel and toe match for the sum of $500 a side, or as much more as may be mutually agreed upon, a distance of one hundred miles, or the distance between the following places, to wit: Walnut Creek, Pa., and Buffalo post office, N. Y. The walk to commence at Walnut Creek, Pa., the same place from which the said Weston started in 1868. The road to be traveled is the one known as the old stage route, or Lake Shore road, leading between the two above named places.

It is further agreed, that there shall be two judges, one chosen by each contestant, and a referee, chosen by the judges, to accompany each party. In case the judges shall disagree, the decision of the referee shall be final between the parties upon all questions arising in this match.

Each of the above named parties shall furnish conveyances with convenience for carrying two judges and one referee, each party to pay his own personal expenses, and the expenses of his judges and referee. The carriage is to be at all times in the rear of the pedestrian for whom the same is intended.

$100 a side is hereby deposited with Messrs. H. W. Burt & Co., bankers, of Buffalo, N. Y., who are to be stakeholders, the balance of the stake to be deposited with the above named bankers on or before twelve o'clock M, on the day before the match.

The party failing to make his stake-good, shall forfeit the $100 now deposited by him, and as soon as the whole stake is deposited, the match shall become a play or pay match, (that is,) either party failing to walk according to this contract, shall forfeit the amount so deposited. It is agreed, that the said Payn shall give the said Weston seven days' notice of the day upon which the match shall commence, and the start shall be made between twelve and two o'clock, P. M., as may be hereafter agreed upon.

King of the Peds

The party first reaching the Buffalo post office, according to the terms of this contract, shall receive from the judges, or referee, a certificate to that effect, which said certificate shall be evidence of such fact to the above named bankers, and upon the presentation of such certificate, the said bankers shall pay over the money on deposit under this contract to the party so presenting it. But said certificate shall not be good, except the same be accompanied by an affidavit of a party to be hereafter appointed by the said referee, that the party receiving sold certificate arrived at said post office first, and that such party shall countersign said certificate.

All the Judges and referees shall, before said walk is commenced, be sworn to do equal and impartial justice between the parties, and to decide the matter according to the merit of the parties, according to the rules of walking.

In witness whereof, the said parties have hereunto set their hands and seals the day and year first above written.

CORNELIUS N. PAYN. (Seal)

EDWARD PAYSON WESTON. (Seal)

Signed, sealed and delivered, in presence of:

M. H. TAYLOR.

FRANK K. SHAW.

It is hereby agreed and understood between the sold parties, that sold match shall commence on, or before the first day of April next. Also, in entering Buffalo, the route shall be up Ohio Street to Main, following Main to Seneca, thence down Seneca to the post office.

CORNELIUS N. PAYN.

EDWARD PAYSON WESTON.

The race was prematurely terminated after 82 miles had been made in 22 hours, when within 21 miles of Buffalo, a dispute between the pair arose as to the time to be allowed to stay at the Cattaraugus Bridge, it having been carried away by the freshet. Payn eventually arrived back in Buffalo by a freight train and Weston went to Girard. *"There was much indignation due to lost bets."*

The abandonment of the race produced the following response from Payn who wrote the following letter to the *Buffalo Courier and Republic*:

BUFFALO, April 1, 1869.

I see that one of the daily papers reflects upon the abandonment of the late walking match between Weston and myself as a humbug upon the people for the sake of taking money out of their purses. In view of the fact,—well-known and acknowledged by all who were present—that Weston deliberately abandoned the match, and that his backer notified me that he would not allow the stakeholder to give up the money, if I completed the walk, and that the judge who was to accompany me on behalf of Weston refused to proceed further, when urged to do so, it seems to me that I was the only sufferer. The walk was to test the endurance and speed of myself and Weston—not on any track where any charge of admission could be made. The public could see what they pleased of it without paying anything towards it, and the position taken by the Weston party of abandoning the walk (which they certainly never would have done, had it not been reduced to a certainty that I must win it), and claiming back their money on the ground that betting was illegal, left me to foot my own bills for all the expenses I had incurred not a dollar of which we contributed by the public in any shape. I always have defeated Weston and am satisfied I always can, and would be glad to walk him for $1,000 or $2,000, if he would find any one to back him who would not sue the stakeholder for his money if I won it; or, if he cannot do this. I will walk him the same hundred miles for nothing, and pay my own expenses, just for the pleasure of walking against him, as I have not the slightest doubt of beating him; or, I will walk him one hundred miles on the track, the entire gate money to be given to the poor of Buffalo, or any benevolent institution of this city.

Yours respectfully,

CORNELIUS N. PAYN.

Payn went on to publish a challenge to Weston to *"pedestrianize with him in almost any manner, and on almost any terms."* About the same time the citizens of Fredonia, where *"Weston was sojourning temporarily, made up a purse of two hundred and fifty dollars for him, in case he should accomplish the feat of walking one hundred miles in twenty-two hours and thirty minutes, going eight times back and forth over a stretch of road twelve and one-half miles in length, beginning in Fredonia and ending in Silver Creek."*

At 5 feet 8½ inches in height, Cornelius, weighing 123 pounds, was described as a lithe, wiry, well formed, unassuming, intelligent young man. He had just celebrated his 22nd birthday on the 11th of the same month when he lined up on the opposite end of the road to the older Weston, at 14:00 on Tuesday, the 20th of April.

There were two small disputes to be settled before the off. Payn objected to starting off on the summit of a steep hill, stating that it would be better to alter the courses direction as it would have to be climbed every 25 miles. Objection overruled! The weather on the day was also not to young Cornelius's liking as it was raining and he asked for the race to be delayed, claiming that both hindrances were in Weston's favour. Again the objection was overruled and the race started on time.

Off went Payn at a *"slashing gait,"* walking flat footed and fast, scoring the first five miles in 56½ minutes, with Weston making the same distance in exactly one hour. *"All along the line of the road were scattered vehicles filled with eager spectators, and each house poured out its last inmate to see the men go by."* Payn reached the turn-around point at Silver Creek at 16:23. *"Near the top of the hill leading into the village, he met Weston, and greeted him with the remark, "Now I have got you, you sardine."* After taking a half a minutes rest in which he indulged in a quick snack of tea and crackers, Payn stormed into Fredonia. *"Here the anxious ones were thronged in the street, in the windows of houses, and on the steps of the hotel. As the white cap of Payn came in sight from the front of the Taylor House, which was the decided centre for the crowd, speculation began as to whether it was Payn or not, and when this became a certainty many a jaw dropped."*

Payn's time for 25 miles was 4h.59m, with Weston making the same distance 23 minutes later. On the *"second leg"* of the contest however, Weston took advantage of a 15-minute break by the race leader, and by the time the younger man reached Silver Creek or 37½ miles into the match at 22:00, Weston was but 5 minutes behind. By the time the top of the hill had been conquered at fifty minutes past twelve the next morning for the second time, that gap had been increased to six minutes. *"Notwithstanding the unorthodox hour hundreds of people were in the streets at the time of arrival, including many staid citizens, whose wives had something to say on the subject when they reached home."*

During the next 25-mile section, Weston took the lead. Payn, having rested for 17 minutes, watched the older man pass him and despite "Ned" taking a nine-minute rest himself, he was the first man to reach Silver Creek at 03:48, 14 minutes ahead of his opponent. On the return journey Weston kept himself in front, his unmistakable figure appearing at the bottom end of the village at 06:30 *"amid tumultuous cheers,"* later reaching the starting off point at 06:52. Turning back down the hill and heading into the village, and on meeting the oncoming Payn, Weston cheekily returned the comment about being a sardine. By the time he reached the summit, and although he was 16 minutes behind, Payn was observed to be in good condition with his *"head well up, and his high-elbow action working like machinery."*

On the last leg of the journey, Weston rested for nine minutes, and by the time he was one and a half miles out from Silver Creek, was still seven minutes in advance of his rival. The leader however, looked weary as he reached the terminus at 09:44 and the advancing *"sight of the sleuth hound so warm on his scent appeared to surprise and discomfort him."*

After a mile and a half of the start of the last 12½ mile section, Payn caught up with Weston whilst the "Walkist" was laid on a sofa in someone's house, covered in blankets at 10:00. He was being examined by a couple of doctors, who advised him that he would be risking his life he went any further. Apparently he was experiencing symptoms of a burning sensation over his chest, followed by an *"almost complete suspension of the functions of the heart."* Following the physician's observations, Weston threw in the towel, having walked 89 miles in 20 hours.

Payn thereafter had a rough ride back to the finish. The weather was atrocious with the wind throwing all it could at him in the form of sleet and rain. When he finally reached the village, there was an air of disbelief that he had prevailed in a race that he had always been considered the likely loser. Still, he was cheered along his way, eventually finishing his tramp in 22h.52m.

Weston later admitted that Payn's time was the best on record, despite recording an *unofficial* record of 22h.19m at White Plains in the previous October; his rationale being that the present course was so demanding, and the weather so bad, that it had to be better than his own.

The irrepressible Weston made a further attempt to walk 105 miles in 24 hours over the same course, starting from Fredonia at 2 o'clock on the afternoon of Tuesday, the 4th of May, accompanied by the judges who oversaw the previous Payn match. He made the first 25 miles from Fredonia to Silver Creek in 5h.1m and 50 miles in 10h.27m, the fastest 50 he had ever made. However, he *"caved in this time,"* owing to *"the indisposition of his left leg."*

The *New York Sun* went on to publish an interesting article about how Weston would be spending his time during the late summer and early fall of that year: "He has concluded a contract with Mr. J. T. Landman of London, the conditions of which are as follows. Weston is to walk 50 miles within ten and one half consecutive hours, on thirty different occasions between July 1 and November 1. During each trial, he is to walk one half mile backward. If successful he is to receive $250 for each success, but failing to walk the half mile backward within the given time, then he is to receive $200. If he fails to make this time and is within eleven hours, then he receives nothing. Should he fail to accomplish the task within 10½ hours on three consecutive trials, then the contact becomes null and void. These trials are to be made on average twice a week, on which tracks, Mr. Landman may hereafter designate."

On the 21st July in Detroit, Michigan, his proposed walk "against time" was postponed due to rain. At Fort Wayne, Indiana, on July 31st, he won $250 for walking 50 miles in the time allocated with five minutes to spare, including half a mile backwards at the Driving Park, Huntington, in front of a *"goodly crowd."* The *Dubuque Daily Herald* was to print the following advertisement many times during late July and early August:

WESTON

-------------------o---------------------

Walking Match Against Time.

-------------------o---------------------

Fifty Miles in 10 ½ Hours.

-------------------o---------------------

One half mile backward – Back inclusive

-------------------o---------------------

For a Purse of 250 Dollars,

-------------------o---------------------

Edward Payson Weston, The Great American Champion and Pedestrian of the World, will undertake the stupendous feat of walking 50 miles in 10 ½ hours, including the most difficult task, (in fact against nature) of walking **one half mile backward,** for a purse of **$250** at the **Dubuque Driving Park**, Saturday. August. 7th, 1869. Mr. Weston on this occasion will wear the splendid uniform presented to him by the people of Westchester Co,. N. Y., and will commence his **arduous task** at 8 A. M. walking the one half mile backward between 3 and 4 o'clock P. M. A sufficient police force will be on the ground, and good order will be preserved.

The day was clear and cool and the track in splendid condition, with a large number of people visiting the above venue to watch Weston, who appeared dressed in a *"tasty uniform."* His first mile was completed in 13m.12s, and he accomplished his task making the entire distance in 10h.25m.30s including a stop of 16 minutes after completing 35 miles and 3,500 feet in 7h.13m.4s. The quickest mile, which was his 18th, was made in less than 11m, and his last mile was made in 11m.30s, with the obligatory half mile walked backwards being accomplished in 8m.32s. Weston said he would be back in the forthcoming October to have a go at making 400 miles in five days.

At the fairgrounds at Davenport, Iowa, on August the 10th, which he had hired for $25, he tried the same feat but failed by 90 minutes. Three days later and starting at 9 a.m. on a very hot day at the Will County Fairgrounds, Joliet, Illinois, he again failed to produce the goods, scoring his 50 miles in 10h.43m.53s, during which time he walked his half mile backwards in 9m.40s.

On Tuesday, the 17th he appeared at the City Driving Park, Niles, Michigan, the result of his effort not being known, and four days later at the Driving Park, Battle Creek, walked the mandatory half mile backwards in *"six minutes,"* completing 50 miles in the allocated time. At the Bristol House Tavern afterwards, he said he had been "confident of success."

The racecourse at Fond du Lac, Wisconsin, on the 27th of August, was another venue on the tour. He failed by 14m.3s to walk the 50 miles in the required time. The usual half mile in reverse however was accomplished in 10 minutes.

Waukesha, Milwaukee, Wisconsin, on the 29th of August was Weston's 13th trial and it proved lucky for him as he made the requisite distance in 10h.25m.45s with no mention being made of the backward bit.

1870

At 12:15 a.m., on the 25th of May 1870, Weston began the unparalleled task of attempting to walk 100 miles in 22 consecutive hours. In consequence of the belief which prevailed among some people that Weston was a *"humbug,"* Mr. W. W. Wallace the proprietor of the Empire Skating Rink in New York, thought he would let the people of that city make up their own minds whether he *"was or he wasn't."*

The track that had been laid out for him was 735 feet 5 inches in length, meaning he would have to go round it 717 times plus 706 feet, to achieve his objective. The men having to judge the monotonous event were Charles H. Winnans, Jerome Phelps, James Burnham, Roswell H. Jerome, Martin England, Charles H. Phelps and Frederick A. Keeler.

Weston was, as always, very confident, telling all he was determined to accomplish the task or, "die in the attempt." By 01:00 he had made 26 circuits of the course, his 50 miles in 10h.35m and was later successful in meeting his target in 21h.38m.15s, in front of 5,000 spectators. He had made nine stops during his feat, all his rests being less than 10 minutes. The *New York Herald* wrote: **The announcement of the result was the signal for a deafening burst of applause from the thousands who had assembled to witness the successful termination of the greatest pedestrian feat ever attempted. Mr. Weston did not seem in the least fatigued, stepping off as briskly on the last mile as on the first, and after the one hundredth mile had been accomplished, he addressed the crowd from the judge's stand, saying that it was love, not money, which had induced him to attempt the feat which he had just accomplished. It was the desire to free himself from the reputation which had been given to him by some of the daily papers of this city of being a "humbug," and to set right before the public those who had befriended and defended him.**

The day after, a challenge was issued to Weston by a man called James Smith, the self claimed "Champion of America," who was obviously not impressed with what he saw at the rink the day before. He wrote:

WESTON, according to the reported measurement of the rink, had to make seven laps for a mile and walk in the centre of the track. On turning he lost two yards on each turn by what we call 'clipping', which would make WESTON walk three and quarter miles short of 100 miles. I know this to be the case, as I tallied and timed him yesterday. Now I want to let the public to see that this man as a walker is a fraud and an impostor. I now challenge him to walk me 100 miles on the same track as he walked yesterday for $1,500 a side. I will allow him five miles start in 100 miles, and my silver cup, valued at $50, which I won at Iventon, shall also be put up, and the winner take all. If Weston can walk, and did walk 100 miles in the time given out, he has another chance in the match with me. I claim he must walk me for the championship in a fair and honorable contest and to let the public see that he can't walk, I offer him the above odds. I also offer to give him one hour start in 100 miles for the same amount.

King of the Peds

Weston must have discounted the above challenge and nothing more was heard from Smith. Then:

GRAND COMPLIMENTARY TESTIMONIAL TO

Mr. EDWARD PAYSON WESTON

THE GREAT PEDESTRIAN

To take place in the Empire City Rink, Third avenue, and Sixty-third street, on THURSDAY, June 2, 1870. On this occasion Mr. WESTON has promised to accomplish the unparalleled feat of walking fifty miles within ten and a quarter consecutive hours. Mr. WESTON will begin his arduous task at noon terminating at 10:15 P. M. During the evening, to gratify the curious, Mr. WESTON will walk one half mile backward. Grand Promenade Concert, both afternoon and evening, by the Empire City Rink full Military Band. Admission 50 cents.

Eight days later, and on the same track, Weston gave another of his 50-mile performances with the usual half mile backward being walked after. However, this time the target was, and as can be seen above from the advertisement placed in the *New York Herald*, in under 10h.15m. According to the *"City Surveyor's measurement,"* he managed his objective with a minute and five seconds to spare, but according to an unofficial time based on *"HORACE GREELEY'S measurement,"* he was a minute and a half over 10 hours. At the end of the show, Weston made a brief speech, announcing that he intended to go over to Europe. The *New York Times* wrote of the achievement: "Mr. WESTON will realize about $1,000 by this feat, besides a reputation which will assist him materially in the future."

In the United States census of October, 1870, Weston was residing in "Ward 21 District 18, New York," informing the enumerator that he owned real estate to the value of $2,000.

Nothing more was heard about "E. P." until November of that year when an announcement was made that, *"for the benefit of science,"* and a purse of $5,000, the man would attempt the *"unparalleled feat"* of walking 400 miles in five days, and 112 miles inside of 24 consecutive hours, commencing at 12:15 a.m. on Tuesday, the 22nd of that month. The organisers of the event had been falling over themselves to make sure the track measured the correct distance and a statement to that effect was released. It read:

Once around the Rink measures 735 84-100 feet; seven times around and 129 12-100 feet make one mile, and to walk 100 miles Weston must go around 717 times and 402 72-100 feet over, and for 112 miles 803 times. The 400 mile walk will be 2,870 times around and 139 2-10 feet over.

The start will be made from the centre of the hall on the Sixty-fourth-street side, and the mile will end a few feet of the opposite the entrance to the Rink. The distance from the centre of track to the door of Weston's retiring room, twenty four feet, was measured also, so that when he goes in and out there to rest and for meals this distance may be counted, From the Judge's stand to that point of the track is 121 75-100 feet. The corners of the track were measured, and it was found that by keeping on the inside edge he would save nearly four feet on every round, or nearly three miles on the 400 miles. To insure a fair, square walk; the measurement was made along the centre, two and a half feet from the inside border.

The above survey, which was carried out by Mr. Jos. L. T. Smith, City Surveyor, was witnessed by fifty people including Dr's. Ogden Doremus and Austin Flint Jr. who were part of a medical committee who had been looking after Weston, the others being Dr's William A. Hammond, J. C. Dalton and William H. Van Bruen.

Weston commenced his walk as advertised after which time every morsel of food he ate would be recorded and weighed and every move he made would be watched, very, very, carefully by the "docs" who would also monitor his physical condition closely. Before he started he weighed 119 pounds.

1st Day: Weston walked 20 miles then went to bed at 04:00 where he slept till 08:00. He then walked 5 miles and breakfasted on mutton chops, egg flip, stale bread and 8 oz of coffee. He went back on the track where he walked till 13:00 after making 41 miles. He was then taken to a private room, offered a meal, but didn't eat it, resuming his walk later. Stopping to eat a beef-steak, he then carried on till 22:58 when he retired to bed on a score of 80 miles.

2nd Day: Awaking at about 4 o'clock for breakfast, he started his 81st mile at 04:58. He appeared to be in fine condition, and showed no signs of fatigue. He managed to complete 100 miles at 11:12, 120 miles at 16:05, and prepared himself for his task of making 112 miles in 24 hours starting at 22:25 when he had already achieved 121 miles.

3rd Day: He didn't make his target but did make 100 miles in 24h.30m, blaming his failure on only being able to get a couple of hours sleep the day before and the inconvenience of a sprained ankle. His diet in that period consisted of three boiled eggs and some beef tea. He only stopped to rest for 1h.35m.

4th Day: By 04:00 he had made 231 miles and had made an undertaking to make a second go of making the 112 miles in 24 hours setting off at 10:13. However, his exertions were catching up on him and despite the crowd urging him on, and the efforts of the band to put a spring in his step, Weston couldn't keep up the strong enough pace he needed to realise his objective, eventually finishing on 277 miles.

5th Day: Weston started his last day with an impossible task of making 123 miles. He actually ended up making a total of 320 miles and lost 5 pounds in weight the process. His medical team however announced that they were satisfied with their findings and that they were "utterly confounded" by Weston's energy in the closing stages of the event.

1871

There then followed a long period of time when Weston's name wasn't mentioned in the press, but six months later the *Freeborn County Standard* of Albert Lea, Minnesota, on the 11th of May 1871, broke the silence when that newspaper reported: That humbug Weston, has been fooling away his time performing another walking feat. This time he proposed to walk 200 miles in 41 hours, and accomplished it. We believe this is the first time his efforts have been crowned with success, and we hope he will now quit. A couple of weeks later on the 25th of May, the *Indiana Progress* stated that: WESTON, the pedestrian, has just completed the feat of walking 200 miles (two of them backward) in 40 hours, 50 minutes, and 45 seconds, at St. Louis. It is therefore presumed that the feat the *Freeborn County Standard* refers to his effort in St. Louis.

Now back in New York, it appeared that the "Walkist" was determined to perform the feat that he failed in the previous year, of walking 400 miles in five days with the 112-mile bit thrown in over 24 hours. He again arranged to do the distance at the Empire Rink and this was hired from Monday, the 12th of June. The track was once again surveyed and certified as being seven *"circuits"* to the mile.

The strategy was, and under the supervision of his new trainer, Mr. Charles H. Winnans, to allow himself just 45 minutes rest for the first 24 hours thus allowing him as much time as possible to make the desired 112 miles. His plan was to make 25 miles, rest for five minutes and then allow himself five-minute rests every 10 miles. If he was successful in achieving his goal in his allocated time, he would then allow himself a rest of 5h.25m. The theory then was that he would have to walk at an average of 3 mph for the next four days in order to achieve 72 miles a day and hopefully, success! At five minutes past midnight, he commenced his journey and walked his first four miles in 12m.24s, 11m.33s, 11m.33s and 11m.44s respectively.

On the 19th of June, the New York correspondent of the *Washington Patriot* wrote: Weston, the "walkist" has again commenced to exhibit himself, attracting crowds to the immense rink on Third Avenue. He made 112 miles in 23 hours, 44 minutes, and 45 seconds, being fifteen minutes ahead of the stipulated time. His fastest mile was in 11 minutes and 6 seconds, and is the swiftest time on record. A band of music enlivened him, but at last, overcome with fatigue, left the pedestrian walking still. Every effort was made to enable him to complete his task. Ice water was dropped on his head, and his weary legs well lashed with a heavy riding whip. After completing the 112 miles, he slept for five or six hours, and reappeared in a velvet suit and blue sash to recommence, exhilarated by an enthusiastic welcome. Many of the most respected people of both sexes congregate to watch this man for no class is quite able to resist the sensation of the moment. In his recent walking feat in New York city, Weston completed the task of walking 112 miles in 24 hours, having 15 ½ minutes to spare. On the 17th he finished his effort to walk 400 miles in five days, having 18 minutes to spare. He made the last mile in 11 minutes 7 seconds, and showed little signs of fatigue.

Following his achievement in New York, and between Wednesday, the 27th and Thursday, the 28th of September, *"the so called pedestrian broke down"* in his attempt to walk 113 miles in 24 hours at the Baseball Grounds in Cincinnati.

Two or three days later he was reported to be performing at the Iowa State Agricultural Fair, before appearing at Macon, Georgia, where, on October the 14th, under the auspices of the city government, he walked 50 miles in 9h.41m.38s and then made an additional half mile backward, completing the whole distance in 9h.49m.46s without a rest.

He then appeared in the same city on at the Georgia State Fair, Central City Park, on Monday and Tuesday, the 23rd and 24th of October to *"illustrate his wonderful powers of endurance which have excited the wonder and admiration of the world."* The *Atlanta Constitution* informed its readers after he had accomplished whatever feat he had performed with several seconds to spare on the Monday: Before entering upon a "long walk," he abstains from smoking four weeks previous to the time, during which he eats nothing salt, no meat, or parsnips, says he never remembered being tired. His manners are polished and easy in his private room, with a ceaseless flow of spirits and humor, is 32 years of age, though much younger in appearance.

1874

From the last week in March to the first week in May, and again under the guidance of John Grindell, the ex-champion 10-mile runner of the United States, Weston *"went into training, not according to pugilistic rules, but merely kept regular hours, ate nutritious food, avoided all spirituous and malt liquors, gave up the use of tobacco, and walked a stated number of miles each day."* The reason for this was that he was about to embark on an ambitious attempt at walking 500 miles in 105 hours and 20 minutes.

On the 7th of May 1874, Weston was at the American Institute in New York, preparing for his forthcoming attempt to walk 500 miles in six days, from the 11th of that month to the 16th. There were a large number of people present, including Professor Doremus and Mr. J. L. T. Smith, City Surveyor, who measured the track as being 754 feet and 1½ inches round, thus requiring seven of its laps to make one mile. The track itself was 40 inches in width and was filled with dry earth. For his attending guests Weston walked briskly round the course created for him 37 times, or five miles in 55 minutes and, for good measure, half a mile backwards. His weight in costume was 128 pounds and the judges for his attempt would be A. J. Vandpoel, Rufus F. Andrews, Colonel Ethan Allen, Judge J. R. Brady, R. J. Cross, Professor Doremus, Lloyd Aspinwall, Major General Alex Shaler, Colonel Josiah Porter, D. A. Curtis, Frank S. Beard, John H. Robins and John Knowles.

The plan of action for the feat was divulged by Weston to the press on the 9th of May. After the public had been admitted, he would start his attempt at 12:05 a.m. and would make his first mile in 15 minutes, his second in 13m and his third in 12m. After that he would make five mph until he achieved 25 miles after which he would indulge in a short 5-minute rest. His plan was to make 115 miles by the end of the day at 23:55 after which he would sleep for five hours. He further planned to complete 200 miles on Tuesday, and during the attempt, make 50 miles without resting on Wednesday and Thursday. By Weston's reckoning, if he could walk 400 miles by 3 o'clock on Friday afternoon, the 15th of May, he had every chance of accomplishing his task. In his calculations, he had allowed himself 29h.20m for sleep, 5h.50m in increments of 15 minutes for meals, 2h.20m in rest periods of five minutes in duration thus allowing him 105 hours and 20 minutes to walk the 500 miles. The time he gave himself for finishing was 22:50 on the Saturday night, or 142 hours and 50 minutes from the start.

Having slept for a substantial part of the day on Sunday, Weston appeared on the track at the designated time in attired in *"full pedestrian costume."* This consisted of a *"loose, black velvet sack coat, black velvet knee breeches, black leggings, high laced walking shoes, a white hat, and a wide, sky blue silk scarf, warn transversely across his person, and in his hand he carried a small riding whip."*

Watched by *"many distinguished professional and scientific gentlemen,"* he proceeded with his remarkable attempt at the time agreed. In the initial few laps he was accompanied by Mr. James Gordon Bennett, proprietor of the *New York Herald,* and went along at a pace of 138 steps a minute, after which he varied his gait between that amount and 160 steps.

The *New York Sun* takes up the next stage of the race: At 4 o'clock, 57 minutes and 7 seconds he finished 25 miles of his journey, and was placed in his bed close to the track and in front of the judge's stand. Mr. Grindell, the trainer, rubbed the pedestrian's legs and the colored servant bathed his head and arms. Dr. Doremus gave him some broken crackers soaked in coffee, and the pedestrian wonder was on his feet in six minutes and one second as happy as a bird.

About 8 o'clock a full brass band struck up a lively air. Mr. Weston seemed not the least fatigued. At 10 o'clock, three minutes and three seconds he had made his fifty miles, and he was fourteen minutes and three seconds ahead of his time. He was rubbed down and given more nourishment, and in six minutes and forty-one seconds was on the track again. He closed his sixtieth mile at 12 o'clock, nine minutes and fifty-nine seconds, and rested a few seconds over five minutes.

"Sometimes arnica liniment was applied. He did not stop while on the track, but took his beef tea and coffee, and buttered his bread while on the go."

He continued on his way taking short breaks and was supported in his effort by spectators who cheered him on. After completing his 80th mile he was hauled off the track, covered in a blanket, and placed on a sofa where his feet were elevated 45 degrees over a supporting chair. Whilst his wrists and face were sponged down by two attendants, a third rubbed his legs briskly using the palms of his hands from his feet towards his body. *"While he was resting whisky was poured through tubes into his shoes, and his stockings were wet with the liquor. He believed the use of whisky in this way made his feet and ankles capable of more endurance."* After two minutes of this he was back out in the ring and performing again in front of the considerable crowd.

At 20:42, Weston completed his 100th mile and his 110th was made at 22:52. It was then touch-and-go whether the pale-looking and exhausted ped would make the 115 miles in the allocated time. After another short rest where his "rubber" had another go at his legs, he went back out into the arena to either make or break. The first mile was made in 12m.1s, his second in 12m.23s, his third in 12m.36s, and his fourth in 13m.24s. There had been heavy betting against him not to make the 115 miles in the time he had allowed himself and the police were on hand to make sure that his fifth mile wasn't interfered with in any way. Three officers were on hand to accompany him on that last mile which he made in 12m.1s, reaching the winning post in 9m.2s less than the specified time! Job done, he made one more lap and went to bed after a hot soak. (It was rumoured that $50,000 was lost in the Union Club by people who had bet that Weston would not make 115 miles in 24 hours.)

Starting off again at 06:38, Weston knew he had a leisurely 85-mile walk ahead of him to keep up with his timetable. Following his admirable effort of the previous day, and looking fit and well, he walked six miles before taking a breakfast of broiled chicken, crackers and coffee between 08:17 and 09:15. Fifteen miles had been made by the time he had his lunch of crackers and cold coffee between 11:34 and midday, and at 13:18, and after covering another five miles, he indulged in underdone cold roast beef, crackers and hot coffee which set him up for his next session. That started at 14:25 and involved walking another five miles till 15:43. He rested 16 minutes and then walked till he had scored 150 miles at 18:17. After supper and an hour's rest, he went back out in front of an ever increasing crowd of eager spectators who spurred him on with the help of the band. The showman, always eager to please the crowd, responded to their attentions with smiles and grateful bows. By midnight he had made 170 miles which was curiously 30 miles short of his target.

He then went to bed and slept soundly till woken up and urged back on the track at 05:09. Initially, he pushed himself along quite slowly on the advice of his trainers, making just 10 miles in three hours before stopping for a break of 1h.26m. However, after his rest he went into top gear and made his 200th mile at 14:31 with only a 10-minute break being taken up to that point. As the afternoon turned into evening, the number of ladies in the swelling audience grew, and they were the perfect catalyst for Weston to show off his prowess as he spurted around the place in quick times, his sixth lap of his 220th mile catching the eye, in a time of 1m.15s. The ladies were beside themselves with excitement, and while the men clapped, they waved their handkerchiefs at the dashing fellow on

King of the Peds

the track. At 20:29, Weston went for his supper and while he was away from the path, he was examined by Prof. Doremus and Dr. Taylor, who both pronounced he was fit and well. It was quite probable that during this break, *"some spirit was poured into his shoes to stimulate the sluggish circulation of the blood in his feet. This softened the inner sole of his shoe, while he walked it worked itself into a roll under the middle of his foot. After a time he began to feel much pain. He stopped, and taking off his shoe, it was found that that the thick skin upon the sole of his foot had become lapped over, making a bad blister."* Unfortunately by 23:00 when he had made 228 miles, he appeared quite exhausted, and it was being considered doubtful that he could go the distance in the remaining time. Only by walking 90 miles a day from thereon could he reach his objective. Weston then went to bed having made 232 miles at 23:57.

On Thursday morning and initially limping before recovering his natural gait, he made 12 miles before breakfast which he took at 09:50, having reappeared back on the track at 06:48. During his 30-minute break in which he tucked into fricasseed chicken, crackers and coffee, he stated he would try and make 100 miles before six o'clock the next morning. However, Weston knew he had his work cut out as his feet were in a bad way, necessitating the use of liniments and salt water baths, as every step he took was described as like *"treading upon coals of fire."* While he walked along during the day he frequently sponged his head and face with ice water, drank beef tea and coffee, and ate crackers. Below is a record of what he achieved up till midnight on his 4th day:

Time started	Miles	Total Miles	Time started	Miles	Total Miles
06:48:30			14:35:37	30	262
08:10:38	5	237	15:41:52	35	267
09:22:11	10	242	16:47:29	40	272
09:50:58	12	244	17:58:04	45	277
10:41:35		Breakfast	19:16:30	50	282
11:48:09	17	249	20:26:10	55	287
12:50:57	22	254	21:34:35	60	292
13:30:28	25	257	22:00:45	62	294
			23:59:55	68	300

Weston now had 48 hours left to make 200 miles. With 8 hours rest per day and by making 5 mph, would he succeed? There were many prepared to bet that he could, but there were also many prepared to bet he couldn't. The ball was in his court.

By the end of the fifth day, and despite being urged on by the masses which flocked into the building to cheer him on, it was quite obvious that he wouldn't accomplish what he set out to achieve. Of the day's highlights, he made one of his miles in 9m.48s and fell down near the judges' stand. Apart from those incidents, he took only two rests, one for breakfast at 07:39 and one for supper at 17:58, and when he was examined by his medical team at midnight having scored 65 miles for the day, they reported his pulse was 84, and that he was distressed by the anticipation of his impending failure. Below is a record of the 5th day's scores:

Time started	Miles	Total Miles	Time started	Miles	Total Miles
05:00:43			14:28:53	35	338
06:17:42	5	308	15:40:47	40	343
07:39:57	10	313	17:15:33	45	348
09:49:34	15	318	17:58:30	48	351
10:49:35	20	323	20:41:45	53	356
11:51:27	25	328	21:45:49	55	361
13:12:17	30	333	23:55:49	65	368

Weston ultimately failed in his attempt, only managing to secure a score of 430 miles by midnight on the last day. It was quite evident that from the moment he set off in the morning he was in poor condition, having taken 3m.39s for his warm-up lap and an appalling 25m.26s to make his first mile, during which he was observed to be limping quite badly. It took a few miles for him to warm to his task, and after frequent stoppages during which he was rubbed with liniment, he soon sped along in his own indomitable fashion. As the brave fellow crossed the finishing line for the final time just before midnight, he was greeted with the wildest applause as the crowd rushed towards the judges' stand to congratulate him. Weston later attributed his poor showing to a foot injury sustained on the third day, but those in the know stated that the first day's exertions had been the cause of his failure.

It was claimed later that Weston had made a nice little $5,000 profit after deducting $3,000 for expenses from his venture. He was also said to have won $7,000 in *"side bets."*

The press then reported that Edward Mullen, the *"champion 10-mile walker of America"* started out to beat Weston's 115-mile walking time at 12:24 a.m. on Monday, the 15th of June, at the Washington Riding Academy on Sixth Avenue and Twenty Sixth Street. Mullen accomplished his task in a time five minutes better, or 23h.48m.45s. The time was made on an inferior and *"heavy"* track, which was 17 laps to the mile, and he made his first fifty in 9h.2m without a rest.

Between June the 17th to the 20th at Philadelphia, Weston accomplished the unparalleled task of walking 200 miles in 40 hours, walking 50 miles within ten consecutive hours each day for four consecutive days, each trial being accomplished without a rest. At the conclusion of each fifty miles, he also walked an additional one-half mile backward. Weston had accomplished his last fifty mile walk in 9h.54m.25s. It must be therefore concluded that he had again been touring the fairgrounds giving exhibitions. Indeed to reaffirm this notion, the following advertisement appeared in the *Port Jervis Evening Gazette* on the 4th of August.

Mr. Edward Payson Weston,
The Famous Pedestrian
WILL APPEAR AT THE
GOSHEN TROTTING GROUNDS
Saturday, Aug. 15, 74

At 1 o'clock p. m, and give a series of illustrations of his **WONDERFUL WALKING FEATS**

MR. WESTON will walk 25 miles, and a half a mile **BACKWARDS**, in five hours; and give illustrations of his various gaits, alternating between his regular pace and his wonderful "spurts" of speed; showing the different styles of walking required to accomplish his great walks of endurance.

An interesting exhibition of Pedestrianism.

MR WESTONS LAST APPEARANCE BEFORE GOING TO EUROPE. GRAND CONCERT on the grounds by the Goshen Cornet Band. Admission to the ground and Grand Stand, 50 cents. Children 25 cents.

On Monday, the 14th of September at 12:02 a.m. at Barnum's "Roman" Hippodrome in New York, Weston began his second attempt at walking 500 miles in six successive days. On the first day, he managed to make 65 miles, and during the time he was actually on the track, he sped along at five mph. On Tuesday he made 71 miles despite having to contend with a large blister, and on Wednesday he walked 70 miles. The hopes that he would make more miles than his last effort in May were dashed when on Thursday he had to be put to bed in the afternoon with a pulse of 140, and what was described as, *"congestion of the brain"*. As a result only 20 miles were made all day. However, on Friday he did manage to make 50 miles without rest in 12h.6m helping him make a daytime score of 52, and after half an hours rest began the task of walking 100 miles in 24 hours at 23:00. His score for five days' work was a miserable 278 miles, and owing to ill health he was unable to make the requisite century, eventually finishing the six days with 326.

In separate letters to Weston and his friends dated the 21st of September, Mr. Barnum said he would let Weston use his facility to have another crack at the distance on October the 5th. Barnum writing from Saratoga reaffirmed that he would give Mrs. Weston $5,000 if her husband completed the task in the time permitted.

King of the Peds

Thus on the date set, the third attempt to secure the distance was began at the usual time. After the first three miles, which were made in 13m.16s, 12m.24s and 11m.44s respectively, Weston rid himself of his velvet suit and red sash and went to work.

The *New York Herald* of Saturday, the 10th of October wrote of, *"Weston's desperate struggle with bunions and impossibilities."* The article provides a clue as to why the pedestrian only walked 16 miles on Thursday the 8th to make up a grand total of 245 in four days: **As the writer entered the Hippodrome last evening Weston was seated in a chair, in front of which was a slat rack upon which his bare feet were stretched upward so as to bring them in convenient position to be manipulated by the half dozen attendants, physicians, timers, and gold laced lackeys gathered about. They were all intent upon a black blister upon the second toe of his left foot. It had sat in judgment between Weston and Time, and decided in favor of the latter. This little patch of extravagated blood had set itself against the pluck, and resolution and endurance of the grittiest man alive, and beaten him. The physicians and attendants swabbed it with lotions and swathed it in cotton; the judges shook their heads at it dubiously and; the anatomized lackey in crimson and gold gazed at it with the solemn official dignity and wooden placidity belittling this occasion, as it befits all others. In the seats above scores of men and women sat with their necks craned eagerly forward, their whole attention absorbed in the contemplation of two swollen feet and ten inflamed toes. The owner of these objects of interest lay back in his chair rather ruefully, reading the time slate, which marked as the total result of his effort 241 miles, and from time to time gazed at his bunions. The general appearance of the man suggests the presence of nervous rather than physical force. His face is thin, his nose peaked, and his chin small and well rounded. He has a mouth full of energy and dogged determination; He is evidently a person - if he had not bent his whole mind and the undivided force of his character upon the production of bunions, and soft corns, and blood blisters on the alluvial bottoms of his own feet - would have accomplished some great thing in the world.**

To the men - and there are many of them - who frequent the Hippodrome during Weston's walk, the condition of the pedestrians feet becomes a matter of absorbing importance; the general color of his corns and, the brilliancy of his blisters, and the temperature of his toes, are subjects of the gravest discussion and the wildest speculations. Weston on his slat stretcher is a monarch. He waves his excoriations with a gesture of command, and controls all about him by the sheer force of his inflammation he is tended and waited on and coodled and combed, bathed and rubbed down and swathed, with all the tenderness imaginable. Everybody seems to bend toward him in sympathy, except the grim, gilt-bespangled lackey, who evidently looks upon him as one of the "properties" of Mr. Barnum's show, which is tinkered up so that it will work again.

Presently the process of tending his feet is finished. Weston rises; after one or two efforts the lines about his mouth deepen into an expression of intense pain. He cannot stand still, but staggers, and rolls and tumbles against his attendants who are pulling to pieces his stretcher and removing the debris of bandages scattered about, he is what is called "groggy." Meantime an attendant is removing the great coat which has been thrown over his shoulders. A small riding whip is put into his hand, and, after a few moments more of shuffling about with that curious coherence of motion, he catches the eye of the timekeeper, throws the butt of his whip into the air and, starts off down the track amid a shout from the crowd. His walk is a strange, shambling, and shuffling gait that suggests a drunken camel walking on hot plates. His body seems to keep well in advance of his feet, and drag them along by the force of superior weight, while they present the appearance of being fixed at inflexible right angles to his legs. The spectator hardly recognizes at first that the pedestrian is walking fast, but he soon observes that the large man who accompanies him is doing his best to keep up with his charge. Up to a few hours before he still had hopes of accomplishing his self imposed task. Now he knows that it is quite impossible. He is hopelessly behind his average. Two hundred and fifty five miles in the two days left him are odds in favor of Time, his untiring antagonist that he knows full well cannot be overcome. Still, after a turn or two, he begins to warm again to his work and goes at it with that dogged determination which seems natural to him. The band in the centre of the great oval strikes up a lively air, and he is soon bounding along over the ground at a lively pace, looking quite fresh and jaunty in his black velvet small clothes, leather gaiters, and canvas helmet. Whenever the band stops, he at once drops something of the rhythm of his stride and he rapidity of his gait, which shows how overtaxed his physical powers have been, and how completely they are dependent upon the force of his will, stimulated by external influences. After a time his legs begin to grow numb with exertion, and then he resorts to the expedient of whipping them with the little riding switch he carries.

On Friday, and by 22:00, he had only managed to make 38 miles from the time he had set off in the morning, and that brought his total up to 286. He did say he would make 75 on the last day but the writing was already on the wall, and the press lost all interest in the debacle other than to confirm that he had failed miserably once again. One newspaper, the *Brooklyn Daily Eagle,* felt compelled to write of the shambles: **Edward Payson Weston has** achieved another successful failure. He has not walked 500 miles in six days, and we doubt that he has ever felt himself able to do so. We think that success would be about as unimportant as failure, in such superfluous undertaking. As for Weston, the necessity or desirability of him is becoming less and less apparent. We have no hard feeling toward him, but we challenge his right to occupy so much attention.

Despite all the criticism which he took from the press, he was still as determined as ever to make the coveted distance in the desired time, and between Monday, the 14th and Saturday, the 19th of December of that year, he once again attempted the task at the Rink in Newark. His previous failures at the feat which had also been attempted in vain by many noted pedestrians hadn't discouraged him to keep plugging away in pursuit of his dream. He underwent a week's special training and his physician Dr. Taylor, after giving him a final medical examination, pronounced him physically in a far superior condition than when he had struggled and failed before. The *New York Times* wrote: Weston was thoroughly cognizant of the immense pluck, endurance and spirit necessary to complete the project and though chafing under a sense of former defeat and public disappointment, he persisted in the assertion that he was equal to the occasion and the task.

He started his great walk around the 16 laps to the mile track on Monday at five minutes after midnight, intending to make the first 115 miles in 24 hours. When he completed his task on Tuesday morning with 58 seconds to spare, he was subjected to a critical medical examination and declared unaffected by it, having rested 4h.59m.12s.

Cheered by the result of the first day's walk, Weston contemplated the idea of making the same distance on the second day. His medical advisers however advised him not to and told him to save his strength for the close of the walk. Accordingly, and on Tuesday, the total number of miles he travelled was only 75, resting 6h.12m.33s. On the third day, he increased this distance to 80 miles resting but 4h.51m.1s.

Toward the close of Wednesday's performance he became disheartened with the small crowds who attended the venue and was adamant he wanted to finish his walk in New York, but sympathetic support from some leading citizens of Newark changed his mind, and continuing his weary tramp, he walked 80 miles on Thursday, resting 3h.45m.12s.

On the track, Weston's medical team was keeping a close eye on their patient, and it was noted that several times every hour one of his physicians would accompany him whilst he made his way round. Nothing untoward was found wrong with him, and if anything he appeared to be growing in strength and spirit.

Toward the close of the fifth day, during which he had completed 75 miles and rested 4h.47m.33s, the pedestrian and his backers were very confident of success and large sums of money were staked on the result. Weston himself was approached by certain people with massive financial inducements of thousands of dollars to throw the race. He told them to go away. He was also convinced there was a conspiracy to stop him by those who were willing to disable him, by throwing pepper and other chemicals at him. So scared was he of the *"New York roughs,"* that he asked for the protection the Newark authorities on the Friday evening. The Mayor responded in a positive way by stating he would call upon the police, and if they couldn't preserve the peace then if necessary, the military would be called in order to guarantee fair play. Indeed on the Saturday morning, Judge Mills issued a warrant, based on information given to him by Superintendent Mills, for the arrest of "Joe" Coburn and *"others"* who were plotting to stop Weston from achieving his ambition.

Weston had now walked 425 miles in five days and retired from the track at 02:12 on the last day. His attendants later got him up and he resumed his walk at 05:03. His first mile after his break was completed in 19m.20s, and after he had completed his 449th mile he was given a rest break of 27m.50s for breakfast. He then set about breaking the 500-mile barrier.

The *New York Times* on the 20th of December wrote: There was nothing in his manner to indicate weariness, or a distrust in his ability to finish his walk. His speech was confident and assuring, his gait was steady and unfaltering and his whole person seemed the embodiment of health and power.

As the galleries filled up and Weston traversed the path at approximately four and a half miles to the hour, there was now real confidence in the record being broken. The scoreboard at six o'clock in the evening showed Weston having made 473 miles, and by 20:00 there was an enthusiastic crowd of 6,000 people in the building cheering the hardy athlete on. Mayor Perry joined the walker on the track for a couple of laps, but withdrew promptly thereafter

King of the Peds

due to the effects of his exertions. Perry, red faced and breathless, was laughed off the track by the ridiculing crowd. Later, the celebrated pedestrian made his 481st mile in 10m.19s.

At around 23:00, he was joined by the chief of police and a captain who trotted along beside him. Behind them followed two policemen and a detective, such was the concern about his safety. Attired in a ruffled white shirt, black velvet knee breeches and black leather leggings, Weston upped his pace to 5½ mph and passed the post, to record the "magic 500" at 23:39:15, walking his last three quarters of a mile in 11m.45s, with the penultimate mile being accomplished in 14m.23s.

Amidst the cheers and the tossing of hats and waving of handkerchiefs, Weston with his hollow cheeks, ruffled hair and unmistakable limp, had achieved the unthinkable. Many had tried before him and indeed he had tried so hard himself, but that day he had accomplished it! Mayor Perry in a speech congratulated him on his success, and the crowd hooted their approval in the direction of the great man. He was then wrapped up in blankets and carried to a coach shortly after 1 o'clock which conveyed him to the Mansion House Hotel on Broad Street, where he slept till seven o'clock the next morning. After breakfast he took a stroll to the rink and back again. He then went to church. Later that week, Weston was presented with a gold watch and a purse of a $1,000 for his amazing feat of endurance and guts.

1875

Weston next appeared on the track at the Hippodrome in New York on Monday, March the 1st 1875 in a six-day match with Professor Judd, for a purse of $5,000 offered by Mr. Barnum. The two couldn't be more different. Whilst Weston totally ignored text book training as regards diet and exercise, Judd was his complete opposite, in that he was fastidious in his preparation. Weston's old trainer, John Grindell, looked after Judd's interests and Mr. T. J. Englehardt, Weston's. The men would compete on two separate tracks. Weston wearing a black velvet suit would perform on the inner, whilst the blue flannel attired Judd walked on the outer.

Judd made the first mile in 13m.19s, his opponent scoring his in 13m.55s. Weston then warmed up sufficiently enough to lead at the two-mile mark with 24m.5s, his opponent 16s in his rear. Weston's time for 25 miles was 5h.21m.36s. He made his 30th mile in 10m.53s, and after scoring 50 miles, he averaged a mile every 13 minutes. By the time Judd retired at 22:00, he was 13 miles behind Weston, who left the track after completing his 108th mile in 13m.02s. The leaders' aim was to complete another 100 miles the next day.

Both men appeared back in the race at 04:00. Although both performed quite poorly initially, Weston did pick up a little in the afternoon and evening. By 23:35, when he retired the Professor had made 64 miles bringing his total to 149, whilst Weston, who had scored 71 up until 12:20 a.m., aggregated 179.

Judd arrived back on the track about two hours earlier than Weston, who began his day at 06:08 on Wednesday morning. Whilst Weston went along reasonably well during the day, Judd performed poorly making more stops than what he had done in the previous day.

Below is a table of times for each contestant in five-mile periods:

| **WESTON** | | **JUDD** | | **WESTON** | | **JUDD** | |
Miles	Times	Miles	Times	Miles	Times	Miles	Times
190	01:23:18	155	01:10:09	220	01:33:50	185	02:08:31
195	01:23:12	160	02:16:50	225	01:15:57	190	02:57:31
200	01:13:33	165	01:27:21	230	01:27:50	195	01:35:43
205	01:38:45	170	01:49:24	235	01:17:29	200	01:26:43
210	01:27:30	175	02:08:54	240	01:12:10		
215	01:18:20	180	01:30:02	245	01:20:01		

Judd retired just before midnight after making an overall total of 200 miles or 51 for the day. The race leader however, kept on until 01:30 going to bed with a score of 254 miles.

Weston's opponent more or less gave up the fight with sore feet on the fourth day, having scored 217 miles by 15:35. He added five more miles, but then retired permanently on 222. Although the match was effectively over there and then, the management, in an attempt to appease the large crowd who were hungry for entertainment, employed the services of the Bostonian, Edward Mullen. As well as taking over Judd's score on Thursday afternoon he was given an extra 35 miles start on top of it and by midnight made 41 miles.

During Friday afternoon, Weston addressed the very large audience and told them about his past pedestrian feats and the build-up to this match. Mullen went on to score an unconvincing 89 miles before making his retirement, attributing his failure to his poor preparation in training and not taking proper care of himself whilst on the track. His place was be taken on by another walker called George B. Coyle at 20:30. Coyle made his first 10 miles in just under 2h.15m and after that plugged away at a steady rate of a mile in every 12½ minutes. Meanwhile, Weston had made 67 miles for his day's work, and that added on to his previous day's score, gave him a total of 371 miles by the end of the night.

On the last day at noon the scores were: **Weston 400; Coyle 55:** Coyle would entertain the crowd until the end of the race, even after Weston had finished his at 23:31 after completing 431 miles. Mullen, who had been given permission to return to the track by the managers to woo the spectators with some fast exhibition walking, was later dragged off by the police after Weston refused to race with him. His forced expulsion apparently caused *"considerable dissatisfaction among the rowdy element in the audience."* The final scores were: **Weston, 431 miles in 6 days; Judd, 222 miles in 3 days; Mullen, 91 miles in 48 hours; Coyle 95 miles in 36 hours:**

A couple of days after the conclusion of the race, Weston returned to the Hippodrome for a complimentary benefit in aid of his children hosted by Mr. Barnum. In front of a meagre crowd of 200, he failed in his attempt to walk 50 miles in 11 hours by four miles, walking his last half mile backwards.

At the Rink in New York in May of 1875, Weston made it his goal to walk 118 miles in 24 hours, 125 miles in 25 hours, 200 miles in two days, and then hoped to score 515 miles in six days. Setting off on his task on Monday, the 10th of May at the usual time of just after midnight, and having made 22 miles, he abandoned his attempt to beat Daniel O'Leary's feat of walking 115 miles in 22h.59m made in Philadelphia on the 23rd of April (as described in Chapter 4) due to cutting his foot on the raised margin of the track.

On the advice of his physicians, who recommended that he should rest, Weston put his feet up at 05:10 and slept for 4 hours before making his reappearance at 09:42. After that, he did something quite remarkable, actually walking 70 miles without stopping, which was considered at the time as being the *"greatest feat of pedestrianism ever accomplished."* Thus, and on a score of 92 miles for the day, he went to bed at 23:20. The mind boggles at the thought that if Weston hadn't hurt his foot, the earlier rest of 4h.32m.32s could have made him an extra 15 to 20 miles or even slightly more.

By the end of the third day, he had managed to make 235 miles, and at an average rate of a mile every 14 minutes, he had only added 65 miles to Tuesday's final score of 170 when he had made 78 miles. Weston had taken seven hours rest during Wednesday; when he left the track shortly after midnight, he was said to be *"badly used up."*

On the 13th of May, the *Brooklyn Daily Eagle* reported that Weston had walked 117 miles in 23h.58m.12s during the race. This feat was also reported in the *New York Times,* but on the evidence of the previous paragraph, this couldn't have been done in a *single* day, so what the newspapers meant was that Weston must have made the new record between whatever time he re-emerged back on the track on Tuesday morning and 09:42 of that day.

On the last day it was reported that he ended his walking day at 23:44 on a miserable score of 370 miles, but there is no mention of when he finished his last mile of the day, evidently adding just twenty during it. However, undaunted by his disappointment, he tried again on the following Monday having only had one day's rest. Beginning his task at 12:25 a.m. he made 78 miles in the first 24 hours and 62 in 48 hours, thus making 139 miles from the start. At the end of three and a half days, and probably through fatigue, Weston was compelled to abandon the attempt, having in that time only walked 200 miles.

Weston had an amazing belief in himself that he could prevail in his forthcoming match between himself and O'Leary. Not many shared his optimistic view but still the people of Chicago looked forward to watching their

King of the Peds

man O'Leary prove he was the best of the pair. The race, which took place in the windy city's Exposition Building between Monday, the 15th, and Saturday, the 20th of November 1875, can be read about in Chapter 4.

CHAPTER 3

What Else Happened in 1875

Between Friday, the 18th and Saturday, the 19th of June 1875, at the Drill Shed in Dunedin, New Zealand, William Edwards, the Australian pedestrian, accomplished the feat of walking 100 miles in 23h.55m. *"After finishing the 50th mile he showed signs of fainting but afterwards revived and continued the walk, though his feet were bleeding very much through the effects of new shoes he wore – a very unwise proceeding on his part."* Edwards made his last mile in good time, though not in the nine minutes that he thought he might, and at the end, was *"thoroughly exhausted."*

Edwards would later attempt to walk 3,150 times round the Oddfellows Hall in Christchurch, New Zealand, to complete a distance of 105 miles in 24 hours. He started his attempt at 20:00 on Friday, the 24th of September. *"He wore canvas shoes with outer soles of india-rubber, similar to that used in galoshes, and inner soles of cork. The India-rubber was, of course, rendered necessary by the unyielding nature of the wooden floor. During the latter portion of the race Edwards was occasionally supplied with brandy and water and some of Gee's calves foot jelly, the latter of which he commends very highly."*

Edwards was examined by Dr. Frankish before starting, at the 12-hour mark, and at the finish. On commencement, his pulse was 76 and his temperature 97. At the half way stage, his pulse was 108 and his temperature 98½, and at the finish his pulse was 134 and his temperature 99½. In the end he successfully achieved the feat in seven minutes and three seconds under the time allocated. Just before he finished, a subscription of £14.6s.1d was collected for him.

CHAPTER 4

The Plucky Pedestrian!

Of Daniel O'Leary, the *Davenport Daily Gazette* on the 7th of March 1887 wrote: He is a muscular looking man, compactly built, about five feet and eight inches in height, smooth face, light moustache, and brown hair. He has the appearance of slenderness, is troubled with no superfluity of obesity and has the regulation pedestrian build. He is of a nervous temperament and moves and acts quickly. Engaging as a conversationalist of good address and intelligent, he is an agreeable person to meet.

O'Leary was the son of a farmer. He was definitely born in, or near, the village of Clonakilty, County Cork, Ireland, on *June the 29th 1846. He worked on his father's farm until, at the age of 19, he sought his fortune in America. He quickly moved from New York, where he couldn't find work, to Chicago, where, after initially working in a lumber yard, he travelled south to Mississippi in 1866. He picked cotton for over a year and then went back to Chicago, where he sold books for a living. O'Leary's personal account of those days can be found below.

*In the United States census of July 1870, he is recorded as being "24" years old. He was living in Chicago Ward 12, Cook, Illinois, with his wife Ann, aged 27, who was also born in Ireland, and who he had married only a couple of months earlier. In the census he was described as working in a *"book store"* and had a personal estate valued at $300.

The following **sketch** of O'Leary's career was published by the **New York Sun** about the time O'Leary travelled *back* to Europe on Tuesday, the 5th of March 1878. It will take us up to that point in Chapter 9.

Mr. O'Leary says he was born in County Cork, Ireland, thirty one years ago. He came to this country in 1866 when 19 years old, settled in Chicago, and claims that city as his residence. With a keen eye for business, he saw that the citizens of Chicago were very much in need of Bibles. He opened a Bible store and did well. "I used to buy my Bibles," he says, "off D. & J. Sadler, of New York, and John E. Potter of Philadelphia, and sell them in Chicago. While the profit was not very great, I made a good living, and felt that I was doing good to my fellow men."

The *Chicago Tribune* wrote: His extraordinary powers of endurance and speed in walking were developed in that precarious manner of living - book selling - which circumstances obliged him to adopt. Early and late he toiled at his calling, and his fare meantime was not, as may be supposed, luxurious. Trying to eke out an existence, he bravely continued his rounds of the city every day, and thus he acquired the strength of muscle and the long-windedness, - necessary qualities of the pedestrian.

"How did you come to leave the Bible business and become a professional pedestrian?" asked the writer.

"When Weston was making a talk by his attempt to walk from Portland to Chicago it set me to thinking in Ireland I was a good traveler, and I bid great experience in rushing for the swinging bridge in Chicago. *One night I was sitting in Gaines' store on Wabash Avenue, when somebody said Weston was talking about going to Europe. I said that if he dropped into Ireland on the way he'd get beaten so bad that he'd never again call himself a walker. Everybody laughed at me. I finally said that I thought I could beat him myself. At that, they all roared, and made sarcastic remarks on what they called me an 'Irish conceit.'

*In the fall of 1873 he went to the dry goods store and found three men discussing the pro's and cons of Weston's proposed walk of 500 miles in six days.

"None but a Yankee can perform such a feat," remarked one of the gentlemen in perhaps, an overconfident tone. "Hold on, hold on," interrupted O'Leary, "perhaps a foreigner might do it." "He won't be an Irishman," chimed in another in the crowd. "Ireland has sent forth good men," calmly suggested O'Leary. "Wonderful fellows, indeed, they can accomplish almost anything with their tongues," was the sarcastic response. "The tongue is the mean member of the human frame," said O'Leary. "Had Cicero and Demosthenes been born dumb, two great minds would have passed away from earth to eternity, like the bird flying through the air, without leaving a trace of their greatness behind."

As the men began to titter, and as he left the store, O'Leary said, "Laugh as you please, gentlemen but bear in mind I will beat Weston in a fair contest."

A Frenchman, offered to bet $250 that I couldn't walk a certain distance in a given time. Nobody had any confidence in me, I had to back myself. I don't suppose I would have done it if I had to stop to think, but my blood was up over the jibing, and I took him up. I don't remember the *exact distance, nor the time, but I do remember that I won the money, and lost five toe nails in doing it. The amount of the business is that I knew nothing about walking. I traveled the distance on solid planks, in every day clothes, and wore common high heeled shoes with my toes pinched and pressed together. As I pulled off the socks the blisters broke and the toe nails came off with them.

*O'Leary is referring to the dates between Monday, the 13th, and Tuesday, the 14th of July 1874, at the West Side Rink, on the corner of Randolph and Ada Street in Chicago, which he had rented specifically for the occasion.

The track had been *"scientifically surveyed"* at a measurement of 400 feet, which meant that a mile was made up of 13.20 circuits of it. Mr. Samuel S. Greely, City Surveyor, certified that to make the required distance of 100 miles, 1,320 circuits of the track would have to be covered. The judges appointed for the event were: Charles Moore, John B. Roche, Capt. Daniel F. Gleeson, John E. Tansey, F. G. Welch and Alderman B. Quirk. The scorers were: Frank. E. McMahon and Leander L. Landers.

Before the event started, the only record of O'Leary competing in any event was a reference to a 70-mile hike on a bad road in one day. O'Leary was described as being *"about 5 feet 8 inches in stature, a genuine Celt, of wiry build and with a resolute cast of countenance."* The Irishman claimed that bets of $1,000 "were up against him," and confirmed that he had wagered $250 on himself succeeding. *"The athlete was not "made up" in professional guise. He was attired simply in a white woollen shirt and ordinary dark pantaloons, but his enthusiasm appeared to be considerable. There was a very good muster of "sons of the soil" at the building, and when Daniel appeared ready for the struggle he was greeted with a hearty round of cheering."*

After completing just 10 miles, the first five of which were made in 1h.5m and the second in 55m, O'Leary was *"advised"* by his trainer to change his costume so that he performed in *"woollen tights,"* which were more *"suited to the task"* he had set himself. His step was measured and averaged during the first two hours at 86 inches. O'Leary eventually covered the distance in 23h.15m which was considered a *"notable achievement for an amateur pedestrian."*

More than a month later at precisely 22:00 on Friday, August the 21st at the same venue, O'Leary, who was said to have wagered $1,000 (of which Frank Agnew was the stakeholder) with Mr. Cerno, that he would be able to walk 105 miles in a 24-hour period, began his new challenge "against time." Alderman Tom Foley was chosen to be the referee and the judges were the same as in the previous event, but without Mr. Welch.

In front of a moderate crowd whose numbers had been dissipated by a severe rainstorm, O'Leary, sporting a swollen hand which had been bitten by a pet monkey, started on his way. He made his first mile in 10m.33s, his second in 9m.3s, his first four miles in 40m, and his fifth mile 10 minutes later. During the first three miles he was accompanied by policeman Maurice O'Connor, and then by his trainer Mr. A. H. Libby, on a wet and slippery track caused by the leaking roof.

O'Leary succeeded in his task and completed the set distance in a time of 23h.17m.58s. The *Chicago Tribune* wrote of the accomplishment: **This performance outdoes Weston or any other man who has set himself up in either hemisphere as the exponent of the art of combining the powers of speed and endurance.** In front of an appreciative crowd who cheered him on, O'Leary sped along at a rate of 7 mph during the closing stages of his walk. There was some concern expressed by the judges that he might have not walked his corners fairly, so to take the doubt from their minds, the athlete walked an extra mile in a time of 9m.35s to make 106 miles in 23h.27m.13s. At the finish, he was rubbed down with alcohol and later presented with a purse which had been collected for the *"plucky pedestrian."* In a later article, the *St. Louis Dispatch* reported: **He now wears the "Championship Pedestrian**

Medal" of the United States, a trophy which was presented him by his many friends on the accomplishment of the tramp.

A week or so later, O'Leary wrote a letter to his local newspaper.

CHICAGO, Aug.28, 1874.

To the Editor of the Chicago Tribune:

SIR:

Perceiving that Mr. Weston recently failed to accomplish his walk of 400 miles in five consecutive days, I hereby propose to walk the above distance in the specified time, either at New York or Chicago, wherever city may be decided upon. My friends and my self are willing to place any sum of money from $5,000 to $10,000 in the hands of a responsible party just as soon as any person believing me to be unequal to the task will inform me of their willingness to put up a similar amount.

D. O'Leary

"That walk," continued Mr. O'Leary, gave me quite a reputation.

Daniel O'Leary

The National Police Gazette (Illustration no: 4)

What O'Leary didn't mention in his interview with the **New York Sun** was the fact that he took himself off to St. Louis to attempt to walk 200 miles in 40 hours, or 50 miles in 10 consecutive hours on each of four consecutive days; a feat which had never been previously accomplished. His shot at the new record would take place at the Rink on the corner of Nineteenth and Pine Street in that city starting on Wednesday, the 30th of September. O'Leary was quite confident that he was up to the task. In its reference to the forthcoming feat, the *St. Louis Dispatch* wrote: That he will have a large attendance, there can be little doubt.

He duly completed the objective in a time of 36h.29m making the first 50 miles in 9h.20m, the second in 9h.17m, the third in 9h.13m and the fourth in 8h.39m. Of the achievement, the *Chicago Tribune* commented: Mr. O'Leary's friends in Chicago are quite jubilant at his success, and in the sporting circles of our city he is and will henceforth be recognized as the champion pedestrian of the world. Of his style of locomotion, the same newspaper later wrote: His style of walking is the purest; there is no deceit in it, heel and toe, straight on. He steps a little more than the military pace, and with such regularity and elasticity that his movements though quick seem smooth. In that he differs from Weston, the Eastern walkist, whose gait is most uneven, sometimes degenerating to the shuffle.

At 14:40, on the afternoon of Saturday, November the 14th, O'Leary, having made a bet with Mr. Libby, his trainer, to the tune of $100, that he wouldn't be able to walk 50 miles in 8h.45m, set off in pursuit of his goal. The timekeeper was Mr. W. B. Curtis and he set his watch as O'Leary went on his way at the West Side Rink, Chicago, and on the same length of track as previously described. To make the 50 in the required time, O'Leary would have to walk 660 times around the path created for him; a path that was in a cold cheerless building, and illuminated by penny candles held in pop bottles spread at wide intervals. He also had to share the track with the occasional trespasser, or, *"every scalawag who thought he could "do some walkin,"* which greatly annoyed the athlete.

Suffice to say, O'Leary failed in his attempt, managing to circle the track 638 times for a distance of 48¼ miles. His best mile was his eleventh, which he made in 9m.12s, and on his 42nd mile, he put in a *"killing spurt"* and kept up the pace for four laps amidst the cheers of the crowd which by this time had numbered 500. At the end, and when Mr. Curtis called "Time!" O'Leary said, "Gentlemen, I have done all I could." Mr. Libby then called for three cheers for the pedestrian. After the crowd had responded to the request, Libby addressed them and said, "Gentlemen, Mr. O'Leary has accomplished a feat which has never heretofore been approached nearer than an hour. In consideration of his performance, I will hand over to him the entrance moneys which amount to about a hundred and thirty dollars."

Below is a record of the average times for covered miles and the accumulated total times:

Mile	Per Mile	Total	Mile	Per Mile	Total
1	10:13	00:10:13	30	11:40	05:23:25
5	09:33	00:49:33	35	10:00	06:17:50
10	09:33	01:38:23	40	10:29	07:15:11
11	09:12	01:47:35	45	10:03	08:07:19
15	11:45	02:29:55	46	10:36	08:17:55
20	09:32	03:28:20	47	12:16	08:30:11
25	11:45	04:26:15	48	12:13	08:42:26
			Fin		08:45:00

Soon after and I came to New York on business and was matched to walk 20 miles in *Barnum's Hippodrome against Mr. Wilson Reid for $500…………………………

*O'Leary refers to the match held on Saturday night the 20th of March 1875 between himself and Reid, who was a New Yorker.

The conditions of the match were that O'Leary would allow Reid a start of 440 yards in the 20-mile race for a stake of $500 a side. Each man would select his own judges, who in turn would choose a referee. Reid selected W. H. Stafford and M. J. Burris, and O'Leary, Daniel M. Sterns and Joseph Carroll, all being members of the New York Athletic Club. After *"considerable difficulty,"* they decided that James Watson would be the referee. Both men were weighed before the start, the muscular Reid weighing in 170 pounds, which was 20 lbs more than his opponent. The start was made at 20:28, and below are the scores for the match:

	O'LEARY			REID			O'LEARY			REID	
Miles	Mins	Secs	Miles	Mins	Secs	Miles	Mins	Secs	Miles	Mins	Secs
1	9	12	1	9	12	11	9	23	11	9	54
2	8	6	2	8	6	12	9	52	12	10	10
3	9	22	3	9	22	13	9	23	13	10	17
4	9	15	4	9	15	14	9	48	14	10	36
5	9	28	5	9	28	15	10	23	15	11	46
6	9	52	6	9	52	16	11	14	16	Stops	
7	10	00	7	10	00	17	12	24			
8	9	58	8	9	58	18	12	42			
9	10	3	9	10	6	19	12	59			
10	9	49	10	10		20	11	22			

…………………………………………………I gave Reid a quarter of a mile start. He was backed by a man named Sullivan, who arranged the match, thinking he had a sure thing. Reid could walk faster than I, but I kept close to his heels for 13 miles, and held him to his work. In one of his spurts to get away from me he broke down and gave it up on the fifteenth mile. At the start I don't think I had a friend in the audience, but they changed toward the close.

King of the Peds

O'Leary by this time had it in his mind that he wanted to take on Weston for the title of *"Champion Pedestrian of the World,"* but he was turned down by the establishment, who told him to make a good record first and then meet him later.

After this match Mr. O'Leary gave John DeWitt ten miles out of 100, and won the match at the American Institute*.

*The reporter refers to a 100-mile walking match between the 28-year-old O'Leary, and the 53-year-old John DeWitt of Auburn, New York, for a purse of $1,000. The race took place between Friday, the 9th and Saturday, the 10th of April 1875 in New York starting at 10 a.m. O'Leary, giving his opponent a 10-mile start, made his first five miles in 49m.55s with his opponent managing the same distance in 1h.5m.5s.

O'Leary completed the distance in 23h.52m.14s, making his last mile in 9m.18s. DeWitt gave up on the 57th mile.

Then he went to Philadelphia………………………………………………

On the 26th of April 1875, under the headline **WESTON BEATEN**, the *Philadelphia Times* wrote: Weston will have to look to laurels, for all of a sudden, in the height of his fame, a competitor springs up who bids fair to throw his best feats into the shade. This wonder bears the common enough name of Daniel O'Leary; and, although he comes from Chicago, it is not known that face bears any blood relationship to the Mrs. O'Leary whose unruly cow kicked over a lamp that started a fire which nearly erased the wicked city from the map of the United States. He said he would beat Weston, and when all smiled he winked knowingly. He is a finely built fellow, with good muscular development, and critical judges made their minds up not to be too rash in venturing their loose cash against his success. On Friday, as the clock struck midnight, O'Leary started at the Chestnut Street Rink to walk 115 miles in twenty four hours, in presence of the judges, twenty in number, who were to relieve each other at intervals. All were fair men, and picked out for this quality. O'Leary started off with an easy gait, but with vigor and rapidity, and after he warmed up it was seen that his powers were not overrated. His step was firm and elastic, and his stretch good. On the seventh mile he made the excellent time of nine minutes, five seconds. He walked steadily all Saturday, keeping up an average which showed by afternoon that if he could hold out he would win easily. He expressed himself as feeling all right, and said he had no doubt of winning. About 8 o'clock he finished his one hundredth mile, and shortly before 11 o'clock completed the task, 115 miles, the time being twenty two hours fifty nine minutes, the best Weston ever made being twenty three hours fifty nine minutes and forty four seconds. O'Leary still walked on, and made a mile and a lap more, the total time being twenty three hours eight minutes, the best on record. Quite a large number of persons witnessed the finish, and O'Leary was heartily congratulated upon his wonderful success.

………………………………………………..and walked 116 miles in 23 hours and 8 minutes.

O'Leary, now convinced of his ability to beat Weston, challenged the celebrated pedestrian to a match, but Weston again denied him the chance insisting he wanted more proof that he was a worthy opponent. O'Leary, although more than capable over 24 hours, still hadn't proved himself over six days. Undeterred, he went back home and once again rented the rink in Chicago, to prove he could walk 500 miles in six and a half days or 156 hours.

On Sunday, May the 16th, Dan and his friends arrived at the rink to find the track that he would race on totally inadequate. The wooden boards which he was due to tramp on were covered in mud which seeped between the timbers, and there was no way he could have walked on that. In an attempt to retrieve the situation, the pedestrian got hold of some extra boards which he placed around the track and covered with sawdust and shavings. The reconstruction delayed the start by over three hours, but eventually he got on his way at 16:31. He was initially accompanied on the track by Officer Connors of the Sixth Police Precinct, who had agreed to walk 50 miles with him on the track, which was surrounded on the outside by a rope, and supported by stakes at its four corners and at other points. It meant that O'Leary had to turn sharply at the corners as he met them.

Walking at a six and a half mile gait, he made his first mile in 9m.5s and his second in 11m.5s. During his third mile, he went along at 7 mph. By this time Officer Connors, who was getting *"fagged out,"* was readying himself to drop out of the time trial, and did so after the third lap. This gave the signal for a young man called Jack Stearns to join O'Leary on the track, but he too struggled against the pace of the Irishman. Of O'Leary's style, the sports reporter for the *Chicago Tribune* wrote: He walks with a light, easy and graceful step. His gait is not long or swinging, but he has a short quick hip-step which gets him over the ground very fast. He carried his arms high, with the elbows thrown far back, and head erect to give his lungs the greatest expansion.

O'Leary made his first 10 miles in 1h.38m, his half century in 8h.56m, his century in 23h.1m and his 130th mile in 30h.27m. Although he was averaging about 11 to 12 minutes to the mile, he made his 115th mile in an unprecedented time of 7m.45s. He went on to celebrate his 200th mile at half past six on Tuesday evening, and before the hour struck midnight, he was 13 hours ahead of the time he had allocated himself to reach his target. O'Leary had allowed himself just three hours of sleep per night between 23:00 and 02:00, but was apparently so nervous that he hardly did so.

On resuming his task the next day he breakfasted on beef-steak, eggs and coffee taking sips of beef tea as he took short rests during the day. In a brilliantly lit building, O'Leary was joined on the track the next evening by Thomas Alcock, the champion short distance pedestrian, for six miles, who managed to keep up with him for the time he was on. During that evening O'Leary suffered a nose bleed, and on retiring to bed at his usual time at 23:00, had made 290 miles.

The lone walker resumed his tramp four hours later and stayed on the track till 10 a.m. After resting for an hour during which time he had his breakfast, he continued on till 17:30 and indulged in a two-hour break. Alcock accompanied Dan around the track for most of the evening, and in front of another large audience patronised by a large number of ladies, he scored 350 miles by 21:00. Going along at a rate of 3½ mph, he was confident at this stage of success.

During Friday he walked just 62 miles, which meant he had scored 412 miles by midnight, thus requiring him to make 83 miles in the 31½ hours which remained in order to reach his goal. The only problem he encountered was a blistered heel brought on by ill fitting shoes in the Philadelphia race, plus stiffness in his limbs after rest. On completion of that 412th mile he was presented with a large bouquet by a lady in the audience. *"He acknowledged it gracefully, and it apparently infused him with fresh vigor as he let himself out somewhat for the general delectation."*

O'Leary retired to bed that night at 23:30, remaining in his *"cot"* till 01:45 on Saturday morning. While he slept, a new track had to be constructed within the old one due to its *"heavy and soggy"* condition. The original one, measuring 480 feet, had to be traversed 11 times to make a mile. The new one was 11 feet shorter and therefore had to be circumnavigated 129 times more just to make up the lost distance. This he achieved by 5 a.m. after which he rested and ate his final breakfast, before setting off to walk 22 miles before noon.

On Saturday evening at 18:10, he had succeeded in crediting himself with 470 miles. At this point, he took a rest until 19:30, during which time his physician Dr. Dunn applied a bandage to the blister on his heel which was considerably inflamed. After being attended to, he went out again and was accompanied by Alcock for a distance of 17 miles, which he managed to walk at a rate of five mph.

Around the hour of midnight, and amid cheering from a 5,000 plus crowd that was beyond itself with excitement, O'Leary, after completing 490 miles, was presented with an elegant easy chair by A. H. Hale & Bros. He was also given $1,000 and a gold medal inscribed with **"Champion Pedestrian of the World"** by his friends. He then went on to complete his objective in tremendous style walking the last ten miles rapidly. Mr. W. B. Curtis and Alcock walked with him for the last five miles and O'Leary's times for those miles were: 11m, 12m, 12m.10s, 11m and 10m.50s. At 01:32:50, he finished his 500-mile walk, making the distance in 2h.28m.10s less than the allotted time of 156 hours. At the end, the new "Champion Pedestrian of the World," was bundled into a waiting carriage and driven to his home on the corner of Lake and Robey Street.

On Sunday, the 30th of May, some days after O'Leary's marvellous achievement, the *Chicago Tribune* wrote the following article. Entitled **PEDESTRIANISM; RESULT OF O'LEARY'S SUCCESS ON THE RESIDENTS OF THIS CITY**, it provides an entertaining insight into how his escapades on the track were influencing people off it:

Chicago is noted as a city of gigantic strides. It has advanced at a tremendous pace. The people of the go-ahead kind, bound to walk away from all rivals, to distance all competitors. It is a fast place: the men go at a rapid gait,

King of the Peds

and the girls are high steppers. It has been called a great blower, but this is now treated as a compliment to its powers of wind.

Curiously enough, most of the comments made upon the garden City have been couched in terms belonging to the pedestrian. Used to indicate its wonderful growth and progress, they have deserved, but Chicago now is peculiarly entitled to the parlance of the heel-and-toe exercise. It has lately become A CITY OF PEDESTRIANS.

Chicago people have, in fact, but just found their legs. This remark is not meant to imply that they are just emerging from a state of infancy, or that their bibulous habits have heretofore deprived them of the proper use of these valuable anatomical appendages. But never until now has Chicago availed itself of their usefulness. A little more than a week ago Chicago rode. It was a city of street-cars, of omnibuses, of private carriages. The nickel dropped into the fare box with an incessant jingle, the click of the conductors punch was heard and the crack of the coachman's whip resounded like the discharge of musketry. Everybody rode. BUT WHAT A CHANGE!

The omnibus still plods along, but the driver howls "all the way up to Thirty First Street," or "West Madison Street to Western Avenue" in vain. People heed him not, or, looking contemptuously upon his deserted vehicle walk, the faster. Nobody gets on; the money box is mute, the driver is sad and an object of compassion because he is obliged to ride. The street-car tumbles along, but the driver and conductor are almost always the occupants. The punch sleeps quietly in the latter's pocket, the upraised finger of the former, soliciting passengers at the street crossings is looked at with scorn and indignation. People are positively angry at the barest suggestion of riding. A man who rides, unless a cripple, is looked upon with contempt, and the woman who rides exposes herself to the suspicion that her limbs are deformed and misshapen. Private carriages not unused in barns, and what provision is to be made for the excess in of horses above those actually acquired for draught purposes is becoming a serious question. It is not at all improbable but that Chicago will follow the example of Paris and eat them.

People dash through the streets with HEADS THROWN BACK, CHESTS THROWN OUT, elbows drawn backwards as if fleeing from some terrible danger, or as if answer to some important summons. Men can be seen with watches in their hands timing themselves as they dart forward, and muttering strange words about minutes and seconds, and distances. The pedestrian mania has even had its effects on FEMALE ATTIRE.

Dresses are now cut loose and allowing to admit of more free use of the limbs. The Chicago woman of the period is not encumbered by any extra clothing or hampered by the "scant effect." She dispenses with the parasol; everything is ordered with a view to the full development of her pedestrian powers. She no longer affects small feet and light boots. High heels are dropped, and the easy, roomy shoe is now the correct thing. Men, women, and children dash through the streets at the most momentous pace, and everybody seems to be walking a match with everybody else.

What has brought such a wonderful change in so short a time? O'LEARY.

Two weeks ago he began his walk of 500 miles in 156 hours at the West Side Rink. Chicago has admired this young mans abilities in the pedestrian line, but had never before been greatly excited thereby. The walk continued day after day. The first 100 miles were completed in a wonderfully short time. People began to go and see him. Still he walked, reaching successively his 200th, 300th, and 400th mile. Ladies in great numbers visited the rink to behold the marvelous example of endurance and skill in walking. It got to be A POPULAR RESORT.

Young men asked their girls to go and see O'Leary instead of Humpty Dumpty, the Minstrels, the circus or McVicker's. His wonderful fast time shown in walking in some of the miles, and his determination to succeed, were the topics of conversation elsewhere. Last Saturday night the crowd at the rink was enormous. The walk was completed in 153 hours amid the greatest enthusiasm. The unparalleled feat was heralded far and wide, and Chicago was converted to pedestrianism. The walk brought Chicago to its feet, - brought it up standing as it were.

Monday morning people ceased to hail the street-car and stage. IMPROMPTU WALKING MATCHES were made by clerks, laborers, business-men, shop-girls, - everybody going to down-town labors. West Madison Street became the scene of hundreds of pedestrian contests. Walks from Western Avenue to State Street were made in incredibly short time by persons who had never walked the distance before in their lives. Bets were made, piles of money were exchanged in sums ranging from a nickel to 25 cents, on the result of these impromptu matches. Clerks, boarding together started down town in the closest imitation of O'Leary in respect to speed and style possible and, neighbors got together for the purpose of testing each others speed in the down-town walk. Those who went it alone all walked against time. It was the same on THE SOUTH SIDE. Michigan and

Wabash Avenues looked as if they had been turned into pedestrian courses. Walks from Thirty Fifth Street to Lake were very commonly indulged in. On the North Side the mania was just as severe. And the disposition to walk, pedestrianize, or O'Leary it, as it is now popularly termed, has continued ever since.

It has wholly transformed the appearance of the streets. The sidewalks are now crowded with hurrying pedestrians all stepping forward, male and female, in true professional style with heads thrown back, and hands held up high, each apparently striving to achieve a six mile gait. Street cars pass along once in a while but if they contain any passengers at all they are cripples, weak and infirm old people, or shop boys with heavy bundles.

A GLANCE AT ANY OF THE CARS passing through State or Madison Streets will confirm this. In them perhaps will be seen a man with a wooden leg, some old lady of great obesity, a club-footed man, perhaps another knotted up with rheumatism, a very small boy with a big bundle, another with a load of pasteboard boxes, and a woman with a child at the breast and two or three at he heels. People of sound body and limb are not to be seen. No one would now patronize a street-car if it called around to the house, backed up at the door, and carried everybody free.

TAKING A YOUNG LADY TO WALK now-a-days means something. She does not saunter around the block, or stroll slowly through the park. She walks at her utmost speed, and as far as she can.

A young man from the East, who arrived here since O'Leary's walk and was consequently ignorant over this excitement over pedestrianism, whilst calling upon a young lady residing near the corner of Eighteenth Street and Indiana Avenue the other evening, asked her if she would not like to take a walk.

"A walk? Oh yes! To be sure I would! I like walking dearly now," she replied. "Since O'Leary's 500 mile walk all of us girls have become great walkers. Oh, dear, you didn't see O'Leary did you? He's just splendid."

The twain started forth. The young man from the East offered his arm, but the young lady refused it, saying: "Oh gracious! No one can walk in that way. You must throw your head back, so as to allow your lungs the greatest expansion. Then throw your elbows back, and hold your hands up so," and she struck the true attitude of the professional pedestrian, and started off at a terrific gait. The young man let himself out, and followed as best he might, although it was with difficulty that he kept up with her. The walk led down Indiana Avenue for a dozen blocks or more, and then the young man ventured to say, "Aren't you getting tired?" "Tired? Why this is no walk at all! We will walk to Hyde Park and the cross over to the boulevards. That will give us a little more exercise an practice."

Chicago ladies seem to be great walkers," remarked the young man.

"Yes, they are now. Since O'Leary everybody walks. Why, I should be ashamed to ride, positively."

"Do you often walk so far and so fast?"

"Oh yes. The other day I walked to Lincoln Park and back and to Western Avenue. Why you would be surprised to see how many ladies walk now. Pa is trying to sell our horse and carriage. We don't use them at all now. I am training for a match with a young lady on Calumet Avenue, and a little walk like this helps me. This isn't fast. See me strike a five-mile gait."

And this brave young lady shot forward at a prodigious rate. The young man struggled to keep up, and perspired and panted, and inwardly cursed O'Leary and pedestrianism and Chicago girls training for walking matches. His boots were tight, his corns pained him, and for several days after this "taking a walk" he wore slippers and bathed his legs in arnica.

This illustrates the present passion for pedestrianism. Legs are of more account than heads, and length and quickness of stride are dearer than length of purse.

MATCHES AMONG ALL CLASSES are talked of. The Alderman and Citizen's Association are going to settle their difficulty by a grand 10 mile walk; the Young Men's Christian Association will walk the Yosefellows a match; the Women's Temperance Union will walk against the good Samaritans; the High School girls are matched against the Dearborn Seminary girls; Field & Leter's clerks will walk Farwell's; different ladies and societies are booked for contests, and the number of individual matches is enormous. There is every prospect that pedestrianism will rival base-ball in popularity, and that ladies will devote themselves to it to the exclusion of croquet.

King of the Peds

Since the O'Leary performance almost everything smacks of O'Leary some way or another. There are O'LEARY COCKTAILS which are said to impart a particular sprightliness to the human legs: there are O'Leary shoes said to be the best adapted for to fast walking: O'Leary shirts, and O'Leary collars, etc. And there are a great many people who attempt by their feeble imitations to palm themselves off on the public as O'Leary himself.

A BRIEF SKETCH of this celebrity will be of interest. He was said to be of Irish extraction before his recent achievement, but since then several claim that he is a descendant of their soil. Spain claims him, contending that his name is of purely Spanish origin. Italy insists that the mellifluous melody of his patronymic could have been derived from none other than her sunny land, while France as vigorously asserts that it is of French deviation. Unfortunately the genealogical records of his family are obscure and incomplete. Hence he is unable to throw any light upon this important matter himself. It is of the greatest importance that the question should be settled. The sporting reporter would be recreant to the duty which history imposes on him should bequeath the unsolved question of O'Leary's lineage to posterity to quarrel and wrangle over, as nations have done over Homer's birth place.

In the absence of all records, this subject must be looked at in THE LIGHT WHICH PHILOGY IMPARTS.

It seems to show that O'Leary is an Englishman, and of royal blood, being undoubtedly a descendent of King Lear. This amused monarch was called Old Lear, or colloquially Ole' Lear, and derisively Ole Leary. This is evidently the origin of the name, and King Lear's pedestrian wanders through England after his daughters went back on him is probably the fountain-head of O'Leary's walking powers. This settles the question of his lineage. He was born in Wankegan, or Walkegau as he writes it, and thence removed to Walkeeha, and thence to Walkonda, of all places in which his early days were spent being suggestive in sound of pedestrian efforts. He began to walk very early in life. He was never a creeping child. He jumped out of the cradle one day when he was but a few months old, and walked about three miles in a little less than an hour. This was looked upon as astonishing, considering his size and years, and it was predicted that he would become a great pedestrian. He never rode, always relying upon his legs to take him from place to place, and early by his peregrinations through the country, established a reputation as a great walker.

THE BOOKS HE READ indicated the turn of his mind. He read Walker's Dictionary with great avidity. The story of the gentleman who wore the seven-league boots, and got over ground so rapidly, pleased him immensely. O'Leary came to this city a few years ago, and engaged in a business which required a great deal of walking. It was that of a book agent. It was very effective in developing his peculiar powers. It is an occupation that more than any other gives a man a chance to walk. Everybody he solicits to buy a book tells him to walk. O'Leary was repeatedly told to walk whilst thus engaged. He did so. He received the greatest encouragement from everybody. Wherever he presented himself to sell a book he was told to walk. All of his efforts to sell books produced nothing but this advice. Finding that there were so many friends interested in his humble efforts at pedestrianism, he determined to take their advice in its fullest meaning. He did so, and turned out, as all know, the most wonderful walker of the age.

O'Leary's next task was to set himself the goal of walking 150 miles in 32 consecutive hours. There were many people who doubted he could achieve this, but there again, there were many who said he could. He booked the Exposition Building for Friday and Saturday, July the 2nd and 3rd to settle the argument. A large number of his friends met at Burke's Hotel on Friday, the 18th of June, to discuss the arrangements, followed by a another meeting at the same venue on the 24th to make further arrangements for the musical entertainment, construction of the six-lap track, appointment of match officials, printing, advertising and organising a band-wagon to parade in the street.

As it was, the track, which was laid out on the boarded floor, turned out to have two sides measuring 336½ feet in length with two half circles at either end measuring 103½ feet. This made a distance of 880 feet, making six laps to the mile. Along with Alcock, he laid out a whitewash streak to the exact length of the track, and thereafter, a line measuring 18 inches from the streak thus making a path of three feet wide. The tracks advantage was that it would be easier to travel round than those smaller at eight laps to the mile. Its disadvantage was that it would be hard on the feet, but the ped was used to this type of track, as experienced in the east of the country. He had already refused the offer of a sprinkling of sawdust on the track, fearing that particles would get into his shoes and make his feet sore.

The pedestrian however, would not be making his trip alone. There were many willing companions wanting to accompany him at various stages of his attempt. Alcock would make the first 20 miles with him. He would be followed by John Eidlemann who would attempt 40. General Sheridan promised him 50, "Tony," the barber on West Lake Street another 40, and J. W. McAndrews, a 13-year-old pedestrian, also offered his services for the effort. Policemen Sprague and O'Connor were among others offering a few miles as well. O'Leary said he would make the first 50 miles in nine hours, and then keep ahead of time until the 125th mile, employing a gait of 4½ mph thereafter till the end. He said he would take little rest, except to "*take a little beef tea or Bass ale occasionally.*"

Wearing a light short sleeved undershirt and light flannel drawers, he set off on his walk at precisely 15:08 as the large crowd looked on. Many sat in seats in the galleries surrounding the track, enjoyed eating ice cream and drinking soda water that was provided by vendors operating from booths in the building. The track on which O'Leary employed his heel-and-toe method of conveyance wasn't protected from the crowd, and the police were present in large numbers ready to expel anyone caught trespassing on it. One young man however, who got slightly carried away with all the excitement, and who tried to lead the walker around for a lap, was berated by the crowd who shouted in unison, "Put him out! Put him out!" And that is precisely what happened to him as the police rather unceremoniously bundled him off the track and ejected him from the building.

The man on the track meanwhile was putting in some good work. He made his first mile in 8m.55s, his second in 9m.26 and his third in 9m.12s. By 22:45 he had scored 40 miles and was six ahead of schedule, averaging at the time a mile every 11 minutes.

Times for the first 40 miles are shown below. The reader will notice how they are adjusted to the nearest 15 seconds *after* the 18th mile:

Miles	Time	Miles	Time	Miles	Time	Miles	Time
1	08:55	11	12:10	21	11:30	31	12:30
2	09:26	12	11:02	22	12:00	32	12:30
3	09:12	13	13:20	23	11:00	33	11:10
4	10:53	14	10:29	24	17:00	34	13:30
5	12:04	15	10:39	25	17:00	35	12:15
6	09:10	16	11:15	26	09:30	36	11:00
7	10:11	17	11:29	27	11:30	37	12:30
8	10:47	18	10:13	28	10:30	38	12:00
9	10:17	19	11:00	29	11:00	39	10:30
10	10:41	20	13:00	30	12:30	40	12:00

Having just completed making his 100 miles in a time of 19h.43m.26s on Saturday morning, O'Leary had an attack of sickness. The *Chicago Tribune* in its report of the walk on the 4th of July commented: **He injudiciously drank some sour ale and egg and sherry during the night which disagreed with him, and at the hour mentioned he was taken with a violent fit of vomiting. He was distressed with sickness of the stomach henceforward to the end of the walk, and had to leave the track several times on account of it. Another impediment to his success was the dreadful chafing of his legs. The seams of his drawers cut deep into his skin before 50 miles had been walked. At the 100th mile he was in a distressing condition and during the walk from that point the blood oozed from several large raw places that had been thus caused, and the pain at every step was acute.**

After making the "ton," he stopped for 1h.27m, walked four more miles, stopped again for 1h.47m, and after taking another break of 48 minutes, carried on marching till advised to quit by a doctor on a mark of 131½ miles at 22:07. By that time though he had another 18½ miles to go and his task with 53 minutes to spare was impossible. *"He relinquished his task very reluctantly, deeply chagrined to mar his past brilliant record by a failure."*

Undeterred by his failure, he decided to have a second go at the distance in the same time on Friday, the 30th of July, at exactly the same venue. This time, O'Leary was prepared to give a purse of $100 to any up-and-coming local pedestrian who could walk 90 miles in the same time he made his 100. The race "against time" began at 15:10, and it was clear he had benefited from his earlier experience in choosing tighter fitting clothes for his effort. His competitors for the $100 were William Hayden, J. Sterns and J. R. Sprague, the latter of whom was disqualified for unfair walking after just four miles.

Times of miles for the first 40, with O'Leary ahead of schedule by 8 miles:

King of the Peds

Miles	Time	Miles	Time	Miles	Time	Miles	Time
1	07:55	11	11:02	21	16:27	31	12:18
2	10:15	12	11:20	22	12:15	32	11:46
3	09:59	13	11:10	23	10:00	33	10:31
4	10:30	14	11:04	24	10:46	34	11:03
5	11:30	15	11:13	25	11:10	35	11:07
6	10:13	16	11:40	26	10:48	36	16:03
7	09:30	17	11:00	27	10:14	37	10:28
8	10:33	18	12:00	28	10:19	38	11:06
9	10:19	19	11:43	29	12:03	39	11:45
10	11:13	20	11:10	30	11:00	40	11:32

His first 50 miles was made in 9h.7m and his century in 20h.14m.

Once again he was doomed to fail. Once again he drank some ale, and once again he was sick, his symptoms causing him to be off the track more than he wished. The state of the hard unyielding boards which put such a strain on his legs and feet, as in his first attempt, were more than a contributing factor in his failure to succeed. He left the track for good at 22:40 on a score of 136 miles, much to everybody's disappointment. O'Leary would later be accused of having *"sold out"* to a gambling fraternity, the allegation of which he totally refuted.

On Saturday, the 16th of October at 02:00, O'Leary met the amateur pedestrian John S. Ennis, in a match at the West Side Rink, for a stake of $500 a side. The arrangement was that Ennis would walk 90 miles as opposed to O'Leary's 100. By the time O'Leary had made his 50 in 8h.52m.18s, Ennis was four miles behind him. O'Leary easily maintained his lead throughout making his century in a new world record time of 18h.53m.43s. Ennis for his part finished with 67 miles.

O'Leary offered Edward Payson Weston a "sure thing" $500 and half the gate money. This, the great Weston accepted, and in the walk at Chicago,……………………………

A six-day walking match was arranged between O'Leary and Weston, the preferred venue of the proven Rink being switched to the larger downtown Exposition Building on Monday, the 15th of November. No bets would be made between the two men but a large amount of money was promised for the winner; the prize to be raised by the people of the city of Chicago.

Two tracks were constructed for the competitors, one of six laps to the mile (O'Leary) and the other one comprising of seven (Weston). The referee was William B. Curtis and the judges for O'Leary were T. A. Alcock, C. E. Hatch, W. H. Thurds and George A. McDonald. Weston's overseers were C. A. Bartis and William Barker of New York, and Captain Shaw and T. F. Shaw of Cincinnati.

Both men entered the arena just before the commencement of their journey. O'Leary wearing a striped tunic, white tights and light walking shoes, carried a pine stick in each hand. The more flamboyant Weston was attired in a black velvet suit consisting of a light coat and *"knee pants,"* boots, a light linen hat, a silk ribbon which was thrown across his shoulders, and carried a whip.

There were two speeches before the race commenced. The Hon. A. Morrison addressed the relatively meagre audience comprising of less than 500 souls, stating he was confident both men would have fair play, and that the visitor would be well treated. He desired that the audience would offer no opinion as the walk progressed, either of approbation or disapprobation.

He was followed by Mayor Colvin who said, "Fellow citizens and visitors, I was invited here by the Committee having this affair in charge to start these gentlemen in the contest. You will all agree with me that my experience in racing, if it be called that, is very limited. (Laughter and a voice saying, "You made a good one once!") "But what we desire is this, and that I hope every citizen of Chicago will endorse, and that Mr. Weston comes to Chicago to go into a contest with a citizen of Chicago. It is to be hoped that there is no man in our city who will not see that he has fair play." (Applause) "If our man can beat him, of course we shall be very happy, and, as much as we like, we who are here, we wouldn't like it to be done in any unfairness whatever." (Applause) "This is a time to most of us. It seems out of place to be here, a little after twelve o'clock at night, to transact any sort of business, but I believe it is generally understood that these gentlemen want to save all the time they can, and therefore they start thus early, and if there is to be any man left it will be at the other end of the race. As we understand it, the man who has walked five hundred miles, he has nothing further to do; he is safe to take a rest. Now it is desired that you gentlemen there will all get back of those benches, to give the gentlemen a fair start. Now gentlemen, when you are ready to start, I propose to start you in this way: "One, two, three," and when you get three you are off. I believe that will be as fair a way as any that can be done. Gentlemen, please get on the other side of the seats." (Crowd retires.) "Are you ready Mr. O'Leary?" O'Leary: – "Yes." Mayor Colvin: – "Are you ready, Mr. Weston?" Weston: – "Yes."

Mayor Colvin: – "One, two, three!"

The race began at 3 minutes and 19 seconds past midnight. The walkers set off with O'Leary hitting the front and staying there to lead the first mile, 11m.3s to 12m.16s, with the second mile once again being in O'Leary's favour; 10m.6s to Weston's 11m.31s.

The *Chicago Tribune* described the two men's styles starting with O'Leary: He has been familiar to Chicagoans, and most citizens interested in sports have seen his straight form, quick stride, and bent arms quite often. He conveys the impression of walking more nervously and with more exertion than Weston, and his crooked arm helps to give him an air of labor that his opponent's style does not indicate. The latter seems rather to drag than throw his feet, and his long, swinging step, with his arms at his sides, is in strong contrast to his friend of the other side of the track. The expressions in the faces of the two men are radically different too; O'Leary holds his head up and looks about him while Weston seems to carry his head on his breast and to see nothing but the dirt before him.

The attending crowd, which numbered between 400 and 500, and which included many women, behaved themselves impeccably, treating the visiting contestant with courtesy. However, when one man in the crowd used insulting language towards him, Weston objected to the tirade and had the offender taken away by the police, of which there was a large presence. They spent most of their time keeping people off the tracks.

O'Leary completed his first 50 miles in 9h.29m.40s, after which he took a rest of 27 minutes. During the accomplishment of his next 50, he took a number of other breaks, and, including those, made 100 miles in 20h.48m.21s with his actual walking time being 18h.27m. At the end of his 110th mile, he was 20 miles ahead of his rival. It was at this stage he left his path to sleep with every intention of resuming his tramp at 02:30 on the second day, having remarked during it that he was determined to "break the back of the journey in two days."

Weston, on the other hand, had plodded along at the same speed taking little rest until he reached his 88th mile after which he retired for a three-hour rest. Returning to his path thereafter, he traversed it for two miles and left it again at 21:45, giving instructions to his team not to disturb his sleep for the next five hours. As it transpired he reappeared back on the course at 02:27, remained there till 03:14, took another rest for breakfast, and stayed on his track till retiring for supper at 17:17 after scoring his 150th mile. During his break which was taken at the Gardner House Hotel, Weston scoffed at reports that he had *"broken down."* On returning to continue with his walk, he appeared in the best of spirits. He was evidently in a good mood *"and his gestures, scraps of song, mimicry of actors, and other recreations, were greatly enjoyed by the audience and seemingly by the actor."*

O'Leary started the second day an hour and a half after the time of his intended return, at 4 a.m. After making a further 50 miles he indulged in an hour's break before scoring another 30 miles. When he'd had enough at 22:30, the score was still well in his favour, at 190 to 168. Below are examples of some of the times achieved for the second day:

King of the Peds

Miles	O'Leary	Weston	Miles	O'Leary	Weston
111	12:38	12:10	140	11:53	13:27
112	13:31	12:38	141	11:03	15:14
112	13:06	12:40	142	11:15	12:27
114	13:37	12:30	143	11:07	11:24
115	13:05	12:20	144	11:05	13:40
116	12:57	12:59	145	11:23	13:06
117	10:32	12:50	146	11:09	13:00
118	11:15	12:34	147	11:21	13:59
119	11:42	12:22	148	11:32	13:57
120	11:30	12:25	149	11:43	14:08
121	16:41	13:24	150	11:37	14:19

O'Leary, who rested three hours during the night, resumed his walk at 01:30. He suffered a nose bleed which inconvenienced him for an hour just after breakfast, and during the rest of the day, covered 83 miles. His second century was made in a time of 20h.48m.21s.

Weston resumed his hike at 06:00 but was off his path an hour later for breakfast. He made 77 miles during the day before retiring to bed at 23:25 having made his second 200 miles in a time of 30h.16m.21s. At the end of the third day, O'Leary led Weston by 26 miles, the score showing at that time, 273 to 247.

On Thursday, the leader retired to bed at 40 minutes past midnight and dozed till 03:45. After making his last mile in a time of 14m.58s, he finished his day at 23:40 after he had scored 350 miles saying to the judges as he passed them, "Gentlemen, I bid you all good night." He left Weston on his path with an advantage of 36 miles, meaning he had gained eight miles on him during the day. Weston completed his fourth day's work on a score of 314 miles, having made 68 miles during it.

The day after saw the largest attendance of the week, estimated to be around 8,000 people, to watch O'Leary put his stamp on the proceedings. When he left the track for bed at 23:30, he had secured 425 miles to his opponent's 390. Barring him coming to grief on the last day, the race was his. Some times made by both athletes on that penultimate day of the contest are shown below:

Miles	O'Leary	Weston	Miles	O'Leary	Weston
353	16:07	13:47	359	12:41	16:03
354	14:38	14:40	360	12:37	15:40
355	14:15	14:12	361	12:10	14:03
356	14:13	15:30	362	12:17	13:35
357	13:31	16:47	363	12:24	14:53
358	13:05	16:25			

O'Leary woke up and resumed his trek at 04:30 looking fresh. Weston joined him on the track at the same time, but the American's appearance gave the impression he wasn't in the same condition as the Irishman, and he was soon back in his quarters after walking for just three quarters of an hour. Nevertheless, the two men plodded on and as the last day wore on, the lines of people seeking entrance to the building increased.

The *Chicago Tribune* described the scenes outside and inside the building: **The approaches to the Exposition Building were surrounded by a surging mass of humanity, eager to procure tickets. Excitement could not have reached a higher pitch, it would seem, for appearances indicated almost a wild delirium of the throng that besieged the building.**

Money takers and door keepers were kept busy alike, and before 8 o'clock the receipts at the various ticket offices figured well up to $4,000 for the day, which up to that time would indicate that over 8,000 persons had visited the building. But, if there was so great an excitement without, it was nothing compared to that within.

The crowd was dense; sweeping hither and thither, - shouting, yelling or cheering. The crowd was motley, but largely respectable; it represented wealth, standing, and brains, and thieves, gamblers and roughs. Ladies were there in large numbers, some with husbands and some with lovers, but all had a terribly hard time of it in the ceaselessly moving and noisy throng.

Children were present in goodly numbers, and they seemed to take a great interest in the walkers, and had a marvelous faculty of just getting where they were not wanted. In front of the judge's stand, the crowd assumed the character of a mob, and was largely composed of the bummer, political, and gambling elements, scattered through which was still a greater portion of thieves, rowdies, and pickpockets, etc, who, no doubt, by pretended crowding, plied their nefarious vocations. The police had trouble with this crowd, and were several times overwhelmed, the mob taking possession of the tracks.

The greater portion by far of the mass within the building, which by 9 o'clock numbered fully 8,000 people, was orderly, and consisted of working men, many of whom who had brought their wives and children with them, and to say the least they must have had anything but a pleasant time of it.

A large crowd of urchins had taken possession of the mammoth fly-wheel at the north end of the building, which by some means began to turn, and in a short time, a dozen or more were sprawling in the pit. They resumed their perches, however, and at different times shared the same misfortunes, but always resumed their places again. The great elevator, the town clock and the pagoda, all had their crowds on top of them, but up in the galleries the loftiest perches presented themselves. Numerous boys and men had climbed up the trusses and squatted on the iron supports near to the roof, and held their places calmly, coolly and deliberately.

Near the large elevator some boys sat down on the planks laid on the iron roof supports, but the planks began to sag, and a fall of over 100 feet was threatened to those upon them, which resulted in a quick retreat and a very bad scare to some.

At 21:55, O'Leary had scored 488 to Weston's 439, and five minutes later, and as Weston was taunted with shouts of "Bully boy!" O'Leary was observed sipping hot tea as he was being given a rub down. It was later announced that the Irishman would complete his 500th mile by 23:00 and that he would continue walking till midnight. That he would ever achieve the 500 at all was a matter for conjecture as many in the crowd were, by now, encroaching on the track. Their antics certainly tested the patience of the city's police force whose job it was to restore order, which it eventually did.

The race finished just before 23:20 with O'Leary accomplishing 500 miles in 143h.13m, the fastest time on record. He made his last mile in 13m.13s, and as hats flew up into the air, and amid the din of the crowd and all the noise made by the band, he was presented with a magnificent basket of flowers by his wife. His final score was 503.2 laps. He had walked 78 miles on the last day as opposed to his opponents 61. Weston's last mile was made in 17m.10s and his final score was 451.4. O'Leary claimed the title of "Champion Walker of the World" at the conclusion of the match when he was presented with a large gold medal.

NB: Many years later in 1885, O'Leary said of the race, "In Chicago, Weston and I walked for the championship and divided the gate money - eleven thousand dollars, evenly. The championship at that time was worth a deal to me."

……………………………………………… **O' Leary beat him 51 ½ miles in a six days match. Weston cleared $5,000, however, by his defeat, viz: $500 from O'Leary and $4,500 for gate-money dividend.**

On the 31st of December, a letter was sent by O'Leary to the editor of *Bell's Life*, 170 The Strand, London, concerning a challenge which had been issued by William Perkins, the English walking champion, offering to walk any man in the world over a distance of 100 miles for a sum between $2,000 and $5,000, the return match to be held in the USA.

768 WEST LAKE STREET

CHICAGO, ILL

Dear Sir

Your issue of the 11th inst., containing a statement from J. Boot, on behalf of W. Perkins, has this day reached me, and I am satisfied with his proposition for a home-and-home match, the first one to be walked in America.

King of the Peds

Herewith I hand you draft No. 538, on Smith, Payne & Smiths, London, Eng., for £100, as a first deposit for the English match. There are several "well known and established sporting papers" in America, and in so an important a matter I do not wish to choose for Mr. Perkins. If he will designate which one he prefers, and forward a deposit, it will be immediately covered. Not knowing Mr. Perkins address, I forward to you this day a letter for him, which you will please read and then deliver to him.

Yours truly,

Daniel O'Leary

According to the London *Sporting Life*: W. Perkins, of London, "is the only man that has walked, "fair heel and toe," eight miles in one hour, and this was accomplished at Lillie Bridge Grounds, London, September the 20th, 1875, in a match against time."

1st mile	6m.46s	**5th mile**	7m.33s
2nd mile	7m.27s	**6th mile**	7m.52s
3rd mile	7m.24s	**7th mile**	7m.27s
4th mile	7m.22s	**8th mile**	7m.14s

Soon afterwards O'Leary went to San Francisco....................................

The background to this was a challenge issued on March 15th 1876 by O'Leary who was in San Francisco, *"to walk against any man on the pacific coast from distances of 100 to 500 miles for as much as $10,000."* If the offer wasn't taken up in a week, he was to walk 500 miles "against time," backing himself to accomplish the feat in 140 hours. An opponent called Harry Roe came forward, and a match for an unknown wager was arranged to take place at the Mechanics Pavilion between Monday, the 3rd and Saturday, the 8th of April.

Eighteen circuits of the building were counted as a "mile," but a mile was a fraction less than a "hall" mile. Therefore to make 500 miles, Dan would have to make 9,173 circuits of the hall to complete his mission.

He began his walk of 500 miles on the morning of the 3rd of April, and at 11:30, completed 30 miles with his opponent scoring 23. O'Leary's fastest mile was made in 9m.4s and Roe's in 11m.11s. Later that evening at 22:00, O'Leary had made 70 as opposed to Roe's 48.

On the second day, O'Leary's score at 21:00, with the places remaining unaltered, was 173. His fastest mile was completed in 10m.16s, and he was said to be very confident of accomplishing his objective.

Third day reports indicated that O'Leary hadn't slept during the contest up to that point, but planned to do so the day after. Roe was said to be 90 miles behind him.

With Roe abandoning his participation in the match, O'Leary was reported to have made 300 miles at noon on the 4th day stating he felt confident of winning his bet.

At 9 p.m., on the penultimate day, O'Leary had completed 403 miles. He predicted he could make the required distance by 23:00 so beating his Chicago time by three and a half hours.

On the final day, April the 8th, and as O'Leary drew near the end of his walk, public interest in his unparalleled performance increased. The crowd in attendance grew larger and it was forecast that as he neared the end of his tramp, the building would be crowded.

During the morning session he had walked for ten solid hours making 46 miles in that time at a rate of just over 4½ mph. It was now known that up to that point he had only slept for a period of 12 hours during the whole event.

At 12:30, and in front of a large crowd, he completed the 463rd mile in 10m.10s and took a brief rest. Including the extra distance on account of the shortness of the track, he had at 13:00, a total of 46 miles to make before 15 minutes past midnight. At that stage, and although he was said to *"appear pale and a trifle haggard,"* he expected to hit the 500-mile mark by 23:20, stating that he would continue walking until midnight to decide certain bets that had been made.

With every confidence of a successful conclusion to the race, the management had organised a magnificent testimonial in his honour. At 8 o'clock in the evening, O'Leary had 18 miles to make in 3h.45m, and went on to make his 495th mile in 8m.58s. At 22:20, he had completed his 9,000th circuit and now had 173 laps to traverse to achieve his goal. O'Leary actually covered the required distance at 23:32 in 139h.32m in front of an immense crowd, some of whom carried him to the stage amid much excitement. He was presented with a magnificent Jurgenson gold watch which sported a gold and quartz chain.

……………………………and walked 500 miles in 140 hours, four hours less than six days.

Sheriff Nunan on behalf of the citizen's presented him with a gold watch and chain. It is the only jewelry he has ever worn.

A six days' match with Henry Schmehl followed…………………………………………………

With O'Leary remaining in San Francisco, reports from there on April the 23rd told of an agreement between himself and Henry Schmehl to walk 500 miles for $2,000 per side at the same venue. Another attempt at walking 150 miles in 32 hours was also announced, the walk being planned between May the 1st and 10th.

The *Oakland Tribune* informed its readers that O'Leary's stride spanned 38 inches, whereas his future opponent Schmehl's stride measured 41 inches.

The match began at midnight on Monday, May the 15th. At 9 A. M., O'Leary had managed to walk 46 miles to his rivals 43½. By 19:49 he had managed to extend his lead to 14 miles, the score at the time being 89 to 75.

As the match was in progress, news was coming in from London that on the 9th of May, in a 24-hour match, and with 14 competitors taking part, a pedestrian called James Miles of Brixton, London, completed 50 miles in 8h.48m.28s, whilst Henry Vaughan, the winner, had knocked 2m.8s off O'Leary's 100-mile record making the distance in a time of 18h.51m.35s. (See Chapter 6)

Tuesday, the 16th: The score recorded at 19:55 was 157 to 128 in O'Leary's favour.

Wednesday, the 17th: With news that a great deal was being bet on the result, O'Leary was seen to be resting at 11:37 having completed his 190th mile. Schmehl, having made his 150th mile at 09:15 in 37h.7m.7s, went on to record a score of 160 miles at 12:28. By this time it was apparent that both Schmehl's appearance and gait were greatly improved. In the evening he placed himself under the care of an experienced trainer *"under whose directions he had developed unexpected powers of speed and endurance,"* promising to greatly diminish the score between him and the race leader. Within an hour, he caught, and passed O'Leary three times.

Thursday, the 18th: The improvement shown by Schmehl had not proved permanent. He was now walking slowly and laboriously and was apparently worn out. There were growing doubts about his ability to complete the walk. O'Leary made 250 miles at 10:45 and Schmehl responded with a score of 200 miles at 11:35.

Friday, 19th: At noon, O'Leary was on a mark of 335. Schmehl on 232 miles was observed to be resting frequently, scarcely able to drag himself along.

Saturday, the 20th: O'Leary failed to accomplish his objective by 69 miles scoring 431. Schmehl had made just *282.

*Correct score.

………………The German walked only 285 miles in the six days, while the Chicago man covered 431.

On July the 13th, John Ennis wrote the following letter to the editor of the *Chicago Tribune*:

In notice in yesterday's Times that O'Leary's friends are anxious to see him on his mettle before he starts for England, and as my match with Fifield is off, through no fault of my own, I wish to remind O'Leary of his agreement to walk a match with me for $500 a side, similar to our first match which he won, providing I beat the time he made in said match. Each of us having won a match, I call on him to carry on his agreement, and

King of the Peds

walk in the Second Regiment Armory, Dexter Park, or any suitable place he may name, from five to thirty days after signing articles, he to name time and place, also stakeholder. From past experience, he knows I mean business, and if he wants a bona fide match he can be accommodated. If not the people will infer that he is following Weston's method of *hippodroming, which will make pedestrianism disreputable. I hope he will have the pluck to carry out his agreement.

JOHN ENNIS

* A term used to infer fixing a match.

Then on the 3rd of August, it was reported in the *Indiana Progress* that O'Leary had been *"badly defeated"* in a four-day match against four amateurs in San Francisco. The Irishman apparently retired on the third day on a score of 217 miles whereas his opponents amassed a total of 351 miles at the close of the contest.

His next performance was a 500 mile walk in the American Institute in New York...............

Daniel O'Leary was cheered lustily by the few spectators who had bothered to turn up to see the start of the race "against time" in his fifth attempt to walk 500 miles in 144 hours. The trial was to be held at the American Institute Building on the corner of Third Avenue and Sixty Third Street, New York, on a four-foot wide, 8 laps to the mile track, composed of sand and sawdust between Monday, the 7th and Saturday, the 12th of August 1876.

He had relaxed the day before as the temperature in the building had meant that training within it was unfeasible. He had already decided what his diet would be during the attempt; beef tea, coffee, tea and the occasional *"Bass Ale."* He appeared on the track at 23:30 dressed in blue body tights, white pantaloons, stockings and undershirt, and light coloured trunks. In his hands he carried two pieces of ivory weighing about a pound each. Mr. F. F. Clark, *"a pedestrian of some note,"* would be his partner on the track till 10 o'clock the next morning. They started around the path at a rapid pace and the first mile was made in 9m.23s. O'Leary went on to make his 10th mile in a time of 12m.10s at 01:44, but, after his 11th, had to rest for 16m.30s owing to the high temperature.

He finished his 20th mile at 04:54, and again, was so overheated that he had to take another rest, during which time he was induced to vomit by drinking a solution of salt and water. He was thereafter given a glass of champagne, ate some eggs, drank some lime water; after which he went back to the track where he completed his 30th mile at 07:56. At this juncture, he was considered to be 20 minutes ahead of his schedule. His 38th mile turned out to be his fastest, completing the same in 8m.49s at 09:25. After sleeping for half an hour, he accomplished his 50th mile in 11m.30s at 12:20. This was followed by another enforced rest of 38 minutes due to the oppressive conditions. Under the careful handling of his trainer James Hanley, he was allowed to continue his tramp and scored 60 miles at 15:35. He went on to make his 70th mile at 18:47, and in front of an ever increasing audience, his 80th at 20:44. After making a score of 86 miles at 21:51, he was given a cold water bath, rubbed down and put to bed.

Having rested for 3h.14m, he reappeared on the track at 01:06, and made his 87th mile in 15m.10s, after which he accomplished his 90th mile at 02:02. He went on to post his first century at 05:01. Breakfast when it was prepared for him consisted of warm gruel and champagne and these two items occupied his diet along with iced tea throughout the morning. Lunch consisted of eggs, milk and lime water, and this sustained him during the afternoon hours, enabling him to register his 150th mile at 17:28. The hungry pedestrian now left the track for his supper and the chef had prepared a hearty meal of chicken, tomatoes, toast and tea, which he tucked into and consumed over a period of 55 minutes. Buoyed on by the enlivening airs of the band which was situated in the centre of the building, he was accompanied on the track by Wilson Reid, who had lost out to him in a previous race. Dan finished his 170th mile at 22:46 despite having a slightly blistered left foot and sustained himself on a diet of beef tea, sherry and egg before retiring to his room at 23:40 on a score of 173 miles. Here he indulged in his customary bath of cold salt water and a rubbing down before going to bed.

A sleepless few hours followed before he re-emerged at 02:57 to make more miles. Breakfast was taken at 06:31, and on the menu was beef-steak, tomatoes, toast and iced tea. That helped him achieve his 200th mile at 10:18 and it seemed enough to keep him going throughout the rest of the day which was broken up by varying periods of rest, one of which lasted 1h.18m, during which time he was rubbed down with bay rum and had his feet bathed in whisky. He stopped for a late supper at 19:44 on completion of his 237th mile during which he consumed toast and drank beef tea. After that the large and enthusiastic audience cheered him on as he completed three quick miles. These were his 243rd, 244th and 245th which he completed in 9m.44s, 9m.21s and 9m.13s respectively. He was accompanied on the track by both Reid and Edward Mullen, and completed his 250th mile at 22:41 in an admirable time of 8m.46s. By this stage he was 7 miles ahead of the time he had set himself to complete his objective. At 23:05, he retired from the track and went to bed after being pampered with his usual alcohol rubs.

After a rest of just under 4 hours, O'Leary went back in the ring registering mile number 300 at 50 seconds past the hour of three in the afternoon. He celebrated this feat by changing his shoes, but was soon spinning round the place in pursuit of the coveted 500. In the evening he was again joined by Reid and while walking around together, Dan asked Wilson whether he would be interested in setting up a wager for a $150 a side that he, (O'Leary) would be able to beat him in the last 25 miles of the contest. Reid said he would consider the offer. It was said that this episode in the race would make the walk *"doubly interesting."* At the end of 95 hours, he had accomplished 333 miles, thus averaging a mile every 17½ minutes, *"a surprising effort of endurance."* At this time, he was reported to have *"wisely abandoned the use of all alcoholic stimulants during his walk, and nourishes himself with chicken soup and nutritious diet of that kind."*

After leaving the track at 22:40, he went to his room and was immediately given a cup of warm tea. After going through his pre-sleep regime, he was tucked up in his bed which had been moved to an adjoining, and somewhat cooler room, in an attempt to help him sleep better. He finally put his head on the pillow at half past midnight and was allowed to slumber for an hour and ten minutes, but this time, he *did* sleep.

Despite having a painful blistered right foot he made good progress during the morning and stuck to his new healthier diet for breakfast when he indulged in more chicken soup. After a good rub, he was back out on the ellipse at 09:25 and walked 10 more miles by 12:12. After completing his 380th mile at 14:22, he ate his lunch consisting of soup and warm tea, and resumed his trek. At 20:35, he made his 4th century in a respectable time of 9m.32s amid the plaudits of the crowd which amounted to about a thousand people, finishing the 5th day on a score of 410 miles at 23:08.

The ped was back out in the ring at 01:32 to begin his last day of plod, doubtless daunted by the mammoth task of securing the 90 miles he needed to be assured of success. Having set off at a lively pace, he took a 15-minute break at 03:22 to change his socks having earlier satisfied his appetite with chicken soup, chicken and strong coffee at 02:00. By 04:16 he had made 420 miles, and by the time he had added a further ten to his tally at 07:07 he was being watched by a large gathering of spectators who were urging him along by the yard. He made his 440th mile in a time of 14m.4s at 10:01 and his 450th at 13:01 in a better time of 12m.5s.

O'Leary had promised that his last 25 miles would be his quickest and when he had completed his 475th mile at 18:30, many people were on their way to the building to watch him keep his promise. They weren't to be disappointed. By eight o'clock, seven thousand souls were present to witness the last hours of the attempt, and they watched in amazement as the Irishman rolled up the miles. He was accompanied on the track by Reid, the Nugent brothers, J. McEwen, his faithful attendant, William E. Harding, and Eddie Mullen, all of whom must have been in awe at the mans dedication to his task. At just before quarter past nine, he completed his 490th mile and as he neared his target, the excited and noisy crowd urged him on his way with the police finding it difficult to keep them off the track. Amid the wildest scenes, the Chicagoan prevailed and completed the 500th mile at 23:29. The time at which each 10-mile milestone was achieved on each of the six days is shown below:

Mile	Day 1	Mile	Day 2	Mile	Day 3
10	01:54:00	90	02:02:08	180	04:40:07
20	04:54:00	100	05:01:37	190	07:51:57
30	07:56:36	110	07:35:22	200	10:18:29
40	09:55:36	120	10:01:15	210	12:53:33
50	12:20:30	130	12:40:22	220	14:45:15
60	15:35:00	140	15:21:46	230	18:19:25
70	18:47:16	150	17:28:40	240	20:32:13
80	20:44:01	160	20:47:53	250	22:41:34
		170	22:46:47		

King of the Peds

Mile	Day 4	Mile	Day 5	Mile	Day 6
260	05:03:25	340	03:02:13	420	04:10:31
270	07:02:30	350	05:11:05	430	07:07:05
280	09:47:12	360	09:12:50	440	10:01:34
290	13:11:04	370	12:12:14	450	13:01:42
300	15:00:50	380	14:22:45	460	15:56:09
310	17:18:04	390	18:13:28	470	17:23:54
320	20:12:13	400	20:35:36	480	19:18:25
330	22:03:49	410	23:08:09	490	21:14:32
				500	23:29:35

....He did it in less than six days.

Frank Clark, who had accompanied O'Leary to New York, wrote a letter to the *New York Sportsman* on August the 14th, claiming the entire press had been duped by the pedestrian, pointing out that the track measured 600 feet to the lap and that 8 x 600 feet did not equal 5,280 feet which measured a mile. He wrote:

Therefore, in walking 500 miles, as this track which O'Leary walked on is 480 feet short to every mile, consequently it would be 45.24 miles short in the 500 miles. Notwithstanding this, every mile that he walked, on average, two laps to each mile were placed to his credit from the whole amount, after deducting the shrinkage of the track. The actual distance walked by O'Leary was 272 miles

- **Frank Clark**

John T. Hayes, one of the judges, denied that there was anything unfair about O'Leary's achievement, stating that the track had been measured by a surveyor who was supposed to be competent. To counter the above allegation, an effort was made to measure the track on the 19th of August by two New York City surveyors, James O'Brien and Frank O'Ryan. However, despite their best efforts, they could not arrive at a conclusion as to its length due to the track having been already removed. Indeed, all the judges made a statement which was printed in the *New York Times* on the 20th of August. It read:

NEW YORK: Aug.18. 1876.

We the undersigned judges in the recent walk given by Daniel O'Leary at the American Institute in this City, pronounce the letter signed in some of the daily papers by one Frank Clark as a falsehood from beginning to end. The "information" supplied the representatives of the journals referred to by a fellow calling himself Plummer or McAuliffe is entirely without foundation. To our personal knowledge, Mr. O'Leary passed in front of the judges stand 4,000 times, which, with eight circuits making one mile, clearly proves that he accomplished the distance he undertook to walk 500 miles, inside of the specified time – six consecutive days.

Thomas H. Cunningham, Hugh J. Drury, John. T. Hayes, James J. Drury, Joseph Daley.

Hayes later told the press that the allegation made by Plummer, the timekeeper, was not worthy of credence and tried to put some light on the situation which had developed. He said that Plummer was visited by a well dressed man on Thursday morning, the 10th of August, had a conversation with him, and when he had gone Plummer turned to him (Hayes) and told him he had a chance to make $500 if he would consent to beat O'Leary. Hayes refused the offer and told of lingering animosity between them both thereafter.

Of the affair, O'Leary told the press that during the walk, Plummer told him he was going to prefer charges against him for "having perpetrated a fraud against the public." He told O'Leary that he would keep his mouth shut if the pedestrian gave him $20. O'Leary told him where to go, and invited him to make the charges. O'Leary then claimed that Plummer acted strangely during the rest of the walk and called time for completion of the required 500 miles with 50 minutes of the race to be completed. Plummer's watch was consequently taken off him and given to Edward Mullen who kept the time of the last mile.

A letter from O'Leary also appeared in the same edition giving his version of events which read:

To the Editor of the New York Times:

The article published some days ago in certain of the morning journals in reference to my late feat of pedestrianism at the American Institute in this City, is as far as the charges are concerned, utterly false in every particular. It is gotten up by Clarke and Plummer for blackmailing purposes, as a careful perusal of the article will show. Believing these men to be unworthy of public notice, I will dismiss them from my mind, feeling that the citizens of New York will place but little confidence in the assertion of such a man as Edward Plummer alias Benjamin Franklin, John Paul McAuliffe, or whatever cognomen may best suit the taste of whom he comes in contact for the purpose of playing his nefarious games. An insertion of the above will oblige.

DANIEL O'LEARY

O'Leary was to later to be presented with an oval shaped medal. Measuring four inches by two and a half inches, it was suspended by gold chains from a spread eagle of solid gold, under which were the American and Irish flags in gold enamel. In the medal's centre was a figure of a walker which was surrounded by a wreath of silver leaves outside of which was a gold band with the inscription; **"Presented to Daniel O'Leary, Champion Walker of America."** On top of the medal was a silver wreath which enclosed a shoe which was generously embedded with diamonds. The reverse of the medal bore the inscription; **"Presented to Daniel O'Leary on the completion of his of his 500 mile walk, at the American Institute Hall, Aug. 12, 1876, by his New York friends."**

The medal which was presented on behalf of the residents of the First and seventh wards by Thomas J. Murphy at a ceremony on the 29th of August, had been made by Tiffany & Co., and was valued at $500.

Just before the above ceremony took place, an article appeared in the London based *Sporting Life* on Wednesday, the 23rd of August. It read: **W. Howes of the city begs to inform O'Leary (the American Champion), Vaughan, and other long distance pedestrians, that he is open to make a match to walk anybody in the world fifty miles or upward. If this challenge is not accepted within three weeks, Howes backers are anxious for him to go to America to walk for the championship of the world, and they will give or take expenses to walk in England or America. An answer and a deposit to the Sporting Life will ensure a match. So that it is pretty certain that O'Leary will be afforded a chance to test the powers of at least of our English pedestrian cousins.**

"Meantime," says O'Leary, "Weston was over in England. I made up my mind to follow him.

It is thought that O'Leary left the USA on Saturday, the 2nd of September for England to compete against the likes of Vaughan and other notable English pedestrians.

After I got there I had the usual difficulty in forcing him to a match. He had made plenty of money, but did not seem inclined to put it up.

O'Leary wrote a letter to editor of *Bell's Life,* the date of which cannot be established, but is estimated to have been around the latter part of September and the early days in October. What is certain is that the letter *was* written in London.

Having arrived in this country a few day's ago, and being desirous of forever settling the question, "Who shall be champion pedestrian of the world?" will you be kind enough to give insertion to the following proposition: For a wager of not less than £100, nor in excess of ten times that amount, I hereby agree to walk against any man in England, Vaughan of Chester, preferred—the following distances: 100, 200, and 500 miles, "best two in three" to be declared the winner. If any pedestrian in this country, or elsewhere, considers to the first named distance too short and the last too long, then I will strike out both, leaving the 250 mile stretch to settle the question of championship. Should Weston be desirous of entering into a side-by-side contest of 500 miles with me, I hereby agree to give him a start of twenty five miles in that distance, and stake two to one on my ability to defeat him, the track to be measured by a competent surveyor, the judge referee, and timekeepers to be selected from the sporting press of London, the money to be competed for to be placed in the hands of *Bell's Life*, and, after all necessary expenses are deducted, the winning man to receive two-thirds of all of the winning money whichever Weston may prefer. Hoping to meet some of your best pedestrians between the hours of 3 and 4 p.m. on Tuesday next at *Bell's Life* office believe me sir.

DANIEL O'LEARY

Whilst O'Leary waited for Weston to agree to a match, he had his first reported public spin on an English track in Liverpool. The race "against time" was at the city's Park Skating Rink between Monday, the 16th and Saturday, the 21st of October 1876.

King of the Peds

The *Liverpool Post* enlightened its readers on the following Monday after the finish of the event on how the Irish-American got on: Mr. Daniel O'Leary, who undertook to walk upward of 500 miles in six days, has not only succeeded in accomplishing the task, but has achieved the still greater triumph of covering 502 miles in fourteen minutes less than the time he allowed himself. This is, perhaps, the most wonderful achievement that has ever been chronicled in the history of pedestrianism, and it is doubly remarkable from the fact that it completely eclipses Mr. E. P. Weston's famous walk on a recent occasion, when it may be remembered, *that pedestrian was successful in "doing" 500 ½ miles in six days. Mr. Sam Hague bet O'Leary £100 that he would not cover more than 500 ½ miles and 48 yards within six days, which was the feat performed by Mr. Weston. O'Leary commenced to walk at the Park Skating Rink, Admiral Street at 12:7 on the morning of Monday last, and particulars have been given in our columns from day to day as to the progress the pedestrian was making in his formidable undertaking. An interest beyond the limits of the pedestrian circle had during the week had been taking in the event; and as O'Leary neared the termination of his task that interest gradually deepened and intensified, till it culminated on Saturday night, in a public demonstration of the greatest excitement and enthusiasm. O'Leary retired to rest at 12:50 on Saturday morning at which time he had finished his 427th mile. He reappeared on the track at 3:50 A.M., and walked on till 9:08 when he retired for about an hour and a quarter. From that time to the close he only rested for a few minutes at intervals. His quickest mile on Saturday was his 493rd which he walked in 11 minutes and 51 seconds. At 11:04:36 o'clock he had accomplished 500 miles and seven laps, but he continued on the track till 11:36 by which time he covered the extraordinary distance of 502 miles. O'Leary has thus beaten Weston's walk by a mile and a half and fourteen minutes to spare, his time not expiring till 11:50 on Saturday night.

During the day there was a numerous attendance of people, the great majority of whom seemed to be Irishmen, who came to give their respects to Mr. O'Leary, who is a native of the Emerald Isle. As the evening advanced, however the concourse of spectators gradually increased, till between ten and eleven o'clock the enclosure was crowded to such a degree that it was almost a matter of impossibility for one to budge from the spot where he located himself. Indeed, so closely packed was the interior of the rink about eleven o'clock that orders were given to the doorkeepers not to admit another individual. Immediately after O'Leary had retired at 11:36, Mr. Sam Hague entered the judges box and briefly addressed the over enthusiastic assembly. It was with considerable difficulty that he could make his voice heard above the cheering and buzz of excitement, but when some degree of quietness had been secured, he intimated that O'Leary had accomplished the task that he had undertaken. "Mr. O'Leary (Mr. Hague continued) is too much exhausted to address you; but he desires me to thank you all for the kindness which has been shown to him during the week; and for the fair play he has received. O'Leary is open to challenge any man in the world to walk 500 miles for £5,000."

*Weston performed the feat between Monday, the 25th and Saturday, the 30th of September.

O'Leary, still waiting for his chance to meet Weston, now began to occupy himself with races against the more learned English athletes who had, by this time, been educated in the art of piling up the miles in six-day events by scrupulous advisors who had been watching Weston perform.

George Parry   **Peter Crossland**

The National Police Gazette (Illustration no: 5)

One of those athletes was the useful Peter Crossland from Sheffield, Yorkshire, who, between Monday, the 11th and Tuesday, the 12th of September at the Royal Pomona Gardens, Colnbrook, Manchester, made a world record of 120 miles 1,560 yards in 24 hours against George Parry of that city. At the time, this was the furthest distance observed in such a contest. What is more astonishing is that Crossland competed the distance **without taking a rest**. Peter won £100 for his efforts, with Parry having scored a respectable 114 miles and 164 yards in the same time.

It was Crossland, who was described as the "Champion of England," and O'Leary who would be matched against each other in *"The Great 300 Miles Anglo-American Walking Match,"* which began on Monday, the 20th of November, again at the Pomona Gardens. The match was originally planned to have been staged at *Lillie Bridge, London, but for unknown reasons was moved to the northern venue.

*Lillie Bridge used to be more or less next to New Brompton tube station on the District line. It was an athletic facility with a running track round it which served as the headquarters of the Amateur Athletic Club, the London Athletic Club and the Civil Service Athletic Club.

Both men *"appeared at their posts looking wonderfully fresh and well"* at 20:00 when the start was made. The 30-year-old O'Leary, weighing 10st.8lbs, immediately went into the lead over his seven year older rival who weighed a couple of pounds more. The American was the first man to complete the opening mile in 10m.11s and maintained the lead thereafter with Crossland following him just a couple of yards behind. The men went on to reach their half centuries in 9h.16m.25s and 9h.26m.15s, the former time being in O'Leary's favour. However, just before six the next morning, the Englishman was forced to retire for a period of 57 minutes due to *"being seized with pain,"* thus allowing O'Leary to open up a six-mile lead.

A military band was in attendance to entertain the five thousand spectators who would pay one shilling for the privilege of watching the two perform during the rest of the day, and they would not be disappointed with the effort both men were putting in. By noon the Irish-American led by 82.2 laps to Crossland's 77½ miles. O'Leary was the first centurion in the match making that distance in 20h.2m.20s at which time he was again, six miles ahead of his opponent. Crossland went on to complete his one hundred at 17:09. Thereafter, and as O'Leary was resting, the Yorkshireman went on to lead the race at the end of the 24-hour stage when the score read Crossland 112½ to O'Leary's 111 miles and 7½ laps.

The Irishman reappeared on the track at 23:05 whilst Crossland was five miles ahead of him. However, from that time, it was clear that the Englishman was suffering from great pain as he began to show signs of lameness. Showing incredible courage, and despite his suffering, Crossland battled away until 10:23. Then, and on a score of 160 miles, he was forced to leave the track by his trainer for a rest of 90 minutes during which time the swelling in his left leg got progressively worse. Unhindered by this, he sought the path again, and in front of 12,000 fanatical spectators recommenced his effort. With the crowd urging him on, he responded to their support by *"sprinting against his opponent in a remarkable manner,"* tactics which O'Leary had no answer to. Making no headway against his opponent, O'Leary left the track at 18:11 on a score of 181½ miles. Crossland took full advantage of his absence and got within 1,200 yards of the Irishman thus forcing his premature return at 20:15. When both men settled down to sleep that night at 22:30, the respective distances were: **O'Leary, 198.4; Crossland, 195.2:**

O'Leary was the first of the men to reappear at 01:03, with his opponent joining him 16 minutes later. Little occurred thereafter until 11 o'clock when the race leader retired for an hour's rest, having covered 236.1 to Crossland's 226.4. After walking on until 12:44, the Sheffielder also rested till 14:53 when he was 14 miles in arrears. Both men now were exhibiting signs of distress, with the man in front appearing very much under the weather. Crossland gained a little, but he was unable to make the impact he was hoping for; and after covering 235 miles at 15:37, left the track, with his *"used up"* opponent who was 16 miles in advance of him, following suit at 15:59.

The champion was the first man to make it back into the ring at 17:51. He walked stiffly and with some difficulty until forced to make a better pace by his rival who joined him bang on six o'clock. Unable to keep up with the pace of Crossland, O'Leary left the track several times thus allowing his opponent to gradually reduce the distance between them. However, the effort finally had a devastating effect on Crossland, who, after he had scored 248 miles at 21:37, *"began to reel about in a hopeless manner,"* and after making a further lap, was forced to *retire, as it was

King of the Peds

obvious by that time he had no chance of beating O'Leary. The Nottingham based backer of Crossland, Tom Noble, allowed the Irishman to continue till he had recorded a score of 264.1 at 22:15 before throwing in his mans towel and informing O'Leary he had won. In a short speech after that, the victor stated that Crossland was the *"gamest man"* that he had ever competed against. His plucky opponent was the recipient of a "whip round" by the spectators and a *"good round sum"* was collected on his behalf.

*In fact Crossland was carried off the track and a doctor was sent for who issued the following certificate: -

"P. Crossland - Head of femur or thigh bone inflamed; painful; unable to walk without great pain; pulse 88."

Later, Tom Griffiths, one of the judges, was to remark, "During the journey, O'Leary subsided on beef tea, oysters stewed in milk, jellies, custards, stout, and champagne; whilst his opponent took beef tea, the yolk of eggs beaten up with port wine, calves foot jelly, broiled chops, and large quantities of buttered toast and tea."

The *Sporting Life* in a column about the two overseas pedestrians informed its readers of the latest developments as regards a future encounter between them: **Some influential members of the Turf Club have expressed a willingness to back Weston against O'Leary for a genuine six day's walking match, to take place at Lillie Bridge, under the management of the A.A.C., and the Smithfield Club show week has been proposed as a most suitable time. If O'Leary and Weston desire to oppose each other in affair and honorable contest, the stake on either side could be made sufficiently large to overcome even the attraction of gate money exhibitions.**

O'Leary responded with the following letter which was published in *Bell's Life*:

Seeing as some influential members of some turf club have expressed a desire of backing E. P. Weston against me for a six-day walk, I beg to say I am willing to except their offer and walk Weston from one mile to 500 for from £100 to £500 a side, the match to take place in the month of January or February next. I only stipulate that the sporting press of London have entire control of the walk, and I will wager all my share of the admission money on the result. One thing I strongly object to, viz: that I will not walk at Lillie Bridge under present management, having no wish to be initiated in the "milking business" at present. In reply to Mr. Lewis's offer to give £250 if all champions try their powers, I beg to say that, with health and a sufficient notice, he may rely on my contending should the prize be given; or, I will put up £100, and let Crossland, Howes, Vaughan, Ide, Parry, and Weston do likewise, the winner to take the whole, including all gate money; the distance a six day's walk. As the management of Lillie Bridge are anxious for something to do, I hope they will deposit £50 at *Bell's Life* **office for Weston, when I will undertake a name, a place to walk that no one can object to, and I will immediately put up a forfeit of $100 in the hands of a stakeholder.**

DANIEL O'LEARY

The backers of Weston responded with their reply which stated:

In answer to Daniel O'Leary's challenge at Liverpool to walk Edward Payson Weston for £5,000, we are authorized to state that, although Weston has invariably declined to engage in any contest for a wager, he, at the urgent solicitation of many influential friends; who have offered to stake the above amount, has yielded to their wishes, and consents to walk a six day's match against Daniel O'Leary, provided O'Leary will walk unattended, and that it shall be one of the conditions of the match that refreshments taken while on the track shall be from a table placed conveniently, and not from the hands of any person; that the stake be not less than £2,000 a side, and that the match shall be arranged to commence on Monday December 18.

Weston was to delay the start of the match by continually making unreasonable propositions in lengthy letters to the sporting press. It meant that there was no agreement in place, and the prospect of a race between the pair seemed a mile off. Meanwhile, as he waited, O'Leary was to be matched up with the *"English champion,"* William Howes in a £200 a side, 300-mile race at the Victoria Skating Rink and Athletic Grounds, Cambridge Heath, London, starting on Boxing Day at 4 p.m. which in that year, was a Tuesday. O'Leary was the 4/5 on favourite to take the honours.

Under a canvas roof, which wasn't sufficiently water-proofed against the drenching rain which intermittently prevailed, there were never going to be any records broken on a track that was exposed to the elements. The fact that O'Leary had been suffering with diarrhoea before the start didn't help matters for him nor Howes, who wasn't really pushed by the American contender, the score on the first day being 95.5 to the Englishman and 77.8 to O'Leary.

William Howes

© *The British Library. All Rights reserved. The Penny Illustrated. (Illustration no: 6)*

Little of note happened on the second day apart from the sight of O'Leary frequently leaving the track to relieve his ailment, and Howes moving uncomfortably around the rain sodden track due a swollen toe, the cause of which was an ill fitting shoe. During the evening he had his toe lanced which greatly eased his distress. Due to the weather and the fact that O'Leary was clearly doing nothing in the race, the attendance for the first 48 hours was only 2,000, the scores at the end of the second day being: **Howes, 162; O'Leary, 141:**

On the Friday, O'Leary, after having completed 209 miles, announced that he was giving the race to his opponent who by then had then just finished his 241st mile, and despite Howes wanting to go on to make the required 300, he was stopped five laps later and awarded the race.

O'Leary was disturbed by the fact that Weston had been telling the English press that during his previous match with him, some spectators in Chicago had threatened to shoot him, and had thrown pepper into his face. There was obviously some suspicion that foul play had been involved, and O'Leary was concerned that he needed to prove that he won against Weston fairly and squarely. After his latest tussle O'Leary finally managed to set a date to once and for all prove which man was the best in the world.

It was not until Sir John Astley offered to back him with £500 that I could get him to walk. I was backed by Mr. Sam Hague of St. James Hall, Liverpool……………………..

The following document was signed by both men on the 3rd of January 1877. A "match" poster containing the words of the agreement can also be viewed in Chapter 7.

MEMORANDUM OF AGREEMENT made and entered into this 3rd day of January between Daniel O'Leary and Edward Payson Weston, whereby they agree to engage in a six days' walking match for £500 a side; the race to take place in a covered building or ground (to be mutually agreed upon by both parties) within a radius of five miles of Charing Cross, at Eastertide, starting at five minutes past 12 a.m. on Monday, the 2nd day or April, and terminating Saturday, the 7th day of April, 1877 at ten minutes to 12 o'clock in the evening (143 3/4 hours from the start). Each man to walk upon a separate track, to be laid down according to his own directions, and surveyed by a competent authority in the presence of the judges appointed. The measurement of each track to be made eighteen inches from the inside border frame. Each man must walk fair - the judges appointed to be sole of fair and unfair walking - and any lap adjudged to have been traversed unfairly to be disallowed and cancelled in the record book. Each man must walk alone, and no attendant to be allowed to go more than twenty five yards at time with either competitor, and then only for the purpose of handing refreshments. The Stakes and two-thirds of the 'gate' money (after all expenses have been deducted) to be handed over to the winner and the loser to take one third. The Editor of the *Sporting Life* is appointed Stakeholder, and the whole of the Stakes must be deposited at the *Sporting Life* Office one calendar month before the time appointed for the commencement of the race. The said parties (Weston and O'Leary) to appoint the four judges at the time of the last deposit and in case they cannot agree in making these appointments, the Editor of the *Sporting Life* is hereby empowered to make such appointments; also, if the men cannot agree in selecting a building or ground for the decision of the match, the editor of the *Sporting Life* to have the power of naming where the race is to be decided. The judges to be four in number, and to have

King of the Peds

full control over the race from the time the men start; the decision of the majority of the judge, to be final and conclusive under any circumstances. Two bands to be in attendance, and play from 5 a.m. till 12 p. m; the bands to be under the direction of both men in alternate hours, and to discontinue playing whilst either man is absent for the purpose of sleeping. In the event of any question arising which may not be provided for in these articles, the judges jointly to have full power to decide such question, and their decision to be final and conclusive. The stakeholder shall in each and every case be exonerated from all responsibility upon obeying the direction of the judges. Either party failing to comply with any of these articles to forfeit the whole of the Stakes.

(Signed)   DANIEL O'LEARY   EDWARD PAYSON WESTON

Whilst the two men waited for their big day to arrive, Biggs of St. Helens, and Smythe of Liverpool, took on O'Leary in a six-day match which started on the Monday, the 29th of January and ended on Saturday, the 3rd of February. The venue was again the Park Skating Rink at Liverpool; and once again O'Leary was victorious seeing off the combined total of the other two by 90 miles, the final score being: **O'Leary, 418: Biggs, 133; Smythe, 195.** The *Liverpool Post* described the closing scenes: The result of the contest was received with great enthusiasm by the large gathering which crowded the rink, and it would be almost impossible to describe the scene. The utmost excitement prevailed and the crowd cheered vociferously, and jostled, crushed, and squeezed each other in the most frantic manner, in their attempt to catch a glimpse of the sturdy, dark complexioned American, the hero of the hour. At the close of the contest, the people shouted vigorously for O'Leary, and several men immediately in front of the box would be satisfied with nothing short of shaking hands with the plucky American, who good naturedly, gratified their desire in this direction.

Just under a month later at 9 p.m. on Wednesday, the 28th of February, O'Leary commenced a return match with Crossland for stakes of £100 per side at the Pomona Gardens. The original conditions of the match were that the two men compete for the *"300 miles supremacy,"* but an amendment later agreed: - **That whichever of the contestants shall have covered the greatest number of miles up to ten o'clock on Saturday night (providing the 300 miles had not been covered within that time) shall be deemed the winner.**

O'Leary, as was expected, hit the front from the start and dashed away from his opponent at a *"warm pace,"* going on to make 15 miles at 23:44:33, with his opponent at the time being a mile behind.

When O'Leary left the track at 11:45 the next morning, he had made 69 miles and 2 laps. Crossland made the same distance at 11:54, and by 14:49, he had extended his lead over the American to a mile and a half, the score being 82 to 78. After 24 hours of competition Crossland managed to increase his advantage to six miles, the terms being 109 to 103, but this lead was decreased slightly by a mile as the men finished the day.

During the night however, with Crossland taking 1h.4m rest as opposed his opponents 30m., O'Leary was able to make up the lost ground, and by midday was able to reverse the previous six-mile deficit into plus four miles, the scores being 166.1 to 162.

As the day advanced, Crossland started to retrieve back some of the lost distance, by employing a series of spurts against his taller opponent *"in a most brilliant manner."* When Dan completed his 200th mile at 19:35, (or 46h.35m.30s from the start) a performance which had never before been accomplished, Peter reduced the gap between them to a little over four miles. Crossland later scored his 200th mile at 20:36 amid *"great excitement, the cheering seeming to make a great effect upon him, as he raced after the American with vigour."* Thereafter, during the night, *"some very "tall" walking was witnessed as the pair came together, "when a neck-and-neck race would ensue for the lead, Crossland invariably coming out the victor."*

Crossland slowly but surely made the necessary inroads into his opponent's score until at 05:09, when on a score of 241.2, he got himself within few yards of O'Leary, who was suffering dreadfully from blistered feet. Then at six o'clock, the Sheffielder overtook the ailing Chicagoan, who must have been very frustrated as he watched Crossland whiz past him. O'Leary thereafter, who was compelled to take a back seat in the race, went on to rest several times during the morning, and at 12:19 left the track having walked 264.8 to his opponents 267.

The Englishman, now sensing victory and keeping to his task, kept on going, making 270 miles at 12:50, and 272 by 13:50, before eventually taking a break at 16:17 on a score of 280. O'Leary returned to the track at 17:04 when Crossland was on a score of 281 miles and 3 laps. *"Although fairly "used up," O'Leary walked on manfully,"* but, after covering 267.7 retired altogether.

Crossland's trainer took him off the track at 18:22 after he had made 287 miles in 69h.22m.22s. The previous record for that distance had been made by Weston in a time of 84h.15m, which meant that the Yorkshireman had secured the same number of miles in 15 hours less!

The attendance at the finish on Saturday, the 3rd of March was very large and Crossland's victory was received with great excitement. *"The result of the match proves what a determined customer Crossland must be, as it was only by sheer pluck and perseverance that he secured a victory which on Friday looked almost hopeless; in fact, as much as 10 to 1 was paid on the "visitor" at one time."*

Peter Crossland

© *The British Library. All Rights reserved. The Penny Illustrated. (Illustration no: 7)*

The **sketch** of O'Leary's career published by the ***New York Sun*** continues in Chapter 7.

CHAPTER 5

Weston Walks in Britain

Weston made his way to England in January of 1876 with the knowledge that no one on the other side of "the pond" could match him in races of endurance. The British press was sceptical of his, and indeed O'Leary's reported achievements, and as a consequence the readers of their newspapers were ready to bet that both wouldn't be able to reproduce the form they had produced in America. *"Five hundred miles in six days? Rubbish!"*

Weston was soon to prove that he was more than a capable athlete when he came up against the *"Champion of England,"* William Perkins, (who had been the only man in that country to have walked eight miles in an hour) in a 24-hour competition at the *Agricultural Hall in Islington, London, on Tuesday, the 8th of February 1876. Perkins, who was born on the 16th September 1852 in the parish of St. Clement Danes, Strand, London, was described as a smart-looking young man. He stood 5 feet 5½ inches high, was broad across the shoulders, and possessed a strong, short back, and very muscular thighs.

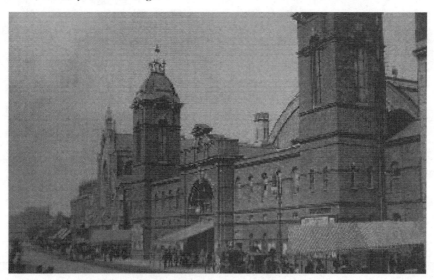

The Agricultural Hall, Islington, London

With the permission of Islington Local History Centre (Illustration no: 8)

*The "Royal Agricultural Hall," which could hold as many as 50,000 people, was built in 1862. It was 75 ft high and covered by an arched glass roof which spanned 125 ft.

The prize was for a silver cup worth £60. Both men had agreed to walk for 24 hours, and Weston spoke confidently of covering 115 miles within the stipulated time. Of the two tracks that were laid out for the race, one of the following judges officiating in the match, (which were, Mr. Atkinson, of the *Sporting Life*, Mr. H. Green of the *Billiard News*, Mr. Thomas Griffith, Mr. Joseph Jenn and Mr. J. Knott of *The Sportsman*, Mr. J. Vandy of *Bell's Life* and Mr. H. F. Wilkinson of *The Field*) wrote in *Bell's Life*: The clear space in the body of the hall (within the pillars) is 310 feet long by 123 ft. wide and the inner track of which the American elected to walk, and which was laid down with a layer of loam and gravel, was stated to be seven to the mile, and the other circuit, six and a half to the same distance; but on measuring both with a steel chain which had previously been tested, it was discovered that Weston's track was three yards over, so that in widening it at the ends. The judge's stand was stationed midway on the north side of the hall, and opposite to it was a board, on which each lap, mile, and mile time, was carefully registered for competitors from the beginning to the finish as we can personally testify.

At the start of the race, and in front of a crowd of 5,000 at 21:35, Weston wore a velvet jacket and trousers, a blue sash, leather leggings, a low crowned white hat, and held his customary riding whip. Perkins on the other hand was attired in the widely known *"University costume,"* of white Guernsey and dark drawers reaching up to the knees. After both men shook hands, Perkins asked one of the judges to address the audience and ask for fair play, the request being received with a *"volley of applause."*

The above illustration shows the two different styles of Perkins on the left and Weston on the right.

© *The British Library. All Rights reserved. The Penny Illustrated. (Illustration no: 9)*

Perkins immediately hit the front, and although inexperienced in the fine art of long distance walking, he steadily increased his lead. At 23:10, and having walked 10 miles, he was leading by about three quarters of a mile. After the Englishman had completed his 15th mile and was a mile ahead of his opponent, it was time for the building to be vacated.

We can now compare the reports of two newspapers about what happened next; - firstly the *Sporting Life*: **Soon afterwards, by order of the authorities, the bell rang for the hall to be cleared of all persons excepting those who represented the Press and judges, and people in office. This however was a matter of some difficulty. The musicians gave a final flourish before they retired, the lights were lowered, and then the great hall gradually was hushed into comparative silence, gloom and vacancy, the only audible sounds being the tread of the pedestrians and the voices of the judges marking the laps and the time.**

The *Islington Gazette* however, offered a different scenario: **It was announced that all visitors must leave the hall by half-past twelve; but though two or three of the servants attached to the building rang hand-bells violently for fully half an hour, few people took their departure. It was found impossible to secure the services of more than four or five policemen, owing to the number drafted off to keep order at the opening of Parliament, and, as may be imagined, these four or five had very hard work. Numbers of people concealed themselves in the gallery and other secluded spots, and a succession of chases and captures helped to pass away some tedious hours.**

King of the Peds

As the night wore on and the cold crept into the place, Perkins completed 20 miles at 01:13, and his 30th at 03:15. Soon after, and satisfied with his lead, the Londoner took a rest of 23m.53s from 03:48, during which time he devoured a chop, had a warm bath, and changed his shoes, while Weston remained on his track attempting to decrease the gap between them. As he walked, the American was observed to summon his trainer, Jack Hopkins of Bristol, with a whistle. This was a sign that he wanted refreshments and as he strode round he contented himself with eating jelly, drinking beef tea, and sucking on chunks of ice which sometimes he rubbed on the back of his neck. After Perkins came back on, he went on to complete 40 miles at 05:08 whilst his opponent, walking in his usual way, finished the same distance some 11 minutes behind. The Englishman went on to make his half century shortly after seven o'clock in a time of 9h.37m.41s, with Weston achieving the same distance in 9h.55m.52s.

The effect of several hours continuous walking now began to tell on Perkins, his feet being in a very painful state due to broken blisters. Having walked on for another nearly nine miles or so, he then rested for more than an hour, and on returning to the track, it was evident that he wouldn't be able do much more. After struggling on a little more, he finally retired at 11:41 having then walked 65½ miles. It was said that due to his feet being so swollen and sore, he was hardly able to walk to his room. Of his predicament, the reporter for the *Sporting Life* wrote: **His boots were filled with blood, and when his socks were cut off, it was found that his feet were in a shocking state, being literally raw.** One of the judges, putting his slant on what he saw stated, "His boots had to be cut off, his socks could not be removed for some hours, and later he had to be carried to a cab being unable to stand."

Perkins's retirement of course went far to destroy the interest in the match. Weston had up to this point walked 70½ miles, and the only remaining question was whether he would be able to fulfil his intention of completing 116 miles in 24 hours. At 19:20, he finished 100 miles or really more than 101 miles. Weston though continued taking very little rest, and although suffering greatly from fatigue, showed great courage to record a distance of 109 miles and 832 yards when the end of the contest was announced by *"report of pistol."* Indeed, when the shot was made, he was being accompanied by one of the judges who wanted to mark the exact spot he was at on the track so that the distance could be recorded accurately. At the end, he had difficulty walking round the track due to the enthusiasm of the crowd who encroached on his path. He was greeted with great cheering, and despite being unsuccessful, his performance was considered *"remarkable."* He was finally carried out of the hall to his lodgings where he was examined by a team of physicians. Below is an idea of what times, in minutes and seconds, the two men made at different stages of the race:

	Perkins		Weston		Perkins		Weston
Mile		Mile		Mile		Mile	
1	11:21	1	12:18	65	13:21	65	12:31
10	10:17	10	11:00			70	12:51
20	10:55	20	11:56			80	13:24
30	10:59	30	11:50			90	13:40
40	11:15	40	12:51			100	14:11
40	11:46	50	12:43			106	13:44
60	12:31	60	11:59			109	13:59

Weston then wrote the following letter to the editor of the *Sporting Life*. What is interesting about it is when it was timed and dated. At 4 o'clock on that day he had just started his 86th mile which he began at 15:57 and which he completed 13m.40s later. Weston was truly a man of many talents!

I hereby challenge any man in England to a pedestrian trial of speed and endurance, at the Agricultural Hall, Islington, to commence at nine p. m., Tuesday February 15, and terminating at nine p. m., Thursday, February 17. The party walking the greatest number of miles in the forty-eight consecutive hours to receive from the loser a silver cup, value not less than £50, and to be acknowledged the Champion Long Distance Pedestrian of England. Each contestant to walk alone, except when it is necessary for the attendant to pass refreshments. The judges to be selected from the sporting papers of London. And in view of the fact that I am in daily receipt of the letters from both professionals and amateurs, proposing to walk various distances from 25 to 100 miles, I will publicly state that I shall hereafter consider no propositions for short distance trials.

Respectfully yours.

EDWARD PAYSON WESTON.
London, February 9, four p. m.

Undeterred by his failure, Perkins wrote the following challenge to Weston on Monday, the 14th of February.

Dear Sir,

I observe that Mr. Edward Payson Weston has undertaken to walk forty eight consecutive hours, commencing on Tuesday night, and has challenged anyone to walk against him, he who walks the greatest distance in the time to receive the cup, and to be styled the long distance champion walker of England. Although not wishing in any way to detract from Mr. Weston's really great performance when he beat me so easily last week – a performance which has never been equalled in this country, I hardly think it is fair for him to challenge any of us at such a short notice as three or four days; as, he having been in strict training for some time, his opponent can have no earthly chance of keeping with him without a proper course of training. Long distance walking is quite new to me, as I have never walked more than eight miles in a match, but I am not going to ask Mr. Weston to come out of his course and walk me a short distance. I will make a match for from £100 to £500 a side, to give him or any man in the world one mile start in fifty, or walk one hundred miles level. If Mr. Weston will not walk for the money I will put £50 to his £50 for the purchase of a cup, the winner to take it. In case of his not agreeing to these terms I will bet £500, or any part of it, that I beat his time of last week – viz. 109 miles 832 yards in twenty four hours, any of these matches to take place in a month from this date, so as to allow us both time to get well. – I am, Sir your obedient servant,

W. PERKINS, Champion Walker

After the match against Perkins, Weston spent some time recuperating in the seaside town of Brighton. He then headed back up to the capital where he had arranged a 48-hour match against Alexander Clark of Hackney between Tuesday, the 15th and Thursday, the 17th for a silver cup valued £50. Clark, who had made the fastest time (9h.24m.16s) in England for 50 miles in the previous October, was 26 years of age as of the previous August. He was described as being *"very wiry,"* 5ft. 4½ inches in height, and weighed 8st.9lb. Weston wore boots and leggings whilst Clark, who wore tights and low shoes, walked on sand instead of the wood that had caused Perkins so many problems in the previous race. Once again the American used the inner track and once again both tracks measured the same distances as in the Perkins match.

The event got under way at 9:45 p.m., again at the Agricultural Hall, and was said to attract little attention, there being only 400 persons to witness the start. At midnight, and as the hall was cleared of everybody but the two pedestrians and judges, the scores were: **Clark, 12.3; Weston 11.5:**

Clark, following his doctor's instructions, gave up the next morning, after walking 54 miles and 6 laps at 09:35, due to the condition of his feet. Of Weston, the *Islington Gazette* wrote: **He went on throughout the day, never resting for more than the few minutes necessary for an occasional rubbing of the limbs with whisky and anointing the feet with oil. For this purpose, a small iron bedstead was kept in readiness, on the margin of the course, and whenever the pedestrian required the attention of his attendants, he reclined upon the bed with body depressed and head and legs elevated. During these pauses Weston displayed his invariable good spirits in a running fire of witticisms and quaint "chaff;" some of his quips, indeed, showed an intellectual power far above the average. One of these rests was enlivened by an interview with his recent antagonist, Perkins, who was complimented by the American on his plucky attempt of last week, Weston quaintly admitting that if the race had been for eighteen or twenty miles he would have been compelled to "hire a horse and buggy" to keep up with the Englishman. It was observed that the American seldom required sponging or icing, as in his last walk, and was so little affected by exertion, that throughout the day on Wednesday he wore his fancy shirt and gay blue necktie with which he started only stripping during the night, when the public marched from the hall.**

Weston, who was a fervent *"anti-tobacconist,"* and hated the smoky atmospheres he performed in, remonstrated with some members of the public who were puffing away at their pipes. He would later go on to make 77 miles by 15:00, 90 miles by seven o'clock, and make his century in a time of 23h.30m.35s after which he bowed to the crowd who applauded the feat. Calling to his attendants, he asked them to bring him his starting uniform. As he walked along, they supplied him with his velvet jacket, which he put on, his blue silk sash, which he draped over the jacket, and his white kid gloves which he put over his hands. After grasping hold of his riding crop, he was then handed the icing on the cake, his famous white hat, which he plonked on his head, much to the delight of many in the audience who couldn't help themselves as they climbed the fence to join him on he track where they chased after him for a couple of laps.

Following the fun, he went back to his quarters where Dr. Thompson examined him: Pulse, 93; temperature, 96. One blister on ball of right foot. Remedy excision! "Scalpel please, Dr. Thompson!" Weston carried out the operation *"skilfully,"* and chatting *"merrily"* to bystanders, immersed the affected limb in a bucket of cold salt water.

"The American, who is said to be a pedestrian, a journalist, a teetotaller, a non-smoker and a Methodist parson "rolled into one,"" retired for the night at 23:30, and as he slept, the building began being investigated for trespassers by men armed with lanterns. Whilst they searched, an intoxicated man called Compton, reputed to be a *Costermonger, fell from the girders at the western end of the building. Apparently whilst avoiding detection he had mistaken one of the gas pipes for a bar, and when he hit the ground he sustained three fractures of the arm, broken teeth, with his face being described as being *"literally cut to pieces."* As a consequence he was taken to St. Bartholomew's Hospital where he arrived in a critical condition.

*A seller of fruit and vegetables from a barrow.

After a rest of four hours, at which time he had covered a little over 107 miles, Weston resumed his walk on Friday morning at 03:27. At 08:44, he *"caused a slight diversion by taking a cornet and playing God Save the Queen,"* and by midday had made 138 miles and 4 laps. By 13:45 he had accomplished a little over 146 miles of ground, and in front of a sparsely crowded hall at 15:40, had made 154 miles. *"His nourishment consisted chiefly of broth, gruel, and tea, at times partaking of a tablespoon of jelly on his rounds."* A few private bets as to whether he could complete 180 miles in the allocated time were now being made. Loud applause greeted the completion of the 175th mile at 20:30. *"180 miles in the forty-eight hours seemed not merely possible but very probable."*

"Barnum's protégé," eventually succeeded in accomplishing his coveted target in 5m.53s under the allocated 24-hour period during which time he rested for 8h.50m.50s. In front of a *"wildly excited"* 5,000 crowd, he made a further 668 yards before the pistol announcing that time was up, was fired. He then mounted the judges' box and made a short speech, during which he praised his attendant Jack Hopkins and announced, "Though I have been walking in different pedestrian matches for eight years, it is only now on British soil that I have met with really fair play." After that he blew on his cornet to "God Save the Queen." He then left the building and later opened the windows at his first floor apartment to address the gathered crowd who listened to his words before quietly going on their way.

A week or so later, beginning at 8:05 p.m. on Tuesday, the 22nd of February, Weston set off in an attempt to walk 275 miles in 75 consecutive hours. With the exception of a slight cold, he seemed none the worse for his exertions during the two previous weeks. In this race, he would come up against the well known waterman and champion sculler of both the rivers Isis and Cam, Charles Rowell of Cambridge. Rowell was a muscular and strongly-built young man who stood 5ft.6in high and weighed 10st.6lbs. Under the direction of Johnny Simpson of Croydon, and given a start of fifty miles, he would be allowed to *"walk or run as he pleased."*

Charles Rowell was born in Chesterton, Cambridgeshire, on September the 23rd 1852. He was the son of Michael Rowell who described himself as a *"shoemaker and publican"* in the census of the year before. His mother Sarah who was originally from Dunkswell in Devon was at 43, the same age as her husband, and the family of two adults and nine children lived in the Queen Victoria Pub on Back Lane in the village. In the winter months in his younger days, he was attached to one of the Cambridge University boat yards helping with the work of getting the crews boated, and for some time he was an attaché of Searle's boathouse where he obtained constant practice with the oars. In the summer he was often seen at Maidenhead, on the River Thames looking after the boats of the officers of the guards. In 1874 he met and defeated Harry Clasper for the championship of the Isis, and in the same year also defeated Logan of Cambridge over the Cam Championship Course. He also won several minor races on the Thames above Teddington. His first public appearance as a pedestrian was on Easter Monday in 1872, when he won a half mile race. In July of the same year at Taplow, Buckinghamshire, he won a race of over a mile. His next encounter took place on the Cambridge Road in February 1874 against David Loadsby. Rowell received 15 yards start in 880 and won £10. The *Sporting Life* described his career from that date: Although passionately fond of athletic sports from his childhood, Master Charley does not have seemed to have entered into any match worth recording until he met Hutchins, of Cambridge, by whom he was defeated in 440 yards race for £10 a side on the Milton-road, Cambridge, December 7th, 1874. The following week he was matched to run nine miles and a half in one hour for £5 a side on the *Trumpington-road, near Cambridge, and on this occasion he was successful, as at the expiration of his journey, the chronometer denoted that he had won by 1min, 52 secs., December 14th, 1874. He next met and defeated the once celebrated ten mile ex-champion (Sam Barker) in an off-hand two mile race for £10 near Cambridge, Feb 15th, 1875. One

D. Loadsby next defeated him in an 880 yards race for a £20 cup in 2min, 6secs, near Cambridge, March 29th, 1875. His next opponent was W. Shrubsole whom he cleverly defeated in a 19 mile race for £50 (1h. 57min, 45 2-5 secs) at Lillie Bridge Grounds, July 3rd 1875. In the following February, he took £50 to £25 that he ran 80 miles in twelve hours, but the backer of time forfeited the deposit down.

*This was run through a snow storm and ankle deep in slush.

Since the finish of his last walk, Weston had been staying at his usual training quarters at Brighton under the care of Jack Hopkins. Again, the match was to take place at the "Aggie," and was set to last till the following Friday evening. On arriving on his seven laps to the mile track, Weston appeared in a velvet coat and breeches, leather gaiters and white kid gloves, whilst Rowell, dressing more conservatively, wore a jersey and flannel drawers when he strode onto his 6½ lap to the mile path. After both men indulged in a hearty handshake, the starter sent them on their way amid a faint cheer from the 200 strong crowd.

In the early stages of the race, Rowell ran along at about 7 mph, whilst Weston, taking matters more leisurely, made his first mile in 12m.9s. By the end of the first hour, the Englishman was a little over two miles to the good, and after two hours he had nearly doubled his advantage. Rowell made 20 miles in 2h.40m.47s, with his opponent, who was wearing lighter clothing, walking just over 14 miles. At 22:47, Rowell stopped for 16m.45s, had a rub down, donned his *"thick boots,"* and re-started on his opponents heels. (Rowell wore thin shoes when he ran and thick boots when he walked.)

Weston, on his part, kept well to his work and made his half century in 10h.18s. During Wednesday morning Weston took neither rest nor refreshment, except fluids, until 14:42, when he took his first break of the race of 10m.27s on a score of 90¼ miles. Twelve minutes earlier, Rowell had recorded 71 miles and 1 lap, having changed his pace and rested at intervals. Weston's 24-hour score was 104.1 with Rowell some ten miles behind him.

By the time the Chesterton man had covered 116½ miles at 22:16, *"it was now pretty well up with Rowell, for, though he was still stout about the feet, his legs were becoming very stiff and sore, and even a Turkish bath did not restore their elasticity."* After this he ate some chops for dinner, was given a good rub down with whiskey and ammonia and renewed his work at 04:24 on Thursday having rested for 6h.7m.10s. *"Later that morning placards outside the hall announced that both men were walking, and that Rowell was in front; but this was scarcely honest, for it turned out that the calculation was based on the assumption—not before disclosed, and as to which some doubt exists, that Rowell had a fifty-mile start, and had, therefore, a lead of ten miles."*

By midday and sensing that the crowd needed to be roused, Weston, now on a score of 149 miles borrowed a *"cornet-a-piston"* and played "Annie Laurie" whilst the band followed him round the track. He then stopped off in front of the judges' stand where he serenaded its occupants with "The Last Rose of Summer."

Weston then tramped on until 2:49 p.m. After completing his 161st mile, he took a late lunch which occupied 19m.50s. At 17:05, he had covered 168.3 and later took a 1h.21m supper break at 18:09 during which, *"Dr Barnes examined him, found his temperature to be 96.8; pulse, 75, and slightly intermittent; heart, healthy, and pupil of the eye highly contracted, and showing nervousness."* Satisfied with the state of his health, the "Walkist" then kept on the track till nearly 1 o'clock on Friday morning when his score was 193.4. Rowell by then was so exhausted that at 23:17 on Thursday night he went to bed for an 11-hour rest, having completed 142.2.

Weston made his 200th mile at 04:41 after indulging in a rest of 2h.46m, and some 10 hours later at 15:00, and although having accomplished more than 239 miles, it seemed doubtful whether he could make the 275 he wanted within the time, (11 o'clock) as that target would require him to go at a rate of 4½ mph. Weston walked his 250th mile in 12m.52s which left him under 25 miles to walk in the remaining six hours. At 18.05, or 70 hours from the start, he had made 254 miles 35 yards. In the next mile he spurted with Rowell, and walked it in 13m.19s which left him 20 miles to make in 4h.46m.56s. During the 71st, 72nd and 73rd hour, his average rate was about 200 yards over the 4 mph. By this time he was being roared on by up to 8,000 spectators who cheered him *"loudly and unceasingly, and ran round with him outside the ropes."* Having scored 4 miles in the 74th hour, he was left with less than 4 miles do in the last hour, which he accomplished with 3m.30s to spare. Rowell meanwhile had covered 175.1 at the expiration of time when it was found that the winner had *"walked fair heel and toe (within seventy-five consecutive hours) two hundred and seventy-five miles."*

King of the Peds

After the race *The British Medical Journal* published the following article entitled **WALKING AND TRAINING**: The surprising feats of endurance which the American pedestrian, E. P. Weston, is now accomplishing in London are capable of affording instruction as well as of exciting interest. He has on a former occasion walked 400 miles in five days, and is now accomplishing, and about to accomplish, feats of endurance even more extraordinary. Athletes generally will be interested to know that he condemns the established rules of training, and that the only preparation which he went through before beginning his present series of walking matches against time was to pass a few days quietly in the country, taking a ten-mile walk daily. His alleged preference for cold meat as an ordinary diet is founded on error. On Tuesday afternoon, before starting his present 300 miles walk, he dined of a broiled steak. He is not a total abstainer, except when he is walking, and then he takes nothing but cold tea, lemons, and oranges to refresh himself; while for nourishment he relies on soup made from extract of beef. Soups made in the ordinary way he considers too heavy for digestion during his protracted exertion and finds himself unable to digest them. His ordinary rate of walking is about four miles and a half an hour; his walking is almost entirely from the hip, the knees being flexed and the knee joint having very little play. During the first hours he rests for about ten minutes at a time every two hours during which time he reclines on a couch so arranged that both head and feet are much elevated, the body being doubled up; he is shampooed during these intervals with Bay rum being rubbed in a direction from the distal end of the limbs towards the trunk. At the end of each 24 hours he takes two hours of sleep, and at this time generally eats a little cold beef. At the end of his greatest walking feats he has never been exhausted or in any way injured. During some of his longest walks in America he has readily submitted himself to rigid scientific observation, and a series of very important conclusions were drawn from the physiological data thus obtained by Dr. Austin Flint in New York which were published in an elaborate monograph, and which Dr. Flint summarises in his newly-published text-book of "Human Physiology." Dr. Pavy is at present checking these results by, an independent investigation, of which he has forwarded us a report up to date, and Mr. Weston, has obligingly consented to facilitate on a subsequent occasion a further series of physiological investigations bearing on the waste tissue which will be undertaken specially on behalf of this journal. He is by profession a writer for the press; he never bets or backs himself, and has a strong desire to make his powers of endurance, useful for the purpose of furthering knowledge of waste and nutrition and the investigation of the vital phenomena connected with muscular effort. Information on this subject is much needed and, when gathered, will have important practical applications to medicine and to physiology.

Weston by now was by now being taken seriously by the British press and public. Ten days after defeating Rowell, and despite having suffered a bad cold which he had caught whilst staying at the hotel adjoining the Sussex County Cricket Ground in Brighton, he was back in action. During his rest he had indulged in short walks along the coast and on the nearby downs. To add to the interest of the occasion, Weston offered £100 to any man who would walk further than himself during the six days and £50 to any two men whose combined aggregate beat his total score.

Alfred Taylor, a 32-year-old compositor who had seen service in India with the second battalion of the 24th Regiment, was the man who he would take on for the £100 prize. It was understood that he had walked 50 miles a day for six days under a tropical sun. The other two were G. Martin, who, at 52 years old, was a member of the London Irish Volunteers of Maidstone. Martin once had the distinction of running the fastest 50 miles on record, (the first 27 miles being performed in three hours) the feat being performed on the London to Hertford road on September the 22nd 1863 in a time of 6h.17m *"against time."* Martin was a war hero having fought bravely at Inkerman, Balaclava, Sebastopol, and the Relief of Lucknow in November of 1857. He had been decorated with the Victoria Cross for a daring feat in India where he had been wounded. Bearing the signs of his injuries in his cranium, which had a silver plate inserted into it, he also had the same metal keeping his ribs together. W. Newman, another *"veteran"* who was from nearby Camden Town, had beaten Charlie Westhall in a 20-mile match for £50 a side, and also E. Ferguson in a similar race for a similar amount on a turnpike road.

The three starters, Martin, Taylor and Weston, would race against each other in the most peculiar of circumstances. Two tracks had been laid with Weston racing on the inner, whilst his opponents raced on the outer, all being expected to walk in opposite directions.

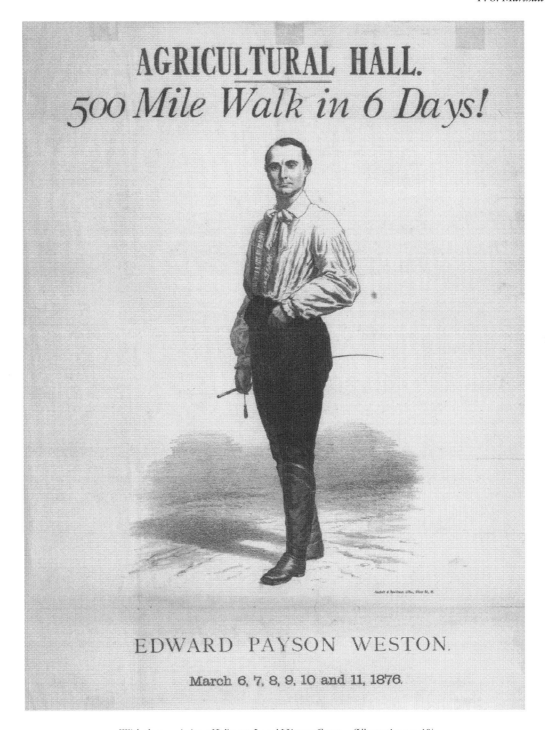

With the permission of Islington Local History Centre   (Illustration no: 10)

The *Sporting Life* informed its readers what happened next and what the men wore: **As the big clock chimed twelve, men stationed at different parts lit the gas simultaneously, and the men immediately came out on to the course, Weston taking up his position on the inner track, and Martin and Taylor on the outer, both standing back to back. Weston was attired in his usual costume, and Martin had donned for the occasion a dark green volunteer's tunic, adorned with several medals, his head gear being an ordinary cricketer's cap. Taylor had on black frock coat, tight breeches, and side spring boots.**

King of the Peds

The men who were given the job of having to adjudicate this most bizarre spectacle were: Mr. Thomas Griffith, of *Bell's Life*, Mr. Atkinson, of the *Sporting Life*, Mr. Wilson, of *The Field*, Mr. Green, of the *Billiard News*, Mr. Mather, of the *Sporting and Dramatic News* and Mr. Jenn. The latter was quick to point out that both Martin and Taylor, despite reports to the contrary, were not being employed to walk against Weston for £100 each. He said the only money they would receive was prize money if either of them should win.

Thus on Monday, March the 6th at the usual time of five past twelve in the morning, Weston began his 500-mile walk very quietly. After having quickened his pace to 5½ mph, he then slowed down to his more customary four and a half. Martin, who started with him, had a spell of giddiness and fell heavily at the Liverpool Road entrance of the building during his seventh mile, and though he resumed the struggle, he went along slowly thereafter. Taylor meanwhile, looped the loop in good style, keeping up well with his American opponent. Indeed, at the end of 20 miles, he was in the lead by a margin equating to seven minutes.

The band entered the arena at 05:00 and did their best to liven things up for the competitors. Weston had his first break at 07:30 for 6m.20s during which time he was given a rubbing down; at the end of twelve hours he had made 57¼ miles as opposed to Taylor's best effort of 54.3.

Towards 3 o'clock, Weston went into his quarters for a rub down and a late luncheon. During his 74th mile he rested on his bed for 16m.40s, and at 17:17, when he was six and a half miles in front of his nearest rival, ate his first solid meal consisting of underdone cold beef and toast. Having changed his clothes, and after indulging in a rest, he was back out on his path, his absence from the race having totalled 2h.22m.16s.

Taylor left the track at 21:58 to put his head on his pillow after scoring 78 miles and was soon joined by Martin, who, on a mark of 50 miles, retired to his quarters at 23:49. Weston was the last of the trio to go to bed, at seven minutes past midnight, having scored 96 miles.

Weston, who had slept for 3h.37m, was at this stage of the race, 12 miles ahead of the distance he had set out to cover at the time. On arising on Tuesday morning, he took an early breakfast consisting of a chop, two eggs, bread, butter and a cup of coffee, and at 03:45 resumed his task going along at about 4 mph scoring his 100th mile in 28h.38m just before 5 a.m. At 08:23, he had another chop, two eggs, half a round of toast, and half a cup of coffee, which took him 25 minutes to consume. When lunch time arrived he sat down to a meal of hot boiled chicken, calves foot jelly, potatoes, bread and butter, and one cup of tea. This fortified and *"freshened"* him so much that he was able to complete his 150th mile in 11m.41s having at 4 p.m. registered a score of 143.4 as opposed to Taylor's 99.4. Martin, although still in the race, was hopelessly behind the other two, and at 16:30 had made only 68.3.

The attendance, estimated at 400, was half of what it was the previous day when Taylor left the track to rest at 17:11 on a score of 103 miles. He was followed by Martin 33 minutes later with 74, and finally Weston at 18:13, when on a score of 153. For tea, Weston ate cold boiled and minced chicken, bread, toast, butter and drank a cup of tea. Comparisons were being made to the *"sparing nourishment"* he took during similar events of old, but he certainly didn't adopt the tried and trusted old "Oxford and Cambridge diet" of beefsteaks and half a cup of tea for breakfast, beefsteaks with a pint of ale for lunch, rusks, half a cup of tea for tea, and bread, cheese and cold meats with a pint of ale for supper.

Whilst Weston appeased his appetite, his competitors, who were both being examined by their doctors, were told they were both in a state of utter exhaustion and unfit to continue. Taylor, who heeded the advice and who *"was so done up, that he was removed from the building by order of his physicians,"* finished his race on a score of 122.1. Martin though, claiming he felt *"as fresh as a daisy,"* and who went back on the track at 18:58, only remained in the race till 20:35, then gave up on a score of 82.2 having rested ten times from the start, his stoppages amounting to 25h.59m.35s. He was replaced by Newman who entered the race at 20:52.

By the time Weston took to his bed at 01:10 on Wednesday morning, he had made 173 miles and 65 yards, by which time he was a good six miles ahead of schedule. Newman at the same time had made 17 miles.

Meanwhile, the medical profession was continuing to take a keen interest in Weston and his accomplishments on the track. During the race *The Lancet* published the following article: **Those medical men who had the pleasure to see Mr. Weston after doing successfully his marvellous feat of walking 275 miles in seventy five hours were** amazed to find him in better condition after the previous walks of respectively, 109 miles in twenty-four hours, and 180 miles in forty eight hours. Without commending, we may admit that he does not appear not to have suffered from his long walks in England. Towards the end of his 275 miles he was walking at a pace which ordinary walkers would find it difficult to keep up with. He did the last 60 miles without a rest, and the last 38 miles at the rate of four miles and a half an hour. Not the least credible and noticeable fact is the perfect serenity in which Mr. Weston is to be found at the close of such an effort, and the good temper with which he greets either friends or medical critics who try to detect flaws in his physical condition. On this last occasion his pulse was regular, and only a little quicker than usual, and his temperature was slightly below the normal figure. His feet and legs were free from swelling, and his feet were unblistered. What makes this feat, and the good physical condition of Mr. Weston at the end of it the more remarkable is that at the onset he laboured under a bronchitic cold, so bad that Dr. Pavy offered to give him a medical certificate of temporary unfitness. But with characteristic pluck and perseverance he went at his great task and accomplished it triumphantly amid the plaudits of thousands of spectators. Mr. Weston disapproves of running. Walking is according to nature in his view; but he leaves running to animals differently constituted. We cannot defend such a long strain upon the muscular and the nervous systems, but we have great pleasure in bearing testimony to the genial and cheerful spirit of Mr. Weston, to the entire absence of coarseness in his athleticism, and his willingness to make his walking feats subservient to scientific purposes. These feats of Mr. Weston, consisting as they do of the performance of such and unprecedented amount of prolonged muscular work may be looked upon as affording an invaluable opportunity of investigating the chemical phenomena concerned in muscular action.

These investigations touch upon the foundation of the principals of alimentation; for according to the actual consumption or utilisation of material, so should the supply be regulated to best maintain the capacity for sustained muscular action. The question at issue as thus a practical bearing in reference to the food, best adapted for armies on a long march, and others engaged in arduous labour. We understand that Weston is still under Dr. Pavy's close observation, and will continue so during and after his six days walk, when it is hoped that more complete results will be obtained than have yet been recorded.

The Yankee joined Newman in the ring resuming his tramp at 04:31 with Taylor adding to the party at 05:00 despite being urged not to by his friends. The score at 08:00 was: **Weston, 191.1; Taylor, 108.6; Newman, 34:**

After his 196th mile, Weston stopped to eat some bread and chopped meat, drink some milk, have a wash and brush up, and have his legs rubbed with bay rum. He then went on to make his 200th mile at 10:46. By this time Taylor was really struggling, and at 11:45, and on a score of 122.1, had to leave the track where he was examined by a couple of doctors who issued the following medical certificate to the judges:

Having co-jointly examined A. Taylor, we are of the opinion that he is quite unfit to resume his walk.

(Signed) John Brunton, M. D., Thomas Hamilton. M. B., F. R. C. S. E

After making 213 miles at 14:00, Weston ate quite a lot of black-currant jelly in an apparent attempt to *"cool his throat."* It was during this day that his pace slackened, and although clearly very tired, he insisted on walking rapidly at times which caused him to slightly sprain one of the sinews in his right knee. This injury forced him to take a substantial rest after which he resumed slowly, but steadily. At the end of the third day, he had walked 243 miles, his poor day time performance causing him to be six and a half miles behind the target he had set himself.

Newman, who had left his path at 21:45 on a mark of 72 miles, returned at 04:11 on Thursday morning. He was joined by Weston 20 minutes later. Having recorded his 265th mile, the ever hungry American took his second breakfast consisting of a mutton chop, toast, half a pint of milk and a light roll and butter at 09:11. He then went on to put in some quick times in the afternoon, his 290th mile being scored in 10m.50s and his 295th three seconds faster. This effort seemed to slow him down so much that about 5 o'clock, after he had instructed the band to play a *"soothing serenade,"* he promptly went to sleep as he walked around the track, thus requiring the services of his attendants to carry him off to bed. Meanwhile, on the other track, Newman went well. After a couple of hours the Londoner was joined by a much refreshed race leader who was by then attired in his full regalia. As he indulged in a spurt with his opponent, Weston went on to record his 308th mile in a time of 10m.50s, going on to finish his 323rd mile at 00:48 next morning at which time he called it a day. An hour and a half earlier, Weston had watched his only remaining opponent retire to his room on a score of 126 miles.

King of the Peds

"Ned" re-entered the arena at 04:07. He was said to be *"sleepy and hysterical,"* and was fed with some mutton chops and buttered rolls after which he still appeared to be in a pitiable condition. However, the plucky American struggled on for nearly another 20 miles before resting again at 09:17. During his break he was shaved, shampooed and given a brush-up following his breakfast which comprised of a mutton chop, bread roll, black-currant jelly and tea. On his reappearance he traversed the track whilst the band played, "The Sleep of Diana." That particular number did the trick, and after being carried off the track again, he slept for 90 minutes reappearing at 12:24. Now on a score of 345 miles, he made his mind up that he wouldn't stop for anything but sleep. That meant that all meals would be taken on the march, indulging firstly in a meal of roast and broiled chicken, calves foot jelly, a cup of tea, and latterly minced chicken, currant jelly and a cup of coffee.

At 18:12, and after accomplishing his 379th mile, Weston's next five miles averaged 15 minutes each. The band did its best to rev him up and keep up his spirit. He was, however, not going very well, and had to go back off the track where he slept for a further hour and a half. At 21:00, in front of 5,000 people, he got back into the race eating his supper which consisted of three ounces of mutton chop, two ounces of minced chicken, bread rolls, toast and butter, black-currant jelly, half a pint of milk and half a cup of tea as he performed. This helped him, and whilst Newman tucked himself up in bed having made 166 miles at 21:19, Weston began to push himself around at 4½ mph, finishing his day on a score of 390 miles at a quarter to one on Saturday, the final day.

The "Walkist" got out of his bed and hit the dirt again at 05:00 making 3 more miles before another enforced rest. And so it went on, and on; Weston walking, resting and walking, his every step watched with interest. It was clear that the cold, which had produced symptoms of catarrh and a troublesome cough, had a detrimental affect on his performance. Dr. Pavy had warned him not to start the race, but Weston being Weston, wasn't going to let anybody down, especially when so much effort had been put in to organise the event.

The *Penny Illustrated* describes the end of the race: **Those who crowded into the hall between ten and eleven o'clock on the Saturday night must have been not a little tickled to see Weston marching round the hall "tootle-tooling" on a cornet, at the head of his long suffering band. The lean and haggard Yankee wore - if not a wreath of roses - a white hat of exceptional character, and round his velvet jacket was a Cambridge blue scarf. When Weston pursued his course alone again it was curious to note the boyish look of gratification that stole over his chin which faced the cheers that encouraged him on his way. He had now taken off his velvet coat, and looked smart as a bridegroom in his white cambric shirt, with the front adorned by a couple of nosegays and a rosette, his hands encased in white kid gloves, and carrying a riding whip with a Cambridge-blue pennon at the end. He would kiss his hands to his fair encouragers. He would smile right and left, and playfully pretend to whip himself on faster. He had indeed put on a very good rate of speed when the hour for closing the hall drew near. He spurted along amid a continued round of cheering. So intense was the excitement when it struck a quarter to twelve that the people jumped over the barriers and would have unquestionably have prevented Weston from proceeding had not the gallant Joe Goss cleared the way valiantly with his umbrella, and so enabled the plucky ped to complete his 450th mile at a little over ten minutes to twelve on Saturday night 16m. 3s. start of the six days. He had thus walked a little more than seventy four miles a day for six successive days; and this great performance, albeit it fell short of the task he had set himself, deservedly won for Weston an enthusiastic greeting, which so far carried him away when he had climbed the judge's tribune he gave expression to the following highfalutin, though questionless sincere, sentiment: - "My heart feels more than I can say; but my prayer this night will be, 'God bless every man, woman and child in this grand old England."**

NB: Newman eventually scored 191 miles making a total for himself and Martin of 273 miles. As he had walked more miles against Weston than any other man in Britain, he was later the recipient of a "subscription" which was headed by the American who donated a sum of £15.

The last day's attendance of 20,000 meant, by that time, Weston had been watched by about 200,000 people in five weeks and was becoming a cult figure. He performed to the audience and when he wasn't racing, would make speeches about the benefits of walking.

A man called Joseph Spencer informed the readers of the *Sportsman,* in a letter written by him on the 20th of March, that he would be attempting to beat Weston's 109 miles at the Agricultural Hall between the 24th and 25th of March which had been *"placed at my service for the purpose."* Spencer, a tall, muscular man was lame in one leg. He had a long stride and *"a peculiar swinging motion of the arms from side to side, as though he were mowing."* Wearing large heavy boots, loose white trousers, a striped Guernsey, and a blue silk sash, he bent forward when he walked, presenting an altogether ungainly appearance. His effort ended in utter failure having managed to walk just 74 miles and 2 laps. *"He was ultimately carried off the track in a helpless condition, the finale being ludicrous in the extreme."*

"Eddy" then took on Manchester's George Parry in a 24-hour walking match at the Pomona Gardens in his opponent's city of abode between Monday and Tuesday, the 10th and 11th of April. Two separate paths had been laid for the men to compete on. During the encounter, and urged on by the Palsca Band, Parry was the first Englishman to *"walk 50 miles without a break"* after which he *"retired for refreshments."* For his part, Weston managed to make 111½ miles in the time allotted. During the race, he had a 10-minute *"tea break"* settling himself down on a sofa to have his temples and legs rubbed. After the match in a speech made from the balcony, Weston congratulated his opponent for his accomplishment of making 97 miles and 3¾ laps.

Weston, who had been staying in Brighton since his appearance in Manchester, had arrived in Birmingham at 20:15 on the following Saturday night, for his next appointment with the British public. Before his appearance, he stayed at the Hen and Chickens Hotel, and while he rested and waited to perform, the printers in the local press had prepared the following advert, which appeared in the morning editions of the Birmingham press on Monday, the 17th of April 1876.

THE WALK BEGAN

EARLY THIS (MONDAY) MORNING

THE RENOWNED AMERICAN PEDESTRIAN
EDWARD PAYSON WESTON,

BEGAN HIS
150 MILES WALK IN BINGLEY HALL.

HE IS NOW WALKING.

SMALLEY, the old Favourite of Birmingham, is exceeding the expectations of his friends. The Race will close at 4 p.m. Tuesday. Gate admission – *One Shilling.* **To long Gallery –** *One Shilling.* **To Ladies' Gallery –** *Two Shillings extra.*

Weston had engaged Henry Smalley, a well known long distance champion, to accompany him on the 150-mile, 38-hour walk, which would start at 2 a.m. The local man would be expected to pick up a prize of £50 if he could beat the American, and there was great interest in the prospect that he just might do the impossible. Smalley, who was the same age as his opponent, had reportedly walked 104 miles from Gosport to Fareham in 23h.30m during the 1860's, and there were claims that he had *"compassed at Cremorne Gardens 100 miles in eighteen and a half hours."* He was also said to have given Thomas, *"the Northern Deer,"* *"a clever beating,"* and that he had been the victor in four 100, and eight 50-mile, matches. Two separate tracks composed of *"fine soil"* had been prepared to accommodate the two walkers. Weston would use the inside track measuring 11 laps to the mile, whilst Smalley would traverse the outer of 10½ laps to make the same distance.

The race didn't actually begin till 03:18. Smalley had turned up at 01:30 expecting to make a prompt start, but unbeknown to him and the privileged few who would witness the start, Weston had taken an extra hour's sleep, his absence initially causing some concern amongst those waiting. Their worries were soon alleviated when a rap at the door of the building informed those inside that he had arrived. Of his arrival, the *Birmingham Daily Gazette* wrote: **He divested himself of his overcoat in a business like fashion, and disclosed to view the smart black velvet paletot and knickerbockers, and the long square toed Hessian boots with which we have been so familiarised by shop window illustrations. He donned the somewhat broad-brimmed white hat, and without further prelude directed his steps to the judge's box. He enquired as to the whereabouts of his opponent, and learning he was in readiness stepped on to his mark and gave the signal to be dispatched at one upon his arduous journey.**

Smalley kept up with Weston for the first hour, the pace being slow, and the American seen to be reversing every five laps. More distance was made in the second hour, and by 06:26, the pair had made 15 miles apiece. Weston went on to make his 50 at 13:44, and much later in the evening, entertained the crowd during the 87th mile by playing the following tunes on his cornet; "Yankee Doodle," "Annie Laurie," "Home Sweet Home," and "God save the Queen." He would take his first break of the match four miles after that when on a score of 91 at 22:53. Whilst he enjoyed his rest, Smalley plugged on until 23:20, registering his 70th mile before he too, called it a day.

Weston set off again at 02:32, but gave in to tiredness almost immediately. Finishing his 92nd mile, he adjourned till 03:40 when he reappeared to make his 93rd in a dreadfully slow time of 19m.24s, complaining *"greatly of the heavy and oppressive atmosphere, which, he said, produced a sensation of drowsiness and lassitude."* Making another three miles, he went back to his quarters where he remained in a state of slumber till 10 a.m., after which he awoke and commenced his task with *"utmost vigour."* He made the coveted 100 shortly before 11 o'clock, and was joined on the track by his opponent 26 minutes later. Smalley had really suffered during the night, his feet being so sore and blistered that they had left him suffering excruciating pain, thus preventing him from falling asleep till seven o'clock that morning. Still, and despite his ailments, he managed to make 93 miles and 9½ laps before time was called at 16:00. For making 75 miles within the time allowed, and as previously agreed, Weston, who himself had made 129 miles, gave his walking partner £10. Added to the £7 that had been collected for him by the crowd, Smalley made a small fortune for his effort. Weston, as was customary, made a speech from the judges' box thanking all for the kind attention given to him. His opponent was then hoisted into the same area to thank those who had contributed to the money that had been raised for him.

Then, starting off at 7 a.m., Weston attempted making 55 miles in 12 hours without resting, at the Trent Bridge Cricket Ground, Nottingham, on Saturday, the 22nd April. After he had completed his 52nd mile, he walked backwards for a half mile in a time of eight minutes. This was the first time such a spectacle had ever been seen in England. He eventually accomplished the feat in 11h.23m, after which he entertained the crowd by leading the band around the field playing "Home Sweet Home," and "The Last Rose of Summer" on his cornet. *"He never seemed in the least weary, and never stopped for food, but drank beef tea and biscuit gruel occasionally when walking."*

After that more challenges to Weston in the sporting press started to appear. Mr. C. Cornforth of the Jolly Tar Inn, Great Ancoats, Manchester, wrote to *Bell's Life* stating that he and W. Sanders would walk six days against the American for a silver cup and £200 a side. Another man wanting a piece of the action was a T. McKelvey who wrote to the same newspaper offering to accompany Weston in a 500-mile hike over six days. He claimed he was being backed for £100 to make 470 miles in the proposed encounter.

The numerous "challenges" were responded to in a letter to *Bell's Life* by Weston's "secretary" Mr. Jenn, who wrote:

Mr. Weston will not undertake to walk against any of the men he has beaten until they have shown themselves 'foemen worthy of his steel' by at least equalling some of the tasks he has set them; and even then, he will walk neither a match for a bet nor in a handicap, but will simply give any of them £100 if they can beat him. So the better plan would be for all challengers to enter Mr. Lewis's Twenty Four Hours handicap, and if the winner can show anything like a respectable performance Weston will let him enter the lists.

On Monday, the 1st of May, Weston, performing at a very cold and under-attended Newhall Grounds in Sheffield, gave an exhibition of his *"walking prowess."* On a track measuring a quarter of a mile in circumference, he made 55 miles, half a mile of which was performed backwards (9m.46s), in 11h.20m.52s, finishing his trial eight seconds before seven o'clock in the evening. He then went on to make a further mile, half of which he walked backwards in a time of 16m.12s finishing his day at 19:16:04. *"Weston took refreshments on the way, in the shape of beef-tea, jellies, hot tea etc."* The weather he had to contend with on the day included strong gusts of wind, and heavy rain intermixed with snow. *"In the 59th lap a heavy shower caused him to use an umbrella and cloak, and later on he was compelled to again mount a "gingham.""* When the entertainer set off in the morning at 07:30, there were barely a dozen souls watching him. By noon, four hundred spectators paid between sixpence and a shilling to watch the extrovert, but by the time of the finish, a thousand members of the public were watching him perform, and at the very end he was heartily cheered as he was driven from the enclosure. It is more than likely that the 17-year-old local lad called George Littlewood, at the time an up-and-coming pedestrian himself, was there to witness the feat.

Weston next appeared at the Kings Road Rink in Brighton on Friday, the 12th of May. At three o'clock in the afternoon, he attempted two goals, the first one being to reach 100 miles without resting, and the second one was to complete 125 miles in thirty hours. It transpired that he failed the first task when at 6 a.m., and on a score of 80 miles, he had to take a couple of hours rest, but he did succeed making the 125 miles with an hour and a half to spare finishing on a score of 130 miles in the allotted time. During his walk he walked two half miles backwards, and during one of his miles, played the cornet much to the delight of the watching crowd, accompanied by the band.

Then on Friday, the 26th of May……………

TODAY! TODAY!! TODAY!!!

THE GREATEST ENDURER LIVING!

EDWARD   PAYSON   WESTON,

The Most Wonderful Illustrator of Long Distance pedestrianism and almost Superhuman Endurance – from Scientific Living - the World has ever known, has been Engaged at GREAT

EXPENSE by the Lessee of the

ROYAL GYMNASIUM

To give one of his unique and exciting Illustrations

In EDINBURGH, on FRIDAY the 26th inst.,

When with an easy, unbroken, and apparently careless gait, he will *without* a rest, WALK within TWELVE CONSECUTIVE HOURS a Distance of 55 MILES, including a half mile backward. A Splendid Band will be in attendance, and everything conducted in the same high-toned and refined manner which characterised Mr. WESTON'S late Popular Entertainments in the Agricultural Hall, London at which on the last day, there was an attendance of over 20,000 Persons, including 5,000 Ladies, and many of the leading Nobility and Gentlemen of England. To accommodate the many Thousands of anxious Spectators to this, the Only Entertainment to be given in Edinburgh by Mr. WESTON, the Lesee has decided to place the admission at the low price of Sixpence, with only Sixpence extra to the Reserved Seats. The Walk will commence at 9 A. M.., and terminate at 9 P. M.

ADMISSION TO THE HALL EXTRA.

On a warm and dry day, and dressed in his usual attire, including, *"white shirt with abundance of frill,"* Weston performed the feat he had been hired for with 40 minutes to spare, in front of an estimated evening crowd of 10,000. At the end of the show, Weston who was carried shoulder high, told the gathered crowd that he would like to give a better exhibition in Edinburgh at a future date.

The London based *Sportsman,* offered *"many points of interest in its description of the physique of a man endowed with the extraordinary powers of endurance shown by Edward Payson Weston:"* He is a tall, slight, and very thin man. His head, hands, and feet are small; his limbs, though well-knit and shapely, are spare. He is remarkably wide in the hips, the pelvis somewhat resembling that of the female, and in consequence his thighs are widely separated, He is of highly nervous temperament; vivacious, but easily depressed; courteous, but (on these occasions least) irritable. His nervous impressibility is well illustrated by the marked effect produced on him by a cheerful word encouragement offered at times when he is fatigued. His face, evidently unconsciously, improves at once. So, too, when the monotony of the walk becomes oppressive he will call upon the band to play one of certain favourite tunes, and under its inspiring influence he saves a minute on the time of the mile. To the wideness of the hips is, no doubt, in part, owing to his peculiar gait. At each step the body receives a slight jerk, which at times of fatigue becomes almost a swagger. The knees are kept constantly flexed at a slight angle—very little movement of the joint can be observed; in consequence the foot is planted firmly and rather flat, and there is very little spring in his walk. But his progression is constant; there is none of the pause which may be observed between each step in ordinary walkers, and on getting a little accustomed to his appearance it becomes plain that his method is eminently serviceable in getting over the ground. The arms are allowed to swing, and are unflexed, in this point differing from English fast walkers. He does not appear to fix the thorax, but lets it move freely. During a walk he takes rest at first at short intervals, and then as the period of exertion becomes longer at longer intervals; and whereas in the earlier part of the journey his period of rest is governed chiefly by the time which he has to spare, later on he is careful not to prolong it; theoretically, because the limbs are then liable to become stiff. Practically, on this occasion he made little difference in the length of his rests. At the end of each twenty-four hours he allows himself two hours of sleep, and it is only during this interval that he takes any solid food. He depends for support chiefly upon Liebig's extract and calves'-foot jelly, and he drinks a great deal of tea to keep off sleep, but this no doubt answers other purposes as well. To these he adds lemons, oranges, grapes, and occasionally ice. As a rule he takes his fluids cold, but when he feels the need of a stimulant he uses them very hot. He is not a total abstainer; but while training he abjures tobacco and alcohol. During a journey he never takes any alcoholic drink, but special reasons led him to break through this custom on the last occasion.

Weston kept his promise and went back to Scotland. He arrived at Waverley Railway Station in Edinburgh on the evening of Friday, the 16th of June, where he was greeted by *"hundreds of people,"* of whom many cheered and tried to shake hands with him.

THE GREAT PEDESTRIAN SENSATION!

THE EVENT OF THE CENTURY!

A WALK OF 500 MILES IN SIX DAY'S

The Lessee of the ROYAL GYMNASIUM is happy to announce that, in response to the cordial and pressing invitation from many of the most prominent citizens of Edinburgh, the world-renowned long distance pedestrian and scientific illustrator of physical endurance from America, Mr. EDWARD PAYSON WESTON, has accepted an Engagement to Walk 500 MILES IN 6 CONSECUTIVE DAYS, INCLUDING 115 MILES WITHIN THE FIRST 24 HOURS On the Pedestrian Track of the

ROYAL GYMNASIUM GROUNDS,

To commence Five Minutes after Midnight,

MONDAY MORNING, JUNE 19th,

And to Terminate on

SATURDAY NIGHT, THE 24TH INST.

During the Grand PEDESTRIAN CARNIVAL, THE Tickets of

Admission will be but ONE SHILLING!

Monday: His intention of walking the 115 miles that had been advertised was abandoned after a couple of dogs got on to the furlong in length circular track, causing him to stumble as he tried to avoid them. As a result, he hurt his foot on a peg which held up the rope around the path, which was protected from the sun by a canvas awning. The *Scotsman* in its report of the first day said: At intervals the monotony of the performance was varied by an attendant appearing on the "track," carrying bowls of porridge, basins of beef tea, and dishes of calves foot jelly, which were heartily partaken of by the pedestrian without the spin being broken. At times, too, he went through his toilet in the most complete fashion, sponging himself, and dressing his hair with the aid of a small mirror. When he retired at midnight the total distance covered was 83 miles.

Tuesday: Sleeping 3½ hours from midnight, he retired Wednesday morning at 00:53, with the total distance being covered up to that point 167 miles.

Wednesday: Having slept 4½ hours he continued his lonely trek. The *Scotsman* remarked in its commentary on the event: At times, as had been the case in the previous twenty-four hours, it seemed as if the pace were about to fall off, but this as will be seen, was never allowed to take place to any considerable extent. At seven o'clock in the evening for example, the look of the performer, as with soiled shirt and sweat-begrimed face he trudged along, evidently fagged, as was shown by the heavy way in which he breathed, was rather discouraging to outsiders; but when after a rest of fifteen minutes then taken he emerged from his tent wearing white linen and a smart blue scarf, with his face washed, and hair neatly combed, he seemed as if he had taken a fresh lease of strength, starting round the track in the 221st mile at a swinging pace, beating time to a lively tune played by the band, and smilingly acknowledging the hearty cheers of the with which his pluck was rewarded. He eventually retired at 22:48 on a score of 233 miles.

Thursday: Weston entertained some of his more distinguished visitors by playing to them on one of his favourite instruments, a small silver cornopean, whilst he tramped over the rain sodden course. Referring to the "soft going," Weston said that when he started on his next 500-mile walk, he might do so wearing a swimming costume or take on the task on a pair of stilts! There is no exact record of when he gave up his hike on that day with the total miles he covered probably being 306.

Friday: Referring to the rain which had delayed his progress earlier in the day, at 21:00, after completing his 350th mile, he addressed the crowd saying, "It was utterly impossible for me to contend against unforeseen circumstances, or the elements. When on Monday morning I entered the track to perform as a pedestrian I had not anticipated that I should also be called upon to exercise my skill as a swimmer." (Cheers and laughter.) "By the rain alone, I have been delayed about eight hours." (Applause.) "Although the accidents that have occurred have prevented me from walking the number of miles I have promised to attempt, I have never been in better physical condition than at present. I promise I will excel on this occasion, the distance covered in the Agricultural Hall, London." (Loud cheers.) He stopped walking at 23:40 on a score of 361 miles.

Saturday: After re-appearing on the track at 03:30, Weston walked 50 miles before taking his first rest of the day at 3 p.m. The 24 minutes break was followed by another 14 miles after which he sat down for 50 minutes. It was during this time that he was presented with a gold watch worth 25 guineas, by Mr. Thomas Mansfield, in the name of a *"few Edinburgh admirers."* Weston initially refused to accept the gift because he had failed to accomplish the task he had set for himself, but, after reading the inscription accepted it as a *"pleasing memorial of his visit to Edinburgh."*

After that it was the American's intention to better the 450 miles he had made in London, but due to the thousands of visitors in the late evening, he had to give up on a score of 435 miles at 22:02 because they hindered his progress on the track by trying to crowd round him and pat him on the back. Weston then stood on a table and gave a speech in which, referring to the watch he had been presented earlier, he said he would place the gift in the hands of Colonel Robeson, the American Consul in the city, until such time that he should accomplish the 500 miles. After the usual pleasantries, he was given three cheers before being carried around the track shoulder high.

During September, Weston spent his time in Liverpool where he made 156 miles between Friday and Saturday, the 8th and 9th of September in a 48-hour walk, blaming his failure to score more on the heavy track, which was partly exposed to the weather. Then, between Wednesday, the 13th and Saturday, the 16th in a 75-hour trial, he scored his targeted 255 miles with 11 minutes to spare. During the event, he made 180 miles in less than 48 hours, and then between Monday, the 25th and Saturday, the 30th September, he finally delivered the goods when he walked 500½ miles at Toxteth Park in Liverpool.

Thereafter, Weston commenced a six-day exhibition of *"long distance walking"* at the Agricultural Hall, London, which began on Monday, December the 18th at five minutes after midnight. He proposed to walk 505 miles, and, as an extra inducement to draw the public, he engaged three of the best long distance English pedestrians to accompany him in his task. Peter Crossland, George Ide and George Parry, would walk for a period of 48 hours each, and for the first inducement for his competitors to put their best foot foremost, Weston guaranteed to give £60 to the man who accomplished the longest distance, provided it was over 160 miles, £30 to the second if he covered 150 miles or more, and £20 to the third if he walked 140 miles or further. The second inducement to the men was an extra prize of £25 per man if their aggregate scores beat his final score.

With the permission of Islington Local History Centre (Illustration no: 11)

Two tracks had been marked out round the hall for the use of the pedestrians. The outer one to be used by the Englishmen measured 6½ laps to the mile, and the inner one of seven laps to the mile, for Weston. The first man to go in the ring with the American was George Ide who walked the first mile in 37 seconds less than Weston in a time of 12m.5s. The American led the Englishman at the 5-mile mark by 200 yards. He then led thereafter and didn't rest until achieving 105 miles and 2 laps before 22:00. His break lasted 18m.10s during which his head and feet were bathed before he went back on. Below is a record of Weston's times of achieving ten-mile distances during the first 24 hours:

Miles	Hours	Miles	Hours
10	01:53:50	70	13:51:48
20	03:50:50	80	15:55:45
30	05:42:59	90	18:05:20
40	07:43:05	100	20:16:55
50	09:43:52	110	22:50:10
60	11:48:25		

The 31-year-old *"strongly built man,"* George Ide, left the show having made 155.5 at 22:50 on Tuesday night with Weston finishing his day on 186. George Parry, the 35-year-old athlete who was then living in Sheffield took his place, and as Weston *"marched as though he had parched peas under his soles,"* Parry finished his 48-hour stint with 163¼. Peter Crossland was the last of the English trio to compete and when he retired from the path at 23:15 on Saturday night, he had registered 170 miles. With Weston only being able to make 460 miles and 251½ yards in 5d.23h.27m.14s, it meant that Weston had to pay £45 to Ide, £55 to Parry, and a nice early Christmas present of £85 to Crossland.

Incredibly at the same venue on Boxing Day, and whilst O'Leary was engaging Billy Howes at Blackwell Heath (See Chapter 4), Weston was at it again at the Agricultural Hall in a five-day attempt to make 400 miles with Peter Crossland and Harry Vaughan, who had both been hired to walk on separate days to accompany him in his goal. Weston failed miserably, scoring a derisory 265 miles before giving it up at 23:27 on Saturday night, the 30th, with the English athletes making a combined total of a hundred miles more.

On Monday, the 12th of February 1877, Weston began an attempt to accomplish the feat of walking 55 miles a day in six consecutive twelve-hour periods, including six half miles backwards, at the Royal Gymnasium in Edinburgh. On the first day on the track, which was in the wooden erection built for the dog shows, he managed his task in 57m.30s.

Starting on the second day at 10 a.m., he covered the required distance in a couple of minutes before time was called. *"Mr. Weston, it may be added, rises at 8 o'clock and takes porridge, a steak or chop and two eggs. During the day he eats a little jelly or drinks some beef-tea. He retires to rest at midnight, after having partaken of a chop or steak and a couple of eggs."*

He managed to make the third day's distance in the same time, but that day registered his fastest mile of the feat, in 10m.30s. During the afternoon he was watched by the *"inmates of the Deaf and Dumb Institution, accompanied by their teachers,"* who had been admitted to the venue, *"gratis."* For everybody else the admission price was one shilling with entrance promised to be halved to sixpence after six o'clock on the last two days.

The fourth day was successfully concluded at 21:58, and on the fifth day he managed to have 2m.27s to spare as he entertained the enthusiastically cheering crowd to a further lap. After the "Walkist" had accomplished his feat on the last day, this time with three minutes to spare, he made a speech saying he would soon be attempting to walk 500 miles in six days, after which he was *"cordially cheered as he left the gymnasium.*

Great 500 Mile Walk.

EDWARD PAYSON WESTON AGAINST TIME.

CORPORAL BRINKMAN AGAINST WESTON.

ROYAL GYMNASIUM LARGE HALL.

March 5, 6, 7, 8, 9, and 10

Weston would give the Corporal of the Army Hospital Corps, Piershill, 50 miles start on commencing his 500-mile trek at five minutes past midnight in the same building he had been victorious in the previous month when he had managed to make 330 miles. The proceedings, which were *"enlivened"* by the presence of a brass band, saw Weston score 106 miles on his first day before retiring at 23:00. Brinkman trailed him by 20 miles in his attempt to achieve a final score of 450.

With a large gathering of people assembled to cheer the participants on, the score at 22:00 on the second day saw Weston adding a further 70 miles with the soldier achieving a quarter of a mile under 70. Thursday night scores: **Weston, 309; Brinkman, 251:** Friday night scores: **Weston, 363; Brinkman, 283:**

Weston could only add a further 59 miles to his overnight score when the match finished in front of a *"meagre attendance."* After thanking the match officials, the American remarked that he had been disappointed that so few people had turned up to witness his walking powers, which meant that he had personally lost £100 on the affair. His opponent in the end managed to make 323 miles.

Sir John Dugdale Astley, Baronet and Member of Parliament for North Lincolnshire, was a veteran athlete and *"ardent supporter of all manly games and contests."* He was known fondly as the "Sporting Baron" because of his links to horse racing and his willingness to aid any project involving athletics he thought worthy. He had been greatly impressed with Weston's recent performances. Later in his life he would write:

After witnessing some of his 'wobbling' feats over here, I offered to match him against any man breathing, to walk six days and nights for £500 a side.

CHAPTER 6

What Else Happened in 1876

On Saturday, the 22nd of April 1876, the 34-year-old *"table-knife cutler,"* Peter Crossland, who weighed 10 stones 2lbs, and who stood 5 feet 7½ inches in height, set off at 8 a.m. at the Newhall Grounds in Sheffield, to see how much ground he could cover in 12 hours. Crossland took on the challenge for two reasons, the main one being in the hope that he would be able to influence Weston, who was due to perform at the same venue on Monday, the *1st of May, into a match which would have proved financially lucrative. The other was for a *"purse of gold."* Peter, who had been working only nine days prior to the event, and who had been trained by George Perry of Birmingham during that time, walked for the whole twelve hours, apart from a brief rest when he changed his *"light pair of boots"* to his *"ordinary elastic side boots"* at the six-hour mark. During the time allocated, the local man walked 57 miles and 208 yards, at the end of which his feet were declared in *"excellent order."* Afterwards Crossland maintained that he could beat George Parry's (of Manchester) **record against Weston only 10 days earlier.

* and ** See Chapter 5.

On Saturday, the 29th of April at 19:38 at the fair ground in St. Helens, Lancashire, George Dootson, a 40-year-old local pedestrian who was an employee at the Sutton Glassworks, succeeded in beating Weston's 109-mile, 582-yard record, by making 218 yards more with 22 minutes to spare. He had started his objective at 20:03 on the previous evening on a ten laps to the mile track. When he had finished, *"he was seized by two stalwart men and carried shoulder high to the Salisbury Hotel, adjoining the fair, amid tremendous cheering from an immense crowd."*

The proprietors of the Agricultural Hall, having seen Weston exhibit his staying powers combined with pace, very spiritedly offered a prize of £100 to any Englishman who could beat Weston's distance in a 24-hour *walking match*. If Weston competed, the prize was to be £200. Numerous applications were received from men from all over the country, but owing to the limited size of the track, only 16 of them could be accepted with 14 actually starting. This "invitation" was made before George Dootson had claimed the world record on the 28th of April in St. Helens.

The following advertisements appeared in the *Sporting Life* on the 1st and 8th of April respectively. The text in **bold** would be repeated at the start of the second advert.

IMPORTANT NOTICE TO ALL LONG-DISTANCE WALKERS: - In order to test the merits of all English pedestrians and to see if England cannot produce a better pedestrian than the American representative, Weston, we undersigned, will give a £100 Bank of England note for first prize, £10 second and £7 10s, third, for a twenty-four hours walk open to the world. £5 will be given to every man not gaining a prize that completes the distance walked by Weston in twenty five hours. As a further inducement we will give 10 guineas to head a subscription for the winner, should he beat Weston's performance - viz., walks anything beyond 109 miles 3 fur. 172 yards within twenty-four hours. Should more than one man accomplish the distance, the money subscribed to be divided we are confident there are many gentlemen, true English sportsmen, who would be glad to subscribe, and support by them presence any English pedestrian who can beat Weston. The match will take place in the Agricultural Hall on Monday and Tuesday, May 8 and 9. The entry will be 5s to be returned to every competitor. The givers of the prizes reserve the right of refusing any entry from old or worn out pedestrians. As regards known good men such as Perkins, Clark, Newman, Howes, Miles, Vaughan of Chester, Golder's Mann, Rowell, Gale of Cardiff, a letter will be sufficient requesting to be entered. The entrance is simply to keep out men with no pretensions to champion form.

King of the Peds

Six acknowledged men must contend, or only half the prizes will be given that is to say; £50 first. If this challenge is responded to by our champions by Friday April 7, arrangements will be made to facilitate the comfort and success of all competitors.

RICHARD LEWIS

WILLIAM ATKINS.

All communications must be addressed either to R. Lewis, 16 Park-street, E. or W. Atkins 4l4, Oxford-street, W.   P. S: - Should Weston or O'Leary contend, the first prize shall increased to 200 guineas, the second to 50 guineas, providing either one week previous to the race taking place.

****

(As above..................) should more than one man accomplish the distance, the money subscribed to be divided. It is fully expected the subscription will amount to over £300, as there are many noblemen who have signified their intention of subscribing. The match to take place in the Agricultural Hall on Monday May 8 at eight in the evening; to finish the same hour on the Tuesday evening; and those not gaining a prize to finish at nine, if they try for the £5 for walking the distance that Weston walked. All competitors must walk on the same wide track, which will be composed of sand and loam, and about seven times to a mile. The start will be made to with the left hand to the to the near edge of the track, and to prevent any confusion, no man will be allowed to reverse the way of walking until he has completed ten miles of the distance. Should he then wish to change he will then have to walk ten miles the other way, and pass on the outside of other competitors that keep the way the race was started. No competitor will be compelled to reverse his way of walking should he think fit to walk all one way. All times will be made opposite the judge's stand, where the start will be made. Invitations will be made to ten gentlemen of the Press to act as time-keepers, scorers, and referee, the latter to be selected by ballot from the ten invited: A separate retiring room will be provided for each competitor. We have been inundated with letters from aspirants to pedestrian fame, and from the tone of some of them we think that young England as well as old England has Weston on the brain. In our first advertisement we reserved the right of refusing any entry from old or worn out pedestrians; we find we must stress a point more, and confine the race to men who have proved they have a claim to compete among champions. There cannot be more than ten men allowed to contend, and among them we have selected the following: - Miles of Brixton, Howes of Haggerston, Perkins of Camberwell, Clark of Hackney, Newman of Camden Town, Vaughan of Chester, Mann of London, W. Gale of Cardiff. The remaining competitors we must select by Wednesday. We have over sixty letters we must return with entrance fee enclosed, which will be returned by Monday's post, with thanks to the senders. All competitors must walk fair; there will be no caution. Should any man infringe the rule of fair play he will be immediately removed from the track. All competitors must compete in becoming costume, with a distinctive-coloured sash which will be provided by the managers. P. S. Should Weston or O'Leary contend, and give due notice of their intention of doing so, we will make the first prize 200 guineas, and 50 guineas the second. We cannot make a separate track for either, but we can guarantee to them an Englishman's boast – "fair play and no favour." Should there be anyone in the above list find that he will not be able to compete with any chance of success, he will confer a great favour by retiring from the contest to make room for others. All communications addressed to R. Lewis, 16 Park-street, Hackney Wick. E.; or W. Atkins 4l4, Oxford-street, W., will meet with prompt attention.

The race was started by the *"report of a pistol"* in front of an estimated attendance of 5,000 people at 9 p.m. on Monday, May the 8th. Miles was the first of the men to complete the first mile, in 9m.15s. The boy from Brixton then led the second mile in 18m.54s, the fourth mile in 39m, and went on to head the field in the first hour registering just over six miles on the *"big blackboard."* After the national anthem was played by the band, the bell rang at 23:30 to signal home time for the spectators, and after the last of them had left by midnight, Miles, on a score of 17.5 was three quarters of a mile ahead of the chasing pack.

The fastest time recorded for 40 miles at that time was 7h.1m.5s. "Jemmy" Miles beat that by 44 seconds and then made his half century in 3m.40s better than the old record in a time of 8h.48m.28s. As the new record holder stopped for a rest at the end of the 9th hour, waiting in the wings to take over was Howes, who, followed by Vaughan, was observed to be going very well. The Chester man bided his time to claim pole position, but by the time the 70th mile had been completed, he found himself a couple of laps in front of second placed Howes.

O'Leary's record for the fastest 100 miles of 18h.53m.43s was broken by the 26-year-old Vaughan, who made the same distance in 18h.51m.35s. Then just after six o'clock in the evening, he passed Weston's 24-hour distance of 109 miles 3 furlongs and 172 yards, with nearly three hours to spare. When that fact was made known, the applause was so deafening that the music of the band occupying the centre platform was rendered quite inaudible.

Both Howes and Crossland, who finished their centuries in 19h.40m.1s and 20h.42m respectively, also went on to beat Weston's total, the former at 18:57 and the latter at 21:55. By eight o'clock, the throng inside the hall was very great, and hundreds more were loitering outside the doors. All three leaders thereafter were *"repeatedly cheered to the echo."* Newman, who was in fourth place, took long rests when off the track, and who kept at a great pace when on it, never stopped smiling *"in a cheery and satisfied manner."*

At 20:08, Vaughan, who on a score of 119.5, and having just indulged in a *"grand spurt"* as he passed the judges' table, all of a sudden staggered and was caught by a couple of the officials, who prevented him from falling down. He was subsequently helped off the track on the back of an attendant; on his return after a rest of twelve minutes, *"his lithe, sinewy form was enveloped in a loose coat."* With laboured steps, and at a painfully slow pace, he crawled around the track. After making a further lap and 25 yards, Vaughan had to stop through sheer exhaustion. Unable to continue, he was carried to his room by four men. Emerging once again, he hobbled and staggered round the path eventually managing to summon enough strength to complete his 120th mile *"amid a deafening roar,"* in a time of 23h.45m. *"It was only by sheer pluck and indomitable perseverance, and the care with which he was looked after by his trainer that he succeeded in accomplishing the distance."*

Howes, who was in a state even more pitiable than Vaughan, was accompanied on the track by a couple of his attendants who fanned him continually as he too staggered round, ready to catch him had he fainted; *"but he kept up, deaf, as it seemed, to the thunders of applause, and wholly insensible to everything but the bull-dog determination not to give in."* No sooner had the pistol sounded to signal the end when Crossland grabbed hold of a hat and began to hand it round.

The winner was 5 feet 11½ inches in height. Although not very well known to the general public, he had performed well at various distances and was said to have walked *"very upright with a long stride."*

Henry Vaughan

© *The British Library. All Rights reserved. The Penny Illustrated. (Illustration no: 12)*

The final score!

Henry Vaughan, (Chester) **120 miles; William Howes,** (Haggerston) **116 and 6 laps less 200 yards; Peter Crossland,** (Sheffield) **113 and 6 laps, less 50 yards; W. Newman,** (Camden Town) **101 miles 5 laps less 50 yards; Arthur Courtney,** (Barnet) **98.1; Nelson,** (Camden Town) **83.5; Cooper,** (Northampton) **71.4; William**

King of the Peds

Perkins, (Camberwell) **70; Henry Smalley,** (Birmingham) **64.1; James Miles,** (Brixton) **62.4; George Ide,** (Woolwich) **54.3; Simmonds,** (Nottingham) **45.2; Alexander Clark,** (Hackney) **38.5; J. S. Robson,** (Liverpool) **16.5:**

Vaughan won the first prize of £100. Howes claimed the second prize of £10 and Crossland was rewarded with £7 and 10 shillings. Additionally, £10 had been promised for any man beating Weston's distance in the same time with a further prize promised to any man completing the task in 25 hours; which Newman couldn't claim as there was no chance of him beating that distance in the time allowed.

On Saturday, the 20th of May, Peter Crossland, the *"sharp Sheffield blade,"* now competing at the Newhall Grounds in his home city, began an attempt to walk 60 miles in 12 hours, having made an announcement that he would try to score the same distance on the following Monday as well. Peter failed to do the distance but he was so, so, close, making 59½ miles in 11h.59m. On his second attempt on the 22nd, alongside his racing partner, C. Hartley who had made 55 miles in 10h.55m.35s on the Saturday, Crossland gave up the attempt early on in the day due to foot trouble, with Hartley retiring through suffering cramp after making 35 miles. However, George Perry, Crossland's trainer came to the rescue by donning his costume and entertaining the large crowd to some *"fast walking"* over a distance of 12 miles.

George Dootson made an attempt to beat Weston's personal best of 112 miles which would, in all probability, have been achieved in Brighton. This time he failed having made 104⅓ miles at the Stanley Grounds in Liverpool between the 16th and 17th of June.

"In the presence of an immense number of admirers of pedestrianism," on Saturday, July the 29th, William Perkins bet £100 at odds of 6/4 that he would be able to walk 8 miles in just one hour. The cinder track at the Sussex County Cricket Ground, Brighton, on which the athlete would compete was measured by one of the seaside town's surveyors and found to be three furlongs and sixty-one yards round. That meant that young William would have to walk 19 times and 381 yards around it to complete the entire distance. Perkins weighing 136 lbs appeared *"at the scratch,"* at 21:16 in the evening with the betting being 7/4 against him reaching his objective. *"At the signal given he went away at a great pace, walking very erect, and taking long, lurching strides, and going exceedingly fair; indeed, his fair style appeared to please the spectators amazingly."*

Perkins in the end won £150 for making the distance in a time of 58m.29s as recorded by Mr. E. Smith, of *Bell's Life*, who was the referee and timekeeper.

At 11:30, on a blisteringly hot day at Lillie Bridge in London on Monday, the 14th of August, William Perkins and William Howes started off on a 50-mile march for £100. Running alongside them were their respective attendants, who carried umbrellas in an attempt to keep the suns rays off them. Perkins, who foolishly went too fast from the off, was the first to buckle under the sun, giving up the chase after scoring 24 miles. That left Howes to finish the distance agreed in a time of 9h.37m.35s.

A great walking feat was attempted at the Royal Gymnasium in Edinburgh on Saturday, the 2nd of September by the "Champion Walker of Scotland," Peter McKellan from Fountainbridge, who decided that he would attempt to walk sixty miles in twelve hours, and when he had done that, run a mile within six minutes.

Mr. J. Milligan, of Portobello acted as timekeeper at the track which was described as being in *"beautiful condition."* McKellan, who was a 42-year-old Irishman, stood six foot tall and tipped the scales at over 12 stones. He had served twelve years in the Scots Guards, and was employed as a labourer at the nearby Indian rubber factory. He began his feat at 8 a.m. and covered the first ten miles in the excellent time of 1h.36m.47s even though he had not trained for the event.

"In the course of the day, he partook of beef tea and a small piece of brandered steak, and toward the finish he was supplied with egg mixed with sherry. At times he refreshed himself with pieces of ice and Rimmel's Vinegar."

After taking just 40m rest during the time allocated, McKellan eventually failed by just 9 minutes to make the sought after 60. Nevertheless, towards the end, a large gathering of spectators cheered the pedestrian *"lustily as he persevered pluckily around the track. The bursts of approbation together with the enlivening notes of a brass band seemed to have a cheering effect on the pedestrian for he sped on his journey to the end with apparently the same elasticity as when he began."* As he stopped, he was carried shoulder high to his tent by those who had stood and watched in awe at the brave ex-soldier who almost made a big name for himself that day.

The *Wellington Evening Post* of New Zealand on August the 25th wrote: As our readers will doubtless be interested in the great pedestrian feat about to be attempted by Mr. Wiltshire, one of our staff yesterday paid a visit to the quarters of that gentleman at the Waterloo Hotel, and had an interview with him. The feat is one requiring enormous powers of endurance. To walk 1,000 miles in 1,000 hours means to keep on walking night and day for 5 weeks 6 days and 16 hours, with no interval for obtaining food and rest of more than an hour and a half at a time. The course is a space boarded in at the back of the Waterloo Hotel. It is 92 yards and 2 feet round, so that 19 circuits require to be made to complete each mile. It is not quite level in all parts, there being a slight slope at the starting point for a few feet. Within the enclosure is a small room, in which the pedestrian will take rest and food at the interval's afforded. He starts at 3.45 tomorrow afternoon, and walks two miles. Then there will be an interval of rest, and a fresh start will be made at 5.45 when two more miles will be accomplished. He proposes to start a quarter of an hour before each of the even hours throughout the 24, during the whole time, and so to time his speed as to do one mile in each hour throughout. Mr. Wiltshire is very confident of successfully accomplishing his feat, though he admits that the strain upon the system through tack of continuous sleep, will be very great. It appears that the prolonged exertion and the short intervals of rest sometimes induce a state of the nervous system which makes perfect sleep impossible. The pedestrian in such cases "dozes" rather than sleeps, waking by fits and starts. Sometimes also, when the exertion has been very long continued, a strong desire for sleep suddenly sets in, which it is hard to resist. The eyes also are apt to be much affected with the continued wakefulness. The food taken during the execution of this walking feat will be nourishing and easily digestible. Eggs, mutton chops done on the gridiron, rump steak, bread, tea, coffee, and corn flour made into a sort of jelly, are the chief articles used to fortify the inner man. No alcoholic spirits or wines are taken, but a fair amount of sound ale, chiefly English, is found advantageous to use. Mr. Wiltshire is a well built man with a chest very remarkable for its breadth and depth. In fact, the upper part of his frame is very well developed, and "hard as nails." Curiously enough, there is not an exceptional appearance of strength about his lower limbs. He walks erect, with a somewhat military action; and the swing and stride are all from the hip. The walking costume is remarkably neat, consisting of white singlet, with a star on left breast black velvet breeches, and light canvas shoes, low-heeled, and tipped with leather. Mr. Wiltshire is a native of Berkshire, and is about 34 years of age. The walking feat will be preceded by several handicaps amongst amateur peds for an electro-late silver cup, given by Mr. Edwards.

At noon on the 7th of October, Wiltshire accomplished his feat, *"finishing without the slightest symptoms of distress."* During the performance he lost a couple of stones in weight, and there was news emerging that he was going to go to Melbourne in Australia to attempt to walk 1,500 miles in the same time.

George Ide won the 50-mile "All Comers Walking Competition" race at Lillie Bridge on Monday, the 16th of October, making the distance in a time of 8h.19m.55s. He beat Harry Vaughan whose time was recorded as 8h.27m. George Parry of Manchester, who was also in the race, came third.

CHAPTER 7

O'Leary v Weston

The **sketch** of O'Leary's career from the ***New York Sun*** continues from Chapter 4.

We walked in Agricultural Hall, London………………………………

As early as the 3rd of January 1877, a correspondent of *The Sportsman* who had signed himself "Anti Humbug," had offered to back an "unknown" Englishman for £500 to challenge Weston in a six-day match. He deposited the money which was matched by Sir John Astley at the offices of that paper on New Years Day. The challenge was accepted by William Howes, who had been second to Harry Vaughan in the 24-hour walk at the Agricultural Hall in May of the previous year (See Chapter 6.) *"For certain reasons Weston did not care to try conclusions with the little Englishman, but as O'Leary stepped in with another offer, Weston sank his scruples about not walking for money."*

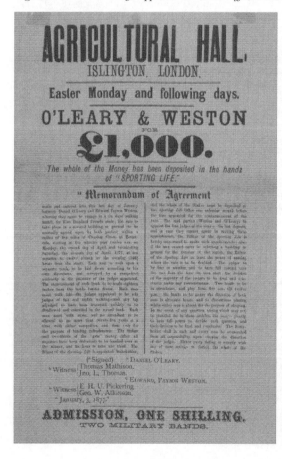 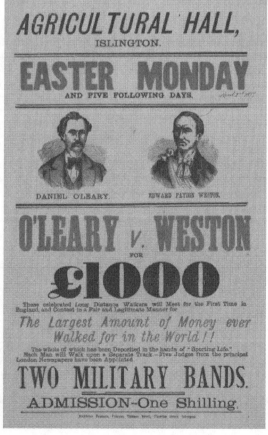

With the permission of Islington Local History Centre (Illustration no: 13, 14)

See Chapter 4 for a transcript of the above "Memorandum of Agreement."

The venue chosen was the Agricultural Hall in Islington, which would be rented out for the week at a cost of £400. The two tracks were carefully measured, and each lap as it was walked would be marked up on a large board in view of the public, as without such a precaution no record could be considered trustworthy. The outside one, which would be used by O'Leary, measured six and a half circuits to the mile, and the one on the inside, occupied by Weston, measured seven laps to the mile. Each man had a tent and these would be situated at opposite sides of the west end of the hall. The judges' stand as usual was on the north side of the building, and the men chosen to adjudicate in the race were: George W. Atkinson and C. Conquest of the *Sporting Life*, J. G. Chambers of *Land and Water*, A. G. Payne of the *London Standard*, J. Watson of *New York Spirit of the Times*, and the famous English Channel swimmer Captain Webb. The first four named agreed to sign the following conditions of walking:

"We the undersigned, who have been appointed judges in the walking match between E. P. Weston and D. O'Leary that commences at the Agricultural Hall on Monday, the 2nd of April, 1877, have mutually agreed to consider all walking fair so long as neither of the two competitors has both feet off the ground at the same time. We consider the distinction between running and walking to be the former is a succession of springs, in which both feet are off the ground at the same moment; the latter to be a succession of steps, in which it is essential that some part of one foot must always touch the ground."

Weston wouldn't sign the above document, stating that a further stipulation should be added that the toes of one foot should not leave the ground till the heel of the other was down.

The match kicked off at five minutes past midnight, and although setting off a full minute later than his opponent, it was O'Leary who went off at a much quicker pace than Weston, who adopted his familiar swinging gait. O'Leary made the first mile in 10m.4/s as opposed to Weston's 13m.2s. After completing ten miles, the Irishman was a mile in advance of him and he went on to complete his 20th mile in 19m.26s quicker than his rival.

"Mr. O'Leary is the perfect opposite of Weston. The latter is talkative and demonstrative; the former is taciturn, and seems to shun notoriety. When walking a match, Weston wears a showy dress and flourishes a gold-handled riding whip; O'Leary, when on the track, dresses very plainly, and carries a corn cob in each hand. Weston craves public applause, and is extremely sensitive to outside remarks; O'Leary plods along apparently without interest in spectators, and neither gibe nor applause affects his gait."

Due to nausea caused by drinking a mixture of bottled beer and seltzer water, O'Leary took his first break of 56m.57s after completing 63½ miles at 11:50. During his rest Weston pulled out all the stops to lead the race by two miles by the time he returned. The American decided to have his first rest of the competition at 14:21 when on a score of 73 miles. This lasted just 17m.5s. By 15:00, both men were level pegging, and the state of their positions remained more or less the same thereafter. Weston made the tournament's first century at 20:11, with O'Leary having to wait a further 19 minutes before accomplishing the same. O'Leary retired at bed at 23:43, and Weston, whose aim it was to make 506 miles, which he believed would be sufficient to win the race, led his opponent by just over three miles, having scored 116 miles 753 yards when he turned in.

The times for each 10 miles covered in the first day are recorded below:

Miles	O'Leary			Weston		
	Hr	Min	Sec	Hr	Min	Sec
10	1	41	43	1	52	55
20	3	27	13	3	46	39
30	5	18	25	5	43	40
40	7	10	30	7	40	34
50	9	11	12	9	48	31
60	11	0	41	11	35	31
70	13	51	36	13	36	37
80	15	55	23	15	54	55
90	18	14	56	17	57	47
100	20	24	1	20	6	10
110	22	57	15	22	36	40

King of the Peds

O'Leary returned to his circle at 01:14 having rested 1h.24m.14s. By the time Weston re-emerged at 02:50 after his break of 2h.53m.40s, the tables had been well and truly reversed by the Irishman, who had put a distance of five miles between them. With Weston making frequent stops, O'Leary steadily began to assert his authority on the race and by 08:45, had secured a 17-mile advantage, his score at the time being 148 miles.

Astley later wrote: **Now, Weston had made out to his own satisfaction that whoever did 506 miles in the 142 hours would be sure to win; so he made out an elaborate table of the number of miles he was to cover each twenty-four hours, and the amount of rest he could take in that time, and when O'Leary led him on the second day, Weston, instead of keeping near him, as he could have done, rested according to his table, feeling quite certain—as he told me—that his opponent would overdo himself and come back to him.**

O'Leary later went on to pulverise his own 200-mile record. The previous one had been made in Chicago and was timed at 53h.49m.34s, whereas this one was made in 45h.21m.33s. By this stage of the proceedings, the leader was still 17 miles ahead of his rival. At 23:12, he went to his bed on a score of 208 whilst Weston continued till 00:16 before ending his day's work on a mark of 194 miles and 720 yards.

The London *Times* described the two athlete's style of walking thus: O'Leary has what may be called a statuesque style, and quite comes up to an Englishman's idea of what walking should be, while, on the other hand, Weston has a very peculiar jerky gait, which is the reverse of graceful. In point of speed also there is no comparison. O'Leary is much faster than his opponent. He has a combination of speed and endurance rarely found in one man. The *Scotsman* on the other hand reported: The two rivals presented a great contrast to each other in appearance, style of walking, and general manner. O'Leary, who is a quiet, unassuming man, is tall and splendidly built and walked in steady, uniform style, and in continuous silence. Weston, on the contrary, is small and wiry, and varied the proceedings by exhibitions of somewhat eccentric pedestrianism, while he indulged in an exchange of jokes with the bystanders. His short "springy" step is quite different from that of O'Leary.

The second day timings again in increments of 10 miles:

Miles	**O'Leary**			**Weston**		
	Hr	Min	Sec	Hr	Min	Sec
120	26	28	30	27	47	54
130	28	47	10	32	31	8
140	30	53	42	34	43	19
150	33	19	5	36	55	8
160	36	5	46	39	8	18
170	38	14	27	41	43	28
180	40	30	26	44	44	26
190	43	6	20	46	56	58
200	45	21	33	52	29	50

O'Leary only slept for a short period of 1h.17m.21s before resuming his battle against his old foe who later rejoined him in the race at about 03:30. At that time, the Chicagoan was 25 miles ahead of Weston who had been off course for 3h.1m.45s, O'Leary maintaining this gap until noon. Despite advice to keep up with the Irishman, Weston, in the belief that leader would burn himself out, refused to hurry. O'Leary went for a rest at 12:03 of 1h.6m during which time the American managed to reduce the deficit to 20 miles; and on his return, the leader maintained this advantage till midnight when the scores showed 294 to 275.

In the betting ring, some punters had been lucky enough to secure themselves odds of even money on an O'Leary victory, but they were few and far between. The best odds that could be got on him were 1/2 but more often than not 2/5 was his general price.

3rd day times recorded at ten-mile intervals:

Miles	O'Leary			Weston		
	Hr	Min	Sec	Hr	Min	Sec
210	48	53	18	55	2	22
220	51	18	25	58	41	10
230	55	33	12	61	1	27
240	57	44	22	63	22	22
250	59	43	26	65	55	18
260	63	15	20	68	21	12
270	65	54	0	70	48	2
280	68	33	15	76	28	3
290	70	49	32	78	55	21

It was O'Leary who was again the first out into the arena having got his head down for a derisory 1h.36m. Restarting his plod at 01:47, he made 300 miles at 03:13. His score gave the signal for Weston, who was still 25 miles in his rear, to return to the fray, having been horizontal for 3h.8m. At 4 a.m. the scores stood 303 to 278. Two hours later it was 311 to 286, and when the clock struck eight o'clock, 319 to 294. The dials at 10:00 indicated 327 to 302, and later at midday, they registered 335 to 309. When O'Leary had made 339½ miles he was persuaded to have a long rest of 4 hours, during which time Weston remained on his path where he was able to reduce the deficit to 11¾ miles.

Rumours were abundant at the time that there was something amiss with O'Leary. *"It leaked out that he had been a little delirious, and his appearance was not altogether reassuring."* The worries of the crowd quickly subsided when he took to his path at 17:10. With Weston away for another break of 1h.13m, the leader increased his lead to 17 miles; this gap was maintained till the end of the day when the scores were: O'Leary 370 miles 704 yards, Weston 353 miles 600 yards.

4th day times:

Miles	O'Leary			Weston		
	Hr	Min	Sec	Hr	Min	Sec
300	75	7	29	81	22	43
310	77	40	18	84	6	42
320	80	7	10	86	34	45
330	82	27	41	90	24	15
340	89	8	18	92	48	5
350	91	12	3	95	7	28
360	93	25	55	100	30	25

Weston left the ring at 00:44 only to surprisingly return some twelve minutes later. *"He was evidently very much fagged and several of his miles occupied longer time than his friends could have wished."* After that, he struggled round his allotted path at a miserly rate of 3½ mph before calling time, and seeking the comfort of his quarters 45 minutes later. Here he put his feet up for 2h.21m returning to his toil 40 minutes or so before O'Leary. The score at five o'clock was 381 to 362.

The *Chicago Tribune* informed its inquisitive readers about what happened next: Weston was getting very leg weary and sought to relieve himself by all sorts of styles in his walk, and as soon as the band put in an appearance at 5 o'clock a. m. he started off in the most suspicious manner, which finally resulted in Mr. Watson, the New York Judge objecting to the tallying of a lap. His associates at the time were Messrs. Conquest and Webb, the former of whom had shown such a partiality to Weston throughout that it was left to Capt. Webb to decide whether the lap should be scored or not. That gentleman contented himself with saying that "It wasn't much worse than he has been doing since he started." After the delivery of this Solomon like opinion the protest was withdrawn and the lap tallied. Weston did not fail to take advantage of the leaning of the Sporting Life representatives, and throughout the day went in a very peculiar gait for walking.

King of the Peds

Following that, for the next few hours it was O'Leary who predictably showed the better method of travel, thus widening the gap between himself and his less than impressive opponent by 20 miles. At 09:30, the Irishman celebrated his 400th mile with a 45-minute break which helped Weston redress the balance somewhat. By 3 p.m. he had been able to reduce O'Leary's comfort zone to 16 miles, the score being 424 to 408. At the midnight hour, Weston had managed to reduce the gap to 14 miles, but at a price, having had no rest whatsoever for 19h.14m. O'Leary's quicker action meanwhile ensured he was able to indulge in frequent breaks, albeit of a short duration. The Yankee finally relented and went to his cabin shortly before midnight, on a score of 439 miles to the leader's 453 miles and 1,143 yards.

5th day times:

Miles	O'Leary			Weston		
	Hr	Min	Sec	Hr	Min	Sec
370				102	52	7
380	98	19	40	105	15	30
390	102	59	57	107	1	30
400	105	23	30	110	7	44
410	108	25	55	112	33	28
420	111	3	3	115	6	12
430	113	34	24	117	33	52
440	116	31	47			
450	118	54	41			

Weston stayed off the track for 1hr.13m. When he returned, he could barely move and made his 440th mile in an exceptionally slow time of 20m.28s. His next two miles were covered in an equally poor time of 38 minutes. Realising the futility of his situation he once again removed himself from the race for another 1h.37m which from all accounts did him the power of good. Astley went on to say of Weston at the time: **When I tried to get him out of bed he went soft, and on my telling him I should chuck some cold water over him, he burst out crying, and that settled the matter; for you can do nothing at any game with a party who pipes his eye.**

His weep must have done him the power of good, for when he returned, Weston performed well covering the next 34 miles without too much trouble. Whilst the American walked with vigour, O'Leary's camp was a little concerned with their man, who was walking along a little lopsided. He was hauled off the track and rested for 3h.9m. On his return, all the worries about his appearance went out of the window as the rest had apparently *"restored"* him. He then went on to complete his 500th mile at 14:49 with Weston 21 miles back. The *Chicago Tribune* told its readers: The 500 miles were done in 5d.14h.49m.20s, amongst a scene of the greatest excitement. Ladies waved their handkerchiefs and gentlemen threw their hats in the air, while the cheering was perfectly deafening for fully five minutes. A clergyman walked up to O'Leary, and taking off his hat, shook the pedestrian cordially by the hand. Then the bouquets began to arrive and soon the front of O'Leary's tent looked more like a florists shop than anything else. The ladies who presented these bouquets would walk quietly past the barriers and hand them to O'Leary, each gift being occasion for more vociferous cheering.

As the day advanced and the excitement increased, the management decided to increase the rate of admission from a shilling to half a crown. The price hike didn't hinder the public from watching the fun, the hall being filled during the afternoon by at least 10,000 people, with the numbers swelling as time ticked on.

The *London Standard* in its account of the closing scenes on Monday April the 9th reported: At 4 o'clock O'Leary had finished 503 miles 3½ laps, but for the last hour he had been looking very queer, and at 4:55 o'clock he retired, seeming very shaky as he as he reeled off the track into the arms of his attendants. This was, perhaps, the most exciting moment in the whole match. Everything, of course, depended on O'Leary's reappearance, and a dense throng gathered outside the door through which he was expected to return. Nor had his friends to wait long, as, after a short rest of 35 minutes, another ringing shout announced O'Leary's return, Weston having completed 485 miles, O'Leary's lead thus being 18 miles. From this point both men went on till 9 o'clock, at which hour O'Leary had finished over 519 miles to Weston's 503 ½ miles. It was evident that the match was now over. Had O'Leary been pressed he could undoubtedly have finished 530 instead of 520 miles, and, as has been said, Weston's backer wisely and humanely declared the match over. The hall, however, was thronged by a by a dense mob, calculated at 35,000 persons. Weston, who was still, comparatively speaking, fresh, continued on, doing his best to amuse those present by his harmless tricks, which seem to have excited so much hostility in some persons against him.

Whilst the loser was making his departure, O'Leary slowly crept around the track adorned in his Ulster overcoat. Accompanied by his backer, Sam Hague, he eventually finished his race on a score of 519 miles and 1,585 yards at 20:55. His tent continued to be besieged with gifts of flowers as the ladies continued to wave their handkerchiefs whilst the gents threw their hats in the air. O'Leary was presented with no fewer than six bouquets by lady admirers whilst Weston received three.

Astley then shook hands with the winner. The Member of Parliament went on to thank the judges for their services and the public for their attendance before making his exit. He was reported to have lost £20,000 on the race. He was said to have given Weston a substantial sum of money for making four miles more than what he set out to achieve. Astley later wrote: **I helped Dan off the track to his four wheel cab at the private exit, and he was that stiff he could not raise his foot to get into the cab; in fact, I lifted one foot and then the other the few inches required to land him in the conveyance. And when I got back into the Hall, there was my man running round the track, pushing the roller in front of him, and keeping time to the music of the band.**

Captain Webb, the hero of the Channel swim, who acting as one of the judges in place of Mr. J. G. Chambers, got up and said a few words: "Gentlemen, I am much obliged to you for calling on me. I can only say in reference to the recent match that I have been here every night all night long, and I guarantee that each man has walked every inch of the way; but as they have both gone to bed, I hope you will all go home as quickly and as quietly as possible." Following the cheering, with the crowd showing no signs of leaving, William Howes, the man who walked 21 miles in three hours the previous Saturday, made a speech declaring his willingness to make a match with either Weston or O'Leary; the distance to be long and the stakes high. It was also common knowledge that Peter Crossland of Sheffield had also thrown out a challenge to walk any man in the world, from 48 hours up to six days, for £1,000 a side.

Weston, *"wonderfully fresh and lively,"* stayed on the track till just before 23:00 amusing and entertaining the crowd by pushing a garden roller around for a lap. He finally finished on a score of 510 miles, and, bowing gracefully to the crowd, then left the hall.

70,000 paying customers watched the event during the week. *"On each day, the spectators could have been counted by thousands and included men of all ranks. At one time on Saturday evening there could have not been less than 20,000 present."* The winner of the match, in addition to the stakes, would also receive two thirds of the gate money after all expenses have been deducted.

Resting times for both men are shown below:

	O'Leary	Weston
Monday	2h.51m.13s	33m.51s
Tuesday	3h.42m.34s	5h.55m.34s
Wednesday	4h.34m.47s	4h.28m.13s
Thursday	6h.23m.51s	4h.42m.19s
Friday	4h.31m.35s	2h.44m.37s
Saturday	6h.2m.55s	4h.31m.48s

King of the Peds

© The British Library. All Rights reserved. The Penny Illustrated. (Illustration no: 15)

Of Weston, Astley continued: **Next day (Sunday) he was as fresh as a kitten, and came down to Lowndes Square just as I was going to morning church, and insisted on going with me, and, I can assure you, played a pretty knife and fork afterwards; whilst poor Daniel, the winner, was all wrong for some days after.**

O'Leary *"was obliged to keep to the sofa, one foot being badly blistered on the heel where a little matter had collected, while the other foot had a bad corn, or rather patch of hard skin, which was gradually reduced by the application of sand paper."*

Of O'Leary, Astley wrote: **Out of the 142 hours, O'Leary had only been off the track 26 hours, and Weston 28 hours. For that matter, I don't believe I had more than two or three hours sleep myself in each twenty four, for I never was more excited over any performance; and the number of cigars I got through was a record—not silly little female cigarettes either.**

O'Leary, in an interview in 1885 said of the race, "For the week's work I received a check on the Bank of London for $14,000. It was a good week's work and I would not mind repeating it."

…I beat him ten miles, and was four hours less on the track than he was. I walked 520 miles in 140 hours, or four hours less than six days, and Weston walked 510, taking more than four hours longer to do it. Since then I have given a few exhibitions but have had no matches of importance."…(End of *New York Sun's* sketch of O'Learys career.)

112

After the contest ended, the *Scotsman* published the following challenge from Weston. This was part of a letter that he had written, which was also published in other newspapers:

My failure was in a great measure due to an accident to me on the second day, and to the fact that I underrated O'Leary's powers of endurance. If I may be allowed to acknowledge my defeat as a fault of my own, I may also state that I entered this contest against O'Leary as I believed him to be in November 1875, without making the least allowance for improvement during the past eighteen months. That he has wonderfully improved I candidly admit; nevertheless, I am anxious to enter a contest with O'Leary as he is in 1877, and for the first time in my life issue a challenge. "I challenge O'Leary for another six days walking contest with me. For a stake of £500, £1,000, or £1,500 a side, as he may elect, the said contest to take place either in the Agricultural Hall or at the Lillie-bridge Grounds, as may be determined on hereafter, and to commence on Monday, May 7, subject to similar conditions to those contained in the articles of agreement for the late match. To make the contest still more interesting, and to settle all controversy on the subject, I would suggest that the plucky little Englishman, Peter Crossland, be allowed to enter this contest, and that it may be a sweepstakes of £500 a side, the winner to take the £1,500, and one half of the net receipts, the remaining half to be divided between the other two. This will give the contest an international character, and prove vastly interesting to the people on both sides of the Atlantic. O'Leary can hardly fail to accept this proposition for a return match, but should he do so, then I will accept the challenge issued by Peter Crossland, and make an international trial of endurance with him for six days for £500 a side, and will wager O'Leary £500 that I excel the distance walked by him during his late gallant struggle. I hope Crossland will find it convenient to postpone his match with Vaughan, so that in either event the contest can take place the second week in May."

Eighty-seven members of Parliament later gave O'Leary a banquet at the Westminster Palace Hotel, at which he was presented with a silver service with the names of all of his hosts engraved upon it.

After the contest was well and truly over, the *Atlas in the World* made the following enlightening observations about the race: When an unfortunate wretch, weary of life and maddened by despair, stands on the parapet of Waterloo Bridge, prepared to end his or her troubles in the heart of the Thames, a humane policeman seizes him or her, transfers the would-be suicide to the police-cells, and the kindly magistrate induces repentance by means of solitary confinement and the ministrations of a prison chaplain. But the illogical law permits thousands of people to assemble, and thousands of shillings to be paid, at the Agricultural Hall, whilst a couple of madmen, under the pretence of sport, shorten the lives allotted to them in the presence of the police as surely as do suicides from the bridges of the Thames. A modern walking match attended by doctors, priests, ladies, and the representatives of English pluck, is about the most sickening spectacle that could well be devised by a nation indignant at cock-fighting, and virtuously outraged at vivisection. Words could not well describe the painful sight of American athletes half delirious from want of sleep, half hysterical with tortured nerves, lollopping along a track with their tongues out, to the brutal applause of the British people. Ears would be shocked to hear the pitiful pleading of the pedestrians wakened from their restless sleep, and compelled to rush out, half slobbering up their food as they pursue their merciless and quite unnecessary course; and for what? Sportsmen tell us, for the sake of showing nature racked to its highest tension, and of proving the sublime endurance of man. Common sense tells us, for the sake of earning a few hundred pounds in the most cruel fashion. It is all over now. The men have done walking, and they have not died; and that is all that can be said. The Catholic youth of London are to give a feast to O'Leary, who fasted throughout Lent, and won a wonderful wager, making himself the while into a miserable spectacle; But "all's well - that ends well." Let us have no more of these walking matches, lest, encouraged by the mercenary applause, the bow is bent too far and the thin string of life is cracked. The doctors, the priests, and the noble sportsmen would not care to see O'Leary drop down dead on the track, or to see Weston walking over the brink of his grave and into it. Society would not hold those spectators guiltless if the next walking match ended in a ghastly tragedy.

O'Leary, who had sailed back to America on the steamer *Wisconsin*, arrived back in New York on May 24th and headed back for Chicago the same day. He was said to be in excellent trim and felt confident about his ability to walk 600 miles in six days. He stated that he would probably challenge any two men from Illinois and New York State to walk against him. *"It is probable that a long-distance match will be arranged between O'Leary and Wm. E. Harding. O'Leary thinks the climate of America is better to walk in than that of England. He says, while walking against Weston in his recent contest in London, he could not eat anything for 146 hours except grapes, figs, and strawberries."*

Back in England between Friday, the 29th and Saturday, the 30th of June at Leeds, Yorkshire, Weston failed to walk 180 miles in two days. He only managed to cover 147 miles when the attempt ended at 9 p.m. Having secured 98 miles on the first day he should have been able to accomplish his objective, but due to illness causing him to take frequent breaks, he could only make 49 miles.

King of the Peds

The next thing which is heard about O'Leary is an attempt to walk 500 miles against Peter Van Ness at the American Institute in New York between Monday, the 2nd and Saturday, the 7th of July 1877 for a wager of $500. His opponent who had walked 450 miles at Philadelphia in the previous month was guaranteed to earn $100 if he walked 260 miles in 72 hours, and $500 if he made 465 miles for the week.

10-mile times: **O'Leary, 1h.53m; Van Ness, 1h.59m**: 20-mile times: **O'Leary, 3h.48m; Van Ness, 4h**: 30-mile times: **O'Leary, 6h.22m; Van Ness, 8h.59m**: 40-mile times: **O'Leary, 8h.50m**: 50-mile times: **O'Leary, 10h.22m**: It was reported later that O'Leary had suffered five hours of vomiting on the first day and his illness was commented on in the *New York Times*: As one of his trainers was very drunk last night, and as his friends kept deluging the pedestrian with champagne and raw oysters all the afternoon, the chances afforded him for recuperation seem to be light.

On the last day of the contest, and despite O'Leary making 74½ miles for the day, the world champion could only make 471½ miles for the six days. However, he did have his excuses for his failure. Dr. Wedder issued a certificate stating that his patient had been suffering from an acute disease from the start "caused by heat and chafing." Although O'Leary had tried his best after having little rest since resuming his tramp at 01:16 in the morning, he couldn't produce enough on the last day to send home happy the 4,000 souls who turned up to watch him. The number of stoppages made by him during the week were forty-eight, the time consumed being 32h.35m.39s. His longest rests were 3h.19m.55s, and 1h.58m.35s. According to the report, the average distance made each hour during the 111h.23m.21s he was upon the track, was four and a quarter miles.

Three days after the walk in New York, it was confirmed in the press that O'Leary had accepted Weston's challenge to a race in London for £2,000 a side in the coming September.

Across the pond during the same month; *"Weston has had rather an unfortunate muddle at Bristol. He undertook to walk 400 miles in five days, doing it well, and he finished the distance within time, when, alas, it found that he had been inadvertently credited with a mile, so that, to his chagrin, when too late he found himself a mile short."*

In the early days of August, a spacious oblong tent had been erected in the grounds of the Northumberland Cricket Club at Newcastle-upon-Tyne on the north east coast of England. Within it, the *"track which is boarded up and raised a little from the level of the turf, is composed of sawdust and soil carefully rolled beforehand to render the going as elastic and as easy as possible."* Edward Weston would have to make 15 laps to the mile or circumnavigate 6,000 laps in order to complete the task of making 400 miles in five days, the effort starting at 9 o'clock in the evening of Monday, the 6th of August 1877. Mr. W. S. Armstrong, land surveyor of 40 Westgate Road, Newcastle, had verified the measurement and certified that one circuit of the track was equivalent to exactly 352 feet or *"533 1/3 links."* The laps would be recorded by post office telegraph clerks.

In the centre of the track was a raised area where Weston's "Full Military Band," (which travelled with him during his exhibitions) would entertain the public, who paid one shilling to watch him perform. They were admitted to the vast marquee at 8 p.m. and waited patiently for the great man to arrive. Weston's quarters were on Princess Street, a quarter of a mile walk from the venue, and it was made known by his manager that the distance would be included in the journey from there. Leaving his place of abode at exactly nine o'clock, Weston arrived at the tent at 21:03 attired in a black velvet jacket, tight fitting velvet trousers, a white *"wide-awake"* hat, and over his shoulder, a large blue silk sash. *"After covering a couple of miles, Weston doffed his jacket, doubled up his sleeves, and went to work in right good earnest."*

The "Walkist" took very little rest during the next 24 hours in which he made 93 miles, completing the century at 22:33 on Tuesday night. As he made his way round the ring he was passed chopped pieces of *"beef or mutton"* which he ate along with rice custard, strawberries, and sugar. Hundreds of people turned up during the day to watch him perform.

On Wednesday the weather was described as *"extremely unpropitious after midday when rain fell in torrents and made the walking track like a quagmire."* Despite the damp atmosphere, the old pro got on with job, his only complaint being to the local newspaper, to remind those watching him to desist from smoking the *"fragrant weed"* while he was on track. Weston made 165 miles at 22:19 that night thus covering 87½ miles for the second day of action.

During Thursday morning at 11:28, he thrilled the crowd by walking his 200th mile in 11m.8s, after which the *"plucky and loquacious"* athlete rested for an hour to get his breath back. The only other incident to note during the rest of the day was when he fell over an iron bar fixed to the floor, the accident causing him some pain. He finally retired for the night at 23:02 with a score of 238 miles.

Weston had made 320 miles when he set off for his apartments to rest his weary frame at 23:00 on Friday night. During the day he had made his 300th mile at 16:27 in a time of 10m.59s, and recorded a minute faster than that for his 285th, having walked continuously from 04:45 till 17:00 without a rest. He would now have to walk at a speed of 4 mph to complete his proposed objective.

Resuming his task at 03:00 after having rested for 2h.40m, Weston's next break was for just one hour at 10:24. From thereon he struggled against the clock until he had achieved what he had set out to accomplish at 20:34 in front of a crowd of 3,500, many of whom were ladies, who *"strewed his path with bouquets thrown from fair hands."* His last laps were made attired as when he started off; when he had finished, he was whisked off to his digs amid the usual cheering promising to return later to make a speech.

Mounting the dais which the band occupied, he said, "I feel felt it is my duty, after taxing the patience of the people of Newcastle for the past five days, to return to you my sincere thanks, and to convince you that the effort I have made, humbly endeavouring to entertain you, has been the same throughout. I have had obstacles which might have been considered insurmountable, but I have succeeded in surmounting them. Very little praise was due to me compared with what is due to those who had been connected with the entertainment. A man needs to know that his efforts, whatever they might be in life, are appreciated, and when that man is governed by a principle to please, then those who encourage him in those simple efforts, is sufficient to strengthen him. If I have done what had been considered superhuman, I have done as a testimony of gratitude on my part to the good people of Newcastle, who have given me pouring storms of encouragement while I have been in your midst. I hoped you would not regard what I have said as conceit on my part, but I think that all the attention and all the praise which has been bestowed on me has arisen from the fact that the English people as a nation love an honest effort, (cheers) and whoever the individual may be, I feel that a man can be an athlete and can make an honest effort without descending to become a creature of a betting clique."(Cheers.) "My efforts to popularise walking as a health-giving exercise have been appreciated more in England during the past eighteen months than experienced in my own country. I was told before leaving America that I would never receive fair play in England, but after an experience of travelling eight thousand miles here, I have yet to receive the first unkind act, or receive the first unkind word." (Cheers.) "There is one great thing to encourage a man in England and that is that misfortune is never considered a crime, even though I have made the most humiliating failures. I have struggled when the elements of success have been against me and have lost, yet, the same kind enthusiasm seems to prevail as I have witnessed tonight. I would like to thank the gentlemen connected with the press — a profession which was my own when in America — who seem to say too much in my praise, and of which I can hardly consider myself worthy. The newspapers in England would rather say a good word of a man than a bad one if they have the chance, whereas in the States, they would rather say a bad word of a man than a good one if they have the chance." (Cheers and laughter.) "Finally, if I can be of any benefit to a charity in Newcastle I would come and tell them to walk four hundred miles!" (Cheers.) The band then played "God Save the Queen," with Weston acting as conductor.

Between the 11th and the 15th of September at the Rifle Barracks in Hull, Weston managed to walk 400 miles in 5 days after having failed in his previous attempt some weeks earlier at the same venue when he broke down at the 375-mile mark. However, this time he succeeded with only two or three minutes to spare.

Back in Chicago on November the 10th at the Exposition Building, O'Leary accepted a challenge from John Ennis to a 100-mile walk for $500 a side which was won by O'Leary.

Weston failed to walk 500 miles in six days at Bristol between Monday, the 26th of November and Saturday, the 1st of December managing to walk only 58 miles on the last day. He retired at 23:00 amid *"demonstrations of dissastisfaction from those who had backed him."*

Then between Wednesday, December the 26th 1877 and Friday, January 11th 1878, he attempted to walk 1,000 miles in 400 hours. On completion of the walk, he fully expected Astley to be there to greet him at the finish.

King of the Peds

The following advertisement promoting the event was found in the *Newcastle Daily Chronicle* on Saturday, the 22nd of December 1877.

NORTHUMBERLAND CRICKET
GROUND
BATH ROAD, NORTHUMBERLAND STREET.

EDWARD PAYSON WESTON

The distinguished American, will give a Second Illustration of his Marvellous Powers of Endurance in Newcastle, by attempting, his Greatest Effort,

WALKING 1,000 MILES
IN 400 CONSECUTIVE HOURS,

Without walking during either hour of the two Sundays, or during the hour preceding each Sunday, thus actually attempting this stupendous task in

THREE HUNDRED AND FIFTY HOURS.

Mr. Weston will start on this Herculean Task at 7o'clock a.m. Wednesday, Dec. 26 (Boxing Day) terminating the task at 11 o'clock p.m., on Friday, January 11, 1878.

GRAND PROMENADE CONCERT
Both Day and Evening by
MR. WESTONS FULL MILITARY BAND.

The Prices of Admission during this Great Trial Will be One Shilling

for every day except Friday, Jan. 11 after 6 o'clock p. m.

After leaving his apartments in Ridley Street, Weston made his way to the track which was enclosed in a tent that had been erected for his attempt, and started on his task at 07:02. The enterprise had been organised by Messrs. Cotton and Custance and they were keen to make the visiting guests as comfortable as possible by keeping them warm with numerous stoves. They were also very keen to encourage ladies to turn up. *"Every accommodation is made for the fair sex."* By 18:20, and with the help of a band to *"relieve the monotony,"* he completed the first 50 miles. Weston told reporters that he enjoyed walking in the cold frosty atmosphere which was to his liking. By 23:00 he had completed 68 miles.

On Friday morning, at a minute after midnight, he had scored 138 miles, and during the day made his fastest mile (180th) in 12m.38s, his 200 being made at 10 p.m.

By 23:00 on the Saturday, and on a score of 270 at that time, Weston had got himself in a position where he had made just over a quarter of the intended distance. His 250th mile was his fastest of the day in a time of 10m.13s. Weston would now rest for the next day as he refused to walk on the Sabbath.

The news from the course on Monday was that *"Weston has consented to be on the track during the first two hours of the New Year so that "First Footers" may be enabled to give him a call and wish him the compliments of the season."* During New Years Eve, Weston's quickest mile was the 275th which he made in 11m.30s for a score of 68 miles and a total of 342 at

11 p.m. As the clock struck midnight, Weston got into party mode and with his cornet in hand, played "Auld Lang Syne" and "God Save the Queen." His fastest mile for New Years Day was the 400th, which he made in 9m.22s, and his total when recorded at 23:55, was 422.

On Wednesday, the 2nd of January, Weston, who started on the track at 04:48, made his 450th in 10m.51s, and by 13:00 had scored 459. Things on the course were going well and according to plan, but off the track there was talk of a rift between the ped and Astley. The "Chit Chat" column from *Mayfair* takes up the story: **I regret to inform of complications that have arisen of two celebrated men. The close intimacy which for sometime has existed between the Hon. Member for North Lincolnshire, and Weston whose walks have been highly creditable to now. But clouds have arisen and I believe that Weston and Sir John Astley do not even "speak." Sir John has been devoting his great natural abilities and his administrative capabilities to making arrangements for a week's pedestrian tournament and rather counted upon Weston going in for it. But Weston won't and Sir John Astley begins to suspect that the tall American is a Russian Spy in disguise.**

Back on the track, amid much cheering in the tent on Thursday, Weston made his 5th century at 08:38. He went on to make his 540th mile in 11m.22s which was his best mile time for the 24 hours. His score at 21:30 was recorded as 543 and his days total was 55. Of the attendance, the *Newcastle Daily Chronicle* wrote that the event was: **Attracting all shades of men, the clergy, the medical profession, and the lower orders of society. Yesterday, a large number of ladies patronised Weston's tent, the polished manners and unrestrained gaiety of Weston rendering him a great favourite with his lady patrons.**

It was raining the next day and Weston made much slower progress on a track described as *"soft to yielding."* Having made his start at 05:06, he was said to have scored his 587th mile at 13:05, and his 600th, which was his fastest mile of the day in 10m.33s, at 17:46. He then gave up his work for the day at 6 p.m.

Of other news, Weston was said to have had a special balcony built for his wife and family who were on their way to Newcastle to join him, and that happened on Saturday because it was reported that he carried his *"pretty little daughter Maude in his arms for upwards of a mile."* That day he made 675 miles by midnight and his best effort for a mile was said to be 11m.17s.

The highlight of the day on Monday, the 7th was when he led the band around the track, apart from recording his fastest mile in 11m.36s. When the last score was recorded for the day at 21:45 it read 743 miles.

On the following day, there was little news of his progress apart from that he started his walk at 06:03 and completed his 800th mile at 21:30 in 10m.5s, which was the swiftest of the day. However, there was some good news coming from the press in relation to Weston's rumoured breakdown in relations with Astley. A letter was published in the press from the M.P. to the walker which read:

ELSHAM HALL, BRIGG, JAN 7.

Dear Weston,

Your letter to hand this morning. I have not seen in any paper or heard that there was any 'rupture in friendship' between you and I; I totally deny that any such feeling on my part exists. We wish you all well. Go it my boy!

Yours truly

J. D. Astley

By 23:00 on Wednesday, Weston had made 871 miles. He had added 61 for the day and his best mile, his 865th, was made in 10m.29s.

On the penultimate day of his feat, Thursday, and having commenced his task at 05:15 in front of an ever increasing audience, he recorded his 900th mile in a time of 10m.2s. By the end of his working day at midnight, he had only 59 miles left to achieve his goal of 1,000 miles.

On the last day he completed his task at 20:46 having started off at 05:55. However, the greatest talking point of the day was his 995th mile which he made in 9m.15s. This was the fastest time he had ever made for a "walking" mile in his life. Weston continued on till 22:41 thus making 1,007 miles and 874 feet, the extra distance covering the distance between his apartments and the track each day. As was customary for him he made a speech the following day at Nelson Street in the evening.

He followed that up with an eye-catching effort of 1,500 miles in 625 hours starting at the Denistoun Skating Rink in Glasgow on the 4th of February finishing at the Bradford rink on Saturday, March the 2nd. The time was actually 525 hours as Weston again would not walk on Sundays and 21 hours following the first Sunday. 436 hours had been spent in Glasgow but the venue had been changed because of lack of appreciation causing the change of scene at the end of the third week.

CHAPTER 8

What Else Happened in 1877

A great feat *"under very dispiriting circumstances,"* was accomplished in the rain at the Powderhall Grounds, Edinburgh, on Saturday, the 21st of April by William Howes of London. The pedestrian attempted to cover 21 miles in three hours, and made it with 37 seconds to spare. The feat was a remarkable one, inasmuch as it had only been achieved by Charlie Westhall of London at Newmarket in 1858, and by G. Davidson of London, at Hackney Wick in 1869.

Walking with a *"medium and unvarying step,"* Howes, the 38-year-old professional pedestrian, weighing 9st.7lb, and standing 5 feet 4½ inches tall, who had been trained for the feat by Hugh Brown of London, went through the task *"with great pluck and perseverance,"* and was repeatedly cheered by those present.

The record of the *"race against time:"*

Miles	Hours	Mins	Secs	Miles	Hours	Mins	Secs
1	0	7	36	12	2	40	25
2	0	15	35	13	2	49	18
3	0	23	41	14	2	58	7
4	0	31	56	15	2	6	47
5	0	40	11	16	2	15	32
6	0	48	33	17	2	24	18
7	0	57	1	18	2	33	7
8	1	5	34	19	2	41	55
9	1	14	12	20	2	50	40
10	1	22	52	21	2	59	23
11	1	31	33				

A match to walk 50 miles, for £25 a side, took place between Walter Lewis of Islington and Arthur Hancock of Hackney, at the Prince of Wales Grounds, Bow, London, on April 30th 1877. Lewis, who was the younger of the two at 20 years of age, was 5ft.11 inches in height and weighed 144lbs. Hancock, at 25 years of age meanwhile, was 5ft. 7 inches and scaled about 140lb. To complete the 50 miles the pair would have to traverse 223 laps and 361 yards to make the whole distance.

Hancock, who led the race till the 19th mile, watched in despair as Lewis passed him and drew away much to the delight of the crowd who cheered him on. However, Walter's supporters were silenced when their favourite *"was seized with spasmodic pains"* after the 34th mile, and began to be caught up by Arthur. With things not looking too good for Lewis he was apparently *"administered"* some rye gin which *"relieved him,"* and he was able thereafter to repel the challenge of his opponent in the 43rd mile. Hancock was persuaded by his friends to give the race up on his 198th lap, (about 44 miles 382 yards) as he clearly had no hope of winning. Lewis was soon after declared the winner finishing on a score of 45 miles 933 yards in a time of 7h.24.9s. Lewis's time from 31 miles (4h.59m.8) to 45 miles (7h.22m.22s) was, at the time, the *"best authenticated public performance"* in England and America.

King of the Peds

A 48-hour walking match between Peter Crossland and Harry Vaughan to see who could cover the most distance, took place between the 17th and 19th of May in the large hall at the Pomona Gardens, Manchester. Both pedestrians were described as being *"in the pink of condition"* at the beginning of the race at 9 p.m. which was witnessed by about 2,000 people, Crossland being the slight favourite to win.

At a quarter to twelve that night, the race was lead by Vaughan with a three-lap advantage over his rival who had scored 14 miles and 5 laps.

The next day at 11:10, the Cheshire man left the race for 11 minutes. This was his very first break of the contest when he had scored 75 miles. His quickest mile up to that point had been 9m.33s and his slowest 13m.4s. Crossland however, who had rested just 20 minutes at 11:00, had recorded a distance of 69 miles, his fastest mile being 9m.54s and his slowest 14m.43s. Vaughan went on to make 122 miles 952 yards in the first 24 hours with his opponent registering 119 miles 1,149 yards for the same period.

"Vaughan who throughout exhibited not only superior speed but much greater stamina than what he was credited with," eventually won the tussle and the £200 stakes money by 17 miles with a final tally of 191 miles. At the end, Crossland was reported to be a suffering greatly with pain in one of his hips which had become inflamed. However, despite his ailment, he stuck on gamely to finish with a creditable 174 miles. The judges were G. W. Atkinson, C. Conquest and C. Haslam of the *Sporting Life*.

At 02:02 on Sunday morning, August the 26th, William Gale, *"the long winded walker of Cardiff,"* commenced his task of attempting to walk at the rate of a mile and a half for 1,000 consecutive hours, till he had made a total 1,500 miles on the cinder track at the Lillie Bridge Grounds at West Brompton in London.

Officiating as judges were: "Exon," (Mr. Charles Mather of the *Illustrated Sporting and Dramatic News* and *Sporting Life*) Mr. Thomas Griffith, of *Bells Life,* Mr. Jewell of *Land and Water,* Mr. J. Vandy and Mr. H. Green of the *Sportsman*. All the aforementioned would walk round with Gale on dark nights or foggy days. Gale, who was 42 years old at the time, stood 5ft.3½ inches in height and weighed 8st.4lb. Born in London, he was a bookbinder by trade and had resided in the Welsh city for the previous 14 years. *"For so small a man for a man with such slender nether limbs, Gale has a good broad chest, as have all great athletes."*

Up to the feat being started, Gale had claimed that he had walked 4,000 miles in 4,000 periods of ten minutes at the Canton Hotel Grounds in Cardiff. Besides that, he had claimed to have accomplished 1,000 miles in 1,000 hours over a turnpike road at Liverpool, 1,000 miles in 1,000 half hours and 500 quarter miles in 500 quarter hours at Preston, Lancashire, in 1856. He had also reportedly made 1,400 half miles in 1,400 half hours, at the Old Cricket Ground in Brighton in March of the same year, 2,000 half miles in 2,000 half hours at Cardiff in 1858, and 2,000 quarter miles in 2,000 quarter hours in 1866.

By the 288th hour he had made 357 miles and by the close of the third week was roundly cheered by the spectators watching the "Podokis" sports on Saturday, the 8th of September as he reeled of a mile and a half in a time of 17m.6s.

Gale completed half of his task by walking 750 miles at 21:22 on Saturday, the 15th of September. A week later, on the evening of the 22nd of September, he walked his 1,000th mile in 10m.31s, the mile and a half being scored in a time of 15m.14s. The overall exertion he had produced accomplishing that milestone in his journey had caused varicose veins on one of his legs to appear and he required the application of a bandage on it to help him round.

The little fellow's routine was always the same. Dressed in a blue shirt, velveteen knee-breeches, brown stockings, and wearing a substantial pair of thick-soled lace-up boots, he would walk over towards the track*, "cross his arms across his chest and doubling his fists in the recognized pedestrian style,"* and heel-and-toe it round the path.

Gale on the move.

© *The British Library. All Rights reserved. The Penny Illustrated. (Illustration no: 16)*

The end of his mile and a half was signalled by a shrill whistle by one of his judges. He would then go back to his small cabin adjacent to the grandstand end of the cinder paths, where, if he wasn't sleeping, he would sit beneath a picture of his hero Captain Barclay.

In its edition of Wednesday, the 3rd of October the *Sporting Life* wrote: Under circumstances of no ordinary difficulty, the Cardiff pedestrian continues bravely to continue his arduous task of walking 1,500 miles in 1,000 hours. In addition to the varicose vein under the left knee, Gale has now to endure the additional inconvenience of severe swelling in the right groin. Still, the little man gamely comes out hour after hour, and, though evidently stiffening much and occupying much longer time on the journey than on the outset, expresses his confidence that his pluck and endurance will carry him through. On Sunday, it is computed that upwards of 25,000 persons passed through the turnstiles. Since Friday night, 22m.35s. in his 880th hour, when he completed his 1,300th mile, has been his fastest time for the mile and a half, whilst 31 min.55 sec., has been the longest - viz., in his 867th hour. Up to half past eleven o'clock on Monday night, Gale had covered 1,329 miles in 886 hours. Dr. Grant of the Royal Free Hospital, has paid him every attention, and is of the opinion that with care, and not attempting to walk faster than is absolutely necessary, Gale's leg may not give way. Gale now, although he seldom gets any sleep in his brief rests, on being called at the commencement of each hour obeys the summons with alacrity. Monday night was very foggy, and it did not clear up until eight o'clock yesterday (Tuesday) morning. As usual, about ten o'clock, Gale had a cold bath, put on a pair of light drawers, and during the afternoon, if anything, he walked decidedly better, and with greater ease than on either of the two preceding days. Once or twice he changed his track, walking occasionally on the outer one (three to the mile), and he maintained a nice steady pace, his slowest mile and a half being 29 min.51 sec. At midnight (Tuesday), on the expiration of the 910th hour, he had walked 1,365 miles, leaving him only 135 miles to complete his task, which, if he keeps on, he will finish between five and six o'clock on Saturday evening next. Gale's appetite still keeps good, but he complains of want of sleep, and once or twice during the last few nights, he has one or two nasty falls when overcome with drowsiness. Between nine and ten o'clock last (Tuesday) night, he fell sound asleep, and one or two more such rests cannot fail to bring about an improvement in his condition. A subscription for Gale's benefit has been headed by Sir John Astley with £5, and doubtless the list will be extensively patronized by all lovers of British pluck.

On Saturday, October the 6th at 17:00, Gale strode out of his hut for the final time to confront the last mile and a half. He was greeted by the applause of 6,000 souls who had gained admission to witness the final moments of the extraordinary feat. *"Cheers followed him round the ground; he warmed to his work, his arms were swung with wonderful vigour, his stride lengthened, and he seemed to skim along the path. And his vigorous action – as cheered to the echo by many, many thousand voices – he ended his unparalleled task in business like style and strode into his hut."*

King of the Peds

Gale walks his last mile and a half in a time of 15 minutes 52 seconds.

© *The British Library. All Rights reserved. The Penny Illustrated. (Illustration no: 17)*

When Gale got back in his hut, he was greeted by Dr. Grant, Dr. McOscar of Argyll Street, and Dr. Farr of Earl's Court Road. They examined him in front of the judges and reported:

"Profuse perspiration – complexion quite natural – pulse 88, regular, and compressible – temperature 106 degrees – heart natural, both in force and regularity of action – no murmurs at either base or apex – pupils of the eyes equal – the inner surface of the eyes slightly congested – eyeballs quite clear, pupils natural, and act under the influence of light – no headache, and perfectly rational – slight cough – varicose veins back of calf of left leg – one spot very thin – external saphoena – right leg unaffected – no swelling of legs, knees or ankle joints – one slight blister on ball of great toe of right foot – no excoriation – toes bend readily back. At the expiration of twenty minutes, the temperature of the axilla was 100 – pulse not up to normal state. Five minutes later the temperature was reduced to 97½ - Weight 8st."

Throughout the walk, Gale's meals were taken when he pleased and they were varied according to his personal requirements. He had a penchant for mutton chops, but interestingly, his four o'clock meal on the last morning consisted of a lobster with bread and butter, fried sole and tea. *"His diet for the twenty-four hours was 16 pounds of meat, five or six eggs, some cocoa, two quarts of milk, a quart of tea, and occasionally a glass of bitter ale, but never wine nor spirits. Strange to say, he suffered from constipation, and took daily a compound rhubarb pill.*

On Sunday afternoon on the 21st of October at the Agricultural Hall in London, William Gale began an attempt to walk 1,000 miles in 28 days at a rate of a quarter of a mile every ten minutes.

A pedestrian called William Hunter managed to beat Weston's achievment of walking 150 miles in 48 hours at Sunderand, Tyne and Wear, England. He managed to add 10 miles to the American's total between Thursday, the 27th and Saturday, the 29th of October. However, unfortunately, he died *"speedily"* on the afternoon of the day after, *"occassioned by over exertion and excitement."*

On the 17th of November, William Gale capped his previous performance of walking 1,500 miles in 1,000 hours by making 4,000 quarter miles in 4,000 consecutive periods of 10 minutes, his last quarter of a mile being made in 2 minutes and 4 seconds! Sir John Astley was one of the many who cheered Gale as he mounted the judges' rostrum to acknowledge the plaudits.

CHAPTER 9

"Go-As-You-Please"

Sir John Astley

© The British Library. All Rights reserved. The Penny Illustrated. (Illustration no: 18)

Astley, who had been the Member of Parliament for North Lincolnshire since 1874, *"was a big, burly, breezy, brazen-lunged old man, fond of strong language and strong drink. Wherever he went he was made conspicuous by his Falstaffian figure, white hair and beard, the enormous cigar, never out of his mouth, save when he was eating, drinking or sleeping, his strident voice and his frequent, boisterous laugh."* Educated at Eton and Oxford, he was formerly a lieutenant colonel of the Scots Fusilier Guards and served with them in the Crimea campaign of 1854 where he was wounded in the neck in the Battle of Alma. He also fought at Inkerman, and later witnessed the taking of Sebastopol. A useful runner over 150 yards, he won four cups for winning races of 100, 150, 200 and 220 yards at Aldershot in 1856.

A great lover of sport, he had been very excited by the performances of O'Leary and Weston and the reaction the public and the press had given them. His enthusiasm for pedestrianism at the time made him decide to inaugurate a series of six-day races for the "Long Distance Champion of the World." However, he would make a significant change to the rules so that competitors could now "go-as-you-please," or, "*do as best pleases himself.*" Competitors would be able to *"walk, trot, run, mix, lift or introduce a new style of pedestrianism if clever enough."* This was a decision made for two reasons, one of which was apparently because of Weston's *"wobbling gait,"* which was considered as not being text book heel-and-toe, and the other was because there was a view that because the American athletes were so much better than their British counterparts, a method of progression was needed to be invented to disadvantage the best of those athletes. It was decided that the winner of the belt wouldn't have to defend it more than once every six months, and also, any man winning the belt *three times in a row* would automatically become its permanent keeper. Sir John would also decide who would be allowed to compete against the holder of his belt, the stipulation being that the race be contested within three months after a challenge had been made for it. The *"Astley Belt races"* as they were called would have the following conditions governing them.

1. The winner will have to defend his claim to the belt for eighteen months and should he wish to have it in his possession he must give security to the appointed Trustees, and undertake take to restore it when called upon in good condition.

King of the Peds

2. In case of the belt being won by any person resident out of the United Kingdom, the Trustees shall, if they think fit, demand the deposit of security to the value of £100 before permitting the trophy to be taken out of the country.

3. The holder of the belt shall not be called upon to compete in more than two matches within each current year, and in the case of his winning it in three consecutive matches or sweepstakes, it shall become his absolute property, providing that the whole of the said matches or sweepstakes have been bona fide in every respect.

4. The holder of the belt must accept all challenges (subject to the above conditions) for not less than £100 a side, and be prepared to defend his right to the same within three months from the issue of any challenge.

5. In the event of a match being made, any body may join in by depositing £100 with the appointed stakeholder within four weeks previous to the day fixed for the commencement of the race, the winner to take the belt and the whole of the stakes; the gate receipts, (after all expenses have been paid,) to be distributed among the competitors as may be agreed upon beforehand with the approval of the Trustees.

6. The committee of the A. A. C. are the appointed Trustees. The editor of the Sporting Life is nominated stakeholder for any matches that may arise for the belt.

7. All appeals upon questions not provided for by these conditions shall be made to the Trustees of the belt, whose decision shall in all cases be final, and subject to no appeal in a court of law or otherwise.

The belt, weighing just under five pounds, was made out of solid silver and gold embossed edges. It consisted of nine plates of solid silver about 3 inches by 4½ inches in size with rustic borders, linked together and mounted upon a broad band of *"Morocco"* red leather. The gold plated centre was gilded, and bore the inscription, **"Long Distance Champion of the World,"** in raised black letters faced with blue enamel. This had two silver plates either side with raised figures in bass relief, the left one being that of a runner and on the other side a walker. The backgrounds of these two links were engraved with sketchy landscapes. The link opposite the only golden link which would be at the back of the belt was engraved with the following inscription:

"PRESENTED BY SIR J. D. ASTLEY. BART. M. P., March. 1878."

The Astley Belt

With special thanks to Miriam Payne. (Illustration no: 19)

When O'Leary left New York for England on the steamer *Idaho* on Tuesday, the 5th of March, accompanied by his wife and Al Smith, he confidently told all his friends, "The man who wins the Astley purse will have to beat the best time on record. Whether the winner beats me or not, my record when I beat Weston last April will have to be improved upon." That record was 519 miles and 1,585 yards, or 175 yards less than 520 miles.

Before he boarded his ship a reporter for the *New York Sun* questioned O'Leary about the great trials of endurance he put himself through: "In my long matches," said the pedestrian, "I generally walk steadily for 24 hours, frequently allowing myself no more than 10 minutes' rest. Of course, I eat and drink while walking. The first pain I feel is a stinging sensation along the shin bone; but it soon goes away. Afterward I feel it here, (rubbing the tendons of the leg). It soon leaves me, and I feel it no longer. My legs never get asleep or become dead, and I am not compelled to whip them, as Weston does, to restore circulation. The greatest trouble I find is to keep my bowels regular. This seems singular, but I attribute it to being laced so tight, and no man can walk without this tight lacing. I find no trouble in digesting my food, provided I can eat it. I prefer beef and mutton. Frequently, on beginning a long walk my stomach feels full, although I know I have eaten nothing. The sight of the food annoys, but does not sicken me, and though I try to forcing it down I find that I cannot eat the beef and mutton. This sensation I lay to a strange feeling of excitement which seems beyond control, and takes away all appetite. I feel myself out of sorts. At such times I keep on walking until I fairly work myself into condition. Along the third or fourth day my appetite begins to increase, and I can eat with a relish. The trouble then is that I want to eat too much, and it is with difficulty that I can keep myself within bounds. There is no trouble about digesting beef or mutton at any time, provided I can get it down. But I can never digest chicken. My stomach absolutely refuses it. Strange fancies seem to control the appetite at certain periods in a walk. Now, during my great walk against Weston, in Agricultural Hall, London, I never ate a mouthful of solid food. For six days I lived on grapes, figs, strawberries, and similar fruits. I only slept eight hours during the week, and rested but 24 hours altogether.

In walking I come down heel first, and then spring from the ball of the foot. The constant pounding makes the soles of my feet very hot, but my legs never swell and never tire. The walk In Agricultural Hall was made of potter's clay, and told terribly on my feet. There was no spring to it and it peeled up like a carpet. For years I suffered for want of an easy shoe. Shoemakers in France, England and America sent me cart loads of them, but they were no good. At last I discovered an Irishman in New York, (Bryan McSwyny of the Sixth Ward) that knew how to make shoes for a pedestrian. He has the shoes with which I won the match in Agricultural Hall in a shoe case fronting his store on Canal Street and Broadway, and today when I came down, there were a hundred people looking at them. I expect him on board any minute with half a dozen pairs."

Reporter: "Why do you always clutch a corn cob in each hand when walking your matches, Mr. O'Leary?"

The pedestrian laughed. "I'm sure I can't tell you," he said. "I think it is habit as reach much as anything else. They probably absorb the perspiration and keep the hands from swelling. In walking I hold my arms up and work my hands across each other toward the opposite shoulder. I used the cobs first because a light grip on them seemed to make me solid, and agreed with the tight lacing. That got me into the habit of walking with cobs and I never have been able to break myself of it. My back is well arched when I walk, and I strike straight out from the hips. The peculiar way in which I carry my hands sometimes creates unpleasant comments. Many think I am showing off, and when I began my walk in Agricultural Hall the reporter of the London Standard took one at me and said, "Well, that infernal fool won't last long."

Here the steamer was cleared and the whistle sounded. Just as the plank was being drawn in, a jerky man with auburn hair ran up it like a squirrel and placed a bundle in O'Leary's hands. It was the pedestrian's shoemaker, who for once in his life was trying to keep a shoemaker's promise. The writer recognized him as the well-known Bryan McSwyny of the sixth ward.

The following notice appeared in the *Sporting Life* two days before the first six-day "go-as-you-please" race for the Astley Belt took place in London's Agricultural Hall, beginning at 1 a.m. on Monday, March the 18th 1878.

Members of the Press, Competitors, and Attendants will be admitted at the Barford-street entrance only by showing their tickets any time after twelve midnight on Sunday, March 17, and the Hall will be opened to the public at six a.m. on Monday, March 18, and five following days. By order of the Commissioner of Police, the Hall will be cleared each night at eleven o'clock of all save the competitors, attendants, officials, and members of the Press. Two bands will be in attendance and play from six a.m. till half-past ten p.m. each day.

Admission, One Shilling: Reserved Seats. 2s. and 3s: Private Enclosure, 10s.

The hall will be open from twelve to four p.m. today (Saturday), in order that the competitors may see what accommodation is provided for them. The tracks are laid, and anyone who wishes to have them measured can do so. Mr. C. B. Walker, landscape photographer, of 26 Baker-street, Lloyd-square, is desirous of taking a large photograph of the men in costume before the race, and he hopes all will attend at the Agricultural Hall at twelve noon sharp today (Saturday), for that purpose. Mr. Walker has kindly offered to present a copy of the picture gratis to all competitors.

*For the convenience of the competitors in this great event huts to accommodate the whole of them, have been erected and fitted with iron bedsteads and every for convenience for comfortable sleeping. A military cooking stove has been provided, so that attendants can in their own way look after the preparation of the provisions of their principals; in fact, in every other way has the comfort of all - officials, pedestrians and attendants – been thoroughly studied.

At twelve o'clock this day the competitors are requested to present at the Hall, in order that every detail of the arrangements may be explained to them and that they may make themselves acquainted with the regulations of the contest.

King of the Peds

*The *"accommodation"* would later be described as by the *Sporting Life* as a: Set of hutches not fit to stable a well-bred cow. Imagine a series of wooden partitions (originally used for dividing the stalls of Mr. Sanger's camels, &c., and smelling accordingly) set up at intervals of about eight feet and covered with open webbed canvas, a thorough draft outside, and from the top, and a noxious odour from the boards, uncleaned since their last use, and these are the hutches provided for our men.

Two tracks composed of a mixture of sifted brick ballast, sand, tan and earth, had been constructed. The one which was ten feet wide and seven laps to the mile would be raced upon by competitors from the British Isles and the eight laps to the mile one would be for foreigners to compete on. The race pitted 15 Englishmen, one Irishman, and a Scot against the undefeated American champion, Irish-born Daniel O'Leary from Chicago. His old rival Edward Payson Weston wouldn't be able to take part due to illness. That meant that O'Leary had his very own track.

The prizes for the race amounting to a guaranteed amount of £750 would be competed for under the following conditions:

There would be a sweepstakes of 10 sovereigns each, for all comers. The man accomplishing the greatest distance in the specified time would receive the championship belt valued at £100 and a purse of £500. The second placed competitor would be rewarded with £100. The third place man would receive £50.

Then: **Any competitor covering a distance of 460 miles would receive back his stake and in addition would receive £10. Any competitor (other than the first three men) covering more than 500 miles would receive £5 for every additional 3 miles over 500 with the amount received not to exceed £40. The surplus receipts over expenses, if any, were to be divided between the competitors who had covered more than 460 miles in the same proportion as the prizes, or to be awarded for the same proportion as the prizes, or to be awarded for further prizes to encourage pedestrianism.**

"A commodious stand has been set apart for the officials and gentlemen of the Press." Right opposite that was the telegraph board which bore the names of each of the contestants. Beneath their names were spaces for figures to be hung which indicated how many miles and laps had been scored, this information being duplicated on the other side of the board.

The judges were Mr. G. W. Atkinson, Charles Conquest of the *Sporting Life* who would be officiating during the day, with Captain Webb doing the umpiring during the night.

Of the original 29 entries, five were thrown out as unworthy of consideration, leaving 24. The name of Daniel O'Leary didn't appear in the original list for the reason that a friend in London, to whom the entrance money had been forwarded, neglected to make the proper entry. However, Astley gave him the go ahead and it was then revealed that Weston had pulled out due to illness and his name dropped from the list along with the following: William Barnett of Leeds, Peter Crossland of Sheffield, Thomas Easthall of Brighton, John Hope of Richmond, William Howes of Haggerston and George Parry of Manchester.

The actual starters numbering 18 in total were:

James Bailey of Sittingbourne: Born at Folkestone, Kent, in 1851: Weight 10st.6lb; Height 5ft.9in: James was described as a good distance runner who had won many races from a mile upwards: Trained at Sittingbourne by W. Collins and attended by H. Steadman and J. Howden of the same town.

Henry Brown of Fulham: Henry was born in Fulham, London in 1843, and that made him between 34 and 35 years of age. He said that he was given the nickname of "Blower" as a small child for a reason he didn't know. However, later in his career the *Boston Globe* wrote of his name: It is only fair to Mr. Brown, who is probably the most modest man in the world, to state that the nickname, "Blower" was not awarded him on account of egoistical eloquence. It appears that in the smithy where he worked in Fulham there were several other Browns and as he was stationed at the bellows he was called "Blower," in order that he might not be confounded with Puddler Brown or Smith Brown: Weight 9st.7lb; Height 5ft.6in: The *Sporting Life* wrote the following resume for him: Won the first prize, a timepiece in a one mile handicap, at Garratt-lane, Wandsworth, December 1, 1862; with 6 ½ min. start, got third prize, £1 10s., in a ten miles handicap, at the Canterbury Rural Fete, May 26, 1863; ran 10 miles in 59 min.48s., winning £10 by 12 sec, West London Cricket Ground, Old Brompton, February 29, 1864; beat Toddy Ray and Joe Spencer in a twenty miles sweepstake, of £5 each, West London Cricket Ground, Old Brompton, April 4, 1864;

with a 5 min. start won the first prize in a ten mile handicap, at the Canterbury Rural Fete, May 17, 1864; beat W. Richards (the Welshman), who gave 2 min. start, in a ten mile race, for £20 a side, at Hackney Wick Grounds, August 8, 1864; with 3 ½ min. start got third prize (£3) in a ten miles handicap at the North Woolwich Gardens, October 1, 1864; beat A. Smith (better known as 'Steeprock,') the North American Indian, fifteen miles, for £15 a side (time, 1 hour 30 min. 25 sec.), West London Cricket Ground, Old Brompton, October 3, 1864; with 5 min. start won £20 in a twenty miles handicap (time, 2 hours 4 min.) at Hackney Wick Grounds, October 10, 1864; with 440 yards start, got third prize (£3) in a five miles handicap at Hackney Wick Grounds, November 7, 1864; beaten by W. Jackson (the American Deer), who had 2 ½ min. start in ten miles, for £10 a side, at Chalk Farm Grounds, June 6, 1865; beat R. Manks, who had 450 yards' start in ten miles for £20, at the Lillie Arms, Old Brompton, April 2, 1866; ran from Mr. J. Smith's, the Manor Tavern, Chiswick, to Mr. G Welch's booth adjoining the Grand Stand at Epsom, in 1 hour 54 min. winning £10 by 6 min., May 27, 1868; beat W. Mills who gave 2 min. start in ten miles, for £15 a side at Bow Grounds, November 30, 1868; beaten by R. Vincent, of Richmond who had fifty yards' start in one mile, for £5 a side, Star Grounds, Fulham, September 12, 1870; beat R. Vincent two miles, for £5 a side, (time 10 min.52.sec.), Star Grounds, Fulham, October 29, 1870; beaten by G. Stephenson, of Battersea, who gave fifty yards' start in two miles, for £10, Star Grounds, Fulham, October 26, 1876; beaten by G. Stephenson again when in receipt of fifty yards' start in two miles, for £10, Star Grounds, Fulham, December 9, 1876; with 6 min. start, got third prize (£3) and £1 5s, for beating 6 min. in a ten mile handicap, Lillie Bridge Grounds, December 26, 1876: He was attended to by J. Smith, senior, ("Regent Street Pet") and Edward Pocock. *"Brown is a thick-set, well-made man, just the build for lasting."*

William "Corkey" Gentleman of Bethnall Green: Born at Bethnall Green in 1833; Weight 7st.6lb; Height 5ft.4in: William, known as "Corkey," thus dubbed for his *"lightness on the path,"* apparently was by trade a *"vendor of cat's meat,"* and who was in the habit of walking twelve to fifteen miles daily on his rounds to deliver the stuff. He was described as having a stooping, awkward gait and raced with a sad look on his face.

© *The British Library. All Rights reserved. The Penny Illustrated. (Illustration no: 20)*

The *Sporting Life* gave their readers a run down on his career up to this race: With 110 yards start, won a silver cup in a one mile handicap, Hackney Wick Grounds, February 10, 1862; beat Bracknell one mile, £5 a side, Hackney Wick Grounds, October 20, 1862; beat Clayton, who had 50 yards' start in one mile, £5 a side, Hackney Wick, May 4, 1863; won the first prize in a three miles race at Weston's Retreat near Highgate, June 25, 1864; with 250 yards' start, won a silver cup in a four mile handicap, Hackney Wick, March 20, 1865; with 400 yards' start, won £5 in a four miles handicap, Agricultural Hall, Islington, April 15, 1865; with 350 yards' start, got second prize (£2) in a four mile handicap, Agricultural Hall, Islington, April 17, 1865; won £1 in a three miles race, Weston's Retreat near Highgate, June 26, 1865; with 560 yards' start , won the "Copenhagen champion belt" in a five miles handicap, Hackney Wick, September, 25, 1865; beat Joe Rowe who gave 30 sec. start in ten miles, £10 a side, Hackney Wick, October 9, 1865; with 200 yards' start, got second prize (£5) in a five miles handicap, Hackney Wick, November 27, 1865; with 650 yards' start, gained second prize (a cup) in a ten miles handicap won by Hazael (650 yards start), Prince of Wales Grounds, Bow, December 26, 1867; beat Joe Rowe, ten miles, £10 a-side, Hackney Wick Grounds, London, May 18, 1868; beaten by J. Cole of Hackney Wick, who had 30 yards' start in 1,560 yards, £5, at Hackney Wick, May 30, 1868; with a 4 min. start, got fourth prize (£1) in a ten miles handicap, Hackney Wick, September 6, 1869; with 1 min. 10 sec. start, won a cup in a four miles handicap, Hackney Wick, September 20, 1869; with 350 yards' start, got second prize (£1 10s.) in a four miles handicap, Bow, Oct. 11, 1869; beat T. Cummings, who had 30 sec, start in ten mile, £10 (time for six miles, 33 min. 20 2-5 sec.), at Prince of Wales Grounds, Bow, April 4, 1870; with 1 min. 10 sec., got second prize (£2 10s.) in a four miles handicap at the Crawley Athletic Sports, Sussex, August 30, 1870; with 350 yards' start, got third prize (£1) in a four miles handicap at Hackney Wick, October 3, 1870; with 25 yards start, won a four miles handicap sweepstakes of £10 each, beating J. Childerhouse (alias boney), 100 yards', J. Mills (brother to Teddy Mills), 350 yards' start, 21min. 3 sec., at Hackney Wick, 1870; with 750 yards' start, won a silver cup in a six miles' handicap at Prince of Wales Grounds, Bow, April 7, 1870; beat W. Virtue of Bedfordbury, six miles for £10 a side at Prince of Wales Grounds, Bow, May 27, 1871; with 6 min. 30 sec., got third prize (£2) in a ten miles handicap at Bow, August 27, 1877: Trained and attended by Joe Woolgar, mostly at the Clay Hall Grounds, Old Ford, and also attended by W. Neal.

W. Gregory of Hoxton: Born on the City Road, London, in 1844: Weight 9st.2lb; Height 5ft.7½in: He had shown average promise as a pedestrian, and up to the commencement of the race, had chiefly been involved in the training of others like Howes and Arthur Hancock: Trained at Chester alongside Vaughan, and attended by Arthur Courtney of Barnet and Mr. E. Isaacs who were assisted by Bill Lang.

Joseph Groves of Oswestry: Born April the 7th 1853: Weight 10st.8lb; Height 5ft.7in: Joe had won many races at short distances including a half mile handicap with 9 yards start at Burnley, the mile race at Wenlock Sports, and the mile and a half champion at the Ryder Sports in South Wales for three years running: Attended by T. Mitchell and W. Ruscoe from Oswestry.

George Hazael of London: George was born on the 22nd of November 1845 in Commercial Road, East, London: Weight 8st.10lb; Height 5ft.6½in: More than fifteen thousand people had gathered at the City Grounds in Manchester on Saturday, the 17th of December 1870, to watch a three-man 10-mile race for £25 a side and the posession of a cup worth £50. The men taking part on the 800-yard track were even money favourite, Hazael, the 5/4 second favourite, J. Fleet of Manchester, and the 5/1 outsider, E. Goulden of Canterbury. Hazael won the race after the other two retired after he went 600 yards clear on the 15th lap, the time being at that stage of the race 39m.59s. For a record of his career in 1872, 1873 and 1875; see James McLeavy below. On Monday, the 6th March 1876 at the Lillie Bridge Grounds, Hazael, (the then current ten-mile champion) had a bet of £20 at odds of 6/4 that he could beat the best time on record for that distance which was created by the American runner Deerfoot in a time of 51m.26s some 13 years earlier at the Old West London Running Grounds (Robert's Grounds). Hazael was to lose his bet, coming in a minute and a second slower than the previous best. George was involved in some controversy in the same year when on the afternoon of Saturday, the 23rd of September 1876, he received, *"loud groans and hisses"* upon retiring from the track after falling over at the mile and a half mark in a four-mile encounter for a prize of £50 with J. Richardson, alias "Treacle," of Whitworth, at the Higginshaw Grounds in Oldham. Richardson eventually completed the designated distance in a time of 20m.12s. What was of concern was that Hazael had done the same thing in a match with the same competitor in London some three months earlier. On Monday, the 10th of December 1877, in an *"International Running Match,"* Hazael took on the Italian *"champion runner of France and Italy,"* Achille Bargozzi, from Forlì, (who had claimed to have run 50 miles in 6 hours) in a 30-mile event for a prize of £50 at the Lillie Bridge Grounds. Hazael, who dashed away with the lead, led the race at the end of two miles by 250 yards, in a time of 11m.21s. With the Londoner thereafter rapidly increasing his lead, Bargozzi, who was two miles behind Hazael, retired within 50 yards of his 15th mile. After going on to complete 20 miles in 1h.57m.27s (best time on record), Hazael stopped and was declared the winner. Then, in a poorly attended contest, George beat Peter Crossland by 28 miles in a six-day "go-as-you-please" for £200 at the Pomona Gardens, Manchester, which started at five minutes past midnight on Monday, the 25th of February, and concluded at 10 p.m. on Saturday, the 2nd March 1878. By 22:00 on the first night Hazael was already 20 miles ahead of Crossland, having scored 91. Hazael's final score was 240 miles.

George Ide of North Woolwich: George was born at West Wittering near Chichester in 1845: Weight 10st.7lb; Height 5ft.8½in: Some of George's previous races have been described in chapters 5 and 6: Attended by his brother C. Ide and Ben Williams, both of North Woolwich.

© *The British Library. All Rights reserved. The Penny Illustrated. (Illustration no: 21)*

George Johnson of Barrow-in-Furness: Born in Barrow in 1848: Weight 10st.5lb; Height 5ft.8in: Trained on the Brighton and York roads, and attended by his brothers Alfred and James.

S. R. Johnson of Wrexham: Born on August the 19th 1849 in Glasgow: Weight 11st.5lb; Height 5ft.7in: Had beaten the amateur, Mr. Bolton, having made 22 miles on the Wrexham to Chester road winning £50 and a gold medal: Attended by W. Williams of Chester who prepared Harry Vaughan for his successful 48-hour match with Peter Crossland, and W. Johnson and W. Mercer, both of Wrexham.

Walter Lewis of Islington (*The "Islington Pet"*): Born in London on March the 4th 1857: Weight 10st.0lb; Height 5ft.11in: Readers will be already aware of one of Walter's performances up to this point (Chapter 8), except for when he had competed against Billy Howes in a 26-hour race only a few days earlier at the same venue where Howes had covered his century in 18h.8m. (A fuller account of this race can be read about in the Chapter 13) He was expected to do well although he hadn't performed in a six-day event. He was attended by Mr. David Broad.

© *The British Library. All Rights reserved. The Penny Illustrated. (Illustration no: 22)*

Mr. Charles C. Martyn (Amateur) of Yatton, Bristol: Born of English parents in Waterford, Ireland, in 1849: Weight 8st.1lb; Height 5ft.7½in: Mr. Martyn was said to have averaged about 35 miles a day (excluding Sundays) between the years 1875 and 1877 which equates to 32,865 miles: Trained at Yatton and Clevedon, and *"waited upon"* by his valet Arthur Carey, and attended by Thomas H. Hargreaves.

Pat McCarty of York: Born in Roscommon County, Ireland, in 1844: Weight 9st.10lb; Height 5ft.6½in: Pat had walked 260 miles in 74h.20m, and had made 400 miles in 5 days at the York Skating Rink, completing the task on the 8th of December 1877: Attended by W. James of Leeds, and W. Crossland of London.

James McLeavy of Alexandria: James was born at Bonhill, Dunbartonshire, Scotland, on October the 26th 1852: Weight 9st.10lb; Height 5ft.4½in: After running several creditable races as a youth he went to London and began contesting with the crack runners of England. His principal winning performances were as follows: **1872:** With a 35-yard start, he won a 1,000-yard handicap in London on March 4th. Then on March the 27th at Lillie Bridge, he defeated George Hazael over four miles in a time of 19m.52s winning £25 and the challenge cup. At the same venue on August the 12th, he was beaten by Hazael who had a 10-yard start in two miles for which Hazael won £100 in a time of 9m.39½s. In Edinburgh on August the 24th, McLeavy won the 6-mile champion cup and £10 in a time of 31m.28s. On September 16th he beat Hazael who had 20 yards start in two miles winning £50 for his efforts. **1873:** Back in London on April 11th, McLeavy again beat Hazael over four miles for £25 a side and the champion cup. At Gateshead on October the 11th, and with a 48-yard advantage, he beat J. S. Ridley and R. Hindle in a one-mile sweepstakes for a challenge cup and £25 each in a time of 4m.21s. **1875:** On May 15th in Glasgow, he won first prize in a two-mile walking race. In the same city on August the 21st, he won the first prize in a 440 yards hurdle race, and on the same day, from scratch, won a three-mile handicap and a two-mile handicap. **1876** *(All in Glasgow)* On June 10th he beat Hazael in a three-mile race for £25 a side in a time of 14m.45s. On July the 1st he won a three-mile handicap from scratch, and followed that up when he won first prize in a two-mile race at the Milngavie Gala on August the 26th. Then in September he won a three-mile handicap in a time of 15m.31s. Later, on November the 4th, he beat A. Clark over a mile for £25 a side and the championship in a time of 4m.25½s. On November the 11th 1876, he beat James Sanderson over four miles for £25 a side and a cup valued at 65 guineas in a time of 19m.58s. In a snow-storm, and a gale, on November the 18th, he beat John Bailey who had 200 yards start in ten miles for £100. **1877:** In Glasgow on March the 10th, he beat Hazael over five miles for £25 a side with £50 added in a time of 26m.6s. On June the 30th he won a ten-mile race for £40 and the champion belt, and on October the 6th, beat Hazael again in a six-mile race for £100 and the championship in a time of 32m.16½s. However, on Saturday, the 20th of October, Hazael got his revenge in another six-mile race for the championship and £75 in Dundee in a time of 35 minutes. Then on November the 3rd, he beat W. Cummings who had 20 yards start in a two-mile event for £50. On November the 10th he was matched to run W. Smith of Paisley for ten miles and £50 for the championship belt, but when Smith was attacked with gastric fever, McLeavy *"ran over."* On November 17th again in Glasgow, he beat James Wood and A. Clark for £75 and the one-mile championship in a time of 4m.28¼s. Then in Falkirk on December the 1st, he beat W. Cummings in a one-mile and a half race for £30 and a cup.

© *The British Library. All Rights reserved. The Penny Illustrated. (Illustration no: 23)*

Daniel O'Leary of Chicago, U.S.A: Weight 10st.6lb; Height 5ft.8½in: Needs no introduction. Attended by Mr. Tansey of Chicago and J. McGee of Liverpool.

© *The British Library. All Rights reserved. The Penny Illustrated. (Illustration no: 24)*

J. Smith of York: Born at Donet (172 miles from Calais) of English parents on June the 17th 1838: Weight 12st; Height 5ft.8½in: He was a whitesmith by trade who had also worked at the N. E. R fitting shops in York. He made 38 miles in 8 hours against another local pedestrian called England who gave the race up. He then attempted to make 400 miles in 5 days, but could only make 398¾ due to bad weather. So disgusted by this, he then set out to make 500 miles in six days which he accomplished *"easily"*: Attended by Charles Simmons and J. Hambury, both from Derby.

William Smith of Paisley: Born at Paisley on the 27th of December 1846: Weight 9st.7lb; Height 5ft.7in: Trained by David Ferguson of Pollockshaws at Salcoats, Ayrshire, he was attended by R. Hindle of Paisley, and Joe Carney of Glasgow.

© The British Library. All Rights reserved. The Penny Illustrated. (Illustration no: 25)

W. H. Smythe of Dublin: Was born on March the 1st 1849 in County Cavan, Ireland: Weight 11st.9lb; Height 5ft.11½in: He walked 2,000 miles in 1,000 hours in Dublin between December the 26th 1877 and February the 1st 1878: Attended by C. Smith of Bethnall Green and Joe Terry of Islington.

© The British Library. All Rights reserved. The Penny Illustrated. (Illustration no: 26)

Henry Vaughan of Chester: Born in Chester on August 23rd 1847: Weight 10st.7lb; Height 5ft.11½in: Henry *"walks very upright, with a long stride, and being thin he has the appearance of being an even taller man than he is."* He was a carpenter by trade. Astley described him as a "clean made and thoroughly respectable man" who had a "long striding giant-like step who paced his races." Vaughan began his career as an amateur walker at Liverpool on June the 16th 1870, where with 30 yards start he won a two-mile walking handicap in a time of 16m.26s. For this one he was attended by Bill "Crowcatcher" Lang and was the ante-post favourite to win.

In the ante-post betting market, much money had been wagered on Vaughan alone, and should he win the match, £100,000 would be taken from the bookies. The starting prices for the men shortly before the "off" were: £50 to £30 against Vaughan; £50 to £20 against O'Leary; £50 to £20 against Lewis. The rest could be had for £50 to £10 upwards.

Emerging from a row of *"poverty stricken and comfortless boxes compared with O'Leary's taut marquee,"* Sir John Astley stood in front of the competitors before him at the start of the race and told them, "You are about to enter in a trying match, in which running and walking and physical pluck and endurance are necessary to compete. Every possible arrangement has been made to have a fair, straight fight, and I hope the best man will win. I appeal to you to second our efforts, for the best man to win, no matter what his nationality, or where he comes from. Now lads, are you ready? A fair, honest, manly race and the best man wins. Ready? Then away you go!"

And away they went at precisely 01:03 with Smith of Paisley going straight into the lead, Corkey and Brown on his heels. They were followed by the race favourite Vaughan and O'Leary. Hazael pursued the four leaders, but in the opposite direction, as the athletes were allowed to do, providing they did so after completing a lap. Smith continued to be the leader after registering 4 miles and 5 laps for the first half hour and 9.1 for the hour's work. Bailey was in the runner-up position on 8.3 and Corkey was a couple of laps behind him.

Hazael, who was in fourth position and a mile behind Corkey, began to intimidate O'Leary by shouting at him as he passed him. On one such occasion he threatened to kill him. The tactics worked, and O'Leary succumbed to the worrying Hazael, who, although walking, began to create distance between himself and the nervous Irishman. Against *"advice,"* O'Leary began to run in an attempt to retrieve the lost distance; his efforts soon bore fruit, and in the third hour of competition, he passed Hazael who then began to drop quickly behind, after which the relieved Irishman resumed his preferred gait.

After two hours of competition, the Scotchman still led the van on a score of 17 miles. Corkey was a mile in his rear with Bailey a mile behind him. Hazael was in fourth place on 14, with O'Leary a mile and a half adrift of him. Brown trailed O'Leary by another half mile.

Corkey's, Vaughan's and O'Leary's performance in the early hours of the race was described in the *Penny Illustrated*: Corkey (who has attracted much attention during the week) was rather laughed at by some as he capered over the track with the lightness of a deer in the early hours of Monday morning. He is a diminutive slip of a man, whom a breath would seem to blow away; and he looked the very image of the familiar pedestrian in old fashioned sporting prints. Clad in ancient garb, little Corkey bounded over the turf by himself, holding a light whip in one hand, and reminding one of those little wan fathers of large families who humbly and meekly walk to and from the City every day of their weary lives, to bring up their too plentiful olive branches with credit. Looking at Corkey, then, as he untiringly ran round and round the hall, and no one could have dreamt that for the first day or so he would lead the famous O'Leary a good dance, and even head the Hibernian American, who trod the earth so firmly that he appeared at times as desirous of stamping the turf flat as of progressing to the 500 miles goal. Now and then, the heavily built O'Leary burst into a run as he turned the corners; but he walked fairly and squarely for the most part, throwing his head well back and moving his arms freely. Handsomest of all was Vaughan, whose style of walking was a model of machine gun regularity.

Corkey was first man to cover 50 miles in 7h.52m.1s, but after 12 hours of competition, O'Leary had moved himself up into in first place with the scores reading: **O'Leary, 66.6; Corkey, 66.3; Brown, 64; Lewis, W. Smith and Vaughan, 61; Bailey and McLeavy, 60; S. R. Johnson, 59.1; Ide, 57.3; Gregory, 55.2; G. Johnson, 54.3; Smythe, 54.1; Groves, 54; J. Smith, 53; McCarty, 51.1; Hazael; 50; Martyn, 41.2:** However, that all changed by 18:00 when the scores of the leading players with Hazael being the first casualty having made just 50 miles, was: **Corkey, 92.4; O'Leary, 87.1; Brown, 81.1; Vaughan, 80.1; S. R. Johnson, 79.5; McLeavy, 78.6; Ide, 76.6:**

Corkey went on to record the first 100 miles of the race at 20:06, with the Irish-American scoring his 42 minutes later. With little change in the positions of the peds at 23:00, the 5,000 people who had watched the race in the evening were politely asked to make their exit from the building. The absence of the spectators made the massive building lifeless, and as there was no reason to play to the crowd, there was all the more reason to get some sleep, and this what Corkey did, bidding the remaining people "Goodnight" as he left the track on a score of 113.1. His departure gave O'Leary the green light to make the best of his absence, and when midnight arrived, he must have been pretty pleased that he, and not the Londoner, was the race leader, albeit by a lap and a half. As the next hour progressed, he went on to pull 4 miles and 360 yards ahead of the snoozing second-placed man, the scores at the end of 24 hours showing: **O'Leary, 117.1; Corkey, 113.1; Vaughan, 102; Brown and McLeavy, 100; Bailey, 94; Gregory, 92.2; W. Smith, 92; Ide, 90.6; S. R. Johnson, 90:**

Whilst the rest of the race contestants took advantage of the peace and quiet, O'Leary, S. R. Johnson and Bailey were the only ones who kept on the track. O'Leary, who had made 124 miles by 02:44, reckoned it was now safe to take his first substantial break of the tournament. Meanwhile, *"Vaughan who was suffering from internal irritation, which he attributed to the change of the water that he drank, sent to Chester for a couple of jars of the same water that he took while training."* That same man was the first of the competitors back on the track, having been out for 3h.7m. Brown was back after a break of 4h.2m, and Corkey re-entered the arena after slumbering for 5h.15m. The above positions had altered when the score at 12:00 was posted and showed: **O'Leary, 148; Corkey, 146.5; Vaughan, 144; Brown, 143; McLeavy, 132.3; Ide, 126.1; Bailey, 123.2; W. Smith, 120; S. R. Johnson, 118.1:**

Of Brown, the *Sporting Life* commented: Plucky and persevering, this wonderful little man has a pace exactly modelled somewhat the reputed speed of a pig, an animal which is popularly supposed to go just a little faster than anything that tries to catch it.

With Corkey putting in a good walking performance, he soon tipped the scales in his favour when O'Leary, on a mark of 160 miles, went for a 45-minute rest in a room in the hall at 15:00. While he was away the meticulously attired amateur Martyn, who seemed to treat the race as a leisurely walk in the park on a Sunday afternoon, left the race for good at 15:25 on a score of 65 miles having *"rested for 38h.20m.7s."* He was the butt of many jokes and many wondered if he would even make it back to Bristol by Easter Monday!

Meanwhile, Corkey had re-grabbed the lead, and at 4 p.m. was two and a half miles in advance of O'Leary, with Brown one lap ahead of pre-race favourite Vaughan on 158.3. However, after his rest, O'Leary caught the little fellow up, and more or less got on level terms with the race leader at 18:00 when the score as displayed on the big board showed: **Corkey, 171.1; O'Leary, 170.5; Brown, 167.1; Vaughan, 166.2; Ide, 148; McLeavy and S. R. Johnson, 143; J. Smith, 139; Lewis, 138; Gregory, 136.6:**

O'Leary then started to take command of the race, and while Corkey rested for 1h.45m, he gained seven miles on him. With Vaughan now taking second position and Brown third, the scores of the first four in the race at 21:00 were: 184, 179.3, 178.2 and 176.4: It was now doubtful that a couple of the athletes who hadn't been seen on the track for some time, Bailey, who was reportedly suffering from *"affection of the sciatic nerve,"* nor William Smith, apparently afflicted with rheumatism, would be competing again. Groves on the other hand who had been thought to have *"jacked it in,"* due to spraining his ankle the day before, came out on to the "Englishman's" path at 21:10, and after walking a few laps, made his 92nd mile in a time of 8m.20s, a performance which *"elicited applause."*

"Mr. J. H. Morgan, the Oxford athlete of a few years ago, who is now a member of the medical profession, examined most of the competitors on Tuesday evening, and recommended some to use an embrocation, to alleviate the stiffening in the limbs from which many of them were suffering."

By 23:30, and with O'Leary doing the business up front leading the two Londoners by seven and ten miles respectively, his earlier odds of 6/4 had been taken and even money was being offered about the Irishman winning. The scores as the clock struck that time and as jotted down by reporters were: **O'Leary, 194.7; Corkey, 187.6; Brown, 184; Vaughan, 182.1; McLeavy, 168; Ide, 160; S. R. Johnson, 158.4; Gregory, 155.5; Lewis, 154.3; J. Smith, 153.2; G. Johnson, 144; McCarty, 136; W. Smith, 134.4; Bailey, 131.4; Smythe, 127.1; Groves, 95.6:**

The leader stuck doggedly to his task, and at 00:40, rewarded himself with a well deserved break after being the first one in the race to complete 200 miles. Whilst O'Leary slept, Brown performed industriously to get within three miles of the race leader by 2 a.m. Vaughan also made much headway pulling himself up to third place with 193.6, whilst Corkey dropped back to fourth "pozzy," 10 miles adrift of O'Leary. The Chicagoan hauled himself out of his cot and back into the arena having rested for 2h.3m, and after a tentative start, began to retrieve the distance lost whilst asleep. Corkey reappeared from his nap at 04:30 but appeared groggy.

As the public started to slowly fill the seats in the hall, an inspection of the bookies' slates showed O'Leary, who was now in pole position, was the favourite at £25 to £15. Vaughan was next in the betting at £25 to £10 with £20 to £7 about Corkey, and Brown at £20 to £4. By 10:00, and with O'Leary really piling on the pressure, he had succeeded in hauling himself a full ten miles in front of his nearest rival, Brown, who was on 220 miles. Vaughan was two miles behind him, and he led Corkey by eight. The rest of the scores were: **McLeavy, 188; Ide, 185; J. Smith, 183; Gregory, 173; S. R. Johnson, 171; Lewis, 165; G. Johnson, 164; McCarty, 160; W. Smith, 142; Bailey, 133; Smythe, 127:**

Smith the Scot shook off his physical woes thereafter by registering almost nine miles in a time of 1h.2m, but despite his improved performance, he suffered, as did many of the home grown peds including Bailey and McLeavy, *"the fleet-footed Scot,"* with sore and blistered feet. That particular ailment had also brought about the downfall of S. R. Johnson earlier that morning prompting a concerned *Sporting Life* to write: Surely, in training for a 500 miles walk; either the pedestrian or his trainer ought to be able to discover what sort of boots or shoes are the most suitable. Had proper care been taken about this small matter, half the likely men would not have been crippled. It is almost incredible to suppose that, if serious attempt is to be made to carry off a prize in a big event, that minor details would not be overlooked. Pitiable in the extreme has it been to see the pain which some of the competitors have suffered from raws and blisters - pain which the judicious outlay of a couple of pounds per head would have in all probability ended. Spoiling the ship for a halfpennyworth of tar is no worse than spending weeks on training, and about and about £50 in board, lodging, entrance, &c., and grudging a few shillings for good boots.

Between twelve and one o'clock, Corkey, who had been resting, came out and thrilled the crowd with a 7 mph performance. As the afternoon wore on, Vaughan replaced Brown for second place, and at 18:00 was 13 miles behind O'Leary with 249 miles to his name. "Blower" was three miles behind. Vaughan continued to pursue the leader, and by 8 p.m., in front of a very respectable crowd of upwards of 7,000, got within 9 miles of him. He also succeeded in doubling the distance between himself and Brown.

O'Leary was given a hearty cheer, when at 22:17, he completed his 280th mile. Three quarters of an hour later, he was one of six others who were still performing for the crowd. Their legs might have felt in better condition that night due to the fact that, *"Messrs. Elliman of Windsor, the proprietors of the celebrated embrocation, sent up on Wednesday a case of their patent liniment. The dozen bottles were divided among the competitors, who have found it of great service to them."* Corkey appeared unwell when he left the path at 23:40, and when he was examined it was found he was suffering from an *"ulcerated throat,"* which begs the question, did he read the bottle right?

At midnight, the score of the athletes stood: **O'Leary, 283.2; Vaughan, 270.1; Brown, 265.3; Gentleman, 254; Ide, 230; McLeavy, 222.6; J. Smith, 220; Gregory, 203.2; Lewis, 199.6; W. Smith, 192.2; McCarty, 183.6; G. Johnson, 179.4; Smythe, 151.3; Bailey, 138.2; Groves, 131.3:**

Astley was said to have placed a substantial bet on Harry Vaughan, and stood to win a large amount if he was successful. However, at 06:09, when O'Leary took a well deserved break leaving his path on a score of 309.3, (Dan had earlier finished his 300th mile in 74h.39m) his "punt" was looking a little precarious. Vaughan, who was then on a score of 286 and resting at the time, was 23 miles behind the leader who had been on the move all night.

During the 3h.20m period that O'Leary was resting, both Vaughan and Brown began to make inroads into his score as can be seen below when the telegraph board at 10:00 indicated: **O'Leary, 312; Vaughan, 301.4; Brown, 296; Corkey, 262; Ide, 253; J. Smith, 243; McLeavy, 226; Lewis, 206.4; Gregory, 203; McCarty, 197.2:**

In the afternoon, a large contingent of people had crowded into the building to watch the sport. O'Leary and Vaughan put on a good show for them by circumnavigating the path at a rate of 5 mph, with a splendid display of fast walking. When O'Leary had completed his 340th mile at 16:01, he had beaten his best time for that distance by 2h.21m.46s.

Just after four o'clock, Corkey reappeared on the course having spent 17 hours in his quarters. He walked for seven miles and then retired again. By 19:00, O'Leary had gained three miles since noon on Vaughan, and five on Brown in spite of their running. At that time, the dials showed O'Leary with 353, Vaughan on 339, and Brown showing 317. By 8 p.m., O'Leary had been competing 91 hours and had beaten the best time on record for that distance which was against Weston in April of 1877. For his effort, O'Leary received a great cheer and many headed to the bookmakers anxious to lay any odds that he would *"win the cake."* An hour later the leader had gained seven more miles on his 91st hour score. Vaughan had gained nine, and Brown eight. Ide moved into fourth with 291, and the fifth man was J. Smith on 277. Corkey, now back in sixth, was given a tremendous reception when he reappeared at 21:18 and began to try and increase the 269 miles he had made for himself. When the hall was cleared at 11 o'clock, the scores showed: **O'Leary, 369.6; Vaughan, 356.1; Brown, 333.2; Ide, 293.1; J. Smith, 285; Corkey, 276; Lewis, 240.1; McLeavy, 236.6; McCarty, 220:**

Vaughan, after resting from 23:55, re-emerged from the comfort of his house at 02:59 on the fifth day, and although appearing a little stiff initially, was obviously refreshed by his break. He was followed 45 minutes later by O'Leary who had been off track since 00:02. Both set to work with gusto and by seven a.m., the two principal players were separated by a distance of 14 miles, the leader having made 387. O'Leary went on to record his fourth century at 10:08, thereafter maintaining the distance between himself and second placed Vaughan with a conveyance of 5 mph, that speed being matched by the Chester man. Both men kept that pace going for two hours, and at one o'clock, O'Leary returned a score of 412.4 as opposed to his opponents 398. Brown at this time was way out in front of fourth-placed George Ide, a distance of some 45 miles separating the two Londoners, with "Blower's" score showing 375.3. The struggle continued with Vaughan really turning the heat up on O'Leary after four o'clock when he began the practice of *"doubling, for a good many laps – "walking along the straights and trotting around the turns."* At 5 o'clock, O'Leary's score was 429.4, Vaughan's was 416.6, and Brown's 391; and the observation was made that Henry appeared in better condition than Dan, who *"was trembling in the knees."* The *Sporting Life* wrote of the leader: His legs are decidedly queer, and he shows great signs of fatigue, but he never has for one moment flinched from his work.

By 19:00, the contest had become a virtual match between O'Leary (438½), and Vaughan (426) who both went along at an average of 4 mph, all the rest being well behind. While O'Leary stuck to walking, Vaughan, who trotted occasionally, consequently reduced the gap between them. Brown completed his fourth hundred at 19:08, and by 9 o'clock, O'Leary had walked 446½, with Vaughan having completed his 433rd mile.

The noisy, and excitable crowd of an estimated 10,000 people, was really helping the pedestrians to put up some good performances, and they were readily cheered as they played to their audience with frequent spurts, Lewis in particular pleasing the eye. Even Groves got in on the act making a mile in 6m.12s. Brown though, who was suffering with stomach cramp, was ordered off by his trainer and was given a warm bath to alleviate the condition. With the remedy doing the trick, he was back on song just before nine o'clock. Vaughan left the track at 11:10 p.m. with both his feet observed to be swathed in cotton wool.

The score at 23:30 with O'Leary just preparing himself to leave for a rest was: **O'Leary, 457; Vaughan, 441; Brown, 416; Ide, 351; J. Smith, 334; Gentleman, 309.2; Lewis, 265; McCarty, 250.3; McLeavy, 244.6; Gregory, 226; G. Johnson, 203.4; Groves, 197; W. Smith, 193.6; Smythe, 175.6; Bailey, 139.1:**

The interest in the match continued unabated. O'Leary returned to the track on the last day at 03:00. Vaughan meanwhile, had rested at regular intervals during the night, but hadn't taken a long rest like the race leader. The scores of the principal performers thereafter were: At 06:00: **O'Leary, 468; Vaughan, 450; Brown, 423:** At 08:00: **O'Leary, 475; Vaughan, 456; Brown, 430:** At 11:00: **O'Leary, 487; Vaughan, 465; Brown, 438:** At that stage, Vaughan seemed fresh and was walking in excellent form. O'Leary however, was somewhat lame. Although suffering from sore feet, he managed to walk along at a steady pace, and it was evident that he was reserving his strength for the last few hours. He had the race well in hand and nothing short of an absolute collapse could prevent him winning. The scores at 12:00 were: **O'Leary, 490; Vaughan, 468; Brown, 443:**

In the early part of the afternoon, and with all the contestants on the track, O'Leary continued to appear in distress but nevertheless walked steadily along. Vaughan ran. Of O'Leary, Astley wrote in his memoirs: **"At one time he was so dazed he could not see the edge of the track, until some fresh white sawdust was brought and laid around the near edge. On another occasion, I fancy he got hold of, or was given, a drop of good old port, which a fond parent of one of the competitors had brought up to stimulate his lad's exertions, and a strong pull at this red wine on an empty stomach made poor Dan's progress decidedly devious."**

The dials at 14:00 showed: **O'Leary, 497; Vaughan, 473; Brown, 447:** O'Leary's 497th mile was walked in 17 minutes whilst Vaughan's 473rd was completed in 1 minute less. The time occupied by O'Leary in completing his 501st mile was 15 minutes whilst Vaughan walked his 487th mile in 13. At 16:00, the telegraph board indicated: **O'Leary, 505; Vaughan, 482; Brown, 458:** O'Leary walked his 505th mile in 14m.52s and slowed down thereafter to complete his 508th mile in 16m.58s.

The scores from 5 p.m. till 7 p.m. were: At 17:00: **O'Leary, 508; Vaughan, 487; Brown, 463:** At 18:00: **O'Leary, 512; Vaughan, 493; Brown, 468:** At 19:00: **O'Leary, 516; Vaughan, 497; Brown, 472:** It was at this time, as the band played *"American airs,"* O'Leary thrilled the audience with spurt after spurt, the spectacle causing the crowd to cheer so much, it *"shook"* the building. Amongst those urging him on were Irish members of Parliament and their lady friends.

The place was now absolutely packed with people wanting to see the action. Their great numbers were causing a few problems and the *Sporting Life* in its post-match write up commented: By two o'clock the hall was crowded, and for hours the click of the turnstiles was continuous, those who passed in late having to take up their positions on the outside of the more fortunate brethren who had arrived early. Locomotion was quite early in the evening

King of the Peds

next to impossible, except in the reserved enclosure, which was well filled while in the stands there were few vacant seats. Great dissatisfaction was expressed by the holders of weekly or press tickets at the way in which they were treated on Saturday. Every rudeness and even violence was offered to them by prize-fighters placed at all the points of ingress, and even the officials and well-known men like Bill Lang came in for some hustling. Every man knows, or should know, best his own business, but to most people it would seem that when four policemen, who are trained to something like civility, and bear about them a little authority, can be obtained for the price paid to one pro, who thinks he has not earned his money unless he makes some bother, a sane man would have gone in for "the force;" policemen a deal cheaper and not nearly so nasty as fighting men, and the presence of these worthies was in every way a mistake.

Vaughan retired at 19:38 after completing 500 miles, and the contest ended prematurely due to many of the 15,000 watching spilling on to the track which made the task of the tired competitors dangerous. O'Leary, lame but game, completed 520 miles and 2 laps and stopped his tramp at 20:10. As the band played "See the Conquering Hero Comes," he was declared the winner amid boundless excitement and enthusiasm. "*Haggard, dazed, staggering O'Leary, his arms no longer knitted in pedestrian form and braced with muscular strength were limp, and almost helpless.*" Brown, "*looking the picture of health, happiness and cleanliness,*" and appearing resplendent in his ultra clean costume which consisted of a spotless white jersey and a pink and white silk neckerchief which matched the colours of his drawers, continued on the track until 20:30, until he too stopped having made 477.2 along with Ide, who ended his race with a score of 405.

The Final Scores!

Pos		Miles	Laps	Pos		Miles	Laps
1	**O'Leary**	**520**	**2**	10	Gregory	231	3
2	Vaughan	500	0	11	Groves	220	2
3	Brown	477	2	12	Johnson	205	0
4	Ide	405	4	13	W. Smith	194	2
5	J. Smith	394	6	14	Johnson	192	0
6	"Corkey"	335	2	15	Smythe	175	4
7	Lewis	270	0	16	Bailey	139	2
8	McCarty	264	2	17	Martyn	65	0
9	McLeavy	250	6	18	Hazael	50	0

Following the race, *The Times* made the following comments about O'Leary's victory on Monday, March the 25th: Without wishing for a moment to deprecate O'Leary's victory, we would point out that he was greatly favoured by one or two circumstances. The fact of his being allowed a separate track is in itself a great advantage. Whatever object the promoter of this contest may have had, there can be no doubt that that it gave O'Leary an incalculable advantage. His track to the end was in capital order while that of the Englishmen was cut up before the close of the second day. In addition to this, the mere fact of the latter having to so often pass and overtake each other is in itself a great drawback. To some minds this is very harassing, apart from the ground which is thus lost. This, in a task so lengthy, amounts to the aggregate to much more than may be supposed. Another advantage was the fact that O'Leary had a commodious tent close to the track, while the remaining competitors were placed in wretched hovels about 20 yards distant, which, even in the wearied state of the men were anything but inviting. We should mention that O'Leary had to walk an extra 50 yards every time he went to his tent. No one, of course, grudges any extra courtesy that may be shown to a man who has crossed from America to expressly to compete. Still it is obviously unfair to strain these courtesies to the detriment of the other competitors, and should another walk be entered on we hope that the men will travel on the same track.

William Howes, who had not appeared in the Astley Belt race, but who had nonetheless won a 26-hour event at the Agricultural Hall only a couple of weeks before, (120 miles in 24h.8m.25s thus beating the fastest previous time made by Vaughan by 43 minutes) issued an immediate challenge to O'Leary of a match for the Astley Belt and £500. Howes had proved his credentials during his latest race where he had succeeded in securing a world record of 100 miles in 18h.7m.57s.

Astley was later to publish a letter in the *Sporting Life* to defend himself against claims that he was making money from his belt:

As some of the sporting scribes imputed all sorts of sordid motives to me, I had all the receipts and expenses verified, which effectually silenced the carping critics for the time; for it dawned on them that a sporting 'Bart,' was a bit more liberal to the men of thews and sinews than the sporting 'Bung' usually was.

Astley at that time was also proposing to introduce a 12-day tournament where £1,000 would be awarded as first prize. The proposed conditions of the race would be to compete from Monday till Saturday as was the norm, then, after resting for 26 hours, continuing from Monday till Saturday again.

The following "Balance Sheet" was found in Astley's book, *"Fifty Years of my Life."*

BALANCE SHEET

RECEIPTS.

By Gate	£	s	d	£	s	d
Monday	267	2	6			
Tuesday	276	11	0			
Wednesday	400	14	0			
Thursday	470	14	6			
Friday	641	13	6			
Saturday	832	1	6			
				2,888	17	0
Entries				170	0	0
Total				3,058	17	0

EXPENDITURE.

	£	s	d
Prizes to Winners and Attendants at Conclusion of Walk	989	10	0
Belt and Medals	130	0	0
Extra Money Prize	498	10	0
Hire of Hall, Gas, Stands, Contractor's Work &c.	455	3	4
Gate-Keepers, Commissionaires, Police	120	9	0
Judges and Scorers	192	4	0
Band	78	0	0
Printing, Advertising &c.	137	3	0
Lavatories, Messengers, Miscellaneous Sundries	56	3	0
	2,656	19	4
Balance at Banker's for Future Prizes	401	17	8
Total	3,058	17	0

News from London, and printed in the American press on the 3rd of April, informed readers in that country that the trustees of the champion belt had decided that O'Leary was entitled to take it to the U.S.A., and anybody challenging him must go there, unless O'Leary would agree to compete in England.

O'Leary gave the following interview to a reporter of the *New York Sun* just before his return home. It gives a fascinating insight into what he went through during the race:

"Eighteen of us started. I had eaten a hearty dinner and got up from a light supper of tea and toast just before the walking began. I tightened my belt, gripped my corn cobs firmly and opened the ball. This cob business is a habit. A firm grip on them seems to gird me up and absorbs the moisture of the hands. I have the same two cobs in my trunk now at the hotel, and always carry some with me. You couldn't get such a thing in England. I ran and walked the first 50 miles, running around the corners and walking the stretches. But I quickly felt the effects of the running in the tendons of my leg and stopped it. It also injured my feet, for in running you spring from the ball of the foot, while in walking the heel comes in play. I walked 208 miles before resting, making 117 miles in the first hours, and changing my shoes twice a day. On the 209th mile I rested an hour and a half, but I

King of the Peds

only slept 25 minutes. In fact, I couldn't sleep. My mind was so excited and my body so sore that I lay moaning, groaning and mumbling, and could get no real rest. So I got to my feet and kept on walking until they told me I was 37 miles ahead of everybody.

Then, at the earnest solicitation of my friend Al Smith of Chicago, I left the track for three hours. I didn't think that it was hardly safe for me to do so, for I didn't feel like sleep, and I was afraid of getting stiff and sore. And it turned out just as I thought. I got a little sleep in the last hour, and that was all. When I again came on the track my nose began to bleed and I found myself very sore and stiff. The bleeding at the nose, however, did me good. It seemed to relieve my head. Then anxiety of the mind came up. I found that Vaughan had gained on me considerably. He was only ten miles behind, and Blower Brown was within 15 miles. Gradually the soreness and stiffness wore away, and my legs got limber, but the right one began to show signs of swelling. Slowly I pulled away from Vaughan, and at 12 o'clock on Thursday night was 15 miles ahead of him."

"Vaughan," continues O'Leary "is a gallant walker and a good square fellow. We watched each other like enemies, but there was no feeling of envy or anger. Of course, Vaughan's friends were by far the most numerous. When they handed him bouquets he would pass them over to me to smell, and on the next turn I would hand them back. The wild applause for Vaughan had no effect upon me. But when a little knot of American's and a few Irish members of Parliament got into one corner and cheered me until they were hoarse, the effect was inspiring. It seemed to put wings on my feet. To inspire him, Vaughan's friends placed the glittering belt under his nose, saying, "Look at it, boy. Don't lose it. Five hundred pounds with it if you win it and thousands more on top of that," On Friday Vaughan was very close to me, and my swollen leg began to trouble me. It was a hard struggle, but after that Vaughan never got within twelve miles of me. When be left the track on Friday night he was fifteen miles behind. I put in two more miles, and was rubbed down and put to bed.

I slept for some time, but Vaughan was ever before me. I told Smith to wake me the instant he appeared on the track, and he did so. All the other Englishmen had given way to Vaughan. They had given him the inside track, and he was putting in his best licks. Before I could I'd get fairly going he had gained two miles, but from that time be slowly fell away. My leg was swollen double its usual size, but I felt no pain. It was very stiff, however, and bothered me considerable in walking. I knew that if I took another rest with so persistent a man as Vaughan behind me it would become so stiff that I might lose the match. So I ended the long agony by walking 18 hours without leaving the track. And that is how I came to get the belt. Vaughan had lots of friends, and he deserved them. If he had won, he would have been the richest pedestrian that ever stood in shoe leather."

O'Leary says that he ate nothing during this long walk. His only sustenance was tea, coffee, and milk, and an occasional suck of an orange. His mind was in much a state that the very sight of solid food him sick. He entered the tournament weighing 148 pounds, and came out of it with a loss of 14 pounds. He rested eight hours altogether sleeping not more than half that time. He lost three toe nails after the match, but the swelling in his leg soon went down, and be now considers himself in excellent condition. He says Sir John Astley was right in ascribing his success to the making of his shoes.

When O'Leary returned home to Chicago on the 19th of May, he showed off the Astley Belt and a large gold medal, which weighed several pounds and was estimated to be worth £500, to members of the press. The medal had a similar inscription to what was inscribed on the belt: **"Presented by Sir J. D. Astley. Bart., M.P., March 1878." "Won by Daniel O'Leary, of Chicago, U.S.A., March 18 to 23, 1878: distance 520¼ miles in 138 hours 48 minutes, beating H. Vaughan, Chester, 500 miles, H. Brown (Blower) of Fulham 477 miles, and fifteen others"**

Below is a conversation he had with a reporter:

Reporter: "What kind of a time did you have?"

O'Leary: "A good time."

Reporter: "How did the Englishmen treat you?"

O'Leary: "Oh, pretty well about as an Englishman would be treated if he walked in America. They didn't like to see the belt leave England, and did all they could to keep it there."

Reporter: "You had to talk for it?"

O'Leary: "Yes, for over a week, but we had justice on our side. They encouraged men to go there from all over the world, and claimed, after I was fortunate enough to win the belt, that it was not to go out of the country. There was no such stipulation in the agreement."

Reporter: "Was there any trouble over the stake?"

O'Leary: "No, that was given up freely. Let me say that Mr. Astley is a gentleman, and a lover of fair play."

Reporter: "Did anything unpleasant occur during the walk?"

O'Leary: "Oh no; I was treated fairly well, but Englishmen don't admire Irishmen. That is sure. They were very quiet on the last two days, didn't have much to say."

Reporter: "Did you enjoy your trip to Ireland?"

O'Leary: "Yes, but it cost me £500 to see Dublin."

Reporter: "How is that?"

O'Leary: "I walked there, and it was very unprofitable. There are five Englishmen in Dublin to one Irishman; but the hall in which I walked was the finest I ever saw. If I had been an Italian or a Bohemian I would have done better."

Reporter: "Why didn't you try Cork?"

O'Leary: "Because I thought Dublin was Ireland, and when I found out my mistake I had enough."

Reporter: "Why is Brown called 'Blower'?"

O'Leary: "Because he blows more than the other Browns."

Reporter: "How does Vaughan walk?"

O'Leary: "He is the best pedestrian I ever saw, and a very decent fellow, but he is not a stayer."

Reporter: "Were you sociable with your competitors during the journey?"

O'Leary: "Yes, we had a laugh once in a while. Some one in the crowd would present a contestant with a bouquet made of cabbage and water-cresses and that would enliven us."

Reporter: "How was your appetite during that week?"

O'Leary: "Appetite? Why, I didn't eat anything for six days."

Reporter: "Not eat anything?"

O'Leary: "No sir, except an orange now and then. I lived on tea, coffee, and milk."

Reporter: "Were you tired when you finished?"

O'Leary: "Pretty tired. I couldn't get into the carriage when I left the track, but if I had stayed on I could have walked several miles more. Stopping was what used me up."

Reporter: "How much longer could you have kept going?"

O'Leary: "I couldn't tell. It pleased me greatly when I saw the others drop out."

Reporter: "Why was it you refused to accept any of the challenges when the match was over?"

King of the Peds

O'Leary: "Because the challengers wanted to walk in London. Having won the belt, I had the say where the walking should be done. I wouldn't walk in London again, but offered to walk in France, Italy, Germany, or Spain. They don't know where America is, and of course wouldn't come here."

Reporter: "You will hold the belt?"

O'Leary: "I'll try to. It is mine if I hold it for eighteen months. Under the conditions, I must accept any challenge within three months after its issue. Only two matches can be walked in a year. Any one who wins it must walk 600 miles. There will be at least one corpse on the track."

Mrs. O'Leary: "Oh! Don't Dan!"

Reporter: "Have you anything in hand just now?"

O'Leary: "No. I tried to get the Hippodrome in New York, but Theodore Thomas had engaged it, and that is the only place I would walk."

Reporter: "Then you will keep quiet for a while?"

O'Leary: "Yes, I shall stay at home for a few months and look after the babies."

CHAPTER 10

Brawn v Brains

On the 1st of April 1878, Harry Hill published a challenge stating that he would back a certain *"poor man"* in New York to the tune of $500 to beat O'Leary's London record. The conditions of the challenge were that the attempt should take place within three weeks, and that the rules would follow the same as the 1st Astley Belt contest in London. The man he was backing was called John Hughes and at the time the *Chicago Tribune* ran the following story on the 16th of April, about the "challenger," who was described as being a *"poor day labourer:"*

He is about the Irishest man I ever saw, and if his travelling wind is as lasting as that which consumes in talk, he ought to run a year at top speed, and then quit fresh. But under the many incrustations of brogue and brag, there is said to be speed that is unequalled and endurance that is wonderful.

He does not profess to be a great walker, but he claims that he can out-run any man in the world. When he heard about the great tournament in London, it occurred to him that there was an opportunity to display his powers to advantage. But he was poor, unknown, and ignorant, and some time elapsed before he could find anyone to back him. At last, however, he met a gentleman who was willing to advance the money for his necessary expenses, but the entries had closed already, and he was shut out. He expresses freely his belief that he should have won that race, and the forthcoming match was arranged to "give him a chance" more than as a money making affair, so his friends say. The race is to be a public one, and will begin at the Central Park Gardens at 8 o'clock on the 21st of this month. The track is to be measured by a city surveyor, and will contain thirteen laps to the mile, which will give the runner some very short turns. But it is claimed that the disadvantage thus imposed is more than removed by the fact that the ventilation is excellent, a part of the track being laid in the open air, outside the building itself.

Hughes was *born in Roscrea, County Tipperary, Ireland, and is now a little over 28 years of age.

*June the 21st 1850.

He is 5 feet and 9 inches high, and weighs 166 pounds, which is considerably less than when he is in the flesh. He is very muscular, and is said to be much stronger than O'Leary. His legs, which are remarkably solid and sinewy, and in a pair of big brawny feet, which are as tough as iron. Great breadth and depth are the noteworthy features of his chest. His face is almost repulsive in its harsh outlines, and denotes the presence of nothing beyond coarse animal spirits. I never knew what "flannel mouth" meant until I heard John Hughes talk. He speaks of "lepping ar-ound the t-h-h-rack," and when he means that he can beat the time made by O'Leary, he says he "caan bet the devil out of him." He has bluish gray eyes, and a coarse, low colored moustache. He is as thick-headed as the Cardiff Giant, and as stubborn as a Government mule, but although he displays all these qualities one cannot hear him talk without believing that that he has attributes which, if rightly directed, will make a great pedestrian of him. But he must be carefully handled, and his excitable nature must be nursed with judicious care. He has a record which is simply wonderful for an amateur, and he is a dead enemy to O' Leary, who, he says, made fun of him because he was too poor to go to London.

When Hughes was yet a boy he showed great speed in running, winning several trials with horses, and successfully keeping close behind the hounds in fox hunts. He claims to have inherited the gift from his father, who, he says, on his 60th birthday, ran a race of *ten miles with him (the son) and won it with the most perfect care.

*His father ran the ten miles mentioned above in 1h.1m.40s.

Hughes landed in this country in 1868, and was at once naturalized by the Tammany Hall process, and put to work in one of the city departments.

King of the Peds

In 1870 Hughes began his career of walking and running and was soon nick-named the "Lepper" due to his *"peculiar jumping gait."* Thereafter, he bet that he could run from 125th Street to McComb's dam in New York, and make the return journey of three miles in 20 minutes. He did it in seventeen. After that performance he met Dennis Murray of Newark who went on to back him in several matches. The first was a run over the same course against Jim Smith. Hughes beat him easily.

Within six months he was matched to run a six-mile race with *John Wild on Harlem lane for $300, Joe Coburn backing Wild and **Ald. Charlick putting up the stamps for Hughes. For this race Hughes did no training, working all day long with his pick and shovel, and on the day of the contest he put in his full time as usual. The race occurred in the evening, and the novice got away with such a splendid burst of speed that Coburn saw he must lose his money unless he adopted some trick. It happened that Hughes was running without any shirt, and that gave Coburn the opportunity to have him arrested for indecent exposure, - which was done in the middle of the last mile. The Captain of that precinct discharged him instantly, and reprimanded the officer. But, of course, it was too late, so the wily Joseph saved his money.

*John Wild would later call himself Patrick Fitzgerald.

** The Harlem Alderman was also joined in backing Hughes with Dennis Murray.

His next match was three miles in length against Harry Munson. It was run in the evening, after a hard day's work, but Hughes won easily, by more than a mile. Hughes best race was run at the Fashion race-track in 1872. It was a ten-mile match for $300 a side, and his opponent was a man called *Martin, reputed to be a first class runner. It was in this affair that the Irish boy developed wonderful speed, winning the race in fifty-four minutes, and coming in a mile and a half ahead.

*James Martin was from New Orleans. Another report claimed that the match at the Fashion trotting course was for $100 a side which Hughes won in slightly over 61 minutes. Rain fell during the race, and Martin, as a result of the exposure, died within three days.

A week after his ten-mile race, an amateur contest for one mile, open to all non professionals, was gotten up by one Hitchcock. Several men who made their livings by running races were allowed to start under false names, but Hughes was recognised and denied admission. After the race was well under way however, he made such a tremendous row that the judges cried, "let that crazy Mick go." He ran like a deer and made a mile in 4:40, but the race was given to the man who came in first, and whose time was 4:47. He has tramped through California like a regular road-beggar, and claims to have saved nearly $30 in a single day by walking instead of patronizing stages and cars.

Hughes is now in regular training and averages forty miles a day. Once he ran to Sing Sing and back, a distance of seventy-two miles. Then he walked to Tarry town and return, about sixty miles. These journeys were made in some unwieldy brogans made by Hughes himself. When he arrived here on the first day, they were found to be full of dirt and gravel, but his feet were so tough that he had not detected their presence. All professional pedestrians are bitterly opposed to him. They say he is a fraud, and brags too much to amount to anything. But he keeps on in the even tenor of his way, and says he'll "make foive hoondered an' fifty moiles in socks days, as stay as nothing."

"Luck a heer," said he to me, with some excitement. "Oi'll bet this divil O'Layry, or bust mi biler. The dar-r–ty ca-r-rr; when Oi was ta-a-lkin' wid him aboot goin' to Loondun, he said he'd have a b-r-r-idge belt for me to walk over, d-a-a-mn his black sowl: But Oi'll be aven wid him. Oi'll bet the divil owt of his tolme, or dole in me th-h-racks. Moinde ye, when I was wance wurrucking for the Anchor Loine, I med a hoondred moiles in nineteen hours. And thaat was whin Oi was wurruking loike the divil. O, Oi'll be thi, Oi'll bet him."

The race will doubtless be an interesting one, and well worth seeing. Should Hughes fail in his task, that will end the matter. Should he win, New York won't be big enough to hold him.

Hughes was said to have made a spectacle of himself before he finished his six-day tramp at 20:23 on the evening of Saturday, the 27th of April, failing miserably to beat O'Leary's London record of 520 miles on a 15-lap to the mile oval track at the Central Park Garden on a score of just under 390 miles. He ran his last two miles in 8m.47s and 8m.1s respectively and was reported to be *"pretty badly used up."*

Soon after this he made 127 miles in twenty-four hours, and after that, Murray went over to London to try and arrange, what was to be later in the year, the six-day match between Hughes and O'Leary for the "2nd International Astley Belt."

At the Tremont House Hotel, in Boston on the 5th of August, O'Leary was interviewed and asked about the possibility of going back England to participate in the then forthcoming Sir John Astley promoted "Long Distance Champion Belt" contest.

"It is very doubtful if I again cross the water, although I see it has been published that I am to be a participant; this, however, is without my sanction. It is not improbable though that at the last moment I might change my mind; but, as I have said before, I shall probably not again visit London. Mr. Weston is entered, and I sincerely trust he will succeed in bearing away the honours, hoping an American will again be the victor."

When asked what his future plans for the future were, he answered, "I am undecided as yet. Possibly I may arrange to give an exhibition in this city, and perhaps also in Chicago and New York. In the meanwhile I am resting and awaiting challenges for my belt, which I must hold for two more years. Holding it now, I have the right, as to locality, etcetera, for the contest, and it would be my intention to make the admission free, or charge a more nominal sum."

He was the asked what his impressions of England and its people were, to which he replied, "No people like to have a foreigner whip them and carry away the prize."

Up to that stage in his professional career it had been calculated that he had walked 9,493 miles, of which 2,055 were made in Chicago, 895 in Cincinnati, 220 in Dublin, Ireland, 960 in Liverpool, England, 1,240 in London, England, 418 in Louisville, Kentucky, 544 in Manchester, England, 1,096 in New York, 116 in Philadelphia, 768 in St. Louis, and 1,181 in San Francisco.

Then, on Monday, the August of 12th at 20:00, O'Leary set off in an exhibition match to cover 400 miles on a 20 laps to the mile track at the Music Hall in that city. Although he duly completed his feat with some 25 minutes to spare on the following Saturday, in an actual walking time of 84h.53m.23s, having rested for 36h.41m.21s, there was a degree of concern that the time-keepers hadn't been doing their jobs properly, and as a result, he was accused of attaining the total fraudulently.

During the walk, the champion was set a telegram which read:

LIVERPOOL., August 16.

Shall I enter you for champion belt of England?

Answer.   GEORGE W. RAMSDEN,

Business Manager Guion line of steamers.

O'Leary answered, "One belt is enough."

In his preparation to challenging O'Leary, Hughes started off on a six days *"walk"* on Sunday, the 18th of August at 11 p.m. at Newark, New Jersey. Finishing it at 22:25 on Saturday, the 24th, he was reported to have made 500 miles *"amid the wildest enthusiasm of a large audience."* However, it was claimed that the track was short, and that he didn't even cover 300 miles.

Then, six weeks later:-

Gilmore's Garden in New York comprised of an oval arena which had brick walls and no roof. Previous to this it was called "The Great Roman Hippodrome." The famous bandmaster Patrick Sarsfield Gilmore who was famous for composing the song "When Johnny Comes Marching Home," obtained the lease and used the building to hold promenade concerts. His "Garden" which displayed flowers, trees, and waterfalls, would be the venue for the "2nd International Astley Belt" race which was arranged to start at one o'clock on the morning on Monday, the 30th of September, and finish on Saturday, the 5th of October.

King of the Peds

The two competitors were the "World Champion" Daniel O'Leary of Chicago, and John Hughes of New York. Both would be competing for the prestigious belt, a purse of $1,000 ($500 per side) and a share of the gate money. The financial arrangements were that the gross receipts would be equally divided between the proprietors of the Garden and O'Leary; the former paying all the expenses out of their share. O'Leary would then give Hughes one third of his share, which meant that O'Leary would get a third of the gross receipts with Hughes receiving a sixth.

Two tracks were laid in the outer circle of the building, one on each side of the inner line of pillars which extended around it. Three inches of earth were laid on top of the asphalt pavement, and on top of this was laid half an inch of damp sawdust. Each track was 30 inches wide and the following certificate was issued to certify the measurements.

GILMORE'S GARDEN, NEW YORK, Sept. 29, 1878.

I hereby certify that I have surveyed the two tracks now being walked upon by O'Leary and Hughes, and that the inner one measures one ninth of a mile, and the outer one, one eighth of a mile.

V. W. SMITH, City Surveyor, No 99 Nassau Street.

O'Leary won the toss for the choice of track and chose the outer. Both men had been provided with *"comfortable"* quarters at opposite ends of the building. The champion's room, which was furnished with a single bed, cooking stove and cooking utensils, was situated under the old circus department, underneath the raised seats near the Madison Avenue main entrance. Hughes would inhabit a small tent along with his wife and two children. The living arrangements for the two athletes had attracted a great deal of attention, and there was some justifiable criticism due to the smoke pouring from the stoves which was very noticeable, and evidently smelly.

The same rules that governed the first match in London applied, and the arrangements for the contest were in the hands of the Harlem Athletic Club, which had assigned forty of its members to oversee its smooth running. A few minutes before the start, Mr. J. D. Riblet, the club's President summoned the two competitors to the score keepers' stand and stated the conditions and rules of the match.

O'Leary, sporting a blonde moustache, admitted that he hadn't trained for the contest. Previously he had stated that he was in excellent condition, and when stripped, weighed in at 150 pounds. He was dressed in a white shirt, tight white trousers with black trunks and wore a heavy towel around his neck.

Hughes, with his darker moustache and close cropped black hair, wore a white shirt trimmed with red, blue trousers reaching to his knees, red and white stockings, a fancy belt around his waist, and a red handkerchief around his neck.

Four hundred people including *"several ladies"* were present to see the start. The men, both grasping 5-inch corn cobs tipped with tin foil in each hand, were then sent on their way; as was expected, Hughes ran at a pace of 10 mph, and O'Leary walked 4 mph slower than his opponent. The champion, who began to suffer with stomach problems, was forced to leave the track to *"vomit"* on four separate occasions. He had eaten about 3/4 of a pound of oatmeal made into gruel, and took his first "sick" break after scoring 15 miles, having to do the same on the 23rd, 40th and 45th mile. He was seen frequently sipping lime water to try and aid his recovery.

O'Leary is on the outer path and Hughes on the inner.

Frank Leslies' Illustrated Newspaper (Illustration no: 27)

Hughes, who made 20 miles in 2h.45m.6s, stopped for a short rest on his 40th mile of 2m.25s. He then went on to make 50 miles in 8h.25m.48s. O'Leary meanwhile, only managed to score 45 miles in 9h.7m.6s. The score at 17:00: **Hughes, 77.2; O'Leary, 70.4:**

Hughes had to leave the track at 19:21 because of the reoccurring sickness he had been suffering from. At 21:00, and in front of 5,000 spectators, the current champion, who then was attracting winning odds of 4/5, was described as being as fresh and lively as when he had started. After receiving treatment for his ailment, Hughes returned at 21:46 appearing lame and weary. He only lasted till 22:02 when he was forced to retire again on a score of 87.7. The press had commented on how the "Lepper," had drank a gallon of milk during the day which had *"soured on his stomach,"* causing him to *be "rather a sick man."* His symptoms greatly disturbed his sleep as a consequence. Indeed, it was reported that he was *"tossing about on his bed suffering with severe colic and cramps in his legs."*

The reporter for the *New York Times* went to investigate how Hughes was getting on: At midnight in his guarded tent, the other gladiator lay howling with the colic. His legs refused to carry him any further, and everybody connected with the canvas establishment was as cross as a bear. The tent is indeed a guarded one. Hughes has great fears of being tampered with. He is suspicious of his food and perhaps drank as much milk on Monday because he thought it could contain no foreign substance but water. This fear is so great that his best friends are not allowed to enter his tent without giving a password that has been adopted. It may be high treason but it shall be told that this password is "Gilmore's Garden." It made a ready entrance for a TIMES reporter early yesterday morning. There was a combination inside of the odors of arnica arid camphor and all the kinds of liniments the mind of man can conceive. Hughes was curled up on the bed in shape that would convince any fair minded person of having an India rubber backbone, and double jointed knees. His face was as pale as the sheets. He did not look like a good subject for an interview, and nobody spoke to him. Joe Goss once tried to pull him out of bed and make him walk, but the doctor interfered and said that he must have more sleep.

Hughes was attended to by Dr. Reich, who managed at least to help him enough so that he was nearly asleep by 1 a.m. There were reports that he was pale and that he might not be able to continue. The management were so worried that they were making contingency plans to replace Hughes with another man called *"Walter Harriman of Boston."* The scores and times up to 100 miles are below:

MLS	O'LEARY H	M	S	HUGHES H	M	S	MLS	O'LEARY H	M	S	HUGHES H	M	S
5		55	14		35	41	55	11	21	46	9	45	22
10	1	47	35	1	15	15	60	12	47	5	10	47	15
15	2	45	35	1	58	47	65	13	42	28	12	1	45
20	3	50	29	2	45	6	70	14	43	51	13	21	47
25	4	56	31	3	35	24	75	15	47	7	15	46	0
30	5	23	26	4	30	21	80	16	59	17	16	37	18
35	7	7	18	5	21	11	85	18	6	25	17	57	15
40	8	18	8	6	19	7	90	19	9	16			
45	9	7	6	7	23	20	95	20	20	15			
50	10	6	10	8	25	48	100	21	39	55			

Whilst Hughes had been attempting to sleep, O'Leary, having made 100 miles at 22:40, left the track after acknowledging the applause of the crowd. Rumours flew around the building that he wouldn't reappear until 3 a.m., and as the band packed up their instruments, many of the spectators made their way home. However, O'Leary reappeared at 22:55 and resumed his effort. He left the track again at 23:55 after completing 103 miles and 3 laps. He was sponged and rubbed down with coarse towels and was reported to fall asleep immediately.

The reporter, having taken a good look at the suffering Hughes then decided to take a peek in O'Leary's tent: About 1 o'clock, he kicked the blankets off, sat up in his little cot and talked with as much glibness as a room full of elderly unmarried ladies over their cups of tea. He was particularly interested in his feet and shoes, two of the most important tools in his trade. The feet were in prime condition, and the shoes were stretched as tight drum-heads over, pair of stretching lasts.

"It don't look very bad, after 103 miles does it?" he smilingly asked, lifting up on foot with as much tenderness as if it were a baby.

The foot was small, high in the instep well arched, and altogether well made. It certainly did not look bad after the tremendous tramping it had done. On the most exposed part of the sole, near the ball of the foot, where it is to be supposed every person who walks at all has more or less of a blister, was a hardened spot about the size of a silver half dollar, not at all sore, but simply rubbed and tramped into hardened skin. This like all such places, might have been shaved off with a sharp knife, as it was entirely without feeling but, as it gave no inconvenience, it was let alone. On the third toe of the left foot was a tiny little blister, or corn, the only spot on either foot that give him any trouble. This was smaller than a pea in size, but sore, although O'Leary said that it was only occasionally that he felt it at all, but that he had ways of his own for curing it, and would soon have it out of the way altogether. "I am the best bunion doctor you ever saw, said O'Leary sitting up a little further in bed. "I never have sore feet myself, but if I did I would soon cure them. The shoes I wear prevent me from getting corns or bunions on my feet." He picked up one of his shoes and pointed out its beauties.

The sole was very wide so that the foot could not, by any possibility, spread out wider than the shoe. Its greatest peculiarity was the heel, only about half an inch high. "I had that put on in London," said O'Leary, tapping a little extra piece that had been put on across the bottom of the heel. "It is to make the heel elastic. When I walk fast I walk almost entirely upon my heels, and this springiness prevents any jar and is a great convenience." The elasticity in the back of the heel is due partly to the extra piece not being fastened at that point and partly to its being slightly wrinkled in the putting on, the effect being that when it strikes the floor, it acts like a spring, trying to straighten itself out with scarcely a sound.

"If everybody would wear shoes of that shape, told O'Leary, "there would be fewer sore feet."

"But you do not wear those low, wide heels, in walking about the street do you?"

"Well, not exactly when I'm walking down Broadway, to show my shape," said O'Leary, smiling; "but they're the best things to wear."

It is impossible not to notice at once the great difference between O'Leary's figure and Weston's. Weston's greatest peculiarity is that he measures as much around the waist as around the shoulders, possibly an inch or two more; and his legs are put on like two toothpicks stuck in opposite sides of a potato. O'Leary's waist, with the aid of a corset, could easily be brought to feminine proportions.

The race leader remained in bed until 03:48 when he was said to, *"spring to his feet as fresh as a lark and after washing and partaking of refreshment stepped from his tent on to the track."* With a nice cushion of 15 miles between him and his rival, the bookies slashed his odds to 1/5.

When Hughes finally emerged from under the canvas at 04:00, he initially limped quite badly, but there was a sense of rejuvenation about him, and as the morning wore on, he made steady improvement. Both men occasionally indulged in a spurt of running, but the exciting spectacle was short lived as O'Leary, although gaining the better of Hughes, re-adopted his familiar walking gait and was eventually passed by his dog-trotting opponent. At 10 a.m. on that second day, the jaded and worn out Hughes, now 18 miles behind O'Leary on a score of 128, left the track for the solace of his tent. The New Yorker by now had stopped drinking milk and was happy to drink beef tea and eat chicken stew well flavoured with onions and potatoes, which was prepared for him by his wife. Joe Goss, his trainer, described his man as having the appetite of an elephant, and that he would eat everything he could get his hands on if given the chance.

The following paragraph from the *Brooklyn Daily Eagle* describes the "Lepper's" character and how he had been observed to carry himself around the track: **He would try to pull himself along if he broke a leg. He is the kind of man who if in fight, if knocked down and held down would begin to chew his adversary's ear. He will never let go; his past record shows this, and he deserves encouragement and sympathy for it, and gets them. Whatever he does will be due in great part to his iron will. He is not built to stand great physical strains; he is not well balanced. It is well known amongst athletes that to exhibit real physical endurance a man must be perfectly well balanced in all parts. Strong lungs will do him little good, unless his limbs are strong enough to carry him through. Head, neck, shoulders, chest, hips, thighs, calves, feet, must fit well together, and belong to each other. Hughes is not this kind of man. In the first place, he is what is described in general terms as "loose-jointed," which is more a habit than anything else. He does not hold himself well together. If he were a horse he would not be put before a stylish carriage. His head hangs down his chest is some inches less than it might have been, although it is still large and his hips are far too narrow. This is one of Hughes' weakest points. His hips would give out, while his chest and lower extremities were still in good condition. His legs are shapely but that is not part of the question– they are fully able to sustain his weight. His calves are marked by several blotches, but they are probably old bruises for he has more sense than to undertake a walk if he were breaking out from bad blood. When he walks the whole upper part of his body leans far forward, so far that the mere lifting of his foot is sufficient to swing the leg forward. It is clear to everybody that he is a runner, not a walker. If he wins the match he must do it by running. He is a remarkable runner.**

Both men were on the track all evening, and although the attendance was smaller than the previous day, they were well entertained by the band who constantly played "My Grandfather's clock," which recalled the fact that while Hughes had been sleeping earlier that day, somebody in the crowd shouted, "Never to go again, when the old man died," – a joke that brought out howls of laughter from his fellow spectators.

The race leader completed his 150th mile in 39h.38m.33s, with Hughes following suit in 45h.35m.53s. When the men stopped for their Tuesday night's rest, Hughes was 28 miles behind O'Leary who waited till the third lap of his 176th to go to his bed at 23:14. Hughes, who went to his hut at 00:07, slept till 04:13 which was 11 minutes after the Chicago man made his reappearance.

On that Wednesday morning, the damp, cold building was not really the most hospitable place to be, whether you were a spectator or a contestant. On the track, both men appeared a little lethargic as they made their way around their respective paths. This was possibly due to the lack of music due to the band's absence, and lack of vocal support from the few that could be bothered to turn up. Very few incidents happened to get anybody excited, apart from Hughes leaving the track at 08:00 for an *"operation"* on one of his legs which was performed by Dr. Craig.

King of the Peds

After it, the physician stated his patient was now in first rate condition and would probably do a little running later that night. Later a smartly dressed lady decided to walk on the track to give O'Leary some advice about his performance. To give him credit, Dan did the gentlemanly thing and paused a while to listen before bowing his appreciation. He then went on to complete his 200th mile in precisely 15 minutes in a time of 58h.7m.20s.

At noon, the champion had made 203 miles. Hughes meanwhile, was completing the fifth lap of his 183rd mile. Despite the 20 miles difference between the pair, the "Lepper's" friends were still pretty confident that under the stewardship of Joe Goss, his trainer, he would ultimately put up a good fight as the race progressed, pinning their faith in his stamina. As the afternoon wore on, it was clear he was getting a great deal of encouragement by seeing his wife and family as they sat outside his tent. At four o'clock, as he ran around his path, his little boy Willie clapped his hands, and shouted, "There goes papa! I know he'll win!"

O'Leary had taken short rests during the afternoon, but his opponent's three breaks were of a much longer duration ranging from thirty minutes to an hour each, the longest stop being 1h.6m at 18:00. As he put his feet up, and enjoyed the company of his family, Hughes tucked into chicken soup. He also, on occasions, drank beef tea and brandy, which was a far cry from the strict milk diet he sustained himself on the opening day. The race leader's diet on the other hand, consisted of oyster stew with finely chopped up onions. Two Catholic clergymen who had visited him earlier in the day, had advised him to drink nothing but champagne in small quantities, and this he did, gulping the fizzy amber liquid at intervals of an hour or so.

The scores below were recorded for both men from the 155th mile to the 240th mile:

	O'LEARY			HUGHES				O'LEARY			HUGHES		
MLS	H	M	S	H	M	S	MLS	H	M	S	H	M	S
155	40	49	56	51	46	51	200	58	7	20	64	15	6
160	42	31	25	53	1	1	205	59	31	45	67	5	9
165	43	43	29	54	10	58	210	60	40	42	68	54	1
170	45	1	3	55	8	58	215	62	14	40			
175	46	7	30	57	17	30	220	63	24	42			
180	52	16	50	58	23	1	225	64	53	37			
185	53	29	43	59	42	58	230	66	47	43			
190	54	44	9	61	31	40	235	67	58	15			
195	56	53	41	63	17	18	240	69	56	49			

During Wednesday, the police had their work cut out in dealing with a group of youths and boys who were trying every which way to steal a glance at the athletes. Their number reached an estimated thousand later in the evening blocking the sidewalks around the building. The *New York Times* revealed how they were dealt with: **Capt. Williams arrived at the scene, in the evening, just in time to see a crowd of several hundred anxiously pushing up toward a hole they had cut through one of the large doors. The Captain approached the crowd with belligerent intentions and with both fists in violent motion. The exact time of knocking down the first 20 was not taken. The Captain then threw his club at the retreating few whom he had knocked over. This ended the disturbance, with no arrests.**

At around 10 p.m., O'Leary was presented with a large bouquet of flowers which he carried around the track several times amid cheering from the crowd. He offered the bouquet to Hughes with a polite bow. The latter accepted them after appearing frightened that O'Leary was about to assault him, but, realising this wasn't the case, took them round the track for a lap himself. Hughes later left for his tent and some sleep at 22:24. At 23:54, O'Leary took himself off the path and headed for his quarters with the knowledge that something would have to go horribly wrong for him to lose his title.

The newspaper reporters commented about the "Lepper's" stockings falling down and told their readers that his shoes were three times too big for him. They suggested he buy some with English style canvas uppers and mocked him by saying he looked as though he was walking about in a couple of *"Whitehall row boats."* Whilst he was being ridiculed, favourable comments were being made about O'Leary's appearance, for example, that his hair was always neat and that he was attired as though he'd just left the dressing room. It was noted that Hughes was observed to be indulging in frequent consumption of alcohol. Indeed, he was overheard saying to his trainer

Joe Goss, "I don't want any of that dollar and a half wine (champagne) but good, cheap American wine, 50 cents a bottle." His comments however, didn't stop his friends from sending him a case of the more expensive version, along with a dozen boxes of condensed meat.

It was reported that Hughes was manoeuvring himself around the track better than he had done, and that he taken fewer breaks and slept less. He was observed to be running well and walking faster. O'Leary, on the other hand, was noticed to have a very slight limp and was showing signs of fatigue. His tiredness might have been partly due to the fact that his trainer Al Smith had allowed his man to drink as much cider as he wished, along with a considerable quantity of claret!

Considering the amount of people in the Garden on Thursday, estimated at 5,000 at any given time, there was very little for the likes of Captain Williams and his police colleagues to do. However, one unfortunate chap, who had far too much to drink, found himself being beaten with a police truncheon about the back and shoulders for running around the track with O'Leary.

At 23:00, O'Leary left the race having made 320 miles and Hughes 279.7, a distance which meant that the leader was nearly 40 miles in the lead. At this time, Hughes was in bed having gone to his quarters at 21:30. Whilst his coach was in the bar, Hughes woke up and told his wife to open one of the bottles of champagne he was given earlier that day. She dutifully did as he asked and he gulped it down. "Ah," he said, "That's the stuff to make one walk! Open me another bottle!" On an empty stomach its effect was predictable and he became rather giddy. Goss was summoned back and prevented his inebriated contestant from performing on the track by forcibly holding him on his bed. After he had calmed down, Goss allowed Hughes out on to the path at 01:12. After 17 minutes, during which time the drunken ped staggered around at less than 2 mph, he was allowed back to his tent where he stayed until 10:04.

O'Leary slept till 04:41. On his reappearance, he appeared bright and fresh. The same couldn't be said for his opponent, who appeared quite sore. Wearing a white shirt, flesh coloured tights and blue silk trunks, which had a heavy gilt fringe around the edge, and which, according to the press, made him look like a circus clown, or a "*hand organ monkey*," he hobbled round throwing his arms about wildly for a couple of laps before disappearing off the track yet again.

Meanwhile, there were rumours circulating that Joe Goss had made arrangements with O'Leary that his man would be instructed to fall. Such talk however, was rubbished by O'Leary's camp. The relationship between Hughes and his trainer was reported to be deteriorating; when Goss tried to enter his tent, he was refused entry and an appeal was made to eject Goss from the building.

The score at noon was: **O'Leary, 339; Hughes, 283:**

The plan for Hughes was for him to stay on the track till his bed-time so as to reduce the gap, but it was expected that by midnight, the leader would be 60 miles in front. At 21:00, he was five miles ahead of that expectation on a score of 365, with his opponent having achieved 300. Hughes went to bed at 21:57 after he had scored another two miles, and O'Leary made another ten miles before he settled down at 23:02.

On the last day, and in front of a constant throng of 7,000 souls, O'Leary continued to dominate the race. Earlier on he had a blister sand-papered off his foot. The "operation" seemed to do him the world of good for he was seen to moving around the track in fine fashion. When O'Leary eventually retired from the track amid enthusiastic cheers and triumphant music, his worn out opponent lay in his room fast asleep, oblivious to the celebrations outside.

The Final Result!

O'Leary, 403; Hughes, 310

King of the Peds

The winner then prepared himself to be presented with a gold medal by Commissioner Thomas S. Brennan at the music stand. On one side of it, the trophy had a figure of a pedestrian surrounded by laurel leaves and the Irish words **Fag au bealac**. On its other side of it were engraved the following words: **"Presented to Daniel O'Leary, the champion long distance walker of the world, by his friends of New York City, Oct. 5. 1878."**

Brennan then made the following speech. "Mr. O'Leary, you have again demonstrated to the world your well established claim to the title of the champion long distance walker of the world. By request of a few of your warm admirers, I have been appointed to present you with this beautiful gold medal. The design is appropriate and emblematic. We sincerely trust that you may live to retain the champion belt, which you have so gallantly won, until every link is inscribed with an additional victory, and that this medal, which I now present you, may serve to remind you of all the well wishes of those who have presented it." The medal was then pinned to his left breast and O'Leary said, "Had I had a better competitor, I could have made more miles, but from the start, I was convinced it was a walk-over. I would have been better satisfied, and so would my friends if Hughes had shown better powers of endurance and better speed. I wish that the only man who ever put me to the top of my speed, Vaughan, of London, had been here, then I could have shown what is possible for me to accomplish."

O'Leary made about $5,000 for his efforts and Hughes about $1,700.

Later that week, Hughes was to appear in court asking for the arrest of his three backers, Murray, Meagher and Deering. He claimed they had persuaded him to believe that O'Leary's friends had conspired to draw all the gate money from the bank in which they said it was deposited, and showed him a paper, which they called an "injunction" to prevent the alleged fraud. As Hughes was illiterate, he made his mark on the document in the presence of witnesses and later learned the document was a power of attorney, which empowered the men to get his money from the proprietors of the Garden whose possession it was in. "They swindled me your Honour," said Hughes, "swindled me out of my heard-earned $1,700. I'm all stoved up. I'm sick. They pizened me milk so that I'd shlape whin I should be walkin', and put all sorts of jobs on me to prevint me bateing that O'Leary. Thin they charged me outrageous in order to cut down me share of the gate money, and thin took advantage of me ignorance and run away wid me share of the gate money." Judge Otterbourg asked him where he lived and Hughes informed him that resided at Eighty Fifth Street and First Avenue. Hughes was informed that he must procure a warrant at the Harlem Police Court. The pedestrian then hobbled out of the court room.

Later the challenges to O'Leary were being written and sent to newspapers in England and America. Here is one.

**10 Pemberton-square,
Boston,
Mass.,
USA**

To the editor of the "Sporting Life"

I hereby challenge Daniel O'Leary, of Chicago, Illinois, U.S.A., to compete with me for £100 a side and the "Astley Belt," which represents the Six Day's Pedestrian Championship of the World. I enclose herewith London exchange for £10, as forfeit. A copy of this letter has been forwarded to O'Leary at Chicago.

CHARLES A. HARRIMAN

CHAPTER 11

Pussy Footing

Astley then sponsored a new competition which was the six-day 'go-as-you-please' "Long Distance Championship of England," race which took place at the Agricultural Hall, London, between Monday, the 28th of October and Saturday, the 2nd of November 1878. The prizes totalling £750, comprised of the "Challenge Belt" valued at £100 plus £500 for the first placed pedestrian, £100 for the second, and £50 for the third. Cash rewards would also be awarded to any competitor making more than 460 miles. The race was also subject to a £10 per entry sweepstakes, and there would be a division of the gate receipts for the best pedestrians.

The conditions of the match would be the same as when O'Leary won the international version of the belt at the same venue earlier in the year, except that all of the contestants would compete on the same seven-lap track. This had been laid out under the direction of John White of Gateshead who, along with the contractors, Messrs. Henry and Wallace of the Caledonian Road Joinery Works, succeeded in producing an *"excellent surface."* The track that the men would walk and run on was 10 feet in width, and was comprised mainly of tan. When resting, the men would have the use of *"comfortably furnished and commodious tents."* These tents were pitched on the north eastern end of the building near a lavatory which was for the sole use of the pedestrians and their attendants. There was a slight problem with their situation however, in that some of the participants would have to walk further to their places of abode as opposed to others. Any arguments about this though were settled by a draw. Interestingly it was the *"Wily Wobbler,"* Weston who won the distinction of having to walk the shortest distance from tent to track. In comparison with the races of the years before, the present accommodation on offer, were *"palaces of luxurious comfort."*

The race judges were: - Mr. G. W. Atkinson and Charles Conquest of the *Sporting Life* and Captain Webb.

The Timekeepers were: - S. Ashbrook, C. Bedford, D. Broad, W. Buchanan, C. Butcher, O. Dowd, H. Green, H. Griffin, T. Griffith, H. Jewell, J. Jewell, W. Mason, F. Richardson, S. Richardson, E. Smith, W. Searle, C. H. Stead, J. R. Sutton, R. Watson, C. Westhall, A. Williams, J. Williams and H. Woods. The Lap scorers were: - H. Andrews, T. Ashbrook, H. W. Barton, J. Boot, J. Buck, D. Edwards, C. Ellison, G. Fenton, T. Harrison, H. Hescott, James Holden, E. C. Holske, D. Isaacs, J. Jerrard, G. Lee, H. Lucas, W. Mellish, W. Perkins, N. Perry, H. Price, H. Shaw-Lucas, T. Sheppard, A. Spalding, R. Stewart, W. Webster, W. White and S. Wisden.

The 23 competitors engaged in the event were:

William Barnett of Leeds: Born in London on October the 8th 1840: Weight 9st.10lb; Height 5ft.5in; Walked 1,200 miles in 18 days at Wellingtown Baths in Leeds: Trained by "Brummy" Meadows of Bow, and attended by J. Read of Poplar.

Henry Brown of Fulham: Born in Fulham in 1843: Weight 9st.7lb; Height 5ft.6in: Since his race in March at the Agricultural Hall, "Blower" had failed to gather 100 stones in 40 minutes for a £5 a side and a "spread" at the Star Grounds, Fulham, on April the 22nd 1878: He was attended to by J. Smith, Snr. and J. White of Gateshead.

William Clarkson of Hull: Born at Oulton near Leeds in 1844: Weight 10st.8lb; Height 5ft.9½in: William, who was a mason by trade, had walked 43 miles in 8 hours, 105 miles in 26 hours, and 332 miles in six days in a 12 hours per day contest at Lincoln in September of 1878: Trained and attended by Robert Smith, Jnr. and George Pickwell, both of Hull.

Arthur Courtney of Barnet: Arthur was born at Islington on July the 4th 1856: Weight 10st.4lb; Height 5ft.9in: He had walked 90 miles in 19 hours, 45 miles in 9½ hours, and 55 miles in 9h.56m. On April the 13th 1876, he beat Arthur Hancock making 28 miles at the Star Grounds, Fulham, and earlier that year on February the 19th, walked 100 miles in 20 hours at the Agricultural Hall. He was trained at Barnet, and in this race, would be attended by Tom Robinson and Mr. E. Isaacs who were both well known promoters of handicaps.

King of the Peds

William Croft of Hull: Was born in 1852: Weight 10st.10lb; Height 5ft.8in: He was a blacksmith by trade. He had beaten both Clifford of York, and Clarkson of Hull, in a 12 hours per day event in his home town, making 295 miles in five days in April of that year. He would be attended by William Chadwell and William Howell, both of Hull, who also trained him.

Peter Crossland of Sheffield: Born in Sheffield on June the 11th 1841? Weight 10st.7lb; Height 5ft.7in: Trained by George Parry from Mr. S. Abrahams the "Nag's Head," Miller Street, Manchester. Peter would be attended by his trainer and William Jones of Manchester.

Samuel Day of Northampton: Born at Kingston-Upon-Thames on September the 17th 1852: Weight 8st.12½lbs; Height 5ft.3½in: His record beginning in June of 1878 reads thus: In a walking match at Northampton against Keeble for £20 a side in a 25 miles race, Sam won by five laps. In the same month in Mr. R. Lewis's tournament at Manchester, in a 14 hours per day contest, he travelled 250 miles and received £5. Then at Lincoln in September he went to compete in a six-day, 12 hours per day contest where he made 335 miles but was beaten by Owen Hancock. For finishing second, he made £10 and was awarded a medal. Then, in a similar event at Hull in October, he received a similar prize, again for finishing runner-up, after scoring 320 miles: He was attended for this match by Joseph Byrnes of Northampton, and Eli Morton of Stratford.

John Ennis of Chicago, Illinois, USA: *"The Hibernian-American"* was born at Richmond Harbour, County Longford, Ireland, on June the 4th 1842: He had lived in Chicago since he was 10 years old. Before that his childhood was principally spent in Greenock, Scotland and Liverpool. Weight 11st.2lb; Height 5ft.8in: Below is an account given by the *Brooklyn Daily Eagle* of his career up to the start of the race: His first public appearance of note (although in 1868 he won & local champion belt, and held it for the required time), was as a pedestrian against O'Leary at Chicago, October 16, 1875, O'Leary gave him 10 miles in 100, for a stake of $1,000; Ennis was compelled to quit after he had made 67 miles. On January 29, 1876, at Chicago, he under took to walk 90 miles in less time than O'Leary covered 100 miles – 18h.53m.43s. In this he succeeded, making the distance in 18h.49m.34s. On May 15 to May 20 following he entered a six-day walk in the same city, but quit early in the race. This walk was won by George Guyon, who placed to his credit 412 miles. In the following winter he gave an exhibition of skating, accomplishing 150 miles in 18h.53m. In 1877 he challenged O'Leary to a 100 mile walk for $500 a side. It was decided November 10, at the Exposition Building, Chicago. O'Leary covered the entire distance; but Ennis broke down by reason of his old stomach trouble. On March 25, 1878, he started at Buffalo to walk 400 miles in 128 hours. Here he broke down again with rheumatism after walking 304 miles in less than five days. He tried the task over again at the same place (Pearl Street Skating Rink), from April 15 to April 20, and accomplished the feat with 9 minutes 34 seconds to spare. In the 36 hour walk for the champion belt, at the Institute Building, May 10 and 11, which was won by Harriman, he was again compelled to pull out, owing to his stomach troubles. On June 6 he took part in a professional walk of 48 hours in the same building. Here he came in third with a record of 142 miles in 46h.21m.35s, George Guyon and W. S. O'Brien leading him. On June 24 he took W. E. Harding into camp in a 100 mile match, for $250 a side, in the same building. From July 15 to July 20 he got a crack at his old antagonist, Guyon, in a six-day walk at Buffalo, for $400 a side, which race he won, scoring 347 miles in 141h.12m.33s. On the first day he covered 100 miles in 20h.20m.28s, and walked 108 miles without rest in 22h.12m.10s. In the same city, September 2 to September 7, for a stake of $800, he covered 422 miles, beating his opponent, Sam Russell, nearly six miles: John was attended by J. De Vere, the celebrated gymnast who was assisted by W. Morris.

William "Corkey" Gentleman of Bethnall Green, London: Born at Bethnall Green in 1833; Weight 7st.6lb; Height 5ft.4in: Trained and attended by Joe Ballam of Bow who used to train Arthur Hancock.

Owen Hancock of Shadwell: Owen was born on the Channel Island of Jersey in 1854: Weight 10st.4lb; Height 5ft.7in: He had walked 50 miles in 8h.25m at Lillie Bridge and beaten Day into second place and Clarkson into third place at Lincoln as described above when he made 350 miles: He was trained by his brother Arthur, the 50-mile champion, who was assisted by McFarlane of his own town.

Joseph Hayward of Billingsgate: Born in Dartford, Kent, on June the 30th 1833: Weight 10st.12lb; Height 5ft.8½in: This was his first appearance in an open competition. He was trained by Jack Hurley of Camberwell and attended by John Snow of the same town.

John Hibberd of Bethnall Green: Born in Wales in 1852: Weight 10st.4lb; Height 5ft.10in: "Jack" was described as a *"splendid walker, and one who will show a great performance, though so far unlucky:"* He was being looked after by Arthur Courtney's team during the race who had trained him.

John Higgins of Hornsey: John was born at Dinton near Aylesbury, Buckinghamshire, in 1852: Weight 9st.7lb; Height 5ft.7½in: He had walked 25 miles in 4h.20m.5s on October the 7th 1878. Other information gleaned about him was that he had run 28 miles in 3h.7m.15s and after that walked a further 8 miles in 1h.4m.25s. He had also apparently made

60 miles in 8 hours. He was trained by James Fincher of Hornsey and attended by Mr. C. Bosher and W. Lutchford of the same town.

John Jackson Holmes of Nottingham: Was born at East Retford on October the 10th 1848: Weight 11st.4lb; Height 5ft.8½in: This was John's first attempt in open competition, though he had made lots of long distances on the open road. Attended by Henry Clark and Samuel Oscroft of his place of abode.

William Howes of London: Had been born at Felthorpe near Norwich on March the 25th 1839: Weight 9st.4lb; Height 5ft.4½in: At the time of the race, "Billy" was described as *"one of the greatest living pedestrians."* He held the 50-mile record. Some of his races up to this date have been described earlier.

George Ide of North Woolwich: George was born at West Wittering near Chichester in 1845: Weight 10st.7lb; Height 5ft.8½in: George has been discussed in races he appeared in previously in Chapters 5, 6 and 9: Attended by his brother C. Ide and Ben Williams both of Woolwich.

G. Pellett (probably **George Pettitt**) of Sittingbourne: Attended by E. Josling of Sittingbourne.

W. H. Richardson of the U.S.A: Was born at Bath, England, in 1851: Weight 8st.9lb; Height 5ft.5½in: Had beaten Walter Lewis twice in pedestrian competitions: Trained at Hoddesdon in Hertfordshire, and attended by G. Freeman of Hertfordshire, and G. Young of Hackney.

Charles Rowell of Cambridge: Weight 10st; Height 5ft.6in: After being beaten by Weston in the exhibition contest at the Agricultural Hall, London, on February 26th, 1876, he was then, according to the *Sporting Life*: Next beaten by P. Speed, of Chesterton, who had 100 yards start in two miles, for £10 a side, near Cambridge, March 5th, 1877. With 60 yards start, won a silver cup in an 880 yards handicap on the University Ground, June 10th, 1878. Beat H. Vandepeer of Sittingbourne, in a six hours contest for £15 a side (time for 32 miles, 4h.) Gore Park, Sittingbourne, October 5th, 1878: Trained and attended by Charles Asplen and Johnny Simpson of Cambridge.

W. H. Smythe of Dublin: Was born on March the 1st 1849 in County Cavan, Ireland: Weight 11st.9lb; Height 5ft.11½in: Apart from walking 2,000 miles in 1,000 hours, he appeared in the 1st Astley Belt contest where he made 175 miles and 4 laps: Attended by C. Smith of Bethnall Green, and Joe Terry of Islington.

Alfred Thatcher of Canning Town: Was born in Surrey on January the 28th 1850: Weight 9st.2lb; Height 5ft.2in: This was Alfred's first appearance in a race of this kind. Attended by H. Thomas of North Woolwich, and John Tucker of Canning Town.

Henry Vaughan of Chester: Born at Chester on August 23rd 1847: (*"Before leaving Chester he scaled, and brought the beam down at 10st.11lb."*) Weight 10st.7lb; Height 5ft.11½in: Attended by Bill Lang and John Snell of Salford. All his races up to date have been described earlier.

Edward Payson Weston: Needs no introduction! Weight 10st; Height 5ft.7½in:

N.B: Although "Lepper" Hughes had sent in a £10 entry fee to compete in the race, he was named a doubtful starter in the *Sporting Life* a couple of days before the event started.

Four days before the "off," Vaughan and Weston were the two "jollies" to win the race at 2/1. The rest could be backed at prices of 6/1 and higher. However, at the start of the race, "Corkey" had been popular with the punters and as a consequence his odds had been tightened in the market to 5/1.

The race, which started at 01:05, was witnessed by a large company of people, which included Astley, his wife, and Lord Francis Lennox. Brown led the first mile in 7m.43s followed by Vaughan, Rowell, Crossland and Ide. Brown continued to lead the men round at the hour stage, his record showing 7.2, with Rowell half a lap behind, and Vaughan a mile and a half away or so in third. The positions, which remained the same for the second hour, stayed that way at the fifth hour, when the Fulham man registered 26.6 in the books, with Rowell three laps in his wake.

The spectators started to drift into the building when the gates officially opened early the next morning, and the men were watched with enthusiasm as they made their respective ways round. There was no change in the positions of the first three as the score of the first nine at noon suggests: **Brown, 64.2; Rowell, 63; Vaughan, 62.5; Crossland and Hancock, 57.6; Weston, 57.3; Ide, 57.1; Corkey, 56.2; Day, 55.2:**

King of the Peds

As the attendance improved thereafter, Smythe was the first man to take a break on a score of 44 miles at about 1 o'clock. While he rested, Weston entertained and amused the crowd with his eccentric antics. Vaughan went on to pass Rowell at three o'clock, and along with Ide and Hibberd, put in some 11-minute miles amid some loud cheering.

Brown was the first to make 100 miles and his effort was noisily received from many of the 10,000 spectators that had passed through the turnstiles that day at 18:59. His time for the century was the fastest on record (17h.54m.14s). Rowell was the next man to accomplish that score at 19:55 followed by Corkey in a time of 19h.28m.50s. Vaughan completed the same task later matched by the fast improving Crossland, and then Weston. Brown went to bed after scoring 111 miles leaving Crossland to plug on to take a decisive lead and score 117 miles at 23:44. By making that amount, the "Sharp Sheffield Blade" had equalled O'Leary's record for the same time.

By the end of 24 hours, the scores were: **Crossland, 117; Corkey, 114; Vaughan, 112.6; Brown, 111.3; Rowell, 106.3; Barnett, 103.5; Weston, 101.1; Hancock, 100; Croft, 99.6; Howes, 94.6; Pellet, 94; Hibberd, 92.2; (No lap scores for the following) Courtney and Richardson, 91; Ennis and Higgins, 90; Ide, 89; Hayward, 85; Clarkson, 79; Day, 77; Homes, 70 (Retired); Smythe and Thatcher, 56:**

There was ding-dong battle for first place during the early morning hours between Corkey, who gained the upper hand at 2 o'clock, and Crossland who regained the lead at 04:00. Corkey however, went past the race leader while he rested. Word got around that there was a really good race going on at the "Aggie," and as soon at the public were admitted to the building at 06:00, large numbers were flocking in to watch the sport. At 08:50, Corkey made 150 miles, but was soon passed again by Crossland who led the men at the 36-hour stage of the race at noon, the scores at the time being: **Crossland, 160.6; Corkey, 160.3; Brown, 153.4; Vaughan, 152.7; Rowell, 146.1; Weston, 135.1; Barnett, 134.5; Howes, 132.6; Croft and Hancock, 130:**

With Weston entertaining the crowd by indulging *"in a lot of buffoonery on the track,"* the scores of the leading six at 16:00 showed that Corkey was in front of Crossland, who had been taking a break, by 2 miles and a lap. Brown led Vaughan by seven yards, both showing 169 and 5, and Rowell was ten miles behind them, with Weston, despite his antics, managing a respectable 149.

Later there was little change, except with Crossland resting for an hour; Corkey remained in the lead which he hung on to until he departed to indulge in one himself at 20:53. Whilst he was away, both Brown and Crossland caught him up, and as the contest between the leading three heated up, it was Corkey who turned out to be the first man to score 200 at 22:40. Brown, on his heels, registered the same mark two minutes later, with Crossland making his second ton six minutes after him.

As usual the band played "God Save the Queen" to remind the crowd that their time was up and they all had to go home. Very few were in the building when the scores were hoisted at the end of 48 hours, these being: **Corkey, 201.2; Brown and Crossland, 200; Vaughan, 195; Hibberd, 183.6; Weston, 183; Howes, 170; Croft, 169.6; Ennis, 168.6; Rowell, 167.4; Courtney, 162.2; Ide, Hancock and Richardson, 160; Barnett, 156; Pellet, 155.6; Clarkson, 155; Higgins, 151.6; Day, 150.4; Smythe, 127.1; Hayward, 105; Thatcher, 87:**

The hall, as usual, was empty in the small hours of the third day when Corkey, who had come back on at 01:37, went into a six-mile lead over his rivals as the clock struck three. The rumours that had been going around that Vaughan had aggravated the sprained ankle that he'd received in training as he tried to avoid colliding with a dog, proved correct. The expected announcement that he would retire from the contest was made at 03:36 after making a lap short of 201 miles. This was a tragic state of affairs for his trainer and his team who had fastidiously prepared him for the contest.

It was absolutely freezing both inside and outside the building, but that said, the men going about their business on the track didn't notice it half as much as the few that sat officiating. The reporter covering the race for the *Sporting Life* put his slant on the chilly atmosphere: **Slowly the still, chill hours wore away, the peds pursuing their endless rounds under the most depressing circumstances, with no spectators of their efforts but the shivering officials, who, cold as charity, and almost too numbed to make a mark, stuck to their figuring till the meagre light of the few gas burners gave way to the scarcely less sickly illumination of a sun striving to make itself visible through rain and fog. More miserable work than this walking, when the attendants even are taking a nap, or those on duty** are huddled around the fire, can hardly be imagined. The nerves get so upset, what with the strain, caused by doing so much work with so little rest, and the grim ghastly, ghostly appearance of the hall, that if any practical joker were to call out "bogey" it is not long odds against a general stampede clearing the place. The devices of the lap scorers to keep up circulation were various and many - one gentleman in particular has taken to himself at night, undercoat, great-coat, and ulster, with as much newspaper as he tied on with string. It only shows how desperate a man may become, for the gentleman in question, though connected, with a high-class but thin journal, has regardless of the fact that he advertises opposition newspapers, gone in only for the heavier but thicker, and therefore warmer high priced organs. As for the telegraph men, they are better off, as they can do as the publican told the mutes who were waiting outside his house in the snow and east wind for the funeral to start, and wanted something to keep out the cold - they are at liberty to jump about and keep themselves warm.

By 6 a.m., Brown had fought back and managed to reduce the gap by 4 miles, the scores at that time showing: **Corkey, 218.2; Brown, 216.5; Crossland, 212:** Vaughan's score of 200.6 was soon overtaken by Weston at 08:00, and as ten o'clock drew closer, Brown had caught up his fellow Londoner. Both he and Corkey were now on equal terms of 233.3 at 10:00. Brown thereafter slowly began to dominate, and by midday, he had put a mile and a quarter between him and his nearest rival, who, at that time had made 244 miles; the front pair both enjoying their comfortable cushion over the third placed "Tyke" who was on 232. The front two then went on to thrill the crowd by swapping positions for the lead on no less than three occasions before six o'clock in the evening when Brown led the race on a score of 262.5 to his fellow Londoners 259.5, the rest of the positions being relatively unchanged.

Reports indicate later that the gas lights were relit after an attempt had been made to illuminate the building with an electric (magnesium) light which was turned on at 21:15. The spectators however, complained that this was unsuitable, and there was general frustration that they couldn't see the peds in action as the contraption flickered, offering bright light one second followed by nothingness the next. Those peds included Weston who hardly left the track, Clarkson and Hibberd, who were putting in their best efforts of the day, Croft walking well, Day, lame but nevertheless raising his score appreciably, Howes, producing the occasional spurt, and Smythe, Thatcher and Ennis, making reasonable gain. Of the new floodlighting system, the *Sporting Life* quipped: **Were this method of illumination the only one shareholders in gas companies have to fear there would not be much reason for the fall in the companies shares. Should this jerky, jumping, dodging illuminator ever be generally adopted, the opticians should present the inventor with a handsome testimonial.**

The 11 p.m. scores: **Corkey, 289.5; Brown, 284; Crossland, 269.2; Weston, 260; Rowell, 255; Hibberd, 253.6; Croft, 239.6; Howes, 236.2; Courtney and Ennis, 230; Higgins, 229; Ide, 220:**

Corkey managed to extend his lead to almost 12 miles by the time he completed his 300th mile at 04:18. Whilst Thatcher retired permanently at 04:57 the race leader went on to increase his lead to 13 miles before the gap was reduced back to eight by 08:00, and then by five at 09:00, after which, Brown made a concerted effort to reduce the deficit.

Of the others, Weston's chances of victory were slowly evaporating, his supporters conceding that their man would need a miracle to win as he was 36 miles behind the leading players at that time. Indeed, Rowell had taken his fourth place, and matters looked hopeless for the American. Hibberd was said to be walking along in the best style, and of Ennis, *The Times* reporter wrote that he looked like *"O'Leary in appearance,"* and, *"pursues the even tenor of his way in a manner that would have charmed the old school of pedestrians."* Owen Hancock, who had been well supported on the first day, was said to be suffering from blistered feet which he had procured the day before, thus ending any chance he hoped for; and Sam Day *"from Birmingham"* was said to be showing a determined effort. With Crossland, who was showing evident signs of fatigue due to hip trouble now losing ground on a score of 297.1, the state of play at noon showed Corkey on 331 miles, five ahead of Brown.

Corkey's lead was further reduced to just three miles by 17:00, and that may have been partly due to the fact that he had changed his footwear from a pair of boots to *"running shoes"* earlier that morning. As time wore on, and as the turnstiles clicked, clicked, clicked away with persistent regularity, the place began to fill up. At 20:00, there were about 10,000 people inside and outside the track, many stretching their necks to and fro, all eager to see the colourful spectacle they had paid their "bobs" to watch, and in some parts of the building, like the enclosure, a hell of a lot more. At that time, the two London men, who were streets ahead of the rest, continued to be separated

King of the Peds

by just three miles. Weston at the time, and due to some fast walking, had moved himself into third place but he was still 30 miles behind "Blower." The "Walkist" had proved popular at this event with the crowd. Always ready to have a joke with them and the scorers, he was in his element whilst being repeatedly applauded as he strode around the place. Accolade to Weston was like a drug which only served to inflate his already bloated ego. If only he would just concentrate on the job in hand – really concentrate, without all the unnecessary diversions he made for himself, he might have been the race leader by then, but that wasn't his style was it?

Meanwhile, the others got on with the job. Clarkson, when he wasn't suffering with cramp, moved well. Croft, even with a bad cold, managed to pile on many a mile. Day showed guts as he hobbled when he wobbled. Howes took on Weston in a battle to be the quickest walker on the track, and won - just! He then set his sights on Brown and ran; "Blower" enjoying the company. Whilst Ide *"persevered,"* and Barnett, Courtney, Hibberd and Smythe struggled, both Rowell and the muscular wiry frame of *"Pellet"* went along gamely.

With the estimated 13,000 spectators being shown the door for the night at 11 p.m., the building reverted from a bustling noisy place of entertainment to the dreariest place in Islington within minutes.

The scores at the end of four days (96 hours) were: **Corkey, 372.5; Brown, 368; Weston, 337; Hibberd, 329; Rowell, 325.3; Crossland, 308.3; Courtney, 300; Howes, 295; Ennis, 293; Richardson, 278; Croft, 274; Day, 270:**

It was a *"cold and cheerless night"* for the pedestrians who stayed on the track, and many of those not remotely interested in finishing in the top half dozen spent much time on their beds. Many of the top six however couldn't afford the luxury of too much time between the sheets, and their rest periods were limited. Corkey rested 2h.30m, Brown, 3h.27m, Rowell, 4h.15m, and Hibberd, Ennis and Hancock, 5 hours each. Corkey made his fourth hundred at 09:27, and Brown celebrated the same score an hour or so later. At 09:45, Rowell announced his intention of running 50 miles non stop. At the time he was about 9 miles behind Hibberd, and as he indulged in that method of conveyance, the two race leaders decided to follow suit. For many a mile thereafter, the ex-boatman was followed in this fashion until the two Londoners both reverted to the more sedate pace of walking, thus leaving Rowell to continue to run.

Weston meanwhile had a good excuse for not putting any more pressure on himself to catch the rest, as it was soon clear that he would be going nowhere, a swollen ankle spoiling his chances of any prize money. He left the track at 13:30: By three o'clock, Corkey, who was "two to one" to win the contest, led Brown by 427 to 422, with Rowell now in third spot on 377. Hibberd, who had occupied that position earlier at 10 o'clock when he was 9 miles in front of *"the waterman,"* was now in fourth place on a score of 374, having been passed by Rowell at 13:33. The ex-sculler, who was described at the time as has having *"the most strongly made legs from the hips downwards,"* had run continuously for 25 miles before walking a lap. He then carried on with his speedier gait to make a further 11 miles, after which he settled down to a walking pace too. Rowell's reluctance to go any faster meant that at 17:00 he maintained the four miles advantage between him and Hibberd when their scores showed 382.6 to 382.1.

By 19:20, the diminutive figure of one "William Gentleman," described as one of the *"feathers"* in the race, had made a distance of 73 miles since 02:19. Of his performance, the *Sporting Life* commented: His light weight is all in his favour, as he seems to be able to trot without causing himself the jarring sensation which disables all the heavy men. Win, lose or draw, the little man is a wonder. As for muscle, there is no room for it on him. His bones are hardly covered with flesh, and if he has any digestive organs, they must be stowed away somewhere at the back of his head, for his heart is so big that it must take up all the space inside his ribs.

There was an estimated 3,000 more people in the building that evening watching the men struggle for dominance. What was noticeable, was that both the centre enclosure with an admission price of 5 shillings, and the reserved stands costing "two and three," were now full, an indication that the "toff's" were in town and enjoying the spectacle as much as those who had paid their shilling to stand. At 10 p.m., Corkey was still at the top of the parapet looking down on at his main rival, from a distance of almost six miles (456.1 to 450.6), and because they were enjoying the "big match" so much, the crowd was reluctant to leave an hour later at "chucking out time."

The scores at the end of the fifth day, with just Rowell and Courtney plodding around were: **Corkey, 457.5; Brown, 450; Rowell, 406.1; Hibberd, 391; Weston, 365.1; (Retired to join the rest of the *"hospital corps"*)**

Courtney, 360.4; Ennis, 360; Howes, 338.1; Day, 335.3; Richardson, 334; Croft, 329.6; Crossland, 320; Ide, 315; Clarkson and Pellet, 305; Hancock, 300; Higgins, 283.5; Barnett, 247; Smythe, 223:

"Blower" was the first man to appear on the track on the last day of the contest, and to protect his eight-mile lead, the *"Bethnall Green wonder"* joined him on the path ten minutes later at 02:35. During the night, the race leader increased the gap between himself and Brown, and by 09:00, had made that gap 15 miles. Despite Brown's brave attempts to reel him in, Corky repelled everything that was thrown at him, and at 13:55 he passed the 500-mile mark. As, at this point he was 5 miles ahead of O'Leary's March time of the same year, there was talk amongst the ever swelling crowd that Corkey might just make a new world record. With very little to entertain the huge crowd on the track, Billy Howes set off to make six and a half miles in one hour, and succeeded in his task with well over seven minutes to spare in a time of 52m.29s. His effort was greeted with the utmost enthusiasm, as was Rowell's attempt to catch up Brown as he ran at a good pace for a mile or two.

Brown made his 500th mile at 18:36, and after that milestone was clinched, it was left to Corkey to satisfy the crowd's thirst to see a new record. At 19:03, the race leader, who by that stage had made 520 miles and 2 laps, thus beating O'Leary's record by 1h.5m.49s, left the track. He rested for a short while and re-appeared attired in a primrose silk costume, and green and white hat carrying a silken flag. *"In this peculiar costume, attended by some of the judges, and several of his less successful competitors, Corkey walked five times round the track, and completed his 521 miles, the band meanwhile playing the "Union Jack of Old England," and "See the Conquering Hero Comes."*

The Result!

Pos		Miles	Laps	Pos		Miles	Laps
1	**Corkey**	**521**	**3**	11	Weston	365	1
2	Brown	506	1	12	Clarkson	357	0
3	Rowell	470	1	13	Ide	355	5
4	Hibberd	440	0	14	Pellet	339	0
5	Ennis	410	2	15	Crossland	335	0
6	Courtney	405	0	16	Hancock	324	6
7	Day	400	1	17	Higgins	302	4
8	Richardson	380	0	18	Barnett	235	4
9	Croft	370	5	19	Smythe	223	3
10	Howes	370	4				

As he walked round with his wife, (who had been given a new bonnet by Sir John Astley), the "little fella," when asked how he felt after having hardly slept for six days, simply replied, "A bit dazed like." There was said to be much enthusiasm amongst the 20,000, *"more or less,"* crowd who were present at the end to witness the closing scenes. Brown took second prize money of £100 and Rowell took home the third prize of £50. The contest was terminated at 10.30 p.m.

King of the Peds

William "Corkey" Gentleman completed the match with a score of 521 miles and 503 yards in a time of 139 hours, which was a new world record distance.

© *The British Library. All Rights reserved. The Penny Illustrated. (Illustration no: 28)*

Astley in his book, *Fifty Years of my Life* said of the race: **I will here put in one more balance-sheet, which shows the receipts were not quite so good, and the expenses were heavier; but the lighting of the hall and the accommodation for the competitors was superior. The winner, Corkey, was a very quaint-looking little old chap, of forty-six: he had won a lot of running matches in his time, and had very peculiar high action. He didn't look a bit like staying, was as thin as a rail, and stuttered very funnily; but in Mrs. Corkey he possessed a real treasure. She never left him day or night and was always ready to hand her sweetheart a basin of delicious and greasy eel-broth, that he loved so well, and which evidently agreed so famously with him. Towards the last, when it was evident Corkey could not be caught, I ordered a lovely suit for him to finish in, and bought Mrs. Corkey an out-and-out bonnet, slightly on the gaudy side; but I can tell you he and she were a striking couple when they did the last few laps arm in arm together, to the tune of the Conquering Hero.'**

P. S. Marshall

BALANCE SHEET

RECEIPTS.

	£	s	d	£	s	d
By Gate						
Monday	317	5	1			
Tuesday	275	14	6			
Wednesday	343	4	0			
Thursday	406	19	0			
Friday	674	10	6			
Saturday	829	5	10			
	2,846	18	11			
Less Banker's Commission	2	12	6			
				2,844	6	5
By Entries				211	0	0
By Burt for 'Right of Sale' of Programmes				31	0	0
By Baker for Standing of Lung-Testing Machine				2	0	0
Total				3,088	6	5

EXPENDITURE.

	£	s	d
Prizes to Winners and Attendants at Conclusion of Walk	867	0	0
Extra Money Prizes	406	0	0
Belt and Medals	130	0	0
Hire of Hall	400	0	0
Gas and Electric Light	125	16	0
Contractor's Work for Track, Stands &c.	109	2	0
Accommodation for Men	40	15	2
Gate-Keepers, Commissionaires, Police	133	3	0
Judges and Scorers	274	0	0
Band	60	0	0
Printing, Advertising &c.	91	0	0
Staff, Messengers &c.	111	18	2
	2,748	14	4
Balance towards Fund	339	12	1
Total	3,088	6	5

CHAPTER 12

Questionable "Sport?"

On Monday, November the 11th 1878, at Bridgeport, Connecticut, Peter Napoleon Campana, alias "Young Sport," the Bridgeport amateur pedestrian, set off at midnight in an attempt to beat O'Leary's London record of 520¼ miles on a 14 laps to the mile track at Hubbell's Hall. The *New York Times* described the venue as: Probably the worst place that anybody ever undertook to walk in. It is on the top floor of Hubbell's brick block a large five-storey mercantile building with so many windows on every side that it could have taken very few bricks to build it. The track follows the walls of the room, except at the corners, where it is slightly rounded and is 158 feet long on its longest sides. It is about four feet wide, and was made by nailing a strip of wood an inch and a half high parallel with the walls, four feet in toward the centre, and filling in the space with sawdust. The hall has heretofore been used only for dancing, and the floor is slippery with wax. The sawdust slides about over this wax with almost every step that is taken on it, and the track is full of bare places the waxed floor showing through where the sawdust has been shoved off. Besides this, the building is not, to say the least more than ordinarily substantial, and the floor gives slightly with every step, a terrible strain in a long walk. The room is very peculiar in shape. About 150 feet long, it is not more than 12 feet wide, and overhead is divided about equally into two sections. The ceiling over one half of the room is flat and not more than 7 feet high. A tall man with a silk hat would almost have to stoop to walk under it. At the other end the ceiling slants, being about 7 feet high at the lowest point, and a few inches less than 10 feet at the highest. In walking from the highest part under the lower ceiling, there is a highly unpleasant feeling, as of want of air a sensation that must be very detrimental to the well being of a pedestrian. A great brick chimney runs up through the ceiling, exactly through the centre of the room. The hall holds not less than 700 or 800 people, sitting and standing, and it is nearly full all the time, the admission being 25 cents. There are several signs of "No smoking," but nearly everybody smokes, and with the tobacco smoke, 700 breaths and the wet sawdust, going into the room from the outer air is like going into a menagerie or a big stable.

Campana had probably always fancied himself as a potential professional pedestrian and may have watched others as they competed for glory. He started to train himself with the objective of being up there with the best, and one day was said to walk to Danbury and back; a distance of 48 miles in 12 hours. On another occasion he walked to New Haven and back, and then beat the milk train from Waterbury to Bridgeport, a distance of 40 miles, prompting the comment *"which may show either that he is a fast walker or the milk train is short winded."*

For this event he employed the services of Sam Merritt, who had proved himself locally as both a runner and walker, and his personal physician Dr. T. F. Martin. The quarters provided for him was a small private room with a bed on the floor which was filled with liniment bottles and lemons.

On the first day of his attempt, he made his half century in 6h.55m (39th mile in 6m.14s) and his first century in 17h.53s, the distance being made in a pair of shoes that didn't fit him. After changing his footwear to slippers, he thereafter went on to make 125 miles at 23:45 (that mile being accomplished in 7m exactly). On the second day, Tuesday, at 06:30, he had scored 150 miles, and later that afternoon, achieved his second ton at 17:32. On Wednesday, the 250 miles mark was reached at 07:00 and he made his third hundred at 16:18 in a time of 6m.32s. That night he retired from the track at 22:15 having scored 325 miles. At this stage, he was 30 miles ahead of O'Leary's London record for the first three days. He apparently insisted upon making another 25 miles before he went to bed, but was advised by his friends not to do so and quit the track.

He resumed his task at 02:20 on Thursday morning and was observed to have been increasing his lead throughout the day. At 07:03, he had completed 350 miles, and at 09:30, 360 miles. He was reportedly *"astonishing professionals"* in the sport, *"by his pace and endurance,"* and his efforts at the time were attracting much interest in that city, and, as a consequence, drawing in large crowds. Although he was said to be in good condition that morning, he nevertheless complained of a soreness extending from his right knee to the foot, due to slipping on the track whilst making a spurt. Campana, who claimed the injury affecting the chords in his ankle wouldn't hinder him in his objective to beat the record, settled down to a dog-trot, a gait with which he felt comfortable. He told the press that he would "do it or die on the track," and satisfied his appetite with a few white grapes, figs and sips of lemonade.

At 12:20, he had made 370 miles, and later in the afternoon, was presented with a *"handsome pedestrian suit"* purchased for him in New York by his friends. 390 miles were recorded at 17:45, and at 20:05, he had amassed 397, the last mile being made in 8m.20s. After making his 402nd mile at 22:00, he rested till 01:40 and resumed his trek. By 12:30 on the fifth day he made 443 miles, and by 20:00 had scored 466 making him 12½ miles ahead of O'Leary's record for the same time.

Campana's remarkable effort was now making headlines in the press, in particular, in New York, where the story was appearing on the front pages. With so much being reported on the outcome, interest was naturally increasing in him and reporters were falling over themselves to get to know more about the man himself.

The *New York Times* enlightened its readers about "Young Sport," his life up to this point, what he looked like, and then gave them some insight how he conveyed himself around the track: **Napoleon Campana, 43 years old**, one of the kind a men who soon made themselves known and felt in any community, was fired by a recent pedestrian match in this city, and determined to undertake a walk himself. He came to this country from France when he was very young and was always interested in athletic sports and soon won for himself the name of "Young Sport." He lived for some time in New York and Philadelphia. In New York he was a member of the Volunteer Fire Department, and was one of the "Fulton Market Boys." When he was young in New York he was a newsboy, and sold the morning papers. About 15 years ago he came to Bridgeport and ever since worked hard for a living going about at times with a peddler's wagon selling nuts and fruit, and at other times keeping a corner peanut stand. He soon became known in Bridgeport as an expert and fearless fireman, and did good service at several large fires. He was always a fast runner, and was noted for his courage and promptness of action in time of danger. He entered the New York Fire Department when quite young as a signal boy for hose Company No. 29. He next joined hose Company No. 2, and signaled his connection with the company by saving the life of a woman at a fire.

About three years ago he stopped a runaway team in East Main Street, East Bridgeport, saving several lives that were in imminent danger, and was severely injured. For this he was rewarded with a handsome gold medal and was presented with a new peddler's wagon, in which he afterward carted about his fruit. The act was one involving so much danger, and one requiring such perfect fearlessness, that a more substantial testimonial was soon given him in the form of a ball. The new peddler's wagon was put in the ball-room and the ball was one of the largest ever given in this city, with highly satisfactory, results to Campana's pockets. He is free with his money when he has any as young as he was 20 years ago, and a great favorite with the young men and boys of Bridgeport.

He went to Philadelphia and challenged the whole Fire Department of that city to run a half mile race. The challenge was accepted by members of three companies and the race took place in the National Circus Building. In this Campana was victorious in 2:30. In 1860 he ran a ten mile race with "Indian Smith" at Powlton Fair Grounds. Smith was a noted runner, but Campana beat him by 1 second; time, 57:26. Within the next few years he ran a number of races among them a 3-mile race at Herring Run Course, Baltimore, in 14:45 and a race against time at Pittsburgh in which he ran 10 miles in 58:30. At Fort Tompkins parade ground he beat William Tell in a half mile race for $10, and soon after beat Amos Saunders of Brooklyn in a two mile race for $50. He won the next race with Matt Cassidy, distance one mile. In his next one mile race he was defeated by Lynbrook, at Lynn, Mass., where the race took place. He at once challenged all New England for a five-mile race and a belt. Five competitors responded. The race took place at Providence, R.I., and was won by Campana. Soon after that one he walked an informal match with Weston at Pembroke Grove, in this city during which the latter claimed that sport had crowned him too hard, and left the track.

Campana looks, in the face, very much like Weston. He might almost be mistaken for Weston. He has the same wrinkles over his face, the same general features, and the same troubled expression; but he is a little larger than the better known pedestrian. He is about five feet eight inches high, very muscular and broader than Weston across the shoulders but smaller around the waist. He has a very slouching gait, not so bad as Hughes but without any of the style or grace of O'Leary. He carries his head usually either thrown away back on his shoulders or drooping lazily down on his breast. He makes an unpleasant jerky motion of both shoulders with each step, and could not by any means be considered a walker. His most natural gait, apparently, is a little dog-trot of from five to six miles an hour, and this is his favorite method of getting along. Sometimes he breaks into a fast run, and occasionally he walks along very slowly. He does not look as old as he is but his remarkable costume has something to do with his youthful appearance.

During the event Campana had attracted much interest, not just for his athletic abilities, but also for his eccentricity. Those paying the admission fee, of which half went to the pedestrian, would have been given the chance of buying a photograph of him at 50 cents a piece. They would have watched him run around the place followed occasionally by one of the three small dogs he kept near the track, which he patently loved to bits. The story goes that just before he commenced on his challenge to O'Leary's record, one of the city's best known citizens kicked one of the dogs. That wasn't a very good idea, because when Campana knew of it, he punched the offender, giving him a black eye. On the penultimate day it was said that he had refuse to race at one stage unless a mirror was hung up, so that he could see himself. At many stages during the event, he was accompanied by someone else on the track to keep his interest up; these people usually being his attendants. On three evenings during the week he had been encouraged by tunes played by a drum corps which must have boosted his morale.

Campana's plucky effort was too good to be true, and there were suspicions something was amiss. A few weeks before the event took place, a 100-mile pedestrian match was held in the same building, between two men called Moore and Laws. The track was measured and it was declared that 14 laps made a mile. The men finished their race and nobody blinked an eyelid about the result. However, and because Campana was attracting so much attention, some prominent citizens in the city of Bridgeport employed the services of the city surveyor Mr. H. G. Schofield and his assistant John P. Bogart to measure the track. They found it to be 18 inches inside the inner edge and $336\,^{3}/_{10}$ feet long, thus requiring it to be traversed $15\,^{5}/_{8}$ laps before a mile could be accurately claimed.

On the last day, Saturday, November the 16th, he went as he pleased around the hall, wearing a red flannel shirt and a matching silk handkerchief wrapped around his neck, beneath a white suit of which his trousers reached his knees. On his head, he wore a blue baseball cap. At 10:30, his score was 521 miles, but because the track was short he still had 10 hours to make the 55 miles to make the record.

Dr. Martin checked his patient over at 15:00 after he had made 497 miles and recorded his pulse at 82. He informed reporters that although Campana's feet were in excellent condition he was suffering from a swollen knee, sore legs probably due to varicose veins, and that he had taken only 10 hours sleep since the start. Of his diet they were informed he had sustained himself on beef tea, toast dipped in the liquid, bread, milk and tea; a poor diet which may have contributed to him suffering from a chill in the upper part of his body. What was more remarkable than anything was the knowledge that the pedestrian was competing wearing a truss which supported two ruptures; one small, one large on either side of his body. He was frequently observed as he walked and ran along adjusting the aid.

"Sport," as he was affectionately known by the people who knew him, altered his gait constantly on the last afternoon, varying from a walk to his more favoured dog-trot, and then to a run. On he went piling up the miles. The news of his impending record-breaking feat spread around the town like wildfire, causing thousands to block the streets around the overcrowded building. On the track at 21:00, he completed his 519th mile and was now but two miles away from glory. *"He was then running along gaily, as if he was just starting, and kicking up his heels like a schoolboy. The crowd was so great that he barely had room to go around, the wall being lined with people all around the building."* Then at 21:39 having completed 521 miles and 54 feet, he was informed that he had broken the old record by three quarters of a mile. *"The crowd cheered him until the walls shook."* He was subsequently handed a number of bouquets before being carried to his room and put to bed. At the end, Campana's appearance indicated that, *"he could have kept on all night. He did not touch liquor during the whole week."* Thirty-seven of the miles he had made had been accomplished since 14:00 and nearly all of them were made whilst running, with one mile being scored in 7m.33s.

Campana made about $500 from admission fees and photograph sales during his trial. He used some of the money to buy himself a brand new suit which he doubtless wore, when on Monday, the 18th, he went to New York seeking out the services of Shook and Palmer to manage a walk for him in the city. He also called on Edward Gilmore, who told him that he was prepared to give a prize of $2,500 to be divided amongst the first two in the race, providing that the runner-up made 450 miles. Gilmore told Campana that he would only consider sponsoring the race providing he and O'Leary competed, but that the race should also be open to all comers. He also told him that he would keep the gate money.

On November the 25th, Daniel O'Leary stopped at the Metropolitan Hotel on his way to Philadelphia, where he was set to walk at the Horticultural Hall in a 400-mile event against time on Monday, the 2nd of December, fully expecting to accomplish the feat in four days. Before he left for Philadelphia on the Tuesday, he gave an interview to the *New York Times*.

O'Leary: "My principal reason for coming on was to get up with Campana. I never saw 'Sport,' but, from the accounts I have read concerning him, he must be a good man. I am ready to bet $2,500 against $2,000 that I can beat him on a six-day walk and run, or trot as they call it. I have seen none of his friends yet. Al Smith, who is at the Gilsey House, is ready to put up the money. He left it at the rooms of Kelly & Bliss last week. I owe New York a good performance and if Sport comes to the front I will give him a chance to stretch his legs."

Reporter: "Can you beat the record he claims to have made?"

O'Leary: "I am willing to wager $2,000 against $3,000 that I will walk 540 miles in 144 hours walking a fair heel-and-toe walk. Of course, the odds are against me."

Reporter: "When does the next contest for the possession of the Astley Champion Belt come off?"

O'Leary: "'Blower' Brown wants the match in February. I have till May 23 to accept, under the Astley rules but I shall accept before that time. Corkey and I have come to no terms yet. He has put up only £10, which is a very small forfeit in a match for £100. I do not propose to walk this match in London, and his offer to pay my expenses there will not cause me to change my resolution. I will hold the belt here as a United States trophy if I can. No one paid my expenses when I won it, and I don't want my expenses paid now. Several pedestrians will engage in the match, and all can chip in and walk together on the same track. It is possible that Harriman of Boston, Guyon, of Milwaukee, and Schmehl of Chicago will enter. I have the right to name the ground and will take them to San Francisco or to Australia if I desire, but, of course, I will take them to the place that suits them best, which will be either Chicago or New York, probably the latter. I am more anxious to meet the Englishmen on account or their good record, than any man in this country. I think Vaughan when in condition, is the best pedestrian in England."

Reporter: "Have you seen your opponent in your late walk at Gilmore's Garden?"

O'Leary: "Oh, yes several times. Myself and Al Smith called on Hughes today. He keeps a place in Twenty Seventh Street, near Gilmore's Garden. He said nothing about walking. He was very friendly. He say's he will run any man in America 20 miles for $500."

Reporter: "You are not accustomed to train before walking?"

O'Leary: "I have never trained regularly for any match, but always took considerable exercise in advance. In my next contest with the Englishmen I shall train and get myself in the best possible condition to be able to make an extraordinary performance. I don't intend to let the belt leave my hands."

Campana used his new suit along with his rather unique personality, to woo a new lady in his life, and they were duly married a week before he was due to challenge O'Leary at Gilmore's Garden between Monday, the 23rd and Saturday, the 28th of December 1878. Articles of agreement had already been signed and stated:

King of the Peds

This agreement, made the 12th day or December, 1878, witnesseth:

That Daniel O'Leary of Chicago, Ill., and P. Napoleon Campana, of Bridgeport, Conn., agree to a six-day pedestrian race, - 142 hours, to commence at 1 o'clock on Monday morning Dec. 23, 1878, and terminate Saturday night at 11 o'clock, to "go-as-they-please," under the rules governing the tournament for championship of the world held by Sir John Astley at Agricultural Hall, London, a copy of which is annexed. The race to take place at the Hippodrome, New York and to be for $2,000, - $1,000 a side which has been deposited with *Wilkes Spirit of the Times***, and either party failing to start will forfeit his stake. It is further agreed that the expenses entailed - namely, rent, printing, advertising etc., etc., - shall be equally contributed by both parties, and those sums shall be repaid to them out of the proceeds resulting from the sale of bar and other privileges, and out of the gate-money. It is further stipulated that any and all moneys received for admission and which may be realized from the sale of reserved seats shall be given to a responsible person to be agreed upon on or before Thursday, Dec. 19, and all such admission and other money's shall be held in trust by the person so agreed upon until the termination of the race, when he shall dispose of the total sum realized as follows: Three-fourths, shall be paid to the winner of the race and one fourth to the loser, provided the loser is accredited with 450 miles. If the loser fails to make a record or 450 miles, the sum total realized from such admission and other moneys shall be paid to the winner. It is further agreed that members of the athletic clubs of the City of New York shall be requested to officiate as judge's scorers, and time-keepers, and in case of any disagreement on the part of the judges, such question shall be submitted to Mr. William B. Curtis whose decision shall be final. It is further stipulated that the person agreed upon to receive and dispose of the moneys realized from the match or the race shall appoint the ticket-sellers who shall be approved by the principals in this match, and their respective backers, the latter to furnish the necessary doorkeepers and ticket—takers. It is further agreed that the tickets received at the door must be deposited in boxes and shall be taken there from once in every twenty four hours and carried in the presence of representatives of the parties to this agreement after which the cash must be balanced and the money paid over to the person agreed upon as aforesaid, who shall receipt for the same in duplicate to the parties to this agreement.**

Nearly 500 people turned up at Gilmore's Garden at noon on Saturday, the 21st of December to inspect the tracks which O'Leary and Campana would compete against each other. There was of course another reason for the meeting of the pair and the sporting men that took so much interest in their coming match, and that was the choice of tracks which would be decided by a toss of a coin. Both of the outer and inner tracks which had been constructed for the pedestrians were said to be superior to any that had been walked on in the history of the city. The ground beneath the two paths had been dug up, levelled, rolled, and covered with four inches of finely sifted loam which had been pressed down a couple of inches before a similar depth of sawdust was scattered on top. Although both competitors were happy with the springy and elastic result, Campana stated he preferred a slightly firmer surface to O'Leary's softer option.

On the afternoon before the start of the match, O'Leary told reporters, "I weigh one hundred and sixty-five pounds, which is twenty pounds too much. I will cover a hundred and ten miles tomorrow and that will reduce my weight."

The man from Bridgeport won the toss, chose the eight laps to the mile outside track as opposed to the nine laps to the mile inside track, and immediately took off his coat and jogged around it for several laps, instructing the men who operated the rollers to press it as much as possible before the start of the match.

At that stage, the betting was 1/2 on O'Leary and 2/1 against Campana even though many thought a price of 5/1 was appropriate for a newcomer to the world professional scene.

Both men had been provided the mandatory accommodation, with O'Leary's superior two winged (main building, sleeping room and kitchen), two roomed *"portable lodge"* situated on the inside of the track, and Campana's smaller quarters on the outside. The athletes were provided with a cot, and a gas stove for heating and cooking.

On the night before the race, the doors were opened to the public at 21:00, and many early birds inspected the two tracks and gazed at the accommodation built for the contestants. By half past twelve, there were 2,000 people waiting patiently for the start of the race, as were the scorers sitting in the judges' stand alongside William B. Curtis of the *Spirit of the Times* who would act as referee.

Then at 00:56, both men, each wearing overcoats, were escorted on to the track by the police and their backers and made their way to the judge's stand amid the weight of the crowd. The *National Police Gazette* takes up what happened next: The throng crowded about the two champions in a way that spoiled Campana's temper. He began in querulous way to tell those about him that he wouldn't walk at all, and would "spoll the hull show if they didn't get back." The police finally cleared the tracks for a narrow passage. Meantime Referee Curtis from the judges' stand told the men that they should regard the scorers as the only judges, and not quarrel with them. "The people of New York," he said, "have paid a good deal of money to see some very poor walking, and now you two men are the champions. We expect to see some good walking. There has been some talk that the tracks are not properly measured. They were measured by a surveyor, and are no doubt right. However, the judge will measure them over on Wednesday night to make sure, and if they are short you will have to make up the distance. It is half a minute of the time."

The men then removed their coats. O'Leary, looking very well, and carrying his trademark corn cobs, wore a white shirt, black knee breeches and white stockings. He was accompanied by his backer Al Smith, and was cheered boisterously as he waited for the call. Campana in contrast, appearing *"worried and haggard,"* was led in by Harry Hill and "George" Englehardt. He wore a scarlet flannel shirt that adorned his knees, black tights, white stockings, black shoes and a similar coloured silk cap which covered a crimson silk bandana. On the front of his shirt was the word "Sport" in black letters and on the back "Old Stag" which was a reference to the fire engine that he used to look after. Ridding himself of his outer shirt, Campana revealed a white undershirt with the words, "Sport 41" on his chest together with three medals, one of which was given to him for saving the life of a woman from a runaway horse in Bridgeport.

DANIEL O'LEARY   **PETER NAPOLEON CAMPANA**

(Illustration no: 29)

King of the Peds

"GO!"
The National Police Gazette (Illustration no: 30)

Campana and O'Leary running
The National Police Gazette (Illustration no: 31)

| Campana; 01:09:31 | First mile | O'Leary; 01:10:42 |
| Campana; 01:18:58 | Second mile | O'Leary; 01:21:16 |

At the end of five miles, Campana appeared *"fagged out"* and ready to throw in the towel. "Sport," however, was very much like "Lepper" Hughes (who was watching the old showman from the stands), in that he appeared *"broken up"* all of the time due to the ungraceful way he pushed himself forward. Appearances however, can be deceptive, and a reporter for the *New York Times* asked the watching pedestrian what he thought might be the outcome of the match. "Ah, but that O'Leary's a caution," said Hughes, "That other feller can't hold a candle to him. Will Sphort stick it out? Av course he will; but where'll he be at the end? Tell me that? He'll be bate worse nor I was, mark that!"

O'Leary was the first to take a break on his 11th mile at 02:54 for 8m.22s. Campana, keeping with his favoured dog-trot, waited till his 31st mile for his first rest of 6m.30s. The Irishman's next stop was for breakfast during which time a blister on his left heel, caused by a projecting welt in his shoe was attended to. The ever growing blister would cause problems for the champion as the day advanced, and he was seen to make frequent little stoppages to change his footwear. The complication however had no bearing on his gait. As ever, *"he walked with a firm step, erect head, and perfect carriage of his body."* The disciplined O'Leary was so, so, different to his opponent who, *"walks and trots with body bent forward, arms hanging loosely, head turned in all directions, and looking as often backward as forward, at any person or object that attracts his attention."* Personal comments made by the crowd at "Sport" were answered by him and this showed how undisciplined and immature he was in the public arena, causing him to lose concentration on the bread and butter issue of focusing on what he was there for; to win the race!

By the time Campana had had enough for the day, the dog-trot that he earlier been using had degenerated into a shuffle, causing a furrow in the path he was performing on. To keep him going, he was constantly accompanied by one of his attendants, who being a step or two ahead, led him round, and at 23:15 he left the track to go to bed having scored 90 miles to O'Leary's 83. The second placed man had left the track a couple of minutes earlier, and his backers were already confidently predicting that their man would be leading by 10 miles by the end of 48 hours.

Campana, who was the first man back in his ring at 01:47, made 100 miles at 04:49. O'Leary on the other hand, having returned from his rest at 03:05, made his initial century at 07:25. After that, he made one more mile and rested till 09:29. After the scores of 110 to 100 in Campana's favour had been posted at 10:00, O'Leary continued on his way at a steady rate keeping the same 10-mile distance behind until early evening when he began to pick up ground on his washed out opponent. At 22:35, Campana left the track on a score of 150 miles (60 for the day) with every intention of sleeping for a few hours. As he left, he turned to the judges and said, "There, that ends my day's work."

That left the ever improving O'Leary to match his score at 23:13 amid a roar of approval from the thousand or so souls who had stayed in the building to watch him take the lead. At midnight, the judges wished O'Leary a Merry Christmas as he continued to put more distance between Campana, and after making 156 miles or 73 for the day, he headed for his splendid little mansion, thirty-six minutes into Christmas Day *"covered with dust and grime."* The press however, was already becoming critical of the champion's performance, rightly pointing out that his two-day score was poor, and that he should have been nearer the 200-mile mark at that stage of the race. They also made the point that, whilst they fully expected O'Leary to win the race easily, they would be surprised if "Sport" would make any where near 450 miles and a claim to a quarter of the gate money.

"The Bridgeport Wonder's" Christmas Day.

Campana left his cottage at 02:07 and traversed his path slowly until 04:00 when he rested for eight minutes. Several short rests were taken before a longer one of an hour starting at 11:17 for breakfast and a rubbing down. *"In his hut during this hour he presented something of a typical racehorse after a heat. The room smelled of drugs and liniment, bandages lay around on all sides, and two men were busily engaging in chafing the limbs of the pedestrian and in limbering the stiffened knee joints as much as possible."*

A large contingent of supporters had chartered a brass band and a train from Bridgeport to cheer their favourite on. However, they were more than disappointed with their hero's performance, and many kept the money they were going to back Campana with at generous odds, firmly in their pockets. The struggling pedestrian walked round the course, his legs swathed in bandages in a great deal of pain, and with obvious difficulty. The news coming from his camp indicating he had a badly swollen left knee which could hardly be bent, due to strained chords in his leg. Due to "Sport's" ailments, the services of Barney Aaron were called upon to do what he could to keep him in as best condition as possible.

Two more short breaks were taken before a further hours rest was indulged in for dinner at 18:24. Thereafter, he went on to make 55 miles for the day, for a total of 205 miles in all at 22:30 when he made his exit for the third day of the match. On his departure from the track, he made a small speech to the judges stating he would run all day on his return and make 125 miles.

O'Leary's Christmas Day.

"Dan, the man", appeared back in the ring at 02:58 looking rather dapper. Dressed in a new white merino shirt and tights, and sporting a white handkerchief around his neck, he looked the picture of health. The blister that had such an affect on his performance earlier in the contest seemed to have stopped troubling him, and he went along in his old indomitable style. His fastest mile of the day, his 202nd, was made in a time of 12m.8s, and when he retired at 23:42, he had scored 20 miles more than his rival.

During the day, the 8,000 tickets that were sold were used over and over again. That meant that between 40,000 and 50,000 people had been admitted, realising just over $20,000, which was more than the management had hoped for. The amount of people tramping about the building caused much dust to circulate, and along with the massive volume of tobacco smoke, it was very difficult for anyone to breathe, let alone the competitors.

With it being Christmas Day, *"beer and strong liquors circulated freely, and nightfall found many victims of a too enthusiastic Christmas celebration stowed away fast asleep in all sorts of queer out-of-the-way nooks and corners of the great building. Fights were also of frequent occurrence and many a tattered and bloody individual was marched off by the Police, of whom a large force was in attendance."*

The *Brooklyn Daily Eagle* was already raising its readers' eyebrows about the performance of the two men on the track, and was beginning to ask questions about that record in Bridgeport: **People are beginning to inquire how is it possible for Campana to have accomplished the Bridgeport feat of five hundred and twenty one and a half miles in six days, if after walking only one hundred miles he shows such weariness and distress. The report that he ever accomplished anything like it is now much questioned. Indeed, the suggestions are now openly made that the Bridgeport walk was not accomplished fairly and was only intended as a preliminary show to the present contest, its purpose being to excite interest in this match. Whether these whisperings are an injustice to the contestants or not the next few hours will tell.**

The thousands that turned up on Christmas Day were followed by thousands more the day after, despite the poor performances of those who had been engaged to entertain them. Many yelled themselves hoarse as they screeched at the two pedestrians making their way around their respective paths. Some shouted at nothing, because there was nothing to see, apart from the thick fog that separated them from *"the farce"* that was going on in the distance.

The event had been heavily promoted in the press, and so much had been promised, but in the end there was much discontent with the whole affair and it was quite evident that Mr. Curtis, the match referee, was thoroughly disgusted with what he was witnessing. Still it went on, and it was the wretched spectacle of Campana, who needed two attendants at the side of him to keep him upright should he fall, which was causing some in the crowd to shout out, "Why doesn't someone stop this?!" *"Every step donates pain. With mouth distended, rives sunken and skin of the color of parched leather, he slowly marched around the track. It was impossible for him at times to raise his left foot from the ground and it made deep furrows in the track. Bent almost doubly and with arms flying to and fro and wearing his radiant flannel outer garment, the old man was a picture to remember."*

Indeed, Campana was now becoming the object of much ridicule from some sections of the crowd. Many taunted him, hoping he would "answer back" as he had done the night before when he had punched someone in the crowd for the awful remarks they were making at him. At one stage, he took off his cap to show off his bald head, provoking many to poke more fun at him. It was a wonder that "Sport" hadn't thrown in the towel already, and the fact that he still stood was attributed to the patient and tender handling of Aaron, who bathed him frequently and built him up with *"champagne and a generous diet."* At least Aaron was interested in Campana's welfare; his backers only appeared interested in whether or not he could make 450 miles to cover their losses on his stake and a quarter of the gate receipts.

"Sport" finished his 260th mile at 21:28, after which he went back to his house, having made just 55 miles since starting his hike at 02:07. During that time he had taken advantage of seven stops of varying length.

The leader, suffering from a cold, had emerged from his posh house at 03:32. He made steady progress with the aid of various people to accompany him around, including Commissioner Brennan. At 22:00, O'Leary completed 285 miles; at which time he was 25 miles ahead of Campana, who was in a much better place, and that was the land of nod. Whilst his opponent slept, the race leader remained on the track, steadily increasing his lead, until at 23:30 he retired for the night, having made ten more miles than his opponent for the day, for a score of 290 and a lead of 30 miles.

On the fifth day of the so-called "contest," Campana came out of his inferior digs just after midnight and proceeded to walk stiffly around the track. He soon warmed to his task however, and it was clear that he was shuffling along much better than he had shuffled the day before. He was joined by O'Leary at 02:18, who, during the course of the day, had to stop no less than 21 times due to the fact he was suffering from a very poorly left foot. His trainer was so concerned about the state of it, that he was scared to take his mans shoes off, stating he wouldn't be doing so until the race was over. The terrible condition of the foot made O'Leary walk very slowly and there was real concern emerging in his camp that Campana, who by now was going along quite well, might just win the race if he ran on the last day, despite his swollen knee. Both men were now being plied with *"stimulants,"* with O'Leary observed to be swigging a lot of whisky. As the evening wore on, both received many floral tributes to keep their morale up. Campana finished his day at 23:00 on a score of 315 miles, and O'Leary left the track for his bed at 23:30 on 361, showing a healthy difference of 46 miles between the pair.

"Sport" returned to the race at 03:56 and was followed by O'Leary a couple of minutes later. He remained on the track till 05:59, choosing not to return for four hours, after which he had numerous rests till the early evening. O'Leary also indulged in frequent breaks, but didn't spend as much time off track as did his opponent. He was said to be in good spirits, his cold not troubling him as much. However, his feet were still a great cause for concern with blisters now appearing on his right foot during the afternoon.

"Well, why didn't you make old Connecticut run fifty miles today as you promised?" said somebody to Barney Aaron during the afternoon.

"He's willin' 'nough," answered Barney, "but then don't you see the old man hadn't the strength left. Why, the old fellow was killed before I took hold of him. They didn't give him anything to eat, and never changed his underclothing until Wednesday. Wasn't that 'nough to kill the old boy? But I never saw a more willin' chap. He's cranky to be sure; but then he'll do what you want, after a while. He only eats what's given to him. Today he's had mutton chops, toast and tea. That was his breakfast. For dinner clam soup, strained was all he wanted, and for supper I gave him a little fish. But too old, too old," concluded Barney, shaking his head and moving off to Sport's quarters.

The reporter of the *New York Herald* then went on to have a chat with Campana.

"I tell you boss, I've had misfortunes in this walk. I have a very bad leg, and I tell you boss, I can go 550 miles in six days; and I can tell you boss I can do it in three months. I tell you, boss, I can go thirty days and not be tired, if my old leg was right. My feet are alright." (with emphasis, his right hand above his head and his eyes sparkling.) "Yes boss, they are as sound as a baby's. Come in and see them! There's nothing a matter with the old man but this knee. Darn the old knee!"

At 17:00, the Bridgeporter completed his 342nd mile, and at 19:00, he struggled through his 345th. At 20:09, he was forty miles behind the leader and off the track, the score being 388 to 348.

Potential spectators, queuing outside the Garden, who were more than willing to part with the 50 cents admission price to see the finale that night, would have heard the familiar cry, "Have yer money ready! Both men now on the track! Walk right in and see the greatest walking match on record!"

King of the Peds

During the evening, and as the band played "Grandfather's Clock," "Johnny Morgan," and other popular tunes, 6,000 people crowded themselves in to the place to watch the conclusion of the *"walking match."* As the excitable throngs screamed, shouted and rushed from side to side of the track to try and catch a glimpse of the performing tramps, Al Smith watching them with a wry smile on his face, rubbed his hands together and said, "Just look at 'em; isn't it beautiful?" as two dollar signs replaced the pupils in his eyes.

The reporter with *New York Herald* continuing with his story went on to comment about O'Leary: After supper and when music had enlivened matters generally, he spurted round the track at a great pace. His 390th mile was made in 13 minutes and 55 seconds and the 391st in 12 minutes and 45 seconds. It was his desire, evidently to round off the 400th mile, and he knew that hard work was necessary to reach these figures. The house was now very enthusiastic, there being fully 6,000 persons present, many of them ladies. O'Leary was walking in magnificent form. His 391st, 392nd and 393rd were each made in 12m.45s., and the 394th mile in the remarkable time of 11m.45s and this with a sore heel and blistered feet. Cheers followed cheers and the house seemed beside itself. Ladies waved their handkerchiefs and gentlemen ruined their gloves in hearty applause of his efforts.

Even "Sport" turned around to look at the heel and toe business of his opponent. During one of these glances of admiration the champion handed him a corn cob; but on the next lap or two the Connecticut walker obtained a bouquet, and when meeting O'Leary the next time handed the floral tribute to him saying, "I go you one better." O' Leary carried the bouquet a lap or two more then returned it with thanks. The five miles from 391 to 395, inclusive were made in 1h.1m.10s, the announcement of which produced intense enthusiasm.

"Oh, ain't he a dandy!" exclaimed Barney Aaron, "Why he beats the world. Look at 'im!"

"He's got another of his cranky fits," shouted Barney Aaron, after "Sport" had rested 34m.30s on his 349th mile, "and he says he going to trot." He kept his word, and managed to finish the mile in 13m.25s. Jogging down the Twenty Sixth street side of the building, some fellow shouted;

"Say, 'Sport' you old bluefish, cheese 'em."

Instantly the old man left the track, but before he could get to the young man who had saluted him so insultingly, Robinson, the trainer of the Harlem Athletic Club, then on the track with him, caught him and remonstrated against this exhibition of feeling.

"Let me go, won't you, and I'll show him what kind of a fish I am!" shouted "Sport"; but Robinson retained his hold and led the Bridgeport pedestrian back to the path.

"Give me two more days and I'd make ninety miles each day," he peevishly exclaimed; and then laughingly continued to hobble along. His 350th mile was made at 8h.41m., and, while apparently in deep meditation, a gentleman stepped in front of him with a bundle and said;

"Here, 'Sport,' just take these; you may want them."

"Sport" took the bundle, and on opening it found two pairs of boxing gloves.

"Well that beats me boss," said the old man; "but here's my hand, and I'm obliged to you."

The boxing gloves were taken by "Sport" to his quarters with evident pride, and much to the amusement of many. "I wish I had that fellow that called me a bluefish here now," said he, "and I'd take his scalp."

The 396th mile was scored for O'Leary in 12m.30s and the 397th in 14m.55s, two minutes of this time being passed in his cottage. If the enthusiasm had been earnest during the previous half hour, it was now most intense. The band was of no account, for deafening cheers drowned the music. In 13m.50s the 398th mile was completed, in capital form, though it was apparent that the strain was at last beginning to tell. A white-haired old gentleman handed O'Leary a candy cane on the sixth lap of this mile, and, carrying it through another lap, he had it laid away in his house. All this while "Sport" was plodding painfully along. His miles were averaging over 16m.30s., and during the 356th he staggered like a drunken man. Bay rum on the back of his neck and thrown repeatedly in his face revived him, and with a gameness worthy of admiration, he pursued his weary way. Many thought that he would drop on the track. But he finally retired in creditable shape.

It required just thirteen minutes for O'Leary to rattle off his 399th mile.

Entering upon the 400th, almost everybody in the Garden was either cheering or clapping his hands. Lap, after lap was done, O'Leary's pace getting hotter and hotter. When eight times round and there was but another circuit to complete the distance, he broke into a brisk run. Hats went into the air, men stood on benches and chairs, and, in their eagerness to see the champion flying over the saw-dust path, fell over one another. The ladies got up to their seats, and men craned their necks to get better views. Mr. Al. Smith stood in front of the scorers stand to tell O'Leary "all right" upon the completion or the lap, and did so; but the determined man did not stop. Once more he bounded around the centre, and the applause became still more vociferous. The 400th mile was finished at 22:43 and a minute later the champion jumped into his quarters.

"Another walk over," he said, and five minutes later he was in a coach on his way to the Metropolitan Hotel. With him went two of his assistants, Harding and Slattery, who intended to go to bed as soon as possible.

Incited by the applause which O'Leary was receiving, "Sport" endeavored to create a little enthusiasm on his own account, and trotted a portion of a lap, but the effort was sickly and he soon abandoned it. He completed his 357th mile at 22:43 and then going two more laps threw up his hands and cried: "I'm done!" The crowd roared in response and one or two Bridgeport acquaintances wanted to hug the old man. He entered his quarters at 22:46 and the tramp ended.

A few minutes later "Sport" came down to the score's stand dressed, and, being raised upon the table, asked if he could make a speech. "Certainly," responded Mr. Curtis the referee, whereupon he removed his fur cap and said:

*"Ladies and gentlemen; this is my first race in New York. I was brought here by two men who paralyzed me by their training for two days. If Barney Aaron had been here from the first I would have beaten O'Leary by fifty miles. Now, I am open to run any man run any man in the world for twelve day's for $5,000 a side. Many thanks and tomorrow, I'll have my pockets full of money."

Cheers followed this speech and one enthusiastic fellow endeavored to pull the speaker off the table by his legs. Then "Sport" made his final bow.

The band struck up a merry tune at 12 o'clock and instantly the loungers were wide awake. Many unfortunate individuals have been in the building since the walk commenced, and upon its completion breathed fresh air for the first time in six days. They could be picked out by their appearance. Dust almost an inch thick covered their clothes, and their faces were in similarly bad plight.

Benches chairs and tables in the garden have largely suffered during the walk, and many of them will require repairing. Vast numbers of men have jumped and stood upon them unmindful of their breaking and policemen were powerless to prevent it.

*Campana was described as being "very drunk" when he made this speech.

O'Leary rested 2d.3h.10m.35s whereas Campana's break times totalled 1d.23h.30m.40s. The next day O'Leary was interviewed by the press:

Reporter: "Well how do you feel?"

O'Leary: "I am not in good trim for a walk at all. My feet are sore, and as you can yourself notice, my voice is entirely gone from a cold. I never was in worse trim for a walk in all my life and cannot make a good score. My feet got sore on the first twenty miles and keep sore. I did intend to make a good walk when I started, but I have learned by this trial that a man has got to take some exercise and a little care of himself before he can enter a contest like this and show any kind of a record. Why even a man has got to train his mind as his legs, and stomach as well as both. In fact, I notice a man's temper is somewhat influenced by the state of his stomach, and why not his nerves? I find my chest so sore I am afraid to cough. I have heard that people blame me for not making a better record here. I say this to the people of the two cities. Give me a man worthy of my steel and I will show you what I can do. What was Hughes? Well the less said about him the better. This man Campana is unquestionably the pluckiest and grittiest I have met so far."

Reporter: "Why do you say so Mr. O'Leary?"

King of the Peds

O'Leary: "Well, of course he won't be able to accomplish his Bridgeport feat here; in fact he is not in the same condition now; but from what I have seen him suffer for the past hundred hours and the manner he kept himself up against it, I conclude he is plucky. His legs are swollen and I can see that the muscles are in a very bad condition; they are so much strained and the man who can persist and contend with such difficulties is worthy of being an antagonist of mine; but said O'Leary smiling he won't accomplish his Bridgeport feat. He has got to walk New York miles now."

Reporter: "Mr. O'Leary, when will your belt be walked for?"

O'Leary: "Not before the middle of *June, and meantime let me say this; I have not been a success in New York in my walking. Now I wish to say for me that I am exceedingly sorry for the poor exhibitions I have given, and now wish to issue this challenge. I offer $5,000 against the same amount that I will walk 540 miles in 144 hours in the city of New York in four weeks from now, and beside this I am willing to give half the profits to be divided equally among all charitable institutions in both cities, they appointing a committee to represent them here in taking and selling tickets. I think they can realise $100,000 on it."

*Earlier, in mid-November, and in response to a challenge by the world record holder, Corkey of London to contest for his belt, O'Leary replied that he was ready to meet Corkey, Vaughan, Weston, Brown, Harriman, or indeed any man in the world, as long as the conditions were complied with and the stakes deposited with the appropriate trustees. He also stated that he had to deposit £100 with the trustees to guarantee that he would produce the belt should he lose his title. However he was adamant that he wouldn't compete for it again in England, unless of course if he was beaten.

At the time O'Leary had said, "Before my contest with Hughes I deposited $1,000 with the *Spirit of the Times*, in New York, offering to wager that the then best on record, made by myself, 520¼ miles, would be beaten, but no one had the courage to accept my proposition. After the race with Hughes, I offered to wager $5,000 that I could cover 540 miles by walking in six days; and I offered to wager $3,000 against $5,000 that by running and walking I could cover 560 miles in 144 hours. None of these propositions were accepted. In conclusion, all I have to say is that in my next contest for the belt, which will take place in January, the American public can rest satisfied, that if I am pushed in the contest, I will accomplish a performance that is the best on record, and that will stand for a number of years without being beaten."

The *Fitchburg Sentinel* of the 30th of December reported that: The receipts amounted to $24,000, of which O'Leary will receive $12,000. According to the agreement, neither party was to receive any of the gate money unless he walked 450 miles. The general impression in sporting circles is that the whole affair is arranged solely as a speculation.

This theory was reinforced by the *Chicago Tribune* who later wrote: Several days before the time for the termination of the contest, it was apparent that under no circumstances could Campana cover the required distance. When this fact dawned upon the minds of "Sport" and his backers, a consultation was held. The time for making a strong bluff had arrived, and the bluff was made. The O'Leary end of the scheme was told that unless matters were "fixed" to the satisfaction of the "Sport" crowd, their man would be taken from the track. Of course, with but one contestant, the race would amount to nothing, and the attendance ditto. Consequently a settlement was made the terms of which, as nearly as can be ascertained were that Campana should receive $2,000 of the gate money in consideration of remaining on the track in some shape or other until Saturday night. He managed to hobble along the required time, and O'Leary completed his victory at the close of the 400th mile. This is the plain truth of the matter, and does the Chicago man no credit. Heretofore he has claimed that in no shape would he would be party to, or in any way entertain hippodromes, but he can make the claim no longer. It now looks as though there never was a match and most people will incline to the belief that the "contest" was gotten up as speculation, the parties to the scheme being well aware that the public was ripe for a humbug.

A little while after the race both men were asked about the amount of money Campana received after the event. Their respective answers prove interesting………………

Reporter: "How much of the gate money does Campana receive, Mr. O'Leary?"

O'Leary: "He gets a pretty good little pile, - about $2,000 I think."

Reporter: "Well, Campana, did you make as much as you lost in the match?"

Campana: "I lost the stake of $1,000 but I made ten times that. I made enough anyway to buy a house and lot for my wife."

The *New York Times* summed up the whole sorry tale up with the following comment: Probably New York has never been more completely sold than in this walk. It was a well conceived job, and has been neatly manipulated from the outset, when glowing reports of the alleged performance of Campana in Bridgeport, where he was said to have walked 521 miles and 54 feet in six days, were forwarded to the New York papers.

CHAPTER 13

What Else Happened in 1878

William Howes won the first 26-hour "Champion of England" race at the Agricultural Hall, London, between Friday and Saturday, February the 22nd and 23rd 1878, when he walked 129 miles in 24h.20m winning £100 and the silver challenge "London Champion Belt." Walter Lewis of Islington was second with 125 miles and 990 yards. Owen Hancock was third with 113¾ miles, and Peter Crossland, fourth, with 110½. Courtney was the only other pedestrian that made above a hundred. Henry Vaughan *"caved in"* after scoring 68 miles and a few laps, and was reportedly *"exhausted."* The twenty starters in the race included George Ide and William Perkins. Large sums of money were wagered on the match and Vaughan went off the favourite.

Hancock led the race from the start in front of 10,000 spectators until he was overtaken by Howes on a score of 38 miles. However, and due to Vaughan's rapid progress on the leaders, the bookies were offering odds of 5/4 that he would win the race. Howes continued to lead with his time at the 50-mile marker being 9h.2m.10s. Hancock was at that stage still second and Ide third. After 75 miles had been walked, an exciting race then materialised between Howes, Ide and Lewis; but it was Howes who was the first of the trio to make one hundred miles in 18h.7m.57s, which was the fastest time on record. Lewis too broke the old record when he too covered the century mark, his time being 18h.42m.35s.

On Monday, the 27th May at the Dublin Exhibition Palace in Ireland, Weston walked 400 miles in six days finishing his task at 10 p.m.

At 10 a.m. on Whit Monday, the 10th of June 1878, Mr. Richard Lewis, who was promoting the event, said the word "Go," and started a 14-hour per day, six-day *"fair walking match"* at the Pomona Palace and Gardens, Cornbrook, Manchester, between 20 men. The carefully prepared track, consisting of loam and sawdust, which the contestants competed on, was seven laps to the mile. The joint 2/1 favourites to win the race were the Londoners, Billy Howes, Arthur Hancock and Walter Lewis. Owen Hancock and George Ide of the capital were next in the betting. The others in the race were Courtney of Barnet, Crossland of Sheffield, Day of Northampton, Fitzpatrick, France, Parry and W. Woodhead of Manchester, Hibberd and Newman of London, Johnson of Barrow-in-Furness, McCarty and Smith of York, McKellan of Edinburgh, and Richardson and Thorold of the USA.

This match was very well attended and was the subject of much interest in the local press. The scores for the first day 23:00 was: **A. Hancock, 73.3; Howes, 73; Hibberd, 70.1; Ide, 70; O. Hancock, 69.5; Lewis, 68.5; Crossland, 66; McKellan, 64.3; Richardson, 61.5; Day, France, Johnson, Parry and Thorold, 60; Newman, 53; Fitzpatrick, 51.4; McCarty, 51; Courtney, 50; Smith, 48; Woodhead, 42:**

The match should have started every day at 09:00, but owing to the hours delay on the first day, the start for the second, third, fourth and fifth day, would be at 08:45. France and Woodhead were both late for the second day and started the race 30 minutes after the rest.

Arthur Hancock beat his brother to be the first in the race to complete 100 miles at 14:00, Owen accomplishing his at 14:04, Hibberd his at 14:44, Ide his at 14:49 and Howes, his at 15:04. With the race leader Arthur Hancock and fifth placed Billy Howes having to leave the track around 21:00 due to suffering with *"evident pain,"* Hibberd was able to take the lead. Crossland, whose chances were *"considered very rosy,"* pushed himself up to a challenging position by the close of the second day when the scores showed: **Hibberd, 140; Ide, 138.3; Crossland, 133.6; O. Hancock, 130.1; A. Hancock and Lewis, 130; Howes, 128; Day, 120; France and Richardson, 118; Parry, 117.1; Courtney, 111; Newman, 108; McCarty, 106.2; Johnson, 105.1; McKellan, 101.4; Fitzpatrick, 100.1; Smith, 100; Thorold, 91; Woodhead, 80.4:**

With Arthur Hancock reported to be back in the capital having retired the day before, and Howes and Lewis also out of the competition, seventeen men started the fourth day of the race on Thursday the 13th. That amount would be reduced even further by 10:00, due to the distress showed by the then race leader, Hibberd, who left the track at 09:59 on a score of 212.1 suffering from symptoms of exhaustion, and *"a bad leg."* His departure left the way for Ide to take control and at 11:00 the scores of the competitors showed: **Ide, 217.4; Hibberd, 212.1; Crossland, 207; O. Hancock, 201.6; Parry, 193.6; Courtney, 181.6; Day, 180.3; McKellan, 174.2; France, 172.5; Newman and McCarty, 171; Johnson and Smith, 161; Fitzpatrick, 158.3; Thorold, 149.1:**

At the same time the day after, Friday, the scores were: **Ide, 286.3; Crossland, 269; Parry, 259.1; Courtney, 241.2; O. Hancock, 240; Newman, 230.1; McCarty, 227.3; McKellan, 225.6; Hibberd, 221.5; Smith, 215.2; Day, 214.2; France, 209.4; Richardson, 207.6; Johnson, 198.4; Fitzpatrick, 193.5; Thorold, 186.5; Woodhead, 168.6:**

Hibberd eventually retired from the race on a score of 223.6 at 13:08, his departure making him the fourth *"crack"* to retire in the event. Just under an hour or so later, Ide recorded his third century at 13:53, at that time being 20.4 in front of his nearest rival. By the end of the day that distance hadn't changed much, as can be seen by the following scores: **Ide, 338; Crossland, 317.6; Parry, 310; Courtney, 288.6; O. Hancock, 269.4; McCarty, 260; Newman, 258.4; McKellan, 252; Smith and Day, 250; Richardson, 232; France and Fitzpatrick, 230; Johnson, 226; Thorold, 224.4; Woodhead, 201:**

George Ide, with a score of 382 miles, eventually won the first prize of £150 *"in coin,"* and a belt worth £100. Peter Crossland took the second prize of £50 over the Pennines, having covered 356 miles. George Parry crossed the winning line in third with 349 miles, taking £20 with him, and Courtney went back to London having won £10 by finishing fourth.

A ten-mile *"running championship"* took place at the Lillie Bridge Grounds on Monday, the 17th of June 1878. Interestingly, the prizes offered by Sir John Astley, included £400, which was the surplus of the gate receipts at the latest contest at the Agricultural Hall, a handsome silver belt, and a medal for the winner, who would also receive a third of the cash, with the second and third men receiving prizes in proportion.

The competitors who entered were the then current champion George Hazael of London, William Smith of Paisley, W. Shrubsole of Northampton, James Bailey of Sittingbourne and Charles Price of Kensington.

A *"gallant fight"* was made by Smith, Price and Bailey, with the Scot eventually winning the race by 40 yards in a time of 53m.42s. A further 20 yards more separated the runner-up Bailey from Price.

The poster below advertised the second race for the "London Champion Belt" between Friday, the 26th and Saturday, the 27th of July 1878. The official record at the close showed that Vaughan had scored 114 miles and 1,1510 yards, Hancock, 93¼ miles, and Howes, 91 miles and 1,320 yards.

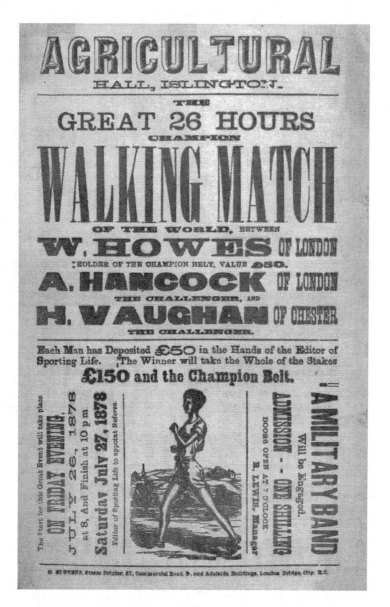

With the permission of Islington Local History Centre (Illustration no: 32)

CHAPTER 14

2,000 Miles in 1,000 Hours

Below is a time-table for a journey of 2,000 miles in six weeks. The reader has just one guess as to who would be embarking on such a trip?

Jan	From	To	Via			Miles
18	London	Folkestone				81
20	Folkestone	Eastbourne	Hythe	Winchelsea	Hastings	135
21	Eastbourne	Colchester	Lewes	Brighton	Arundel	192
22	Colchester	Winchester	Portsmouth	Southampton		242
23	Winchester	Wareham	Salisbury	Poole		306
24	Wareham	Honiton	Weymouth	Dorchester	Bridport	368
25	Honiton	Plymouth	Exeter	Totnes		435
27	Plymouth	Grampound	Liskeard			482
28	Grampound	Redruth	Truro	Falmouth	Penzance	546
29	Redruth	Hatherleigh	Bodmin	Launceston		622
30	Hatherleigh	Tiverton	Barnstable			675
31	Tiverton	Bristol	Wellington	Taunton	Bridgewater	746
Feb						
1	Bristol	Worcester	Gloucester	Tewkesbury		807
3	Worcester	Shifnal	Droitwich	Bromsgrove	Birmingham	860
4	Shifnal	Whitchurch	Wellington	Whitchurch		900
5	Whitchurch	Ormskirk	Chester	Warrington	Liverpool	970
6	Ormskirk	Preston	Wigan	Bolton	Manchester	1,037
7	Preston	Shap	Garstang	Lancaster	Kendal	1,098
8	Shap	Haydon Bridge	Penrith	Carlisle		1,158
10	Haydon Bridge	Darlington	Newcastle	Durham	Stockton	1,232
11	Darlington	Pickering	Thirsk			1,284
12	Pickering	Great Driffield	Scarborough	Bridlington		1,337
13	Great Driffield	Market Weighton	Beverley	Hull		1,380
14	Market Weighton	Huddersfield	York	Leeds	Bradford	1,449
15	Huddersfield	Worksop	Wakefield	Barnsley	Sheffield	1,540
17	Worksop	Nottingham	Retford	Lincoln	Newark	1,567
18	Nottingham	Leicester	Derby	Burton		1,622
19	Leicester	Peterborough	Stamford			1,673
20	Peterborough	Swaffham	Wisbech			1,731
21	Swaffham	Lowestoft	Norwich	Yarmouth		1,792
22	Lowestoft	Needham	Wickham	Ipswich		1,847
24	Needham	Cambridge	Stowmarket	Bury St Edms	Newmarket	1,890
25	Cambridge	Newport Pagnell	St. Neots	Bedford		1,936
26	Newport Pagnell	Oxford	Buckingham	Bicester		1,977
27	Oxford	Windsor	Dorchester	Reading		2,024
28	Windsor	London				2,047

King of the Peds

On Saturday, January 18th 1879, Edward Payson Weston started a six-week walking tour of England. At five minutes after midnight, at the Royal Exchange in London, and initially accompanied by Charlie Rowell, he promised to deliver 50 lectures *"What I know about walking,"* on the 2,000-mile hike en route, in 1,000 hours. Weston made a £100 bet with Sir John Astley who offered odds of 5/1 that he wouldn't make it. The American was accompanied by Astley, Lord Francis Gordon Fenner, Colonel Goodlake and a number of others including Messrs. A. G. Payne, G. W. Atkinson and Herbert Jewell (the judges) as he set off down King William Street.

Travelling over London Bridge and keeping to the middle of the road, he walked down Great Dover Street onto the Old Kent Road at a brisk pace of 6 mph. He reached East Greenwich at 01:20 where the judges accompanying him in an omnibus changed horses. Weston then made the wrong turning at Woolwich, thus losing 200 yards, but was recalled to get back on the right road for Dartford. Many mishaps happened on the way. A lamp fixed to the front of the bus malfunctioned at Greenwich, and the judges had to rely on a box of *"lucifers"* to enable them to work. Then the inadequate stature of the horses meant that they couldn't pull the vehicle up the *"loose and flinty"* hill at Belvedere, which meant that all riding in the carriage had to help push it up.

© *The British Library. All Rights reserved. The Penny Illustrated. (Illustration no: 33)*

The party was accompanied by a couple of bicyclists, who both fell off their bikes as the group sped down the now conquered hill, in pursuit of Weston and Rowell, who were a fair way in front. The procession made another wrong turning at Bexley Heath, going down the wrong road for a mile before being put right by a sleepy local resident, who had the misfortune of being *"knocked up"* by the group. The consequences of the mistake meant that Weston was nearly an hour late when he reached Dartford at 05:00. Nevertheless, and undeterred by the night's misfortunes, he firstly reached Gravesend at 06:45 and then marched on through the snow and cold to Strood, which he reached half an hour late at 08:00. The horses were changed at Rochester and "E. P." arrived at Chatham at 08:30 where it was snowing heavily. Here, he and his entourage were received with curiosity, but nevertheless given a good reception. The vehicle struggled thereafter towards Sittingbourne, which was reached at 10:50 by the two peds who were going at a fair old clip ahead of the rest.

The tired horses needed to be changed and a telegram was sent to Canterbury to make sure they were ready when the group reached Faversham. Eventually everybody arrived in Dover via Canterbury at 18:45. Arriving fifteen minutes ahead of time, and with the aid of a police escort to guard their passage through the town, the pair were mobbed by the hoards of onlookers. The household names went on to reach Folkestone, 81 miles from the start, at 20:30. Here they were preceded by a band until he reached the Town Hall where Eddy gave his first lecture.

Weston rested all day Sunday and set off with Rowell at 03:00 on Monday morning from the West Cliff Hotel where they had been staying. Walking at a speed of 4 mph, the "Walkist" reached Sandgate at 03:43, Hythe at 04:25, Dymchurch at 05:53, New Romney at 06:45, and Rye at 09:45 where a meal was taken at the Cinque Port Hotel.

Setting off at 11:20, he then walked the next three miles in 40 minutes. As he passed them by, many onlookers were heard commenting about his eccentric gait. "Why, he is lame?" said one. He arrived at Winchelsea at noon, and was met with curious crowds on the way to Hastings which he reached at 14:30, passing the town's memorial 10 minutes ahead of time. He reached Pevensey, his next stop on his tour, at 17:30. Here he stopped for an hour and a half for dinner leaving for the Devonshire Park Estate in Eastbourne where he lectured and stayed overnight.

The next day, Tuesday, the party set off at 06:20 on a cold and frosty morning, arriving in Lewes at 10:35 where they breakfasted. After that Weston was escorted a mile out of town by the police, on his way to Brighton. He was followed by thousands of people to the Sussex coastal resort, where he was greeted by so many admirers that he had to seek refuge in a shop, where he stayed for a couple of hours to avoid the crush. It was only with the greatest of difficulty that he was able to force his way through to Ginnet's Circus where he gave another talk. He was apparently smuggled out of there afterwards and was joined by the pedestrian, George Ide, as he continued his way westwards to Arundel, and then Chichester, where he slept for the night.

He carried on his trek at 06:10, Wednesday, and headed for Portsmouth where he was mobbed on his arrival at noon. After delivering his speech at the Princes Theatre, he carried on to Southampton where he arrived at 18:55, thereafter making his speech at the Victoria Rooms. Some of these unwelcome *"interruptions"* were creating quite a lot of concern about his safety en route. The London *Times* wrote: It is very probable that in laying down the plans for his long walk Weston did not take into consideration the interruptions that would happen through being met by crowds of people at the various cities and towns on his journey. His experience, however, has before now taught him that this is an important factor in the affair. At several places during the past week he has been greeted enthusiastically; but the kindly attentions of the people and their excess of curiosity have well-nigh proved fatal to the undertaking. On one or two occasions he has had recourse to strategy, and a fictitious Weston has been sent off to draw the multitude, while the real man has made good his escape. No sooner was this discovered than at one or two places the mob resented the little deception and their curiosity turned into rage, which found vent in pelting the omnibus with stones. It is hoped there will be a continuance of this kind of thing, as already it has caused the American to lose several hours. Indeed, when he then headed off towards Winchester, it was reported that, *"some roughs behaved very brutally"* to him, and in an attempt to keep the "undesirables" away, one of his attendants, William Begley dressed up as the pedestrian, so that he could make his way safely to the George Hotel where he took refuge. He later arrived in Stockbridge at 04:30 on the morning of Thursday the 23rd, where he rested till 09:20, before hiking on to Salisbury.

Leaving Cranborne at 18:00, he reached Wimborne Minster at 20:42, where again he was surrounded by those desperate to catch a glimpse of him. It was here that he fell on the floor due to the crush, and where he cut his hand and hurt his knee. Still undeterred, he continued his march to Poole, where he delivered a shorter address at the Assembly Rooms, due to the late hour of 22:30.

He left Poole at 00:40 on Friday and headed towards Wareham via Lytchett, a distance of about 10 miles, arriving three hours behind time at 03:00. From Wareham, which he left at 07:00 after just 3 hours sleep, he headed towards Honiton which was 62 miles away, planning to lecture at Axminster on the way. Reaching Weymouth at noon on *"roads of a trying nature,"* he kept on to Dorchester, where the police had to link arms to keep the *"mob"* off him. Passing through there, he strolled on to Bridport via Winterbourne, which he passed through at 16:00. He arrived in Bridport at 19:00, and as he passed through Charmouth before 22:00, he was met by a brass band and escorted through that place by men carrying torches. Having passed through Hunters Bar at 22:48, he eventually reached Axminster three hours behind time, and apparently far too exhausted to give his promised lecture.

At 05:15, he was again on the road after a sleep of five hours. The wind on the bleak, cold, Saturday morning which he marched against, made him sleepy, and he had to stop in the village of Wilmington for an hour. After his rest, he continued on to Honiton three miles away, turning up there at 08:45. By that time though, he should have been in Exeter, a distance of 17 miles away, but, resuming his tramp at 10:15, he went on to reach the old city at 14:00. It was here that he gave the lecture that he should have delivered in Axminster, at the Victoria Hall at 15:30, having passed through the street safely, thanks to the local constabulary, who adopted the same techniques to keep the crowd at bay as their colleagues had employed at Dorchester. It was in Exeter that Weston alluded to the idea of telegraphing Astley, for his permission to ride the omnibus out of town, in an attempt to stop himself being hurt. He said he would make up the lost time spent being driven by walking the extra distance when things were quieter. After he left Exeter, he made his way to Newton Abbott where he stayed all day Sunday.

King of the Peds

Predictably, at five minutes past midnight on Monday morning, Weston left Newton Abbott and pointed his compass in the direction of Totnes, covering the unsuitable road at a steady gait of 4 mph. From there he then set out for Plymouth, and whilst tramping towards Modbury, missed his route, meaning that he went a quarter of a mile out of his way. Not too much inconvenienced by that, Modbury was conquered at 05:30. From there he trudged on through the cold night air towards Yealmpton where he stopped for an hour for his second nap of the morning, having previously indulged in 25 minutes of shut-eye before he arrived at Yambridge-gate. Turning up at Plympton at 09:30, he thereafter made good progress towards Plymouth, where he was met by ever increasing crowds and escorted by the police to the Globe Hotel; where he made an appearance before his admirers on a balcony. From there he passed over the Tamar at 12:55, and headed towards St. Germans, which his distinguished feet graced at 15:15. From there he trudged to Liskeard, a distance of 454 miles from the start, arriving in the town at 17:45.

Whilst the party stopped to dine at the Webb's Hotel, the crowd increased outside so much that Weston found it impossible to leave the premises at 19:30. He was therefore allowed to mount the carriage by Astley before being driven slowly through the cheering throngs, till he reached the 3rd milepost. He then set off a brisk pace, but because he was persistently followed by the crowd which caused him to stop, he made an appeal to them to leave him alone.

The next we hear of Eddy's exploits is when he stayed in St. Austell, having walked into that town at 00:40 on Tuesday morning, the 28th of January. The sleety, snowy weather he encountered after he had set off at 06:05 made his task of walking the six miles to Grampound very difficult. In the end he made it in a time of 105 minutes. Reaching Truro via Tresillion before ten o'clock, he marched into Falmouth at 13:00. Up to this point, the man on a mission had gone very slightly over a quarter of the distance he had intended, accomplishing it in 252 hours. He remained for a couple of hours indulging in horizontal rest for an hour, before moving on and reaching Helston at 18:15; five and a quarter hours behind time. Beating a retreat from the back of the hotel for the usual reasons, he headed for Penzance which he reached at midnight; the last quarter of a mile being spent on the omnibus to protect himself from the hoards that came to greet him.

Back on the trail the next day, Wednesday, he headed north towards Hayle (08:00) via Camborne, and reached Redruth at 10:40 where he lectured at the Town Hall. He then followed his nose to Blackwater (13:20), St. Michael (15:20), and finally reached Bodmin at 20:00. By that time he had covered 46 miles for the day and was 575 miles from the start of his tour of England. He had also ridden six and a half miles, and this amount needed to be deducted from his overall total.

On Saturday, the 1st of February, the great traveller left Bristol, reaching Berkeley about 10:00. Appearing fatigued, he arrived at Gloucester at 02:00. After a rest of an hour, he went on to deliver his lecture to a vast crowd at the Skating Rink. Resting till 4 o'clock in his hotel, he was once again driven out of the cathedral city in the direction of Worcester, due to the heightened interest of the vast crowds who wanted to see him.

Wearing his arm in a sling, the *"father of pedestrianism"* met a couple of its sons as he headed into Tewkesbury, being met and escorted into the town by a young ped by the name of Hughes, who was the then *"Champion of the Midlands,"* and the famous Manchester based athlete, George Parry. Not bothering to stop for refreshments, Weston left the town at 18:47 as sleet was falling, and, as he tramped on, he went on to encounter roads which were three inches deep in snow.

It took the walker and his party a total of four hours to reach Worcester. On the city's outskirts, and walking along the Bath Road, he was met by the usual throngs of *"well behaved"* onlookers. The police kept with him as he entered the city on top of his accompanying carriage from the Berwick Arms Inn, to the Star Hotel where he would stay over the Sabbath. Just before he entered that establishment, he was reported to have addressed a vast cheering crowd, explaining to them how he had badly bruised his arm after being knocked over in Wimborne. That night he was joined by his wife, who, during the next day, accompanied him to the Sunday service in the cathedral.

Continuing to wear his arm in a sling, we pick up Westy's trail at Droitwich on Monday, the 3rd of February where he arrived at 02:18, having set off from Worcester at 12:25 a.m. By now, the *"Weary Wobbler"* had found himself some miles in arrears, so to make some of them up he walked back to Worcester, and when he left there again at 04:00, and upon checking his calculations, he found himself 65 miles behind his official time-table. Striding out again from Worcester, and working his way through drizzling rain, thick fog, and slippery roads containing pools of water, he made his way to Bromsgrove via Fernleigh and Droitwich, arriving at Bromsgrove at 07:20. Here the horses were changed and a brisk walk ensued to Birmingham.

The *Birmingham Daily Post* told its readers what happened next: About noon the Bristol Road bore a much more animated appearance than usual, and the Horse Fair, Suffolk Street, and the approaches to Bingley Hall were thickly lined with spectators. The vast multitude would have not stood so patiently in the slush and mire of our filthy streets if they had known that the indefatigable Yankee had arrived a couple of hours before his advertised time, and was taking advantage of the interim afforded by his extra exertions by taking a comfortable nap at the Bingley Hall Tavern.

A vast crowd of between 3,000 and 4,000 had paid an undisclosed amount to listen to the American wearing a soft cloth broad brimmed hat and black coat thrown over his shoulders on account of his sling. Addressing his audience, Weston, referring to the fact that Sir John Astley didn't believe that he could accomplish his walk at that time of year, admitted that he hadn't taken into account how long it would take him to pass through any given town owing to the amount of people that wished to see him, thus blocking his path and causing subsequent delays. Referring to having to pass through such places using the sanctuary of a carriage, and the mobbing he received, he said he would rather lose the contest rather than be the victim of an accident. He did not care what the newspapers said of him. He was used to having his name kicked about by the press, and it really mattered very little to him whether they called him a clergyman or a pickpocket.

He then went on to talk about a particular newspaper's comments about the judge who had pulled out of the walk (a "gentleman whose intellect would disgrace an ordinary Government mule"), when it stated that the judge was right to withdraw from the affair rather than facilitate it by prolonging its *"discreditable imposition on the public."* He thought that men who wrote such stuff "were sadly in need of exercise, for their digestive organs must be out of gear." They could attack him all they liked, but he would tell them that the next time he heard from them he would put the matter in the hands of his solicitors.

Weston then went on to talk about diet and using walking as the perfect exercise, going on to advise his audience, not to eat apple tart and Devonshire cream — even though it helped him in his task! He then told his captivated listeners of his experiences and the confusing information he got when asking various people on the way what the distance was from A to B, stating, "These are some of the little encouragements which are calculated to make a man amiable."

"Weston has a quaint style of lecturing, and occasionally indulges his audience with a bit of crisp Yankee humour."

After telling the gathered that he fully intended on making up the lost time, he was loudly cheered before waiting for the hall to clear. He made his way out to the waiting carriage; the pedestrian having mounted the top, acknowledged the *"boisterous manifestations of the motley multitude beneath."*

Speech over, he then made for Wolverhampton. On slushy roads due to melting snow, he sped through Handsworth at 15:35, and from there encountered a rough set of characters who threw snowballs at him. Undeterred by their antics, he plodded on to West Bromwich (16:25), Hill Top (17:00), Wednesbury (17:20), Bradley (17:45), and Bilston (18:00), where he was met by Inspector Evans and five constables. The law accompanied him to Wolverhampton where: At Monmore Lane which was reached at half past six, Major Hay and the Chief Constable of Wolverhampton, Superintendent Lavery, and a body of police were in readiness, and it was with the greatest of difficulty that a path could be cleared from Monmore Green into the town, the streets the whole of the distance being lined by people all anxious to get a glimpse of the celebrated walker. The route was by Bilston Road and Cleveland Road, and by the time the "procession" had reached the Agricultural Hall an enormous number of people had congregated. Metcalfe's brass band was here in waiting to lead Weston to the Exchange, where he was announced to lecture; but the party had only proceeded about 150 yards - to the end of Bilston Street - when a dead-lock resulted from the pressure of the enormous crowd. Fortunately a four wheel cab was on hand, and Weston was placed within it, and it was in this manner he was conveyed to the Exchange, the band marching in front and the crowd increasing at every step.

Weston made the last 200 yards of his journey in the carriage before entering the building, resting half an hour, and then delivering his talk to the meagre audience. On completion of his lecture, he was taken to the Coach and

Horses Hotel, Snow Hill, where he *"complained of his head,"* and, *"wrapped in blankets,"* rested for five hours till just before 02:00 on Tuesday. He was then woken up and took some tea and toast before resuming his journey towards Shifnal arriving there at 05:00 after a journey of three hours.

He only intended to stay at Shifnal for a couple of hours, but was so tired, *"the cause being a recurrence of the prostration caused by the excitement of the previous day,"* that he had to put his feet up for an extended six, leaving that place at 11:00 before embarking on the rest of his journey towards Shrewsbury. It was about this time that an amateur walker called W. G. Gilbert of the Irish Champion Athletic Club (who had walked from Manchester overnight in an *"ordinary walking costume,"*), duped some of the gathered throngs into believing *he* was the Yankee yomper. They consequently followed him, thus leaving the lucky few to see the real McCoy pass through their communities.

And so it was that the authentic American passed Prior's Lee at 11:45, and about noon reached the Oaken Gates, at which point he had conveyed himself exactly 800 miles. It was on this leg of his journey that he was greeted by further masses of intrigued souls as he continued through the colliery district, passing through Ketley, but bypassing Wellington (12:35), Atcham Church (14:30), and Lord Hill Column (15:15), on his way up to Shrewsbury where he arrived at 15:30. It was here that he was *"invited to take luncheon"* by the proprietress of the Lion Hotel, Mrs. Roberts, who provided an excellent meal for him, along with *"some other gentlemen,"* and city magistrates. Just before he left the inn, he was visited by the high sheriff of the county, the Hon. Mr. Herbert, brother to Earl Powis, Miss Herbert, and the Rev. R. K. Salisbury, who *"tendered their hearty congratulations and good wishes"* to the man everybody *just had to meet.*

At this stage of his tour, he had walked 812 miles from the start. He left Shrewsbury at 17:05 under the escort of Superintendent Davies, and made for Chester via Preston Gubbals (19:20). At the agricultural town of Wem (20:20), his escort left him, and he arrived in Whitchurch at 23:00, where yet another large congregation were on hand to get a glimpse of the enigmatic Yank. Their presence again caused him to hitch a ride on the top of the carriage, and a mile was sacrificed to get him to his destination at the Victoria Hotel safely, at 23:30.

Having taken light refreshment, there was little rest for "Ned" as he resumed his plod at 01:30 on Wednesday, the 5th. After being bundled out of the back door of the "Vic," he was accompanied by the sergeant of the borough who took him as far as Grindley Brook (three miles), where he was left *"to his own resources."* Pushing himself forward at the comfortable rate of 5 mph, Weston stumbled into Chester, the home of a certain Henry Vaughan, who greeted him three miles from the city centre, which they both entered at a fair clip at 06:10. Weston thereafter enjoyed a short nap of 90 minutes duration at the Queens Railway Hotel, during which time he didn't undress because he was anxious to keep his lecturing engagements later in the day before he headed up towards Warrington.

Initially the weather had been cold and frosty as he set off, but that soon changed, and the bitingly cold February weather brought with it more sleet and snow to hinder the plucky fellow on his way. Still, the human locomotive persevered in his task, and despite the awful weather, he passed through Frodsham at 10:40 on his way to the Lancashire town, which he reached 45 minutes late at 13:15. Having delivered the first of his talks in Warrington, and because he hadn't the time to keep his engagement to give his promised lecture at the League Hall, Liverpool, he took the 16:40 train to convey him the 18 miles to the port's Central Station, where he arrived at 17:15. He was then driven to a hotel, where he waited to fulfil his engagement at seven o'clock. Afterwards, he used the same method of travel to go to Ormskirk, 12 miles away, where he spoke at the town's Institute. This must have been within the rules, as it was said that Astley *"wasn't complaining."*

Whilst Weston was busily sitting on trains and delivering lectures, there was said to be a lot of *"ill feeling"* being displayed by the thousands who had turned up to see him walking trough their villages and towns. The driver of the omnibus which followed him everywhere must have been petrified at times. The howling mobs who had previously been so excited at the prospect of seeing the celebrated American, turned their anger on him by following the carriage for miles, as it made its way firstly from Warrington to Liverpool and thence to Ormskirk. The inhabitants of Prescot were reported to be *"especially annoyed"* by the invisible hero. The driver eventually caught up with him at Ormskirk where he elected to stay at the Wheatsheaf Hotel instead of going straight on to Wigan as he had planned. It was here that he settled down for the night and was reported to have slept from 23:00 till 04:00 the next morning.

The day after, Thursday, he left Ormskirk at 04:50. Travelling at a good rate of 4 mph in totally unsuitable and dangerous conditions, and with the weather being described as frosty and the road being described as a *"sheet of glass,"* he was reported to have fallen with his full weight onto the elbow and shoulder of his right arm, whilst descending a steep incline on a slippery road, near the White Cross Colliery Works near Skelmersdale. The accident had caused him to sustain *"some severe contusions besides a heavy strain on his nervous system,"* thus requiring him to take a rest of 30 minutes before continuing slowly on. The injury however, had knocked the stuffing out of him so much that at 06:35 the bus was halted again at Tawd Bridge, to give him time to recuperate in the back, whilst he laid on *"one of the cushions."* After an hour he set off again, but this time at a swifter pace in the now pouring rain, passing Holland Moor at 07:45 and Upholland at 08:30. He later told reporters that he believed he would have broken his arm had it not already have been in a sling. When he arrived in Wigan at 09:30, where he took breakfast at the Big Lamp Inn, he was reported to be about 96 miles or so behind time. He set off from there at 10:27 and walked to Bolton followed by a few hundred people. The throng accompanying him increased to about 5,000 as he made progress towards his goal, and it was estimated that he was met by 60,000 locals who cheered him on his way. Only half a dozen or so policeman were employed to see he got a safe passage through the town, and leaving Bolton via Moses Gate at 13:45 and Halshaw Moor ten minutes later, he faced a 13-mile tramp to Manchester.

Passing Kearsley at 14:15 and the Seven Stars Hotel (which was the half-way house between Bolton and Manchester) 20 minutes later, he arrived at Pendleton at 15:35, where encountering the same sized crowds as had welcomed him in Bolton, *"locomotion became a matter of considerable difficulty."* However, the law came to his aid again in the form of Captain Torrens, who, with the assistance of Inspectors Little and Shuter and thirty constables, delivered him safely to Keith's Circus, where he made a further speech about the benefits of walking to some eager listening natives of that industrial city at 4 p.m.

After his talk, Weston was driven to Victoria Station where he had to take yet another train journey, the "ten past six" to Blackburn, where he would address more listeners, before recommencing his journey to Preston by foot. His popularity up to that stage had been his downfall, as he had by that stage walked 905½ miles, and ridden 120. The *"fagged,"* limping, pedestrian arrived in Preston shortly before midnight. As he walked down Fishergate, his every step was guarded by his police escort, who kept the jostling crowd away from him as he headed for the Corn Exchange, where he would address an audience of 600. That night Weston stayed at the Stanley Arms Hotel where he slept soundly till 09:30 the next day.

Clad in a white mackintosh, Weston left Preston just after ten o'clock on Friday morning, the 7th of February during a heavy downpour. Everybody thought he would take a breather in Garstang when he arrived there just before 13:00, but he didn't, preferring instead to push on towards Lancaster where he arrived at 15:30. It was here he gave himself the luxury of sitting down for an hour.

The next stop on his travels would be Burton, and on his way there, he passed through Slyne at 17:40 and Carnforth at 18:45. When he reached Burton, he had been on the road for 500 hours, and at this stage of his trek was just 49 miles short of what he had hoped to achieve in the time. Crooklands was conquered at 21:09, and he arrived at Kendall 20 minutes later. After speaking to the townsfolk, he retired to bed having given up his attempt to walk on to Shap due to the rain and mud which was prevalent on the road.

The weary and daunting walk uphill to Shap 15 miles away was made in four hours in the pouring rain. He had set off from Kendall at 09:00 on Saturday morning, and when he reached the isolated village he just had to go to bed for a couple of hours. This made him late for his forthcoming lecture, and because the roads were so bad, he took the train at Shap and went on to Carlisle from there, missing an intended stop and a lecture in Penrith. A telegram was sent stating that he would be turning up in Carlisle at 19:30 as opposed to the time he should have reached there on foot at 14:30. With that information in mind, many people who had walked ten miles out of the town on the south road to meet him were disappointed to find out later how he had really arrived.

Arriving at the railway station at 17:00, he dined at the Bush Hotel, lectured to an exceedingly small audience at the Victoria Hall, and at 21:00, accompanied by Mr. Mackay, the Chief Constable, and some policemen, continued his journey towards Haydon Bridge. On a fine night, and travelling along at a fair old pace, he crossed Warwick bridge before proceeding on to Corby hill at 22:25. Eventually reaching Brampton at 23:30, the *"unruly mob"* which welcomed him, severely hustled him so much that the frightened American had to take refuge *"under the friendly*

King of the Peds

portals" of the Howard Arms Hotel, where he was picked up an hour later by the carriage which had journeyed from Shap. Weston was then driven 20 miles to Haydon Bridge which he reached at 5 a.m. It was here that he slept all day on his "day off" till 22:30 and left that town just after midnight on Monday, the 10th of February to walk to Hexham where he arrived at 01:45 and Corbridge at 02:35.

The *Newcastle Daily Chronicle* takes up the next bit of his journey as he finally began to head south: **Weston reached Newcastle at 6.30 a. m., and whilst his omnibus proceeded to the Douglas Hotel, new Grainger Street, Weston bid good-bye to the two amateurs who had accompanied him over this, the first 28 miles of his day's journey, and proceeded without stopping by way of Collingwood Street, across the High Level Bridge to Gateshead, where he stopped for ten minutes and partook of a cup of tea at Lockhart's Cocoa Rooms. Up to this time not a dozen people had recognized him as he passed through Newcastle, the wet weather probably keeping most people indoors, and notwithstanding that he had his right arm suspended in a sling, the American stretched out freely in his usual style of walking, and appeared little distressed by his previous efforts over the bad roads between Haydon Bridge and Newcastle. Birtley was reached at ten minutes to nine o'clock, and here a large assemblage of people had congregated along the whole length of the village to see him pass, and loud cheers were given for him, which he courteously acknowledged. Here he was rejoined by the judges and the omnibus. Chester-le-Street, eight miles from Newcastle was reached at 2.15, and here an immense crowd had turned out to see Weston pass. Inspector Collins and his constables were present, however, and they rendered good service as he passed up the village street by clearing the way in front of him, and in preventing the crowd from pressing upon him, whilst he bowed his acknowledgement of the plaudits which greeted him from time to time. The road after leaving Chester-le-Street was much worse than any he encountered since leaving Haydon Bridge, particularly at Chester Moor Colliery, where both the footpath on which he walked and the roadway were a complete quagmire, but Weston never altered his pace. Pity Me, three miles from Durham was reached about twenty five minutes past ten o'clock. Here a large crowd of people assembled, and although the policeman stationed at Framwellgate Moor did his utmost to keep the crowd off, Weston was very much hampered by them. Framwellgate Moor was passed at about thirty minutes past ten o'clock, and the end of the North Road, Durham, was reached at about forty four minutes past that hour. Large numbers of people were assembled along the whole route through Durham streets, and three constables, whom Head-Constable Duns had deputed to preserve order, closed round the pedestrian, and kept the crowd from pressing upon him, and on reaching the door of the Waterloo Hotel in Old Elvet, he raised his cap in acknowledgement of the cheer that was sent up for him by the crowd, and disappeared into the hotel, at ten minutes to eleven o'clock, having accomplished 42 miles from Haydon Bridge in 10 hours 50 minutes. He was accommodated in an upstairs room of the Waterloo Hotel, where, after resting some time, he partook of a light lunch. Several persons were introduced into the room during his stay, including one or two clergymen and a number of ladies were anxious to see the famous walkist. After a delay of one hour and a quarter, at five minutes past twelve o'clock Weston left the Waterloo Hotel and took the Stockton road, by way of New Elvet and Shincliffe. Weston showed little effects from his long walk of the first half of his day. At Shincliffe and Coxhoe he was greeted by large crowds of people, and was keeping up the good pace he had shown when entering and leaving Durham.**

After that he passed Sedgefield at 14:30 and reached Stockton at 17:00. Owing to confusion about the time he was due to address his audience at Swallow Circus, Weston lost an hour's walking time, and as he waited to start his lecture at 18:00, he dined at the Black Lion.

Having given his talk, he left for Darlington at 7 p.m. initially accompanied by Superintendent Bell and 30 constables. Travelling towards that town at a smart pace, he passed through Heartburn at 19:30, Long Newton at 20:15, Ludberge at 20:50, Houghton at 21:30, and arrived at his destination at 10 p.m., having made a respectable distance of 74 miles for his day's work. After making his way through the usual throngs of excited townsfolk, and delivering his second lecture of the day at Livingstone Hall, Weston thereafter, and contrary to expectation, pushed on to Northallerton at an hour before midnight, arriving there at 03:40 on Tuesday morning. This meant he had walked 91 miles in 28 hours, over some very heavy roads.

He had now competed 1,077 miles and had racked up 171 miles in arrears due to his rides in the carriage. After taking a few hours rest at the Railway Hotel, and to make up some of the lost distance riding, Weston walked 20 ½ miles in 4½ hours, ten of which were made along the Boroughbridge road, and back, to the Railway Hotel through Otterington, Rewsham, Sandhutton and Busby Stokes, returning there at 16:40. After dinner and a short nap, he recommenced his journey proper towards Thirsk at 18:45.

Accompanied by the town's fife and drum band, which escorted him through its streets at nine o'clock, Weston relieved by the splendid behaviour of its occupants, headed towards the *"most difficult hill in Yorkshire,"* the infamous "Sutton Bank" after spending a *"pleasant half hour with Mr. Cassand at Brook House."* Of his journey up the bank, *"the Yankee made little of it, and took the rise all the way in his stride, speedily putting a gap between himself and the omnibus, which made very slow progress up the steep ascent, a mile in length."* Continuing on, he reached Helmsley, 14 miles from Thirsk, at 01:25 on Wednesday morning, and then pushed on to Pickering where he stayed at the Black Lion Hotel from 04:40 till 08:30. After breakfast he hurried himself on his way to the beautiful seaside town of Scarborough, which he reached at 13:45. It was here that he gave a lecture at the Town Hall before heading in the direction of the smaller coastal resort of Bridlington at 15:20.

"Brid" was conquered at 19:45, and whilst the rest of the party indulged in a pint at another Black Lion Hotel, but this time, in the seaside town, Weston made a speech at the Temperance Hall before joining his travelling companions. It may have been at the Black Lion where Weston lost another of his judges. This time it was Mr. H. Etherington of the *Bicycling Times* who left the party for good after some words were exchanged between him and the pedestrian. The group stayed at the hotel till 23:00 and then re-commenced their journey inland on the road to Great Driffield, which was reeled in at two o'clock on Thursday morning.

The Keys Hotel was the place where Weston would spend the next few hours before once again pounding the road to Beverley at eleven o'clock. Passing though Cranswick at 11:35 and Watton at 11:55, he was joined by the celebrated Hull pedestrian William Clarkson, who joined him on his journey just before he entered Leconsfield. The winner of a six-day pedestrian contest in his home town some months earlier accompanied his more famous counterpart towards Beverley, which the pair reached around 14:00. It was at the Mechanics Hall where the American chatted to his audience about the benefits of walking, before heading off to Hull, accompanied by a posse of Beverley based constables. Weston was glad to have the police with him because it took him and his protectors a full hour to get from the city limits to the Public Rooms, where in front of a much larger crowd, he would reiterate what he had said at Beverley before dining at the town's Imperial Hotel. The time lost battling through the large crowds in Hull meant that he wouldn't be able to keep his appointment to lecture in Market Weighton. Disappointingly for him he had to be driven there, thus losing the distance he gained in Northallerton of 20½ miles.

The "Walkist" arrived in Market Weighton, having been driven in the bus through the rain which had persisted since he left Hull at 20:20. After addressing a poor assemblage of interested people at midnight, he left that town on foot in the direction of the walled city of York at 01:20 on roads, described as, being *"very heavy."* Notwithstanding the time of morning when he passed through Pocklington Riverhead, the inhabitants of that place six miles from Weighton turned out in numbers, carrying lanterns and lamps to guide him through the village. A slight delay occurred thereafter when the party reached Barmby Bar, due to the turnpike keeper being fast asleep. However, when he was woken from his slumber, he at once removed the obstacle which prevented the group from continuing its journey to York.

Weston arrived in the old walled city at 06:15 on Friday the 14th having walked 1,227 miles. Very few people were about when he slipped into the White Swan Hotel, where he put his head down for a couple of hours. On resuming his hike at 08:20, he was joined by another celebrated local pedestrian, Pat McCarty who walked briskly alongside his more illustrious counterpart towards Leeds via Tadcaster, where they entered the former named place on the York Road and were met by hundreds of *"working men"* near the Dog and Gun Inn. Thereafter, they were escorted up Quarry Hill and Lady Lane by the borough police, before arriving at two o'clock, and on time, for Weston to deliver his "talk on walk" at the Grand Opera House before leaving for Bradford at 15:20. After his speech, which was of 20 minutes duration, and which was given to between two and three hundred people, he was escorted by a strong force of mounted constables under the charge of Superintendent McWilliams down New Brigate, through Upperhead How, Guildford Street, Park Lane, and St. Paul's Street, before being followed to Bradford by the usual large crowd of hangers-on, arriving there at 17:45 where he gave a lecture at St. Georges Hall.

It was on the same day that the following article appeared in a Sheffield newspaper asking the citizens of the city to allow him some space when he passed through. It read: **With regard to the flying visit of this celebrated walkist, a correspondent writes as follows: - "As E. P. Weston, the American pedestrian, is to pass through Sheffield on Saturday next, it is to be hoped that the people of Sheffield will give him a hearty welcome, and at the same time** do all in their power to clear a course for him, and not crowd round and hinder him on his long and tedious journey. The distance he is now behind has been caused by people in towns he has passed through pressing too closely about him. It is to be hoped that this kind of thing will not take place in Sheffield. Being personally acquainted with him, and knowing him to be a perfect gentleman, is the reason for my bespeaking him fair play.

By Friday evening he had made his way to Halifax, where he lectured at the Drill Hall. He then travelled by omnibus to Huddersfield where he *"was received by a rough mob of persons who would keep no kind of order,"* consequently finding it extremely difficult to enter, and indeed, leave the *"Gymnasium"* where he gave another address at midnight. After taking 10 hours rest the next day, Saturday, he used the train again to get to Wakefield, where he gave a further talk at the Theatre Royal at 11:30 before hitting the road, this time on foot, to Barnsley at noon. It was there he was later met by another disorderly crowd causing him to take refuge once again in the security of the wagon. After lecturing in Barnsley at the new Public Hall, he boarded a carriage at three o'clock, and headed to Sheffield where he was to deliver his third lecture of the day.

The *Sheffield Telegraph* takes up what happened next: **He was preceded by his omnibus, and when within five miles of the town large crowds were met with. They could not be persuaded that he was not in the bus, and a good deal of strong language and threats of personal violence were used to the occupants of that vehicle if they did not permit the little man to get out and walk the rest of the journey. The Wicker and all the approaches to the Alexandra were well nigh impassable by reason of the dense crowd that had assembled. At ten minutes to five, after many false alarms, Weston drove up and immediately there was a terrific rush, and it took the united efforts of twenty policemen to clear him a passage into the building. He at once proceeded to the wardrobe, where some tea and toast was provided for him, and where also he had a shave.**

Weston looked very haggard and weary, and it is evident that his protracted walk has told upon him. The distance he had covered by foot up to that time was 1,277 ½ miles, and he was 209 miles to the bad. In the meantime a fairly large audience had assembled who were kept in good humour by the band under Mr. Parkin.

Weston was ushered on to the stage to the strains of, "See the conquering hero comes," and he received a most enthusiastic welcome. Before commencing his lecture, "What I know about Walking," he apologised for his appearance. His right arm was in a sling and his apparel was certainly very travel stained. He explained that he had been so jostled by the people in Huddersfield in their desire to see him that when he awoke that morning he felt a fitter candidate for a future world than he was for reaching Sheffield. He should like in Sheffield, a place which took such a great interest in pedestrianism, and a place which had given him such a kindly welcome, to make an explanation personal to himself with regard to that trial.

Weston then went on to tell his audience of the journalist who had tried to discredit him following the publication of Mr. A. G. Payne's (the first judge to leave the trial) letter to the press, in which that man had accused Weston of violating the conditions of the feat. Weston then read out the letter from Astley which challenged him to cover the distance in the time stipulated, asking the audience if they agreed that he broke the conditions. Cries of "No!, No!," rang out from the gathered followed by applause. He then went on to say that he would try and make up the lost distance from Monday, gave examples of humorous incidents en route, talked of the advantages of walking and left the stage promising to do his best to accomplish his task, amid much cheering: **There was such an immense crowd around the Alexandra, that Weston was shown out of the back way and slipped unobserved up Exchange-lane, where his carriage was waiting. He was then driven to the Royal Victoria Hotel where he had dinner. Afterwards he took a train to Attercliffe, and started on his walk to Worksop, where he arrived at three minutes after eleven, being 212 miles behind his time.** The following is the official timetable for the ensuing week: -

Feb - 17th	Time	Miles	Feb - 20th	Time	Miles
Retford	04:00	1,512	March	10:00	1,690
Lincoln	10:00	1,535	Wisbech	14:00	1,700
Newark	15:00	1,554	Kings Lynn	19:00	1,715
Southwell	17:15	1,556	Swaffham	00:00	1,731
Nottingham	20:30	1,569			

Feb - 18th			Feb - 21st		
Derby	01:00	1,584	East Dereham	08:00	1,743
Burton	05:00	1,596	Norwich	13:00	1,759
Ashby De-La-Zouch	20:00	1,605	Yarmouth	20:30	1,781
Leicester	00:00	1,623	Lowestoft	00:00	1,791
Feb - 19th			Feb - 22nd		
Billesdon	08:30	1,632	Blythburg	10:00	1,807
Uppingham	11:30	1,642	Saxmundham	13:00	1,817
Stamford	15:00	1,656	Wickham	15:00	1,825
Market Deeping	17:45	1,664	Woodbridge	16:15	1,830
Peterborough	20:00	1,672	Ipswich	19:30	1,838
			Needham	23:00	1,847

Always looking to make money out of his ventures, the following advertisement appeared in the national press on a regular basis:

WESTON'S MATCH AGAINST TIME. - 2,000 miles in 1,000 hours, - Now ready, 6d, ; post free, 6 ½ d. - "WESTON'S ROUTE AND TIMETABLE," giving route, times of arrival, distance, conditions, &c., together with a record of his principal performances; his life, with incidents, and a full length photograph of his costume. May be had at all Newsagents, Booksellers, &c., or of the Publishers, ETHRINGTON and Co., East Temple Chambers, Fleet Street, E. C.

Weston's rest on Sunday, the 16th of February in Worksop, evidently did him the power of good, for he was described as appearing much refreshed when he started off from the Nottinghamshire town to walk to Lincoln at midnight. In an attempt to make up his arrears, he walked to the sixth milestone on the road to Lincoln, turned back, walked to the first milepost out of Worksop, and then continued on his journey on to Lincoln, thus taking ten miles off his deficit.

On his way, he passed through Retford at 04:30, where a large crowd gathered to witness his passage, Markham at 05:33 and Saxilby at 08:20. Realising he was ahead of time as he passed the fourth milestone from Lincoln, he went back to the fifth and returned to the fourth thus adding a further two miles to his *"back score"* before recommencing his journey. As he entered the city, he was met by a large contingent of police at the Grand Stand. They escorted him trouble free to the Pavilion where he arrived to give his lecture at 10 o'clock. After that, he set off to tramp to Newark at 11:30 arriving there in time to offer his second talk of the day at 15:15.

From Newark he set off for Nottingham at 16:20 where he had an engagement to give his third and final sermon, reaching that city at 19:45. Entering Nottingham over Trent Bridge, Weston was met by huge crowds, which caused so much bother that he had to seek refuge in a shop for a time. Eventually he reached the Mechanics Hall, informed those listening about the real benefits of walking, and after having dinner and indulging in a welcome rest, he left there at 23:35 in his omnibus and was driven a mile out of the city. He then stepped on to the road again, making Derby his next port of call.

When he eventually reached Derby at 03:30 on Tuesday morning, Weston had walked a total of 92 miles in 27 hours. The bed provided for him at the Royal Hotel must have been a welcome sight. However, he didn't have the luxury of sleeping in it for long as he needed to make up some of his lost distance, and that meant setting off at 08:50 to walk to the tenth milestone on the Nottingham Road and back again to Derby, which he did in a time of 4h.25m, before lecturing at the Temperance Hall in the town at 13:30. When he started off for Burton on Trent at 14:50 he had covered 1,403 miles of his journey, his arrears accumulating to 181 miles.

We next catch up with him when he arrived in Ashby-de-la-Zouch, where, after giving a lecture at the Masonic Hall, he rested in the town until midnight and then set off on the road to Leicester.

His journey that night wasn't helped by the fact that he had to struggle through a snow storm. He arrived in Leicester at 04:40, rested till 07:40, and plodded on to Billesdon, arriving there an hour behind schedule. However, on reaching Uppingham, he had managed to make up 40 minutes of the time lost and must have been in his element as he lectured to an *"aristocratic audience"* at the Falcon Hotel, *"Sir H. Fletcher presenting."* From there he set off for Stamford at 12:30, and on his way, passed through South Suffenham at 2 p.m., arriving at the *"little Lincolnshire town"* about 16:00 on Wednesday, the 19th of February where he lectured at the Assembly Rooms before pointing his nose in the direction of Peterborough via Market Deeping.

At 21:05, he was escorted by a *"body of constables"* to the Town Hall, where, after giving his address, he took refuge at the Bull Hotel leaving there at a quarter past four on Thursday, the following morning. After passing through Whittlesey, he complained of drowsiness, and shortly after, allowed himself a chance to recuperate on his arrival at Eastrea at 06:25 by getting his head down for 45 minutes. Then it was back on the trail to March where he told the citizens of that town about the benefits of his chosen profession at the St. Johns Hall before leaving for Wisbech via Guyhim at 10:50. From Wisbech, which he vacated at 14:15, he tramped to Kings Regis (Kings Lynn) where he lectured at 20:00. From there he moved on to Swaffham, where he informed the press on his arrival at 03:00 that he had accomplished the task up to that stage of walking 1,540 miles, albeit 175 of them being in arrears.

The weather was bad when he set off for East Dereham 2h.15m later on Friday morning. Before entering there, he turned at the second milestone and went to the third, and back, before arriving in the little Norfolk town where he told the locals about his exploits at the Corn Exchange. An hour later he recommenced his journey in a snow storm towards Norwich. On the outskirts of that town he was *"met by a number of stalwart men bearing long poles, who rendered sufficient to the police, under Superintendent Bernard, in forming a square, and thus keeping back the people who thronged on all sides in great numbers."* In this manner he was safely conveyed to the Victoria Hall, where, after lecturing again, he settled himself down to lunch and rested at the Rampant Horse Hotel. Weston had now made 1,566 miles with 173 to make up before he reached London.

We pick up his progress the next day, Saturday, at 05:15. Having delivered his 50th lecture in the coastal resort of Yarmouth, he headed in the direction of Lowestoft in the most appalling of conditions, during which time he had to contend with falling sleet and extremely heavy roads. It was as he was passing through Lowestoft that he complained of feeling unwell. Nevertheless, he persevered with the task in hand, and waited till he arrived in Bythburgh before taking a rest of an hour at 10:25. He then hiked through Saxmundham at 14:35. After that he trod on to Woodbridge where he went back on his ground between milestones thus recovering another two.

Pushing on towards Ipswich, he was escorted by a posse of constables under the direction of Colonel Russell and some 60 soldiers of the 1st brigade and the Royal Horse Artillery, *"the two services working admirably together in piloting him through the immense concourse of people."* After he delivered his address at the Lecture Hall, he was off on his toddles again to Needham Market, having to take the bus in from half a mile out, finally arriving on Saturday night at 23:00.

During Sunday he stopped at the Swan Hotel. It was here that he undoubtedly made intricate plans on how he was going to recover the lost ground due to the interest his great romp around the shires of England had been creating. His plan was to knock 40 miles off the deficit starting the next day, and this he set out to do at one minute past midnight when he set off for Scole in Norfolk 16 miles away; firstly via the Coddenham Road, and then the Norwich High Road. Retracing his steps, and walking an extra four miles on the way back, Weston achieved his objective and arrived back in Needham at 08:45. Many expected him to stop there for a while, but the plucky pedestrian had other ideas and kept pounding away later passing through Stowmarket at 09:30, Woolpit at 10:50, and finally arriving in Bury St. Edmunds at 12:40 having travelled over 59 miles *without a rest,* which was his best performance, bar the very first day, in the five weeks he had been walking.

The *Isle of Ely and Huntingdonshire Gazette* in its edition of March the 1st 1879 described Weston's visit to Cambridge: Mr. Edward Payson Weston, the celebrated American pedestrian, who undertook the task of walking 2,000 miles in 1,000 consecutive hours, over the turnpike roads of England, reached Cambridge last Monday night having walked from Needham Market. The town was in a state of excitement, and hundreds of people were anxiously waiting in the vicinity of Newmarket road for his arrival some time before the appointed time. Weston was timed to reach Cambridge at eight o'clock, but he was half an hour before time. He came from Newmarket, leaving the latter place (after lecturing there) just before five o'clock. On reaching the last mile on the Newmarket road, opposite "The Priory Tap," he entered a fly which had been provided for him and he proceeded by way of Emmanuel road, to the Guildhall arriving there about a quarter to eight. Some time before this, hundreds of people were waiting about in the neighbourhood of Jesus-lane, in which direction it was expected he would come, eager to catch a glimpse of the plucky traveller. About half past seven o'clock a ruse was played by some undergraduate, who dressed himself up something similar to Weston and went into the Pitt Club. It was generally thought that this was the real tramper, but the crowd were soon informed in which direction the pedestrian had proceeded to the Guildhall, and a rush was made down Sidney-street and Market-street to the Market hill, where a large crowd had already assembled. Immediately the fly conveying Weston drove up in front of the hall, the crowd gathered round it and pressed forward to get a good look at him, and the police had great difficulty in making a clear passage. This having been done, Weston stepped from the conveyance and was heartily cheered as he walked up the hall steps. He afterwards partook of some tea and toast before delivering his lecture. After Weston had entered the hall there was a rush at the doors for admittance, and the large room was soon filled with undergraduates and townspeople, the audience however being chiefly composed of the former. The Gallery was also filled. About eight o'clock the occupants of the shilling seats made a rush, and stepped over into the reserved seats. Otherwise the proceedings passed off very orderly. At about five minutes past eight Weston mounted the platform and was wildly cheered. After the applause had subsided, the Mayor, who presided briefly, introduced the pedestrian: - Weston began by saying that in order to fulfil his engagement that evening, he had walked a distance of eighty-five miles since 12 o'clock on Sunday night, and as he had several miles further to walk that night he hoped they would excuse him if his remarks were somewhat short and disconnected. Why had he undertaken this walk? Some people may be ready to answer, "To make money," but when he told them he received £300 if he accomplished the task and had to pay £800 away for expenses it could not be said that he did it simply for pecuniary gain. This was only partly the reason. He had no other reasons, however, and one was to show that man was not the poor creature some would make him. He did not wish to be thought a champion, and he did not claim to have accomplished a task which other men could not do, if they did but live and sat properly, and - obeyed their parents, [Laughter] Referring to Charles Rowell, who accompanied him at the commencement of the journey, he said he, as well as every one else, was astonished that Rowell showed so little effect from having done so much work. He was gratified and surprised, and he only hoped that Rowell would have the same fair play in America as had been shown to him (Weston) during the time he had been in England. He must say that if Rowell had a fair trial and was as well as when he last saw him, he ought to bring the championship belt back to England. [Applause.] With reference to training, he said he always abstained from smoking or taking any stimulating drinks, and also abstained from eating any false food, such as pastry. After speaking of the preparation of the feet against blisters, he stated he felt perfectly well, and anything but weak. During the day he had knocked off 40 miles of the arrears that were against him on Saturday, and he had to walk from 41 to 43 miles a day until the end of the week to complete the distance in the specified time. A week ago that morning, he was 213 miles behind, that morning he was 172 behind [applause]; during the day he had knocked off 40, so that at the moment he was 182 miles behind. He stated that the roads over that he had passed that day were in good condition, which had enabled him to accomplish such a good day's work. - Weston thanked those present for the kind reception they had given him, and left the orchestra amid loud cheers. - There were a large number of people waiting outside the hall, which Weston left about 8.40. Mr. Stretten, the deputy chief constable of the county and one of the Judges accompanying him for a mile out in a cab, to avoid the crowd. On dismounting to continue his journey on foot, he went very stiffly, his previous exertions during the day telling on him. He appeared both leg weary and drowsy, and at the Caxton Cross-roads, the omnibus was brought to a standstill, and at 11.5 he lay extended on the cushions. Weston had covered ninety-three miles in twenty three hours which was his best performance during the trial. He rested till midnight, when he proceeded on his journey. Still going very stiffly, he arrived at St. Neots at 2.20. He stayed at the New Inn till 9.50, when he left and walked 2 miles out and in before lecturing at the Public Hall. He resumed his journey at 11.35 and travelled on to Bedford.

The journey is then picked up after he had delivered his lecture in Bedford at 14:45 on Tuesday, the 25th of February. His time-table had indicated that he was due to lecture in Newport Pagnell at 19:30. However, due to his excellent progress, even on the snow covered roads, he arrived in the town with an hour and three quarters to spare. Taking full advantage of the situation, he subtracted eight miles from his arrears by passing through the town, walking to the fourth mile post and retracing his steps. Satisfied with that, he dined at The Swan after his talk and went to sleep till midnight. Thereafter a further 30 miles were knocked of the deficit when he thought he would take an early morning stroll on Wednesday to Buckingham, via Stoney Stratford and back, a distance of 30 miles in 6h.50m, the return journey proving difficult for him due to the cold north westerly wind blowing in his face.

After eating a hearty breakfast, he started off for Buckingham again at 08:30. After reaching the Town Hall, he entertained the locals for half an hour before pushing on to Bicester, where a repeat performance at the town's Corn Exchange was undertaken at 15:20. He was met there by a large contingent of undergraduates, who accompanied him to the university city of Oxford, which was a distance of twelve miles away. The plan was to get him to the *"Theatre"* as quietly as possible, but the word was out that the great man was on his way, and when he realised that he was in for another mobbing, he sought refuge on a *"drag"* which whisked him to his lecture. After completing that, he started off for Wallingford. The American had now covered 1,871 miles, and at that time, had 92 miles of arrears to make up.

Weston arrived at Wallingford at 02:30 on the morning of Thursday the 27th. Taking a longer rest there than was expected, he resumed his journey to Reading via Pangbourne at 09.10. The drizzling rain which fell all the way didn't help his cause, and after walking a couple of extra miles, he reached Reading at 14:15. An hour was spent in that town before leaving for Windsor at 15:15 having covered a distance 1,914½ miles. He now had just over 24 hours in order to accomplish his task, but alas, the signs of failure were beginning to stare him straight in the face.

Despite the inevitable negative conclusion of his unprecedented effort, the brave Yank tackled the heavy roads with relish, going on to pass Binfield at 17.05. When he approached Windsor at 19:30, a very large crowd awaited his arrival. On reaching the town's Theatre, where he addressed a moderate audience which included Sir John Astley, Colonel Goodlake and the Mayor, he unwisely walked down to the Castle Hotel where he was jostled in the crush. After resting till 23:40, he then took a ride in a closed carriage, accompanied by one of the judges, to the 22nd milestone on the way to the Metropolis on the London and Bath road. From this point he walked to the 14th milestone from the capital, and then retraced his steps as far as the 21st at 03:20 on Friday morning, having completed 15 miles in 3h.40m.

On starting again, he only got about half a mile before having to halt once more and take another 50 minutes rest as it *"was now evident that he was suffering from great prostration."* At 05:30, he once more attempted to proceed. *"Weston was now palpably done up and reeled all over the road like a drunken man. His attendants had twice to catch him to prevent him falling into a ditch. Accordingly the cab was once more brought to a standstill and he slept restlessly till seven at which period all chance of completing the distance had vanished.*

By 08:50 and with 40 miles still to be made, Weston, realising that he had no chance of success, stopped at Mr. Ellinson's for breakfast, and didn't resume his tramp till 10:25 when he wobbled three miles out, and in, on the Maidenhead road, turning and repeating the exercise, thus making twelve miles. Repeating his steps again, he walked two and a half more out and in, and then an extra half mile down to Mr. Ellinson's once again.

When the thousand hours were up at 16.10, Weston had managed to walk 1,977½ miles. He thereafter walked on to the Royal Exchange, London, where he arrived at five minutes to twelve thus completing the desired distance eight hours late.

The *New York World* later wrote: **The walk as a speculation is said to have been a success, for although his bet of £100 against £500 made with Sir John Astley is lost, Weston did so well with his lectures and by the sales of photographs and pamphlets on walking, that it is thought he will clear several hundred pounds. Another cause of failure may be attributed to bad weather, either snow or rain having fallen nearly every day during the journey.**

CHAPTER 15

Rise and Fall

Charlie Rowell did most of his training on the roads around his home village of Chesterton near Cambridge. He was reported to run to Ely before breakfast accompanied by his dog which, and apparently, he had to carry much of the way. It was claimed that Lord Balfour and the Prince of Wales had recommended Rowell to Astley who was said to have wanted a home grown athlete to go to America to bring the his belt back to Britain. Sir John agreed to pay Rowell's £100 ($500) entry fee for the forthcoming contest, and the $1,250 needed to cover his handler's costs. If Astley would have had his way, Rowell, the "Maidenhead Waterman," as Astley referred to him, would have been accompanied by "Blower" Brown, "Corkey" and Harry Vaughan, but the three absentees had been put off by the crossing even though Astley had offered to pay their expenses too.

In his book *"50 Years of my Life,"* Sir John would later write: **The third man in the late competition, C. Rowell, took my fancy much, as he was a very clean-made, muscular young fellow, and had formerly been our boat boy at the Guards' Club at Maidenhead. He had since that time run long distances well, and was real fond of the business, though he had not made any great score. However, I fancied he could, if properly looked after; so I posted £100 for Rowell and entered him for a six days and nights competition at Madison Square Gardens at New York; and I bid Rowell get himself fit, and I would pay expenses of himself and two friends (to look after him) in the land of Stars' and Stripes. In due time he reported himself in proper fettle for the contest; so I wrote to him to come down to Elsham, and I would see him run four or five hours. He duly arrived, and the next morning, having measured off the requisite number of laps to the mile on the gravel walks in our kitchen garden, I set him going, and told him to run at the rate of eight miles an hour till I bid him stop.**

He ran the first sixteen miles with such ease in two hours that I went away, telling one of the gardeners to score up the laps with a bit of chalk on the garden-wall. In about an hour I returned, and he seemed going easier than when he started so I let him continue another hour, and when he had covered thirty-two miles—just under the four hours had not turned a hair. I stopped him and advised him to have a good rub down between the blankets; but he ran off to the stables, and stripping, got two of the helpers to chuck three or four buckets of the coldest spring water over him; he was then rubbed dry in the warm stables, put his things on, and asked me to let him go and shoot some rabbits, and away he went. I was satisfied that he was good enough to send over to try and bring back the champion belt to England, and I duly sent him and his two mates over to New York, lending him £250 to cover all expenses.

Rowell was probably virtually unknown by the American public when he arrived in New York on the steamship *Parthia* which, having set sail from Liverpool via Queenstown, Ireland on the 15th of February, docked at her berth at a few minutes before nine o'clock on Friday the 28th.

He and his trainers, Charlie Asplen and Johnny Simpson were met at the pier by one of the contestants in the forthcoming race, the then present world champion Daniel O'Leary, who had been permitted by the Customs officers to be the first man on the gang plank. The newspapers of the time reported that Rowell had been given a hearty reception by his American hosts, and after a chat of fifteen minutes, passed through customs and was driven by O'Leary to the St. James Hotel at Twenty Eighth Street and Broadway.

Rowell had turned up at the offices of the *Turf, Field and Farm* in the *"World"* building, New York, on Saturday the 1st, with every intention of signing the articles of agreement for the race that had been drawn up in London. He was expecting the three other pedestrians who would be appearing in the race to do the same, but there were objections to the rules affecting the distribution of the prize money by the other three competitors, Daniel O'Leary, Charles Harriman and John Ennis. Consequently it was agreed that they all should wait for the arrival of Mr. Atkinson before they signed them. The following was drafted to meet the wishes of those taking part:

If only one man does 450 miles, he shall take all the money; two men do 450 miles, the winner shall take three quarters and the second man one quarter of the money; if three men do 450 miles, the winner shall take one half, the second man 30 per cent., and the third man 20 per cent.; if four men do 450 miles, the winner shall take one half, the second man 25 per cent., the third man 15 per cent., and the fourth man 10 per cent.

On the following Monday afternoon, Rowell was watched by a large contingent of people, including O'Leary and Harriman, as he trained for the forthcoming "3rd International Astley Belt" race at Gilmore's Garden. Dressed in dark blue tight fitting trousers, a brown cardigan jacket, and a multicoloured cap, he firstly ran around the track at 8 mph, and then changing his gait from a walk to a fast trot, maintained that pace for a couple of hours.

Betting on the morning of Tuesday, the 4th was as follows: **O'Leary $75 to $100; Rowell, $100 to $45; Harriman, $3 to $1; Ennis, $10 to $1:** Rowell continued to impress at the Garden as he prepared himself for the race by putting in 7½ mph around the track, whilst O'Leary limbered up with a brisk walk to the High Bridge and back.

On the next day, the pedestrians, minus O'Leary and Rowell, their backers, and Mr. Atkinson who represented both the London *Sporting Life* and Astley, met at the offices of the *Turf, Field and Farm* to once again talk about the distribution of the gate money. The amendment that had been proposed at the previous meeting was discussed and found to be acceptable. It was expected that the articles of agreement would be signed later that day at the St. James Hotel, where other arrangements would be finalised for the race. Mr. Atkinson, Astley's agent, stated that Rowell was in excellent condition.

All the contestants visited the Garden on Saturday, the 8th of March. The 10-foot wide track, which was laid outside the pillars supporting the roof, was described as being in *"excellent condition,"* and was measured by Mr. Hammell the civil engineer, who gave the following written statement about it.

Having measured the course for the competitors for the belt of Sir John D. Astley for the long distance championship of the world in Gilmore's Garden, in this city, I certify that at eighteen inches outside of the inner curb it is exactly 660 feet in length. I am,
CHARLES H. HAMELL.

The competitors watched the workmen erecting their accommodation, which were four tents situated at the four corners of the track. A draw had been made for who was to occupy which property. Three of the tents had just one room, but the best of the lot, No. 1, which O'Leary drew, had three. Ennis drew No. 2, Rowell, No. 3, and the least attractively located tent, No. 4, was drawn by Harriman. Rowell asked what arrangements there were for cooking and when told gas stoves would be provided, was anxious to know if they were suitable to broil chops on. The carpenters had also been hard at work, boarding over the entire space within the track to cut down on the dust that had been so problematic for the athletes in prior events, and the 17 furnaces which kept the building warm, were lit in preparation for the big event.

The competitors.

Daniel O'Leary   **Charles Rowell**   **John Ennis**   **Charles Harriman**

The National Police Gazette (Illustration no: 34)

Daniel O'Leary at 32 years of age was 5 feet 8½ inches in height and weighed 148lbs.

Charles Rowell was 26 years old. He was 5 feet 6 inches in height and weighed 137lbs.

John Ennis at 36 years of age was 5 feet 8 inches in height and weighed 156lbs. Since his last appearance in the London race won by Corkey, he had skated 100 miles on January the 6th of 1879 in 11h.37m.45s, which at the time, was the best on record.

Charles Harriman was born in Whitefield, Lincoln, Maine, on April the 22nd 1853. He was 6 feet 1 inch tall, weighed 168lbs, and had no experience in a six-day race. His career as a pedestrian commenced in 1868 at the Jefferson (Maine) Trotting Park in a 200-yard foot race, which he won, defeating seven starters. At the country fair at Hingham, Massachusetts, he came in second in a half mile race. Then in April, 1872, he won a $50 a side, 210-yard race over the bridge between Auburn and Lewiston against Paxton Allen of Auburn, Maine. In the spring of 1873 at Lewiston, he covered 100 miles in 21h.30m. At Haverhill, Massachusetts, on February the 19th 1878, he walked 100 miles, square heel-and-toe, in 18h.48m.40s without resting, thus beating Henry Vaughan's 100 miles record of 18h.51m.35s. He followed that up by making 150 miles in 36 hours at the same place and in the same fashion. His next walk of note took place at the Music Hall, Boston, on April 11th in an attempt to beat O'Leary's *American* record of 18h.53m.43s. At the ninetieth mile he was forced to stop, which he finished in 17h.26m.45s. Then, between the 10th and 11th of May at the American Institute Building, New York, in a professional 36-hour heel-and-toe race for $200 and the champion belt, he beat Guyon, Ennis, W. S. O'Brien and ten others, covering 160 1/8 miles in 34h.29m. In this contest, he also walked 100 miles without a stop in 19h.36m.52s, and after resting 17 minutes, continued on the track until the finish. From the 120th to the 160th mile, he made the best time on record in the USA. At the Pearl Street Rink, Buffalo, on July the 3rd 1878, he walked 100 miles again without resting in 20h.43m.40s. His next appearance was at Gilmore's Garden, New York, between October the 7th and 8th, when, during a 24-hour walk, he won the first prize of $200, scoring 106 3/8 miles in 22h.35m.11s. This turned out to be the greatest distance ever walked in America without resting. On November the 25th, he was beaten by C. P. Daniels for the 25-mile championship of New England at Boston. Since then Harriman had been giving exhibition walks throughout the country, including one in January of 1879 at the Mozart Garden in Brooklyn, he walked 50 miles a day in 10 hours per day for three consecutive days (See Chapter 23).

Amongst the large contingent of visitors that afternoon was Norman Taylor, the "Vermont pie eater" and runner. Mr. Walton of the St. James Hotel bet him $10 that he couldn't make 5 miles in 30 minutes. Norman, accepting the wager, pulled off his boots (he always ran either barefoot or in his stocking feet), went on the track and completed the distance with 10 seconds to spare, after which he was heartily cheered by curious onlookers.

All was now ready for the start of the match. The huge blackboard at the lower end of the enclosure had been painted and the names of the participants added. The track had been rolled and the railings protecting the track were described as being solid and strong. A high picket fence had also been erected around the scorers' and press stands to protect the individuals working there.

Three hours before the contest started, 1,200 people had gathered inside the building. There were massive problems developing outside as the masses tried to gain entrance, and by 23:30 the figure had swollen to 3,000. The amount of people present in the crowd was about 5,000 when Peter Van Ness, famous for his recent achievement of making 2,000 half miles in 2,000 consecutive half hours, turned heads as he was helped through the crowds to his box at midnight. He was readily applauded by many who stood up in tribute to his achievement. The story of his achievement which was tainted by an incredibly exciting incident can be read in Chapter 23. If the reader can't bear the suspense, I suggest they go and investigate what happened right now!

Rowell, wearing a blue and white striped shirt, lavender coloured tights and low shoes, received courteous recognition in the form of quiet clapping when he sauntered out of his tent at 00:30 and walked a lap with his trainer to test the state of the track. When he went back in, John Ennis, the stocky Chicagoan, wearing a white sleeveless undershirt and blue trunks atop a pair of white tights, and accompanied by his wife, did the same. His appearance however, was welcomed with much more enthusiasm than the challenger from "across the pond."

Tickets couldn't be sold fast enough to supply the demand, and by 00:45 a quarter of an hour before the start, police Captain Williams ordered the doors to the building closed and ticket sales suspended. This action caused much consternation amongst the waiting crowds, and their anger increased so much that they began pushing up against the entrance doors, causing those in front of them to be in danger of becoming crushed. Some people were beginning to yell out in pain as a result of their distress and the situation was becoming bleaker by the minute.

King of the Peds

As the time came close to the start inside, the noisy and unruly throng drowned out the efforts of the brass band to entertain them all.

Cheers greeted the appearance of the belt as it was displayed near the judges' stand and William B. Curtis of the New York Athletic Club summoned the race participants from their booths and read them the rules. Here is an example of some of them:

All will start with the left hand toward the inside of the track, but any competitor may turn and go in the opposite direction at the completion of any mile by giving notice of his intention to do so to the scorers a lap beforehand.

No competitor shall leave the track without giving notice to the scorers a lap beforehand.

Men with the left hand toward the inside track shall have the right of way; those meeting or passing them must go outside and no man passing another shall take his ground until two good paces ahead.

Before the race started $2,000 had been deposited with the bookmaking firm of Kelly and Bliss, $1,500 of which was bet that O'Leary, Rowell and Harriman would make 500 miles and $500 that Ennis wouldn't. O'Leary was the favourite to win the race in the pre-match betting at odds of 4/6. Wearing a white shirt, similar coloured pantaloons, black velvet trunks, and sporting a handkerchief around his neck, he came out of his hut five minutes before the start of the race and was given a huge ovation by the masses. As he made his way to the starting line, he was pursued by a female admirer who presented him with a silver horseshoe which he inspected as he took his position on the inside of the track.

The crowd cheered tremendously when the word "Go!" was given at one o'clock sharp by Mr. Curtis. All the men set off at a brisk walk and O'Leary was in the lead after the first lap. Rowell was second, Harriman, wearing a white shirt and tights below a pair of purple trunks, third, and Ennis fourth. The Englishman then started running and Ennis moved up behind him followed by O'Leary. Rowell scored the first mile in 9m.25s, O'Leary in 10m.27s, and Harriman and Ennis dead-heated in 10m.40s.

Meanwhile, outside the building, the yells from within signalling the start of the match had only served those attempting to gain entry like a red rag to a bull. The *New York Times* described the ensuing pandemonium materialising in the streets: **A few minutes after the start the outside mob made frantic by the cheering inside, charged on the closed doors of the Madison Avenue entrance with such force that in a moment the outer doors were burst from their hinges and crashed inward. Rushing through the lobby, the dense mass of human beings was knocked against the inner barrier with such force that it shook and cracked. Timbers were hastily placed against it from the inside and men planted themselves firmly against it in a vain effort to oppose the force on the opposite side. One charge, another, and still another from the outside and, with a crash, the frail partition was torn from its fastenings and burst in. The two policemen at the entrance could do nothing toward stemming the torrent, and were being overpowered, when from a distant part of the Garden, Capt. Williams and a squad of a dozen men of the Twenty-ninth Precinct, rushed to the rescue. For a moment the crowd held their own, but the terrible blows of the clubs, rained without mercy on heads and bodies told at last, and the mob suddenly fell back until the lobby was cleared and the partition replaced. The Police did not rest here, but drove the crowds back until all of Madison Avenue from Twenty Sixth to Twenty Seventh Street was cleared. Beyond these limits they were held in check by strong bodies of Police until after 2 o'clock, when they gradually dispersed.**

Things inside were no better, with the police being described as having to *"beat"* back some spectators who had leapt over the barrier surrounding the press and judges' table. Indeed, it was so bad that many people dared not leave the building as they were frightened that the mob outside was out of control.

THE GREAT WALK - GO AS YOU PLEASE.

A cartoon of the time shows Daniel O'Leary, the defending champion, with corn cobs in his hands setting off in the four man race at the start of the race. Behind him are Rowell, Harriman and Ennis. *Library of Congress, Prints & Photographs Division, (reproduction number: - LC-USZC2-2537) (Illustration no: 35)*

The *Brooklyn Daily Eagle* commented on each of the men styles of locomotion: The style of the pedestrians differed greatly. Rowell with his closely cropped head, queer jockey cap and excellent form was undoubtedly the chief object of interest, as it rested with him whether the belt should be taken across the water. His limbs were finely shaped, his shoulders rested perfectly natural, even when exerting himself to the utmost. He carried himself with more ease than his competitor, yet a briskness showing that he meant business characterised his movements. Perspiring freely and mopping his face industriously he went around the track. He did not run, he did not walk, but only took little jog-trots around the track. He took little steps, keeping his feet all the time under him. When he did undertake to speed up, he kicked his heels high, thereby calling more on the muscles of the under thigh. Ennis's style of walking was not in the least showy, and his manner of on the track was very different from that of the Englishman. His figure was excellent, yet not so square and flat on the shoulders as was Rowell's, but firm and well put together nevertheless. Harriman's style of walking attracted much attention. He slowly but surely forged ahead, always with the same long stride. All the bones in his body seemed to be brought into play as he swept over the track, and occasionally would carry a toothpick in his mouth. When O'Leary started he wore a very earnest cast of countenance. He swung his arms, balanced by the corn cobs he each hand, with steady regularity, his back was straight, and his head set at just the most favourable angle. The articulation of his every joint seemed perfect, and he stepped so regularly and even that no sawdust was displaced.

King of the Peds

The early scores:

	Rowell			O'Leary			Harriman			Ennis		
Hrs	Miles	Laps	Yds	Miles	Laps	Yds	Miles	Laps	Yds	Miles	Laps	Yds
1	6	7	110	6	2	25	5	4	80	6	1	165
2	13	1	130	11	7	85	10	6	110	12	3	40
3	18	6	70	17	3	200	15	5	150	18	0	30
4	24	5	0	22	4	200	20	4	190	22	7	0
5	30	0	160	27	3	50	25	0	0	26	2	150
6	35	3	50	31	2	50	29	6	50	30	0	0
7	41	1	70	36	1	70	34	6	0	32	0	0
8	46	2	200	41	1	200	39	5	110	36	0	30
9	50	0	0	46	2	0	44	3	150	40	6	50

After the 12th hour of competition, O'Leary, on a score of 59, was 7 miles behind the score that he made in London the year before. His indifferent performance was put down to suffering from colic and sickness. As a consequence, his odds of winning had drifted out to even money as the morning wore on, and by 14:00, Rowell, was out in the lead with 68.7 miles, which was 5.3 ahead of O'Leary. Harriman had made 61.6, and Ennis was the back-marker on 53.7.

The Englishman introduced a new stalking strategy called "dogging." The first person he practiced it on was O'Leary hoping the tactic would demoralise the champion. The tactic was simple; Rowell would catch O'Leary up and follow on his heels. If O'Leary altered his pace or gait, Rowell would copy him. The theory was that any advantage gained earlier could be consolidated as long as the person being followed wasn't allowed to pass his pursuer. However, not content to stick behind O'Leary, Rowell was said to race alongside him, *"give him a patronizing look,"* run away from him, re-catch him, and start the whole process again!

O'Leary continued to appear sickly in the afternoon and was off the track a number of times between 15:00 and 21:00. Apparently he had eaten some rich food and his trainers admitted he was suffering from a *"disordered stomach."* As a consequence he had vomited on several occasions. He wasn't the only one to be complaining of gastric problems. After earlier completing 33 miles, *"Honest John"* Ennis had also become ill, the same ailment forcing him to stop frequently thereafter.

Rowell's English supporters had planted themselves near his quarters. Here they shouted enthusiastic encouragement to him all day and whenever he passed by. They would refer to the freely perspiring individual as the *"small un"* and *"the little feller."* His trainers, the diminutive figure of Simpson and the taller Asplen, were said to be *"perfectly satisfied"* with his performance on the first day. They were confident he would take the belt back to England and with him, a *"big pot"* of dollars. Both were constantly watching and assessing his progress and were said to be spending a lot of time concocting drinks and cooking for him on the small gas stove situated in a corner of his tent.

Rowell leads Harriman with O'Leary on the inside of Ennis.

Harpers Weekly (Illustration no: 36)

The *New York Times* told of the efforts being made by some youngsters desperate to catch a glimpse of the action inside the great hall: One of the most interesting features of this match is the great crowd that, without a hope of obtaining admittance, haunts the outside of Gilmore's Garden. In Madison Avenue they line the curb opposite the main entrance four and five deep, and patiently wait for hours, with what object, "no feller can find out," for they cannot by any chance catch a glimpse of what is going on inside the Garden. On Twenty Sixth street, crowds of street boys continually hang about the low doors that used to afford egress to the animals of Barnum's Museum and work industriously to tug holes through the thick panels with their jack knives and after cutting them, fight for a chance to look through them. The prospect after all this labor is one of utter darkness; but each boy imagines that he sees something, and so is satisfied.

Rowell moved along in a steady jog-trot clocking his century at 20:34. He was at this stage 12 miles ahead of Harriman, the *"Steamboat,"* as the crowd called him, because he moved himself along in a mechanical way. He went on to match the leader's speed making 95 miles at 22:12. O'Leary had made 90 miles at 20:35 and Ennis had scored 80 at 20:41. O'Leary left the path for his bed at 22:48 on a score of 93.6, and Rowell waited till he had completed his 110th mile before leaving to go to his hut at 23:16 where he had a light supper before falling asleep. Harriman was the third man to go in on a score of exactly 100 at 23:31, whilst Ennis plodded on at a steady pace until 00:43, when he too called it a day with 95 miles to his credit. John slept soundly thereafter secure with the knowledge that he wasn't in last place anymore.

King of the Peds

Later scores:

		Rowell		Harriman		Ennis		O'Leary	
Time	Hours	Miles	Laps	Miles	Laps	Miles	Laps	Miles	Laps
11:00	10	55	6	47	0	45	3	50	7
12:00	11	60	1	52	3	48	0	55	1
13:00	12	64	0	56	7	51	5	59	0
14:00	13	68	7	61	6	53	7	63	4
15:00	14	73	7	65	3	59	1	67	7
16:00	15	78	1	70	0	62	1	71	6
17:00	16	83	0	74	5	66	3	73	4
18:00	17	87	5	78	5	71	4	77	2
19:00	18	92	4	82	2	73	0	81	3
20:00	19	97	1	86	0	76	7	84	5
21:00	20	100	1	90	0	80	0	87	6
22:00	21	104	3	94	1	83	0	91	1
23:00	22	108	6	97	6	86	7	93	6
24:00	23	110	0	100	0	91	1	93	6
01:00	24	110	0	100	0	95	0	93	6

The actual time of all the men on the track omitting breaks was: **Rowell, 21h.28m.11s; Harriman, 20h.52m.49s; O'Leary, 19h.21m.38s; Ennis, 19h.22m.10s:**

At 02:00, and with only O'Leary in the ring, there were a surprising number of people milling about the building, estimated to be in the region of 2,000. Amongst the house guests were a large number of *"club men"* attired in full evening dress, and group of actors who had just stopped work. Many of the Garden's residents were using the place as a cheap form of accommodation. The admission price of 50 cents would give them a relatively warm and dry place to spend the rest of the week in. One told a reporter, "I had but a dollar, and I paid half of it to get into this place. Here I can stay till next Saturday night. The seats are comfortable and I can get a good night's rest. I can go downstairs and for ten cents I can get a sandwich; which is a better dinner than I can count on many days of the year. In the meantime I can have as good entertainment as the people who have thousands in their pockets to bet on Rowell."

The man he mentioned, who was now the race favourite at 1/2, stayed in bed till 02:11. He then reappeared along with Harriman to put on a further 9 miles. After that he rested for just over eight minutes before recommencing his effort until 07:11 when he spent a further 34 minutes "off track," having made 133 miles. Harriman waited till 09:22 till he sat down for his breakfast (34m), having rested earlier on his 118th mile for 12m. Ennis slept until 04:14, and returning to the track, he competed till 06:50 before spending 24 minutes at the dining table, later indulging in a further rest of 24m at 10:10. O'Leary meanwhile had slept for 2h.24m.24s. After his return to the track at 01:24 he took frequent rests, which caused much concern amongst his backers and those who had bet on him winning. Reports suggested he had then been able to keep down a little food, which consisted of calves foot jelly and mutton stew. At 03:14, he left to rest for 1h.5m whilst on a score of 101 miles. He returned to make two more miles before resting another eight minutes during which time, and before his attendants could stop him, *"swallowed 2 large bumpers of champagne."* He went back out at 05:04 but came back in again only 8 minutes later. Further rests were made until his 107th mile.

O'Leary was clearly not going very well and was consuming much too much brandy, which was being given to him as a *"stimulant."* His face was described as wearing a dazed appearance, and bets were already being placed on him to come in last. However, he did have one supporter. "Old Sport" Campana, the eccentric pedestrian wearing two gold medals, came to the Irishman's defence, stating he was willing to bet every cent he owned that O'Leary would come from behind and win the race. He spoke of O'Leary's staying powers, stating the champion was keeping himself in reserve for the last hours of the contest, "when you may rest assured," he said, "that he will come out in his true colours."

Rowell, who the crowd fondly nicknamed *"Sawed-off,"* so called because he was short in stature, continued to please the spectators with his quick gait. Appearing flushed and perspiring heavily, he carried a wet sponge which he frequently mopped his brow with. The bookies continued to offer 1/2 about him winning and there were many takers. As the leader sweated, Harriman, whose step had been measured at 39 inches in length, walked steadily. Meanwhile, Ennis made his best mile in a time of 8m.20s at 09:45.

Mr. Kelly reported that up to 10 o'clock, a total of $11,000 had been taken at the ticket office. There was tremendous enthusiasm for the event tantamount to mania. So many people wanted a part of the action and everybody just wanted to be there and watch the amazing spectacle that was "the pedestrian match." *"The walk has brought out a tremendous stock of note-books. Everybody has turned reporter. Gentlemen with high hats and white ties, sportsmen in chequered shirts and with cigars growing out of their mouths at angles of 45 degrees, young clerks with shining collars, shop boys, clergymen, physicians, policemen, and people of all sorts, crowd up in front of the bulletin boards, jostling against youngsters not much bigger than their pencils, all with note-book in hand, to take the last recorded mile of the man who has just passed the judge's stand."*

Rowell began to make frequent trips to his apartment starting around ten o'clock. Apparently a blister had formed on the outside of his left heel, and after all efforts to soothe it had failed, it was decided to cut the counters from the heels of both shoes and cover the outside with an improvised form of leather legging which could hardly be noticed. Although Rowell's left leg was reportedly swelling, painful, and was *"giving way,"* there didn't seem too much concern on his face and his stable denied they knew anything about the "dodgy" limb.

The champion was observed walking with dogged determination. He was seen to be glancing up at the big blackboard frequently and when he did so at 10:20, he saw the following scores: **Rowell, 145; Harriman, 131; Ennis, 120; O'Leary, 116:** Harriman had rested on his 130th mile for 34m.20s and made his 135th mile in 13m.57s at 11 o'clock. O'Leary took nearly 22 minutes to complete his 120th mile at 11:20, and Ennis completed 125 miles at 11:42. At noon, the score was: **Rowell, 149.1; Harriman, 139.2; Ennis, 126.2; O'Leary, 122.3:** Rowell was reported to be very sleepy and required much motivation to fight his tiredness. The perfect tonic came from a dispatch from Sir John Astley which read:

LONDON, March 11.

To Rowell, Gilmore's Garden:

Go it, my boy. Don't overdo it. Tell Atkinson to put on a century for me.

Mr. Atkinson, who was looking after Rowell's interests, had been talking to the press about his reservations about the track, stating it was getting in very bad condition and that "it was too soft and yielding" and "afforded no spring or resistance to the foot." He went on, "In England, we had the best track ever laid down, and it was done under my own personal supervision. We first laid out ground and then rolled it well and spread a coat of tan over it, pressing it well down. This was watered and a slight sprinkling of sawdust put over it; this was brushed off, and a finer track a pedestrian never stepped upon."

King of the Peds

The morning scores for the 2nd day:

| | | Rowell | | Harriman | | Ennis | | O'Leary | |
Time	Hrs	Miles	Laps	Miles	Laps	Miles	Laps	Miles	Laps
02:00	25	110	0	100	0	95	0	96	0
03:00	26	113	4	103	6	95	0	100	1
04:00	27	118	7	108	1	95	0	101	0
05:00	28	122	7	112	3	98	2	103	5
06:00	29	127	7	116	5	102	5	106	7
07:00	30	132	1	119	7	106	0	108	4
08:00	31	134	0	124	1	109	1	111	0
09:00	32	138	7	128	3	114	0	114	3
10:00	33	143	7	130	2	119	1	116	2
11:00	34	146	2	135	0	122	0	119	0
12:00	35	149	1	139	1	126	2	122	3

As the race entered its second afternoon, the bookmakers were chalking 2/1 next to the name of Ennis on their blackboards. Rowell however, was still in command, and at 12:10 his 150th mile was made in 12m.28s. Prior to that feat being accomplished, the race leader had spent varying periods of time in his quarters indulging in rests of 35m.7s on his 145th, 5m.5s on his 146th, a similar amount of time on his 148th, and 11m.5s on his 149th.

Harriman meanwhile, made his 150th mile at 14:44 and appeared to be going along just fine and dandy! He was very confident of successfully overhauling the leader and was the favourite of the crowd, due to being the only true American in the race. He continually circled the sawdust carrying a floral tribute, many of which were thrust into his hands by his female admirers. A lady admirer presented him with six brightly coloured silk handkerchiefs, one of which he wore around his neck with the others being stuffed into his pocket.

Harriman's camp knew that Rowell was having serious trouble with his leg. Every time the "little un" went in to have it attended to, they instructed the "tall un" to increase the heat on the track. The general ten-mile gap would be ultimately be reduced by a mile or two, and when that heat got too hot for Rowell's team, they would send him scurrying back on to cool things down. Ennis would also unsettle Rowell by cruising up alongside him thus forcing to exert himself further. The third placed man had evidently got over his gastric troubles, and while his wife cooked his favourite dishes in his house, the man himself was putting on a creditable performance, putting in a sizzling time of 8m.20s on his 118th mile. Later, around 13:00, he went in for his lunch after knocking up his 130th mile. On the menu was broiled chicken, and after devouring that and cat napping for a few minutes, he went back into the fray following his hour break. Later on he began to increase his speed and eventually secured his 150th mile at 18:13.

O'Leary's trainer, Barney Aaron, stated that his man was in good condition and would do some *"tall"* walking the day after. The champion, who had earlier been drinking a mixture of lime water and eggs, even indulged in some spurting with Rowell. However, and earlier on, there had been much concern expressed about his condition. *"His hands were allowed to droop, his chest was not held as high as of yore, and his stride fell eight inches short of its old time length."*

Rowell left the track at 18:25 reportedly suffering from several painful blisters and badly swollen calves. At that stage, the Chesterton man led the contest on a score of 180 miles, with Harriman in second position, just over five miles in his rear. Rowell reappeared at 21:30 full of running, and the bookies made the two race leaders joint favourites, at even money to win. Harriman's backers were now confidently claiming that their long striding athlete would take over the lead by midnight. *"He is walking according to a carefully prepared schedule, and plods along with an unvarying stride of immense length, seemingly as untiring and regular as a machine."* Meanwhile, O'Leary's odds to win had drifted out to 4/1.

The efforts of the pedestrians were well received by the audience and many were riveted to their seats. There was no repetition of the disgraceful scenes of the night before when someone could have easily been killed. Many in the audience had spent a little more on the price of admission by buying from the ticket touts at 10 to 30% above their original price, but at least they didn't have to fight their way through the hoards who queued patiently for theirs. Many of the onlookers were *"ladies in the height of fashionable attire, wearing camel's hair shawls, and other expensive wraps, and bedecked with valuable jewelry."* All classes of people were watching the fun with the *New York Times* reporter observing amongst the crowd: The millionaire, the black-leg, the hard working mechanic, the common laborer, the tramp, the thief, and the street urchin were the component parts of the vast mass of human beings that framed the track or jostled each other in the excitement of a common impulse on the inner floor.

Thankfully there was no trouble during the day, but it was reported that between eleven o'clock and midnight, a gang of men who were assembled on the Fourth Avenue side of the Garden got hold of a heavy beam of wood and used it to batter one of the entrance doors down. Three policemen were powerless to stop the torrent of gatecrashers. Some arrests were made, but after instant justice was meted out by the police in the form of a good hiding a few blocks away, the trespassers were set free.

The rest of the day's scores on that second day:

Time	Hrs	Rowell Miles	Laps	Harriman Miles	Laps	Ennis Miles	Laps	O'Leary Miles	Laps
13:00	36	153	0	142	7	130	0	126	2
14:00	37	157	8	146	4	130	3	129	3
15:00	38	162	2	151	2	135	4	132	5
16:00	39	167	1	155	5	139	7	136	7
17:00	40	172	2	156	3	144	4	141	1
18:00	41	177	4	162	6	148	6	143	4
19:00	42	180	0	167	1	152	5	147	5
20:00	43	180	0	170	3	157	6	150	3
21:00	44	180	0	174	5	162	4	153	7
22:00	45	182	1	178	7	165	0	157	5
23:00	46	187	5	181	7	167	4	161	0
00:00	47	192	1	185	5	171	1	161	0
01:00	48	197	6	188	3	173	7	164	3

In the early hours of Wednesday morning, Ennis had employed a new trainer named Jim Cusick (who had some success with the professional boxer Heenan in his great fight with Sayers) to help his slow but gradual improvement in the race.

O'Leary had made a valiant effort the day before to keep up with the pace, but continued to lose ground against all his rivals. As the morning progressed, it was O'Leary who was off the track more than any of the other pedestrians. He left for 10m at 02:30, 9m at 03:15, 24m at 04:00, a further 4m at 06:30, and finally indulged in a 20-minute break at 07:00. Any excuse was given to get off the tanbark and there was clearly something amiss with him.

The *Brooklyn Daily Eagle* wrote the following article on the Wednesday, the 12th of March. It commented on Daniel O'Leary's penchant for alcohol during the race:

O'Leary and His Bacchus

According to Brigadier General Atkinson, commanding the army of attendants upon Rowell, the English pedestrian, the comparatively poor time that has been made by the leading contestants in the now extremely interesting match is due to poverty of the track. At the end of the forty eight hours Rowell, who led well, had accomplished but 197 miles or seven short of the distance walked by Corkey in London in that time. Atkinson declares that the English track was kept in superb, springy condition, which that at the Garden is not. However that may be, Rowell has obtained a good and constantly increasing lead over O'Leary, while the long person from Maine, has walked away from the champion and presses pretty closely upon the leader. Even Ennis of Chicago, has left his fellow townsman behind and O'Leary brings up the rear with novel and rather unpleasant reflections. It is quite possible that the failure so far of every man to beat the record of the great match is possibly due to the fact that there is nobody to force the pace. O'Leary if he is to win must do so by coming up fresh at the end and showing his strength, as he did before in the final forty eight hours.

But there is an excellent chance that he will not. THE EAGLE pointed out during the Madame Anderson walking match that a contest of this kind, demanding endurance, depends in a very large measure upon the stomach. Nothing is more apt to interfere with the proper operation of that important organ than what in vulgarly call "tod," and according to his friend, backer, trainer and adviser Al. Smith of Chicago, "tod" is a pursuit to which O'Leary has been assiduously devoting himself. In other words, his stomach will not retain its food or do its duty, because Mr. O'Leary has been on a protracted spree, and is even now keeping it up on the track. To shut off at this moment would be fatal to his chances. He must keep his system toned up with wine, and by and by it will be brandy. It may be that the tone can be gradually restored to his stomach but all this time the waste of the body incurred by such energy as he puts forth is not being repaired. Alcohol, as has been shown, in small quantities checks that waste, and if he will consent to a moderate use of stimulants he may yet brace up and work like a steam engine. Rowell's appetite is said to be enormous. So long as it holds out he's the safest man to predict success for. He is already stiff, a little, and has a blister, but that will not trouble him much. Harriman is developing unexpected staying quantities and is rapidly walking into the good graces of the spectators. At 3 o'clock this morning he was seventeen miles behind Rowell but later bulletins show that this distance has rather been increased than diminished, although at one time he was within four of the leader.

There is a certain providence that takes of inebriates, as everybody knows a sort of lurking belief that O'Leary will yet come out ahead. It would require a tremendous interposition to straighten out his disordered stomach, though the discovery of a new beverage might do it, and little short of a thunderbolt would dispose of the three men who now lead him, but since O'Leary has put himself in the hands of the god Bacchus, to the defiance of his merely mortal backers, nobody would feel astonishment if that popular divinity exercised his customary watchfulness on the champion's behalf.

There were about 2,000 people watching the proceedings on the third day of the match at 11:00. Rowell, still in the lead, trotted nicely around the ellipse, even though it was reported that his heel was blistered. Harriman kept up his magnificent stride, whilst Ennis frequently broke into a run to entertain those present. The poor unfortunates outside could only attempt to glimpse at their heroes through cracks in the doors and relied on people leaving the building to tell them the state of play inside. At noon, they would have been informed that Rowell was on a mark of 236.4, Harriman was credited with 222.7, Ennis, the 8/1 outsider, was a good third, having achieved 209 miles, and the 3/1 third favourite, O'Leary, was in last "pozzy" on 203.7.

Good news was coming out of the tail-ender's camp. Reports that his stomach was much better had shortened his price, and he moved himself around with more determination, grasping his corn cobs tightly in his hands as he walked.

Rowell's left ankle was so swollen that it had to be lanced, and after that operation was performed, he wore a leather stocking to keep the swelling down, offering him some support. It was written at the time that, *"Rowell is commencing to have redness of the face. He follows on Harriman's heels and the crowd frequently whistle at him as if he were a dog."* Rowell was also reportedly *"hissed frequently by several crowds of roughs, but was heartily applauded by all decent persons present."*

The fastest miles made by each athlete from midnight to noon on the third day were as follows: **Rowell, 230th mile in 10m.5s; Harriman, 209th mile in 11m.20s; Ennis, 179th and 198th mile in 11m; O'Leary, 199th mile in 12m.15s:**

A summary of the morning's scores:

| | | Rowell | | Harriman | | Ennis | | O'Leary | |
Time	Hours	Miles	Laps	Miles	Laps	Miles	Laps	Miles	Laps
02:00	49	200	6	188	3	175	0	164	7
03:00	50	203	6	188	3	176	0	172	5
04:00	51	205	8	188	3	177	3	176	3
05:00	52	209	6	193	6	182	0	178	4
06:00	53	214	3	198	3	186	4	182	2
07:00	54	219	4	200	5	191	3	186	3
08:00	55	219	6	204	3	194	6	188	4
09:00	56	225	0	209	2	199	4	192	5
10:00	57	231	0	213	7	200	0	197	0
11:00	58	235	0	218	4	204	4	200	5
12:00	59	236	4	222	7	209	0	203	7

The good attendance over the first days of the match meant that $20,000 had been taken at the gate up till 10 o'clock in the morning. Outside, in the afternoon, a large crowd had gathered. The *New York Times* reporter takes up the story: Several hundred boys and men stood on the north side of Twenty Seventh Street watching the operations of a very small and very ragged boy, who, at great danger to his unwashed neck, climbed the fancy brickwork of the wall to a ledge about 25 feet above the sidewalk, walked along the ledge till he reached one of the upper circular windows, and peered through a hole in one of the panes. He had been enjoying himself thus for a quarter of an hour, or more, and the crowd had been enjoying the momentary expectation of seeing him break his neck, when a policeman came in sight. The sympathies of the crowd were with the boy, as against the policeman, and they shouted him much bad advice, to "Jump, boy, jump," and "Stay where you are, Johnny he can't get you." The policeman, when he reached the place, called to the boy to "Come down out of there," and the boy was considering the situation when suddenly the circular window opened a few inches, a mysterious hand grabbed the boy's coat collar, and the boy was whisked through the window into the building, and nobody knows to this minute what has become of him. The boy's unexpected disappearance left the policeman in rather an awkward situation, and when he started away he was followed by the jeers and laughter of the crowd.

Rowell's 240th mile was made in 8m.10s. Ennis made his 215th mile in the same time. These transpired to be the fastest miles made in the day.

At 15:31, O'Leary, who had been walking in fair form, left the track for what was intended to be a brief rest having accomplished 215.5. *"He hardly walked a single yard without swerving from side to side,"* and his trainer Barney Aaron told reporters, "He was walking on pure courage." He returned to the track at 15:33, walked one lap and retired from the contest at 15:37 having made 215 miles, 6 laps and 110 yards. He was said to fall into the arms of Aaron, who helped him on his bed where he fell into a dazed state, his eyes being half closed and appearing glassy. *"O'Leary looked like a corpse. His face was terribly flushed, and his neck and chest were as red as a beet."* His pulse was 88, his tongue parched and furry and his skin cold and dry. *"He was the personification of a man who had walked himself to death.* Many in the crowd realised what was happening when an immense basket of flowers was conveyed along the track and taken into his room. The *National Police Gazette* wrote: Ladies rose in their places and with flushed cheeks and glistening eyes waved handkerchiefs high in the air, while the men swung their hats and shouted themselves hoarse. Some one proposed "Three cheers for O'Leary," and they were given the voice of a mighty multitude.

Dr. Robert Taylor was summoned, and after examining his patient, declared that it would be suicidal for him to continue. *"His stomach, head, feet, mouth, tongue and entire body seemed to have given away. It is very doubtful whether O'Leary will ever walk again in a pedestrian match. Doctors say rumors of O'Leary having been under the influence of stimulants of late and that his breakdown is attributed to that are untrue, and that his failure to keep the track was simply because he was used up."*

At 17:36, the ex-champion reappeared on the track and walked gingerly towards the judges' stand. He was heard to say to them, "Gentleman, I have finished," after which he was driven off to the Metropolitan Hotel. O'Leary's trainers stated that they had done everything possible to help him. They said that his sickness gradually increased since the start of the contest and that because he couldn't eat anything, he had kept going on stimulants and that their reaction on his empty stomach was too much for him. They said they had forced him to retire despite him wanting to remain in the race. The *Brooklyn Daily Eagle* commented: Indeed it is likely that, without the stimulation he received from the champagne, the unfortunate pedestrian would have given in hours before exhausted nature removed him. It is one of the properties of alcohol to interrupt waste of tissue, and by focusing all his energy and drawing largely upon his reserve strength, the wine he drunk unquestionably benefited him.

There were wild rumours flying around the city that O'Leary had died at the hotel he was taken to. These were quashed however, when it transpired that Coroner Wolfman and Police Captain Brogan found O'Leary in the upper room of Gilmore's Garden suffering from an *"extreme bilious attack,"* and that he was *"in an almost unconscious condition."*

The *Chicago Tribune* was scathing in its criticism of him: The complete collapse of Daniel O'Leary, the Chicago pedestrian, and his withdrawal from the contest in New York is calculated to still further lower toward absolute disrepute the business of getting up walking matches for the gate money that can be squeezed out of a silly public. O'Leary's downfall would excite sympathy and commiseration among his former friends and admirers in this city were it not for the very strong impression prevalent that his breaking down is the result of dissipation and excess. The man who but recently commanded the admiration of a musical worshipping world by reason of his extraordinary capacity as a pedestrian is reduced to the condition of a pitiful wreck, partly through the indulgence of gross appetites, but largely on account of the terrible strain his system has undergone in previous contests. He might have lasted longer if he had had the brain and will-power to withstand temptation, but the end was sure to come, and was only hastened a little in consequence of his failure to get and keep himself in condition for such a test of endurance.

Men in this city who bet on O'Leary attribute his failure to champagne, which he drank to excess. Perhaps this is so. If it is, we hope every ambitious pedestrian in the land will go to drinking champagne. We would recommend large drinks, and a short time between drinks. This practice of drinking should commence at an early age. When a child displays a peculiar genius for pedestrianism, his mother should take him in hand, and dose him with extra dry champagne instead of paregoric. There, is nothing like a mother's care in bringing up children. This may be a rather expensive way of killing off such muscular idiots as O'Leary, but it is effective. Laudanum would hasten the business, but there is a deep-rooted prejudice against that fool-killing drug.

It will be observed that we have no sympathy for O'Leary. He is only one of a large class of bullies who have nothing to boast of except feats of physical endurance. He is one of that kind that the world would never miss. True he has caused a flutter of excitement in his time, but is the world grateful for the sacrifice? Did it pay him to ruin a fine physical organization for the plaudits of the gambling world? Did the paltry gate-money pay him for a ruined constitution and the disgrace among the sports that followed? Had he directed half his energies at the wood pile, instead of misdirecting them as he did, he might today have a prospect of long life. But what's the use of talking? Men will keep on making fools of them selves as long as they can get gamblers to back them. We beg pardon for having mentioned the subject.

At 17:30, Harriman had lessened the gap until Rowell only led him by 6 miles. The American led Ennis by 20. Both were walking admirably, and both were loudly cheered when making spurts. With O'Leary out of the race, Rowell now needed someone else to follow around the path. He turned his attention to Harriman. The tall long striding young man from Maine had the effect of making the stubby legged Rowell run after him. The name callers and fun pokers in the crowd had a field day with him. "Get a chain for Harriman's dog!" and "There's Harriman's pup!" were but two of the many wise cracks coming from the crowd.

Then at 20:30, as the three remaining men in the race were doing some work on the track, a crash and a roar was heard as a long section of the temporary upper gallery at the Madison Avenue end suddenly collapsed on top of the heads of people sitting below. The immediate fear was that they had been crushed to death under the fallen timbers that had given way under the tremendous weight of those that had occupied the structure. Whilst some women fainted, piercing cries accompanied the horrific sight of falling bodies, planks, broken timbers and other debris. Amid absolute pandemonium, and with cries of "Fire!" and the "Walls are falling!" panic ensued and a host of people rushed frantically towards the exits.

Mayhem!

The National Police Gazette (Illustration no: 37)

Fearing for their lives, all the building's windows were smashed and people were seen to jump out of them, cutting themselves badly as they pushed their bodies through the broken glass. Meanwhile, at the opposite end, four or five thousand people found easier opportunities to escape as they made their bid for safety. Fearing a serious crush, more controlled people in the place, including match officials and the police under the admirable direction of Captain Williams, urged calm by waving their hands in front of the delirious crowd telling them to, "Go Back, go back; for God's sake go back!" When the crowd realised the building wasn't about to collapse, calm was restored, and they did what they were told and returned to their seats.

Mr. Kelly, the manager, ordered the band strike up a lively tune, and Rowell, Harriman and Ennis, who had previously stopped their tramp, continued on the track at the urgent request of those trying to allay the panic. After the accident, the atmosphere at first was quite subdued, but after 21:30 when the scores read, Rowell, 269, Harriman, 259 and Ennis, 243; the place started to liven up again. Within an hour, it was as if nothing untoward had ever happened.

It was later reported that there had been a hundred people in the gallery and that its occupants fell onto the heads of those standing some eighteen feet below. However, due to the timbers of the construction being new, the gallery didn't collapse at once thus giving those below a chance to escape. Louisa Ahern, aged 40, broke her wrist. Mr. and Mrs. Martin Bates received painful, but not dangerous injuries. Richard L. Denzel, was hit by a falling beam in the back and was admitted to Ward 10 at the Belleview Hospital. John Foley suffered *"congestion of the brain"* after being struck by a timber and was also hospitalised. Warren Harrigan, the 16-year-old son of the comedian Edward Harrigan, suffered a dislocated collar bone, and Mary Lewis, John Mahler, Frank Mosher and Daniel Ring were also hurt to some degree.

Ennis left the track for the comfort of his bed at 23:51. He was followed by Harriman at 00:39. Rowell also bid "goodnight" at the same time having made 283.4.

King of the Peds

The rest of the third day scores:

		Rowell		Harriman		Ennis		O'Leary	
Time	Hours	Miles	Laps	Miles	Laps	Miles	Laps	Miles	Laps
13:00	60	237	5	226	6	212	3	207	3
14:00	61	243	1	230	5	218	0	215	0
15:00	62	247	0	235	0	221	4	215	5
16:00	63	250	3	238	0	223	4	215	6
17:00	64	250	3	242	3	228	3	Ret	
18:00	65	253	0	245	0	233	7		
19:00	66	258	3	248	3	235	0		
20:00	67	263	7	253	3	238	3		
21:00	68	267	0	257	2	241	4		
22:00	69	271	2	260	0	245	0		
23:00	70	275	4	263	4	246	3		
00:00	71	280	6	267	6	250	0		
01:00	72	283	4	270	0	250	0		

Ennis reappeared on the track at 03:45. Harriman, with bloodshot eyes and a stiff stride, followed him at 04:01, and the plucky Briton joined them both 21 minutes later. All the men crept along in the comparative silence of the place, and at 06:00 the big blackboard gave the following information: **Rowell, 291; Harriman, 275; Ennis, 261.1:**

Scenes from the race: Ennis leads Rowell with Harriman following. As portrayed in *Frank Leslies Illustrated Newspaper* **on the 29th of March 1879.**

Library of Congress, Prints & Photographs Division, (reproduction number: - LC-USZ62-88335) (Illustration no: 38)

Harriman later took nearly two hours to eat up his breakfast, after which he indulged in numerous short rests. Ennis meanwhile, remained on the path for the duration of the morning, a fact which impressed many in the building. The Irishman was observed constantly chewing on beef sandwiches made for him by his wife, who fastidiously prepared his food and drinks. Rowell had a few problems, in that he required constant attention for his swollen leg, which required its dressing to be changed, along with treatment for blistered feet, and a *"chafe"* on his left thigh.

Following a request by the three remaining pedestrians about the effect that the tobacco smoke was having on their health, the management issued an edict banning smoking in the building. Harriman in particular was very sensitive to it. On the subject he asked the press for help. "Please ask my friends as a favour to desist from smoking while they are in the Garden," he appealed.

Neither the withdrawal of O'Leary, nor the increase in admission price from 50 cents to $1, caused any abatement of interest in the race. Huge crowds gathered at newspaper offices and business premises where the score was constantly displayed. The police patrolling the sidewalks had great difficulty in making space for those who wanted to pass. The match was said to be the sole topic of conversation wherever people congregated. However, the previous night's incident had put the ladies off, and they were very few of them in the audience. The part of the gallery which had fallen down was being fixed by the carpenters who were busy at work strengthening the structure by adding fresh posts and beams. The workmen were very busy in other parts of the building too. The *"mob"* had broken down two doors on the Fourth Avenue and Twenty Sixth Street side of the building, and they, along with the broken windows, were being fixed as well.

The morning's scores:

		Rowell		Harriman		Ennis	
Time	Hours	Miles	Laps	Miles	Laps	Miles	Laps
02:00	73	283	4	270	0	250	0
03:00	74	283	4	270	0	250	0
04:00	75	283	4	270	0	251	1
05:00	76	286	1	274	1	256	0
06:00	77	291	0	275	0	261	1
07:00	78	295	7	275	0	265	4
08:00	79	298	1	279	2	270	7
09:00	80	303	1	283	1	276	2
10:00	81	308	6	287	3	281	3
11:00	82	313	7	290	3	286	0
12:00	83	319	3	293	3	290	0

As the "little un," and "honest John," occasionally ran round together, Harriman continued with the same method of conveyance, and at 13:29 he made his 300th mile at in a time of 13m.44s. To mark the event, a lady presented him with a silver horseshoe, the now weary ped accepting it with a gracious bow.

Rumours were abundant as to the fate of O'Leary. The great man was eventually found at the *"Hippodrome Building"* where he had hired some rooms. Sat on his bed in his under-suit accompanied by one of his trainers, Barney Aaron, he told the press that the reason he had broken down was because of the enormous amount of walking he had done in the previous year. He dismissed the notion that he had been drugged by his attendants saying, "Why, Barney Aaron would as soon cut off his right hand as to try and make me lose the match." The *Commercial Advertiser* stated the general opinion was that he wouldn't be ruined by withdrawal from the race.

There were disturbing reports concerning the assistant referee, Mr. Edward Plummer, an Englishman, who stated that he had been the target of threats by friends of Harriman and Ennis, and as a consequence, was afraid to leave the building. The accusation against him was that he favoured Rowell, who was alleged to receive many valuable hints from him. Plummer told a reporter, "The other night when going to my hotel for something to eat and a bath, an unknown ruffian attempted to stab me in the back, but only succeeded in cutting the brim off my hat." He showed the reporter the three-inch cut and insisted that he didn't favour any of the pedestrians.

At 14:00, there were 10,000 people in the old Hippodrome. The seats were all full and the main topic of conversation was the withdrawal of O'Leary. Many who had indulged in a wager on him were now contemplating their move in the betting market. Rowell, the 1/4 favourite, continued to jog along nicely during the day whilst

Harriman, at odds of 4/1, struggled, his face wearing a tired and anxious expression. Ennis, the 8/1 outsider, kept up his steady quick walking gate and was slowly creeping up on the faltering "Steamboat."

Rowell realised that the American was in all sorts of trouble and switched his attention to his only real threat in the match, John Ennis. At 15:05, the Englishman began a run and flew past the Irishman, who, after momentarily hesitating, realised there was a race on. He sprinted after the leader, and within the next mile, overtook him, finishing his 300th mile in 8m.5s, which was the quickest of the contest, and a full 30 seconds faster than Rowell, whose previous best mile for the day had been his 291st in 9m.40s. (Harriman's quickest was his 279th mile in 11m.20s.) The crowd loved it and the band showed its appreciation by booming out "Hail Columbia." Ennis responded by making the next lap in 55 seconds. This fast time was made at a stage of the race when the Irishman had successfully reduced the gap between himself and Harriman from 25 to 5 miles. Indeed Ennis's 4th day performance was the subject of much comment and the *Brooklyn Daily Eagle* attempted to explain why in this interesting piece found in an article about the race ....the circumstance is explained by Ennis's stomach trouble. It seems that his digestive apparatus is not perfect and that the organ becomes impaired. Whether this is due to exhaustion affecting it or to the motion is not apparent. At all events, it only proves once more what the EAGLE showed some time ago, namely, that the ultimate test of endurance is normality of the stomach, and that so long as that organ can retain its condition the athlete whose endurance is being tested may be pronounced in perfect trim, no matter how many blisters torment him, or how raw his limbs may become. The stomach is, in one sense, the athletic conscience for it regulates his pluck. The moment it gives way seriously the athlete must surrender his chance. The rarity of sound digestive apparatus is moreover demonstrated by this match for Rowell's internal economy alone seems to be normal. He ate ferociously, as he ought to have done, to repair the waste of tissue which was inevitable. O'Leary ate nothing and soon exhausted his capital. Ennis had an insufficient amount to start with, and lost distance until his system became used to the new condition, and since then the supply of nutriment exactly equaled the outlay in force.

The 4 p.m. scores: **"Sawed-off,"** 332.1; **"Steamboat,"** 307.1; **"Honest John,"** 304.1:

At 16:41, and with Rowell heading for his tent, Ennis, who had been blazing a trail around the place, was exactly one mile behind Harriman on a mark of 309.6. For the next five minutes, with many of the 10,000 plus crowd behind him, the Irishman sped around the circle with the intention of finally passing the poorly performing American. Mrs. Ennis gave her husband his tea at 17:05. *"It consisted of a small beefsteak and roll. He was then just in the rear of Rowell. He refused to go into his room to eat it, but grasped the plate in his hand as he passed. As he walked along the track he ate his steak in his roll, using the only implements known to civilization, his fingers. When he had covered three laps of the track his supper was ended and he tossed the plate to his trainer, somewhat as a lord would toss a package to his retainer. The audience applauded this act as loudly as they applauded the race between Ennis and Rowell."*

The leader was now 25 miles ahead. When he returned to the track at 17:21 wearing a purple and red jockey cap and woollen jumper, he was said to be brimming with confidence. Ennis, on witnessing Rowell reappear, began running after the leader who had been walking for 3 laps. The leader initially took no notice, but the reaction of the crowd to his rival's efforts must have made him slightly envious, and he began to trot, then run, then sprint past the Irishman. *"One grand howl of exultation arose which must have been heard at the Fifth Avenue Hotel."* The two thrilled the crowd so much with a spurt of two laps that hundreds of eager spectators rushed around after them. Then after another two riveting laps, Ennis's knees began to weaken and he dropped back into a rapid walk. Rowell responded by keeping behind him exhibiting his renowned persistent trot. Ennis was clearly uncomfortable with the "little fella's" attentions and responded by, once again, trying to break free with a run. Rowell followed suit, and the pair once again careered around. Ennis then slowed down and so did Rowell. "Eee's breakin his eart!," came the cry from the English supporters. The tactics were working and Ennis knew he couldn't go on like this for much longer. He slowed down to a gentle walk but the rapid four miles he had added to his score meant he had been able to reduce the massive gap between himself and the "Steamboat."

After the fun had subsided, a quick glance of the score showed Rowell to be on 338, Harriman, 313.5 and Ennis 313.1. The ailing runner-up then left the course, this move giving Ennis the opportunity to go one up on him. Now on his 314th mile, what had been thought as "mission impossible" had finally became "mission accomplished." *"Every step that he took was signaled by a cheer, and every movement of his hand called forth applause. The band tried to play, but the music was fairly drowned in the tumult of human voices. Baskets of flowers were handed to Ennis as he passed around the track. He took them as he walked, gave a slight inclination of the head to the right in recognition of the donor, and passed on until he reached his cottage, when the flowers were transferred to one of his attendants."* John's wife was heartily proud of her husband's achievement. As she prepared his next meal and arranged all the floral tributes he had received, she managed a wry smile.

Ennis, not content with his new position, remorselessly pressed forward, and after a quiet walk of two laps, again broke into a run. Rowell responded by gluing himself on to his heels, and when the second placed man sprinted at 18:06, the "little un" went with him. For the next five minutes the place was in uproar as the Irishman tried to shake the Englishman off. Alas it wasn't to be, and, as the pace slowed, John was content to amble along whilst Charlie trotted, covering two laps to his one.

Rowell's odds had drifted to 1/2 and Ennis's had been clipped in to 6/4. The *"weary and dragged out"* Harriman's chances had drifted out to 10/1. He was rumoured to have broken down, but more reliable reports emanating from his camp implied he was drowsy and would fall asleep as soon as he fell on to his bed. Mr. Lathrop, his trainer, had to work really hard to get the "Steamboat" away from the quayside and back on the river where he knew the engine might cut out before it had made the 450 miles journey to safety and a slice of the gate money.

At 19:30, Harriman, looking much better, was greeted with feeble applause when he emerged from his den. *"His eyes were bright and his step elastic."* However, he soon put the timidity of his reception behind him as he put in some good strides around the path, and the crowd soon warmed to him again. His reappearance caused the other athletes and the place to explode into life again, and all three were soon moving rapidly around the tanbark. Harriman though just couldn't keep it up, and after registering 320 miles, he went back to his room at 20:18 following Rowell who left at 20:00 with a score of 350 miles.

Ennis, who had been on the track on his own for quite a while, was joined by Rowell when he was on all the threes. He then finished his 335th mile and left the track at 23:08. He was followed off by the leader on a score of 355 at 23:35. Meanwhile, Harriman, wearing a miniature American flag around his neck, had returned for another crack of the whip just after eleven. He staggered around until 00:13 and went back indoors on a score of 325. The bookies took note and extended his odds to 20/1, at the same time offering 1/5 on Rowell and 3/1 on Ennis. Rowell finally called time for the day at 00:40 on a mark of 360:

The rest of the fourth day's scores:

		Rowell		Ennis		Harriman	
Time	Hours	Miles	Laps	Miles	Laps	Miles	Laps
13:00	84	320	0	290	0	297	7
14:00	85	323	4	294	2	300	0
15:00	86	328	3	299	3	304	3
16:00	87	332	1	304	1	307	1
17:00	88	335	6	308	5	310	0
18:00	89	339	1	314	0	314	1
19:00	90	344	5	316	7	315	0
20:00	91	350	0	321	4	318	7
21:00	92	350	0	325	7	318	7
22:00	93	350	0	330	1	318	7
23:00	94	352	0	334	4	320	0
00:00	95	357	0	335	0	324	0
01:00	96	360	0	335	0	325	0

The *New York Times* was always keen to tell the readers of the conditions within the building: **The atmosphere in the Garden was vile; but the atmosphere in this bar room was much worse; it was horrible. It reeked with smoke, with the odors rising from the mire of beer, tobacco juice, cigar stubs, and bits of bread, with which the floor was covered and with the foul breath of drunken men, many of whom slept in odd nooks and corners. A tour of the Garden and of the darkened recesses with which it abounds, made during these small hours, led to many queer revelations. The space left by the removal of the debris of the gallery that had been crushed by its weight of human beings the night before, afforded so comfortable a resting place that it was fully occupied with recumbent figures. As they lay perfectly still, with most of their faces hidden beneath low-drawn slouched hats,**

King of the Peds

they were horribly suggestive of the recent accident that had nearly cost so many lives, In the dim light afforded by the low-burning gas these motionless bodies, contorted and drawn into strange shapes, but unmistakably human, recalled vivid recollections of the old market Morgue in Brooklyn just after the great theatre fire. In the long rows of red leather covered seats lining two sides of the building, hundreds of persons slept peacefully, and in the dark recesses of the artificial rock work at the lower end of the Garden where many more sleepers, most of whom were boys huddled together in ragged heaps.

The "pleasant" man that Captain Williams was, must have enjoyed himself as he and his men had a jolly old time of flinging the sleepers and *"bummers,"* out on to the street. By six o'clock, and as daylight presented itself through the dirty windows, he and his men had managed to reduce the number of spectators to 400 from an estimated 1,000 that had dozed there about three hours earlier.

Rowell, having rested for 3h.27m during the night, made a further 15 miles, took a quarter of an hour break, and then pushed himself around for another ten miles in his pursuit of first prize, before breakfast, and the removal of a chafe that had been troubling him. He re-emerged at 10:29 having spent 1h.19m eating his meal, having earlier completed his 386th mile. He was quickly presented with a gift of an oversized jockey cap which he looked ludicrous in, but nevertheless insisted on wearing around the path. Ennis, who had indulged in a longer night's rest of 5h.1m, emerged from his hut at 03:55. He took his first sit down meal of the day at 09:07 and was off course for 1h.6m. On his return, *"He looked as fresh as a daisy, and stepped off with a quick, springy gait that drew forth a storm of applause all around the amphitheatre."* Harriman was content to have the least amount of rest of the trio taking in just 2h.43m.

The management had decided to open the roof windows in an attempt to rid the building of the lingering stench of stale tobacco. This made the place chilly and the men on the track attired themselves accordingly. Rowell and Harriman donned woollen cardigans, whilst Ennis wore a blue Guernsey shirt. Rowell moved around the path varying his gait from a quick stepping walk to a trot as Ennis stuck to a regular walk. Harriman continued to struggle and had a painful expression written all over his face as he shuffled himself forward.

From midnight till 11:00, the fastest times on the track for all three men were: **Rowell's 387th mile in 9m.55s; Ennis's 357th mile in 13m.23s; Harriman's 344th mile in 13m.13s:**

The crowd thereafter numbered over a thousand, most of them being ladies, one of whom presented the diminutive Rowell with a blue silk cap just after he completed his 390th mile. After he had acknowledged receipt of it he then proceeded to speed around the track for a lap, much to the pleasure of the fairer sex who constantly sent bouquets of flowers to the pedestrians.

Rowell carries a bunch of flowers round the track. As portrayed in *Frank Leslies Illustrated Newspaper* **on the 29th of March 1979:**

Library of Congress, Prints & Photographs Division (reproduction number: - LC-USZ62-88335) (Illustration no: 39)

The scores up until midday:

		Rowell		Ennis		Harriman	
Time	Hours	Miles	Laps	Miles	Laps	Miles	Laps
02:00	97	360	0	335	0	325	0
03:00	98	360	0	335	0	325	1
04:00	99	360	0	335	3	329	2
05:00	100	364	4	339	5	333	2
06:00	101	369	6	343	7	335	4
07:00	102	374	4	348	1	339	4
08:00	103	378	6	352	4	342	0
09:00	104	384	0	356	4	342	0
10:00	105	385	0	357	8	345	4
11:00	106	387	7	360	3	349	7
12:00	107	392	0	364	6	354	2

It was literally "jackets off" for the two leaders as they entertained the crowd with a spurt of a mile which was started by Ennis at 12:10. John made that one in 8m.25s, the fastest of the day, Rowell making the same distance in 8m.38s whilst his discarded jacket lay on the track waiting to be retrieved. Ennis made another attempt to incite Rowell into a dash a few minutes later, but the offer wasn't taken up. Ennis was thereafter given a huge basket of flowers and struggled to show it off due to its size. Rowell had the numbers four zero, zero, placed next to his name at 13:31, and at 14:20, *"the men swung their hats and canes, the women waved their handkerchiefs, and the crowd on the floor were to and fro yelling like Indians"* as Ennis scurried around the sawdust.

Throughout the day Harriman was the recipient of many telegrams congratulating and encouraging him. One, was from some fair admirers at Baltimore, and read:

FRIEND CHARLIE: - You don't know how crazy we all are over your walk. The ladies here are just as much interested as the gentlemen. We watch the papers with interest, and we only hope that our side will beat, for we don't want the belt to go over the water.

The *Port Jervis Evening Gazette* on the 15th of March reported: During the afternoon and evening the boxes were filled with richly dressed ladies whose interest in the match seemed to equal, if not exceed, that of their escorts. Senator Blaine, Senator Jones of Nevada, General Baring of Ohio, General Chester A. Arthur, Mr. Edwards, the British Vice Consul, General Sickles, and many other gentlemen of distinction were among the spectators. Nearly all the local celebrities of every sort were present at some time during the day. Senator Blaine's visit was unfortunately timed. He had a basket of flowers for the representative of Maine, but Harriman was resting and the Senator could not wait until he returned to the track. The number of bouquets and other floral offerings showered upon the contestants during the day was something enormous. Rows of tables had to be placed in the track opposite the several rows of cottages to contain them all.

The spectators continued to pour in the Garden and there were 6,000 present to watch the drama unfold on the penultimate night of the race. Many of them hissed Rowell, but he ignored them. They instead cheered Ennis who altered his style between running and walking, and who made the fastest mile of the contest in 8m.3s when he completed his 382nd mile. Soon after, *"A beautiful little girl stepped onto the track, and timidly held up a button-hole bouquet toward the approaching pedestrian. Ennis, stopped, smiled, took the flowers, and after patting the child on the head, passed on."* A short while later, a gift of a gigantic loaf of bread wrapped in red, white, and blue ribbons, which was addressed to *"the successful walker in Gilmore's Garden,"* was placed on the scorers' desk. It had been sent from a Sixth Avenue baker, and when it arrived, it caused much hilarity amongst those who received it.

Evidently the lap counters generally weren't a happy bunch as they had started to complain they were wearing away and were fed-up with the predictable diet of sandwiches, coffee and cake which the management was feeding them with. Meanwhile, the *"used up"* Harriman walked slowly and with great difficulty. The *Port Jervis Evening Gazette* continued: Poor Harriman tottered around the track like a dead man all day. It seemed impossible for him to go on, but four electric shocks gave at intervals, and numerous doses of milk punch, champagne, brandy, and other stimulants poured into him in rapid succession, kept him going until far into the night.

King of the Peds

NB: The shocks were administered from an electric battery!

At around 20:00, all three men put on a show of fast running, which fully satisfied the crowd's appetite for entertainment. Harriman, who started a spurt, stopped it when Ennis took up the chase and passed him. The race leader, now itching to get involved, scampered after Ennis, and as the pair raced along, *"the spectators became a mob of howling lunatics."* The spectacle continued for three laps until Rowell dropped his pace down a couple of gears.

In a sporting gesture, the two leaders publicly stated that if Harriman remained on the track, and if either of them won, they would give him back his entrance money at the end of the contest. Indeed Rowell wrote out the following on a piece of paper whilst resting.

GILMORE'S GARDEN, MARCH 14.

In case I am fortunate enough to win the race for the championship belt, and should the third man fail to cover 450 miles, I shall be glad to return him his stakes, £100.

CHARLES ROWELL

Ennis made his fourth century at 21:41 in a time of 9m.28s. He then left the track to rest. At 23:00, Harriman, now racing alone at this stage had made 387 miles. He left for his bed three miles later in poor condition. Mr. Frazer, his assistant *trainer and a member of the Scottish American Club, openly stated, that in his opinion, Harriman was drugged by the other trainers. Reports suggested that the matter would be fully investigated. It was also stated that the electric shocks Harriman had received earlier had proved *"beneficial"* to him, and these would be continued every time he left the track, being one of the few remaining remedies available to enable him to accomplish 450 miles. *"Stimulants"* given to him earlier had failed to do their expected job, and the expected increase in his speed had not materialised. His trainer was busy calculating the number of half hour rests his man could take to achieve the objective, and was angry because Harriman was preoccupied with making arrangements that the band would be playing all night to help him with his quest. "I wish the fellow would walk instead of talk," he said. The plan was to give the American a half hour rest after every two hours of effort.

*It is understood that the man that took overall charge of Harriman during the race was the well known English trainer Joe Robinson, Professor of Gymnastics at Harvard College, *"who has a reputation of being better posted in pedestrianism than any other man in the country."*

Ennis came back on at 23:37 sporting a green sash around his waist. "How do you like that?" he asked his friends. Looking fresh, he started off amid great applause at a rapid gait. Rowell joined him at 00:23 after slumbering for 2h.38m, and like Ennis, walked fast. News from the Chicagoan's camp that he would be worked steadily till he broke the 450 and then *"be pushed for all he was worth."*

The afternoon and evening scores for the 5th day:

Time	Hours	Rowell Miles	Laps	Harriman Miles	Laps	Ennis Miles	Laps
13:00	108	397	0	369	5	358	0
14:00	109	400	0	371	6	358	4
15:00	110	401	1	376	0	362	7
16:00	111	405	3	380	0	364	4
17:00	112	409	5	380	0	368	6
18:00	113	410	5	383	6	372	1
19:00	114	414	5	387	7	373	2
20:00	115	420	0	392	5	376	4
21:00	116	422	1	396	5	380	6
22:00	117	425	3	400	1	383	0
23:00	118	425	3	400	1	387	2
00:00	119	425	3	400	1	390	0
01:00	120	427	7	403	5	390	0

On the last day of the race, and at one o'clock in the morning, Rowell's score was 30 miles behind Corkey's London time of November 1878. At 2 a.m., Gilmore's Garden was unusually quite full as the chandeliers high above the crowd jingled in response to the din created by the noisy masses congregated below. *"The band varied from its usual course and instead of playing a dirge, indulged in a rollicking selection from "Pinafore."*

On the track, the object of the crowd's attention was the red faced Rowell, who, dressed in a dark cardigan cotton drawers and a silk cap, moved confidently along. With him was the gangling figure of Harriman, who, having stepped back on the circle at 02:20, and now apparently refreshed by his midnight rest, steadily increased his momentum. The tall Yankee wearing a knit jacket, purple velvet trunks, long leggings and white hat looked at the scoreboard. He knew that at this stage that if he wanted to be paid handsomely for his efforts he needed to make another 58 miles before the close of the race. A score of 450 miles would secure him gate money beyond his dreams, and that was for finishing third!

John Ennis, meanwhile, was sat contemplating his share of the money in his tent. He had slipped off the track at 01:55, and when he returned 29 minutes later, the band played "Yankee Doodle" as the crowd stamped their feet, whistled and cheered relentlessly. Even those lingering outside joined in the fun. Ennis then began running and Rowell went after him. The excitement went on for 5 laps, and as the pace got faster and the crowd got louder, poor Harriman could only look on in envy as the two leaders passed him continuously. His despair was evident, and as his legs trembled, his eyes appeared sunken and his face pale. The two runners then settled back into a walk, but at 02:49 Rowell broke into another run and the battle was re-ignited as Ennis took up the challenge, the pair mesmerising the crowd for a full 57m.35s in which time they both covered 5 miles and 5 laps each. During the encounter the Chicagoan overtook Rowell who, not to be outdone, chased after his foe, caught him up, and put him firmly back in his place.

Harriman kept up his steady walk until 03:52, and while the band played "Yankee Doodle" in his honour, he sought his quarters for a short rest of 24 minutes. Just before he left, many in the crowd were shouting, "Three cheers for the Yankee!"

Ennis entered his room at five o'clock in front of a much smaller audience, leaving the little Brit all alone to wobble around the path. At half past six, it was reported that a *"drunken loafer"* had attempted to assault Rowell. The culprit, an Irishman, had vaulted over the fence on to the track, swore at Rowell (who ignored him), and raised his arm in an attempt to hit him. The police quickly subdued the would-be assailant and threw him to the ground. *"Roundsman Kelly"* was quickly instructed to get himself on the path and follow the leader around.

Further up the track ahead of Rowell was Ennis, who stopped and went back to remonstrate with the mob. He joined Rowell, shook his hand and shouted at them, "Gentlemen! I don't know if you are friends of mine or not. If you are, you can best show your friendship by respecting this man." He then pointed his finger at Rowell. "You see this man," he continued, "I want you all to understand that if this man is injured, I will leave the track and not walk another mile. He is an Englishman and I am an Irishman, but that Englishman has done the square thing ever since this walk began. If he wins it, it will be because he is the best man. Give him fair play gentlemen. If you don't, I'll give you foul play by leaving the track." The two athletes then shook hands, and then holding each other's, covered a lap together amid the din. When they reached the scorers' stand Rowell disengaged from Ennis and sped away. Kelly was instructed by the police commander to continue to follow Rowell around for a further two laps, and thereafter kept a watchful eye on the vulnerable athlete for a considerable time after.

Ennis shakes hands with Rowell. As portrayed in Frank Leslies Illustrated Newspaper **on the 29th of March 1879.**

Library of Congress, Prints & Photographs Division, (reproduction number: - LC-USZ62-88335)   (Illustration no: 40)

The leader was now on a score of 448.6. He was a full 23 miles in front of Ennis, who, in turn, was 17 miles ahead of Harriman, who 25 minutes later, and appearing distressed, went to his hut for a rest of 1h.5m. When he reappeared, he shook Rowell's hand and walked around the course with him for a lap. Ennis arrived back on the scene at 08:16 after a rest of just six minutes and walked with Rowell until the race leader left the ring at the end of his 458th mile at 09:08 to have the water in his blisters drawn off with a siphon.

With Ennis and Harriman having headed back to their cabins at 10:15 and 10:30 respectively, Rowell had the path to himself. He was joined by an ill looking Harriman, wearing a brown cardigan jacket and a mouse coloured *"wide awake hat"* at 11:01. The hobbling American almost fell over, had it not been for Rowell who supported him. Both were presented with floral baskets and the gifts seemed to raise the spirits of Harriman, who smiled in appreciation. The band also offered support to the exhausted pedestrian. They played "Yankee Doodle" and "Marching through Georgia" whenever he was perceived to falter.

Up until 10 o'clock in the morning, the gate receipts for the whole of the contest up to that point were $45,000. Some people who probably didn't pay to get in were the British minister Sir Edward Thornton and his wife, along with the Russian minister Baron Shishkin. The attendance increased from 3,000 to 4,000 by noon, and many floral tributes were given to the athletes. One such, a large crown of flowers and laurels was presented by a lady to Rowell, but he refused custody of it until the Union Jack flag it bore was replaced by the Stars and Stripes, fearing that he would be attacked if he'd accepted and carried around the former. He had no such reservations however, when presented with a gold medal by another lady admirer which he pinned proudly to his chest.

Rowell was now 1/20 to take the belt. Mr. Atkinson, in conversation with the press, denied his man had a varicose vein in one of his legs, but did confirm that his man was suffering from blisters on his feet. He informed them that the leader's diet was good and that he had a fondness for oranges which he ate in amounts of up to twenty per day, telling reporters of their slight laxative affect. They were also told that when Rowell was at home in his cabin, he was chatty and vivacious! Atkinson also revealed that Rowell had received some threatening letters during the race. One of them read:

(Private)

Should your man, Rowell, be so far ahead Friday night, or especially Saturday morning as to make it impossible for him to lose, you cannot be too watchful, as there is a party contemplating some dirty work to prevent him from winning. If the attempt is made, it will be done where the grotto is situated or else on the south side of the building near the saloon entrance, there is where they are likely to be. On the north or west sides the game little fellow has nothing to fear. Depend upon it, sir, this information is true and I assure you that you cannot have too many policemen in the localities above mentioned. Wishing you all success and knowing the little fellow cannot be beat if he has only fair play, I remain.

(Signed)   AN AMERICAN LOVER OF FAIR PLAY

The press reported that early in the morning, attempts had been made to interfere with Rowell on the track, and that such were promptly suppressed by the police who were stationed around it. Extra sections of police were ordered to be on duty at the Garden that night to prevent any attempt at a riot, and Colonel Clark of the 7th Regiment had denied the rumour that his command had been notified to be in readiness for service. He did say however, that several hundred fully armed men could be turned out at a moments notice. *"Policeman leaned against every rail, and guarded every crossing and appeared in every unexpected place. If a man stepped on your toes, and you looked up to give him a chance to apologize, it was a policeman; if something hit you a whack on the shoulder, and then went on like a flash, it was a policeman; if your struck head unexpectedly against something hard, and saw stars whilst the sun shone, it was a policeman's club. There never was a nicer turn out of policemen, with polished clubs and very stern countenances. They stood like Roman statues, except when they leaned against the fence. Many of them used their official note books to keep the score in and kept it as regularly as the hours rolled by."*

The last day scores up until noon:

		Rowell		Ennis		Harriman	
	Hours	Miles	Laps	Miles	Laps	Miles	Laps
02:00	121	432	7	410	1	392	0
03:00	122	435	7	412	6	396	2
04:00	123	441	3	417	2	400	0
05:00	124	444	0	420	1	402	6
06:00	125	445	5	422	4	406	2
07:00	126	449	6	426	6	410	0
08:00	127	453	5	430	0	410	0
09:00	128	457	3	433	2	413	7
10:00	129	459	5	437	1	418	0
11:00	130	463	4	440	4	420	0
12:00	131	467	3	443	5	423	5

As midday passed, it was fully expected that Harriman would make the desired 450 miles. At 13:00, he only needed to make another 23 miles to make his objective. When Ennis neared his 450th mile, he ran around the path *"like a deer"* causing the excited throng to go berserk. Ladies standing on chairs waved their fine handkerchiefs and men lost the hats they had thrown in the air. With his arms up to his chest, and head bent well forward, the pumped up pedestrian made the mile in 7m.16s at 13:26, the fastest of the match. Even Rowell was impressed with the Irishman's performance as he watched him literally run to his hut where his wife had an "honest" meal waiting for him. Harriman crept to his room at 13:35 for a nosh up followed by the peckish Rowell, who nipped in for his lunch 21 minutes later.

The attendance began to increase with rapidity in the early afternoon. With all the men off the course, and the band silent at 2 p.m., many of the Garden's patrons headed for the bar whilst there was a lull in the proceedings. The *New York Times* was on hand to describe what was witnessed: **A half intoxicated crowd were already making themselves still more unsteady by taking in more draughts of whiskey. There was a fine crush at the bar, sporting men in gorgeous apparel and sparkling with diamonds vying with roughs and poorer sports to get the next drink. The lunch counters did a thriving business at the same time, selling a compound called clam chowder by the gallon whose principal components were water and pepper. The clams had all disappeared long before. The waiters could not make sandwiches fast enough to satisfy the hungry crowd. It was evident that the 4,000 or 5,000 people who had paid $1 for admission early in the day intended to see the conclusion or the match. Men ate hard boiled eggs by the half-dozen and sandwiches on which the shadow of ham had fallen, and drunk the most despicable coffee. But the eatables disappeared just as fast as if they had been better and cheaper. The crowd was at a loss for something to do while the track was empty, and hundreds appeared to feel an irresistible attraction for the pen provided for reporters and hung over the fences reading the note-books.**

The battle to attract readers was in full swing. The *Brooklyn Daily Eagle* gave a fascinating insight into what spectators ate and drank, and how some tried to gain free admission to the building: **Early in the afternoon the crowd in the Garden began to grow. A constant stream of men and women poured in at the entrance on Madison**

King of the Peds

Avenue. Within the building it spread like an overflowed torrent to every part of the vast structure. It was a thoroughly representative metropolitan assemblage. In it were hundreds of well known men about town. A throng of fashionably dressed women occupied the front seats in the gallery and brightened them with shimmering silks and diamonds flooding in the sunlight. The space inside the big circle was blackened by a surging, jostling throng. As the pedestrians left the track this mass of bipeds made a mighty rush for the bar and lunch room. There they charged valiantly upon mountains of sandwiches that melted before them like snow in the sunshine. Then they besieged pyramids of eggs, and captured them amid a crackling of shells that would have discouraged all the hens in creation. Turning their attention upon the big kettles of a compound called "clam chowder" made of invisible clams, hot water and seasoning, they took them by storm and poured the steaming fluid down their throats until THEY LOOKED LIKE GEYSERS.

Shallow pies and tough sponge cakes were swept away by the cart load. Then the beer fountains were turned on and nearly exhausted, while fire water flowed into the guzzles of the older and more hardened drinkers.

Most of the people who had seats had evidently come to stay. They passed the time in munching sandwiches and pork and beans, drinking beer brought to them by flitting waiters, and staring at their neighbors. In the nooks and corners of the building various enterprising youths drove a profitable traffic. One shocked his patrons with a galvanic battery. Another weighed his customers in the balance of an enormous pair of scales. Pop corn and candy vendors offered their seductive wares on every hand. Many photographs of the pedestrians were sold by a young man whose peculiarity was the contrast in his eyes, one being pink and the other blue. Policemen and firemen dotted the great auditorium. The former were exceedingly ornamental. They formed a pleasant addition to the decorations of the interior. With the utmost composure they stood on peoples corns and buffeted innocent spectators about. Any individual who unfortunate to enough to lose his bearings and steer into the forbidden precincts about the markers' stand or the judges' coop was quickly brought to realization of his position by a thwack on the head from a locust.

While the audience was killing time and awaiting the appearance of the pedestrians, the unwashed without were not idle. A detective high up in the gallery was startled by a crash of glass and a boy, with a wart on his nose, jumped through the sash. He had scaled the height by climbing up the drain pipe, fifty feet from the sidewalk. Before the officer recovered from his surprise, the boy had whisked out of sight and was lost in the throng. Another gamin followed him through the window, but he was promptly led to the door and put out with a kick as a parting token. The gallant police, in order to get even, glowered at all the very small boys in the garden and became more austere than ever.

Harriman, wearing a broad brimmed hat, a handkerchief around his neck, purple trunks and leggings, appeared on the track at 14:19. The band was quickly summoned back on duty, and it was pretty evident from their red faces that they had been drinking heavily. Nevertheless, they struck up the popular "Hail Columbia," and as the tall fellow went on his way, he was chased round by many within the track who shouted their encouragement.

Rowell made his appearance at 14:49 wearing a red and blue silk cap, new silken tights, a drab woollen shirt and a red and blue handkerchief around his neck. The leader soon caught up with the back-marker and kept him company, to the delight of the chasing mob of over-enthusiastic fans, who continued to run around after them inside the railings.

Ennis rejoined the race at 15:20 and was immediately presented with a basket of flowers by a small boy. Everybody clapped, stamped their feet and shouted, "Hi, yi, yi, yi!" repeatedly. The men continued on their way in Indian file with Ennis at the front and Rowell at the rear of the trio. They continued like this for a mile. Ennis went on to thrill the crowd during the rest of the afternoon by making spurt after spurt. He left the arena at 17:38 on his 460th mile to inspect the many bouquets of flowers that had been thrown at his feet. They had been gathered by his attendant and placed in and around his house.

Captain Williams, along with a group of 110 policemen, entered the Garden at 18:00 and marched into the centre of the building. From there they were observed to surround the entire track with their intimidating presence. They were stationed six feet apart whilst another force of reserves was packed in the *"long caves"* under the seats near the Madison Avenue entrance. Altogether there were 330 defenders of the law on duty under the control of Commander Dilks.

Harriman, now in his cabin had a *"ghastly pallor,"* which *"whitened his countenance; his eyes were dull and sunken and his lips almost bloodless."* He returned to the track without his hat at 18:15 having rested for just under 90 minutes after making his 440th mile. He was greeted on his reappearance with applause which continued for a full five minutes as he crept wearily along.

At 18:30, all three men were on the path together. Rowell chatted with Harriman as they linked arms and went round together. They were joined by Ennis, and the sight of the three in very close proximity brought a noisy response from the crowd. *"The situation was too much for Harriman. His eyes filled with tears, and he would have been crying with emotion if somebody had not presented him with a beautiful basket of flowers, which distracted his attention."* The judges however, took a dim view of the practice and docked Rowell and Harriman two laps each because they were perceived to be aiding each other.

A cartoon shows Ennis pushing the *"fagged out"* Harriman as Rowell leads him along. The feet of O'Leary are seen in the background sticking out of his tent. *Library of Congress, Prints & Photographs Division, (reproduction number: - LC-USZC2-2536) (Illustration no: 41)*

Whilst Ennis broke away in a run, Rowell stuck behind Harriman urging on the Maine man, a gesture that was very much appreciated by the crowd. *"In this style the procession went – little Rowell with head erect and eyes bright, but bobbing painfully on tender feet; tall Harriman, pale, hollow eyed, thin almost to a skeleton, and looking as though every tottering step would be his last; and sturdy Ennis, stiff and tired, but plodding with determined gait – for six laps."* Somebody in the crowd shouted out, "Three cheers for the Englishman!" and everyone joined in. Ennis was later to be accompanied by his three-year-old son, dressed in a black velvet suit, who thrilled the crowd as he walked round the track for a couple of laps with his father.

The Yankee, nearing his objective quickened his pace. *"Harriman his face brightening for the first time in many weary hours was nearing the long sought goal. People stood up, ladies and all."* After completing his 450th mile at 20:42, he was presented with several immense bouquets presented by his lady friends which he helped carry around the track whilst wearing an American flag around his shoulders. *"Then came the first ramblings of a mighty thunder of cheering………How the vast throng yelled and strained their throats and yelled and yelled again, till the air seemed charged with an electricity of delight that made men stand on end and caused even the women to shout involuntarily, "Hurrah for Harriman!" "Brave Harriman!" "Down-east Yankee Harriman!" "Grit to the last!" Now, he comes past the judges' stand, streamers of red, white and blue flowing from his* shoulders. *Then carrying the American flag, he makes the last two laps, and the great Garden is a volcano of applause.*" He then left the track for the last time having completed a further three laps and 140 yards at 20:45.

During one of his very last laps Rowell carried the monster sized loaf of bread wrapped in ribbons, which had been presented to him earlier. It was so big, that he could only carry it on his shoulders. At 20:57, when the figures 500 were put up next to the leader's name, the excitement that prevailed in the building could scarcely be imagined. Rowell donned his Ulster coat, and carrying an American flag over his right shoulder, and an immense bouquet in his left hand, marched around the track accompanied by his trainer and Captain Williams whilst the band played "God Save the Queen." His last mile was made in 13m.37s.

After receiving handshakes and congratulations in his cabin, and a farewell from Harriman, he then left the building for good at 21:15 heading off for the luxury of the Ashland House. The "Steamboat" was then driven off in a carriage for the safety of the dry dock at the St. James Hotel, accompanied by his doctor, after shaking hands with the judges. He was in a feverish state when he was put to bed, and like on the track many times before, he fell asleep as soon as his head hit the pillow.

Only John Ennis remained on the path and he was there in order to win $1,500 from a bet he had placed on himself to complete 475 miles by 22:30. It was also reported that Al. Smith had placed $3,000 at odds of 13/8 for Ennis to make the said score, and he had apparently promised "Honest John" $1,000 if he did it. Nobody left the building and at the end of his 474th mile, many of the spellbound spectators found themselves sharing the track with the brave Irishman. Ennis informed the judges and scorers as he passed the stand that he wished to run the last mile and stop at 475 miles. "Alright," said William B. Curtis, "I'll give you the word." The encroaching crowd gave the Irishman the space he needed to accomplish his task.

The *Franklin Gazette* on Friday, the 21st of March recorded what happened thereafter: **He came up with his body thrown forward and in his free, light footed motion there was nothing to indicate the long strain in which his body had been subjected. He passed the line with a dash and as the group of judges, scorers and police captains about the score discussed the general aspects of the race the last man on the track doing the last mile was doing it in a style which put all preceding intervals in the shade. While Rowell was content to walk for a whole day before the finish, Ennis had been doing some running, and now the matter of his freshness, he put in this rattling mile, which the majority ordinary people would not be able to equal under the best of circumstances. Seven times the Flying Irishman skimmed over the scratch which had been made in the sawdust track. The packed audience filling the boxes set apart for four and provided with forty tenants shouted lustily, as though Ennis was doing all the finish there was to the race, and as Ennis passed in line for the eighth time and a young man who had been watching with his face vis-a-vis with a chronometer dial called "Six fifty-five!" as the time of the mile, there went up one rending shout, and the record of the third Astley belt contest was completed.**

After receiving another bouquet, he left the electric atmosphere of the Garden for the more sedate setting of the Putnam House, wearing an overcoat and a fur cap.

 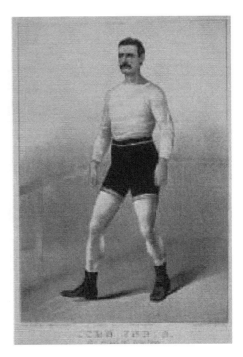

The Winner   and   Runner –up

Library of Congress, Prints & Photographs Division (reproduction numbers: - LC-USZ62-8835 and LC-USZC2-2710) (Illustration no: 42)

Captain Williams meanwhile was presented with a bouquet of flowers. He held it aloft and waved it triumphantly on the end of his club towards those who hated him. As the multitude left the building, the band played "Home, Sweet home!" and the people sang along.

The Final Score!

Rowell, 500 miles and 180 yards; Ennis, 475 miles; Harriman, 450 miles and 800 yards:

Back at the Ashland House, and having been met and congratulated by twenty ladies, the winner drank a bowl of beef tea before being given a salt water bath and a rub down. He was then put to bed by his trainers. Information received from Mr. Atkinson indicated he would be wakened every 2 hours thereafter and "exercised."

Plans had already been made to hold a banquet in his honour on the following Monday night after which a *"social hop"* had been organised. Mr. Atkinson also revealed that Rowell was puzzled why the crowd called him "Sawed-off," and concerned that he had only been allowed to drink half a glass of champagne daily. He stated that whilst the current champion was encouraged to eat 20 oranges a day, he had been permitted to drink only the smallest quantity of anything during the six days, stating that the water Rowell had drunk had been the pure and unadulterated "Croton" variety which had been brought over from England with him.

Meanwhile, the hotel where Ennis was staying was mobbed by his fans, some of which invaded the lobby attempting to find their hero. Back in his room, having been rubbed down, he was interviewed by a reporter. "I feel first class," he said, "They have given me a scrubbing and I am as fresh as a lark. I have no blisters to speak of. There are three or four little fellows on my feet, but they'll be all right by Monday morning. Rowell is a good man - a tough man, but I think I can beat him, nevertheless. He did not worry me in the slightest by keeping so close on my heels. I returned the compliment, I believe, once or twice. He broke up O'Leary completely, however. O'Leary didn't have a head enough on him to see the game that the Englishman was playing. Harriman is a good fellow, but hardly built for long walking. For a three days walk he is the best in the land, but a six-day tramp is too much for him. He isn't built for it."

King of the Peds

"My wife," he continued, "has stood by me right along and I am proud of her. I'm going after the Astley Belt, and am going to challenge Rowell next week, before he returns to England. I'm positive I can beat him, and if there had been one more day to the match, I think I could have carried off the belt. Cusick didn't take charge of me until Wednesday, and I begun to pick up right away. If I had had him the first two days of the walk, the result would have been different. I shall get a good nights rest tonight and tomorrow will take a walk around town."

What the tally sheets indicated for those last few hours:

		Rowell		Ennis		Harriman	
	Hours	Miles	Laps	Miles	Laps	Miles	Laps
13:00	132	471	2	447	4	427	5
14:00	133	475	0	450	0	430	0
15:00	134	476	0	450	0	432	0
16:00	135	480	1	453	2	436	7
17:00	136	484	1	457	4	440	0
18:00	137	488	0	460	0	440	0
19:00	138	492	0	462	5	442	5
20:00	139	496	0	466	0	447	0
21:00	140	500	0	470	0	450	3
22:00	141			474	0		

The total number of miles completed by each finisher on each of the six days of competition was:

	First	Second	Third	Fourth	Fifth	Sixth	Total
Rowell	110	87	86	77	68	72	**500**
Ennis	95	78	78	85	69	70	**475**
Harriman	100	86	84	55	65	60	**450**

The total resting times for the whole six days were as follows:

		Rowell Time Off				Ennis Time Off				Harriman Time Off		
Day	Stops	H	M	S	Stops	H	M	S	Stops	H	M	S
1	8	2	58	39	11	4	37	54	9	3	31	54
2	14	6	39	22	6	7	4	7	9	4	15	3
3	13	6	57	50	11	5	52	20	8	5	48	59
4	9	10	16	59	8	6	20	14	10	12	1	29
5	6	9	22	36	8	7	35	34	8	7	37	42
6	3	2	27	2	4	4	31	24	5	4	46	14
TOTALS	**38**	**42**	**28**		**36**	**1**	**33**		**38**	**1**	**21**	

Below is a table comparing the positions of the first and second contestants in the races in England and America for 1878 and 1879.

	ENGLAND 1878					AMERICA 1879			
	FIRST		SECOND			FIRST		SECOND	
HOURS		MILES		MILES	HOURS		MILES		MILES
16	Corkey	88	O'Leary	82.6	16	Rowell	78	O'Leary	72
24	O'Leary	117	Corkey	113	24	Rowell	110	Harriman	100
40	Corkey	167.2	O'Leary	166.4	40	Rowell	166	Harriman	155
48	O'Leary	200	Corkey	190	48	Rowell	197	Harriman	186
64	O'Leary	257.6	Vaughan	246.1	64	Rowell	250	Harriman	238
88	O'Leary	344.4	Vaughan	333	88	Rowell	332	Harriman	307
96	O'Leary	369.6	Vaughan	356	96	Rowell	360	Ennis	335
112	O'Leary	429.2	Vaughan	416.6	112	Rowell	405	Ennis	380
120	O'Leary	457	Vaughan	440.2	120	Rowell	432	Ennis	410
136	O'Leary	508.6	Vaughan	486.6	136	Rowell	480	Ennis	453
End	O'Leary	520.2	Vaughan	500	End	Rowell	500	Ennis	475

No sooner had the match finished when Weston sent the following letter to Astley.

London, N.,
March 15.

Sir John D. Astley, Bart., M.P.,
4 Lowndes-square,
London, S.W.

MY DEAR SIR,

As it is a foregone conclusion that Charles Rowell had won the Championship of the World Belt from O'Leary, I hereby challenge him to enter into a contest with me for it.

I shall be obliged if you would at once inform him of this challenge, that he may name the time and place for the contest.

Faithfully yours,

EDWARD PAYSON WESTON

Sir John responded to that by sending the following dispatch to Rowell:

Well done my boy. Pay O'Leary £100 deposit on belt. Weston has challenged you. Match to take place in London May 5.

The *Fitchburg Sentinel* on the 18th of March gave the following account of those arrangements along with other news in the pedestrian world: Greatly to the surprise of every one with whom O'Leary has talked, Harding, one of his trainers, said on Monday that O'Leary had determined to enter for the London race and would probably send out his challenge on Tuesday or Wednesday.

Ennis says that he will go to England to compete for the belt, and win or lose, will make a record America need not be ashamed of.

Concerning his English match Rowell said: "I'm entirely ready if they want me. I'll be all right and as good as new in a couple of weeks, and I have five weeks before that time. I'd be glad to have Ennis there, but I'll bet him the whole gate money that he doesn't win."

The Sun says that O'Leary's claims $2,000 of the money received at the late walking match. He says that he intends to find a man who is equal to the task of bringing the belt back from England. He proposes a contest for an American belt, with twice the inducements offered by Astley, and pick out from the contestants a man to fight for the Astley belt. He thinks that 500 miles will yet be made.

King of the Peds

The day before the above report, news had emerged that Harriman had managed to leave his room at the St. James Hotel. O'Leary meanwhile, had been settling up his debts. He had backed himself to win the race and had also bet that Harriman wouldn't make 450 miles. With both bets failing, he had lost $4,000, a lot of money! A quarter of a million dollars had been bet on the race. One of the big winners was said to be Astley himself who had reportedly won a cool $25,000!

The total gate receipts per day were as follows: **First day**, $3,576.75; **Second day**, $7,270.00; **Third day**, $9,156.75; **Fourth day**, $11,466.15; **Fifth day**, $11,447.20; **Sixth day**, $8,690.50: **Other profits**, $2,707.05; **Total**, $54,314.40.

At a meeting of the successful pedestrians which was held at the Turf Exchange, Twenty Eighth Street near Broadway on the 19th March, the *Brooklyn Daily Eagle* reported: **The meeting decided that O'Leary was not entitled to the $2,000 which he claimed, and agreed to give him $1,000. It is thought this will cause considerable difference of opinion, which may cause a reconsideration.**

On the following day, the same newspaper went on to say: **The division of the profits was made yesterday in the international walking match, and a statement was made by manager Kelly as follows: Total receipts, $54,314.40; expenses $12,908. $40,487.80 was clear profit. Rowell received $18,398.31; Ennis, $11,038.98; and Harriman, $3,679.66. Manager Kelly received $2,000 and Mr. Walton, Harriman's backer, $3,679.66. *Two thousand dollars was left in the bank to cover any contingencies which might arise, but the prevailing opinion is that $1,000 will be left for O'Leary. If this is not done, the final balance will be divided on the basis of fifty, thirty and twenty per cent. Harriman and Ennis refused to allow O'Leary the $1,000, and Rowell declined to commit himself either way, the majority having settled the matter. The question was discussed at length during the settlement of the trouble, and afterward it was the opinion that a change would be made and that the successful men would give O'Leary the $1,000.**

*Out of the expense account, the scorers who weren't paid for their efforts nevertheless received $1,500 collectively for expenses, and the door men and *"special policemen"* received $15.

A report in the *Chester Daily Times* on the 25th of March said: **Rowell, the champion pedestrian, will visit Concert Hall, Philadelphia, tomorrow, and will run for two days against time.** The result of his efforts there were that he ran 8 miles in 55m.9s on the first night, and on the second, he ran 10 miles in 1h.10m.57s, running the last mile in 6m.50s.

Rowell left New York with Asplen, Simpson and Atkinson on the Cunard mail-steamer *Sycthia* at 15:00 on Wednesday, April the 2nd. There were many well wishers at the Jersey City Wharf to give him a parting cheer.

It is believed that Rowell arrived back in Cambridge on Sunday morning, the 20th of April. He was received at the station by crowds of enthusiastic admirers, and a band which escorted him as he travelled in an open fly to Chesterton. The day after his arrival, there were reports that John Ennis had sailed for London that day to engage in the forthcoming pedestrian contest with Rowell, and that Peter Panchot and Sam Merritt, a couple of up-and-coming American athletes, were following him later.

On the 17th of May, the *Cambridge Chronicle* gave an account of Rowell's *"welcome home"* reception. Charlie's brother Michael was the licensee of the Bleeding Heart Public House, on the corner of Chesterton High Street and Chapel Street. He ran the place from 1858 till 1888 until he took over the running the Scales Hotel, which is now the Portland Arms. The newspaper said of the event: **On Monday evening last, the Rowell Reception Committee brought their labours to an end. At nine o'clock the chairman presented to Charles Rowell a clock, to C. Asplen a tea pot and cream jug, and to "Johnny Simpson" a clock, in the name and with the best wishes of the Committee and Subscribers. After the recipients had returned thanks, several other toasts were drank with great enthusiasm, and the evening was spent in great harmony.**

John Norfield, a shoe maker who practiced his craft on Chesterton High Street would doubtless have been in the pub that night. It was he who had made Rowell's running shoes. They were described as being *"extra broad in the sole,"* and *"particularly light."*

CHAPTER 16

Flags, Flowers and Femininity….

He walked into the affections of a pretty woman, the wife of a New Yorker and the result has been domestic discord, a suit for divorce and a suit by the injured husband for $10,000 for "alienating his wife's affections and breaking up his home.

The above paragraph was part of a much bigger story concerning an affair between one Charles A. Harriman, and a Mrs. Katie Stackhouse, which was printed in the *Philadelphia Times* on the 20th of July 1879. Mrs. Stackhouse, who was the sister of the proprietor of the St. James Hotel, was reported to have become *"infatuated"* with Harriman during the contest for the "3rd International Astley Belt," *"going there nightly, strewing flowers before him, and nursing him when the contest closed."* The 22-year-old was described as being a very pretty woman. *"She is tall, slender, and graceful, has large black eyes, well cut features, and a complexion clearer than the "Bloom of Youth" itself."*

It was Mrs. Stackhouse who was observed sitting in a box marked "Harriman," on numerous occasions. From there she would send her favourite baskets of flowers and occasionally wave an American flag over his head as he made his way round the track wearing the *"beautiful"* red, white, and blue sash that she had made for him.

After the contest had finished, the physically broken up athlete was carried to the St. James Hotel, where, prostrate with exhaustion, he was confined for some days to his room. It was during her frequent visits while he lay recuperating, that she became *"indefatigable in her attentions"* towards him. She is said to have carried dainties to the convalescent, and to have relieved the weary hours of recovery by reading newspaper reports of the match to him. It is said that by these means a *"tender feeling sprang up in the bosoms of both Mrs. Stackhouse and Harriman. In short, Mrs. Stackhouse had become fired by Harriman's heroic efforts in the ring. While the pedestrian was rendered doubly susceptible to womanly sympathy by his exhausted condition, she loved him for his struggle and pains, and he loved her that she did pity them."*

As soon as Harriman recovered, he embarked on a tour through the eastern states whilst Mrs. Stackhouse entered into partnership with George Brown, the well known English restaurateur. On his return to New York in May, the "Steamboat" received an anonymous letter, which had obviously been written by a woman, inviting him to a meeting at the Hotel Brunswick. The woman was Mrs. Stackhouse. This meeting turned out to be a precursor to many subsequent liaisons, and both he and she were later seen riding in Central Park and visiting *"places of amusement"* together. Mr. Stackhouse was informed of their meetings, but he treated them as defamatory, and not only refused to listen, *"but admonished the informant that a repetition of the tale might possibly result in a severe castigation with a rawhide."*

This state of affairs continued till the 1st of June when Harriman toured the southern states of the country. While he was away, *"several tender epistles are said to have passed between Mrs. Stackhouse and the absent pedestrian."* Mrs. Stackhouse was said to be showing signs of distress, and despite receiving much support from her friends, she appeared despondent. Her husband, who was aware something was amiss, suggested that she take a trip to Philadelphia to stay with her parents. Accepting the offer, she left for that city on July the 2nd and then stayed with her parents for four days before leaving without telling anybody where she was going on the morning of the 7th.

Mr. Stackhouse, who was promptly informed of the situation by telegraph, packed a bag and immediately went to Philadelphia. Following a line of enquiry, it was soon discovered that his wife had made the journey to Richmond, Virginia, where Harriman had been contesting in a race. When she reached the city, *"she had her trunk sent back to Philadelphia by express, to be left until called for,"* directing that the receipt and key should be sent to her at the Mystic

King of the Peds

Hotel in Boston under the care of Harriman. Mr. Stackhouse caught the next train for that city, but when he reached there, he couldn't find his wife or the famous pedestrian.

What he didn't know was that the couple had made the journey to Massachusetts together. A report from Haverhill stated that they stayed in the city's Eagle House Hotel on the same evening that Mrs. Stackhouse had left her parent's house. Harriman checked in first and the name immediately following his on the register was said to be of a lady calling herself *"Katie Wilson"* from *"Philadelphia."* Dispatches at the time suggested that the pair went to the Isles of Shoals on the steamer *Bartlett* on Wednesday, the 9th. Katie was said to be *"dressed in the height of fashion."* They left the hotel on the morning of Friday, the 11th of July, and returned to Boston the same day at 2 p.m.

Reports from New York on Monday, July the 14th suggested that the two had eloped on the 7th. Mr. Stackhouse was said to have enlisted the services of a private detective who tracked the pair to Medford, Massachusetts, and then on to Boston where, on Thursday, the 17th, Harriman had been *"summoned before a referee and his money in the Boylston Bank attached."* However, and to add a further twist to the story, another report later said; *"The statement that Harriman's money at the Boylston Bank in Boston has been attached is denied by the bank officials, who say that Harriman has never had an account with them."*

On the 19th of July, Mrs. Stackhouse went to collect her trunk, but unable to produce the receipt, she had to call on some of her old friends to identify her. *"Almost simultaneously with the arrival of Harriman's letters at the Mystic House Hotel, Mr. Stackhouse arrived there. Harriman and Mrs. Stackhouse were out at time and the latter says her husband took charge of the letters, and opening them all, retained the key and receipt."*

Mrs. Stackhouse, giving her version of events to the *Philadelphia Times* said: "**My name is Katherine Stackhouse, and I am the wife of George W. Stackhouse recently the steward of the St. James Hotel, and a brother in law of Theodore Walton once Recorder of Deeds of this city, and now proprietor of the St. James in New York. The relationship was established by Mr. Walton marrying Mr. Stackhouse's sister. I was married in this city, where I was formerly an operator on shirts, and went with my husband to New York and heaven knows he was a good husband then and gave me every care and attention, and we were very happy. Well, we lived a good deal at the hotel of course, and when the walking match was started we heard a great deal of it, for Mr. Walton was very much interested, and my husband was, too. Mr. Harriman don't you know was backed by Mr. Walton and when he walked I heard nothing but Harriman. I had never seen him in my life, but it was Harriman at breakfast table, dinner and tea table, Harriman in the parlor at home, and at night too when they used to bring dispatches to the house when we were in bed, telling how Harriman was getting along. It was all Harriman, till I got weary of the name. Well, I went to see the walk, and I saw Harriman. After the walk was over I met him at a masquerade ball to which I went with my sister and her husband. I talked to Mr. Harriman and I didn't know my husband was there although he was right along side of us, and we were making fun of his dress, Well, we went into the wine room, and just then my sister's husband came in and he says: 'Who do you think is out there threatening to expose you?' 'Nobody can expose me, and nobody is doing any threatening, except my husband,' and I went right out to him. He was like a crazy man. He raved and swore, and picked me up bodily and threw me into a carriage and home we went. Well, I give you my word, all his charges were false.**

"**Shortly after that I was in Boston and Mr. Harriman was there. One day he went down, to the bank to draw some money, and the Cashier laughed at him and said: 'Your money is attached; we can't pay you any.' Mr. Harriman thought that it was because of the accident at the Garden, You know the seats broke down, and all the people who were hurt had to be paid by the walkers. All of them put $2,000 in the bank against possible claims. So Mr. Harriman said: 'Why, there is money in New York against the claim,' and they told him to see Lawyer Bragg. He went there and asked for an explanation, and the lawyer said, 'You haven't any broken seat business, to attend to now. It's for breaking a family, you villain, amid you ought to be ashamed of yourself.' and Mr. Harriman laughed in his face. Well, I came back to New York, but I must tell you, Mr. Harriman had about $7,000 in the bank. Well, I came to New York, and I went to my house, and my husband—I mean Mr. Stackhouse—had sold out every blessed thing—my piano and everything—and he had sent for the landlady to come and take my pictures for the rent. I went to his place of business, and I told him, I'd make things warm for himself and his family if he didn't instantly withdraw the attachment from Mr. Harriman's money, and he turned white, for you know people who live in glass houses shouldn't throw stones. I had been served with the notice of the divorce suit, and had filed my answer of denial of the charges in New York. Then it was agreed that I should come on here to my family. I came and stayed four days and then I thought I would run down to Richmond. That was about the 7th of July. I went there to visit my friends, and I met Mr. Harriman there. He was walking there. Then I came back to Boston, and that's where Mr. Harriman was sued. Now, my—I mean, Mr. Stackhouse—has had all sorts of publications made about me, and I think it only right that I should tell the story just as it is I have been an abused woman.**"

The situation of affairs at the time was that a suit for divorce would be called on August the 4th in New York, and that some time in September, the suit against Harriman would come up for decision in Boston. Mrs. Stackhouse stated that she would prosecute her husband *"on all these charges concerned, and make it hot for him unless he abandons the suit against Harriman."*

Then, on the Saturday, Mrs. Stackhouse returned to her husband at his place of business acknowledging that it was all her fault, and sinking to her knees, begged to be taken back. Finding her husband obdurate and unforgiving, Mr. Stackhouse refused, and ordered her to leave, stating he would have nothing to do with her, reiterating that he had began proceedings for a divorce and a suit against Harriman for damages.

On the 17th of October, Mr. Stackhouse, who placed the *"damage to his alienated affections,"* at $10,000, instigated a suit for that amount in the Supreme Court, and secured an order for Harriman's arrest in which the pedestrian's bail was fixed at $5,000. It was stated that Harriman's friends *"patched up the matter,"* and Stackhouse withdrew the case and Harriman was released. Nothing more was reported of the affair thereafter.

CHAPTER 17

American Championship Belt

The advertisement below appeared in the *Brooklyn Daily Eagle* on the day before the commencement of the next race to tantalise the taste buds of New Yorkers, who, by then, had been well and truly hooked on the new phenomenon of "Pedestrianism." The match was scheduled to begin at 12:05 a.m. on Monday, April the 14th 1879.

GILMORE'S GARDEN.

A. R. SAMUELLS..	
THOMAS O'RORKE...	Managers
WM. F. McCOY...	

The most exciting contest that ever took place in America will commence at 12:05 tomorrow morning for the

SIX DAYS' CHAMPIONSHIP OF THE UNITED STATES

go-as-you-please, for the purpose of producing the best man to enter the International Match to come off at London, England, in June next, for which the management offer the following bone fide prizes:

> 1st Prize, Massive Gold and Silver Belt and $1,000 cash
> 2d Prize $750
> 3d Prize $500
> 4th Prize $250

For the above, forty men have entered, and each man has paid his £100 cash to Mr. Frank Queen, editor Clipper. The New York Athletic Club will have entire charge of the scoring, and Mr. W. B. Curtis will act as referee, so that no question can arise as to the fairness. Contestants or their representatives will meet at the Garden at 4 o'clock this (Sunday) afternoon to draw for tents and receive instructions.

The massive gold and silver belt which was being competed for was described as being composed of eight heavy plates of silver of which four, on either side, were large curved gold plates bordered with silver. On the central plate was the inscription **"Championship Pedestrian Belt of the United States."** On the smaller plates were embossed figures of pedestrians, both walking and running, winged feet and wheels, and on the central plate, there were two large figures representing Liberty and a North American Indian.

The *New York Times* gave its readers an idea of the preparations being made for the *"most exciting contest ever to take place in America:"* Even a person familiar with the aspect of the Garden on all previous occasions, when it was, in succession, a circus, a tabernacle, a skating rink, a ballroom, and a dog show, will hardly be able to form any correct idea of its present appearance without seeing it. The great change is in the main circle, the boarded ball-room floor. This has been divided into two nearly equal parts, by a fence run from the reporters' stand to a point near the entrance to the bar-room. Between the fence and the Madison-avenue end the floor is clear and open to visitors, but eastward of the fence, and between it and Fourth avenue, 41 tents have been erected, and a stand has been put up for the accommodation of the band. The large number of entries for this match which is not only for the championship of the United States, but for the selection of a man to enter the international match in England, on June 16, made it necessary to provide extraordinary means for their accommodation. Two dozen of the tents are included in four rows of six tents each. Two rows on each side of the Garden, and the remaining 17 into a semi circle. This display of canvas gives the Garden something of the appearance of a military encampment. Each tent contains a little cot bed, a table, a gas stove and one or two chairs. A few of the pedestrians provide their own furniture, and their quarters are more handsomely fitted up. Each of the tents is abundantly large enough to accommodate a contestant in the match and his attendants and the canvas cannot fail to be a blessing to the pedestrians, for it will strain a little of the dust and the tobacco smoke before it reaches their lungs. It will be an open question among pedestrians whether the present track is an improvement on the one last used or not. It is well provided with sawdust, and, if kept properly rolled and packed, can hardly fail to please the tender footed. The arrangements for scorers and reporters are excellent, and everything possible has been done for the public accommodation and safety, with the single exception already mentioned.

The two score of walkers met in the garden yesterday afternoon at 5 o'clock to draw lots for choice of tents and each man, as he drew his number, selected his tent. The numbers of the tents are consequently in disorder, the figures being scattered about promiscuously.

The 40 entries for the race were: **Charles Armstrong,** New York: **George Barber,** Jersey City: **David Bradley,** New York: **Clement Britain,** New York: **Stephen Brodie,** New York: **M. J. Byrne,** Buffalo: **Thomas Callaghan,** New York: **W. H. Davis,** New York: **James Day,** New York: **William H. Dutcher,** Lee, Massachusetts: **Peter Fenlon,** New York: **William Flitchcroft,** New York: **John W. Goodwin,** New York: **John Hall,** Brooklyn: **Harry Howard,** Glen Cove, Long Island: **John Hughes,** New York: **Edward Kennaven,** New York: **Frederick Krohne,** New York: **Ludwig M. Kyleburg,** New York: **Frank E. Leonardson,** New York: **James McEvoy,** Brooklyn: **Michael Mahoney,** Norwich, Connecticut: **Sam Merritt,** Bridgeport: **Gustav Meyer**, New York: **J. B. Murray,** New York: **Frederick W. Nash**, Brooklyn: **Thomas Noden,** Brooklyn: **William S. O'Brien,** New York: **Timothy O'Burke,** New York: **Peter J. Panchot,** Buffalo: **John G. Raine**, New York: **David M. Rankin,** New York: **Edgar H. Reeves,** Brooklyn: **W. H. Spear**, New York: **David Scanlon,** Brooklyn: **A. B. Sprague,** New York: **G. L. Stanley,** New York: **Cornelius Sullivan,** New York: **Samuel Tiers,** Paterson, New Jersey: **H. L. Willis**, New Millford, Connecticut:

There were about 2,000 people in the Garden as the clock struck midnight. People were still coming through the doors fully expecting that the race would start on time. However, and with the 40 competitors waiting patiently in their tents, it was announced that the "off" wouldn't be made until 1 o'clock. *"The Garden was damp, chilly, and uncomfortable, but the crowd amused themselves by walking over the floor, peering into the tents and starting the week's supply of cigar smoke."*

At half past the hour, the pedestrians emerged from their tents, gathered in front of the scorers' stand, and listened intently to a Mr. Wade, who made a five-minute speech, during which time he repeatedly told the crowd that the winner of the forthcoming race was to go England to bring back the Astley Belt to its rightful home. However, he was interrupted by a large group of newsboys who had occupied the seats on the terrace opposite the scorer's stand, who began to chant "Brodie! Brodie!" and "Brodie's the man!" Undeterred by the noise, Mr. Wade continued, "The winner of this match when he comes back from England with the belt will get the grandest ovation in New York that any man ever got." (Cat-calls, and cries of "Brodie! Brodie!")

After the speech, the band, which was occupying the platform, played "My Mary Ann" as the contestants sauntered back to their tents past the excitable crowd who stood behind the heavy timbers which served as rails.

At 00:53, the *"Forty Thieves,"* as the men were referred to, were recalled back on to the eight-foot wide track, and formed themselves into ranks of five in front of the scorers' tables. Nearly all those taking part, *"presented such a ridiculous appearance at the start with their wonderfully constructed and motley hued costumes,"* They were all dressed in tights and trunks, and wore fancy caps. *"The peculiar appearance and costumes of some of the men created great merriment. Flitchcroft wore a yellow upper garment, much resembling a nightgown; Mahoney's appearance was such as to call out loud calls of "Pat Rooney!" Scanlon was trying to imitate O'Leary's gait; Meyer walked with the grace and general appearance of a rheumatic camel."* As the objects of ridicule waited, many were taunted by the crowd, who also jeered them and made derogatory remarks.

King of the Peds

"Where's Hughes?" came the cry from the stands. After a short time, the "Lepper," wearing a *"very pretty pair of red stockings,"* emerged from his tent to occupy the No. 1 spot on the path. As the time neared for the start, the number of spectators increased to about 2,500, and *"at exactly 1 o'clock the signal was given, and the men started off like a flock of sheep, stumbling over each other."* Harry Howard was the first man to make a lap, followed by O'Brien and Brodie, with Hughes seventh past the post.

Howard was the first of the men to score a mile and considering the conditions did well to make it in 7m.23s. O'Brien was a whisker away in second place. Of the others, Sprague was reported to walking boldly with a giant stride, and Merritt and Bradley were observed to be swinging themselves about wildly, whilst the well supported 16-year-old newsboy Brodie, who had previously been reported to have walked 90 miles in 24 hours in February, went along his way with a *"pleasant, graceful gait."* He would be presented with a handsome bouquet after he completed his first mile by members of his fan club.

At noon, the score of the leaders was: **Panchot, 62; Flitchcroft, 55; McEvoy and Merritt, 52; Brodie, Byrne, Goodwin, Howard, Krohne and Raine, 49:**

The only withdrawal from the race on the first day was No. 15, Callaghan, who made his departure on a score of 42 miles, and the first man to score a century was Panchot at 20:23. The Buffalonian at the time was 9 miles in front of the 21-year-old Merritt, and he led Brodie, O'Brien and Krohne by five miles. Apart from the *"dark skinned wiry little Frenchman"* who led the race, the fourth placed O'Brien took the eye. Brodie however, was limping along, and there were doubts about him getting any further. Krohne, *"the raw-boned German,"* moved himself forward *"with a curious gait, in which each of his legs seems to act independently of the other."* Of the others, the 26-year-old graceful walking, 5ft.7 inches tall, Dutcher, weighing 150 pounds, who had gone so well during the day, had to be carried to his cabin *"insensible."* He returned a few minutes later apparently cured. Kyleburg had to be forcibly removed from the track due to drunken behaviour and put to bed after *"raving like a crazy man."*

The midnight score with Flitchcroft now out of the race having made 76 was: **Panchot, 104; Merritt, 100; Krohne and O'Brien, 91; Dutcher, Fenlon, Hall, McEvoy, Merritt and Murray, 90:**

On the morning of the next day of competition, the press complained that because of the miserable arrangements for score-keeping, it was nigh on impossible to get an accurate report about many of the participants in the race. What *was* gleaned was that the Buffalo postman, Panchot, most definitely remained in the lead by ten miles over his nearest rival, Merritt, on a score of 149 miles. The *"puffy"* looking Hughes who appeared in poor fettle, and who had bet $100 on himself to cover 500 miles by the end of the event, was hopelessly out of contention with a mere 103, and Rankin was the debacle of the event as he struggled round on a pathetic score of 61. Of the others, Mahoney, *"a typical Irishman,"* came in for ridicule from the crowd who poked fun at the way he circumnavigated the ring. The 42-year-old, 5ft.3in. tall Noden, weighing approximately 100 pounds, caught the attention for his fragility. He was described as *"the little bundle of bones"* and the *"living skeleton which had escaped from a museum."*

The leader however, still progressed smoothly on his way, and by 21:00, employing a mixture of running and walking, had covered 180.1, the distance being a furlong more than Rowell had travelled in the same time in the previous contest. By 22:00, this feat had been bettered by a mile and 5 laps, and his effort was being duly recognised by the crowd who clapped him on his way. The betting at the time was: **Panchot, 1/1; Dutcher, 4/1; O'Brien, 5/1; Merritt, 6/1; Krohne, 10/1; Murray, 15/1; Bar these, 20/1 to 100/1:**

After 48 hours of play, and with just 29 men left, the score was: **Panchot, 190; Merritt, 180; O'Brien, 171; Murray, 169; Dutcher, 165; Krohne, 163; Noden, 160; McEvoy, 154; Fenlon, 152; Mahoney, 150; Hall, 148; Byrne, 145; Brodie, 143; Sullivan, 142; Spear, 140; Howard, 137; Hughes, 132; Bradley, 131; Goodwin, 127; Day, 124; Willis, 121; Raine, 117; Scanlon and Stanley, 115; Kennaven, 113; Sprague, 111; Kyleburg, 108; Davis, 89; Armstrong, 44:** Panchot, who had gone to bed at 23:30, was now seven miles behind Rowell's record.

With the "Lepper" making his exit from the contest at 09:00 on a score of 149.4, the score at 11:30 showed that Panchot was still leading with 219 miles to his nearest rival Merritt's 213. O'Brien remained in third place with 206. The *"great Dane"* Krohne, had catapulted himself up to fourth with a mile to make for his second century.

 The youngster **Stephen Brodie**, *(Illustration no: 43)* who stood 5ft.7½ inches high, surprised everybody with his brave display. He was the recipient of many floral gifts as he continued to please the many fans that had warmed to him. His appetite was immense, and he was often observed chewing away at a large sandwich as he plodded around the path. As the day wore on, and as the crowd increased to 3,000 during the evening, they were entertained by Willis who amused them with his *"remarkably deliberate"* method of conveyance. He had replaced the *"comical"* Mahoney who had retired, much to the disappointment of his enthralled admirers earlier. The other retirees during the day were Sullivan for 167, Kennaven for 113, Goodwin for 127, Bradley for 131, Raine for 120, and Sprague who had managed 111. As the belt was being displayed by Frank Whitaker in the centre of the track for all curious to see, the betting on those trying to win it was: **Panchot, 1/3; Dutcher, 4/1; O'Brien, Merritt and Krohne, 10/1:**

With Fenlon and Davis withdrawing later in the evening, a field of 19 were left in the tournament and the score at the end of three days read: **Panchot, 260; Merritt, 250; Dutcher, 243, Krohne, 241; Murray and O'Brien, 240; Noden, 230; Byrne, 214; McEvoy, 200; Howard, 199; Hall, 198; Brodie, 193; Spear, 186; Willis, 174; Scanlon, 170; Day, 156; Stanley, 155; Kyleburg, 152; Armstrong, 70:**

During the 4th day, Panchot, now wearing moccasins, stepped around the track in splendid fashion keeping the good lead he had built up during the race. The second and third positions were now occupied by Merritt and Krohne, the latter mentioned having managed to promote himself due to Dutcher's demise, that man suffering from badly blistered feet causing him to *"drag himself around the track with the greatest of difficulty."* Dutcher then fell back to sixth position and later retired altogether on a score of 286 along with five others for the day. These were Murray with 256, McEvoy with 201, Hall with 198, Spear with 186 and Armstrong with 73. *"The men who left the track were utterly used up, some of them presenting a most wretched appearance."*

The *New York Times,* as always, referred to the efforts of those not wishing to pay to get in to watch the contest: **The street boys began the practice of the game of climbing up the outside of the Garden, smashing a window, and then effecting entrance in which they were so successful during the Rowell walk. It was no little amusement to the spectators to watch the various appearances or hands at the broken windows, the stealthy entrances, and the sudden and ignominious ejection of the culprits from the gallery they had attained with infinite pains by the Police officers who lay in wait for the rascals as a cat does for a mouse.**

The midnight scores of the thirteen left in the contest: **Panchot, 337; Merritt, 324; Krohne, 321; O'Brien, 310; Noden, 296; Byrne, 280; Howard, 256; Brodie, 231; Scanlon, 221; Willis, 218; Kyleburg, 198; Stanley, 197; Day, 196:**

The fifth, and penultimate day, saw no change in order of the leading men, but there were three more retirees in Howard, Scanlon and Kyleburg who withdrew on 283, 221 and 215 respectively. Merritt, although appearing distressed, made much ground on the leader, whereas the man behind him, Krohne, lost a little. Brodie meanwhile continued to inspire everybody who saw him in action. At 20:55, Panchot ran the last two furlongs of his 400th mile, and not long after was confronted by ten letter carriers who were employed at Station F in the New York Post Office. They had just entered the building in Indian file carrying a floral piece in the shape of an "F" which was three feet in length and made up of white rose buds, carnations, calla lilies and smilax, with the letters "N. Y. P. O." in blue violets. The leader of the men, who were all dressed in grey uniforms, then presented the design to Panchot, who, although not stopping to receive the gift, nevertheless bowed graciously in his acknowledgment of it.

There were 2,000 watching when the scores were announced at the end of 120 hours (1 a.m.): **Panchot, 407; Merritt, 401; Krohne, 396; O'Brien, 366; Noden, 362; Byrne, 352; Willis, 265; Stanley, 244; Day, 224:**

During the early hours of the last day, the only cheering the competitors received was on the Twenty Sixth Street side of the building, as the mainly empty seats on the other side were reserved at a price of 50 cents more. Panchot managed to keep the seven-mile gap between himself and Merritt, and at 09:00, he led the lad from Bridgeport 439.5 miles to 432.6, with Krohne falling back even further behind the second placed contender on a score of 425; the rest of the positions remaining the same. At 11:30, the race leader had knocked up 444 miles. Merritt had scored 437 and third man Krohne, 426. As the day progressed it was clear that barring anything serious happening to the front three, that's how the race would end, with Panchot booked as the ultimate victor.

Krohne was the first man to withdraw from the contest at 20:50. He had easily secured third place and the $500 that went with it. Celebrating his fortune by ridding himself of his walking costume, and carrying two large American flags around the path whilst dressed in his ordinary clothes, he said he was very tired and planned to use the money to open a beer saloon.

"The incidents were lively and the tumult uproarious during the last two hours of the race. The contestants literally went as they pleased. At one time, they all carried American flags, the band whanging out, "Yankee Doodle," and "Hail Columbia," while the crowd yelled at the top of their voices."

Panchot, wearing a United States Post Office cap, remained on the track until 22:07 in front of 6,000 spectators to win the race easily with 480.1. Not only did he carry off a prize of $1,000, but he was immediately offered $5,000 to give exhibition walks throughout the USA. He was presented with the belt by W. B. Curtis of *Wilkes Spirit of the Time,* after traversing a lap draped in the Stars and Stripes and carrying two others in his hands. Curtis, upon presentation of the belt said to the winner, "You came amongst us a stranger, Mr. Panchot. We know nothing of you, but you have earned the belt, which I am pleased to have the opportunity of handing over to you, and the money you will receive on Monday."

Merritt, who had previously *"been going like a freebooter under the skilful training of Andy Sheehan,"* left the track at 22:23 with the knowledge he would receive $750 for his wonderful effort. He had scored just five miles less than the winner but looked so much better than either Ennis or Harriman had done in the last Astley Belt contest. The eccentric figure of Napoleon Campana had accompanied him round the track for a lap, claiming young Sam as his protégé, and telling reporters after the lap, "Why the boy beat his old boss." Campana told the press that he had just returned from Canada where they had tried to kill him in a walk saying, "But I beat them all easy." Of his former protégé, he continued, "If I'd stayed here Merritt would have won. He's my orange peddler and the best boy that ever yelled." Commenting on the news that Merritt had reportedly slept for only seven hours since the start, "Old Sport" said, "What do you think of that for a boy only twenty-one years old?"

O'Brien finished fourth. The day before he had to be kept up to his work by the copious use of brandy, and his physician had told him in the early hours of that day that if he didn't retire, he would likely die on the track. His trainers and attendants, ignoring this advice, plied him with even more of the liquor and told him to continue. This he did and with a *"seriously impaired constitution,"* went on to win $250. Byrne and Nodin, who came in fifth and sixth respectively, both saved their deposits having made over 425 miles. Brodie, the seventh placed athlete, entertained his fans to the end. His friends were said to have raised a tidy sum of money for him from the crowd, and he himself went round the track selling newspapers at exorbitant prices to anybody who would buy them. Willis finished in eighth with nothing and was said to be *"badly used up."* Having been advised to leave the race earlier in the day he was said to have replied, "No sir; I've paid a hundred dollars to spend six days on this track, and I'm going to get my money's worth, even if I don't make a cent. The man from New Milford in Connecticut eventually made 310 miles and 5 laps.

The Final Score!

1st **Panchot, 480.1;** 2nd, **Merritt**, 475.5; 3rd, **Krohne**, 455; 4th, **O'Brien**, 435; 5th, **Byrne**, 427; 6th, **Noden**, 426; 7th, **Brodie**, 375; 8th, **Willis**, 310; 9th, **Stanley**, 280; 10th, **Day**, 243:

The Winner!

Peter Panchot

Frank Leslie's Illustrated Newspaper. (Illustration no: 44)

Peter Panchot was born in Buffalo on the 10th of December 1852. Previous to this event, he defeated William Hoffman over a distance of 25 miles in the *"alleged"* time of 4h.22m.30s in Buffalo in January of the previous year. At the same venue on March the 24th of the same year, he beat Cyrenius Walker in a 50-mile match for $200, his time being 9h.5m.40s.

CHAPTER 18

2nd Long Distance Astley Belt

AGRICULTURAL HALL, ISLINGTON.
CHAMPIONSHIP OF ENGLAND.
Great International Contest
[Under the Patronage of Sir J. D. ASTLEY, Bart., M.P.]

4 COMPETITORS
W. CORKEY, (Holder).   GEO. HAZAEL.
"BLOWER" BROWN,   E. P. WESTON,
                             Providence, U.S.A.

APRIL 21st to 26th, 1877
INCLUSIVE.

The above Race will commence on MONDAY, the 21st inst., at 1.5 a.m., terminating SATURDAY, the 26th inst., at 10.30 p.m. The man covering the greatest distance in the specified time to be declared the Winner.

From previous performances of the Men it is contemplated that Record Time will be Beaten.

DOORS OPEN AT 8 a.m.   FULL BAND.
ADMISSION TO HALL 1s; ENCLOSURE 2s. 6d.
Weekly Tickets to Hall 5s., To Hall & Enclosure 10s.

With the permission of Islington Local History Centre (Illustration no: 45)

The *second contest* for the "Long Distance Championship of England" for the prize of the Astley Challenge Belt, was advertised as above. Brown and Hazael were joint favourites at 2/1 to win the event. Corkey was priced at 5/2, and Weston at 4/1 was the outsider. There had also been a lot of money placed on Brown to make 125 miles in the first 24 hours before the race.

The winner would receive the whole of the stake money of £100 each. The gate receipts, after the payment of expenses, would be distributed as follows:

"If three men start, winner takes half; second man, two thirds of the remaining half and the third man the remainder. If four men start; second man, one fourth of the whole; third man, one sixth of the whole; fourth man the remainder. No man will receive any money who does not accomplish 450 miles."

George Atkinson of the *Sporting Life,* who had accompanied Rowell back from America after the 3rd "International Astley Belt" contest, was the referee, whilst Charles Conquest and Captain Webb were the judges.

The track, which was six feet wide and eight laps to the mile, and made up of spent bark sawdust, and *"a slight admixture of broken glass to make it bind,"* was described as being *"as good as any other that had been laid down in the building."*

Each competitor had been provided with a double-sized *"commodious"* tent, each of which was situated at each end of the ellipse.

There were other attractions to get the public in through the doors of the big building; the general admission price of which was a shilling, or "two and a tanner" for the extra comfort of the reserved inner circle. A punching machine could be battered, cocoanuts could be bowled or thrown at, and there was also a hammer hitting test for those who wanted to show off their strength to their friends.

Much was expected of **Henry Brown** who had won third prize in the race won by O'Leary in March of 1878 when he had scored 477.2, and who had also finished second to Corkey in November of the same year on a score of 505.3. He had been hard at it in training at his base at the Manor Tavern in Chiswick, where a cinder track had been constructed for him in an orchard nearby. His interests in the race would be looked after by the "Regent Street Pet," John Smith, David Broad, the landlord of the Prince of Wales Tavern, Turnham Green, and Sam Smith.

"**Corkey**," who was the *"feather"* in the race, had been trained at Oxford and Cambridge, and for this race was attended by Professor Austin R. Smith of Hackney, Mr. R. Moore who looked after a pub called the Morpeth Castle, and his brother R. Gentleman.

George Hazael, following his embarrassing performance in the *first* "International Astley Belt" contest, was said to be determined to prove himself in this match, and there was a lot of pre-race expectation that he might well win. He had been making his preparations at the Sussex County Cricket Ground at Hove near Brighton for six weeks. He was being assisted by Jem Howes, W. Mills and W. King. Since competing in that match at the "Aggie," George had been involved in a few events up and down the country. The following is his *resume* up to the race: With the thermometer registering 69 degrees Fahrenheit in the shade, and Mr. Atkinson refereeing, Hazael won a 50-mile, *"best of way, run or walk,"* race against 11 other opponents at Lillie Bridge on Monday, the 15th of July 1878. Hazael won the event easily in a time of 7h.15m.23s. Three miles back in second was Sittingbourne's Vandepeer, whilst A. Dickenson of Edenbridge passed the post in third and A. Flaunty of Woolwich fourth. The distances of the last two mentioned men when Hazael crossed over the winning line, were 45½, and 44 miles respectively. The victor won the Astley "Champion Challenge Belt," valued at £50, a gold medal valued at £5 and £25 *"in specie."* Vandepeer got £7 and a silver medal whilst Dickenson received £3 and a silver medal. Some other notable competitors in the event were Corkey of Bethnall Green, McCarty of York, Simpson of Cambridge, and Smith of Paisley. Between Monday, the 4th and the 9th of November 1878, Hazael made 403 miles and 6 laps at the Agricultural Hall, as compared with the 521 plus miles that Corkey had made in the previous week. This race was for *"second class men,"* ie, those who had entered, but had been excluded from the first contest. The starters were, T. Beaven of Islington, E. Butler of Lambeth, A. Dickenson of Edenbridge, A. Flaunty of Woolwich, France, W. E. Green, of Clerkenwell, W. Gregory of Hoxton, T. Hamilton of Homerton, G. Hazael of Camberwell, E. C. Holske of New York, U.S.A., A. Houghton of Islington, G. Martin of Camden Town, J. Miles of Brixton, S. Miles of Cardiff, E. Nichols of Rotherhite, H. Norman of Holloway, G. Parry of Manchester, J. S. Robson of Liverpool, J. Sexton of South Wales, A. Smith of Brompton, H. Vandepeer of Sittingbourne, and Whitley of Hyde. After a delay to the start, Hazael, who shot off into the lead, and who gradually increased it during the day, completed firstly 90 miles in the then new record time of 15h.30m.45s, and then 100 miles in the new record time of 17h.4m.6s. Hazael went on to win the first prize of £100 and indeed was the only man to complete 400 miles thus securing a prize for covering that required distance. George would have made a better score, but for some reason could only manage to make 12 miles in the last 23 hours of the contest. France finished second, Robson third, Martin fourth, Flaunty fifth and Norman sixth, having made 383, 377, 352, 302 and 262 miles respectively.

Edward Payson Weston, only the week before, had engaged himself in a 150-mile walk over two days, starting at 1 a.m. on Easter Monday, the 14th of April at the Pitville Gardens in Cheltenham. He completed his task on the heavy track with lots of time to spare at 22:47 the following day. For this match he was being cared for by Mr. R. Lewis, the donator of the 26-hour "Championship Belt."

The *London Times* wrote of the large crowd attending the event that night: One would had almost thought that the public interest in this description of sport would have by this time on the wane, if not entirely exhausted; but judging from the number of persons who witnessed the start, it does not seem to have abated in the least.

After the usual words of caution regarding fair play which were given by Astley, the men rushed away from the start at 01:00. By the first strides, it was clear that the promising Hazael meant business as he went on to secure a full half mile advantage over Brown in the first hour of the race. "Blower's" score was eight miles and he was half a mile ahead of Corkey. Weston was the last of the quartet on a derisory score of 4.5.

Hazael was the first man to score a "score" in 2h.17m.12s. At 4 o'clock, he had made 26.5 as opposed to Brown's 23.2, Corkey's 22.5 and Weston's 14.6. Hazael's tally after four hours was 33 miles 1,650 yards. After five hours, when he had made 40 miles 1,100 yards, he was almost five miles ahead of Brown, but wasn't expected to maintain his electrifying pace. He went on to make 47 miles 1,210 yards in 6 hours, 50 miles in 6h.14m.47s, and 54 miles and 935 yards in 7 hours. By 09:00, he was going so well that he had beaten the best 60-mile record by *two* hours, claiming that distance in a time of 7h.57m.10s.

Hazael's suicidal pace was beginning to take its toll by midday, and he had to go for a lie down for 22 minutes just before noon, after complaining of stomach cramps. The scores at that time were: **Hazael, 75.5; Brown, 67.5; Corkey, 65.5; Weston, 57.6:** Although slightly slower on his return, Hazael quickly made up the lost ground of two miles whilst he rested, and by three o'clock, having made his 83rd mile in 6m.51s, and now going as well as before, was able to show a score of 91 as opposed to Brown's 83.1. The leader went on to complete his 100 at 16:35 in 15h.35m.31s thus beating his previous record for the fastest century ever made, by 1h.28m.35s. Brown was next to pass the landmark at 18:14 with Corkey claiming his 34 minutes later, and Weston having to wait till 21:44 to celebrate his. The score at 23:00: **Hazael, 127.6; Brown, 121.5; Corkey, 116.3; Weston, 105:**

With Hazael and Brown seeking their beds after the spectators had left the hall just after eleven o'clock, there was only Corkey and Weston plodding around the empty building. Corkey, who had been out of the race for 1h.25m, now went along with renewed vigour. He was the only one on the track when Weston summoned his attendants to prepare his bed for his forthcoming occupation at 00:41 after making 111 miles without a break. At the end of play for the first day then, the telegraph board showed: **Hazael, 133; Brown, 126; Corkey, 119.4; Weston, 111:**

After Weston had made his reappearance, he not only complained of a headache, but also of a slight stoppage in his bowels. Apart from those ailments he looked as *"gay as a sparrow,"* and at that stage of the race he was fully expected to make 530 miles. Hazael continued to lead the race during that morning session with the score at 08:00 showing that he was still almost 5 miles ahead of his closest rival on a mark of 155.3; Brown having made 150.6. Corkey had made marvellous progress and had the second placed ped in his sights with 149.1. Weston continued to trail them all with an indifferent score of 126.1.

Things went pretty smoothly thereafter for Hazael, for as the records show, he maintained the five or so mile cushion over Brown. However, and as the afternoon progressed, the latter took two miles out of the leader's score as he rested. "Blower" continued to hack away at the leaders tally, and at 14:44 got up level with the over-enthusiastic and by now *"spent"* Hazael. When the three o'clock scores were raised, Brown had earned himself a lead of a mile, the score at the time being: **Brown, 183.2; Hazael, 182.2; Corkey, 174.4; Weston, 147.7:**

Hazael had displeased his trainers by taking a prolonged rest, which had cost him dearly. He had stayed under the canvas till well after 5 o'clock, and when he reappeared, he had been passed by Corkey who had gone three miles ahead of him. Worst still, was that Brown had gained an eleven-mile advantage over him at 18:00, and was now leading the race on a score of 197. After a slow stiff start, Hazael soon got back into top gear, and as the *"feather"* rested, he swept back into second place between the hours of seven and eight o'clock. The 9 p.m. scores: **Brown, 210; Hazael, 200.2; Corkey, 197.5; Weston, 174.7:**

"Blower," who was now the hot favourite to win the race, was noted to be going smoothly. Hazael was looking dangerous in the runner-up spot and he too was looking impressive. As the men started to indulge in their nightly rests, there was only Weston on the path at 1 a.m. when the telegraph board showed: **Brown, 221.4; Hazael, 211.1; Corkey, 205.4; Weston, 191.7:**

With the American out of the ring, the other three competitors started to return to the fray starting with Corkey at 01:41, then Brown eight minutes later, and finally Hazael at 02:10. Weston returned at around four o'clock appearing better for his break and plodded on with the rest of the jaded looking bunch. The third day was always regarded as the crucial test of the staying powers of those involved in these type of races, and Hazael's attempts to lessen the gap with the leader didn't materialise until he made some headway after eight o'clock. In the next four hours up until noon, and having made his 250th mile at 11:03, he took almost two miles off the distance with the returns showing: **Brown, 262.4; Hazael, 254.1; Corkey, 248.3; Weston, 221.4:**

The men had been given many bouquets during the day but the luckiest ped of the lot was Blower, who was given a pair of gold earrings for the *"missus"* as well as a smoking cap, which he wore for a lap before giving it to *"Mrs. Blower."*

The two front-runners had put on a fine show to entertain the London crowd. Corkey went on to register his 250th mile at 12:26, and by 3 p.m., the gap between the Brown and Hazael had been further reduced by nearly another two miles as Brown enjoyed being pampered inside his tent. However, in the following two hours he soon made up what distance he had lost, and by six o'clock in the evening enjoyed a nine-mile gap; the books at that time showing: **Brown, 285.2; Hazael, 276.3; Corkey, 272.1; Weston, 242.7:**

The impression was that Hazael would attempt to stay within a reasonable distance of the leader and wipe out the arrears on the last day with a fine running performance. Meanwhile, Weston, although observed to be walking gamely, was apparently having problems with his stomach.

Using a Benson's chronograph, the London *Times* correspondents timed one lap circumnavigated by each pedestrian between the hours of seven and eight o'clock. The results showed; Brown, 1m.40s; Weston, 1m.47.25s; Hazael, 1m.57.25s; Corkey, 2m.2.50s: More lap times were taken an hour later and they showed the following results: Brown, 1m.43.75s; Weston, 1m.47.50s; Hazael, 1m.54.75s; Corkey 2m.19.25s: From these results we can deduce that Brown and Weston were travelling along at the rate of about 4.5 mph, Hazael at just under 4 mph and Corkey averaging about 3.5 mph. The score sheets at 21:00 showed the following results: **Brown, 297.2; Hazael, 287.2; Corkey, 282.1; Weston, 255.2:**

Brown had achieved something that no one had achieved before, and that was the feat of scoring 300 miles within three days in a time of 68h.32m.10s. For accomplishing that, and while being heartily applauded by the boisterous crowd, he was not only presented with a couple of silk handkerchiefs, but also a bouquet which he ran around with for a lap or two.

Edward Weston, as predictable as a second hand on a clock, was once again the only man on the tanbark as the contest entered its fifth day. Very few people were in the building as he trudged around, apart from the race officials, the pedestrians, their attendants and the cleaners. Some would have looked at the scoreboard and familiarised themselves with the latest figures compiled by the scorers. At 01:00, they showed: **Brown, 311.4; Hazael, 295; Corkey, 287.4; Weston, 272:**

Weston went for an hours rest at 02:00 and little changed thereafter in the performance of the all the athletes. By 10:00, Brown had not only managed to make another 33 miles for the day, but had also surrendered another 4½ miles to Hazael. Corkey, now plodding slowly along on, appeared to be wanting his bed, and Weston, although going well, was clearly not in a position to be winning the race, the scores at that time being: **Brown, 340.5; Hazael, 333.4; Corkey, 320.1; Weston, 293.6:**

Brown had lost further ground to Hazael by a distance of a mile by 11:30, and at noon, another quarter of a mile, thus reducing the gap between them to 5¾ miles. The situation got worse for the leader as he indulged in short rests, Hazael further eradicating his lead to 3¾ miles by 1 p.m. as the following record shows: **Brown, 352.2; Hazael, 348.4; Corkey, 330.3; Weston, 306.5:** *"Encouraged by his success, Hazael persevered in his endeavour to overtake Brown, and although the latter, thoroughly on his mettle, gained ground, Hazael by his performance showed undoubted pluck – a quality in which many have hitherto considered him deficient."* Hazael however, couldn't maintain his challenge, and as he rested at 15:00, Brown, on a mark of 362.5 started to gain some ground and went along over four miles ahead of his fellow Londoner who was on 358.2. Corkey still went slowly on 335.1 and Weston went better on 315.1.

Comparisons were already being made with the recent Astley Belt race in New York where at the same hour (87th), Rowell's score stood at 332. Brown was a full 29 miles ahead of Rowell, and big things were expected of him. He then began to apply the pressure on Hazael, the pair thrilling the crowd with an exhibition of sprinting which they both maintained for several laps. Brown was advised to cool the hot pace which he did, and by 17:00, he had gone ten miles clear. With Hazael taking a further longish rest of 1h.12m, the *"Fulham Pet"* was beginning to stamp his authority on the race. By 20:00 he had moved further ahead as the returns at that time show: **Brown, 387; Hazael, 372.3; Corkey, 353.2; Weston, 330.2:**

When Brown crushed the previous 400-mile record time by eleven hours at 22:57 or 93h.56m.10s from the start, he received such an ovation *"enough to shake the building."* The celebratory mile, which was made in 9m.40s, was achieved in front of many lines of spectators crowding round the barriers estimated to be in the region of 7,000. *"Excitement and reason for excitement there was galore, and judging by the cheering and shouting of the evening, this must be the most popular of all the competitions held at Islington."*

By three o'clock in the morning on the fifth day of the contest, Brown had blown himself further into the lead as he sailed 18 miles in front of Hazael, the scores at the time being recorded as: **Brown, 403; Hazael, 385; Corkey, 365; Weston, 347:**

The last man in the race was the first man back in the ring, at 03:22, after his customary early morning rest, which in his case had been started at 00:11. Brown joined him a couple of minutes later having been prostrate for just under 3½ hours. Corkey joined them at 03:27, and Hazael was the last to gate-crash the party in the cold and dimly lit hall at 04:08. Nothing much happened thereafter until Hazael joined the four centuries club at 08:18, and at 09:40, and with both the leaders going well, the leader managed to gain more ground on his main rival. Weston had just arrived back on the track after a long rest and was reported to be looking *"queer."* He moved slowly and did the same pace as the poorly performing Corkey. As the large crowd glanced at the scoreboard at that time they would have noted the following credits: **Brown, 427; Hazael, 403; Corkey, 389; Weston, 362:** Corkey eventually got his act together just after midday, when he too made the psychologically important distance of 400 miles.

The pedestrian contest at the Agricultural Hall attracted over 10,000 spectators in the afternoon. After their delight at watching the leader complete 450 miles at 15:38, many of those watching witnessed the same man falling into one of his attendant's arms at 16:47, after running his 455th mile briskly around the track. He was helped back to his tent by the young man who caught him, John Smith. While he was being cared for in his tent, the score at 5 p.m. was: **Brown, 455; Hazael, 430.5; Corkey, 414.2; Weston, 370.5:** Any fears that he had broken down were quickly dispelled when he reappeared on the track at 17:12. However, he did appear quite dazed and his first few steps were akin to a toddler taking its preliminary unassisted walk. Looking a bit groggy, he gradually increased his speed, and when all was well, continued on his way. At 20:00, and having made a full recovery, Brown, although coming back to Hazael slightly, still looked to be the man who would be victorious at the end: The scores at that time were: **Brown, 465.7; Hazael, 442; Corkey, 424.1; Weston, 387.4:**

Whilst Hazael had been off the track resting, Brown was able to increase the gap between them. The race leaders time had beaten all past records, and he was *"greatly lionized"* by the cheers and shouts of the 20,000 spectators that filled the building. Weston, who had walked nearly the whole time, had covered a greater distance than he ever did before at this stage in a race. Although he was suffering terribly from blistered feet, he gamely struggled on in order to try and complete 450 miles and thus receive his share of the gate money. The strain on Corkey's frame was quite evident and he was described as being the most *"used up"* of the quartet at 20:00. Brown ran several of his miles during the evening, at an average speed of 6 mph, despite appearing feverish. Although his left leg was badly swollen, it was thought barring him breaking down altogether he was almost certain to be victorious; whilst Hazael, who was in better condition than Brown, was expected to indulge a great running performance on the last day.

News of the race was in high demand and every mile scored was being telegraphed all over the country. Reports also suggested that Brown intended to complete 560 miles before the end. At 23:00, the scores of the contestants stood as follows: **Brown, 477 miles; Hazael, 453.2; Corkey, 435.5; Weston, 397.2:**

At three o'clock in the morning of the 26th, the contestants had made the following scores: **Brown, 480 miles, Hazael, 454, Corkey, 438, and Weston, 400:** There was a little betting on Corkey for second place as Hazael was ill. Again, there were comparisons being made with the New York race where at the same time, Rowell had made 441 miles. As Brown completed his 500th mile at 09:13, the crowd showered him with bouquets of flowers which he acknowledged with *"becoming modesty"*. The 10 o'clock scores: **Brown, 503 and going well; Hazael, 472 and going wearily; Corkey, sore and stiff on 454 and Weston resting on 427:**

"All along during the afternoon, Brown showed his superhuman endurance, looking like the specimen of a of a well formed healthy man which he is, and exhibiting what he has shown from first to last, an unwavering good temper." At 15:00, the leader, who was grafting on the path, had added another 15 miles to his score. Hazael had to have his painful right foot lanced, but the operation didn't have too much effect in that he still went along slowly. Corkey was 20 miles in his rear, and Weston who had been entertaining the crowd with his eccentric behaviour, continued to enjoy his rest under the canvas on a score of 430. When he rejoined the race, he was said to be *"playing monkey tricks"* around the track. Brown was later to be seen walking round with his little boy and later at 18:00 the scores showed: **Brown, 532; Hazael, 485; Corkey, 467; Weston, 437:**

With Corkey stopping his tramp at 20:00 and Hazael shortly after, the match terminated at 21:21 when Brown had beaten the fastest record— by 21 miles in a time of 140h.21m.42s. Corkey, the previous champion then handed him belt, which the winner carried around the hall in triumph in front of an estimated attendance of 14,000 people.

The Final Result!
Brown, 542.2; Hazael, 492; Corkey, 473.2; Weston, 450:

In his book, "50 Years of my Life," Astley later wrote of the winner: **Brown had early distinguished himself by the rapid manner he trundled his barrow of bricks to the kiln, and back again or another load, and, like all brick-makers (I have ever heard of), he was wonderfully fond of beer therefore, when old Jack Smith wished to get an extra spurt out of his *protégé*, he used to yell at him on the track, and the same exhortation and promise was enumerated whenever his instinct told him encouragement was needed; "Well done, Blower! Go it, Blower! You have got 'em all beat, my beauty! Yes! Blower shall have a barrel of beer all to himself if he wins; Go it, Blower!" One day Blower showed signs of shutting up, and as he was more an animal than an angel, Smith and I agreed that it would be a good thing to wake him up a bit by putting him in a hot bath—quite a new sensation for him—so we took him to my lodgings hard by, and I ordered two chops to be got ready for him, and then put him into a hip bath of real hot water, which livened him up considerably, fairly making him sing out. When we had got him nicely dried, the chops appeared, and whilst I was helping Blower into his running-suit I was horrified to observe old Smith busily employed gobbling up all the best parts of the chops, leaving only the bone, gristle, and fat, and when I expostulated with him on his greediness and cruelty to his man, he replied "Bless yer, Colonel Blower has never had the chance of eating the inside, he likes the out side," and, sure enough, the brick-maker cleaned up the dish, with the result that he won first prize, doing 542 miles, a grand performance, and, what is more, his appetite and thirst were in no way impaired.**

CHAPTER 19

4th International Astley Belt

Rowell had arranged to compete against Weston in the 3rd international contest for the Astley Belt which was due to start on May the 5th 1879 at the Agricultural Hall in Islington. Rowell had met John Ennis on Thursday, the 20th of March in America to sign the articles of agreement to compete in the same race. Ennis had deposited $500 (£100) with Mr. Atkinson of the *Sporting Life* in conformity with the rules laid down by Astley. However, because "Blower" Brown, George Hazael, and other notable athletes had been entered in the *second contest* for the "Long Distance Championship of England" which was destined to be held between the 21st and 26th of April at the same venue, their participation in that event would virtually rule them out of the international match, since the intervening time was seen to be too short for recuperation. Mr. Atkinson had therefore influenced Sir John to postpone the date of the "Long Distance Championship of the World" to start on Monday, June the 16th.

With the permission of Islington Local History Centre (Illustration no: 46)

The stage was set for the most fascinating of contests between some of the world's greatest athletes. Charlie Rowell, the holder of the international version of the Astley Belt would face the holder of the English version, Henry Brown of Turnham Green, John Ennis of Chicago, Richard Harding of Blackwall, London, and Edward Payson Weston of *"New York."*

Weston was having a spot of bother finding the £100 necessary to enter the race. His reputation as a *walker* had even influenced Astley into refusing his request of a loan, the M. P. justifying his decision by stating that the 40-

year-old hadn't a hope in hell of competing against the modern *runners*. Weston took no notice and persevered with his quest to find the funds, and after being granted a week's extension by the other competitors, he finally got the cash from his wife's inheritance money.

Two or three days before the race started, a disturbing rumour regarding Rowell's participation started to hit the sporting pages of the worlds press. The unthinkable news that he might have to give up his newly earned title as the world's greatest pedestrian, was reported in an article in the *Sporting Life* on Saturday, June the 14th: **Even money was taken about "Blower" Brown yesterday in consequence of a rumour being circulated that Rowell had broken down. Upon enquiry we found that Rowell really had been compelled to stop work. It appears that while at exercise on Wednesday last, his left heel was punctured by a peg (or small stone). The heel subsequently gathered, and he could not put his foot to the ground without causing intense pain. The matter has now been extracted and it is just on the cards with proper treatment he may be patched up to start in tolerably sound condition though anyway the accident is to be regretted.**

The next day, the preparations for the forthcoming race had been completed. The track, measuring eight laps to the mile, was composed of tan, faced with fine sifted garden loam.

As the spectators waited for the start, it was revealed that Rowell would not be in the line-up. That meant a change in the odds offered by the bookmakers who chalked up the following prices as the men prepared themselves for the race: **Brown, 4/6; Ennis, 5/1; Harding, 6/1; Weston, 10/1:**

At 1 o'clock, and in front of a crowd of about 500 spectators, Astley shouted "Go!" and watched from the sidelines as Harding rushed past the post to score the first mile in 6m.5s. Brown made the same distance 15 seconds later whilst Ennis took 8m.5s to register his. Weston, *"the game old ped"* meanwhile, took 10m.10s to see out the first 8 furlongs. The Blackwall man kept up the gallop to lead the contest at the hour registering 9 miles to Brown's 8.6. Ennis made 7.6 and Weston was at the back of the pack on 6.7. After 2 hours the score was: **Harding and Brown, 16.6; Ennis, 15.2; Weston, 13.5:** Though Harding led Brown by 5 laps at 04:00, the *"Fulham Pet"* led *"Dick"* by 6 laps at 05:00. He went on to be the first man to make the half century in seven and a half hours with Weston, the *"weary wobbler,"* surprising everybody by making the same distance 17 minutes later.

Astounding everybody watching, the "Walkist" was actually running! Not only was he running, but he was looking cool and confident as he did so. Gone was the aloofness one normally associated with him, and gone were the flashy clothes he had worn in previous contests. Dressed in red worsted tights and a light white shirt, he now looked as though he meant business. His easy stride caught the eye as he moved effortlessly along, and he alone looked to be the danger to the gritty Brown.

At 09:30, Harding, who was on a score of 42.4 when the first reports of the race were being telegraphed around the world, was already being talked of as being the first casualty in the contest when he had previously headed for the comfort of his tent on a score of 30 miles. At the same time, and on a score of 56 miles, the race leader had gradually built up a small lead over the rest. The graceful figure of Weston viewed his progress from three miles away, whilst Ennis, who was *"seized with cramp of the stomach,"* plodded on eight miles behind him.

The Chicagoan later became quite sick at 14:00 when the telegraph board showed Brown was still the leader with 79 miles, a couple of miles ahead of Weston. At the same time, the *"queer"* looking Harding, who was toiling on the track on a score of 58 miles, was four miles behind Ennis. The Irishman's chances of victory were said to have been materially lessened by straining his back, whilst attempting to rescue a couple of women who had been at great risk of drowning days before the race at Teddington. He managed to save the pair, whose small boat had been smashed into by a tug, as he was training beside the river. Unable to get a ride back to his hotel, he walked the five miles in wet clothes; and the cold he caught as a consequence, ruined his chance of winning.

Some other first day scores: 16:00: **Brown, 89.5; Weston, 87.3; Ennis, 70.1; Harding, 65.5:** 18:00: **Brown, 99.2; Weston, 97.1; Harding, 75.1; Ennis, 70.4:**

Brown was the first man to make the coveted first hundred in 17h.13m.7s, and when he accomplished it, *"he was greatly cheered, almost everyone in the building joining in the applause."* Weston achieved the same feat 23 minutes later making his last lap in 7m.56s. The American went on to take the lead whilst "Blower" let his sails down for a rest,

King of the Peds

but as Eddy took his turn to put his feet up, the Brit re-hoisted them to retake the prime position just after seven o'clock. The score at 22:00: **Brown, 116; Weston, 113.7; Harding, 87; Ennis, 70.4:**

Midnight saw the Londoner continuing to lead the race on a score of 125.3 to Weston's 123. Ten minutes later, Brown left the path for a rest. This gave Weston the opportunity to take the lead, and that he did, scoring 127.3 before heading for his tent at a few minutes past 1 o'clock. At 04:00, and with Brown back on the track since 02:40 and Weston since 03:50, the score stood: **Brown, 131.2; Weston, 128; Harding, 87.4; Ennis, 70.4:**

Brown made 150 miles just after eight o'clock. Weston was to secure the same score an hour or so later, by which time the Fulham man had adopted the notorious "dogging" tactic on his opponent. However, the proven method of stalking one's opponent in order to break their spirit would fail in Brown's case. Weston countered the tactic by simply notifying the lap counter that he was about to reverse his direction. This strategy was well within the rules and Weston used it to perfection. Weston knew when he was about to reverse, but Brown didn't. As the American quickened his pace with the Englishman at his heels, he would suddenly yell out his intention to the official at the last second, turn around, and head the other way. Brown, due too his momentum, would find himself a few yards over the lap marker before realising what his opponent had done and thus lose valuable yards in the process. Of the spectacle, the *Sporting Life* wrote: **Considerable amusement has been caused by the strict way in which Blower sticks to his principal of dogging Weston, and being with him. Faithful as "Mary's little lamb," wherever Weston is there Blower with him goes. Weston walks; Blower walks. - The Yankee does a double; Blower cannot double like Weston, but he can and does run at an equal pace. When Weston turns his companion also reverses the direction of his route; and if Weston had a fit, it is a question whether Blower would not ask his mentor (Mr. John Smith) whether he would like him to have a fit too.**

The feature of the morning was the reappearance of Ennis (who was attended by John De Vere, the celebrated gymnast), who it was thought had permanently retired. He came on the track at 08:55 looking thoroughly refreshed by his 16 hours of rest. It appeared that he had entirely recovered from the sickness that he complained of the day before and he went along really well.

At noon, it was reported that there was much interest being shown in the match due to the splendid performance of Weston, who, prior to the contest, had distinguished himself as the *"great American failure."* At this stage, he was now 5 miles and 2 laps behind the leader on a score of 163.1. Again, comparisons were being made with the New York match, when Rowell at the same stage had made 153 miles. Weston's preparation was being touted as the reason for his promising performance. He was now being seen to be adopting a jog-trot in preference to his more favoured form of conveyance, the fast heel-and-toe walk, and it was this change of tactics which was making the punters think what was previously thought impossible, the possibility of a Weston victory. Harding, who was still in his tent, was miles back in third on 87.4 and Ennis was on 85.2.

Harding reappeared on the track after lying on his bed for 13h.9m at 14:42, and at 15:00 the score showed: **Brown, 182.3; Weston, 175.6; Ennis, 100.2; Harding, 91.2:** The leader went on to extend his lead. By 5 p.m., he was 7 miles in front of his nearest rival, going on to register his 2nd century at 18:29 with Weston scoring the same distance at 19:52.

It had generally been expected that Weston would then overtake Brown, but the Londoner showed tremendous resilience in not allowing that to happen. His gritty performance must have pleased the 2,000 crowd who cheered him on and the bookies made him 1/2 favourite to take the spoils.

Later scores: At 22:00: **Brown, 216.3; Weston, 209.5; Ennis, 131; Harding, 109.1:** At midnight: **Brown, 226; Weston, 218.6; Ennis, 137.4; Harding, 109.1:** (By this time, Dick Harding had left the building and it was wholly expected at the time that he wouldn't be returning).

Brown left the track at 00:18 and reappeared at 02:25. At 03:00, Brown, on a score of 227.1, led Weston by a lap under 7 miles, and Ennis, who had made 140, led the fourth placed, and by now absent Harding, by 31. The race leader went on to increase that gap to 13 miles by 07:00 due to the enforced absence of his main rival who hadn't been going too well due to a poorly and stiff right leg, the actual scores at the time being: **Brown, 242.5; Weston, 229.4:** That distance was maintained until noon when the leader board showed: **Brown, 265.6; Weston, 252.5; Ennis, 167:** When Brown later left the path for 30 minutes at 15:30, Weston, buoyed on by the band, managed to erase 3 miles and a lap from his deficit. At four o'clock, and with Brown back in the thick of it, the scores were: **Brown, 281; Weston, 271; Ennis, 180:** The American was raising many an eyebrow with his performance. He appeared fresh and was said to be confident of winning.

Ennis finally threw in the towel at 16:30 on a score of 180 miles as he had no chance of making the 450 miles necessary for a share of the gate money. Although he appeared better than the day before, his feet, which had blistered during his hike back to his apartment following his heroic attempts at the river, festered, and he could go no further.

At 20:00, Brown's score was 300.1, Weston being 11 miles in his rear. At 22:13, and with 69h.13m of the contest completed, Weston watched the number 300 hoisted next to his name alongside the figures 311.2 which were next to the leader.

Both men had beaten all previous records by the time the score went up at three o'clock the next morning, when the credits read: **Brown, 318; Weston, 311.3:**

The leader, having rested from 23:50, reappeared looking somewhat jaded at 03:16. By 4 a.m., Weston was only 5 miles behind his rival. However, the Fulham man was able to increase that advantage as the morning wore on, but whatever extra distance he did build up, his previous odds on status was to be wiped off the bookmaker's slates during the morning as his rival, now running really well, ate into his lead. At one stage, the American was seen to run two miles without a break. At 08:10, Brown went off the track. His break meant that "Ned" was able to reduce the gap between them to 6 miles and 5 laps. On his appearance some thirty minutes later it was quite evident that the Englishman was in trouble.

At 09:30, Brown led Weston 343 to 339, and 45 minutes later he left the track on a mark of 346.2 appearing unwell. This state of affairs caused his supporters to become quite anxious about his chances. Weston meanwhile, who was going really well and seemed strong, then took full advantage of his absence, equalling his score a few minutes after eleven o'clock. He then took the lead in the best time for the distance ever accomplished, and as he did so, the Americans in the crowd gave a mighty shout, making the building *"echo and re-echo."*

At 2 o'clock, Weston led Brown by 3 miles and 3 laps, and the impression that prevailed was that he now stood an excellent chance of taking the coveted trophy back over the Atlantic. Weston stated that if he won he wouldn't be competing in England anymore, telling reporters, "I intend taking the belt to America and whoever wants it must go there for it." He also stated this would be his farewell performance in London, and he intended to mark it by making 550 miles.

At 15:15, and when the score stood 361 to 356, Brown, who was wearing elastic supporters on his right knee which had given way, walked very slowly. At 4 p.m. Weston, who was now 6 miles ahead, spurred on by the ringing cheers of the spectators, while the band played "Coming through the Rye," ran briskly. At six o'clock, both men were resting. Weston was on his 369th mile, and Brown having accomplished 360 was being attended his physicians. Later, the 10 p.m. score showed: **Weston, 385; Brown, 360:**

Astley paid Weston a visit in his tent; the meeting of the two men reported to be *"of the most cordial character."* Sir John told him, "You are doing nobly Weston, and eclipsing anything on record. I hope you will husband your forces sufficiently not to become exhausted too soon." Weston replied laughingly, "I am going to do my level best to take back your belt to the States. The boys would be glad to see it once more. They did not feel over glad when little Rowell took it away on the Cunarder." Sir John then said, "Well you look in good fettle. Now I'll tell you what I'll do so that this tournament shall be a memorable one. I'll wager five hundred pounds to your one hundred pounds that you don't cover 550 miles by Saturday night. Do you take me?" Weston replied, "Certainly, Sir John. The five centuries will make a good lining to the belt," after which two men shook hands and parted.

Brown, who had been cautioned by his physician not to over-exert himself, took frequent rests of short duration, although he was told by his physicians to remain off the track for four or five hours. Whenever he appeared he was hailed with vociferous cheering. For his part, Weston retired to his tent at 23:40 intending to come out again at 02:30. However, his trainer let him sleep until 04:40 and this seemed to annoy him, although apparently the long rest did him much good.

After six o'clock, many people began to make their way to the hall, and during the morning, the excitement grew more intense with every additional mile added. The *Brooklyn Daily Eagle* in an article of the 20th of June commented: At noon today the leader was 20 miles ahead of Rowell's time (419 to 392) with only 34 hours left him to accomplish the necessary 132 miles, which would necessitate his averaging a trifle less than 4 miles an hour. In the 108 hours preceding he has not averaged quite 4 miles an hour, and to accomplish the feat he must maintain his actual rate of speed, which at this stage of the contest he is not likely to do. The odds given by Sir John Astley about fairly represent the chances. The bet undoubtedly intended to spur the pedestrian on. At all events, whether he reaches that figure or not he will almost certainly beat the best time made in any belt contest It is perhaps, to be regretted that Brown has broken down, for it will not give half the satisfaction to American's for their champion to beat a man who has collapsed as it would to vanquish an able bodied rival. However, the giving out of Brown's knee is not an accident. The walk has truly intended to test knees, stomachs, ankles, lungs, nerves and heels as any other parts of the human walking machine, and the swelling of Brown's knee, and the failure of Ennis's stomach are quite as truly incidents of the match as would be the rupture of a blood vessels or the failure of Weston's courage. Ennis has clearly shown that he is not a good six days walker, for his stomach unfits him for such trials. Brown's discomfiture in a lesser degree proves that he is not sound, wind and limb, and therefore that Weston is his superior. But all this apart, Weston is making better time than anybody but Brown has ever done. Weston's pluck is as great as his endurance. He has done what Rowell feared to do—met the great Brown.

The building was choc-a-bloc with spectators at 2 o'clock when the score was: **Weston, 425.1; Brown, 397.5:** At 15:00, the telegraph board showed: **Weston, 428; Brown, 400:** At 4 o'clock, with the score showing: **Weston, 433.4; Brown, 400;** the leader was described as, *"as fresh as a lark,"* whilst Brown was still troubled with his leg. At 18:00, Weston had added another nine miles to his tally against nothing from Brown and at 8 p.m. the returns were: **450 to 407.** The 10 p.m. score, when displayed showed: **460 to 414;** whilst the 1 a.m. record showed: **473 to 420.**

Weston's rest during the night amounted to 1h.50m, *"and when his trainer called him, he left his bed in the best of humour. Fresh and confident, he reappeared on the track, and very determinedly resumed work."* At 10 o'clock in the morning, the end of the 129th hour, and with the score showing **491 to 429;** Brown, although reported to be feeling well, *"was much downcast at the position of affairs."* Both men made the same amount of distance between ten o'clock and noon when the score was: **498.2 to 436.2.** Weston went on to crack his 500th mile at 12:20 in 7m.39s, and thereafter the American bounded along in an enthusiastic fashion adding even more distance between him and the ailing Londoner, whose only reward from the affair was the probability of making the requisite 450 miles to share in the gate money. At 2 p.m., and with the score showing **507 to 442;** Weston needed to make 43 miles in nine hours which meant he had to achieve at a rate of 5 mph to succeed in his objective. From that hour, and indeed for the next two hours, he really enjoyed himself on the track as, *"he ran lap after lap at a pace that had never before been seen. The spectators cheered wildly, and were lost in astonishment at the sight of the flying human machine."*

On the 21st of June, the Nevada based *Reno Evening Gazette* reckoned the belt was already Weston's. The paper reported: By our telegraphic dispatches it seems Weston has the belt as good as won in the great walking match in London. He and Parolo will be received with honors when they return to this country, for,

> "They are A-mer-i-can
>
> For every one has said it,
>
> And it's greatly to their credit
>
> That they are A-mer-i-can.
>
> For they might have been Roosian
>
> Or Arabian, Turk or Proosian,
>
> But in spite of all temptation
>
> They remain A-mer-i-can."

During the afternoon, it was predicted that Weston would easily beat Brown's six-day April record of 542 miles. By 4 o'clock he had made 517 miles and at 17:00 he was described as, *"going wonderfully. When the band plays, he trots along at five miles an hour,"* with Brown, *"merely limping along."* At 17:17, Brown earned his gate money when he made the required 450 miles, and at six o'clock, he was said to be running. Weston however, who was 75 miles ahead of Brown, was running much faster. He made his 526th mile in 7m.37s, the fastest of the match. *"His muscles seemed of steel, and as elastic as India rubber. Often he would recognize a friend, and then smiling dance away at a brisk pace for some distance, as if to assure him that everything was alright."*

At 18:30, the leader had covered 530 miles to Brown's 458. Shortly after 8 o'clock the band began to play popular American airs in Weston's honour, and in response he increased his speed. At 9 o'clock, he was going along at a tremendous pace and the cheering crowd urged him to get his name written into the record books. At 21:10, and having made 541 miles, he was only 10 minutes behind Brown's record. As soon as he was informed of that fact, he ordered the band to play "When I go in I'm bound to win!" And win he did, for at 21:30 he succeeded in beating it by about 40 seconds. His achievement stirred him sufficiently to challenge for the unprecedented feat of being the first man to make 550 miles in six days, and when the announcement was made that he was going to try from the judge's stand, he was greeted with a tremendous roar of approval. The building was packed, and as he made his way round, the track was covered in flowers which were thrown before him. His tent was surrounded by his fellow countrymen including Peter Panchot (who had travelled from New York to watch the match), John Ennis, Edward Hanlan, the celebrated oarsman, and Sir John Astley who shouted out, "Well done, my boy!"

At 10 p.m., Weston, having completed 546 miles, kept to his task, and by 22:25 had added two miles to his score. He now had 35 minutes in which to make 550 and win his bet. At 22:35, he completed another mile, and after stopping to receive a large bouquet while the band played "Hail Columbia," he resumed his effort. *"As Weston passed his tent for the final lap, he was given the British and American flags, which he carried around the ring waving them amid the deafening cheering and the din of the music. The band first played "Yankee Doodle," and ended with "Rule Britannia."* Then finally at 22:55, and as the crowd shouted "The champion of the world!," Edward Payson Weston completed 550 miles and 110 yards in a time of 141h.55m.

The Winner!

© The British Library. All Rights reserved. The Penny Illustrated. (Illustration no: 47)

Weston then made a speech, saying the people would not believe he could walk in America, but he had won the belt and was ready to defend it! Victory gave him the coveted trophy, £500 in stake money, the same amount for winning his bet with Sir John, and approximately £132 in gate money.

> **There was an old fellow named Weston,**
> **Whom critics made many a jest on;**
> **But he picked up his feet,**
> **And he went in to beat,**
> **And astonished us all as he pressed on,**
> **This plucky old fellow named Weston.**

Brown "blew" his sweepstake money, but did manage to cover 453 miles. His last few laps were made wearing a scarlet jacket covered in medals. Ennis stated he would be returning to the United States a fortnight later, and although he was $2,500 out of pocket, he was ready to start his preparation to contest the 5th Astley Belt.

Of the contest, the *New York Tribune* wrote: The difference between English and American patronage of pedestrianism matches is shown by the fact that while there was $35,000 to be divided between the contestants in the match in New York in March, Weston gets only $2,000 as his two thirds share of the proceeds of last week's contest in London. It is stated that Gilmore's garden has been engaged for pedestrian contests in September, and that probably the next contest for the Astley belt will take place at that time.

At the garden last night it was rumored that $6,000 had been offered for the lease of the place for the last week in September, that the persons making the offer proposed having the Astley belt contest take place in that week, and that they would bring over from England. Brown, Hazael, Corkey and Rowell, on the other hand, O'Leary's friends said that the lease of the garden, which he holds for the entire month of October at $8,000, contains a stipulation that the place in the meantime shall not be leased for any pedestrian or athletic contest which would interfere with his project.

The *New York Herald* wrote: It was a sight to see the great crowds gathered about the Herald building, where cable dispatches were bulletined every hour of the day regarding the progress of the walkers, and at night the bulletins were made conspicuous by aid of the electric light, and the crowd was always larger than during the day. The difference between New York and London before the Johnny Bulls knew of it. The match closed at midnight Saturday, and the cable dispatch announcing the result was published in an Evening Telegram fore half-past nine o'clock. A few years ago it would have taken at least six days before we could have known of Weston's wonderful victory. Last Saturday we knew it three hours before it was known in London. New York yelled itself hoarse in rejoicing over the great American victory.

Weston would breakfast with Astley on the Monday after the race, and under his patronage, made a farewell speech at the complimentary performance of the Mohawk Minstrels the following day.

This interesting article turned up on June 22nd in *The Mercury* which published a sensational story to the effect that: A sporting man here, who lost $80,000 on O'Leary, determined to relieve his losses through Weston and went to England and had Weston to go into secret training. He staked $150,000 on this recent match, getting great odds on Weston. Weston was promised half of his patron's profits if he should win.

The *Decatur Daily Republican* of Illinois followed this story on with an interesting article on the 3rd of July 1879:

WESTON'S SECRET.

"It is now generally believed that Weston's extraordinary feat is the result of a long cherished determination on his part to regain the laurels," observed a well know wealthy gentleman of sporting proclivities to a Mercury representative. In a measure it is. But there is more than that in it. I know to an absolute certainty that it is one of the best laid and carried out plans to scoop a big winning that was ever concocted. I dare not give you names, but I will tell you a story, for the truth of which in its minutest details, I pledge you my honor.

"A friend of mine, a club man and a passionate sportsman, was a heavy backer of O'Leary against Rowell in the international match at Gilmore's garden. Even when things looked darkest and most desperate for his man he stuck manfully by him. The consequence was that he came out a loser of over $80 000. His bets were private ones in most cases, and except for a few heavy outside ones, his losses remained unknown to the general public.

"My friend went to England on business immediately after the match. He there met Weston, whom he had known before. Weston expressed himself warmly in regard to America's losing the belt and said, "If I had a couple of month's training I believe I could win it back." My friend became convinced by his enthusiasm that he did not over estimate himself and suggested to him to try it. After some talk Weston agreed to go into training at once. Then the idea struck my friend to recover his losses. Previous to that he had, as he told me himself, been only actuated by a desire to see the belt return to America.

"Weston's popularity as a walker was deep in a decline, and the betting in any match he entered for was sure to be against him. If he was known to have been in training it might be more favorable, but if his preparations were kept secret betting men would regulate their investments by his old record.— Any one backing him under these circumstances could get long odds, and my friend, firmly convinced that the veteran walker could win, determined to indorse his convictions. His losses on O'Leary had seriously crippled him. He deliberately, and at no little sacrifice raised $150,000 in cash, mortgaging a quantity of his real estate to do so. — Every dollar of this money he applied to the one purpose. The victory of his man meant a fortune to him or nearly absolute ruin, and he told Weston so without reserve. "I am putting nearly every cent I own on you," he said; "if you win, half of what I gain is yours. I only ask two things of you — one is to keep quiet with your training, the other to do your best."

"Weston did so. No soul outside of the plot knew that the ex-champion was laying himself out for a big victory and fortune by rigorous training. — When he went on his pedestrian tour through England people spoke of it as showman's dodge. It was really a part of his preparation for the contest on which he and his backer rested their hopes. My friend meanwhile went quietly to work laying out his $150,000 where it would do the most good. He worked so quietly that scarcely any one knew what he was about. Every one thought that Weston went into the contest with no preparatory training. It was not until he began to show up in the match that people began to think that he had been preparing himself for the task, and to find out that some one had quietly been putting up money on him all along, and held nine-tenths of the bets laid against Weston in the race. I don't know how much the thing has netted him, but it is safe to say the scheme has cleared a big profit. There isn't a sporting gentleman in London who is not bit to a greater or less extent, for my friend is hand-in-glove with all of them, and had bets booked with all. He has called twice with his brother, each time giving the amounts of his books."

"Half of the money, of course, goes to Weston?"

"My friend has promised it. He is well known as a man who never breaks his word."

The above story however was more than likely a load of old bunkum, because in the 4th paragraph of the following letter from Astley to the *Sporting Life*, he claims that Weston was in much financial trouble due to his past walking commitments in Britain. There again, who knows; the *"Wily Wobbler"* might have been hiding such a secret!

4, Lowndes-square, S.W., June 24, 1879

Sir,

I venture to think that very many of your readers will agree with me that the feat accomplished by Edward Payson Weston at the Agricultural Hall last week, 550 miles in six days and nights, in the 'go-as-you-please' style is a marvellous performance. Weston tells me he has now covered on foot something like 53,000 miles in America and England, and I verily believe he is at this moment in no way worse for his exertions, and he certainly looks better than he did on Monday, the 16th, when about to start.

I have read in many newspapers, from time to time, of the fearful sufferings, of the certain ruin of constitution, of the probable mental aberration, and so forth, caused by over-exertion on "the track," but the present condition of Weston is the best proof of the utter ignorance displayed by these poor scribes, and confirms me in my opinion that many more men die from not taking exercise enough than from taking too much.

I have known Weston about three years, and have always admired his great powers of endurance and his energy of character, and yet up to this last performance he has never had the good fortune to succeed in the task set before him, ergo, the farther he goes the better he gets. His failure in accomplishing 2,000 miles in 1,000 consecutive hours on the roads of England was to be entirely attributed to the awfully severe weather and the consequent state of the roads, as well as to the enormous crowds that beset him and hindered his progress through the towns on his route. Still, the performance was a most astonishing one, and though Weston did not win, he was far from disgraced.

The expenses attending his walk through England, including the conveyance of his judges and attendants over 2,000 miles for six weeks, were so heavy that his failure cost him over £500. This, coupled with serious losses previously, have placed him in pecuniary difficulties from which the poor receipts of the late week's "wobble" (caused by the breaking down of the four other competitors) are not sufficient to extricate him. It is, therefore, proposed by some of his friends and admirers that we should assist him out of his difficulty by organising a complimentary testimonial on his behalf, and Messrs. Betram and Roberts have generously put their theatre at the Alexandra Palace at our disposal.

I must wind up my long-winded epistle by asking those who agree with me in the above sentiments to take as many tickets as they can afford, particularly impressing on those who have benefited by Weston's instruction in the art of long-distance progression to lend a helping hand to one who has striven to teach the world what the powers of man are capable of when governed by pluck, perseverance, and abstinence from overindulgence in the so-called pleasures of dissipation. I shall be glad to supply any one who wishes to assist in the above testimonial with tickets if they will apply to me.

Yours faithfully,

J. D. Astley.

At the aforementioned testimonial, Weston received a gold watch from his friends during the ceremony at the Alexandra Palace. The inscription on the watch read: **"Presented to E. P. Weston by some fifty of his admirers as a mark of their appreciation of his great powers of endurance, energy of character, and honesty of purpose, July 5, 1879."**

On the 3rd of July, the *Daily Constitution* of Atlanta wrote: Weston, the pedestrian, is an upside down specimen of physical culture. He never eats meat, indulges largely in pie, has flabby muscles, runs in his stocking-feet, and lunches on custards and cheese while walking; in fact, anything that sporting man ought not to do, according to accepted rules, he does with impunity.

The same paper wrote the following article on the 17th July 1879: Mrs. Weston, wife of E. P. Weston, pedestrian, writes to a Brooklyn friend that her husband had very little sleep or rest before the six-days' walk in which he won the belt, and that he has had but little since. He is busily engaged with Sir John Astley every day, and his leisure hours are occupied in receiving calls. A number of his admirers are arranging for a concert, to be given in a few days at Alexandria hall in his honor. It is not probable that Weston will return to New York for several weeks.

The following article was written in the *New York World*, in July of 1879, and, entitled **Man's Walking Powers**:

Weston's performance in covering 550 miles in rather less than six days may be of no particular importance from a patriotic point of view. If Weston had been a new man the fact that he had "beaten the record" by ten miles or so would have furnished any occasion for the American eagle to display himself, but Weston has engaged in so many matches that his victory will not create nearly the same excitement in New York as if his achievement had been made by Ennis. It has always been Weston's weakness to set his mark a little higher than he could reach, and his remarkable performances have been overrated, simply because of the impossibilities he has undertaken. Nevertheless, what he has now done is a very remarkable achievement. Rowell in Gilmore's Garden, and Brown at the long-distance walk in Agricultural Hall, seemed to those who saw them to have exhausted the limits of human endurance. What they did has now been so badly beaten that there is more difference between Weston's performance and Rowell's than between Rowell's and that of the second man in this race. Rowell made barely 500 miles and Ennis made 475, whereas the winner in this race in making 550 miles has beaten Rowell by something like fifty miles. There is every reason to expect that within a very few years a long-distance walking match of six days will be won with a record of not less than 600 miles, or 100 miles a day. This would be an excellent performance for a horse. In fact, so far as we remember, it has never thus far been equaled or even approached by a horse. People who have studied the powers and performances of horses and men have long been of the opinion that in point of endurance the biped was much to be preferred to the quadruped. They are justified by the result of the recent long-distance matches. The owner of a horse who should subject his animal to the extreme tests to which Weston and Brown have submitted themselves would probably come under the official notice of Mr. Bergh. The record of any six days' walk is regarded with consternation by every man who has walked enough to know what fast walking means, and who has yet not walked enough to know how much exertion the human system will bear. There is no reason to believe that any professional pedestrian could come nearer to Weston's record than his opponent in the present match has heretofore done, but there is reason to believe that professional pedestrians will hereafter succeed in beating Weston's time even more than Weston has beaten the time of his predecessors. At all events, if the present race is repeated in this city, there is reason to expect that the record will be beaten, and that the winner will be obliged to surpass a feat of pedestrianism which now seems to be the limit of human perseverance and endurance.

A remarkable insight into the race was given by John Ennis when he returned to America. His story told of his heroic feat on the river and the incident's effect on his performance. Ennis talked about admission prices at the Agricultural Hall, financial rewards, Weston and his tactics in the race, and his defence of the title in the USA. The article was printed in the *New York Times* on the 27th of July 1879:

Among the passengers who arrived in this City yesterday in the Inman steamer, City of Berlin was John Ennis, the pedestrian, who, in the great international match at Gilmore's Garden in March last, came in next to Rowell, the winner. He has been in Europe with his family for the last two months, and he competed in the international match in London last month, when the Astley belt was won by Edward Payson Weston. He is the first of the pedestrians to arrive in this country since that event, and he brings with him information which was not cabled during the contest. He looked strong and healthy yesterday when he greeted the TIMES reporter, and the unusually large size of the shoes which he wore was the only mark which reminded one of his profession. These spoke of ease and comfort in walking, and they were of such ungainly proportions that no man but a pedestrian would wear them. In accounting for his failure to make a good record in the late match, he said to the reporter;

"I don't want to be understood as attempting to apologize for, or explain my failure. But the facts may as well be told as an extenuation, if not as an excuse. I was taking my training exercise on the banks of the Thames near Hampton. About a week before the great match began, as I was walking for practice, I saw a tug run down and sink a row-boat. In the boat were two ladies and two gentlemen. I plunged into the river to save the ladies, and I did save them both. One of them weighed at least 180 pounds and in saving her I strained my back. When I came from the water I had to walk four miles and a half before I came to a place whom I could change my wet clothes. During that walk I caught a severe cold and blistered my feet very badly. The result was that I could not properly train myself during the last week before the match, and when I went upon the track, I knew that I could not win the belt, and I told my friends so. I did hope however, to make creditable record on the English track, and when I found myself obliged to retire, I felt very sore about it. I had gone a long way to do good work, and found myself unable to do any work whatever. That would make any man feel sore, and especially one who had made the record which I made in New York. The match was, to the best of my knowledge, a perfectly fair one. I have heard that the American people doubt that Weston really made 550 miles. I have heard no such doubts expressed in England, and I believe that he honestly made it. It was as surprise across the water as it was here. But I can easily understand it. Weston has remarkable powers of endurance, and for the first time in his life he gave himself a fair show. For the first time since I have known him, he went on the track to win and not to win the admiration of the ladies. He discarded his frilled shirt his fancy sash, and the other trumperies which have generally distinguished him on the track. He was dressed in red worsted tights, a thin white undershirt, and ordinary trunks. He was dressed, in fact, to walk, and not simply to make a show of himself, and he did walk, and he won the belt, I believe, honestly and fairly. I have told you one reason for Weston's success. Now I will give you another, and this is the principal one. In this walk he displayed more strategy than he has ever shown before. 'Blower' Brown attempted to follow the tactics which Rowell so successfully used in this City. He tried to break the heart of Weston by following close on his heels, by dogging' him. Weston saw the game, and he was equal to the emergency. It is a great trick of his to reverse in walking – that is, to turn around and walk in the opposite direction. He practiced this to Brown's disaster. He knew just when he was going to reverse, but Brown did not. He would he walking at a rapid pace with Brown at his heels, when suddenly he would turn about and go the other way. Brown would get some paces over the line before he realized what Weston had done. In this way he lost several yards each time. Weston turned, and at the end of the race these yards counted up into miles. I don't mean to say that Weston would not have won the race anyway, for his performance is a wonderful one, but I do say that Browns performance would have been better but for these tactics of Weston. He started in the contest with the intention of worrying the American, and while the American may have been worried somewhat by the continual dogging of his footstep, he turned the Englishman's tactics to his own advantage and gained much more than he lost."

"How does the encouragement given to pedestrianism in England compare with that given to it in this country?" asked the reporter.

"There can be no comparison," was the answer. "The receipts at the international match in London were about £800 ($4,000) just about enough to pay the expenses. Weston's gate money amounted to absolutely nothing. All that he made by his great feat was the sweepstakes, $2,000, and what few bets he may have made outside. Admission to the hall cost only a shilling, (25 cents) while in America you pay 50 cents and $1. Then the principle of class comes in England. Very few ladies will patronize a pedestrian contest, because they fear to meet there people who are supposed to be inferior to them. There is none of the enthusiasm that you find in this country, and I am heartily glad to get out of England. Of course, the people over there are very much disgusted. They have been beaten this year at rowing, walking and racing. They are not more disgusted, however, than the pedestrians from his country who have visited them. So far as I am concerned, I hope that the Astley belt will remain here, for I don't want to go to England to walk again for it. America is the only country in which pedestrianism is appreciated, and it is here that I want to do my walking in the future."

"Then you intend to compete for the belt in the next match?"

"Most certainly I intend to compete for it, but nothing is definitely arranged about the next match yet. It is in Mr. Weston's power to name the time and place for it, but up to this time he has named neither. I am afraid that there will be trouble about it. Rowell has challenged him, as has also George Hazael, the champion 50 mile walker of England. He must name the time within three months of the challenge, but there are no conditions imposed on him as to the place. He says now that unless he is allowed to manage the match to suit himself, he will decide to have it in a town of 1,500 inhabitants. Now, the rest of us think that we ought to have something to say about the management and the probability is that there will be trouble before the match is definitely arranged. You know what Weston is. He was airy before his great feat, and he is more airy now. It has been customary for the winner of the belt to deposit $500 as security that it will be ready when called for. O'Leary did this, and so did Rowell. Mr. Atkinson, of the Sporting Life called on Weston to make the deposit and he refused. He said that he was a gentleman, and they must take his word. Sir John Astley was appealed to, and he decided that Weston's word was enough. This fact was simply added to his self conceit and there is no knowing how far he will go before he gets to the end of his string."

"Can you tell me when Weston will return to this country?"

"I saw him just before I left London and he told me then that he should sail for New York about the middle or last of August. He is now delivering a course of lectures, throughout England, the subject being 'What I Know About Walking!' I don't know who his backers were in the last walk. He applied to Sir John Astley and that gentleman refused to back him. There has been some talk about Weston's having been allowed to enter for the race after the regulation time. I want to explain that to you. Weston was fairly in the race. He wrote to us who had entered asking for a week's time to get the money, and we allowed him to enter on those terms. He paid in the money at the end of the week, and the stated time had passed then, but it was a fair agreement between him and us, and he was as legitimately in the contest as Brown, Rowell, or myself."

Mr. Ennis will remain in this City for a week, and then go to Chicago to visit his friends. As soon as the next competition for the belt is arranged in some definite shape, he intends to enter as a contestant; but the articles are not yet signed between Weston and Rowell, and Mr. Ennis seems to think that there will be some trouble before they are signed. But if Weston does not name a time and place within three months of Rowell's challenge, giving to all the competitors four weeks for training, Mr. Ennis thinks that Sir John Astley will take the matter in his own hands, reclaim the belt and offer it to be competed for by the men who have challenged the champion.

Weston as portrayed by The National Police Gazette **on news of his victory** *(Illustration no: 48)*

CHAPTER 20

5th International Astley Belt

The London *Sporting Life* of August the 2nd 1879 commented: The next contest for the World's championship belt (Sir J. D. Astley's) of which Edward Payson Weston is the holder and Charles Rowell the challenger, is definitely fixed to take place at Madison Avenue Gardens (late Gilmore's), New York, during the week commencing Monday, September the 22. The articles will be signed today (Saturday) at our office, and all those who wish to join in the match with Weston and Rowell must deposit £100 in our hands on or before Friday, August 22.

The two pedestrians put their signature to the following document.

Memorandum of agreement made and entered into this second day of August, 1879, between Edward Payson Weston, of New York City, USA, party of the first part, and Charles Rowell, of Chesterton, Cambridge, England, party of the second part, witnesseth: Whereas the party of the first part is now the holder of the "Long-Distance Championship of the World Belt," won by him at Agricultural Hall, London, in June, 1879, and the party of the second part has duly challenged him to a pedestrian match therefore pursuant to the conditions upon which the said Belt is held. Now, therefore, this agreement witnesseth, that the parties hereto hereby agree to compete for the said Championship Belt, won by the party of the first part, and the sum of 100 pounds a side. Twenty-five pounds a side is hereby deposited by the parties hereto in the hands of the editor of Sporting Life to bind the match, and the remaining sum of seventy-five pounds a side must be deposited in the hands of the editor of Sporting Life, or his authorized representative, on or before Monday, the first day of September, in the year before mentioned. The match is to take place in a covered building or ground known as Madison Avenue Gardens, New York, USA, which is mutually agreed upon by both parties, and is to commence at one o'clock a.m. on Monday, September 22, 1879 and terminate at eleven o'clock p.m. on Saturday, September 27, the party covering the greatest distance during that time, by either running or walking, without assistance, to be declared the winner. The match is to be subject to the same conditions as that at which the said Belt was won by the party of the first part, and the Belt is held by the winner on the same terms and conditions on which it is now held. In the event of any other person or persons joining the match, they must each deposit the sum of one hundred pounds with the appointed stakeholder, within four weeks previous to the fixed date for the commencement of the race; and by subject to the conditions and terms of this agreement. The editor of Sporting Life, London, England, is hereby authorized to appoint three judges, and the editor of the Turf, Field and Farm, New York, is hereby authorized to engage and appoint the requisite number of lap scorers and timekeepers. A stipulated sum for incidental expenses is to be allowed for each person officially engaged during the contest, beyond which no allowances will be made to them for any purpose whatsoever. All matters of dispute or appeals from questions not provided for by these conditions are to be referred to the trustees of the Belt, whose decision shall be final in all cases. The gate receipts (after all expenses have been paid) are to be divided as follows:

If only one man completes 450 miles (or more), then the whole of the gate receipts (less expenses) to be paid over to him; if two competitors complete 450 miles the winner to receive two-thirds of the receipts, and the second man one-third; if three men complete 450 miles, the first to get one-half, the second 30 percent, and the third 20 percent; if four men complete 450 miles, the winner to receive one-half, the second 25 percent, the third 15 percent, the fourth 10 percent; if five men complete 450 miles, the winner to receive one-half, the second 25 percent, the third 12 percent, the fourth 8 percent, and the fifths percent; if six men complete 450 miles, the winner to receive one-half, the second 25 percent, the third 12 percent, the fourth 8 percent, the fifth 6 percent, the sixth 4 percent; should more than six men complete 450 miles, the winner to receive one-half, and the balance to be distributed among the other competitors in proportion to the miles completed as may be directed by Sir John Astley, Bart M.P., the giver of the Belt. Should there be only two competitors, each man to walk on a separate track, to be laid down according to his own directions, and surveyed by a competent

authority in the presence of the judges appointed. The measurement to be made eighteen inches from the border frame on the inside, which is three inches higher than the mold. Should there be three (or more) competitors, all to go on one wide track (not less than ten feet wide). Either party failing to comply with any of these articles to forfeit all moneys deposited.

"Blower" Brown, George Hazael and "Corkey" were some of the other English pedestrians expected to take part. John Ennis, Peter Panchot, Frederick Krohne, Samuel Merritt, George Guyon, Norman Taylor, Yuma, a Mexican Indian residing in Los Angeles, who was said to be a *"remarkable pedestrian,"* Daniel O'Leary, and a protégé of his, Frank Hart, the black American champion from Boston, were some of the American athletes who were probable starters. The then current champion, Weston was still in England by the time Rowell set off for New York on the 10th of August with his trainer Charlie Barnsley, on the steam-ship *Bothnia* from Liverpool.

Meanwhile, some problems were being encountered over the staging of the event, which clashed with a similar one organised by Daniel O'Leary. The up-and-coming entrepreneurial figure had made arrangements to rent the Garden out some months before, and his "O'Leary Belt" match was due to take place from the 6th of October.

The Garden had been rented to the Kuntz brothers from May the 30th till September the 30th at $1,000 per week. As they had had difficulty holding events to recoup and profit from their investment, they were naturally enthusiastic about staging the Astley Belt race at the Garden when approached by Mr. Hess, Weston's agent. The brothers initially agreed to take a quarter of the gross receipts after paying all of the expenses. A meeting between the agents of the principal contestants and the lessees of the building, Messrs. K. Botsford and Louis F. Kuntz was held in *"parlor No. 68"* at the St. Denis Hotel, New York, on the 17th of August to plan a reception for Weston. Mr. Hess, the English Opera Troupe manager represented him, and Mr. Busby saw to the Englishmen's interests. During the meeting, Mr. Hess accused O'Leary of whipping up controversy in the newspapers, saying that Weston would meet with legal difficulties in endeavouring to carry out the contract with the present lessees, the Kuntz brothers. The *New York Times* wrote: **The contract with the present lessees of the Garden is simply an undertaking on the part of Mr. Hess to furnish an entertainment, the lessees agreeing to hand over to him a portion of the entrance money, which some will be made into a gate money pool. Mr. Hess said that as far as he had learned all the talk about the courts being called upon to prevent the walk was based on either bold rumor or spite. The lessor of the Garden suggested no difficulty of this sort and complimented Dodworth & Co, because they kept their engagements in spite of a bad season, although they did not ask for sympathy.** The problem would have to be sorted out; in the meantime, O'Leary asked the millionaire, Cornelius Vanderbilt, to help him.

Five days later, in an interview with one of the lessees of the Garden, and in reference to the conditions of the lease and the arrangements of the match, he said; "We hire this troupe of walkers, with Mr. Hess as manager. We could not take a fixed sum for the rent of the Garden, for that would be subletting, which is forbidden by our contract with Mr. Vanderbilt; but we can hire the men and pay them with a percentage. We get twenty-five per cent of the proceeds and the men on the track get seventy-five per cent, to be divided according to the terms specified in the agreement under which they walk. The conditions have been accepted by Weston and Brown and they could make no better. We would not listen to the offer of a fixed term, not even of fifteen thousand dollars. We are perfectly satisfied and so are the men. We provide the building, the gas, and the music. We lay down the track under their orders or allow their men to do it. We pay all the doorkeepers, cleaners, ticket sellers and other employees. The walkers each provide his personal attendants, and provides also for the scoring and timing. The bar is out of our control and out of theirs as well. It was leased when we took the Garden to the man who runs it, and his lease runs out after the walk. We shall not change the interior of the garden much. The track will be as before, and the side seats and the interior square will be given up entirely to spectators. There will be three lines of entrance and each will have an iron turnstile, and according to the registry of those stiles, we shall pay the walkers their proportion. There will be one hundred policemen on duty, and a charge of a least one dollar will be made for admission. We do this to keep away an undesirable crowd. We don't intend the garden to be a lodging house either. Every morning at three o'clock it will be cleared of all loungers and sleepers."

On Wednesday, the 27th of August, Rowell arrived back in New York. He was met by Hamilton Busby and Mr. Brockway of the Ashland House Hotel where he would be staying. The *New York Times* wrote of him: **His physical appearance is moderately good although his face is thinner and more sallow than it was six months ago, and his eyes have a weary and haggard expression that is scarcely in harmony with his easy and rather phlegmatic temperament. His shoulders are not broad, and at first glance he appears to be deficient in the heart and lung** power essential to great endurance. But his great depth of chest corrects this impression on second thought, and one mentally registers him as a hard antagonist to beat in a long race. This last conclusion is rendered indubitable by the easy and supple movement of his compact and splendid muscular limbs. To the stereotyped salutation respecting his health, by no means superfluous when estimating the prospects of a pedestrian, Rowell replied that he was in excellent condition. But the boat had been crowded so that there had been no opportunity for training. His feet have troubled him or late, being tender, easily blistered, and not sufficiently hardened by exercise. In ordinary life he wears soft, thin soled shoes, and this custom though contributing to ease of movement, impairs the resistance of the foot, and renders the skin moist and subject to bruise and blister. Owing to this trouble with his feet, Rowell has done very little walking since the contest in this country, and was prevented from starting in the recent London race. As it has been intimated that his ability to start on that occasion was an "understood thing," his own explanation of the affair may be interesting to his American admirers. "I had blistered one heel by wearing a pair of old shoes," he said, "and a day or two before the opening, I put on a new pair. Something in the leather acted like a poison on the blister, and made me so lame that it would have been folly to start against a man like Weston, who was in first-class condition. I shall start this time, though, and I mean to win, feet or no feet." Rowell's general condition is not very good. He feels very well he says, but the voyage was a rough one, and he has had no exercise of any consequence, he will recover from this in a day or two, however, and lose the fatigued expression that his countenance wore on landing.

The *New York Evening Post* sent a reporter to interview Rowell that afternoon:

Reporter: "I suppose you are ready for the match?"

Rowell: "I intend to be when the time comes. For the next three weeks I shall run and walk everyday, the distance to be regulated by my feelings. I shall eat what I feel like eating. Mr. Barnsley, my trainer, is with me."

Reporter: "Will you run in this match as much as you did in the last?"

Rowell: "Yes; I will adopt the same method."

Reporter: "If you are pressed can you make more than five hundred miles?"

Rowell: "Barring accidents, I think I can do so."

Reporter: "Whom do you fear most?"

Rowell: "I can't say that I fear any of them. Weston and Ennis are the only men of whom I can judge, and Weston is a better man than Ennis."

Reporter: "How much running did Weston do in the big match in England?"

Rowell: "About as much as I did here."

Reporter: "Will he run as much as you will in the coming match?"

Rowell: "Yes, I think he will."

Reporter: "Where are the other contestants?"

Rowell: "Blower Brown left Liverpool on the same day as I did on a National steamer. It is uncertain whether Corkey or Hazael will come."

Rowell stated that he intended to train in Central Park, but if his appearance drew too many crowds he would find himself a much quieter place in the country. The day after he rose early and after breakfast and a quiet stroll through the streets, headed off to the Garden where he donned his walking costume, and *"got down to business"* by *"spinning around the track at a lively pace."* The ex-champion admitted that he had some superfluous fat to get rid of and after dinner that night went back to the building to try and shed a bit more.

His main obstacle to reclaiming the belt was Weston, who arrived back in his home country the day after on Thursday, the 28th on the steamship *Nevada*. He was accompanied by his wife, his three children: Lillie aged 11,

Allsworth aged 8, Maude aged 5, and a valet. The voyage had taken one day longer than expected on account of head winds and fogs.

Mr. Busby was back at the piers again, along with Mr. C. D. Hess and Rufus F. Andrews. They had originally hired the steamboat *Harlem* to take them out to meet the *Nevada*. However, after waiting for six hours on pier No. 38, and with no sighting of either the *Harlem* or the *Nevada*, the party hired the funeral tugboat *William Fletcher* to sail out to meet the great man. Laden with the managers, a small party of reporters, six kegs of beer, two baskets of wine, and a large basket of sandwiches, the tugboat set off.

The boat soon encountered the ship, which was covered with national flags two miles below the Upper Quarantine; and as soon as the tug blew her whistle, the ships passengers crowded around her side. The party on board the tug gave three cheers for Weston and toasted him with glasses of beer as the world champion, dressed in *"black diagonal clothes,"* low shoes and red stockings, stood on the deck waving his low crowned stiff black hat to them. Some in the party then boarded the ship with the intention of taking the fit looking ped to shore, but he declined the offer, instead taking them to the ship's card room where he told reporters:

"Actions speak louder than words, but there's nothing succeeds like success, gentlemen. I have seen the time in this city when I could not borrow $25 to keep the Rink open another day when I was walking, I did not care to bring this belt back to New York. In fact, when I went away I had made up my mind not to walk any more in this city. While in many quarters I always received the kindest treatment here, in others I did not. There was a time when I would have considered it the proudest event in my life to bring this belt back to America, but I have got over that. Still I am glad to bring it back for the sake of my friends here. If I had my way about it, this next walk would not be in New York, but in Australia, but my wife and Sir John Astley overcame my wishes.

"One thing you can set down for a certainty. I will not walk in that Garden if smoking is allowed there. It is too hard on the lungs to breathe that foul atmosphere for six days, and I do not intend to do it, and Rowell will not walk if I do not.

"Whose make of shoes did I use in the London walk? I have no idea. I bought them and paid for them as anybody would, without inquiring who made them. I did not train at all for the walk, and have never trained an hour in my life. I was in perfect health when I went into that walk, and am now as sound as a dollar. I was shown every attention in England, and could not have been better treated if I had been a prince. Sir John Astley is one of the kindest and noblest men I have ever met.

"I must show you my watch. Don't think that this is the Newark watch, for it isn't. Oh no, this is not the Newark watch. I have no Newark property about me. You've heard of the Newark watch, I suppose? After I walked there, the Mayor told me that he and some of the prominent citizens had been appointed a committee to present me with a gold watch as a memento of my long walk. I heard nothing more of it for about a month, and then I met the Mayor one day, and he told me the watch was being prepared, and was almost ready. I told him it was no matter, I was satisfied with what I had done. A few weeks after that one of the 'prominent citizens' said to me, "I don't know about the watch; there was a little dispute about the figures, you know." One old Newark citizen said to me, "You ought to come here and live, Weston; this is a splendid place to live." Yes it is. If I owned a house in perdition and another in Newark, I'd rent the Newark house.

"About the next walk? Well, I have nothing to say about that. I shall do my best, whatever that may be. How many miles will I make? I'll try to make a good many. I do not care to say anything about the profits of the London walk, as that would not interest the public."

By now Weston had signed his declaration form for the Customs officers and the ship had arrived at the pier, where hundreds had gathered to welcome him home. Thousands more had congregated outside the gates, and they cheered as he and his family were driven away to the Rossmore Hotel where later, sitting on a small rocking chair in the parlour, he said:

"Before the big walk in London, I went to Sir John Astley and asked him to put up the £100 entrance fee for me. 'My dear boy,' said he, 'why not let well enough alone. No walker can compete with these runners, and I'm not going to let you throw £100 away in that way. I'll lend £100 for anything else, but not to waste on this walk.' I did not say any more about it to him, but entered myself for the race. While I was in this country I never believed that running could hold out against walking, but when I saw the easy pace of some of those runners, I changed my mind. Some of the men ran a ten-mile gait with less apparent exertion than a man makes walking four miles per hour.

"You want to know whether this walk is going to be 'square?' I have been accused of making unfair walks, but I will give any man $100 for every inch he can prove I claimed without making it. I never made an unfair walk in my life, and would not degrade myself by thinking of such a thing. As to the running, I like it. I fell accidentally into an easy running race, just as I did in walking. I never ran a mile in my life till a month before the last London race. I hardly knew I could run.

"Dr. Newman, of New York, preached a sermon about the "brutality" of walking matches. I have walked 53,000 miles in the last fourteen years, and I don't look much like a used-up man, do I? If the ministers would pay more attention to theology, and less to walking, there would be less ministerial scandals."

Weston then announced that he would leave the Rossmore Hotel on Saturday night and hide himself till the beginning of the race. The day after he was said to be thinking about what he would eat in the forthcoming contest, and although he indulged in meals of "good beef" and fruit, the latter would be off the menu when he raced. In the afternoon, he took his family to see his father-in-law's grave in Stamford, Connecticut, and accompanied his wife to the theatre at night. Meanwhile, he was defending some of the cutting comments that he was perceived to make about his fellow countrymen the day before whilst being interviewed. "No man loves his country better than I do," he said, "but I was nervous and felt annoyed yesterday because certain professed friends who had sent me word that they would meet me, did not do so. I had counted upon seeing their faces, but they failed to welcome me at all. I suppose in speaking of them I may have spoken too hastily, and given the reporters the impression that I was 'down' on all Americans. But I am certainly not."

The steamship *California* of the Anchor Line carrying "Blower" Brown, docked in New York on the 29th of August. The famous ped wearing a plaid suit, a red silk handkerchief around his neck, and donning a Glengary cap, went through immigration at Pier 21, accompanied by his trainer John Smith. He immediately enquired about Daniel O'Leary who was supposed to meet him there, and was said to be disappointed when he discovered he wasn't. He went on to walk to the Ashland House Hotel where Rowell was also staying. The two English stars of the tanbark would both be attending the reception laid on for Weston at the Garden that night. It was already ascertained that Brown would not be taking part in the forthcoming Astley Belt race and instead would compete in a similar event a week or so later, the "1st O'Leary Belt" contest. Brown stated that Weston had given him the idea that the belt wouldn't be walked for in America, so he entered the O'Leary belt contest instead. He wasn't happy with what he called Weston's "bad faith," and pointed out that it would be silly to compete in both events when they were so close together.

That night, Brown, who was described as having "the appearance of a prize fighter", along with Rowell was given a box at the Garden. Brown drank lager as they watched the build-up to the event. Among other pedestrians present were Ennis, Harriman and Panchot. At 8 p.m., both men were invited on to the track to march round while Dodworth's band played a waltz. An hour later, the large crowd of 3,000 *"cheered lustily"* when welcoming the world champion, who made his appearance in full evening dress, bowing to them.

After Weston had taken his seat, Professor Doremus made the opening address. Doremus equated pedestrianism with the great arts of the world, and spoke about it from a physiological standpoint saying that it had given many people a new lease of life, by encouraging them to walk instead of taking street cars and carriages. After welcoming speeches, Weston tried to explain the negative remarks he had made and said that they had been greatly exaggerated. He then went on to say; "Of all the objects or pity that London ever saw, I was the one great object on the morning of June 16th. The amount of sympathy showered upon me would have sufficed to stock several funerals. It was 'Poor Weston! I'm sorry for him!,' all over the great city. But I started in that race with the firm intention of meeting the most sanguine expectations of the few friends that I had and I think that I met them!" (Cheers.) "Any young man can accomplish the same task that I have accomplished, if he will live in the same way that I do. Now I have one word to say to the young men of this City. If you will abstain from smoking in this building during the next match, you will see one of the greatest pedestrian contests ever attempted in the world.

It will be a performance second-to-none ever seen here. I shall do my best to keep the Astley Belt in America. I stand here tonight a hundred eighty per cent better physically than when I won the belt in London. Only give up your smoking while we are walking and I promise to keep the belt where it belongs, in America."

Weston was heartily applauded thereafter. There were calls for Rowell to make a speech but he modestly declined and went. Weston was later serenaded at his hotel by the Washington band.

The *Daily Kennebec Journal* of Augusta, Maine, reported on the 1st of September what Weston got up to on the following evening: PROVIDENCE, August 30. E P. Weston, the champion long distance pedestrian, was given a reception tonight, and greeted with cheers on his arrival at the depot, and was escorted by the crowd to the hotel. In the evening he appeared at the Park Garden, where he was presented to 5,000 or 6,000 people, as a Providence boy. Weston made a short speech and then walked and ran a few miles, giving specimens of walking and running, gaits. He was serenaded at the Hotel after the reception.

The *Daily Constitution*, of Atlanta, Georgia, on the 3rd of September, and possibly in reference to Weston's appearances amusingly wrote: If Weston could walk with his tongue he would make seventy-five thousand miles a day, and then have time to show his friends the presents he received from the nobility of England. The queen didn't give him anything, but she is naturally of a very retiring disposition.

The bookmakers were already offering odds on some contenders for the belt: **Weston and Rowell, 6/4; Hazael, 3/1; Brown and Guyon, 4/1; Ennis, 6/1; Panchot, 7/1; Krohne, 8/1; Taylor, 10/1:**

Meanwhile, rumours that a proposition to postpone the contest for between 30 and 60 days, and that the match was to take place outside of New York, were being quashed by the press who confirmed on the 5th of September that the race would start on the 22nd. It was also confirmed that Mr. Hess, the manager of the event, had hired Mr. Busby to have a supervisory control over the match and organise the scoring and time-keeping facilities for the race. Mrs. Weston was said to be busily dealing with hubby's entrance fee as he was too busy in training to attend to the matter, and finally it had been agreed that smoking would be been banned while the race was on.

There was said to be a lot of *"misunderstanding"* amongst the pedestrians entered into the race. Of the two principal countries organising and holding the event, both the English and the Americans mistrusted each other; the latter seen to be causing the division by alleging that the trustees namely, Atkinson, Astley, Busby and Hess, along with Rowell and Weston, (who was perceived to be in the English camp), were in partnership with the intention of *"hippodroming"* the match. The belief was that the English were making arrangements and securing contracts for the event to suit themselves, without asking the natives what they thought. All these problems needed to be sorted out and a *"Pedestrian Congress"* was organised for a start time of two o'clock on the afternoon of September 7th at the Glenham House Hotel on Third Avenue and Twenty Fourth Street, and invitations to attend were sent to all the competitors and their backers. Those who turned up at the arranged time were Mr. Charles E. Davies, backer of George Guyon, *"a Newburg gentleman,"* backer of Norman Taylor, Thomas Scannell backer of Sam Merritt, who was only pedestrian present, and James Cusick trainer of John Ennis.

After waiting one and a half hours for a representative of either Weston or Rowell to show up, without anyone arriving, they began the meeting. The first to speak was Thomas Scannell.

"I am sorry for it, but it is a fact, nevertheless, that this contest is now in a muddle. We don't know for sure even whether it is to come off at all or not, although we have paid our five hundred dollar entrance fee and the other expenses of training. The English claim to be the grand patrons of sport. Humbug. They seem absolutely incapable of managing a contest of any kind fairly, and there's no trick in the world they won't play to beat an American. This Sir John Astley is a smooth one. He's on the "hippodrome," he is. He has got up a sharp set of rules about this belt that allow him to be the final judge in all matters in dispute, and even to make changes in the proceedings after the making of the match.

"When Rowell took the belt back and twenty thousand dollars besides, it raised a craze among the English pedestrians and showed Astley a new field for making money out of his belt. That's all he got it up for. I believe that Rowell hasn't got a cent. I believe Astley took all his twenty thousand dollars and put it in his own pocket. These English walkers are all too poor to pay their way over here. Astley takes them in hand, offers them wages and expenses for coming over, sends his own referees and agents along to see that they do their work, and that the money is divided fairly, and then just scoops in the cash himself. Why, Rowell is just as poor now as when he first came over. Sir John it was who made the speculation out of the little fellow's legs.

"Here's the situation. Weston has the belt. He is credited with having made 550 miles. I don't believe he did. Brown had made 542 miles, and in the last match, Brown being in it, a score better than his had to be put up to allow Weston to win. Astley wanted him to win so that the belt would come over here, and he could send over some more hired pedestrians and make another rake. You'll see. I'll bet almost any amount of money that neither Weston nor Rowell will make any five-hundred and twenty-five miles here. After Weston won the belt, Rowell at once challenged him, and the match was made. The Astley rules allow the holder of the belt and the challenger to make the match, agree upon the date, arrange the division of money, and choose managers.

"Weston and Rowell are both protégés of Astley, and he can cook up any nice little job that he likes. How have they done? After fixing everything up to suit himself, he allows as many other contestants to enter the match as pleased to, providing they all pay as entrance fees the sum of five hundred dollars at least four weeks before the day set for the match, which the rules require. Ten Americans, excluding Weston, paid, making five thousand dollars. After they all paid their money what did they find? Why, that they were likely to be swindled right and left.

"Every contestant covering four hundred and fifty miles in the match was entitled to a share of the receipts and the return of his fee. At least five American's can make four hundred and fifty miles. Guyon, Merritt, Krohne, Ennis and Panchot have all surpassed that score. These men, and in fact, all who pay the fee, are interested in the management of the match, and have a right to have a voice in the selection of the treasurers and ticket-sellers, in order to protect their interests and secure the true total of the receipts for division. But the English interest is playing a double game, and will not permit it.

"Astley, Weston and Rowell have made the arrangement without consulting any of the other walkers; C. D. Hess to manage the walk and supervise all the other arrangements. He is to have twenty-five per cent of the entire receipts and the Garden privileges, such as the bar, cigar stands, restaurant besides. The expenses of timekeepers and judges are to be taken out of the remaining seventy-five per cent, as also are the expenses of the three friends of Sir John Astley who are to come over as referees. These gentlemen are very anxious to come to the United States on a little picnic with their expenses all paid. They will not provide themselves with enough pleasures to foot up a bill of two thousand dollars anyhow. What money remains will be divided between the contestants.

"I tell you Hess has a soft thing. I'll give him seven thousand dollars for the bar privilege alone. Of course, I have no idea what percentage of his share he has agreed to divide between Astley, Weston and Rowell. But we will insist on one thing, to be represented at the box office and at the doors, in order to save ourselves from being defrauded in the matter of tickets sold and receipts. But every proposition we make to the English interest on that score is quietly ignored."

George Guyon's backer, Charles Davies agreed saying, "The Americans have a right to be represented in the box office, a moral right if not a technical right. The English interest could probably claim that technically Weston and Rowell had a perfect right to make that match and the arrangements to suit themselves, and the other contestants were merely 'joiners in' after the terms were made. But such a position was not an equitable one, and if Weston and Rowell should adhere to it, their conduct would certainly justify the suspicion that they were 'hippodroming' the match.

"Weston and Rowell had no right to accept the money of other competitors if they intended to deny them all a voice in the management. Whoever paid an entrance fee, paid it for the privilege of a chance to win the belt or a certain share of the gate receipts, and they were entitled to every opportunity of seeing that the amount divided was the true and whole amount. So long as Weston and Rowell resisted this proposition, they were justly liable to a suspicion of intending to juggle in their own interests with the receipts. Weston and Rowell have acted unfairly toward the other pedestrians in giving Mr. Hess such liberal terms without their consent. If these terms had been published, probably a great many of the contestants would have refused to enter the match."

The well known trainer for the boxer John Heenan, and then trainer of John Ennis, James Cusick, followed.

King of the Peds

"I know these Englishmen; I've been among them. They try every time they can to play us. The English have eaten so much bull beef as to have become a race of bullies. That's a fact. I think they want to make all they can by any means out of this contest. The Americans ought to have a voice in the management of the financial affairs of the match. If they don't get it, they'll be cheated.

"The English interest should consent to a meeting of all the representatives of the contestants. At this meeting each contestant should have an equal vote. And then a treasurer should be elected. The meeting should appoint the ticket-takers and sellers. Watchers should be placed in the ticket office and at the entrances to prevent fraud. At the last Astley Belt contest in this city it was notorious that the ticket-takers used to pass large numbers of tickets to confederates outside to be sold on joint accounts. In this thousands of dollars were made, and that is the reason why the receipts in the box office did not tally with the crowds in the building.

"Another thing should be prevented. At the last contest the walkers allowed each of themselves to take out of the receipts one thousand dollars, allowed certain members of the management to take a similar amount, and then place away some two thousand dollars as a contingency fund, to meet unforeseen or unprovided for expenses. Such business is all 'skin' business, and should not be allowed. The contingent fund had never afterward been heard of. If Weston and Rowell refused to consent to such propositions their conduct would be construed as very singular, to say the least."

The forthcoming match then came in for discussion. Many in the meeting believed that the match wouldn't take place on the 22nd and that would be a good thing for the Americans. It was known that Vanderbilt had expressed a wish to stop the match at the Garden, *"even if he had to pay the penalty."* It was also known that Mr. Hess had made a threat to take out a Writ of Prohibition stopping Vanderbilt's injunction, and it was mentioned that the millionaire offered to give the pedestrians the venue in November for nothing but the bar privilege, if they would postpone the race till then. He further threatened to withhold the liquor licence if they refused, and make them accountable for every infringement of the law if they proposed to continue with the venture. Sir John Astley was approached on the question of postponement and he had submitted the matter to his lawyers to look into; they advised him to continue as planned, and the Hess camp agreed. The O'Leary camp however offered the pedestrians favourable terms if they agreed to postpone the match until October, which the Americans wanted to do. Rowell's and Weston's camp refused to entertain any such notion. Thereafter the meeting broke up.

The National Police Gazette (Illustration no: 49)

George Hazael arrived on the 9th of September on the steamship *Montana* accompanied by his trainer Isaac Sullivan. They headed off to Sweeny's Hotel, and after checking in, went to visit Rowell at the Ashland. On their arrival, Rowell was just about to set off for Jones's Wood to attend a *"Police picnic"* and invited the newcomers along. They accepted and Hazael was said to be given a good reception. During the intermission games at the picnic, George, wearing a cutaway coat and vest, lavender coloured close fitting pantaloons, an easy fitting pair of congress gaiters, and a small Derby hat, walked and ran around the enclosure scoring a mile in 7m.45s. Hazael, described as being 34 years of age, about five feet seven inches tall, and weighing 125 pounds, was said to be round shouldered due to walking and running. *"His gait is a peculiar one, and, when running his knees bend forward as though he were about to fall down."*

Asked about his voyage over, Hazael told reporters it had been a pleasant one apart from the first two days when there had been storms and the wind blew a gale. He stated he kept fit on board by walking around the deck and admitted that he had done so 100 times the week before, covering a distance of 11½ miles. George had probably sailed over on a steamship operated by the Guion line. The company was used by most of the professional peds crossing the Atlantic due to the *"unusual facilities afforded to them by the officials, who provide special baths and other means for the men continuing their exercises on board."* He said he "was not" friends with Sir John Astley and that he had nothing to do with him when arranging his participation in the forthcoming match. "Sullivan and I are here alone," he said, "and are going to look out for ourselves." His trainer said he would try and find a suitable place for George to train.

A week after, he was observed running ten miles at Green Point Grounds on or around the 13th of September employing an awkward but nevertheless easy gait, which he had calculated in doing in an just one hour. However, the distance was accomplished in 62 minutes and Hazael told those who watched that his effort was a little exercise rather than an exhibition. The diligent reporter evidently had taken his stopwatch along for he recorded the following times for each mile.

Mile	1	2	3	4	5	6	7	8	9	10
Time (mins:secs)	05:10	11	18:08	23:20	29:55	36:25	42:40	49:05	54:30	62

He later told the reporter (who confirmed his weight to be 133 pounds) whilst training at the grounds on Van Cott Avenue, that he never felt better in his life and was confident of winning the belt and the large sum of money which accompanied it. He admitted that the only man he feared in the race was Weston and stated he hoped to be leading the field at the end of the first day. He then mentioned he would follow in the leader's wake like a shadow and "break their hearts." He stated that he would be giving an exhibition run of 50 miles later that week on Thursday the 18th which he proposed to complete in five and a half hours.

On Saturday the 13th, after a meeting at the Gilsey House Hotel, the Kuntz brothers, the Garden lessees, Mr. Hess, the manager of the contest, and Mr. Kelly and Mr. Smith, representing Daniel O'Leary, a compromise was agreed upon by which the O'Leary party were to receive a large sum of cash to withdraw their objection to having the match at the Garden. On the 16th of September, the *Daily Miner* of Butte, Montana, then reported:

At the meeting of the pedestrians and their backers interested in the international walking match, a copy of the letter to Mr. Vanderbilt was read; setting forth that all the differences between various parties had been settled, and requesting that opposition of the New York and Hudson Railroad Company be withdrawn to the use of the Madison Square Garden. A reply from Vanderbilt was also read stating that the arrangements were satisfactory to the company and permission to use the Garden was granted for the match on the 22nd.

On Wednesday, the 17th, many of the athletes engaged in the forthcoming race met at the *Turf, Field and Farm* office to read and sign the articles of agreement. Ennis, Guyon, Hart, Jackson, Krohne, Merritt, Panchot, Taylor and Rowell were present. Mr. Atkinson, who presided, deputised for Astley.

The American camp once again stated they were unhappy with the management of the event by Mr. Hess. Speaking on behalf of Weston, Mr. Busby reminded them that as the current champion he could choose who he wanted to run the affair. He also informed them that Mr. Hess had put in a considerable amount of money into the venture already, and referring to the articles of agreement signed in London, reminded them as "other" contestants they were bound by the conditions within them.

John Ennis asked if they had any say in who managed the match. Atkinson responded by saying that those who had signed had the undoubted right to manage it. Ennis suggested that each signatory select a representative who would then form a Board of Managers, who would, in turn, elect a chairman. He would have control over matters relating to the match subject to two thirds of the board members.

Mr. Hess offered to continue the management of the contest as President of the Board who would appoint track, door, and finance committees, and the men agreed to his request after further discussion. The resolution was further amended to include Mr. Atkinson who was appointed to become chief referee, and who would therefore belonged to the Board of Managers. The document was then signed by all except by Mr. Busby who represented Weston and Rowell.

The *Daily Constitution* of Atlanta, in its run up to the race on the 21st of September wrote: NEW YORK, September 19 – The contest for the Astley belt, now that there is no prospect of litigation which will prevent its occurrence, promises to be an event of extraordinary interest. Money is freely being placed on Weston, Hazael, and Rowell. All of the contestants are hard at work training. Weston is in seclusion in Connecticut, getting his legs in trim. Hazael is walking in Green Point, and Panchot and Rowell in this city. The track is being made in the Madison Square Garden of tanbark, sawdust and earth. Cottages for the walkers are being constructed under the seats, away from the annoying gaze of spectators, who are apt to follow their favorites to their cottage door. Weston's request that there shall be no smoking in the garden is to be heeded, and smokers, if allowed at all, will be confined to a smoking gallery.

Ample arrangements have been made for the great throngs that are expected, and separate entrances and exits to the garden have been provided. As it is not now necessary to adopt the subterfuge of presenting the walk as a feature of the Dodworth band concerts, these will be suspended, but there will be music both afternoon and evening. The basis on which the dispute about the garden was settled is now said to be an agreement by the present lessees to pay $10,000 for the bar privilege during the O'Leary walk. Panchot being lame, it is probable that he will not enter, and it is said that the number of entries will be reduced by ruling out those who have not a record, but as this is not permitted by the rules of the Astley belt, it will probably not be done.

Before the race started there was another problem to be sorted out. Weston and Rowell, holder and challenger, had been afforded the choice of situation of the tents on the course, at a previous meeting of the contestants during which John Ennis hadn't been present. He latterly objected to the arrangement, and to stop any further wrangling it was decided to hold a lottery for the accommodations. Mr. Atkinson picked the balls from the hat and Mr. Scannell, Merritt's backer, picking number one, announced he would give it to Weston. Scannell then informed the meeting that Rowell desired the tent nearest the corner of Fourth Avenue and Twenty Sixth Street so that he could run over to the Ashland House whenever he desired and hoped that the pedestrian drawing that tent, number 11, would let him have it. Hazael later drew number 11 and gave the tent to Rowell.

At the end of the draw, the allotments stood as follows. Beginning at the Fourth Avenue and Twenty Seventh Street corner, and running westerly around the ellipse: No. 1, Weston; No. 2, Dutcher; No.3, Jackson; No. 4, Hart; No. 5, Federmeyer; No. 6, Guyon; No. 7, Ennis; No. 8, Panchot; No. 9, Krohne; No. 10, Merritt; No. 11, Rowell; No. 12, Taylor; No. 13, Hazael.

On the 22nd of September, the *New York Times* described what was happening behind the scenes in preparing for the contest, and in the same article, the scenes within the Garden prior to the race starting: During the interval between Saturday afternoon and yesterday morning, the interior of the garden underwent an extraordinary transformation. At 8 P.M on Saturday, after the carpenters had laid the floor, Mr. Atkinson, John Astley's representative, was given 100 laborers, and at daylight yesterday morning they had completed a track which the maker says is one of the best whose construction he ever superintended. It is several feet narrower than that used in the last match and has two feet less width than the specifications called for, but the pedestrians and their backers have said that they are satisfied with it. The ground was first dug up to the depth of a foot all around, and broken fine, all pebbles being removed with a rake. Over this earth was placed a covering of tanbark and loam, and this was sprinkled with sawdust. All day long and just before the pedestrians appeared, men were drawing heavy iron rollers over it. A space of about 18 inches, guarded by a raised wooden string piece separates the track all around from the floor. This is an improvement, and will go far toward preventing the contestants from being annoyed by evil-disposed spectators. As in the previous match, the floor on both sides at the track has been boarded over for the use of the public. The floors are bordered by wooden railings, apparently stout enough to resist any pressure that may be brought against them. At this point ends the resemblance of the interior arrangements to those of the last match.

The scorers and reporters are provided with a raised stand with a triple row of desks, one above the other, twenty seven feet in length. Opposite these has been erected a board fence six feet high, and on this has been tacked a long and broad muslin sheet, divided into thirteen spaces. Each space is headed with the name of one of the contestants. Below is painted a double circle with the numerals from one to eight inclusive, the number of laps to the mile. A large black indicator turns on a pivot in the center. A peg goes through a hole near the point, and corresponding holes are bored into the dial at each numeral. Between the names and the dials are pegs on which small placards bearing numerals are hung to denote the number of miles accomplished. This novel scoring arrangement is excellent in every respect save one.

None of the spectators, except the few who can crowd immediately in front of it, and the reporters, judges, and scorers, can see anything occurring at the starting point. On the edge of the central floor, between every two alternate pillars supporting the roof, are pitched the tents of the competitors, facing the track. These are surrounded by stout wooden railings to keep off interlopers. All except Weston's are of blue and white striped canvas, with white roofs. Weston's has black and yellow striped sides. They are all wall tents, but are not of equal size. The largest is twelve feet square. All have ventilating holes in the roofs. An enterprising furniture-dealer has fitted each one with a cot and mattress, a table, a washstand, two chairs, a gas stove, and a strip of carpet, in return for permission to hang his advertisement, surmounted by the name of the occupant, on each ridge-pole. Weston has gorgeously furnished two rooms in the corner of the building near his tent, and here he will take luxurious rests, using the tent only for short rubbings-down. He has substituted a lounge for the bed there, in his other quarters he has two beds, one for himself and the other for his trainer; while, in another small room adjacent, are accommodations for a second attendant. During the evening the trainers and backers of men were busy dragging in little extra comforts and appurtenances, and the several tents now look quite cozy and homelike. Guyon indulges in a refrigerator, and Ennis in a bath tub.

As may be imagined, this arrangement of tents is a very unfortunate for spectators. From no point in the building can more than a succession of glimpses of the track be had. After the tents were put up, the managers were struck by the stupidity of the plan, and they sought to change it by placing the contestants in the space under the seats on the Twenty Seventh Street side. Another wrangle was the result of Ennis and Guyon refusing absolutely to consent to the change. It was finally resolved to leave them as they were.

On the central floor near the Fourth Avenue side is a raised platform on which are eight tables for the use of the bookmakers, and fronting the boarded grotto is a tall blackboard, visible from nowhere, on which the record of completed miles is hung. The Garden is lighted at night by electric lamps, which have been specially furnished with extra thick and large globes so as not to injure the pedestrians' eyes. There are numerous petty apple and cake stands, weighing machines, soda-water fountains, and other contrivances for catching stray pennies all around the enclosure and an extra bar has been fitted up in the north corner. The new decorations consist of advertisements that placard the walls in all directions, and notices to the effect that smoking will not be allowed on the floor.

As early as 7 o'clock Sunday evening there were many hundreds of people congregated around the Garden, despite it being generally known that the doors would not be thrown open until at the very earliest 9 o'clock, and the start would not take place before 1 a.m. Some of the adjacent streets were said to be impassable due to the gathering throngs of would-be spectators. Meanwhile inside, George Guyon, accompanied by his trainer Jim Smith and his backer Charles Davies, was the first of the contestants to arrive. George had arrived early with the sole intention of getting some sleep, and by 19:30 was doing just that. As he dreamed of glory, the rest of the trainers and attendants were busy arranging bottles and making their respective contestant's beds on which were laid the costumes which, in many cases, wouldn't be donned until a few minutes before the start. About 200 or so officials milled about the place, and all apart from one were men; the exception being the woman who operated the 5-cents-a-go weighing machine. Many of the employees were German bartenders and Irish waiters who would work under a large floral cross which read, "THY WILL BE DONE." The *Brooklyn Daily Eagle* wrote: **The interior of the vast building was brilliantly illuminated with electric lights making it as bright as day within the amphitheatre. It has been claimed that the American public has grown very weary of these six days contests and that no such enthusiasm will be aroused here as was called out in March, but the reverse seems to be the case. Should the race be close towards the end we may expect to find the building densely thronged, day and night, the air hideously foul, and the neighborhood of the garden noisy and disorderly.** At that moment however, the air in the vast place was quite clear as the final preparations were made before the doors would be thrown open at 10 o'clock at which time the public would be admitted.

The venue was well policed on that opening night. Captain Williams had prepared for the event with military precision and had placed twenty of his officers at each entrance. The rest fiddled with their truncheons as they walked down the huge lines of people eager to get into the building. Then at 22:00, the gates opened. There was little pushing and as a consequence little disorder. As he watched the customers pass through, manager Hess rubbed his hands together and exclaimed, "Oh this is the way to do it! Here we have an orderly, quiet, nice crowd of people, and I'd be gratified if the house was only half full, instead of being jammed by a howling mob at fifty cents."

King of the Peds

All the arriving pedestrians were cheered by the crowd as they turned up. Norman Taylor was the first of them to arrive in the building and make his way to his tent at ten o'clock. "I feel first rate," he said as he opened the canvas door. By eleven o'clock, and with William Dutcher now sitting inside his quarters, all the good seats and standing areas had been occupied and there were between six and seven thousand *"well dressed and respectable looking persons in the building."* Peter Panchot arrived at his quarters for a pre-race rub down at 23:30, and Ennis strolled into his tent fifteen minutes later, followed by Leon P. Federmeyer *without* his trusty wheelbarrow. Weston arrived from the Rossmore Hotel at midnight and was directed towards a room at the Fourth Avenue end of the building. Frank Hart, who had been staying at the Brunswick Hotel, arrived with O'Leary and was smuggled into the Garden.

The *"roller men"* received loud applause by the awaiting crowd as they pulled the heavy metal cylinder around the ellipse; despite the no smoking rule, many in the place ignored it and lit up. At thirty minutes past the midnight hour the band played *"Pinafore Airs,"* and when the time finally arrived for the start, the thirteen contestants lined up for the chance of glory and a big pay day at the end of it all. An estimated 12,000 to 13,000 people paying $1 a head had given up the chance of a normal night's sleep to witness the start.

It had already been agreed that Mr. Atkinson would not have to caution the competitors against breaches of the rules governing the track, by telling them to, *"turn outside their competitor's line of progress, to allow nothing to turn them from the rail when they chose to follow it, or the simpler caution about treading on one another's heels or interfering with each other in anyway."*

The scorers and judges wearing *"gay badges"* were in their seats, and the pedestrians who had been called in front of the scorers' stand, organised themselves four deep on the track. All were cheered heartily by the crowd. Mr. Busby, who was to start the race, stood with a watch in his hand. The other judges were Mr. Atkinson and Mr. C. H. Pierce, president of the New York Athletic Club.

Scenes before the start.

The National Police Gazette. *(Illustration no: 50)*

THE LINE UP:

Note: A pedestrian's starting price is followed by his odds for a (place) to finish 1st or 2nd:

CHARLES ROWELL: Chesterton, Cambridgeshire, England: 6/4: (1/2): 139 LBS: Colours: Blue and white striped shirt, trunks and jockey cap. **Best six-day record:** 500 miles: **Pedestrian profile:** The 26-year-old was 5ft.6in tall. *"Physically he is a splendid specimen of manhood, and his broad shoulders, deep chest and tremendous calves at once indicate great powers of endurance. He has got a pleasing but anxious face and sticks to his work without turning to the right or to the left. He is both a graceful runner and walker and his every movement indicates great reserve force. He is an enormous feeder and does most of his feeding on the track. There is not the fullness about Rowell's face and neck as there was a year ago. He is a modest, undemonstrative little fellow."* **Career:** Accounted for.

EDWARD PAYSON WESTON: Rhode Island, USA: 5/2: (1/1): 140 LBS: Colours: White shirt, red trunks and tights. Cane: **Best six day's record:** 550 miles: **Pedestrian profile:** At 40 years of age he was 5ft.7½in tall. He was reported to have trained long and hard for this race. Anybody witnessing his style of locomotion for the first time would have noticed how he would work his head shoulders more than any of his rivals. He was expected to win or come in a close second. *"He had filled out in flesh without any apparent loss of solidity, and looked as though, beneath his weather bound skin, he was made of finely wrought steel."* **Career:** Accounted for: **At the start:** *"Besides Charley, his valet, his old friend Deputy Sheriff Henry B. Ford of White Plains who was with him when he won his first 100-mile race, accompanied him. He thought Ford would bring him luck."*

GEORGE HAZAEL: London, England: 3/1: (5/4): 138 LBS: Colours: White shirt and green trunks: **Best six day's record:** 492 miles: **Pedestrian profile:** At 33 years of age, poor old George who stood 5ft.6½in tall would never have won a beauty contest with his "bull dog face," short cropped hair and almost deformed stooped shoulders which gave him the most displeasing appearance. His trainer stated, "He was a lazy man if not pushed but when he is he can move himself forward at a tremendous pace." **Career:** A record of George's achievements has already been mentioned previously.

GEORGE GUYON: Chicago, USA: 10/1: (4/1): 152 LBS: Colours: White shirt, blue trunks, white drawers: **Best six day's record**: 480¼ miles: **Pedestrian profile:** George was born in St. Cecille, Milton County, Shefford, Canada, on September the 11th 1853. He stood 5ft.6½in tall. He was described as the most handsome and finest built man to take part in the race. He was described as walking upright with a quick elastic step which moved him along at a good rate of knots. He moved his body around economically thus preserving his stamina. He was a pleasant chap and was well liked by the spectators: **Career:** At the Exposition Building in Chicago between the 15th and 20th of May 1876, George won a six-day walk scoring 412 miles. Then, two years later between June the 6th and the 8th at the American Institute Building in New York, he won the belt in a 48-hour match for scoring 187½ miles in 46h.31m. He was then beaten a month later by John Ennis in a six-day walk in Buffalo, New York, between the 15th and the 20th of July. Then, in a 26-hour walk on August the 2nd and 3rd of the same year at Utica, he stole the honours by beating Peter McInernay with a score of 106½ miles. Eleven days later in a 75-hour match at Rochester, New York, he beat Jas. Smith who gave up on the 41st mile. In 1879, and between April the 25th and 26th, he won a 24-hour walk at Gilmore's Garden "easily." and then at the same venue starting May the 5th, won the six-day heel-and-toe walk with a score of 480 miles and 2 laps in a time of 142h.15m.5s. **At the start:** *"He had his hair cut just before he went on the track, and looked trim and in good form."*

FREDERICK KROHNE: Germany: 15/1: (8/1): 168 LBS: Colours: White shirt, belt and drawers, navy blue trunks, and blue silk neckerchief: **Best six day's record:** 461 miles: **Pedestrian profile:** Fred, who was known as *"the grenadier,"* was born in Prussia ("which *never produced a more awkward man")* in 1841, but hailed from New York. He stood 6ft.1in tall. An ungainly walker, he ploughed his way steadily along in his races and was confident of making the necessary 450 miles in order to take home place money. **Career:** Fred had taken third prize in the match won by Panchot in April of that year, and then in the month after between May the 5th and the 11th, took second prize money of $750 by making 461 miles in 140h.51m.25s in a six-day heel-and-toe match at Gilmore's Garden. **At the start**: *"Krohne towered above all the others by nearly half a head, and showed his height far more than when in citizen's dress. He stepped off with a slight limp, which is permanent lameness."*

FRANK HART: Boston, Massachusetts, USA: 20/1: (10/1): 140 LBS: Colours: Grey shirt, black cap and trunks: **Best six day's record:** 425 miles: **Pedestrian profile:** At 5ft.7½in, Frank, originally called Fred Hichborn, was *supposedly* born in Haiti in 1858 but the *Boston Globe* stated he was born in France and arrived in America when he was very young. It was claimed he had arrived in the USA in 1877, but is likely he arrived in Boston at that time where he worked in a grocery store before starting to compete professionally. The *Daily Constitution* of Atlanta, Georgia, which was to write an article about his athleticism *after* the race, suggested that he had been in the USA a few years: Hart is a Georgia raised darkey. He lived for a number of years in Lagrange and on many occasions has walked over to Columbus from his home, a distance of 40 miles, to attends frolics, danced all night, and then walked back reaching home in time for breakfast the next morning. Hart won the twenty five dollar purse at the fair of the North Georgia Stock Association last fall. There were eleven entries, all colored. Hart walked the mile in magnificent style easily distancing his competitors. Indeed the dark walker led them so far and with such astonishing ease that their efforts to catch him took on the form of burlesque. **Career:** He won his first race in a 30-hour, go-as-you-please which finished on Saturday, the 26th of April 1879 at the Boston Music Hall. During the event, which Hart had led since the sixth hour, a spectator tried to throw pepper in his eyes. Frank made 119 miles and 13 laps in 29 hours and received $100 and the "Englehardt Gold Medal" for his win. John F. Manning of Brighton was second scoring 112 miles and 7 laps and winning $50. Hughes followed him home in third place on a score of 106 miles and 9 laps receiving $25. Apparently, Hart, who hadn't trained for the event, lived *"at Strong place off of Cambridge street"* at the time of the race, and although he had been one of the contestants in an amateur race at Silver Lake as an oarsman, he had no previous experience as a pedestrian, nor had he trained for the race! His second race was at Lowell, Massachusetts, when he won $75 in an eight hours walk covering over 50 miles. The next time he raced was on Wednesday, the 21st of May when he competed on the third day of the 2nd contest for the "Silver Bean Pot," again at Boston at the corner of Huntingdon Avenue and Newton Street. This was an event where teams of professional pedestrians from Massachusetts, Rhode Island and Maine, (who won the first contest a week earlier) competed against each other in a six hours per day go-as-you-please competition. Frank, who was paired with another Bostonian called DeForrest, would make the highest score of 39 miles and 5 laps in the six runner event with his partner making 34.2. Levery of Providence was second best with 37 miles and a lap. For this effort Hart won $45. His first attempt at a six-day go-as-you-please contest was in the *"big tent"* on the Back Bay, Boston, between Monday, May the 26th and Saturday, May the 31st. At the end of five days, Lacouse was ahead with a score of 355.5, Coughlin of Erving was second with 354.5, and Hart was third with 348.2. During a spurt with Coughlin, who tripped and fell on the track, Coughlin's trainer accused Hart of deliberately flooring his man whilst Hart claimed the incident was accidental. It was deemed by the rules of the race Hart was to blame but Coughlin sportingly withdrew his protest, with the remark that he "did not want it to happen again." The most *"closely contested match of its kind"* finished at 11 o'clock, with the result showing a win for Lacouse who scored 427 miles making $300. Hart took home $150 with an effort of 424 5/8 miles, and Coughlin got $100 for scoring 400. His next race was an O'Leary sponsored go-as-you-please, 75-hour race which started in the Music Hall at Boston at 20:16 on the evening of Wednesday, the 23rd of July. During the first 24 hours, Hart made 102 miles and five laps and took only 2 hours rest, covering three miles more than he had planned to. At the 28-hour stage, he was 10 miles ahead of his nearest competitor, Arthur Croft of Little Falls, New York, on a score of 117 miles, and later led the same opponent 183.4 to 178 with Campana just two laps behind him in third position. Hart would eventually finish as runner-up in the race with a total score of 263 miles and 16 laps winning $150 for his efforts. The winner, Croft, who made 271.6, was rewarded with a silk purse containing $250 in gold and the O'Leary medal. Campana took $100 on a score of 262.8, and Lacouse, with 256.6, got $75. It was estimated that 45,000 watched the match from beginning to end. On the 7th of August, the *Reno Evening Gazette* informed its readers: The brutality to which pedestrianism has sunk was illustrated by a seventy-five-hour race in Boston. Near the close of the third day, three of the contestants were so close together that the struggle for the lead became desperate. Croft, a young man from New York, became temporarily crazy from fatigue and want of sleep, and quitted the track; but his trainers forced him to return and he eventually won by completing 271 miles, on a course so small that nineteen circuits were required for a mile. Campana, the old man whose feats in Gilmore's Garden were awkward and ridiculous, also fell into a condition of mental derangement, and frequently stopped to talk incoherently with spectators; but he was forced to continue, although he sank on the track exhausted, and at the last moment relinquished the second place to Hichborn, a negro. Hart then won the O'Leary and Englehardt promoted 75 hours, at a 12½ hours per day, go-as-you-please pedestrian contest, which was held at Providence, Rhode Island, between the 8th and 13th of September 1879. Frank made 362 miles in this one, winning the grand sum of $300, a handsome gold chain, and a belt made of solid silver which held eight clasps and a shield. One of the clasps had the words, **"Providence, R. I., September 8 – 13. 1879"** engraved on it while the other read, **"Presented by Fred J. Englehardt and Dan O'Leary."** The race attracted a field of 30 contestants which included Peter Crossland, O'Leary's old adversary. The race, which was watched by 20,000 people on the final night, attracted so much interest in surrounding cities that carrier pigeons were dispatched with messages about the latest scores. As the race reached its finale, all the remaining contestants on the course received several floral tributes each, with Hart's tent being *"literally strewn with flowers."* The crowd was also entertained, when at 20:45 "Old Sport," an earlier retiree, ran 5 miles in 34m.40s. Earlier, and in a separate match, Crossland had raced O'Leary, square heel-and-toe, but lost to the race promoter. Alfred Elson came in second with 252.7 ($200), John Dobler was third on a score of 340.3 ($100), John Colston was fourth. He made $50 for making 318.5. Mohr was fifth with 312.6, and Robert Vint took home two pairs of McSwyny's walking shoes for achieving 297 miles and 4 laps.

After showing all the above "form," Hart left his job and hired trainer Fred Englehardt to coach him. Hart's earlier performance in Boston had attracted the attention of Daniel O'Leary who was looking for a protégé. It is not clear when O'Leary approached Frank, but when he did, instead of gradually introducing him to the big time races, he entered him in this one, the most important pedestrian event of the year. O'Leary was said to have taken great interest in the lad, and Frank had imitated O'Leary's gait and manner to perfection, even carrying the corn cobs that his mentor swore by. Due to the similarities in style Hart gained the nickname, "Black Dan."

Frank was not expected to win the race and a decent "place" was only a dream, but, with diligent coaching, O'Leary said he would get his man right one day and get him up there with the best. "Gentlemen in sporting business sometimes keep their men back to make money and other things, but I don't want that," he told O'Leary. "I must go straight and win or I'll go back to groceries." Hart was married and had two children. **At the start:** *"Looked extremely well."*

JOHN ENNIS: Chicago, Illinois, USA: 30/1: (15/1): 164 LBS: Colours: White striped shirt, trunks and cap: **Best six days' record**: 475 miles, 800 yards: **Pedestrian profile:** Apart from Guyon, John at 5ft.8in in height was possibly the next most physically perfect of the contenders. His camp were said to be pleased with his preparation. He had showed good form in the last Astley Belt contest, but his run in London was poor. More was expected of him now and he was an interesting outsider. John was married and his faithful wife carefully managed his training. **Career:** Accounted for.

PETER PANCHOT: Buffalo, USA. 30/1 (15/1) 138 LBS. Colours: White balbriggan shirt, blue trunks and drawers: **Best six days' record:** 480 miles: **Pedestrian profile:** Peter was 5ft.4½ inches in height and weighed 128 pounds *"when in condition.* He had been a postman on the outskirts of Buffalo, and was compelled to walk long distances to perform his duties. He was described as *"very good looking with a dark complexion"* and *"ran gracefully."* He was described as having a nervous, but quick step, possibly from learned experience when escaping from pursuing dogs on his post round. He was known for getting over the ground quickly, and took frequent short rests in his races. Panchot was said to have trained diligently and was frequently observed exercising from Prospect Park to Coney Island and back. It was here that he sprained his ankle a few days before the race whilst out walking, and to his credit, he had warned his friends not to back him. **Career:** Accounted for.

SAMUEL MERRITT: Bridgeport, Connecticut, USA. 35/1 (18/1): 166 LBS. Colours: White shirt and tights, blue trunks, scarlet cap: **Best six days' record:** 475 5/8 miles. **Pedestrian profile:** Sam was born in Havanna, Schuyler County, New York State on March the 4th 1858. At the time of the race, he was residing in Bridgeport, Connecticut. At six feet tall, he was a tall ungraceful looking young man, who was described as having a shambling gait bringing his arms in front of him with each step. However, with that method of progression, he was expected to make good ground and would *"run like a deer"* when it suited him. He was expected to be in the frame at the end as he appeared well and showed no signs of anxiety about the task ahead of him. **Career:** He was said to have made 400½ miles in a six-day championship tournament for the State championship at the Lyceum Hall in Bridgeport between the 3rd and 8th of February.

WILLIAM DUTCHER: USA. 50/1 (20/1) 145 LBS. Colours: Red shirt and drawers, white cap and belt. **Best record**: 286 miles in 4 days. **Pedestrian profile:** William, who was 27 years old and 5ft.7in tall, was described as *"a nice-looking young man with a German cast of countenance and a German build, with a round smooth face and small bright eyes, broad and deep chest and large legs."* **Career:** His record for a six-day event did not amount to more than 350 miles, but having said that, he was considered to one of the best men in the field as he had showed promise in training in nearly covering 450 miles in the permitted time. **At the start**: *"His eyes sparkled and the cheeks were full and rosy."*

LEON P. FEDERMEYER: France. 50/1 (20/1) 138 LBS. Colours: Grey shirt and hat and red tights: **Best six-days' record**: 407 miles pushing a wheelbarrow: **Pedestrian profile:** The long haired Frenchman had been born in Lorraine about 40 years earlier. He sported a brown bushy beard and moustache, and was known the *"Rip Van Winkle"* character of the race for pushing a wheelbarrow in a race from San Francisco to New York before entering the competition. He was said to have *"a mincing step"* which wouldn't help him achieve any prize money. **Career:** Federmeyer took on Lyman Potter for a prize of $2,000 in the above mentioned race. Both held daily workouts before it and these were watched by the public. The rules of the race were that each of the competitors was to push their wheelbarrows with contents not weighing less than 100 pounds at all times. Each man had to supply a referee to validate the weight at various points on the way. Federmeyer left San Francisco on December the 8th 1878, and arrived in New York on July the 23rd 1879. What happened to his opponent is not clear. **At the start**, *"His hair had not been cut nor his beard trimmed, and he stood bent forward as if he held an imaginary wheelbarrow and was endeavoring to catch up to it."*

HIRAM JACKSON: New Bedford, USA. 50/1 (20/1) 125 LBS. Colours: White shirt and drawers and blue trunks: **Best six days' record**: None. **Pedestrian profile:** The sallow faced and emaciated figure of the 27-year-old Hiram, the mill operative or "spinner" from Fall River, Massachusetts, was being talked of fondly by his father, who referred to his son as, "My boy Hiram." Dad told reporters that he was confident that his son would be in the mix by the finish. **Career:** None to report.

NORMAN TAYLOR: Vermont, USA. 50/1 (20/1) 148 LBS. Colours: Linen shirt, pantaloons, and stockings. **Best six days' record**: None. **Pedestrian profile:** Norman was born in Vermont, and at the time of the race, was said to be about 48 years of age. This was his first ever long distance contest. He was described as a very strange character because he had not eaten meat in many years. *"He has a wonderful physique, and great endurance. His skin is clear, red and drawn over his bones with the tightness of parchment over a drum."* Norman liked his pies and was not expected to do much in the race, except, that was, to retire early. **Career:** He was more a runner than a walker and had excelled in 20-mile races. He was reported to have lost but one race in his career. **At the start:** *"He had told his friends these clothes never failed him, and he had a superstition that any other dress would bring certain failure."*

The pedestrians, who all wore large numbers painted in red on black oil skin on their chests, looked at the judges. After a short pause, Mr. Busby shouted to the men, "Are you ready?"

Lining up for he start of the 5th Astley Belt race. **They're off!**

The National Police Gazette (Illustration no: 51)   *Frank Leslie's Illustrated Newspaper. (Illustration no: 52)*

Then, after a much, much, longer pause, and precisely at 1 o'clock, he shouted, "Go!" A tremendous din erupted, and as the band played up, the thirteen brave fellows set off on their journey amid encouraging shouts, clapping hands, waving handkerchiefs and stamping feet. Hazael, as expected, went straight to the front making the first mile in 6m.10s with Panchot almost a lap in arrears and Rowell, Taylor and Jackson following in that order.

In the early stages, the progress of each one of the pedestrians was being watched closely. The following observations were made. **Ennis:** Was *"swinging his arms as if plying a bucksaw."* **Federmeyer:** Walked for the first three miles, his long hair floating behind him. *"He tramped as though every step would give him headache but he paid no attention to his competitors as they passed him in rapid succession."* **Guyon:** Was *"graceful"* in every movement. **Hart:** Chewed his toothpick as he moved along. **Hazael:** Was a *"revelation."* He *"almost skimmed over the earth."* Holding himself as *"awkwardly as an ape,"* he swung his shoulders to and fro independently of his body: **Jackson:** Was described as being *"like a scared child."* **Krohne:** His movements were described as being *"awkward."* **Merritt:** Glided easily along when he ran, but walked with considerable effort. **Panchot:** Held his head high in the air and took tiny steps. **Rowell:** Bent well forward and ran with the ease. **Taylor:** Ran upright with wonderful ease carrying a stick. **Weston:** Operating toward the outside of the track, he reversed his direction at the end of every alternate mile. Carrying his head very high, he swayed his body to and fro, clutching his cane with a tight grip as he ran along.

Weston sheds his coat and gets down to business.

The National Police Gazette. (Illustration no: 53)

After 30 minutes Hazael continued to lead the way with four miles to his credit. Dutcher was half a mile behind in joint second place along with Jackson, Taylor and Rowell, who were a lap ahead of Guyon. He was a lap up on the slow walking, but long striding Krohne who had Hart a lap behind him. Ennis had 2.6, Weston 2.3 and Federmeyer was the last man on 2.1. As the men went round, some in the crowd would shout out at their favourites………… "Go it Ennis old boy!" "Stick to him Hart!" "Go it Rowell!" Hazael made the first five miles in 32m.57s and went on to score 8.7 in the first hour when the other scores were: **Taylor and Jackson, 8.1; Panchot, 7.6; Dutcher, Guyon, Hart and Rowell, 7.5; Krohne, 7.2; Weston, 6.5; Ennis, 6.3; Merritt, 6.2; Federmeyer, 5.4:**

Dutcher, who had broken down in a race at the Garden during the spring, was the first to show signs of distress. He fell and fainted on the last lap of his 22nd mile and was immediately taken to his tent. He reappeared on the track at 04:52, but fainted again on the fifth lap of his 23rd mile after which his physician hoisted the white flag and surrendered his patient's further participation in the race. The young man was said to have, *"sobbed like a baby,"* and later, when interviewed, said, "Well, I've got some trouble with my heart. I chewed a lot of tobacco while training and that brought on the trouble. Why, my heart beat like a trip hammer. If I had gone on they said it would have killed me." His biggest mistake in the race was to follow Rowell around for 20 miles or so. He had been a major disappointment, especially to the hoards of people who had their fingers burnt backing him.

Dutcher faints for the second time.

The National Police Gazette. (Illustration no: 54)

At 05:00, Guyon moved swiftly into second place and was a lap up on Rowell. As Merritt slowly gained ground at the back of the field, Panchot, Taylor, Krohne and Jackson were putting in indifferent performances. The latter named had been involved in a slight scare when he had become quite ill after his father had allegedly given him eggs laced with brandy. However, he quickly recovered and went along nicely thereafter.

Just after 08:00, and now on his 43rd mile, Rowell took second place from Guyon. Later whilst Hazael took an hours rest around 09:00, Charlie took full advantage, and powered himself into the lead; the crowd responding to the change in positions with great applause. Dutcher's dial, as expected, was placarded with word "withdrawn" at 10:00, and by 11:00, Ennis passed Hazael and went into second spot. The betting on winning the belt at that time showed: **Rowell, 1/2; Weston, 4/1; Hazael, 5/1; Hart, 10/1; Ennis and Guyon, 12/1; Krohne, Panchot and Taylor, 50/1; Merritt, 60/1; Jackson, 80/1; Federmeyer, 300/1:**

Panchot's foot had troubling him and he made poor progress around the track in the morning in front of the many spectators who had watched the proceedings from the start. *"He rolls his shoulders around as other men roll their eyes. He runs hardly any, but keeps up hour after hour, his peculiar, quick, nervous walk and violent swinging of the shoulders."* Rowell kept up the same easy trot as he did in the last race. Weston walked at a lively pace, and occasionally ran a few laps. Ennis walked a number of laps in each mile and then ran the last three laps very quickly, thus making good time.

He looked in fine condition and didn't appear to be troubled as in previous contests with his stomach. Hazael walked a little, and took long strides when running.

In the style of his preceptor O'Leary, the corn cob carrying Frank Hart amused the crowd by walking, sprinting and running in sync with Rowell. He also aped his style. *"Rowell does not seem to like it, and runs frequently; but Hart also runs, and Rowell cannot shake him off."* However, some saw Hart's attempts to disconcert the leader as playing into Rowell's hands and thus increase his score. *"Rowell is up to all the tricks in his profession, and occasionally smiled at the silliness of the colored boy."* The show really revved the crowd up. Because of their admiration for Hart's mentor, O'Leary, the Irishmen in the crowd took Hart's side, whilst Rowell's supporters encouraged their favourite to repel the Bostonian's challenge. "Go for him Frankie!" "Shake him off Rowell!" The *New York Herald* wrote of Hart: **He carried his head high, with a quill toothpick between his lips, observing that when the band played his favourite tune "Baby Mine," Frank would make a spurt.**

Hart "dogs" Rowell

The National Police Gazette (Illustration no: 55)

Whilst Rowell was being hounded by Hart, Ennis was chasing the Boston boy, and the quips from the crowd inferred that Ennis was also dogging Hart. "Hold on to him Ennis!" "That's right, go get him!" The remarks seemed to annoy Ennis who responded by passing Hart and concentrate his efforts on chasing Rowell instead. The move was cheered *"to the echo"* by the crowd who appreciated the change of tactics. Ennis sustained his pace for a few more laps, but when he began his 61st mile he slowed down allowing Hart to recapture him.

At this time, Panchot was observed to be walking rather stiffly, and showing evidence of lameness, stating his foot was severely troubling him. None of the men leading in the race had been off the track for any length of time. They took occasional rests for five or ten minutes and re-entered the fray looking fresh. Rowell made his 70th mile at 12:28 making that distance at a speed of 6 mph. Up to that stage, he had only rested for meals, and walked and ran alternately, apparently doing so with ease. *"Rowell has lost in great part that plumpness which peculiarly characterized him in the previous contest for the belt. His face is cadaverous, but otherwise he looks in excellent trim."*

The 1st 12 hours scores, the 12th hour being 13:00:

HR	Rowe	Guy	Hart	Merr	Ennis	Panch	Haz	Jacks	West	Khro	Feder	Tay
1st	7.5	7.5	7.5	6.2	6.3	7.6	8.7	8.1	6.1	7.2	5.4	8.1
2nd	14	14.4	14.2	11.6	12.3	14.6	17.4	14.6	13.2	14.6	10.6	15.7
3rd	20.7	20.3	20.4	17.1	18.5	20.1	24.2	20.6	18.7	20.1	15.6	21
4th	26.4	26.1	25.7	21.6	24.6	25.1	29.7	25	23.4	22.4	20.6	26.7
5th	31.7	32.2	31.1	26.3	28.3	28.2	33	27.4	27.7	25	22	30.1
6th	37.6	37.7	36.7	31.3	36	33.1	39.4	28.4	31.4	27.5	24.2	33.9
7th	43.5	43	42.3	36.1	40.6	37.3	45	31	35.5	32.3	29	39.4
8th	49.3	48	47.3	39.6	45	42.4	50.2	39.7	41.1	36.6	33.2	41.1
9th	55.1	53	53.1	43.2	51.8	47	54.3	44	46	41.7	37.6	44.3
10th	61.2	58.3	57.7	48	57.1	50	56.6	49.3	50	44.7	40	49.7
11th	67.1	63	61.6	52.4	63.2	54.3	60	50.4	53	49.3	41.5	50.4
12th	73.2	67.4	64.5	58.2	69	58.5	64.3	55.6	57	53.1	46	55.7

At 13:00, all the men, except Guyon, were entertaining the crowd. Ennis finished his 75th mile at 14:08 and Rowell finished his 80th mile at 14:20. Whenever the two came together, the crowd cheered, the noise spurring both on to break into a run.

Hazael, described as looking *"more like an elongated monkey,"* was already being attacked by the press as being *"another disappointment."* His doctor stated that George was ill in the morning due to drinking Croton water and milk, neither of which he was used to. His trainer however, said he was just plain lazy and told the press that he was disgusted with him, and that he had thrown his chances away. He said he showed no desire to accomplish anything and that he would be in his tent half the time if he could. *"The question is often asked, "What is that thing?" when Hazael goes around, but the questioner is always awed into silence when told that is one of the best runners in England.* He stooped as he moved himself along, *"his shoulders bent and his arms jerking laboriously."* There was obviously something wrong with him and he appeared to be in some degree of pain.

The building was filling up nicely in the afternoon. On their way to the match, the more observant spectators surrounded and cheered Campana and O'Leary, as the pair made their way to the building to watch the proceedings, where the bars were awash with customers, many of whom were in a *"state of merriment."* Some of the more inebriated made their way to the side of the track where they made unpleasant remarks at the contestants. They were quickly sought out and ejected.

The bulletin boards outside the building, like in Printing Square, were being closely monitored by *"eager crowds, forgetting business and everything else for the sake of learning how the changing record stands. In the cars, on the ferry-boats on the streets, in the offices and in the parlors, the walk and the walkers are the uppermost topics of conversation."*

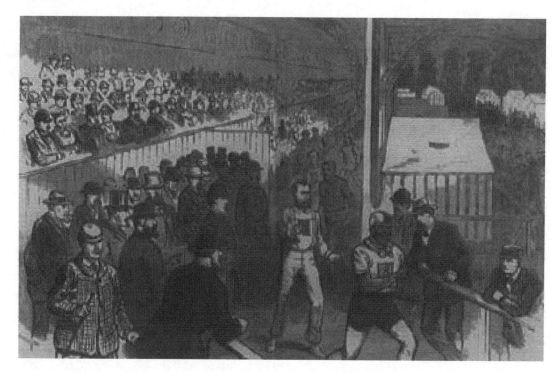

The view from the Madison Avenue side - the "Star of Africa in the Ascendant."

The National Police Gazette. (Illustration no: 56)

The atmosphere within was particularly pleasant with the many ladies present watching their heroes at work. All the windows were open and there were few patrons smoking which must have delighted Weston who told reporters at the press stand, "Thanks for what you said about the smoking. The air is pure and fresh here now, quite as fresh as what it was at the Agricultural Hall." His attitude however, didn't last long. As he left the path at around three o'clock, he was seen remonstrating with a man in the crowd who, whilst standing close to the side of the track, deliberately blew cigar smoke in the champion's face. Whilst making a formal complaint to the managers about the incident, he lost valuable time and distance as the police moved in to feel the collars of those observed breaking the rules.

The *Brooklyn Daily Eagle* commented about Weston's miserable display: The latter's excuse, that the tobacco smoke is responsible for his failure is so far, probably absurd. At the same time there is a tendency on the part of the newspapers to belittle the evil effects of the use of tobacco in the building. Even confirmed smokers know that at certain times one cigar is apt to affect them unpleasantly, while the smell of tobacco in a street car is frequently distressing to stomachs hardened to nicotine. Weston does not smoke, and is peculiarly susceptible to the smell of tobacco, and it is likely that he is seriously troubled. One of the essential requisites of good circulation is pure air. The atmosphere of the Garden is sufficiently vitiated by the exhalations from thousands of lungs without adding to its impurity the foul fumes from such atrocities as are sold over the bar under the alluring but deceptive title of cigars. The police, therefore, ought to see to it that that smoking shall be strictly prohibited and should expel from the Garden such selfish an ill mannered persons as insist upon filling the lungs of the pedestrians with suffocating and sickening stench.

At 15:30, and now on his 70th mile, the *"lazy"* Hazael started a run and kept it going for seven miles right through till well after 4 o'clock. Whilst he thrilled the crowd, the Londoner received a bouquet of flowers which he held aloft as he sped around, *"giving the large audience that had assembled a fit of temporary madness."*

Merritt's positive track performance meanwhile was being scribbled into the notebooks. He looked in first rate condition and didn't appear to be fatigued in the least. As Hart chewed away at another quill and rattled off the laps at an enthusiastic pace, the whip carrying Federmeyer plodded along at the back of the field as though missing his wooden companion. Taylor, although running easily and gracefully, was not expected to stay the distance even at that early stage of the race, as he was spending far too much time in his cabin. He seemed incapable of making a prolonged effort. The ill looking fellow had the crowd's sympathy and there were those in the crowd who desired to see him win more than anyone else.

Weston reappeared on the track at 17:40 and went straight back to work in an apparent cheerful mood. During the race, and when the band struck up, he had been observed on occasions dancing to the music it produced. He was also seen to toss his cane in the air and even placed a cup on the end of it which he walked round with for a lap. He *"walks and runs prettily, working his shoulders and head, and frequently reversing, a system of tactics that compels him to travel on the outside of the track, and, consequently, to cover more ground than the others. On nearly every turn he had some antic to perform, skipping about the track sometimes when Hazael was running, or poor little Federmeyer was trying to walk fast, going up behind them and imitating their gait."* News from the Weston camp indicated that their man was saving himself for the latter part of the contest when his competitors would be tiring.

Hart caught the eye of many, and those in the know put it down to O'Leary's influence. *"Englehardt and O'Leary are almost constantly in front of his tent, and with four attendants, all the lad needs is a pair of McWhacktery and O'Shaughnessy's celebrated pedestrian shoes to win the match."* He was said to be the freshest looking ped on the ellipse in the evening. He dogged Rowell, persistently keeping within 4 feet from the leader's heels. Rowell however, who had made his century at 17:49, was said not to mind the stalking as much as he had done earlier in the race when Hart annoyed him, taking all the Bostonian's attention in good humour. At this stage, the centurion was 6.7 ahead of Guyon, 14.1 ahead of Ennis, 16.6 ahead of Hazael, 19.3 ahead of Hart, 19.4 ahead of Merritt, 22 ahead of Panchot, 24.2 ahead of Jackson, 26.7 ahead of Taylor, a whopping 31.3 ahead of the disappointing Weston, 31.3 ahead of Krohne and 40 ahead of Federmeyer.

Guyon, who looked very much like Rowell, went along at a 5½ mph clip. *"He walks erect and with a quick elastic tread, swinging his arms freely and doing wonderfully quick time."* The Chicagoan made his century at 19:56. The great crowd pleaser that he was, George responded positively to those who encouraged him with smiles and nods. The race leader, who at this time was twelve miles in advance of him, disappointed the expectant crowd when he failed to put himself into the record books when his then current score of 116.6 was one lap shorter than the previous record for the time.

During the evening Rowell took few rests, and those that he did indulge in were short. He seemed determined to put a good distance between himself and the rest of his competitors. By the time Ennis made his century at 20:47, for which he received *"tremendous"* applause, 7,000 people were in the Garden. The band played "Kitlarney," and a basket of flowers was handed to him. The next for 100-mile honours was Merritt at 22:09, and as the figures were placed on the blackboard, all of his supporters from Massachusetts shouted themselves hoarse. He later treated them by running a lap at break neck speed. The appreciative applause had scarcely subsided when cries of "Hart! Hart!" went up after he had scored his ton at 22:15. Ennis then retired for the night at 22:27 when his stomach began to trouble him. As he moaned in his tent, Panchot celebrated his century at 22:39 and Hazael his at 22:49.

The leader's intentions were thought to be to make a big distance during the first day, so that he could take a long recuperative rest in the early hours of the second, preferably in the quiet surroundings and pollution free environment of the Ashland House which was only a block and a half away. However, Rowell made for the canvas instead on a score of 127 at 23:00, where, after he was disrobed, he was rubbed down and put to bed. Before he closed his eyes he stated that he felt "first rate" and that, had he been pushed, he could have covered 145 miles. During his last mile one punter approached Kelly and Bliss pitch at the bookmakers' stand and made a bet $5,000 at odds of a little over 5/4 that Hazael would not finish first or second. Merritt's camp, satisfied with their man's day's graft, called him in at 18 minutes after midnight.

Below is summary of some of the competitor's performances for the first day:

Rowell: Was reported as being in superb condition. He had a good appetite and there was no evidence of aches or pains. **Weston:** Had vomited on many occasions. He had initially covered the ground at five mph, but later crawled round the track at half that speed complaining incessantly about the tobacco smoke. He was described as *"fretful and nervous,"* his eyes *"wild and staring."* He took a poor diet, but was observed moving along better much

King of the Peds

later in the evening. **Guyon:** Was described as being in *"prime condition."* He was eating and working well, and he was feared by Rowell as being his main threat. **Ennis:** Expressed fears that his stomach would "go back on me," and was reported to be quite sick later. **Hazael:** Was rumoured to be refusing to follow his trainer's instructions by eating, drinking and sleeping as he liked.

After 24 hours Rowell found himself in a commanding lead of 12 miles. The little known Guyon was attracting a huge amount of bets, particularly from backers in Chicago. He had made a respectable 115 miles and *"O'Leary's dark horse,"* Hart, as the "wags" called him, who was described, *"as supple as an eel and full of go,"* was in third spot on 110 with Merritt in fourth

Of the attending crowd's behaviour for the first 24 hours, the *New York Times* reported: The first day passed without the slightest disturbance in the garden, owing, in great part to the admirable police arrangements of Capt. Williams. The crowd in the garden however was not of the kind to create disturbances. There was a large force of police present, and some of the officers were kept on duty for 24 hours on a stretch, with very short intermissions, for meals.

The scores from the 13th till the 24th hour (01:00):

HR	Rowe	Guy	Hart	Merr	Ennis	Panch	Haz	Jacks	West	Khro	Feder	Tayl
13th	77.3	72.7	69.1	61.7	74.3	63.3	67.4	60.1	62	55.6	50	60.1
14th	83.1	78	74.2	67.1	77	68.1	69	65	66.1	59.7	53.5	65.5
15th	89.3	82.4	78.4	72.1	81.2	70	Unav	68	66.1	64.3	53.5	68.7
16th	95.1	88	80.6	77.2	85.2	74	Unav	73.2	68.4	68.5	56.1	72.3
17th	101	94.4	81.1	81.7	87.2	78.4	Unav	75.7	69.5	72.1	60.6	73.2
18th	106	95.5	86.2	85.1	91.6	83	85	81.4	72	75.4	64.3	76.2
19th	111	100	90.5	90	96.1	88	85	87	77	77.6	68.5	80
20th	116	105	94.3	94.4	99.7	94.4	89.5	89.7	80.1	82.3	71.3	80
21st	121	109	98.6	99.2	100.7	96.4	Unav	Unav	Unav	Unav	Unav	80
22nd	127	113	103.2	103.4	102.6	100	100	Unav	Unav	Unav	Unav	80
23rd	127	113	107.3	108.4	102.6	100	100	Unav	Unav	Unav	Unav	80
24th	127	115	110.1	109.4	102.6	100	100	98.7	95	90.2	85.5	80

The tired and stiff looking Hazael re-entered the race around 01:00. Shortly after, Krohne took up the bit at 01:18 having been away from the circle since 23:25. Meanwhile, the *"disappointing"* Weston had made only 95 miles, and comparisons were being made to the same stage of the London match when he had mustered 123 miles. Although clearly unwell, he wasn't sufficiently poorly enough to leave the track for any length of time. He was observed carrying a small atomizer and often sprayed its contents of perfumed water into his face. There was considerable doubt that he would even make a good place and his poor show tightened Rowell's odds to 1/4. The punters flocked round the bookmaker's tables like pigeons being offered seed in Trafalgar Square. Many would stick their $40 on to make a quick ten bucks by the end of the week, but life was full of ifs and buts, and the big players steamed in on the favourite at the prospect of making some serious money. Other odds: (Placed odds to finish 1st or 2nd are in brackets): **Guyon and Hazael, 10/1 (5/1); Ennis, 25/1 (9/1); Weston, 30/1 (15/1); Hart, 40/1 (20/1); Merritt, 100/1 (10/1); Panchot and Jackson, 100/1 (50/1); Krohne, 150/1 (50/1); Taylor, 200/1 (100/1); Federmeyer, 500/1 (200/1):**

Jackson bounded back on to the stage at 02:11 after a rest of 2h.13m. Rowell returned to continue his task at 02:30 dressed in a more becoming plain outfit. He was followed firstly by Merritt, and then Guyon, who had been sleeping since 23:25. Hazael, possibly still feeling the pain in his legs, took some more time out between 02:16 and 03:10. Federmeyer, who had plodded on till 01:07, rested till 03:22 when the lonely and *"ghostly looking"* figure of the long haired Frenchman reappeared and moved himself slowly around again obviously missing the company of his wheelbarrow. *"He is a ridiculous looking creature at any time but he looks so miserable now, that he excites everybody's sympathy. He seems stiff in every joint and every motion seems to give him pain. Several of the walkers are queer specimens of humanity, but he is the queerest of all. Part of the time he wears his shirt tucked in, and part of the time he wears it out. When he wears it in, he looks like a stuffed doll, and when he wears it out he looks like a ghost on a spree."*

O'Leary decided he wanted to see his young star Hart in amongst the action, and he duly woke the lad up about 04:00 and prepared him for his re-entrance in the quest for fame and fortune. Wearing a long woollen shirt over his black velvet trunks, he ran back on at 04:06 having slumbered from 01:41. After he warmed up, he discarded his extra clothing revealing a suit of gauze and velvet. Weston, who had left the track at 00:30, and who had slept for 3h.30m, returned at 04:20 and thereafter walked and ran intermittently.

The reporter for the *National Police Gazette* wrote the following paragraph about what Hiram Jackson was getting up to at that stage of the race: A strange scene was witnessed shortly after five o'clock, Jackson, the youngest and smallest of the pedestrians, appeared on the track with a Reina Victoria in his mouth. He puffed away, and seemed to take intense comfort from his smoke. It was the finest smoke he had had for several days, and his appreciation of it was complete. Only to a smoker was the appreciation or his face significant. He fairly beamed at the weed as he twirled it between his thumb and forefinger. He let the blue smoke steal out of his mouth while his eyes were fixed up amongst the rafters, as one elated. Dan O'Leary looked in amazement at the boy, but the boy was wrapped in the contemplation of heaven, and gave no heed to the veteran's surprise. The narcotic soother had an immediate affect on his face. The careworn look that had had been noticeable entirely departed, and his face was BEAMING AND HAPPY.

An announcement to the effect that the Garden would be closed from 5 p.m. till 6 o'clock in the morning, to clean the building, had been made earlier on. That decision never happened despite the efforts of some of the police, of whom the reporter for the *Brooklyn Daily Eagle* wrote: Occasionally one of Captain Williams ornamental policemen would arouse from his graceful pose long enough to punch some snoring sleeper in the ribs with his locust, or to remind a somnolent drunkard that he would do well to seek the seclusion of his home if had one or the bracing air of the street If he had not a dwelling place.

Shortly after six o'clock, Hart had suffered stomach cramps which caused him to become dizzy and fall. It had been said that he had taken a glass of soda water from a stranger and rumours abounded that he had been poisoned. He was rushed off to his cabin where he was tended to. Feeling better, he was soon back on the tanbark going nicely enough. Peter Panchot, always an early riser due to the fact that he had to deliver the mail at home in Buffalo, had been given a good chance to recover by his attendants, and he was shaken up and sent on his way at 06:24, having caught flies since 23:27 the previous night.

Later at 08:00, there were around 200 spectators, most of them vagrants, milling around the place, amid the smell of fried beefsteak and chops. The aroma of food being cooked gave Norman Taylor, the "pie eater," an excuse to eat a hearty breakfast, which was said to make him feel slightly better. He arrived back on the scene at 09:25, and as ever carried his whip which he wrapped around his hand. Apparently, when he left for his quarters at 00:50 he had every intention of not making an appearance on the course until 05:00, due to suffering symptoms of nausea and sickness. However, his enthusiastic running effort after he had warmed up quashed the rumours that he was all *"used up"* and would as a consequence retire altogether. He also said he was very pleased with his patent stockings and buckskin and canton flannel soles, which he thought were very neat and light.

This drawing, which appeared on the front page of *Frank Leslie's Illustrated Newspaper* **is dated the 4th of October 1879. Hazael leads Jackson, Guyon and Hart.** *(Illustration no: 57)*

The giant six-foot figure of Krohne took yards and a half strides around the path, carrying a large sponge which he frequently mopped his brow and neck with. Weston meanwhile swung his arms, his ivory headed cane as ever in his hand. He didn't appear to be troubled in the least by his performance. The negative whispers from his followers showed they doubted that he cared about breaking his own record of 550 miles. There was a lot of discontent in his camp. His friends and backers were disgruntled with his lacklustre performance and there was talk that he had *"sold out,"* and was *"playing false."* The negative accusations never bothered the champion. He did his own thing, reversing his laps frequently and keeping himself refreshed with drinks of beef tea and sucking on lemons.

The track was coming in for a little criticism and was described as being quite inferior to that of the Agricultural Hall, which it was supposed to duplicate. *"The London track is much better in the quality of garden mold used and as prepared is harder than the New York path and level as a floor, while the latter is uneven, rutty and too soft on top."* Hazael said it was the worst he ever saw.

When the *"fagged out"* Federmeyer, sporting *"dull eyes blinking with weariness,"* eventually left the track on a score of 111 at 11:06, he was met at the entrance of his tent by his burly six-foot tall trainer who blocked his path. The insensitive soul attempted to push the contestant back towards the track, to the spectators' cries of "Shame, Shame!" After "Rip Van Winkle" pushed him aside, the weary "barrow man" went inside to hit the sack and was said to be asleep within seconds.

Several minutes later, and with approximately 800 souls in the audience, Rowell, who had been continually sucking at a sponge, led the men who were all on the track, with a score of 167.6. The second placed man, Guyon, as he glanced at the board knew he had a hard job on to close the gap, which was exactly 14 miles to the Englishman's advantage. Every time he passed the structure he would hurry his pace. Merritt, who wore a pink jockey cap, was seven miles or so back in third and Hazael was a couple of miles behind him. Hart was next on 138.3, Panchot on 134, Weston on 129.3, Jackson on 127.6, Ennis with 122.1, Krohne, sporting a red flannel shirt and black trunks on 116, Federmeyer on 111 and Taylor on 88.

The betting market at midday with Rowell's name not on the bookmaker's boards was: (Placed odds to finish 1st or 2nd are in brackets): **Guyon, 10/1 (1/1); Hazael, 20/1 (3/1); Merritt, 25/1 (4/1); Weston, 30/1 (8/1); Ennis, 50/1 (10/1); Hart, 50/1 (20/1); Panchot, 75/1 (30/1);Jackson and Krohne, 150/1 (50/1); Taylor, 200/1 (100/1); Federmeyer, 400/1 (150/1):**

The Garden began to slowly fill up after the clock struck twelve. The newcomers were greeted with the sight of Weston running speedily around the track, wielding his cane and tossing his head from side to side. The crowd loved it and he responded to their adulation by blowing kisses at those who cheered him along. After running a while, he heeled-and-toed and then ran again. Rowell, who had been watching him from a distance, chased after him as the crowd went mad with delight. The rest could only wish they could thrill the throng the same way, especially the "pie eater" Taylor, who looked ghastly. The poor man looked as though he was a corpse being conveyed towards a cemetery bolt upright on wheels. With his bloodless lips, pale face and dull eyes, only the coffin covering his sickly frame was missing. So much for eating pies!

At the end of 36 hours, at 13:00 Rowell had made the best time on record by one sixth of a mile, having completed 176 miles. At the same time with Weston showing impressive improvement, the bookmakers recalculated their odds and amended their boards accordingly: (Placed odds to finish 1st or 2nd are in brackets): **Guyon, 10/1 (1/1); Hazael, 25/1 (5/1); Merritt, 25/1 (3/1); Weston, 20/1 (5/1); Ennis and Hart, 50/1 (15/1); Panchot, 75/1 (30/1); Jackson and Krohne, 150/1 (50/1); Taylor, 200/1 (100/1); Federmeyer, 400/1 (150/1):** Whilst some of the punters were eyeing up the new odds at the track side, Ennis, now feeling much better, had a running race of seven laps with Hart who couldn't keep up with the man from the windy city.

During the afternoon, and indeed for several hours, Guyon led Hazael (who had scored his 150th mile at 12:24) and Rowell around the path of glory with Ennis occasionally joining on the end of the trio. The two race leaders were seen chatting at one stage about their chances of success. Meanwhile, Mr. Jackson senior was with the rest of the family and some friends urging the ailing Hiram on as he moved himself around the track chewing away at what appeared to be a piece of bark. *"His cheeks are hollow, his eyes sunken, and he looks as if he had a sudden attack of consumption."* Other "chewers" included Hart who when he got fed up of exercising his jaw, carried the quill he was gnawing at behind his ear, giving him the appearance of a *"hard worked entry clerk!"* Hazael was another one who liked to crunch away at a quill and he had a particular penchant for one of the goose type!

The second day scores from 2 a.m. in the morning till 3 p.m. in the afternoon:

HR	Rowe	Guy	Merr	Haz	Hart	Jacks	Panch	Ennis	West	Khro	Feder	Tay
25th	127	115	110	105	110.1	95	100	102.6	103.2	93.1	86	81
26th	130	117.5	110	106	110.1	95	104.2	102.6	106	96	86	81
27th	134.1	122.8	116.5	109.4	113.1	95	109.1	102.6	107.2	96.3	88.4	81
28th	138.4	126.7	120.7	114.2	117.4	101	109.1	102.6	110.2	96.3	92.3	81
29th	143.6	131.1	125.2	118.6	121.7	105.7	113.5	102.6	112	98.1	96.1	81
30th	149.3	135.3	130.5	123.7	125.6	110.5	118.6	105.2	115.3	101.3	100.1	81
31st	154	140.4	133	129.6	128.5	115.1	122.5	109.6	117.5	104.5	100.1	81
32nd	157.1	144.1	138	135.4	132.1	119.4	125.6	114.1	121.6	108.2	102.3	81
33rd	162	148.7	141.5	140.4	133.2	123.4	128.2	116.7	124.8	111.6	106.3	85
34th	166.5	152.6	145.6	143.4	137.4	128.3	133	121.2	126.6	115.3	110.5	88
35th	171.4	156	147.7	148.2	141.7	131	137	125.4	131	119.1	111.3	90
36th	176.2	159.7	152.4	150	146.1	135.6	138	130	134.7	122.3	115.4	93
37th	178.5	163.7	156.1	150.4	150.1	140.1	142	135	134.7	125.4	119.2	93
38th	183.1	168	160.2	156.4	152	145.2	145.1	140.1	137.7	127.7	123	97

The continual hisses that had followed Rowell by those who had backed others in the race had all but disappeared. Many of the clever ones who sat in the upper tier, and who had taken odds of 6/4 in favour of him recapturing the prize, shouted at him, "Go in Rowell and push ahead!" The "jolly" moved along easily and some in the crowd were already counting their winnings in their heads.

King of the Peds

Hazael persistently snapped at the fast walking Ennis's heels, which the American didn't like. In response, every now and then, he tried to break free from the Briton's attentions by breaking into a fast run; but after his attempts proved futile, he gave up. Hazael then diverted his attention to his compatriot Rowell, employing the same dogging tactics on him.

The race leader, who had made 188 miles by 17:00, was followed by Guyon on 175 and Merritt on 167. Weston, who had made 150 at the time, was behind both Hazael and Hart. With all the rest going pretty well, Panchot limped out of his cabin. He was joined on the course by Taylor who re-appeared wearing shoes. The pie-man was still on the verge of making his century. The crowd held its breath and *waited and waited*.

As the clock struck the hour of six, with Merritt continuing to wear his pink jockey cap and Jackson rejoining the action, Ennis quickly walked passed the two British performers who raced along together. This move inspired Panchot, who stoked up his engine room and injected more power into his action. Taylor joined in the chase and Weston, never wanting to be the party pooper, hit the gas pedal. The fun continued for a few minutes as all had a jolly good time sprinting round the circle. The frenzy was all too much for Panchot whose face said it all. He'd had enough and fell back into his former slow walk. As the rest eventually slowed down, Taylor continued to sprint, keeping the attention of the crowd, until he saw the number 100 on his dial at 18:23. After that, and after adding two more laps, the old fellow trundled back to his house, giving the inspired spectators a chance to give their sore palms and hoarse voices a well deserved rest.

Krohne was likened to a *"blue heron, whose movement is that of a jumping jack,"* and who, *"continues to stride around the ellipse in four or five steps. He was no doubt sent to this world as a sample of the most awkward man that could be created. There are times when his long legs get twisted into knots that it seen impossible for anybody but a sailor to untie them. He has not done very much, and is too old and ugly to receive any sympathy from the ladies."* He was said to be in good condition. The lameness which affected him during the early part of the day had disappeared and he had steadily piled up the miles. However, when he had made 138.7, and with some evidence that he wasn't quite himself, he left the path.

At 18:30, Guyon caused quite a stir in the crowd as he walked along at a good rate with the two Englishmen trotting along in his wake. Rowell was now nearing his 200th mile, and when he completed it on a run at 19:19, he fairly shook the rafters. He was then 15 miles ahead of Guyon, 27.2 ahead of Merritt, 28.2 ahead of Hazael, 31.2 ahead of Hart, 37.6 ahead of Weston, 41.7 ahead of Ennis, 45.2 ahead at Panchot, 51.4 ahead of Jackson, 57.3 ahead of Krohne, 64 miles ahead of Federmeyer, and 99.6 ahead of Taylor. Since the completion of his first hundred miles he had gained 8 miles and 1 lap on Guyon, 7.6 on Merritt, 11.4 on Hazael, 11.7 on Hart, 6.5 on Weston, 23.2 on Panchot, 24 miles on Federmeyer, 26 miles on Krohne, 27.2 on Jackson, 27.6 on Ennis, and 72.7 on Taylor.

As the excitement grew in the building, many outside who couldn't afford the $1 admission tried any which way they could to gain entrance. The *New York Times* revealed some of the strategies employed to see the race: In the early part of the evening a man standing in of the upper circular windows on that side of the building let down a rope, and it was soon filled with climbing boys. A policeman appeared, and the man let the rope drop. It was a wonder that some of the boys were not seriously injured, as two or three of them fell from a height of nearly 20 feet. This gave the crowd a hint and there were many efforts to climb up the door casings and water drains. The ascent was too much for most of the youngsters, but at length one lot succeeded in getting into one of the lower windows. In the meantime the employees of the Garden had, as one of the crowd expressed it, "tumbled to the racket" and the agility with which the interloper darted out again was proof that a sharp stick had been in waiting for him. Soon afterward somebody discovered that one of the coal covers was unfastened. Twelve or thirteen boys quickly let themselves down, and then a joker put on the cover. For half an hour the yells and pleads of the imprisoned lads afforded intense amusement to the assembled thousands.

Back in the building, George Guyon was heard to quip, "That beats my record!" as he passed the dials which had the number 188 next to his name at 20:30. Just before nine o'clock, "Blower" Brown appeared on the track and presented Frank Hart with a crimson and white bordered silk handkerchief. When questioned about the gift, Brown said, "They're my colours," and of Hart, "I never saw him before, but he's plucky and I like him." Hart was also presented with a handsome bouquet by a pretty young lady called Miss Muller, along with many other tributes which he constantly carried around with him. With all the walking and carrying, the young man needed to keep his strength up. Englehardt, his trainer, reported that he had eaten nearly a pound of raw minced beef for his supper. O'Leary said that he had not entered Hart into the match to "dog" Rowell. Krohne meanwhile, raised a few eyebrows when he indulged in a run which as expected, didn't last long.

Weston had been attracting attention to himself all evening by pulling silly faces at the crowd and generally acting like an unruly child. At one point, he knocked Mr. Atkinson's hat clean off his head as he was walking past him. He eventually went off at 21:54 after completing 173.1. He announced that after his present rest he would commence running, stating that he would run continuously to the end of the race and avoid walking altogether. Federmeyer now competed, having cut about a foot off the length of his hair. Panchot, who had left the track at 19:08 on his 164th mile, was so much disturbed by the noise in the building that he left the Garden and went to sleep at a hotel. A number of lively races occurred thereafter between Merritt, Ennis, Guyon and Hazael, who had obviously something wrong with him. With his left foot troubling him, George walked along rather stiffly in a certain degree of pain, wearing only his right shoe, his left foot enclosed in a strong stocking.

At 22:00, and with about 5,000 or so at the venue, the police were busy outside clearing the streets of those who loitered and consequently blocked the streets around the place while waiting for the news of the race inside.

Rowell went off at 22:56. At 23:30, Guyon scored his 200th mile and five minutes later went to bed. He was now just 15 miles behind the race leader. Merritt, who went to his couch after making 193 miles just before midnight, was summoned back on to the track by his trainers to take on Hart, who was after his second place and running in fine form on a clear track. The two battled it out for a while and Ennis reappeared to do some good running about the same time.

The 2nd day scores from 4 p.m. in the afternoon (being the 39th hour); to 2 a.m. in the morning (being the 49th hour) with *laps omitted*:

HR	Rowe	Guy	Merr	Hart	Haz	Ennis	West	Jacks	Khro	Panch	Fede	Tay
39th	187	171	164	157	160	141	148	141	132	148	124	97
40th	188	175	167	161	161	146	150	143	135	149	128	97
41st	193	179	167	166	165	151	157	144	138	152	131	97
42nd	197	183	170	167	169	156	161	147	140	154	135	100
43rd	202	186	175	172	174	161	164	150	145	154	138	100
44th	206	190	180	177	176	163	170	154	149	154	140	100
45th	211	194	184	181	176	166	173	155	154	154	142	100
46th	215	197	188	185	180	171	173	159	157	154	146	100
47th	215	200	193	189	184	175	173	160	160	154	149	100
48th	215	200	197	193	186	180	173	160	160	154	150	100
49th	215	200	200	198	186	185	173	160	160	154	150	100

Many of the men had had a decent rest during the night. Rowell came back on at 01:21, Guyon at 01:51, Panchot returned at 04:18 and Weston at 06:49. Ennis only took brief breaks during the early hours of the third day.

Off and on times for rest: **Taylor**, 18:30 till 08:33; **Hazael**, 23:30 till 02:14; **Krohne**, 23:35 till 02:10; **Jackson**, 23:30 till 02:29; **Federmeyer**, 00:24 till 02:48; **Merritt**, 01:37 till 03:50; and **Hart**, 02:29 till 05:34:

With very few people watching the unfolding saga in the track, there was little atmosphere in the Garden as dawn broke. Many of those using the building as a doss house would have been woken up by the army of *"colored"* cleaners wearing bandana head dresses and armed with hot water, soap, and scrubbing brushes which they used to attack the filthy seats, benches and rubbish laden floors. The invasion gave a few spectators an excuse to view the men's tents, where they would they stand and gawp at the huge floral gifts which surrounded them. Horseshoes and stars were the main themes on offer along with the usual baskets, bouquets and wreaths. The popular *"copper faced darkey,"* Frank Hart, was one of the main recipients, as was Rowell. In fact, the leader had accepted an ornamental six-foot high floral cross surmounted by a star upon which was inscribed his initials from his fellow guests at the Ashland House only the night before. Many of the other runners received their fair share too. Only Weston, Taylor and Hazael, described as the ugliest of those taking part, were neglected. The Londoner seemed to revel in his appearance, and was indifferent to any negative banter thrown his way in relation to how he looked.

King of the Peds

The outside temperature had fallen and there was a steady drizzle as the cleaners went about their work; the daylight becoming more intense as it made its presence felt through the apertures of the roof and along the walls. The disgusting stench of stale tobacco smoke crept out of the place and all the athletes welcomed the clean fresh air as it penetrated their lungs.

The band was summoned into action resuming its concert of well worn ditties in an attempt to inject a bit of fun into the place. The men on the track appreciated their efforts, especially Hazael, who forged ahead of "Black Dan." A well dressed young lady who had too much to drink caused a stir annoying her fellow spectators by lavishly bestowing applause on the men on the track and then having a go at those who jeered at her with some *"choice"* language. Captain Williams, the hard man that he was, took a dim view of her behaviour and promptly had her taken away to the station house to sleep it all off.

Whilst the leader traversed the path at a steady 5 mph, the back-markers 14-hour festival of sleep didn't appear to help him. When he returned to continue his effort, he simply crawled round at less than half the pace of the leader. Taylor had spent the night in a local hotel and had told one of the scorers he feared one of his ankles had been sprained. However, many thought he wouldn't last out until the end of the race and that he would retire in the next day or two. *"I am going to make 300 miles if I can, and that will be creditable for the first trial,"* he said.

Weston was the complete opposite to the "pie eater." His nine hours of rest appeared to have perked him up considerably and he maintained the same speed as the day before. However, it was later learned that he had hardly slept and was mad with himself for being so far behind. *"His backers were disgusted at his failure to make an effort and complained that they had been "skinned." Weston walked around the track with a grin upon his weazened face and indulged in all sorts of flippant extravagances. He drank enough ginger ale on the track in the forenoon to satisfy the most ardent of teetotalers for a month."*

Guyon, *"the favorite of the ladies and the shapeliest man in the ring"* looked *"pucker"* on his reappearance and some in his team insisted he would eventually be ahead of Rowell. His backers were more cautious after witnessing his steady heel-and-toe gait, stating they were hopeful he would make second place. His trainer reported his appetite was good.

Although appearing *"used up,"* young Hiram Jackson continued to maintain his good record. Hazael ran continually on his return and was making excellent progress in his pursuit of reducing the gap between himself and his opposite in the beauty stakes, Guyon. The friendless Cockney started to run just before seven o'clock and went on to score six miles between then and 08:00, at which time he had made 208. He then passed Hart on his 210th mile and thus went into fourth place.

Despite being relegated to fifth, Hart was pleasing his trainer, O'Leary who was now oozing confidence that his protégé, who was walking along rapidly at 5 mph, would make a good place. Earlier in the morning he took Frank to a Turkish bath where he had him rubbed down. The gangly German, Krohne, having only rested three hours during the night, plodded along relentlessly, never running, always walking. Panchot, who had been suffering with painful blistered and lacerated feet, showed great bravery in running many laps after sunrise.

While Rowell "dogged" Guyon, "Honest" John Ennis claimed his 200th mile at 09:42 at a rattling pace to the strains of "Yankee Doodle." *"He kept on his way with a steady, determined tread, his eyes fixed squarely in front of him, seeing nothing but the track and the scores."* Rowell was literally miles ahead of the Irishman, and at 09:56, produced a positive and very noisy response from the crowd which was said to *"shake the building"* when the board man placed the number 250 next to his name. *"He seemed as vigorous as ever but there was not so much color in his face as yesterday, and his eyes were sunken and encircled by black rings."*

The betting shows at 10:00: (Placed odds to finish 1st or 2nd are in brackets): **Guyon, 7/1 (1/1); Hazael, 15/1 (5/2); Merritt, 30/1 (2/1); Weston, 50/1 (10/1); Hart, 70/1 (8/1); Ennis, 100/1 (15/1); Krohne, 200/1 (100/1); Jackson and Panchot, 500/1 (100/1); Federmeyer and Taylor, 1,000/1 (500/1):**

The "pie eater" astonished the crowd at 10:30 by actually running! His decision to do so reverberated around the track, and soon all the men, including Krohne, joined in the dash which lasted 15 minutes or so. Guyon continued walking until 10:49, when, on a score of 234 and 7, he went to his tent for a well deserved break. George Hazael continued to impress, and earlier, between nine and ten o'clock, assembled another seven miles. By 11:00 he had credited himself with 222 miles and the bookies stands were being inundated with punters eager to back the lively "limey" at place odds of 2/1.

Ennis was soon back in his tent feeling unwell. Hart too was under the weather and he spent a lot of time with his trainer in his tent. Weston appeared a little lame. He was observed carrying a piece of ice which he occasionally sucked at or rubbed his wrist with. Merritt however was going really well, and at 11:29, and carrying a sponge to mop a temporarily bleeding nose, he was only six laps behind Guyon. The usual noisy accolade was offered by the crowd when he passed the sleeping Chicagoan's score. As a result, the bookies tightened Merritt's price in from 30/1 to 25/1. Guyon drifted out four points to 11/1 and Hazael's price was pushed out to 20/1 from 15/1. The bookies were not impressed with Ennis's chances and they responded by knocking out his price to 75/1 whilst Hart was on offer at 60/1. Rowell's name however, was not seen on the boards. 1/5 had been taken by the punters and the bookies were cursing themselves for being so generous.

The gritty Brit, Hazael, *"looking neither to the right, nor to the left as he ran along, his head bowed and his eyes fixed upon the track,"* put in three quick miles in astonishing times of 6m.37s, 6m.43s and 6m.55s just after midday. Guyon, who had reappeared at 12:01, and Merritt, with *"his thin face as calm as a summer pool,"* battled it out for second place. At 12:27, they were level pegging whilst the band responded to Krohne's 200th and Rowell's 260th miles by playing "Hail to the Chief." As the crowd shouted themselves silly, the eccentric figure of Weston smiled, bowed and waved his cane at them as he too broke the 200-mile barrier 13 minutes later. Panchot rejoined the race at 12:30 after he had gone back in before noon to rest his poorly feet. However, on his return, he continued to suffer, and hobbled along the sawdust much as before.

The betting shows at 14:00: (Placed odds to finish 1st or 2nd are in brackets): **Merritt, 10/1 (1/2); Guyon and Hazael, 15/1 (5/2); Weston, 50/1 (25/1); Hart, 70/1 (7/1); Ennis, 100/1 (15/1); Krohne, 200/1 (100/1); Jackson and Panchot, 500/1 (100/1); Federmeyer and Taylor, 1,000/1 (500/1):**

The third say scores from 3 a.m. in the morning; (being the 50th hour) to 2 p.m. in the afternoon (being the 61st hour):

HR	Rowe	Merr	Guy	Haz	Hart	Ennis	Khro	West	Jacks	Panch	Fede	Tay
50th	217.7	200.1	200.4	188.6	200	189.7	163.7	173.1	162.1	154.6	150	100
51st	222.3	200.7	204.5	193.7	200	189.7	167.2	173.1	165	154.6	155.1	100
52nd	226.7	205.3	208	198.1	200	190.6	170.7	173.1	169.1	158.4	159.3	100
53rd	231.2	209.4	212.5	200	201.2	193.6	175.7	173.1	173	163.1	162	100
54th	235.7	214.1	217.2	202.4	205.1	193.6	179	173.7	176	166	164.6	100
55th	240.5	218.6	222.1	208.3	208.7	194	182.5	178.4	180.4	169.3	169.3	100
56th	245.3	222.7	228.2	215.2	212.3	197	186.7	183.5	185	175	174	102
57th	250.2	227.4	231.1	219.5	216.5	201	189.7	187.6	186.6	178.1	176	105
58th	255	232.1	234.7	222	218.6	203.4	194.5	192.3	190	183.4	178.6	108
59th	259.2	235.5	234.7	224	222.7	205.2	198	198.5	193.6	185	183.1	110
60th	260.1	239	238.6	230.2	226.7	206.7	201.4	201	197.4	187.4	184.1	115
61st	263.2	243.3	242.5	235.3	231.2	211	205.1	203.2	200.1	189.1	186.4	117

Panchot went on to secure his double century after three o'clock, and Weston, who had earlier only been a mile or so up on the smallest pedestrian on the course, Jackson, ran much better than he walked. However, his eccentric behaviour displayed by his constant habit of reversing was a cause of concern for his trainers and the spectators, who thought he was a bit of a *"fruitcake."* He had also earned a reputation for himself as being *"off his nut."*

With some 6,000 encircling the ring in the early evening at 18:00, nine of the men were busy wobbling around the path. A number of bouquets were showered upon the pedestrians, including a floral horseshoe which was handed to Hart bearing the inscription "Go it Black Dan" in purple immortelles upon a bed of white carnations.

Weston went on to astonish everyone in the building at 18:50. Having circled the track slowly for a long time, he suddenly burst into life and covered a mile in six minutes! For his achievement he was roundly applauded. He stopped to acknowledge the praise, reversed his course, and then walked along the track like *"a man thoroughly broken down."* Picking himself up, he was soon running again before altering his gait to walking, then back to running for which he was cheered. Hart, noticing the reaction of the crowd, decided to stalk the "entertainer" with an unlit cigarette in his mouth. Ever the complainer, Weston trudged off the track and complained to the referee who ruled Hart should discard the offending article. Weston was greeted back with generous applause as the band offered another rendition of "Hail to the Chief" and the champion set off running again.

Of the scenes outside, the *New York Times* made the following observations: **All day long the streets in the neighborhood of Madison Square Garden were filled with loiterers, and every approach to the building was surrounded by crowds of gaping boys and men, who looked as if they would pawn the clothes they wore if they could but pass the vigilant doorkeeper. These persons inclined to talk about the "outrage" of charging the public a dollar merely to see a dozen men.**

Inside, there were queues of thirsty people half a dozen rows deep lining the bars trying to get served, and *"beer was flowing out of the kegs like water out of a broken Croton pipe."* The alcohol fuelled atmosphere didn't cause Captain Williams any bother however, and the men under his command reduced their efforts to stopping people lighting up on the first floor where smoking was prohibited.

At 8 p.m., and continuing to keep up his good lead, Rowell had made 290.4. This score left him just 9½ miles behind "Blower" Brown's best time on record. The strenuous efforts of his opponents failed to close the gap, and at 20:30 he had a massive lead of 25 miles over Merritt. Weston moved around the track at a blistering pace and was said to care more for gaining applause from his occasional bursts of speed than for decreasing the nearly 60-mile gap between himself and Rowell. At 20:50, the Englishman went for a short nap, and while he dozed, another beautiful floral tribute consisting of a star of flowers resting in a basket with the word "Rowell" worked in white on a blue background was left outside his tent. Again it was from the Ashland House.

Some 13,000 people were present and they were screaming themselves stupid as Hazael got nearer and nearer to catching Guyon. The noise was deafening as both men ran two laps level pegging, but then on the 6th lap of the 269th mile, Hazael won the argument to move into the third spot. As Guyon left the track disgusted with himself, the Londoner stuck his head down and went after Merritt, who was four miles further up the road. The constant clapping of hands and stamping of feet continued up to the point when Rowell scored his 300th mile at 21:51. When he did it and the number was pinned up, the place went barmy, and with the band playing "God Save the Queen," Rowell ran eight laps of honour. *"The deafening cheer that shook the building was taken up by the outside crowd and carried around the block like a whirlwind,"* the leader's effort being second only to Brown's London record of 307.7 laps in 72 hours.

Ennis, who had left the track at 16:04, had not returned until ten o'clock, owing to suffering from nausea, and it was thought he was out of the race. Guyon who retired after completing his 270th mile, was said to *"take stimulants freely."* Taylor attracted attention when he carried a pie around in his hand.

At eleven o'clock, the 70th hour since the start, Weston was 57 miles behind his London record and Rowell was nearly 30 miles ahead of his own record when he last won the belt. The smoke in the building was so thick that it was difficult to see to the far side of the track, causing Weston to feel sick to his stomach. He promptly left for his house, but did make another half-hearted appearance five minutes later as the band played "The Swannee River." He initially bounded on to the track, but soon gave up the ghost due to the effects of the smoke which descended from the galleries unable to escape into the cold night air due to the skylights being closed.

The lingering smoke gave the perfect cover for the pick pockets to ply their trade. Captain Williams deployed his men in an effort to thwart their progress in the murk but the Garden was so packed that he had difficulty keeping the crowd safe from the criminals.

At 23:30, Hart put on a strong burst of speed walking, *"swinging his arms from side to side as his body swerved."* For his efforts he received much applause, hurrahs and yet more bouquets. Weston also got a good hand when he made his 250th mile at running pace at 23:38. Hart accomplished 270 miles at 23:45 equalling the sleeping Guyon's score, and as a result moved, into fourth place.

Rowell had already arranged to spend three hours in bed at his hotel. However, his trainers had told him that to earn this little luxury they wanted him to make 310 miles before midnight, which would be a new record for three days. The gutsy athlete set to work to earn his reward, and with five minutes to spare before the allocated time, he needed just two more laps. With visions of a comfy bed waiting to be occupied, the little fellow sped on and achieved his goal at 23:58. He was afforded the usual accolade on completion of his objective, and having their thirst for excitement satisfactorily quenched, many spectators started to leave the building in their droves.

Here are some details of some tallied up rest periods during the day: **Rowell, 1h.13m.55s; Hazael, 3h.23m; Weston, 2h.2m.50s; Federmeyer; 3h.48m:**

The third day scores from 3 p.m. in the afternoon (being the 62nd hour); to 1 a.m. in the morning (being the 72nd hour):

HR	Rowe	Merrit	Haz	Hart	Guyon	West	Khro	Jacks	Fede	Ennis	Pan	Tay
62nd	268.2	247.5	239.4	235.3	243.5	208.5	207.3	203.7	189	213.1	197.6	121
63rd	272.2	250.6	244.2	239.1	248.4	213.5	211.5	208.6	191.3	215.4	197.7	124
64th	277.4	255.2	246.1	243	253	218.7	213.6	212.7	193.2	219.5	201.7	127
65th	282	258.7	251.6	247.4	257.4	223.5	217.3	217.4	197.5	220	203.7	130
66th	286.2	263.5	254.3	250.4	260	228.4	221.6	219.7	201.6	220	205.1	132
67th	290.4	267.4	260	255	263.2	233.7	224.3	222.2	205.5	220	205.1	136
68th	293.7	270.3	265.5	258.6	266.6	238.4	227.7	226.3	209.6	220	205.1	138
69th	300.7	274.7	270.7	262.7	270	241.6	231.3	229.7	211.1	220	205.1	143
70th	305.1	279.2	275.2	266.4	270	246.3	233.7	229.7	214.5	220	205.1	145
71st	310	282.7	276	271	270	251.1	233.7	230.2	218.4	220	205.1	150
72nd	310	287	276	272.7	270	251.1	233.7	230.2	220.6	220	205.1	150

As early as 01:00 the next day, and having not been seen on the track since the previous evening, Panchot on a score of 205.1, sent word to the judges that he had quit the race due to the dreadful condition of his feet. At 02:35, Hazael rushed out of his tent and challenged Hart to a race. Despite appeals from O'Leary to avoid the confrontation, the pupil ignored his teacher and engaged the Englishman in a speedy duel. This lasted for several laps until the exhausted Bostonian fell in a heap on the ground. His attendants rushed to his aid, carried him to his house, dosed him with stimulants, and rubbed him down. It was later ascertained that he had given his ankle a severe twist.

Off and on times for the remaining contestants: **Ennis,** 17:06 till 02:07; **Guyon,** 22:55 till 03:53; **Hazael,** 23:10 till 02:29; **Weston,** 23:51 till 03:38 (Was said to have slept well); **Rowell,** 23:57 till 02:11 (Stayed at the Ashland House); **Taylor,** 00:00 till 07:52; **Merritt,** 00:54 till 03:04; **Federmeyer,** 12:25 till 03:07; **Hart,** 02:50 till 04:35:

Word from John Ennis's camp indicated that he was now over his stomach problems and was expected to go well from there on. Ennis told the press that since the race began he had *"felt badly,"* and that on Monday and Tuesday night he had been unable to sleep due to the noise from both the crowd and the band. Following advice from his wife and physician, he went to a hotel where he slept well. "My physician declares that my stomach is stubborn, and if it had not been for that I would have won the race." As his wife watched from his tent, her husband bravely moved himself forward in a determined manner, occasionally running rapidly. She never failed to check his progress every time he passed the scorers' stand.

In a general report about the progress of the race, the *Brooklyn Daily Eagle attempted* to explain how the scorers at the Garden tallied up the laps and miles: The manner in which THE SCORE SHEETS are kept is a source of general complaint. The official timekeeper sits in the centre, and half the score sheets are kept on one side of him and half on the other. They are kept in an entirely different manner, and there is an hour's difference in their way of recording. For instance, on one side when a man quits the track say at 11 o'clock he is recorded as going off at 10 o'clock and on the other side the actual time is recorded. The reason of it is that on one side they counted the day commencing at 1 A.M. on last Monday and on the other they began it from 12 o'clock. This leads to the greatest possible confusion.

King of the Peds

It then went on to inform its readers about what happened to Hiram Jackson: **Another to instruct the judges to place the word "Withdrawn," over his name was Hiram Jackson at 07:49. There had been much sympathy for him as he struggled round in obvious distress suffering from raw and blistered feet. The ointment and liniment that had been previously administered to his blisters had initially removed them but he was then to be troubled with sore ankles. At 02:00, he had gone to his room to be worked on by his "rubbers," and came back out 24 minutes later. After that he walked along and rested for short periods until 05:10 and his 231st mile. On a score of 232, his father walked over to the scores stand and said, "I guess I'll have to take my boy out." Young Hiram was later observed in the crowd watching the race at 09:30 dressed in street costume and wearing a heavy overcoat and muffler. He was later whisked away to a hotel to recover. When asked about his condition, he told reporters he had had problems with his feet caused by his shoes and sought a solution by wearing a new pair which inevitably chafed his ankles making every step excruciatingly painful.**

The band celebrated George Guyon's third century at 09:47 with the 20th rendition of "Yankee Doodle" during the entire contest. The number of times that was played easily beat "Captain Jinks" which was aired 15 times, "Rocky Road to Dublin" 5 times, "Hail to the Chief" three times, and "God save the Queen" once. However, all of them were eclipsed in the music stakes by "Pop Goes the Weasel" which had been blasted out on forty occasions, along with many repeats of "Pinafore" numbers.

Some nasty rumours were circulating around the building to the effect that O'Leary and Panchot were to challenge the winner of the present contest, in order to keep up interest in a similar forthcoming event, in an attempt to increase the gate money. *"Weston's ridiculous antics on the track were said to be part of the same scheme which also involved the present race managers and some of the principal pedestrians. He is a very nervous man, and every trifle worries him. He did not look well in the morning, although he continues his antics which have been called kittenish, but are much more monkeyish. His face was pinched and sallow. He chews a great deal of ice and gargles his throat with cold water which he slobbers all over himself, soon ruining the clean linen in which he frequently appears. He has no more chance of winning the race than Taylor has, but he keeps on smiling as ever."* Indeed, at 10 a.m., Weston was involved with Hazael in one of the best spurts seen in the contest, during which they passed, and re-passed each other in an 8-furlong sprint. George eventually beat Eddy who later tossed a cup he had been sipping from on the ground when he saw someone in the crowd smoking a cigar. That sort of behaviour was unusual for the champ as he usually shook his cane in disgust at the offenders.

The mid-morning betting with no price for Weston: (Placed odds to finish 1st or 2nd are in brackets): **Hazael and Merritt, 20/1 (4/6); Hart, 30/1 (5/1); Guyon, 35/1 (6/1); Ennis, 100/1 (50/1); Krohne, 500/1 (125/1); Federmeyer and Taylor, 1,000/1 (500/1):**

At 11 a.m., 82 hours into the game, the leader was on a score of 345.3. At the same hour, and during Weston's win in London, Brown and Weston were within a lap of each other on a mark of 346.2 and 346.1 respectively.

Hart, who had returned to the track just before 05:00, was suffering with the effects of his sprained ankle. The lad's face was said to be distorted with pain, and O'Leary was concerned the boy would lose his deposit. However, O'Leary worked hard on his protégés foot and sent him out again. It was soon evident that he had done a good job as Frank moved around the place in less discomfort.

Hazael though was really going for it, and while he did the business, Merritt was glancing over his shoulder nervously. The lanky Yankee decided he would take a break at 11:45, and while he had his legs up on his couch he was given the news that the plucky Briton was within five laps of him. His trainer shoved him out of his tent and on to the path, but it was hopeless to expect his man to make any immediate impression. "Make no mistake about him," said Mr. Leslie Bruce, the chief of the scorers, "he will be here Saturday night and in a good place too." *"Merritt showed a good color in his face and a comfortable expression in his eyes."* The tall American wore a little, black silk cap, a clean white shirt, blue trunks, white tights and was the picture of neatness.

Hazael on the other hand presented an altogether disreputable appearance. Sporting close-cropped hair, his flushed perspiring face exhibited an unsightly growth of stubble on his chin. He was said to stand up *"in pugilistic fashion"* like a *"stiff brush."* The white flannel shirt and brown drawers he performed in were evidently filthy, the only bit of colour showing through the grime being a pair of green trunks that appeared far too small for him. *"Hazael does not change in appearance, but he runs with as much ease at least as at the start. Indeed as far as his appearance goes, there could not be any great change in him for the worse. If he would lie down flat on his face and have a few tons of old iron piled on his stooping shoulders, to straighten him out, he would have more the appearance of a human being. He would hardly be a representative of England to be proud of in case he should win the belt. He is said to have a sore foot and to suffer from some terrible, mysterious disease, but nobody know what is and it is altogether probable that it exists principally in somebody's mind."* The race was on……………

Hazael continually flew past Merritt, and finally at 12:06 the writing was on the wall for Sam as George took second place amid the usual hullabaloo. The race's ugly ducklings wings had flown him an astonishing 31 miles and 3 laps during the six hours before midday, causing the heavily perspiring Rowell and his backers to get nervous. In response to Hazael's profitable exertions, the race leader increased his pace from his jog-trot to a speedier gait, and then began to try to dog his fellow countryman, which didn't work as Hazael was simply too fast for him. Whilst all this was going on, Rowell had made his 350th mile at 11:55 and the noise made by the crowd due to the race for second place was said to startle the leader. Sullivan, Hazael's trainer said, "Hazael will take first place if he can get it you know; the reason he won't be first will be because he can't."

The fourth day scores from 2 a.m. (being the 73rd hour); till noon (being the 83rd hour):

HR	Rowe	Merrit	Haz	Guy	Hart	West	Khro	Ennis	Fede	Jacks	Tay
73rd	310	287	276	270	276	251	233	223	220	230	150
74th	310	287	279.3	275.2	279.5	251	237	228.1	220.1	231.2	150.3
75th	314.1	290.7	281.3	279.2	279.5	252.6	241.1	232.2	223.1	231.2	150.3
76th	318.1	295.1	286	283.3	279.5	256	242.3	237.4	224.2	232.1	150.3
77th	322.7	299.3	291.2	286.5	281	256	245.3	241	225.4	232.1	150.3
78th	327.2	302.6	295.7	289.3	282.3	259.4	250.2	244.2	229.5	232.1	150.3
79th	333	306.7	300	292.6	285.5	264.4	253.2	248.1	234	Withd	150.7
80th	336.4	311.2	304.7	296.6	289.2	269.2	257.2	251.7	238.1		154.7
81st	341.3	315.4	310.1	300	291.6	273.7	260.1	256	240.2		158.5
82nd	345.3	319.7	316	303.4	294.6	278.5	262.6	258.3	244		161.1
83rd	350.4	322.4	322.3	308.2	298	283.2	265.6	263.5	247.2		161.2

There was a little amusement on offer after twelve o'clock when Weston, ever the attention seeker, stopped next to the score dials and put up the figures of 364 miles instead of 164 next to the name of Norman Taylor. As the back-marker walked passed them, some spectators shouted out to him to look at his score, but ignoring their taunts, he continued on his way with many in the audience giggling at his response. Even the clean shaven Rowell was seen to have a crafty chuckle at the sight.

Merritt was relieved to see Hazael go to his den for a well earned rest. With the brave Brit sleeping, the tired and listless American was able to reconnect with second spot. "Go it, Merritt, you're the hope of the country," somebody shouted at him as he passed the scorers' stand.

Rowell went to his cabin at 13:30 on a mark of 357.5 and had a snack. He was said to have a *"fierce appetite"* and ate fruit, fish, oysters and meat in liberal quantities as well as drinking copious amounts of beef tea. When the peds weren't eating indoors they ate on the track, from little dishes which were shaped like gravy bowls that had long thin spouts which could be drank from without spilling the contents all over themselves.

Meanwhile, Hart continued to limp away on his sore ankle, whilst the retired Panchot slept blissfully in the Putnam House, oblivious to the drama he had left behind (Panchot's tent was taken down giving race-goers better views of the track, as Jackson's tent was being investigated by the curious). The punters who had wagered on Hart were dejectedly cursing themselves as they watched him *"crawling around the track at a snail's pace. His lips were bloodless, his eyes dim, and his limbs trembled beneath him at every step."* Fred Englehardt, his assistant trainer, and his backer O'Leary, decided to call in the suffering youth at 13:15. They helped him to his bed which he fell on after entering his tent. They had tried to encourage him to do more and had given him a diet of beef tea and cocoa, but his problem wasn't his stomach, more his foolish "brush" with Hazael earlier in the morning, which had strained the muscles in his leg.

King of the Peds

News from the betting ring around mid afternoon was that there were no takers of Rowell's odds of 1/4. The bookmakers knew that Rowell seemed invincible and was going to be a tough nut to crack, and as a consequence, refused to take bets on the rock solid favourite: (Placed odds to finish 1st or 2nd are in brackets): **Rowell, 1/4: Hazael, 10/1; Merritt, 15/1 (1/2); Guyon, 25/1 (6/1); Weston, 25/1 (4/1); Hart, 30/1 (5/1); Ennis, 100/1 (25/1); Krohne, 100/1 (50/1); Federmeyer and Taylor, 1,000/1 (250/1):** The only changes to the betting later were Merritt's and Guyon's odds being pushed out to 25/1 and 40/1 respectively. Many of the other outsiders also took a walk in the market.

The expectation was that Rowell would win the race and take a purse of $25,000 back home to England with him. As the fans of the sport headed towards the great building for the evening entertainment, they were full of eager expectation. Many had worked hard to save up for the $1 admission price, but it was a price worth paying. They also knew that that their contribution to the final gate money would probably end up across the water in Europe.

There was a lot of anger being directed at Weston. Nobody but the present champion himself could see the point of him constantly reversing and thus wasting time and distance. The least expected of him was to come fifth or sixth and maybe save his stake money. The man himself arrived back in the ring at 18:10 and raised a few claps which he acknowledged by raising his whip. Smiling and jerking his shoulders, he immediately challenged the passing Rowell to a race and the offer was taken up by the leader who chased after him. Rowell overtook him and the pair sped round to the delight of the gathered. The band tooted "Tommy Dodd" and Weston responded with a lively effort. The two men kept it going for 3 laps, and then the inevitable happened as "Ned" stopped at the line, reversed, and continued his effort by walking. As he came face to face with the running Rowell on the other side of the path, Rowell saluted him military style and Weston responded by again raising his whip.

At about 18:40, Hazael, on a score of 348.7, and now with his eyes on the runner-up position, began to run slowly. To accomplish his objective, he had to get past Merritt who was two laps in advance of him. Catching him up on the bend, Hazael quickened up nicely and effortlessly overtook him. Ten minutes later he equalled his score. Two laps followed with the men in close proximity, but eventually the Briton prevailed and moved comfortably into a lead of two laps, leaving the shattered American looking second rate in his rear.

At 19:20, Rowell, Ennis and Guyon also *"got the fever"* and joined the second placed man in a spurt; all four spurting round abreast while the band played their respects to Queen Victoria. Rowell won the race after three laps of capital effort, and then on a score of 386.6 settled down to his familiar gait. By that time Hazael had put almost two miles between him and the resting Merritt. Those on the track who took no part in the spurt included Hart, *"the best walker on the track,"* and the indifferent Weston, who had been walking in the opposite direction *"swinging his arms and jerking his head nervously"* as the quartet thundered around. At the end of his lap, Weston left the arena at 19:31 returning ten minutes later, to an enthusiastic response from the crowd which clearly humbled him. As "Tommy Dodd" blared out again, Eddy responded with a run as Hart, egged on by even louder cheers, chased after him.

News from the attendants of the *"Adonis"* indicated that not only were Guyon's feet a mass of blisters, but his legs were also very sore. This meant that he was hauled off on a regular basis to have his dressings renewed, the interventions taking between 20 and 30 minutes.

In front of 10,000 souls, half of which apparently smoked, and with thousands said to be milling about outside, Ennis went on to make his 300th mile in a time of 7m.58s. At 20:15, and on a score of 299.1 as he was passing the scores stand, a friend shouted out, "Now go it Ennis!" The athlete broke into a brisk run and helped by the noise of "Yankee Doodle," he completed the needed seven laps in 6m.30s. The foundations of the building once again shook as the three centuries were recorded on his dial; the spectators going positively delirious with delight. Ennis then slowed down to a walk and everyone calmed down.

Forty-five minutes later, Rowell was reported to be stalking Hazael with *"wonderful persistency. He dogged him around mile after mile and some of the crowd shouted at him, "Come off doggy!" He paid no attention to them whatsoever."* At 21:30 the race leader indulged in a two-lap race with Hart, who eventually overcame him. There was some concern that the excitement produced by the fun would cause the huge crowd to spill on to the track. People were packed in like sardines, and it was very difficult to see the action on the course. As the men spurted loud cheering would ensue; everybody wanted to see the spectacle which caused a huge strain on the police who encircled the track.

At 10 p.m., Rowell's score was 393. This put him 6 miles and 6 laps ahead of Weston's London record for the same time. It also made him 43 miles and 1 lap ahead of his own record when he won the belt at the Garden previously. Hart left the action at the same time and his departure meant the race lost its interest, with many of the participants slowing their pace. However, the despondency wasn't to last for long, because after five minutes, Hart reappeared, and along with Rowell, both began to run. They were joined by the flagging figures of Merritt, Ennis, Krohne and Hazael for a two-lap jaunt which reinvigorated the crowd.

As the race progressed, it was confirmed by Rowell's team that their man would make his 400th mile by the end of the day. Denying the rumours that the current champion had broken down, his attendant stated he was suffering with the smoke and would re-enter the race before midnight.

Merritt meanwhile was planning to fool the 2nd placed Hazael (who was a mile and three laps in front of him), into thinking he was *"all used up,"* so he began making his rounds with an apparent downcast look. His demeanour had also attracted the attention of the bookies, who responded to his *apparent* distress by allowing his name to slide down their slates. The American had made up his mind that he wanted to spoil the party of those predicting an English 1/2 race result. His plan was simple. He would break into a run, catch Hazael up, quickly pass him, demoralise him, and, with a prolonged effort, steal his runner-up position. What he didn't bargain for was that the plucky Englishman would respond positively to his challenge, and the inevitable eruption of noise from the crowd, by giving chase. As the band played "Tommy Dodd" *yet again*, the two ran their hearts out for a mile, after which Merritt gained absolutely no advantage on his opponent whatsoever. Some party pooper!

A little later, Rowell made his fourth century at 23:36. As happy as Larry, he then covered his next mile in 9m.34s carrying a gift of red and white flowers in the shape of a pedestrian's shoe. As the band played "God Save the Queen," he was greeted with justifiable appreciation from the English contingent, who bellowed their approval. After he made another mile and two laps he went to bed and that move gave the perfect excuse for half of the crowd to do the same as they headed home.

At 23:49, the limping Weston returned to the fray. He had been going well all day and had won over many neutrals who had been giving him as much support as the rest of the pedestrians. The band had also helped him by *once again* playing "Tommy Dodd" which encouraged him into a few laps of running. He then settled down to a walk after making six laps of his 319th mile. He had been suffering from the smoky atmosphere all day and caused some derision in the crowd when he refused to accept a bouquet of flowers from a young woman. This happened at half past midnight and caused much bad feeling amongst some spectators, who increasingly hissed at him as he made his way round. It was later claimed that the incident greatly worried Weston at the time.

About the same time, Fred Krohne's stable revealed their star was expected to make the desired 450 miles and reported that he had only managed to eat eggs and drink milk and beef tea since Monday as his stomach was refusing to retain any solid food. Krohne himself said, "I am solid as a rock, and my nervous system could not be improved. I am suffering from throat disease which prevents me from swallowing solid food. Since the race began I have been living on liquids."

With the leaders head safely on its pillow, there were only a few of the athletes performing out on the track including Ennis, Merritt, Hart, Hazael and Federmeyer. The fight for second place continued and around 00:45 as Merritt and Hazael raced together, a large stone was thrown at George by a spectator standing near the Fourth Avenue entrance, which just missed him. The Thirteenth Precinct police arrested a man who was pointed out to them by Hazael. The detained man was called Ephraim Holland, who told his captors that he was from Cincinnati and was stopping at Red Leary's Hotel near Fort Hamilton. The alleged reason for attempting to stop Hazael was due to a bet of $1,500 which had been placed on Rowell, Guyon and Merritt for the first three places. He denied the charge. Hazael went to bed almost immediately after the incident and this gave Merritt the impetus to snatch second spot, which he eventually did at 01:15.

King of the Peds

More fourth day scores from 1 p.m. till 1 a.m:

HR	Time	Rowe	Haz	Merrit	Guyon	Hart	West	Ennis	Khro	Fede	Tay
84th	13:00	355.5	326.6	327	310.5	301.1	287.3	268.7	269.2	251.3	166.2
85th	14:00	357.5	326.6	330.2	314.5	301.1	290.3	276.7	273	252.2	170
86th	15:00	361.1	328.7	334.2	318.6	305.4	295.1	279	277.1	256.7	170
87th	16:00	366	334.3	338	320.7	309.1	299.3	281.2	279.6	260.2	170
88th	17:00	371.4	338.6	342.3	325.1	312.5	304	286	283.1	263.4	170
89th	18:00	377.1	344.1	346	328.4	315.5	306.2	290	286.5	267.7	170
90th	19:00	383.3	350.2	350.1	331.4	319.4	311.1	293.4	289.3	270	170
91st	20:00	386.6	354	350.6	335	321.7	314.4	297.5	290	270.6	176
92nd	21:00	388.6	355	350.6	338.3	325.4	317.3	301	294.2	275.2	177
93rd	22:00	393.1	359.2	354.5	340.2	329.2	317.3	302	298.1	279.3	180.3
94th	23:00	397.3	360.2	358.7	343.6	331.7	317.3	305	301.6	280.3	180.3
95th	00:00	402	364.5	363.4	345	335.4	318.4	309.2	304.5	284.7	180.3
96th	01:00	402.1	368.3	367.2	345	339.1	322.6	310	307.7	288.6	180.3

Off………and………on times: **Guyon**, 00:20 till 02:36; **Hart**, 01:10 till 03:15; **Rowell**, 00:06 till 03:18; **Krohne**, 01:15 till 03:20; **Ennis**, 23:14 till 03:28; **Hazael**, 00:52 till 03:48; **Merritt**, 02:12 till 03:57; **Federmeyer**, 01:19 till 03:58; **Taylor**, 21:45 till 07:56:

As can be seen from the above off and on times, the first man back in the ring was Guyon, who was followed by a very weary Hart, wearing an overcoat and cap. Rowell, showing no signs of stiffness or fatigue, his eyes bright and clear, then bounded on the track bidding the scorers, "Good morning." The cheery chap smiled, bowed to the crowd, ate his breakfast on the track, and went on his way at 4 mph. Krohne, dressed in scarlet was next man out. As he stepped on to the track a policeman was dealing with two brawling drunks. The limping Weston was next to emerge at 03:30 with a cup in his hand which he drank from; and as Guyon warmed up, the long legged Prussian *"blue heron"* was presented with a floral tribute by some friends.

The announcement "Hazael back on track!" was made at 03:49. The figure of George actually wearing a *clean* costume raised a few eyebrows in the crowd. He had also treated himself to a wash and shave. His trainer said of his revamped star: "He's as shiny as a dollar and as clear as a bell." When he hit the sawdust however, and despite his trainer's positive rhetoric, Hazael limped badly on a swollen leg which was bandaged. As he warmed up, and just after four o'clock, he engaged with Hart in some serious running for about a mile, the pace increasing in the last two laps of the said distance. Merritt, wearing an overcoat and black cap, and who had earlier arrived back from his bed three miles up on Hazael, watched his rival closely as he kept up his pace to keep the advantage between them. Federmeyer raised cries of, "Go it, go it Federmeyer!" and, "Do you see him run?!" as he cantered along on his return. Then, Hart, who had been walking for an hour, deposited his coat with an attendant and went after Hazael who responded by breaking into a run. The race caused a few spectators standing in the middle of the track to run from one side of the ring to the other shouting encouragement. As Hart dropped back after relentlessly pursuing Hazael for a mile and a half, the chase was maintained by Guyon. With Ennis now back on the path, the Englishman was soon joined by Merritt and the two were pursued on the inside of the fence by a hoard of enthusiastic runners from the public. The time was now 04:40.

The *New York Times* described what was happening inside and outside the building on that fifth day of the race: Three o'clock by the chronometer that stands before the time-keeper in the walking match for the Astley belt, and the City streets are deserted, save in the immediate neighborhood of Madison-Square Garden. Even here, where so many curious loiterers, hang about from day light until midnight there were very few of the hangers-on left in the neighborhood. The few who did remain were clustered about the entrance to the Garden or just opposite to it, kept a respectful distance by the shivering policemen. Ten or a dozen cabs waited on Madison Avenue or on Twenty Sixth Street to pick up the fares that might drop into the cabby's hand from those who had lingered in the Garden beyond the early morning hours. The men at the gates wore a tired look, as if they were just about leaving or had just come upon their posts, and were full of sleep. Inside the Garden, the electric lamps were burning as brightly as ever, but there was chill in the air that the brightness of the light did not dispel.

The crowd had been thinned down to less than 1,000 persons, and 300 or 400 of these were stretched on chairs in the most comfortable positions they could assume. The more wakeful occasionally amused themselves by imitating the snores of the poor devotees who had preferred to sleep out the worth of the dollar they had paid to be admitted, and to assure them an opportunity to see the race as it appeared today rather than take the trouble to go home. In the bar-room there were two or three dozen men and a few of the women who remained through the night, sometimes venturing out to the Garden to exchange the freest salutation with the walkers and with men who were not more noble than the women themselves. Within the lines of fence separating the path used by the walkers from the central space there were perhaps 50 melancholy looking spectators, who hung over the rail watching the lights above them, or talking over the prospects of the men who were sleeping in the dingy tents near by, in most of which the lights were burning dimly. Around the circle outside the track, and in the red back seats, were distributed part of the diminished crowd, curled up as comfortably as it was possible to dispose oneself in such cramped quarters.

As the clock clicked away into the early hours of the morning the drunks at the bar were getting quite loud necessitating police intervention. Some flashily dressed ladies with blonde hair who had been drinking themselves silly just escaped being arrested by the law as they were escorted away from the building by their male companions.

The *Brooklyn Daily Eagle* described the place at dawn: **The sunlight streamed through the skylights and circular windows, piercing with golden shafts the shadows in nooks and corners and driving them out forever. Bracing Autumnal atmosphere replaced the foul air, and rippled the waters in the fountain until they sparkled like jewels. Hundreds of little boys on the sidewalks without, having exhausted their ingenuity in vain efforts to effect surreptitious entrance to the tournament flocked around the doorways looking as though they wanted to follow the sunlight. A strong force of policemen kept the gamins in awe by an occasionally gallant charge and a sound of thwacking clubs.**

As the clock indicated five o'clock, Hazael on 374.6 was following the race leader who was on a mark of 409.7. The second placed Merritt, on a score of 376.1 dogged Hazael with pertinacity but this only lasted for just over a mile when Hazael broke free of his American shackle, and thereafter, and with an impressive burst of speed, began to reduce the existing gap by the minute from the 378th to the 383rd mile. Hazael made those six miles in the remarkable times of 9m.8s, 8m.18s, 8m.2s, 7m.47s, 7m.36s and 8m.37s. That sound effort which ended at 06:36 left Merritt a lap behind his English rival on a score of 382.7. A minute earlier, and as the band played "Marching through Georgia," Merritt went off course for a break of five minutes. Soon after his return, a massive shout went up to celebrate Federmeyer knocking up his three hundred at 06:47.

By seven o'clock, Hazael, now running at 7 mph, was half a mile in front of Merritt. Hazael's come-back however, was to be short lived. At 07:44, he decided to go for his breakfast and a nap, and no sooner had he left the track than Merritt, still wearing his overcoat and hat, began to attempt to regain the initiative, by using a tactic of consistently walking seven laps and running three. This strategy was paying the dividend Merritt had hoped for. When he glanced at his dial and compared it with Hazael's at 08:00, he saw he was six laps in the clear; as a crowd gathered to see a group of policemen deal with a drunken brawler, he continued to widen the gap by 2 miles at 08:17. When Hazael returned having rested till 09:04, he ran his heart out after Merritt, who was now 4 miles and 2 laps in front of him. The Londoner however, could make no impression, and to his dismay, his rival extended his lead to five miles at 09:44. Later, after chewing at a pear and tossing the core aside, Merritt finished his 400th mile with a promising quick run at 10:54. The band played "Pop goes the Weazel" once more, to everybody's dismay. *"The band is known as a "Go-as-you-please band," which means that each performer blows as he pleases, independent of all the others."*

Of Merritt, the *Brooklyn Daily Eagle* wrote: **He has a sleepy look about the eyes, and his naturally sallow complexion is gradually assuming a bilious hue, but there is a determination about his gait that augurs well for the reliance his backers place upon him. As Merritt walks he moves his arms as though he was swinging a scythe across one of his native Connecticut meadows. His dark brown eyes looked out from beneath the visor of a black silk cap. His costume was a white flannel and drawers and sky blue trunks. He wears a sky blue silk handkerchief about his neck. The front of the Yankees tent is covered with flowers. His trainer Ed. McGlinchey, sat before it this morning in a confident frame of mind. "Merritt is alright," he said to an EAGLE REPORTER. "He has a good appetite and there isn't a blister on his feet. I prescribed a regular diet for him before the match, but I let him vary it as much as he pleases. He is headstrong with strangers, but with one who knows him he is as easy to manage as a child. I feed him on beef tea, steaks, chops, and fruit in moderate quantities. His nerve is something wonderful. Why, think of it, he is only 22 years old. He is full of pluck, and there has been no time since the match began that, he could not get out and walk four miles an hour. He told me today that all he wanted** to do was to show that we had as good men in this country as any other. With careful training he is confident that in a year or two he will be able to compete with Rowell or any other man on the other side."

Whilst Merritt celebrated his achievement along with the crowd, there was a rumour that the race leader was under the weather and being attended to by two doctors at the Ashland House. Rowell's absence was on everybody's lips but his camp was as usual silent about their star, other than saying he was in his tent and that, "He is sick, but he will be alright soon." The leader had been away from the fray three times during the night and early morning, the second time being from 04:04 till 05:12. Then at 06:17 he left again appearing most unwell. A further story circulating about the place made reference to the fact that he had been poisoned by a stranger, who had secreted a drug into a bunch of grapes which he had given to him on the track. Another rumour was that the same trick had been tried on both Ennis and Hart but they had refused to accept the fruit. The management was so concerned that they summoned a meeting to investigate the claims. Mr. Atkinson quickly made a statement to the press that Rowell had been affected by a rush of blood to the head, and that his stomach *"had gone back on him."* The news soon reached the competitors and many of the leaders responded by increasing their pace. They watched with interest as they passed the ailing athlete's tent, observing several bottles of brandy and other *"stimulants"* being passed in. Taylor, on hearing the news about Rowell exclaimed, "Ha, ha! Then I must come out!" as he dipped his head into a basin of water.

As the news spread like wildfire into the streets, hundreds of people sprinted towards the Garden to get in and see the unfolding drama themselves. Some who had backed Rowell were incredulous with rage, and the betting was that if the perpetrators were caught, they wouldn't live very long. As the time approached midday the building began to fill up and unusually by that time, it was already three quarters full.

Meanwhile, Eph Holland, the notorious "Cincinnati blackleg" and well known gambler and politician, accompanied by his counsel, Peter Mitchell, was making an appearance before Justice Flammer at the Jefferson Market Police Court in New York. Mr. Henry B. Davis, the lawyer who had been assisting Hazael's trainer, Isaac Sullivan, appeared on behalf of the pedestrian. A charge of assault and battery had been made against the prisoner. The motive given, but never substantiated, was that Holland had put a bet of $1,500 on Rowell to beat Merritt and Guyon in that order at 10/1, and that Hazael's position in the race at the time was likely to lose him his bet.

Otto Lechla of No. 67 Second Avenue had witnessed the alleged assault. He stated that he had seen Holland, who was about six feet away, throw a brickbat at the two runners when they were only four feet apart; the object in question not actually striking the pair.

Mr. Mitchell moved for the discharge of the prisoner on the grounds that it had not been shown that he had intended to hit either man but the judge refused to grant the motion. Mr. Davis then told the court that for 36 hours, Holland had attempted to get into Hazael's tent and interfere with his food and that Hazael had him driven away. The judge ordered that a double complaint should be drawn up against Holland on behalf of both pedestrians.

Back at the Garden, the usual noisy reception greeted Hazael's 400th mile; the ped, who was complaining of sore ankles, pleaded with his trainer for a glass of ale. The request was granted and as he hobbled around the path, he gulped it down and smacked his lips. The doorman standing guard at Hazael's tent quipped, "He oughter be out here now running instead of walking. He's no good at walking, and the crowd's just disgusted at his not showing 'em how he can run."

As the clock struck midday, Mr. Rowell was still nowhere to be seen. Somebody in the crowd was heard shouting "Rowell's sick. It looks bad." He was now only 16 miles ahead of Merritt and those who had bet their houses on his victory were beginning to get very nervous. The bookmakers were unsure what to do. They waited anxiously for news from his handlers; there were no names chalked up on their boards as the silence continued.

Then at 12:11, and wearing a cardigan and jacket, the sickly figure of the Englishman walked slowly from his tent on to the track, carrying a glass of milk laced with brandy, half of which he later spat out as he walked gingerly along. As he crept around, looking pale and weak, to thunderous encouragement from the crowd, many who had backed him to win ran alongside him, to check for themselves that he wasn't on his last legs. What they would have noticed was the state of his eyes which had dark rims around them. With his head bobbing up and down on his chest, he stayed on the path for 19 minutes during which time he added a mile and a lap for a score of 421.3.

The bookies had at last something to go on and the names of the men taking part reappeared on their boards. "One to five Rowell!" some shouted. "Two to one Merritt!" screamed others. Hazael's price plunged to 3/1 and Guyon and Weston's odds were clipped in to 20/1. Hart was on offer at 40/1 and 50/1 was available on Ennis, whilst Krohne became a 100/1 shot. The prices were quickly rubbed out as more rumours emanating from Rowell's camp suggested that he had been "nobbled." Mr. Atkinson, who had been sent for by his trainer, was seen entering Rowell's tent, and the suspicion was that someone had tampered with his food.

Meanwhile, all eyes were on Merritt, who at 13:15 was thirteen miles behind Rowell. To the urgings of the crowd, he conveyed himself along with economy of movement, but occasionally spoiled the crowd with a spurt of three laps. The *New York Times* was on hand to give their readers an account of how he was reacting to the news of Rowell's predicament, and their impression of the pedestrian's overall temperament: **As he walked around the track he was greeted by loud and enthusiastic cheers on all sides, but his face showed no recognition of the applause. He is a peculiar man for a pedestrian – enthusiasm seems to have no effect upon him, and he appears to be indifferent to all his surroundings. He walks as well in the stillness of the early morning hours, to the music of the snores of the lodgers who have made a home of the Garden this week, as in the early evening, when thousands are cheering him on and the band is playing inspiring airs to encourage him. Rowell might challenge him to a run from morning to night and unless he felt like running and knew that it was best for him to run he would not vary his pace a particle. It is this perfect indifference to all the excitement which has surrounded him that enables him by patient work to secure the second place from Hazael, and which now gives good promise of winning him the race.**

Whilst some of the other *"tramps"* were going about their business in admirable fashion, the performance of another was causing concern. As Hart and Ennis were performing as they were expected to, with hard work, pride and dignity, a certain Mr. E. P. Weston was again bringing the sports' *good* name into disrepute. The *New York Times* made the following observation about his behaviour: **Weston was ambling around the track, playing queer antics, and twisting his body into all sorts of apish forms, to the great amusement of a few and to the great disgust of the many. The opinion was freely expressed that the man was insane, and that he would never walk another race. He was hissed and cheered alternately as he passed around the track, and in some instances, insulting epithets were hurled at him by ruffians in the crowd. He did some very good running at times, but the effect of it was sadly marred by the ridiculous antics which he played, and the silly grimaces which he made at his scorers and the spectators. No flowers were offered him during the day, and the applause which he, of all men, covets and requires in his walks, was bestowed upon him very sparingly.**

As the attendance continued to increase, the news from the Rowell camp got worse. Dr. Mott, one of his physicians made a statement informing the press that Rowell had had a fit and was suffering from convulsions, but denied that he had been poisoned. He said that Rowell's stomach was bad and that his patient had coughed up heavy phlegm. Dr. Mott also said he was getting better even though he had been previously been *"out of his head."* No sooner had the doctor spoke when at 13:15 the brave little fellow again walked gingerly back onto the track and continued with his participation in the race. By 14:00 he had made two miles and three laps. He was soon observed to be walking steadily, then *"easily"* as he chewed away at a piece of ice, and at twenty minutes past the hour challenged Merritt to a run. The American accepted, and the two men set out on their way as the band, recognising Rowell's pluck, played the English national anthem. The men were soon joined by Hart, and as the crowd yelled its self hoarse, Weston, not wanting to be out of the party spirit, joined in the festival of speed; when it was all over after two laps, Rowell resumed his previously employed gentler walking gait and the rest followed suit.

King of the Peds

The fifth day scores for the twelve hours from 02:00 till 14:00:

HR	Time	Rowe	Merrit	Haz	Guy	Hart	West	Khro	Ennis	Fede	Tay
97th	02:00	402	371	368	345	339	327	307	310	288	180.3
98th	03:00	402	371.5	368	346.3	340	327	308	310	288.6	180.3
99th	04:00	405	371.6	369	351.4	341.2	330	310.5	310	290	180.3
100th	05:00	409.7	376.1	374.6	354.1	345.2	332	314	312.3	293.6	180.3
101st	06:00	413.7	380.2	378.6	358.3	348.6	336	317.7	317.3	296.5	180.3
102nd	07:00	419	384.4	385	363.2	352.7	337	323	322.3	301	180.3
103rd	08:00	420.1	388.7	388.1	367.4	356	341.7	324.4	326.4	306.2	180.3
104th	09:00	420.1	392.1	388.1	370.3	359.3	346	327.4	330	309.7	184.3
105th	10:00	420.1	396.1	392.1	374.4	362.7	351	331.4	330.7	314.1	186.3
106th	11:00	420.1	400.3	396.7	378.4	366.5	355.2	335	335.1	315.3	186.3
107th	12:00	420.1	404.4	400	383.2	370	360.4	338.3	338.3	318.4	188.1
108th	13:00	421.3	407	402.2	387.7	374.3	364.3	341.7	341.7	322.6	193
109th	14:00	423.5	411.1	405.1	389.5	378	369.4	346.6	345.6	325.3	193

Hart, after having completed his 380th mile at 14:28 was called in to his tent by a rather humbled Daniel O'Leary, where four men were waiting to meet him and the following letter was read to him.

BOSTON Mass, Sept. 25, 1879.

Messrs O'Leary and Englehardt:

GENTLEMEN: At a meeting of the Young Men's Club, (colored) of Boston, held this morning, it was voted that your interest and gentlemanly politeness and kindness to Mr. Frank Hart, the colored pedestrian are more the object of our thoughts than you, perhaps, imagine, and that we return our thanks to you, many and sincere for the same use, that Messrs. O'Connell, Ruffin, W. H. Davis, and Chauncey Jacobs be appointed a committee to wait on you personally to deliver this communication, and also a floral offering to Mr. Hart.

C. RUFFIN

President

NB: The floral offering consisted of a monster horse shoe. O'Leary also received a large bouquet from the group. This incident pleased Frank so much that he bounded out of his tent and ran three laps to a boisterous reaction from the crowd.

With concerns being expressed about the future of Rowell's health preoccupying the bookmaking firms, below are the odds that were being offered to the swarms of would-be backers at 14:30 as Weston stepped off the sawdust for a break. The wise owls surrounding the tables were already grabbing the 1/3 on "the limey," who was just about to pass the post for his 426th mile. Other odds: (Placed odds to finish 1st or 2nd are in brackets): **Merritt and Hazael, 3/1; Guyon, 30/1 (5/1); Weston, 20/1 (10/1); Hart, 40/1 (10/1); Ennis, 100/1 (10/1); Krohne, 100/1 (20/1): Any contestant making 550 miles, 100/1:**

Weston's rest amounted to four minutes. When he returned he insisted that the band play the monotonous "Tommy Dodd." To everybody's disappointment they did. Off on a run went the champion to the tune he loved, and off after him went Hart, whose shadow annoyed Weston so much, he turned round and *"puffed his face"* at him. Hart responded to this moment of incredulity on Weston's part with a simple smile, but nevertheless continued to stalk the angry man. Weston responded by reversing. Hart to the delight of the throng followed, thus increasing Weston's rage. Frank chased Eddy for another six laps and, unbelievably after another reversal of course, Weston having this time escaped the boy's attentions, complained to O'Leary that his pupil should desist from dogging him. Hart's master agreed and sent word to Frank to stop.

Ennis received an ovation for scoring his 350th mile at 14:36 in a time of 14m.40s, and three minutes later Merritt made his 414th in a time of 15m.35s. A minute before that, Rowell left the circle on a mark of 426.1 which meant he was now only 12.1 in front of Merritt, who immediately began a spurt of two laps. Again, the band played, "Yankee, Doodle" amid the racket.

Manager Hess had told reporters during the day that that the final receipts would be at least seventy thousand dollars. "I calculate on twelve thousand dollars for both Friday and Saturday. It won't come far from that. I believe the large receipts are owing due to the dollar admission. I have been in the business for a good while, and I find when you cheapen a thing you hurt it. People find that they can come here and be in a quiet, decorous throng. There's no such scenes here as were at the other match. So gentlemen come and bring their wives and children."

"What do you imagine the winner will get of the seventy thousand dollars?" asked the reporter.

"It is impossible to tell. First there is twenty-five per cent, to come out, and then the expenses. They are large. There will be however, be a very pretty sum of money for the winner, who will get half the net proceeds."

Back in a packed court house at three p.m. Eph Holland and his counsel were waiting along with Judge Flammer for the start of the examination of another witness, Frank Creamer, of No 60 South Second Street, Williamsburg. However, although they waited for an hour, neither Creamer nor Mr. Davis bothered to turn up and the Judge ruled that Holland should be released.

Rowell, looking shaky and carrying a wet sponge in his hand and showing *"no signs of insanity,"* was reported to have been suffering from a *"rush of blood to the head along with nausea, colic and chills,"* after he had returned to the track at three o'clock. His physician reported that his sickness was due to indigestion, caused by eating some grapes that disagreed with him. He added that his patient was alright and would continue till the end of the match.

As Merritt's score on the dial showed 415.4 at 15:10, Norman Taylor, now recording 193 miles next to his name, crept slowly about the place. Many in the crowd poked fun at him and so did Weston, who again was up to his old tricks by replacing the number one in Taylor's score with a number four. Many in the crowd fell about laughing, but when the place fell quiet, someone in the crowd shouted out at Weston, "Was that the way you did it in London?" The angry looking champion responded by slithering back to his tent.

At 16:00, Rowell completed his 428th mile alongside Hazael, Merritt, Ennis and Taylor who were all walking in a bunch; the audience cheering him along with Merritt who made his 419th mile at the same time. Guyon, Hart and Weston were also walking but none of them were making very good time. The leader went off course again at 16:15 on a score of 429, but only remained away for a short time when he realised Merritt was only 8½ miles behind him. Rowell was able to increase the gap to 10 miles between the time Merritt left the track at 16:37 and his return at 17:00 when he reappeared munching on a bunch of grapes whilst, *"Rowell was walking as though in a dream, with his mouth partly open, his eyes closed, and his body so limp that it seemed as though a trifle more relaxation of the muscles would cause him to drop into a heap."*

Guyon's feet were so sore when he put in his reappearance at 17:15 that he winced every time he put them on the ground. Rowell went back off at 17:20 followed by Krohne who re-emerged ten minutes later donning an overcoat. In the interim, Weston had been showing off again angrily remonstrating with a scorer who had crossed his path. A cry of "Rowell back on track!" went up at 17:30 to greet the sickly leader as Hazael accepted a challenge from Guyon, who confounded everybody by running the Englishman into the ground; so much so, that the latter retired to his tent with his tail firmly between his legs at 17:41.

After six o'clock, various contestants were running about the place. Weston started the fun with a lap spurt. Hart appeared at 18:05 and ran merrily round the ring for several miles before resting a short time and was then inspired to do so again as the band struck up "Going back to Dixie." At 19:00, Rowell ran a lap but couldn't keep it up and immediately sought his couch. The bookies responded by extending his odds to 1/2. *"He kept his gait and his legs manfully when he did come on the track for his evening's work. That he was a very much weakened man was easy to see from the sunken pallor of his cheeks."*

Guyon hobbled off at 19:02, and Taylor surprised everybody when returning to the track at 19:13. He made a couple of laps and then started on a run. Isaac Sullivan sent Hazael back on at 19:15 after a rest of 1h.34m during which time the gap between George and Sam had increased to eleven miles in Merritt's favour. Hart ran the last two laps of his 397th mile and was loudly cheered. He then went to his cottage, but returned at 20:05. Rowell was back on at 20:10 and the run which Taylor had earlier instigated produced a marvellous total of six miles and four laps up till 20:17. Hart made four centuries at 20:36.

King of the Peds

Whilst the story was unfolding on the inside, Captain Williams and his men had, as ever, to deal with the problems outside of the building. A minority of those unfortunate enough not to possess the minimum amount of money to gain legal entrance to the premises tried every way they could to get in free. One young boy was observed sprinting across the street and climbing a drain pipe at the top of which a helping hand appeared at a window. He was duly chased by a host of policemen. As they tried to unsuccessfully to batter his legs from below, they were jeered by those who hated the ground they walked on.

The throngs of those who couldn't afford admission interfered with those who could, and soon there was a sea of bodies congregating around the entrances, either attempting to get inside, or waiting for news as to what was happening on the track. Some of the luckier ones watching the match were shouting down the scores from windows at the top of the building as well as answering questions from the inquisitive crowd below. "How's Merritt's stand?" "Is the darky keeping up to biz?" "Is Weston as big a lunatic as ever?"

The bookies were doing a roaring trade in the street as well as inside, and the clerks' pencils were busy scribbling away as the punters handed in their dimes and quarters. The photograph vendors were also doing brisk business, with pictures of Hart and Merritt being in particular demand.

Later on, Merritt was getting a lot of attention from the crowd, who made him their favourite; they continually showered him with noisy encouragement. One of his attendants said of him at the time, "Merritt has collared Hazael and kept him right there all day. He is in a better condition than when he started. He is not lame in either of his feet although be has a small blister on the little toe of his right foot. He didn't notice it however till I pointed it out to him. His appetite is excellent. He's a good feeder, the boy is. Beef tea, chops, and steaks have disappeared rapidly whenever he walked into 'em. He thinks a great deal of calves foot jelly and within a few minutes he has just disposed of two cup custards, some bread and butter and calves foot jelly. When he goes off the track about 10 o'clock, he will turn in and take about three hours sleep, he hasn't slept any since 4 o'clock this morning, and is a bit tired. He'll do a big day's work tomorrow."

The bookies, recognising the danger that Merritt was in, shortened his odds to 6/4 and 1/5 a place; 6/4 was also being asked for Merritt to beat Hazael. Rowell was a steady 1/3 to win with 100/1 having been taken on 550 miles being scored. That unlikely event now attracted a quote of 10/1.

(Illustration no: 58)

    Go! Go! Go!
  Go to the walking match; go!
   "Scoop" the pedestrian show!
  Dollar admission, but "nary" seat,
Jostled and hustled by bummer and beat,
Wedged in a crowd, with no chance for retreat,
   Stifled with stenches, but-oh!
   Go, fellow citizen, Go!
   Go, if you die for it, go!

> Go! go! go!
> Seldom if ever you know,
> Such an astonishing show!
> What though multitude, noisy, profane,
> Act as if chaos were coming again,
> Officers bawling and clubbing in vain;
> Friend, keep your temper, for so
> Rumpus and wrangle will go,
> Simply as part of the show.
> Go! go! go!
> Go where the trampers you know,
> Trip the competitive toe:
> Rowell the plucky, who leads from the start,
> Merritt and Hazael, Guyon and Hart,
> Taylor, the Green Mountain "man of the tart,"
> Weston, eccentric and beau,
> Ennis with nary a show,
> Think of it, wonder and go!
> Go! go! go!
> Put up your money and blow,
> Swagger and swell at the show:
> Tip your hat sidewise and "taffy" the boys,
> Bully the verdant, and tell him he "loies;"
> Bet your last dollar and kick up a noise;
> Nay be a nuisance, but-oh!
> Don't stay away for the show!
> Go fellow citizen, go!

Hart was given a magnificent floral ship by the "Colored Republican Club" at 21:13. Soon after, one of the many admirers of the remarkably handsome chap, Guyon, placed a huge floral horseshoe around his neck. After that he left the building for a bath and bed at 21:43, on a score of 415 miles. That effort meant that he had just 35 miles to muster on the final day to earn some money.

On a score of 440 miles, Merritt went to his tent at 21:55. Five minutes later, and 117 hours into the contest, Rowell had scored 449.4 and was 10 miles behind Weston's London record. Weston himself made 400 at 22:06, and a minute later the race leader scored 450. Hazael went in at 22:11 and Rowell followed him two minutes later.

Weston and Hart caused quite a stir later in the hour (22:35) as the champion tried to shake off the stalking youngster who had followed him mile after mile. Weston reversed often, but Hart also reversed and stuck closely behind him. Whilst all this was going on, some in the crowd shouted, "Shake him up Weston!" "Stick to him Hart!" The pair then knocked against each other whilst reversing, and as the two contestants' trainers argued about the incident, Weston's appeal to the judges was turned down and no foul was allowed. The crowd *"applauded with vigor." "It was the excitement of the evening."*

Ennis returned to the match just after eleven o'clock, but lasted only minutes, while Weston disappeared at 23:14. At 23:30, the only men on the track were Krohne and Hart. Hazael returned to the track on a score of 431 at 23:34 stiff, lame, and seemingly pretty well used up after having rested for 1h.23m.

The Garden was packed with people in the crowd anxiously expecting the other walkers to appear. Gossip was rife that Rowell had had a relapse, but the bookies, apparently indifferent about the rumour, licked their chalks and altered the odds accordingly: (Placed odds to finish 1st or 2nd are in brackets): **Rowell, 1/6 (1/12); Merritt, 2/1 (1/7); Hazael, 7/1 (2/1); Hart, 40/1 (20/1); Weston, 100/1 (20/1); Guyon, 100/1 (20/1): (40/1 was also being offered about a competitor making 550 miles and 5/1 about the successful completion of 540 miles).**

King of the Peds

By 00:25, Guyon had almost reached Hart's 415-mile score, and 13 minutes later, Rowell's return to the ring was met with positive acknowledgement from the 10,000 plus throng. Ennis followed him in and within a minute, the stiff walking Merritt, wearing a thick overcoat and jockey cap joined them to cries of "Bravo," *"and for a few minutes the Garden was in uproar."* Merritt initially walked round, but after a few laps he began to spurt and led the bunch around. Hazael responded to the challenge, and with an extraordinary turn of foot, ran away from them all. Guyon tried to stay with him, but it was useless as Hazael was simply too good for them all, as he sprinted around showing the best of them the soles of his feet.

The fifth day scores from 15:00 till 01:00 on the last day:

Hour	Time	Rowe	Merrit	Haz	Hart	Guy	West	Khro	Ennis	Fede	Tay
110th	15:00	426.1	415.3	408.1	393.6	382.4	374.3	349.2	351	329.6	193.1
111th	16:00	428.3	419	413	398.5	386	379.2	352.5	353	334.2	198.4
112th	17:00	431.6	421.5	416	400	389.1	383.2	356.5	357.3	337.7	200.2
113th	18:00	434.4	424.3	418.7	402.6	392.7	388.1	358.7	360.2	340.7	200.3
114th	19:00	438.2	428.7	418.7	406.1	397.4	390.3	362.7	363.2	344.6	200.3
115th	20:00	442	432.4	422.3	409.7	398	390.3	364.7	367.5	346.3	206.2
116th	21:00	445.5	436.3	426.5	413	401.2	394.5	368.6	371.7	348	208.4
117th	22:00	449.4	440	430.3	415	404.1	399.3	372.2	373	348	213
118th	23:00	450.2	440	431	415	408.1	404	375.1	374.5	348	213
119th	00:00	450.2	440	432.1	415	411.2	405	378.4	375.4	348	213
120th	01:00	452.4	442.1	436.2	415	415	405	382.2	377.4	348	213

After the one o'clock scores were scribbled down by the eagerly departing reporters anxious to get the latest situation back to their offices for the early morning editions, Merritt, Rowell and Hazael were all moving round the track in the order named. Rowell had to pull out all the stops to keep up with the pace by trotting along. The crowd yelled out at Merritt, "Shake off the dogs!" The American "dogged" the Englander incessantly causing someone in the crowd to shout out "Go on Hazael, break his heart!" George however, had had enough of being shadowed and left his ghost on the track. *"The anatomical curiosity from beyond the Atlantic lugged his awkward collection of bones into his tent at 01:53, upon the completion of his 440th mile. He looked as uncouth and as dirty as ever, but was in good spirits, and inclined to boast of his ability to beat Merritt."*

The 22-year-old Merritt, who had rested for three hours between 22:00 and midnight, continued to wear his stout jacket to ward off the cold night air. He told his trainer, "I have done sleeping until the end of the match, and I intend to win the belt if I can." *"Merritt, the only native of the soil who has done his duty, persevered during the early morning with the possibility of earning a snug fortune and the championship luring him forward. His angular beak was carried at a proud and lofty angle as he passed the scorers' stands and marked the steady advance of his needle on the dial. Toward three o'clock it told him that he was nearing his 450th mile, and he marched gaily around the track with a pleased and eager flush on his dark face."* Cheering reverberated around the building like claps of thunder as the doughty young man passed the line at 02:48. The house guests stamped their feet in appreciation.

With the pedestrians showing very little interest in their beds, Rowell, who had earlier taken an hour's rest from 23:30 which had refreshed him considerably, and a further seven-minute break at 02:54, was 10 miles and 4 laps in front of Merritt, who in turn was 10.6 in front of Hazael.

"Taylor, the pie biter, was slumbering in his tent dreaming possibly of the huckleberry season, and Krohne, the gigantic Prussian grenadier, whose legs hang over the end of his cot when he reclines, was snoring a pleasing version of "Die Wacht am Rhein" from beneath a breastwork of blankets."

Just before 03:00, as the buildings windows were opened to allow the cool outside air to enter it, Federmeyer had announced his permanent retirement from the race, having left the track at 20:28 the previous night on a score of 348. His trainer announced that his man's feet were in a terrible state and that he had suffered from soreness and blisters after putting on new shoes on Wednesday. During the race he had rested 30h.10m. His tent would soon be taken down and carted away from its position on the home stretch and stored alongside those used by Dutcher, Jackson and Panchot, thus making for a better view of the course.

Later on in the morning, and after a rest of 2h.9m, *"Hazael kicked the knots out of his crooked legs at 4:02:30 o'clock and reeled out to the sawdust feeling very stiff and sore. He soon limbered up, however, and loped down the stretch with the amble of a spavined nag. He is a queer looking customer, and grows queerer as the hours pass. His costume does not vary from the clownish breech cloth and dirty tights which have grown so familiar. When he begins a running spurt, he lowers his head as if he intended to butt something, throws his hands backward, and lurches forward like a drunken man."* As George's limbs responded to a few laps of plod, he was soon moving smoothly along and engaging in a bit of a tussle with Hart, who was now showing better form. Wearing a long woollen over-shirt and velvet trunks, Hart bounded along as *"light as a rubber ball,"* and a *"satisfied grin overspread his shining copper countenance."* However, the smile soon disappeared as the faster Hazael left him standing. The perky Brit went on to make his 443rd mile in 9m.15s.

At 04:10, Rowell left the track for a few minutes; when he made his reappearance he looked quite pale. He carried a large sponge which he sucked iced water from, and used it to bathe his head and temples. As the leader dabbed himself and walked slowly round, Merritt, Hart and Hazael, who was suffering from the effects of a swollen tendon in his leg, raced against each other. The Englishman was evidently indifferent to his injury, as he led the trio round playing Catch Me If You Can.

"The personification of wretchedness," described a certain Mr. G. Guyon as he emerged from under the canvas at 05:25 with 428 miles above his dial after an absence of 47m.20s. The poor chap hardly slept at all with the pain he was experiencing from his badly strained leg muscles and the sores and blisters that covered his feet.

A large contingent of people had remained in the Garden during the small hours, estimated to be about 1,400. The management had threatened to clear the place between three and six o'clock in order to make as much gate money as possible on the final day. The lucky ones who stayed would remain till the end and save the re-admission fee. Many had been drinking heavily but there had been no trouble during the night. Of the type of people that had frequented the place during that time, the *Brooklyn Daily Eagle* wrote: **There were women there whose bleached hair, cheeks flushed with rouge, gaudy costumes, and "loud" manner showed them to be fast; there were gamblers with big diamonds and dyed moustaches, and there were dwellers in the lower strata of society; but these collectively only formed a minority of the crowd, for with them sat hundreds of respectable people, intent on seeing every feature of the great walk.**

All through Friday night the apoplectic Germans in the band gallery blew well worn airs through their tarnished instruments. The spectators seemed unwilling to leave, for was it not their last opportunity to enjoy sleep with a walking match thrown in for at least ten days? The electric lights threw a cold glare upon the ellipse lengthening the forms of the walkers on the track into gigantic shadows prancing and dancing in all directions as the positions of their objects changed. The squatters squatted all the more closely to their chairs as the hours wore on and tried to sleep, but the cheers of the wakeful spectators and the horrible clangor of the band roused them out of their lethargy and fixed their attention upon the tournament.

Weston, who had kept up his queer swinging walk until 02:49, had a short kip and then indulged in another rest from 03:46 till 06:38. After making three laps, he began to complain about the smoke yet again. Somebody in the crowd who knew him, and who had invested $500 on him to win the event, told a reporter, "I'll tell you the trouble with him. Weston is an insufferably conceited man, and if he had been encouraged right straight along, by popular applause, he would have shown up in front." Meanwhile, the man with no friends ran around the place looking, as ever, immaculate, wearing purple tights, carrying a whip in his hand, his hair shining from a recent shampoo. On occasions, if he really was seen to be trying, there would be a courteous ripple of applause, and *very* occasionally someone in the crowd who had backed him would shout out "Go it Weston!" As he and Merritt passed the scorers' stand together, somebody shouted to Merritt, "Say, don't have anything to do with that fellow there!"

As eight o'clock approached there was much activity going on in the building. The police and scorers who had worked all night handed over to their counterparts on the day shift. The bookies sat talking about the race in the bar, and while the band revved up, the men on the track stuck to their tasks. Merritt led the way, followed by the sunken cheeked Hazael, who carried a sponge smelling strongly of ammonia, which he frequently pressed to his nose. Rowell, following him, was kept awake by the perfumed smell of the shampoo he had washed his hair in earlier that morning. Perhaps he'd borrowed some of Weston's?

The clean shaven Krohne, who had left his room at 03:23, moved himself stiffly forward using his familiar long striding gait, hardly moving his arms, and always looking indifferently ahead. He had originally appeared wearing a coat and a black felt hat to protect himself from the cold, but these had been discarded as he warmed to his work, revealing a scarlet flannel costume. During one lap, he dropped a small sponge which he was carrying on the track. *"The effort to pick it up required him to come to a full halt, and his grimaces as he stooped to get it provoked a burst of laughter."*

The race between Ennis and Krohne excited the crowd of 2,000 or so around nine that morning when the two were on 405 and 404 respectively. Ennis had earlier completed his 400th mile at 07:11, and at that stage was just two laps behind. Krohne was determined to put into check any attempt that Ennis made to increase his, by then, mile lead; the pair bounded round the place together, with the tall Prussian staying close to the Irish-American.

Three thousand people were gathered watching the sport at 10 o'clock. That was the highest attendance for that time of day for the whole week. They watched everything on the track with the utmost interest. Hart however, was oblivious to their presence as he walked round like a zombie, his eyes tightly shut. Only the shakes from his trainers and the presentation of an American flag could wake him. Of all the men on the track at the time, Weston appeared the freshest, but as had been the case during the contest, he was being derided by the many in the crowd.

At 10:36, and on a score of 480, Merritt, wearing a scarlet silk hunting cap, dark blue silk trunks and a red handkerchief around his neck, was 10 miles and 3 laps behind the leader. He was however, well ahead of third placed Hazael, who was off the track and eating his breakfast, by 14 miles. One of Hazael's attendants was still hopeful he would be the runner-up by the end of the race. "We hope he will get second place. He is taking his breakfast now. His appetite is good, and he is docile enough to please anyone. We had a little disagreement with him at first, but it is all over now. The sea voyage had a bad effect on him, and so did the change of climate. It upset him for a while. If it had not been for that you would have seen six hundred miles on that blackboard tonight. He has cleared off three miles off Merritt's lead, and may still beat him yet. He began to take stimulants yesterday, and in the afternoon drank three pint bottles of Bass Ale, which did him a great deal of good. Today we will give him champagne. He is eating heartily of chops and stewed chicken, and he is drinking tea with it."

While Taylor was reading the morning papers, his trainer told a reporter, "No one expected the old man to do much. He is over fifty years old and pretty good for a twenty-mile run, but he stands no show in a tournament like this. His long sleep keeps him in good shape, and he keeps on the track more to amuse himself than anybody else." After digesting both his breakfast and the news, the "pie man" ambled on to the path at 10:58 wearing the same old linen suit and clutching the familiar riding whip in his hand. *"A countryman would have taken him for a farmer in harvest time, but the city people said he resembled a ghost more than anything else. He went along now with a mincing walk, now with a light skipping run. He ran like a woman. When Weston capered up behind him and challenged him to a run, he accepted the challenge and ran the faster, pursued by the champion. The weazen faced holder of the belt, giggled and gurgled as he ran at the pie eater's heels, but the latter took it in good part, and astonished every one by running until Weston was glad to drop into a walk."*

Krohne at this time was focused on two things. One was the close proximity of Ennis, but more importantly, he was looking forward to seeing the hopeful sight of the figures 4-5-0 above his name on the dial. Only then would he afford himself the luxury of a wry smile. Ennis had taken only a short nap between 02:56 and 03:49 before reintroducing himself, to make the necessary distance to bring a smile on the face of his bank manager. When he got himself into top gear, he *"swung his limbs in a sturdy stride,"* and by noon, had wiped away any thoughts of a smile that *Krohne* was thinking of supplying for the crowd when he led him by seven laps. His trainer attributed his failure to the condition of his stomach. "He has lived on beef tea all the week, but this morning he ate a piece of steak; he will make 450 miles without doubt. If his stomach was as good as his legs it would have been 550 miles instead."

Rowell was still the king of the castle, and barring an absolute crisis, was looking forward to retaking his title and picking up a cool sum of money for his efforts. Having stopped and breakfasted between 09:11 and 09:40, he joined his main rival at 11:10 after indulging in a further rest of 29 minutes, wearing a tight fitting jockey cap, dark brown cardigan and a blue and red silk handkerchief around his neck. He was given an American flag which he carried round the place with a smile on his face to the delight of the crowd. His trainer said, "He is feeling as well as ever. The stories about his sickness are absurd in the extreme. Why, there is no possibility of poisoning him and no attempt at such has been made. He is too carefully looked after to render anything possible in the shape of foul play, even should it be made. We think he is certain to win the belt." Of the leader, the *New York Times* commented: **One old sporting man, speaking of Rowell's temporary break down the day before, said it fell** like a thunder clap on the book-makers, not only in the Garden but throughout the City and country. "They had put so much on him that his failure to win would have completely ruined half of them," said he. "I have heard it broadly hinted that if Rowell couldn't win by fair means, the bookmakers were determined he should by foul. Rather than see him lose, it was sad that they would turn out the gas and break up the walk in the evening when the critical hour arrived."

Hart, wearing a lilac handkerchief about his neck, a similar coloured shirt with black facings, the sleeves of which terminated at the elbows, black velvet trunks and white tights, created a stir in front of 3,500 onlookers when, after returning at 10:58, he flashed across the line to complete his 450th mile at 11:14. *"The band played a negro ditty for his encouragement, and it made him redouble his speed."* He was now sure of financial reward in the form of gate money; the only question being how much? His final placing would influence the answer.

The bookies were offering odds of 75/1 that 550 miles would not be made and 5/1 that 540 would not be achieved. Odds of 20/1 were being offered on Guyon to finish 1st or 2nd. Hazael, Hart and Weston were being touted at 30/1 for the same outcome. Ennis commanded a price of 35/1 and Krohne was the 100/1 outsider. Many people surrounded the bookies' table eyeing up the odds and large amounts of cash were being handed to the layers, who stuffed the notes and coins into their bags. The firms had earlier made the popular announcement that all winning bets would be paid out on Monday. No bets were being offered on Rowell.

Hazael returned to the track at 11:35.

The scene inside the Garden at the time was described by the *Brooklyn Daily Eagle*: **From high noon forward a human torrent poured into the Garden. It flowed in eager but good natured processions at the Madison and Fourth Avenue entrances, and even the little side door on Twenty Seventh street was besieged by a multitude anxious to obtain admittance. The torrent divided as it surges reached the interior, a third rolling off to the seats at the left and the rest into the oval amphitheatre. Soon the seats were filled and there was little standing room upon the central flooring. About the time there was a rush for the big lunch and bar room on the Twenty Sixth Street side. There were piled up mountains of sandwiches, destitute of butter and spliced with imaginary slices of ham; thousands of eggs, boiled as hard cobblestones; tons of pork end beans, which the boys called "stars, and stripes;" chickens that had lost their "Spring," and other attractions or a cheap lunch counter. With shirt sleeves rolled up to the elbow and big aprons tucked under their chins, the regiment of bartenders strove to keep alive, the gurgle that sounded in hundreds of thirsty throats. Beer ran in copious streams, and there was plenty of fire water for the older and more hardened drinkers. The bar did a bigger business than all the gin mills in Brooklyn did yesterday, and that is saying a good deal.**

Fully five thousand persons were in the Garden by noon, and after that the attendance increased at the rate of a thousand an hour. There was little smoking, and except up under the roof, where the squatters sat, the air was as clear as it would save been in a twenty acre lot. The sunlight made every one cheerful, even to Taylor, the most hopeless of all the walkers. The management early began to complete their preparations for managing the vast assemblage. It was feared that in the excitement of the evening the crowd would break through the frail wooden rails on either side of the track and break up the match. Extra stanchions were provided to strengthen the railing where it was weakest, and the track keepers were placed at frequent intervals to restrain the curious public, from getting in the way of the walkers. Captain Williams command was strengthened by platoons drawn from other precincts, and a squad of detectives was scattered through the multitude to look out for the light fingered.

The only person who could topple Hart from fourth position was Guyon, and at midday, the *"Adonis of the Ellipse"* was only three miles behind him on a score of 448. The race for fourth place was now well and truly on and the crowd realised they were about to witness a real old battle between the two to finish in that position.

Hart, now carrying a sponge which he rubbed vigorously over his face, used questionable tactics to protect his lead; and as George ran lap after lap, Frank kept close to him. The Illinoisan kept in the centre of the track where the ground was softer rather than on the inner, where it had been packed harder by the feet of the contestants. The Bostonian attempted all the tricks under the sun to spoil his opponent's run and take his ground, until finally the indignant Guyon appealed to the match referee. Mr. Atkinson told Hart to stop his questionable methods of running or he would have him temporarily taken from the track. Frank was informed that if he wanted to pass Guyon he would have to do so on the outside. After the lecture, Guyon frequently reversed attempting to fool the former grocery boy who watched and copied his every move faultlessly. *"The band played a very suggestive tune, while the race continued. It had reference to a monkey chasing a weasel; and Hart was doing the chasing."* Guyon eventually

King of the Peds

completed the yearned for 450 miles at 12:38 whilst Hart was resting. *"Men arose and waved their hats, and women fluttered handkerchiefs and ribbons in the air."* As he moved rapidly around the path making his next mile in 7m.23s, he was a different man to the one who emerged from his tent in the early hours of the morning, when he had been so stiff he could hardly move.

Daniel O'Leary was watching Guyon's progress closely from the door of Hart's flower festooned tent where earlier, a stylishly dressed young blonde lady named Miss Maria C. Firmbach, a gardener's daughter, handed him an elaborate basket of roses. An immense floral horseshoe bearing his name in immortelles was also presented to him from "The ladies of the St. Omer Hotel." The appreciative recipient was said to have doffed his cap upon presentation and carried it around the track. O'Leary quickly dispatched his protégé back into the ring to take on the improved Chicagoan. After Hart had caught him up, the pair ran two laps and then a mile in 7m.23s at 12:46, and then with the two reversing, a further mile in 9m.26s.

Guyon then left the path. With Hart just over a mile in front of him, O'Leary said of his athlete, "If he had not sprained his ankle, he would have done much better, but as it is he is making a good race. His record is saved and that is all I expected after his bout with Hazael the other morning. He is receiving telegrams and letters from all over the country and flowers and presents are pouring in by the bushel. Hart is a good boy and I am fond of him. He will make his fortune at walking. His appetite is good, and his general condition is first rate."

At the head of affairs, the three leaders went around in Indian file about a yard apart; and all advanced at a rate of 4 mph. Hazael's chances of gaining second spot had already evaporated. *"With face suggestive of anything but intelligence, or the finer feelings of humanity and bent shoulders, from which swung a pair of ungainly arms, he dragged one leg after the other."*

Rowell caused the band to blow "God save the Queen" for the fourth time during the tournament, when at 13:02, he finished his 500th mile. Many in the crowd stood on their seats to cheer and their hands were sore with clapping. "Rowell! Rowell! Rowell!" The leader responded by doffing his cap at them and carried it in his hand as the band played, respectfully replacing it back on his head at the end of the anthem. Minutes earlier when the leader had scored 499.6 at 13:00 after 132 hours of the contest, he was three miles and one lap behind Weston's London record.

The last day scores from 02:00 up until 14:00:

Hour	Time	Rowe	Merrit	Haz	Hart	Guy	West	Ennis	Khro	Tay
121st	02:00	456	446	440	417	416	405	382	383	213
122nd	03:00	461.2	450.6	440	422.1	420.6	409.2	386.2	383.4	213
123rd	04:00	464.7	454.7	440	426	424.7	412	387.1	386.1	213
124th	05:00	468.5	458.7	444.6	429.5	428.6	412	391.1	390.1	213
125th	06:00	472.5	462.4	448.7	433.1	432.4	412	395.1	393.6	213
126th	07:00	476.5	466.4	453.3	436.3	434.3	413.4	399.1	397.4	213
127th	08:00	480	470.6	457.5	439.5	437.4	417.7	401.2	400.5	214.4
128th	09:00	485.2	474.7	462	442.7	440	421.6	404.4	404.1	220.1
129th	10:00	489.5	478.7	466	446.1	442	425.4	406.7	407.5	220.1
130th	11:00	491.5	481.8	467.3	448.5	445.3	428.2	411.2	411.4	220.2
131st	12:00	495.6	485.4	471.4	451	448	430	414.2	413.5	225.7
132nd	13:00	499.6	488.3	473.5	453.2	452.1	434.2	418.3	417.5	226.4
133rd	14:00	503.7	492.4	477.5	457.1	453.6	438.2	422.5	421.4	226.4

In the afternoon, the match reporters were as busy as usual trying to gain what information they could to write in their columns. One visited Sam Merritt's quarters, which was covered in floral tributes. Ed. McGlinchey, his trainer, said his man felt in tip-top condition after his sleep of three hours the previous night. "Do I think Sam will win the belt?" he replied to the reporters' query. "Well, I believe the probabilities are against it. Rowell, you see, has come up fresh and strong after his sickness. I don't propose to kill Sam in an effort to win it. He is young yet, and the people can feel assured that he will be heard from again. He is sure of getting second place, unless an accident befalls him. Hazael is beaten out. We broke his heart last night. If Rowell goes to pieces again we may save the belt, but it don't look like it. Rowell has a high opinion of Merritt's ability as a pedestrian. He told him that he believed he was the best heel-and-toe walker in the world."

Rowell was presented with a large floral ship, which he struggled round with before depositing it in his tent. He then continued his slog whilst reading a telegram from Astley. Meanwhile Hazael had been drinking wine, and as he wobbled out of his house at 14:36 in a new pair of emerald green trunks, it was noticeable that he had had another wash and a shave! He was followed by Merritt at 14:41, who had to cover another seven or so miles to make his fifth century, and after competing 495 of them he did some fine running. He was followed by Taylor who always made the crowd laugh with the way he conveyed himself. As Rowell cajoled his struggling, and now limping fellow Brit, Hazael along, Guyon hobbled, as he was followed by the strong walking Weston. Ennis meanwhile, left them all behind, as he ran as if on hot coals in his pursuit of a prize.

Off track, and in the crowded bars where patrons weren't able to drink their beer in comfort, *"Fifth Avenue prices were charged for Bowery rum,"* and the buildings restaurants were doing splendid business but again at an over-inflated cost to their customers. Hundreds of messages were being sent by those who continually surrounded the telegraph office, and all the boxes were occupied with many handsomely dressed ladies. Outside, the streets were described as impassable. They were occupied by thousands amongst who were many *"street boys and young ruffians,"* and *"unwashed crowds,"* who were required to be driven away from the surrounding entrances. Many businesses used the opportunity to advertise themselves, by giving people scorecards, with the name and address of the firm that they worked for and how they could serve them, on the back.

As the tramps plodded round, the bookmakers were more interested in taking money on the winning race distance than who would win. Odds on offer were: **535 miles, 1/1; 540 miles, 5/1; 545 miles, 15/1; 550 miles, 100/1:** With Rowell not on the boards, Merritt was 30/1 to win, Hazael 40/1, and Hart, Guyon and Weston 500/1 to take the belt. Other novelty bets were, (without Hazael and Merritt) Guyon and Hart 50/1 to be placed second, and in the same circumstances, Weston was 100/1, Ennis 200/1 and Krohne 500/1. Even money was also being touted that Ennis would beat Krohne. On one of the bookies boards, a notice was put up. It read; *"Tickets on Rowell first and Merritt second and third, cashed immediately; commission 5%."*

Between two and three o'clock, Taylor was at the back of the Indian file of pedestrians who constantly circled the track. Merritt led them along, and as the magic 500 beckoned, he quickened his gait. The expectant cheers rang out and a basket of flowers were given him. He ran with them to his tent, and then hand in hand with Hart, Hazael and Rowell, marched around the path until the roar went up "Merritt five hundred!" The band joined in the deafening noise of approval emanating from all corners of the building and played "The Star Spangled Banner!" By then, Rowell was on a mark of 512, and the ailing Hazael, who was suffering from swollen tendons of his right leg, on 482. Young Sam went off the track to celebrate, and when he returned some eight minutes later, he was greeted with cries of "Go it Merritt!" and "Good boy Merritt!"

Captain Williams marched in front of one hundred of his officers into the arena at 17:25, his presence bringing about mixture of hisses and cheers. Thereafter, and for a good few minutes, his friends and enemies had a competition in the crowd between them to see who could make more noise. Of the other people employed in the building; *"Everybody about the place, the attendants, the bar-tenders, the scorers, the young women who attend the scales, the telegraph operators, the ticket takers, and even the policemen looked almost as much fagged out with their week's work as the walkers, and they all congratulated themselves that the strain was nearly over. The bar-tenders had as hard work as anybody, for they were kept as busy drawing liquors, all day long, as men could be."*

When Weston completed his 450th mile and found he hardly received any applause, he began to cry. He was helped away from the track and taken to his tent where he became *"quite hysterical"* causing his attendants to think he had been suffering convulsions. However, he was said to make a quick recovery, and was seen to be laughing when he made his reappearance.

The six o'clock scores: **Rowell, 519.6; Merritt, 506.3; Hazael, 491.3; Hart, 470.4; Guyon, 466; Weston, 453.7; Ennis, 438.1; Krohne, 435.4 and Taylor, 240.2:**

After six o'clock, Rowell resumed his efforts to tow his friend Hazael along. He somehow managed to persuade him to run behind him and the spectacle could have been called "Beauty pulls the beast." Hart initially joined in the chase but soon slowed to a walk whilst Krohne, now firing on all cylinders, passed the resting Ennis who was given a sharp nudge by his trainer and advised to get back in the melee and win back 7th spot. He duly obliged and was soon tearing round the ring to recover his former position which he accomplished. Hazael continued to follow Rowell the sight akin to the ugly duckling following its mother. His bravery impressed many in the crowd and a few sympathetic souls presented him with flowers. The grateful Londoner smiled in humble appreciation as he received a basket, then a horseshoe, and then a bouquet, all of which he took to his dull little house to brighten its interior which probably only contained a few empty beer and wine bottles and some old smelly running costumes next to his bed.

Weston left the path very quietly after finishing his 455th mile at 18:17 and stood around his tent dressed in an overcoat, looking disgusted with himself. The story was that he would rejoin the race only if either Ennis or Krohne threatened to displace him from sixth position. The ex-champion was ignored as everybody's attention was focused on the events on the track; as the four leaders dashed around, the excitement grew more intense.

At 19:00, a glance at the score sheet showed Rowell on 523, Merritt on 509, Hazael with 495 and Hart credited with 473. The leader, who had left the track at 19:09, rejoined the race and began running. He was joined by Hart who challenged his pace. As a spurt materialised, Hazael and Merritt followed the two pace-makers who pulled the other pair along at a ten-mile an hour gait for several laps. The building exploded with a deafening roar, which not only rattled the windows of the Garden, but those in nearby buildings; and, if the press is to be believed, some blocks away! Hazael kept on going and only Rowell could keep in his wake. Merritt meanwhile, was happy to slow himself back down to a walk as O'Leary called Hart in. *"The race was terribly hot and perspiration poured from all."* Whilst the building quivered, Taylor came on the track to jeers and taunts from the crowd.

At 19:24, Mr. Atkinson said, "Rowell cannot now make five hundred and fifty miles, but he will remain on the track as long as the contest requires, and roll up as many miles as he can. As the matter now stands, he will make the best record ever shown in this city and will show the American people that it is possible to make five hundred and fifty miles in six days. They know his condition yesterday. They will judge from what he does what he might have done had he been well throughout the six days."

Guyon limped back to his tent on a score of 470.3 at 19:56, and four minutes later, Rowell was being acknowledged as the champion on a mark of 526.1. Merritt was next with 514.2, then Hazael with 499.6. Hart had scored 477.5 and both Ennis and Krohne on 444 with the latter just edging it.

With Weston and Taylor off, Hazael became the third man in the field to have the number 500 put up below his name at 20:05. The usual noisy reception followed his courageous effort. He made one further lap and retired. Hart meanwhile was putting on quite an exhibition of graceful walking for his adoring fans. Swinging his arms, he put his chest out and threw his head backward. He was a totally different man to the one some in the crowd had seen in the early hours of the morning, when he had practically slept as he walked slowly around the track.

Rowell made his 530th mile at 20:28. A couple of minutes later, Merritt, carrying the Union Jack over his shoulders was followed around the track by the new belt holder, who repaid the compliment as he waved the Stars and Stripes, Hart close by him. The band played "God save the Queen," and respect for it was observed by all including Hazael who bowed his head and giggled to himself. "Yankee Doodle" followed, and the three leaders then held hands. With Merritt in the centre towering above the first and third, all walked slowly to the tune "Columbia, the Gem of the Ocean." The dense crowd which was by now cheering, whistling, and clapping their hands, was spilling onto the track and the police were finding it difficult to maintain a clear course for the pedestrians to walk on. *"The scene beggars description. The enthusiasm went beyond all bounds. Crowds in the street outside took up the roar and the mighty sound was carried away far on the balmy air."* The winner was then offered a magnificent floral trophy bearing in immortelles, with the inscription, "To Charles Rowell, by the Albion Society." The trio stopped opposite the time-keeper's stand and Rowell said, "Gentlemen, I thank you, I am through."

After shaking hands the three parted. Rowell was ushered out of the building under the watchful eye of Captain Williams wrapped in a plaid Ulster overcoat and wearing a Derby hat. *"As he walked along, hands were thrust out to his and he shook one now and again with a pleasant "Thank you," and an abundance of pleasant nods to the persons behind the rail."* He was helped into a flower filled carriage where he was whisked off to the Ashland House. The carriage, which was driven rapidly, was followed by a large crowd which congregated outside the hotel, requiring considerable effort on the part of the police to hold them back. Accompanied by Dr. Naylor, his physician, Rowell was helped up to his quarters, parlour no 61, on the second floor. Sat looking pale on a sofa, he told a reporter, "I feel much better than I did after the last walk. I am more hungry than tired, and I am going to get something to eat as soon as I can." He then reminded Mr. Brockway, the proprietor of the hotel, that he wanted corn bread for breakfast and then expressed a desire to retire. Dr. Naylor stated that his patient was in as good condition as could be expected after such an effort.

Some punters, who had bet on Rowell to go beyond 530 miles, and even 540, were very, very, angry. He had had two hours and twenty minutes to spare in which to add to his total. "I knew him," said one man, "when he was running on the tow path for twenty five shillings a week, he is now worth from $45,000 to $50,000; but if I were in his place I would rather be back on the tow path than to stand in his shoes tonight."

Merritt was dressed leisurely in an overcoat and hat when he emerged from under the canvas after a brisk rubbing down. He received a *"perfect ovation"* and was subsequently driven to the Glenham House where the plan was for him to take a hot bath and put him to bed at two o'clock. Reports indicated he would leave for Bridgeport on the following Monday or Tuesday, where he would be received by the Mayor and Common Council.

Weston, who had hurried out of the place accompanied by his wife, was driven away to the Rossmore House where he had stayed since his return to New York.

Back at the Garden, the only men wobbling away were Ennis and Krohne, who were hoping to save their entrance fee and make gate money. Guyon, for no other reason other than he may have been a masochist; and why Hart and Taylor remained was anybody's guess? The "Pie-Eater" took just 8m.2s to make his 250th mile at 21:20 with a horseshoe of flowers over his arm, and after he had finished with his gallant lap, he was presented with……………… a pie!

At 21:24, Ennis finally achieved the desired distance, which was 200 miles beyond Taylor's. The effort produced a massive roar that could be heard by the retreating crowd. The successful athlete made one more lap just to be sure and made haste back to his tent. Hart left the game at the same time. He left the building ten minutes later attired in a fashionable suit, accompanied by O'Leary and Englehardt. The trio threaded their way through the crowds, with Hart smiling and holding his head aloft proudly. The boy bowed to the crowd and shook some of his supporters' hands. He was driven to the Omer Hotel on Sixth Avenue.

Guyon left the track at 21:25. After being presented with a bottle of cologne, he was taken to his hotel where a bath was prepared for him, which it was hoped, would help the dreadful pain he was suffering. He was then put to bed.

Krohne finally made the required 450 miles at 21:48, the last lap being made at a blistering pace. Ennis had joined him on the track just in case the former tried to take 7th place, but the tired Prussian had done enough and permanently retired after making one last lap. After Ennis had made sure of that seventh spot, he hurried back to his tent and quickly left the building to go to his residence in Seventy Seventh Street. Krohne was taken to his home on Sixty Seventh Street in company with his trainer. He was expected to go to Fort Lee after recuperating.

Hazael left the Garden at about 22:10 after he had been bathed and his swollen legs attended to. His trainer Isaac Sullivan wasn't too happy with his arrogant player. Sullivan stated that if George had proved a little more tractable, he would have carried off the belt. The two were whisked off to the Grand Street Ferry, and an hour after their journey, Hazael was reported to be fast asleep in his boarding house in Division Avenue.

Rumours were beginning to circulate that Taylor had stayed till the end to win a bet of $1,000 for his backer at 5/1 that he would stay on the track for a week. His backer had won the bet and Norman was assured of a slice of the dollar cake he had won for him. He was later whisked away to Scott and Earle's Hotel in Sixth Avenue accompanied by his trainer, Mr. Sprague.

The band then played "Home, Sweet Home" after which the audience began dispersing.

King of the Peds

At eleven o'clock, Eben's band arrived beneath the window of Rowell's rooms, where they serenaded him. The champion who was resting at the time opened the curtains at the window and waved to the crowd. He then went to bed.

The Final Scores:

Hour	Time	Rowell	Merritt	Hazael	Hart	Guyon	Weston	Ennis	Krohne	Taylor
134th	15:00	507.6	495.3	479.5	459.6	456.4	442.3	426.1	425.1	228.1
135th	16:00	511.5	409.2	483.2	463.1	460	445	428.1	428	233.2
136th	17:00	515.5	502.4	487.2	466.5	463	449.5	432	432	235
137th	18:00	519.6	506.3	491.3	470.4	466	453.7	436.1	435.4	240.2
138th	19:00	523	509	495	473	468	455	439	438	240.2
139th	20:00	526.1	514.2	499.6	477.5	470	455	444	442.7	244.4
140th	21:00	530	515	500	481.2	470	455	448.2	446.6	247.4
141st	22:00	**530**	**515**	**500**	**482.4**	**471**	**455**	**450.2**	**450.1**	**250**

NB: The track was later to be found to be 7 feet 5 inches short of an eighth of a mile thus leaving a discrepancy of 59 feet 4 inches to the mile. This meant that Rowell's official distance was actually **524 miles and 7 yards**. The other pedestrians' scores were also affected, meaning the likes of Ennis and Krohne were lucky to get a share of the gate money as they had officially had been under the required 450 miles. This anomaly will be dealt with in Chapter 21.

The day after the conclusion of the race, many of the men who competed spent a quiet day recovering from their week's exertion. The winner declared he felt "first rate," but appeared *"pale and haggard."* He was up with the lark at six in the morning, appeased his voracious appetite, bathed, and then went for a run in the park. He told the press that he intended to defend the belt back in England and thanked them for their uniform kindness, admitting that the English pedestrians were largely ignored by their English counterparts, apart from the sporting papers.

Merritt was up at eight o'clock feeling *"clear headed."* He went out, ate a hearty breakfast, had a shave, and relaxed for the rest of the day indoors. He had a few blisters on both feet but otherwise felt well. Of his performance, his backer Scannell said, "Merritt has shown what he can do, and he has done even more than I expected. I believe, with good training, he will yet astonish some pedestrians." Merritt confidently stated that third placed Hazael could beat any man in the world over six days.

Hazael for his part was made to wake up by his attendant and walk around his room during the night. He was then allowed to sleep till he woke which he did at 09:30. He went for a ride later in the afternoon to Coney Island, informing reporters that he wouldn't be taking part in any more like contests, but was willing to compete in future one-to-one matches.

A hotel waiter had brought the ordered meal for Frank Hart to consume, but the fourth placed man was so fast asleep when it arrived at 23:30, that Fred Englehardt, his trainer, sent it back refusing to wake his young star up. It was Fred who was woken up in the morning by his voracious athlete who *demanded* to break his unwanted fast. Hart went back to Boston that evening, leaving huge amounts of flowers which had been sent to him by his fervent fans, which had adorned one of the parlours of the St. Omer Hotel. His trainer said Hart would be given a long rest of three or four months and would then be targeted at the next Astley Belt contest. Frank was the subject of an article in the *Brooklyn Daily Eagle* on Sunday, the 28th of September:

THE PEDESTRIANISM OF OUR COLORED FRIEND MR. HART

The very excellent performance of our colored friend, Mr. Hart, in the pedestrian contest which ended last night may be cited as proof that those who think the negro necessarily degenerates physically, when transferred to this latitude, are mistaken. He did not win the belt but he came in ahead of several white competitors, and he started under the serious disadvantage of having but recently undergone a severe strain. It is true that one swallow does not make a Summer, and that the achievement of one colored man does not prove that other African citizens have the stamina of the average Celt or Anglo Saxon, but it is equally true that whatever any representative of a race accomplishes must be held as illustrative of what that family can do under fair conditions. There is a not uncommon notion that the colored man, while possessed of many estimable qualities such as good nature kindness of heart and great fidelity to those who treat him well, lacks courage and endurance. In the opinion of the majority of the American people, he does not make a good soldier, and among the vulgar it is a settled conviction that he is destitute of that stolid determination which secures victory in the prize ring. Now Mr. Hart has shown conclusively that there is nothing in a black skin or woolly hair that is incompatible with fortitude, and there have been several proofs afforded in the English prize ring that the negro can hold in any rough and tumble contest. It may seem to some that demonstrations of this kind are unimportant. It does not seem so to the EAGLE. As the world goes, truths are enforced by rude illustration rather than by resort to the niceties of the syllogism. The man who cannot see what is involved in the proposition that "all men are created free "and equal" will not misapprehend the significance of a prize fight, a pitched battle, or a pedestrian contest. The idea that our colored brother is an inferior will never sustain so severe a shock at the hands of the logician as it will when a colored man proves his physical equality as Hart has done; his intellectual possibilities as the negro blood in the elder Dumas did; his martial spirit as the Zulus have done, and his ability to take and give punishment as did several ornaments of the prize ring, whose names we forget. In the contest which ended last night there were American's, Englishmen, Irishmen and Germans and this colored boy showed that he was above their average.

Coupled with the significance of Mr. Hart's commendable effort should be put the kindly feeling of the audience for him. He was undoubtedly the most popular man in the list. Rowell's pluck was admired; Merritt's Yankee perseverance elicited much applause, and the calm, sober efforts of Krohne store witnessed with appreciation but over and above all, the spectator took delight in giving encouragement to Hart, and would have been especially pleased to have seen him crowned with the victor's wreath. In this there is a lesson for our colored readers to remember. The average American citizen is not only not "down" on the negro, but he has a spirit of chivalry in his breast that will force him to encourage by double manifestation of approval every colored man who appears as a worthy competitor in a fair field.

Considerable might be said in this relation touching the opinion long prevalent in the Old World—that men on this continent deteriorated both in mind and body. Edwards, Webster, Emerson, Hawthorne and Longfellow have abundantly proven that there is no falling off in mind, and our yachtsmen, our riflemen, our pugilists and our pedestrians show that there is no decline in physical stamina. White and black, we are doing admirably.

George Guyon slept till 13:30, had breakfast, and then went for a walk calling on Sam Merritt on his way. He then went for a ride. He said he would definitely be competing in the next event. He was reported to have lost eight pounds in weight during the contest. Ennis was up bright and early at seven, and stated that due to his persistent stomach problems, he thought it might be a good idea to retire now.

Weston was up at ten in the morning, ate breakfast, read the papers, visited Rowell and then accompanied his wife to their home. It was reported that he had expressed the greatest mortification at his poor showing in the late match and was dismayed with what was being said about him in the press. One such report read: **Weston was a thorough disappointment to his friends and a laughing stock early in the week to the spectators who jeered him for his buffoonery. Later, when the old ex-champion went along the track with a pinched face, unsteady gait and straining eyes, the picture of a broken down and miserable man, the people remained silent, realizing that he badly broken down utterly, bodily and mentally. The sight was pitiable, and the silence of the crowd as he passed by alternately laughing and crying deepened the sadness of the scene.** He stated that he was not in condition for the contest, and was subject to many inconveniences after the match began. He said that the immense crowd on the first night had disconcerted him, and that he had been nervous during the race, where the smoky atmosphere irritated him, along with the match scorers. Referring to his "frivolity" on the track, he said this was due to a "desire to distract his mind from the thought of walking," and that he "did not intend to trifle with the people." One of his friends told reporters that Weston's failure to retain the belt was due to the amount of walking he had carried out in England before his arrival in America and the constant excitement thereafter, claiming that had he not held the belt, he would not have entered the contest. He added that anyone who wagered money on him under these circumstances deserved to lose. His friend also said the death of several dear friends, including his mother, had affected the ex-champion. Weston refused to say whether he would take part in the next contest for the belt.

The *Brooklyn Daily Eagle* produced an interesting piece in its edition of Monday, the 29th of September, in which Rowell and the local bookies were accused of unscrupulous behaviour. The article's headline **Sharp Practice in the Walking Match** stated:

King of the Peds

It was fondly hoped that the reports of the last hours of the great walking match, to which the EAGLE and its contemporaries surrendered much space yesterday, would be the last of that six days agony, but it appears that a side issue has sprung up and one which involves the ethics of the track in a distracting degree. It will be remembered that Mr. Rowell retired permanently from the track at about eight o'clock on Saturday evening with a score of 530 miles to his credit and that simultaneously Messrs. Merritt and Hazael quitted the ring with scores respectively of 515 and 500 miles. They could all of them have added to the scores between the time of retiring and the hour of closing the match, but they preferred not to. Intervals of fifteen miles separated the first, second and third men, which it was hopeless for them to attempt to close within the specified time, and when they saw the further attempt to alter their relative positions was useless, they gave up the struggle together, completing their distances on the same lap, hand in hand, amid much enthusiastic uproar.

Incidentally, an esteemed contemporary declares that Rowell has tarnished his reputation by this act, and proceeds to give the why and the wherefore. It seems that industrious bookmakers had offered bets against Rowell completing more than 530 miles in the 142 hours, and that they had found many takers who were willing to accept the wager. When Mr. Rowell departed for home with only 530 miles and not a lap more to his credit the takers of those bets were exceedingly wroth and declared him to be a cheat and a swindler, and our complaining contemporary goes so far as to state that he did this shameful deed in collusion with the bookmakers aforesaid, wilfully an dishonestly to prevent betters making money.

If it is true that Rowell was in collusion with the bookmakers, he certainly did not act honorably in arranging a given distance beyond which he would not go. If, on the other hand, he had been in collusion with the men who took the bets offered by the bookmakers, and had made the necessary lap in addition to his 530 miles it would have been equally dishonorable, and the bookmakers would have raised an uproar. There are, however, several things to be borne in mind. Mr. Rowell was entirely and completely in the hand of his backers, and implicitly obeyed their instructions. If any collusion was had, it was between the backers and the bookmakers. If the former told him that 530 miles were quite sufficient, it was his duty by previous agreement to desist from making more, and if those who bet on his making more, simply because he could evidently have done so, without considering the probability of bets being made on a sure thing, lost their money, they have simply themselves and their own stupidity to blame. They ought to have remembered that in dealing with organized sharpers they are at a disadvantage. Again all the men were thoroughly worn out with six days racing. Rowell may have retired of his own free will when he found himself in position to do so safely, and he may not in any case may have not known anything at all about the betting. Why should he have tortured himself still further in order to win money for strangers, since he was compelled neither by the conditions of the match nor by honorable feeling to do more than win it if he could? If the bookmakers bet on a sure thing they were out and out sharpers, and those who bet with them were out and out ninnies for not taking heed to themselves. But, granting that all this is true, we fail to see how it compromises Rowell any more than sharp practice on the turf ruins the moral reputation of a horse who wins by a nose instead of half a mile. The moral seems to be that greenhorns should avoid betting against professional bookmakers.

Some interesting facts about the amount of food sold at the lunch stands were to appear soon after the race. Ten men were constantly employed serving; $1,000 was taken daily from the public who consumed 3,000 sandwiches made from 400 loaves of bread every day along with 5,000 pigs' trotters, 5,000 oysters, 6,600 pickled sheep's tongues, 100 pounds of roast beef, 200 chickens, 250 pies, 200 pounds of corned beef and 2 barrels of eggs; 170 gallons of clam chowder were sold, and 2 barrels of sugar were used to sweeten customer's coffee. Four men were kept busy preparing salads all day and opposite at the bar, 200,000 glasses of lager were sold along with 15 barrels of liquor and 8,000 bottles of soda.

The total gate receipts for the week were: Monday by 8 a.m: **$6,329**; Tuesday by 8 a.m: **$8,665**; Wednesday by 8 a.m: **$8,713**; Thursday 8 a.m: **$10,120**; Friday 8 a.m: **$10,977**; Saturday 8 a.m: **$17,065**; Saturday 11 p.m: **$12,063**. Total: **$73,932**: The Board of Managers held a private meeting on Sunday, the 29th. They revealed that the receipts for the week were $73,932.00, of which 25% or $18,480.75 went to the Kuntz Brothers. After deducting expenses, $39,000 was divided amongst the successful competitors thus: **Rowell (50%), $19,500.00; Merritt (18.75%), $7,312.50; Hazael (10.75%), $4,192.50; Hart (7%), $2,730 00; Guyon (5%), $1,950.00; Weston (3.5%), $1,365.00; Ennis (2.75%), $1,072.50; Krohne (2.25%), $877.50:** In addition to the gate money, Rowell also took possession of a silver card-receiver worth $200 and $6,500 in stake money, which at the time was being held in London by Astley.

Two attachment orders were presented at the meeting, against Weston's share of the gate money by David E. Saunders of Salem, Massachusetts, for $4,000, and by Abraham Avery of New York for $613. The Board decided to pay no attention to them because the money belonged to his wife who had paid the entrance stake. It was revealed that Saunders had been stalking Weston in Britain in his relentless pursuit of recovering the money from the former champion, and that Weston had spent $5,000 in defence costs in the courts there.

Excursion

WITH THE GREAT PEDESTRIANS

THURSDAY, OCTOBER 2.

MERRITT TO BE RECOGNIZED

The friends of Mr. SAMUEL MERRITT, having determined to make a triumphal entry with him to the city of his home, BRIDGEPORT, have chartered the largest steamer in the world.

THE GRAND REPUBLIC

On which occasion, and at the invitation of Mr. Merritt, he will be accompanied by his late competitors and their friends. The steamer will be greatly decorated with the flags of all nations.

CONTERNO'S CELEBRATED MILTARY BAND

Will discourse the finest music the entire trip. The celebrities will be welcomed at Bridgeport by artillery salutes which will be answered from the steamer, two brass bands, and thousands upon thousands of the citizens of Connecticut.

STEAMER LEAVES West Twenty–fourth at 9 A. M.: Leroy st, at N. Y., 9:15 A. M.; Pier 1, N. R., 9:30 A. M.; Jewell's Wharf, Brooklyn, 9:45 A. M.; Twenty-third at East River, 10, A. M.

FARE FOR THE WHOLE EXCURSION, 50 CENTS Refreshments and dinner to be had on board at reasonable prices

The above advertisement appeared in the *Brooklyn Daily Eagle* on Tuesday, the 30th of September. That night, a presentation of the Astley Belt was to be made to Rowell in front of 3,000 onlookers at the Garden, followed by an exhibition by the pedestrians who had starred in the recent match. However, there had been a rumour beforehand that the belt had been *"attached"* by one of Weston's numerous creditors, and would be retained pending future court proceedings. Of the problem, the *New York Times* reported: Rowell said he went to Tiffany's about 5 o'clock in the afternoon, after the belt, and they refused to give it up. They said it had been attached by one of Weston's creditors, and would be retained, pending the decision of the matter by the courts. It was too late to do anything about it last night, and it was concluded to let the matter rest until today, when legal steps are to be taken to get possession of the belt. Both Atkinson and Rowell said they had no fears as to the result, and that they were certain the belt could not be permanently detained, for the good and sufficient reason that it was not, and never had been the property of Weston.

The rumour was correct and therefore the belt would not be presented that night as planned. However, the exhibition did go ahead and many of the pedestrians took part in entertaining the crowd. The "Pie Man," Taylor, who was originally matched to run against Hazael, the latter named unable to compete owing to lameness, started by running five miles in 33m.44s. When he left, both Merritt and Guyon then entertained those present with a quarter of a mile exhibition of walking. They were followed by William Dutcher who, attired in a flaming red costume, then made two miles in 14m.34s. Ennis was next on track with an effort of a mile in 6m.17s and then Peter Crossland, *"the champion 75-mile walker of America,"* had a two-mile walking challenge match of $50 with John Dobler of Chicago. Although Crossland won in a time of 18m.56s, he was disqualified on a claim of a foul by his rival. Rowell finally treat the crowd to a mile in a time of 5m.27s. A speech was then read during which Leonard Grover presented Rowell with the extra 24-hour prize, after which the crowd dispersed.

The belt was finally delivered to Mr. Atkinson the day after, who handed it over to Rowell. However, Atkinson had to deposit $500 as security to the sheriff, pending the decision of the disputed ownership by the courts. On the 4th, both Rowell and his trainer Charlie Barnsley were entertained in a flower and flag festooned lodge-room of the British Provident Association headquarters at No. 26 Delaney Street. After the belt had been inspected by those present, Rowell was elected as an honourary member. A couple of days later, the champion was again in demand when he was presented with a membership badge of the Albion Society by the president, Mr. E. Driver at the Steuben House Hotel. The dinner was said to take place in rooms *"profusely decorated with flags and flowers,"* and was attended by 100 ladies.

Rowell confirmed that the belt would be deposited with Astley on returning to England because he didn't want to be accused of just wanting to make money from large attendances in the USA, and that the next race would be in England. He hoped too that the rules would be changed, from making 450 to 500 miles in future events, in order to claim gate money.

Finally on October the 25th, the *Isle of Ely Herald and Huntingdon Gazette* was able to let many of the people of Cambridge who read its pages know what had happened in relation to the legal proceedings: - THE ASTLEY BELT; Litigation has arisen in New York with reference to the right of property in the Astley Belt. On Monday, Oct. 6, a Sheriff's Jury met to try the claim made by Weston. At four o'clock Rowell, Mr. Atkinson, and Mr. Potter, entered the court room, and took seats beside their counsel, Mr. Blandy. Rowell was the first witness, and testified to the terms of the agreement under which the belt was held. He said, further, that Weston had no money to receive on account of the belt; that although his wife had deposited £25 in London, and £75 in New York, that amount was practically refunded to him for his entrance fee in the late pedestrian contest. He was sure that Weston had no interest or property in the belt, and that no one had any property in the same until he had won it three times consecutively, when it became the absolute property of the winner. Mr. Atkinson was then called, but his testimony was for the greater part corroborative of Rowell's. At the conclusion of the evidence, the Sheriff's jury promptly decided in favor of Rowell.

CHAPTER 21

1st O'Leary Belt

Daniel O'Leary decided to sponsor a series of races, for the purpose of finding and developing an athlete who was good enough to bring back and keep the Astley Belt in the United States. His other reason for holding this particular race and the forthcoming races, was to give something back to the sport that had been so generous to him. Thus the *"O'Leary Belt Race for the Championship of America"* would be held at the pedestrians' *"Mecca,"* Madison Square Garden, between Monday and Saturday, the 6th and 11th of October 1879.

By the terms of the contest the first man to pass the post would own the belt and win $5,000. The runner-up would secure $2,000, the third placed man $1,000, and the fourth, $500, the prizes being deposited with the *Spirit of the Times*. However, to win any prize, a competitor would have to make a score of 450 miles. To anybody not winning either of the main four prizes, a bonus of $300 would be awarded to any man who covered 475 miles, and for anyone making 465 miles, $200 would be theirs. All those making 450 miles would have their entrance money returned.

The conditions of the O'Leary Belt competition were:

1. All matches for the belt shall be for $500 a side.

2. The belt shall be subject to challenge from any man in the world.

3. Challenges may be sent to the stakeholder, accompanied by $100 and the remaining $400 must be made good when articles are signed.

4. Challenges shall date from the day of their receipt by the stakeholder and the holder must arrange race with the first challenger.

5. The holder of the belt must name date place, sign articles, and deposit his $500 stake money four weeks from the date of challenge.

6. The holder must name a day not less than three months nor more than six months from date of challenge.

7. The holder must name either New York City or Chicago, Illinois, as the place for the race provided that by consent of the stakeholder and all the contestants, it may be agreed to hold the race in some other American city where a suitable building may be procured.

8. After a match is made any person can join in the race by agreeing the articles and depositing $500 stake money with the stakeholder four weeks before the date set for the commencement of the race.

9. The winner shall receive the stake money and must give the stakeholder satisfactory security for the safe keeping of the belt and its prompt return when called for.

10. No share of the gate money shall be given to any competitor who does not cover 450 miles.

11. All necessary and reasonable expenses shall be paid from the gate money and the remainder shall be divided among those competitors who go 450 miles or further in accordance with the following rules: If only one man finishes 450 miles he shall take all. If two men, the division shall be two-thirds and one-third. If three men, fourth-sevenths, two-sevenths and for all other numbers the division shall be on the same principal, each man receiving twice as much as the man behind him.

12. The holder must deliver the belt to the stakeholder ten days before the date of the race.

13. The belt will become the personal property of any man who wins it in three successive races, or holds it for eighteen consecutive months: provided that if at the completion of the eighteen months, he shall be under challenge, the match must be contested and won by him.

14. The editor of the *Spirit of the Times*, New York City shall be the official stakeholder. In all contests for the belt, shall appoint all officials and decide all questions not expressly provided for in these rules.

The prize belt which was on view at a jewellers shop before the race was described by the *National Police Gazette* thus: It is far superior in artistic execution and elegance of design to the Sir John Astley belt. It is composed of fifteen chains, each thirty-six inches in length and three and a half inches wide, upon which is placed six medallions. The center shield is eight inches long and six inches wide, and over it is the name "O'Leary" in diamonds; underneath is the inscription, "Championship of America. Six-days-go-as-you-please;" below this, on an oval shield in blue enamel, are the national colors of England, France, Ireland and America. In the center of the shield is a gold figure representing O'Leary walking on a tan-bark track. The shield is also surrounded with eight Solitaire diamonds, in stars, and on the lower part of the shield is an American eagle, on branches of laurel leaves, and the words "Strength and Endurance." The two shields on either side of the center shield have pedestrian gold figures, one of which is representative of Rowell's "jog-trot," and the other of a runner. All the shields are bordered with Scotch thistles, American ferns, oak, ivy and acorns. The material is sterling frosted silver. The belt is valued at about $800. It weighs nine pounds, and has about one hundred pennyweights of gold in its manufacture.

The O'Leary Belt

The National Police Gazette (Illustration no: 59)

The 35 contestants were:

01. Joseph Allen lived in Renfrew, Massachusetts: He was born in Carlisle, England, in 1850. Weight 133lbs; Height 5ft.8in: Joe's best six-day record was 348 miles made at Adams, Massachusetts, in August of that year. What was interesting about that performance was that he started the race with a lame leg but made 87 miles on the last day. A couple of weeks after that, and at the same venue, he made 100 miles well within a day.

02. John Henry Behrman lived in Jersey City: He was born Germany in 1838. Weight 156lbs; Height 5ft.10in: He was reported to have won several 100-mile races in his home country and one 250-mile race. His record in the USA was 100 miles in a day.

03. Charles Boyle lived in Montreal: He was born in Donegal, Ireland, in 1851. Weight 132lbs; Height 5ft.6in: He was a well known snow shoe champion and the president of the Emerald Snow Shoe Club of Canada. He had made 91 miles in 21h.40m on May the 9th of the same year, and the month after made 50 miles in 10 hours.

04. E. Brand of Asbury Park, New Jersey: He was 30 years old. Weight 137lbs; Height 5ft.7½in: He was "Sullivan's unknown," and had made 25 miles in 4 hours in private trials. With that record was considered in with a good chance of winning.

05. J. Briody resident of Greenpoint, Long Island: He had been entered by Judge Charles B. Elliott, who hadn't forwarded his race history.

06. John Albert Brondgeest resided in Toronto: The 33-year-old compactly built and sturdy Irish/Dutch scout had been born in Montreal: Weight 148lbs; Height 5ft.7¾in: He had been a mail carrier and trapper, and was an officer of the Hudson Bay Company. Apparently he had made the following distances wearing snow shoes: 124 miles in 30 hours; 133 miles in 32 hours; 155 miles in 36 hours; 332 miles in 6 days and 946 miles in 21 days:

07. Henry Brown of Fulham, England: Weight 133lbs; Height 5ft.6in: "Blower" needs no introduction.

08. Michael M. Costello of Fishkill-on-the-Hudson, New York: 26 years old: Weight 151lbs; Height 5ft.8in: He had scored 127 miles in 24 hours.

09. Thomas T. Costello: (Called "**R. Dugan**" in the race due to there being two Costellos competing). With a record of 438 miles, he was known as *"The Rat Catcher."*

10. Richard Cromwell from San Francisco: Known as the "Californian Scout," he was a trapper *"from the borderland."* He claimed he was a doctor worth $100,000 and that he had written three books on walking. He stated that he went into the race to discover *"whether it was hydrogen or carbon that made muscle."* He weighed 170 pounds, was 35 years old and had a record of 463 miles in six days.

11. Peter Crossland of Sheffield, England: Another in the race who needs no introduction.

12. Benjamin Curran of New York: At 46 years old, he was also known as the "Longshoreman." Weight 146lbs; Height 5ft.6in: "Old Ben" had made 438 miles in 141h.59m at Gilmore's Garden between May the 5th and 10th of that year.

13. Edward Davis of Kerry, Ireland: With no record to speak of, he was described as the *"Soap Man"* of former contests. He was said to be the same as Norman Taylor, in that he slept for 16 of every 24 hours he competed in. The story was that he had come from Ireland *"expressly to win the belt,"* and had been in training at the Manhattan Grounds for the past two months.

14. John J. Dickenson of Philadelphia: Had a record 407 miles in six days made in the previous spring.

15. John Dillon: With no identifiable record, he was a baggage-master of New York Central Railroad.

16. J. P. Dushane of New Castle, Pennsylvania: His record was thus: In 1868, he had made 614 miles in 12 days at Montana. In 1869, he had scored 100 miles in 23h.30m and 50 miles in 9h.29m at Vancouver Island. In British Columbia he had walked 402 miles in 8 ½ days, and at New Castle on September the 14th of that year, he had made 100 miles in 24 hours.

17. Walter Eckersall living in Chicago: Was born in Glossop, Derbyshire, England, in 1847. Weight 131lbs; Height 5ft.6in: *"A well known English pedestrian, with no long distance record."*

18. Frank L. Edwards of New York: Aged 24 years. Weight 161lbs; Height 5ft.6in: Frank was described as being one of the few good looking men in the match. His best effort was when he won the "California Diamond Belt" making 371 miles in six days at San Francisco in July of that year.

19. Alfred Elson lived in West Meriden, Connecticut: Alf was born in Northampton, England, and was 47 years of age. He was described as being a *"little wiry fellow."* He was remembered for walking from Providence to Woonsocket four times a day in a week in 1875, averaging 68 miles per day. He then walked from Norwich to New London, walking back and forth at the rate of 65 miles per day, also for a week. On the 10th of March 1879, he took on Professor Washington of Baltimore in a six-day walk at Wright's Hall, Poughkeepsie, for $500. At 23:00 on the first day, and after he had completed 93 miles in 22h.49m, his opponent gave up on a score of 77 miles made in 21 hours. In July he beat Campana in Waterbury, Connecticut, in a 26-hour walk for $250. In his next contest he beat Sam Merritt in a 50-mile race in a time of 8h.32m. He then walked in an exhibition match for six days making 65 miles in 12 hours, and at the end of the week had covered 300 miles. He then won $150 for coming second to Harriman with 274 miles at Providence, Rhode Island, in a 75-hour event which ended on the 17th of August. His final race was when he came third to Hart in the O'Leary-Englehardt sponsored, 12-hour event, between the 8th and 13th of September, when he made 352 miles and 7 laps securing $200 for his time on the track.

20. Christian Faber of Newark, New Jersey: Born in Germany in 1848. Weight 148lbs; Height 5ft.4in: The 33-year-old was the man who had famously been drugged and survived in a previous contest at the Garden. In his home city in February of that year he had walked 107 miles in 24 hours; and then between the 5th and 10th of May, made 450 miles in 142h.25m.25s.

21. Patrick Fitzgerald of New York: Pat was the champion 10-mile runner who had *"exhibited some astonishing bursts of speed on the Manhattan Athletic Grounds."* He was *"tall and burly, with the muscular development of a champion oarsman."*

22. Charles Fox of Austin, Illinois: Charles was 37 years old. Weight 135lbs; Height 5ft.4½in: His best record was 80 miles in 18 hours in July, and 57 miles in 9 hours in September of that year.

23. Harry Howard of Glen Cove: Weight 9st.12lb; Height 5ft.6in: Much more on the 29-year-old who was born in Lancashire, England, but had resided in the USA for ten years, can be gleaned in Chapter 23 - when he attempted to make 450 miles at the Mozart Gardens at Brooklyn, New York, between Monday, the 20th and Saturday, the 25th of

King of the Peds

January, 1879. The *Glen Cove Gazette* in the 18th of January edition in its lead-up to that race wrote of him: Howard is an exotic from the kingdom upon which the sun never sets, and for seven years a resident of this place. Is a butcher by trade, a wrestler by profession, having contended in many a tough and successful contest; and withal is a dog trainer, owning his own hounds and "thoroughbred" horse, and in top boots and plug hat rides with the proudest of the Queens County Hunt after fox or aniseed bag, as the case may be. He is a typical young Englishman, tough and plucky, and is said to have trained faithfully for the task he has set himself to perform taking a daily morning walk of thirty miles or more over the rough roads of this section and doing up his day's work after finishing the exercise. Then in a *"Grand Six-Day Walking Contest"* which commenced at the Central Pedestrian Hall, 635 and 637 Fulton Street, Brooklyn, on Monday, March the 17th in the same year, he took on John H. Bush for a purse of $500; Howard to make 450 miles before his opponent made 425. Harry won the match with 429.6, Bush making 370.12. He then made 283 miles in 110h.40m at Gilmore's Garden when he competed for the "Championship Pedestrian Belt of the United States," between the 14th and 19th of April. (See Chapter 17 for a full account of this race which was won by Peter Panchot). Then in May at Allegheny City, Pennsylvania, he made 400 miles in 6 days. Finally at Cincinnati, Ohio, in June, in a 7-day, 15 hours per day contest, he made 410 miles.

24. Martin Kemmerer of Lock Haven, Pennsylvania: Martin was just 21 years of age. Weight 163lbs; Height 5ft.10in: His record was: (All in 1879) In March in his own city, he made 100 miles in 27h.30m. At Revere, Pennsylvania, he made another 100 miles in 24h.10m. Then at Lock Haven on May the 9th he took 21h.5m to make the same distance. At Williamsport, Pennsylvania, on the 21st of May, he made 141 miles in 30 hours. After that at Milton in the same state, he scored 187 miles in 50h.30m on June the 18th. Finally on July the 21st he made 450 miles in 140 hours again in his own city.

25. W. H. McClane of Philadelphia: With no record, he was known as *"Professor"* McClean; a well-known baseball umpire.

26. David McKee of New York: No record.

27. James McLeavy of Bonhill, Scotland: Age 27 years. Weight 122lbs. Height 5ft.4½in. James needs no introduction.

28. James Mahoney of New York: Weight 163lbs. Height 5ft.8½in. In private trials had made 197 miles in 48 hours, and 253 miles in 75 hours.

29. Nicholas Murphy of Haverstraw, New York, was a young man of 18 years old who was said to have run 184 miles in 2 days.

30. John Perkins of Brooklyn: 25 years old. Weight 145lbs. Height 5ft.8in. As well as having made 50 miles in nine hours for six consecutive days, John had made 189 miles in 52 hours.

31. Albert Pierce of New York: At 23 years of age, Albert was the only *"colored man"* in the contest: Weight 139lbs; Height 5ft.9in: He was known as *"the pride of Sullivan Street,"* and was reputed to have made 100 miles in 16h.29m.40s.

32. Samuel P. Russell of Chicago: His best record was 432 miles in six days in 1877.

33. Timothy Spellacy of Millerstown, Pennsylvania: Tim was 25 years old. Weight 157lbs. Height 6ft.1in. At Petrolia, Pennsylvania, he made 260 miles in three days and 364 miles in 4 days.

34. William Tait of New York: Weight 136lbs. Height 5ft.5in: He was the smallest man in the race. In a private trial, he had made 113 miles in 25 hours.

35. Cyrenius Walker of Buffalo was 39 years old. Weight 168lbs. Height 6ft.1in. On April the 7th of that year in Buffalo, he made 105 miles in a day. Then on the 30th of the same month, he made 318 miles in 72 hours, and finally on May the 24th he scored 434 miles in 142 hours.

One final note to mention is that a special prize was to be awarded to the *"neatest, cleanest, best appearing man on the track."*

O'Leary gave the following interview to the *Brooklyn Daily Eagle,* the text of which appeared in their Sunday edition on the 5th of October 1879:

O'Leary; "I came in just to see that you newspaper men were supplied with as many tickets of admission to the walk as they might wish."

"We are glad to see you Mr. O'Leary. What do you think of the prospects for your great contest? You know this is close after the walk in which Rowell carried off the Astley belt again. Do you think that the public will have as much interest in this one, or enough to warrant your great expenditures?"

O'Leary; "I have no doubt that there will be more interest in this match than in any walking match that ever took place either in this country or in England."

"What makes you think so?"

O'Leary; "Well, in the first place just see the number of entries. We first limited the number of entries to twenty five, but the applications were so numerous that we had to select ten more. Then the men who take a pecuniary interest in it are business men. They know what they are about. For instance, one man pays $4,000 for the bar privilege; another man pays $800 for the lunch counter; another pays the same amount for the cigar stand. The privilege of that kind, sold to men of good business judgment, amount to $6,400 cash. That is one good indication that we are going to have the biggest crowd that was ever in the building to see a walking match.

"How about your track? Have you the distance accurately surveyed?"

O'Leary; "Yes sir, by the best engineer we could find. Now I'll tell you something, there's going to be trouble about the money awarded to the winners in this last walking match and we don't propose to have any of that kind of difficulty when we get through. The track the contestants in this last match walked on was short fifty nine feet and four inches as you have just heard. In a six days walk that makes a great deal of distance. The conditions of that match were that to secure anything, a man must have made 450 miles. Ennis was short in his 450, five miles and 307 feet. Weston was short 597 feet, Krohne, 5 miles and 14 feet, yet all these received a share of the gate money when they were not entitled to it. All those who made the distance were defrauded - not intentionally - by just the money the others received. What I was going to tell you is that Hart, the young colored walker, in whom I was interested, has retained General Butler to sue for his money. He is entitled to $390 more than he got."

"Well, that is the case with Rowell and Merritt, in a greater degree is it not?"

O'Leary; "Yes, but Hart is only looking out for his own rights."

"You took a great interest in Hart. How did that come about?

O'Leary; "Oh, I happened to get acquainted with him, and found him a fine walker. Mr. Englehardt first got him to walking. I was with him a couple of months, giving him information about walking, and advancing his interests. I sent the money over on the third of August, to enter him for the Astley belt just won by Rowell."

"Rowell got away with the Astley belt pretty easily. Will you challenge him?"

O'Leary; "Yes. But I don't propose to go to England and walk. If it cannot be walked for in this country, I won't trouble myself about it. Walking six days is very laborious. I don't propose to do it for nothing, as I would have to do in England."

"Who, in your opinion is the greatest pedestrian we have, Rowell?"

O'Leary; "Rowell is the best in the 'go-as-you-please' contest, I think, although Blower Brown is a good one, if not quite so good, very nearly. I know of another colored man who may beat Rowell."

"You say a good many more entered for the O'Leary belt than you could admit?"

O'Leary; "Yes there were 98 applications to put up the money and walk. Mr. Curtis, of the Spirit of the Times, who has charge, compelled to accept of more than 25 and more than he intended to.

"How compelled?"

O'Leary; "Well, not actually forced, you know, but big pressure was brought to bear upon him. Behind one man would be Mr. Mayor this, and Mr. Govenor that behind another. There was a tremendous scramble to get into the race. We have made all the preparations for thirty five contestants."

"The prospect then is for good walking?"

King of the Peds

O'Leary; "The very best. Blower Brown, you know is champion of England. He is a most extraordinary walker and runner. He is not a pretty man, and not a pretty walker, but he gets over the ground very fast and stays. Then there is a man by the name of Pierce, who is said to be a great walker. Then there is a Scotchman by the name of McLeavy - I think that's his name - who has done some big walking, and is one of the most graceful runners I have ever seen. The other men I don't know so much about, Wild, of New York, is spoken of as a great runner for one hundred miles. *Wild, a great runner for an hour. He ran eleven miles in one hour. What he can do in six days I don't know."

*Patrick Fitzgerald.

"You are a pretty good walker yourself, Mr. O'Leary. As you don't take part in this contest suppose you talk about your own powers a little. What have you done and what can you do?"

O'Leary; "I don't like to talk about what I think I can do. What I have done is on record. I have had fourteen matches of more or less importance. The principal ones are my match with Wilson Reid in New York four years ago in Barnum's Museum. We walked 20 miles a side for $500, and I was innocently drawn into giving him one fourth of a mile. I say innocently, for before I got through, I thought he would beat me. I beat him, however. My next was with DeWitt also in New York. We walked 24 hours, and I gave him ten miles and beat him. The next was with Ennis in Chicago, where I first met him. I gave him ten miles in one hundred. When he was 67, I was 77 miles and he gave up. I walked the match out. The next was with Weston in Chicago. He quit at 451, and I was then 505. I walked with Weston again in London fifteen months after that, and he made 510 to my 520. Thirteen months after that I won the Astley belt in England. These are the principal matches although there were several others of less importance in which I won."

There was to be no view blocking by unsightly tents in the middle of the track for the O'Leary's races. The contestants would set up their temporary, 10 feet by 7 feet homes under the gallery on the Twenty Seventh Street side of the Garden. All the rooms were numbered from 1 to 35 and contained a cot-bed and mattress, stoves, gaslight and two tables and two chairs. When Peter Crossland realised that his cot was devoid of bedding, the Yorkshireman challenged Mr. Curtis, the manager, about the problem. Curtis response was said to reply to him, "Why, my dear fellow, you wouldn't want to sleep in another mans bed clothes?" Crossland replied, "That's so." Off went Peter with his trainer to cover his nest, and the rest of the peds followed suit.

Two separate tents would be provided for all the men so that it wouldn't be necessary for them to enter their main accommodation other than for sleep. The other tents would serve as places where the contenders could be rubbed down rather than have to trudge to their rooms.

The reporters and judges' stands would also be situated on that side of the building, which meant the scoreboard would replace the space that they vacated. The actual scoring would be done by members of the various athletic clubs within the city and vicinity. The dials as used in the previous contest would be replaced by the old system of names and numbers, with the laps and miles printed on strips of black cardboard. A large clock had been placed in front of the scorers' stand to help the judges and reporters carry out their duties with the utmost efficiency.

The pre-match betting: (Placed odds to finish 1st or 2nd are in brackets): **Brown, 4/6 (1/3); Faber and Kemmerer, 4/1 (2/1); Allen and Cromwell, 5/1 (5/2); Elson, 6/1 (5/2); Russell, 6/1 (3/1); T. Costello, Curran and Walker, 7/1 (7/2); Fitzgerald, 12/1 (6/1); Bar these, 10/1 and above:**

Mr. Haswell, the City Surveyor, confirmed that the track was 7 feet five inches short of an eighth of a mile—thus leaving a discrepancy of 59 feet 4 inches to the mile, or a difference of one mile in every 100. The track construction had been entrusted to a carpenter employed by Mr. Atkinson, Astley's representative for the previous competition a week earlier. When asked about the track, Rowell apparently smiled and said that Atkinson would make it alright next time. When the discrepancy was pointed out to Brown, he remarked, "All I ask is what is fair and just. I never had any favours shown me, and never want any. Why just look at the favours that were shown O'Leary when he walked in London and won the belt. He had a separate track all to himself, and no one was allowed on it to bother him, while the rest of us had to walk on one. And there were seventeen of us too. Do you suppose they would do that with me here? Instead of that they are going to allow thirty-five men to start here on one track; that notwithstanding the fact that the original agreement specifies that there should be twenty-five starters. I don't think its fair, and it will be impossible to make a record if all those men continue on the track. But I intend to do my best, and I shall certainly beat Rowell's record. I never felt better in my life, and was never in better condition for a contest than I am at the moment."

The track itself was said to be far superior to the old one. Under the direction of Mr. Alfred West, loam, four inches in depth, had been covered by tanbark and sawdust, doused with water, and then pressed with a heavy roller. The result was said to be *"kinder"* to walkers than runners, who preferred a spongier surface. "Blower" Brown, when asked about to comment on its condition stated, "We runners have an advantage over you walkers that makes up more than what you gain in having this kind of track." He went to comment about the *current* cleanliness, and the purity of air in the building. "If the building could only be kept in this condition until next Saturday night," he said, "you would see some of the best walking ever done. But before tomorrow the air will be heavy with tobacco smoke, and I don't care how good walker or runner a man is, the smoke is bound to affect him in a six-day walk. Give us the good pure air that we've got here now and I tell you some of us would astonish you." However, when Mr. Curtis the manager was asked later if an attempt would be made to ban smoking in the building, he rather ignorantly replied, "Oh, we all smoke. I shall give orders that no man pass the door without a cigar in his mouth!"

The *New York Times* described the scene in the street on the day *before* the start of the contest. That newspaper also wrote about what lengths one man went to to gain free entry: A crowd of 200 or 300 men and boys had gathered at noon yesterday in Madison-avenue, in front of the Madison Square Garden, where the walk for the O'Leary belt began this morning. On the curb stone on the west side of the avenue sat ragged boys and bare-legged girls, ranging in age from 6 to 15 years, in a long line. Behind them, idle men stood in a row staring stupidly up at the bare walls of the Garden. The side walk in front of the main entrance was blocked with men, all eager to get into the building. Cards by the dozen were sent in to Mr. Curtis and Mr. Kelly but very few of them had the desired effect. Tickets had been issued on Saturday to the trainers of the pedestrians, and all persons whom the managers cared to allow within the building before the doors were opened to the public, and the door-keepers had been instructed to admit no one without a ticket. The majority of those who attempted to enter yesterday were, Mr. Kelly said, the regulation lodgers, who were anxious to get into the building without paying, and take up their quarters there for the week. Once in, the managers would have no power to put them out, because the exhibition was advertised to last six days and one admission entitled a spectator to see the entire exhibition. But the managers were determined that the lodgers should pay 50 cents for their six nights accommodation, and they thought that this was cheap enough. Numerous devices were adopted to affect an entrance, but they generally failed. One seedy looking man, with a nose of the color of a boiled lobster, presented himself at the door with a package of tacks, which he said the carpenter had sent him out to get. This dodge did not work and that man has probably been lamenting all night the loss of the drink, the money for which he had recklessly squandered on the tacks.

When the doors were opened at 21:20, many of those who were old enough headed straight for the bars where, *"the lager and the whiskey began to flow freely."* For those not interested in consuming alcohol, other attractions within the Garden included shooting galleries, scales, punching, lifting and trial of strength machines. Those operating the various attractions had paid the managers the following amounts for the privilege of doing so: The bar to the Kuntz brothers for $4,000; the lunch counter to Mr. Kerns for $800; the cigar stand for $800; candies, soda water and fruits, $125; the shooting gallery for $80; the paper stand and flower stand for $20 each.

The reduction in admission price to 50 cents had the desired effect of attracting many to the match, and by 20:30 there was a huge gathering of about a thousand souls waiting to get in. Captain Williams was on hand to keep everybody in order, but he wasn't expecting trouble stating that by Wednesday, the services of doctors and surgeons would be in greater demand than that of his men. He quipped, "By that time you will see a string of ambulances drawn up in front of the Garden!"

By 23:00, nearly 2,500 people were already in the place, and many watched with interest as each of the competitors arrived with his baggage. When Frank Hart turned up and headed for Albert Pierce's room, he was roundly cheered. "Old Sport" Campana entered the building, and as usual, the eccentric fellow was followed wherever he went. As he arrived, John Ennis told waiting reporters that he predicted there would be few withdrawals in the match, and that he expected at least a dozen men to make 450 miles. With the spectators increasing to over 6,000 by midnight, Captain Williams was keeping an eye out for any trouble. *"The crowd was rather a rough one, and the band played a number of lively airs in the endeavor to keep them quiet."* However, the police didn't intervene to stop the *"crazed man, dressed as a labourer"* who thought he was a pedestrian, from walking round the fountain for an hour, much to the amusement of the crowd who egged him on.

The bookmakers had been given an area in the centre of the track on the eastern side of the building where their 13 tables could be found. The betting on the competitor's chances just before the start was: (Placed odds to finish 1st or 2nd are in brackets): **Brown, 1/2 (1/4); Faber, 8/1 (4/1); T. Costello, Cromwell, Kemmerer and McLeavy, 10/1 (5/1); Allen, 12/1 (5/1); Elson, Crossland, Curran, Fitzgerald, Fox, Pierce, Russell and Walker, 15/1 (7/1); Briody, 20/1 (8/1):**

As the time drew closer for the "off," Brand was the first of the men to appear on the track. He was followed by the swaggering figure of Peter Crossland, who was yawning as he made his way to the start wearing a pair of red tights, red shirt and a blue silk cap. The Englishman was followed into the ring by the 41-year-old, German born, Behrman, who was said to have made 100 miles in a time of 21 hours, and then by the hot favourite "Blower" Brown, attired in a red and white scull cap, white tights, and sporting a red handkerchief around his neck. *"Dillon wore the clover leaf of the First Division of the Second Army Corps on his cap."* The rest joined in and stood in seven lines of five, according to the numbers that they displayed on their chests. After quick handshakes (Pierce, dressed in dark blue and stood on the last row, was the only man to get only one hand shake and that was by Sam Russell of Chicago) all round, history was made as the first ever "O'Leary Belt Race" was got under way by the starter, Mr. W. B. Curtis at one o'clock prompt.

The only person who didn't set off running was Crossland. Brown made his first lap in a minute. Fitzgerald was the top man in the race after the first mile which he made in 6m.25s followed by Eckersall, Allen, McLeavy, Mahoney and Cromwell, whilst Brown blew round in eighth position. After an hour of competition the scores were: **Fitzgerald, 9.3; McLeavy, 8.2; Brown, 7.7; Fox, 7.4; Tait, 7; Elson, Howard and McClane, 6.6; Briody and Walker, 6.5; Allen, Boyle, Dillon, Costello and Edwards, 6.4; Dickenson and Brondgeest, 6.3; Kemmerer and Mahoney, 6.2; Curran and Davis, 6.1; Dugan and Spellacy, 6; Crossland, Faber and McKee, 5.7; Dushane and Pierce, 5.6; Brand, Cromwell and Murphy, 5.5; Eckersall and Perkins, 5.4; Russell, 5; Behrman, 4.7:**

The start of the "1st O'Leary Belt Race"

The National Police Gazette (Illustration no: 60)

There were quite a few people that stayed in the Garden throughout the night to watch the throng of men bustling around the track, and they yelled and cheered at the colourful sight before them. Many had scraped together the admission price. *"They were a hard looking crowd, and the hard benches in the Garden seemed soft and downy beds for them. Many of them belonged to the "Gems and "Toughs" who are accustomed to sleep in street wagons, on the docks and under door stoops."*

In the early stages of the race, the reporter for the *Police Gazette* observed that: **Peter Crossland did not show any of his wonderful running powers and fell behind the foremost division or thirteen. His face is of the same color** as his dress. J. H. Behrman is a curious looking old fellow. He was dressed in dark blue flannel and had his breeches hitched up with an old-fashioned pair of suspenders. He is evidently an old sport and has somewhat the appearance of one not un-remotely connected with the oyster trade. E. Brand is tall and ungainly. He takes long strides and gets over a good deal or ground in a short time but does not look as if he had good staying qualities. Dickenson is a wiry red-headed little man with, a decidedly Celtic coat of countenance. T. Dugan, another of the short ones appeared to take things very quietly. A. Elson plodded steadily around looking neither right nor left. C. Fox also means business. He was continually on the track and frequently broke into a run. Howard is a peculiar looking walker. He carries his head on one side and appears to be continually chewing. D. McKee is well made and adopts the O'Leary style of throwing his body well back. Tait had a determined look and appeared in good condition.

Fitzgerald ran all the way to make his 50th mile with only a few moments of rest. The race favourite, Brown, just couldn't keep up with him, and at 05:11 left the track with 23 miles and 2 laps to his credit. Of Brown, *"He was taken to his room and remedies were applied, but with very limited success for a very long time. He vomited freely, and it appeared as if the pace had broken him to pieces. Finally he got to sleep and did not appear again on the track until half past ten in the morning. He was then last in the race, Dushane alone being behind him."*

The *Brooklyn Daily Eagle* described what the peds ate on the course: THE APPETITES of the grand army of walkers are as various as the colors they wear. Behrman is an old man, and wears a blue flannel shirt and a pair of blue pants with red braces, and he looks like for far all the world like a ships carpenter. Some of the men eat custard, pumpkin, or even mince pie, when they walk around; others drink lager beer or ice water, while not a few are constantly lifting small black bottles to their mouths with evident relish. All kinds of vessels are used, and frequently a pedestrian comes round with a large tin pot at his mouth, large enough to hold corn beef and cabbage sufficiently to supply the wants of an extensive family. Some of them pass along eating pork and beans. All carry sponges which they use frequently.

"Blower" reappeared on the path at 10:30. He responded to the applause that greeted him with a *"ghastly smile and it was evident that he was sick."* Fitzgerald, appearing lame, gave up the lead, and at 11:00, the unknown Nicholas Murphy became the new race leader and subsequent favourite at 3/1 with a two mile advantage over "Fitz." Brown, now appearing much better, finally got down to some serious work, and his trainers told the press that he was determined to overhaul those ahead of him. He ran three miles in 23m.30s and then carried himself along with a rapid walk. Having made 32 miles and 4 laps, he went back to his tent at 12:10. At that stage of the race, he was a hopeless drifter in the betting market at 12/1. At 13:00, Murphy was still in charge on a score of 65 miles. Faber trailed him by a mile, Fitzgerald by three and Fox by four. Faber was now the new favourite at 3/1 and Murphy went out to 6/1. The rumour that Brown was *"disabled"* began to gain respectability as the afternoon passed. His trainers denied any attempts to see him, and his physician Dr. Naylor stated he was suffering from *"costiveness."*

The scores at 15:00: **Faber, 73; Curran and Murphy, 72; Fitzgerald, 69; Walker, 67; Allen, Brondgeest, McClane, McLeavy and Spellacy, 65; Crossland and Elson, 63; Russell, 62; Dillon, Edwards and Howard, 60; Boyle, 59; Mahoney and Pierce, 58; Tait, 57; Briody, 55; Perkins, 53; Brand and Dickenson, 50; Costello, 49; Behrman, 45; Dugan, 43; Eckersall, 37; Brown, 32; Davis, 21:**

The first three in the race at 19:00 were Murphy who, *"has the advantage of youth good looks, good nature, and good legs,"* with *"arms as white and plump as a girl's,"* on 93 miles, Faber on 88.5 and Fox on 85.1. The betting at this time was: (Placed odds to finish 1st or 2nd are in brackets): **Murphy and Faber, 2/1 (1/1); Crossland, 10/1 (4/1); Walker, 12/1 (5/1); Allen, 20/1 (8/1); Brown, 25/1 (15/1); Tait, 30/1 (15/1); Fitzgerald, 75/1 (35/1):**

The *New York Times* was, *at last,* able to report on Brown's condition: At 7:30 a TIMES reporter entered the room occupied by Brown. Brown was lying on his bed asleep. His face looked well, but he rolled and groaned as though suffering intense pain. All the medicine given him had not relieved his costiveness and his physicians were much more worried over him than his friends. Their advice was that he should not be allowed to go upon the track again. Mr. Kelly, at whose house Brown lives, said that Brown's illness was mysterious, and that he might never be able to walk again. He had not made as many miles on the track in this walk as he had made every day in training before the match. But his trainers insisted that he would be on the track all right again in a few hours and that he would win the race.

Back in the ring, Murphy completed his 100th mile in a time of 8m.40s at 20:49. Despite protests from his medical team, Brown was eventually coaxed out of his room by his trainers at 21:21, and thereafter, and to the

King of the Peds

disappointment of those who backed him, walked slowly around the track. Whilst grimly crawling along, the Londoner couldn't fail to notice Curran's century being recorded on the scoreboard at 21:30. He responded by moving up a gear. Faber was the next of the men to make the ton at 21:38. The disappointing Brown went back to his bed at 22:00 after making just a mile and a quarter; whilst he pulled a blanket over him, it was the turn of Fox to hit 100 three minutes later.

Crossland got himself into the *"first spurt of the night"* with Pierce, who, although putting up a gallant fight, eventually succumbed to the Englishman. The Yorkshireman then went on to challenge McKee who also lost out to him; the applause by the 7,000 spectators which followed seemingly *"shaking the building."*

At the end of the first day, the scores at 01:00 were: **Walker, 111; Murphy, 110; Faber and Spellacy, 105; Fox and Russell, 102; Allen, Curran and Pierce, 100; Crossland, 96; Brondgeest, 95; Elson, 87; Fitzgerald, 85; Mahoney, 83; Howard, 81; Dickenson and McLeavy, 80; Briody, 79; Boyle and Dillon, 78; Edwards, 75; Costello and Kemmerer, 73; McKee, 70; Tait, 68; Perkins, 64; Brand, 62; Dugan, 59; Behrman, 56; Brown, 34:**

Brown was woken from his slumbers when the above scores were registered. The Englishman made a further 3.3 before going back to his tent at 01:35. The last betting show of the first day had shown him as a hopeless outsider at odds of 30/1. Faber was the 6/4 favourite and the race leader was on offer at 4/1.

The state of the pedestrian's accommodation was described by the *New York Times*: The sleeping rooms provided for the men under the seats on the Twenty-seventh-street side are not arranged on strictly hygienic principles. On the contrary, any man who had regard for his health would hesitate to sleep in one of them, even if he were under no great physical strain. A platform has been built over the water tank that was used for the skating rink last winter, and the rooms are built on this platform, each room being about 10 feet square, or less. There are no closets and there is not a window for ventilation; at least one gas-light is kept going in each room, night and day, and every room, has, besides, its gas stove. The stench in the long low corridor into which these rooms open is almost intolerable. The gas stoves alone make the air impure; the cooking, the slops, the scores of attendants, and the tables loaded with bottles of medicines and liniments all do their share until the air the pedestrians breathe when they rest is almost thick with dampness and smells. In front of one of the doors was a pile of more than 30 ginger-ale bottles that had all been emptied by one of the walkers. Blower Brown's room, which, together with Brondgeest's room was separate from the rest, had better ventilation but it was very damp. Crossland's room was in one of the old cloak-rooms with a wall of empty pigeon-holes looming up on each side, and only room for a little bedstead between them. In the absence of the walkers from their rooms the trainers and attendants regale themselves with draughts of beef tea and stronger beverages, and sleep on the walkers' beds. The entire lodging-house for the pedestrian's is on the site of Barnum's old stables, when the Garden was known as the Hippodrome, and the men have hardly as comfortable quarters as the horses had, but none of them have far made serious complaint of the accommodations; and, indeed, there is no place else to put them if they should, for the tents that were used in the last walk were as bad for the spectators as the present quarters are for the walkers.

By the start of the second day, eight men had dropped out of the race. When Davis left at 05:30 on a score of 21.5, the only thing that could be found in his tent was a medicine bottle with a label on it saying, "Take 3 times a day." Richard Cromwell, who wore a *"somewhat aboriginal costume on the track"* had only managed 25 miles and had left the race at 06:20. No reason was given for his withdrawal, but he did say his trainer was drunk, and that he couldn't rely on his wife to take over his training! Dugan left due to sore feet, and J. P. Dushane withdrew at 10:30 complaining of the same ailment. He claimed that earlier in the race, Cromwell, who he said he had been on bad terms with for years, *"seriously injured him by picking him up and throwing him to the ground."* He stated he would *"get even"* with him one day, and that as a result of his injuries sustained by the "Californian Doctor," he was covered in plasters. He then left the race, having swallowed some liniment which his trainer gave him to drink, in large doses by mistake. Eckersall left at 10:39 with 37.7 due to stiffness in his legs and a *"disordered stomach,"* whilst Edwards was said be *"too fat"* to continue. Fitzgerald, who had done so well earlier in the race was reported to be *"utterly broken down,"* the last score recorded for him being 88 miles at 03:00. An enquiry made about him at midnight revealed that his knee had been troubling him greatly, and it was probably this that contributed to his downfall. Also out was Tait, who was said to be *"tired of his job and left it."* None of the above had informed the scorers of their intentions of withdrawing from the event. All their names were still on the scoreboards, and some bookmakers ignorant of their respective decisions to leave, still had their names up at long odds on their blackboards.

Meanwhile, the three leaders were traversing the tanbark in glorious style. *"Nearly all the walkers ate their breakfast while on the track, taking it out of the spouts of little tin tea pots."* The by now 50/1 shot, "Blower" Brown, who was still on a mark of 37 and 6, having been in his room all night suffering from *"inflammation of the bowels,"* made another appearance, covering just two miles. He went back off and reappeared at 09:47 looking sick, pale and *"broken down."* With his *"eyes sunk in his face,"* he walked painfully around till 10:05, finally giving notice of his withdrawal from the event at 11:00 on a score of 40.4. Brown later told reporters that his problems initially began when half a dozen men leaning over the railings on the track insisted on blowing smoke into his face, which made him feel sick. Complaints to have them stop to the police proved fruitless, and from then on his condition deteriorated. What he didn't say was that his withdrawal *"was due to cramps in the stomach, caused by too free use of ginger beer."*

The scores for the first 12 hours of competition on the second day:

Hr	Time	Mur	Fab	Curr	Spel	All	Russ	Walk	Pier	Brond	Fox	How	Brio
25	02:00	110	109	105	105	101	105	111	100	98	104	86	83
26	03:00	114	112	110	105	108	109	111	100	100	104	90	89
27	04:00	114	116	112	109	112	110	114	100	100	104	94	93
28	05:00	122	120	116	114	116	110	115	104	100	106	96	97
29	06:00	127	124	121	116	120	113	119	109	102	109	99	101
30	07:00	132	127	126	121	120	118	121	113	107	112	102	105
31	08:00	137	131	131	122	125	122	125	116	111	116	107	109
32	09:00	140	136	135	126	127	126	128	120	115	121	112	113
33	10:00	145	140	138	131	128	130	133	125	119	123	117	116
34	11:00	150	145	143	135	133	135	137	130	123	128	119	121
35	12:00	155	149	147	138	137	138	140	133	127	132	125	125
36	13:00	160	153	148	142	140	142	141	135	132	135	130	130

Peter Crossland, who was on a score of 100.1, and who had been away from the track since 03:00, was refusing to have his name erased from the scoreboard. A doctor had been sent for to examine the painful swollen glands underneath his arms, which his trainer thought had been caused by the manner that he *"swings his arms, like a windmill."* After examining him, the doctor told Peter to throw in the towel as it would be madness to continue. Following that advice, his name was removed at 12:10. Another pair to hand in their notices to quit were Dillon and Perkins on scores of 78 and 64.2 respectively. Their departure left 23 to trudge round the place. Boyle the Canadian was the next man out, due to the blistered condition of his feet on a score of 93. His defection left Christian Faber of Newark as the even money favourite to win the race, whilst Curran was 2/1 to succeed and Murphy a 3/1 shot.

After young Murphy completed his 200th mile at 22:13, he walked a lap and went to bed. Of his gait it was written, *"He is very solidly built and in running keeps his shoulders well braced and his arms closely pressed to his sides. Of all the runners who have appeared in this city, he is the most graceful."* Nick was a full 10 miles out in front of Faber and eleven miles behind Rowell's record for the same time competed.

At 23:25, Behrman, after scoring 100.1, told the judges that he had had enough. However, all was not lost for the *"Ancient Mariner"* of the race. It was reported that the only reason he stayed in it for so long was, that by making the ton, he won for himself a keg of lager!

King of the Peds

The dozen leaders' scores till the end of the second day's play were:

Hr	Time	Mur	Fab	Curr	Spel	All	Russ	Walk	Pier	Brond	Fox	How	Brio
37	**14:00**	164	158	148	147	144	145	145	136	136	138	134	134
38	**15:00**	168	160	152	150	149	149	148	141	140	140	139	137
39	**16:00**	173	163	157	153	150	152	152	145	144	142	143	142
40	**17:00**	178	169	162	156	155	157	156	148	148	142	147	147
41	**18:00**	182	172	164	161	159	161	158	150	148	143	150	151
42	**19:00**	186	177	169	165	164	163	162	153	148	148	154	156
43	**20:00**	191	181	174	167	167	167	164	158	148	151	158	160
44	**21:00**	195	185	179	170	171	170	168	161	148	155	162	165
45	**22:00**	199	189	180	173	176	171	170	165	153	159	167	169
46	**23:00**	200	190	180	176	180	171	174	168	157	160	171	171
47	**24:00**	200	190	180	180	184	171	175	168	161	162	175	171
48	**01:00**	200	190	180	184	187	171	175	168	165	162	180	171

The *"used up"* Elson, who *"was in a wretched condition and tottered like a drunken man,"* withdrew from the race at 05:49 after an effort of 162.3. He had made several attempts to gain entry to his room, but these had been thwarted by his trainers: "Happy" Jack Smith, who obviously failed to see the funny side of his exploits, and George Magee. Unable to get in his quarters, Elson sought the help of the police, which angered his coaches so much that, *"they roughly seized him and gave him a violent shove that nearly threw him head foremost down the platform leading into the corridor where the men's quarters were."* His incredulous trainers told him to get out of the building pronto or else he would be leaving on a pair of crutches! The penniless Elson hurriedly got dressed and told reporters that he would try and find his old mate Napoleon Campana, who, he hoped, would give him the fare back to Meriden, Connecticut, where his wife and eight children who were apparently living in destitute circumstances, awaited his arrival. He also told the press that after finishing second to Hart in the Providence race three weeks earlier, the two promoters of the present race, Englehardt and O'Leary had offered him the chance to appear in this one, and was promised half of his winnings if he did so. He claimed his efforts in the previous race had undermined his present performance, and that by Sunday night he was suffering badly. He also said when he could go no further he was threatened by Smith and Magee. Englehardt however, told a different story. He stated that he and O'Leary had been duped by Elson with pathetic stories of his inability to feed his family and gave him a chance to make some honest money. He told reporters that Alf had been well fed and well cared for, but had been drunk continuously for the week during which he should have been training. He further informed them that the pedestrian had constantly fought his trainers, and that there was nothing wrong with him, other than sheer laziness.

Brondgeest left the track for good at 06:15 on a score of 178.4 suffering from constipation. *"All the remedies applied failed to relieve him."* By 08:00, there were only 18 of the original 35 men competing around the ellipse.

The constantly running 18-year-old Murphy, who earned $6 a week *"trundling a wheel barrow in a brickyard,"* was by now 10 miles ahead of his nearest rival, Faber, who was patently struggling as he limped around the ring. The Newark man himself was gradually being overhauled by the 46-year-old longshoreman Curran. In fourth place was Pierce. *"Pierce does not resemble Hart. He is at least two shades darker and runs with a more jerky nervous gait.......................... He has not been allowed to take much sleep by his backer, and the poor fellow can scarcely keep his eyes open while on the track. He dodges into his room whenever the entrance is clear and his backer away, but his repose is short for he is pulled off the bed and shoved out on to the track the moment he misses his dusky form from the track."* Of Albert, the *Chicago Tribune* wrote: **The colored boy Pierce goes around the track with his eye partly closed, and suffers for want of rest. Near 11 o'clock, he made a rush for the entrance to his room, intending to go to sleep, but the stout and brutal looking fellow who is his backer caught him by the arms and flung him out on the track. He insisted on the colored man's keeping along, although it was apparent to everyone that he was staggering from exhaustion. He threw bay rum and perfume in his face to keep him awake. The poor fellow trotted along, and his efforts to keep his eyes open were painful.** Of his insatiable thirst and his penchant for the finer things in life; *"He seems to be always dry and is ever ready to swallow whatever liquid his trainers give him. He is supremely happy when they present him with a large dose of an amber colored liquid, and the way it disappears down his throat is a caution. He then starts off smiling, and at a good run, when the brandy warms him up."*

The *Brooklyn Daily Eagle*, which had been concerned about the antics of the official scorers, put its worries about the recording of the race into the following paragraph: The scoring on the scoreboards still continues to be altogether at variance with the score sheets, and in several cases laps and even whole miles of difference exist until "straightened out" and made to tally to suit the wishes of the sleepy and stupid young fellows, to whom this important work is entrusted. They sit chatting with one another, or chewing tobacco or smoking strong cigars, all supplied free to them by the managers and at times utterly oblivious of the pedestrians as they walk by. The consequence is that laps fail to be recorded, or worse still, one more lap is put on another mans score. When remonstrated with, these young "gentlemen amateur athletes," as they profess to call themselves, get indignant and use anything but choice language. It is no uncommon thing for a walker to see his score, say 170 miles, on passing the boards, and after making several laps additional he finds his score down to 169 or 168 making him seem to go backward instead of forward.

The bookies' boards at noon indicated the following odds on offer: **Murphy, 4/5; Faber, 5/4; Allen, Russell and Spellacy, 6/1; Curran, 7/1; Briody, 12/1; Walker, 15/1; Howard, 20/1: The rest, 40/1 and above:** The punters piled in on Murphy, and the bookies consequently tightened his odds in to 1/4. Faber was eased out a point to 6/4. The 7/1 offered on Curran's chances had been grabbed, and his price was squeezed into 3/1. Allen had also being heavily bet upon with his price adjusted to 4/1. Meanwhile, Russell took a walk out to 8/1 whilst Howard drifted out ten points from 20/1 to 30/1.

The top scores for the first 12 hours in the race on the 3rd day were:

Hr	Time	Murphy	Faber	Spel	Allen	Curran	Howard	Walker	Briody	Russell
49	02:00	200	192	183	185	185	180	175	171	176
50	03:00	205	196	185	188	190	180	175	174	180
51	04:00	210	200	187	188	195	183	177	180	185
52	05:00	214	204	190	189	200	185	181	183	189
53	06:00	218	209	194	194	203	189	186	188	193
54	07:00	220	213	198	199	208	193	190	195	197
55	08:00	225	217	201	203	212	196	192	197	201
56	09:00	230	220	205	208	217	200	197	202	203
57	10:00	235	225	210	211	221	202	203	206	207
58	11:00	240	229	214	216	226	206	207	210	210
59	12:00	242	233	218	217	230	209	210	214	214
60	13:00	247	236	223	222	232	211	213	218	218

James McCleavy was the third man to call it a day on a score of 150.1 at 12:15 having not been seen on the path since 04:30. *"He was attacked with violent pains in the thighs, the result, he believes, of cold contracted in the miserable quarters furnished by the management."* Kemmerer was the next man to put his civvies on at 12:50 after an effort of 201.7. Murphy went on to make 250 miles in 13h.29m.14s, but his time was 14 hours behind Weston's London time, and he was also a full ten miles behind Rowell's record time made in the Astley Belt contest.

At 15:30, Pierce, who had been making attempts to obtain rests using varying excuses including pretending to have *"bad diarrhea,"* suddenly, *"threw up his arms and fell flat on his back."* After being helped to his feet, he rushed round the track at great speed and made a quick dash for his room. Desperate for sleep, Albert knew the only way he could get into his tent, which was being guarded by his attendants, was to create a diversion. Only then would he be able to lie on his bed which he so dearly wanted to do. He was seen by a doctor who gave him the all clear to continue and he was soon back on the tanbark wearing a new blue shirt. A half an hour later, a man from the crowd got on to the track and ran for a while alongside the competitors. He was taken hold of by one of the trainers who *"threw him,"* after which he was ejected from the building by the police.

Dickenson indicated he could go no further at 18:00 as he was suffering from *"badly suppurated heels."* He had scored 201 miles. By now Rowell and Brown were among the spectators in the Garden and were said to be offering advice to their fellow athletes on the track. By 8 p.m. there were 4,000 or so spectators watching the men parading around the track in their *"finest toggery."* Pierce drew rapturous applause when he began performing like a *"steam engine,"* his effort which gained him 225 miles at 21:00, seemingly helped by copious amounts of rum which apparently rendered him *"as drunk as a lord."* Murphy left the track shortly after to rest on a score of 282 miles. At around 22:00, both Russell and Howard completed 250 miles. Whilst the boy from Haverstraw slept in the ramshackled and smelly room provided by O'Leary, the race promoter waltzed into the Garden at about 22:30 telling reporters, "Boys, the fun is only just commencing. This race will narrow down to the ten best men, and there will be excitement." As he spoke, Faber left the building, but it was to only to sleep at the nearby Putnam House which he was in the habit of doing. Twenty minutes later, Spellacy moved into third place, passing Curran who was suffering with the ankle which he had sprained on his 150th mile; the latter leaving the track soon after to have the cause of his pain attended to by a couple of doctors. There were no such problems for Joe Allen though. He impressed as he flew around the place devouring the laps one by one, giving the impression he would be sharing the winners podium at the end of the race.

At 02:00, Murphy was leading the field of 14 on a mark of 285.6. He was 10.3 ahead of Faber who was 5.3 ahead of Spellacy. He had meanwhile opened up a nice little gap of two and a half miles between himself and Curran.

The scores of the nine leaders for the remainder of that third day were:

Hr	Time	Murphy	Faber	Spell	Allen	Curran	Howard	Walker	Briody	Russ
61	**14:00**	252	238	227	226	237	217	217	223	221
62	**15:00**	255	242	231	231	241	222	221	227	225
63	**16:00**	259	246	236	235	246	226	225	232	229
64	**17:00**	264	251	237	239	251	231	230	235	230
65	**18:00**	268	255	241	243	254	235	232	237	236
66	**19:00**	270	259	245	246	256	236	236	241	240
67	**20:00**	275	263	249	247	256	241	241	242	243
68	**21:00**	279	268	254	252	256	246	245	242	246
69	**22:00**	282	272	258	255	259	250	245	246	250
70	**23:00**	282	272	261	257	260	254	249	251	250
71	**24:00**	282	272	265	260	260	258	253	254	250
72	**01:00**	282	272	269	262	261	260	256	255	250

Fox was the next contestant to leave the race on a score of 200.1. He *"was a thoroughly used up man and was nearly crazy from the pain he suffered from the blisters on his heels."* He hadn't given notice of his withdrawal to the scorers, but had had taken his belongings from his room which had been discovered to be occupied by a few down and outs when Englehardt and three policeman carrying *"their big night-clubs,"* went round the building removing the undesirables from their sleeping places.

On the fourth day, and with barely anybody in the building watching the contest in the early hours of the morning, the only noise heard in the place, apart from the snoring, were the voices of the lap scorers as they called out the names of the men that filed by. *The New York Times* commented: **The Garden was deserted and lonely throughout the morning, but the air was not as bad as it often is, after a night of dust and tobacco smoke. The quarters of the men were in worse condition than on any previous day, and they cannot help becoming worse and worse every day. The smell is enough to send many of the home sick and there is dampness enough to give rheumatism to a regiment of cork-legged veterans. There is little doubt that these unhealthy sleeping rooms have a great deal to do with driving so many of the men off the track.**

On the path, Murphy, watched by his widowed mother whom he had supported for several years, continued to pursue the $5,000 first prize. For a young man earning $6 a week, he would have to work 16 years to get that sort of money. It was learnt that this was his first ever six-day match and that he walked the eight miles to work every day.

There were those in the crowd and on the sidelines that had bet on other competitors who would have liked to see the boy fall from grace, by either breaking down or by other sinister means. Indeed before the start of the race, young "Nic" was as high as 50/1 in the market. His family and friends watched him closely and prepared all his meals themselves to make sure anything he ate would not be tampered with. The lad continued to move nicely along and showed no signs of weariness or lameness. Later on in the morning, he was applauded by many people who had made their way from his home town, most of whom who had brought their lunches with them. At 11 a.m., he received a telegram from the postmaster at Haverstraw saying: **"I congratulate you on your success thus far, and hope it may well continue to the close of the race."**

Scores of the leaders during the first dozen hours of the 4th day:

Hr	Time	Murphy	Faber	Howard	Allen	Spell	Briody	Curran	Walker	Russell
73	02:00	286	275	260	267	270	255	267	258	254
74	03:00	290	279	264	269	270	257	270	262	258
75	04:00	294	283	268	272	270	258	274	265	262
76	05:00	298	287	271	276	274	263	277	265	265
77	06:00	300	291	274	280	278	268	280	266	269
78	07:00	305	295	279	280	281	272	280	269	271
79	08:00	310	299	281	285	286	277	280	274	275
80	09:00	314	300	285	290	290	281	283	279	279
81	10:00	319	304	290	291	294	285	287	284	283
82	11:00	322	308	294	294	298	290	291	286	286
83	12:00	327	313	299	294	302	293	293	289	290
84	13:00	331	317	300	298	305	297	296	290	294

Murphy, now 14 miles in front of his nearest rival, was 1/3 for the title. His nearest rival Faber, who was a 2/1 shot, appeared weary and was gradually dropping back. He was gradually being caught by the gangly figure of Spellacy, who was aptly nicknamed the *"locomotive lamppost."* His odds of 4/1 were being nibbled at by the punters eager to get some value; whilst the hobbling Curran, struggling to keep up with the leaders with an increasingly swelling and painful sprained ankle, was drifting remorsefully out to 10/1. Even money was being offered that a score of 500 miles would not be made.

"Blower" Brown, wearing a big red silk handkerchief around his neck, was followed, as was Rowell, around the Garden, until they found some sanctuary from their admirers as they prepared to watch the match. Rowell, who was described by the press as a, *"very quiet, sensible and pleasant man,"* told reporters that he had no intention of going back to England the following week and that he might appear in an exhibition match in Chicago if the money was right. He informed them that O'Leary had told him that he wouldn't be going to England again to compete and thought that was unfair as he had made the effort to compete twice now in the United States. Brown's request to rejoin the race later that day was declined by Mr. Curtis; the decision apparently annoying the ex-champion.

A lot of people in the audience in the afternoon were women, many of whom were elderly and, *"whose appearance and deportment left no doubt as to their respectability."* Their numbers were swollen in the early evening with many arriving in *"stylish carriages accompanied by male escorts."* They watched as the youth, Murphy, continued his impressive work on the track. Running for three laps at a time, they cheered along with everyone else as they viewed some of the crowd in the inner circle, rushing to and fro to get a glimpse of him in action.

Pierce had finally been allowed some quality resting time in his bed. *"His trainers had been using him pretty badly, forcing him to keep on, and calling him hard names. They tell him that if he does not keep up to the end, they will feed him to the dogs. He is "broken hearted," and says that he will never start in another six-day match."* Albert, who at the time was on a score of 270.6, was subsequently disowned by his trainer who was reported to leave the building in disgust. Brand left the race at 23:26 with 221 miles and 5 laps to his credit. He was said to be so angered with his performance, that he gave formal notice to the scorers of his withdrawal from the race at 00:15. With his feet a mass of blisters, he said he had been sick since the beginning of the match and for the past couple of days had been unable to eat.

King of the Peds

The rest of the 4th day scores:

Hr	Time	Murphy	Faber	Howard	Allen	Spell	Briody	Curran	Walker	Russell
85	14:00	335	321	304	303	307	300	298	294	298
86	15:00	339	325	309	308	309	302	302	298	300
87	16:00	344	329	312	310	314	307	302	300	303
88	17:00	346	331	313	315	317	310	303	302	304
89	18:00	350	333	319	317	321	315	308	305	306
90	19:00	354	337	321	320	325	318	312	307	310
91	20:00	358	341	321	323	329	318	313	312	313
92	21:00	360	345	321	326	331	318	318	316	317
93	22:00	363	349	326	330	334	321	321	320	321
94	23:00	366	350	330	332	334	326	321	322	323
95	24:00	366	350	334	336	334	329	325	323	323
96	01:00	366	350	338	337	337	333	327	327	323

With Murphy back in his room, and Faber relaxing in the comfort of his more salubrious surroundings of his hotel, there were only two and a half thousand souls watching the goings on at that time. The field was now reduced to twelve. Spellacy was withdrawn from the race at 01:30 on a score of 340.3 after complaining of a sore throat and an inability to draw breath. He was seen by a physician, who stated that his lungs were so badly affected the phlegm nearly suffocated him. The doctor warned him that if he didn't retire immediately, he wouldn't be responsible for his life.

Having spent the last seven hours lying down, Pierce, appearing positively resplendent in his new outfit, went wonderfully well after he *"bounded"* out of his accommodation around 02:00. One man in the audience quipped, "Give that man enough sleep and plenty of whisky, and he will win the race!" At the positive end of the field, the *"brick man,"* now 15 miles out in front, brought about a hearty cheer from the crowd when he scored his fourth century at 10:30. The money was as good as in the bank as he ran his 399th mile as well as he had done his first. Meanwhile, Howard went along very, very well, and was climbing the positional ladder to great effect. Pierce celebrated his 300th mile at 10:51 with a rest, and an alcoholic drink perhaps?

Early scores for the 5th day:

Hr	Time	Murphy	Faber	Howard	Briody	Allen	Mahoney	Walker	Russell	Curran
97	02:00	366	352	342	336	340	329	330	326	331
98	03:00	371	356	347	336	342	329	331	329	333
99	04:00	375	360	351	340	343	334	331	333	335
100	05:00	379	363	353	343	346	337	331	335	335
101	06:00	382	367	356	345	350	341	332	338	335
102	07:00	385	370	361	349	352	344	336	341	339
103	08:00	389	374	365	353	356	348	340	341	343
104	09:00	393	378	368	358	360	352	344	348	345
105	10:00	398	382	373	360	362	356	348	352	349
106	11:00	403	387	378	362	365	359	351	356	354
107	12:00	407	391	381	366	366	362	352	360	358
108	13:00	410	394	385	370	369	367	356	363	359

When Pierce re-emerged from the 'bar' in his room at 13:21, he and Mahoney walked around the track arm in arm, much to the amusement of the crowd who screamed their appreciation amid the din the band was contributing to the spectacle. The fun continued as the black boy was presented with an immense bouquet, after which he *"made a steep drink of brandy disappear."* Albert was also partial to egg flips which he drank in abundance, and it was said he was consuming three pounds of beefsteak at every meal, which didn't help him.

McKee, the good looking lad that he was, kept making his female fans' hearts flutter with excitement every time he changed his costume; and that's precisely what he did almost every hour. For his vain efforts he was positively rewarded by his swooning admirers with a plentiful amount of flowers accompanied by messages of admiration. If there ever was to be an odds candidate to take the prize for the best turned out "ped," he was a certainty to get the gold medal! On the subject of appropriate attire for the men, the race promoter had offered cash inducements to the trainers of the competitors to get their lads to dress smartly. The *New York Times* had earlier commented: **And the men are nearly all dressed in outrageous costumes. A lady might almost as well be a spectator at one of the free swimming baths. The tights are cut so very tight that there is no decency about them, and the men would look very much the same, if they were painted, instead of covered with their flannel.** O'Leary told reporters, "The hundred-fifty dollar trainers' prizes have been thrown away because the object I had in view was not attained. The men did very well so far as cleanliness was concerned but the prizes were not meant merely to make the men wash their faces. I wanted them to have appropriate costumes, such as Frederick Englehardt furnished to Frank Hart in the last race. The bathing drawers and circus trunks worn by the majority of the men on the track are not fit for a pedestrians dress. There should be a small pair of regular pantaloons coming part of the way down the thigh. In the race next week I intend to supply every contestant with an appropriate costume at my own expense."

*For $75, $50, and $25 respectively, this was given for "the best looking men on the track" during the contest.

When Allen completed the 3rd lap of his 370th mile, he went for a rest. *"When he laid down his legs became muscle bound as it is termed. The muscles in the calves of both his legs became knotted and cramped, and all efforts to straighten his legs or get him on his feet, proved unavailing. His trainers are now applying hot vinegar and water to them, and expect they will relax within an hour."* With Murphy now flagging, Faber was exuberant, when at 14:00 after thirteen hours of continuous movement he won a bet that he would make 50 miles without resting. When he completed his task, he went and sat down for 20 minutes before resuming his struggle again. He was now 11 miles ahead of Howard, who at 20:00, was being offered at 20/1 (2/1 a place) to win by the bookmaking firms.

Other odds at that time: (Placed odds to finish 1st or 2nd are in brackets): **Murphy, 1/6; Faber, 10/1; Briody, 100/1 (20/1); Allen, Curran, Mahoney, Pierce, Russell and Walker, 100/1 (50/1); Evens, that 510 miles would not be made: 2/1 that 520 miles would not be made:**

Miss Eva Fisk presented Murphy with a miniature wheelbarrow containing three bricks of flowers at 21:00, which he subsequently pushed round for a lap when on a score of 440.5. At this stage of the race, he was 5 miles and 3 laps behind Rowell's distance in the last six-day race at the Garden. Pierce at this time was fast asleep, and when he didn't respond to attempts to rouse him by shaking and pinching him at 21:30, a doctor was sent for. The quack placed two leeches on his legs causing him to jump out of his bed. Despite his rude awakening, he refused to go back on the track. However, he was later persuaded to return an hour or so later when, looking bleary eyed, he walked slowly around the path wearing a jumper and a black cap. Mahoney was *"advised"* to take a rest at 23:30 by his trainer as he appeared *"broken down,"* and there was some doubt expressed whether he would be seen again in the race. Ten minutes later, Curran limped away from the forbidding stench of the men's quarters and took a full three minutes to make just one lap.

With half of the gas lights off in the building, the place had a gloomy feel about it in the wee small hours of the morning. Some of the Garden's permanent guests tried in vain to enter the unoccupied rooms left by the failed pedestrians, but they were sent packing by the vigilant coppers. Little else happened apart from an occasional shout from an inebriate and the sight of the tramps steadily plodding their way around the course.

King of the Peds

More 5th day scores:

Hr	Time	Murphy	Faber	Howard	Briody	Allen	Mahoney	Walker	Russell	Curran
109	14:00	413	398	387	374	370	371	360	367	364
110	15:00	417	400	392	378	374	375	362	370	367
111	16:00	421	404	396	382	377	379	367	374	369
112	17:00	426	408	400	385	380	381	370	375	373
113	18:00	430	412	405	388	383	383	372	375	377
114	19:00	432	416	407	391	388	383	376	377	380
115	20:00	436	420	407	394	390	383	380	378	382
116	21:00	440	425	407	390	390	387	383	378	387
117	22:00	444	429	410	400	394	389	387	379	387
118	23:00	446	430	413	401	399	391	388	382	387
119	24:00	446	430	417	406	403	394	392	386	388
120	01:00	446	430	420	409	403	397	394	389	392

The silence was interrupted about 05:00 when a quarrel occurred between the race leader, who always wore large moccasins, and the third placed man Harry Howard, who accidentally stepped on his heels. *"The young brick carrier turned on him savagely and threatened to "Smash him in the snout!" if he repeated the performance. "I'll just give you one dollar to strike me" said Howard, and things looked threatening."* The situation was quickly defused by Murphy's family and friends and Mr. Maxwell Moore, assistant manager, who had *"words"* with the offenders. *"He warned them that that the result of a conflict would be the disqualification of both men from the race. This seemed to act as a damper on the pugnacious ardour of the two men."* Murphy did state however, that he would attend to him later, and Howard for his part stated he looked forward to whatever Murphy was going to try to do to him. With the argument over for now, the two men resumed the race with Murphy running on and Howard setting off at a fast walk.

It was quite apparent to all who watched him that Faber was struggling. At 10:00, Howard was only 2 miles and 5 laps behind the German, and the way he was going, it looked a cert that he was going to take his second place.

Both Curran and Briody looked destined to make the necessary 450 miles to be assured of prize money and keep their entrance fee, whereas the *"lame and used up"* Mahoney barely kept going. Pierce went well if supplied with his favourite tipple, but denied the drink, slinked away to his pad in *"supreme disgust."*

The inevitable happened at 11:22. Howard, *"a man so fresh and in so fine condition,"* eventually caught up with Faber, and with Murphy alongside, the three walked along briefly chatting away. Four minutes later when the conversation ended, Howard slowly pulled away to become second man in the race to applause from the crowd. The two race leaders now ran along briskly, leaving the ailing Faber to contemplate what might have been. Howard was now 4/1 to win the race.

News from Murphy's camp indicated that they were expecting their boy to make 535 miles by the end of the contest, but the wise ones in the crowd were betting that would not be the case and "even money" was being offered by the bookies that he would score 525 miles or more. The firms were also offering odds of 2/1 against Faber, Russell, Curran, Briody, Walker, Mahoney, Pierce and McKee for first or second place. 50/1 was being offered about Allen and Russell to win, and 100/1 against Mahoney, McKee and Pierce to do the same.

By 13:00, and with Murphy now on a mark of 490.5, the brick mover was now exactly nine miles behind Rowell's record for the same time. However, due to the short measurement of the track in the previous race, this distance was reduced to just four miles.

With 3,000 people watching the contest at 2 o'clock, the man at the head of proceedings, now reported to be suffering from blisters and sore feet, was circumnavigating wearing just his stockings and no footwear. Apart from the three leaders, all the men left in the contest were entertaining the crowd of 3,000 at 3 p.m. The argument for second place had finally been won by Howard who, wearing a light brown suit and red trunks, was 2 miles and 2 laps ahead of the wilting Faber who was 26.7 ahead of Briody.

As the afternoon wore on, and with all the seats taken by eager spectators, the plucky teenager Murphy amassed his 500th mile at 15:51, his last eight laps being scored in an agonizingly slow time of 26m.17s. The usual lively applause followed the lad's remarkable effort, and the delegation from Haverstraw was particularly noisy in their recognition of their athlete's performance.

Mahoney cracked the tough 450-mile nut and so saved his entrance money at 16:53. He was followed by Curran who scored one lap more at 18:56, Allen at 19:50, and Walker finishing his race with a further three laps at 20:00. After "Old Ben" had finished his painful struggle, the longshoreman who had a wife and six kids, made his way off the track. This is what the *Boston Globe* said of his performance: **With his feet cut almost to pieces and his system shattered terribly by the enormous strain, the performance of Curran, a man 46 years old, may be counted as one of the greatest feats in the history of courage and endurance. He stood in his costume of red, with his gray hair matted over his forehead, and his racing cap in hand, in front of the scorers stand. He thanked the press, the scorers and the public for the kind consideration they had given to him, and added that if he could he would have done better. The plucky old man was cheered to the echo and overloaded with flowers, as he went to his room.**

At 20:37, and having earlier been presented with a pair of the coveted "Bryan S. McSwyny pedestrian shoes," the race leader went to his quarters. When he re-emerged eight minutes later, he was wearing the O'Leary belt and pushed an old fashioned clay covered wheelbarrow full of bricks and flowers. As Mahoney walked behind the new champion carrying an American flag to the strains of "Yankee Doodle," the audience responded by shouting themselves hoarse. After completing a couple of more laps the winner went back to his room at 20:5, having completed his task in 139h.51m.30s for a distance of 505.1. He was then whisked away to the Putnam House, where, after having a bath, he received the congratulations of his friends and went to bed.

Allen also finished his race at the same time with 452.1. He was followed home by Faber who retired at 21:14 after completing 488.5. Russell saved his entrance money amid a storm of applause eleven minutes later after making 452.2. Mahoney was the next off the course at 21:45. He was well pleased that he had secured a reward of $200 for making 465 miles as per the rules of the race. He eventually made 467.3. Pierce left the path at 22:15 having tottered around for 343.1. The judges were officially informed five minutes later that McKee, *"the Adonis,"* had retired, even though he hadn't been seen on the track since 19:52. Briody stayed on till 22:21 until he had completed his 475th mile and then quit leaving Howard all alone in his quest to complete 500 miles before time was called. He did as he had wanted with Pierce for company for his final lap at 22:42, and after the tremendous applause he received died down, the band played the inevitable, "Home Sweet Home." Thus ended the first ever contest for the O'Leary Belt.

Nick Murphy

The National Police Gazette   (Illustration no: 61)

The final scores and prizes!

1st: Murphy, 505.1 ($5,000); 2nd: Howard, 500 ($2,000); 3rd: Faber, 488.5 ($1,000); 4th: Briody, 475 ($500); 5th: *Mahoney, 467.3 ($200); 6th: **Russell, 452.2 ($150); 7th: Allen, 452.1 ($100) 8th: Walker, 450.4 ($100); 9th: ***Curran, 450.1 ($125); 10th: Pierce, 343.1; 11th: ****McKee, 302.2 ($75):

*For making 465 miles + a pair of McSwyny shoes + a silk suit. **Including 2nd 'Neatness Prize' of $50 + a pair of McSwyny shoes + a silk suit. ***Including 3rd 'Neatness Prize' of $25. ****1st 'Neatness Prize' + *"Suit of Silk Tights"* + $8 pair of walking shoes.

King of the Peds

The last day's scores:

Hour	Time	Murphy	Howard	Faber	Briody	Mahoney	Allen	Curran	Russell	Walker
121	02:00	447	425	434	412	400	404	397	393	397
122	03:00	451	430	438	412	404	404	400	395	397
123	04:00	455	432	442	412	409	407	400	395	400
124	05:00	459	437	446	416	411	410	404	396	402
125	06:00	462	441	450	420	415	412	405	399	404
126	07:00	467	446	454	423	419	415	409	402	404
127	08:00	473	451	458	427	422	419	414	406	407
128	09:00	475	455	460	431	425	420	416	408	411
129	10:00	478	461	463	435	429	424	420	411	413
130	11:00	482	467	467	438	432	427	425	414	415
131	12:00	486	471	471	442	435	430	428	417	419
132	13:00	490	475	475	446	438	430	430	421	423
133	14:00	493	478	478	449	441	433	434	424	426
134	15:00	496	482	479	452	443	437	437	428	431
135	16:00	500	484	479	454	447	438	440	431	435
136	17:00	500	484	479	458	450	442	443	435	439
137	18:00	500	484	479	461	453	443	446	438	443
138	19:00	500	485	479	464	456	446	450	441	445
139	20:00	502	489	483	467	460	450	450	444	449
140	21:00	505	493	488	470	464	452	450	448	450
141	22:00	505	497	488	473	467	452	450	452	450
142	23:00	505	500	488	475	467	452	450	452	450

Day to Day Scores of the Finishers:

	Mon	Tue	Wed	Thur	Fri	Sat	TOTAL
Murphy	110	90	82	84	80	59	**505**
Howard	80	100	80	78	82	80	**500**
Faber	105	85	82	70	88	58	**488**
Briody	76	94	85	78	76	66	**475**
Mahoney	82	80	86	77	72	70	**467**
Allen	106	83	74	75	66	49	**453**
Curran	100	80	84	63	65	58	**450**
Walker	111	64	81	71	67	56	**450**
Russell	102	70	78	73	66	63	**452**
Pierce	100	68	68	34	43	30	**343**
McKee	70	67	51	52	33	29	**302**

Below is a table comparing the five six-day go-as-you-please events up to and including Murphy's win starting with Rowell's Astley Belt triumph in March of 1879.

HOURS	Rowell 03/79	Brown 04/79	Weston 06/79	Rowell 09/79	Murphy 10/79
26	113	127	127	**130**	114
50	200	**224**	220	217	205
74	283	306	**313**	310	290
98	360	**403**	390	402	371
122	435	**480**	473	461	451
142	500	542	**550**	530	505

P. S. Marshall

The following tongue-in-cheek article which was found in the *Brooklyn Daily Eagle* on the 12th of October 1879, poked fun at the pedestrian mania sweeping the country:

IN ANTICIPATION.

The Walking Match of a Hundred Years from Now.

What the Walkers of the Future may do and What the Brooklyn or the Future may Be.

To the Editor of the Brooklyn Eagle:

Brooklyn, October 27th 1979

The 146th International contest for the pedestrian championship terminated at 3 o'clock today, and Shang Smith retains the belt and earns $98,762.52 as his share of the gate money, exclusive of $26,000 of entrance fees.

Shang was an easy winner and left the track an hour before the time was up, with 1,905 miles to his credit and 104 miles ahead of the next best man. He scored his miles, at the rate of about 15 an hour, and his best record was made on the 8th day when he ran without stopping 262 miles and a quarter.

High Brown came in a pretty fair second with 1,601 miles, and will make $58,000 in money.

We ought to say, parenthetically, and in explanation of Mr. Brown's being so far behind the champion, that he broke his kneepan earlier in the race, and was compelled for nearly eight days to make his way on crutches. And, beside, he was bothered with the rheumatism, had a cold and was troubled with blisters on the soles of his feet. These were quite serious pullbacks, and handicapped Mr. Brown throughout the entire race, discouraging very much as well they might.

The much talked of champion from the Pacific slope, Blower Kearney, who walked from San Francisco to Brooklyn in four days, seven hours and twenty-three minutes, came in third, completing only 1,601 miles— thus needing forty-nine miles to entitle him to a share in the gate money.

We thought from the send off that Kearney was over praised and his score shows we were right.

He is too young, being only 57 to have the experience necessary to make a long distance walker; as he grows older he may do better.

The Australian champion showed himself to be a neat heel and toe walker, but not much of a runner. He scored 1,402 miles.

Our climate did not seem to agree with Ching Lung the representative from China. He walked with great effort and gave much time to rest. When he gets acclimated he may make a tolerable success in short walks of six days.

The dusky African Adonis showed himself to be any thing but a novice, and would no doubt, have made a good record, had he not dropped dead of consumption on the seventh day of the tournament.

Of the remaining eighteen contestants it will be but charity to say nothing, as they made such small scores and showed such poor training that we wonder they were allowed to continue in the race.

We hope in the future, that the managers of the Coliseum will not accept the entrance fee from any one not showing a record of at least 250 miles in twenty four hours. We cannot expect good scores to be made by young and inexperienced walkers, and (we repeat) we hope they will barred in future contests.

The tournament, as a success, was fully equal to its predecessors, the attendance aggregating two millions.

The managers say that the day the King of England was present was the best day. On that occasion nearly 230,000 people were present.

His majesty caused the greatest enthusiasm by walking five miles arm in arm with the champion amid the roar of artillery and music from eight hundred musicians.

King of the Peds

The good will thus exhibited by his Majesty not only added great éclat to the match but goes a great way toward preserving the entente cordiale, now so happily existing between his nation and ours.

A rumor prevailed this morning to the effect that our champion intended to retire from pedestrian matches, in compliance, so the rumor ran, with the urgent request of his mother, to whom he promised he would stop when he reached his seventieth year, and, by a curious coincidence, Mr. Smith's seventieth birthday occurred yesterday.

We hope this is merely a rumor, for should it be true, we fail to see at the moment any one capable of taking his place.

High Brown might be the man, but he has got to hump around pretty lively if be expects to amount to anything. He is still young being but fifty eight, and in time may make himself worthy to be called the champions successor.

The championship belt and a crown of diamonds was presented to Mr. Smith at the close of the contest, amid the plaudits of the multitude. Mr. Smith accepted them gracefully and modestly, and declined to make any remarks saying he was somewhat tired and desired a rest.

He soon after left the Coliseum, intending to walk to his home in Kansas, where he hoped to arrive in five days, barring an accident.

AN INTERVIEW WITH THE CHAMPION

Our sporting reporter walked with Mr. Smith as was he was completing his last 10 miles and when the enthusiasm of the audience permitted, had the following talk with him.

Reporter-Well Mr. Smith, it seems pretty certain that you will win the race, and all that that word implies, and I desire to congratulate you on your success.

Mr. Smith: Thanks; shake, my lad.

Don't you feel tired?

Well, yes, somewhat. I've traveled quite a number of miles during the past two weeks, and kept on the track very nearly all the time. I've rested only some fifty-six hours, and as for sleeping, why bless you, I haven't done anything like that in for fourteen days. So you see, I ought a feel somewhat tuckered out.

I should say so; I don't see how you stand it as well as you do.

Oh, you shouldn't mind such a small trifle as the loss of sleep –it's too insignificant in an affair of this kind.

Has your appetite been good?

Only so so. I wish it had been better, for then I would have made a better score; my stomach went back on me at first and I was compelled to nurse it a little. I had to stop running on the third day after making only 241 miles, when I intended to do much better. A fellow can't run very well when his stomach shaky.

You made, however a good score on the 8th day - 265 miles.

Yes, I did but that should be average during a race and if I could always depend upon my stomach, I could do it too.

How much do you eat at one meal in a contest of fourteen days?

It varies according to the condition of the stomach. A fair specimen is the one I ate this noon. It consisted of soup, roast beef, sirloin steak, oysters, pork chops, cutlets, potatoes, pie, pudding and beer. This isn't much of a meal, but then, in order to win we have to diet ourselves somewhat.

You look hearty, even if you have been deprived of your food.

Yes I suppose so. I feel pretty good.

Shall you enter for the next match?

No sir. It commences to-morrow morning too soon to admit of getting the proper training to do myself justice, and besides I don't know but that I will stop this walking business altogether. I've got plenty of money and can afford to quit and enjoy a dignified seclusion in my library for the rest of my days.

Here the champion completed his task and giving our reporter a hearty hand shaking, he retired to his tent and began his preparations for a speedy departure.

A RETROSPECT.

We have been examining the flies of the EAGLE for the past 150 years and find some interesting data as to walking matches, which we will here present, in the hope that they will prove interesting to our rising generation.

As far back as 1879, one hundred years ago, it seems that those matches were in vogue. They however conducted in a primitive way, and very meager scores were made.

A person by the name of Weston made the highest score up to 1879—550 miles.

Their walking tournaments were carried on in a structure in the Forty first Ward of Brooklyn, called "Gilmore's Garden."

The exact location of this building we are at present unable to determine, but we can safely put it, we think, as part of the site now occupied by the Brooklyn Electric Lamp factory. Why it was called a garden is to us a mystery, but we suppose it must have resembled one in some respects, or our ancestors would not have so termed it.

It was not until 1904 that the capabilities of the human frame began to be known and appreciated.

Then or about then, our magnificent Coliseum was erected, and good scores became the order of the day, or rather the match.

Murphy was given the full treatment when he returned back to Haverstraw three days later. The entire population of the city turned out to see him and a committee welcomed the victorious youth at the pier. He rode through the streets in a carriage bedecked with flowers, proudly displaying the O'Leary belt in his hand amidst firing cannons, ringing bells, and the din of factory whistles.

CHAPTER 22

Rose Belt

There were an astonishing number of competitors for another six-day go-as-you-please contest which started on Monday, the 22nd of December 1879. The race, which was held at Madison Square Garden, New York, would be competed for right through the Christmas holiday period till Saturday, the 27th of December.

A total of 65 men would fight each other for the privilege of carrying off the first prize of the "American International Championship Belt" or the "Rose Belt" which comprised of seven sections, and was described as a *"handsome piece of work."* Six of the sections consisted of frosted silver with the seventh central section sporting a globe in full relief with enamelled coloured flags of several nations surrounding it. This globe had the word "Rose" and above the word was a large star with a *"brilliant set"* in the centre. At each side of the globe, in niches, were the figures of runners in full relief, wrought in bright and dead gold. The words **"American International Champion of the World"** were inscribed on scrolls at the sides. Apart from receiving the belt valued at $500, the winner would also receive 50% of the gate money. The second placed man would get 20%; 3rd, 10%; 4th, 7½ %; 5th, 5%; 6th, 4% and 7th, 3½ %.

An estimated $20,000 had been invested on the race before the off and the bookies were laying Nick Murphy at 5/1 to snatch a quick double, the lad from Haverstraw having won the 1st O'Leary Belt earlier in October. Sam Merritt of Bridgeport also headed the market at the same price. Harry Howard was 6/1 to succeed with Frank Hart the next in the betting at 8/1. The slates operated by the firms were surrounded by hundreds of punters some of whom were looking for 11/2 and better for the two favourites.

Whilst Captain Berghold and his army of policeman cleared the track at 23:45, the competitors were getting their final instructions from their trainers inside the small wooden cabins and tents that had been provided for them during the tournament.

It was bitterly cold outside, but inside, and in the packed arena, the spectators were settling down. Some read their programmes, some chatted, and some gazed at the scenes within the track where the shooting galleries and other fairground type attractions were doing a roaring trade. Many were in the bars swilling down the last few drops of lager before they staggered out into the main hall where the athletes were slowly starting to make their way on to the track. Miss Howard, the winner of the ladies' six-day event in the same venue which had finished only the day before, sat in one of the boxes along with some of her fellow contestants, Cook, Massicot and Rockwell. They all watched intently as the army of athletes dressed in brightly coloured costumes walked on to the track.

They were: **C. Berdan,** Philadelphia; **Fred Brandes,** New York; **Thomas Briody,** Brooklyn; **Steve Brodie,** New York; **Daniel Burns,** Elmira, New York; **Peter Napoleon Campana,** Bridgeport; **Ephraim Clow,** Prince Edward Island; **M. Crawford,** Salaman, New York; **A. Croft,** Little Falls, New York; **Richard Cromwell,** California; **Richard Davis,** New York; **W. H. Davies,** New York; **George Dufrane,** New York; **Christian Faber,** Buffalo; **Patrick Fitzgerald,** Long Island; **Dan Fitzpatrick,** New York; **I. Gilloon,** New York; **P. Gebring,** Rahway, New Jersey; **Ed Geldert,** Worcester, Massachusetts; **T. N. Gorman,** Peoria, Illinois; **George Hanwaker,** New York; **Frank Hart,** Boston; **D. A. Hennessy,** Troy; **George T. Hilton,** Brooklyn; **Clarence G. Howard,** Huntingdon; **Harry Howard,** Glen Cove; **John Hughes,** New York; **Frank Johnson,** New York; **Fred Krohne,** New York; **Richard Lacouse,** Boston; **John Lowery,** New York; **Joseph McCormick,** New York; **David McKee,** Boston; **J. McLellan,** New York; **Benjamin Madden,** New York; **P. Madden,** Marlborough, Massachusetts; **James Mahoney,** New York; **Mathews,** Haverstraw; **Samuel Merritt,** Bridgeport; **Philip Mignault,** Boston; **Paul Molineaux,** Boston; **Charles Murphy,** New York; **J. Murphy,** Stamford, Connecticut; **Nicholas Murphy,**

Haverstraw; **P. O'Brien,** Covington, Kentucky; **A. Panchot,** Minnesota; **H. Panchot,** Minnesota; **Peter Panchot,** Buffalo; **August Paris,** New Jersey; **William Pegram,** Boston; **J. Rae,** Canada; **David Reid,** New York; **Samuel P. Russell,** Chicago; **William Ryan,** New York; **Thomas Shannon,** New York; **William Sprague,** Chicago; **James Steel,** New York; **A. Thompkins,** Armonck, New York; **Patrick Toomey,** New York; **Robert Vint,** Brooklyn; **Cyrenius Walker,** Buffalo; **D. Weaver,** Stroudburg, Pennsylvania; **Isaac Webster,** Wallacebury, Canada; **W. E. Wheeler,** Boston; **Edward Williams,** New York:

There was a loud roll of the drum at 23:55 after which the contestants started to appear on the track. Hart, chewing as ever on a toothpick, and wearing a *"black and white striped shirt, very like a State Prison jacket,"* underneath his Ulster overcoat, strode into the arena sporting a grey fur cap. All the men were applauded as they made their appearance and were directed where to stand on the path to future glory.

Mr. Whitaker shouted, "A minute and a half!" thus giving his indication that he wanted the trainers off the track; after watching the men organise themselves in rows of three, he gave the signal for the start of the race at five minutes past midnight. William Ryan was the first of them to pass the winning post on the first lap. Peter Panchot was the first man to make a mile in about nine minutes, followed by John Hughes a minute or so later. The same Panchot lead the field at 01:00 on a score of seven miles and he was kept up to his work by Byrne and Fitzgerald.

The crowded track lost its first casualty when, surprisingly at 06:38, one of the race favourites, Sam Merritt indicated he could go no further when on a score of just 29 miles. He had earlier showed a lot of promise in the race and was observed running speedily and appeared in good shape. Toomey was next to fall out at 08:50 on 37.7 and Steele followed him at 11:48 with 45.1.

The scores at 13:00 on the first afternoon of the contest: **P. Panchot, 76; N. Murphy, 73; Faber and Hart, 71; Berdan and Hughes, 69; Weaver, 68; Briody and H. Panchot, 67; A. Panchot, 66; Krohne, 65; Fitzgerald, Geldert, Lacouse, P. Madden, Pegram and Vint, 64; Hilton and Russell, 62; Crawford, Fitzpatrick, Mahoney, Mignault and Webster, 61; Davis, C. G. Howard, O'Brien and Sprague, 60; Campana, Gilloon and McLellan, 59; Davies and Dufrane, 58; Mathews, Gebring and Shannon, 57; Clow, McCormick, Ryan, Walker and Williams, 56; Hanwaker, C. Murphy, Reid and Thompkins, 55; Hennessy, Johnson, B. Madden and J. Murphy, 54; Brodie, 53; Croft and Rae, 52; Wheeler, 51; H. Howard, Molineaux and Paris, 50; Brandes, 49; Gorman and Lowery, 48; Steel, 45; Cromwell, 44; Burns and McKee, 42; Toomey, 37; Merritt, 29:**

The amphitheatre had been filled from the moment the race had started, but as soon as Nick Murphy announced his retirement from the competition at 15:30, many who had put their money on him and many others who hadn't, called it a day and went home. Many thousands of dollars had been made by virtue of his early departure by the bookies and they were delighted with his withdrawal. He had made 82 miles and one lap. There was no formal reason given for his premature retirement, but the rumour was that he had lost heart in his performance, and was disillusioned with the effort being made by race leader Peter Panchot and the gap he had created between them.

With fewer spectators now watching the proceedings, C. G. Howard was the next man to leave at 16:46 on a mark of 75 miles. The impressive Buffalo postman, Panchot, was the first man in the tournament to make 100 miles at 18:02, the distance being made in an "on track" time of 17h.47m.5s which was a new American record. Frank Hart shared the honour 1h.10m later followed by Hughes, and then Faber. With the place starting to fill up again, the bookmakers were offering 1/2 that Panchot would eventually prevail and win the belt. Hart was 6/4, and Faber 10/1 along with Harry Howard. The other Panchot's in the field were both 15/1 shots.

With Gorman's name being added later to the list of withdrawals for the first day (Johnson also left the track for good but failed to inform the referee till the next day), the "centurions" for the first 24 hours in the race were:

P. Panchot, 120; Faber and Hughes, 112; Hart, 107; Fitzpatrick, 105; Mahoney, 104; Briody and Davis, 103; Fitzgerald, 102; H. Panchot, O'Brien and Russell, 101; Campana, Geldert, Krohne, Gilloon, Hilton, Mignault, Vint and Weaver, 100:

King of the Peds

Peter Panchot, who had been leading the then 60 competitors up until midnight, withdrew from the race for no apparent reason at 02:00 on a score of 126.1. Two reasons were later given for his disappearance. The first one was that *"the same old foot had again gone back on him."* This was a reference to the foot that had given him trouble in the 5th Astley Belt race in September and which apparently had once again proved his downfall in this race. The second was the claim that the bookmakers had some sort of hand in his premature disappearance, along with Murphy and Merritt.

With 55 still left in the race, Frank Hart got himself into a real old tussle with the other O'Leary protégé and stable-mate, Faber, for the leader's position at noon. This was watched with much interest and excitement by a small audience when the scores of the leading dozen men were as follows: **Faber, 160; Hart, 159; Briody, 158; Krohne, 154; Hughes, 147, Fitzpatrick, 144; Fitzgerald, 142; Geldert and O'Brien, 140; Mahoney, 139; Gilloon, 138; Campana, 138:**

With the hard work of Krohne, Williams and Pegram being noted by the reporters, Campana was also the subject of their attentions. Whatever he did and whatever he said was followed by the press and consequently written about. The subject matter for the evening was "Old Sport's" diet. Apparently his trainer was making some sort of suggestion as to how the old athlete should convey himself around the track to which Campana retorted, "Oh give me some fish balls and I will fly!" He was said to be particularly fond of them during the race, along with hard boiled eggs. Dufrane's *"queer"* gait was also commented on thus earning him the nickname of "Spasms."

The bookmaker's slates during the evening were showing the following odds: (Placed odds to finish 1st or 2nd are in brackets): **Hart, 1/3; Faber, 5/2 (2/5); Krohne, 7/1 (5/2); Briody, 15/1 (6/1); Fitzpatrick, 20/1 (8/1); Howard, 25/1 (8/1); R. Davis, Geldert, Hughes, Lacouse, O'Brien, Mahoney and Pegram, 50/1 (25/1):**

Hart eventually took the upper hand in his race with Faber for top spot. Frank was the first man in the race to make 200 at 20:10, Christian scoring the same distance at 20:52. "Black Dan" went on to make 15 more miles before hitting the sack at 23:16 having accomplished a new 2-day record, having just beaten Rowell's by an eighth of a mile.

When the clock struck midnight, and with only 43 of the original 65 men who lined up for the start still in the race, the scores of the leading 22 were: **Hart, 215; Faber, 208; Krohne, 193; Briody, 191; Hughes, 189; Fitzgerald and O'Brien, 186; Fitzpatrick, 185; R. Davis, 182; Campana and Pegram, 180; Vint, 177; Lacouse, 176; Gilloon, 175; Clow, 173; Dufrane, 172; Mignault, 171; Geldert and Russell, 170; H. Panchot, 167; Williams, 166; Mahoney, 163:**

The *New York Times* wrote an amusing paragraph about one of the underperforming competitors: Mr. Curtis, the referee said last night that W. H. Davies, one of the pedestrians, who had only made 84 miles up to midnight yesterday, was a truck driver in the employ of a soap manufacturer down town, who had some confidence in his ability to walk, so he gave Davies a week's vacation, with full pay, on the condition that, however poor his score may be, he should remain in the race until the finish on Saturday night. Yesterday, Davies received notice from his fellow workmen at the factory that they were going up to the Garden today to cheer him on. Having told this much, Davies said he was ashamed of having made so small a score, and begged Mr. Curtis to "put the figure '2' before the 84 for tomorrow," while his friends were there. "Of course it won't mean anything," he said, "and you can take it down when they are gone." Mr. Curtis said he would "think of it."

The scores at noon: **Hart, 256; Faber, 252; Krohne, 245; Briody, 235; Hughes, 232; O'Brien, 228; Pegram, 224; Fitzgerald, 221; Campana, 217; R. Davis, 216; Fitzpatrick, 215; Geldert, 213; Clow, 211; Gilloon and Vint; 210; Russell, 208; Dufrane, 204; Croft, 203; Ryan, 202; Williams, 201; H. Panchot, 200; Reid, 197; Webster, 190; Hennessy, McKee and Walker, 189; Mahoney and Roe, 188; Mathews, 184; Brodie, 178:**

Hart gave Faber an unexpected Christmas present when he allowed his fellow protégé to not only equal his score, but pull four miles ahead of him by midnight. Faber, who had always been about four miles in the rear of Hart during the day, took full advantage when the race leader took to his bed at 20:43, equalling his score of 291.6 at 21:30 in front of a full house. The cynics in the crowd were already crying foul, believing that Hart had *"sold"* the race to those bad bookies.

At midnight, the scores of the top 30 on the big blackboard showed: **Faber, 295; Hart, 291; Krohne, 286; Briody, 274; O'Brien, 269; Pegram, 262; R. Davis, 261; Fitzgerald, 260; Geldert, 259; Hughes, 258; Campana, 255; Vint; 251; Russell, 250; Williams, 249; Dufrane, 244; H. Panchot, 243; Clow, 240; Ryan, 239; Reid, 235; Rae, 222; H. Howard, 220; McKee, 215; Brodie, 214; Mahoney, 213; Hanwaker, 211; Gilloon, 210; Mathews, 200; Hennessy, 190; Lacouse, 188; Mignault, 172:**

A further nine men decided to spend their Christmas otherwise occupied. Their names and scores were: Byrne, 114; Croft, 226; Fitzpatrick, 217; Gebring, 105; McCormick, 177; P. Madden, 147; Shannon, 151.7; Walker, 189.4; Webster, 190.6:

Hart reappeared ten minutes into the start of Christmas Day and immediately set about retrieving the four miles he had lost to Faber. However, his progress was slow, and by 05:00, Frank had lost a further two miles to his adversary who was on a mark of 306. As Hart plugged away, the other contestant in the race who was making good progress was Fred Krohne. The tall German, who because of foot trouble had changed his shoes for slippers with socks drawn over them, actually took the lead between three and four o'clock in the afternoon. His lead didn't last long, and by nine o'clock both Hart and Faber overtook him, the Bostonian eventually getting the measure of his rival and going a mile in front of him. The scores at that time were: **Hart, 368.2; Faber, 367.2; Krohne, 366.5; Hughes, 345; Briody, 341; O'Brien, 340:**

It can be seen from the above record that the "Lepper" was going great guns. He had pulled out all the stops during the day to advance his position from tenth to fourth. At 21:30, and along with Brodie, Fitzgerald and Hart, he thrilled the crowd with a fast run when the band struck up "Wearing of the Green." Hart was now 4/6 on favourite to take first prize with Faber a 2/1 shot.

By the end of Christmas Day, 14 more pedestrians had had their dials taken down. The casualties were: W. H. Davies, on a score of 84.1; Gilloon for 210; Hennessy on 190; Lacouse with 188; Lowery showing 168; McKee, 215; Mathews, 200; Mahoney, 213; Molineux, 177; Mignault, 172; H. Panchot, 258; Reid, 256; Russell, 289; Ryan, 250:

With 19 competitors remaining at midnight, Frankie Hart was within a mile and a quarter of Weston's time when he made his 550-mile world record in June. The race leader was also 12¾ miles in front of Rowell's best record with both Faber and Krohne having bettered that too. The scores at that time were: **Hart, 381; Faber, 377; Krohne, 370; Hughes, 352; O'Brien, 349; Pegram, 345; Briody, 344; Fitzgerald, 341; Geldert, 340; Campana, 335; Williams, 331; R. Davis, 326; Vint; 325; Dufrane, 323; Clow, 315; Rae, 300; Howard, 293; Hanwaker, 276; Brodie, 275:**

Hart, who had rested from 1 a.m. for a couple of hours, maintained his advantage over Faber, who was observed to be stiff and sore. Pegram passed Hughes at 02:00, and Krohne, moving along with dogged determination, steadily made ground on Faber and passed him at around 04:00. It was at this time Harry Howard indicated to the match officials that he could go no further; the numbers 296 next to his name. He was followed by Hanwaker who, having made 188.5 some minutes later, sent word he too could no longer stand the pace. Meanwhile, Pegram continued his excellent progress snatching O'Brien's fourth place at 05:00. The contestants changed positions frequently as the morning progressed, and the field was further reduced as Brodie was the latest Boxing Day casualty, departing at 11:00 on a mark of 280.6. In front of an enthusiastic crowd, the fortunes of the pedestrians continued to excite all during the evening hours and bets at even money were being sought by the bookmakers that the winner would make 530 miles. 2/1 was being asked for 532 miles and 5/1 for 540 miles.

At midnight, the score of the remaining 16 pedestrians on the fifth day (24-hour distances in brackets) were: **Hart, 465.6; (84.6) Krohne, 459.7 (89.6); Faber, 456.7 (79); Pegram, 444.3 (98.6); Hughes, 440.3 (88.7); Fitzgerald, 431.1 (90.2); Geldert, 429.4 (80); O'Brien, 420 (80.2); Williams, 418.2 (87.3); Campana, 417.4 (82.4); Briody, 408.4 (64. 4); R. Davis, 407.3 (80.5); Dufrane, 399.7 (76.7); Clow, 398.2 (82.6) Vint, 391 (65.5); Rae, 375 (74.7):**

NB: Clarence G. Howard was reported to have died at his residence in Huntingdon, Long Island, during that afternoon. His demise was thought to have been due to his exertions on the track, and was it was stated that he died of *"prostration."*

King of the Peds

A lame looking Faber appeared back on the course at 01:40, but he soon limbered up, and went round in good style in front of a large crowd who stayed in the building throughout the early morning. They cheered Pegram as he walked around the track for four laps asleep until he woke up. By 3 a.m., Krohne had reduced the deficit with Hart to five miles. With Richard Davis retiring altogether from the race at 04:19 on a score of 450.2, Krohne went on to get within one mile of Hart's score by 8 o'clock, and by 10 o'clock he had equalled it. However, as he rested, Frank went on again to grab the initiative and put two miles between them.

During the afternoon Hughes was said to have been plied with champagne. The fizzy *"stimulant"* had been prescribed him in an attempt to alleviate his apparent suffering on the track, where the day before he had been reportedly suffering with bronchitis. He, along with Fitzgerald, Pegram and Williams, frequently ran amid the foul tobacco smelling atmosphere in front of an ever increasing crowd.

The scores at 18:00: **Hart, 522.6; Krohne, 519.3; Faber, 514.7; Pegram, 508.3; Hughes, 504; Fitzgerald, 496.6; Williams, 484.6; O'Brien, 484.1; Campana, 481.7; Geldert, 462.7; Clow, 460.2; Briody, 450.2; R. Davis, 450.2; Dufrane, 448.7; Vint; 443.6; Rae, 436:**

The afternoon's withdrawals were: Geldert at 14:28 on 462.7; Clow at 16:02 with 460.2; Briody at 16:33 for 450.2. Both Briody and Davis retired having reached the needed 450 thus regaining the $100 entrance fee they had paid, and their example was followed by Dufrane at 18:21.

Both Hart and Krohne stopped in front of the judges' stand where the belt was on display and *"waved over it the national flag, to the intense delight of the immense crowd which cheered and stamped in the most frantic style,"* and *"the rails about the track kept back a crowd of men ten or a dozen deep."* By eight o'clock in the evening the place was described as being almost impossible to move about in, *"with women and children being jostled mercilessly in the crowd."* The police had real problems keeping people off the track where Hart, wearing a white flannel suit and a *"natty blue jockey cap,"* moved himself around it *"swinging his arms as regular as clockwork,"* in typical Dan O'Leary style with his head thrown back *"like a conqueror."*

At 21:00, both Hart and Krohne headed towards their tents and there was speculation that they had finished their work for the tournament, their scores being 534.1 and 529.1 respectively. However, Hart only stayed off the path for five minutes after which he re-emerged to sprint round the track for three laps. He had already beaten Rowell's record of 530 miles, but it was now impossible for him to beat Weston's world record of 550. Meanwhile, Fitzgerald was intent on taking Hughes's fifth position in the race, and now running, set about the task in earnest at 21:10 making a lap in 1m.2s with the next being made in a minute flat. However, he had much work to do as he was five and a half miles behind the tottering "Lepper" who was described as *"short nosed, with a drooping jaw and a short bristling beard growing savagely over his lantern jaw."*

As time went by, the men on the track started to retire having reached their personal goals for the night. Campana was one of them and he left the track at 22:18 on a score of 500. *"As he reeled up to the scorers' stand, he dropped into a chair and pulled off his shoe and stocking, displaying a sole covered in blisters. A cheer went up as he staggered back to his tent carrying his stocking."* Hughes crawled off at 22:23 on a score of 520.1 and Williams won a slice of the cake at 22:25 having made 502.2. Faber withdrew for the final time at 22:27 on 531.6 and Rae finished his 450th mile at 22:31. Pegram left the scene a minute later on a final mark of 527.

At 22:35, Hart, wearing the belt, was seen running around the track carrying an American flag in both hands, having scored 540.1, amid cheering *"that fairly shook the building."* Whilst the winner left the track for his tent accepting the adulation of the crowd, only Fitzgerald and Krohne were left performing. Khrone on 536.2 then made his departure leaving Fitzgerald as the only man on the track, and with the police struggling to keep people off it, he continued to run at a lively pace of 8½ mph until he managed to reach his goal of beating Hughes at 22:47 for which he received the appreciation of the plaudits.

The Final Score!

Pos		Miles	Laps	Pos		Miles	Laps
1	**Hart**	**540**	1	9	O'Brien	484	1
2	Krohne	536	2	10	Geldert	462	7
3	Faber	531	6	11	Clow	460	3
4	Pegram	527	0	12	Vint	450	4
5	Fitzgerald	520	3	13	Briody	450	2
6	Hughes	520	1	14	Davis R	450	2
7	Williams	502	2	15	Dufrane	450	0
8	Campana	500	0	16	Rae	450	0

The pedestrians' share of the gate money which amounted to $7,000 was distributed as follows; $1,000 was shared amongst those making 450 miles. That left $6,100 to be shared amongst the first seven past the post. Hart therefore received $3,050; Krohne, $1,220; Faber, $610; Pegram, $457.50; Fitzgerald, $305; Hughes; $244; Williams, $213.50:

FIRST **SECOND** **THIRD**

Frank Hart **Fred Krohne** **Christian Faber**

The National Police Gazette (Illustration no: 62-64)

CHAPTER 23

What Else Happened in 1879

MOZART GARDEN.

FULTON AND SMITH STREETS

Under the direction of A. R. SAMUELS and J. H. WEBB

GRAND WALKING CONTEST

Between E. HOLSKE, of New York, and HARRY HOWARD of Glen Cove, and the coming champion long distance walker of America, CHAS. A. HARRIMAN, walking day and night for one week, starting January 20, at 12:05 A. M., and closing, January 25 at 12 P. M.

ADMISSION, TWENTY- FIVE CENTS

There were three good reasons to visit the Mozart Gardens at Brooklyn, New York, between Monday and Saturday, the 20th and 25th of January. Harry Howard, the Lancastrian from England, would set out to make 450 miles in six days. Edward Holske, a New Yorker, and the champion short distance walker of America, would start off at the same time as Howard attempting to walk 180 miles in 48 hours, and Charles Harriman would attempt to walk 50 miles in ten hours on the last three days of the event. Harriman had got himself the reputation of being the next best walker in the USA and had got his name down to compete in the next Astley Belt competition having already issued a challenge to walk any man, any distance, from one to six days, for $500. Harriman's shot at the feat would be beyond what anybody had ever done before in America, and if he succeeded, the man promoting the event, Mr. J. H. Webb, promised to introduce him to the English public.

The events would take place on a loam and tanbark track, which would be laid out on the ground, not on the wooden floorboards. For their admission price the public were promised they would be entertained by piano players in the afternoon and a band in the evening. During their trials, all the men would be accommodated in portioned off areas at the corners of the track. *"They contain cots, bed clothing and the necessary appurtenances for preparing the pedestrians meals."* As for the interior of the building, the walls *"have been decorated with gay coloured flags and streamers."*

The *Brooklyn Daily Eagle* described what happened before the pair began their respective journeys: **Three minutes before the time set for starting, Howard and Holske came out of their cabins on to the track, and walked up to the judges stand, which is situated at the edge of the track midway in the garden, just opposite the big clock. Howard is five feet six inches in height, weighs 140 pounds, and has turned his twenty ninth year. He is compactly built, square shouldered and muscular. He wore a white flannel shirt, black velveteen knee breeches, and a pair of baseball shoes laced tightly across the ankle. A black slouch hat covered his head, and a blue and white silk handkerchief was tied loosely around his neck. Holske's light trim figure offered a strong contrast to his companion's rather clumsy form. He is five feet nine inches, and he strips 132 pounds. He is scarcely 21, and his smooth clean shaven face, make him look even younger. His costume consists of scarlet trunks, white drawers, and a brown knit cardigan jacket. His feet were encased in low quartered shoes, while a close fitting skull cap crowned his head.**

Both contestants suffered with their feet in their attempts to achieve their objective, particularly Holske who suffered with blisters. This handicap caused him to fail in his bid to make the required *180 miles and he fell 20 short of this when he left the track; his best time for a mile being walked in 9m.30s. Howard, on the other hand, was one mile ahead of his planned itinerary by the time the clock clicked on to midnight at the end of 48 hours and a score of 151 miles. His feet however, although sore, were blister free and he was confident he could make 230 miles by the end of the third day; but in the end only made 214 at that time.

*It later transpired that Holske had agreed to complete 160 miles in the articles of agreement he had signed before the race, thus completing his task with nearly half an hour to spare.

At 14:00, on the fourth day, Harriman appeared on the track amid some excitement, to begin his ambitious attempt. The *Brooklyn Daily Eagle* wrote of him: He is built like a racehorse, his limbs long and clean cut seem to be made for just the style of work that is laid before him. He stands fully six feet in his stockings and tips the beam at 169 pounds scant. He is just in his twenty sixth year. He has a pleasant face expressing both will and good humour, while his mouth, rather firmly set in its expression, seems to indicate a great deal of determination. He wore light colored tights, and blue silk trunks covered with silver spaugles. A white gauze shirt enveloped the upper part of his body, on the front of which the letter "H" was worked in blue silk. Just below the legend he wore an enormous sapphire pin, and in a hip pocket a chocolate colored silk handkerchief peeped out. Harriman walked with a firm, elastic step up to the starting point, holding a corn cob tightly clenched in either hand, and chewing on a wooden toothpick that he shifted nervously from side to side between his sharp, white teeth. When he got the word Harriman shot away with a wonderful stride, swinging his arms rapidly backward and forward with a powerful action which seemed to greatly accelerate his speed. His easy graceful movements showed him to be a beautiful walker.

Harriman went on to complete his first 50 miles in 9h.11m.44s and his second half century in a time of 9h.39m.16s. Howard meanwhile, on the penultimate day of his attempt, was behind time, and there were severe doubts whether he would be able to make up the lost distance. In the end he failed to complete what he had set out to achieve by some 39 miles. He did, however, through his grit and determination, make many friends in the large audience who greatly appreciated his efforts as he alternated his gait firstly running then walking, but never failing to entertain them as he whizzed past Harriman on the home stretch. Howard eventually gave up at 23:21 leaving Harriman to complete the unprecedented feat he had yearned to accomplish, and that he did when he walked his last fifty miles in a time of 9h.38m.31s.

On *"an exceedingly narrow"* 33 laps to the mile track at the Coakley Hall Walking Rink at 162 Pacific Street, Brooklyn, David Scanlon of South Brook, Brooklyn, the Irish ex-amateur pedestrian, who in 1870, *"had performed a far more difficult feat at the exhibition at the Crystal Palace in the city of Dublin,"* failed in his bid to cover 450 miles in six days ending on Monday, the 27th of January 1879. Scanlon, who was *"tall in stature, raw boned, and full of pluck and muscle,"* and not only looked like O'Leary, but walked like him, actually covered an amazing 405 miles in that time. With little preparation, and no training, it was said that if he had competed at the Mozart Garden, he would have easily had made the required distance. Had he done so at the Coakley Hall, he would have earned himself a cool $1,000.

A 26-hour walking contest on a seven laps to the mile track for the "London Champion Belt" and £150, was started by Mr. Lewis at 8 p.m. in front of 3,000 spectators on the evening of Friday, the 14th of February 1879, at the Pomona Large Agricultural Hall, Cornbrook, Manchester. The pedestrians taking part were Harry Vaughan of Chester, who was the holder of the belt; the 5ft.4in William Howes of London, and 5ft.11in Walter Lewis also of the capital, were the challengers. *"The conditions of the belt are that it shall be a challenge and the winner shall have to defend his claim for it for 18 months before becoming his own property; three months to elapse between each match."* This was the third competition for the trophy, which had been previously won on the first occasion by Howes on February the 23rd 1878 at the "Aggie" when he walked 129 miles in 24h.20m. The second contest, which was held at the same venue in late July of the same year, was won by Vaughan (See Chapter 13 for accounts of both races.)

22:00 scores: **Howes, 13.1; Lewis, 13; Vaughan, 12.4:** 01:00 scores: **Howes, 30.4; Lewis, 30.2; Vaughan, 30:** 04:00 scores: **Howes, 47.3; Lewis, 46.5; Vaughan, 46.2:** 07:00 scores: **Howes, 63.3; Vaughan, 62; Lewis, 57.2:** 10:00 scores: **Howes, 80.4; Vaughan, 77.6; Lewis, 61.4:**

King of the Peds

The contest was brought to a premature close at 13:42 the next day by Vaughan's trainer T. Williams who announced his enforced retirement through *"an attack in the right leg"* (the same one that had failed him in the match in the previous November which Corkey won), at 12:19 having scored 90.3 in a time of 16h.19m. Howes would eventually win the race with a score of 100.2 in 17h.42m.19s. Lewis finished 3rd on a score of 61.4 in a time of 13h.3m having been pulled out of the race at 10:45 by his representative, Mr. Capes of Hull, as a consequence of the stomach cramps and sickness that he had been suffering since 06:00. The winner had been trained by J. Howes at the Surrey County Cricket Club at Brighton.

For our next snippet, we have to go back to five minutes past midnight on Monday, the 27th of January 1879, when Edward Belden of Milwaukee, Wisconsin, and Peter L. Van Ness, of New York began an exhibition at the Fifth Regiment Armory, Hester Street, New York. The conditions of the match, which was for $500 a side, was that Van Ness would have to make 2,000 half miles in 2,000 consecutive half hours, whilst Belden was to make the same in 2,000 consecutive periods of 20 minutes. On commencement, both men were reportedly in fine condition with Belden displaying a number of medals on his chest.

On the 2nd of February, Belden had made his 431st half mile while Van Ness had completed his 287th half mile. Twelve days later on the 14th, the *New York Times* reported: **As they go round and round, they have not only the inspiriting notes of a piano to keep them in time and tune, but the additional aid of gorgeous and plentiful decorations of all sorts about the walls, such as flags, big posters, time announcements, and many mysterious notices about "laps" and "half miles" and "best times." Van Ness and Belden, the walkers, are almost as gorgeous as the walls. Belden appears in a flannel suit, that makes him as red as the orthodox stage devil, and he walks well. Van Ness is in something of a Sing Sing costume. The men are nearly the same size, and their styles of walking are very much the same. At 9 o'clock last night Belden had finished 1,287 half miles, and Van Ness 858 half miles.**

At midday on the 17th, Van Ness accomplished 1,033 half miles, and Belden 1,540 in their *"test of endurance."* That night, Belden, who was said to be under the influence of *"injudiciously administered"* opiate, would have had to leave the track had he not been helped by his physicians. By 23:00 on the 22nd, Belden had walked 1,942 half miles and Van Ness, 1,233. Belden completed his feat at 18:24 the next day. *"Making his last half mile in 4m.36½s, he walked three additional half miles and was presented with an onyx ring by Dr. Swan. He was greeted with great enthusiasm, and was lifted upon the shoulders of some of the assemblage and carried entirely around the track."*

On the 4th of March, the *Brooklyn Daily Eagle* wrote: **Yesterday, the nervous wear and tear to which he has been subjected seemed to render him preternaturally irritable.** After completing just over 1,700 miles, Van Ness wouldn't respond to his trainer Joe Burgoine who tried to get him back on the track. Complaining of burning sensations in his head and throat, and suffering from swollen legs and ankles, he knocked Burgoine over after completing 1,718 half miles: **In addition to other uses of tons of excitement, he partook for the first time of alcoholic stimulants, and rather overdid the thing, for after behaving like a madman on the track he rushed into his room seized a revolver, which had been presented to him, and fired several shots at random. He then shot Burgoine in the arm.** The proprietor of the hall narrowly escaped being killed, for one bullet went through his hat; two female pedestriennes in an adjoining apartment were frightened by a bullet whizzing past them. The deranged athlete then continued to fire indiscriminately as the spectators swiftly made their exit. After emptying the chambers of his revolver, he was overpowered by the police, causing him to faint and require the administration of morphine in *"hot drops."* After coming round he continued on his way and managed to make 1,721 half miles by 21:30: **This is a whim which threatens to imperil spectators and will materially reduce the probable profits of the exhibition. It is quite clear that Van Ness being deprived of sleep is in a state of cerebral irritation which bodes ill for his reason. How long he can keep up his present work without producing inflammation or softening of the brain, is a question which his friends would hardly care to see tested at his expense.**

Interestingly, there appears to have been no further reporting of Van Ness's attempt thereafter, but as readers will have already gathered, he did complete what he had set out to achieve, doing so on the 9th of March.

With much less fuss, Bartholomew O'Donnell, an octogenarian pedestrian, successfully walked 80 miles in 26 hours at Phillip Casey's track on the corner of Court and Baltic Street, Brooklyn, between the 19th and 20th of March, having failed to walk 75 miles in 24 hours a few weeks earlier in the same city.

The result of the 16 competitor, six-day, heel-and-toe "Championship of the World" match, inaugurated at Gilmore's Garden, New York, on Monday, the 5th of May, was a win for George Guyon, the well known Chicagoan. The conditions of the match were that in order to gain a cash prize, a contestant would have to walk 400 miles. To get back his entrance fee of $100, he would have to make 425 miles. As an incentive to score 450 miles, an extra award of $50 was offered. The men were accommodated in quarters on the Twenty Seventh Street side of the building which had heavy red curtains for doors which meant that *"no tobacco smoke could intrude."* Each *"little"* room was furnished with a cot-bed, blankets, a table, a chair, wash bowl and pitcher.

Guyon, who the bookies offered at a price of 3/1 before the off, made an impressive total distance of 480.2 which was a lap more than Panchot had made in the go-as-you-please event three weeks previously. The winner, who was rewarded with a cash prize of $1,000 and the champion belt (made by Tiffany & Co and composed of gold and silver) worth $1,000, left the track at 22:19 suffering little from the week's exertions in front of a disappointing crowd of 1,500.

George Guyon

The National Police Gazette. (Illustration no: 65)

Fred Khrone was the runner-up earning $750 for walking 461 miles. John P. Colston, the *"big Swede"* from Hoboken (who had succeeded in walking 1,018 miles in 500 hours in his home town), and who started the race with his feet encased in medicated cotton, made 452 miles, took third prize of $500. Faber grabbed fourth money of $250 for traversing 450 miles, and Curran, who made a respectable 438 miles, had a collection made for him which raised $50. He beat Campana who scored 401 miles.

Peter Crossland sailed for New York on the 6th of May 1879 on the steam-ship *Nevada* to participate in the forthcoming 75-hour walking match in Chicago. He arrived at 17:00 on Thursday, the 15th of May. Of Crossland, the *New York Times* commented: He is of medium height, but of magnificent physique. His shoulders are broad, and his form is perfect. Crossland comes from Sheffield, Yorkshire County, England. He brings no trainer with him. He is 40 years old, and began to walk in matches three years ago. Previous to that time he had worked at his trade, a cutler. At the match in the Pomona Palace, in Manchester a walk of 72 hours, he beat O'Leary 19 miles. He walked at that time 120 3/4 miles and 200 yards without a rest. This was September 11 and 12 1876. He has made the best record in England for 242 and 284 miles having made the former in 57:02:37, and the latter in 68:40:19. He has made the best 33, 34, and 35-hour times in England making in 33 hours, 151 miles and 4 laps; in 34 hours, 156 miles and 1 lap, and in 35 hours, 160 miles and 6 laps. Crossland has received the Champion Cup of the Midland Counties in Nottingham, England, for making 322 miles in a six day's walk of 14 hours a day. He says he comes to this country to walk, not to run.

He reached Chicago on the next day and immediately went into training in the vicinity of the South Park Hotel for the match at the Exposition Building which would start on the evening of Wednesday, the 28th of May. The race initially attracted 16 other entries. Crossland was expected to win, as his performances in England were considered *"remarkable ones."* Along with him, Banks, Parry and Burns were the other favourites for the contest. Before the race took place, Daniel O'Leary, who was promoting the event, thought it pertinent to explain himself to his fellow townsmen. The following letter sent to the *Chicago Tribune* explains why:

To the Editor of the Tribune.

CHICAGO. May 23rd - Having learned from reliable sources that considerable dissatisfaction prevails amongst the competitors for the seventy five hour championship belt of the world, owing to my being entered for the much coveted prize, will you be good enough grant me brief space for an explanation? When the belt was offered by me I thought the contest would be confined to local or home pedestrians; but perceiving that foreigners – one of them an old rival – had entered, I once concluded to enter also, with a view of settling for ever the question of superiority between Mr. Crossland and myself. No other motive ever induced me to be a competitor, and I feel much pleasure in saying that Mr. Crossland was not only willing but anxious to try issues with me in the present contest. Now, however, that home pedestrians and betting men have declared that it would be bad taste for me to compete for a prize given by myself, I hereby withdraw my name from the list of competitors promising, however that the winner of the belt will hear from me at an early day. In conclusion, allow me to express the hope that every courtesy will be extended to my old rival, Mr. Crossland. In the coming match, by our citizens whose love for fair play has never been, and I hope never can be, impeached.

Respectfully yours.

DANIEL O'LEARY

Dr. N. Rowe, editor of the *Chicago Field,* would manage the contest, and the following rules would govern the tournament:

1. The match to be a fair-heel-and-toe walk. The winner will have to defend his claim for the belt for twelve months, and should he wish to have it in his possession, he must give security to the appointed stakeholder as a guarantee to restore it when called upon in good condition.

2. The holder of the belt shall not be called upon to compete in more than two matches in one year, and should he succeed in winning in two consecutive matches or sweepstakes, it shall become his absolute property, providing that said matches or sweepstakes have been bone fide in every respect.

3. The holder of the belt must accept all challenges, subject to the above conditions, for not less than $500 a side, and be prepared to defend his right to the same within three months from the issue of any challenge.

4. The man walking the greatest distance in the specified time to be the champion seventy-five-hour pedestrian of the world, and to have entrusted to his keeping a belt, value $800, and receive $1,000 in cash; second, $500; third, $250; fourth, $150, and any competitor other than the first four men covering a distance of 260 miles to receive back his stake, together with an additional sum of $10 for every five miles walked in excess of the above distance.

5. In the event of a match being made, any man may join in by depositing $500 with the appointed stake holder within two weeks previous to the commencement of the race.

6. The editor of the *Chicago Field* is appointed stakeholder for any matches that may arise for the belt.

7. All appeals upon questions not provided for by these conditions shall be made to the referee, whose decisions in all cases shall be final.

Each of the 21 pedestrians was provided with *"a little cottage convenient to the track,"* where he could go in at intervals and *"receive nourishment and proper treatment from his trainer."* It was from these small apartments the 22 walkers emerged on to the 14-foot-wide track on the evening of the race, wearing cards attached to their backs and shoulders. They were then observed walking slowly around the course until they were all called in front of the judge's stand where they had the rules of the walk read out to them. *"They were a motley looking crew at best, but after being labelled looked like a gang of prison birds waiting to be sent into the stone yard."*

Below is a list of those taking part and the number beside their name was the one given to them just before the "off:" 1: **John Banks;** Chicago: 2: **Frank Benton;** Lake, Illinois: 3: **George Brandsetter;** Chicago: 4: **"Capt. Harry;"** Chicago: 5: **P. Van Castella;** Chicago: 6: **Peter Crossland;** Sheffield, England: 7: **John P. Dammers;**

Chicago: 8: **A. M. Dana;** New York: 9: **John Dobler;** Chicago: 10: **R. H. Dodge;** Escanaba, Michigan: 11: **John J. Geraghty;** Mendota, Illinois: 12: **H. L. Goodman;** Chicago: 13: **George Guyon;** Chicago: 14: **"Guy Burns;"** 15: **William. H. Heine;** Chicago: 16: **William H. Hoffman;** 17: **"Iowa George;"** Tipton, Iowa: 18: **James McAndrews;** Chicago: 19: **George Parry;** Manchester, England: 20: **Albert Schock;** 21: **John Sherry;** Waukegan, Illinois: 22: **Otto Salman;** Galena, Illinois: The race in front of 5,000 people, for the prizes amounting to $2,000, started at 20:50, after a considerable delay, due to the administration of the numbers.

The *Chicago Tribune* in its story about some of the performing peds, also commented on the good natured and humorous crowd which was being added to by the minute: "Iowa George," who is a brawny young man with excessively red hair, was the first to attract attention, and cries of "Go it sorrel top!" cheered him on his way. No. 9 was a solemn looking little fellow, who brought up the rear of the procession at a funeral pace, and "Look at him run!" resounded through the building as soon as he came in sight. No. 15 was also an object of special consideration, from the fact that he walked very carefully, as if in constant fear of stepping on a chunk of red hot iron. No. 16 had elegant knee action, but didn't seem to cover the ground very rapidly. There was nothing particularly noticeable about the others, except that No. 18 was a very tall youth with too much daylight underneath him to last out a long race, and No. 16 wore a perpetual smile, appropriate remarks concerning which were frequently made."

After the first mile, the fastest man on the track was Banks with a time of 8m.32s. The Indianan, Geraghty was next in 8m.57s and Goodman next in 9m.18s. Six miles were accomplished by Guyon in 1h.14s, by Parry in 1h.2m.30s and by Crossland in 1h.15m.47s. At midnight, the man leading the pack was Guyon on a score of 19 miles with Dammers, Dobler, "Iowa George," Parry, Schock and Sherry in joint second place a mile behind. However, Guyon was to quit the race on 25 miles due to *"inflammation of the kidneys."*

At 14:45, the score of the prominent competitors stood as follows: **Parry, 82; Van Castella and Dobler, 73: Burns, 71; Sherry, 70; Banks, 69; Goodman, 65; Crossland, 64; Dana, 62:**

Crossland, who had been resting a long time in the afternoon, regarded the gap between himself and Parry as of *"little consequence,"* and after 24 hours of competition, the slim, light haired, Van Castella, would be the man to the lead the race on a score of 94 with Dobler and Parry on 92, Banks on 91, Sherry with 89 and Crossland getting closer on 86.

The spectators up to that point had been kind and indulgent to the foreigners with Crossland and Parry being afforded a limited amount of applause. Captain Turtle (who was in charge of Crossland) was doing all in his power see that his man wanted for nothing in the way of attention, having received a cable dispatch from Astley who told him to, *"spare no expense in providing proper attendants, etc, for the Sheffield man and that he (Astley) would bear all expenses."*

The midnight scores of the first ten men in the race on the second day with Benton, Dammers, Dodge, Guyon, "Iowa George," Salman and Heine all retired: **Dobler, 102; Parry, Sherry and Castella, 100; Crossland, 97; Burns, 96; "Capt. Harry," 92; Goodman, 90; Schock, 88; Brandsetter, 86:**

The knees of the impressive German, Van Castella, swelled badly as he rested, causing him to be the next casualty in the race. His departure left Johnny Dobler and George Parry to lead the way. As the day progressed though, Dobler started to dictate matters and asserted his authority on the event. Of the others in the race, *"Banks, who at the start was dubbed "The Corpse," on account of his cadaverous appearance, resembled one more than ever last night, his bright black eyes being in great contrast to the white face and hollow cheeks which surrounded them, was suffering from blistered feet but limped bravely along, now and then wiping his face and forehead with a wet sponge."* At 19:30, and with Dobler stalking Parry, Dana appeared to be the liveliest competitor on the path, and in the absence of "Captain Harry," McAndrews, and the smiling Hoffman, the field had been reduced to ten.

After 48 hours of hard slog, the local lad, Dobler (real name Dolan), was 5 miles in front of Parry on a score of 174. Banks was in third "pozzy" on a score of 162 and Sherry was close behind him with 161. The contest must have been very exciting thereafter because, as the midnight score shows below, Parry made up much ground to take the joint honour of being the race leader. During this part of the race the press commented that the noise made by the crowd could be heard a block away: **Dobler and Parry, 183; Banks, 175; Sherry, 171; Dana, 163; Goodman, 153; Crossland, 152; Burns, 151:**

King of the Peds

The match finished at 23:53 with the last four hours being full of developments and controversy, and although trouble had been anticipated, nothing serious occurred. The Exposition Building had been packed and the track had to be kept clear by a string of policemen stationed within a few feet of each other.

The trouble had started with an attempt to stop Dobler who was in the lead on Friday afternoon. The story goes that as he took a rest in his cabin, his bed had been mysteriously saturated with chloroform, and as a consequence he lost four hours in the race whilst he recovered from the stupor induced by the drug. The charge was made that Jerry Monroe, a notorious sporting character tried to deny Dobler the race, and although Monroe denied the accusation, there was pretty strong evidence that he had instigated the whole affair. As a result trouble had been threatened thereafter by Dobler's friends, but nothing untoward occurred.

Following that incident attempts to stop Parry from winning the belt followed. At 18:00 on Saturday evening, Schock, who had previously left the race after scoring 100 miles, unexpectedly re-appeared on the track and walked slowly in front of Parry causing him to slow down. There was so much concern amongst the managers that, *"fresh relays of police were summoned"* because Schock's behaviour was having an adverse effect on the crowd. After comparative quiet had been restored, Crossland appeared back in the ring to lend his support to his fellow countryman and shield him from some of the hostile spectators.

At 9 o'clock, both Englishmen had pepper thrown in their faces, the brunt of which was taken by Crossland causing him to retire permanently. However, following an investigation, it was stated that there was nothing wrong with Crossland's eyes. The story that Captain Turtle had found a package of red pepper on the track couldn't be verified, and Dr. Rowe, one of the managers, then made an announcement that any repetition would mean that the contest would be closed and the belt would be awarded to Parry. A tall policeman was then employed to follow him and guard him against further attacks.

The **final scores** of those still left in the race which closed at 23:53 were: **Parry, 268; Dobler, 265; Banks, 254; Sherry, 242; Dana, 221; Brandsetter, 202; Geraghty, 185; Crossland, 158:**

A protest against awarding the belt to Parry, on account of alleged wrong scoring and violation of the rules, was lodged with the judges by Dobler's friends. One of the objections was that Parry's trainer walked alongside him, but it was said that it wouldn't be entertained. Dr. Rowe went on to read out the score, and said that to give the matter proper consideration he would not give his decision on the first prize until the week after.

Following the enquiry on 3rd of June, all objections were overruled and Parry was awarded the belt and $1,000: Dobler received $500; Banks $250, Sherry, $150 and Dana, $100: The following letter then appeared in the *Chicago Tribune* on the 5th of June.

To the Editor of the Tribune.

CHICAGO. June 5. – Now that the contest for the O'Leary champion belt has been decided, I feel that a few words from me will not be considered out of place by your citizens. I came here from England for the express purpose of competing against my old rival, Mr. Daniel O'Leary, and, owing to the short time given me for the late seventy five hour contest, I was in no condition to compete against the 21 pedestrians with whom I was obliged to contend. Having met Mr. O'Leary on two occasions in honourable combat, and having defeated him once in a 75 hour match, I hope the American people will bear with me when I say I am not fully satisfied with the result of the recent walking match in this city. I therefore challenge Daniel O'Leary to walk against me in a third or final seventy five hour match, in any city in the world, for any amount of money from £1,000 upward, the match to take place whenever the champion so desires, as I am ready to meet him or any other champion, at any time.

In conclusion, I tender my heartfelt thanks and gratitude to Mr. O'Leary for the unexpected courtesies bestowed on me since my arrival in this city, as also to Capt. Turtle for the great kindness shown me since I have had the pleasure and good fortune of meeting him. My money and myself can be found at Capt. Turtle's office, on Lake Street, at any time, and I hope the question of superiority as a 75 hour walker between Mr. O'Leary and myself will be settled at an early day.

PETER CROSSLAND

That letter inspired Mike McDonald, the backer of George Guyon, to write another challenge to O'Leary on the 9th of June, the same appearing in the *Chicago Tribune* on the 10th.

To the Editor of the Tribune.

CHICAGO. June 9. – Learning that Messrs. O'Leary and Crossland are anxious to make a seventy five hour match at fair heel-and-toe walking, I hereby offer to back George Guyon against either of them for $5,000 a side; or will enter him in a sweepstakes, open to all, each entry to put up $5,000. In case this challenge is accepted by either or both of these parties to whom it is addressed, Mr. Guyon will require ten weeks time in which to properly prepare himself. In regard to forfeit, I would suggest $2,500 per man as a suitable sum, the same to put up in any National bank or in the hands of any responsible man as stakeholder; the remaining $2,500 of each mans stake to be made good one week before the date fixed for the race. The winner of the race to take all the gate money, and in order that there be no chance for hippodroming I agree, on behalf of Guyon, that, in case any underhanded work is discovered, the entire stake and gate money shall be divided among three charitable institutions of this city. Man and money ready at 176 South Clarke Street.

In addition to the above, I will bet $500 that Sir John Astley is not backing Crossland.

M. C. McDONALD

On the 12th of June 1879, O'Leary and Crossland met at the Burke's Hotel along with Guyon's backer McDonald (who failed to get his man into the contest), to sign the articles of agreement for the match they had arranged between themselves and which was to take place within thirty days. The articles stated the following:

1. The match to be a seventy five-hour contest fair heel-and-toe walk, for a wager of $5,000 a side, which sum must be placed in the hands of a responsible party at least seventy two hours previous to the start taking place.

2. Fifty per cent of the amount to be competed for being already in the hands of a reasonable party, the balance must be placed in possession of the appointed stakeholder three days previous to the commencement of the match.

3. By mutual consent of the parties to this agreement, George E. Gooch, Esq., is hereby appointed stakeholder to the match.

4. The party failing to have the entire amount of his portion of the wager deposited with the stakeholder at least seventy two hours previous to the start to forfeit all claim to the 50 per cent placed as earnest money.

5. Each man to walk on a separate track, the composition and construction of which shall be as himself may select or approve of.

6. Should either party, during the process of the match, use disrespectful language toward the other, the competitor so offending shall be expelled from the track, and will not be permitted, under any pretext whatever to further compete in the contest.

7. Neither competitor will be granted the privilege of "coaching," but each pedestrian will be allowed one attendant, for the purpose of giving food and drinks on the track; provided, however, that such attendant shall not attempt to accompany his man more than fifty yards from the place where he offered such nourishment.

8. The winner to receive all the stakes and two thirds of the gate money after all expenses have been paid.

9. The stakeholder to retain in his possession the full sum competed for until such time as he receives a written decision on the result of the contest from the referee, when he will hand over all the stakes to the party declared the lawful winner of the contest.

10. The expenses of the match to be deducted from the gate receipts, the balance (if any) to be divided between the competitors in the manner herein before provided, namely, two thirds to the winner and one third to the loser.

11. All questions not provided for in these conditions to be decided by the referee, from whose decision no appeal shall be taken to a court of law.

(Signed)   **PETER CROSSLAND**   **DANIEL O'LEARY**

King of the Peds

It was reported in the press on the 21st of June, that the match between the pair would take place between Wednesday and Saturday, the 25th the 28th of the same month. In the meantime, both men had been in training. O'Leary had been practicing at Sunnyside and Crossland at Austin. The stakes of $5,000 a piece, were said to be the highest ever competed for in the United States.

The race started promptly at 8:15 p.m. in front of 2,000 spectators and a record of each man's performance can be found below up until 23:45 on the first night of competition:

O'Leary		Crossland		O'Leary		Crossland	
Miles	Time	Miles	Time	Miles	Time	Miles	Time
1	09:45	1	09:05	10	11:50	10	11:55
2	10:20	2	09:55	11	22:10	11	11:50
3	10:35	3	10:00	12	12:30	12	11:20
4	10:50	4	10:05	13	15:00	13	11:50
5	11:05	5	10:10			14	11:40
6	10:50	6	10:50			15	12:00
7	11:30	7	10:55			16	12:10
8	12:30	8	11:00			17	12:30
9	11:30	9	11:15			18	12:30

On the second day up until 08:00, O'Leary had been off the track 36 minutes as opposed Crossland's 7 minutes an hour later. The visitor was the first man to make 100 miles in 22h.29m.30s, whereas the Chicagoan made his in 26h.15m.20s. When the score was recorded by the press that night at 23:00, Crossland was 13 miles ahead of O'Leary on a score of 113 miles. O'Leary seemed unconcerned by the large gap however, and was confident of ultimate success. Many in the crowd of 3,000 felt differently; there was much dissatisfaction with the Irishman who they thought was taking far too many breaks. O'Leary was blaming his stomach for his poor performance but there were no complaints from Crossland, who satisfied his appetite with dry toast and roast beef washed down with the occasional glass of *"Bass Ale."*

On Friday morning, O'Leary, after having three hour's sleep, started to close the gap, and indulging in little rest during the day, managed to catch up the ailing Yorkshireman at 19:26 when both men's scores registered 170 miles apiece. When the news broke that O'Leary had passed his rival, the public flocked into the building to watch their man slowly take control of the race. By 22:00 the place was packed with 5,000 spectators all willing O'Leary on as well as giving his rival some support too. Both men received flowers from the crowd, and both were sent telegrams wishing them well in their efforts from all over the American continent.

With little to change the obvious result barring catastrophe on the part of O'Leary, the outcome was an emphatic win for the Irish-American. The stomach problem that had caused him misery in previous days had disappeared thus allowing him to beat his opponent with ease. During the day, Crossland didn't help his cause as he took numerous rests after which he appeared progressively stiff and sore. The score at the end was announced to the crowd by Mr. St. Clair, one of the umpires, who said, "Ladies and Gentlemen, the great race between Daniel O'Leary, of the United States and Peter Crossland of England has now terminated. The scores stand as follows; O'Leary two hundred and fifty miles; Crossland two hundred and twenty-five and three laps. Time, seventy-four hours and forty minutes for O'Leary. Unless objections are raised between this and ten o'clock on Monday morning the stakes, ten thousand dollars will be handed over to the victor."

After the announcement much noise and three cheers were given to the both pedestrians after which Crossland made a small speech thanking the people of Chicago for their support and intimating that he may try again to take the belt. He then gave way to O'Leary who made the usual positive comments about the fairness of the contest, giving his thanks to all who had supported him in his victory. Both men were then driven away, O'Leary to his home and Crossland to his hotel. On their journeys both men may have been aware that they would have made a small fortune from the gate receipts, with O'Leary alone making between $7,000 and $8,000. Crossland would get between $2,000 and $5,000, which would be welcome recompense for the amount he lost on the unsuccessful adventure.

Henry Vaughan of Chester won a 14 hours per day, six-day contest *"with comparative ease,"* when he defeated Pat McCarty of Leeds for first prize money at the Agricultural Hall, Islington, London. Vaughan's score was 399 miles. McCarty scored 377 for second prize money. George Pettitt of Sittingbourne having mustered 361 miles took third booty. Woolfe of Chichester claimed the fourth prize on a score of 328 miles.

The contest, which began at 09:00 on Monday, June the 30th and finished on Saturday, the 5th of July, had attracted eleven competitors including Clarkson of Hull, Day of Northampton, Freeman of Australia, Hibberd of Bethnall Green, Ide of Chichester, Richardson of the USA and Robson of Liverpool.

In San Francisco on July the 15th, over 10,000 people assembled at the Pavilion in the evening to witness the finish of the six-day *"walking match."* With the greatest enthusiasm prevailing, the diamond belt and first prize money of $1,000, was won by Frank Edwards who made 371 miles. $750 was won by the runner-up, McIntyre, with 366 miles. He beat Bowman, who won third prize money of $500 after scoring 367 miles.

On Saturday night, August the 17th, a 75-hour, go-as-you-please race finished at 12 o'clock, at Park Garden, Providence, Rhode Island, in the presence of 15,000 enthusiastic spectators. Of the 40 men who started, only eight held out to the end. The first prize of $250 and a gold medal was awarded to Charles Harriman, who made 283.2. The second prize of $150 went to Alfred Elson of West Meriden, Connecticut, who made 274 miles, the third prize of $100, to Jimmy Albert of Philadelphia, who made 270 miles. The fourth prize of $30 went to J. P. Colston of New York, who made 262.3. Robert Colbert of Chelsea, Massachusetts, who scored 261.3, received his entrance money back. Trainers' prizes of $20 each went to Campana who made 210.4, and to G. R. Daniels, a 16-year-old boy who finished the race with 200.

At Baltimore, Maryland, on October the 4th 1879, the "O'Leary and Englehardt" 12½ hours per day, 75-hour go-as-you-please pedestrian contest, which started on the 29th of September at the Academy of Music, was brought to a close at 10:30 p.m. In front of about 1,500 witnesses, John Hughes won the race with a score of 376.1 and was awarded $300 in gold and the "Pimlico Gold Medal." Redding was the second placed athlete on a score of 357 ($200), followed by Colston on 348 ($100), Harmer with 347 ($75), and Campana with 329 ($50).

There was a crowd of less than 400 to witness the 40 men participating in the start of the O'Leary sponsored 14 hours a day, six-day go-as-you-please match, which began one hour later than advertised at 11 a.m. at Madison Square Garden on Monday, the 13th of October. This match had followed the 1st O'Leary Belt contest won by Murphy which had ended only two days earlier. The race had been promoted by O'Leary, as a means of trying to cover the costs of the building which he had leased for a month. Each starter was required to sign an agreement to retire if he didn't make an average of fifty miles per day. One of the major attractions was the fact that the renowned English pedestrian, Henry Brown, was in the line-up, along with Charles Harriman and John Hughes.

The competitors organised themselves four abreast in front of the scorers' stand to await the word "Go!" from the starter, "Pop" Whittaker. Hanlon made the first mile in 6m.10s, but it was "Blower" Brown who led the race after an hour, making 8.1 with Harriman and Cole traversing 7.6. In recognition of the Englishman's impressive start, Brown was quickly installed as the even money favourite. Harriman was next on the list at 4/1; Fitzgerald attracted a price of 6/1, and Campana, 8/1. Half of those odds mentioned could be obtained for a place first or second. Those who had backed Brown would have been pleased with his second hour performance, as he led the race by a mile on a score of 16 miles. Fitzgerald, Hughes and Hilton followed with Cole a mile behind them. However, the smiles of the Londoner's backers were to be wiped off their faces when at the end of the fourth hour, and on a score of 26 miles, Brown began to complain of feeling sick and started to fall behind.

King of the Peds

The leading scores at 1 A. M., the close of the first 14 hours with 14 men already out of the contest including Fred Krohne for 44 miles, stood: **Woods, 81; Harriman, 77.3; Preuss; 71.5; Hughes, 71.2; Fitzgerald, 71.1; Campana and Vint, 71; Cahill, 70.2; Hilton, 69.2; Colston, 65.1; Dufrane, 64.2: (Brown, in 19th position was on a score of 57):**

It was obvious that Brown had retired from the race the next day when he failed to turn up to take his place in the line up for the start. His absence prompted the following comment in the *Brooklyn Daily Eagle*: His miserable performance in the O'Leary Belt contest proved that for the first time being, at least, he was out of trim, and his collapse yesterday indicated that his pedestrian days were over.

On the second day, Hughes, one of the prominent runners in the race, fell back from a leading position to seventh by the evening. Harriman had raced with Woods most of the day, but the latter named fell by the wayside too when he started to retreat down the field as well. The score at midnight with just 15 men left on the track, eleven having retired during the day, was: **Harriman; 137, Vint, 134.4; Fitzgerald, 134; Campana, 133; Colston, 130; Woods, 128; Hughes, 127; Preuss; 125.4; Dufrane, 121.3; Waters, 116.4; Hilton, 114; Perrin, 113.1; Barber, 112.1; Hanlon, 110; Ring, 110:**

At noon on the third day, and with the field further reduced to 13, Perrin being the last man out, Vint led with a score of 146 miles, demoting the poorly performing Harriman, the overnight leader, to third place. Harriman would be the third casualty of the day, following Hanlon who had given way at 12:16. The "Steamboat" retired at 13:00 on a score of 147.2 due to blistered feet. Meanwhile, Hughes had been complaining of being cheated and tried to leave the track but had been prevented from doing so by his trainer. O'Leary and his protégé Hart had entertained the crowd with a six-mile walk during the evening, but on the whole, and although the management was doing well out of the event, the attendance hadn't been up to scratch. At the end of the day, when time was called, *"there were few spectators present at that hour, and they were mostly dead-heads."* The scores at midnight: **Fitzgerald, 199; Vint, 198.4; Campana, 196.1; Colston, 193; Hughes, 181.4; Waters, 176.4; Preuss; 176.2; Hilton, 175; Dufrane, 172; Woods, 168.4; Barber, 165:**

The event had been poorly attended during the mornings, and the start of the fourth day was no exception. The few who watched saw Preuss removing himself from the race altogether at 10:44 for a score of 178.5 followed by the emaciated figure of Woods who held out till 15:15 with 184.5. Hilton also gave his excuses and left the scene at 19:17 when on a score of 210.6. As the evening progressed, that attendance grew considerably, and by ten o'clock, a couple of thousand or so were milling about the place, many of whom, would have watched another O'Leary-Hart exhibition match as an alternative to the sport on offer. With the *"Williamsburg shoemaker,"* Vint, now having *"foot problems"* of a kind he wished he didn't have in the form of a limp, Patrick Fitzgerald was now taking command of the race. Campana was now his nearest challenger. The 56th hour scores: **Fitzgerald, 265.5; Campana, 259.4; Colston, 256.6; Vint, 254.1; Waters, 235.1; Hughes, 232.3; Dufrane, 223.2; Barber, 220:**

At noon on the penultimate day, Fitzgerald maintained the lead over "Sport" in front of just 30 spectators, having covered 10 miles more than the previous night's closing score. The highlight of the day was Hughes's withdrawal from the race at 18:19 having made 248 miles and yet *another* contest between the race sponsor and the star of his stable, "Black Dan." By the 70th hour, and with "Fitz" still leading on a mark of 330.6, Colston, who had 321.4, headed Campana by a lap with Vint back in a comfortable fourth registering 310.3. Of the rest, Waters led Dufrane and Barber with 288, 279.6 and 275.1 respectively.

It was inevitable that the *"not widely known"* Irishman, Fitzgerald, would, bar catastrophe, win the race. *"The men toward the finish looked very wretched. Every step seemed to give them pain."* In the end when the contest finally folded up at 22:25, the **final score** was: **Fitzgerald, 377 ($1,200); Colston**, 370.1 ($600); **Campana**, 363.1 ($400); **Vint**, 350.0 ($200); **Waters**, 333.1; **Dufrane**, 325.3; **Barber**, 319.3:

Patrick Fitzgerald **John Peter Colston**

The National Police Gazette   (Illustration no: 66, 67)

"Charley" Harriman went on to win a 12 hours per day, 72-hour, *heel-and-toe* walking match, this time on a 16 laps to the mile track (as measured by Messrs. Van Duyne Young, surveyors) at the Rink in Newark, New Jersey, against 31 other opponents out of 48 original entries. The race, which started at 11 a.m. on Monday, the 3rd of November, was under the management of Daniel O'Leary and Fred Englehardt. Harriman, who won a gold watch and $500, scored 342 miles and 9 laps which, at the time, was the best ever distance in such an event. Christian Faber, who had led the way until the 36th hour, dropped out leaving the race at the mercy of the amorous fellow from Haverhill. Cyrenius Walker received the $300 second prize, his score being 336.2. Thomas Noden of Brooklyn picked up third prize money of $200 for making 332.2, and Harry Armstrong, the New York champion amateur, got fourth pickings of $100 with 321 miles. J. M. Rae of London, Ontario, came fifth with 305 miles and 13 laps and Charles A. Preuss of Newark, sixth, having scored 303.

On Monday, November the 17th 1879, the Australian newspaper, the *Sydney Morning Herald* reported: During Saturday the Exhibition building in Prince Alfred Park, the scene of the go-as-you-please pedestrian tournament, was visited by large numbers of people, and as the evening drew on and the conclusion of the contest approached, the building was literally packed by eager and excited spectators. A brass band was again in attendance, and if it did not exactly discourse most eloquent music, its strains, at any rate, sufficed to afford some relief to the senses of those who had narrowly observed the tournament during the day and needed relaxation. As the hands of the timekeepers' clock approached 10, the excitement became intense, and each succeeding lap of the contestants was watched and noted with marked interest. The form of those competing was scrutinised and loudly commented upon, and the exertions of the attendants in encouraging their friends were unremitting. Edwards, throughout the evening, was the subject of much admiration, and the freshness and vigour of his style won for him loud plaudits and a host of new friends. At 10 o'clock the tournament concluded, and amid uproarious cheers, Edwards was pronounced the winner, he having traversed 153 miles and 5 laps in the 48 hours. J. C. Williams came next with 148 miles and 9 laps.

At 10:50, on Monday, the 29th of December 1879 at Cooke's Circus, Bridge Street, Aberdeen, Scotland, a 12 hours per day, six-day go-as-you-please race for the "Champion Belt of Scotland," and promoted by the Dundee Sporting Club, began. Out of 16 original entries, only 11 started the race. They were: **Bell, W. Bisset, P. Dickie, W. Gibb, J. Leith, J. Salisbury** and **A. Shewan** of Aberdeen, **J. Bruce** of Arbroath, **D. Ferguson** of Pollockshaws, **J. S. Robson** of *"Berwick,"* **P. McKellan** of Edinburgh and **W. Smith** of Paisley.

King of the Peds

The match, which was won by Smith, was tarnished by the fact that Robson, who came home in fourth place, was disqualified after a protest was sustained on the grounds that he was *"not of Scotch nationality."* The winner was followed home by Leith, McKellan, Robson and Ferguson. Robson, who scored 293 miles and 23 laps, would have won £3 for his efforts but went home to England penniless. The referee Mr. Watson of the *Sporting Life* presented Smith with the £20 first prize and the belt for scoring a distance of 351.35. Leith made 320.2 for his £10, and McKellan got £7 for traversing 304.14. Ferguson who came in fifth was considered a rather lucky laddie, having only made 237.23.

CHAPTER 24

3rd Long Distance Astley Belt

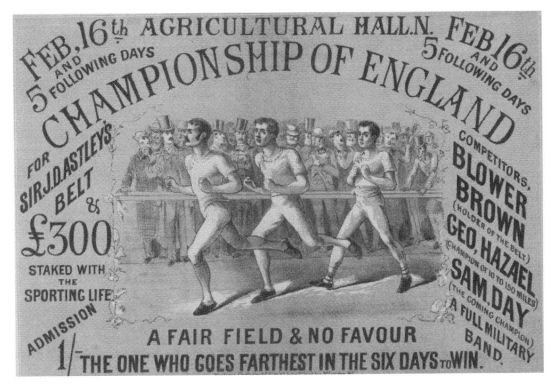

With the permission of Islington Local History Centre (Illustration no: 68)

The *third* competition for Sir John Astley's Challenge Belt which the giver gave the title "Long Distance Champion of England," commenced at the Agricultural Hall, Islington, on Monday, the 16th of February 1880 for a sweepstakes of £100 each between **Henry Brown** of Fulham, **George Hazael** of Deptford and **Samuel Day** of Kingston. All three competitors were reported to be in *"first rate condition."* Brown, it will be remembered had a disastrous time during his brief visit to America in the latter part of the previous year. He and his backers were confident of success though, and had bet £100, at odds of 5/1, that he would beat Weston's record of 550 miles of the previous year. Indeed, "Blower" would *"strain every effort to do so."* Hazael's supporters were also said to be, *"full of confidence"* that their man would be victorious due to that man having ran well in some private trials before the start. Day's backers meanwhile were described as being *"sanguine in consequence of his recent victories in the north of England."*

At this stage, it is well worth the time to have a look at the third competitor, Sam Day's career, *after* he had picked up £10 for making 400 miles between the 28th of October and the 2nd of November 1878 in the "Championship of England" match won by Corkey. The details of his career *before* that race can be found in Chapter 11. Sam then travelled back up to the north of England where at Hull between December the 12th and 17th 1878, he got the second prize of £20 for making 383 miles in a 14-hour per day contest which was won by George Parry. In the following year in March, he made his way back down to London, where at the Lambeth Baths, he took 4th prize money of £2 for scoring 313 miles in another 14 hours per day competition. Staying in the capital, he *"broke down"* having made 208 miles in a similar competition promoted by Mr. Alden. He then crossed the border and travelled to Dundee, where he was one of the principal contenders in yet another 14-hour a day, six-day go-as-you-please contest which was under the direction of the Dundee Sporting Club. This race took place at Newsome's Circus in that city between Monday, the 18th and Saturday, the 23rd of August 1879. Those taking part were, J. Bailey of Sittingbourne, W. Clarkson of Hull, S. Day of Northampton, A. Flaunty of London, J. Leith of Aberdeen, P. McKellan of Aberdeen, J. H. Palmer of Plymouth, J. S. Robson of Liverpool, J. Simpson of Cambridge (who was one of the men who accompanied Rowell to America in April of the same year), and H. Vandepeer of Sittingbourne. At the end of the first 14 hours, Day held the lead on a score of 85.21. By the end of the fourth day Sam still led the race with 278 miles, his nearest rival Clarkson trailing him by about 15½ miles. Palmer was in third place at that time with 246.24. Those positions were maintained until the close of the contest at 23:00 when Day finished as the winner of the £50 first prize, the final scores being: Day, 402.5; Clarkson, 386.10 (£20); Palmer, 340 (£7); Leith, 333 (£3); Robson, 316.26; McKellan, 254: He then took the top prize of £60 at Bingley Hall at Birmingham making 405 miles between the 6th and the 11th of October before winning a six-day 13-hour a day race at Wolverhampton between November the 10th and 15th. Since then he had won £50 in a match against "Time" covering 82 miles and 26 laps at the Lambeth Baths on the 20th of November. The story behind this "trial" had its origins back in Dundee, when on the first day of that race; Sam made an astonishing total of 80 miles and 29 laps for the first 14 hours of the competition. Because the track in Scotland had been 36 laps to the mile, there were some misgivings amongst the sporting fraternity that the score could not have been achieved. One of the doubters was a man called Sullivan who not only backed George Hazael, but trained him as well. He would be the man to put the money up. The track at Lambeth was exactly 49 yards in circumference, so that for every recorded mile, Sam travelled an extra 4 yards, or 340 yards over the total of 82 miles and 26 laps which was his final score. After this, Day then went on to receive £23 for making a distance of 66 miles in ten hours at Kingston, his home town. Finally, and before this race, and from London, he ventured up to the Pomona Gardens in Manchester, where he was beaten by Harry Vaughan in a 75-hour walking match, the scores being, Vaughan, 229.3 (£55) and the belt; Day, 216.7 (£25); Hibberd, 204 (£10):

Astley himself gave the word to "Go," and the three were sent on their way at 01:00 with Hazael leading the way followed by Brown and Day. After one hour of competition the positions remained unaltered and the distance which each of the runners covered was 8.5, 8.3 and 8.1 respectively. George kept up his pace and after five hours was three miles ahead of "Blower," the scores recorded being 38.5, 35.2, and Day, who at the time was complaining of rheumatism in one of his legs, the last of the trio, on 28.2. When Hazael went for a rest, Brown took full advantage by reducing the deficit and taking the lead. However, he relinquished his mile advantage when, on a mark of 49.1, he too sought his tent at 08:00 leaving the way open for Hazael to resume his lead.

At 13:00, the men's scores were: **Hazael, 76.4; Brown, 75.5; Day, 58.6:** Hazael was reported to be going poorly probably due to a blister on his left foot as was third placed Day, and just before 15:30, George went to his house for almost an hour's rest. While Hazael was being attended to, Brown took a commanding five-mile lead. At 5 p.m., he led the van with 96 as opposed to Hazael's 89.2, Day trailing the field on a paltry 68.3. Brown went on to make the first 100 at 17:45. The two leaders rested frequently thereafter with the race leader beginning to assert his superiority. By 20:00, he was way out in front on a score of 107. Hazael had 92.1, and Day, now making steady ground on the ailing Londoner, 80.

Hazael had been resting from 18:00 when the scores were hoisted at 22:00. They showed that Brown was still way out in front on 114.3, and with Hazael's record remaining the same, Day had advanced his to 86.5. Sam passed George at 22:50, but by the time the figures were hoisted on the scoreboard at midnight, Hazael, who had returned back to the track at 23:00, had recovered his second position and led the man from the Midlands by just under three miles, the figures at the time showing: **Brown, 125; Hazael, 96.6; Day, 93.7:**

TUESDAY: At 1 a. m., and with all the men on the move, the telegraph board registered: **Brown, 130.7; Hazael, 109.7; Day, 103:** 10:30 score: **Brown, 163; Hazael, 139; Day, 120:** 14:30 score: **Brown, 183; Hazael, 153; Day, 123:** At 3 p.m., and with Day apparently *"outclassed,"* Hazael was compelled to make more use of his tent as Brown added more distance between himself and the other two contestants. The 17:00 score: **Brown, 196; Hazael, 165; Day, 129:** Brown was to complete his second 100 miles amidst great excitement, although it is only fair to add that he made that second century before a poorly attended hall. The 22:00 score: **Brown, 215; Hazael, 182; Day, 150:** At midnight, and with Brown on 225.6, Hazael on 193, and Day with 150.2, the leader was one mile behind his own record of the previous June which was the best two-day record.

WEDNESDAY: As the match entered its third day, and with the men having rested, Sam Day reappeared on the track at 01:10 running in better condition. Hazael came back to the ring at 02:10, and Brown, likewise at 03:17.

At 4 a.m., and with Brown moving along at 4½ mph, he was 28½ miles ahead of Hazael who had just recorded his second century. Four hours later, the leader added a further 4 miles to the distance that separated him from the slower Hazael, and he was now on a score of 247. Day on 178 was 27 miles adrift of the second placed man. Between nine and ten o'clock, Brown ran 5½ miles and Hazael took to his bed at 09:48 on a score of 230 miles. As he slept, the leader increased his lead to 34¾ miles when the score was recorded at 11:30. After his rest Hazael was observed running along at a speed 8½ mph at 12:45.

When the score was hoisted at 13:00 (60th hour), Day, now running occasionally, was doing much better than on the first day of the contest. Brown's score was 269.7 (270.4 being the greatest distance in the time), Hazael was on 237 and the improving Day was 4 laps short of his 2nd century.

At 4 p.m., Brown's score of 285.1 meant that he had made a new record for 63 hours. With Hazael having cracked the 250, all the men were progressing around the path in Indian file. Day occasionally indulged in a spot of spurting and the challenge was answered by Hazael, who was observed to run away from his opponents, and then settle in behind them after he had caught them both up. At 19:15, Brown completed his third century having run the last two miles in 8m.56s and 8m.2s respectively. The 22:00 score: **Brown, 310; Hazael, 265; Day, 238:** The 23:00 score (70 hours): **Brown, 314; Hazael, 269; Day, 242:** The 01:00 score: **Brown, 315; Hazael, 270; Day, 242:**

THURSDAY: As there was no action on the track till the reappearance of Day at 01:43, the officials had the place to themselves. Hazael joined Day on the path at 02:01, and Brown re-entered the race making up the trio at 02:57. The 05:00 score: **Brown, 324.2; Hazael, 282.5; Day, 252:** The 11:30 score: **Brown, 356.6; Hazael, 310.6; Day, 273.6:**

After going along *"exceedingly well"* all morning, Brown was to progress 9 miles and 825 yards past the previous "best on record" time at noon, when his score stood at 359.4. Whilst he rested, Hazael, who was now running around freely on the track, recorded a score of 318.2 and Day 279. However, at 15:00, Blower, on a mark of 367.6, was now only four miles and seven laps ahead of the best time on record. As the leader ran, Day walked and Hazael, *"as usual,"* ran for three quarters of a lap then walked.

During the evening, and with Brown going along in *"even better style than ever"* at 19:00, or 90 hours from the start, he was 44 miles ahead of Hazael. At 10 p.m., and on a score of 397, Blower was six miles ahead of the best record. Hazael was on 347 and Day had 308. The midnight score: **Brown, 405; Hazael, 350; Day, 313:**

FRIDAY: The score at 04:00: **Brown, 408; Hazael, 350; Day, 315:** 08:00 score: **Brown, 420; Hazael, 366; Day, 330:** 11:00 score: **Brown, 433; Hazael, 375; Day, 344:** At noon, Brown's right knee cap was slightly swollen and Hazael was reported to be in a *"pitiable condition limping around with his head down and back bent."* However, despite George's appearance, there was considerable confidence that he would make the requisite 450 miles so as to share in the gate money. Day was sleepy, and there were doubts as to whether he could also make the 450. A couple of hours later, and 109 hours from the start, Brown, on a score of 446.5, was now only 2 miles and 1,155 yards ahead of the world record distance with his closest rival in the race, Hazael, having made 386.1 and Day, 356.2. With the second placed man on a score of 390 at 14:28, Day challenged him to a spurt, but as the pace increased, he soon gave way and Hazael went on to complete the mile in 8m.43s. Brown left the track at 14:44 having made 450 and resumed at his task of attempting to break the world record at 15:30. The score at 17:00: **Brown, 456; Hazael, 393; Day, 367:**

Just after seven o'clock, there was a little excitement manifesting on the track as Day and Hazael took on each other in a running race. Both were observed to be circling at a good pace. An hour later, Brown was 20 miles ahead of Weston's distance at the same stage when the latter made the world record in the previous year. The 22:00 score: **Brown, 475; Hazael, 418; Day, 389:** Hazael retired to his room at 23:12 with Brown making the same decision 14 minutes later looking *"wonderfully fresh."* With the midnight score showing Blower leading comfortably on a score of 481 miles against his name, he was now only one mile ahead of his own best record. The expectation was that he would make now make a new world record and thus win his bet. Hazael's score was 423 when he retired at 23:12. Day decided to wait until he had scored four centuries before making for his bed at 00:06.

SATURDAY: The race leader returned at 02:44 running at a fairly good pace with Hazael resuming business at 03:31, and Day, likewise, at 04:47. The score at 05:00: **Brown, 493.4; Hazael, 430; Day, 401:** 11:30 score: **Brown,**

King of the Peds

516; Hazael, 450; Day, 422: At 12:25, Brown on a score of 520 miles needed just 30 miles in 11 hours to equal the best record.

The event on the last day was better attended than the previous days despite the fact that the belt, barring catastrophe, would be placed around Brown's waist at the end of the race. *"The band did its best to drive everyone mad with its discordant braying. There was also during the week, "all the fun of the fair," rifle shooting, bowl, roll, or pitch, for cocoanuts, a six legged horse on view in a tent, and other attractions (?) too numerous to mention."*

Hazael retired at 19:50 having *"mixed"* 480 miles and 22 yards. A minute later Brown succeeded in equalling the best record and then took a short rest. Day retired at 21:09 on a score of 456 miles and 504 yards.

Brown finished his day at 21:10 with a brand new six-day world record of 553 miles and 168 yards. For his wonderful effort he won £200 from his rivals and £500 from his bet, the £700 being a nice little "earner" for him. There is no record of how much gate money he earned.

The Final Score!

Henry Brown: 553 miles and 168 yards.

George Hazael: 480 miles and 22 yards.

Sam Day: 456 miles and 504 yards.

Brown's mileage per day:

	Monday	Tuesday	Wednesday	Thursday	Friday	Saturday	Total
Miles	125*	100	90	90	76	72	**553**

* plus 168 yards.

His time on the track:

	Monday	Tuesday	Wednesday	Thursday	Friday	Saturday	Total
H:M:S	20:02:42	18:39:26	18:07:23	18:05:20	17:21:43	14:47:09	**107:03:43**

And off it………

	Monday	Tuesday	Wednesday	Thursday	Friday	Saturday	Total
H:M:S	02:57:18	05:20:34	05:52:37	05:54:40	06:38:17	06:22:51	**33:06:17**

Interestingly, "Blower" could have stayed on the track till 23:00 (the 142nd hour), but he chose to give up his race after 140h.10m. At the rate of speed he was going (about 5 mph), he could have added about 9 miles to his score in the permitted time.

CHAPTER 25

2nd O'Leary Belt

The following advertisement for the "Second O'Leary Belt" race appeared in the *Brooklyn Daily Eagle* on the 3rd and 4th of April 1880.

THE O'LEARY BELT

The second contest for the trophy.
THE AMERICAN SIX-DAY PEDESTRIAN CHAMPIONSHIP.
A sweepstakes of $9,000, one-half the gate money and a special prize of $1,000, takes place
AT MADISON SQUARE GARDEN,
Commencing at 12:05 A. M.,
MONDAY, APRIL 5.
EIGHTEEN OF AMERICA'S BEST LONG DISTANCE MEN WILL START.
GRAND SACRED CONCERT.
SUNDAY EVENING, APRIL 4, AT 9 P. M.
Doors open at 8 P. M.
ADMISSION, 50 CENTS.

A sum of $10,000 was paid to Mr. W. H. Vanderbilt for a ten-day lease of Madison Square Garden. The race was to be managed by Mr. F. A. Abell who had *"observed"* the administration of a previous contest, and who gave his assurance was that the affair would be "on the dead level." Mr. William B. Curtis, of the *Spirit of the Times* would act as referee, and as in the first contest, the judges and scorers would be chosen from the amateur athletic clubs of New York.

There were many improvements to make both the contestants and spectators happier. The pedestrians' accommodation would revert back to canvas, and in the space usually occupied by the waterfall and grotto. Under that canvas was an *"uninviting cot bedstead, a small deal-table, a small looking glass and two chairs"* which were provided courtesy of the management. The race participants were expected to provide their own gas stove, bed sheets and other necessities. The relocation of the accommodation would mean that all parts of the circuit would be seen by the spectators. The athletes' trainers and attendants would be confined to this area, and would not be allowed to accompany the men as they circumnavigated the track, except when offering their men food and drink.

The stand housing the race officials would be situated on the northern edge of the inner circle, and lap scoring would be done on dials opposite by inserting a red headed wooden pin in a hole for every lap achieved. A huge blackboard for marking the score would be situated at the eastern end of the building and this would be linked by telephone with the scorers' stand. The bookmakers' tables would be located behind the officials' stand where the press would also operate from. The track, which was slightly narrower than of late, was declared in fine condition, and when measured by Mr. Curtis, was an eighth of a mile.

The standard of refreshments offered by the bars and restaurant would be improved and a team of *"polite ushers"* would deal with the Gardens patrons, with special arrangements being been made to accommodate ladies without escorts. A $1 over the admission price would reserve one of a 150 balcony chairs, and the holder of such a seat would be able to enter and leave the Garden as they pleased till six in the morning of the next day.

After deduction of expenses, half the gate proceeds would be taken by the management and half would be given to the pedestrians. Half of that figure would be given to the winner, and after the second placed man was awarded half the balance, the rest would be divided proportionately amongst by the others. The $1,000 "special prize" would be given to any man who could beat "Blower" Brown's record of 553 miles and 168 yards.

The full race card was as follows: **Joe Allen,** Carlisle, England; **J. F. Brown,** New York; **John Dobler,** Chicago, Illinois; **John Ennis,** Chicago, Illinois; **Chris Faber,** Newark, New Jersey; **George Hanwaker,** New York; **F. H. Hart**, Boston, Massachusetts; **James Henry,** New York; **Harry Howard,** Glen Cove, Long Island; **"Mr. Jaybee,"** New York; **W. H. Kerwin,** Tarrytown, New York; **F. Krohne**, New York; **P. McIntyre,** California; **Sam Merritt,** Bridgeport, Connecticut; **Nick Murphy,** Haverstraw; **W. Pegram,** Boston, Massachusetts; **E. Williams,** New York; **J. Woods,** Jersey City:

Frank Hart, who was 2/1 favourite to take the trophy, was one of 18 contestants who had paid the $500 entry fee for the race. Before the race, the confident pedestrian told the press, "I'll break those white fellow's hearts, I will - you hear me!"

"Nic" Murphy, the holder of the belt, entered the building at half past ten limping ever so slightly. He told reporters, "I was at a fire up in Haverstraw about six weeks ago, and the boys turned the hose on me. I caught cold and got rheumatism, and for four weeks didn't do anything but doctor myself. I have only been in training for two weeks and am still pretty lame in one knee. I am going to start though. Maybe the lameness will wear off. If it does, then I will keep it up till the end."

There was a good 6,000 people waiting to watch the start of the match by 23:30, and many cheered the arrival of the *now* 3/1 favourite Frank Hart when he briskly walked up the track towards his quarters wearing a drab overcoat and seal skin cap. At 23:55, when the pedestrians appeared in their costumes, the place was packed. *"The mere sight of the men set the people crazy."* The size of the audience had never been seen at the start of such a race since Weston success at the Third Avenue Rink.

With Hart's price continuing to drift, the starting prices of the leading contenders at the off was: **Hart, 7/2; Merritt, Pegram and Krohne, 6/1; Murphy, 8/1; Ennis, 15/1:**

The men lined up wearing the *"gayest of colors,"* and when the word was given to "Go!" at the advertised time, it was the New-Yorker, Brown, who shot into the lead. Hart overtook him to make the first lap but his lead didn't last long as Williams went on to control affairs at the front of the pack, which contained the confidently running belt holder. Some in the crowd shouted, "Go it Murphy!" Others shouted, "Good boy Murphy!" and "Wade in, old Haverstraw!" As the young lad *"increased his speed and gradually overtook Williams, the Garden echoed with the cries of "Murphy, Murphy!"*

Observations of how some of the pedestrians performed in the early part of the race follow: The emaciated **Allen**, looking like *"the living skeleton in museums,"* and the only Englishman in the race, having recorded a previous best of 452 ½ miles, started off well. It was reported on the 1st of April that **John Dobler,** the Chicagoan, had sprained his ankle. Having made a personal best of 340 ⅜ miles in 75 hours, Dobler was described as a, *"beautifully formed young fellow, solid in breast and limb,"* who in the early part of the race, *"walked with the grace of a gazelle."* **Hanwaker,** whose previous best form was 288 ⅝ miles, was described as a little fellow, and **Woods,** who had tried to withdraw from the race days before, but denied the request, *"a thin man."* **Williams**, one of three *"colored"* athletes in the race with a personal best of 502 ¼ miles, was described as *"very dark, and his face,"* and *"when warmed up with the exercise, shone like a table."* **William Pegram**, the *"dark horse"* of the race, who had made 527 miles in his second ever match, was the other black contender apart from Hart. He *"looked as if he might be anywhere from 20 to 60,"* but, *"handled his lower extremities very deftly."* The red headed **Kerwin,** wearing a similar coloured shirt to his hair, *"warmed up into a state of redness of the face."* The tall, slim **Sam Merritt's** (who had made 515 miles before the event was one of the youngest men in the race), *"Connecticut fed legs spun around the track with great rapidity."* The very conspicuously attired tall and thin **McIntyre,** the champion of California, dressed in green and white silk, with a reputed 500 miles credited for his best ever score, moved around the path *"lightly and swiftly."* **Mr. Jaybee** was his assumed name, his initials being J. B. He was said to belong to a prominent family and daren't make his real name known. He was mystery to all. He had neither trainer nor backer. He was 5 feet 7 inches tall, was about 50 years of age, sported a full beard, and continually wore glasses. During the few days before the match, he had been busily acquainting himself with other pedestrians in the race and had given them all photographs of himself in walking costume. At the start of the race, he was dressed in a, *"gorgeous suit of white, with a blue dart worked across the breast, and a blue horseshoe on the back. He was greeted everywhere with invitations to "brace up," "strike out bold" and "pull down his vest."* He was the first man to go for a rest on a score of 2.5, but returned full of running ten minutes later.

The score at 01:00: **Pegram, 8.3; Hart and Williams, 8.2; Kerwin, McIntyre and Murphy, 8.1; Woods, 7.7; Brown and Howard, 7.6; Allen and Faber, 7.4; Dobler, 7.2; Hanwaker, 7.1; Henry and Merritt, 7; Ennis, 6.3; Krohne, 6.2; Jaybee, 5:** And an hour later at 2 o'clock: **McIntyre, 15.5; Hart and Pegram, 15.4; Faber, 15.2; Woods, 15.1; Murphy, 14.7; Howard, 14.6; Allen, 14.4; Brown and Henry, 14; Williams, 13.7; Dobler, 13.5; Merritt and Ennis, 12.4; Krohne, 12.3; Kerwin, 10.5; Hanwaker, 10.4; Jaybee, 8.4:**

Up till 10 o'clock on the Monday morning, 7,928 tickets had been sold. Those staying during the night would have witnessed the early departure of the belt holder after just 15 miles. Nicholas Murphy called it a day after just two hours of pounding the sawdust, a very costly failure considering it had cost him $500 to enter. The next retiree was John Ennis, who, after scoring just 38.3, left the track at 10 o'clock. He was last seen leaving the building at noon, carrying his stove wrapped up in a copy of the *City Record*, the presumption being that he had the inevitable problems with his stomach. He never gave notice to quit the race to the managers.

Scenes from the race

The National Police Gazette (Illustration no: 69)

The first man to hit the ton was Faber at 16:53, and the second man to make the same was Hart just over five minutes later. Dobler joined the two "centurions" at 17:19 and McIntyre admitted himself to the club at 18:48. He was followed by Woods at 19:05 and the Briton, Allen, at 19:13. Faber had actually made the fastest 100 miles ever in the United States having earlier notched his 50 in 7h.35m.30s.

By the time Williams, who was described as *"as black as a length of stove pipe and in appearance resembles a Zulu on the warpath,"* made his 100 miles at 22:30, Frank Hart, who was going along easily, was already opening up an impressive gap between himself and second man, the New York confectioner, Christian Faber of about 7 or 8 miles. However, Dobler, who was another of O'Leary's protégés, was going as well as the Haitian, and by midnight, was within striking distance of first place on a score of 129 miles to the leaders 131. The Californian, McIntyre, also went well. Hart was ahead of "Blower" Brown's effort when he made his record, but well behind Hazael's 133 miles and 110 yards for the same time. He could have passed the latter's record but decided to put his feet up at 23:20 thus leaving his fans disappointed.

The scores at 01:00 at the beginning of the second day: **Hart, 131; Dobler, 130; Faber, 122.1; McIntyre, 121; Allen, 120.1; Merritt, 115.1; Pegram, 109.1; Woods; 102.7; Williams, 100.1; Howard, 99.3; Hanwaker, 90; Krohne, 85.5; Henry, 83.3; Kerwin, 54.6; Jaybee, 52.3:**

Hart returned to the track when the above scores were recorded. He immediately set about trying to put some distance between him by dashing around the track at 5 mph. While he grafted, it was learned that James Henry was the next permanent retiree at 02:25. By 03:00, and in front of a meagre audience, the race leader had managed to increase his slender advantage by a mile. He left for a rest at 04:00, and 20 minutes later, and while he snoozed, Brown became the fourth man in the race to hang up his boots; that left 14 competing on the circuit. When Hart returned at five o'clock, he amused himself by walking a few laps with Mr. Jaybee, whose real name was now found to be John Brinkerhoff. Whilst Hart walked along impressively, Sam Merritt appeared in poor condition and tramped along wearily. Woods was no better. He limped and looked in need of a good kip.

The six o'clock scores with the man from Chicago now heading the field: **Dobler, 151.5; Hart, 147.6; Faber, 145.1; Merritt, 127.3; McIntyre, 121; Allen, 120.1; Pegram, 120; Howard, 118.6; Williams, 116.5; Woods; 106.6; Hanwaker, 105.7; Krohne, 99.3; Kerwin, 59.5; Jaybee, 56.7:**

While Hart employed "dogging" tactics on the new race leader, Faber was the subject of a rumour that he had broken down. His trainer confirmed, "He went off at eight thirty for good, with a hundred and fifty-one miles and one lap. His left leg was badly inflamed and there was no use in working a cripple, particularly when it was so early in the race and no hope of keeping him up." It was later established that he had strained his back and hurt the tendons in one of his legs.

Dobler kept up his slender lead of just over a mile and a half in front of Hart up until noon on a score of 177.1, as Allen moved himself into 3rd place on a score of 158.7. Pegram, with 157, kept his fourth place, whilst McIntyre slipped back to fifth on 156 and 5. Merritt was sixth man, with a score of 151.7 next to his name.

What the scorecard said at 14:00: **Dobler, 185.1; Hart, 183.5; Allen, 167.1; Pegram, 165.5; McIntyre, 161.4; Merritt, 159,2; Howard, 155.1; Williams, 143.1; Woods; 128.5; Krohne, 136.6; Hanwaker, 136.1, Kerwin, 78.7; Jaybee, 78.6:**

The betting shows at the time:(Placed odds to finish 1st or 2nd are in brackets): **Hart, 1/2 (1/4); Dobler, 3/1 (6/4); Pegram, 8/1 (2/1); Merritt, 10/1 (3/1); McIntyre, 10/1 (4/1); Allen, 10/1 (5/1); Howard, 15/1 (5/1); Krohne, 25/1 (10/1); Williams, 30/1 (15/1); Woods, 50/1 (15/1); Hanwaker, Kerwin and Jaybee, 100/1:**

There was little to report during the afternoon. The three black athletes spent some time running along together, and the story goes that both Williams and Pegram gave Hart much encouragement. Other reports suggested Williams was having trouble with his left leg, along with McIntyre, who limped along with a troublesome sore foot.

As the crowd increased in the evening, it was "Black Dan" who was causing a little concern on the track even though he had clawed the deficit back between himself and Dobler. As the evening wore on, he appeared rather tired, and it was the Chicagoan who was worrying the bookmakers with his lively and fresh performance. He had been as much as 20/1 at the start of the race and his performance was something of a revelation.

Both race leaders left the track just after eleven o'clock. With Woods being the latest race casualty, there were now only eleven men's names on the blackboard. At midnight, and with not one of the competitors gracing the path, the score was: **Hart, 225; Dobler, 224; Allen and Pegram, 200; Merritt, 196; Howard, 195; McIntyre, 181; Krohne, 178; Williams, 175; Hanwaker, 165; Jaybee, 101:**

As the clock ticked on after 01:00, most of the contestants started to return to the ring. The only two still snoozing were Howard and Jaybee, the latter having been in bed for four hours. At 03:00, Hart was just half a mile ahead of his nearest rival. The strong, well built African, Pegram, who was much heavier than Hart, joined the leader an hour later and kept him company. It was remarked that Hart's fellow Bostonian was *"coaching him."* He didn't appear to do a very good job however, because by 06:00, Dobler had retaken the lead, albeit by a slender 2 laps on a score of 243.1. The ever improving Pegram now took over third spot on 221.3 and the slow walking Allen fell back to fourth on 217.2. Merritt was five miles adrift of him. Howard kept up a steady jog-trot and Krohne, the *"Prussian jumping-jack,"* who had a bright look on his face, was said to be working *"like a mill."*

The eleven went down to ten as McIntyre gave up the fight after succumbing to *"badly swollen feet."* At 09:20, the *"fat"* Mr. Jaybee, finally woke from his slumbers and bounded from his tent appearing fresh and rested. As he went around the track, the managers were counting the tickets and money, and as was customary, the figures were released to the press. On Monday, the admission receipts amounted to $3,964, on Tuesday $3,533, and Wednesday $2,931, meaning 20,532 people had paid to watch the match. Half of the money would go to the mangers and half would go to the pedestrians' fund.

At 22:00, and after 70 hours of play, Hart, on a score of 313.7, was just an eighth of a mile short of Brown's record for the same time. The tired leader took to his bed on a score of 315.4, but Dobler, deciding he wanted to beat "Blower's" 72-hour record, kept on and made 318.4 before leaving the path at 23:30. He was now a full three miles in front of the fast asleep Hart. Pegram scored 300 miles at 23:33, and it was being speculated that if he continued his work rate, he might make a score of 565 miles by the end of the contest. Of Jaybee, *"his score is less than 130 miles, not withstanding frequent spurrings from an electric battery, handled by his special electrician, at great expense."*

At this stage of the race, the resting times of the three leading men were: **Dobler 5h.41m, Hart 7h.19m and Pegram 11h.57m:** The rule of thumb was that one hour was equivalent to four miles in this type of contest, so it was interesting to note that by this time Brown had taken just under 14h.10m of rest in his record breaking race when he made 315 miles by the end of 72 hours. If Pegram hadn't had taken more rest than the race leaders, he would have been bang up there with them both, and well in contention for first place. The midnight score: **Dobler, 318.4; Hart, 315.4; Pegram, 300; Howard, 284.7; Allen, 280; Merritt, 271; Krohne, 267; Williams, 255; Hanwaker, 240; Jaybee, 127.5:**

Hart returned to the empty track at 01:59 followed by Howard 15 minutes later. Three toiled round the path when Pegram came on at 02:18, and Allen made a quartet at 02:26. They were soon joined by Dobler, who quickly got into his stride and reeled off the laps. He was chased by Hart, who, finding it difficult to keep up went back to his room at 04:00. Dobler quickly put 10 miles between himself and Hart, but gave up after a nose bleed forced him off the track at 05:00. The 6 a.m. scores: **Dobler, 334.2; Hart, 326.2; Pegram, 316.7; Howard, 302.4; Allen, 290.3; Merritt, 287; Krohne, 282.6; Williams, 273.7; Hanwaker, 255.7; Jaybee, 127.5:**

Hart returned at 7 a.m. and began to address the deficit that had been created by the Chicagoan. At 08:08, Merritt announced his retirement from the race due to suffering from exhaustion. Having *"broken down"* on a score of 294.2, his withdrawal meant there were just nine left in the race. The scores at 09:00 were: **Dobler, 345.2; Hart, 341.3; Pegram, 321.1; Howard, 314; Allen, 303.6; Krohne, 295.6; Williams, 286.3; Hanwaker, 267; Jaybee, 130.1:**

The latest betting: (Placed odds to finish 1st or 2nd are in brackets): **Hart, 1/2; Dobler, 6/4 (1/3); Pegram, 4/1 (1/2); Howard, 15/1 (5/1); Allen, 15/1 (7/1); Hanwaker, Krohne and Williams, 50/1 (25/1):**

King of the Peds

When the tickets were counted at 10 a.m. for the previous day's attendance, 7,306 people had passed through the gate (equivalent to $3,653 in receipts). At 11:40, news was announced that Jaybee had withdrawn from the race for good, but just before noon he ambled down the track announcing it was his intention to stay the course till Saturday, and that he would astonish the crowd on the last day. Whilst Dobler was off the track, Hart made massive inroads into his score, and at noon the scores were: **Dobler, 356.6; Hart, 355.7; Pegram, 338; Howard, 326.6; Allen, 322.1; Krohne, 308.1; Williams, 300; Hanwaker, 275.6; Jaybee, 133.2:** At 13:00, half a lap separated Dobler and Hart and the battle for overall supremacy was enthralling the crowd which at 2 p.m. stood at 2,000.

During the afternoon, Dobler's ankle *"gave out."* It was badly swollen, causing him to lose his chance in the race. Hart took full advantage, and as the day progressed he slowly but surely, put more distance between himself, Dobler and Pegram.

Between four and five o'clock, a lot of smoke was observed in the building and after the walkers complained, the skylights were opened. This however, didn't eradicate the problem; indeed it became worse. It was soon discovered that smoke was pouring from cracks between the floorboards under the scorer's box. The incident was investigated, and a small smouldering fire was discovered in an open space beneath the seats, which was quickly extinguished. It was suspected that a watchman had built himself the fire as the place was very cold and had neglected to put it out. It was predicted that if the fire had took hold, the building could have been destroyed as there were many old boards and lumber in the area where it was situated.

At 23:42, Hart completed his 400th mile, and at 22:00, Mr. Jaybee left the Garden. A carriage was seen taking him and his wife, his doctor, his electrician and the *"battery"* away. It was reported that he would return on the last day of the race to try and win a prize of a chair, for making the most miles during it. Hart retired at 23:03 exactly equalling Brown's record. Dobler was being vigorously rubbed down at midnight and his ankle to his knee was not a pretty sight being twice the size it normally was. It was still hoped however, that he might still make the required 450 miles for a share in the receipts. His trainer Smith reported that his leg was in a terrible condition and that his man had sprained his ankle a month previous. Only Krohne and Pegram were on the track at midnight and the score at 01:00 was: **Hart, 405; Pegram, 392; Dobler, 391; Howard, 375; Allen, 365; Krohne, 352; Williams, 350; Hanwaker, 312:** At 3 a.m., it stood: **Hart, 407.1; Pegram, 393.2; Dobler, 391.5; Howard, 379.3; Allen, 368.3; Krohne, 356.3; Williams, 352.5; Hanwaker, 319.5:**

For mile after mile, Pegram had dog-trotted relentlessly around the track in the latter hours of the morning. Hart had noticed that his nearest rival in the race was going along smoothly and stalked him closely, following him within inches of his heels. "Hart will win or die on the track," said one of his backers as the two went along. Then as Hart was just about to tuck in to a cup full of soft boiled eggs, Pegram set off running. Hart put the eggs down and made after him. His rival stopped running and Hart followed suit, thereafter resuming his meal.

The race leader, wearing a blue and white striped shirt, black velvet trunks, white stockings, grey and black cap, and sporting a bright scarlet handkerchief around his neck, had made excellent progress all morning as his score at midday testifies when the following records were announced: **Hart, 447.6; Pegram, 432; Dobler, 428.1; Howard, 416.2; Allen, 404.1; Williams, 393; Krohne, 386.4; Hanwaker, 342.1:** When he made his 450th mile at 12:29 he nodded approvingly, and with reference to Pegram, said, "I'll beat that darkey if I have to run him into a hole to do it." At this stage of the race, he was the 1/2 favourite to take the belt and was about five miles ahead of Brown's time for the same stage. Many *"sporting men"* who had been regular attendees at the pedestrian events over the years said that they had never seen any contestant looking in such splendid condition on the fifth day of any race. *"His eyes are bright and full of ambitious fire. He swings around the ellipse with a gait as the vibration of a pendulum. He is as dignified as a Fifth Avenue dandy."*

Whilst Hart went exceptionally well, Pegram attired in purple trunks, white shirt and drawers, and a pink bordered blue scarf, now a 6/1 shot for first place and a 1/3 chance to make 2nd in the race, was on a score 434 miles. Dobler, the 15/1 third placed man, had just completed the last lap of his 430th mile. *"He moved around the Garden in a doleful state. He looked like a ghost."* Wearing a long white undershirt, white drawers and black trunks, *"his movements were slow and painful; his face wore a look of disgust and hopelessness."*

Howard, wearing a white shirt and red neckerchief, was 12 miles behind Dobler. Harry was reported to having some resemblance to the *"crab-like Hazael,"* and was pencilled in to finish in third "pozzy" ahead of the struggling Chicagoan. Perspiring as he laboured, the sweat he created caused the dye in his neckerchief to make pink streaks down his shirt. He appeared cheerful however, and was confident of making 500 miles. The bookies offered odds of 6/4 that he wouldn't make second place. Meanwhile his fellow Englishman, Allen, who moved painfully along, was offered at 15/1 to gain second spot, and at 13:00, he had scored 407 miles. Of the others, Krohne, attired in bright purple trunks and scarf, wobbled along as he neared his 400th mile. Williams, in seventh spot indulged in some rapid running, whilst last man, Hanwaker, appeared poorly, and on a score of 345 miles, it was thought unlikely he would make the needed 450 miles.

Pegram scored 450 miles at 16:16, Dobler doing likewise at 18:15. Hart made 490 miles at 22:35 and was circling the ellipse at a lively pace. *"He moved like a machine, making no apparent effort."* Pegram, having done some very good work for the day, left the track at 22:46. The midnight scores: **Hart, 492; Pegram, 473; Dobler, 460; Howard, 453; Allen, 445; Krohne, 438; Williams, 436; Hanwaker, 386:**

The rest times for the whole of the match for the remaining pedestrians up till this time were as follows: **Allen, 29h.29m.40s; Howard, 25h.14m.22s; Krohne, 24h.51m.28s; Williams, 23h.52m.35s; Pegram, 22h.43m.19s; Hanwaker, 21h.41m.40s; Dobler, 18h.38m.57s; Hart, 17h. 28m.34s:**

As the clock ticked on into the last day of the contest, only Khrone, Williams and the poorly performing Dobler, were making their respective ways around the track. They were joined by Pegram at 01:20 who began to make an impression as soon as he stepped into the ring. His trainer whispered to him, "Go and win the belt!" to which Pegram replied, "Dat's what I'se after!" with a smile so broad that his ivory white teeth positively shone within his *"dark countenance."* Whilst Pegram put on a splendid show to amuse the watching crowd, Hart slept soundly in his tent and there was much anxiety around the place as to when he would make his reappearance. "Where is that Pegram?" asked the sleepy race leader on being woken by his trainer just after two o'clock. "Happy" Jack Smith replied, "On the track and going like the devil." Within seconds, Frank was back on the path shouting to his attendants, "I'll win it, sure!" as the crowd clapped for him as he began his 493rd mile.

With Hart back in the ring and seemingly booked for the gold medal position, many of the spectators finally started to make their way home. They left behind 300 or so of the permanent squatters that had been in the Garden since day one. *"They were a sorry lot of creatures, unkempt and befouled with the fumes of tobacco and the odors of stale whiskey."*

Howard soon rejoined the race and made it his objective to pass the faltering Illinoisan once and for all. *"His ruddy face flushed and his bright eyes beamed as he saw his score creeping up to that of Dobler."* Within no time, young Harry passed the faltering *"Johnny"*, his left leg being, *"frightfully swollen and showed through his trunks much larger than his fellow. From his face, pale and haggard, his eyes looked out sunken and glassy. He showed great pluck."* O'Leary said of Dobler, "That boy will make his mark yet. I'm ready to back him at any time for ten thousand dollars against the field, a walk to take place three months from now. Up to Thursday morning we felt certain we had the race in our own hands. I thought Dobler was the best man on the track, and I think so yet. The only trouble with him is that he needs experience. In a six-day walk a man must have confidence in himself. Dobler's sprained ankle frightened him and he began to lose heart. Then, on Thursday, the windows were opened, creating a draught through the tents that gave him a bad cold. I think inflammatory rheumatism set in, and that gave him a set back that proved fatal to his chances of first place. He will be heard from again, and, when he is, you can bet that it will be in a way that will justify confidence in him."

Of the others, Allen went along much better stating he was going to fight all the way to try and take fourth place from Dobler. Whilst the gigantic Prussian grenadier, Krohne, and the ex-waiter, Williams, kept to their task, the *"ghostly"* Hanwaker, who was described as having the appearance of a *"hospital patient,"* struggled on, saying that if he didn't make 450 miles, he would give up pedestrianism altogether.

Hart waited till he made 500 miles at 04:22 before he went off for a rest eight minutes later. He was now a full two miles ahead of "Blower's" record. On his return at sun-up, and wearing his favourite blue and white striped shirt, he was greeted with words of encouragement by the ebony faced cleaners who were just starting to use their scrubbing brushes and soapsuds to rid the building of the filth it had accumulated. He immediately began to dog

King of the Peds

Pegram, who wore a white shirt and tights, purple trunks, and a blue and white cap. As the morning wore on, Hart maintained a good 12 miles in front of the second placed man.

Jaybee was formally withdrawn from of the race by the managers at 10:00, having turned up on the track wearing an overcoat. He was subjected to a series of cheers, cat calls and jibes which he took in good humour as he made two laps of the track. Dobler, to rapturous applause, made his fifth century just before noon, and this wonderful feat encouraged him to lengthen his stride so much that the former cattle driver actually started to decrease the distance between himself and third placed Howard. The scores at noon were: **Hart, 528; Pegram, 516; Howard, 503; Dobler, 500; Allen, 490; Krohne, 483; Williams, 481; Hanwaker, 416:**

As the men toiled at lunchtime, the *Brooklyn Daily Eagle* described how the crowd's appetite for food and drink was catered for by the restaurants and bars: **With the growth of the crowd, the business of the bar and restaurant increased. The presiding genius of this important department expressed satisfaction with his week's work. He paid $6,000 for the privilege of supplying the hungry and thirsty. Patronage of his store was to some extent compulsory. No return checks were given at the door and visitors were obliged to patronize the garden restaurant and bar or else starve and thirst. At noon a raid was made on the refectory, by the increasing multitude. Then there was a marvelous disappearance of sandwiches with shadowy bits of ham between wafer like, slices of bread; of eggs boiled as hard as grapeshot; of chickens that might have flourished before the flood, of bullet like beans and chunks of greasy pork. A continuous draft was made upon the beer kegs, and fire water vanished like dew before the rising sun. The waiters and bartenders, from noon on, were kept s busy as the walkers, and they put in their fine work like old hand at the trade.**

Hart was attacked with a slight fainting episode just after midday, but he was soon revived by his attendants who gave him a *"stimulant"* and then the "magic sponge" which had the desired effect of reviving him. At 13:00, and now wearing a gauze under-shirt, and blue and maroon silk cap, his score was 531. In the next hour he added another four miles to his tally followed by five more in the hour after that. When O'Leary was asked what he thought of Hart, he replied, "Hart is a wonderful walker. That boy will make six hundred miles yet. He has the strength and vim to do anything, and I am sure that he has not yet put his best foot forward. Look out for him in the next match and see if he does not do better than he has ever done before."

Dobler went better than at any stage in the two preceding days. At one point, he indulged in a little spurting with Howard, whilst Allen, with his *"face as bright as the noonday sun,"* and running swiftly along in fifth position, made his 500th mile between two and three o'clock. Whilst the Englishman went well, Khrone, wearing a pair of royal purple trunks, and Williams, donning his old *"Zouave"* pantaloons, were involved in a little duel between themselves as to who would take sixth place in the race. The grenadier, on a score of 492, responded when Williams, on a mark of 490, forced the pace. Both ran for many laps for a whole hour entertaining the crowd who were cheering wildly.

Then at just after four o'clock, on his 542nd mile, Hart *"gave a magnificent exhibition of his pedestrian skill. His head was poised as gracefully as a swans; he threw his chest back, moved his arms with a long, easy swing and made his vigorous legs fly until they fairly twinkled. His brow was unwrinkled; his eyes glowed with pride. Every hand clap made him go faster."*

Two peds who had really been entertaining the crowd were Williams and Krohne. Both had managed to put on 8 and 9 miles respectively in their two-hour duel with the black athlete, who was forced to slow down to a walk as he succumbed to the German's superiority. However, at 16:50, a smile appeared on the African's face when he hit the magic 500. Ten minutes later, and when the credits were hoisted for the men's scores, seven of whom had manoeuvred themselves to the same milestone, the record at 5 p.m. stood: **Hart, 546; Pegram, 531; Howard, 523; Dobler, 518; Allen, 509; Krohne, 504; Williams, 500; Hanwaker, 435:**

As Hart put more distance between himself and the chasing Pegram, he was showered with the usual floral gifts. One such was an enormous horseshoe which was hung on his dial. His tent was described as *"a bower"* with dozens of pretty flowers presented in all forms adorning its outer. The other pedestrians also benefited from their adoring fans, in particular Dobler, who was the recipient of many bouquets and messages of sympathy and encouragement. During the afternoon, Howard, when receiving one of the gifts bestowed upon him, was seen to blush when an elegantly dressed woman gave him a basketful of blooms.

At 17:50, Hart recorded the second best ever score made in a six-day event. He celebrated his 550th mile along with the 6,000 plus crowd, by running around the circle carrying a broom which had a small Stars and Stripes flag wrapped around it. The building which shook with applause nearly fell down due to the din created when "Black Dan" went on to beat "Blower" Brown's Astley Belt record of 553 miles at 18:33 in a time of 138h.33m. As the place went crazy with delight, even Hart's fellow competitors cheered him. As he went to his tent for a brief rest, the bookies evaluated the odds on the new champion making 560 miles, and offered 2/1 that he wouldn't. The punters flocked in and took the price. At 7:30 p.m., whispers abounded that Hart would make 565 and call it a day. The bookies had been offering 3/1 on him beating that score, 6/4 that he wouldn't beat 567 and 6/1 that he wouldn't master 570.

Just before 8 o'clock *"Father Jaybee"* appeared back on the track wearing black velvet tights and a flesh collared shirt embroidered with an arrow and a horseshoe. *"He strutted like a peacock, throwing his attenuated form into a variety of ridiculous postures."* He was greeted with both cheers and jeers.

At 20:11, Hart, clad in blue and ash, and wearing a scarf in the colours of the American flag, minus the stars, completed his 560th mile. As he did so the desperate figure of Hanwaker did what he could to make the required 450 miles, and a few minutes later, wearily passed the post to secure the few dollars he would receive. *"He seemed more dead than alive."* He was given a loaf of bread mounted on a pole which was pierced with rosebuds and this he held aloft in glorious affirmation of his achievement.

Pegram thought he'd finished his race at 20:22 after completing his 543rd mile and went wearily to his house. Howard thought otherwise and persuaded him to reappear. The two of them went round again and Hart caught them up. Pegram then stole Hart's cap which he ran down the track with. Frank went after him, but couldn't catch the cheeky chap who threw it into the box containing the O'Leary Belt. Hart was not amused! The spectators loved every minute of the spectacle before them and roared their approval at every opportunity. They also cheered when Dobler was presented with a huge basket of flowers surmounted by a dove, bearing the inscription, "Gallantry" by a woman called Miss Nixon. Hart was presented with a pair of fine walking gaiters which rested in an elegant basket of cut flowers; and at the same time he received a written challenge for the O'Leary Belt which read:

NEW YORK, APRIL 10th, 1880

To Frank Hart, Boston, Mass; - I hereby issue you with a challenge for any "unknown" for the O'Leary belt, six days go-as-you-please contest, according to the specified rules governing the same."

BRYAN G. McSWYNY

Then, one by one, the men began to retire from the race. Williams was first off at 20:45 followed by Hanwaker who made a formal announcement a minute later. Pegram followed at 21:01, Allen at 21:04, Howard at 21:06, Dobler at 21:09 and Krohne at 21:11. Joe Allen made the best record for the last 24 hours of a six-day match with 88¼ miles beating both Hart and Rowell who had made 78 and 75 miles respectively.

Only Hart was left, and after he completed his 563rd mile, he ran around the track for two more miles with an American flag and the belt secured around his waist to the strains of "Yankee Doodle" and the inevitable adoration of the crowd. He then left the track abruptly at 21:24 and there was a sort of disbelief in the audience when he didn't re-emerge from his tent, everybody expecting that he might do a couple of miles more. The rumour quickly spread that Hart had capitulated to the bookmakers for apparent gain and there were some nasty things said about him. The *Brooklyn Daily Eagle* in an article on the 12th of April wrote a very pertinent article about what happened at the end of the race: It is to be regretted that Hart, the successful pedestrian, did not retire from the track without, at the last hour raising suspicions that he had, by agreement, enabled certain professional betting men to fleece certain incautious individuals, who, at the height of excitement, backed with money their opinion of the distance he (Hart) would travel. The professionals bet that he would not go 567 miles. He could have gone that length easily, for when he stopped with something over 565 to his credit he had an hour remaining in which to walk. It will be remembered that the same trick was played by Rowell in the match for the Astley belt. Perhaps there ought not to be any sympathy extended to fools who thus persist in the face of experience, in staking their money on "a skin game;" but, whatever be thought of them, it is to be deplored that such Laurels are won on the tanbark track should be defiled by knavery.

King of the Peds

As the band played "Home Sweet Home," the winner was whisked away to a nearby Turkish baths where he was given a good rubbing down and later put to bed at the residence of his business agent, J. J. Gottlob, No. 214 East Twenty Ninth Street. Dobler, accompanied O'Leary to the Metropolitan Hotel, and Pegram and Howard both journeyed to the comfort of the Putnam House.

MILES PER DAY OF THE TOP EIGHT FINISHERS AND FINAL SCORES:

	Monday	Tuesday	Wednesday	Thursday	Friday	Saturday	TOTAL
Hart	131	94	90	90	87	73	**565**
Pegram	104.6	95.2	100	91	82	70.7	**543.7**
Howard	97.4	97.4	89.7	90.1	78	81.5	**534.5**
Dobler	129	95	94	73	69	71	**531**
Allen	119.5	80.3	80	85	80	80.2	**525**
Krohne	83.2	94.6	89	85	86	78	**516**
Williams	100.1	74.7	80.3	93.5	87	73.3	**509.5**
Hanwaker	90	75	75	73	69	68.3	**450.3**

AMOUNT OF TIME THE TOP EIGHT FINISHERS RESTED DURING THE WEEK: **LONGEST RESTS:**

	Hours	Minutes	Seconds	Hours	Minutes	Seconds
Hart	23	23	0	3	33	25
Pegram	32	18	37	2	58	45
Howard	31	23	19	3	53	20
Dobler	23	7	17	3	3	40
Allen	34	44	49	3	25	15
Krohne	27	18	15	2	58	
Williams	29	4	18	4	24	
Hanwaker	27	11	40	2	32	45

The distribution of the prize money: **Hart,** $17, 967 ($7,967.86 gate money, $9,000 sweepstakes and $1,000 for beating the record); **Pegram,** $3,480.93; **Howard,** $1,741.91; **Dobler,** $970.96; **Allen,** $434.98; **Krohne,** $217.74; **Williams,** $108.87; **Hanwaker,** $54.49:

Hart also is purported to have made $3,600 on bets on himself at long odds thus giving him an overall total of $21,567.86 for just under 6 days' work! Of the fact that three men *"of color"* had done so well in the race, one reporter concluded, *"They kept up well with the others and demonstrated their constitutional right to walk in public, without regard to any previous condition whatever."*

Finally, this small article appeared in the *Fitchburg Sentinel* on the 14th of April 1880: O'Leary has deposited $500 with Frank Queen, and issued a challenge for a match with Hart and Dobler to any two men in England for $10,000 to $20,000 a side, the match to be in New York three months from the signing of the articles, the agreement and challenge to remain open two months from today. O'Leary says there are several men in England supposed to be superior to any in this century, and he expects expert. Rowell, Brown or Hazael will promptly accept.

The Winner and New World Record Holder!

Frank Hart

The National Police Gazette (Illustration no: 70)

CHAPTER 26

A New Kid on the Block!

George Littlewood was born on the 20th of March 1859 in Church Street, Rawmarsh, near Rotherham, in the county of Yorkshire, England. The census of 1861 indicates that the boy was living at 58 Shirland Lane in Attercliffe, a suburb of Sheffield, and at the age of two was probably already showing a great enthusiasm for walking around the house.

His father Fred Littlewood won a couple of Sheffield handicaps, the first at Hyde Park in the great "City of Steel" in 1857 and the second at the same venue on November the 30th 1864 when he was awarded £30 for winning *"Boothroyd and Milner's Sprint Handicap Race"* of 125 yards. The young George was more than likely to be present when his father competed in the latter race and Fred would have probably urged his son to take a keen interest in the sport from an early age.

When Littlewood junior was eight years old, he began showing an aptitude for running, whilst chasing the hounds in the local hunts of that time. He also excelled in other sports including boxing, wrestling and cricket, but it was in the field of athletics, and in particular running, which he displayed a real talent for. His father knew his son was something "special" and took on the task of training him seriously. The regime he fashioned for him was both daunting and vigorous, and when the boy complained to his dad that his muscles were sore one day, Fred offered him the carrot of a financial reward. "If you can catch me, you can have this halfpenny. If you really want it, you can get it." His father set off and the lad set off after him. When he caught him up and passed him, he was given his prize for his effort. He had proved to himself that he could overcome the pain barrier to reach his goal and that experience would prove valuable for his future career. The punishing training regime that he went through built up his stamina no end and this was noted by many who took a keen interest in the sport of both running and walking.

The *Sporting Life* in its edition of the 30th of October 1880, described George's earliest races: When nearly nine years of age, he ran *G. Charlesworth (twelve years of age) of Brightside, 100 yards, level, for £5 a side and a supper for twenty. He got half a yard advantage in the start, and won by that distance. In the subsequent week, they ran a second time, on the same terms, for a like sum, when Littlewood was defeated by ten yards. Five months subsequently he **won a half-mile £15 sensational handicap, with 30 yards start - for which twenty-nine started - by forty yards. In the next encounter, in 1871, he met W. Woodhead of Oughtibridge, in a match three times around Hyde Park (distance about 1,512 yards) level, for £15 a side, Woodhead being 14 years of age. Each led alternately, but eventually Woodhead won by ten yards.

*Beat Frank Hewett, champion half mile runner of England, at Queen's Grounds, Sheffield.

**This is the race the *Birmingham Daily Gazette*, on the 2nd of October 1882 *might* have been referring to when it stated: His first appearance on the track was when he was nine years of age, and with a big start, he then won a half mile £15 handicap, beating F. Hewett of Millwall, the then champion. This was race against older boys at the Hyde Park Ground in Sheffield.

Littlewood's dedication to perfection in the art of race walking soon paid off, when at the age of 16, he won his first long distance event and was given a silver cup donated by several city publicans. A judge at the time said this of the lad as he performed on the track, "He is completely genuine, without any deviation from the strict laws of walking." As he progressed during the next four years, the up-and-coming youth won various races in both disciplines in his local and county area. His preparation involved both running and walking over 200 miles a week. He would train by running to Doncaster and back three times a week in a 38-mile round trip. Many youngsters would initially run along with him, but alas, he would always be on his own by the time he reached Rotherham. On his arrival in Doncaster, he would call into a local butcher where he would buy mutton which he would run back home to Darnall with. There were reports that he had a food fetish and that his mum used to go to his races and cook for him to see that he ate properly! One of his trainers Fred Bromley said of him, "If you want to raise a lot of steam and power, you must stoke the coals on the fire!"

The *Sporting Life* article continued: **About twelve months ago he competed for a cup given by E. Gill, at Hyde Park, in a three mile handicap, in which he met Hornby, a noted local walker, G. Nill and others. He received a start of 3 min, 10 sec, of the giant Hornby; he also conceded 20 sec. start to Williamson, whom he defeated somewhat easily by ten yards.**

That takes us nicely up to November of 1879, when Littlewood, then aged 20 and weighing in at 11 stones, made his first appearance into the world of professional pedestrianism. A *"suitable race"* was found for him to make his appearance, and he made his way down from Sheffield to Wolverhampton, near Birmingham, to take on 27 other men in a six-day, 72-hour, go-as-you-please pedestrian match at the towns Agricultural Hall, where, along with the 27 men competing against him, he would have to circle the track 19 times to make a mile. The match would begin at 10:00 on Monday, the 10th of November. The race would start at that time every day except for Wednesday, the 12th when the men would *"toe the mark"* at the later time of 5 p.m. due to that day being *"corn market day."* That meant that for 5 days, the race would last from 10:00 till 23:00 except on Wednesday when it would end at midnight. Littlewood's performance would be monitored by the promoters of the race Messrs. Ashford and Devey of the Bricklayers Arms, Walsall Street. They were offering prize money amounting to £80 with the winner getting £50, the second £20, the third £7 and fourth £3. One of the conditions of the race was that any man making 250 miles would get his £1 entry fee back.

George was up against some of the *"principal pedestrians of the day."* One of his opponents would be Sam Day *"of London,"* who, if he won this race, would be on a hat-trick of victories in similar contests in just under 3 months, the others being at Dundee and Birmingham. Day, the odds on favourite for the contest, was described as, *"having a good chest, a hardy frame, and the toughest of legs and feet."* Other formidable figures in the race were the Leeds based Pat McCarty who came second in the aforementioned Birmingham race, George Parry, the Mancunian, who beat John Dobler in the 75-hour event in Chicago, and William Smith of Paisley, winner of the "Astley Ten Mile Championship Belt."

The Agricultural Hall, Wolverhampton.

From the collections of Wolverhampton Archives and Local Studies. (Illustration no: 71)

The 28 contestants were: **J. Brighton,** Moston; **George Cartwright,** Walsall; **William Clarkson,** Hull; **James Cliff,** Cardiff (*"long-distance champion of Wales"*); **Sam Day,** London; **B. Forth,** Dewsbury; **Grant,** Islington; **Richard Harding,** Blackwall; **Jack Hibberd,** Bethnall Green; **John Hope,** Richmond; **Hurst,** Sittingbourne; **Ives,** St. Lukes; **George Littlewood,** Sheffield; **Pat McCarty,** Leeds; **McCormick,** Bolton; **J. H. Palmer,** Plymouth (*"long-distance champion of the West of England"*); **George Parry,** Manchester; **E. G. Perry,** Birmingham; **George Pettitt,** Sittingbourne; **W. H. Richardson,** USA (*"winner of the Beckwith and Taylor belt"*); **J. Smith,** Hackney; **William Smith,** Paisley; **R. H. Stevens,** London; **E. Thomas,** Wolverhampton; **Henry Vandepeer,** Sittingbourne; **F. White,** Wolverhampton; **B. Willis,** Maidenhead; **Ted Winn,** Swindon:

The Willenhall Brass Band would help entertain the many spectators who attended the race to watch the start at 10:07. An hour after it had commenced, the first half dozen men on the scoreboard was headed by the Bolton boy, McCormick who led with 9 miles. He was in front of Cliff of Cardiff who had made 8.11. The third man was the Walsall contender Cartwright who was on 8 miles, and he was followed in the race by McCarty with 7.13. A couple of laps behind him was Winn, and he was being followed by the Scot Smith who was a further three laps adrift. *"All the men were going at a good trot, and appear little the worse for their exertions."*

With McCormick and Forth having already retired on 14 and 11 miles respectively, the scores at 16:00 were: **Brighton and Cartwright, 36; Cliff, Hope, Hurst, Winn and W. Smith, 35; Day, Clarkson, Hibberd, McCarty, Pettitt, J. Smith and Vandepeer, 34; Harding and Palmer, 33; Littlewood, Parry, Stevens, Thomas, White and Willis, 32; Perry, 31; Ives and Richardson, 30; Grant, 28:**

Brighton was the only man not to start with the rest at the beginning of the second day leaving his reappearance for the afternoon. Little was mentioned in the press about that second day except, *"the men appear to keep up well and the order of going with most of the competitors is a good "trod.""* With the competition continuing *"to excite a great amount of interest,"* and with the hall well filled with spectators, the telegraph board on the second day at 18:00 indicated: **Hope, 112; W. Smith, 110; Hibberd and Vandepeer, 109; Day, 107; Hurst and Harding, 106; Littlewood, 103; Clarkson, 102; J. Smith, 100; Stevens and Winn, 99; Cartwright and Richardson, 96; McCarty, Parry and Pettitt, 91; Palmer, 87; Thomas, 86; Cliff and Willis, 85; Perry, 84; Ives, 80; White, 76; Brighton, 60; Grant, 50:**

As previously mentioned, the race started later on the third day owing to the market being held there. Four hours into that day, Vandepeer had rushed himself up into first place and led Hope by a mile, his score being 152. The Scotsman, Smith, described as *"of the thin and wiry kind,"* was five miles back in third position. He led the Londoners, Hibberd, Harding and Day; three miles, two miles, and one mile respectively. Clarkson and Littlewood meanwhile, were both on 141 miles which was seven ahead of the nearest challenger, Smith of Hackney.

Littlewood was already beginning to show much promise and did surprisingly well, keeping up close to the race leaders in the first two days of the competition.

By Friday on the fourth day, there were only 12 men left in the race. One of the retirees was George Cartwright who reclaimed his £1 entrance money when he abandoned the race on a score of 250 miles at 18:30. At 20:00, the match was headed by Sam Day on a score of 290 miles. William Smith followed him on a score of 287, and it was reported that both of the principal leaders were going along in a most determined manner. Clarkson claimed third spot on 270, whilst the relatively unknown Yorkshire lad, Littlewood, had crept into the prize winning position of fourth place with a hard earned 244 miles. George was actually 12 miles ahead of the more experienced Londoner, Harding, who had been up against the likes of Weston, Brown and Ennis, in the 4th International Astley Belt contest which had been held in June of the same year.

On the last day of the race, there were only two miles separating the competitors from England and Scotland. However, even at that early stage of the day, it was clear that the younger man Day would win if he kept to his task as Smith was suffering badly with his feet. Indeed, the Scotchman had to take a couple of substantial rest periods during the day, the first of which was just after four o'clock which lasted for 32 minutes to have them dressed. On his return, he ran 8 miles in the preceding hour in an attempt to make up the 3.3 miles he had lost whilst being attended to. Whilst the front two fought out the lead, Clarkson and his fellow "Tyke," Littlewood, took their time and didn't overexert themselves due to the fact that their positions were secure.

With the Paisley representative falling behind the leader by eight miles, he ended his race at 21:15 leaving Day to stay on the track till 23:11 to win the event with a record score of 360 miles and the £50 first prize. Of Day's performance, the reporter for the *Birmingham Daily Post* wrote: He is evidently endowed with exceptional stamina. When the competition was proclaimed to be at an end, he was going as strongly and well as when he started, and, far from exhibiting the least traces of fatigue, looked the very picture of ruddy health. Smith was the runner-up securing for himself £30 for a score of 346.5, with Clarkson taking home £7 for making 335.2. George Littlewood had his name placed in the frame in fourth place with a respectable 275 miles, taking back to Sheffield a prize of £3, plus the £1 that he had deposited at the beginning of the race. The same reporter observed: Littlewood is a very well built young fellow and such a good natural walker, that he ought in time to make a name for himself. Another eminent sports journalist of the time wrote, *"With more experience, Sheffield's George Littlewood will make the top grade and challenge the best in the world."*

The Final Score!

Pos		Miles	Laps	Pos		Miles	Laps
1	**Day**	**360**	**0**	3	Clarkson	335	2
2	Smith	346	5	4	Littlewood	275	0

Sam Day

The National Police Gazette (Illustration no: 72)

The advertisement below, which appeared in the *Nottingham Evening Express*, announced a somewhat novel six hours a day, go-as-you-please, beginning at 16:35 on Saturday, the 7th of February 1880 in the presence of a large number of spectators.

TO-DAY

EXHIBITION BUILDINGS
ARKWRIGHT STREET, NOTTINGHAM
GREAT SEVEN DAYS' PEDESTRIAN CONTEST.

Open to the World. Go-as-you-please. Hours of Running Half past Four to Half past Ten, p.m. Commencing on Saturday, February 7th, and finishing the following Saturday. Prizes £55 in money: First, £30; second, £13; third, £7; fourth, £3; fifth, £2. Admission Sixpence and One Shilling. The prizes have been deposited in the hands of the Editor of the *Sporting Life*.

Each man appears on the track in proper Pedestrian Costume. Ladies accompanied by Gentlemen will be admitted to the Reserved Seats FREE.

The promoters of the race were Messrs. Wood and Turner of Wolverhampton, and the race would take place on a track which consisted of loam, tan bark and sawdust which measured just under 14 laps to the mile. Mr. H. C. Taylor of Nottingham was in charge of the arrangements as well as officiating as timekeeper and referee.

The 19 contestants were: **T. Ashbourne**, Nottingham; **E. Barker**, Rotherham; **T. Bateman**, Birmingham; **G. Cartwright**, Walsall; **H. Crawley**, Grantham; **A. Flaunty**, Woolwich; **W. Garnham**, Bullwell; **G. Hilton**, Derby; **J. Hope**, Richmond; **W. Horton**, Croydon; **F. Hughes**, Birmingham; **G. Littlewood**, Sheffield; **"Brummy" Meadows**, London; **J. Merryweather**, Grantham; **H. Mundin**, Hull; **T. Shipley**, Birmingham; **G. Noremac**, Edinburgh; **W. Padley**, Nottingham; **H. Vandepeer**, Sittingbourne:

Of the competitors, Henry Vandepeer had proved himself by winning a recently run three-day contest in Wolverhampton, with John Hope (also appearing in this contest) coming in second. Vandepeer would be attended to by John Bailey, the holder of the "Astley 50-Mile Championship Belt." George Cartwright, the "Midlands 50-Mile Champion," who featured so prominently in the race that Day won in the previous November, was also in the field. George Noremac, the Scottish challenger, was also a leading fancy to win as he had won a £20 race in Aberdeen in the previous summer, firstly scoring 138 miles in 26 hours, and three weeks later, 150 miles in the same time. Littlewood was also mentioned in the press as a man that had shown recent promise. He was being handled by Powell of *"Sheffield handicap notoriety."*

Cartwright was the man who made the early running. He had set off at a blistering pace and was chased along by Hughes. However, it was Mundin who made the best time for the first mile in 6m.3s. At the three-mile mark, Hughes was in the lead in a time of 18m.27s, and when the five-mile mark was passed, the time recorded for Cartwright, who led the men, was 33 minutes, the rest following in three divisions. With Hughes on his heels when his score registered 8.13, the *"Walsall candidate"* upped the tempo, and at a blistering pace attempted to shake him off. Hughes though was up for the challenge and gamely stuck closely to the leader, but gradually fell back by the 10-mile stage of the race when he recorded a time of 40 seconds slower than Cartwright who made that distance in 1h.8m.20s. Mundin followed that pair with a time of 1h.10m, and Hilton made the same distance two minutes later. As the notoriously speedy race leader was accomplishing 15 miles in a time of 1h.45m, *"the Attercliffe representative now began to come through his men"* and was gradually gaining on Mundin who had established for himself second place. Mundin, who had gone in front of the fifth lap of the 16th mile, was still the race leader at 20 miles recording the effort in a time of 2h.25m. At 25 miles, the positions in the race changed yet again. Littlewood now led the pack, and he continued to do so at the 30-mile stage of the contest making that distance at 20:32. Cartwright was now second and Vandepeer third. Littlewood clung on to his lead as he passed the 35-mile mark at 21:22, but the *"Walsall Flyer"* caught him up again to lead the men on the 39th mile. Vandepeer then passed Littlewood thus taking his second position, and it was his and Cartwright's spurts *"which worked the onlookers into a state of excitement."*

By the end of the first day the score stood: **Cartwright, 42.10; Vandepeer, 42.2; Littlewood, 41.9; Hilton, 41.6; Flaunty, 40.1; Meadows, 39.13; Noremac, 39.8; Hope, 38.11; Garnham, 37.8; Crawley, 37; Mundin, 36.4; Ashbourne, 34; Bateman, 33.12; Merryweather, 33.2; Horton, 32.6; Barker, 26; Hughes, 23.10; Padley, 23.9:**

The *"wretched weather"* in Nottingham on the second afternoon of the contest prevented many from attending to watch the men commence the next stage of the race. Two of the competitors were missing when the seventeen men lined up to begin the day's business. They were the local lad Padley and Shipley of Birmingham.

Cartwright set off from the starting post at a hot pace followed by Vandepeer, Hilton, Noremac, Littlewood, Hope and Hughes. Pressed by Hughes, who was trying to make up the distance he had lost due to illness the previous day, Cartwright made 45 miles at 16:45, the same distance being made by Littlewood a couple of minutes later.

The band's arrival perked up the competitors. As they played, many of the men raised their game according to the tempo offered by their musical counterparts in the field of entertainment. Their presence certainly spurred on Cartwright, for he was the first of the men to register the half century at 17:21, Vandepeer following suit 7½ minutes later. The two principals in the race then kept close order, but it was the Walsall man who surged on to make the first 60 miles at 18:30, with Vandepeer registering 58.10 in second spot and Littlewood five laps behind him.

With Cartwright flagging a little by the end of play on the second day, Henry Vandepeer went to bed that night knowing he had done well to snatch pole position from the overnight leader: **Vandepeer, 86.1; Cartwright, 85.6; Hilton, 83.11; Flaunty, 83.3; Littlewood, 82.8; Meadows, 81.10; Noremac, 79.10; Hope, 78.3; Garnham, 75.4; Mundin, 73.7; Ashbourne, 69.3; Horton, 66; Bateman, 50.13; Crawley, 47.2; Hughes, 40 (Retired); Merryweather, 35.7; Barker, 34 (Retired):**

On the third day of competition, Vandepeer consolidated the lead he had gained on the previous day. At the resumption of proceedings, he went away at a *"rattling good pace,"* and despite his best efforts to keep up with the man from Kent, Cartwright failed to overhaul him. Of the others, Hilton, who was handled by Mr. T. Vernon of the Belvoir Inn in Derby, made eye-catching progress and was reported to be walking in splendid form. He was expected to get a place or even win the race itself. Noremac, on the other hand, suffering with rheumatism in his right knee, lost considerable ground as a result of being forced to be off the track for four and a half hours. The end of the 3rd day scores: **Vandepeer, 128; Cartwright, 126.6; Hilton, 124.1; Flaunty, 121.5; Meadows, 120.3; Littlewood, 116.7; Hope, 114.5; Mundin, 109.6; Noremac, 102.7; Horton, 100.6; Ashbourne, 84.7; Garnham, 77.8:**

Just before the start of the 4th day, there was disaster for the race leader as he was severely afflicted with cramp and wasn't able to compete. That unfortunate circumstance allowed Cartwright to capitalise on a two-mile lead, and along with Noremac, he made a good showing during the race. Owing to Flaunty's lameness, both Meadows and Littlewood were able to advance up the leader board, and by the end of the day at 22:30, the indicators showed: **Cartwright, 165.3; Hilton, 160.3; Meadows, 158; Littlewood, 153.3; Hope, 152.4; Flaunty, 150.7; Mundin, 148.10; Noremac, 144.13; Ashbourne, 117.3; Horton, 104.9:**

There was another large attendance on the fifth evening to watch the sport on offer. Apart from the main event, the promoters had hired Vandepeer's trainer John Bailey, the "20-mile champion," to attempt to make 19 miles in two hours. Starting the challenge at 20:00 and coaxed on by Vandepeer himself, who, having left the main contest, made the running for five miles for him, John failed by just six seconds to complete the feat. Had he not slipped up on the corners of the track, he would have undoubtedly won his substantial £25 bet that he would accomplish his daunting task.

In the 7-night contest, all the main leaders except Hilton, who had to retire due to lameness, went along in splendid form. In particular, "Brummy" Meadows caught the eye as he made relentless progress up the field. Hope initially looked in fine fettle as well, but apparently overexerted himself, and had to rest after fainting on the track. Mundin had also made excellent progress having pushed his way up from 7th to 3rd position during the time allowed. The scores at the end of the 5th day: **Cartwright, 201; Meadows, 193.9; Mundin, 189.10; Hope, 189; Littlewood, 185.10; Hilton, 184.5; Noremac, 184.4; Ashbourne, 150.2:**

While Cartwright maintained the momentum that had kept him out in front of the chasing pack, the Londoner, Meadows, brave effort of the previous evening, petered out on the 6th day of competition just after completing his 209th mile. He was thereafter forced to retire from the contest due to exhaustion and his withdrawal left seven men in the contest. As can be determined from the finishing scores on the penultimate day of the race, Mundin made the best score of the day, gaining 4 miles on the leader who was reported to be *"taking it easy:"* **Cartwright, 237.8; Mundin, 230.4; Hope, 227.5; Hilton, 225.5; Littlewood, 218.13; Noremac, 217.10; Meadows, 209.5; Ashbourne, 181.6:**

On the last day, Cartwright, who was in such a commanding position, went quietly about his business knowing that barring accidents, he would be the eventual winner. That attitude served him well for the rest of the evening for he eventually did win it and win it well, ignoring Mundin's persistent challenges to induce him into a race. Mundin, who had walked from Hull to take part in the race, and who had been *"badly handled"* during it, worked really hard to close the gap, eventually finishing a creditable second. As the racing got underway, Flaunty soon passed Hope to take, and keep, third position till the end, despite the latter's brave attempts to regain that position by indulging in frequent running. George Littlewood eventually finished in fifth place earning £2 plus a £1 for completing 220

King of the Peds

miles, as did six other contestants. His performance prompted a reporter from one of the Nottingham newspapers to say, *"Littlewood of Attercliffe, who gave promise at the outset, had to be content with a more backward position towards the end of the week in consequence of the failure of his knee."*

At 10:30 p.m. the final score was:

Pos		Miles	Won	Pos		Miles	Won
1	**Cartwright**	270	£30	5	Littlewood	252	£2
2	Mundin	265	£13	6	Noremac	230	
3	Flaunty	264	£7	7	Meadows	220	
4	Hope	263	£3	8	Ashbourne	214	

George Cartwright

The National Police Gazette (Illustration no: 73)

After that Littlewood competed in what was described as a "Great Six Days Pedestrian Tournament" promoted by Mr. J. Hagan of the Dundee Sporting Club at Newsome's Circus, Cookridge Street, Leeds, Yorkshire, *"when fifteen of the fastest men in the world will compete."* The twelve hours per day, six-day go-as-you-please race, commenced at 12:40 on Monday, the 29th of March 1880 in *"the presence of a fair attendance,"* and attracted the likes of Sam Day of Northampton who, had up to that point, had won a number of other races of the type. Indeed Sam had covered 4,328 miles in various competitions in the previous 22 months.

Those taking part were: **William Barnet** of Leeds, **William Clarkson** of Oulton, **B. Forth** of Dewsbury, **J. Fitzpatrick** of Manchester, **F. Hardie** of London, **John Hope** of Richmond, **George Littlewood** of Attercliffe, **Pat McCarty** of Leeds, **H. Mundin** of Hull, **W. Neville** of York, **T. Newton** of Holbeck, **George Parry** of Manchester and **J. S. Robson** of Liverpool.

On a track that measured 38 laps to the mile (of which one lap equalled just over 46 yards), Littlewood made a good impression on the first day of competition being well in the lead when the scores of the following leading competitors were recorded at midnight: **Littlewood, 67.8; McCarty; 64.24; Day, 60.10; Hope, 60.2; Fitzpatrick, 59.24; Parry, 57.20; Newton, 57; Robson, 53.18; Mundin, 52:**

On Tuesday morning, with Neville failing to turn up, and with Barnet and Newton only travelling for a short distance before both packing in, it was Day, Fitzpatrick and Mundin who shone as they continually passed the others. Day was particularly impressive conveying himself in that fashion for 7h.10m without a break. In the process he passed McCarty at 13:30 to take his second position. Littlewood passed the 100-mile post at 17:37, Day at 18:00, Hope at 19:28, Mundin at 19:47 and Parry at 20:37. However, when "Time!" was called at the end of the day's proceedings, and despite his Herculean efforts during the day, the Northamptonian could only manage to make a couple of miles on the race leader which was still Littlewood as the scores illustrate: **Littlewood, 133.2; Day, 128.6; Hope, 121; Parry, 114.34; Mundin, 113.29; McCarty, 113.14; Robson, 109.18:**

On Wednesday, the race leading *"youth,"* Littlewood, scored his 150th mile at 14:40, with Day the next man in line to take that honour at 16:20. McCarty, who had done so well to be second at the end of the first day, *"occupied the sixth "shop""* by the end of the third day's play, the scores at midnight showing: **Littlewood, 200.13; Day, 186.12; Mundin, 179.4; Hope, 175; Parry, 172.9; McCarty, 167.16; Robson, 159.11; Fitzpatrick, 152.7:**

Thursday saw the three overnight leaders all employing a trotting gait, rapidly overtaking the rest who appeared happy to walk. Day, Mundin and Parry went on to complete their second centuries at 14:15, 15:42 and 17:53 respectively. When the scores went into the reporters notebooks for the end of the fourth day, they showed: **Littlewood, 262.17; Day, 246.14; Mundin, 236.4; Parry, 224.34; McCarty, 221.25; Hope, 214.1; Robson, 210.6; Fitzpatrick, 204.22:**

Hope and McCarty were absent for the start of fifth day of competition which ended with Littlewood still well in the lead. Day remained in second spot with Mundin third and Parry fourth. The scores were: **Littlewood, 318.6; Day, 302.13; Mundin, 284.9; McCarty, 271.29; Parry, 270; Robson, 258.13; Hope, 255.37; Fitzpatrick, 251:**

The last day saw the leader consolidating his well earned lead by following Day around the track, and when "Time!" was eventually called for the end of the race, he won the £35 first prize plus £10 for beating *Sam Day's previous record by over 14 miles. George was asked later why he had had been so determined to beat the record, his answer apparently being, *"because I wanted that tenner!"* Day took £15 for coming second. In the opinion of Frank Dale, his backer in a future contest some years later, this was Littlewood's "greatest race."

*At the same time that this race was in progress, there was a similar contest taking part in Edinburgh, Scotland. Although that "tenner" was safe in his pocket, George would have been disappointed to learn that his new record score had already been beaten. However, it had been beaten on a 14 laps to the mile track and had therefore had been much easier to crack than the "ring" he had struggled in! To find out who did it, see Chapter 28.

The Final Score!

Pos		Miles	Yards	Pos		Miles	Yards
1	Littlewood	374	277	5	Robson	308	1,005
2	Day	362	973	6	Hope	308	864
3	Mundin	327	1,452	7	Parry	306	812
4	McCarty	317	252	8	Fitzpatrick	302	1,757

Littlewood then made the trip to London to make his first appearance at the Agricultural Hall in Islington. The 72-hour go-as-you–please race, which commenced every day for six days at 11:00 and finished at 23:00, would take place between Monday, the 6th and the 11th of September 1880, on a track seven laps to the mile, *"which measured a foot from the inner edge all the way round."*

King of the Peds

With the permission of Islington Local History Centre   (Illustration no: 74)

The "Champion Gold Medal," which was a gift from Sir John Astley, and a cash prize of £50 would be given to the winner. An extra £10 was offered to the first man to score 405 miles and a further £10 was given to any man who could make 420 miles. The second placed competitor would receive £20 with an extra £5 if the winner didn't succeed in getting more than 10 miles ahead at any time. The competitor finishing third would get £10 and an extra £5 if not beaten by the winner by more than 8 miles. Fourth man past the post would receive £5. Every contestant who made a score of 300 miles, irrespective of whether they got a prize, would receive £3.

Mr. Atkinson of the *Sporting Life* and Mr. R. Watson were the judges. Messrs. S. Ashbrook and Williams were the time-keepers, and Mr. W. G. Begley was in charge of the lap scorers. Before the contest started at 11:20, *"Mr. Nicholls of Stamford took a portrait of the competitors in a group,"* and the 29 participants who bunched up for him for that moment of prosperity were:

S. Burdett of Derby: Age 24. Weight 9st.13lbs. Height 5ft.6in. Trained at Derby by J. Messenger and attended by S. Phillips of Clerkenwell.

H. Carless of Millwall: Age 29. Weight 10st.4lbs. Height 5ft.7½in. Attended by G. Gray.

G. Cartwright of Walsall: Age 32. Weight 9st.11lbs. Height 5ft.5½in. Trained at Cannock Chase; Attended by *"Old Miles"* of Newmarket.

W. Chillman of Streatham: Age 24. Weight 9st.5lbs. Height 5ft.8in. Attended by W. Bryant.

S. Day of London: Age 27. Weight 9st. Height 5ft.3½in. Attended by J. Sedoff.

J. Dean of Winchmore Hill: Age 22. Weight 9st.½lb. Height 5ft.7½in. Attended by his brother.

M. Fox of Dundee: Age 28. Weight 11st.7lbs. Height 5ft.10in. Trained at Dundee. Attended by J. Gibbons.

W. Franks of Marylebone: Age 29. Weight 9st.4lb. Height 5ft.6in. Trained at Lillie Bridge. Attended by R. Seward.

R. Harding of Blackwall: Age 31. Weight 9st.4lbs. Height 5ft.3in. Trained at Bow. Attended by W. Whale.

H. Hill of Swansea (No information):

J. Hope of Richmond: Age 34. Weight 10st. Height 5ft.5½in. Attended by G. Baker.

H. King of Rotherhite: Age 31. Weight 10st.6lb. Height 5ft.7½in. Attended by W. Bryant.

G. Littlewood of Sheffield: Age 21. Weight 10st.10lbs. Height 5ft.7½ in. Attended by T. Higginbottom.

W. Lockton of Haggerston: Age 20. Weight 8st.1lb Height 5ft.4½in. Trained at Bow. Attended by J. Lockton.

G. Mason of Ratcliffe: Age 29. Weight 8st.9lbs. Height 5ft.6in. Trained at Bow. Attended by A. Flaunty.

H. Mundin of Hull: Age 32. Weight 10st.3lbs. Height 5ft.7in. Trained at Arbroath, Scotland. Attended by E. Walker of Arbroath.

G. Noremac of Edinburgh: Age 26. Weight 8st.10lbs. Height 5ft.3½in. Trained in Edinburgh. Attended by George Beattie.

H. Palfreyman of Leeds: Age 37. Weight 11st. Height 5ft.9½in. Attended by A. Wilson.

J. H. Palmer of Plymouth: Age 18. Weight 8st.12lbs. Height 5ft.6½in. Trained at Plymouth. Attended by A. Manning.

W. Robinson of Bow: Age 28. Weight 9st; Height 5ft.4in. Trained at Gravesend. Attended by R. Tuckerman of Woolwich.

J. Simpson of Cambridge: Age 27. Weight 8st.12lbs. Height 5ft.4in. Trained at Cambridge. Attended by Charles Rowell and Alfred Langford.

C. Smith of Hackney: Age 19; Weight 9st.7lbs. Height 5ft.4½in. Trained at Bow. Attended by W. Gregory and J. Moseley.

J. Smith of Dalston: Age 19; Weight 9st. Height 5ft.4in. Trained on the Epping Road. Attended by J. Adkins.

R. J. Smyth of Islington: Age 43. Weight 9st.8lbs. Height 5ft.6½in. Trained on turnpike roads. Attended by S. Baker of St. Luke's.

W. Smith of Paisley: Age 33. Weight 10st. Height 5ft.7in. Attended by A. Pearson of Brighton.

J. Spicer of Hertford: Age 30. Weight 11st. Height 5ft.8½in. Trained at St. Helena Gardens. Attended by W. Barnett of Leeds.

R. H. Stevens of Paddington: Age 24. Weight 9st.4lbs. Height 5ft.6in. Trained round Regents Park. Attended by C. Connelly.

C. Thomas of Kilburn: Age 19. Weight 11st.4lbs. Height 5ft.8½in. Trained on the Bedford and Cambridgeshire roads. Attended by C. Crossley of Holloway.

H. Vandepeer of Kent: Age 29. Weight 9st.10lbs. Height 5ft.6½in. Trained at the Sheerness Royal Hotel Gardens. Attended by E. Clackett of Sittingbourne.

Starting prices: **Noremac, 4/1; Cartwright, 5/1; Mason, 7/1; Littlewood and Vandepeer, 8/1; Simpson, 10/1; Franks, 15/1; Up to 100/1 bar these except for Smythe, Hill and Robinson who were all 1,000/1:**

With the going on the track described as *"rather soft, consequently, heavy going,"* all, apart from Palmer, went off a brisk pace. Lockton registered the first mile in a time of 6m.7s with Noremac eight seconds behind. It was all change just before the end of the third mile with the ever impatient Cartwright leading the gang around, headed by Noremac, Littlewood, Chillman and Stevens, in that order. The *"flying collier"* was still tugging them round by the end of the tenth mile, registering that distance in 1h.1m.22s, 15 miles in 1h.36m.48s, 20 miles in 2h.10m.38s, and 26 miles in exactly 3 hours. Mason by this time was itching to show what he could do, and a ding-dong battle ensued as the two scrapped it out for superiority from the 27th mile. Cartwright retook premier position at the end of the 28th and stayed there to register the first 30 miles in the race in a time of 3h.37m.30s. The scores when recorded at 16:30

were: **Mason, 40.2; Cartwright, 39.2; Vandepeer, 38.4; Littlewood and Stevens, 38.2; Franks, 37.2; Fox, 37; Simpson, 36.4; Day, 35; Mundin, 34.1; Noremac, 33.5; W. Smith, 33.3; Hope, 33.2; Dean and Harding, 32.1; King, 31; C. Smith, 30.3; Burdett, 30; Palmer, 29.6; J. Smith, 28.3; Thomas, 27.1; Carless and Spicer, 27; R. J. Smyth, 25.4; Palfreyman, 24; Chillman, 23.4; Lockton, 21.5; Robinson, 16.3: Hill, 13.1:**

The Ratcliffe man had led from the 33rd to the 50th (6h.56m), but the scales were tipped in favour of the midlander between the 51st and the 73rd which was registered in a time of 10h.53m.36s. It was Mason however who took control from the 74th mile till "Time" was called when he went in as overall leader with a score of 79.4 next to his name.

Twelve-hour scores: **Mason, 79.4; Cartwright, 76; Simpson, 74.3; Noremac and Vandepeer, 74.1; Littlewood, 73; Fox and Stevens, 70; Day, 69.5; Mundin, 68.2; W. Smith, 65.4; C. Smith, 65.2; Harding and King, 65; Palmer, 60.3; Franks and Hope, 60; J. Smith, 56.2; Dean, 56; Spicer, 55; Palfreyman, 51.2; R. J. Smyth, 50.2; Burdett, 50; Chillman, 38.1; Carless, 27.1; Lockton, 21.5; Robinson, 16.3: Hill, 13.1:**

When the men came to answer the roll-call at the start the next day at 11:00, Burdett, Cartwright, Day, Dean, Fox, Franks, Harding, Hope, King, Littlewood, Mason, Mundin, Noremac, Simpson, Spicer, Palfreyman, Palmer, C. Smith, J. Smith, W. Smith and Stevens confirmed their presence. After the "off" it was the young "Tyke," Littlewood who forced the pace taking the fourth position off Noremac at 11:45 and then passed Simpson to take third "pozzy" 30 minutes later. At about this time, there was some *"commotion"* on the track when Day fell over. He required some assistance and was taken to his tent where, after spending four minutes recovering, he rejoined the fold only to retire more or less straight away with 82.3. Spicer followed him out of the building with 69.6 as the rest got on with the job of trying to be the quickest man to make the first century. That honour went to Mason in 15h.35m.35s. He was followed by Cartwright in 16h.10m.7s, and then by Littlewood in 16h.28m.36s. Mundin celebrated his 31 minutes later.

At 16:30, and in front of few spectators who offered *"little encouragement,"* the telegraph board showed: **Mason, 108; Cartwright, 107.4; Littlewood, 105; Mundin, 103.1; Noremac, 101.5; Simpson, 100.2; C. Smith, 98.1; Stevens, 93.5; Harding, 92.4; Fox, 90.4; King, 90; Hope, 88; Palmer, 87; Day, 82.3; J. Smith, 81.6; Franks, 76.3; Palfreyman, 73:**

Littlewood, who was going like the clappers, took second place at 18:44 when he "nicked" that position off Cartwright on the 3rd lap of his 120th mile. At this time, he had gained 5 miles and 4 laps on Mason who was walking when he passed him 20 minutes later to take the lead again in the third lap on the 124th mile. Of Littlewood, the *Sporting Life* commented: "Unlike some of the men in the competition, he is a splendid walker as well as a good runner, and as he is but a youngster, he will do a good performance some day."

Up to the end of play on that second day, Littlewood's score of 144.6 laps was well below John Dobler's at the same juncture when the American scored 150.5 on August the 10th 1880. The scores in this one however, were: **Littlewood, 144.6; Mason, 139; Cartwright, 138.4; Noremac, 135.2; Simpson, 131; Mundin, 128.1; Harding, 120.3; C. Smith, 120.2; Stevens, 119.5; J. Smith, 113.3; Palmer, 110; King, 109.4; Hope, 109; Franks, 101.5; Palfreyman, 100.1; Burdett, 94.6; Day, 84.2:**

The 18 remaining participants reported for duty at 11:00 on the third day of the race. George Cartwright was the first person to throw in the towel at 11:40 with an injury to his instep. The gritty little Scot, Noremac, from Edinburgh, took his place in third spot but lasted only 50 minutes before he informed the match officials he was retiring after breaking down on the track having made only 5 miles and 5 laps since the start of the day. Previous to this he had complained of *"shin ache"* and the injury had forced him to turn up 15 minutes late for the start. Under the watchful eye of one of his trainers, Charlie Rowell, Johnny Simpson replaced Noremac for third; and no matter how much the second placed Mason tried, he couldn't make any impression on the Yorkshireman, who went impressively at the head of affairs. The marker board at the 16:30 showed the following positions. **Littlewood, 179; Mason, 171; Simpson, 161.2; Mundin, 159.3; Harding, 145.4; C. Smith, 144.1; J. Smith, 134.6; King, 134.3; Stevens, 134.2; Hope, 133; Palmer, 130.6; Fox, 127; Franks, 126.6; Palfreyman, 120.2; Day, 120.1:**

The large crowds that the management believed would watch the ongoing race were virtually non-existent. However, the young Sheffielder shrugged the disappointing atmosphere off and motivated himself towards his objective to win the race and secure that extra "tenner" for making the coveted 405. It was a real shame for Littlewood that in his first race in the capital there was a lack of support for him. The London crowd were notoriously patriotic to the men from their area and news of a northern boy in the lead would not have sent them scurrying along to the great hall to spend their hard earned money. Having made 71.5 in the 12 hours, George went to bed that night about 400 yards short of Dobler's best distance for 36 hours. Interestingly Sammy Day who had been off the track on Tuesday due to illness, had returned that day and had made a couple of laps more than the race leader. Littlewood was 6 miles in front of Mason and 20 ahead of Simpson. Things were looking good for the northerner whose mouth must have been watering at the prospect of earning the phenomenal amount of £50 in those days, and possibly even £70–– if only he could make the coveted 420…

The 36-hour scores: **Littlewood, 216.4; Mason, 210.4; Simpson, 196.4; Mundin, 176.3 Harding, 172; C. Smith, 170.4; J. Smith, 165.5; King, 163; Palmer, 160; Day, 156.2; Hope, 155.1; Franks, 147.5; Palfreyman, 147.2; Stevens (retired), 144.3; Fox (retired), 127:**

When the muster roll was called for the start of the fourth day's proceedings, there were only twelve others accompanying Littlewood to face the starter. The two trainers of the famous pedestrian Charlie Rowell, Barnsley and Asplen, who were both watching the contest, were both in agreement that there was something special about the Sheffield lad, and both thought he would be a future champion. But first he had to win; when the starter shouted "Go," he went on his way in a determined fashion. At 12:30, he had added a further 9 miles to his score in contrast to his nearest rival Mason, who, content to *"jog-trot,"* added 8 miles and a lap. Simpson, who had made 4 laps more than Littlewood in that time, was now 15 miles and a lap behind the Ratcliffe man whilst heading in the opposite direction, a tactic he had employed since 11:35.

It took just four hours for Littlewood to move himself another 22 miles and 6 laps further along. The quest to secure second prize money urged Johnny Simpson to decrease the deficit between him and Mason. In the same amount of time, the Cambridge candidate scored a healthy 19.6 which was seven laps better than the man he was chasing. Mundin meanwhile, was in fourth place on 203.3, and Harding in fifth, wanted one more mile to make a double century. The others left in the race were C. Smith with 193.2, J. Smith on 190, Palmer with 182.6, Day on 179.3, King having negotiated 174.4, Palfreyman with 167.1, Franks having traversed 154.3 and Stevens, the tail-ender, with 144.3.

Whilst Palfreyman limped along, Mason, who had previously been reported to have been *"very dotty on his pins all day as if suffering from weakness in the knees,"* moved along much better later and managed to make 54.1 by the end of the day. Simpson though did really well to secure 60.3 whilst Mundin went five miles up on Harding.

Shortly after 22:30, Littlewood made a little bit of history as he beat Dobler's 48-hour record of 282.2 which the American achieved in the previous month at Buffalo, USA. At the end of the day, he was just over 2 miles better off on a score of 284.6 and was now 20.1 in front of Mason. The Sheffielder had made 68.2 for the day and his friends were asking the bookies for even money that he might make an extra £20 by making 420 miles in the time allowed.

Those 48-hour scores: **Littlewood, 284.6; Mason, 264.5; Simpson, 256.3; Mundin, 234.3 Harding, 228.5; C. Smith, 220.5; J. Smith, 220; Palmer, 210.6; Day, 197.4; Hope, 197.1; Palfreyman, 186.1; King, 185.3; Franks (retired), 154.3:**

On the penultimate day, a dozen men faced the starter. After they were dispatched on their way, the "top man" continued to go well and initially maintained the 20-mile gap between himself and Mason by following in his footsteps. This state of affairs continued till after the second hour when the race leaders, barring Simpson, enlivened proceedings with a series of spurts. During the fun, Littlewood managed to make his third century at 13:33, but the real interest thereafter was whether Simpson could catch Mason, who subsequently increased his speed when the former got within four miles of him.

The 16:30 score: **Littlewood, 313.4; Mason, 293; Simpson, 285.3; Mundin, 268.1; Harding, 250.2; C. Smith, 241.5; J. Smith, 237.1; Palmer, 231.5; Day, 223.5: Hope, 219.5; King, 212.4; Palfreyman, 199.6:**

King of the Peds

Later at 18:12 Mason managed to make the 300. More importantly, he had kept his rival at bay at least for the time being whilst the others in the race went along well, the following all expected to make the necessary 300 miles to receive the *"talent money,"* Palmer who had just finished his 250th mile in good style, Day, and *"the Smiths."* Hope and King were both expected to miss out.

The faltering Mason, who had struggled remorsefully during the day, was finally caught and passed at 22:35 by Simpson. Littlewood meanwhile, was to fail by just over half a mile to equal Dobler's 60-hour record for the same time; when he left the track on the penultimate night of the contest he had bagged 349 miles and 1 lap. The 60-hour scores: **Littlewood, 349.1; Simpson, 320.4; Mason, 310.4; Mundin, 280; Harding, 272; C. Smith, 266; J. Smith, 263.6; Palmer, 257.1; Day, 256.2; King, 245.1; Hope, 240.2; Palfreyman, 218.5:**

By noon on the last day of competition, Littlewood was 28 miles ahead of Simpson, and although the leader slowed down somewhat during the rest of it, he achieved his goal of getting paid the extra £10, as he scored a memorable 406 miles in 72 hours. The name of George Littlewood was now being mentioned as a potential future champion in the world of professional pedestrianism. Time would tell how well he would perform in one of the cruellest of sports.

The Result!

Pos		Miles	Laps	Won	Pos		Miles	Laps	Won
1	**Littlewood**	**406**	**6**	**£60**	7	Smith C.	300	1	£3
2	Simpson	371	3	£20	8	King	300	1	£3
3	Mason	350	4	£10	9	Palmer	300	0	£3
4	Mundin	317	1	£5	10	Day	300	0	£3
5	Smith J.	303	0	£3	11	Hope	217	4	
6	Harding	300	1	£3					

George Littlewood

(Illustration no: 75)

CHAPTER 27

The Master v The Apprentices

As early as the December the 13th 1879, there had been reports in the press that the next match (the 6th) for the international version of the Astley Belt, would take place on Monday, the 5th of April 1880 either in London or Manchester. In May of 1880, Charlie Rowell wrote to the *Sporting Life* in reply to a letter he had received from John Dobler of Chicago, who wanted to match himself and his fellow countryman, Frank Hart, against any two Englishmen:

Dear Sir,

I am ready to compete with Hart, Dobler or any other man in the world for £500 or £1,000 a side, but the match must be open (nobody barred) and the winner to take the entire stake and half the gate money. An international match between Hart, Dobler, Brown and myself in New York cannot be arranged at present, as Brown's backers are unable to leave England and wish to look after Brown themselves in any race wherein they put up money on him. Hart, Dobler, or any other American pedestrian would have a good reception in England, and as Brown's backers offer to stake £500 I shall be glad to stake the same amount and make a £500 sweepstakes with Hart, Pegram, Dobler or anybody in the world at the Agricultural Hall, London, three months after signing articles. I agree to allow the American representatives £100 altogether for expenses. After my last victory in New York I left a deposit of £100 in your hands. Anyone covering it can rely upon having a match.

CHARLES ROWELL

The articles of agreement were described as being exactly the same as governing the last contest in New York. However, it was reported that Astley had objected to increasing the entrance fee or the minimum distance of 450 miles, where the contenders could take a cut in the gate money. He also declared that he regretted the withdrawal of Panchot and O'Leary from the future match. It was further claimed that Rowell had suggested a wager with O'Leary of £300 or more, if that man was willing to cross the Atlantic to compete. The following document was then drawn up and signed.

MEMORANDUM OF AGREEMENT made and entered into this eighth day of September, one thousand eight hundred and eighty between Charles Rowell, of Chesterton, England, party of the first part, and William Pegram of Boston, Massachusetts, USA., party of the second part: Witnesseth, whereas the party of the first part is now the holder of the "Long-distance Championship of the World Belt," won by him at Madison-square Gardens, in September, one thousand eight hundred and seventy nine, and the party of the second part has duly challenged him to a pedestrian match therefore, pursuant to the condition upon which the said belt is held: Now, therefore, this agreement witnesseth that the parties hereto agree to compete for the said Championship Belt, and the sum of one hundred pounds a side (£200) which is hereby deposited by the parties hereto in the hands of the editor of the *Sporting Life* to bind the match. The match to take place at the Agricultural Hall, London, which is mutually agreed upon by both parties, and is to commence at one o'clock a.m. on Monday, November first, one thousand eight hundred and eighty and terminate at eleven o'clock p.m. on Saturday, the sixth of November, one thousand eight hundred and eighty, the party covering the greatest distance during that time, by either running or walking, without assistance to be declared the winner. The match is to be subject to the same conditions as that at which the said Belt was won by the part of the first part, and the Belt is held by the winner on the same terms and conditions on which it is now held. In the event of any other person or persons joining in the match, they each must deposit the sum of one hundred pounds (£100) with the appointed stakeholder within four weeks previous to the day fixed for the commencement of the race, and be subject to the terms and conditions of this agreement. The *Sporting Life* is hereby authorised to appoint the judges, and to appoint the requisite number of lap-scorers and time-keepers. All matters of dispute or appeals from questions not provided for by these conditions to be referred to the trustees of the belt, whose decision shall be final in all cases. The gate receipts (after all expenses have been paid) to be divided as follows: - *(These are exactly the same as in the Articles of Agreement for the 5th Astley Belt race which* can be found on the first page of Chapter 20):

To go on one wide track (not less than ten feet wide.) Either party failing to comply with any of these articles to forfeit all moneys deposited.

(Signed)

Witness.   MICHEAL ROWELL, for CHARLES ROWELL

            J. SMITH, for "BLOWER" BROWN

            T. DAVIES, for {W. PEGRAM
                          {H. HOWARD

            CHARLES E. DAVIES, for JOHN DOBLER

            GEO. W. ATKINSON, for G. LITTLEWOOD

Witness to the above. W. Potter.

William Pegram and Harry Howard were the two other *"American"* athletes who had sailed for England from New York on September the 18th on the steamship *Maine* to compete in the race. They were accompanied by their backers Tom Davies and Henry Selkman, along with "Happy Jack" Smith, *"who will care for the boys in the race."* Howard told reporters, "I am going to win that belt and shake up Rowell. I am fully prepared to cover five hundred and eighty miles and six hundred if necessary. The man who wins must cover five hundred and eighty miles. I'll do as I never did before to win." Howard was employed by the Montclair Hunting Club as *"runner in,"* and due to his job was said to be in splendid condition. Pegram, who had been in training at his home in Massachusetts, and who was also reported to be in good condition, said that he, or Howard, would take the belt from Rowell. Mr. Davies said he was also confident of success and had $10,000 to bet that they would both come in first or second. Later, on October the 5th, Daniel O'Leary accompanied John Dobler on the steamship *Wisconsin* which sailed for Liverpool to compete in the competition.

On October the 20th, the *Sporting Life* reported: Littlewood, of Sheffield, completed on Monday last his deposit for the pedestrian championship. He is reported to be in splendid condition, as are all the other competitors. "Blower" Brown has proved, in private trials that he can stay as well as ever. Rowell has also been making long journeys daily. Pegram and Howard have worked off the eight pounds they gained during their voyage from America and are now again in proper weight. John Dobler, of Chicago landed in England on Monday in the best of health. At a meeting of the competitors, or their representatives on Monday, articles of agreement and a contract for the use of Agricultural Hall were signed. The start is to be made at 1 o'clock on the morning of Nov. 1. Nobody was present on behalf of Dobler, but, possibly neither he nor his agent were able to reach London in time.

It was fully expected at the time that one or more of the pedestrians would cover 600 miles during the race which would commence on the 1st of November 1880. The contestants taking part were:

"Blower" Brown of Fulham, London, England, who was the present holder of the "Long Distance Champion of England" belt which he had won twice by making 541, and 553 miles and 168 yards respectively, both victories being achieved with any amount in hand. The oldest participant of the present contest at 37 years of age, he stood 5ft.6in, and weighed 9st.7lbs.

John Dobler of Chicago, Illinois, USA, was 21 years old having been born in the "Windy City" on the 25th of May 1859. He had been credited with making the best score on record for a 12 hours a day, six-day event, and this performance in Buffalo, USA, between the 9th and 14th of August 1880 can be read about in detail in Chapter 28. Dobler's weight before the contest was 11st.6lbs, with his height being recorded at 5ft.9½in. John had been employed as a shipping clerk and timekeeper at the Union Stock Yards in Bridgeport, south Chicago, up to the time he entered the pedestrian arena: His first race was allegedly a six-day affair in Chicago in 1878 where he came in third place winning $150. More definitely, he starred in a 75-hour contest when he lost by three miles to George Parry of England between Wednesday, the 28th and Saturday, the 31st of May 1879 at Chicago's Exposition Building (See Chapter 23). He then went on to defeat George Guyon and Charles Rier in a 75-hour heel-and-toe race for a sweepstake of $1,500 and the "Champion Cup of America." This match, which again took place at the same venue, began on the night of Wednesday, the 30th of July and finished on Saturday night, the 2nd of August 1879. The final scores when the referee Dr. N. Rowe called "Time," were Dobler, 229.3; Guyon, 188.4; Rier, 160: *"Rier showed himself to be about the worst pedestrian that ever took the track. He hadn't the pluck of an infant. His doctor said there was nothing whatever the matter with him but sheer cowardliness. He could eat and sleep a match against anyone, and that is his proper vocation."* At Providence, Rhode Island, in a 60-hour walking match finishing on the 24th of September 1879 between himself and Peter Crossland, Dobler lost to the *"Sharp Sheffield Blade,"* the Englishman cutting out for himself a score of 206.20 as opposed to Johns 202.3. On Tuesday, September 30th 1879, a two-mile walk for $50 between Dobler, and Crossland, was won by the American in 18 minutes, after an objection to Crossland (who actually passed the post first) was sustained. At Bridgeport, Connecticut, on October the 4th, Dobler came second in a 20-mile square heel-and-toe contest against William O'Leary of that city who made the said distance in 3h.10m. Following that, he came third in a 72-hour go-as-you-please race at Providence, Rhode Island. He then travelled to New Orleans where he won the O'Leary 60-hour race, and secured the "Champion medal of Louisiana" and a stake of $500 in a race of 17 competitors, winning by 25 miles. A 22-lap to the mile pedestrian match staged at the McCormick Hall, Chicago, for a sweepstakes of $200 each, with the winner receiving a substantial amount of the gate money, terminated at 23:15 on the 27th of December 1879. Four contestants entered walking twelve hours daily in the six-day, go-as-you-please match, with the result being a win for George Guyon, who scored 331 miles. Dobler finished in the runner-up position on 325.13. Crossland made 280.1 with Pierce coming in last on 259.2. At Racine, Wisconsin, he scored 125 miles when winning the O'Leary 24-hour go-as-you-please race before making 531 miles in the 2nd O'Leary Belt contest in New York between the 5th and 10th of April 1880 (As described in Chapter 25). After this he took part the 72-hour O'Leary Belt contest in Buffalo in August as mentioned above. Then, between the 5th and 11th of September he took part in a 156-hour go-as-you-please against horses at Chicago. After that was involved in a 75-hour walk arranged by O'Leary the venue being the pavilion on the Lake Front, again at Chicago, against Sherry, Olmstead and Banks which finished at 22:00 on September the 18th 1880. The score was Dobler 227.6 to 213 miles for Banks. *"The pouring rain soaked through the tent and absolutely water logged the arena. For an hour preceding the close of the contest the walkers were trudging around in saturated sawdust and locomotion became increasingly difficult. During the last hour of the walk the spectators, under the shelter of umbrellas, swashed about the ring in mud and water, which in many places was several inches deep. Nevertheless, quite a number of the ladies were in at the death, and as the contestants left the track the crowd cheered, the band played with dampened energy, and the walk was over."* For his efforts Dobler won a massive silver belt worth $500 which was encrusted with gold, the plates of which were composed of polished silver with a fretwork border, the centre piece of which contained a bas relief of a pedestrian on a track.

Much more on **Harry Howard,** who was born in Lancashire, England, but had resided in the USA for ten years, can be gleaned in, Chapter 23. He was living at the time of the race in Montclair, New Jersey. In the 2nd O'Leary Belt contest in New York between the 5th and 10th of April in the same year, he made 534½ miles (See Chapter 25). Harry was 30 years old, was 5ft.6in in height, and on weighing in before the match, tipped the scales at 9st.12lb.

George Littlewood of Attercliffe, Sheffield, Yorkshire, England, like Dobler, was 21 years of age, and had never participated in a race of this type. However he had won two 12-hour six-day events, the last time covering 406 miles. As his victories were secure and nobody was pressing him, it was thought he could have covered far greater distances. George, who weighed in at 11st.9lbs, and was 5ft.7½in tall would be attended to by the veteran, Bill Lang, otherwise known as "Crowcatcher," from Middlesborough, Higginbottom of Attercliffe, and his father Fred.

William Pegram, an ex-paver from Boston, Massachusetts, USA, was a 35-year-old black athlete who had made two fine scores of 527 in the "Rose Belt," and 543.7 in the 2nd O'Leary Belt. He tipped the scales at 10st.10lb and was 5ft.5in in height.

Charles Rowell of Chesterton, Cambridgeshire, England, and holder of the international version of the Astley Belt will be remembered for his two successful trips to America, where he won the championship of the world on both occasions and consequently netted upwards of £10,000 for both performances. In the two races in question he covered 500 miles 180 yards and 530 miles respectively. He had been in a class of his own on both occasions and it was difficult to estimate how much further he could have travelled had he been pressed at the time. Rowell weighed 10 stones and was 5ft.6in tall. He would be looked after by C. Asplen, J. Simpson, C. Langford and C. Barnsley during the race.

There was some regret that Frank Hart, along with Weston, couldn't make the event. Hart had recently covered the longest distance on record of 565 miles 465 yards in a six-day race, and Weston was considered the *"father of long distance pedestrianism."* Hart, who had recently suffered an attack of *"*brain fever,"* had not fully recovered, whilst Weston had been described at the time as being, *"very quiet as of late."*

*Hart, speaking to a reporter in late July at his house in North Anderson Street, Boston, about his illness which was described by the *Boston Globe* as *"congestion on the brain,"* said, "I feel much better today, but my physician says I must keep quiet. Ice seems to be the only comfort that I have. My head worries me considerably, but I am satisfied that I will come out all right. It, however, annoys me, as I fear that it may hurt my chances for holding the O'Leary Belt, for should I be challenged I may have to go on the track before I can properly recover from this attack. But you can tell my friends that I hope to get out of present sickness, and show them that Boston's representative will not be behind at the next race."

Unfortunately the weather in London had been so bad as to prevent the athletes from taking much exercise outside. Indeed, Dobler would be starting the race 10 pounds over his normal racing weight. It was a well known fact at the time that Brown, Rowell and Littlewood were the best athletes in England. Each man had staked £100 on the race which meant there was £600 in the pot. It was estimated that the gate receipts could be as much as £5,000. After deducting expenses on completion of the race the remainder would be divided thus: One half to the winner, 30% for the second and 20% for the third.

A *"very good track"* of seven laps to the mile composed of sifted garden mould, tan and a top dressing of sawdust, had been laid down under the supervision of Jack White, *"the once famous Gateshead Clipper."* It was described as having, *"beautiful rounded turns and with a little use would provide splendid going."*

The accommodation for the men also came in for some praise. *"The arrangements for the men were excellent, and having been provided with "Humphreys" galvanized iron houses, in lieu of the wretched cold tents usually provided, they were very well satisfied, the house proving both snug and warm."* The *"zinc cottages"* which had been erected by J. C. Humphrey, Iron House Builder, 15 Albert Gate, Knightsbridge, had red curtained windows on either side of the door which gave them an *"inviting aspect."* Littlewood and Dobler had one each at the Liverpool Road end of the building whilst Rowell had one close to the press stand and Brown's was situated half way down between the Barford and Upper Street entrances. The other two Americans were accommodated in a doubled-up version near Rowell.

Just before the start of the race, the management had been described as *"useless"* for providing just three policemen, who were powerless to keep the disorderly crowd gathered at the Barford Street entrance waiting for admission, *"in order."*

The *Sporting Life* in its coverage of the race commented on the betting market at the start: In the betting, of which there was a good bit, Rowell and Blower ran a closish race for favouritism. Howard was knocked out at 50 to 1. Of the others, Littlewood found friends at 6 to 1, while Dobler and Pegram were backed at a point less each. There was more money for Rowell than Brown, and at the finish he may be quoted at 7 to 4 while Blower went back to 9 to 4. Just at the start Sir John Astley offered to clear the market at 6 to 4 about the holder of the belt, but did not make any business whilst Rowell tried to bet £100 that Blower did not lead him a mile at any part of the competition.

The race, which was being judged by Mr. Tom Griffiths of *Bell's Life* and Mr. G. W. Atkinson of the *Sporting Life*, began in front of a small audience of about 300. Starting precisely at 1 o'clock in the morning, Sir John Astley (who was accompanied by General Goodlake, V. C., Hon, Seymour Egerton and Sir Seymour Blane), offered the men a few words of caution before he sent them on their long journey.

Dobler initially led the men, but after half a lap, Littlewood settled himself in the lead. After three laps he was followed by Pegram who had moved up from last place, then Dobler, Rowell, Brown and finally Howard. The black American was observed to be sweating profusely in his efforts to keep up with the pace at the half mile stage. The first mile was made by the *"Sheffield Blonde"* in a time of 6m.10s, and after being overtaken by both Pegram and Dobler at the three-mile stage, he went on to reassert his former position by going on to make the first five miles in a time of 36m.39s. However, it was Pegram who led the first hour with a score of 8 miles and 1 lap. The American, who had taken control of the race from the seventh mile, was the first of the runners to score 10 miles in 1h.14m.3s, with Littlewood, Rowell and Brown close behind.

Rowell went on to be the man to make the first 20 miles in 2h.30m.51s, Littlewood close at his heels. At 30 miles, Littlewood retook the lead but was challenged almost immediately by Rowell, causing the Sheffielder to fall back. Rowell then moved away to complete 40 miles in 6h.15m.20s and 50 miles in 7h.38m.44s. Brown made his half century in 7h.44m.44s, Littlewood in 7h.50m.10s, Dobler in 8h.3m.5s and Howard in 9h.2m.4s. Rowell left the track momentarily when on a score of 52, but Littlewood stuck to it like glue. The others took short rests allowing the two leaders to open a considerable advantage for themselves. Brown left the track at 08:10 for 15 minutes, and it was quite apparent on his return that something was amiss, as he walked along as if in considerable pain. Rowell, who had made 70 at 10:32, was four miles in front of his nearest challenger, Littlewood.

Dobler is just ahead of Brown and Littlewood.

© *The British Library. All Rights reserved. The Penny Illustrated. (Illustration no: 76)*

At 13:00, Rowell began to put more distance between himself and Littlewood, who by that stage, had started to walk at times. The "Tyke" then took thirty seconds rest, but it was just enough to see Dobler overtake him, and as the Englishman walked, the American began to create a considerable gap between them both. Rowell went on to complete his 90th mile at 13:28 whilst Brown, who had left the track at 12:35 having been told to rest by a doctor, was compelled to withdraw altogether, as a consequence of the swelling of a vein in the groin. Blower left the hall at this time assisted by his friends having scored 73.5. It was stated later that he had been *"incapacitated through his clothing rubbing him sufficiently hard to bruise and inflame the flesh and muscle."*

At 14:57, Rowell achieved his century, much to the pleasure of the approximate 2,000 watching spectators who cheered him enthusiastically. He had smashed the record for the fastest century created by Hazael (15h.37m.1s) on the 21st April 1879 making the same distance in 13h.57m.13s (At the same stage Hazael had covered 91 miles in the same time). Dobler, who was leading Littlewood by two miles, accomplished his century in 14h.52m.48s whilst the Sheffield man gained his in 15h.19m.30s. Dobler's trainer, O'Leary, was very pleased with his man's performance stating that John had a great reputation for courage, and that if he had only one leg left, he would still walk. His main fear though was Dobler's notorious requirement for sleep.

Pegram and Howard continued plodding on, and it was said of the former that he had no intention of covering 100 miles in the first day anyway.

King of the Peds

At 18:15, and in front of an estimated audience of 5,000, Rowell had hit the 120-mile mark. At that stage of the race, he was 6½ miles in front of Dobler who went on to enjoy an eight minute break shortly after 7 p.m. Rowell, wanting some of the same, followed him off the track for a welcome break of 14 minutes. With Pegram having left the track just after eight o'clock and now taking it easy in his hut, Littlewood also left the race for 43 minutes making his return at 21:30 to plug on gamely thereafter until he had completed just over 124 miles for his first day's graft. He then went to bed. Dobler went back to his hut at 23:13 having mustered a very commendable 138, and 14 minutes later, and having accomplished a brand new world record of 146 miles and 250 yards in 22h.27m, Rowell drew the curtains on his performance. Goodnight!

The first day's scores:

TIME	11:40	13:00	15:00	16:00	17:00	20:00	21:00	23:00
Rowell	77.1	87.5	100	106.3	112.4	128.3	137	142.5
Littlewood	73.2	82.2	93	98	104.4	117.4	120	124.1
Dobler	72.1	82.1	94	100.2	106.1	122.2	130	137
Brown	69.3	73.5	Ret					
Howard	62.4	69.5	74	82.2	86.5	98.5	105	105
Pegram	58.1	63.5	71	74.5	78.1	83	83	85

Whilst the "big match" was in progress in London, there was another six-day go-as-you-please contest entertaining the crowds 270 miles away up in Newcastle-Upon-Tyne. This one was being promoted by Mr. L. Barlow, and the venue was the Circus Royal, Percy Street. The track was 34 laps to the mile, and the prizes on offer were £50 for the winner, £20 for the second, £10 for the third, and £5 for fourth place. An extra £20 was promised to any man who could make 553 miles or £10 for traversing 500. The competition attracted the likes of Carless, Cartwright, Corbett, Day, Noremac, Ferguson, McCarty, Robson and Vandepeer. The two races gave the punters a chance to have a "double" on both outcomes. Day and Noremac would have been the favourites for the match "up North," so when midnight scores for the first day were later received in the capital, they showed the following: Vandepeer, 102.22; Carless 102: Cartwright and Corbett, 100: Many backing both the favourites to win would by then have been getting a little nervous.

The resting times for the athletes during the night were: **Rowell, 2h.25m; Dobler, 2h.13m; Littlewood, 3h.51m; Howard, 2h.32m:**

Dobler was the first of the peds back on the track at 01:26. He was followed by Rowell at 01:53, and with both men moving along well, they began to open up quite a substantial margin between themselves and the rest who were still headed by the frequently resting Littlewood.

All the remaining men left in the competition were reported to be suffering greatly in the early morning from the intense cold, in particular Pegram who was laid up with rheumatism in his thighs. He was also said to be suffering from a cold. The American would only last another five or so miles before retiring permanently from the event shortly after 6 a.m. on a final score of 88 miles. The temperature was so low in the building that the competitors had to put on further layers of clothing, in an attempt to keep the freezing conditions at bay. Littlewood, who was walking at this stage, was steadily being reeled in by Howard, who was continuing with his now familiar "jog-trot."

At 12:43, the leader of the pack completed his 200th mile in a time of 35h.43m.10s from the start. This achievement had bettered the previous record set in February of the same year by Brown by 5 hours. When he had made it, he was 9 miles and 3 laps in front of Dobler and 36.1 in front of Littlewood, who, later at 1 p.m., was going along better than he had done for a while.

Rowell's *"persevering antagonist,"* Dobler, also completed his 2nd century at 14:28. The amazing thing about this was that he had also beaten Brown's record by three hours. Littlewood again left the track at 15:35 and returned seven minutes later during which time Howard had recouped several laps on the Sheffielder. When George sauntered off again at 16:07, Harry had reduced the gap between them both from an original deficit of 17 miles to just 6½ by teatime (17:00).

The two leaders were now running and walking alternately. Both moved well; out of the two, the young American seemed more at ease. His trainer, O' Leary, had bet £100 at odds of 5/1 that his protégé would cover 600 miles in the allocated time.

Just after 19:00, Dobler had made 220; five minutes later Rowell had amassed a score of 230 miles for himself. When Littlewood returned at 19:44 he appeared to be shaking, and when he started to propel himself forward, appeared quite stiff. The bad news for him was that Howard was just half a mile behind and closing in rapidly. The writing was definitely on the wall for George; soon after 20:00, Harry overtook him as the suffering Sheffield youth ventured yet again to his quarters, due to his feet being in such bad shape.

Whilst the two leaders settled down to an evening of walking, with Rowell making the occasional spurt to increase his advantage, it was obvious that Littlewood didn't appear too happy about having being demoted to fourth place. To redress matters, and with the help of some fast heel-and-toe walking, which he used impressively to outpace the running Howard, he pluckily plodded on until he retook the third position he yearned for at 21:30. The thousands in the supportive crowd had egged him on till he got there, and duly cheered him when he did. The gutsy northerner was the first of the quartet to head for bed at 23:31 followed by Dobler five minutes later. Rowell followed soon after and Howard ended his day's work at 23:49 after getting on the same terms as Littlewood on a score of 200 miles.

A record of some of the scores on that second day:

TIME	02:00	04:00	10:00	13:00	15:00	17:00	20:00	23:00	00:00
Rowell	146.1	156.5	187	201.5	210	219.5	232.6	245.5	248.3
Dobler	140.3	149.4	177.1	192.1	201	210.4	222.5	235.3	238
Littlewood	124.1	130	152.3	165.1	172	177.5	184.1	196.3	200
Howard	110	116.4	136.2	153.1	160	171	183.6	196.4	200
Pegram	85	86	88	88	Ret				

The midnight score from Newcastle was: Carless, 182.10; Corbett, 172.13; Day; 163.13; Cartwright, 155.14:

At one o'clock in the morning, the path was devoid of action until the *"Sheffield Flyer"* re-emerged from his house at 01:33 having rested for 2h.3m, the break apparently having done him the world of good. Dobler came back at 02:37 and started to jog-trot. Whilst Rowell slumbered till 03:31, his nearest rival had reduced the margin between them. Howard awoke and resumed his efforts at 03:49 by which time Littlewood had opened up a considerable gap between the pair. Both he and Rowell went best thereafter and constantly lapped the other two. At 04:35, Littlewood went to his room for an hour and a half, and while he dreamt of glory, Howard was unable to make any impression on him due to his slow progress. When Littlewood returned, he put on a grand show of heel-and-toe walking for the newly arrived spectators, who shouted their approval.

At 09:52, Rowell's score sheet showed 280 miles. At the time he was a dozen miles ahead of Dobler, and although Charlie took a 23-minute break during which time he lost two of those miles, he returned full of running in order to retrieve the lost distance. Whilst he went much faster than Dobler, Howard lost more ground to Littlewood who persevered with the cause.

All plodded on monotonously until the arrival of the band which served to inject some pace into the race, and as always, the man who responded best to the music was Johnny Dobler. At 14:02, and with Littlewood having conquered 250 miles, he took a well deserved 35-minute break having done some excellent work in the morning. Rowell graciously accepted the round of applause given to him after completing his 300th mile in a time of 64h.10m.55s, it beating all previous performances by a staggering 25 miles!

Dobler was now 13 miles behind the leader, and was finding the going tough. He followed the sturdy Sheffielder around at a walking pace, and by 5 o'clock it appeared his legs were giving him trouble. The other "American," Howard, wasn't fairing much better either and was clearly struggling. The two Englishmen though both went well, Rowell with a trot and Littlewood bounding on with long telling strides. At 17:10, Dobler also made his 300th mile, and at that stage was 10 miles ahead of the old record. Soon after however, he went very lame and had to take a series of rests, whereupon Rowell was able to increase his lead by 19 miles.

After having scored 240 miles and a lap, the American *"second string,"* Howard, finally threw in the towel at 18:19 and made his exit from the race having broken down completely, the back tendon of his right leg being the culprit. His departure left just the one "visitor" in the race. The two "home" players had really been piling on the pressure on Dobler, Rowell gaining 5 miles on him and Littlewood knocking 5.6 miles off the distance between them. *"During his absence however, *Dobler's attendants had been most assiduous in their efforts, and the gallant young American on continuing his work was most enthusiastically greeted by the public. He went very slowly at first, but afterwards he gamely stuck to the track, though still going lamely. As the evening wore on, the walking area was surrounded by a ring of spectators standing three and four deep, amounting to several thousands."* Urged on by them, Dobler did a little better just before 20:00 but at the stroke of that hour he was still 19½ miles down on Rowell. His performance however, didn't stop O'Leary from betting £10 at odds of 3/1 that his man would beat Littlewood. O'Leary must have been worried that he would lose the wager as ten o'clock approached, when his star really began to struggle despite his urgings. After enduring a few more minutes John sought the comfort of his hut clearly in much distress at 22:09.

*Apart from O'Leary, Dobler was being cared for by Charles Davies, J. Smith (after Tom Davies's pair Pegram and Howard had retired), and George Guyon.

George Littlewood meanwhile was going very, very well. Indeed, it was at this time that a few in the crowd were thinking maybe, just maybe, the gritty lad from "up norf'" might just make it into second place? He went to his iron dwelling at 22:51, leaving the leader alone on the course, till he too decided to rest his weary legs at 23:07, having made five laps short of 340 miles.

Those third day's scores:

TIME	01:00	13:00	17:00	19:00	23:00
Rowell	248.3	293.4	313.3	321.1	339.2
Dobler	238	281	298.5	305.6	315.3
Littlewood	200	243.5	259.2	268.1	286
Howard	200	231.4	239.6	240.1	Ret

The interest in *"Charley"* Rowell's progress was so intense back home in Chesterton, that every night someone from the village would get the last train from London to Cambridge *"arriving well after the village pub is closed"* and make his way to a barn nearby, where, every night, a group of people were waiting to hear the latest news about the situation on the track. The villagers would have been well pleased that night with their lad's performance during the day.

The news from Newcastle wasn't very good for favourite backers. George Noremac had retired from the race at 9 o'clock on Wednesday morning with 164 miles and 16 laps, and he had been followed later by Day who had covered a distance of 208.3. The midnight scores from Percy Street therefore were: Carless, 272; Corbett, 250; Cartwright, 240; Barrow, 215.8:

The path was empty at midnight on Wednesday. Dobler later occupied it after an absence of 2h.51m.15s at 01:02, and proceeded to walk very stiffly due to a swollen knee. Littlewood would later join him at 01:41 after a rest period of 2h.49m.32s which put him in good heart. He then resumed his efforts to reduce the margin between him and the struggling American. Rowell, having gone to bed at 23:09, reappeared having rested 3h.10m.13s. The ex-boatman appeared a little stiff as well, so he took himself off for another break at 03:12 which amounted to 2h.16m.32s.

Whilst the champion slept, Littlewood proceeded to make fantastic amounts of ground on the struggling Dobler who was now forced to take frequent breaks. Having covered 300 miles at 05:05, he went on to make serious inroads into the second man's score during the morning. The Yorkshireman was reported to be changing direction every few laps, and, *"the breaking down of Dobler and Howard is attributed to not reversing direction whereby both right legs in both cases have given way."*

At 10 a.m. the score stood at: **Rowell, 361; Dobler, 335; Littlewood, 319:**

At 11:48, Littlewood, who at that stage had made 325 miles, was joined on the track by Rowell after which, for mile after glorious mile, the privileged few in the building were treat to the spectacle of the two Englishmen running constantly on the fourth day of a six-day *"go-as you-pleaser."* Indeed, during this time, Littlewood ran his 335th mile in 6m.49s (this had been the fastest mile by 3 minutes since the start), with Rowell simultaneously making a comparable effort in his then 376th. *"Between 11 and 1 p.m. the third man, who seemed endowed with a new lease of strength, dashed along at a rare pace."* At 13:20, and shortly after the band started to play, Littlewood sprinted away from the champion, who, although chasing after him, couldn't keep up with his fellow countryman's pace. To put what was happening on the track in perspective, Dobler, who was dragging his right leg behind him, took a full 36 minutes to cover a distance of one and a half miles!

Clearly in distress, Dobler took time out in his hut at 13:30. Sixty six minutes later, Littlewood took a 65-minute break and on his return at 15:42, it took him just 10 minutes to reach the then resting second mans score. Then at 15:54, on the 5th lap of his 342nd mile, and as the crowd screamed their approval, George moved himself effortlessly into second place. As all this was happening, Daniel O'Leary was keeping his fingers crossed as he waited for his protégé's swollen leg to dissipate so that he could bring him back on and hopefully reclaim his former position.

There were whispers around the building that Littlewood might eventually beat Rowell, as he was going well, and at that time was a clear match for the champion.

Dobler emerged from his rest at 17:49 and looked in poor shape. Littlewood meanwhile, was about to make his 350th mile at 18:02. He was going quite well but appeared to be suffering from a bad cold and as a consequence, *"wore a respirator."* Rowell made his 4th century at 19:13, and although apparently lame, stuck well to his task. Dobler on the other hand had made an amazing recovery and moved well considering his predicament, but once again vacated the track at 20:20. After being besieged with flowers along with Rowell, Littlewood left the track at 20:53 to nurse his *"violent"* cold. That left just Rowell on the track. He was subsequently joined by Dobler to entertain the large company of spectators.

The score at midnight: **Rowell, 416; Littlewood, 360.3; Dobler, 360.2:**

George Littlewood returned to the track at 00:23 after being absent from it for 3h.30m.50s. Dobler meanwhile had only rested 1h.22m.17s, and on his reappearance went very slowly. His intention of course was to make the necessary 450 miles to enable him to get some money from the gate receipts. As he struggled, Rowell was still asleep. The race leader returned at 03:42 having rested since 23:15 the previous night. On his reappearance he looked quite fresh and he and his fellow Brit went to work covering about 4 mph. At 07:16, after completing his 430th mile, and after two short breaks, Rowell nipped out for a Turkish bath. On his return at 09:03, it was obvious his dip had put him in fine fettle, with the lameness he had been suffering with on the previous day having seemingly disappeared.

At 10:00, the scores of the remaining pedestrians were: **Rowell, 432; Littlewood, 387; Dobler, 379:** Dobler was much better by this time and going fairly well, as were the others. On account of the intense cold and fog that was prevalent, Littlewood continued to wear that respirator!

The news coming from Newcastle about the fourth day's racing was quite intriguing. Carless's lead of 22 miles at midnight had gradually been whittled away by some enterprising running by the Scot, who got within a couple of miles of him by 05:00. However, the effort had taken its toll on Corbett, and from thereon Carless increased the gap again going on to register his 300 miles in a time of 83h.17m.23s from the start. Drama was to follow when the leader was carried out of the building at 22:02 suffering from exhaustion, when in the lead by 14 miles.

At the eleventh hour on the fifth day, the scoreboard showed: **Rowell, 436.2; Littlewood, 390.3; Dobler, 381:** At 12:00, the score was: **Rowell, 442; Littlewood, 394; Dobler, 381:**

When Dobler emerged from his iron hut where he had spent the last 1h.25m at 12:05, he was wrapped up in a heavy great coat and wearing gloves. It seemed to all watching that this strange attire seemed to hinder his poor progress even more. The Agricultural Hall was described as an unfit place to hold such an event with the temperature varying between 40 and 50 degrees Fahrenheit. The others too obviously felt the cold, and Rowell wore a cardigan jacket and Littlewood, an overcoat.

Littlewood ran at the end of his 399th mile. He then ran in snatches until he completed his 400th at 13:14. He then went to his house, followed by Rowell at 13:40 after he had completed his 450th mile. Of the race leader, the *Sporting Life* reporter covering the match observed: **His tongue was clean, his eye bright, and his feet without a mark of a rub or corn, and there was not a trace of a blister. Despite all the miles traversed at a fast pace, and in heavy clothing, Rowell had not been chafed, and as for waste of tissue, he had gone the other way.** Both men had left the ellipse for 50 minutes or so. On resuming business again Littlewood pleased the crowd with some fast walking, but all attempts to entice Rowell to join him failed; the leader, having none of it, preferring to indulge in his own method of conveyance instead.

The 3 p.m. scores (110th hour): **Rowell, 458.1; Littlewood, 404; Dobler, 391:**

Dobler made his 400th mile at 18:50, and in spite of his lameness, he kept to his work resolutely. He now had to make 50 miles at a rate of 18½ minutes per mile to entitle him to a share of the receipts. The crowds continued to flock in; despite little going on within the confines of the track, people still showed a lot of interest in the proceedings. They were joined by the Marquis of Queensbury, Lord Marcus Beresford and General Goodlake V. C.

Littlewood and Rowell increased the pace as the close of the day approached and their spurting was thoroughly appreciated by the crowd. The "Tyke," now going really well, brought much excitement into the arena when he made six miles between 8 and 9 o'clock. Rowell also caught applause when he made 480 miles just after 21:00.

The Sheffielder vacated the track at 22:52 and Dobler left two minutes later. The champion however, kept going with the purpose of beating Frank Hart's five-day performance in New York that same year. At 23:54, he too retired, having passed Hart's score by a few laps, thus securing the fastest time on record.

At 01:00, the three remaining competitors had recorded the following distances: **Rowell, 492.1; Littlewood, 426.1; Dobler, 410.3:**

In the Newcastle race, news had emerged that Carless had been 2 miles and 32 laps in front of Corbett when he re-entered the race at 01:17. From thereon the Londoner increased that lead, and when the scores were announced at midday, they showed that he led the race on 377.22 with Corbett having made 368.19. Cartwright was 34 miles back in third spot and Barrow 18 miles away in fourth. The leader later went on to make 400 miles in 116 hours, which was considered an *"excellent performance."*

The gallant young Chicagoan was the first to appear at 02:21 after an absence of 3h.27m. He walked stiffly at first, but afterwards showed great improvement to go better than he had done since his knee failed him on the previous Wednesday evening. Littlewood, who was away for 5h.46m, reappeared at 04:38. He also moved along impressively, putting in several fast miles. Rowell's absence amounted to 5h.29m, the champion coming back into the ring at 05:24. He went in *"capital form"* and completed 500 miles at 07:13 (126h.13m), which was 20 minutes behind the fastest time ever made. At this juncture, he retired to take another Turkish bath and was away 2h.35m.

At 11:30, the positions and distances in the "big match" stood as follows: **Rowell, 507.2; Littlewood, 443.1; Dobler, 433.5:** Rowell continued running at a good clip in the hope of catching the record again, his second long rest that morning making his objective somewhat doubtful. To achieve his goal he would have had to run nearly 6 mph which was an unprecedented performance for the last day of such a contest. Littlewood left the path at 11:45 and returned about 12:00, evidently not meaning to exert himself much further. Rowell was still going at good rate of knots when he completed 520 miles at 13:50. Just afterwards, Littlewood finished 450 miles at 13:52, thus earning the right to participate in the division of the gate receipts. Although this was considerably behind record time, it was altogether deemed a splendid performance considering his youth. He left the track soon after for his lunch.

Dobler limped round until 14:05 and then left the hall, his friends suggesting it advisable to let him have a Turkish bath as well. Littlewood continued to be absent until 15:35. Having been away for 1h.1m, he then returned, and as he walked round enveloped in a top-coat and continuing to wear his respirator, the public cheered him on his way. Dobler returned after 1h.10m looking better for his bath and recommenced his quest to secure the gate money. By 4 o'clock Rowell had scored 530.6 which was the best distance ever made in the time. However, he still required to make 35 miles to beat Hart's world record. Littlewood later returned from over an hour's break at 17:36 adorned in a *"clean white costume which showed his natty figure of to advantage."*

This interesting article entitled **Modern Pedestrianism** appeared in the *Ohio Democrat* on the 11th of November 1880 a few days after the finish of the contest: **The contest now in progress in London between six-day pedestrians, says the New York Sun, promises to add another surprise to the list of records, which has risen higher and higher, with rapid steps, during the past six years. First Weston scored 431 miles; then O'Leary raised the figures in quick, successive marches to 501, 519, and 520 miles; next little wiry Corkey popped up to 521, followed by his light-legged countryman, Blower Brown, who raised the peg to 542. Weston then plumed himself with eagle wings, and swooped the record up to 550 on English soil. Blower Brown, not to be outdone, inflated his balloon and soared to 553 miles. This was believed to be the top notch of pedestrian flight until young Frank Hart, in the great race for the O'Leary belt last April, during which seven men left the 500-mile post far behind them, climbed up to the 565th peg. It is quite possible that Rowell will surpass Hart's extraordinary performance. The tough little Englishman's first spurt of fifty miles in six hours and a half would have wrecked ninety-nine out of one hundred amateur or professional pedestrians. His 300 miles in sixty-two hours seven minutes, and his 340 miles inside of three days, throw all former efforts into the shade. If Rowell holds out until Saturday night he may verify the report current on his first arrival in this city that before starting for America he had placed 600 miles behind his flying feet, and that this induced Sir John Astley to back him heavily and send him to America.**

Rowell's mind was set. His aim was to beat the old record, and in the next 3h.15m made 21 miles before taking but the shortest of rests. By 21:38, he was on a score of 560 miles, and by 22:29, he had equalled Hart's record. At the close of the match, and after some game running by the champion who frequently enjoyed the applause of the estimated 10,000 crowd, he succeeded in beating the record distance by a mile at 22:39:08. After completing another 165 yards, he turned at the entrance and left the building aided by the police who accompanied him to his apartment in Barford Street.

"The result proved that Charles Rowell is undoubtedly at present the champion of this branch of pedestrianism, as he not only succeeded in winning very easily indeed, but also proved that he would have "smothered" the best on record if he wanted."

Henry Carless won the Newcastle match and £60 with an impressive 500 miles in the time allowed. Corbett who was 43 miles behind won £20 and Barrow took third prize of £10 coming home 105 miles behind the Londoner.

The Final Score!

© The British Library. All Rights reserved. The Penny Illustrated.   (Illustration no: 77)

TIME OFF

ROWELL
Time Off

	Miles	H	M	S	Rests
Mon	146	0	51	34	8
Tue	102	2	59	31	7
Wed	91	4	44	51	4
Thu	76	7	10	40	5
Fri	76	7	8	46	7
Sat	74	8	43	6	7
	566	31	38	28	38

LITTLEWOOD
Time Off

	Miles	H	M	S	Rests
Mon	124	3	6	52	13
Tue	75	6	56	28	10
Wed	86	5	28	29	14
Thu	74	8	12	51	17
Fri	66	8	52	38	25
Sat	43	13	14	38	8
	470	45	51	56	87

DOBLER
Time Off

	Miles	H	M	S	Rests
Mon	138	1	1	38	5
Tue	100	2	11	58	6
Wed	77	6	26	48	13
Thu	45	8	5	13	21
Fri	50	7	39	16	9
Sat	40	8	37	53	9
	450	34	2	46	63

BALANCE SHEET

	RECEIPTS	£	s	d		EXPENSES	£	s	d
By Gate	Monday	382	0	0	To	Hire of Hall, Track, Gas, Tents, Police, &c.	503	13	2
	Tuesday	205	14	0	"	Gatekeepers, Money-takers, and Staff	67	18	8
	Wednesday	200	8	0	"	Judges, Scorers, and Timekeepers	66	16	8
	Thursday	186	19	9	"	Bands	46	0	0
	Friday	188	8	0	"	Printing and Advertising	102	8	0
	Saturday	210	6	0	"	Posting & Distributing Window Bills, Misc	35	2	6
By Read	Programmes	15	15	0	"				
					"		£821	19	4
						Balance for distribution amongst men	517	11	5
		£1,389	10	9			£1,389	10	9

DISTRIBUTION OF GATE RECEIPTS

	£	s	d
Rowell (winner) - one-half	£258	10	0
Littlewood (second) - 30 per cent	155	2	0
Dobler (third) - 20 per cent	103	8	0
	£517	0	0
The winners share, (including the stakes, £600)	£858	10	0

On returning to the USA on board the steamship *Nevada* on the 29th of November, the five passengers who had been involved in the race, O'Leary, Davies, Dobler, Guyon and Pegram, told awaiting reporters of the conditions they had encountered during the race. The Agricultural Hall was described as being in *"miserable condition – damp, badly ventilated, and permeated with all pervading fog which the men found troublesome."* Edward Hanlan the famous oarsman of the time who had visited the Americans during the race had said of it whilst he was there, "They fought dogs in Canada in a better place than that." John Dobler told reporters, "Why, the old place was so damp and wet, that I had to walk one day with my overcoat on. The fog was thick enough to cut with a knife."

CHAPTER 28

What Else Happened in 1880

A *"fair heel-and-toe"* walking contest which attracted 23 starters, took place over six evenings between the hours of 5 p.m. and 11 p.m. at the Lambeth Baths in London from Monday, the 9th till Saturday, the 14th of February 1880. The match, under the management of Messrs. Beckwith and Taylor, was won by Jack Hibberd of Bethnall Green, who took the first prize of £25, having scored 201 miles and 19 laps in the allowed time. G. Say of Haggerston won the runner-up prize of £10 with a record of 196 miles, and J. Woolfe of Chichester earned the £5 third prize having achieved a tally of 193. McCarty of Leeds with 185.18 finished fourth. A. Booker and Harry Carless of Millwall both made 180, with Robson of Liverpool scoring 177.20.

Whilst the above race was taking place in London, a similar six-day competition took place at Cooke's Royal Circus a few hundred miles away over the border in Aberdeen. George Parry of Manchester earned £30 by winning this one with a score of 355.23.

Out of the thirty men that started the 70-hour walking match at the Music Hall in Boston, Massachusetts, between the 16th and 21st of February 1880, only seven finished. The winner was Peter Panchot with 345 miles. Jimmy Albert came in second with 330, Clow, third with 326, McEvoy fourth with 321, Dufrane, fifth with 318, Campana, sixth with 300, and Barrett seventh with 304. During the early part of the match, Albert had denied charges that he had been abusive in language towards a Mr. Hanson, who he allegedly struck with a cane.

Between Monday, the 23rd and Saturday, the 28th of February, at Newsome's Circus in Glasgow, George Noremac won £50 in a 12 hours per day, six days per week "pedestrian competition" when he made 357 miles. McKellan who had finished 3rd in the recent Aberdeen race was second with 348. Smith of Paisley followed him home on 335, and J. S. Robson of Liverpool took fourth prize with 309.

The Scottish pedestrian scene was really busy at the time, and the next six-day go-as-you-please race in that country started at Perth on the 8th of March, again, and most probably in a circus ring. Out of the 12 starters, G. D. Noremac, the victor in Glasgow, beat W. Clarkson of Hull, P. Marshall of Dundee, and J. S. Robson of Liverpool, the final scores being 344.34, 324.37, 319.5 and 314.33 respectively.

Whilst they were running round in small circles in Perth, the much touted O'Leary v Weston *"walking match"* for a stake of $5,000 a side, was being competed for on the Pacific coast at the Pavilion in San Francisco. The match began at 01:00 on Monday, March the 8th 1880, and it was contested according to the Astley rules. Baldwin, the *"millionaire turfman"* had backed Weston, who had been in training for three months for the race, whilst O'Leary had put up the money himself. Weston had always been insistent that the match should take place in England or Ireland, whereas O'Leary preferred the USA. In the end Weston agreed on San Francisco, providing the duel took place in the second week of March.

There was a small attendance at the start, but during the next report available on the 10th, the crowd had increased only a little in size due to the *"cold and boisterous weather."* Weston was said to be troubled with colic and had to stop frequently, whilst O'Leary, the favourite, was said to walk steadily. The 01:00 score was 187 to 175 in O'Leary's favour and later in the morning, the leader increased his lead further when the score of 214 to 199 was announced at 09:00. As the day progressed however, Weston began to make inroads into his adversary's lead, and in front of a *"substantial"* audience, reduced the deficit to ten miles by 21:00 when the score read 253 to 243.

On the 11th at 01:00, Weston had managed to reduce that deficit even further, and by that time the distance between the pair was just 3 miles. As the day progressed, O'Leary ran, with Weston who looked the fresher, content to alter his method of travelling along. The score at 21:00 with both men reported to be *"free from soreness of feet or joints,"* and in front of a large audience, was 344 to 335.

Since 3 a.m. on the morning of Friday the 12th, Weston had been off the track about three hours against O'Leary's two, and reports suggested that O'Leary had not ran at all during the day. As the day wore on there was mounting confidence that neither man would make 550 miles, and during the evening due to the increasing closeness of the contest, the 3,000 people present watched the race with interest and enthusiasm.

The score at 7 p.m. was O'Leary, the 7/10 favourite, 420, Weston, 411.

On the last day at 02:00, and with O'Leary on a score of 437, the Irishman increased the gap between himself and his old rival to 12 miles. From thereon he proceeded to stamp his authority on the match by increasing the distance to 18 miles by 09:00, and 24 miles by 18:00, by which time he had accomplished 500 miles. In front of a packed pavilion, the race leader kept on gamely to clinch a satisfying victory, with the final result being 516 to 490 when the contest came to an end at 23:00 on Saturday night.

Jimmy Albert was awarded $300 and a gold watch for winning a 75-hour go-as-you-please match (12 ½ hours per day) which took place at the Opera House in Brockton, Massachusetts, between Monday, the 22nd and Saturday, the 27th of March. The scores at the end were: **Albert, 435; Hughes, 423.16 ($200); Clow, 411.6 ($100); Hourihan, 385.14 ($75); Geldert, 361.4 ($50):** The *Boston Globe* in its report on the match stated: **The track not having been measured by a professional the above records will not stand as it is undoubtedly short.** Campana, Colston and Mignault were also in the race.

George Noremac scored an incredible hat-trick of wins between the 29th of March and the 3rd of April in the Show Hall at the Royal Gymnasium in Edinburgh, when he won his third six-day go-as-you-please in 5 weeks on a score of 384 miles. The performance was even more remarkable in that he also broke the then present day 12 hours a day record made by Sam Day at Wolverhampton having made 360 miles in the allocated time. The track that the men competed on was 125 yards and 2 feet and 6 inches in circumference, its two straights being 56 yards in length, meaning that the competitors covered 1 yard and 2 feet extra for every "mile" made. Interestingly, this match was also competed for at the same time that George Littlewood beat Day's record in Leeds by 14 miles. That however, was on a dizzying track of 38 laps to the mile.

Noremac's last mile, which was made on the run, was timed at 6m.30s, brought him victory (£40) over *David Ferguson of Pollockshaws who made 376.5 (£15). Peter McKellan came third with 309.12 (£7), and J. Dalziel of Dalkeith grabbed fourth place with 236.1 (£4), his last mile being accomplished in less than six minutes. At one stage before the finish, he had trailed Ferguson by nearly four miles.

*Ferguson, by trade a quarryman, was born at Barrhead, Paisley, and at the time of the race was 40 years old. He stood 5 ft.5 ½ inches tall and weighed 10st.2lb.

The *Sporting Life* informed its readers about Noremac's racing career up to that point: **Noremac was born at Edinburgh, May 18, 1854 - height, 5ft.3½in; weight, 8st.10lb, being 5lb heavier than when he won at Perth. By trade a lithographer. His principal performances are as follows: - Won a weeks competition of four hours a day at the Aberdeen Recreation Grounds, July, 1879 (prize £20); won a two days' competition, (twelve hours a day),**

Drill Hall, Perth, December 30 and 31, 1879 (prize £8); (See above for next two wins): In addition to the above, he won first prize (£20) in a mile handicap at Strathbungo; won a £5 mile handicap at Powderhall Grounds, Edinburgh; won a £7 mile handicap at Royal Gymnasium, Edinburgh; received £3 for running second in a two miles handicap at Powderhall Grounds; received £2 for running second in a four miles handicap at Shawfield Grounds, Glasgow; beat Watson of Roswell, in a ten mile match, conceding 30 secs. start for £20; received £2 for running second in a two miles race at the Vale of Clyde Grounds, Glasgow; beaten by P. Corbett, 10 miles, for £20 at Shawfield Grounds, Glasgow; ten miles, for £20 at Shawfield Grounds, Glasgow; received £1 forfeit from P. Corbett, they being matched to run 10 miles.

SAN FRANCISCO: April 10th. It was reported that Weston's walk "against time" had attracted scarcely any attention. He was said to have been troubled with vertigo during the feat, which accounted for his poor performance. On the last day of his effort at 13:00 he had covered only 334 miles, and by the finish, his final score was 365 miles.

A twelve hours a day, 72-hour *"foot race,"* which started on Monday, the 12th of April at the Infantry Hall, Providence, Rhode Island, ended at 11 o'clock on Saturday night, April 17th 1880. John Sullivan of Saratoga with 385 miles and 2 laps won $500 and a gold and diamond medallion. He beat George Guyon of Chicago who made 378 miles and collected $200. Robert Vint of Brooklyn took $100 for scoring 370 miles and John Colston of Hoboken, Sweden, who made 365 miles, collected $50. Daniel Herty of Revere, Massachusetts, who came in fourth, took $25 plus an extra $25 for making the best record on the last day of 66 miles.

In the 75-hour go-as-you-please contest at Lowell, Massachusetts, which finished on Saturday, the 24th of April, O'Toole won the first prize of $300 and a watch when he made 380.7, beating Clow, Colston, Fitzgerald and half a dozen others. The winner created excitement by running several laps carrying the American and Irish flags.

Before the O'Leary six-day, 72-hour, 12 hours a day, go-as-you-please contest, commenced at the Pearl Street Rink, Buffalo on Monday, the 26th of April, the race promoter was interviewed by a reporter. This is what he had to say:

O'Leary: "The men will only walk twelve hours a day, and each day will be nearly equivalent to a new race. They will go on the track at eleven o'clock in the forenoon, and, leaving it at eleven o'clock at night, will be able to renew their work feeling rested and vigorous. They can score just a many miles as they may be able to cover during those twelve hours, and the people of Buffalo may confidently expect some really exciting sport. Some of the best men in the country will enter the race, for it is open to all who wish to compete for the prizes, no matter what their record may be. It is not unlikely that some of the contestants will be men of whom very little has been known, and that they will distinguish themselves. This innovation of walking only twelve hours a day is original with myself, and was first tried in Providence. It proved a success, and has been in public favour ever since. It was the means of originally bringing out Hart, Ennis, Harriman, Rowell, Dobler, Merritt and Murphy. I expect that Edward Walker and Panchot will be among the entries here. During the week Hart, Dobler and myself will give exhibitions, both afternoon and evening."

Reporter: How long do you suppose this walking mania will last?"

O'Leary: "Three or four years. There are now two champion belts in the field, - that offered by Sir John Astley of England, which Rowell holds, and the one given by me which Frank Hart won in New York last week. There is one other O'Leary belt for the score in a seventy-five-hour heel-and-toe walk, which George Guyon holds. Just so long as they are open to contest they will be challenged, and the pedestrian fever will be manifested. New men will be constantly springing up."

Reporter: "Who is the best man now before the public?"

O'Leary: "Well, sir, that is a difficult question to answer. Hart, of course, has the best record now of any man in the world, but he could have made it still better by fifteen miles had he so desired. Dobler is a young man of whom I have great expectations, and had he not met with an accident I am not so certain that he would not to-day be in possession of the champion belt of America. It was his first practical experience in a walk of the kind, and in the next big walk you may be certain that six hundred miles will be made. You will see by the *Clipper* of this week that I have so much confidence in these two men that I call them the American team, and propose to match them against the two best pedestrians that England can produce for any sum that may be agreed upon, from $10,000 a side upward, the duration of the contest to be 142 consecutive hours and to take place in New York three months-from, the date of signing articles of agreement. This challenge was issued on the 12th Inst., and is to remain open for two months. The two best men that England has now are "Blower" Brown and Rowell. The former has the best record, but the latter is the most reliable. He is long headed, sensible and takes good care of himself."

Reporter: "What has been the effect of Hart's achievement?"

O'Leary: "What might naturally be expected. The coloured, boys are all crazy to walk, and darky pedestrians will probably soon be almost as numerous as blackberries in summer. You may look for several in the Buffalo race, among whom will be one from Chicago, another from Corry, Pennsylvania, and possibly Pegram, the only coloured man besides Hart that has gained any prominence as a pedestrian. He is the homeliest negro you ever saw. One great difficulty has been encountered in handling this class of men, and that is their desire for sleep. It gives the white man a decided advantage. The moment that night comes on a terrible drowsiness is experienced that they can not shake off without making a very great effort. With all his great score Hart had to have his sleep, no matter how close the race might be."

Reporter: "Are there not certain elements which will depreciate the popularity of pedestrian contestants?"

O'Leary: "There is just one. If the gambling fraternity have much to do with pedestrianism it will kill it. They have been mixed up in it slightly, in New York, already. Walking is a fine exercise, and a manly sport, and just so long as pedestrians do justice to the public it will be as much thought of as it is now, so far as these contests are concerned. Otherwise it will sink into contempt and ridicule, and there, will be no interest in it. The doctors, I know, are somewhat against these long walks and say they will damage a man's constitution, shorten his life, and all that sort of thing. But I don't agree with them. There is Weston, who has probably walked more miles than any other pedestrian living, but be is in perfectly good health, and shows no signs of decay. Jim Smith of New York, the best trainer I know of is fifty years old and has been racing ever since he was twenty. Though having myself walked a great many mile, I am in as good condition physically and feel just as rugged, if not more so, than if I had never tested my powers of endurance. A fifty mile walk is far more injurious than the matches which last a week, because the speed has to be so great; if you want to win. In a long walk, it is steady plodding, and the man who is constant and can stay on the track the longest is bound to succeed. There are two fortunes to be gained by pedestrians between this time and next December, in the contests for the Astley and O'Leary champion belts, to say nothing of the challenge for the American team, if the Astley Belt be contended for, however, it will have to be brought to this country voluntarily, and that probably will be done. I would not encourage any man to go after it, and it is not likely that any one will. There is no money in the venture, for in England the people do not turn out as they do in America. I am looking for an unknown man to compete for that belt, and to add to my American team, I have some idea that I may be able to find him among the men who enter for the walk here. If a man of promise should turn up I'll take good care of him. I expect one hundred miles will yet be walked in seventeen hours and walked and run in fifteen hours."

Five thousand people were present during the first day to watch **Bluett, Byrne, Campana, Faber, Fitzgerald, Guyon, Harding, Herty, Hooker, Kraft, Panchot, Roller, Robinson, Smith** and **Walker** race against each other. At the end of it, Faber had beaten the best twelve hours record by three miles with a score of 78 miles and 4 laps. The rest of the scores were: **Herty, 73; Panchot, 71.4; Fitzgerald, 71.1; Walker, 70.3; Guyon, 67.5; Bluett; 63.6, Robinson, 61; Campana, 59; Hooker, 51 - withdrew; Smith, 46.9 - withdrew; Harding, 46; Byrne, 42.8 - withdrew; Roller, 17.4 - withdrew; Kraft, 15.4 - withdrew:**

King of the Peds

The score at the end of the second day was: **Faber, 150; Herty, 139; Panchot, 136; Fitzgerald, 132; Walker, 131; Guyon, 121; Campana, 117; Bluett, 116; Robinson, 109:** Faber, Herty and Panchot had all beaten the previous best time by 14 miles.

On Wednesday, the 28th, George Guyon ran 50 miles in 7h.56m.45s which was the fastest time on record in the world for the third day in such a contest. He later went on to make an unprecedented 71.7 for the 12 hours. The closing scores for that third day are as follows: **Faber, 212; Panchot, 205; Herty, 200; Walker, 196; Fitzgerald, 192; Guyon, 182; Campana, 178; Bluett, 163:** Up to that stage, there had been 13,050 tickets sold.

Before the racing started on the fourth day, a quarrel occurred between the trainer of Faber, James Smith and "Happy" Jack Smith (no relation) who looked after Herty and Panchot. The *Buffalo Evening Republic* told its readers what happened next: Happy Jack was still smarting under the crowing of the rival trainer, and told him half jocosely, half ironically, that he needn't look for a piece of the prizes, as Faber would not make a place. "I told you," he said, "that you hadn't got a race until your man had won it; what do you think now?" "Bob!" said the gentle James with considerable asperity, "what glory is there in taking a piece away from a man with a swelled knee? His stake is no object to us, anyway." "I think there is some glory in putting two men on the track the fourth day of a race in as good condition as these are," retorted Happy Jack with a look of affectionate admiration in the direction of Panchot and Herty. "If I blowed about them as you did about your Dutch failure two days ago, you'd think me smart wouldn't you?" James had something better to say and for a few minutes the air was blue at the western end of the rink. It would be a good thing it some of the *quidnunes the smarties who know every thing, and who have been whispering mysteriously that the two trainers have been laying their heads together over the race, could have heard this passage at arms. It was a demonstration in regard to the honesty—the bitter honesty—of the race which was beyond refutation.

*Gossips.

Eight men toed the line for the start, and Robinson wasn't one of them. Faber could only walk due to a swollen knee and Fitzgerald's affected tendon still bothered him. Panchot meanwhile, took advantage of the ailing German's predicament and started the slow process of eating into his considerable lead. Faber could do no more than walk at as brisk a pace as his painful joint would allow him; his angry glances at the local lad as he passed him time and time again, saying it all.

Guyon felt so ill and weak that he withdrew from the race at about 16:30 after completing 207 miles, *"his stomach refusing food."* It was reported that he *"drank whisky freely."* News of Guyon's withdrawal was like music to the ears of Campana, and *"like a surgeon be delighted in the crippled condition of his unfortunate companions of the sawdust. He joked poor Faber unmercifully and spared not the others. When Guyon departed he shouted exultingly and wanted to know who the next man was that he was going to kill. When he heard the *rain on the roof he raised an umbrella and ambled along with a grin that was childlike and bland."*

*The rain flooded the main floor of the rink.

During that 4th day, as O'Leary was showing the pedestrians the medal they were competing for, in an attempt to spur them on to *"make greater efforts,"* Campana wrenched it from his hands and ran away with it. O'Leary tried to catch him, and for three laps "Sport" kept possession, but finally was captured and *"gave up the prize gracefully."*

Panchot passed Faber at 20:28. Meanwhile, Walker was almost a total wreck and the expectation was that he wouldn't be racing the next day. The score at the close of the fourth day was: **Panchot, 270.3; Faber, 269.4; Herty, 266.6; Fitzgerald, 256.7; Walker, 246.8; Campana, 239; Bluett, 216.6:**

At the start off the penultimate day, only six men *"appeared at the score,"* and Walker wasn't one of them. Faber's trainer had done wonders to reduce his man's swelling in the knee which had prevented him from running the previous day, and Chris himself was very confident of making up the lost ground. Much money was reportedly being bet on the race in New York, and when a telegram arrived from there asking "Happy Jack" whether the money should be laid on Panchot, Faber retorted, "Tell them to bet their pile on me!"

"Happy Jack," who trained both Panchot and Herty, gave them instructions to allow Faber to make the pace, and this is what they did as they fell in behind him forming part of a running chain around the track, of which Campana was one of the last links. Assured of fifth place money, "Old Sport" shouted over to O'Leary laughingly,

"I'll box a couple more of em' before night, Danny, lord, what a graveyard I have got!" as he cast a triumphant glance at Cyrenius Walker, who was sitting among the spectators. "Poor Panchot," he continued, "I expect to kill him about four o'clock this afternoon."

Herty's pace dropped off in the afternoon, but his form didn't worry his trainer who told reporters that he was saving him for the last day when he would be pushed to make the best record thus winning him some hefty bets. Of Herty's appearance at the time; *"His thin, hollow face and stiff walk had a bad look for his chances, and many recollections of rash spurts earlier in the week came up like accusing spirits between our eyes and the drooping figure."* However, later, he positively beamed when he was handed a silver cup and some flowers, the gifts cheering him up. As Fitzgerald made good progress, occasionally running, Bluett nearly gave it up and would have done so if Frankie Hart hadn't stepped in and gave him a pair of his McSwyny's shoes, which seemed to help him later on.

As the crowd swelled in the evening, Daniel O'Leary who was obviously very impressed with the performances of the pedestrians on the track said, "I tell you, this sawdust track is the finest I ever saw, and I am going to try to spur the men on to make a record which will astonish the world. I am going to give to every man who beats the record of three hundred eighty-five miles twenty five dollars; to the winner, if he beats four hundred miles, and I believe it will be done, I will give fifty dollars extra. Besides, this, to spur the men still further to their work, I will give fifty dollars in place of twenty five if he beat the best sixth day record. I am bound to give Buffalo the fastest race ever known, perhaps the fastest which will be ever walked or run."

"Campana, as usual, furnished a chapter of amusing incidents. He received among other bouquets one made from cabbages and radishes, and ate it with relish. And when his long-wished-for moccasins were handed him, a present from Capt. MacLeish, the old man was as happy as a school-boy."

Faber had been quietly making some gain on Panchot's score during the evening, but it was the Buffalo postman who went to bed that night with the knowledge that he was still top dog in the race, and before he left the track, he thrilled the audience by sprinting round his last lap. The fifth day scores: **Panchot, 342.4; Faber, 341; Herty, 320; Fitzgerald, 326.9; Campana, 295; Bluett, 266:**

On the last day, Faber ran every lap apart from one and scored 72 miles in the process. Panchot, in the end, just held on, but not before staggering around the track on the last mile when he fell down in sheer exhaustion, as a consequence cutting his face. The finale was watched by 8,000 paying customers who were part of an overall total of 27,000 for the week, *"and there were over 2,500 complimentary tickets given away besides enumerable nods from Mr. O'Leary's head to the gate-keeper in the direction of small boys and impecunious countrymen."*

Panchot, with a score of 406 miles and 5 laps won $600, the O'Leary medal, and an additional $25 for beating the best previous record of 385 miles. He was also awarded $50 for going over 400 miles. Faber, the runner-up, who scored 405.4, who won $300 and $75 for the same reasons as those given above, also took $50 more for making the best sixth day record. Fitzgerald, who was back in third place on a score of 386 miles, won $200 and $25 for beating the best previous record. Herty won $100 for finishing fourth with 369.2, and Campana's 340 miles won him $50. Bluett, who came in sixth having made 312.7, won two pairs of *"McSwyny's champion walking shoes."*

In the J. H. Haverly-Fred Englehardt promoted contest which ended at the Industrial Art Hall in Philadelphia in the same week as the above race, Jimmy Albert won the six-day 72-hour (12 hours per day) race with a world record score of 412 miles. He beat Hughes, who was 8 miles behind. Redding finished in third on 387 and Harriman was fourth with 378. For making the best performance in the last 12 hours of the race, Harriman also received a diamond scarf pin, the costume prize and a *"costly silver cup."*

A fifty-hour walking match closed in Bradford, Pennsylvania, on Saturday night, the 1st of May. A. S. Leifeld of Jackson, Michigan, entered as the "unknown," scored 198 miles, carrying off the first prize of $350. M. Crawford of Salamanca, New York, with 193 miles, took second money of $150. Tim Spelling of Bradford with 180 miles was third, and Curtis of Jamestown, New York, with 176 miles was fourth.

Peter Crossland's last race in Chicago was probably the O'Leary sponsored 12 hours per day, six-day, heel-and-toe race which started in the McCormick Hall between the 10th and the 15th of May 1880. The 16 laps to the mile track, *"calculated to admit the fastest possible time,"* consisted of a sawdust bed and was seven feet wide. Prize money was set at a limit of $1,500 with a special award of $50 being offered for beating the best six-day, 12-hour, time on record of 342 miles. An attraction for the public to attend the event would be the display of Frank Hart's belts and trophies including the "O'Leary Diamond Belt" which that athlete had won.

The 22 contestants were: **John Banks,** Chicago; **Allen Blake**, Chicago; **George Brandsetter**, Chicago; **Napoleon Campana**, New York; **Charles H. Caustin**, St. Charles, Illinois; **William Crowley**, Freeport, Illinois; **Peter Crossland**, England; **Sam Elder**, Chicago; **W. H. Gilbert**, Freeport, Illinois; **George Guyon**, Chicago; "**Capt. Harry,**" Chicago; **Harriman's "Unknown,"** Boston; **John Hefferman**, Chicago; **William Houran,** Chicago; **Kelly**, Pittsburgh; **"McDonald's entry,"** Chicago; **Gus Olmstead**, Chicago; **"Panchot's entry,"** Boston; **Otto Salman,** Chicago; **John Sherry**, Waukegan; **Walpole's "Unknown,"** Austria; **Michael Walsh**, Chicago:

The race started promptly at 11:00 and it was the 20-year-old Austrian, otherwise known as Walpole's "Unknown," who went careering into the lead at a rapid pace. His lead however, fizzled out quickly, and the *"handsome"* George Guyon soon took a slender lead over Crossland, Crowley and Sherry. But it was the 19-year-old Gus Olmstead who came from midfield to chase the leaders along with *"the finest exhibition of heel-and-toe traveling seen in this city since the day's when O'Leary was at his best."* Traversing the circle at a rapid pace of 5½ mph, he soon passed Crossland then Sherry. He then took on the game Guyon for the lead which he eventually took, and kept up his grand performance putting a mile between him and Crowley who had grabbed 2nd spot. By 20:00, Gus had walked his rivals ragged and was the first man in the match to make 50 miles. News coming from his camp suggested he would force the pace and make good use of the mandatory 12 hours rest to prepare him in his quest to maintain his well earned lead.

Of the rest, Crossland went well enough to give his friends *"encouragement,"* whilst Campana, who was dressed in a *"fantastic suit,"* was dutifully fed and watered by his young wife. "Captain Harry" went slowly and the young Austrian, although appearing well enough, complained that he felt unwell. At the end of 12 hours, the top ten in the race were: **Olmstead, 64 (New record); Crowley, 63; Gilbert, 61; Blake, Guyon and Sherry, 60; Campana, 58; Crossland, 56; Houran and Salman, 56:**

There was just one withdrawal during the night, that of Walters, the *"big German cloth cutter"* (who was one of the "Unknown's"). Olmstead kept up the rapid pace he had used to such good effect the night before and maintained his lead well. He was hotly pursued by Crowley, Gilbert and Guyon for the first couple of hours.

The next man to head for home was Brandsetter at 14:00, his excuse; sore feet. He was followed half an hour later by Gilbert who complained of back pain due to a strain he had received some weeks earlier. As he left the building, Guyon began getting chest pains and thought it wise to vacate the track having spent so much time on it in recent months. Banks would be the last man to withdraw from the match when it was learned that his brother had died in hospital.

Crossland went much better on this second day, but the man that got the tongues wagging was John Sherry. He sped along at a good clip scything through the field in masterly fashion. His performance, along with Campana's crowd pleasing antics, was very popular with the large crowd.

At 22:40, Olmstead had succeeded in beating Harriman's best score in the O'Leary walk in Newark of the previous October when that man had made 120¼ miles. By close of play on that second day, he had exceeded that distance slightly more to continue to lead the race on 122 miles. The next five men in the shake up were: **Crowley, 121; Sherry, 118; Campana, 114; Crossland, 111; Banks, 110 (Guyon had rejoined the race at 21:00, but was 35 miles adrift of the race leader).**

When the word was given to "go" on the third day, Crossland initially took the advantage, but not being able to keep up the spectacular fast gait of the other leaders', he soon gave way and watched at a distance whilst the younger men fought out for the privilege of being in the lead. After four hours of sticking together in a bunch, Sherry eventually started to pull away from young Olmstead, and with the 19-year-old well and truly cracked, he soon fell back and started to lose distance, not only to Sherry, but also to Crowley who went after the second placed man. As the afternoon passed into evening, with the race capturing the imagination of those who watched it, the score at 21:30 was evenly balanced. It showed Olmstead on a score of 174, leading Crowley by a mile. He, in turn, led Sherry by the same distance.

With the best three-day record of 179 miles up for grabs, it was always going to be possible for one, two, or even three of the leading players to break the existing one. With all three men going like the clappers, Crowley was the first of them to succeed at 22:45, followed by Olmstead and then Sherry. The crowd loved it, and when the whistle was blown for full time on the third day the scores stood: **Crowley, 180; Olmstead and Sherry, 179; Campana, 169; Crossland, 161:**

The tendons in Olmstead's right leg were found to be swollen after his third day exertions, and his trainer had put a lot of effort into trying to reduce the inflammation during the night. On resumption of the race the next day it was Crowley's right leg that was giving cause for concern, this limb being badly swollen. Crossland must have spotted the leader's problems and set off at a murderous pace, *"a burster"* as he called it himself. Predictably Olmstead, and especially Crowley, struggled badly with the former seemingly able to shake off his injury after an hour thus passing Crowley with ease, but not as easily as Sherry who found himself in front. Of the others, "Old Sport" shuffled himself around the course in his customary awkward gait, but nevertheless, he made good ground during the day. It was to Crossland's relief that the foreigner, "Walpole's Unknown," suffered from nausea in the afternoon thus losing much ground to the Yorkshireman. Walsh spent most of the evening off the path and Caustin, who went well all day, made significant progress. However, due to his previous day's performance and being so far behind, he was deemed as not being a threat.

Frank Hart and race promoter Daniel O'Leary were on hand to make sure the crowd, which included a large contingent of ladies, were suitably entertained with exhibitions of running and walking during the evening. At the close of the fourth day, and with Sherry looking particularly tired as he left the ring, the score read: **Sherry, 234; Olmstead, 233; Campana, 228; Crowley, 226; Crossland, 216; Walpole's "Unknown," 211; Caustin, 200; Hefferman, 180:**

The start of the fifth day brought dismay for the friends of Crowley, whose poorly leg caused him so much trouble, that he had to give the race up after a couple of hours. Of the other leaders, Olmstead made some impression on Sherry during the morning. However, due to a dodgy stomach, he couldn't sustain his challenge, and the leader once again pulled further away as the day progressed. By 21:00 he went three miles ahead of his rivals and his victory at that stage seemed secured. With the withdrawal of Crowley, Campana was promoted to third spot, and out of all the remaining competitors, he was the one who impressed, not only in walking, but in amusing the crowd. They showed their appreciation of him by showering him with gifts, one of which was a *"beautiful silk walking cap, which he prizes greatly."* The end of the fifth day scores: **Sherry, 291; Olmstead, 288; Campana, 282; Crossland, 271; Walpole's "Unknown", 263; Caustin, 251; Hefferman, 210:**

As predicted, John Sherry won the race after spending his day grittily increasing the gap between himself and the plucky young Olmstead. The race winner was presented with a magnificent floral cross at 22:00, and when he beat Harriman's 342½ mile record, the crowd of 2,000 that filled the hall roared their approval. When the match finished at 22:45, all the prize winners assembled on the platform and were presented with their rewards. Sherry received $500 *"in gold,"* a $250 gold watch, plus an extra sum of $50 for breaking the record. Olmstead was awarded $300, Campana, $150, and Crossland $100. The young Austrian *"Unknown"* earned himself $50 and Caustin a couple of pairs of walking shoes.

The final scores were: **Sherry, 347; Olmstead, 337; Campana, 327; Crossland, 315; Walpole's "Unknown," 305; *Caustin, 275:**

*In the United States Census enumerated on the 9th of June 1880, Peter Crossland was found living in Saint Charles, Kane, Illinois, with the family of a fellow pedestrian in the above race, Charles A. Caustin. He would eventually set sail for Liverpool on June the 23rd 1880 on the steamship *Wisconsin*.

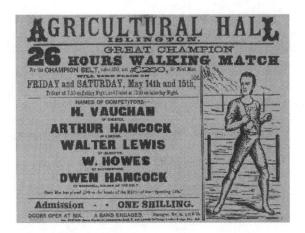

With the permission of Islington Local History Centre (Illustration no: 78)

William Howes, on a score of 101.2, was proclaimed the "26 Hours Champion" without having to walk for that amount of time in the *fifth* competition of its kind. The race was brought to a premature conclusion the next day at 14:26 when all his rivals had retired. Lewis came in the runner-up position with 83 miles. Vaughan, who made 77.3, was third. Arthur Hancock came fourth with 67.2, and his brother Owen, fifth, with 64.1. The prizes were presented by Mr. R. Lewis who was the race promoter.

Pearl Street Rink!

May 31 to June 5.

THE

O'LEARY

Tournaments
Fourth Race of the Circuit, and Second of the

Heel-end-Toe Series,

6 DAYS! 12 HOURS DAILY!
From 11 a.m. to 11 p.m., under the Management of

DANIEL O'LEARY,

For the Following Prizes:

FIRST PRIZE..$600

And a Gold Chronograph Watch, Value, $200.

SECOND PRIZE... 300

THIRD PRIZE... 200

FOURTH PRIZE 100

FIFTH PRIZE... 50

SIXTH PRIZE, Two Pairs McSwyny's Walking Shoes.
Additional prizes: $50 to the winner, provided he excels
the best performance on record made in similar contests;
$25 for the greatest distance traveled on the last day.

OPEN TO PRIZEWINNERS ONLY.

EXTRA ATTRACTIONS

Each Afternoon at 3.30 o'clock and Evenings at 6.30,
Exhibitions in Running and Walking will be given by

DANIEL O'LEARY,

Ex-Champion of the World, and his American Team

FRANK H. HART,

Of Boston (Colored), Champion of the World, and
Winner of the O'Leary Belt; record, 565 miles,
Excelling all Previous Records 12 Allies, and

JOHN DOBLER,

Of Chicago, 76 Hour Heel-and-Toe Champion of America.

GUSTAVUS OLMSTED.

The "Boy Wonder," will also give Exhibition.

Special provisions have been made for the comfort of ladies and children

ADMISSION . . . . 25 CENTS

The above advertisement was inserted into the *Buffalo Evening Republic* to attract the public's attention to the forthcoming event. Before that one commenced, a couple of more contests, which both ended on the 29th of May need to be commented on, these being the "O'Leary 72 Hour Pedestrian Contest" which took place at Pittsburgh, the result of which was: **Mignault** of Lowell, Massachusetts, **378 miles; Herty, 370; Bevers, 358; McEvoy, 348; Campana, 336; Freeman, 282:**

Then at the Armory at Syracuse, New York, a 50-hour go-as-you-please race was won by Charles Harriman with a score of 204 miles and 6 laps ($300). Curtis was the runner-up with 186 ($150), whilst James McCann ($75) and Ratigan ($25) took third and fourth places, with 168.10 and 151 respectively. The men were all handed envelopes containing their prize money. Billy Pegram, who was also in the race, gave a couple of exhibitions where he impersonated the gaits of Weston, Hart and Guyon.

Now back to that intriguing advertisement! Eighteen competitors entered the race and these were: **Bluett, Bolstridge, Byrne, Davis, Driscoll, Faber, Guyon, Hoffman, Koelble, Krohne, Kraft, Kunz, Landin, Otto, Patterson, Robinson, Walker** and **Walty.**

At the end of the first day, the scores were: **Guyon, 66.6; Faber, 66.2, Bolstridge, 64.8; Davis, 61.7; Krohne, 60.9; Walker, 60.3; Kraft, 57.4; Bluett, 57; Robinson, 55.8; Walty, 54.9; Byrne, 51.7; Otto, 50.6; Hoffman, 48; Landin, 43; Patterson, 38.5; Kunz, 25.2; Driscoll, 25; Koelble, 12 (Driscoll, Koelble and Kunz were all first day casualties):**

King of the Peds

Charles Harriman, the winner of the Syracuse race only a couple of days earlier, attended the race on the second day where 3,000 people had paid to watch the sport. The following pedestrians pulled out at various stages of the day: Patterson made his exit at 14:00 for 41, Davis at 17:00 with 82.4 and finally Landin at 19:00 on 67.1. Their withdrawals left twelve competing, and at the call of "Time," the scores were: **Guyon, 129.9; Faber, 128.10; Walker, 116.10; Bolstridge, 112.3; Krohne, 111.10; Kraft, 108.10; Byrne, 107.7; Bluett, 106; Robinson, 105.5; Hoffman, 90.3; Otto, 86; Walty, 80:**

By the end third day, the spectators had been more or less been watching two separate races. In the first race, and at the head of affairs, Guyon was leading Faber by a mile, which he had achieved by indulging in a series of spurts; the effort allowing him to get away from that rival. In the other race, Walker, who had a similar physique to Krohne, eventually created a reasonable distance between the pair after a tough battle of wills during the day. Of the others, the diminutive, but sturdy *"boy wonder"* from Newburgh, Bolstridge, impressed along with Hoffman, who although far behind the rest, made 54.2 in the 12 hours, a score which was only 4½ miles less than the race leader. Byrne withdrew from the race at the 30th hour with 124.7, and *"Poor little Walty, whose only trainer has been a lad with drinking water bravely stuck to his hopeless task and actually made twenty-seven miles before leaving the track."* The third day scores: **Guyon, 189.6; Faber, 188.2; Walker, 174.5; Krohne, 170.7; Bolstridge, 160.2; Robinson, 155.5; Kraft, 155.4; Bluett, 152.6; Hoffman, 144.5; Otto, 131.10; Byrne, 107.7; Walty, 107:**

On the fourth day, Walty was the only man missing from the line up. The $200 gold watch, which along with the $600 cash prize that would be presented to the winner, arrived at the track from *"Barton and Rice's establishment in New York city,"* and was shown to the competitors. On its lid was the inscription: **"O'LEARY; Tournament, Buffalo, N. Y. May 31st to June 5th, 1880; 72 Hour Heel and Toe; Won by   ."**

Fred Krohne would have been one of those who would have admired it, but he had a more immediate task to accomplish, and that was to pass Walker and gain third place. Otto threw in the towel and lost his entrance money after completing 2 miles and a lap, and Bluett, *"the gritty walker from Black Rock,"* later put on a sterling performance to pass Robinson, who had been a mile ahead of him within an hour of the start.

The two race leaders meanwhile were having problems. *"Both are in serious danger of a collapse; both are walking with ulcerated feet; Guyon's stomach is playing him very false."* Faber struggled around the place with a limp whilst his opponent in the glory stakes, Guyon, *"vomited violently"* at midday. *"Round and round he went with his body bent over, and his head drooped forward on his chest. His gait was a rambling, shaky one and sent dismay to parties who had money bet on him."*

Khrone, who had earlier set his mind to pass Walker, managed to do so at 16:00, the effort of closing the 3-mile 9-lap gap seemingly invigorating him as he strode on to create distance between them. Kraft, employing some rapid walking, passed Bluett after 9 p.m., and what was interesting about his performance for the day, was that he covered exactly the same distance that he had the previous day. Robinson later walked with difficulty; and Hoffman accomplished the task of passing that *"colored"* competitor by the end of the day, eventually leading him by just one lap. The end of the fourth day scores: **Guyon, 248.3; Faber, 247.1; Krohne, 233.1; Walker, 229.7; Bolstridge, 216; Bluett, 204.6; Kraft, 201.9; Hoffman, 190.3; Robinson, 190.2:**

Khrone must have been rubbing his hands together with glee as he was told by his trainers of the plight of the two leaders in the walking match on the fifth day. The tall German had made some gain into their scores on the previous day, and considering their respective plights, he must have thought that he had a good chance of being thereabouts by the end of the contest. All he had to do was keep up the steady 14-minute miles and he just might be in there with a shout.

Charles Harriman was on hand to offer the ailing Guyon some medicine to help his stomach, which was described as being in a *"wretched condition"* all day. The previous night, Guyon's trainer Merritt, had given his man something to help him, and he was warned not to repeat the practice if he ever wanted to attend to a competitor in an O'Leary race again. The Harriman remedy seemed to help George whose face returned to a fresher colour. His corresponding improvement helped him gain a few laps on Faber during the course of the day, and he went on to make 300 miles in 58h.46m, with the second placed ped making the same distance 19 minutes later.

Of the days other events, Kraft *"ran away"* from the track in the afternoon only to be brought back where he continued his struggle in an apparent state of inebriation. Hoffman withdrew after following Krohne around for a while as the rest soldiered on in the hope of keeping their positions. The scores at the end of the fifth day: **Guyon, 305.7; Faber, 304.3; Krohne, 293.2; Walker, 279; Bolstridge, 267; Bluett, 254.4; Kraft, 236.8; Robinson, 219.9:**

The last day of competition was played out in an atmosphere of indignation due to the rain outside. Perhaps the weather had contributed to the dispiriting gloom inside where just 2,000 people were present to watch the end of the race. The men on the track must have felt betrayed by the attitude of the visiting public who seemed to tire of the predictability of the proceedings. *"There was scarcely a ripple of applause to cheer the men on their way, and they had nothing but the lazy playing of an uninspiring band to break the terrible monotony of their journey."* O'Leary must have taken note of the reaction of the spectators to the six-day walking event because he was already proposing a six-day go-as-you-please event to be held in the coming August.

It was George Guyon with a score of 356 miles who won first prize of $600, the gold watch and the extra prize of $50 for beating the best previous record of 347.5. Faber with 355 miles won second prize of $300. Krohne, after making 346.3, landed the third prize of $200 and an extra prize of $25 for making the greatest number of miles on the last day. Walker (327.4) won the fourth prize of $100, Bolstridge (315.1), the fifth prize of $50 and Bluett (302), the sixth prize of *another* two pairs of McSwyny's shoes.

A three hours per night go-as-you-please "pedestrian tournament," which started on Tuesday, the 22nd and concluded on Saturday, the 26th of June 1880, for prizes of £5 and a silver medal for the winner, £3, £2 and £1 for the next three places, took place at the Corn Exchange in Alloa, Scotland. Collins of Methven won the tight finish, beating his nearest competitor E. Thomas of Wolverhampton by 2 laps, with a further 3 laps separating him from third placed Clarkson of Hull. McManus of Dundee was fourth, the final scores being: **124.7; 124.5; 124.1; 117.19:**

Whilst there was a thrilling finish in Alloa, George Noremac, was notching up yet another win, this time in a *reportedly* 26-hour (more than likely a 48-hour race?) go-as-you-please *"pedestrian competition"* held at the recreation grounds at Inches in Aberdeen. The race finished on the same Saturday night as the above event with the winner making 204.3. George was awarded an extra prize of £10 subscribed by *"two local gentlemen"* in addition to the £20 first prize. W. Smith, who took the £10 runner-up prize, ended the race with 201.1. H. Mundin of Hull made £7 with his effort of 180 miles and D. Ferguson of Pollockshaws took £3 fourth money with a score of 165.4.

At the Garrison Hall, Dunedin, New Zealand, between Friday and Saturday, the 2nd and 3rd of July, Brookes of Christchurch (who was one of the pre-match favourites with the eventual runner-up), claimed the £50 first prize when he won the 24-hour walking competition there with a good score of 116 miles. Swan, from the same city as the victor, won £10 with a creditable second on a score 114.1, and Malcolm came in third to secure a prize of £5 for his effort of 113.7. In addition to the above prizes, and because of a £1 sweepstakes contributed to by all the contestants, Swan secured an extra £12 (two thirds) more to make his take home pay £22. Malcolm also received an extra £6 (one third). All three had surpassed Joe Scott's score of 113 miles in his walk against time at the same venue only a week earlier, details of which can be read in Chapter 58. The match had been witnessed by about 4,000 people. McKewan, who came in fourth with a score of 106 miles, had £8 collected for him.

John Dobler went to Buffalo in August of that year to take part in a six-day, 72-hour, go-as-you-please match at the Pearl Street Rink.

The contest for the O'Leary "Championship Belt of the World," opened at 11 a.m. on Monday, August the 9th. The belt, which was made of silver and gold, was described thus. *"In front is a large plate with the American and Irish flags on one side and the English and French flags on the other. Perched upon the top between the flags is the American eagle overlooking* *the following inscription, "**O'Leary Champion Belt of the World. 72 hours go-as-you-please, 12 hours a day, from August 9th to August 14th, 1880.**" A gold laurel wreath surrounds the entire face of the front. Outside of the flags are two figures in the attitude of running. The cost of the belt was $300."*

The newly laid track was highly praised by the pedestrians, and the novel idea of having a narrow track for attendants to run along inside of the other was applauded, for it *"kept the trainers away from tobacco smoke of unmannerly spectators and relieved them from one of the greatest inconveniences of their task."* Although not competing on this race, Daniel Burns of Elmira had made a fast time on the same track in a 25-mile race on the previous Thursday evening.

Before the race to which bookmakers were not invited to attend, O'Leary drew up the following:

RULES OF CONDUCT.

1. No coaching will be allowed.

2. No jostling or interference will be permitted.

3. Any competitor striving, for the lead must take the outside, and must have a lead of at least ten feet.

4. A competitor following a leader must be careful to keep sufficiently far in the rear to avoid treading on his heels or otherwise injuring him.

5. Leaders in order to remain entitled to the advantage of holding the pole, must keep within two feet of the inside track line.

6. No two or more competitors will be allowed to travel together abreast when they are deemed to obstruct the progress of other contestants in the race.

7. Competitors who are judged guilty of infringing the rules will be penalized by distances from one lap upward to permanent removal from the track, at the discretion of the manager or his representative.

8. Competitors are held responsible for the conduct of their trainers and attendants, and if either through misbehavior or infringement of the rules make themselves objectionable to other competitors, they will be removed from the building.

9. Two badges for the exclusive use of their attendants will be furnished each competitor; if otherwise used will be forfeited.

10. Competitors must be properly costumed, and it shall be the duty of the manager to remove any competitor from the track who shall be so negligent in his costume as to offend the eye of modesty.

11. Gentlemanly and sportsmanlike conduct on the track will be insisted upon under penalty of forfeiture of distance or of the right to continue in the race.

12. At the close of the day's racing time will be called and only completed laps will be counted.

Apart from Dobler, some of the other more notable contestants competing in the race were: **Jimmy Albert** of Philadelphia who had made the then world record of 412 miles in that city; **Eph Clow,** the then Canadian champion of Toronto; **John Cox** of Petrolia, Pennsylvania; **Chris Faber** of Newark, New Jersey, who had only just shaken off his title" of "Unlucky Chris" in Pittsburgh; **Dan Herty** of Boston; **Charles Harriman** of Haverhill; **John Hughes** of New York**,** who had recently made 407 miles in a similar contest; **Richard Lacouse** of Boston, and **Robert Vint** of Brooklyn. The rest of the runners were, **C. H. Curtis** of Cleveland; **Sanfield Dawson** of Canada; **Michael Flandon** of Niagara Falls; **William Hatchjin** of Buffalo; **Jerry Hourihan** of Boston; **Arthur Layton** of Schenectady; **James McCann** of New York; **Phillip Mignault** of Boston; **Thomas O'Leary** of New York, and **White Eagle** the Indian from Warm Springs.

Before the start of the race, *"the band very wisely had been placed in the gallery, and neither pedestrians nor spectators were troubled by the unpleasant resonance of it's too propinquity."*

Of the nineteen competitors who started on the first day, one of the first retirees was White Eagle, who scored 25 miles. John Hughes went on to beat the best 50-mile record in a time of 6h.55m. *"With far too much flesh on his bones for athletic comfort,"* and with *"a heavy ungainly stride, muscle rather than brain is Hughes reliance. He does his best all the while and seems to have no notion of husbanding his strength."* By the end of the permitted time, Dobler, *"who had been running a beautiful race throughout the day, his clean upright pace carrying him steadily and rapidly onward,"* had covered 78.7 thus making the best time on record, beating Faber's previous one by two laps. He was reported to be going along at an average speed of over 6½ mph, whilst the man he had stolen the record off, Faber, had to withdraw on his 62nd mile. The other first day withdrawals were; O'Leary who left the track on a score of 14.1, Albert, on 23.2, Flandon for 26.2, Hatchjin, having made 38.9 and Layton for 57.4.

The end of the 1st day scores: **Dobler, 78.8; Cox, 76.5; Hughes, 76.1; Harriman, 75.5; Mignault; 75.1; Lacouse, 70.8; Dawson, 70.3; Herty, 69.2; Hourihan, 67.1; Clow, 63.7; Curtis, 63.4; McCann, 60.3:**

On the second day, Layton, who had rejoined the race after supposedly retiring the first day, was the first to man to withdraw after 40 minutes of competition on a score of 61.5. Dobler was the first competitor to claim the century which he did in 15h.14m, his time knocking off a full 12 minutes from the old 72-hour record. Mignault claimed his 100 in 15h.35m, Harriman, his, in 16h.2m, Cox, in 16h.7m, and Lacouse in 16h.54m.

At 14:30, Dawson, realising he had no chance in the race, wisely gave up the chase and left the building on a score of 84, as did the "Lepper" who *"caused the sensation of the day"* when he succumbed to rheumatism shortly before five o'clock having made 106.9. Earlier, Mignault had received monetary gifts from some in the crowd and was also given a silk handkerchief from a lady admirer in the gallery. Also receiving gifts, but of the floral kind, were Lacouse, and Curtis, *"the giddy pedestrian,"* the latter evidently being a favourite of the ladies who he entertained by covering the ground by hopping, walking, running and waltzing! Evidently, when he was told that the females in the audience left, he *"drooped and wilted."*

McCann and Hourihan for their part, *"helped to relieve the occasion of monotony"* by indulging in frequent spurts. Later Hourihan's stomach, *"had become rebellious,"* and as he dragged himself around the path, he *"hung his head, and his pale face indicated sickness."* He later perked up though, and woke up the crowd with a display of rapid running. Things however, weren't looking too good for Herty, who, at 21:08, decided enough was enough when he left the race altogether having managed 120.2.

When time was called for the end of play, Dobler, who had made 150 miles at 22:54, led Mignault the Frenchman by seven miles, his departing score being 150 and 5. Mignault had passed Harriman soon after 8 p.m. Both had been involved in a rare old ding-dong battle for second place during which the American had been exhibiting his stereotypical heel-and-toe method of conveyance. He followed Mignault back to the dressing rooms some half a mile or so behind. Lacouse, who was the next man in the race with 139, just led Cox when the bell rang.

On Wednesday, there was real excitement on the track when Mignault, Harriman, and Lacouse, fought bitterly for second position. As the lanky figure of Harriman and bronzed form of Lacouse slowly encroached upon his territory, the thin Bostonian scrapped to repel them. Then at 16:15, Harriman passed Mignault. An hour after that Lacouse passed him, in spite of the giant's best efforts to keep him from doing so. Thus, it was in that order that Dobler was pursued. It was also in that order that the first four men on the leader board at the end of 36 hours were: **Dobler, 216.8; Lacouse, 208.3; Harriman, 207.3; Mignault, 206.5: (Dobler made his 200th mile in 32h.50m; Lacouse in 34h.32m; Harriman in 34h.36m and Mignault in 35h.35m):** Behind them all was the little pug-nose Irishman, Hourihan, who ran like a deer most of the day. He accumulated 71.9 making 50 of them in the astonishing time of 7h.56m. That effort entitled him to claim the record for the best third day's time. The others all did good work during the day with the exception of Clow, the so called *"Champion of Canada," who raised a few eyebrows when he eventually left the race for good with only 175.10 at 20:00. When the men left the track for the night, both Mignault and McCann were said to be in poor condition. Cox finished the day in fifth position with 210.2, Hourihan in sixth on 194.9, Curtis in seventh having made 186.7, and finally McCann, the back-marker in eighth "pozzy" with 184.8.

*In the 72-hour go-as-you-please "Toronto Walking Tournament" which started on the morning of June the 7th 1880, Clow of Prince Edward Island had beaten Faber's celebrated record in Buffalo. Panchot, who was also in the same race retired on his 40th mile with a sprained ankle.

N. B: During the evening, and in a separate 10-mile race on the track for prize money totalling $60, the Scot James

McLeavy, in a time of 59m.30s beat White Eagle who he had pursued around the track until the last lap. Daniel Burns and a man called Ross also competed, with the latter named finishing several laps behind the Indian in third place. The winner won $40.

At the start of the fourth day, Dobler decided that he would insure his position by following in second man Lacouse's steps, and that was the strategy he stuck to and tried to maintain throughout. Meanwhile, initially, Mignault made some inroads into those who had passed him the day before. His effort however, petered out, and as the day grew older he found himself being passed by Cox and Hourihan, thus relegating him to sixth place. Harriman, the long man from *"Massachuse,"* spurred on by his adoring fans who handed him fresh bouquets, eventually headed his darker skinned rival Lacouse, who, for his part, had shook off the attentions of the race leader. By the end of the day, Cox got within striking distance of Lacouse and Hourihan who continued his fine form by running 50 miles in 8h.21m. Of the Irishman whose gait was likened to Campana; *"He has a queer way of hanging down his head, and he picks out his steps as daintily as if walking on eggs not unlike Old Sport's celebrated "dejected gait,"* and, *"he is constantly making numerous remarks in broad Hibernian to his fellow tourists. Hourihan is a man who should be cultivated both for his social and his speedy qualities."*

At the back of the pack, Curtis continued to show off to the ladies with spurts and *"unexpected gyrations,"* whilst the industrious little fellow McCann, the New York news-boy, struggled on in rear in an attempt to save his entrance money. He was observed picking up money tossed at him by the sympathetic crowd, which had been noticeably much better than the preceding days.

At the end of that fourth day, the scores were: **Dobler, 282.2; Harriman, 273.2; Lacouse, 271; Cox, 270; Hourihan, 265.3; Mignault; 258.9; Curtis, 251.2; McCann, 244.9:**

After ten minutes into the penultimate day of competition, Phillip Mignault, whose ankle was severely troubling him, pulled out of the contest on a score of 259.5. That left just seven men from an initial entry of nineteen. The twinkling stars in the early hours of the day were Cox and Hourihan who sped along the course in sparkling fashion. As the afternoon progressed, Cox took Lacouse's position on the leader board. He went on to progress into second place leaving Harriman to take retrograde steps back into fourth as Lacouse recovered his composure to hang on to third. Dobler had tried to keep up with both Cox and Hourihan, but their combined pace proved too hot for him, and he had to watch nervously as the pair constantly gnawed away at his lead. Indeed the plucky little Irishman, who in the morning had been 7 miles and 10 laps behind Harriman, gained seven miles on him during the day.

Nearly a thousand ladies had witnessed the action from the galleries during the evening. Curtis must have been in his element!

In a separate 15-mile race in the evening, there were eight entries, who were Daniel Burns, Philip Dufrane, Riley's "Unknown," James McLeavy, R. D. Ross, White Eagle, and John Hourihan. Burns was the easy winner in 1h.36m, beating White Eagle, Dufrane and Riley's "Unknown."

Before setting off that morning, Harriman had shouted to his wife, "Charley is going to run seventy-two miles today!" As the following record shows for the end of the fifth day, he had miscalculated by seven miles: **Dobler, 349.7; Cox, 342.7; Lacouse, 339.2; Harriman, 337.2; Hourihan, 336.3; Curtis, 312.2; McCann, 309.4:**

On the last day, Cox was said to be elated when he heard the news that Dobler's knees were giving way. Both he and Hourihan were determined to capitalise on the previous day's performance, and it was the Irishman who set off in tremendous style to firstly, pick off the walking Harriman, and then secure a lap under 8 miles for the first hour. The *"flying Paddy"* then went on to make 15 miles at 12:55 much to the pleasure of the watching public, whilst Cox only managed to gain a few laps on the race leader.

As the weather outside improved, and the earlier rain was replaced by blazing sunshine, many left their houses and headed for the rink to watch the afternoon's entertainment. News from the track indicated that Hourihan was going all out to get third place from Lacouse. As it transpired the effort used during the previous day told on the Irishman, because just after two o'clock, *"his face grew pale and his eyes glassy."* That being the case, and his race seemingly over and done with, he later failed to make any further impact on the contest thereafter.

Cox, who had made a commendable effort chasing after Dobler, eventually settled into a walking pace after 19:00, accepting the inevitable after the leader had gamely resisted his challenge.

At the finish, Dobler had his name written into the record books by scoring 414 miles to claim the first prize of a purse of $700. What was more important was that he had won the championship belt, which he wore around his waist as he made his last two laps. He was then hoisted on to the scorers' table, where along with the other prize winners, he received his money. Cox, who made 409.4, received $350 for following him over the line. The third prize of $200 went to Lacouse who scored 400 miles. Hourihan claimed fourth spot with a total of 396.2 securing $100. Harriman, who was fifth, made $50 with his effort of 379.5. Sixth man was Curtis with a mark of 370 and 3 who was paid $25. Finally, McCann who made 352.1 was given his entrance money of $25 back by the race promoter, Daniel O'Leary.

Whilst Dobler was traversing his last mile, Hughes created quite a disturbance at the scoreboard claiming that the peg board was crediting Dobler with fraudulent laps. *"He was pushed from the track by Assistant Manager Davies. Late last night Hughes and his irate wife were searching for a warrant against Davies."*

A six-day *walking* match that had taken place at what is presumed to have been at the Rifle Drill Hall, Bristol, England, between Monday, the 30th of August, and Saturday, the 4th of September had been, contrary to expectations, won by the fifty year old plus veteran, Williams, who won the belt valued at £50 and a cash prize of £40. He had gradually overhauled George Parry and finally defeated him by an impressive 19 miles, his final score amounting to 412 miles and 10 laps. Parry had recorded a score of 393.18. The rest of the scores were as follows: **McKellan, 351.16; Clarkson, 323; Barrow, 218.6; Pettitt, 177.4; Hibberd, 174.18; McCarty, 163.2; Higgins, 148.7:**

That irrepressible Scot, Mr. G. Noremac secured the first prize of £50 with a score of 383.1 for winning a 14-hour, six-day, go-as-you-please contest for prizes adding up to £150. The match, on a 19-lap to the mile track, definitely did take place at the Rifle Drill Hall in Bristol, between Monday, the 11th and Saturday, the 16th of October. Sam Day (the then 75-hour champion) finished second with 380.4, Henry Vandepeer finished third with 346.9, Harry Carless was fourth with 320.2, and George Mason finished fifth with 305. The other starters included Cartwright of Walsall, Hughes of Birmingham, McCarty of Leeds (258.10), McKellan of Scotland, Mundin of Hull and Robson of Liverpool (292.3).

On the morning of December 30th, William Gale *"broke down"* having covered 2,233 miles of his proposed feat of walk 2,500 miles within 1,000 hours, which he had commenced on November 20th at Lillie Bridge.

CHAPTER 29

1st O'Leary International Belt

The American Institute Building situated on Third Avenue and Sixty Third Street, New York, was the venue for the first *"O'Leary International Belt Championship of the World"* which was to begin shortly after midnight on Monday, the 24th of January 1881 and end the following Saturday night.

The trophy they would be competing for was made of predominantly silver, with a gold centre oval shield surmounted with branches of oak and laurel, bearing lettering in relief and enamel which read: "**International O'Leary Champion Belt of the World.**" The upper part of the of the shield was decorated with the flags of America, Britain, Germany and Ireland, and there was an American eagle holding a shield, at the centre of which three diamonds were set in the shape of a trefoil. The aforementioned branches were held together lower down by another shield containing, in blue enamel, the inscription, "**Six Days Go-As-You-Please. Jan. 24-29. 1881.**" The shields either side, which bore figures of a man running and another trotting were both in gold relief. The rest of the shields, held together by oval links, were left blank for the engraving of the names of future winners.

The entrance fee for the match was $100, and 65% of the gate money received would be divided amongst those competitors making 480 miles or more in the allocated 142-hour time-frame. The gate money would be divided as follows:

If only one competitor managed to complete 480 miles, he would take all. If two completed, the winner would receive 60% and the runner-up 40%. If three men completed, the division would be 50%, 30% and 20%. If four completed, then 40, 30, 20 and 10% would be shared, and if five men all made the distance, then they would divide 40, 25, 17, 10 and 8%. Every contestant, except the five sharers of the gate who covers 480 miles shall receive $200 to be deducted from the gate money.

A special prize of $1,000 would be given to the man who beat the best record held by Rowell of 566 miles and should he cover 600 miles, an extra $1,000.

All the men contesting the event were to be accommodated in a little wooden room measuring 10 by 6 feet containing a wash stand, gas stove, wooden chair, wooden bed, mattress, blanket, pillow and small mirror. They would be expected to go as they pleased around an elliptical shaped track measuring one eighth of a mile, made up of a mixture of clay, tan bark and sawdust to a depth of three inches atop a concrete base. The thirty competitors were: **James Albert**, Philadelphia; **George Barber**, Jersey City; **J. Bruchs**, Burlington, Iowa; **T. Burke**, Brooklyn; **Daniel Burns**, Elmira, New York; **Peter N. Campana**, Bridgeport; **J. E. Coughlin**, Orange, Massachusetts; **John Cox**, Bradford, Pennsylvania; **Ben Curran**, New York; **John Dillon**, New York; **George Dufrane**, New York; **Alfred Elson**, Boston; **O. Feeney**, Haverstraw, New York; **Patrick Fitzgerald**, New York; **George Guyon**, Chicago; **C. A. Harriman**, Haverhill, Massachusetts; **Harry Howard**, Glen Cove, Long Island; **John Hughes**, New York; **Frederick Krohne**, New York; **Richard Lacouse**, Boston; **C. P. Lewis**, Lowell, Massachusetts; **Ira D. McCoy**, Cleveland, Ohio; **Philip Mignault**, Bradford, Pennsylvania; **J. Moore**, New York; **Richard Moore**, New York; **P. O'Leary**, South Amboy, New York; **William Pegram**, Boston; **E. Phillips**, Boston; **Frederick Swemling**, New York; **Robert Vint**, Brooklyn:

The pre-match betting: **Burns, 6/1; Albert and Cox, 7/1; Pegram, 8/1; Howard, 10/1; Feeney, 12/1; Harriman, Krohne and Lacouse, 15/1; Bar these, 25/1:**

By midnight there were between eight and ten thousand spectators in the building. Many had been given complimentary tickets which had been given out in the city's bars, pool rooms and bookmaking establishments.

The crowd was entertained by a *"sacred"* concert which had played since the place opened at 9 p.m. Seats on the north side of the Rink were non-smoking and were reserved for the ladies who were accompanied by gentlemen. At the start of the race they had a clear view of the track, which was occupied by the 30 contestants in 10 rows of three. Each athlete had his number plastered on his breast. Swemling, number 31 was in the front row along with number 30, Hughes and number 28, Moore. On the back line were numbers 1, 2 and 3, Krohne, Howard and Cox.

The word was given at five minutes past the hour and the thirty hopefuls were on their way, with Fitzgerald taking first lap honours, followed by Campana and Hughes. Barber finished the first mile in 6m.20s followed by Elson and Campana.

The 11 o'clock score: **Albert, 68; J. Moore and R. Moore, 67; Elson and Hughes, 65; Vint, 64; Guyon, 62; Harriman and Krohne, 61; Coughlin and Mignault, 60; Lacouse, 59; Curran, Dufrane and Fitzgerald, 58; Cox, 57; Feeney and Howard, 56; Barber, 55; Phillips, 54; Campana, 52; Burns and Dillon, 51; Burke and Pegram, 50; Swemling, 47; Lewis, 45; Bruchs, 43; McCoy, 37:**

The midnight score: **Hughes, 134; R. Moore, 127; Albert, 125; Elson and Mignault, 123; Cox and Vint, 120; Krohne, 115; Feeney and Coughlin, 113; Fitzgerald, 108; Dufrane, 106; Howard, 105; Burke, Burns, Curran, Lacouse and Phillips, 100; Campana, 94; Barber, 93; Dillon, 90; Pegram, 88; Bruchs, 79:**

After scoring 113 miles and 7 laps, Patrick Fitzgerald gave up the race on the second day at 05:15, for *"no apparent reason."* The following retirements were also announced by the referee at 10 a.m: Guyon, Harriman, Lewis, J. Moore, McCoy, P. O'Leary and Swemling. Lewis however, continued to race despite his formal withdrawal, and after consulting with Referee Curtis, he was allowed to continue with his task.

At noon, Hughes, who up to this point had had little sleep, leapt around the path with his face appearing *"pinched and worn."* He was in the lead on a score of 177.7, and at this stage of the race, was four miles or so ahead of Albert, who, in turn, was leading Richard Moore and Cox, the latter pair being involved in a neck-and-neck battle for third place. The rest of the scores at that time (no lap returns) were: **Albert, 173; Cox and R. Moore, 167; Mignault and Feeney, 166; Krohne, 161; Vint, 160; Howard, 153; Elson, 149; Lacouse, 142; Campana and Curran, 139; Phillips, 135; Coughlin and Dufrane, 116; Barber, 111; Pegram, 110; Burke, 106; Burns, 103; Dillon, 102; Bruchs, 100; Lewis, 71:**

Hughes made his second century at 16:56, and in doing so beat Hart's record for the same time by a mile and 175 yards. Others who went on to knock up their 200's were, Albert at 19:01, Cox at 19:34, Krohne at 20:27, and Vint at 20:53.

There were 1,500 paying customers watching the men go about their business on the track at 21:00. The band's efforts to entertain were clearly appreciated by the likes of Howard and Cox, who skipped around the place with more vigour every time they played. Howard must have enjoyed the moment at 22:01 when he too joined the double centurions traversing the place. A couple of minutes later, the race leader, Hughes, wearing a scarlet costume, bounded back into the ring, and that gave the signal for the equally colourfully attired Campana to do what he did best in pedestrian contests, which was play to the crowd. This he did by *"throwing his body about with most curious motions, and out-rivalling the careless, slip shod gait of Hughes."*

The race leader led a charge around the path at about 23:15. He was immediately followed by half a dozen of his rivals including the black boy Phillips. He was also trailed by Feeney, who was encouraged at every opportunity by a gang of his supporters from Haverstraw, and the whip carrying Jimmy Albert, who looked so impressive with his method of conveyance, that the bookies put him up as "the jolly" on their boards at midnight when the scoreboard showed the following totals: **Hughes, 229; Albert and Cox, 220; Vint, 213; Krohne, 206; Howard, 205; Feeney, 199; Mignault, 193; Curran, 185; Campana, 180; Phillips, 176; Lacouse, 170:**

Elson withdrew from the event at 03:12 on Wednesday morning having made 164 miles. Between five and six o'clock, the three race leaders dashed along at a rate of 7 mph keeping the few spectators that were still awake very much entertained. Feeney was the next man to dress into his civvies at 06:32 after making 216, and then it was the turn of Burke to have a word with the "ref" and declare his intention to depart after an effort of 155 miles.

King of the Peds

Mignault was next in the queue to hoist the white flag when he announced he was quitting at 10:58 on a score of 193, and the presumption was that Barber had left the premises as he had not been seen on the track since the previous night.

Hughes remained in the lead on a score of 280 at 14:00 and appeared in the same condition as the previous day. Cox continued in second position, with Albert in third place, keeping up a light trot. Krohne, back in fifth, plodded along on in characteristic fashion behind the improved looking Howard. They were watched by very few spectators, who were undemonstrative in their support. However, as day moved into night, the place began to gradually fill up, and with the seats half filled at 21:00, the record showed: **Hughes, 312.4; Cox, 298.3; Albert, 298.2; Howard, 297.7; Vint, 290; Krohne, 280.6; Curran, 265.1; Phillips, 257.3; Campana, 244; Lacouse, 237.3:**

Hughes, who had a look of determination upon his *"flushed countenance,"* hurried himself along with his fists clenched and arms swinging. He raced against all but Lacouse, who was resting. He was joined in the men's quarters by Cox and Albert after they had both completed their 300 miles. Howard by now was becoming a real alternative to the punters who were seeking the solution as to who would finish in second place. As Cox and Albert put their feet up, he remained on the track, and at 21:30, took second place. Continuing with his commendable effort till 22:40, when on a score of 305, he too left for a break. Hughes left the path on his 319th mile; and while some of the leaders slept little Vint thought he might try for third spot. Hughes reappeared after snatching only 16 minutes of rest at 23:01, and appearing worn out, anxiously eyed up the scoreboard. He soon got himself going after a stiff start, and after throwing off his *"blouse,"* ran around the loop briskly. At 23:10, Vint, after firstly achieving 300 miles, then went on to accomplish his objective of securing the bronze medal position three minutes later, after which he sought the comfort of his cot. Half an hour after that, Krohne, who had been making steady inroads on all the race leaders, found himself overtaking Vint at 23:45. Whilst Phillips *"jumped around the track with a peculiarly ungainly stride,"* Campana pulled faces at the crowd as he slowly walked around it wearing an old white slouch hat. The spectators as ever loved his eccentricity and greatly appreciated his efforts to make them smile. Lacouse gave word of his retirement at 23:46 leaving just nine of the original thirty in the race. With Hughes beating the best American record for 72 hours by 7¾ miles, the midnight score read: **Hughes, 325.6; Howard, 305; Albert and Krohne, 301; Vint, 300.1; Cox, 300; Curran, 278.1; Phillips, 270.7; Campana, 255; Lacouse, 243:**

There were a few raised eyebrows about the "Lepper's current performance as he was one of the outsiders at the start of the race. There was some suspicion as to the correct measurement of the track; because of these worries, Mr. Joseph. L. T. Smith, a city surveyor, was asked to attend the building to allay any misconceptions. After completing his work, he issued an affidavit sworn before a notary public that the track was up to scratch, measured 18 inches from the inner curb, and was the required distance of exactly 660 lineal feet in circumference.

The *New York Sun* wrote: A great deal of money has been placed on the leaders during the week. It is said that dodges and rascally tricks are being resorted to in order to disable the probable winners. About 9 a.m., a stranger persisted in entering Howard's quarters, against the wishes of his backer, Tom Davis. Davis knocked the fellow down, causing quite a commotion for a short time.

With the record showing that Hughes was beating the best ever recorded world record by nearly six miles and the then current American record by eleven miles, the noon score showed: **Hughes, 368; Cox, 349; Albert and Howard, 348; Krohne, 340; Vint, 339; Phillips, 317; Curran, 307; Campana, 289:**

The aforementioned newspaper went on to write of an incident which occurred at 13:00: Mr. W. H. Harding, who is assisting Mrs. Hughes in the care of her husband, has gone without sleep until he is more livid in the face than the Lepper. Mr. Harding says the constant vigilance is needed to keep villains from laying out his man. One finely dressed gentlemanly appearing fellow presented Mrs. Hughes with three nice, fresh eggs for her husband. Upon his wife saying that John did not relish eggs, the stranger brought, her some deliciously flavored soup. Mrs. Hughes ate some of the soup before giving any to John. The soup made her violently sick for hours.

Other reports suggested that the soup was brought to his tent by a waiter who said one of "Jack's" friends had sent it to him. Mrs. Hughes was later given an emetic by her husband's trainer to ease her plight.

John Hughes being attended to by his wife

The National Police Gazette (Illustration no: 79)

The 3 p.m. score: **Hughes, 379.1; Howard, 361.6; Albert, 360; Cox, 359.2; Krohne, 358.7; Vint, 349.6; Phillips, 330.2; Curran, 318.5; Campana, 300:**

When the 6 p.m. score was hoisted, Hughes was eight miles ahead of Hart's record, and eight miles behind Rowell's score for the 90th hour: **Hughes, 391; Howard, 374; Albert and Cox, 372; Krohne, 366; Vint, 363; Phillips, 343; Curran, 331; Campana, 304:**

The second placed Howard left the track at 19:30, and the "Lepper" completed 400 miles 13 minutes after his departure. *"A wave of cheers rolled around the track when the figures appeared on the blackboard,"* after which Hughes immediately left the path for a nap. The 9 p.m. score: **Hughes, 404; Albert, 387; Cox, 383; Krohne, 378; Howard, 377; Vint, 376; Phillips, 349; Curran, 341; Campana, 315:**

Howard returned a couple of hours later but looked tired. Whilst out of the ring, Jimmy Albert had taken his second position, but Cox who had duelled with him for quite a while, proved too good for the Philadelphian, and at 21:52, the *"dark featured shapely young man"* from Bradford, Pennsylvania, took the runner-up position in the race 19 miles behind the race leader. Cox remained in the race till 22:21 and then left the building for a Russian bath on a score of 392.

Whilst Krohne trudged around the place wearing a dark blue woollen costume, Vint, the pale faced, heavily perspiring ex-cobbler from Brooklyn, crept around hoping for nothing more than a share of the gate money. By 22:30, and in front of a crowd of 4,000, he was two miles ahead of the now sixth placed Howard. Phillips meanwhile, munching away on peanuts, barely made progress, as he struggled along suffering with painful swollen feet. Another in the fray was the middle aged, moustache sporting, Curran, who made steady progress around the track. The back-marker was "Old Sport." He seemed more committed in entertaining the crowd by providing them with a fashion show than any display of athleticism, and frequently changed his costumes. A *"world too wide"* dirty suit of a merino undershirt and red tights was swapped in no time for a *"gorgeous"* crimson suit and black silk hat. He had for a rest at 22:25 for 1h.10m, and when he came back, *"ambled around like a lame camel."*

At 23:47, Hughes passed Rowell's 96-hour record of 416 miles. His last mile, made in 11m.12s, beat Rowell's record by a mile and 165 yards, and Hart's by 12 miles and 165 yards. At midnight, the leader board read: **Hughes, 417; Cox, 392; Albert and Vint, 390; Howard, 388.1; Krohne, 385; Phillips, 354.7; Curran, 351; Campana, 320:** Hughes at the time was "even money" to take the title. Howard was on offer at 2/1 with Albert at 3/1, Krohne at 15/1 and Vint was a 25/1 shot.

With Ben Curran being the latest casualty in the race having retired on a score of 360.3, there were malicious rumours circulating the building that John Hughes's progress within its confines had, *"not been squarely earned."* The managers were very concerned about the accusations being made and gave their assurance that not one lap more had been added to the race leader's total during the match. They defended the integrity of both the referee Mr. Curtis, and the chief scorer Arthur Ellam, whom they insisted were both *"upright men."* They stated that it would be impossible for them to *"doctor"* the record and that the scoring system in operation prevented the scores from being fraudulently marked.

O'Leary stated he had wagered $5,000 to $3,000 that Hughes would beat Rowell's record of 566 miles. Hughes himself sped around the track with relative ease, and the knee that had been causing him some concern earlier in the race ceased to bother him.

The battle for third spot between Cox and Vint had been fought all morning; at 11 o'clock, the pair passed the lap marker on 430 miles apiece. Vint slowly began to win the argument thereafter and pulled half a furlong clear of his adversary, but the sturdy and plucky Pennsylvanian soon fought back and quickly drew half a mile in front of the little man. The midday scores: **Hughes, 457; Howard, 441; Cox, 434.4; Vint, 434; Krohne, 432; Albert, 428.6; Phillips, 394.2; Campana, 344.2:** At 13:30, Hughes made his 466th mile and kept to his task well dogging the second placed and *"over trained"* Howard relentlessly.

At 22:00, the "Lepper," attired in a red costume, and on a score of 496, was 8 miles ahead of Rowell's best record. The men that were left in the race were described as *"forlorn, jaded animals, pushed on by their trainers, and wishing apparently for the exhibition to come to an end."* To brighten up events on the course, one man could always be relied upon to cheer the hearts of both spectators and fellow contestants. That man was of course Campana. It was said that he was actually paid just to remain in the race as a side attraction. O'Leary, the race promoter, knew that whenever things were a bit dull in the arena, he could rely on "Old Sport" to get the crowd going, and with his help, and whilst Hughes and the rest of them toiled on the track, that's just what happened. O'Leary also put himself on the track and ran around with the old stager, much to the delight of the amused throng who were said to be ecstatic at the sight. *"It made a sensation!"*

Hughes made the magic 500 at 22:53 amidst the usual hullabaloo from the fans that went wild with appreciation. "He's a great man, aint he?" remarked O'Leary as the race leader went off to his room to think about all the dollars he was about to be showered with should he prevail. The midnight score: **Hughes, 500; Krohne, 488; Howard, 485; Albert, 484; Vint, 473; Phillips, 425; Campana, 385:**

Phillips, the Bostonian, was the next man to remove his running shoes for good at 04:20 having made 437.3. The only real excitement of the rest of the morning occurred when Khrone indulged in some running with Howard, which in itself was a very unusual sight. They went around the tanbark at a terrific pace for three quarters of a mile and the rare event proved too much for some spectators, some of whom were beside themselves with excitement as, *"men jumped up on the benches and cheered lustily."* The 10:00 records: **Hughes, 538; Albert, 525; Vint, 518; Krohne, 516; Howard; 513; Campana, 401:**

Howard withdrew from the race at 11:29, stiff, sore and in great pain due to bruising on his left foot which had developed into an abscess having achieved a score of 515.1. Although disappointed that he could go no further, Harry was safe in the knowledge that he would secure a share of the gate money. At noon, the scores of the remaining five participants were thus: **Hughes, 546.4; Albert, 532.4; Vint, 527; Krohne, 524.1; Campana, 401:**

The spacious rink was quite full in the afternoon, and, as usual, there were many female fans of the sport in the audience, which was estimated to be about 4,000 people. The word had got around the city that some impressive scores were being made and people from all walks of life made their way to see for themselves. Many knew that both Hart's American record of 565 miles and 165 yards, made on April the 20th of the previous year and Charlie Rowell's world record, completed on November the 6th of the same year in London, were both there for the taking. The scores at 5 o'clock: **Hughes, 562; Albert, 544; Vint; 537; Krohne, 527; Campana, 411:**

Hughes leads Albert

The National Police Gazette   (Illustration no: 80)

"Lepper" Hughes, the star of the show, was the only man in the place who could break those records and at 17:43 he equalled Hart's score. Then, at precisely 17:56:20, he made the necessary distance to surpass the 566 miles to tie the record made by Rowell. When his score was put up on the big blackboard, there was a hearty round of cheering and deafening applause. After making one more lap, he sought rest after his fantastic accomplishment. Albert was then in second place with 547 miles, Vint, third with 539.1, Krohne (resting), fourth with 527.5, and Campana, having made 419.1, was in sixth spot. Indeed "Sport," after completing just one more mile, was announced as the next retiree much to the disappointment of the crowd who now had no one to *"clown around"* for them. The audience, due to its numbers began to encroach on to the track, but they weren't interfering with the progress of the competitors.

Now lying on his bed in his tent, and surrounded by a crowd of ladies, Hughes told a visiting reporter, "Why, I could have made six hundred miles, and will do so yet, but there was no necessity. I have beaten the Englishman, and I am satisfied."

With the building filled to capacity by 7 o'clock, there were only two men on the track running their way through a huge cloud of tobacco smoke. They were Albert, who had made 550.1 and Vint, who, wearing a black jockey cap and crimson silk neckerchief, was on a score of 542.6. Incidentally, Albert at this time still believed he could beat Hughes, despite being 16 miles behind him. With Hughes still off the track, any rumours that he wouldn't return were quickly denied by Mr. Curtis. Krohne arrived back on the track at 19:12 having been out of the race since 15:00. He appeared refreshed after taking a bath and changing his costume and immediately began running three laps to Albert and Vint's one. After the tall Prussian had been running for two miles, he then began limping and finally retired altogether from the race having achieved 529 miles.

Hughes left his quarters at 19:40 and was greeted with enthusiasm by the crowd. He wore a black and red suit and carried on his chest a placard saying, "Police Gazette." He made two awkward laps and appeared to limp, but as the band started to play once again, his gait improved, the music appearing to inspire him and his weary fellow pedestrians. He made 567 miles and went back to his hut. Again, it wasn't known if whether he would reappear. Whilst taking some time out, he doubtless would have been read some of the many telegrams of congratulations that had been sent to him, one of which informed him:

King of the Peds

BRADFORD, Pa., January 20, 1881

Pedestrian Hughes, American Institute:

Accept congratulations from the boys of the first bay resort. We are proud of your record, beating the English record. Although our two entries were unsuccessful you're many friends hope to see you in our city soon, when a warm welcome will be extended to you.

(Signed)   MANY FRIENDS.

Campana appeared at the scorers' stand at 19:55 complaining he had only been taking a drink earlier, and that he had been misunderstood by Mr. Curtis, who had officially posted him as retired at 18:16. He insisted on taking part in the match again. Vint and Albert were both given flowers which they ran around with, and Campana followed Albert imitating his gait. Ten minutes later the Bridgeporter raided the case holding the prized belt and ran around the track with it. He was chased by the *"attaches"* and the crowd enjoyed his eccentric antics. Campana had been placing small bets on himself in the last two days that he would make initially 400, then 425 miles. Consequently he was the only man on the track at times *"entertaining"* the crowd.

A prize of a *"handsomely"* upholstered rocking chair would be given to the pedestrian covering the most miles in the last 24 hours of the contest, by The Brooklyn Furniture Company. It was said that Vint had set his heart on it and that he had made some sort of arrangement with Albert that he would set the pace that would give Albert second place.

Hughes came back on the track at 20:58 followed by "Sport" who was carrying an old broom, which he held above the champion's head. Campana disappeared from view after making his 425th mile giving one last grimace to the man who operated his dial. Meanwhile, Vint, clenching his teeth, ran around the track like a deer, passing and re-passing Albert.

John Hughes

The National Police Gazette   (Illustration no: 81)

On the last lap of his 568th mile, Hughes donned an American flag while the band played "Hail Columbia." Amidst utter pandemonium during which Hughes got caught up in a procession of messenger boys, O'Leary rebuked Bryan G. McSwyny for attempting to place the belt around the race winner's waist. "Hang it, man!" he shouted at him, "the race isn't over yet." Indeed, Albert and Vint were still toeing it around the track, and both were finding it difficult to move themselves through the gathered masses which blocked their way. When those two left the path for the last time, Hughes was finally presented with the belt by O'Leary at 21:24. After he had been formally declared the winner of the contest at 21:32 he left the track to join his wife at the Metropolitan Hotel, after completing two more unrecognised laps of the track. Bookmakers were reported to have lost a fortune on him winning the match.

The prize of the rocking chair that had preoccupied Vint was eventually won by him having scored 76.6 against Albert's 72 and 5 in the last day of competition.

Since his participation in the Rose Belt race in late December of 1879, Hughes had been 2nd twice to Jimmy Albert, firstly in March of 1880, in a 75-hour event at Brockton, Massachusetts, then in a 72-hour event at the Industrial Art Hall at Philadelphia, where he covered 404 miles in April. Then at Cincinnati, in another J. H. Haverly-Fred Englehardt promoted go-as-you-please contest held between May the 16th and the 24th, on a 14-lap to the mile track, he covered 548 miles in 100 hours (12½ hours per day). Storms interrupted the match and it was frequently stopped and postponed. Later in August, he scored a paltry 106 miles after withdrawing from the 72 hours O'Leary Champion Belt of the World on the second day, the race being won by Dobler.

Six-Day Scoring Records and Final Result:

		Monday	Tuesday	Wednesday	Thursday	Friday	Saturday	TOTAL
1	Hughes	134.2	94.7	96.6	91.2	83	68.2	**568.3**
2	Albert	125	94.7	81.1	89	95.3	72.5	**558**
3	Vint	120	93.6	86.2	90	83.2	76.6	**550**
4	Krohne	115.1	91.5	93.2	84	95.4	49.4	**529**
5	Howard	105.7	99.3	99.6	83.1	95.7	31.1	**515.1**

A record of each of the first five contestants on and off track times during the week is as follows:

		On Track	Off Track
1	Hughes	116:09:51	25:50:09
2	Albert	119.25.01	23:14:50
3	Vint	121:22:17	23:17:43
4	Krohne	117:44:12	21:44:48
5	Howard	108:23:46	22:58:14

The financial rewards for the first five past the post were:

		Gate Money	Special Prize	Sweepstake	TOTAL
1	Hughes	$4,219.52	$1,000	$3,000	$8,219.52
2	Albert	$2,414.64			
3	Vint	$1,207.32			
4	Krohne	$804.28			
5	Howard	$402.44			

On the following afternoon, the victor was found in his hotel room at the Metropolitan with his wife, the manager of the *National Police Gazette,* and his trainer, Harding. Asked how he was by a reporter, the "Lepper" replied, "I have nothing to trouble me but my throat. For some time past, I have been suffering from bronchitis, and on Wednesday night, owing to the chilliness of the rink, I have received a fresh cold, otherwise I am without a blemish. Of course I am somewhat stiff in my legs. If pushed, I could have covered six hundred miles, and, what is more, I will do so in the next race that I enter." He added that he may enter for the third O'Leary Belt contest due to take place on the 28th of February at Madison Square Garden.

Frank Hart was also visited by a sports correspondent. He told the reporter that he hadn't been surprised by Hughes's score, adding, that if the track hadn't been so hard, and if there hadn't been so much tobacco smoke to contend with, he would have made a better score. "In fact," he added, "You can bet that if Rowell and I ever come together the winning man has to cover six hundred and fifty miles, and I think it can be done with ease."

CHAPTER 30

3rd O'Leary Belt Race & a "Four-Cornered Event"

There would be two races held at Madison Square Garden in the first two weeks of March 1881. The first race was the *third* contest for the six-day go-as-you-please "O'Leary Belt" race starting on Monday, the 28th of February, and the second, starting exactly a week later, which was dubbed a "four-cornered contest," was a race in which George Littlewood was being aimed at. On 11th of February, the *New York Times* reported that: **Littlewood, the pedestrian, of Sheffield at the suggestion of an American gentleman, who was struck with his recent performance with Rowell, has, entered for the walking match which will begin in Madison Square Garden, New York on Monday, March 7th. He will set sail for New York in the Inman steamer, City of Richmond, from Liverpool today.**

In this second race starring the illustrious English pedestrians Charlie Rowell and Henry Vaughan, *"the two Englishmen's scores are to be added together, and pitted against the combined scores of the two Irish-Americans, so that if any one were to be taken ill or drop out in any way the game would be up."* The identity of one the Irish-Americans was of course O'Leary whereas the other man's name wasn't mentioned. Although it was more than likely John Hughes, a report in the *Washington Post* on the 20th of January subsequently suggested that the other man would be John Dobler.

Charles Rowell: *Frank Leslies Illustrated Newspaper: Library of Congress, Prints & Photographs Division, (reproduction number: LC-USZ62-88335) (Illustration no: 82)*

Both Rowell and Vaughan had arrived in America on the steamship *Abyssinia* on the same day as Littlewood's departure from England on the 11th of February. The *Sporting Mirror* referring to his pedestrian engagements in America said: "Old England could not have been better represented or leave her honour and glory in better hands than those of Charles Rowell." Both men were seen with their attendants, Ashel and Landsworth driving up to the Ashland House Hotel. Rowell, attired in a dark *"fitting suit and jaunty hat,"* who was observed to have *"gained considerable in flesh since his last visit,"* stated he would be going into training at once and anticipated doing some *"heavy work"* in his preparation for the match. The day after, it was confirmed that Vaughan would be matched against O'Leary in a heel-and-toe contest, whilst Rowell was reported to be lined up against O'Leary's "Unknown" in the go-as-you-please event. All the contestants would deposit $2,500 in a sweepstakes, and articles of agreement would be signed the following Wednesday, on the arrival of Mr. Atkinson from England on the steamship *Wyoming*.

A sports journalist working for the *Washington Post* was sent up to New York to report on the forthcoming event. The following is his report which appeared on the 14th of February: **Rowell retired at about 9 o'clock last night after receiving a rubbing down. His spin around the track at the American Institute has, he says, done him considerable good, and helped him to get rid of his sea legs. The champion slept soundly, and awoke this morning at 7 o'clock before his trainers were fairly astir. He was soon after given a thorough rubbing, which made his body glow like a lobster's. His breakfast, which was the next thing to be discussed, was simple, but extremely appetizing and** nourishing, comprising delicate mutton-chops, followed with marmalade and toast. No tea or coffee was taken by either Rowell or Vaughan. The dinners to be furnished the pedestrians will consist of some kind of roast meat, together with bread and vegetables, while the suppers will be simply of toast and tea. After breakfast the walkers, with their trainers went around to the Madison Square Garden and made an inspection of the large enclosure. Vaughan, who had of course never seen the building before, was delighted with it advantages for the coming struggle for the championship between himself and O'Leary. The party spent over an hour in a walk around the track, and discussing among themselves subjects connected with the match. The men then returned to their hotel, sitting in the rear of the bar-room and entertaining their visitors. No stimulants, either tobacco or liquor, are used by Rowell or Vaughan. The latter is a fine looking Englishman, tall, well built, with dark hair and dark, piercing eyes. When together in the street, such a disparity appears in the height of the two men that Rowell looks like a boy. The course of training with which the men are being put in condition is, without doubt the best which the most experienced trainers could give. Under these circumstances and considering the stamina of the men, the American champions will at least find it no child's play even to compete with these Englishmen.

As the days passed, there was much disenchantment about the forthcoming four-cornered event. The suspicion was that the contest would fall victim to hippodroming. The suggestion was to divide the gate money so that two thirds went to the winning team and one third to the losers. This was said to be further evidence that the event was of the *"hippodroming"* type, because in a fair contest the winners, and not the losers, would be the ones to claim the profits.

It was said that O'Leary was unfit for the match and that Vaughan would easily beat him. There was still no word as to who Rowell would be running against. Frank Hart's name had been mooted, but he was said to have refused. John Hughes, Jimmy Albert and John Dobler were said to have been approached but they too declined. "None of them would go into the match," said a prominent *"turfite,"* "and now O'Leary is reduced to the necessity of scouring the country to find someone who can make an appearance of holding his own against Rowell, that is if the latter tried to win the race."

The critics, who had doubtless been watching Rowell closely, claimed that he had *"too much superfluous flesh"* and hadn't trained in the same style as he had in previous contests. One of them stated, "Rowell is hog fat, and he has been to balls and wrestling matches since he got here. That doesn't look as though he was training for a very tough contest, does it?"

Rowell and O'Leary denied all the negative accusations, declaring the contest to be a *"perfectly straight forward affair, and one that will be contested to the utmost by all the parties. Bryan McSwyny says that the talk against O'Leary and Rowell is actuated by pure malice that the O'Leary Belt walk will be contested only by fourth rate pedestrians like Ennis, etc, and will in all likelihood prove a failure. McSwyny also denies the charge brought by Hart's friends that O'Leary tried to borrow five thousand dollars off the colored boy to match against the Englishman's money in the forthcoming struggle. Smith, Hart's trainer, says that the latter will produce five thousand dollars at an hour's notice that he can beat Rowell if the latter will enter for the O'Leary belt."*

When Mr. Atkinson arrived in New York on February the 18th, he was whisked off to the Ashland House where he answered some questions about Rowell's forthcoming engagements, in particular his future defence of his Astley Belt against Weston (See Chapter 32).

Reporter: "Will the walk between Rowell and Vaughan on one side and O'Leary and his unknown on the other take the precedence of all of Rowell's other engagements?"

Atkinson: "I know of nothing to the contrary now. Mr. Kuntz tells me that the Madison Square Garden has been engaged for this event, and it is on O'Leary's challenge that Rowell came over here. However, the arrangements will all be definitely settled on Monday when representatives of the press will be invited to attend."

Reporter: "How about Weston's challenge to Rowell for the Astley Belt?"

Atkinson: "Of course as Weston has made the necessary deposit of £20, Rowell as holder of the belt, will have to accept it. But it should be borne in mind that Rowell has the naming of the place where the walk will take place, and Weston, I am informed objects to walking in this country. However, this is a matter for further consideration. In the meantime I have written to Sir John Astley asking him if the entrance fee cannot be raised to more than £20.

King of the Peds

Reporter: Is not Rowell also under promise to Mr. Abell to enter his six day's tournament the last week in May?"

Atkinson: "Yes; but of course Rowell will have to defend the Astley Belt. After this engagement with O'Leary any challenges to compete for that belt comes first and foremost. This is one of the matters that will be talked over on Monday."

The last that is heard of Rowell and Vaughan at that time was on the training front, and where it was reported that the former was reducing his weight to *"fighting condition,"* and the latter, for his part, heel-and-toeing 50 miles a day.

On Saturday, February 19th, at the *Spirit of the Times* office, referee William B. Curtis said, "There will be no hippodroming in the O'Leary belt contest," as he exhibited the list of entries for the O'Leary Belt contest which would commence at the Garden on Monday, February the 28th. The winner of the contest would win the belt, the $2,000 or so entrance money, and 4/7ths of the gate money, after expenses, the remainder going on to be divided among those who would be placed.

The 19 contestants in the race were: **Joe Allen** of Adams, Massachusetts, who had a best distance of 523 3/8 miles, was 31 years old, weighed in at 135 pounds, and was 5ft. 8in tall. **W. Bendigo** was from Haiti and lived in Boston. He had never walked in a six-day race before. **W. Bolstridge,** New York. **Daniel Burns** of Elmira, New York, had been matched against horses and always won. His best record was 578 ¾ miles which he made in 156 hours. He was 22 years old, weighed 140 pounds, and stood 5 feet 10 inches. **Napoleon Campana**, *"the clown of the last race in the Garden claimed Bridgeport as his home, much to the disgust of some Bridgeporters who had wagered money on him. They said he was quite old enough to die."* He said he was 45 and said he weighed 112 pounds. He was 5 feet 8 inches tall and his best distance was 500 miles. **Benjamin Curran** of New York, had made a personal best of 450 1/8 mile. **John Ennis** of Stamford, Connecticut, weighed 156 pounds for this race. **Thomas Goulding,** New York. **George Hanwaker** of Boston, had a best record of 451 3/8 miles. **Frank H. Hart,** also of Boston. "Happy Jack" Smith and Dr. Robert Taylor would attend to his well being. **Harry Howard** of Glen Cove, Long Island, had been originally touted as **Thomas Davies's "Unknown:"** Harry weighed in at 145 pounds, and the furthest distance he had made in a race of this kind was 534 5/8 miles (Tom Davies was originally going to introduce George Littlewood to the American pedestrian scene in this race, but as it transpired, waited till May of the same year). **John Hughes**, New York. **Frederick Krohne**, New York. **Richard Lacouse** of Boston had made 425 miles. **J. McCarty,** Manayunk, Pennsylvania. **John C. Mulgrew,** New York. **Peter J. Panchot**, Hastings, Minnesota. **Pierce Ryan**, New York. **John Sullivan** of Saratoga Springs. The slimly built athlete would be attended by James Riley, the oarsman. He was 27 years old and was 5 feet 4 inches in height. *"He is of rather slight build, but well developed in the chest and legs."* He had been a factory operative, a driver in a team and then a clerk in a hotel until he was successfully entered in a number of country walking matches. He competed in his first race at Hall's Opera House, in Whitehall, New York, in September of 1878 which he won, thereafter taking part in many 72 and 27-hour races during the next two years. His best record to date was when he made 385.2 in a 72-hour go-as-you-please race at the Infantry Hall, Providence, Rhode Island, in April of 1880 when he beat Guyon, Vint, Colston and Herty in that order. **Michael Tynan**, New York.

The bookmakers were giving the following odds on the race: **Hart, 1/1; Hughes, 3/1; Allen, 7/1; Howard, 10/1; Panchot and Sullivan, 12/1; Burns, Krohne, McCarty and Ryan, 15/1; Bar these, 20/1:**

The *New York Times* described the start of the race: In spite of the prospects of a thorough cleansing by the prevailing rain "the great unwashed" rallied in force at the Madison Square Garden last evening. Mingling with it in the line which led into the building was a modicum of gentility as represented by young clerks and business men. Fully 5,000 persons were beneath the roof when the pedestrian match opened, and every seat and every box was occupied.

At 12 o'clock Referee Curtis gave the word "go," and the 19 shot away like a pack of hounds that had struck a scent. Krohne brought up the rear, working his legs as fast as it was possible to move them. He does not shine as a trotter and, conscious of that fact, never breaks his heel and toe gait if he can avoid it. Campana ran like a deer, and was first around to the judges' stand. Curran was next and Hart was a good third. Bendigo, the other colored man was packed in a group which came down the track together at a headlock gait. Mulgrew's was a contemplative gait, such as a truant school-boy would adopt after the day's fun was over. Burns finished his mile first and Hart was only 10 feet behind him. The excitement among the spectators found vent in uproarious cheers and Rowell and Vaughan, the two doughty little English walkers, applauded the men as they passed the box in which they sat.

McCarty, the light-weight wrestler, was the first man to drop out of the race. He lasted exactly 2h.16m for a score of 13.5. Mulgrew was next in line for a premature retirement on an equally pathetic score of just 14 miles at 04:50. This left just seventeen men to fight out for the prizes on offer.

Hughes, who was in the lead at 06:00 on a score of 42 miles, led Burns by just seven laps, with Hart 10 laps adrift of him. The "Lepper" then settled himself down to some solid work, and actually broke the American record for the ninth hour, when he made a distance of 6 miles and 40 yards, thus beating Faber's record in the 2nd O'Leary Belt contest made on the 5th of April of the previous year.

Hanwaker was the next man to give in at 09:30 having made 34.6. After that, and much to the disappointment of his connections, Hart, who was in sixth position at 11:30, retired on a score of 63. Earlier in the race he had complained that he felt unwell, stating he was suffering from a cold that he had contracted through *"getting overheated,"* and that his lungs were *"paining him."* He had hardly been able to walk between 04:00 and 05:00, but had recovered sufficiently well to be seen to be going along pretty nicely at 08:00, and even better at 11:00. Of his withdrawal from the race, the *New York Times* commented that Hart: Created a vast deal of talk and the suspicion was very general that he had been bought off. As the bookmakers are believed to be the wickedest class of sporting men known about the Garden, they were charged to having conceived and executed the purchase. The hows and wherefores for such a transaction, however, were a mystery which the rules of logic even could not assist in solving. If *Dr. Alexander B. Mott of No. 62 Madison avenue, is to be believed - and his standing in the medical profession confirms the correctness of his opinion - Hart was really too ill to continue on the track.

*This is to certify that I have examined Frank Hart and find that he is suffering from intercostal neuralgia, caused by taking cold during the walk from wearing too light clothing, and the trouble would be increased by his continuing to walk, but will be relieved with by rest and treatment in a few days.

ALEXANDER B. MOTT. M. D.

By noon, Hughes's effort of 74.5 had beaten Jimmy Albert's American record by a lap. Punters could now get 6/4 on him winning the match, 1/3 for him to come in first or second and 1/5 a place, 1st, 2nd or 3rd.

The score at 13:00, with Hughes ahead of the American record by a mile and 220 yards, was: **Hughes, 80.3; Panchot, 76.4; Sullivan, 76; Burns, 74.7; Krohne, 71.3; Lacouse, 65.7; Howard, 65.1; Curran, 64.1; Allen, 63.4; Tynan, 59.2; Campana, 56.1; Ennis, 58.4; Bendigo, 55; Ryan, 42.6; Goulding, 42:**

Three more of the pedestrians fell by the wayside as the afternoon progressed starting with Bendigo the Bostonian at 13:10, having amassed 55.4. He was followed out of the ring by Goulding at 15:35 with 49. The last man to leave around teatime was Ryan with 57.1 at 17:13. By this stage Panchot had hauled himself to the front, and was going along just fine and dandy. Hopes were high that he would beat the "Lepper's" American record of 134 miles and 220 yards made on January 24th in the same year, which was far below Rowell's 146 miles and 251 yards world record made in November of the previous year.

The scores at 21:00: **Panchot, 121; Sullivan, 113; Hughes, 112; Burns, 109; Howard, 107; Allen, 102; Krohne, 100; Curran, 97; Campana and Lacouse, 88; Tynan, 82; Ennis, 77:**

When Hughes was the next competitor to leave the race, the press's disillusionment about the possibility of the contest being fixed was reinforced. It was obvious that he hadn't rested sufficiently since his previous race before embarking on this latest battle for glory, *"acute rheumatism of the stomach"* being touted as the official reason for failure. The *New York Times* wrote: It is a sad commentary on the honesty of pedestrians that a physician's certificate is necessary to relieve them, when they drop out of a race, of the suspicion of shamming.

When the news of Hughes's collapse got around the suspicion strengthened that there was something somewhere that made the match an awfully crooked one. Hughes skipped into his box for good at 9:59 P. M., having made 115 3/8 miles. Inquiries were made for his physician's certificate, but it remained invisible. He is alleged to have had *"cramps in his stomach." Hughes lay on his cot, the very picture of a man in perfect health. Whether the interest in the race will now disappear remains to be seen.

King of the Peds

*Hughes also complained of "swimming in the head."

Charlie Rowell, who was in the building, told reporters that he thought that "Oward would win the race," even though Panchot was doing so well on the track at the time. The leader was to be seen to break the American record at 23:25 and retired for the night a few minutes later on a score of 135 miles and 145 yards. Meanwhile, the punters were piling in on Sullivan. The "knowing" ones had managed to get 12/1 before the start of the race, and it was claimed that $23,000 had been bet on the Saratogan to take the belt. Campana was also advising one of his friends to put his mortgage on him saying, "I've fooled all my life, but I'm going to win this time." The old eccentric stated he would make an average of 96 miles a day and beat all records; but the advice wasn't heeded.

Later, the midnight scores read: **Panchot, 135; Sullivan, 125; Howard, 120; Burns, 116; Allen, 114; Curran, 105; Krohne, 104; Campana, 99; Lacouse, 95; Ennis and Tynan, 85:**

At 00:40, Tynan was the ninth man to withdraw permanently with 87.7. Within four hours "Honest" John Ennis succumbed on a mark of 90, with problems with his stomach being quoted as the excuse for his premature departure.

The three men at the head of affairs all went well during the early hours of the next day. Sullivan, who was three miles ahead of Howard in the morning, raced a few yards behind the Glen Cove *"wrestler."* The Saratogan himself was persistently followed by Panchot, who, at eleven o'clock, was exactly a mile ahead of the best American record made by Hughes. The scores at that time were: **Panchot, 174; Sullivan, 163; Howard, 160; Krohne, 156; Allen, 151; Curran, 145; Campana, 132; Lacouse, 127:**

Burns, who had not been seen since 22:34 the night before, advised the match officials at 13:27 that he too would not be seen again on the track. He had made 116.4 and his withdrawal left just eight in the race.

At 14:00, the scores were: **Panchot, 187; Sullivan, 178; Howard, 172; Krohne, 168; Allen, 165; Curran, 157; Campana, 144; Lacouse, 139:**

Joe Allen was the next man to offer his resignation at 22:05. He had made 179 miles and that left a remaining total of seven to fight for the prizes and the paltry amount that would be offered by the management from the gate money due to the ever dwindling attendance brought about by the withdrawal of Hart and Hughes. Of those still competing, Howard went about his business in good style. It was said that he was getting the most careful attention from his team who were said to, *"watch every movement of Sullivan's team as a cat would watch a mouse."* Krohne lurched forward as ever, his gangly legs evenly stepping out the same distance giving his followers confidence that he might finish the race in top position. Likewise, Curran, wearing a pink shirt and blue overalls, with the lower half of the legs cut above the knees, covered the ground impressively.

Panchot, whose face wore a *"fagged expression,"* gave some the impression he may not last the week due to the scintillating pace he had made in the past two days. He settled down to an impressive heel-and-toe race with Sullivan at 11 o'clock, having just equalled the best 48-hour score on record 50 minutes earlier. When he went to his bed at 23:30, the betting on the boards showed: **Panchot, 1/1; Sullivan, 5/2; Howard, 3/1; Krohne, 5/1; Curran and Lacouse, 50/1; Campana, 100/1:**

The returns at midnight were: **Panchot, 235; Sullivan, 220.7; Howard, 213; Krohne, 203.5; Curran, 200; Campana, 144; Lacouse, 174.5:**

It was with great surprise that the Glen Cove *"boatman,"* Harry Howard gave up the chase a few minutes after six o'clock in the morning, after travelling 226 miles and a lap. No explanation was offered for his demise, apart from the speculation that this race had come too soon after his epic encounter with the likes of Hughes and Krohne in the race at the American Institute Building, which had ended only a month before.

Having said that, Krohne was still going strongly in this race and it might be a good idea to familiarise ourselves with the form of the three men over a period of 18 months starting from September of 1879 till this race.

	Dates							Totals
Krohne	79/09		79/12	80/04		81/01	81/03	
Howard		79/10	79/12	80/04	80/11	81/01	81/03	
Hughes			79/12			81/01	81/03	
	Distance							**MILES**
Krohne	450		536	516		529	???	**2031**
Howard		500	296	534	240	515	226	**2311**
Hughes			520			568	115	**1203**
	Position							
Krohne	8th		2nd	6th		4th	???	
Howard		2nd	Unp	3rd	Unp	5th	Unp	
Hughes			6th			1st	Unp	
	Earnings							**DOLLARS**
Krohne	$877.5		$1,200	$217.74		$804.28	???	**$3,099.52**
Howard		$2,000	0	$1,741.91	£0	$402.44	0	**$4,144**
Hughes			$244			$8,219.52	0	**$8,463.52**

Looking at the table above we see Fred appearing in five races, Harry in six and the "Lepper" in three. Fred's final score for this race is not included, but we can see for ourselves the frequency of competitive racing they indulged in. Harry's six-race record is particularly interesting. The reader will notice how each score of 500 plus miles is followed by a race where that distance is followed by a mediocre effort, whereas Fred's more economic method of conveyance is rewarded with more consistent scores of 450 plus every time he competed. Fred may have not been a pretty sight as he strode around the track, but he always managed to pick up prize money. The tall Prussian was also more comfortable employing a walking gait and rarely ran. John Hughes on the other hand, was predominantly a runner, and using this method of locomotion did manage to pick up a pretty prize of $8,219.52 for his sole win. Yes, six-day go-as-you-please racing was tough, but for those at the top of their profession, the rewards were there to be had. Fred, Harry and John did very well for themselves.

The old place lacked any sort of atmosphere as the remaining six trudged round its inside, and there were very few people watching the sport on offer. The restaurants and bars were lacking in custom and the only thing which offered the paying public anything in the way of interest was a five-mile running race between Panchot and Sullivan during the afternoon after which, the leader headed for his house for a rest. Just before the excitement, the scores at 2 p.m. read: **Panchot, 288.2; Sullivan, 272.7; Krohne, 264.3; Curran, 243; Campana and Lacouse, 232:**

Of the others, Krohne lumbered along in his stereotypical ungraceful way. Lacouse, although appearing well, projected himself forward slowly. Curran, for all his grim effort, appeared *"decidedly played out."* The only other player on the field to comment on was "Old Sport," who, *"continued to furnish jests and amusement for the crowd by his oddities. He hobbled around the track, bobbing his head first to one side and then the other, much after the manner of a harmless lunatic on Blackwell's Island who imagines himself a horse."* It was a well known fact that the old stager was being paid to amuse the crowd, and with the state the race found itself in, whatever he was paid was worth its weight in gold.

Fred Krohne must have raised a few cheers when he ambled past the winning post to register his 300th mile at 22:14, his supporters still convinced he could overcome the two lads performing respectfully in front. He was still on offer at 3/1 with the bookies who sat in front of their tin boxes twiddling their thumbs as they watched the match scores being hoisted up at midnight. With Panchot having left the track at 23:35, followed by Sullivan 20 minutes later, they showed: **Panchot, 327; Sullivan, 317; Krohne, 300; Curran, 280; Campana, 269.6; Lacouse, 264.5:**

At 10 o'clock the next morning (82nd hour), Panchot was a mile ahead of Rowell's record distance made in London in the November of the previous year. However, when his total of 364 miles appeared on the telegraph board, the information was greeted with *"feeble applause"* by the few souls that made up the audience in the building, many of whom were described as *"corner loafers,"* with the females amongst them of the *"lowest class."* Following his success, the leader immediately left the track for a change of clothing and a good rubbing down. Whilst he enjoyed the attentions of his team, Sullivan went hell for leather out on the course in an attempt to gain some ground on him, managing to lessen the gap by a couple of miles. Another of the athletes who was hell bent on making solid progress during the day was Krohne. He had set himself a task of competing a 100 miles a day but his trainer had other ideas. Fearing that Fred was a bit deluded in his thinking, he hauled the lanky German off the track at 11:30 and locked him in his cabin until he reluctantly agreed to have a bath and allow the rubbers to go to work on him. Krohne, despite the remonstrations of his attendants, went back to work at 12:17 to make up the lost ground after being washed and massaged.

It was about 12:30 when Panchot received the adulation of the crowd as he stopped his fellow competitor Sullivan on the track, and tenderly removed something from his eye which had been annoying him. When the Saratogan had been relieved of the foreign object, he continued to trot around the place with Panchot, as usual, snapping at his heels.

The scores at 2 p.m: **Panchot, 381.4; Sullivan, 368.1; Krohne, 353.1; Curran, 324.5; Campana, 316.2; Lacouse, 303.7:**

Despite the poor attendance, the men on the track wobbled along with much determination. Panchot, the top dog in the race, alternated his gait all afternoon, and up till eight o'clock in the evening, maintained his positive assault on Rowell's record. Sullivan brightened up the dullness of the place after his reappearance at 21:10, when he ran around the path wearing pink tights for a couple of miles—much to the appreciation of the 1,500 patrons watching. Later on, as the band played "Tommy Dodd," Krohne and Sullivan amused the smaller crowd of 500 or so with a 10-minute burst of speed, but the effort soon petered out. Panchot meanwhile, slept in his room having knocked three miles off Rowell's record.

The state of play at midnight: **Panchot, 420; Sullivan, 407; Krohne, 377; Curran, 360; Campana, 355; Lacouse, 343:**

Barring absolute catastrophe, it was a foregone conclusion that Panchot would prevail in the *"walking match."* That sense of inevitability and the rain kept many away from the Garden in the morning during which a 100 or so people witnessed the events on the track. The few that were watching, witnessed Panchot complete his 450th mile at 09:46 which meant he was the first of the pedestrians who would profit from the gate money. He was also four minutes ahead of Hughes's January record at the same stage. The 1/3 shot was now a mile ahead of the best ever record, and the bookies responded to that fact by offering even money that the Buffalonian would beat the current record by the end of the match.

The midday scores (100th hour): **Panchot, 459.3; Sullivan, 440.3; Krohne, 427.6; Curran, 404.4; Lacouse, 386.3: Campana, 374.3:**

What the score sheets stated two hours later: **Panchot, 464; Sullivan, 448.2; Krohne, 434.7; Curran, 413.5; Lacouse, 391.7: Campana, 375:**

As the fifth day wore on, the only event that tempered the dullness of the affair happened at nine o'clock in the evening, when a dozen uniformed letter carriers entered the building carrying a large bouquet of flowers with the letter "P" in the centre. When Panchot completed the fifth lap of his 500th mile, this was presented to him. The gathered throng of 1,500 cheered as the postmen blew their whistles. To celebrate his achievement, Panchot left the building in search of a relaxing Turkish bath, probably glad to leave the tobacco laden atmosphere, but also possibly a little reluctant to leave behind the *"usual number of women, gorgeously clad in furs and rouge,"* who *"filled the boxes."*

What wasn't commented on by the press was Sullivan's demotion to third spot in the race. No reason was given for the fact that from two o'clock in the afternoon, the Saratogan could only make a paltry 10 miles in the 10 hours between that hour and midnight. Of course, the reliable plodder that Fred Krohne was took full advantage of whatever was ailing John, and by the end of the fifth day, he had managed to pull himself 13 miles clear. Ben Curran, who had been making eye catching progress in the day, was now closing in for third place.

Midnight information: **Panchot, 501; Krohne, 471; Sullivan, 458; Curran, 449; Lacouse, 422: Campana, 400:**

At last, the newspapers were able to offer some insight into the rapid demise of Sullivan on the previous day. He was said to have been suffering intense agony during the night, his right knee being swollen to almost twice its usual size with both his feet being *"frightfully blistered."* Further to that, his *"blood"* was reported to have been in *"poor condition"* from the start of the week with *"eruptions"* being visible upon his face and neck during the race; and when he offered his resignation from the race at 06:07 on a score of 461½ miles, his eyes were bloodshot and his face had a purplish hue. He was carried from the building to the Putnam House and put to bed by his trainer, who it was said would try and induce him to walk later.

Sadly, Panchot's early promise of a record-breaking performance fizzled away after midnight, as he only travelled 10 miles in the race since then until 08:44, when he was recorded as being 14 miles behind the best record made by Hughes. The reason given for his failure was that his feet were sore and swollen. The race leader was evidently determined not to punish himself by doing any more than win with a fair score.

Meanwhile, Curran plodded on in a dogged manner, and it was expected that a large group of his fellow dock workers were going to turn up at the Garden that evening to shout him home. Lacouse, who had suffered with his stomach the day before, was now over his problems, and showing more energy and speed than any of the rest, moved along sweetly in fourth position, with the old campaigner Campana bringing up the rear.

The 9 a.m. scores: **Panchot, 520; Krohne, 486; Curran, 483; Lacouse, 460; Campana, 428:**

Later, the scorers' returns at 14:00 showed: **Panchot, 526.5; Krohne, 501.2; Curran, 484; Lacouse, 467.7; Campana, 435.3:**

It was at his time that the bookmaking firms of Kelly & Bliss, H. Snedeker, Brown and Jahr, William Atkinson, Duryea and Co, Wandle & Co, Gould, Sillack & Co, Nelson & McClean, T. B. Johnson and H. Stanford announced that all bets on Panchot for first place would be paid on presentation of winning tickets. Friends of Sullivan who had been compelled to spend nearly all his time in his quarters the previous day, stated that they had made a considerable loss on their man. The bookmakers declared that they had lost little on Panchot at 20/1, and whatever losses there were, they had been made up for by the failure of Hart and Hughes at the beginning of the match.

At 3 o'clock in the afternoon, the record showed: **Panchot, 530; Khrone, 505.3; Curran, 487.2; Lacouse, 472.3; Campana, 438.2:**

An hour later the scores were: **Panchot, 534; Khrone, 508.2; Curran, 491; Lacouse, 477; Campana, 442:**

At 5 p.m. the indicators showed: **Panchot, 534.5; Khrone, 510; Curran, 492.2; Lacouse, 484.4; Campana, 445.4:**

An hour later at 6 o'clock, the scores were: **Panchot, 535.5; Khrone, 512.2; Curran, 496.4; Lacouse, 484.4 and Campana, 448.7:**

Just before Campana fell out of the race with 450 miles and one lap to his credit at 18:20, Charlie Rowell jumped out on to the track and accompanied him for a lap talking to him and urging him on. The gesture brought much praise from the crowd, who showed their appreciation by roundly applauding the Englishman. The old fellow, who had made a further 25 miles than he had accomplished in his last race, apparently appeared as fresh as when he had started out.

There was faint ripple of applause when Curran accomplished 500 miles at 18:58 in front of a light attendance of about 1,200 people of which about 250 were women and children. At that time, the record showed: **Panchot, 534.5; Khrone, 515.3; Curran, 500; Lacouse, 484.4; Campana, 450.1:**

A lot of money had been bet on Lacouse getting third place, and Curran had been offered $1,500 of pool tickets to make sure that happened. The people behind the bribe were said to be a group of Canadians, who had placed $6,000 on Lacouse at long odds to come in one of the first three positions. One of Curran's backers took the tickets,

King of the Peds

and the affair was reported by Mr. Curtis, the chief scorer, to the management. Curran, although exhausted by his efforts, declared that he would compete until he dropped rather than give up his third place. For his honesty and pluckiness, Mr. Curtis gave a $500 bill to Curran; Curtis later telling reporters, "I do not wish this to be misconstrued. I have paid this $500 out of my own pocket, as I did not wish injustice to be done."

When the conspirators found out that the scheme had been discovered, they cursed Curran for his honesty, with one of them remarking, "The dastardly fool will lose over seven hundred dollars, which he could have easily made!" The *New York Times* put its slant on the story by writing: **About 7 o'clock it leaked out that a large sum of money had been bet that Lacouse would win third place, and that an effort had been made to buy off the longshoreman and allow the Frenchman to pass him. Unfortunately for the longshoreman's reputation he was about to accept the $1,500 bribe, when Manager Kelly heard of it. That gentleman sent Barney Aaron down to Curran's box to learn the true inwardness of the affair. One of Lacouse's backers stepped up and said if Barney didn't stop coaching the longshoreman and "get out" he'd hit him in the nose. "My son" replied Aaron, leaning his elbow upon the speaker's shoulder, "I'll give you $10 to come out with me out behind these boxes where nobody but our selves can witness such an occurrence." The speaker hurriedly retreated. When Aaron made his report to Mr. Kelly, that gentleman threatened to bring the reporters down to Curran's box to show them, in the doctor's presence, that the old man was perfectly able to go on. If he cared to be exposed, he could accept the bribe. Curran decided that he wouldn't leave the track, and Mr. Kelly then gave him $500. To those who only knew that Curran had declined to be bribed, the five hundred dollar bill which he carried around the track on the end or a stick had all the significance of a reward for Roman virtue.** (At 8:10 p.m. Curran made two laps holding a truncheon with the $500 note given to him; as the report of the reason why he had received it spread he was much applauded).

Lacouse finally retired at 19:40 with a score of 489.1. Five minutes after the announcement was made, Khrone and Panchot sprinted around the path for a couple of laps with the long legged Prussian outperforming the leader who fell back into his dog-trot and commenced to stalk his adversary.

With the attendance rising to about 1,600 by 20:00, Sullivan, who had withdrawn from the match earlier in the day, appeared *"all broke up"* when he was observed in front of the reporters' stand, having rested and slept. At this time, the record showed: **Panchot, 537.7; Khrone, 518.5; Curran, 503.4; Lacouse, 489.1:**

At 8:30 p.m., there were about 2,000 spectators present. Panchot and Khrone had another dash for a lap or two, they being the only two remaining on the track. Khrone was much the fresher of the pair, and the remark was made that he looked good for 48 hours more. Curran called it a day at 20:40 with 504.4 for his record, and 20 minutes later at 9 o'clock, the score was as follows: **Panchot, 539.3; Khrone, 521.1:**

Krohne walked past the scorers' stand in his street clothes at 9:35 p.m. having retired with 523.3, and a few seconds after Panchot came around with the belt clasped around his waist. At 21:45, Sullivan joined the winner on the track who withdrew from the race at this time with 541 miles and 3 laps. The three principals in the race were showered with floral tributes from their lady admirers; and as the band played "Hail Columbia" followed by "Home Sweet Home," Panchot was said to have had a good look at his hard earned trophy.

The Final Score!

Pos		Miles	Laps	Yards	Pos		Miles	Laps
1	**Panchot**	541	3	165	4	Lacouse	489	1
2	Krohne	523	3	165	5	Sullivan	461	4
3	Curran	504	4		6	Campana	450	1

Mr. Curtis reported that that there had been 21,101 tickets sold during the week. Panchot would therefore receive the belt worth $500, the $1,900 entrance money and about $300 as one-half of the profits, which would aggregate over $650. The winner would therefore receive $2,100 exclusive of his own $100 entrance money. Khrone would receive $150 as his share of the gate money, Curran $75, Lacouse, $37.50 Sullivan $17.25 and Campana $8.62.

On the last day of the contest, the 5th of March, the following article concerning Michael Tynan, who had competed in the match, appeared in the *Brooklyn Daily Eagle*:

P. S. Marshall

A Man Who Entered the O'Leary Belt Contest, and Thrashed His Wife on His Return Home.

"You are fined $20, and if you can't pay it you had better send to Napoleon Campana asking him to pay it for you."

Those words were addressed by Justice Ferry this morning to Tynan, the pedestrian who entered the O'Leary Belt contest at Madison Square Garden, and let the track after a tramp of twenty four hours, during which he made eighty five miles. He was induced to enter the match by his "friends and admirers" in South Brooklyn, who thought he possessed wonderful powers of endurance, and who were prepared to give him a token of "appreciation and esteem" in case his efforts came up to their expectations. Mr. Tynan lives at No 440 Smith Street, and there was a profound feeling of disgust among the neighbors when it was found that their hero was vanquished in such a summary manner. But Mr. Tynan is something more than a pedestrian. As shown to the entire satisfaction of Justice Ferry, he is a most expert and accomplished wife beater, and the way in which he blackened the eyes of his inoffensive spouse and tore away much of her hair would have done credit to the most experienced and proficient of his class. Alice is Mrs. Tynan's Christian name. She made complaint against her husband, and the result of the examination was the imposing of the fine, which was paid not by Mr. Napoleon Campana, better known as the "Sport," but by the prisoner's employer. It was shown that Mr. Tynan was of irritable temper, especially at times when he was in training, and that it was customary for him to throw dishes around the house, break glass and raise the wind generally. He promised to reform before leaving the court, and marched down Butler Street with stately tread, followed by two of his misguided backers in the recent contest.

------------------0------------------

To begin coverage of the four-cornered race, we have to cast our minds back to mid February of that year, when all sorts of accusations were flying about regarding the promotion of the contest. Interestingly, the following article appeared in the *Evening Auburnian* on the 22nd of February. No other newspaper followed the same theme and it provides very interesting reading: SPECIAL DISPATCH TO THE AUBURNIAN: New York, February 22.—James Albert of Philadelphia is O'Leary's "unknown." He is pitted against Rowell in the four cornered walk to begin March 6th. Albert won second money by making 558 miles in the late walk where Hughes eclipsed the record. O'Leary thinks that the name of his unknown is safe, and he will curse when it is telegraphed from your columns throughout the country.

Only three men in this city know who is to be Rowell's opponent, and one of them is O'Leary's representative and the man from whom this information comes to me. Rowell is still in ignorance as to who is to be his enemy and O'Leary wants to keep it dark to draw a curious crowd on the first night to learn who he is.

I disclose this because the race I am convinced is thoroughly and scandalously crooked. I believe I know now just who are to be the winners, though this is a point still somewhat in doubt. The reason of the hitch is that one of the men objects to being beaten in the eyes of the public, though he will get his share of the divvy.

This man who rebels is Vaughan. The slate is made up for Rowell to win the go-as-you-please and O'Leary, the heel-and-toe. Vaughan don't like this and hence the delay. The bookmakers and gamblers are to have the "tip." And the public are to be fleeced.

There are betting men amongst your readers. Let them be warned to let this thing alone. They cannot bet on merits with any safety. If they choose to stake their stamps on their ability to guess how the thing is to be "fixed," well enough. I give them the slate as it is now. If so I think I shall know it before the start. If Albert shows signs of beating Rowell, he will be curbed. His chance on the square is to be when Rowell walks next for the Astley belt.

This is not an international walk. It is a match race with $10,000 in the pot as stake money, ostensibly, I say ostensibly because I don't believe that the stakes are honest. It is said there is not even any money up, but this is not so. Money was staked for the looks of the thing but it all goes back to the man who put it up, no matter if he wins or loses.

Frank Hart, the colored boy, is my authority for the statement that O'Leary came to him last fall on his return from England and said: "I have put you against Rowell and myself against Vaughan for a four cornered match. You give me $5,000 to put up for a while. It's all safe for the money all comes back whether we win or loose, but we must make some show before the public." Hart refused. O'Leary then went to "Al." Smith, the sporting man, and he refused. He finally got a brewer named Kuntz who is a blustering ass.

King of the Peds

Vaughan says: "I came over here to walk O'Leary and under the London agreement made last fall." O'Leary says he can beat Vaughan and his "unknown" (Albert) can beat Rowell, but O'Leary will not consent that the winners shall have all the gate receipts.

When Dobler's challenge went to Rowell with his stakes last summer, Rowell would not name date or place till he knew who his opponent was. Now Rowell has traveled 3,000 miles and won't up to this minute know who he is going to walk. He knows the thing is safe, for the bargain was made in London last fall.

The thing is a big job and hippodrome to squeeze money out of those who go see these walks, and a rascally plan to swindle those in the habit of totting.

I send these discoveries by wire for this reason: The facts are to be sent to a Boston paper by mail tonight, their correspondent thinking he has it exclusively. This matter will appear Wednesday and thus, we get a clean "beat."

M.

The writer of the article was correct. *Jimmy Albert *was* the "Unknown," and of him, it was said he looked impressive during the previous fortnight. Other reports suggested that he had also been resting and sleeping a great deal in order to recover from the strain he had put himself through when he came second against Hughes in the previous January. His backers felt confident with the score he made in that race, and the feeling was that he would give Rowell a good race.

*Jimmy Albert was born in Brooklyn in 1854. He was five feet 7¼ inches, and weighed 148lbs. He began his pedestrian career in Philadelphia at the Arcade Garden on April the 7th 1879, where he made 460 miles winning first prize money in a six-day walk. In a 75-hour walk, at the Industrial Art Hall in the same city on May the 31st, he secured second prize making 225 miles. In a 75-hour race at Providence, ending on August the 17th, and on a score of 270 miles, he was third to Harriman who made 288 miles. On February the 6th 1880 at Dover, New Hampshire, in a 27-hour race, he secured first prize for making 136 miles in 25 hours. At Brockton, Massachusetts, ending on March the 27th, in a six-day 75-hour, 12 hours per day race, he won first prize with 435 miles. Again at the Industrial Art Hall in Philadelphia in a six-day 72-hour race contest ending on May the 1st 1880, he made a new world record of 412 miles. Later that month, he took part in another race at Providence, Rhode Island, where he made 275 miles in 75 hours. He then *"won with ease,"* the six-day, 12 hours per day, go-as-you-please O'Leary tournament at Boston in June, scoring 387 miles. *"It was a great performance, in view of the fact that his right leg was injured while saving the lives of three ladies and two children who were on board the Narragansett."* After that in January of 1881, in the first contest for the "O'Leary International Belt," he came second to Hughes, with a score of 558 miles.

A little betting had been done on the contest which began in the early hours of Monday, the 7th of March, the odds of 1/6 being offered by the bookmakers against Rowell, 7/1 against Albert, and in the heel-and-toe match, 1/3 against O'Leary, and 2/1 against Vaughan. Rowell and O'Leary were both being looked upon as *"sure winners."* However, there had been a rumour of a *"sell-out"* on the Sunday evening when the press reported *"that an absurd rumor gained credence which put a stop to all betting."* The story circulating around was that Rowell had arranged for Albert to beat him 20 miles into the contest, and that O'Leary would allow Vaughan to beat him. It was further speculated that when the match was over, Rowell, after a proper period of training, would be invited to try to beat 600 miles.

The indications were that there was going to be a lot of interest in the match, much more than any preceding pedestrian contest that had taken place. One of the managers had stated that if none of the contestants broke down in the early part of the week, the receipts would probably aggregate $75,000 during the term of the contest.

The men were all reported to be in excellent condition from their trainers. It was learned that Rowell hadn't been doing too much exercise, thus allowing him the chance of *"running his feet off"* during the race, and it was confidently stated that Rowell, if pushed, would try to make 600 miles, *"barring accidents."*

O'Leary was reported to be in better form than ever before, and having *"obtained plenty of vitality"* during his long rest from walking, was expected to beat the record by at least 30 miles, and then go for 550 miles which would make it very hard for Vaughan to beat him.

Vaughan, for his part was said to be in fine condition, and as the weather had been cold since his arrival, the news from his camp was that he had acclimatised himself. It was also reported that he had exercised more than Rowell and was expected to sweat off his *"superfluous flesh"* during the first 48 hours of his match against O'Leary.

Nearly 7,000 people were present at the opening of the competition despite the fact that the admission fee had been raised from 50 cents to $1. The match itself was for a total stake of $10,000; half of which was to be given to the winner of the heel-and-toe competition.

At the start of the contest between America and England, all four men shook hands vigorously. The referees would be Hamilton Busby of the *Turf, Field and Farm*, Joseph Elliott of the *New York Herald,* and George Atkinson of the London *Sporting Life*. The track was 8 laps to the mile.

Busby gave the word at midnight and the men went on their way. As expected, Rowell made the first mile in a time of 6m.32s. This was just one second ahead of Albert. The slower walkers made the same distance in 9m.29s and 9m.53s, Vaughan ahead. Albert hung at the heels of Rowell, and was less than a dozen feet behind him when he finished his fifth mile in 32m.45s. Vaughan had up to that time had walked 3.2 and O'Leary 3.1. After an hour, Rowell and Albert were neck-and-neck on 9.1, with Vaughan beating his opponent by just under a quarter of a mile, his score being six miles during which time he beat the old record by 33 yards.

After two hours, Albert kept up with Rowell and they were both on an equal footing of 17½ miles, but, as the pace became too strong for him, the American fell back, and when he went in for a rest of 14 minutes, the Englishman took control. By the end of the third hour, Rowell had the advantage of a two-mile lead. His fellow countryman meanwhile, maintained the couple of furlongs gap he had created between himself and O'Leary. At 08:00, the scores were: **Rowell, 59.4; Albert, 48.2; Vaughan, 43.3; O'Leary, 42:**

At 09:17, Vaughan made his half century and was a full 4 miles ahead of his opponent. Due to O'Leary taking half an hour rest for breakfast, this margin was doubled by 11:00 when the scoreboard showed the Englishman on a score of 59.1 to 51.1. O'Leary was said to be not in the best of condition due to stomach trouble. Rowell meanwhile, had made 80 miles to Albert's measly 63. The Philadelphian, who was said to have a perpetual smile on his face, kept lightly springing along grasping a short cane in his left hand, whilst the man he hoped to catch persisted with his, oh so very familiar dog-trot which he never varied, except that is, for short spells of rapid walking.

Vaughan, holding on to cornstalks, hurried himself along like *"a steam engine"* as he worked his arms in a frantic fashion, a style which observers concluded would be his downfall insomuch that it would sap his energy levels quickly. His opponent was much the graceful of the pair adopting his vintage method of conveyance. At 11:10, Vaughan rested for 28 minutes. On his return he followed O'Leary around in the opposite direction to the go-as-you-pleasers. At 12 o'clock, he was 1,787 yards behind O'Leary's best walking record of 63 miles 957 yards, which the Irishman made in London in 1877.

The one o'clock betting: **Vaughan, 3/5; O'Leary, 1/1; Albert, 5/1:**

The two o'clock scores: **Rowell, 99.6; Albert, 78.6; Vaughan, 72.5; O'Leary, 63.7:**

At 18:56, Albert made his century, but by then he was over 25 miles behind Rowell. After making a lap, he rested for 31 minutes, and on his return, walked lame. It was reported that he was suffering from a strained tendon which hindered him so much, it took him 20 minutes to make a mile and two laps. He was hauled off by his trainer who immediately set to work on the troublesome left foot at 19:47.

As he limped off, Henry Vaughan made the first hundred miles in the walking race, his last mile being achieved in a time of 11m.35s. O'Leary meanwhile, was 15 miles behind, and the two races were certainly not going America's way. O'Leary was the only man on the track at 2 a.m. on the second day when the scores showed: **Rowell, 147; Albert, 103; Vaughan, 116; O'Leary, 100:**

Official notification was given at 06:40 that Albert had succumbed to the pain caused by his strained tendon, and much interest was lost in the affair as a result of his withdrawal. However, O'Leary was still in with a shout, and he was going along nicely hoping that the match could be at least drawn. During the morning he had managed to pull Vaughan back a little. The score in their race at 9 o'clock was 139.5 to 127.5.

At 14:00, and when there were only 200 people in the building, the admission prices were halved to 50 cents, and owing to the first day's excellent attendance, $13,000 had been taken at the gate up to that point. The score at that time: **Rowell, 183.3: Vaughan, 159.6; O'Leary, 147.6:**

During the evening, both Englishmen spent a lot of time off the track much to the disgust of the 2,000 spectators, the boredom being relieved by a couple of events, the first being Rowell's 200th mile at 20:57, and the second, a big fight which broke out near the press stand which required the intervention of three policemen to quell the subsequent disturbance. Meanwhile, the Irish-American impressed on the track, and because of that, his odds of 3/1 had been snapped by the punters hoping for a victory over Vaughan. By 22:00, "even money" was being chalked up next to his name on the bookmaker's boards. Bets were also on offer that Rowell wouldn't make 555 miles and the two walkers, 500. At midnight, the scores showed: **Rowell, 213: Vaughan, 206; O'Leary, 193:**

With the withdrawal of Albert and rain persisting outside, there was little incentive apart from a surprise victory for O'Leary to entice New Yorkers to the race, thus the meagre attendance that watched the story unfold on the track. At 15:00, O'Leary was just 11 miles to the rear of Vaughan on a score of 232. By this time, Rowell, who had slowed right down due to a swollen leg, registered 243. O'Leary was to get within 5 miles of Vaughan later on in the evening but by the end of play on the 3rd day, the scores showed: **Rowell, 272: Vaughan, 273; O'Leary, 263.2:**

O'Leary walked throughout the early hours of the morning while Rowell and Vaughan slept. By 03:00 he was within two miles of his opponent. Rowell emerged on the track at 11:20 having slept at the Ashland House all night, but not in his racing costume. Instead he wore a chequered cloth business suit and a black Derby hat. He headed towards the rail at the press stand which he vaulted and told the press that his race was over, and that he intended saving himself for the Astley Belt contest in nine weeks time. He did say however that he would be going back on the track of an evening to give the audience some exhibitions of walking and running.

The two o'clock score in the afternoon: **Vaughan, 310.6; O'Leary, 306.8:**

Rowell did show up in the evening and made seven miles in 41m.45s, that effort apparently being just for *"practice."* Vaughan by midnight had put some more miles between himself and O'Leary who disposed of his trainers declaring, "I am boss!" At midnight, he was 17 miles behind the Englishman, the score being 342 to 325 with O'Leary's drifting odds of 3/1, being representative of his diminishing chances of winning.

Vaughan continued to keep his nose in front the next day as the following scores indicate:

09:00: **Vaughan, 357; O'Leary, 350:** 12:00: **Vaughan, 364; O'Leary, 358:** 15:00: **Vaughan, 372; O'Leary, 367:**

During the evening, and in front of 4,000 spectators who were being serenaded by a German band, the Englishman had repelled everything O'Leary could muster to try and demoralise him. The Irishman had initiated spurt after spurt, but it was to no avail. Later on at 20:40, Rowell entertained the spectators with a 3-mile run, 4 laps of which were raced with a seven-year-old boy.

The scores at 22:00: **Vaughan, 398; O'Leary, 387:** 23:00: **Vaughan, 400; O'Leary, 387:** Midnight: **Vaughan, 405; O'Leary, 390:**

During the day, O'Leary had walked 65.1 whilst Vaughan had walked 62.4, before both men retired at midnight. The gate receipts up to that time were $20,000.

Some final day scores for the morning and afternoon: 09:00: **Vaughan, 424; O'Leary, 414:** 12:00: **Vaughan, 433; O'Leary, 424:** 15:00: **Vaughan, 440; O'Leary, 430:**

During the afternoon, Rowell did his best to entertain the crowd by running five miles in 33m.20s, and later made his first mile of the evening in 6m.52s as he started off on a 20-mile trot. His backers had offered to bet him that he couldn't make 100 miles without stopping, and when it was said that he couldn't do it, Rowell offered to bet $5,000 to $2,000 that he could, saying, "I means run, you know; no 'arf way business, but run."

When eight o'clock in the evening arrived, O'Leary had played all his cards, and not being able to offer any more, handed his notice to quit in to the referee on a score of 450 miles. He was *"completely broken down,"* and his backers said he *"had his heart in his boots."* He was seventy miles behind his best walking record, and many said he had seen his best days. Vaughan eventually stopped going when he had made 461.1 at 21:32.

$16,000 was to be shared amongst the "peds." Rowell won a *"handsome chair,"* supplied by the New York Furniture Company, and Vaughan would also win the same prize for making the most miles in the walking race along with a suit of clothing from *Max Stadler's New York* store.

CHAPTER 31

2nd O'Leary International Belt

The young English hopeful George Littlewood made his first trip over the Atlantic with his father Fred on the *City of Richmond* which had set off from Liverpool on the 11th of February 1881, arriving in New York on the 22nd. He was under the management of Tom Davies of that city, the man who had previously brought the American athletes Dobler, Pegram and Howard to the British Isles. His first race in America was for what was being placarded about the streets as the "Second International Tournament for the O'Leary Belt" at Madison Square Garden, between Monday, the 23rd and Saturday, the 28th of May 1881.

MADISON SQUARE GARDEN *(Illustration no: 83)*

There was a certain amount of cynicism about the O'Leary belt races of the time. They were perceived as a money making racket on behalf of the man who promoted them, and for the people who benefited from the money that was made from them. The races were better received in the winter and spring, but not during summer, when they were seen as nuisances. There had also been problems with scoring in races with miles and laps having been credited to some pedestrians when they hadn't achieved the distances. The only positive the races could offer, were the prospect of more records being broken.

One cause for the waning of interest in these races was the fact that in nearly all the late contests, most of the men perceived as potential winners had dropped out *suspiciously* early, thus destroying the confidence necessary for their success. Reports suggested that after spending more than $300,000 on six-day races during the last few years, New York was apparently tired of them. All of the four matches which have followed each other in that city within as many months had been financial failures, compared with the earlier successes which enabled the winners to walk off with what appeared to them large fortunes.

Thus, there was much indifference shown to this particular race by the press. Consequently, the limited reporting there was, tended to concentrate on the scores of the contestants. The *Boston Globe,* whose reporting of the race was to be far superior to its counterparts in New York, Chicago and Washington, was the only newspaper to offer its readers any real insight into what happened.

Fourteen men therefore started in the second contest for the *"last in the season."* The race would last six days and the winner would get receive the international version of the O'Leary Belt and the same percentages of the gate money as described in Chapter 29. Extra cash prizes would also be given to any man beating the previous record. Several of those taking part wore the names of those who were backing them in the race and all of the contestants sported large letters on both the front and back of their running jerseys.

They were: **H. F. Brown, Eph Clow, John Cox, Ben Curran, P. Dalton, Donovan (Dr. J. B. Perry's "Unknown" of Boston), George Dufrane, Patrick Fitzgerald, George Hazael, Harry Howard, "Lepper" Hughes, George Littlewood, John Sullivan** and **Robert Vint.**

On the events first night, there were about 3,000 people who had made the journey to the Garden. The local press claimed that there had been a liberal distribution of free passes which helped secure the large attendance. Despite the collective cynicism, there was another good reason to watch the race, and that was because "Levy's cornet" was providing some of the entertainment.

When the race began at midnight, Curran was the man to make the first lap amid the usual enthusiastic din. Then, the *"light haired, boyish looking Littlewood, Tom Davies' importation,"* made the fastest mile in 5m.50s. Sullivan was five seconds behind with Hughes a further six seconds in his rear. Littlewood, who made two miles in 12m.13s, was followed around closely by George Hazael, and based on the evidence they were presented with at that time, the bookies were displaying the following odds 15 minutes into the contest: **Littlewood, 2/1; Hazael, 4/1; Hughes and Vint, 5/1; Cox, 6/1; Curran, Howard, Sullivan, 8/1; Fitzgerald, 15/1; Brown, Clow, Dalton, Donovan and Dufrane, 25/1:**

The English pair went on to make 4 miles apiece in 22 minutes, Littlewood making the first five miles in exactly 30 minutes. The young Yorkshireman then went on to smash Hazael's best time for an hour (9 miles and 735 yards), by adding another 660 yards. However, and as was expected, that sort of pace in this sort of race just couldn't be maintained by the young lad, and when the third hour came to an end, Hazael had employed his maturity and experience to take the lead. Littlewood also went on to make new 2nd and 3rd hour records with 18 miles and 1,635 yards and 26 miles and 1,490 yards respectively.

The 6 a.m. scores: **Hazael, 44; Hughes, 43; Littlewood, 42; Vint, 40; Clow, 38:**

This state of affairs was maintained until the eighth hour when Hughes overhauled Hazael (who had made a new 60-mile record in 7h.47m) to take the pole position in the race. It was about this time that the little Irishman, Vint, started to creep a little closer to Littlewood, his hard effort being rewarded at the 14th hour of the race when he exchanged places with him, the score of the first four at midday being: **Hughes, 80; Vint, 76; Littlewood, 75; Hazael, 73:**

Harriman, who was sitting in the 2,000 strong audience, *"his face white and as transparent as wax after his great walk in Chicago,"* must have been impressed with the performance of the nine men who had made their centuries. At 20:00, and with Dalton, Brown and Cox now out of the race, their scores being 27, 29 and 40 miles respectively, the scores read: **Hughes, 119; Littlewood, 116; Vint, 115; Sullivan, 109; Clow, 108; Fitzgerald, 107; Howard, 104; Hazael, 103; Donovan, 100; Dufrane, 90; Curran, 84:**

Then, shortly after nine o'clock, and amid an appreciative din by his supporters who had put a lot of money on him to succeed in the race, Vint re-passed the by now limping Littlewood and moved into second place. Along with the Englishman, who also appeared to be struggling, Hughes nevertheless pursued his goal relentlessly, and maintained a healthy four-mile lead between himself and the ex-shoemaker as the following record for 22:00 suggests: **Hughes, 128; Vint, 124; Littlewood, 123; Sullivan, 118; Clow, 117; Fitzgerald, 114; Howard, 112; Hazael, 110; Donovan, 100; Dufrane, 93; Curran, 89:**

A couple of hours later, the midnight score in *"the alleged walking match"* was: **Hughes, 137; Vint, 133; Littlewood, 130; Sullivan, 126; Clow, 125; Fitzgerald, 114; Howard, 112; Hazael, 110; Dufrane, 107; Donovan, 105; Curran, 98:**

Hazael returned during the early hours of the morning and began to do what he was good at, run! Littlewood meanwhile, was paying the price for his unprecedented first day record, his contracted and aching muscles twitching as they carried him around the big circle. As the he toiled uncomfortably, the *"condensed cobbler"* went about his work with regularity, his tiny legs kicking off the miles at a constant rate of five an hour.

A scorer at the event was caught adding another mile on to Vint's score sheet. Apparently this incident led to Hughes protesting loudly, and inevitably his behaviour got him into an altercation with the Brooklyn mans trainer who had insisted that the score was indeed correct. A judge ruled that Vint's total should be reduced from 169 to 168 and the race continued.

Hughes kept the premier spot until 10:15, and it was likely that he was resting when Vint robbed him of his lead. At noon, the score was: **Vint, 180; Hughes, 177; Littlewood, 173; Sullivan, 167; Clow, 163; Hazael, 159; Fitzgerald, 156; Howard, 151; Donovan, 146; Dufrane, 143; Curran, 135:**

Hazael finally gave up running after completing his 168th mile, his time for 50 miles in that period being a commendable 9 hours. As Hughes began to flag, the *"midget,"* now eating his dinner on the hoof, kept up his relentless pace. At 16:00, he had created a considerable gap of 10 miles between himself and his fellow Irishman as the record at that time testifies: **Vint, 200; Hughes, 190; Sullivan, 189; Littlewood, 184; Hazael, 180; Clow, 179; Fitzgerald, 172; Howard, 170; Donovan, 185; Dufrane, 156; Curran, 152:**

The disdain of the press towards the contest was emphasised in their reporting of the race. They described the contestants as *"eleven wretched looking men,"* and would later question the validity of a claim by the management who had told them that 500 people had paid for admission during the day and more than double that number after seven in the evening.

Whilst the press bickered, two men on the track were making some fine entertainment for the paltry few who had bothered to turn up to watch the fun. Hughes by now was taking longer rests, and his decision to do so gave the opportunity for Littlewood and Sullivan to improve their positions, the former going particularly well. One man who wasn't faring well was Fitzgerald, his swollen feet causing him huge problems.

The record at 21:00: **Vint, 220.3; Sullivan, 210.4; Littlewood, 209.5; Hughes, 208.4; Clow, 201.6; Fitzgerald, 195.1; Hazael, 194.3; Donovan, 187.3; Howard, 184; Dufrane, 175; Curran, 173:**

George Hazael had an arrogant streak in him. More often than not, he was a law to himself, and rarely, if ever, took any notice of his trainers, attendants, and backers. He would go on and off the track *as-he-pleased* and showed complete indifference to their wishes. Still, and by midnight, the Londoner had done well, achieving his second century when the positions were: **Vint, 233; Littlewood, 225; Sullivan, 221; Hughes, 220; Clow, 215; Hazael, 206; Donovan and Fitzgerald, 200; Howard, 197; Dufrane, 186; Curran, 184:**

Despite Vint being eight miles in front of the young "Tyke," the bookmakers were calling "Even money, Littlewood!" The rest of the odds were: **Vint, 5/4; Sullivan, 4/1; Hazael, 7/1; Hughes, 8/1; Clow, 15/1, Howard, 40/1; Fitzgerald, 50/1:**

Vint, who only slept for less than a couple of hours, was back on the track at 03:00 and continued pegging away in his now familiar fashion. Littlewood looked much better than he had previously in the contest and was now running with more fluidity. Hazael *"crawled around the corners,"* but *"ran like the wind"* on the straights. While Sullivan, Clow and Donovan went well, and Dufrane and Curran stuck grittily to their tasks, the pale haggard and gaunt Fitzgerald, although game, walked slowly around the course with his hands *"paddling slowly behind him."*

The hard working Hughes eventually took the Saratoga man's third place before noon. After that, the race was dictated by Vint, who, inspired at times by the musical contribution of the band, controlled the actions of the other competitors. If the *"midget"* walked, everybody walked. If he ran, they all ran, and so it went on just like a long drawn out version of follow my leader, mile after mile, the only respite being when one of the peds went off for a rest.

With just one hour before the end of the third day, five of the men in the contest had scored 300 miles, and by the time the following scores were recorded *"by the professional scorers"* at midnight, Vint was 10 miles or so ahead of Hughes's American record for the same stage of that race: **Vint, 335; Littlewood, 319; Hughes, 315; Sullivan, 310; Clow, 301; Howard, 291; Fitzgerald and Hazael, 290; Donovan, 277; Curran, 275; Dufrane, 270:**

When the race leader began his fourth day's work at 01:17 having rested for 2h.25m, he was five miles ahead of Rowell's London record made in November of the previous year. Jogging along, it took him till 08:00 to equal the English champion's feat, and when he had accomplished that, he treat himself to a breakfast of mutton chops and calves foot jelly.

At midday, on Thursday, the 26th of May, the scores were: **Vint, 380; Littlewood, 362; Hughes, 360; Clow and Sullivan, 352; Hazael, 344; Donovan, 341; Howard, 338; Fitzgerald, 333; Curran, 311; Dufrane, 300:**

And at 14:00 they were: **Vint, 391; Hughes, 371; Littlewood, 368; Sullivan, 363; Clow, 362; Howard, 345; Fitzgerald, 340; Hazael, 331; Donovan, 321; Curran, 319; Dufrane, 310:**

At 3 o'clock, Littlewood was seen to be staggering around the track and appeared to have *"broken down."* He was taken off the ellipse and spent an hour in his hut, but after going as badly as before when he returned, he was given a longer rest by his trainer. His backers admitted that they had little hope of him finishing within the front rank at the finish. Whilst the Englishman suffered, the Irishman, Hughes, increased the distance between the pair. Meanwhile, Clow renewed his effort to increase his chances of making a better place. The leader who had not rested since breakfast, scored his 400th mile at 15:58 and was now not only 10 miles ahead of Rowell's best time, but was also 20 miles ahead of his nearest rival, Hughes.

At 6 p.m., the records showed: **Vint, 410; Hughes, 389; Clow, 381; Littlewood and Sullivan, 377; Fitzgerald, 359; Howard, 358; Hazael, 344; Donovan, 341; Curran, 335; Dufrane, 329:**

Vint, the *"diminutive specimen of humanity,"* had made 233 miles in less than 48 hours. His trainers and backers now seemed sure of his success as he showed little sign of fatigue. Between 8 and 10 p.m. when the score below was recorded, it was estimated that the match attendance was in the region of 10,000, the increase partly due to the attraction of another race on the track between letter carriers, policemen and firemen. The huge crowd apparently really galvanized the pro's on the track to put in some wonderful performances with the likes of Fitzgerald and Hazael showing off their speed to full advantage. However, the man who was really making heads turn was Clow who made an incredible score of 95 miles from one o'clock in the morning till nine o'clock in the evening when the following scores were recorded: **Vint, 420; Hughes, 402; Clow, 400; Sullivan, 389; Littlewood, 381; Fitzgerald, 376; Howard, 364; Donovan and Hazael, 356; Curran, 335; Dufrane, 346:**

At 22:20, Vint was a mile and 3 laps to the good of Rowell's world record score of the year previous. Littlewood then returned to the race after a four-hour absence at 23:35, the excuse for it being due to *"inflammation in his hips."* *"He limped painfully around, evidently suffering great agony."* Whilst he moved along with the utmost difficulty, Ephraim Clow continued to make his way round the track in sparkling form. Indeed, his effort of 104 miles in the preceding 24 hours was the best distance ever made on the fourth day of such a competition. Not only had he made a most marvellous record for himself during the day, but he had lopped off a total of 16 miles from an original 34 miles which was the distance between himself and Vint 24 hours beforehand. The bookies, whilst recognising that achievement made him a 6/1 shot to win the race, but wouldn't take any bets on a Vint victory.

The midnight score: **Vint, 428; Clow and Hughes, 410; Sullivan, 396; Fitzgerald and Littlewood, 383; Howard, 373; Donovan and Hazael, 367; Curran and Dufrane, 351:**

Littlewood was described as being a *"marvel,"* this being only his second attempt at a 142-hour race. Some of the men at times showed evident signs of pain and fatigue, but John Sullivan certainly didn't fit in with them. *"Sullivan is closing the daylight between him and third place. He looks trim and well preserved, and has some steam to spare, even after the high pressure he has been carrying during the week. His legs work like piston rods and he holds his head up well."*

The race leader however, was on a roll, and at this stage of the contest many were saying of the little fellow that, *"he is incapable of exhaustion."* The plucky Irishman was in a different class to the rest, and at one stage during the morning, was 18 miles in front of the record and going like a train. It was thought that if he could go into the last day 25 miles ahead of it, he could well be on course for a final score of 600 miles.

At noon, when the scores below were recorded, the little ped was 17 miles ahead of it: **Vint, 475; Clow, 458; Hughes, 455; Sullivan, 447; Littlewood, 425; Fitzgerald, 420; Howard, 414; Hazael, 400; Donovan, 397; Curran, 384; Dufrane, 379:**

With all eleven men still hard at work, the race was described as the best which had ever taken place on the tanbark. In comparison with previous events, when all the contestants appeared *"fagged out"* at the same stage, the athletes in this one were running around the course at a high rate of knots. It was therefore not surprisingly predicted that all of the men on the track would make the necessary 480 miles in order to save the money they had spent participating in the race.

John Hughes belligerently arrived at the start of the race believing he was the *"greatest pedestrian living."* He soon came down to earth with a very big bump! He hadn't been the most pleasant of characters whilst competing, seemingly finding fault with everything and everybody. For example, having consumed raw eggs washed down with beer at the start of the race, he had the audacity to complain about his poor protesting stomach thereafter!

Hazael had been very disappointing and many were blaming his age for his poor performance. Ben Curran, who was also getting on a bit himself, was a revelation and was said to be performing well. Last man in the field, George Dufrane came in for special praise from the reporter of the *New York Times* who wrote: "**The handsome Dufrane looks as pleasing as ever and has a smile for everybody. He takes quite a pride in having the rearguard of such an admirable squad of runners looking in good form. He beguiles the monotony of the walk by numerous anecdotes, which set the other pedestrians in a roar. He is the funny man of the tanbark, the comedian of the sawdust."**

The plucky pedestrians were really going for it, *"their faces streaming with perspiration, and their tight garments clinging to their almost exhausted bodies and weary limbs."* The leader's performance when he secured his 500th mile with seven hours to spare before the end of the 5th day was a defining moment in the history of the sport. Indeed at 17:13, he had beaten all previous records by 25 miles. The question now on everybody's lips was could the little fellow make the coveted 600?

The score at 18:00: **Vint, 500; Hughes, 484; Clow, 475; Sullivan, 467; Littlewood, 449; Fitzgerald, 445; Howard, 434; Hazael, 420; Donovan, 420; Curran, 402; Dufrane, 399:**

There were 5,000 people watching the contest, but some childish reporting in the press said they were there to watch the boy's five-mile go-as-you-please race which they claimed was the *"feature of the evening."* They then went on to inform their readership that four of the youngest lads were ordered from the track by Officer Chardi of the Society for the Prevention of Cruelty to Children. The truth of the matter was that the paying audience was enjoying the spectacle before them. The *Boston Globe* wrote: **The enthusiasm amongst the spectators during the evening almost reached fever heat, and the cabin doors of the pedestrians were covered in floral horseshoes and baskets.**

The 10 p.m. scores: **Vint, 513; Hughes, 497; Clow, 484; Sullivan, 479; Littlewood, 459; Fitzgerald, 457; Howard, 444; Hazael, 432; Donovan, 430; Curran, 413; Dufrane, 407:**

After Hughes had completed his 500th mile at 22:45, Daniel O'Leary in conversation with a reporter said he firmly believed that the then present record would be beaten by 20 miles. When Vint went for a quick nap of 30 minutes on a score of 520 miles at 23:20, he was 18 miles ahead of the old record. At 23:30, Clow's trainer Oscar Durgin said his man would definitely finish in second place as he watched him move around the track effortlessly on a score of 492 miles. The backers of Hughes though disagreed, and were looking for even money that their man would finish as the runner-up to Vint.

The midnight scores at the end of the fifth day of the contest: **Vint, 521; Hughes, 502; Clow, 495; Sullivan, 491; Fitzgerald, 467; Littlewood, 462; Howard, 450; Donovan and Hazael, 440; Curran, 420; Dufrane, 415:** At this time, Vint was 20 miles ahead of the best record in the world which belonged to Panchot for the 120th hour. Hughes was 2 miles ahead of the record he made in January.

The 3 a.m. scores, with Curran having just repelled a 20-minute spurting challenge by Dufrane who was carrying a furniture company advertisement on his back: **Vint, 530; Hughes, 513; Clow, 501.2; Sullivan, 500; Fitzgerald, 473; Littlewood, 465; Howard, 460; Donovan and Hazael, 440; Curran, 422; Dufrane, 418:**

A statement was issued to the press stating that Clow's withdrawal at 03:30 was a result of him being bought off in the race by the backers of Hughes. He is believed to have received from between $5,000 to $10,000 for *"playing his little game,"* and later that morning rumours were rife that Clow's backers had been offered $12,000 to retire him from the contest. Apparently a large amount of money was bet on Hughes to secure second place. The story goes that Clow, after overexerting himself to take second place in the contest, began to flag and retired from the track having made 502 miles stating he wouldn't return. His trainer was apparently furious, and after a few harsh words during which he accused Clow of *"selling out,"* punched him in the face. Clow then went quietly to his quarters, dressed, and went outside. He returned shortly after when his friends tried to get him to back on the track. Clow stated that there was no money in the race and he "wasn't going to walk for nothing." The *Graphic* takes up the story: O'Leary was sent for, and in response to his enquiries why he had quit the track, Clow said he was afraid he would not get his share of the gate money, and, if that was so, why should he make a fool of himself any longer? "I'll stay till the finish," he said at length, "if you give me $500 cash in hand." O'Leary replied that he would see that he received the $500. "That won't do," said Clow, "I want the money plonked down right here before I take another step." O'Leary declined to accede to his request, and the malcontent left the track and sat down near the main entrance, where he whined he had been penniless, and had not enough money to take him back to Boston. Later he left the Garden.

In a race in which he could have certainly have finished as runner-up, Clow would have received at least $1,300 had he finished third. It was the general feeling that he had deliberately sold the race in exchange for pool tickets or a cheque. In an unusual report it was also established later that promises had been made by Clow to his backer the day before that he would finish in front of Vint.

The 8 a.m. scores: **Vint, 543; Hughes, 532; Sullivan, 520; Fitzgerald, 495; Littlewood, 479; Howard, 477; Hazael, 467; Donovan, 464; Curran, 438; Dufrane, 433:**

Littlewood meanwhile was really feeling the strain, and gave up the race on a score of 480 miles about 08:45 thus recouping his entrance fee. It was said that he had been over-trained and badly handled, but many people watching the race at the time formulated the impression that he would have won barring the problem with his foot. The attending physician diagnosed a *"broken guider"* and told George that his days as an athlete were unfortunately over. At the same time as his withdrawal, Fitzgerald recorded his fifth century.

At 09:20, and amid much celebration among the ever increasing audience, the race leader recorded 550. Shortly after, Howard, who was in a playful mood, grabbed hold of Mr. Plummer, the chief scorer, and wrestled him to the ground in front of the scorers' stand, a move the official was reported to not be very pleased with! By 11 o'clock, Sullivan, now doing some splendid work on the track, was on a score of 533 miles which was just nine miles behind the second placed Hughes whose legs had apparently *"gone from beneath him."* The Saratogan, seeing his chance to move himself up the list another place, made another five miles in the next hour to get himself within five miles of the Irishman until, at noon, the record showed: **Vint, 557; Hughes, 543; Sullivan, 538; Fitzgerald, 510; Howard, 495; Hazael, 480; Donovan, 474; Curran, 451; Dufrane, 449:**

By 12:30, Sullivan's objective of overtaking Hughes was now looking quite realistic. He was now just two and a half miles away, and barring catastrophe, it was an absolute certainty that he would make his effort pay. The scorer's sheets for 13:00 certainly show he was level with the "Lepper," and as the record testifies below, he indeed became the second man in the race when the scores were hoisted at 14:00. Indeed Hughes was reported to have given his opponent a *"savage look"* when he was passed. Alas, there was nothing he could do but hope and pray that he had done enough to keep the third prize money on offer: **Vint, 565; Sullivan, 545; Hughes, 544; Fitzgerald, 518; Howard, 503; Hazael, 490; Donovan and Littlewood, 480; Dufrane, 457; Curran, 456:**

The little race leader, running swiftly for a lap, passed the old record at 15:21, and then, after walking several more, went to his tent for rest. By this stage he had given up hope of achieving the 600 miles which, had he done it, would have given him another $1,000. Howard announced he had enough at 19:30, and Hazael, who had not been on the track since 16:00, made the same announcement three quarters of an hour later.

King of the Peds

Curran then put on a fine show of speed at 20:20, but the others couldn't keep up with him. Hughes, to give him credit, did try, but the old legs just didn't respond. Sullivan meanwhile, who shot round the ring round at 7 mph, was not only cheered by the crowd, but also bombarded with bouquets as was Curran. Dufrane retired from the track at 20:40 with 482 miles, and shortly after at 20:53, Curran followed suit after making 480.1 thus saving his entrance money. Then, after he had made 569 miles Sullivan called it a day at 20:55.

The contest ended at 21:03 with both Vint with the top score of 578.2 and Sullivan with 569, beating the previous record. A large audience witnessed the end of the race and lustily cheered the jaded men as they crept along the home stretch. The press admitted that the contest had seen some extraordinary performances during the week, but then went on to question whether the scores were to be believed.

The contest had been seen as a financial failure because the receipts were estimated to be less than $8,000. Because the management refused to divulge the figures offered to the pedestrians, I have attempted to calculate what each man who finished in the race received. According to the conditions of the race, 65% of the $8,000 gate money would be divided among the men. Assuming this was $5,200, and taking $1,200 off that figure to be divided amongst six of the eleven finishers who couldn't share in the gate, that left $4,000 to divide among the top five. That meant that Vint's 40% would give him $1,600, Sullivan's 25% would give him $1,000, Hughes's 17% would net him $680, Fitzgerald's 10% would earn $400, and Howard's 8% share would reward him with $320. Vint would also receive $1,000 for beating the record, and it was also reported that Sullivan made an extra $1,000 for doing the same.

Robert Vint

The National Police Gazette   (Illustration no: 84)

Robert Vint was 35 years old. He was born on the 12th of November 1846 in Ruthfriland, County Down, Ireland, leaving the shores of the Emerald Isle travel to the USA in 1866 where he settled in Brooklyn. He was described as being 5 feet 2 inches tall, but *"wide"* in proportion. He weighed 103 pounds, and due to his stature, was sometimes called the *"Infant Pedestrian."* At the time of the race, he was the proprietor of a liquor saloon in Fulton Street called the Vint House. His first contest was a 75-hour go-as-you-please event at the Park Garden, Providence, between September the 8th and 13th 1879 won by Hart, where, after scoring 297 miles and 4 laps, he took the sixth prize. He then took the fourth prize of $200 in the fourteen hours a day, six-day go-as-you-please match at Madison Square Garden on Monday, the 13th of October after covering 350 miles, Fitzgerald being the winner that time. Making 450 miles in the Rose Belt won by Hart at Madison Square Garden in December of 1879 wasn't enough to win him any prize money, but between the 16th and the 22nd of February 1880 at the Baldwin House, Cincinnati, he made the best record in the Englehardt promoted, 84-hour (12 hours per day) contest, when he scored 432 miles 550 yards beating Harriman by 11 miles, Guyon by 17 miles and O'Brien by 26, thus beating the old record by 27 miles. At Providence, between April the 12th and 17th 1880, he came third to Sullivan, scoring 370 miles in a 72-hour go-as-you-please event. He then went on to accomplish the same position, this time making 507 miles in an 8-day 12½ hours per day, 100-hour, Englehardt promoted contest, which Hughes won with a score of 548, and which ended on Monday, May the 24th. Vint then came third yet again in January 1881 when he came in 18 miles behind Hughes who made a world record of 568 miles.

The Final Score!

Pos		Miles	Laps	Pos		Miles	Laps
1	Vint	578	2	7	Donovan	500	1
2	Sullivan	569	0	8	Hazael	500	0
3	Hughes	552	2	9	Dufrane	482	1
4	Fitzgerald	536	3	10	Littlewood	480	2
5	Howard	518	5	11	Curran	480	1
6	Clow	502	0				

Day by Day scores

Pos		Mon	Tue	Wed	Thur	Fri	Sat	Total
1	**Vint**	133	100	101.1	94.4	92.3	57.2	**578.2**
2	**Sullivan**	126	95	89.1	86.4	94.6	77.5	**569**
3	**Hughes**	137	83	95	95	92	50.2	**552**
4	**Fitzgerald**	114	86	90.3	92.7	83.6	69.3	**536.3**
5	**Howard**	112.6	84.4	94	82.1	76.5	68.5	**518.5**
6	**Clow**	125	90	86.5	108.3	85	7	**502**
7	**Donovan**	105.2	94.6	77.5	90.3	72	60.1	**500.1**
8	**Hazael**	110	96.3	83.5	76.6	73.2	60	**500**
9	**Dufrane**	107.2	79.1	83.6	80.7	64	67.1	**482.1**
10	**Littlewood**	130.4	94	94.6	63.4	80.1	17.3	**480.2**
11	**Curran**	98.3	86.1	90.5	75.7	69	60.1	**480.1**

CHAPTER 32

7th International Astley Belt

On the 25th of March 1881, Rowell and Harriman both gave exhibitions at the walking match at Bradford, Pennsylvania, where the Englishman made 5 miles in 34m.25s. When he returned to New York a couple of days later, Rowell stated that although he personally wasn't bothered where the next contest for the Astley Belt took place, and although he knew it highly unlikely, he had hoped to influence his challenger Weston not to object to New York being the venue. Both parties met the next day the 28th, but owing to a *"misunderstanding,"* the articles weren't signed. Incidentally, it had been agreed that if America had been chosen to hold the event the contest would begin on May the 30th in Chicago, Cincinnati, Philadelphia or Boston.

On the morning of the next day, both Rowell, the holder, and Weston, the challenger, met at the office of the *Turf, Field and Farm*, in New York, and signed the articles of agreement. Rowell was accompanied by his brother in law and trainer, Charlie Asplen, and William H. Hixby representing Weston. During the meeting it was definitely settled that the race should take place in England in a city to be decided upon by Weston before May 23rd, and according to the articles, the contest was to begin at 1 a.m. on Monday, June the 20th, and end at 11 p.m. the following Saturday. The stakes of £100 for each entry had been deposited with the London based *Sporting Life*, which, along with the New York based *Turf, Field and Farm*, were to select the referees, timekeepers and scorers for the match. The two journals were also to decide all questions of dispute and appeals.

However, not everybody was happy about the arrangements that had been made to contest the event. In fact George Hazael wasn't happy at all. It transpired that a letter had appeared in a morning paper signed by a Mr. Davis, stating that Rowell was afraid to race against a couple of Englishmen (Littlewood and Hazael?) that were presently in the country. Referring to the letter which had apparently annoyed him, Rowell had remarked, "To show that I am not afraid to walk against either of these two men, I will give Mr. Davis five hundred dollars if he will match his two men against me for five thousand pounds each. I don't want to boast, but I shall be ready to make a match on those terms as soon as the Astley Belt affair is settled."

The *Brooklyn Daily Eagle* sent one of its reporters to meet Hazael to find out why he wasn't pleased with recent events. The following headline was inserted into the paper on the 31st of March: **Hazael has an Interview with Rowell, Who Declines to Run for the Belt in This Country or Make a Match with Him – What Hazael and his Friends says About the Matter.**

George Hazael, the English pedestrian who came to this country a week ago to enter the lists, as he supposed, for the Astley belt, was surprised and disappointed to learn a day or two ago that Rowell had determined that the race should take place on British soil; so he waited upon the champion accompanied by Counselor H. B. Davis and Harry Martin, at the Ashland House last Monday night to arrange for a match.

In order to ascertain the result of the interview, an EAGLE reporter visited Hazael at the Williamsburg Athletic Club grounds, and found the pedestrian on the track making about ten miles an hour. He was apparently in fine condition and ran without any visible effort. His friends declared that he was in excellent trim and prepared to go on the track at any moment. After Hazael contested for the belt in the Madison Square Garden a year ago last September, when he came in third, he ran in a six-day go-as-you-please in England, and took second place. When he had completed his seventeenth mile he came off the track, made his toilet and said, in answer to the reporter's enquiries:

"I waited on Rowell for the purpose of bringing on the contest for the Astley belt in this country. Before Rowell left England, I challenged him for the belt in the usual way, and deposited £10 in the office of the Sporting Life.

Rowell made a mis-statement when he asserted that I withdrew the money, for it is there yet. When I deposited the money on a Friday nothing was said to me about Weston having sent a challenge, and I knew nothing of it until I saw it in the paper the next day along with my challenge. I came here to contest for the belt as I understood it to be run for here, especially as Rowell brought it with him. I was informed that Rowell was not going back to England until June; consequently he must have intended to contest for the belt here. Under a technical construction of the rules, he has forfeited the belt, as he has failed to deposit a sum equal to that of the challenge inside of ten days. Immediately after coming here I notified Rowell through the press of my presence and desire to meet him. Then he changed his program and instead of coming to terms with Weston, whom he preferred as the first challenger, he has been playing fast and loose, evidently wanting to avoid a contest here where I would be a competitor. I was determined when I called on him to bring on a contest for the belt or make a match with him on any terms he chose to name - from one mile to two weeks. Finding, after a long conversation that Rowell who has the right to declare where the belt shall be contested for, had decided that the race shall take place on British soil, where it would be unprofitable for a dangerous competitor to go, I tried to get on a match and let the contest for the belt slide. I told him to name any place in this country he liked and the winner could pocket all the gate money, but he refused. Judging from our conversation, I am forced to the conclusion he is afraid to meet me, and all this talk about my challenge being a game of bluff is merely the cry of stop thief repeated. Charles Asplen, Rowell's brother in law and trainer, was in the office of the Sporting Life when I made the challenge and put up the money."

WHAT HAZAEL'S FRIENDS SAY

Mr. H. B. Davis, who was with Hazael at the Ashland House, said that Rowell could not have spoken truly when he said he had no idea that Hazael was coming here to contest for the belt, as he must have been aware of the challenge, as Mr. Atkinson had spoken to him (Mr. Davis), about it after coming here. "When Rowell stated," he continued, "that he had never any intention of contesting for the belt in this country, I reminded him of a conversation he had with me, in which he said that he would not return to England until June. I told him also that I did not see why Weston's challenge should be preferred to Hazael's, and that if that if he had any regard for public opinion he would drop Weston, as people generally understood that there was nothing into it, and that he only wanted to forego a match here. He declined to run in New York at all, and said he would leave the country next Tuesday. I pressed him to name a later date for the Astley belt contest in England, and make a match with Hazael, but he declined. I made up my mind that he was not very anxious to meet Hazael, notwithstanding all his talk about Hazael's challenge being a game of bluff."

Mr. Harry Martin corroborated all that Hazael and Davis had stated about the interview with Rowell.

On the 11th of May it was reported that Frank Hart and "Blower" Brown were in training at Turnham Green in London, and Rowell at Chesterton, Cambridge, for the match announced for the third week in June. For whatever reason, Brown never entered for the race, but it was known that Frank Hart had thrown his hat in the ring by staking £100 to enter the contest. However, drama was to follow, for in a report in the *Penny Illustrated* on the 11th of June, he was reported to have appeared at the Marlborough Street Police Court on the 4th of June for assaulting a French woman during which time he was alleged to have stolen 25 shillings from her. He was committed for trial at the Middlesex Court of Sessions and bail was fixed with two sureties for £40 each.

On the same date that Hart appeared in court, the *Sporting Life* reported that Rowell intended to make 600 miles in the match, and would accept odds of *"£200 to £1,000"* that he would succeed. It was also reported that the race would be his final one and that he intended to retire after it. Should Rowell prove successful in the race, he would have absolute ownership of the belt as it would mean his third successive win. The match would take place at the Marble Rink, Clapham Road Athletic Club Grounds, 143 Clapham Road (at Clapham Junction adjoining the station), on a track which was eight laps to the mile. *"In formation the track is sort of oval, and is from 8ft to 10ft wide. One half of the track is through a covered building, the remainder is out of doors, but the path is roofed in."* The only pedestrians competing for the prize would be Rowell and Weston. The accommodation on offer for both pedestrians was described as being, *"well up to their requirements."* In reality they were housed at opposite ends of the track in corrugated iron huts, Rowell's being under cover and Weston's in the open air.

Weston had advertised himself to walk 400 miles in five days at the Concert Hall in Brighton between the 6th and the 10th of June. That feat and the subsequent training he did at the seaside town would set himself up nicely for the forthcoming struggle with his opponent who had trained at home.

King of the Peds

The two men were sent on their way by Captain Astley, brother of Sir John Astley for the "Championship of the World" at 1 a.m., on Monday, June the 20th 1881, amid great applause. It was reported that Frank Hart, Daniel O'Leary and many American's were present in the 600 plus audience who were cheering loudly when the two men started. Rowell, *"showing as usual, lots of muscle,"* and wearing a jersey, jogged into the lead straight away, whilst Weston, donning a long tailed overcoat and wearing an uncustomary beard and moustache walked.

In the first hour, Rowell led with 9 miles and 6 laps as opposed to Weston's 7.1, and after 90 minutes the score was 13 to 10.4, again in Rowell's favour. In the second hour, the little Englishman, sticking rigidly to his jog-trot, continued to increase the gap with the American who walked and ran intermittently, so that at the end of that hour the scoreboard showed 17.2 to 14.3. By 7 o'clock that distance had increased to 10 miles (47 to 36.6). It was later reported that Weston had *"turned very queer,"* and had to retire to his hut repeatedly suffering from a bad attack of diorreah. This helped Rowell, the then 1/10 favourite, secure a long lead, and at 11:00, his total was 72 miles to Weston's 49

The "Cambridge Wonder" made his first 100 miles in 14h.40m.58s whilst the "Weary Wobbler" could only watch 40 miles in rear. The next three hours saw the race leader adding a further 13 miles to Weston's eight making the score at 18:00 read, 113 to 68. There was a good attendance at the rink for the event in the evening, but it was felt much interest was lost due to the American's illness. By 23:33, when he retired to his house, the Englishman had scored 140.1. On his way to his bed, Weston's midnight score was recorded as 85 miles. Weston's total rests for the day, which had amounted to 12 in all, had worked out at 6h.56m.2s whilst Rowell's four rests had occupied 1h.9m.5s.

On the second day, Weston, who was first on the track at 03:07, went on to cover his ground at a rate of 5 mph. Rowell meanwhile, who re-appeared at 04:34, continued to dominate, but, Weston, having got over his tummy troubles, appeared to be in fine condition and going well. Rowell completed 150 miles in 28h.48m.8s with Weston getting his century shortly after 6 o'clock in the morning. The score at 11 a.m. was 174.7 to 124.5, at 3 p.m. 196.1 to 147.1, and at 6 p.m., 212.6 to 160.7.

The hall was quite full during the evening with both men getting cheered equally for their efforts. The general feeling at the time was that despite Weston's much improved performance, the race was already very much in his opponent's bag. The score at 9 p.m. was 226.5 to 173.6 and at 11. p.m., 236.7 to 180.5. Rowell retired to bed at 23:40 having made 240.1 which meant he had made 100 miles for the second day. Weston was said to be somewhat light-headed when he headed for bed twenty five minutes later on a score of 185 miles.

On the third day, Weston left his tent at 03:19 and after a period of limbering up at walking pace, began running. The race leader joined him on the track at 04:20. A minute after 8 a.m., when the scores were 255.5 to 195.5, Weston retired to his hut till 09:19. By the time of his departure, Rowell had increased his lead to 60 miles due to the frequent rests that his opponent had been taking. On returning, the American walked along *"gingerly"* till 10:02, when he left again. This time he wasn't to be seen again in the race having offered his formal retirement from the contest at 16:20 due to being *"utterly unable to continue."* His score at the end was 201 miles and 3 laps. Whilst he lay in his hut in a *"delirious"* state, Rowell continued on his way *"looking perfectly fit and well"* until he had made a score of 280 miles at 15:17.

After the match, Mr. Duryea of New York offered to match Rowell against any three men in the world for a six day's race for a purse of $10,000, the winner to take the whole of the gate money. Rowell was now absolute possessor of the stunning Astley Belt having won it three times in succession.

Reproduced with kind permission from John Weiss (Illustration no: 85, 86)

CHAPTER 33

Ennis International Belt

There were to be two pedestrian contests promoted by "Honest John" Ennis during 1881.

The *first* one, which had taken place between the 9th and the 14th of May at the American Institute Building in New York, started with nine entries who were: **George Barber** of Jersey City who was known as "Cast-iron George" and who had covered 480 miles in six days; **Daniel Burns** of Elmira with a record of 578 miles in six and a half days; **Eph Clow** of Massachusetts with 460 miles; **Ed Geldert** of Worcester, Massachusetts, who, at the Wood's Athletic Grounds in Williamsburg between the 25th and 26th of April of the same year had made 133 miles and 2 laps in 25 hours; **George Hazael** of London with a record of 500 miles, **John Hughes** of that city who won the "1st O'Leary International Contest;" **Phillip Mignault** of Boston with a record of 481 miles, **John Sullivan** of Saratoga who had a record of 461½ miles; **Henry Weekman** of Newark:

The referee was W. B. Curtis, and the scorers were selected from the athletic clubs of the city.

One of the conditions of the race was that sixty per cent of the entire gate money would be divided up amongst the first four who made the required 500 miles, with 40 per cent going to the first man, 30 per cent to the second, 20 per cent to the third and 10 per cent, to the fourth. Any competitor not making 500 miles would not be entitled to a prize. Another condition was that the race promoter would pay the $500 entrance fee for the Astley Belt contest, passage to England and go with him to assist him in trying to win the world championship provided that the winner beat Hughes's record of 568 miles and 825 yards

"At 11 o'clock there were possibly about 300 people in the great hall, and a brass band was giving what purported to be a sacred concert which consisted of choice selections from "Billee Taylor," "Ollivette" and other popular musical trifles interspersed with medleys of Irish airs." When the word was given to "go" at 12 o'clock, all of the competitor's, apart from Weekman, started on an easy run with Barber heading the field on the first lap in front of 2,000 or so spectators. Mignault was second and Hughes and Hazael third and fourth. Weekman made his appearance fours minutes after the others had started and when he did, the crowd laughed at him as he made his way round with an *"ungainly gait."* Mignault was the first man to make a mile in 6m.18s, with the second made jointly by Hazael and Hughes in 6m.22s.

Very little was subsequently reported about how the race developed and this was probably due to the fact that so few people attended. The *Brooklyn Daily Eagle* wrote: **The public seems at last to have made up its mind that the six-day go-as-you-please contest for all sorts of nominal trophies is more or less fraudulent. The match under the management of John Ennis, in New York, came to grief in forty eight hours, mainly because the attendance was mournfully slender.**

What is known is that by noon on Tuesday the second day, and in front of only 40 spectators, of the three remaining contestants, Geldert led Clow 170 miles to 160 with Sullivan having scored 133. Hazael was the sixth man to have left the contest that morning giving the reason that no money was being made to pay for his trouble. He was followed by Sullivan on a score of 163. That left just two in the race and by midnight Geldert with 207, led Clow by 20 miles.

The *Washington Post* in its short report of the race on May the 12th said: **New York. May 11. - The six days go-as-you-please tournament at the American Institute building at 10 o'clock this evening had four men and a negro woman for an audience. At that hour Geldert went to bed with a record of 280 miles. Clow reappeared on the track now and then, and at midnight had a record of 219 miles.**

The score at midnight on the fourth day, Thursday, was Geldert, 356; Clow, 338: The leader had left the track at 22:45 to sleep. As he left the building Clow stated that he wouldn't return the next day. With his promise kept, that meant Ed Geldert was left alone in the race. John Ennis informed the press that he couldn't close the race as long as long as one pedestrian remained on the track, *"all bets made on the race would be declared off."* What was also worrying for "Honest John" was the fact that very few of the 6,000 people who were issued complimentary tickets to the match ever bothered to turn up to watch it.

The *Chicago Tribune* on May the 14th wrote: **New York, May 13.** - In his solitary walk at the American Institute, Geldert had 400 miles scored at 3 this afternoon. There was not a paying spectator in the building. A reporter asked Geldert what his intentions were. He replied: "To make 500 miles, and I shall accomplish that by 4 tomorrow. I am as fresh now as when I started, because there has been no incentive to attempt anything extraordinary. Want of patronage and competition make it a dreary task, but I am taking Mr. Ennis at his word. By completing 500 miles I shall get 60 per cent of the receipts." The reporter asked as to the receipts and was told; "At 11 o'clock yesterday there had been $557.60 taken in. Since then the ticket taker has received 50 cents that makes $558.10."

"Where does the odd change come from?"

"Oh we are accommodating here. I suppose some boy has been admitted for 10 cents."

Of the sum, Geldert will get 60 per cent or $331.80, less his entrance fee.

Geldert at 10:37 finished 432 miles and retired to rest till 2 o'clock.

The last report on the contest stated that Geldert left the track just before eight o'clock in the evening on Saturday night having made 501 miles in an "on track" time of 115 hours. For his efforts he was awarded just over $300 out of which he had to pay his trainer and attendants about $150. Only about a dozen spectators were present at the finish.

For the *second* event, Ennis attempted to follow O'Leary's example, and organised the "Grand World Championship six-day go-as-you-please Tournament" which he arranged to take place between the 26th and the 31st of December again at the same venue. He was convinced that the dates he had chosen would be financially rewarding as the race would take place in the week of the Christmas holidays. The promoter would add five extra prizes to the sweepstakes of $100. A silver cup worth $200 representing the *"Long Distance Championship of the World"* would be awarded to the winner of the race, but only if the victor succeeded in beating Robert Vint's world record distance of 578 miles. The financial rewards were a prize of $1,500 to the winner, $800 to the second, $400 to the third, $200 to the fourth and $100 to the fifth. In order to be awarded any prize, the race contestants would have to make 500 miles. The cup itself was most impressive, its base representing the very first Astley Belt race in the USA showing the figures of the four contestants, Ennis, Harriman, O'Leary and Rowell. On top of this was a silver globe with the countries of the world set in gold and flanked either side by the flags of America and England. On top of the globe was an allegorical figure of a winged Mercury.

The plan was that after the doors of the great building had been opened at 20:00, the waiting spectators would be entertained by a *"sacred concert" which would offer listeners comprising airs and melodies from nearly all the "sacred" opera bouffes which have become popular in this City."* By 10 p.m. the place was filling up nicely and most of the seats were taken. Outside the touts were doing a lively trade selling *"complementary tickets."*

Whilst people milled around inside, some admiring the splendid cup which was displayed on an elevated stand beneath the scoring dials, there was a noticeable absence of any bookmaking firm within the place. Ennis had seen to it that, this contest at least, would not be under the influence of *"sporting men."*

The track, which consisted of loam and sawdust to a depth of three inches, was exactly one eighth of a mile in circumference. It had been laid on the concrete floor of the Rink and was said to be a *"remarkably springy road bed which will favor the sore feet of the pedestrians as much as possible."* The inner part of the track which could be reached by a wide seven-foot high bridge and divided in the middle by a railing, was surrounded by a picket fence giving easy access to the spectators to that part of the arena without interfering with the pedestrians. A number of chairs and settees were provided for patrons around the outer edge of the track and a large number of seats were provided for spectators of the *"fairer sex"* near the entrance, but only if accompanied by gentlemen.

Arrangements for scoring the laps and miles would be carried out by officials selected from the amateur athletic clubs from New York. The *"lappers"* would sit opposite the scorers and their findings would be recorded on two dials for each contestant, the upper dial being for miles and the lower for laps which were situated on a large board at the northern end of the track.

There would be no tents on the track to hinder the view of the spectators. The athletes' accommodation would be provided inside a series of rooms alongside the main entrance. The rooms provided the men with the usual bare necessities including an iron bedstead, mattress, wooden chair, and cooking stove.

There were 15 entries in the race, these being: **J. Cox, B. Curran, A. P. Curtis, P. Edwards, A. Elson, J. Ennis, P. Fitzgerald, B. Gettings, F. Hart, D. J. Herty, H. Howard, F. Krohne, R. Lacouse, G. D. Noremac** and **W. Waldo.** Some of these names are instantly recognisable but Gettings and Waldo had not starred in a six-day match before. Dan Herty was Frank Hart's protégé having been induced into the race by the famous "ped."

The start was made at one minute past midnight when William B. Curtis gave the word "Go!" The men sped off in front of approximately 2,000 people and the first mile was made in 6m.15s by Curtis who was followed by Cox, Fitzgerald, Hart and Howard. At half past the hour, Curtis had scored 4 miles and 3 laps. Cox was second and Fitzgerald third.

With about two and a half thousand people watching the contest, Ennis, the race promoter was the first competitor to retire after completing 30.1. Gettings also went after 45.3 and Curran after 79. The reason for their withdrawals is unknown. Hart went well and took first place in the afternoon. Later, the race returns as recorded at 21:00, were: **Hart, 111.5; Fitzgerald, 109.7; Herty, 107.3; Edwards, 103.6; Lacouse, 102.3; Howard, 100.6; Elson, 100; Waldo, 100; Cox, 99.6; Curran, 74; Curtis, 60.4 (N.B. No score is given for Noremac or Krohne.)**

On the second day, Curtis was the first retiree of the day after completing 68 miles. He was followed by Waldo who retired on a score of 109.7 but only after much amusement when his wife appeared on the track declaring she could beat him walking. After pulling up her skirt, she skipped around the track making a lap, and after proving her point, she grabbed her husband by the arm and dragged him out of the building. Edwards was the last to retire on 150 miles.

Meanwhile, both Herty and Noremac made pleasing progress. The former preferred his own company on the track and rarely got involved with the other pedestrians. Noremac jog-trotted along at the same pace, and by midnight, found himself in fourth place, the scores of the leading contenders at that time being: **Fitzgerald, 223.5; Hart, 221.7; Lacouse, 213.2; Noremac, 207.4; Howard, 207.2; Herty, 205.7; Cox, 186.2; Krohne, 180.2:**

On the third day, Hart was the first big name casualty of the race. He retired early in the morning on a score of 229.4, putting down the reason for his failure as an attack of pleurisy brought on by catching a cold. Up to that point, he had been going well and was catching the race leader Fitzgerald who, to his credit, stood his ground and held off the challenge. Howard was the second competitor of the day to pack it in on a mark of 258.6 at 14:28. Noremac, although moving along gamely, was observed to have a perceptible limp during the afternoon. In the evening, Herty and Fitzgerald battled it out up front and in reaction to his positive performance, the young American was being backed off-course to win the race. After indulging in a good rest later, Noremac re-entered the race as stiff as a board, but having limbered up, later went along with his usual enthusiasm. The midnight score: **Fitzgerald, 328.2; Herty, 314.7; Lacouse, 308.5; Noremac, 292.4; Krohne, 270; Cox, 258.5; Elson, 244:**

Cox was the only retiree on the fourth day, Thursday, having made 283.5 a little after 12:30. His departure left just six men in the competition. Lacouse briefly took second place, but after Herty rejoined the fray after a good sleep, he retook that position and thereafter pulled away creating a three-mile gap between them within an hour. At that stage of the race, the leader Fitzgerald was 8 miles and 5 laps behind Vint's record and the pressure was on him to pass it. Ennis curiously was the man to be seen to be putting that pressure on the Irishman to claim that new world record, and despite Fitzgerald's trainer advising his man not to overexert himself, the race promoter tried to make a bet of $500 with anyone that he would do so, promising to give the money to Fitzgerald should he achieve the required distance. This decision was made by Ennis even after he had banned betting on the event in the building, but his reasons were probably from a business perspective. If he could induce the race leader to step on the gas and aim for a new world record, the response from the public would mean one thing, higher attendances and more gate money. He clearly wasn't stupid and $500 was a big enough incentive for Fitzgerald to put his foot down. The $500 bet was taken up by George H. Bailey of Boston and the money was deposited with William B. Curtis. At 18:00, the score stood: **Fitzgerald, 404.6; Herty, 383.2; Lacouse, 370; Noremac, 345; Krohne, 311.1:**

An hour later, Fitzgerald had made the same number of miles that Vint had made in the same number of hours. He was now on course for the world record, and by 23:00, was a full six miles ahead of it on a score of 428. The midnight score: **Fitzgerald, 430; Herty, 411.5; Noremac, 398; Lacouse, 372; Krohne, 347.5; Elson, 280.2:**

On the fifth day, Elson retired quite early in the morning on a score of 294.7. That left just five in the game playing for the money. At noon, Fitzgerald, now 4½ miles in front of the best record, continued to run the show with 480 miles on his score card. Herty was next in line on 456, and Noremac was nine miles behind him on 447.1.

Charlie Rowell was at the match. He told the press that he was going into training for the contest against Hughes in February at the start of the forthcoming week. He also stated that he had neither seen nor heard anything to make him wonder that there was anything wrong with the scoring of the current contest. He also confirmed that his next match was positively his last here or in any other country.

Herty left the path with lameness for a well deserved break at 22:30 having added seven laps to the fifth century he had just conquered. *"Herty's feet were in a terrible state and it was a wonder that he could keep on the track."* Fitzgerald followed suit seven minutes later having amassed 522 miles; and while those two rested, the plucky Scot, Noremac, played catch up on the track. Herty was soon summoned back to the ring and nearly fell over as he tried to defend his second spot. Realising the futility of it all, he went back to his apartment and that move meant Noremac moved up into the runner-up position. The midnight scores: **Fitzgerald, 522; Noremac, 505; Herty, 501.1; Lacouse, 453.2; Krohne, 440:**

On the last day of the contest at 17:23, Fitzgerald completed 578 miles, thus tying Vint's record. He then tramped around the hall till 20:15 before he retired for rest with a new world record score of 580.6. Earlier, Krohne and Lacouse left the circle for good at 17:42 and 17:43 respectively, with scores of 509 miles and 1,595 yards for the former and 501 miles and 275 yards for the latter. Noremac made a respectable 60 miles during the day and at 9 p.m., and with his score showing 563 miles under his name, he began to sprint around the path making his 564th mile in 7 minutes and his 565th in 8 minutes after which he walked an extra 495 yards and retired from the contest altogether. Herty left the track 21:10 with a final score of 556 miles and 275 yards.

The race leader didn't put in another appearance until 21:35 until all the other contestants were off track and then dragged himself tiredly around it a few more times to bring his tally up to 582 miles and 55 yards. At 21:58, in front the 500 people who had gathered to see the conclusion of the race, "Fitz" left the path for good having secured just $2,000 for his efforts. The *New York Times* remarked: **There was very little enthusiasm, no presentation of flowers or trophies, and though the band played some lively airs, they did not tend to arouse Fitzgerald sufficiently to move him out of an ambling sort of gait.**

The Final Scores!

	Miles	Yards	Prize	#
Fitzgerald	582	55	$1,500	$500
Noremac	565	495	$800	
Herty	556	275	$400	
Krohne	509	1595	$200	
Lacouse	501	275	$100	

For making a new world record:

King of the Peds

The new world record holder was born at Hill O'Listuff, County Longford, Ireland, on December the 5th 1846. He stood 5 feet 10¾ inches tall and at the beginning of the race weighed in at 165lbs. He initially began his career on the track in Canada at the age of 12 years old winning a two-mile race against a field of nine. He then arrived in New York, taking up the occupation as a cattle drover. Whilst doing this he carried on his interest in athletics as a short distance performer making some fast times in the process reportedly running 11 miles in 59m.50s.

His first crack at a six-day event was between the 6th and 11th of October 1879 at Madison Square Garden, where, in the first hour, he ran 9 miles 416 yards and led the race for five hours having to retire the day after with a badly swollen knee on a score of 88 miles. Seven days after that failure, he lined up for the 14 hours a day, six-day go-as-you-please match which started at the same venue on Monday, the 13th of October. Incredibly he won this with a score of 377 winning the first prize of $1,200. He then came fifth to Hart in the Rose Belt in December of the same year recording an impressive score of 520 miles. After that he made 132 miles in a 72-hour, 12 hours per day event, which began in Providence on April the 12th 1880. He then went to Lowell, Massachusetts, where he finished out of the frame in a 75-hour race which ended on the 24th and which was won by O'Toole. Two days later on the 26th, he started a 72-hour event at Buffalo when he came in third behind race winner Panchot and runner-up Faber with a score of 386 miles. At Boston, in the John Ennis sponsored 130-hour walking match at the Music Hall between the 27th of December 1880 and January the 1st 1881, he withdrew after making 352 miles, the final score being Lacouse, 425, Wilmot, 400, in a time of 127 hours. Billy Pegram was also a competitor in that one, having retired after making 211.1 in 59 hours. Patrick, who had been initially going well, had made 131 miles in 24 hours and 306 miles in 72 hours. Then at the American Institute Hall between the 24th and 29th of January of 1881, and after scoring 113.7, he gave up the race early on the second morning. His last race was when he finished 4th to Vint between May the 23rd and 28th having accumulated a total of 536 miles 660 yards.

CHAPTER 34

What Else Happened in 1881

The 75-hour world champion, George Parry, of Manchester, and the 50-mile champion, Arthur Hancock, of London, entertained a large crowd who had gathered to watch a three-hour walking match for £50 at the Aylstone Park Grounds, Leicester, England, on the afternoon of Saturday, February the 7th. Parry, although given a seven-minute start by his opponent, lost the match due to being inferior in fitness, and when passed by Hancock, realised there was not much point in carrying on. *"Hancock's efforts were a truly magnificent performance – indeed it was frequently remarked by those who knew him that he has never done better anywhere, or at any time."*

The race in the O'Leary 142-hour heel-and-toe match held at the Exposition Building in Chicago between Monday, the 9th and Saturday, the 14th of May 1881 was interesting in the sense that very little was reported about it in the press. The little information gleaned about the "in running" scores, and the outcome, was picked up from smaller city newspapers. Even though the match was held in Chicago the predominant newspaper in that city, the *Chicago Tribune,* failed to mention anything about the race apart from offering scathing criticism about the event on the 9th of May. The whole article is reproduced below and gives a fascinating insight into the how the sport of pedestrianism was being viewed by an extremely cynical press at the time:

DIZZY TRAMPS. – The Stupid Walking Match at the Exposition Building. – An Exhibition That Ought to be Closed by the Police.

One of those rare and delightful athletic novelties (?) which periodically blossom forth in large cities, remain for a week, and then vanish, leaving life a blank behind them, was inaugurated last night in the Exposition Building, with a small crowd of spectators, in which the gambler, confidence man, bummer, and prostitute element was conspicuously predominant, and with Bill O'Brien as the oratorical ornament of the occasion. The novelty alluded to, which was introduced into this country some eight years ago, is known as the "six-days' pedestrian contest," and as there may be readers of THE TRIBUNE who are unacquainted with the peculiar charms of this peculiar entertainment, a brief explanation may be in order.

The necessary adjuncts of the contest are a sawdust track and a number of patient plodders who are willing, in the hope of securing a money prize, to pound it and keep on pounding it at a slow and melancholy gait, - the man who does more pounding between Monday morning and Saturday night receiving a larger amount of the money which has been taken in from a strangely curious public than the man who does less. Of the interest that attached to a genuine pedestrian contest, where swift men compete in which muscle and lungs are for a reasonable time exerted to the utmost, and the result trembles in the balance, with varying results, to the close, there is none. It is simply a question of dogged and brutal perseverance, with the feature of swiftness - the essential element of a race – lacking from beginning to end. A much finer display of pedestrianism can be seen at any time near the Madison street bridge than that now offered at the Exposition Building, and why people should be willing to pay for admission to a poorer show is a matter of wonder.

The exhibition just inaugurated is being conducted by Mr. Daniel O'Leary, a broken down pedestrian, who having worn out his own legs to poor purpose, is seeking to gain a livelihood, if not a fortune, by promoting the disability of the legs of other people. Twenty seven willing victims placed themselves at his disposal yesterday evening, and began pounding sawdust for his benefit, and, although the race was announced as an amateur contest, several of them are of the profession, - persons who have never greatly distinguished themselves in the pedestrian world, but whose presence nevertheless in a contest from which professionals ought to be excluded stamps the whole affair as a fraud. The alleged race, in fact, is nothing more or less than a piece of hippodroming gotten up by Mr.

O'Leary for the benefit of Mr. O'Leary and such persons as may be "In with him" in the undertaking. Occasionally the long-distance pedestrian succumbs to misfortune. Varicose veins sometimes cause him TO VANISH FROM THE SAWDUST TRACK; at other times it is bunions; and again the straining of a tendon will end his career; there is one thing, however, which never interferes with the practice of his business, and that is professional dishonor arising from palpable dishonesty in a race. Thus it is that the old hippodromers appear again and again, taking part even in amateur contests, where the prospect making a professional one day is most promising. Over and over again it has happened that the pedestrian who is the favorite in a race, and upon whom, the backers plumbed their money, has succumbed to contestants so notoriously his inferior that the fraud was palpable, yet the same favorite comes up again smiling, and smiled upon, and the pocket of the sucker is again depleted.

Of the race which started last night, but little needs to be said. Shortly after midnight - the solemn music of a sacred concert having preceded the melancholy event - some twenty-seven - most of them slab sided, narrow chested, stork legged waddlers with about a much "nation" to them as a duck on dry land were started by the oratorical Bill O'Brien on their six days task. In five minutes the whole crowd were strung out all over the track, so that to the spectator the enjoyment of a race which consists in watching the movements of the more advanced in it was not possible. All there was to see was a string of men walking at a very moderate gait along a track of sawdust. Which was first and which was last no one but the scorers knew, and they had not the time to tell. And so it is all through such contests. Occasionally a "brush" will be gotten up between two of the walkers, just to keep the flagging public interest, but when the public learns that the man who is doing the pushing is in reality some twenty five miles ahead of the man who is being pushed, its interest eases on the instant and it feels that its quarter has been lavished upon one of the sorriest delusions that ever prostituted the game of sport to its purposes.

There is no need to give any particulars regarding last nights walking further than to mention that fact that the gentleman who was in the lead half an hour after the start was known as the "Police Gazettes entry." His name was not learned. The gentleman, who may or may not be a foreign aristocrat, is traveling around (the sawdust track), as is the fashion with foreign aristocrat's. He wore a tight fitting blue flannel suit, and the fact that he was the "Police Gazettes entry" was blazoned in yellow flannel letters across his bosom. He was a favorite with the crowd, and, judging by the appearance of those who composed it, their intimacy with the delectable sheet he represented was THE FOUNDATION OF HIS POPULARITY. Taken altogether, the affair is a disgusting fraud, and one well worthy of police interference, both on account of the brutal nature of the exhibition and the decidedly immoral character of the audience which it brings together.

The reporter who wrote the above article must have been choking on his words as early in the match, Charles Harriman's $117^1/_5$ miles was the best on record score for 24 hours beating the best previous performance by *"about"* two miles, his 200 was accomplished in the best time ever made, and his final distance of 530 miles was a *new world record* for which he won $1,000. Edward Tracey of Cincinnati, with 523 miles, came in second winning $750. Frederick Krohne claimed the third prize of $500 with 520 miles. In fourth place was Antoine Strokel having made 458 miles. He won $200. Finally, Napoleon Campana got nothing for a score of 375 miles.

Charles A. Harriman
The National Police Gazette (Illustration no: 87)

There was no sharing of the gate receipts, probably due to the fact that there wasn't enough money in the pot after expenses had been paid out.

In New York on the 28th of June 1881, William Gale started his attempt to walk 6,000 quarter miles in 6,000 consecutive ten minutes in an *"open lot"* at Madison Avenue and Eighty Sixth Street. A couple of weeks before the end of his objective, he moved the venue to the old Bowery Garden where he continued on a 12-lap to the quarter mile sawdust track which had been constructed on a stage. On August the 8th at 18:40, he finished his great feat continuing on the track until he had added 14 additional quarter miles to his record. His fastest quarter of a mile was made in 2m.2s, and his slowest in 8m.12s. At the finish, Gale wanted to bet $5,000 to $1,000 he could cover 500 miles within seven days and he wanted to start straight away!

William Gale, the world's "endurance pedestrian."

The National Police Gazette (Illustration no: 88)

Between the 6th and the 11th September, a six-day go-as-you-please tournament was held on a 16-lap to the mile track under a large canvas tent on a piece of land near the Haymarket in Sydney, Australia. Nine competitors started the contest. They were: **Edwards, Baker, Williams, Swan, Le Petit, Rayner, Campbell, Cotton** and **Palmer.** The first three mentioned were the more experienced contestants with Williams being the oldest at more than 50 years old.

The race started at 01:00 on Monday morning. Edwards, Swan, Rayner, Baker and Campbell soon settled down to a lively pace, while Williams enlivened proceedings with his frequent bursts of running. By 09:00 on Tuesday, Swan had taken the lead having run more than 127 miles, which was a mile more than Edwards in second place.

By the last day, the 26-year-old Swedish born Swan still had the lead, and any hope of an exciting finish was dashed shortly after 21:00 that evening when Edwards retired after scoring 423.3.

Swan was declared the winner at 23:00 having completed 434 miles and 5 laps thus entitling him to collect the first price of £100 and a gold stopwatch.

In a 75-hour contest which ended on Saturday, December the 10th, 1881 in Memphis, Tennessee, Frank Hart and Daniel O'Leary, who had mustered a combined total of 607 miles, easily beat Harriman and Schmehl who could only manage 518 miles between them.

In London, on the 26th of December 1881, G. A. Dunning made 25 miles in 2h.33m.44s.

CHAPTER 35

There once was an Ugly Duckling.....

On August the 24th 1881, it was reported that Charlie Rowell had arrived back in the USA, accompanied by Montague Sherman and Ainsworth, the English athlete. All three were said to be visiting friends and thereafter taking a tour of the country. Rowell said he had no intention at the time of indulging in any racing.

However, just three months later, the *Chicago Tribune* in its edition of the 27th of November, stated that there would be a $1,000 a side, 26-hour go-as-you-please contest between Rowell and Dobler at the McCormick Hall in that city between December the 5th and 6th. The original choice of venue, the Exposition Building, was rejected by Rowell because it was too cold and that meant that the stage would be removed from the favoured venue to create a sixteen-lap to the mile track. It was further stated that Dobler was already in training for the match, and under the direction of "Happy Jack" Smith, he was regularly running thirty-five miles a day at the Exposition Building. Rowell meanwhile, was limbering up at on one of the east coast athletic grounds and would arrive in Chicago later on in the week.

The 26-hour race between them began at 21:00 on the evening of December the 5th with about 400 people present at the start. Both men were said to be in excellent condition, and the friends of each were said to be equally confident of success. *"Both the contestants stripped well, Rowell especially so. Dobler's countenance was clearer and brighter than usual, and he seemed to be in the best of spirits. Both his trainer and himself thought his condition excellent. Rowell stripped and rubbed down is a glowing picture of health and of muscular development from head to his heels. The sinewy tendons and muscles of the legs, when at full tension, betray his marvelous strength and endurance of limb."*

With no appreciable distance between the two men, the first mile was made in 6m.32s and the first four miles were accomplished in 34m.54s.

Dobler was said to have over-trained for the contest, and as a result *"vomited and purged freely,"* putting him far behind. At 01:00, he was off the track on a score 21 miles with Rowell 9 miles in advance of him. The match was called to a halt at 1:47 a.m. when it was announced that Dobler was too ill to continue the contest. Rowell was therefore declared the winner on a score of 35 miles.

As early as January the 16th 1882, news was surfacing that Vint, Panchot and Hughes were among the first pedestrians to place $1,000 in the hands of Mr. Hamilton Busby, the referee and stake holder, to join Rowell in another six-day event at Madison Square Garden between February the 27th and March the 4th 1882. The huge sum was to ensure the contest attracted only the most serious competitors. It was thought at that stage that six other men would add their money to the pot for entry to the race, the closing date being three weeks before the start.

The other incentive to enter was the additional prize of a diamond studded whip. The principal materials of the trophy were coloured gold and precious stones. The handle consisted of red gold, and within that, in yellow gold, was the figure of the famous E. P. Weston in pedestrian costume carrying a whip. Below him was an American eagle supporting a wreath of laurel leaves which were wrapped around the handle. This had an inscription enclosed within it. Below all of this was a second band of gold encircling gems, including a blue tourmaline from Maine and a red jacinth from Arizona. The whip was surmounted by a crown of precious stones in the form of a cap which was a mass of diamonds, rubies and sapphires thus forming the national American colours of red, white and blue.

The rules regarding the division of the gate money are explained below:

"No man completing less than 525 miles will be entitled to any part of the $9,000 sweepstakes or gate money.

The gate money after the expenses have been paid is to be divided as follows;

If only one man completes 525 miles or more, the whole gate receipts, less the expenses, to be paid over to him. If two men complete 525 miles or more, the winner is to receive two thirds of the gate receipts, and the second man one third. If three men complete 525 miles or more, the winner to take one half, the second man 30 per cent, and the third man 20 per cent of the receipts. If four men complete 525 miles or more, the winner is to take one half, the second man 25, the third man 15 and the fourth man 10 per cent, of the receipts. If five men complete 525 miles or more, the winner to take one half, the second man 25, the third man 12, the fourth man 8, and the fifth man 5 per cent of the receipts. If six men complete 525 miles or more, the rate of division shall be 50, 20, 12, 8, 6 and 4 per cent."

Rowell

The National Police Gazette (Illustration no: 89)

Rowell, having deposited his thousand bucks, was busily training at the American Institute Building where he was putting in 40 miles of practice daily. He was sharing the facility with John Hughes who was backed by *The Police Gazette* under the mentorship of William E. Harding. Another contender training alongside Rowell and Hughes was George Noremac, the Scotsman, who was seen spinning round the track, but only for short periods, 15 miles a day being his preparatory regime. Patrick Fitzgerald, the world six-day distance record holder who was also to compete, was slightly lazier than the British holder of the Astley Belt. He was running around Wood's Gymnasium in Brooklyn and reported to be doing 25 miles a day. Robert Vint, who Fitzgerald had deposed as the record holder, worked out at the same venue, and thought that 13 miles of exercise during his three-hour training sessions would bring him victory in the coming event.

Below is an interesting article that was doing the rounds in many of the newspapers of the time about the training of professional pedestrians for a race:

The training of a walker for a long walk requires the skills of a dedicated and intelligent trainer. It is the trainer who devotes himself to getting his athlete just right for the big race.

There are no set rules to govern the training of a walker, and each man has his own peculiar methods. Training begins about a month before the start of the race. The athlete is run distances of between 25 and 35 miles each day. There is the usual rubbing down and gymnastic exercises, with careful attention to the diet and habits of the contestant. Special attention is given to the development of the muscles of the leg, and they are hardened as much as possible.

The diet though is the most important for success or failure depends on the condition of the stomach. It goes through its own peculiar and special course of training. Barley and chicken broth, beef tea, and similar constitute the main diet of the walker for the few days previous to the race. The athlete is also given any soft, easily digestible food he may desire. On the track many of the men content themselves in a measure with jellies, raw tomatoes, and foods of that character. Liquor also forms a very important factor in a race. Doses of brandy mixed with iced tea, form the principal drink of the walker, although some use champagne. Whisky is rarely ever used.

Take the diet of "Old Sport" Campana for example; He eats anything but meat and was fond of barley soup and beef tea and when walking around the track frequently carried a little can with a small spout containing one or the other which he sipped at. His diet was described as "light" and he eats plenty of oysters. Another athlete, Lewis eats from a cup as he goes round. His trainer gave him beef tea with eggs beaten up, tomatoes, milk and sometimes a little sherry.

When the race starts, the trainer must watch his contestant closely carefully all the times and be a mentor for him both physically and mentally. He is the doctor who soothes his aching limbs, the housekeeper who prepares his food, the nurse who watches him in his sleep, and, in fact must do everything for him, except the walking.

Some men are easily handled, while others are very hard, and it requires threats and sometimes an appeal to brute force to keep them to their work.

The interior of a walkers hut is like a study. There are usually two beds in it, and a small gasoline stove, always heated, while the shelves contain an array of bottles that would go a long way to stocking a village apothecary shop. There are teapots, kitchen utensils, sponges and buckets of pulverized ice with bottled drinks in them. There is a washing line with shirts, stockings and handkerchiefs on it. Liniments and lotions of all kinds are there in abundance, plenty of alcohol in which to bathe the runner (the runner is bathed carefully in alcohol every time he leaves the track and his legs well rubbed. The rubbing, however, must always be from the hips towards the feet, and there is no reverse motion of the hands), and a supply of salves, court plaster, bandages and other little things that come in active use during the week.

On the track the runner usually carries a small sponge to moisten his mouth, and takes nearly all of his refreshment while on the move. His trainer has to constantly study to maintain a certain gait, for nearly all of them run by a certain time schedule, and aim to accomplish a certain number of miles each day.

The most trying time in a trainers experience is when he arouses his man from his sleep to go on the track. Exhausted nature has to be fought against and the runner is willing to forego his chances of victory for a few more hours sleep. The inexorable trainer, however, has to make him go upon the track, and sometimes it is necessary to stick needles into a man to thoroughly arouse him. Others on the contrary wake easily and are as docile as lambs.

Charlie Rowell wasn't in Peter Duryea's office, Room 4 in the Gilsey Building, 1193 Broadway, New York, when a newspaper reporter called to interview him on Saturday, the 25th of February. Mr. Duryea, the race promoter was though, and after pleasantly introducing himself, this is what he said about the race he had organised and Rowell's participation in it.

Mr. Duryea: "I have already expended $18,000 in making necessary arrangements, and I estimate the entire expense for the race at $21,000 or $22,000. For the use of the Garden for one week, I pay a rent of $10,000. In every way much more money has been laid out on this race than ever before. I have Gilmore's band of fifty performers, with Mr. Gilmore himself as leader, to be present throughout the week, and that is $1,500 more than was ever paid for music during a match before. Altogether I do not see how the whole expense of the race to me can be less than $22,000. The pedestrians of course pay their own expenses, so that there will be so much in addition to what I have to pay. Everything else has to be paid for beforehand, and is charged to me. In return, I am to receive fifteen percent of the gross gate receipts, which is to be paid me before anyone else receives anything. The rest of the income from the match is divided among the pedestrians who cover more than 525 miles. Each man, you know, puts up a stake of $1,000. The winner takes all this except $1,000 besides half the gate receipts. The remaining $1,000 goes to the second man together with 25 per cent of the net gate receipts. The remaining 25 per cent of the net gate receipts is divided among the other pedestrians who go over 525 miles. Besides the gate receipts and the sweepstakes money there is considerable income from the sale of 'privileges.' The right to keep the restaurant bar and cigar-stand, I sold to Thomas Kearns for $6,000, the right to keep the shooting gallery I sold to J. Donovan for $205. The flower privilege was bought by Mr. Brown for $75, the fruit privilege by Mr. Connors for $105, and the right to sell periodicals by Mr. Snowdon for $50. Besides these other privileges brought considerable sums. The admission fee will be $1, and there will no season tickets. Of course, once inside the Garden, a visitor may stay as long as he likes."

He then went on to talk about Rowell.

"When I brought Rowell from England, he had no intention of going into a sweepstakes race under any circumstances. I had offered to match him against any man in the world for $5,000 or $10,000, but nobody was ready to take me up. Then the newspapers began to talk about the proposed stake being too large, and said that if I would make it a sweepstakes race, with an entrance fee of $1,000 for each man, everybody would go in. I did this, and Rowell finally consented to enter. After beating Dobler in Chicago on December the 5th last year, he came to New York, where he trained at the American Institute. He has been doing in all about forty miles a day. In the morning, before breakfast, he will do about five miles, and then after breakfast take a spin of twenty miles or so at the rink. Then a slight lunch, and a fifteen-mile run on the road would finish up the day. His handlers during the coming race will be Asplen, Barnsley and Longford, all of whom have come over from England to look after him. These three will take entire care of him during the contest. He took his last run today. He is in perfect condition and says he never felt better in his life. He was over at the Garden a short time ago….. Ah! There he is now!"

Spotting his man rushing by outside on Broadway, Duryea opened the window and shouted, "Charlie!" Within a few minutes the man himself appeared at the door wearing a short walking jacket and carrying a cane. After a hearty handshake, the reporter commented on how difficult it was to get the Englishman to talk about himself.

Rowell: "Yes, I feel in first rate condition, and as far as confidence in the result of the race goes, I think I may give my competitors some trouble before they beat me. Have I got through training? Oh yes, I stopped running today. Tomorrow? Well, I shall stroll about a little I suppose and take a rest. I don't mean that I shall go to bed and stay there all day, and I suppose to some people my "rest" would seem fairly hard work but comparative rest I mean. I don't suppose I shall go over to the garden much before 12 o'clock Sunday night."

Reporter: "How do you feel with regard to Hart's application to be allowed to compete?"

Rowell: "Oh, I want that and everybody who wants to shall start, Albert too, if he applies. As for Hart, I put my name down for $100 towards his entrance money. I think he will come in. Sullivan? Yes, it is a pity he is a little off. No, I never was sick a day in my life; never had the toothache, the earache or anything. The trouble is people eat too much, and don't exercise enough. If a man lives plainly and takes plenty of exercise he ought never be sick."

Reporter: "It must take a strong constitution, though, to endure the strain of a six-day race?"

Rowell: "Well the strain doesn't hurt me. A man gets tired, but all he needs is rest to bring him back again. A couple of days rest after the race and I am alright once more. Which day is the worst in the race? Well it grows harder and harder every day, I think."

Reporter: "Have you made up any plan in this race?"

Rowell: "No, I never take any notice of time or work on a schedule (pronounced schedule). I go according to what the other men are doing. My game is to beat the other men. I shall only attempt to win if I can, and shall not make any effort to cover 600 or any fixed number of miles. But I expect, if I do win to have to cover 600 miles."

Reporter: "Who do you think will be second man, if you should take first place?"

Rowell: "Well, I never saw Scott, and I know nothing at all about him. As for the rest, you might put there names in a box and draw lots. I have no choice."

Reporter: "What plan of living shall you adopt during the race?"

Rowell: "I shall eat oatmeal, beef, tea, chicken, broth, eggs, chops, oysters and nourishing food of that kind. My drink will be ginger-ale and sometimes bottled cider. I have no regular hours of eating, but eat when I am hungry – that is pretty much all the time (with a laugh). I eat a lot of food during a match like that. As for sleep, it depends on how hard I am pushed. If I can, I mean to go off every night at 12 o'clock. Yes, my sleep rests me a good deal at such times. I sleep sound, and it makes me feel much better. Go without sleep? Well, I think I could keep on without my rest after Thursday night till the end of the match. I should try that if I were pushed."

Reporter: "How far shall you go on the first day?"

Rowell: "One hundred and fifty miles. My best first day's record is 146 miles, in less than twenty-two hours. That was in November in London. The second day I shall go as I find it necessary. It depends altogether on how much I am pushed. I am going to try hard to win, and if I can I shall do it."

Mr. Duryea: "I don't know that I ever heard Charlie talk so much before!"

The carpenters had been making quite a din in Madison Square Garden during the week before the contest while getting the interior ready. *"The main flooring was as smooth as wax as though put in condition for a ball."* Several strong truss bridges had been constructed over the track to prevent the spectators from walking on it. In previous contests, the track had been made up of loam, sawdust and tanbark. However, on this occasion, only the first two ingredients mentioned would be utilised. The change was made after Rowell had recommended that the new surface would be faster without the tanbark. The men would be accommodated in *"neat single room houses"* which were 15 x 15 feet in size, and were furnished with the usual items.

The building was to be heated by steam and lit by 30 electric lights, and the race managers made it known that the hordes of ticket touts who had plied their trade and made good money at previous contests, were to be suppressed. Many parts of the building had been boarded up to prevent gatecrashers from entering it.

With just one hour to go before the start of the race, the place was filling up rapidly and an estimated 6,000 were milling around the place. The north side, part of which was non-smoking and reserved for ladies and their consorts, was already full as were the south side seats. At the Madison Avenue entrance, the vendors at a book stand were shouting out, "Lives of all the walkers!" and "Programme of the race!"

Frank Hart arrived in the place much to the delight of many in the building, and his appearance as he strode along the track caused a buzz of excitement. Referee Hamilton Busby and Manager Peter Duryea instructed Mr. Bruce to telephone the board scorer to put Hart's name up on the big blackboard. Rowell followed Hart into his cabin, but before he did, he was clapped by a Mrs. John Morrisey who wore the English champion's colours in the form of a handkerchief around her neck.

The bookmakers with their tin boxes were sat at their small tables and were operating alongside the scorers, time keepers and reporters. They had obtained a court injunction preventing the police from interfering with their business. They offered the following odds on the contestants before the off:

Charles Rowell: 2/1: He was 29 years old, and although he was probably better known and had been more successful than any of the other competitors, his personal best distance was only 566 miles and 63 yards. He was 5 feet 6 inches in height, and weighed 138 lbs. His chest measured 36 inches, his calves 15½ inches and his thighs 20 inches.

NB: Just after Rowell left England to participate in the contest, it was reported that Sir John Astley made a wager of £10,000 that he would cover 600 miles. After the money had been put up, Sir John cabled Rowell saying, "If you cover 600 miles I'll give you half of my wager of £10,000."

Patrick J. Fitzgerald: 4/1: He was 35 years old. In December 1881, he covered 582 miles and 55 yards, a new world record distance. He stood 5 feet 10¾ inches *"in his training shoes,"* and weighed 165 lbs. His chest measured 42 inches, his calves 16 inches, his thighs 22 inches, and his feet were exactly 12 inches long. He was a round shouldered man like John Hughes and always appeared as though he was about to throw in the towel after a few miles. *"He throws his head away over almost on his chest, throws his elbows far out from his body, working his arms in the air, thus giving the impression that he is wasting exertion."*

George D. Noremac: 6/1: He was 28 years old and only weighed 115 pounds. George had arrived in the U.S.A on June the 10th of the previous year having won many races in Britain. He had scraped the entrance fee together courtesy of a group of friends who had all pitched in with a $100 each. He was 5 feet 3½ inches in height, and weighed 118 lbs. His chest measured 35 inches, his calves 13 inches and his thighs 18 inches.

Since his arrival in America, he had entered the Rose Tournament at Coney Island on July the 3rd where he won the $80 first prize. He then ran several sprint races thereafter beating Garrett Fitzgerald in a 25-mile race for $100 a side at the Scottish-American Grounds in New Jersey on September the 26th. He then covered 565 miles and 495 yards in the Ennis sponsored race at the American Institute Building in December.

Frank H. Hart: 7/1: In April 1880, at Madison Square Garden, he had made 565 miles and 165 yards. He had never been able since then to equal this feat. He was 25 years old, and weighed 150 pounds. He was a late entrant in the race due to a dispute with fellow runner John Hughes whom he owed money to. However Hart paid Hughes half of the $100 he owed him and said he would pay the rest out of his winnings.

Peter Panchot, 7/1: He was described as very good looking with a dark complexion and was graceful when he ran. He was trained by "Happy Jack" Smith. Panchot, backed by Tom Davies, had proved he was a capable sort in the arena and had notched up a personal best of 541 miles and 825 yards in a "six-dayer." He was 29 years old, was 5 feet 4½ inches tall, and weighed 141 pounds. His chest measured 33 inches, his calves 13 inches, his thighs 17½ inches and he wore a size 7 shoe.

George Hazael, 8/1: He was 5 feet 6½ inches tall, and weighed 140 lbs. His chest measured 37 inches, his calves 13 inches, and his thighs 18 inches. He wore a size 7 shoe. The best distance he had covered had been 500 miles and 165 yards. *"He assumes a more and more curious shape as a six-day walk progresses, and makes the last 100 miles with his body bent like a jack knife a quarter closed, with one shoulder up and his head on one side."*

John Sullivan, 8/1: At 27 years of age, he was the youngest competitor in the race. He was born at Whitehall, Washington County, in the state of New York on September 1st 1854 and lived in Saratoga Springs where he had been in training for the race. His father died when he 12 and his mother passed away when he was 17. He had been employed for ten years in a sash, blind, and door factory, where he was in charge of the horses. He had also worked at Saratoga racecourse as a special policeman. Only the week before, he had had his jaw broken by a *"vigorous dentist,"* who he had employed to remove a tooth. It was reported that Sullivan telegraphed these facts in an attempt to have his entrance money returned to him. He was 5 feet 4 inches in height, and weighed 125 lbs. His chest measured 37 inches, his calves 14 inches and his thighs 19 inches.

After his victory at Providence, Rhode Island, between the 12th and 17th of April 1880 when he scored 385 miles and 2 laps against the likes of Colston, Guyon, Harriman, Herty, Jerry Hourihan, Panchot, Vint, and fifteen others, he headed west with Fred Engelhardt and during that summer won most of his races. His first six-day race was for the third contest for the O'Leary Belt which started at Madison Square Garden on February the 28th 1881. During the first four days, he made some good scores, on Monday covering 125 miles; Tuesday, 90 miles; Wednesday, 96 miles, and Thursday, 90 miles, after which he broke down entirely, his final score of the race being 461½ miles. He also contested the "2nd O'Leary International Belt Contest" which began on May the 23rd 1881 at the same venue. In this race, John, with a score of 569 miles beat the old record and finished runner-up to Vint who gained a new world record. His last performance was at the Town Hall in Saratoga Springs on January 11th and 12th 1882, in a $100 a side, 24-hour go-as-you-please handicap race against Daniel Ireland which he allowed his opponent 15 miles. He won!

John Hughes: 12/1: He had been trained by ex-pedestrian, William Harding. He was confident of winning despite only managing to cover 15 miles daily in training. He had told the press he would "win or die on the track!" He was 5 feet 9 inches in height, and weighed 150 lbs. His calves measured 13½ inches, his thighs 19 inches, and he wore a size 9 shoe.

William H. Scott: 20/1: Was a 38-year-old Californian based pedestrian and champion of that state with a record of 505 miles in a six-day go-as-you-please made in San Francisco from the 23rd till the 28th of June where he beat Reid, Eaton and Callaghan (500, 471 and 460 miles respectively). He had backed himself, and was being trained by two friends who had come with him from the Pacific coast. He was 5 feet 9½ inches in height, and weighed 155 lbs. His chest measured 36 inches and his calves 15½ inches. *"He is a fair walker and neat and fast runner."* He carried himself *"as straight as a soldier,"* and looked as though he strained himself to keep erect but he said the position is involuntary and natural.

Robert Vint: 25/1: The 35-year-old ex-shoemaker from Brooklyn had a record of 578 miles and 603 yards. Vint was 5 feet 2 inches tall and weighed 117 lbs. His chest measured 36 inches, his calves 12 inches, and his thighs 18 inches. He wore a size 3 shoe. What he lacked in muscular build and speed was made up in stamina. He leant forward when he walked and moved along taking *"tiny little steps."* Though an excellent athlete, he had claimed he was unfit to race because of rheumatism. He asked for his entrance fee to be returned and issued his fellow contestants with a supporting letter from his doctor. This all fell on deaf ears and he took his position at the start.

Since the days of Daniel O'Leary, the six-day events on show were still as popular as ever, and this particular race was to be no exception. The match, which began at five minutes after midnight, had 10,000 people witnessing its start.

A hearty welcome was given to Scott who was the first man to arrive at the scratch. He was followed by Hart, Hughes, Vint and Rowell who got the biggest cheer. Just before the start, Hart took hold of Hughes hand and shook it vigorously. Mr. Busby wearing a huge sunflower type badge shouted "Go!" and set the athletes on their journey. Hughes went into the lead on the first lap. An Indian file followed, and the first to head it behind the leader was Noremac followed by Hart, Rowell, Scott, Vint, Fitzgerald, Hazael, Panchot and Sullivan. Hughes finished the first mile in 6 minutes and was still in front when he completed his second mile in 6m.25s. The third mile took him 6m.35s.

As many of the men were finishing the sixth lap of their tenth mile, some in the crowd were shouting, "Clear the track Hart!" At the time, Hughes was trying to overtake a bunch of contestants who were three laps behind him, and as he passed the judges' stand, the "Lepper" shouted, "I want Hart to come out!" The perception was that Frank was holding up the progress of many of the pedestrians as he ran alongside Rowell, thus causing anybody trying to pass them to have to go very wide of the pair. The cynics were under the impression that Hart had been put in the race to help Rowell, but his critics were soon silenced when Hart passed the Englishman and ran away from him. Referee Busby, who was called upon to adjudicate on the issue, ruled that Hart wasn't doing anything intentional. That decision pleased those in the crowd who supported Frank; every time he passed the scorers' stand for the next few laps, they cheered him to the echo. Hughes however, was hissed!

The early scores: At 01:00: **Hughes, 8.6; Fitzgerald and Noremac, 8.3; Hart, Hazael, Rowell and Vint, 8.2; Scott, 8.1; Sullivan, 7.5; Panchot, 7.4: At 01:30: Hughes, 13; Hazael and Rowell, 12.4; Noremac, 12.1; Hart and Scott, 11.7; Sullivan and Vint, 11.3; Fitzgerald and Panchot, 11.1: At 02:00: Hughes, 17.1; Hazael and Rowell, 16.4; Fitzgerald, 16.1; Noremac, 15.6; Scott, 15.5; Hart, 15.3; Vint, 15.1; Sullivan, 14.7; Panchot, 14.4:**

Retiring on a score of 19 miles, the diminutive figure of Robert Vint was the first casualty of the race two and a half hours after the start. The poor chap had lost $1,000 in no time, despite futilely protesting to his opponents only the day before that he was in no fit condition to race due to rheumatism.

Hughes maintained his lead up until 04:00, but then Rowell took his customary position at the head of affairs with his *"friend"* and fellow countryman Hazael chasing. Hughes went on to have a further altercation with Hart who had bumped into him whilst passing him. The New Yorker took exception pointing to the Bostonian shouting, "I rule this man out!" Hart explained his side of the story to the referee and was roundly cheered by the crowd, who, taking exception to Hughes's unsportsmanlike behaviour hissed him at every opportunity. However, Mr. Busby took a different view than that of the crowd and ordered Hart to stop harassing Hughes or he would disqualify him. Hart consequently left the belligerent Irishman alone.

At 07:00, Rowell, then with 50 miles to his credit, went along splendidly and was able to secure a handsome margin of 10 miles between himself and the rest of the field a couple of hours later. Then as was the norm for Charlie, he fell in behind the rest. He knew from experience that if anything untoward should happen during the race, for example, an injury, he could rely on the distance that he had created for himself to give him time to get it sorted out. He also knew he could call on his reserve strength for the final part of the race when the others were on their knees.

Hughes ran much better after taking a forced rest at 09:00 due to stomach cramps. Fitzgerald tramped along in a glorious suit whilst Noremac, with his mouth wide open, puffed and panted his way round. As Sullivan raced along like a *"startled goat,"* Panchot's odds tumbled as his right hip gave way to rheumatism. Scott appeared to be going the same way as the Buffalo postman - back home! Hazael too was in the doldrums, the Londoner complaining of a stiff right knee. Hart was not at all impressive, and the promising athlete that he had been just a year earlier, now appeared to be history. He was dubbed *"mischievous"* and a *"chronic kicker."* *"His once splendid form has given way to a wasted figure, and he has apparently lost pride in his work."*

The midday scores: **Rowell, 90; Hazael, 81.4; Hughes, 76.3; Sullivan, 70.3; Fitzgerald, 69.1; Noremac, 65.1; Panchot, 62.5; Hart, 59.7; Scott, 59.3:**

It was rumoured that some massive bets had been made on Rowell and the bookies weren't accepting another penny on him. However, they were freely offering *place* only betting on the rest which equated to: **Hazael, 2/1; Noremac, Panchot and Sullivan, 3/1; Fitzgerald, 7/2; Hughes, 5/1; Hart, 6/1; Scott, 12/1:**

Rowell broke his own 100-mile record in an unbelievable time of 13h.26m.30s thus beating his previous record by 29m.8s. It may be a good idea at this juncture to familiarise the reader with the evolution of the 100-mile race record as Charlie's amazing achievement would not be *bettered for many, many years to come! Below is a table reflecting its progress from 1870:

Time	Name	Date	Location	Style
21:45:00	Edward Weston	25.05.1870	New York	Walking
21:01:00	Edward Weston	12/13.06.1871	New York	Walking
20:38:00	Edward Weston	11.05.1874	New York	Walking
18:53:43	Daniel O'Leary	16.10.1875	Chicago	Walking
18:51:35	Henry Vaughan	08/09.05.1876	London	Walking
18:48:40	Charles Harriman	19.02.1878	Haverhill, Mass	Walking
18:07:57	Billy Howes	22/23.02.1878	London	Walking
17:54:14	Henry Brown	28.10.1878	London	G.A.Y.P
17:04:06	George Hazael	09.11.1878	London	G.A.Y.P
15:35:31	George Hazael	21.04.1879	London	G.A.Y.P
13:57:13	Charles Rowell	01.11.1880	London	G.A.Y.P
13:26:30	**Charles Rowell**	**27.02.1882**	**New York**	G.A.Y.P

17:00 scores: **Rowell, 125.7; Hazael, 113; Hughes, 104.1; Sullivan, 100; Fitzgerald and Hart, 94.6; Noremac, 88.5; Panchot, 85.2; Scott, 77.2:**

9 p.m. scores: **Rowell, 140.7; Hazael, 126.4; Hughes, 120; Sullivan, 110.6; Fitzgerald, 107; Noremac, 103; Hart, 100.5; Panchot, 97.1; Scott, 86.4:**

At 22:30, Hughes was *"sad eyed and gruff as he passed the scorers and looked savagely at the markers. Sullivan in green velvet, walked like a Tammany Hall politician who had just been ruled out of the State convention and who was disposed to protest. Noremac flew by like a gust of wind and Hart jogged around the ellipse as though on his way to a funeral."*

Rowell went on to make **150 miles in 22 hours and 30 minutes. The band celebrated by striking up a "Pinafore" air, and "He's an Englishman." The applause from the mass of spectators was loud and enthusiastic.

* and ** See "Summimg Up" at the end of the book.

At the midnight hour, when the race was about as exciting as watching paint dry, the big blackboard indicated that Rowell, who was asleep in bed, had made 150 miles and 220 yards. Hazael was in second place having made an impressive 135, and the "Lepper" behind him by a mile. Hart, although not disappointing at the end of the first day in fourth place on a score of 124 miles, was drawing criticism from the crowd who had earlier appealed to his backer Jacob Gottlob for information about his performance. Gottlob stated Frank had been under the weather due to a cold contracted at the opening of the race, and that because of his late admittance to the race, his problems were compounded due to not having quarters to operate from. However, Hart was now using Vint's old accommodation. Sullivan was fifth with 120 and Noremac followed him in sixth with a respectable 115.4. The world record holder, Pat Fitzgerald, having 111 miles in the bag, was in seventh.

Rowell, still way out in front, was also way out in front in the betting market. At odds of 2/5, no one wanted to know.

King of the Peds

With the desperate figure of Hughes being the only man on the track at half past midnight, the buildings clientele had very little in the way of entertainment. Many called it a day and headed off home. That left the pedestrians, their trainers and handlers, the usual crowd of down and outs, and the drunks in the bar, the sole occupants in the Garden. The boredom however, didn't last for long. Rowell reappeared after his rest at 01:32, and his re-emergence back into the race was greeted with applause from the 300 bleary eyed souls who were still awake.

Peter Panchot forfeited his $1,000 entrance fee at 02:05 due to suffering from rheumatism in the ankle which had evidently been troubling him even before the start of the race. None of his attendants, nor his backer, Tom Davies were anywhere to be found at the Garden. Panchot had made a score of 102.5 when he bade farewell.

The *"ridiculous Californian champion"* Scott, who had retired for good at 21:00 the previous evening, didn't formally notify the managers till 04:30 the next morning. His score on withdrawal was 86.4. The man had angered his backers so much, that they had told reporters the previous afternoon that they would back the female pedestrians Howard and Tobias to the tune of $1,000 to beat him in a distance of his choosing.

It cost $1 to get into the building for the morning session, and as a result the few who had paid that large amount wouldn't be returning as frequently as what they would like to in the future. The ladies section contained but two and both were described as being *"very pretty."*

Early scores on the second day of play:

Hour	3		4		5		6		7		8		9		10	
	M	L	M	L	M	L	M	L	M	L	M	L	M	L	M	L
Rowell	157	5	163	3	168	5	174	1	180	2	185	3	188	1	193	7
Hughes	145	0	150	3	155	6	161	2	167	5	172	3	176	4	182	4
Hazael	143	2	147	5	152	5	157	4	164	1	168	2	174	0	178	4
Hart	129	6	134	0	138	2	140	4	144	7	149	2	152	4	154	2
Noremac	123	7	128	4	133	2	137	3	139	7	145	1	147	6	151	7
Sullivan	121	6	126	3	131	0	136	1	140	7	145	6	150	1	155	3
Fitzgerald	121	2	124	5	129	2	133	5	138	2	142	5	147	7	153	5

At 10:30, about a thousand people were enjoying the entertainment on offer. Rowell had adopted his classic stalking tactics and jogged behind Hazael. The race leader made his 200th mile at 11:09 and was rightly cheered for his effort in a time 35h.09m.28s which would be another entry for the record books.

Hart followed the first three whilst Fitzgerald and Sullivan tramped after him. The second trio would catch the first about every mile, and the six of them would be more or less abreast for a lap going their separate ways, at least that is, till the next time. These tactics went on mile after mile. News from the Rowell camp indicated that their man would trot along until tired and rest when he felt like it.

At 11:30, Hazael went to his cottage. On observing the move, Rowell walked behind the fresh looking Noremac. Fitzgerald blew his way around and Hart kept alongside keeping him company. When Hazael returned, Rowell left the track to change into a new striped silk shirt. He waited for his fellow countryman to come round before continuing to remorsefully dog him.

More scores from late morning till mid afternoon:

	11		12		13		14		15	
	M	L	M	L	M	L	M	L	M	L
Rowell	199	1	204	5	209	6	215	2	218	0
Hughes	187	6	193	0	198	1	203	5	207	0
Hazael	183	1	188	7	193	5	196	5	202	0
Fitzgerald	158	5	164	1	169	1	174	3	179	5
Sullivan	160	4	163	2	168	3	173	1	178	5
Hart	158	3	164	0	169	4	172	2	177	3
Noremac	155	1	157	0	159	2	162	3	167	2

At about 16:00, the three race leaders, who had been moving along for some time together, began running, and carried this on for a mile and a half. When it was over, and as Hughes passed the scorers' stand, he *"pranced along like a young colt, jumped, and kicked his heels about, and appeared in other ways as kittenish as a schoolboy."* The reason given for Hughes abounding energy was apparently the fact that he had been under instructions by his trainer, William E. Harding, to drink a beverage which he had concocted. It was called *"Harding's Lightning Exhilarator."* Of the potion Hughes commented, "Beggora, I have something now that that would make a dead man walk. It lays over the stuff I have ever tried, and since I began using it, I feel like a new man." Time would reveal the drink's long term effects on the famous "Lepper."

The 6 p.m. scores with the match leader out of the ring having gone to his cabin at 17.07. **Rowell, 230.1; Hughes, 223; Hazael, 220; Sullivan, 194; Fitzgerald, 191.7; Hart, 190.7; Noremac, 175.5:**

The race was going well for all the *"tramps"* and their connections. The expectation was that big scores were going to be made, and the hoped for 600 miles would be attained. Hazael was 40 miles ahead of his previous record, and even the poorly performing Hart was within five miles of his best showing. Pat Fitzgerald too was in tip-top form. At 21:00, when the scores showed: **Rowell, 243.2; Hughes, 237.2; Hazael, 232.1; Fitzgerald, 206; Hart, 204.4; Sullivan, 203; Noremac, 188.5;** "Fitz" was only 5 miles behind his best record made in the previous December

At around 22:00, *"Among the spectators on the Twenty Seventh street side were several hundred women, and the size and quality of their diamonds and the profusion of golden yellow hair with many proclaimed them to be the kind of women who would naturally be attracted by such an event. The bar lessees were doing a thriving business on this side of the house as well as in the bar proper and the frequent popping of champagne corks and the clinking of glasses made music when Gilmore's band was silent."* The silence of the band wouldn't last for long though because they would be called upon to play a tune suitable enough to celebrate the little Englishman's victorious completion of his 250th mile at 22:24. Six minutes later, Hazael grabbed his 240th, and then went to rest on his sofa.

The 48th hour scores: **Rowell, 258.3 (new record); Hughes, 251; Hazael, 242.4; Hart, 219; Sullivan, 215; Fitzgerald, 211.4; Noremac, 200 (made his 200 at 23:44):**

The bookmakers were making their calculations as to the outcome of the race as they saw Hart pass 48 hours in fourth place, 39 miles behind Rowell. Noremac, in last place, was 19 miles in arrears of him but the bookmakers gave him preference in the betting as opposed to Fitzgerald who was in fifth spot.

After 48h.24m of gruelling plod, Rowell sought the comfort of his room having moved himself a distance of 260 miles. During that time he had only rested for just over 6 hours, which was a very impressive performance in strength and endurance. After he had been tucked into bed, the word was out that his stomach had been giving him problems and that, although he *had* been suffering from nausea, he had overcome that ailment and felt much better.

Hughes had confounded his critics having done some sterling work to reduce the gap between himself and the Englishman to just over seven miles. As well as covering 121 miles for the second 24-hour period, he had been observed lapping Rowell during the latter stages of the day; both he and Hazael were apparently determined to both catch, and overtake, the leader. They both knew that just one hour on the sidelines could leave Rowell

King of the Peds

clinging on to the lead, and 2 hours rest could alter the whole complexion of the race. This scenario was in the minds of his two rivals as they chased *"ansome Charley"* along. Hazael was looking in great condition and Hughes had bettered his previous best.

Rowell returned just after 2 a.m. and plodded along in his familiar dog-trot. Just before he re-entered the fray, Fitzgerald took 4th place from Hart.

During those early hours on that third day it was raining outside, and amid the precipitation and gloom of the dark streets, hardly anyone asked what the scores of the athletes were inside, where many of the tired 500 or so paying customers slept. They were joined in their states of slumber by the only visible policeman on duty who had very little else to but wile away the hours likewise.

All the participants were on the track at 10 a.m. and Sullivan was trying desperately to quell bleeding from his nose, albeit unsuccessfully. Noremac was going the best, and he raised an odd cheer as he followed Hazael round aping every action his fellow Briton made. Hughes, who was two thirds of a lap behind Rowell, jogged along and listened to the crowd as they acknowledged the fact that the race leader had made his 300th mile at 10:17 or 58h.17m.06s with a tremendous cheer. That feat was yet another incredible record by a most incredible athlete. The "Lepper's" trainer, Mr. Harding, told reporters that his man would be in the shake-up on the final day.

Rowell began dogging Hazael who was 5 miles and 754 yards behind him at that juncture. Hazael later completed his third century at 11:38, and when he did it, he was rushing himself along at a pace of 5 mph which was quicker than Noremac's four. Rowell towed along behind so as not to lose any ground, and both Sullivan and especially Hart, went nicely.

Hughes left for his house at noon. He was limping and news emerged he had a blister on his foot. He amazingly bounded back on the track 20 minutes later and resumed his effort with a jog-trot and went on to make his 300th mile at 13:56, albeit in a very poor fashion. After the numbers were hoisted next to his name, he literally staggered back to his apartment. The future for the "Lepper" was looking grim; his connections knew they had to do something miraculous to rescue the situation. He was whisked off to a local Russian baths and returned at 15:20 looking only a shade better.

Some local youths had got on the roof and were running around it in an alternative contest. The noise they created was heard below and the police moved them off rapidly. Rowell at this point was 1/3 to win the race.

Some further morning and afternoon scores:

	3		4		5		6		7		8		9	
	M	L	M	L	M	L	M	L	M	L	M	L	M	L
Rowell	262	4	267	1	272	3	278	0	282	4	288	1	293	1
Hazael	255	4	259	5	265	4	271	1	277	3	283	1	286	6
Hughes	255	0	260	0	264	2	270	1	274	5	274	5	279	1
Fitzgerald	224	6	229	7	235	0	240	0	244	6	249	4	254	4
Hart	221	7	224	7	228	7	233	4	237	7	242	4	247	5
Sullivan	216	2	221	1	226	0	229	5	234	3	238	7	243	3
Noremac	203	3	208	2	213	5	217	5	221	0	223	7	229	0

	10		11		12		13		14		15	
	M	L	M	L	M	L	M	L	M	L	M	L
Rowell	298	2	301	2	307	6	313	2	318	2	323	7
Hazael	290	2	295	4	301	7	306	2	307	0	312	4
Hughes	284	2	289	1	290	0	295	1	300	0	300	0
Fitzgerald	259	0	263	7	269	1	273	3	277	5	282	0
Hart	251	0	256	5	261	6	266	0	271	0	275	6
Sullivan	246	9	251	7	256	6	260	0	265	0	270	2
Noremac	234	1	239	0	243	0	245	4	250	0	255	1

Hart and Sullivan put on a spirited display for fifth place for the crowd watching the evening performance. Both appeared quite fresh, and between six and nine o'clock, continually indulged in a series of spurts much to the delight of those watching. At one stage, they ran a mile together at high speed. The audience they were playing to was a large one. By eight o'clock, every seat was taken and the space within the track was crowded, making movement for those within its boundaries very difficult. The roar of the crowd made it hard to be heard and the stench of the smoke made it nigh impossible to breathe properly. Oh those poor "peds!"

Fitzgerald had made 300 miles a little after seven o'clock. When Rowell hit his 350th at 20:42, he was 17 miles ahead of the best record. Even the then resting Hazael was one mile ahead of it on a score of 334. At 20:45, both Hart and Sullivan, more or less, celebrated 300 miles at the same time. Poor old Hughes meanwhile appeared to be in a right state when he hobbled around the path at 21:00; and with Hazael back on the course at ten o'clock, and the return of Rowell at 23:25, the betting on the result looked like this: (Placed odds to finish 1st or 2nd are in brackets): **Rowell, 1/3; Hazael, 5/1 (1/1); Hughes, 20/1 (6/1); Sullivan, 25/1 (4/1); Hart, 25/1 (5/1); Fitzgerald, 30/1 (4/1); Noremac, 75/1 (15/1):**

The midnight scores: **Rowell, 353.1; Hazael, 342.3; Hughes, 331.4; Sullivan, 314.3; Fitzgerald and Hart, 313; Noremac, 284.5:**

Quite an extraordinary incident had occurred during the night and one indeed that would have literally "brought the house down." While Hughes's attendants were heating some alcohol, the pot containing it fell over and ignited. The small hut caught fire, but was put out quickly using pails of water. The management, taking note of the debacle, put in extra measures to make sure there was no repetition, as the incident could have proved more serious.

The match reporter on night duty for the *Brooklyn Daily Eagle* described his observations in the Garden during those early hours of that next day: **The crowd lingered in the Garden until the small hours of the fourth day began to lengthen. Then it parted and rolled itself tiredly homeward through the muddy streets. Of the spectators, only those who staying qualities last a week remained on the stiff backed opera chairs. Even these packed themselves away in the corners and composed themselves for slumber. Their slumbers replete with tramp like indifference as to attitude and nasal trumpetings, remained unbroken until the glowing sunshine of opening spring bedimmed the electric lights and turned to a pallor the colored gas jets that flickered and faded in the golden rays shot through window and skylight. Then the permanent lodgers were rudely awakened. The circular apertures in the extended walls were opened and floods of cool crisp fresh air poured into the great structure dissipating the tobacco smoke and foul odors of the night. A troop of colored damsels, armed with scrubbing brushes and soap sufficient to demoralize any tramp, entered and made cleanly preparation for the multitude certain to come with the new day.**

On the track, Rowell, wearing his blue and white jersey, continued to maintain his lead into the early morning. At 01:17, he ventured into his tent and napped for 1h.40m.40s after which he rushed around till 05:55. He then took a similar rest break and was back in the ring at 06:38. At 07:00, having made a score of 375.5, and having pleased his team, his trainers allowed him a further rest at 08:17. While Rowell rested, his nearest rival, Hazael, even with a troublesome knee, had made ground on him during the night. Despite exhibiting his unusual eccentric and ungraceful gait which was more akin to a mobile windmill, his arms wildly beating the air, George, wearing a purple silk suit and matching cap impressed *"those in the know."*

King of the Peds

Hughes on the other hand was performing rather poorly. With sunken eyes, and a look of desperation on his face, he had spent a lot of time in his quarters during the night. His gait was poor and he limped along, coughing productively as he did so. Whereas the bookies had been inundated with people placing hopeful bets on him when he zoomed around the track early in the contest, there was now only interest in wagering on whether he would finish at all!

The very determined Fitzgerald saw his chance of making a place, and he trotted along in pursuit of his goal of overtaking the shattered Hughes on the scoreboard. In an attempt to retrieve the lost cause, Hughes was summoned from his tent and went back into the fray at 09:24. Although he moved slightly faster, he lasted at that pace for just five minutes. He then tried to stalk his fellow Irishman, but his effort was to no avail. "Fitz" soon succeeded in his goal at 09:30, and the crowd, now gathered in all parts of the Garden, clapped him for his commendable effort.

Watching the "Lepper" wilt, Sullivan, wearing a velvet cap, also saw a chance of moving up the leader board, and chased after the two sons of Erin who were ahead of him. Not too far from the Saratogan was Hart, who stuck to his tried and trusted *"cake walk"* method of transport. Noremac meanwhile, wearing a pink satin cap over his cropped head along with a pair of baggy tights made up of the same material, moved swiftly around the path. His trainer said he would score 600 by the time the contest had finished.

With a clear complexion, bright eyes and clad in a pair of scarlet trunks, Rowell, looking the picture of health, resumed his quest for glory at 10:13. Earlier on he had been indulging in heel-and-toe, but with Hazael so close, and erring on the side of caution, he now began to run. The rest of the men, barring Hughes, who appeared decidedly ill as the sweat poured down his face and saturated his sky blue hanky that he wore knotted around his neck, followed the charge. The crowd loved it. *"Rowell bobbed away like a cork. Hazael, Sullivan, Fitzgerald, Hart and Noremac bobbed after him. Hughes alone of all the company lacked the buoyancy to do more than drift."*

Well after ten o'clock, the crowd started to increase. Many in the growing audience were women. *"They were principally well dressed and comely. A few wore rustling silks and fluffy seal sacques and blazing diamonds and kid gloves with innumerable buttons clasping there arms almost to the elbows. None in the garden were more interested than they; and they showed their interest in many ways. Chief among their expressions of favor and approval were the floral tokens that bloomed on the huts of the walkers. Rowell had the largest show. A dozen great floral horseshoes billowed their buds into a fragrant cornice for his lowly roof. Harps, stars, wreaths and bouquets covered the front of the structure. Hart's house displayed many emblems of regard; and the rest, even the diminutive Noremac, were not forgotten. About all the bouquets were from women. "H'ive thought as some of 'em would like to 'ave Rowell for a husband," remarked the man of the plaid and pipe, as he approvingly surveyed the arrangement of the flowers."*

At that time the bookies were fully expecting Rowell to win the event. Accordingly, he was a very warm favourite. Here's how the odds looked on the blackboards. (Placed odds to finish 1st or 2nd are in brackets): **Rowell, 1/3; Hazael, 15/1 (1/1); Hughes, 15/1 (3/1); Sullivan, 25/1 (3/1); Hart, 25/1 (4/1); Fitzgerald, 25/1 (7/1); Noremac, 40/1 (7/1):**

At 12:08, Rowell went to his room. *"The English champion was given refreshments, and was put in bed with as much care as though he had been a tiny infant. He closed his eyes at once, and without apparent fear of the other English champion, who was still loping around the track, fell asleep."* With the leader now laid prostrate in his tent, Hazael stole the show with a positive display of running which ate mercilessly into the score of his fellow countryman. When George looked up at the leader board at one o'clock he must have a broad grin on his face for it was he who was the race leader by two laps! Rowell was nowhere to be seen. His trainers sat outside his house, arms folded and said, "Oh he's alright," whenever anybody enquired about his welfare.

Meanwhile, the failing Hughes was having an absolute nightmare on the path. He was seen barely crawling along, and by doing so was rapidly losing places. At 14:00, he was overtaken by Sullivan. At the same time, Hazael had gone six miles in front of Rowell.

The scorecards from the match from 03:00 for the next 12 hours showed:

	3		4		5		6		7		8		9	
	M	L	M	L	M	L	M	L	M	L	M	L	M	L
Rowell	358	7	364	0	368	6	374	0	375	5	381	5	383	2
Hazael	348	5	350	1	351	2	358	7	361	1	362	2	370	1
Hughes	339	5	344	5	349	9	352	1	352	6	353	1	353	4
Fitzgerald	320	3	325	7	330	6	336	3	340	6	346	3	350	7
Sullivan	316	3	321	6	326	4	330	0	334	2	338	7	343	7
Hart	315	3	318	3	321	7	325	5	330	3	335	2	340	5
Noremac	294	5	300	2	303	3	308	1	310	0	314	5	320	5

	10		11		12		13		14		15	
	M	L	M	L	M	L	M	L	M	L	M	L
Hazael	375	3	380	5	386	2	392	7	398	1	402	0
Rowell	383	2	386	6	391	4	392	5	392	5	392	5
Fitzgerald	356	1	361	0	365	5	372	9	377	3	381	1
Sullivan	348	0	352	1	357	2	362	5	366	6	371	2
Hart	345	0	349	0	352	6	356	7	361	5	366	6
Hughes	354	4	359	1	362	1	363	2	363	2	365	4
Noremac	321	6	328	7	335	3	341	1	345	7	351	1

On his return to the track at 15:47, the gaunt figure of Rowell, 14 miles behind Hazael and now attired in a new costume, walked briskly on to the track and tried to muster some sort of a challenge to the new leader. He appeared concerned as he looked at his score and quickly settled into his favourite dog-trot. His efforts however were forlorn, and after having spent just over an hour on the track, had to leave again. The bookies were beside themselves with joy and they quickly signalled their concern at his plight by allowing him to go for a walk in the market. Rowell was now "even money" favourite and a few punters took the price placing some hefty wagers on him.

Hazael left the track and left his attendants to monitor the situation while he dozed. With a nice cushion of 14 miles, the hard working Londoner deserved a bit of a break. The score at 18:00, with Hazael back on course and Fitzgerald just about to fill second slot in the race was: **Hazael, 414.7; Rowell, 398.7; Fitzgerald, 397; Sullivan, 382.2; Hart, 381.4; Hughes, 370.3; Noremac, 366.4:**

Rowell's faltering situation was compounded when Fitzgerald moved into joint second spot at 18:19. When the two scores corresponded at 398 miles and 7 laps, the spectators, who had been cheering for several minutes in anticipation of a change in order, finally let rip when he took the runner-up position. It was only then that Rowell's team admitted their lad was seriously ill. The bookies ran to their blackboards, having made their renewed calculations, and scribbled the new odds up. Rumours then began to fly around the building. Rowell was said firstly to have a dodgy stomach, then *"brain fever,"* then he had been poisoned, and then that he had *purposely* surrendered the lead so as to attract more people to the Garden to swell the gate receipts after which he would resume his winning ways.

The 19:00 score: **Hazael, 420.1; Fitzgerald, 402.1; Rowell, 398.7; Sullivan, 387; Hart, 386.7; Hughes, 371.6; Noremac, 371.6:**

At 21:13, the improbable happened as Rowell stepped gingerly back into the ring. *"His eyes were bright and his features bore a bold determined expression."* Everybody said, "He looks as fresh as a daisy." At this time he was 33 miles behind the leader who had already beaten the best four-day record, and was 14 miles behind second placed Fitzgerald. Hart and Sullivan were only two miles behind him. Rowell went on to finish his 400th mile at 21:27, and later while he rested in his tent, the two men who had been behind him, passed him at 23:15 thus condemning the ailing champion to fifth place in the race.

King of the Peds

The midnight score, with Hazael marching round the place as though he *"meant business,"* was: **Hazael, 433.5; Fitzgerald, 413.3; Hart and Sullivan, 409.4; Rowell, 406.3; Noremac, 392.4; Hughes, 381.1:**

Rowell landed back on the track at 01:06 after a rest of 2h.17m much to the relief of those who had backed him to win. He was obviously in some distress and appeared disgusted with himself. After making just three miles, he went back to his room.

Hazael meanwhile, with *"his sharp features, his face flushed to a deep vermillion, his costume of fiery red and his slender legs made such a figure of Mephistopheles as might be expected to appear upon the operatic stage,"* easily outshone the rest of his competitors. He seldom rested, and during the hours from midnight to dawn, whilst most of the buildings occupants slumbered, the *"bravest of the brave,"* as he was labelled, moved relentlessly around the track reinforcing his superiority. *"His gaunt frame was evidently tireless as the pendulum of a well wound clock."* At 03:50, and now relaxing in his tent, Hazael had registered his 450th mile. Up to that point he had rested just 23h.46m.10s. He was back at 04:20 with a new mode of travel having disposed of his *"long, slashing gait."* He was now trotting around the course increasing his advantage. *"Long after the German musicians of flamboyant visage and wide expansion of waistcoat had blown themselves voiceless, long after the thousands of excited evening spectators had gone out under the starlight, when the trainers dozed and even the keen eyed keepers of the record were uplifting with difficulty their burdened eyelids, the angular Englishman hurried on his way. His fiery costume flashed around the ellipse brightly as the glare from a Pittsburgh blast furnace, and incessantly as a pertinacious book agent."*

Rowell, having left the track at 01:50, kept out of the race until 03:23. He had made 413 miles by 04:00 and was in a pitiful state. He left again at 04:44 until 05:11. He then returned to the cold arena to try and shake off whatever was troubling him, but after a promising start, his body just wouldn't respond to the demands he was making of it. The initial faint applause encouraging his efforts disappeared as the crowd realised the man was spent. After completing just 16 laps, the once race favourite was back in his stable being attended to by his lads at 05:30 on a score of 415.3.

Fitzgerald, the second placed man, clocked up his 450th mile in the morning. His handlers were pleased with his progress and the prospect of a second place in the race.

At the start of the fifth day's proceedings, Hart had been going well. By 07:00 he had managed to pull six miles ahead of his main rival, the stamina driven Saratogan oarsman, John Sullivan. As time wore on, Hart, chewing a toothpick, and who was constantly changing his bright coloured costumes, pulled himself further away, whilst Noremac, the wee man from Edinburgh, continued on his way with the same stride.

Hughes, who was in a similar condition to the struggling Rowell, said he was determined to make the profitable 525 mark. Wearing a brilliant green cap embroidered with yellow silk, he started to quicken up, much to the amazement of the crowd. The score at 09:00: **Hazael, 476.3; Fitzgerald, 453.3; Hart, 438.1; Sullivan, 429; Noremac, 426.6; Rowell, 415.3; Hughes, 407.1:**

Meanwhile, substantial amounts of money were being placed on Hart to get second place: (Placed odds to finish 1st or 2nd are in brackets): **Hazael, 5/3; Fitzgerald, 2/1; Rowell, 4/1 (5/2); Hart, 8/1 (2/1); Sullivan, 10/1 (3/1); Noremac, 35/1 (4/1); Hughes, 50/1 (25/1):**

At 08:50, Mr. Duryea and Mr. Busby went over to Rowell's quarters to find out what was happening with him. At 09:55, after they were jostled by the inquisitive, they gave instructions that Rowell's name be taken down from the scoreboard. They then went on to make the dreaded, but somewhat inevitable announcement that he was out of the race.

Just before that information was relayed to the public, Rowell, wearing his civilian clothes, was observed leaving his flower festooned hut. He was pale and looked a sorry sight as he gazed forlornly up the home straight. Hughes, his face distorted with pain, who was limping past at the time of the announcement shouted, "I've gained one point. I've broken him up!" *"His face lighted up and his features broke out into a broad smile and he stopped as though going to execute a clog dance."* The realisation that Rowell would no longer be in the race spurred the "Lepper" on and he increased his pace maintaining it for a half mile. The bookies were on top of the world as they wiped the Englishman's name off their slates, having collectively won in the region of $100,000 by his retirement.

One of the reasons given for Rowell's failure was a story that during his last visit to his tent, and whilst his physician Dr. Taylor examined a scratch on his leg, Rowell asked for some beef tea. His brother-in-law and attendant, Charlie Asplen, apparently, and mistakenly, gave him a cup of warm vinegar which was supposedly to be used on the scratch. Rowell consumed it in one gulp and then exclaimed, "Why, that's nasty! That's not beef tea." He then went back on the track. After initially going along well, and within an hour of his return to the arena, he was soon back in his quarters vomiting. After that, and after having been offered food and drink which he wasn't able to keep down, he suffered greatly and vomited many times. There were those however, including one of the match judges, who believed that the story had been invented by Rowell's attendants to cover up the real reason for their man's demise. Many thought that a mixture of overtraining, along with his earlier devastating performance in this encounter, had coupled to have a detrimental effect on his body, which could simply, go no further. The same judge said that Rowell's consumption of ginger ale, ice and "slops," as he termed other liquid refreshments, hadn't helped him either.

Accompanied by his attendants, Rowell left the building through the Fourth Avenue exit just before one o'clock. He headed for his hotel where he stayed a short while and was then driven to Mr. Duryea's stables. Interviewed by reporters at Duryea's home later, Rowell gave the following explanation for his retirement.

Rowell: "I was taken sick on Wednesday night. I was sick at the stomach and couldn't eat. I went out on the track and tried to do all I could but my stomach refused nourishment. The doctor then informed me that I would make myself worse if I did not take sufficient rest. I could not bear the idea of losing time, but he said I rest. My feet and legs were as good as when I started."

Reporter: "Through whose advice did you leave the building?"

Rowell: "Dr. Taylor's."

Reporter: "What threw you out of condition?"

Rowell: "I can't tell."

Reporter: "Do you think you trained too fine?"

Rowell: "No, no. What do you think Charley?" turning to Asplen, his brother-in-law and trainer.

Asplen: "I don't think you trained too fine. The two big runs on Monday and Tuesday, 150 miler, followed by with 110 is what did it. The long runs used you up."

Rowell: "I don't think so."

Asplen: "The reports that Charlie ate heartily the first day of the race were wrong. The fact is, he ate scarcely anything, but had a craving for fluids."

Rowell: "I never felt better in my life than I did on Monday night after finishing the 150."

Reporter: "How were you on Tuesday night after the 110?"

Rowell: "In excellent condition."

Reporter: "You were taken sick on Wednesday then?"

Rowell: "Yes, my head felt hot and feverish and I could not rest."

Reporter: "Your failure was a bitter disappointment?"

Rowell: "Aye." He then began coughing stating he had a cold and a sore throat.

Reporter: "Did Hughes have anything to do with forcing your pace at first?"

Rowell: "No. I paid no attention to anybody on the track, but went on with my work."

Reporter: "Did you drink vinegar by mistake?"

Rowell: "Yes. There was a new preparation of beef tea. I had just gargled my throat. I thought the taste was strange, and said so, but the others, supposing I had the tea, said, 'Go on and drink it. It will do you good;' so I take several swallows more. I felt worse on the stomach after drinking the vinegar."

Mr. Duryea: "Rowell desired to go on and get a place in the race, but that I, as well as the doctor, advised him not to do so. Charley was then informed that there were some who declared that he had sold the race."

Rowell: "There isn't money enough in the world to have made me sell it. If I had wanted to sell out, I should have kept on until Saturday."

Mr. Duryea: "For myself, I would rather have lost both of my hands than have had Rowell lose the race. We have been together like brothers here and amongst his people at home. I feel worse over Charlie's breaking down than he does himself."

Reporter: "Is it true that Sir John Astley telegraphed that he had wagered £5,000 that Rowell would make more than 600 miles and that, if he did he would give Rowell half the bet?"

Mr. Duryea: "No. We have had one message from England, and that was from a neighbour."

Rowell was then asked his future plans, to which he replied that he didn't know, and that hadn't thought about it.

Mr. Duryea: "If, Charlie ever feels like racing again, I'll put any reasonable amount of money against man or men who *may* desire to compete with him."

Dr. Naylor, a young English physician who attended to Hazael during the race, and who knew Rowell well, had looked after him since he retired from the race. He said that Rowell had failed for no other reason than he was overstrained on the first two days. He said, "He was not so bad that he could not have remained in and won a place in the race, but, being a very proud little man he could not bear to be in the rear ranks."

That morning, there was another athlete in trouble. Sullivan appeared pale and he moved himself along with faltering steps. His trainer said that he had been suffering from rheumatism since the start of the race. Both the graceful walking Hart, and the energetic Noremac, passed him and pulled away from him, as having sought the sanctuary of his house, he lingered within its cramped confines feeling unwell. The Scotsman was a revelation. He had begun running at a real old clip at 11:25, and as he continued with his impressive display, he got within 10 miles of Hart in third place.

As they moved along the ellipse, none of the men rested and they all ate on the hoof. Whilst Hazael demolished custard puddings, Hart drank coffee, Hughes guzzled ginger beer, Fitzgerald ate oranges and Noremac was content to gulp down beef tea.

At 11:40, Hazael went in for a break having covered 490 miles. At that stage, he was 11 miles ahead of the previous record. The man now in second position, Fitzgerald, stayed on the course to reduce the gap, which he slowly did. By then there was talk of another surprise waiting to happen. The noon score was: **Hazael, 490; Fitzgerald, 468.4; Hart, 450.1; Noremac, 442.4; Sullivan, 433.3; Hughes, 422.5:**

At 12:26, and after a rest of 1h.45m, the timekeeper shouted out, "Hazael on!" The leader, wearing a grey shirt, dark blue trunks, red tights, light blue neck handkerchief and a dark black skull cap, appeared confident and looked well as he took his first steps. He was 21 miles ahead of Fitzgerald and his trainer was confident of making the 600 by the end of the sixth day.

Hart, now wearing a blue cap and nibbling at a chicken leg, moved along with much more urgency as he responded well to Noremac's efforts to catch him. He was joined by Noremac wearing a crimson cap, and they walked quickly around together at 12:30. The betting at the time was: (Placed odds to finish 1st or 2nd are in brackets): **Hazael, No offers; Fitzgerald, 2/1; Hart, 6/1 (2/1); Noremac, 8/1 (2/1); Sullivan, 10/1 (3/1); Hughes, 25/1 (5/1):**

At 13:00, and with the match now being watched by John L. Sullivan the renowned prize fighter, Hazael was cruising around the course. When Fitzgerald arrived back on track, he carried a large sponge which he mopped the sweat from his brow with.

Hazael made his 5th century at 14:14 in a match time of 110h.14m.30s thus annihilating Fitzgerald's previous 500-mile "best" which was scored in a time of 113h.8m.10s. Fitzgerald's distance for 110 hours was 486 miles, but in this race Hazael had scored almost 13 miles more.

The 5th day scores from 3 a.m. till 3 p.m:

	3		4		5		6		7		8		9	
	M	L	M	L	M	L	M	L	M	L	M	L	M	L
Hazael	450	7	453	2	456	5	463	2	465	0	471	0	476	3
Fitzgerald	427	2	430	0	435	0	439	1	443	1	448	5	453	2
Hart	412	5	417	1	421	5	425	4	429	4	433	6	438	1
Sullivan	411	5	416	1	420	0	423	6	423	6	426	5	429	0
Noremac	400	0	403	6	409	4	412	6	418	7	422	5	426	6
Rowell	410	4	413	0	413	2	415	3	415	3	415	3	415	3
Hughes	382	0	384	3	388	0	392	4	397	2	402	4	407	1

	10		11		12		13		14		15	
	M	L	M	L	M	L	M	L	M	L	M	L
Hazael	480	3	485	3	490	0	492	6	498	1	503	6
Fitzgerald	456	1	462	1	468	4	470	3	475	2	479	4
Hart	442	6	445	4	450	1	453	5	456	4	460	0
Noremac	431	5	436	3	442	4	445	7	450	7	456	0
Sullivan	431	0	431	3	433	3	435	4	438	1	440	1
Hughes	412	0	417	1	422	5	425	0	425	2	430	0

Hart found himself in a bit of a dilemma. He was aware that the lean figure of George Noremac, who had been creeping ever closer towards him, was ready to pounce and grab his 3rd place. Should he attempt to repel the challenge or seek the warmth of his bed, rest, and recover the lost ground later? The need to rest his tired body won the argument. While he dozed, the plucky Scot overtook his score of 464.1 some 24 minutes later at 16:11. Whizzing around the circle impressively, Noremac quickly put distance between himself and Hart, and when the latter resumed his tramp at 17:25, he was exactly 2 miles adrift of the Brit who was now in fourth position. After that Noremac really started to motor as he went on to increase the gap by the minute, with Hart offering little resistance.

The *Fitchburg Daily Sentinel* in its report about the race on the 3rd of March stated: At about 6 p.m. Hughes succeeded in taking the fifth position from Sullivan. Bouquets were literally showered on the walkers, Friday night, and at one time each was given a pillow of flowers with his name inscribed on it, and as each passed around the track amid wild cheers from not less than 8,000 throats, it looked as though the six men were carrying off a large flower garden in sections.

Early in the evening some very practical friend handed Fitzgerald a crisp $50 note, which he bore aloft, waving it over his head as he made one lap, his face indicating that he thought a $50 bill better than all the bouquets and baskets of flowers his friends could give him. Manager Duryea placed $200 in the hands of Referee Busby, last night, as a forfeit to challenge the winner in the present contest. It was understood the challenge was to be made by Rowell.

King of the Peds

"Fitz" made his five hundred at 19:30. Half an hour later the score showed: **Hazael, 522.2; Fitzgerald, 502.2; Noremac, 478; Hart, 473.6; Hughes, 454; Sullivan, 449.5:**

The Garden was reminiscent of the days when the place used to be packed to the rafters, and like the previous night, its patrons found great difficulty in moving around the place. The bookmakers' stands were attracting the curious would-be punters, but little business was being done. Hazael was the hot "jolly" at odds of 1/3 but no one took the price. Fitzgerald was 4/1 to triumph, but at a distance of twenty miles behind the leader, people were looking for more favourable odds. 12/1 was found against Noremac. Hart was being touted at 25/1, and the other two, Hughes and the struggling Sullivan, attracted odds of 60/1.

Later, there was a rumour going round the Garden that Rowell had died!

Little happened on the sawdust during the rest of the evening except for a seven-lap sprint around 10 p.m. between the race leaders. *"As the three men passed the scorers' stand, a great cheer went up on the other side of the building and rolled around the ring in a deafening volume."* Hart at 22:30 was now 8 miles adrift of Noremac and back-pedalling all the time. He repeatedly stopped for breaks, during which time, he would change his costume. At midnight, the big blackboard showed: **Hazael, 540; Fitzgerald, 513.4; Noremac, 498.3; Hart, 490; Hughes, 470; Sullivan, 464:**

There were 2,000 spectators in the Garden at the opening of the 6th and final day. Many of those who had used the place as a permanent doss house since the beginning of the race were cold and dirty. They nevertheless watched the proceedings with interest alongside the many genuine fans of the sport.

Hazael had gone in to put his feet up at 23:37 having scored 540 miles in 120 hours. He had complained of feeling sleepy, and having eaten a large meal, slept like a baby till 01:49 when the announcer called his name as he arrived back on the path. The Londoner, looking radiant as he acknowledged the cheers of those watching, continued his journey on the yellow coloured pathway at a rattling good pace. He was joined by the equally enthusiastic Fitzgerald who had been out on the course since just before 01:00. Fitzgerald's *"gait was, if possible, more ungraceful than ever, and his face was cadaverous with its outfit of sharp cheek bones, lantern jaws and sunken eyes."* Things then started to hot up as the men covered 6 miles and 7 laps between 02:00 and 03:00. The crowd was beyond itself with excitement and the building erupted with the sounds of appreciative applause. Even the *"low life,"* which used the place as a home for the week, joined in the fun and dragged themselves to peer at the wonderful show that was the race between two brave men. But what indeed was happening? Why after 5 days of hard slog were these two men going at such an incredible pace? The answer was quite simple. It was Fitzgerald's last opportunity to win the race.

Whilst the excitement on the track gripped the crowd, one of the blackboard markers called Roberts was being attacked by a mob, who accused him hoisting incorrect marks, for which he received *"a bruised head and discolored eyes:"* The *New York Times* took up the story: **Many in this crowd were intoxicating and insulting. Being unable to quietly rest under these aspersions upon his character, he descended the ladder from the platform where he was on duty, and undertook to reason with the excited men. They pitched upon him and beat him unmercifully. The police officers were at the other end of the Garden, and the ruffians only desisted in pounding Roberts when they were satisfied with their work.**

As Roberts nursed his wounds, Hazael, then on a score of almost 548 miles, was 22 miles ahead of Fitzgerald. Pat knew he had one last chance to break George, who, when the challenge was issued by the Irishman, responded to it by sprinting away from him, thus thwarting the aspirations of the hardy *"son of Erin"* to pass him. The scene was reminiscent of a *"saw mill operating at top speed as the dust flew in the air."* Hazael went on to knock up his 550th mile, and thereafter, and until 05:28, covered the ground at 5 mph. He then rested for 58 minutes before resuming his slog.

After the encounter with Hazael earlier, where the two had run themselves ragged, a note was sent to the Irishman saying simply, "From an Astoria friend." It contained a $100 bill and was said to have been sent by his backers to encourage him.

Two places below the front runners, Noremac had rested between 00:52 and 01:44. He had continued to go well and had surprised many with his pluck. *"He was as tough as iron and as steady as a Mississippi tugboat."* He was determined to keep his third place as he moved swiftly around the track wearing a crimson coloured silk jockey cap and a blue and white jersey which fell just above his knees. Noremac ran the last mile necessary to complete his 500th mile in 9m.26s. Frank Hart, his nearest rival, kept up with the pace as he walked round with determination as if to send a clear message to his critics who muttered that he was as "lazy as a pig." Hughes meanwhile, made a remarkable recovery, and maybe that was because, just for once, he was sticking to drinking ginger beer. Poor John Sullivan on the other hand was just hopeful of making the sought after 525. He continued to perform poorly and looked ill. *"His face was a sickly pallor, his form was attenuated and his haggard movement proclaimed huge suffering."*

Day-break was always a welcome sight for the pedestrians, as usually, the management would give the nod to open the windows, which would allow the cold crisp outside air to penetrate and circulate around the stuffy old building. Although good for the competitors, it was bad for the hoards of black women cleaners, who, after initially going about their business, demanded that they be shut as the now draughty environment made working conditions for them unbearable. That meant that the stench of stale tobacco smoke and other smells continued to linger on as they couldn't now be moved away by the prevailing breeze outside.

Amid the filth, the traders who sold food to the hungry hoards exhibited their wares in attempt to cajole the hungry into buying them. What were described as beef or ham sandwiches, were really two bits of bread filled with more mustard than meat. Along with hard boiled eggs, and pork and beans, there was little else on offer to entice people to part with their money, apart from the numerous bars which were a gigantic attraction and an easy means of making lots of money. *"The proprietors say their profits from the sale of liquor in the match have been enormous. They believe that the Moderation Society, whatever their achievements in other directions, has failed to wrestle successfully with the class of people who attend walking matches."*

Hazael went off the track again between 08:11 until 09:20 when he had 570 miles in the bag. Noremac and Hart, in that order, were continuing to battle for third place. Hart had stopped wearing the colourful jacket he had competed in during the cold night. To give him credit, he had attempted to break away from the tiny Scot, but try as he might, he couldn't shake off the ultra-attentive George who dogged him remorselessly. *"Hart stepped more proudly when he detected in the in the most conspicuous portion of the gallery a troop of admiring colored men. They were dressed in the extreme height of fashion, and attracted attention by their lofty bearing."*

When the 09:00 scores were released, Sullivan, who was so disheartened by this time said, "I'm afraid I won't make it:" **Hazael, 570; Fitzgerald, 547.1; Noremac, 526.1; Hart, 512.1; Hughes, 500.1; Sullivan, 489.2:**

It was after ten o'clock, when, wearing what was described as an ordinary English business suit, Rowell turned up at the building to be greeted with a loud clapping of hands. Due to the fact that he was being mobbed, he was compelled to seek the sanctuary of the office where he chose to remain during his visit. He looked weak and quite ill but a rumour suggested that he would probably be participating in a match in autumn after all.

The score at 11 o'clock: **Hazael, 576.3; Fitzgerald, 550.5; Noremac, 530.4; Hart, 518.7; Hughes, 507.6; Sullivan, 497:**

At 11:19, the race leader had gone in for a rest. A minute later, Sullivan, wearing a suit of Lincoln green, made his 500th mile clutching a sponge to dab some blood on his face. He was readily cheered for his effort.

Just before noon there was a disturbance in the south east section of the Garden when a drunken man was evicted by a police sergeant. On the track meanwhile, and apart from the Hazael and Sullivan, the rest were running around the tanbark. Fitzgerald stood out amongst them. Wearing a coarse flannel undershirt and blue tights, he perspired profusely and was clapped as he made a spurt. Hazael reappeared at 12:20, limped slightly, then retired back to his tent after spending only 11 minutes on the track. Fitzgerald, on seeing the leader depart, employed a jog-trot to propel himself forward. As Noremac readied himself in his house for the effort to come, Sullivan returned to the track after an hour's rest at 12:30. His face plainly showed the great suffering he endured due to rheumatism in the limbs, and he appeared to walk *"very lame."* Hart secured his share of the gate money at 12:45 when, with a rapid run, he finished the lap which made his 525th mile. He was now 10 miles behind Noremac who was said to be suffering from severe bleeding of the nose. The race leader arrived back at 12:59 appearing tired and distressed. Fitzgerald noticed his condition and forced him into a run. They were both accordingly warmly applauded by the crowd which was growing in anticipation of the finish.

King of the Peds

The scores at 13:00 were: **Hazael, 578.5; Fitzgerald, 556.5; Noremac, 535.5; Hart, 526.3; Hughes, 515.5; Sullivan, 502.6:**

The bookies offered even money Hazael wouldn't make 605 miles and 2/1 that he would fail to make 610 miles.

In an attempt to see the men in action, many a person tried to evade paying the entrance fee, but their efforts were thwarted by the huge police presence at the doors of the Garden. *"Unmindful of the clouds of dust that filled the air and choked pedestrians, they stared at the blank gray walls of millionaire Vanderbilt's show house as if they would pierce them with the effort of visual powers. A gigantic policeman lorded it over the urchins round about and, so far as he could go without the use of his club, made them confine themselves to the bounds of propriety."*

All the boxes were taken, and all the folding chairs in the galleries that were so popular with the opera goers had someone's backside occupying them. The box seats meanwhile were mainly sat on by women, who showed off in their beautiful costumes and expensive jewellery. *"Diamonds of great size and value flashed in their ears with every turn of the head and every beam of sunshine."* The enterprising ushers were out to make a fast buck as always and used the opportunity of a full house to their advantage. People who tried to get a seat in the gallery boxes were unable to advance any further without paying the going rate of between 50 cents and a dollar. If they refused to pay, they were shown to the rear seats.

After rushing around the track, and when he had contented himself with smashing all previous records in six-day events, Hazael *"returned to his cot and gurgled beef tea"* at 13:57. Indeed, by the end of the 134th hour, he had managed to pulverise Fitzgerald's previous record and was 19 miles and 220 yards in advance of it. The veteran circus man, "Pop" Whitaker climbed on a table in the reportorial stockade and tried to tell the amused crowd of the new achievement. Alas, he got all his facts and figures wrong informing all that the race leader had beaten the record by 13 miles.

Whilst "Pop" made the crowd laugh, the sad spectacle of the "Lepper" continued to drag himself around the path. *"His cheeks were depressed, his eyes almost sunk from view, and his chops hung down like those of a tired hound after the chase."* With blood pouring from his nostrils intermittently, and although expected to collapse at any moment, he nevertheless continued on his way, collecting bank notes given to him by sympathetic spectators, which he waved triumphantly at the crowd.

The arrival of Gilmore's band inspired "Black Dan," and on listening to the music, he thrust his head back, and lengthened his stride. As he did so, Mr. Gilmore instructed his band to play along to the *"exhilarating passage:"*

```
"We're all noddin',
Nid, nid, noddin
We're all noddin
And dropping off to sleep,"
```

Hazael emerged from his cabin at 14:59 and darted onto the ellipse. Of an enquiry about his contestant's welfare, one of his attendants replied, "He's pretty well except a trifle 'cavy around the eyes." He immediately dogged Fitzgerald with his formidable stride and some in the crowd shouted "Go it George old boy!" As he kept up to the task, he looked absolutely wasted but his mind was focused, and staring at the sawdust, he continued with his quest of winning the race.

The leader board at 3 p.m. gave the following information: **Hazael, 584.2; Fitzgerald, 562; Noremac, 542.3; Hart, 532; Hughes, 523.3; Sullivan, 511.5:**

Hughes, wearing a green and yellow cap miraculously made the magic 525 at 15:21. Recognising the fact, Mr. Gilmore, instructed his men to play "Wearing of the Green" as the crowd screamed its approval of the man's accomplishment. The "Lepper," having made one more lap, then went to his tent where he was greeted by his rubinesque wife who simply said to him, "Good boy John!"

As the going got tough, Noremac dug deeper, and although his jaw dropped further towards the track, he plodded on. When Sullivan realised that he was very close to his goal on a score of 518 at 16:00, he positively beamed with delight. Although the rheumatism he was enduring was playing havoc with his body, he somehow mustered enough strength to continue. "It's the longest part of the journey though," he said, "I feel very, very tired." Hazael took another rest at 16:30 when on a mark of 591 miles. As he cat-napped, the diamond whip was exhibited at the judges' stand where Hazael's attendants went over to inspect it.

Three quarters of afternoon session ticket holders did not want to give their seats up, and as the evening drew in, there was trouble brewing in the crowd as many did not want to leave the building, the most adamant being the females! There was a significant presence of the undesirable and notorious in New York society, and the drunks in the crowd were making their presence felt.

A Boston caricaturist by the name of Davis had drawn a mocking cartoon representing Rowell with a handkerchief pressed to his eyes. Entitled, *"Rowell Weeping Over a Lost Cause,"* over the pedestrian's head were the words "I'm beat, but there's 625 miles in my legs yet!" Davis had posted it on the referees' stand. A cane was pushed through it by an angry backer of Rowell which tore it up, but the determined artist replaced it and guarded the new drawing for all it was worth.

The *Brooklyn Daily Eagle* was already looking at the possibility of prospective matches in the future as a result of Hazael's expected win: **Considerable talk was going about as to the result of several challenges already directed to Hazael. Mr. Curtis, one of the judges in the match and an eminent sporting personality, said to an Eagle reporter on this point: "Any one can challenge Hazael, but he is under no obligation whatsoever to compete. There is nothing in the articles of agreement which requires him to accept a challenge. Of course, he can do as pleases concerning another match. Next fall he can go and make an arrangement with any pedestrian for a contest, draw up articles of agreement and then the others, if they want to, can come in. I am authorized to say on behalf of Mr. Hazael that he will pay no attention to any of the challenges made at present.**

By six o'clock the Garden's electric lights were on. Higher up in the roof they were complemented by the flickering yellow gas lights. Fitzgerald probably didn't notice them as he tarried with a score of 569 miles. Hazael, who was 5 miles short of what had never been witnessed in the world of professional pedestrianism, was now back in his den. Noremac also sought his bed, having notched up 550. Worried about the near presence of Hughes, Hart delayed his visit to the Turkish baths till amassing a score of 539 and 3 laps. On his return he wore a heavy jacket and the thickest of skull caps. *"His features were almost frightful, and his step was slow and weak. He coughed like a consumptive, and would have groaned, no doubt, if he had had the strength."* On one of his laps, he picked up a mouse off the track and held it up by the tail as he walked around before dropping it mischievously on the reporters' table.

The men at the wrong end of the scoreboard somehow managed to remain erect and Hughes looked particularly unsightly as he groped his way round, his face covered in blood. He soon took advantage of a free shower as he pushed his head underneath a watering can held by a track walker. As he passed his tent wearing a green silk cap which sported a gilt shamrock on its peak, he shouted to his wife in a hoarse voice, "We're not dead yet and don't yer forget it!"

Sullivan achieved what was deemed the impossible only a few hours earlier by scraping together the last miles, which meant that he achieved the coveted 525 at 18:55. As he was helped to his hut after making another 175 yards, *"the men cheered, the boys yelled, and the women clapped their gloved hands and waved their handkerchiefs high in the air."* Noremac resumed his travels four minutes later wearing red white and blue. He looked the freshest contender on the track, and as he skipped along, he was given a magnificent floral basket.

Wearing his favourite suit of purple and grey, the man at the head of the leader board made his penultimate appearance in front of the excited crowd at 19:26:35 precisely. Before he made his reappearance, his trainer, the famous English heel-and-toe walker, Harry Vaughan, had said that George would run ten miles, "Just to show the nobs that he was alive you know." *"The champion again had been freshly groomed. A barber's blade had given him a smooth and shining visage, and plastered his flaxen hair close to his head. His eyes, brightened by consciousness of victory, twinkled brightly in their little caverns."* As he passed the judges' stand on the home stretch, Miss Ada Wallace, a pedestrian in the crowd, gave him a blue silk handkerchief. He waved it, put it around his neck, knotted it, and revelled in the applause he received from the exuberant audience, who were entertained by the band with selections from "Patience," "Pinafore" and

King of the Peds

"Olivette." He was later handed a basket of flowers from a mother and child, courteously acknowledging the gift with a bow.

A *Brooklyn Daily Eagle* reporter had a word with Hazael's trainer Vaughan:

"How is your man feeling?"

"He's as uncomplaining as ever. A better fellow to handle I never saw," was the answer.

"Does he feel weak at all?"

"Oh, he's a bit sore in the feet, but not anything to speak of. Why, I believe if he had another day, he could do another hundred."

These words seemed justified by the action of the champion on the track. His swinging pace pushed him along about as swiftly as on the first night of the race. His arms worked like cranks in a piece of machinery driven by steam.

Noremac wore a rosebud on his chest as he plodded around. Fitzgerald, now donning green silk trunks, dark tights and a scarlet scarf around his neck, ran along with a massive floral horseshoe that he had been presented with, to the delight of the small boys watching him at trackside. Frank Hart, now attired in a striking outfit of sky blue and black sash, enjoyed the moment too as he waltzed along with anybody else who could still stand. One of those who could was Hughes, who ran around the place for seven laps, after which he and Hart stopped in front of the scorers' stand and shook hands *"in the most cordial manner,"* much to the approval of the crowd who roared with delight as the two made a further lap together.

As Rowell looked on from the seats contemplating what could have been, Hazael took himself back to his hut at 20:08 at the end of his 598th mile. All the men now on the track busied themselves entertaining the crowd. Even the indefatigable Sullivan, as shattered as he was, joined in the party and covered a few more laps.

Mr. Gilmore's band was in a real old dither as they excitedly played their numbers seemingly back to front. Thus, "Home Sweet Home," was followed by "We Won't Go Home until morning." At nine o'clock, they played "He is an Englishman" in contemplation of the inevitable result. Then to the strains of "Auld Lang Syne," Hazael, wearing a light brown silk shirt, dark trousers and girdle, and light blue and scarlet neckband, ran around the course with Fitzgerald, amid the sounds of clinking beer and champagne glasses and the inevitable noise of the delirious crowd. Both trotted around the track for fifteen minutes before stopping in front of the scorers' stand.

It was at that point, at precisely 21:15:45, George Hazael of London, England, became the first man to cover a distance of 600 miles in six days or 142 hours.

Barney Aaron opened the box containing the winning trophy. He handed the whip to referee Busby who then handed it to "Pop" Whitaker who stood on the scorers' stand. The band, who were in full flow, were making such a din that Busby shouted out, "Somebody stop the band!" Whitaker screamed, "Shake your handkerchief at them!" Eventually Mr. Gilmore got the message and he instructed his enthusiastic players to pipe down.

"Pop," well used to making speeches in circus rings, said to the winner in front of the hushed crowd, "Mr. Hazael, your great performance of six hundred miles in one hundred and forty-two consecutive hours, in one of the hardest contested races in against the best men of two continents, makes the trophy presented by Mr. Busby entirely emblematic of the championship of the world. It is our wish, and the wish of all who hear you, that you may long enjoy the honours you have so gallantly won."

Hazael, who was said to blush with embarrassment, firstly bowed to the crowd before taking his prize. After receiving the mandatory three cheers from the crowd, he went away on a final lap showing the whip off to the crowd. Fitzgerald followed him around, accepting the accolade that was given to him by his admirers in the audience. When Hazael had completed his triumphant lap of honour, he was given an extra award of a pair of *"handsome shoes"* which had been named by the maker, *"the champion shoes of the world."* Hazael was informed that he would also be getting a chair. With that done, the new world record holder was escorted to his tent where he quickly got changed and was then driven to the Gilsey House Hotel.

George Hazael
Frank Leslies Illustrated Newspaper (Illustration no: 90)

The Final Score!

	Time of finish	Miles	Yards
Hazael	**21:15:45**	**600**	**220**
Fitzgerald	21:15:45	577	220
Noremac	20:48:14	555	0
Hart	20:44:00	542	440
Hughes	18:43:00	535	0
Sullivan	18:55:35	525	175

King of the Peds

Table of resting times:

DAY	1			2			3			4			5			6			TOTAL		
	H	M	S	H	M	S	H	M	S	H	M	S	H	M	S	H	M	S	H	M	S
Haz	2	55	10	6	58	40	6	18	35	6	25	0	3	16	35	9	27	35	35	21	35
Fitz	3	45	40	4	36	35	3	55	3	5	49	15	4	46	5	6	30	40	29	23	16
Nor	4	42	20	7	33	12	6	41	11	3	17	7	2	30	20	7	20	10	32	5	20
Hart	2	51	8	5	35	28	4	25	2	3	51	12	6	34	53	7	23	40	30	41	28
Hugh	2	50	33	3	0	58	8	14	40	10	37	40	5	52	15	5	15	35	35	51	41
Sull	3	54	5	4	50	15	5	0	35	5	1	20	10	42	25	3	45	5	33	13	45
Row	1	24	30	7	8	13	7	0	35	13	30	0	3	49	0	Retired			32	52	18
Pan	5	58	40	Retired															5	58	40
Sco	3	21	0	Retired															3	21	0
Vint	0	0	6	Retired															0	0	6

The last day scores from 3 a.m. till 10 p.m.

	Hazael		Fitz		Noremac		Hart		Hughes		Sullivan	
	M	L	M	L	M	L	M	L	M	L	M	L
03:00	547	7	525	7	507	7	497	3	474	0	470	2
04:00	552	5	530	0	510	0	497	3	479	6	470	2
05:00	557	5	533	0	513	1	501	0	484	1	473	5
06:00	560	0	537	6	517	3	504	6	488	4	477	4
07:00	563	2	542	4	522	4	509	4	491	6	480	6
08:00	569	0	543	7	523	7	509	5	496	1	485	0
09:00	570	0	547	1	526	1	512	1	500	1	489	2
10:00	572	1	550	0	527	4	514	0	504	0	492	4
11:00	576	3	550	5	530	4	518	7	507	6	497	0
12:00	578	0	552	6	534	4	522	6	511	4	500	0
13:00	578	5	556	5	535	5	526	3	515	5	502	6
14:00	581	1	562	0	538	4	529	4	520	0	507	4
15:00	584	2	562	0	542	3	532	0	523	3	511	5
16:00	588	0	564	4	544	5	535	0	526	0	515	0
17:00	591	0	567	1	546	2	539	3	530	1	518	0
18:00	595	0	569	4	550	0	539	3	531	0	521	3
19:00	595	0	570	0	551	7	541	0	534	0	525	1
20:00	597	0	572	0	552	4	541	0	534	0	525	1
21:00	598	1	575	1	555	0	542	2	535	0	525	1
22:00	600	1	577	1	555	0	542	2	535	0	525	1

A meeting was called by the management to divide the spoils of the race at the Astor House Hotel on Wednesday, the 8th of March. All the pedestrians who were to benefit financially from the race turned up for their pay day.

A limping George Hazael carrying a cane, wearing *"ill fitting clothing"* and *"an unsightly piece of red flannel around his neck,"* was followed by *"several hungry looking men,"* into room 111. Inside to greet him was the manager of the race, Peter Duryea and referee Hamilton Busby. The expressionless winner sat himself down, and as he did so, Deputy Sheriff Shells entered the room, holding an attachment which a court had issued on behalf of a Thomas C. Lyman, a brewer, against Hazael's recent earnings. The attachment was for the sum of $118 for ale provided to Hazael by Lyman. The pedestrian claimed the bill was a mistake saying, "I owe nufink to nobody y'know?" He also stated that it was a case of forgery and that someone should be sent to "joyal."

When the room went quiet, John Hughes, who was also there, made a threat against one of his trainers, Mr. Plummer, stating he would drive him through the floor like a hammer hitting a nail. He was angry because, in his reckoning at least, Plummer was after some money from him for services rendered during the match. Whilst the other peds and their backers looked on in some discomfort, the "Lepper's" wife had to intervene to stop her husband from striking the first blow as she stood between him and the object of his angry intention to hurt. Mrs. Hughes had the desired effect and "good boy John" was brought to heel.

There was known hostility between the race participants, the management of the event and Mr. Duryea, who was probably as frightened as the hotel staff at the prospect of a brawl ensuing in their establishment, quickly moved on to business and announced the race receipts, which were $45,674. By deducting his percentage of 15%, $38,822.90 was left. Expenses totalling $20,061.28 meant that the amount to be shared to the pedestrians was $18,762.12. According to the race's articles of agreement, the sweepstake money of $10,000 would be shared by the winner and the runner-up, with Hazael therefore receiving $9,000 and Fitzgerald $1,000. The rest was subdivided as indicated below:

	Gate Money	Sweepstake	Total
Hazael	$9,380.81	$9,000	$18,380.81
Fitzgerald	3,752.82	1,000	4,752.82
Noremac	2,251.39		2,251.39
Hart	1,500.93		1,500.93
Hughes	1,125.70		1,125.70
Sullivan	750.47		750.47

Here is what the *New York Tribune* said of the race: The triumph of Hazael is a step downward in a rivalry that was low enough already. The defeated champion had little to recommend him except a stout heart and legs of uncommon size; but he was a cheery, amiable little fellow, who, if his ambition did not rise higher than the keeping of an alehouse on the proceeds of his races, at least had few vicious qualities, and with his compact, sturdy figure and bright, resolute face, was not an unpleasant object to look at while he was on the track. His successor is morose and sullen, with no single redeeming trait in mind or person. He has no friends, and never had any. He was put in this match by a speculative gambler, who had no more personal interest in him than he might have in a gamecock on which he had laid a wager. This gambler paid all Hazael's expenses, furnished him with a trainer, was responsible for everything, and of course will take nearly all the profits, the poor creature who has done the work getting only money enough to support himself until another match is arranged. Before this race was begun it was known everywhere among persons interested in such matters that Hazael was wholly without means, and that if he failed to get a share of the spoils at the garden he would be forced to take up some honest labor like shoveling dirt or sweeping up the streets. He has no brain for anything higher. But now that he has reached the highest score on record he will be able to live on his backer until he gets beaten.

His performance was a marvelous one, as showing what a terrible strain can be put on the human machine without destroying it utterly. He has suffered torments during no small part of the last six days than which those of the rack could hardly be more severe. What a procession of wan and weary ghosts was that which staggered around the track on Saturday last. The leader's face was distorted by pain, pinched and worn by the killing work of six days and nights, seamed and furrowed by the agony which he was undergoing. Fitzgerald the second man in the race, blundered on, so stupid and dull from lack of sleep and excessive exertion that he was almost insensible to what was going on a round him. His face at the best is ugly; but it is now sickening. More pitiable wretches than the last two men in the race, Hughes and Sullivan, it would be hardly possible to conceive. To look at them was to feel a shudder of disgust and horror. For such an exhibition as this as this thousands of men gathered in the foul smoky air of Madison Square Garden day after day and night after night. It was a gathering in which the lowest elements were most conspicuous. Every pick-pocket, every sneak thief, every gambler, every criminal of any class in the city whom fear of the police did not keep away was present. The ruffian's who crowd around the pit at every dog and cock-fight, the fellows to whom Sullivan and Ryan are heroes, the heelers and bruisers and swindlers of every grade and every sort, were out in force. A few women were there, but they were of chiefly of the class that consumes peanuts in public. Some club men with an idle hour stepped in occasionally and lounged about for a short time. In the main the attendance at the match, from the first hour to the last, has been made up of the people who waited impatiently for the first news from the recent prize-fight near New Orleans. Here and there was a representative of the respectability of the community, but he seemed sadly out of place.

King of the Peds

The Globe writing for the inhabitants of Atchison in Kansas on the 9th of March was not very complimentary about the new champion: The New York papers find nothing in the walking match lately concluded at Madison Square Garden to praise, but much to condemn. The dissatisfaction begins with the champion, Hazael, who is described as "repulsive in form and face, dull, brutish features never lighted by a gleam of intelligence, lack-luster eye, loose, lop-sided, shambling figure—the least heroic figure that ever bore off a championship of any kind." The garden was the resort of the low and vile, with only now and then a representative of the better class, and the exhibition throughout is described as brutal, disgusting and demoralizing in every respect.

The following advertisement is one which appeared in many different newspapers around the United States after Hazael's victory.

How Hazael Won the Race.

The great race is over; the champions have returned from the arena; one by one the lights have gone out in Madison Square Garden; the sporting fraternity now sum up their gains or losses, as the case may be, and the only question now to be decided is, how the race was won. This we propose to show. We are going to prick the bubble; we are going to conduct our readers behind the scenes and prove to them how Hazael, now the world's champion pedestrian, became such.

Who is Hazael, the winner? George Hazael was born in London. He is five feet six and a half inches in height, and weighs 122 pounds. He is the recognized champion runner of England, from six to fifty miles. He now caps the pinnacle with six hundred and a half miles, and comes off winner of nineteen thousand dollars, a fortune in itself, the result of a week's work; and why? The writer of this, who is an "old-timer" (to make use of a pedestrian expression), and has assisted at several walking matches, waited on Mr. George Hazael, the world's champion, in his cabin, immediately at the close of the race. He was one of the favored few who were permitted to enter, and he saw that which gave him a "pointer" as to how the long fought and heroically contested race was won. He imparted his ideas to Mr. Harry Vaughan, a gentleman who came from London, England, five weeks ago, purposely to act as trainer for Mr. Hazael. That gentleman spoke freely, and bade the scribe meet him at Joe Bowler's Ram's Head Hotel, Greenpoint, L.I, on the following day, and see Mr. Hazael in reference to the matter. In accordance therewith Mr. Hazael was met on the following day, March 5. Mr. Hazael was found to be in excellent condition, and had just partaken of a splendid dinner, and was preparing for his afternoon siesta. After some introductory remarks, the writer observed: "George, when I entered your cabin at the close of the race last night, my olfactories were pleasantly assailed and my vision greeted the former by smelling ST. JACOB'S OIL, the latter by seeing it. I came to ask if the world's champion racer had found the world's champion remedy the proper thing for his valuable limbs?"

"So," said Mr. Hazael, laughing, "you saw my stock of ST. JACOB'S OIL, did you? It is a wonderful medicine, sir, wonderful! I do not know what pedestrians would do without it; it is their best friend. A rub of ST. JACOB'S OIL after leaving the track makes a new man of one, and gets him again for the contest." Mr. Henry Vaughan, who was standing by, broke in at this juncture as follows: "I was never so surprised at anything in my life as I was to see the effect of ST. JACOB'S OIL on George. It did George a power of good, and but for its use he might have had a different ending." "Yes," exclaimed Joe Bowler, just entering with a bottle of Piper Heidsick, "you can safely say that ST. JACOB'S OIL won the race for the champion, made a fortune for Mr. Hazael, and prepared him to win the greatest race on record." The secret was out; and Mr. George Hazael, a Briton of whom all England may be justly proud, and of whom America is justly proud also, has shown not only phenomenal endurance to such an extent that it awakens our wonder and surprise, but he has shown that he tempers wisdom with pluck and energy; that he not only knows how to "go," but that he knows what is best for him while going. Mr. Hazael has won for himself fairly, honestly, and above board, the title of Champion Walker of the World. George is a perfect gentleman, and in his pleasant manner awards the championship to ST. JACOB'S OIL, the great German Remedy, over all other remedies.

Mr. Bowler is willing to back Mr. Hazael in any sum from $l,000 to $5,000 against any man in the world, for 100 miles running, and give the opponent five miles out of the 100. We will back ST. JACOB'S OIL against all medicines at rates as liberal.

Hazael eventually left the United States on the 14th of March for Liverpool, having evaded being taken into custody on the warrant of arrest by direction of Judge Neilson, following an action by a former trainer of Hazael's, Henry Martin. He was the man who claimed that he made a contract with Hazael on the 1st of May 1881 whereby he would house, train, and prepare him for any contest which he might enter, claiming the pedestrian would give him one-half of all winnings received. Hazael however, left his care and went into training with Al Smith and Barney

Aaron in early January of 1882. When Martin approached Hazael at the Astor House Hotel, he was threatened with violence. Martin claimed he had spent $2,000 of his money on Hazael and he wanted it back.

CHAPTER 36

Walking on Top of the World!

The original venue for this *"great walking sweepstakes"* contest was to be the Bingley Hall in Birmingham, England, but owing to the contractor leasing out that venue for another event, it was changed to the Drill Hall, Clough Road, in Sheffield, Yorkshire, between the Monday and Saturday, the 6th and 11th of March 1882. The building was described as being *"well adapted for long-distance races."*

By permission of Sheffield City Libraries. (Illustration no: 91)

Quite a while before the race, Harry Carless of Millwall, London, had issued a challenge to *"the world,"* for a six days heel-and-toe match for £100. George Littlewood accepted it, and in order to make the race as competitive as possible, an open sweepstakes of £25 was decided upon. All five contesting the race had paid that amount to enter it. Corkey, the *"veteran,"* had lost his deposit of £5 by failing to put up the rest, so the total prize money was £130. In addition to that prize money, the winner would receive 50% of the gate receipts, less expenses, whilst those covering more than 400 miles expected to receive proportionate awards. The second placed man would get 25%, the third, 12%, the fourth, 8% and the fifth 5%.

Those taking part were:

Henry Carless of Millwall: **Odds: 5/1.** Attended by his brother and his friends.

Peter Crossland of Sheffield: **Odds: 6/4.** Attended by Mick Kelly, Harry Shaw (the dual Sheffield Handicap winner), and others.

Jack Hibberd of Bethnall Green: **Odds: 1/1.** Attended by Mr. Isaac Sullivan of the Walter Arms, Addy Street, Deptford, and "Brummy" Meadows.

George Littlewood of Sheffield: **Odds: 6/4.** Trained by Thomas Higginbottom in Sheffield, and attended by his father Fred and others.

H. Williams of Gloucester: **Odds: 5/1.** Attended by his wife and Mr. W. Vaughan of Newport, Monmouthshire.

The track was thirteen laps to the mile and measured between seven and eight feet in width. It was said to be in *"faultless trim."* Messrs. G. W. Atkinson and R. Watson, of the *Sporting Life* were the referees.

Although the contest wasn't due to start till after midnight on Monday the 6th, eager spectators were already congregating outside the building to make sure they got in to see the contest. The entrance fee was sixpence for basic admission. Those willing to pay a "bob" could sit on an elevated platform which was capable of seating 900 spectators. The estimated attendance at the "off" was in the region of 3,000, and due to the amount of time it took to get them all in, there was a delay to the start of about an hour. Also, the more expensive platform seats had been occupied by those paying a "tanner." For the many who had paid the correct amount, well, as a Sheffielder would say, it was "just 'ard lines" for them.

The first man to appear from his tent on to the track was Crossland. He was followed by Hibberd, Williams, Littlewood and Carless in that order. They all took their positions at the starting post and set off at 02:00 when the starter said the word "Go!" As they did so, an enormous roar went up that *"will long be recollected by those present."* Amid the deafening noise, Hibberd flew to the front and remained there after the first circuit with Littlewood a few yards behind him, and his fellow Sheffielder Crossland in third. The oldest competitor Williams, who was in last position, was soon lapped by the leader after half a mile had been made. Hibberd led at the end of the first mile which he made in a time of 9m.35s. Those positions soon changed; by the end of the second mile, Littlewood was the "leader of the pack" in a time of 19m.21s. From thereon it was the local lad who dictated as the race continued.

At 02:30, the scores stood: **Littlewood, Hibberd and Crossland, 2.9; Carless, 2.7; Williams, 2.4:**

Crossland was the first of the men to show signs of distress having to leave the track at 05:45 due to suffering stomach cramps. The doctor who had been summoned to attend to him must have given him the OK to continue, for at 06:04 he was back in the fray and noted to be having to put in a lot of *"arm work"* to keep him up in contention with the rest. Littlewood however, performing wonderfully, never left the track and was able to put some distance between himself and Hibberd. Meanwhile, the veteran Williams was putting in some sterling work, his attitude proving very popular with the local crowd who gave favourable encouragement to all the competitors.

The scene in the hall was described by a reporter for the *Sheffield and Rotherham Independent*: A narrow track skirting the walls of the hall, and in the centre space, an assemblage of humanity about as miscellaneous as regards social position as could well be imagined. Lawyers, doctors and clergymen were there jostling on the edge of the track with ragged, besotted, ill looking fellows, and all breathing an atmosphere redolent of tobacco smoke and of the shell fish and oranges which numerous hawkers were vending in all corners of the building. Around the retiring quarters of the pedestrians were gathered groups of their attendants and friends; and on the platform the officials were busy recording each circuit made by the men.

After 12 hours the score was: **Littlewood, 67.2; Hibberd, 64.7; Williams, 61.10; Carless, 58.12; Crossland, 55.8:**

The crowd in the afternoon witnessed the Londoner, Carless, initially and repeatedly lapping his opponents. He later settled down to a more sedate pace. The crowd then really appreciated what they were witnessing on the track as Hibberd constantly challenged Littlewood, and as the numbers in the audience swelled, the atmosphere became more exciting. Littlewood completed his century in 18h.23m.2s, his last lap being made with a *"fine spurt."*

King of the Peds

At this point, he was 3 miles and 4 laps ahead of Hibberd, 9.6 ahead of Williams, 15.3 ahead of Crossland and 16.6 ahead of Carless. Hibberd achieved the same milestone shortly after 21:02 and Williams accomplished the same feat at 23:03.

The scores at 23:45 were: **Littlewood, 117; Hibberd, 110; Williams, 103; Crossland, 99; Carless, 97:** (Crossland went on to make his century at 23:58 just before he retired to his tent).

Up to this point Littlewood hadn't stopped *except for necessary purposes,"* waiting till he had completed his *120th mile (22h.18m.55s) to *"allow himself that luxury."* If he had gone on for another three quarters of a mile he would have beaten Crossland's record of walking 120 miles and 1,560 yards, *without rest*, made at the Pomona Palace, Manchester, between the 11th and 12th of September 1876. It was probably during this welcome break that the race leader had his badly blistered feet attended to, during which time the painful things (blisters) were cut off. At 00:30, Williams, who was on a mark of 107, and on the track on his own, made another 3 miles before making for his quarters at 01:05, when the scores were: **Littlewood, 120.1; Hibberd and Williams, 110; Carless, 100.12; Crossland, 100.4:**

*Before he went bed, Littlewood would have been aware that he had beaten Harriman's best distance for 24 hours of 117 and 1/5 miles made the year earlier.

No one occupied the track for 15 minutes until Carless reappeared. Initially moving around it in a cramped style, he gradually improved his posture until he was soon bounding along splendidly. Hibberd then emerged from his tent. When Littlewood re-entered the arena at 02:35, he proceeded to move swiftly in a manner which put the rest to shame. Meanwhile, Hibberd had also been reported to be suffering with blisters that he had accumulated on his right foot. After these were excised, he made rapid improvement.

Littlewood soon started to break records, going on the beat Henry Vaughan's fastest time between 143 and 165 miles, which he achieved at the Pomona Palace at Manchester on the 18th of May 1877.

By the time Crossland had completed his 143rd mile just before 14:00, or 36 hours into the competition, the leader, who was then on a score of 177 miles, set about annihilating the opposition by continually lapping them. At this time, he was 13 miles ahead of Hibberd. By the time it came to make his second century, he found himself 20 miles ahead of the 2nd placed man, making the distance in a time of 40h.46m.30s. Thus George made a new record, which had smashed the previous one set by Harriman between the 10th and 13th of May 1881 at Chicago by 3h.28m.30s! *"Then the crowd rose en masse, and the shouts, waving of hats, and cheering lasted for several minutes."*

When the building was quite full at 20:00, all the men were walking vigorously, Crossland in particular catching the eye with a fine exhibition of *"grand heel-and-toe"* progression. He was fully expected to overtake Carless, and when this didn't materialise due to him taking a short rest, his supporters were disappointed. However, their belief in him was rewarded when he later swapped positions with the resting man from Millwall.

Littlewood later went on to set yet another world record when he walked 218 miles within 48 hours, the score at 23:00 being: **Littlewood, 219.5; Hibberd, 198.11; Williams, 180; Carless, 178; Crossland, 172.3:** The race leader made one more lap before heading for his tent. That same privilege wasn't allowed his closest rival until he had made his 200th mile fifteen minutes later.

Crossland later came back on to complete 182.5 miles and went back to rest. The 31-year-old Harry Carless, now on his own, was soon joined by Williams, who, having rested for 3h.41m after achieving a score of 180, was cheered by the 600 souls in the crowd when he came back on to the scene at 00:16. He was an inspired man after his sleep, and promptly put himself back in to third place with some tremendous work. Carless too made a place on Crossland, who *"amidst great excitement"* returned to work at 01:29. At 02:00, the scores were: **Littlewood, 219.6; Hibberd, 200.1; Williams, 188; Carless, 184.4; Crossland, 182.5:**

Hibberd re-emerged at 02:21 followed by Littlewood at 02:35. Carless went off at 03:22 followed by Crossland at 03:42. Hibberd went off again at 03:55 returning very shortly after, and then leaving again at 04:01. The 22-year-old Littlewood was left in the ring with the 53-year-old Williams and was trying to lap him, which he succeeded in doing at 04:03. Crossland arrived back on the scene followed by Carless; then Hibberd, also wanting a piece of the action, returned at 04:05. Williams made his 200 at 04:44, the same score being achieved by Crossland at 06:25, with Carless making his eight minutes later.

Littlewood accomplished his 250th mile at 09:12, and during the 58th hour, the leader bagged his 270th. Hibberd was 20 miles in his rear on 250, but was six miles ahead of the others who were almost neck-and-neck.

At six o'clock in the evening, and with many hundreds of people outside trying to gain admission, *"the money takers not being able to take money fast enough,"* the Drill Hall was jam-packed with up to six or seven thousand spectators. By this time the two leaders had been on the track together between 16 and 18 hours and still they went for everything, the Bethnall Green man being particularly impressive.

Williams went easily in third. This *"military looking individual"* went about his business in splendid form with his head erect, shoulders square and chest thrown out manfully. He was the less distressed of the quintet and moved along impressively. At 19:30, Littlewood made his 300th mile in 65h.30m, and despite pleas to leave the track by his attendant, he just kept on walking. He was then tackled by Williams and a hot race ensued between them both for quite a few laps. The leader initially and gallantly kept pace with the southerner, but had to give way retiring to his tent at 21:40. During that time he had covered almost 86 miles which had contributed to his total of 305.4. His efforts were rewarded with yet another record, as at that stage he was 6h.30m in front of anything previously accomplished.

At 23:00, the score was: **Littlewood, 305.4; Hibberd, 286.9; Williams, 261.9; Carless, 259.4; Crossland, 259**: Carless did some major work, and despite his troublesome blisters, he kept on lapping Hibberd who had set about reducing the gap between himself and the man in the premier position. Before he went to bed at 11:53, Jack had managed to reduce the gap between them to 15 miles as the 01:00 (the 71st hour) scores testify: **Littlewood, 305.4; Hibberd, 290.3; Williams, 270.4; Carless, 268; Crossland, 260**:

At 01:14, and after having rested for 3h.34m, Littlewood joined Carless and Williams. At 02:00 (three days into the contest), he was 18 miles and 5 laps better off than Hibberd. Eighteen minutes later, Crossland and Hibberd, who had been out of the ring for 2h.36m, resumed their labours. The *"Bethnall boy"* was observed at the time to be the best performer, and he certainly showed his plucky character by lapping Littlewood, who if anything, was going along faster than he had done before. The Londoner however, began pulling away and must have felt elated when, at 04:35, his name registered 300 miles on the scoreboard. Twenty minutes prior to his achievement the match totals were: **Littlewood, 318.9; Hibberd, 298.5; Williams, 281.2; Carless, 276.7; Crossland, 267**:

At 06:20, Carless managed to fly past Williams who was resting at the time. Apart from that very little happened on the track during the day, except that all the contestants kept up their excellent work rate. In doing so they managed to maintain the distances between each other, apart from Carless, who had almost doubled the distance between himself and Crossland.

As evening arrived, hopeful spectators in a *"seething crowd clamoured for admission"* as they jostled each other outside the building to get near the entrances. This state of affairs necessitated the hasty opening of a new gate where the money takers were working as fast as the pedestrians on the track. There, Hibberd plodded on admirably, his objective now being to make sure he kept the second position well away from Williams. Hibberd went to bed at 21:30 thus joining Littlewood who had done the same 50 minutes earlier. The scores at 23:00 were: **Littlewood, 387.1; Hibberd, 370.2; Williams, 345; Carless, 335.11; Crossland, 318.11**:

The track was deserted until 23:20 when the Gloucester man reappeared dashing along for a mile and six laps. Littlewood emerged from his tent to a tumultuous welcome by the gathered throng of at least 2,000 after resting 3h.20m. Hibberd followed him having been urged by his mentors to return to the track and *"walk Littlewood down."* Moving stiffly along at first, he soon limbered up, and he and Littlewood exchanged places on numerous occasions as the pair battled it out, with Williams tagging himself on behind. The crowd, enjoying what they were witnessing, cheered the men along. Many waved their handkerchiefs and hats as the unbelievable spectacle just never seemed to stop. During all the excitement, Williams went on to make his 350th mile. Hibberd's trainers later ordered him to walk in reverse so that the pace wouldn't be forced by his adversary.

King of the Peds

At 01:00, the scores were: **Littlewood, 391.10; Hibberd, 375.6; Williams, 350.10; Carless, 336; Crossland, 320:** The tactics of the two principal pedestrians in the contest apparently brought some ill feeling between their respective supporters, who either cheered or *"hooted" the men as they bounded along."*

The 02:00 score at the end of the fourth day was: **Littlewood, 396.3; Hibberd, 379.10; Williams, 352.12; Carless, 337.8; Crossland, 331.9:**

At 02:10, and after nearly falling off the track, Hibberd was helped back towards his tent. Incredibly he was vehemently cursed by his entourage who refused him admission to his quarters, the unfortunate man having to be cared for by Crossland's attendants instead. On top of what had just happened, there was a negative rumour going round the hall that he wouldn't last the six days against the likes of the formidable Littlewood. At 02:51, and with Hibberd still off the track, the "Tyke" completed his 400th mile. Many people had stayed to watch him accomplish the milestone, and when he did, they certainly made their appreciation heard! Of the race leader's efforts, the reporter for the *Sheffield and Rotherham Independent* commented: The scoring board showed that Littlewood maintained his position far in front of the other competitors, and as, at a smart pace, he perambulated the track he was repeatedly cheered. Walking in a not very graceful manner, but with an easy swing he got over the ground at a wonderful pace. Considering that he had travelled 400 miles, with but the shortest of intervals of rest; and, although his cheek bones seemed unduly prominent, and his eyes had a weary look, he showed no other signs of fatigue.

The score at 04:15 was: **Littlewood, 405.7; Hibberd, 380.5; Williams, 361; Carless, 347.6; Crossland, 328.8:**

When Hibberd resumed his efforts at 05:04, he continued at a snail's pace and his performance was pitiable to witness. He dragged one foot after the other and the news from his team was that *"both his ankles were out."* There was clearly something very wrong with him as he hobbled round, with one of his attendants at his side waiting to catch him should he fall. It was he and his unfortunate predicament that was attracting the attentions of the watching audience, who seemed fascinated by his plight.

Inevitably, Williams soon claimed his second place. He wasn't the quickest on the track but boy, had he got stamina! The veteran soon created quite a gap between himself and the ailing figure of Hibberd, who at 16:30, was just a mile ahead of the ever encroaching Carless. Meanwhile, Littlewood continued to ply his trade at the front with the same indomitable spirit he had shown throughout the contest, *"his eyes being as bright as a star, and complexion ruddy and devoid of haggardness."* The 40-year-plus Peter Crossland also moved quite well. It was obvious, that he too, was preoccupied with the task of passing the 400-mile mark so as to secure gate money. Carless, who had been suffering considerable discomfort with his feet had altered his style of walking, and by that time, appeared more comfortable as he progressed.

The crowds kept pouring in and the officials were working extremely hard in preventing people spilling on to the track thus impeding the progress of the men circling it. At 20:00, and with Williams having made his fourth century, the building was so full that the management had to lock the gates, thus disappointing the hundreds outside who were waiting for the privilege of being able to see the incredible story unravelling within. As they stood in the cold and cursed, Littlewood kept his relentless pace up. He was now 48 miles in front of Williams who walked with him, and at 18:15, had made 450 miles. It was at this juncture that Hibberd resumed his task of trying to make the badly needed 400. To cries of "Bravo old chap!" he traversed the path at a funeral pace having earlier stubbornly resisted advice from the public to retire.

The crowd was now occupying the track, and the officials taking a dim view of the prevailing circumstances, asked the athletes to enter their tents. Estimates of between 5,000 and 6,000 spectators were occupying the place at the time. The *Sporting Life* in its commentary on the race was keen to inform its readers that due to the prevailing conditions: "It is also worthy of notice that owing to deficiency in ventilation and plentiful supplies in tobacco smoke, the atmosphere was stifling and heat intense." When the situation was put back in order the band played up, and at 23:00, with Hibberd now on the track alone moving along slightly better, the scores were as follows: **Littlewood, 463.8; Williams, 411.10; Hibberd, 391; Carless, 390.1; Crossland, 378.6:**

With Hibberd trying to mend his broken body back in his tent, Carless, who reappeared at about 23:25, had the track to himself. He was later joined at 00:15 by Littlewood and Williams. The house greeted their entrance with the now customary roar of approval. Both continued on their way, and as they did, Carless created an extraordinary loud cheer when he too joined the ranks of those who had scored the money spinning figure of 400 miles. But it was Littlewood who set the place with his blistering pace. He was just plainly sensational in the manner he ate up the laps, and so quickly too, in comparison with the others.

At 01:00, the score was: **Littlewood, 466.7; Williams, 414.6; Carless, 400; Hibberd, 393; Crossland, 378.12:**

At 02:00, and at the end of the fifth day with the two principals and Crossland competing on the track, the score stood: **Littlewood, 470.10; Williams, 418.7; Carless, 400; Hibberd, 393; Crossland, 383.2:**

Both leaders left the track at 02:24. The word was out that Littlewood would attempt to break more records on the last day, and at 03:53, and after a nice little rest of 3h.18m, Carless made his way onto the ellipse and carried on. The other rumour was that Williams had backed himself repeatedly to make 450 miles by the end of the race.

The reporter again left the Drill Hall around 04:30 to type his story, but before he did, he took a note of the score at 04:15 which was: **Littlewood, 472.10 (resting); Williams, 420 (resting); Carless, 401.5; Hibberd, 393 (resting); Crossland, 390:**

Such was the pandemonium experienced the night before that the worried officials decided to clear the building of every single spectator at six o'clock on Saturday morning. This was done on safety grounds, the other reason being that many men and boys had been in the building since the start of the contest. The new admission price was one shilling, and although the decision was unpopular with the crowd outside, this was readily paid by many who were said to be a *"different class"* of people than those who had frequented the previous day's entertainment. Indeed for the rest of the day, although the attendance was large, there was little or no crowding.

During the morning Hibberd made 400 miles and 7 laps and later retired for good, content in the knowledge that he would get something back for his efforts, that being 5% of the gate money. Jack was then whisked off to the Earl of Arundel and Surrey Hotel, where under the care of the host, Mr. Joshua Biggin, he was said to be recovering. Indeed, it was thought at the time, that he would have to stay there for quite a while!

Crossland, who had been ill and had been bent over at times with abdominal pain, recovered sufficiently enough to go on to walk as *"erect and straight as a gun barrel,"* inevitably passing Hibberd into fourth place. Meanwhile, at the head of affairs, the two top men in the event continued with the hot pace. The leader was observed to walk with *"unexampled vigour and sprightliness,"* and was said to be spinning round the track at 5 mph. Whilst putting on this amazing performance, some prominent members of the crowd, which included magistrates, gave him sovereigns whilst the less affluent passed him silk handkerchiefs, five of which he received in a very short time. George was then given a *"handsomely worked"* smoking cap which he wore to the amusement of the crowd in a cock-eyed fashion on his head.

Littlewood's ambition was now to beat Harriman's American record of 530 miles and, with the track to himself, did this in great style at 20:47:15 in **5d.18h.47m.15s** from the start. At this juncture, he was 2h.7m.47s in front of Harriman's time, and as the crowd went delirious, the band played "See the Conquering Hero Comes." This went on for several minutes, and as it did, Littlewood did the unthinkable. His last mile for the race was covered in 9m.17s which was the quickest mile covered in the whole of the competition! After that, the band played "For he's a jolly good fellow!" and the crowd joined in with the chorus.

When it was over he went to his tent, which was besieged with people offering congratulations. The contest at 21:30 was, more or less at an end, apart from all the men making a few laps arm in arm, much to the appreciation of the audience. They all then stopped opposite the stand where three cheers were given for the "Champion" and for "Glorious old Sheffield," after which the band played "God Save the Queen."

"Littlewood has proved himself the champion of the world!" said the speaker above all the din and mayhem ensuing in the Drill Hall, and continuing, "This ought to be a proud moment for every true Sheffielder!"

King of the Peds

The final score!

	Miles	Laps	Time	
Littlewood	**531**	**5**	**138h.48m.30s**	**World Record**
Williams	456	1		
Carless	426	8		
Crossland	416	3		
Hibberd	400	7		

It was later reported that the amount of money taken on the gate amounted to £700.18s.4d. Proceeds from the refreshment bars were £6.18s. Expenses amounted to £207.16s.4d. The profit of £486, which was divided amongst the men, meant that Littlewood was supposed to get £243 plus £130 stake money. Williams received £121. Carless got £58. Crossland received £38 and Hibberd £24 thus losing £1 on the venture.

Authors note: As far as I am aware George's six-day record **still stands today.** I have not been able to find any record that beats it and would be surprised if anybody ever does!

Below is a table recording Littlewood's mile by mile performance as reported in the *Sporting Life* on the 14th of March 1882. *The 1st mile time is actually Jack Hibberd's and this was the only one which was led by another competitor. I have included it for two reasons. The first reason is because it gives a comprehensive account of the whole of his race, and secondly, and more importantly, a world record that has stood for over 125 years deserves to be illustrated in detail.

Finally, the *Sporting Life* wrote this post-match summary of Littlewood's achievement:

Though Littlewood has accomplished such a marvellous performance, it is by no means unreasonable to suppose he will not do better on some future occasion, for had he now been pressed he most probably would have covered 550 miles.

*1	00:09:35	50	08:54:49	99	18:11:10	148	30:13:45	197	40:08:00	246	53:20:25
2	00:19:21	51	09:05:57	100	18:23:02	149	30:25:11	198	40:21:00	247	53:33:59
3	00:29:22	52	09:15:56	101	18:34:47	150	30:36:28	199	40:32:03	248	53:46:29
4	00:39:22	53	09:26:52	102	18:45:37	151	30:51:49	200	40:46:30	249	53:58:59
5	00:49:15	54	09:37:38	103	18:58:47	152	31:02:47	201	41:03:30	250	54:12:22
6	00:59:14	55	09:48:27	104	19:10:05	153	31:13:36	202	41:15:00	251	54:24:50
7	01:09:33	56	09:59:15	105	19:22:00	154	31:25:19	203	41:27:05	252	54:37:10
8	01:19:59	57	10:10:03	106	19:35:40	155	31:38:56	204	41:40:00	253	54:50:09
9	01:31:18	58	10:21:00	107	19:45:55	156	31:50:42	205	41:52:45	254	55:02:00
10	01:40:47	59	10:32:03	108	19:58:49	157	32:01:55	206	42:04:06	255	55:14:25
11	01:51:00	60	10:43:59	109	20:08:25	158	32:13:46	207	42:16:30	256	55:27:00
12	02:01:23	61	10:54:00	110	20:20:06	159	32:26:01	208	42:23:35	257	55:51:26
13	02:11:46	62	11:04:16	111	20:32:05	160	32:38:40	209	42:40:25	258	55:55:20
14	02:22:43	63	11:14:00	112	20:44:40	161	32:53:17	210	42:54:03	259	56:07:13
15	02:33:10	64	11:25:00	113	20:55:28	162	33:05:35	211	43:06:00	260	56:19:20
16	02:43:52	65	11:36:24	114	21:07:15	163	33:17:36	212	43:18:45	261	56:33:10
17	02:54:38	66	11:47:30	115	21:19:28	164	33:28:33	213	43:32:24	262	56:47:00
18	03:05:35	67	11:59:00	116	21:31:23	165	33:39:00	214	43:46:04	263	57:00:00
19	03:16:36	68	12:09:45	117	21:43:26	166	33:50:36	215	43:00:00	264	57:12:03
20	03:27:40	69	12:21:02	118	21:55:29	167	34:01:40	216	44:13:17	265	57:25:14
21	03:38:35	70	12:32:45	119	22:07:21	168	34:13:00	217	44:27:51	266	57:39:17
22	03:49:54	71	12:44:22	120	22:18:55	169	34:24:30	218	44:40:17	267	57:54:07
23	04:00:42	72	12:55:27	121	24:46:33	170	34:36:24	219	44:54:58	268	58:07:26
24	04:11:04	73	13:06:40	122	24:59:54	171	34:48:07	220	47:41:18	269	58:19:32
25	04:21:39	74	13:18:00	123	25:15:02	172	34:59:56	221	47:54:52	270	58:33:15
26	04:33:45	75	13:29:20	124	25:27:10	173	35:11:26	222	48:06:03	271	58:51:04
27	04:44:41	76	13:41:40	125	25:39:33	174	35:24:01	223	48:20:03	272	59:08:47
28	04:55:45	77	13:52:35	126	25:52:54	175	35:36:25	224	48:33:07	273	59:21:45
29	05:05:43	78	14:04:01	127	26:04:16	176	35:49:56	225	48:47:07	274	59:34:48
30	05:21:56	79	14:14:56	128	26:16:36	177	36:00:00	226	48:59:14	275	59:48:49
31	05:28:58	80	14:26:40	129	26:28:37	178	36:11:25	227	49:12:22	276	60:01:30
32	05:39:11	81	14:38:20	130	26:41:40	179	36:23:04	228	49:26:37	277	60:14:05
32	05:50:20	82	14:50:08	131	26:53:51	180	36:37:00	229	49:39:59	278	60:27:37
34	06:01:07	83	15:02:20	132	27:05:05	181	36:49:34	230	49:53:37	279	60:42:05
35	06:11:40	84	15:14:06	133	27:16:46	182	37:00:18	231	50:07:40	280	60:55:00
36	06:22:26	85	15:26:55	134	27:28:45	183	37:14:15	232	50:20:06	281	61:08:56
37	06:34:27	86	15:37:45	135	27:41:12	184	37:26:03	233	50:34:37	282	61:23:00
38	06:44:05	87	15:49:25	136	27:53:18	185	37:38:12	234	50:47:02	283	61:36:31
39	06:55:34	88	16:01:15	137	28:05:35	186	37:51:30	235	51:02:27	284	61:50:15
40	07:04:43	89	16:13:00	138	28:16:49	187	38:03:02	236	51:14:55	285	62:03:36
41	07:15:36	90	16:25:06	139	28:29:45	188	38:16:00	237	51:27:02	286	62:18:32
42	07:26:06	91	16:37:08	140	28:41:17	189	38:28:36	238	51:41:19	287	62:34:00
43	07:36:37	92	16:49:53	141	28:53:45	190	38:40:59	239	51:53:58	288	62:48:26
44	07:47:34	93	17:01:12	142	29:04:24	191	38:53:00	240	52:06:39	289	63:01:50
45	07:59:36	94	17:12:06	143	29:15:49	192	39:04:56	241	52:18:20	290	63:15:00
46	08:09:40	95	17:23:00	144	29:27:14	193	39:17:38	242	52:31:58	291	63:29:20
47	08:20:47	96	17:34:58	145	29:39:43	194	39:30:30	243	52:44:25	292	63:44:30
48	08:32:47	97	17:47:08	146	29:50:20	195	39:43:58	244	52:56:08	293	63:59:00
49	08:43:47	98	17:59:15	147	30:02:04	196	39:56:20	245	53:08:45	294	64:10:30

295	64:23:25	344	79:04:30	393	96:16:10	442	111:16:12	491	129:27:40
296	64:36:46	345	79:21:04	394	96:30:14	443	111:28:36	492	129:41:50
297	64:50:03	346	79:34:00	395	96:45:06	444	111:47:03	493	129:56:37
298	65:03:48	347	79:49:07	396	96:57:45	445	112:01:47	494	130:09:30
299	65:16:30	348	80:02:36	397	97:09:50	446	112:14:56	495	130:23:46
300	65:30:00	349	80:15:05	398	97:22:18	447	112:24:15	496	130:37:50
301	65:43:00	350	80:29:08	399	97:37:26	448	112:45:00	497	130:56:00
302	65:56:05	351	80:52:37	400	97:51:03	449	113:01:10	498	131:08:00
303	66:09:25	352	82:05:10	401	98:10:15	450	113:15:06	499	131:22:30
304	66:21:13	353	82:19:53	402	98:25:02	451	113:28:10	500	131:33:45
305	66:34:35	354	82:32:49	403	98:40:02	452	113:44:17	501	133:21:40
306	70:24:41	355	82:57:00	404	98:57:11	453	113:58:59	502	133:34:40
307	70:38:29	356	83:00:35	405	99:11:58	454	114:12:50	503	133:48:00
308	70:52:21	357	83:14:00	406	99:26:38	455	114:25:30	504	134:00:56
309	71:05:03	358	83:28:00	407	99:41:49	456	114:40:00	505	134:14:24
310	71:19:52	359	83:42:00	408	99:57:03	457	114:55:03	506	134:26:00
311	71:33:51	360	83:58:03	409	100:10:19	458	115:09:55	507	134:39:25
312	71:48:10	361	84:11:30	410	100:24:36	459	115:24:00	508	134:51:30
313	72:02:07	362	84:26:00	411	100:37:02	460	115:37:30	509	135:02:21
314	72:15:31	363	84:49:10	412	100:50:11	461	115:52:20	510	135:15:13
315	72:28:08	364	85:03:20	413	101:04:27	462	116:05:20	511	135:23:00
316	72:41:42	365	85:17:27	414	101:18:07	463	116:24:08	512	135:41:55
317	72:54:38	366	85:30:20	415	101:30:42	464	119:24:20	513	135:54:52
318	73:06:14	367	85:42:53	416	101:44:09	465	119:41:00	514	136:06:50
319	73:19:04	368	85:58:30	417	102:08:52	466	119:54:01	515	136:20:01
320	73:32:33	369	87:12:15	418	102:22:47	467	120:07:16	516	136:32:50
321	73:45:53	370	87:26:05	419	102:36:50	468	120:20:31	517	136:46:30
322	73:58:32	371	87:42:00	420	102:51:05	469	120:34:11	518	136:59:35
323	74:10:05	372	87:55:35	421	103:43:00	470	120:49:02	519	137:12:45
324	74:23:02	373	88:09:30	422	103:58:00	471	121:05:00	520	137:21:20
325	74:35:11	374	88:25:00	423	104:12:50	472	121:19:07	521	137:38:32
326	74:49:17	375	88:38:30	424	104:28:35	473	125:22:19	522	137:53:28
327	75:02:28	376	88:53:55	425	104:43:20	474	125:37:19	523	138:05:43
328	75:15:30	377	89:07:20	426	104:58:20	475	125:52:00	524	138:19:28
329	75:28:40	378	89:23:05	427	105:13:00	476	126:05:27	525	138:32:40
330	75:41:46	379	89:37:20	428	105:37:30	477	126:18:02	526	138:46:20
331	75:58:08	380	89:52:00	429	105:42:20	478	126:31:03	527	138:59:35
332	76:11:23	381	90:18:01	430	105:59:30	479	126:45:15	528	138:12:46
333	76:24:22	382	90:24:15	431	106:15:05	480	126:58:30	529	138:26:15
334	76:38:37	383	90:33:14	432	106:28:40	481	127:11:00	530	138:39:13
335	76:52:27	384	90:52:23	433	106:44:30	482	127:25:27	531	138:48:30
336	77:12:00	385	91:06:40	434	106:59:50	483	127:39:00		
337	77:25:15	386	91:21:30	435	107:12:30	484	127:52:00		
338	77:39:25	387	91:31:16	436	107:25:45	485	128:05:08		
339	77:52:55	388	95:13:55	437	107:40:29	486	128:19:30		
340	78:05:30	389	95:24:15	438	107:54:33	487	128:34:45		
341	78:20:00	390	95:36:08	439	108:09:10	488	128:47:02		
342	78:36:37	391	95:50:28	440	108:24:05	489	129:01:40		
343	78:50:04	392	96:03:45	441	111:08:30	490	129:14:30		

CHAPTER 37

1st Astley Challenge Belt

Of the forthcoming race which was to commence on Monday, the 24th of April 1882, the *Sheffield Telegraph*, in an article entitled, **DRILL HALL, SHEFFIELD, GREAT SIX DAYS' GO-AS-YOU-PLEASE CONTEST**, wrote: The contest, for prizes amounting in the aggregate to almost *£100, in connection with Sir J. D. Astley's **championship of England challenge belt, value £100 (to be won three times before becoming the property of anyone), will commence at the Norfolk Drill Hall this day at twelve o'clock. From the large number of entries received, and the well known excellence of a great many of the intending competitors, it is no wonder that conjecture is quite rife as to the probable winner. After the exceptional performance shown by the well known Sheffield pedestrian, George Littlewood, in the last six days' walking contest, held at the Drill Hall, and as he is claimed by his supporters to be as good as a runner as he is a walker, it is not surprising that he is looked upon to possess a chance second to none. At the present time he is looking well, and expresses himself confident as to the result. In Mason of Ratcliffe, Cartwright of Walsall, Ferguson of Pollockshaws and Mundin of Hull (the late winner of a similar contest held in Scotland) he may meet some foemen worthy of his steel. The pedestrian honour of Sheffield will likewise be upheld by P. Crossland, L. Pinder, J. Roebuck, N. Baxter and S. Jones, but with the exception of Littlewood and Crossland, the rest are fresh aspirants to pedestrian fame. The entries total 29, and from present indications it looks as though the field of competitors will number above twenty.

* The first prize was £50, second prize, £20, third prize, £10, fourth, £6, fifth, £4 and sixth £3. A consolation prize of £2 would be given to all competitors making 300 miles.

**This was the same belt (the "Long Distance Astley Belt") that was first won by "Corkey" between the 28th October and the 2nd of November 1878, and "Blower" Brown between the 21st and the 26th April 1879 and the 16th and 21st of February 1880. It was originally raced for over 142 hours but for some unknown reason was reduced to 72 over six days, 12 hours per day.

The competitors were:

1	**Lewis Armstrong**	Huddersfield	14	**David Ferguson**	Pollockshaws
2	**T. Ashbourne**	Nottingham	15	**T. Fitzpatrick**	Manchester
3	**H. Baker**	Dover	16	**John Hope**	Leeds
4	**N. Baxter**	Sheffield	17	**S. Jones**	Sheffield
5	**J. Bergin**	Brighton	18	**H. King**	Rotherhite
6	**Henry Carless**	Millwall	19	**George Littlewood**	Sheffield
7	**F. Cattle**	Holloway	20	**Pat McCarty**	Leeds
8	**W. Cattle**	Holloway	21	**George Mason**	Ratcliffe
9	**George Cartwright**	Walsall	22	**H. Mundin**	Arbroath
10	**William Clarkson**	Hull	23	**J. W. Raby**	Huddersfield
11	**William Corbett**	Aberdeen	24	**T. Roebuck**	Sheffield
12	**Peter Crossland**	Sheffield	25	**C. Thomas**	Kilburn
13	**Sam Day**	Birmingham			

A bridge had been erected from the entrance to the building over the track to make sure that the two thousand spectators watching the event would not interfere with the progress of the athletes. Once again Mr. Begley of London had been called upon to lay out the path and the men would have to traverse it 13 times in order to score one mile.

King of the Peds

The crowd waited patiently for the 25 men to start the race for the "Championship of England Challenge Belt" at five minutes past twelve in the afternoon, and the men competing waited nervously at the starting post for their chance to be the very first pedestrian to clip it round their waists. The absentees were Alderton, Cooper, Hibberd and Pinder. Mr. Atkinson, the referee had the privilege of shouting the word "Go!" and the men set off on their way. *"It was laughable to see the various styles in which the men got over the ground, some running, whilst others walking, all getting over the track manfully."*

Out of the mass of contestants, one man was sure to be up there at the front dictating the pace, and that man, of course, was the irrepressible Mr. George Cartwright! The 5/2 shot in the betting market moved along, as he always did, at a fast pace, and soon took command. Another thousand or so people crowded into the hall, and between two and three o'clock, they watched the men running lap after lap, except for the celebrated walker Raby from "up't road in Uddersfield" who comforted himself with his familiar mode of progression.

After *"half time"* the pace relaxed and the men slowed down. With the ventilation being described as *"totally inadequate,"* the leader slightly increased the distance between himself and the chasing pack headed by the race favourite Littlewood, of whom it was commented, wasn't in the physical condition his friends would wish. The famous "ped," Sam Day, made his move on the Sheffielder at 20:00 giving him the *"go by."* George Mason of London, and the Scotchman Ferguson, followed the three leaders along. Cartwright's previous exertions were beginning to catch up on him and he decided to slow the pace down, adopting a brisk walk to carry him around the course. With Baker, Burgin, Hope, Mundin and Raby all out of the race by ten o'clock, the scores at the end of the first day showed:

Pos		Miles	Laps	Pos		Miles	Laps
1	Cartwright	76	6	11	McCarty	61	0
2	Day	73	8	12	Fitzpatrick	60	3
3	Mason	70	8	13	Clarkson	58	4
4	Corbett	68	0	14	Thomas	57	4
5	Littlewood	67	0	15	Carless	54	10
6	King	67	0	16	Cattle F.	54	1
7	Crossland	66	6	17	Cattle W.	52	0
8	Armstrong	64	0	18	Ashbourne	51	1
9	Ferguson	62	2	19	Roebuck	51	1
10	Jones	62	0	20	Baxter	50	2

Around 600 people had made their way to the building to watch the start of the second day of competition, and with Thomas missing from the line up there were 20 men ready to toe the line. The attendance later increased to 1,500, and all present must have very excited as they watched the two *"midlanders,"* Cartwright and Day alternate their positions at the head of affairs. However, many of them had come to see the local lad Littlewood, and he wouldn't let them down as he flicked the sawdust in the air in a determined effort to gain on the two front runners. Within the first three hours, the ex-steel worker, running as though he was being chased by someone brandishing a hot iron from his old foundry, gained two miles and two laps on Cartwright alone.

The scores at 2 p.m: **Cartwright, 87.1; Day, 87; Mason, 82.12; Corbett, 79.7; Littlewood, 79.2; King, 77.5; Crossland, 77.2; Ferguson, 75.7; Jones and McCarty, 72.7:**

The 16:00 scores: **Cartwright, 98.4; Day, 98; Mason, 91.9; Corbett, 91.2; Littlewood, 89.1; King, 86.8; Crossland, 86.3; Ferguson, 85.2; Fitzpatrick, 81.7; McCarty, 81.5:**

Cartwright was the first of the runners to hit the ton which he made in a time of 16h.18m, Day making the same tally 3m.5s later. Needless to say, both men were given the usual hearty applause by the appreciative Sheffield crowd.

With Cartwright languishing for some reason in his tent around teatime, Day took the lead and Littlewood rushed himself up to take third place. Mason was behind him though, and as the local lad walked, his namesake passed him. The other George, Cartwright, emerged from his tent at 17:55, but he only stayed on for three laps. After leaving for a short time he came back on again but by then it was clear there was something wrong with his feet, and again, he went off.

The scores at six o'clock: **Day, 109.1; Cartwright, 103.5; Mason, 102.6; Littlewood, 101.9; Corbett, 99.3; King, 95.8; Crossland, 94.1; Fitzpatrick, 92.10; McCarty, 91.6; Jones; 88.1; Ferguson, 86; Clarkson, 85.11; Carless, 82.7; Ashbourne, 79.10; Roebuck, 75.11; Armstrong, 71.9; F. Cattle, 60.7; Baxter, 60; W. Cattle, 57.7:**

"The band now played, which seemed to rouse up the contestants, and with a lively tune, all went merrily," especially Fitzpatrick, *"who caused some fun by dancing as he was going round until the music ceased."* The music wouldn't have been helping George Cartwright however, the Walsall man having to give up the race on a score of 105.7 for reasons unknown.

By 20:00, nine of the contestants had made 100 miles. Three thousand people were now crammed into the hall, and conditions again were said to be appalling due to the poor ventilation. Whatever the circumstances they competed in, the pedestrians knew that they had no choice but to carry on and do their best; they needed to make a living after all. With all the filth they had to breathe in, it wasn't a very pleasant way of doing so; their predicament reminding us of the old Yorkshire saying, "Where there's muck, there's money!"

As can be seen below, when the scores at the end of the second day were hoisted, the progress of one or two of the competitors was quite spectacular. McCarty in particular appeared to be going along like a streak of lightening, thus enforcing his claim for a prize by advancing through the ranks from ninth "pozzy" to fourth. Pat had made as many miles as the leader Sammy Day in the last six hours of the race. Another to catch the eye with his relentless progress was Corbett who made over 29. The local *"blade,"* Peter Crossland had also sharpened his act together so that he too was scything through the field. Mason also impressed, and it was forecast that if he continued in the style he was progressing, he was going to prove a very troublesome customer indeed.

Pos		Miles	Laps	Pos		Miles	Laps
1	Day	141	7	8	King	117	2
2	Mason	135	6	9	Jones	113	6
3	Corbett	130	0	10	Clarkson	110	1
4	McCarty	123	3	11	Carless	101	1
5	Littlewood	122	0	12	Ashbourne	100	2
6	Crossland	121	11	13	Ferguson	100	1
7	Fitzpatrick	117	2	14	Roebuck	80	7

As the men who wished to compete in the third days proceedings *"were marshalled in front of the scoring board,"* one of the most noticeable absentees, apart from Cartwright, was Littlewood. The others who stayed away from the ring were Armstrong, Baker, Barker and the Cattle brothers.

Day, who held a commanding lead, and who had a reputation for being a *"good stayer and a most determined opponent,"* was thought to a safe bet to eventually take the first prize. Alas, nothing in life is certain, and because the likes of Corbett, Crossland, McCarty and Mason were all part of a pursuing pack that was waiting to pounce should their quarry fall in the chase, many punters who were "on the jolly," prayed that he could last the course.

As the men got into their stride, Crossland's classic style of heel-and-toe progression was bringing him favourable comments. Peter was going along very, very well, his performance being so much better than that displayed in the last *"walking"* competition. Ferguson, on 105.6, was the first casualty of the afternoon and he was soon to be followed in the loser stakes by Roebuck with 91.10. Whilst those two were busily gathering their belongings up, McCarty was carrying on with the wonderful work which he had indulged in the night before, and continued to make the relentless progress that had so captured the imagination of the paying public.

Later, Mason was forced to take an enforced rest between five and six o'clock, as his attendants busied themselves trying to alleviate the discomfort caused by blistered toes. He was then sent back into the fray only to have to come off again ten minutes later. Ferguson, *"although virtually retired from the contest,"* reappeared and ran around the track at a blistering pace, his efforts being loudly applauded as he thrilled the audience with his evident speed.

King of the Peds

The 19:00 scores: **Day, 180.1; Mason, 165.8; Corbett, 164.11; McCarty, 161.1; Crossland, 155.6; Fitzpatrick, 151; King, 150.8; Jones, 147.4; Carless, 135.11; Clarkson, 134:**

The strange habit of returning to the course when all hope had gone of picking up a prize seemed to afflict another two of the starters in the race. Cartwright, for reasons no one could offer, made his reappearance at 19:45, despite being officially declared as retired, and proceeded to race around the ring as if chasing a hare. One theory for his return was that he was enticed by some punter who had bet that he couldn't make so many miles in such and such a time. Another of the original line-up who decided he wanted a piece of the action again was Mundin. A dim view was taken about his presence on the track because he hadn't scored the required 50 miles on the first day of competition; a distance that was necessary to be able to continue on the second. He was asked to leave, but ignored the request. Later, finding himself being ignored by the scorers, he eventually left the track.

Whatever his trainers had done to him to alleviate his previous suffering, they had done the trick, for Mason was later able to make quite an impression upon the score of race leader, Day, who at 22:48, was the first man to make his second 100 miles of the event.

The scores at the end of the third day:

Pos		Miles	Laps	Pos		Miles	Laps
1	Day	205	6	7	Fitzpatrick	170	2
2	Mason	195	0	8	Jones	168	8
3	Corbett	188	11	9	Carless	157	2
4	McCarty	186	10	10	Ashbourne	151	0
5	Crossland	178	12	11	Carless	134	0
6	King	171	0				

At midday, 400 people watched 11 men start the 4th day's business, Ferguson being the only one from the above table not to gather at the scorers' stand. The veteran, Fitzpatrick, was the first of them away, and he maintained that position for quite a while before being overtaken by McCarty, who, after Mason had registered himself as the next man to make 200 miles at 12:43, overtook Corbett to become second man in the race.

Thereafter, very little happened of note except Crossland had created much approval amongst his supporters, of whom there were many, when the number 200 appeared next to his name at 16:40. Whilst resting, Mason was then overtaken by both McCarty and Corbett, and just before six o'clock, *"Fitzpatrick was walking the track with a glass of whisky in his hand,"* the alcohol proving to have a positive effect on his performance, for he too would later celebrate passing the 200th milestone shortly before 8 p.m.

The usual furious pace ensued in the last hour as the participants jockeyed for the best position before their forthcoming hours of slumber, and their respective performances in the final 60 minutes was greeted with cheering that was *"loud and long."* With Mason having a poor day, the scores at the end of the fourth day were:

Pos		Miles	Laps	Pos		Miles	Laps
1	Day	268	2	7	Jones	222	11
2	McCarty	251	9	8	Fitzpatrick	210	3
3	Corbett	242	10	9	Carless	210	2
4	King	232	3	10	Ashbourne	195	3
5	Crossland	231	8	11	Clarkson	185	4
6	Mason	226	2	12			

The attendance at the start of the penultimate day's competition was noticeably less than in the previous days. This was probably due to the fact that none of the local lads competing were among the major prize contenders, and what with the early withdrawal of Littlewood, interest in the event was on the wane. Still, there was a chance that Crossland and Jones might improve their respective positions; that notion, along with a chance to see some of the best pedestrians performing in the country, kept the turnstiles clicking, albeit a little more slowly.

Those in the crowd hoping that Crossland would make a better show were rewarded with their faith in him as he soon elevated himself from fifth, to fourth position at 2 o'clock due to King taking a rest. Day continued with his splendid form, achieving 300 miles at 18:42. But it was Mason who put in the performance of the day by *"running in grand style."* George made 24.4 in the first four hours to take him from sixth to fourth passing Crossland as he did so, his actual day time score being a stunning 68 miles and 4 laps.

The monotony was later broken by the first three hours of a two-night six-hour go-as-please race between Mundin and Ferguson for £8 which started at 6 p.m., the former winning the first leg of this one easily after scoring 22.4 to 18.1.

The 5th day score at midnight with Clarkson's name missing from the ranks:

Pos		Miles	Laps	Pos		Miles	Laps
1	Day	326	12	6	King	272	2
2	McCarty	304	11	7	Jones	270	9
3	Corbett	297	7	8	Carless	264	2
4	Mason	294	6	9	Fitzpatrick	251	1
5	Crossland	283	6	10	Ashbourne	217	9

When Mr. Atkinson gave his final command to "Go!" at noon on Saturday, Fitzpatrick, as predicted, sped away from his field which he lapped on several occasions to win the first mile of the day easily. Mason scored his 3rd century at 12:46, and whilst the "Championship Belt" was being *"exhibited behind the bar,"* the first Sheffielder in the race to make the corresponding score (Crossland), did so at 15:30, the last lap of it being walked at a *"tremendous pace."* This performance obviously warmed the cockles of one of his many female admirers in the audience so much, that she gave him a beautiful silk handkerchief. Oh the delights of being a professional pedestrian! Later at 17:40, Jones, the other local lad, brought forth a *"storm of applause"* when he broke the same barrier, but alas, there is no mention of him receiving any gifts from any ladies, which may give us some indication that perhaps he wasn't as handsome as his fellow townsman. Just before that, at teatime, McCarty, Mason and Fitzpatrick all indulged in a sprinting race against each other *"amidst the wildest excitement."*

Then in front of a packed audience, with the rain teeming down outside, shortly after 9 p.m., the "Championship Challenge Belt" was brought out on to the track and placed around Day's waist. Having initially walked a few laps wearing the trophy to the strains of "See the Conquering Hero Comes," and "Auld Lang Syne," he ran his last few laps at a fast pace, presumably with it off. The winner who had been trained for the race at the Reservoir Grounds, Edgbaston, *"finished wonderfully strong and well."* The men *"came to an arrangement,"* and the affair ended at 21:25. Had it gone the full distance, Corbett would have probably passed McCarty to take second honours in the race.

The Final Score!

Pos		Miles	Laps	Prize
1	Day	373	5	£50
2	McCarty	353	2	£20
3	Mason	335	12	£10
4	Corbett	335	3	£6
5	Crossland	321	9	£4
6	Jones	315	1	£3
7	Carless	304	3	£2
8	King	302	0	£2
9	Fitzpatrick	291	1	

King of the Peds

A day to day breakdown of the finisher's scores:

	Mon		Tue		Wed		Thur		Fri		Sat		Total	
	M	L	M	L	M	L	M	L	M	L	M	L	M	L
Day	73	8	67	12	64	1	62	7	58	10	46	6	**373**	**5**
McCarty	61	0	62	3	63	7	64	12	53	2	48	4	**353**	**2**
Mason	70	8	64	11	59	7	31	2	68	4	41	6	**335**	**12**
Corbett	68	0	62	1	58	10	53	12	54	10	37	9	**335**	**3**
Crossland	66	6	55	5	57	1	52	9	51	11	38	3	**321**	**9**
Jones	62	0	51	6	55	2	54	3	47	11	44	5	**315**	**1**
Carless	54	10	46	4	56	1	53	0	54	0	40	1	**304**	**3**
King	67	0	50	2	53	11	61	3	39	12	29	11	**302**	**0**
Fitzpatrick	60	3	56	12	53	0	40	1	40	11	40	0	**291**	**1**

Mundin eventually won the six-hour go-as-you-please race, beating his rival Ferguson by a score of 44 to 39.1. The winner received £5 and the runner-up £3. In the other race that night for £7, which was a two-hour square heel-and-toe event, Raby of Huddersfield with a score of 12.11 beat Hibberd of Bethnall Green on a score of 12.4.

CHAPTER 38

2nd Astley Challenge Belt

The *second* "Six Days Pedestrian Contest" for Sir John Astley's go-as-you-please "Long Distance Championship Belt" which had previously been won at Sheffield by Sammy Day in April of the same year, commenced at the Bingley Hall, Birmingham, England, at eleven o'clock on Monday morning, the 25th of September 1882. The conditions of the race were that those taking part should move around the 160-yard, 11 laps to the mile track (as prepared by Mr. Begley of London), twelve hours per day, for six days. The prizes on offer were exactly the same as the previous contest in Sheffield. There was also a £1 sweepstakes on the race, and of the original 18 entries, Watson of Newcastle was the only absentee. Mr. G. W. Atkinson of the *Sporting Life* would officiate as judge and starter, and Mr. Ashbrook would be the timekeeper.

On the first day, 1,500 spectators watched the start and double that amount attended during the day to see the 17 competitors "wobble" around the track.

1	**Harry Carless**	Millwall	10	**Pat McCarty**	Leeds
2	**George Cartwright**	Chasetown	11	**George Mason**	Ratcliffe
3	**William Corbett**	Aberdeen	12	**H. Mundin**	Arbroath
4	**Peter Crossland**	Sheffield	13	**H. Pettitt**	Walsall New
5	**Sammy Day**	Birmingham	14	**Albert Pierce**	York, USA
6	**W. Hyde**	Birmingham	15	**J. S. Robson**	Liverpool
7	**H. Isaacs**	Tottenham	16	**Charles Sabin**	London
8	**B. Lion (Alias)**	Chepstow	17	**Walter Whale**	St. Lukes
9	**George Littlewood**	Sheffield			

Of the men called to the mark by Mr. Atkinson, Cartwright, Corbett and Mundin looked the pick of the paddock along with the black contender from America, Albert Pierce, whose *"eyes fairly glistening with good health, whilst his smart and clear white jersey and a particularly gay coloured cap gave him a rather prepossessing appearance."* Day, who had been the race favourite before the off, was the second favourite when the race commenced; Littlewood being named as market leader at odds of even money.

When the word "Go!" was shouted, apart from Crossland and Corbett, all the competitors set off at a jog-trot. The *"darkey"* initially led the race, but Littlewood robbed him of the position, and before the first lap was over he was followed in Indian file by Cartwright and Mason, those positions remaining for the next three miles. George Cartwright though couldn't restrain himself any longer; on commencing the fourth mile, he whizzed past Littlewood, going on to take a commanding lead. Of Cartwright," the *Sporting Life* commented: **It is simply astonishing how this ped will persist in recklessly destroying his chance of success in contests of this kind by bursting himself at the outset. Time after time he has had splendid opportunities of success, and has thrown them away through his own foolhardiness.** According to one local reporter, *"some smart running was done in the first hour"* at the end of which Cartwright led the pack on a score of 9.4 with Mason and Littlewood following in his wake a couple of laps behind.

After two hours, the *"Flying Collier"* remained in the lead with 17 miles and 10 laps. Mundin had also joined in the argument at this stage, and he was a close second on 17.8 with the two Georges, Littlewood and Mason following in third and fourth places on 17.7 and 17.5 respectively. By 14:00, Cartwright was beginning to assert himself in premier position leading Littlewood by 7 laps, his score registering 26.2. Mundin had dropped to third and he

King of the Peds

was a mile and a lap behind the Sheffielder with Mason one lap adrift of him. Cartwright went on to complete 40 miles without a rest in 4h.54m.45s. Littlewood made the same distance just over 21 minutes later.

It was in the leaders 44th mile that the watching spectators witnessed a most remarkable incident. The race was going quite smoothly when, at 16:30, Cartwright, who had a large amount of money bet on him winning, left the track to punch a spectator who had been jeering him. It was not clear who attacked who first, or if the same spectator retaliated, but apparently George was struck between the eyes with a bamboo cane causing blood to flow freely from the wound the blow had created. Initially it was thought that the injury suffered would necessitate his early withdrawal from the event, but after encouragement from his associates, and assistance from his trainer, he returned to the track still wiping blood from his face as he continued with the task in hand. The incident which had caused considerable consternation amongst the audience was the subject of much gossip. Some witnesses claimed that the assailant, who had been barracking Cartwright, was afraid that the runner was just about to hit him, so getting in the first blow. The police arrested one man, but it was doubtful he was the real culprit.

At five o'clock, Cartwright was still in first place with a score of 46.10 which was six laps in front of the Sheffield lad. Mundin remained in third on 42.8, whilst Mason, who was now in fourth "pozzy" on 41.5, looked anxiously over his shoulder. The reason for his nervousness was that both Whale, and Day, were now getting a little too close for comfort as a result of their eye-catching progress: **Whale, 38.9; Pierce, 38.6; Day, 38.5; Carless, 38.2; Corbett, 38.1; Lion, 35.9; Isaacs and Hyde, 35; Crossland and Pettitt, 34.10; McCarty, 33; Sabin, 32; Robson, 28:**

In September of 1880, Mason had made 79 miles and 1,005 yards in the first 12 hours of a similar event, but this was easily beaten by the race leader in a time of 11h.33m.42s. Cartwright later went on to cover 82 miles and 320 yards by the close of the first day at 23:00 when the scores were:

Pos		Miles	Laps	Pos		Miles	Laps
1	Cartwright	82	2	9	Whale	65	0
2	Littlewood	77	3	10	Sabin	60	1
3	Mason	74	2	11	Hyde	60	0
4	Day	73	5	12	Lion	59	6
5	Mundin	71	0	13	Carless	58	2
6	Corbett	68	3	14	Pettitt	57	7
7	Crossland	65	0	15	McCarty	51	6
8	Pierce	65	0	16	Robson	51	6

The day after, and with Hyde, Isaacs, Lion (real name H. Williams who came in a creditable second to Littlewood in the "Walking Sweepstakes" in Sheffield in March of the same year), McCarty, Sabin and Whale not turning up, *"having had enough of it,"* the press reported that Cartwright, not only indulged in some splendid running, but that he was able to fully maintain his early advantage. Littlewood and Day also impressed with the latter mentioned, soon passing both Mundin and Mason, thus taking third place.

The scores at 17:00 which was the 18th hour: **Cartwright, 119.8; Littlewood, 113.4; Day, 109.8; Mundin, 102.8; Corbett, 101.4; Mason, 99.6; Pierce, 94.1; Crossland, 93.3:**

The times of the first four centuries made were: **Cartwright, 14h.34m.9s; Littlewood, 15h.41m.23s; Day, 16h.18m.10; Mundin, 17h.23m.10s:**

There was little change in the race during the evening but later on, and due to *"spraining one of his legs slightly,"* Cartwright, who at the time was leading the van by three miles, left the track on completing 146.2 a half an hour before the designated time to stop proceedings. This gave the signal for Littlewood to run, and that's what he did, eventually ending the day as overall leader, as can be deduced below:

Pos		Miles	Laps	Pos		Miles	Laps
1	Littlewood	146	5	6	Crossland	121	6
2	Cartwright	146	2	7	Pierce	120	0
3	Day	138	1	8	Carless	113	2
4	Corbett	136	0	9	Mundin	112	5
5	Mason	131	6	10	Robson	105	0

On the third day, and with an even further reduced field of 10 men turning up due to Pettitt's absence, Littlewood continued to be well supported in the betting at even money. Day had drifted out to 3/1, but punters still had some confidence in him and were willing to take that price on him.

Cartwright's exertions over the first two days had taken their toll, and the midlander had fallen to the rear of the chasing pack, which Littlewood comfortably led despite his somewhat indifferent performance in the first 22 hours. He was jogging nicely on the track and looked very confident in demeanour. George Dickenson, his attentive trainer was pleased with how the race was developing for his man. The northerner, who covered an amazing 8 miles in the first hour of the day, and who had created the new record of making 150 miles in 24h.26m.24s, slowed down thereafter to between 6 and 7 mph. Cartwright, who'd had a second wind in the first hour, again fell back and was clearly exhausted when he left the track promptly at 13:00 due to blistered feet. His enforced absence allowed Day to eradicate the 8 miles difference that separated the pair at the start of proceedings. Day meanwhile lobbed along trusting that his stamina would prevail and that he would ultimately catch Littlewood. The other athletes on the track, Corbett, Mundin, Crossland, Mason and Pierce, all moved well, especially the Scot, who at that stage was expected to do very well in the race. Pierce then succeeded in overtaking Crossland.

The spectators, whose numbers gradually increased as the afternoon progressed, witnessed Cartwright falling further behind, this time to the *"quiet and unassuming"* Scot, William Corbett, who, as the record for 17:00, the 30th hour shows below, wasn't too far behind Day: **Littlewood, 185.10; Day, 173.8; Corbett, 169.10; Cartwright, 162.7; Mundin, 149.6; Mason, 149.4; Pierce, 148.6; Crossland, 147.10; Carless, 146.2; Robson, 135.6:**

In a cold hall, the lighting of the gas not only illuminated proceedings, but warmed the crowd, who must have been unhappy about the announcement of Cartwright's enforced retirement caused by wearing *"narrow-toed shoes"* on a score of 162.7. Still, there was plenty to look forward to, and one event was Littlewood claiming his 200th mile which he duly accomplished at 19:12.

Another part of the entertainment for the evening an advertisement in the match programme concerning W. Franks of Marylebone who was hired by the management to attempt to make a total of 8 miles in an hour. To do this he would have to pass all the peds in the long distance race, and it became clear after he started at 21:00 he wouldn't make it. Franks eventually lost his challenge against "time" in a time 1h.2m.3s. Still *he had tried* and for that he was greeted *"with a perfect storm of cheers."*

Littlewood, who had covered 7½ miles in the first hour on Wednesday, went on to score just over 76 miles during the day. His score of 222.6 easily beat the previous record set by Dobler in the USA in August of 1880 when that man covered 216 miles and 1,280 yards in the same time. In fact George's record was made in 30 minutes short of the 36 hours. By the end of the third day then, the scores read:

Pos		Miles	Laps	Pos		Miles	Laps
1	Littlewood	222	6	6	Crossland	173	8
2	Day	207	3	7	Pierce	171	1
3	Corbett	200	9	8	Robson	159	3
4	Mundin	180	2	9	Mason	149	4
5	Carless	176	0				

A lot of people from Sheffield had made their way down to Birmingham on the train to support the efforts of both of that city's subjects on the fourth day. The race was also proving popular with the local "Brummies" and they turned up in great numbers to witness the amazing feats of endurance prevailing within the building. Littlewood

King of the Peds

continued to make relentless progress as he went further ahead with each step taken. His nearest competitor was Day and he was 24 miles behind. The only flaw in his performance was that he was now travelling at less than 7 mph! Mason had now retired through exhaustion on a score of 155 miles and 610 yards having been reduced to being the back-marker. Mundin, now back-pedalling, was also in the doldrums, and the chances of him winning were a big zero!

Meanwhile, Littlewood had broken another record. In the aforementioned race in the USA, Dobler had covered 284 miles 1,508 yards in 48 hours. Littlewood made the same distance in 45h.50m.12s which was 2h.9m.48s less than Dobler's time. Interestingly the *Birmingham Daily Gazette* in its coverage of the race wrote: **The interest of this contest as it goes on increases greatly owing to the extraordinary performances of Littlewood, the Sheffield man. In the first two days he was handicapped by illness**............and later, they informed their readers that the championship belt he was competing so hard to win was: **On view at the warehouse of Messrs. Elkan and company, cigar merchants, The Quadrant, New Street,** noting that: **His average for the four days is almost seventy five miles a day, and as he apparently is able to keep up so going till the finish of the contest, he will barring accident cover a distance that should hold pride of place for many a day.** Of Littlewood's track performance, it was written at the time, *"His style is very superior to any of the other men, as he gets over the ground with certainly less waste of power, whilst his stamina has never been open to doubt."*

The score at the end of that 4th day was:

Pos		Miles	Laps	Pos		Miles	Laps
1	Littlewood	296	2	5	Crossland	225	0
2	Day	272	8	6	Pierce	220	0
3	Corbett	257	0	7	Robson	207	6
4	Carless	238	1	8	Mundin	203	1

On the penultimate day, Mundin, who had the day before overexerted himself in his quest to catch Corbett, and who had failed miserably, paid the price as he left the scene having made 211.7. Meanwhile, Day, who had stopped dogging Littlewood, contented himself with the knowledge that, barring a mishap, he would finish in second place as Corbett and the Millwall "ped," Carless, were locked in a battle for third place. Carless would initiate the occasional spurt, but the gallant Scot, who had recently fought off illness, was more than a match for him and he responded positively by matching the former's speed. The other Sheffielder in the race, Crossland, like the American Pierce, had walked steadily for most of the contest. Pierce had been issued instructions by his team to convey himself along using the heel-and-toe method. Albert however preferred to run, and gave the slower style of locomotion up as it was ruining his chances of making a good score. Littlewood later broke another Dobler record of 349 miles in 60 hours making the same distance in 58h.42m.28s.

The score at the end of the fifth day:

Pos		Miles	Laps	Pos		Miles	Laps
1	Littlewood	355	7	5	Crossland	278	0
2	Day	328	6	6	Pierce	260	1
3	Corbett	310	1	7	Robson	253	2
4	Carless	295	1				

On the last day (during which 5,000 had paid for admission) at 18:30, Day ran fast for five laps amidst loud cheering. Seventeen minutes later, Littlewood reached his 400th mile after being on the track for 67h.47m.28s. A few minutes after accomplishing the feat he rested, only to reappear later wearing his *"gala costume."* At 21:22, he broke yet another record making 414 miles in 70h.22m.55s, thus beating Dobler's record in America of 414 miles for 72 hours. He then went on to run a mile in 6m.14s, achieving this after completing well over 400 miles, a truly incredible feat! Day, who stayed on the track till the end of time, came second with a score of 377 miles, but he was the only man to take advantage of the full 72 hours. Corbett came in third with 347 having left the track along with the rest at 10 p.m.

Below is a breakdown of the last few hours' scores of each of the remaining athletes:

AM/PM	17		18		19		20		21		22		23	
	M	L	M	L	M	L	M	L	M	L	M	L	M	L
Littlewood	390	1	395	6	400	6	405	10	410	10	415	6	**415**	**6**
Day	352	10	355	10	359	8	364	0	368	4	372	3	**377**	**3**
Corbett	332	0	335	9	340	3	342	8	345	7	347	0	**347**	**0**
Carless	318	9	322	7	326	0	327	1	331	1	333	0	**333**	**0**
Crossland	301	7	305	9	308	0	312	2	316	5	320	0	**320**	**0**
Pierce	284	5	288	7	292	9	295	9	300	0	303	7	**305**	**8**
Robson	280	6	284	9	289	2	293	6	297	7	301	0	**302**	**8**

Individual records of the first six, final scores, and prize money:

	Mon		Tue		Wed		Thur		Fri		Sat		Total		Won
	M	L	M	L	M	L	M	L	M	L	M	L	M	L	
Littlewood	77	3	69	2	76	1	74	0	59	1	59	10	415	6	£68
Day	73	5	64	7	69	2	65	5	55	9	48	8	377	3	£20
Corbett	68	3	67	8	64	9	56	2	53	1	36	10	347	0	£10
Carless	58	2	55	0	62	9	62	1	57	0	37	10	333	0	£6
Crossland	65	0	56	6	52	2	51	3	53	0	42	0	320	0	£4
Pierce	65	0	55	0	51	1	48	10	40	1	45	6	305	8	£3
Robson	51	6	53	5	54	3	48	3	45	7	49	6	302	8	£2

At the end, Mr. Normansell presented the winner with *"a handsome gold pin."*

"Littlewood was looked after by his father and J. Dickenson during the race. Corbett was attended to by D. Scott of Arbroath and Edward Skellett of Birmingham; Day by H. Swann of Birmingham and others; and Carless as usual by his wife."

CHAPTER 39

Did he Fall or was he Pushed?

On the 15th of July 1882, the *Chester Times* of Chester, Pennsylvania, published the following article entitled: **NEWS FROM THE PEDESTRIANS**: LONDON, June 28. The English pedestrians are already preparing for the foot race which is to come off in New York next October. Rowell has been here for two weeks with Mr. Peter Duryea. The pedestrian takes a run of ten miles every morning, just to keep his muscles flexible.

Peter Duryea

The National Police Gazette (Illustration no: 92)

In the afternoon he and Mr. Duryea drive a team of American trotters through Hyde Park. As the team work magnificently, and can trot close to the twenties, they attract a great deal of attention. Rowell and Mr. Duryea are going to Paris for a week, after which Rowell will go into regular training for the race. He has a private track on his country place, near Chesterton, of seven laps to the mile. Rowell promises to be in better condition than he was last spring. He has an unknown pedestrian that will train with him for the race. They will start for New York on the Alaska, August 26th.

Hazael is training steadily at a quiet retreat a few miles out of London. He looks in excellent condition, and says that he will make the man who beats him go long way beyond six hundred miles. George also drives an American trotter. He spins out to the races occasionally, and, while enjoying himself, takes care of his physical health.

George Hazael arrived in New York from England in the steamship *Wisconsin* on the morning of the 30th of August, accompanied by his wife and two children. Hazael stated to awaiting journalists that he expected to take part in a proposed six-day walk and said that he had come over to go at once into training. He said he was in excellent health, and on his arrival, went to Greenpoint, Long Island.

Rowell arrived in New York on the 4th of September with Charlie Barnsley and Peter Duryea. Reporters described him as looking the *"picture of health and youthful vigor."* He said that besides himself and Hazael, he expected Sam Day, who was then currently racing in England, to take part in the forthcoming race (Sam actually didn't turn up as Rowell predicted, instead preferring to remain in England to take part in the Birmingham race which was won by George Littlewood between the 25th and 30th of September, as described in Chapter 38). Rowell told reporters how pleased he was with the three American trotting horses he had purchased and taken over to England and that, "they were doing finely and he expected to raise some good stock from them."

On the 10th of October, the *Olean Democrat* of New York State reported: **Never were pedestrians in finer condition for a protracted struggle. Since Hazael and Fitzgerald became capitalists through their defeat of Rowell last March they have taken excellent care of themselves, and have improved in appearance without gaining superfluous fat. They, with Vint, Noremac and Herty, are training in Wood's Athletic Grounds Williamsburg. Either one of the five can spin ten miles an hour without signs of distress. Frank Hart returned to Boston yesterday afternoon. He will resume his training there under the cheerful influences of Happy Jack Smith. Vaughan, the champion English heel and toe man is coaching Hazael, and faithful James Smith is attending to Fitzgerald. John Hughes takes care of himself in the Polo Grounds. He laps around the whole field before some of the ball players make first base. Rowell has returned from climbing mountains, and will stride over the easier paths of Central Park while taking outdoor exercise.**

The carpenters had been making quite a noise as they prepared the interior of Madison Square Garden for the contest which had been booked to take place between the 23rd and 28th of October. Indeed, the building was now exhibiting quite a few changes since the last go-as-you-please event held there. Two bridges had been created; one under the first row of seats opposite the main entrance in Madison Avenue, and the other on the Twenty Sixth Street side. The structures would facilitate easy transit from the inside of the track to the bar-room and lunch counters without stepping on the track, thus leaving a clear space for the pedestrians below. The restaurant on Madison Avenue had been transformed into a billiard saloon, and the beer and lunch counter was on the Twenty Sixth Street side, as in all former matches. Added to the hundreds of gas jets were many electric lights, which made the scene a brilliant and picturesque one. There were also the old familiar weighing machines, rifle gallery and numerous stalls that were reminiscent of a country fair. That same side of the building was now reserved for ladies. It was separated from the rest of the building by a wooden fence, the gate of which would be attended by a keeper to prevent all men unaccompanied by ladies from passing. No smoking would be allowed on that side of the building.

As usual the track was made up of a bed of clay and loam with an added slight sprinkling of tan bark, and this had been topped off with sawdust. Eight laps constituted a mile and the workmen had been busy raking and rolling it vigorously. The track was enclosed by a picket fence leaving a broad pathway on the outer side.

The pedestrians who were to compete for the "Championship of the World," met at the Garden with their backers in the afternoon on the day before the race. Hamilton Busby, the stakeholder and referee, presided over the meeting. The principal business was to draw for the houses which the men would occupy. Another decision to be made was whether Peter Panchot should be allowed to deposit his money at the last moment and enter the contest. He had not appeared at the stipulated time and nothing short of a unanimous vote would admit him at the eleventh hour. Hughes was the only man opposed to Panchot joining in and the general belief was that he would remain firm in his attitude.

Slips numbered from 1 to 8 were placed in a hat. The numbers represented eight huts and they were situated on the Fourth Avenue side of the track. Each was about 10 feet by 6 feet and plainly furnished with a bed, a wooden chair and a gas stove. Hart was the first of the men to enter the draw. He wore a brown overcoat which was turned up over his ears, and his head was covered with low crowned Derby hat. Rowell, who went second, was attired in an English cut walking suit. Carrying a small cane, his face was bronzed and fuller than when he started in his last race, and he looked the *"picture of health and youthful vigor."* Hazael also wore a well made suit. He was described as having a clear and rosy complexion, and it was commented on that his bright hazel eyes actually made him appear handsome! Fitzgerald, dressed in his working suit, appeared the picture of *"endurance and tenacity of purpose."* Hughes seemed to be in excellent shape for the race, his looks contradicting his late assertion that he wasn't in training. His eyes were restless however, and he seemed ill at ease. Bobby Vint came to the front with his hands in his overcoat pocket. He looked healthy, contented and confident, a different man to what he was seven months earlier when he *"twitched with rheumatism,"* when he had unsuccessfully requested to withdraw his $1,000 entrance money. Noremac had also trained well. *"His skin was clear and his eyes shone."* Herty had trained steadily, and like all the others, expected to make a great score. The result of the lucky dip was that Hazael took hut number 1, Vint, 2, Fitzgerald, 3, Hughes, 4, Noremac, 5, Hart, 6, Herty, 7 and Rowell 8.

After the draw, Hughes announced that he was willing to allow Panchot to enter. "Wait gentlemen," said Vint, "When I desired to withdraw, Mr. Panchot voted against me, but, I will not retaliate. Mr. Panchot can enter without any opposition from me." That settled the matter and Panchot was the ninth man in the race. Panchot then stepped to the front and deposited his $500 sweepstake money in the form of a crisp new bill to Mr. Busby.

The *Brooklyn Daily Eagle* summed up the newspapers somewhat cynical attitude to the forthcoming contest: **For the remainder of the week these trained pedestrians will undergo hardships from which brave men would shrink. They will deny themselves proper rest, take their meals while they are running, hobble round during the last few days of the race with torture to themselves and distress to the spectators and finally wrangle over the gate money, a share of which they hope to obtain.**

The man who covered the greatest distance in 142 hours would be entitled to 70% of the stakes which amounted to $4,500, the second man 20%, and the third 10%. The gate money, after all expenses were paid, would be disposed of as follows. If only one man completed 525 miles, the entire sum would to go to him. If two men covered the distance, the winner would take two thirds and the second man one third, and if more than two men were entitled to a share, the winner would take one-half and the others a proportionate share.

Edward Hanlan, the champion Canadian oarsman would act as a judge and start the men. The other judges would be L. C. Bruce, editor of the *Turf, Field and Farm,* and E. L. Myers the short-distance runner of the Manhattan Athletic Club.

In front of the judges' and scorers' stand was an immense clock, the timepiece being the major instrument used to regulate the records. The match scorers had been instructed to hang a number on a board for every lap made. This would be done by an attendant who operated opposite the starting point where there stood a row of boards with each competitors name on. The attendant would call out the contestant's number as he passed that point. Each competitor had their own scorer. This replaced the old dial system, which had been discarded for this meeting. The new system was instigated in an attempt to stop mistakes from being made, and if there were, they could be more easily detected and corrected.

As early as 7 o'clock on the evening of the match, crowds began to assemble in the vicinity of the vast building. By 8 o'clock, there was a steady stream of people entering the Garden from the Madison Avenue sidewalk which was full of those quietly queuing up for the event. The public knew they were going to be watching some established class athletes racing, many of whom had created a record or records in their professional careers, and the expectations were high of more to come. By 10 o'clock the house was three quarters full. It was a comparatively orderly gathering, but not as large as at former contests. The management explained that the custom of giving away some 3,000 passes had not been carried out this time, and as the hours passed by, and as the crowd swelled, they appeared happy with the attendance.

On the Twenty Seventh Street side, the spectators were nearly all women, many of them using the opera-glasses they had taken with them to scan the crowds below. Most had been influenced to attend because of assurances from the management that they would be well looked after and that they would be well away from the rowdy mobs who frequented this type of event. A ladies parlour was also provided for them in which a female attendant was always on hand, and they were in an area of the building which was relatively smoke free.

The 78th Street Band was situated on the stand on the Twenty Sixth Street side of the building and they began to play at 21:00. However, there was a degree of consternation that the so-called *"sacred music"* they were engaged to play wasn't at all "sacred" when the musicians played "La Mascotte," "Patience" and "Squatter Sovereignty."

The activities of the ticket touts who operated outside the building were being suppressed and any betting that was done was done in private as bookmakers had been banned from the building. It was thought that the chance of fixing a race was less likely if the firms were kept away. Despite all that, Rowell was the still the "Jolly."

The familiar Captain Williams was in charge of the large police presence. He kept his men on a low profile due to the fact the attending masses were behaving themselves and looking forward to the ever nearing start of the race. At midnight, all the seats were occupied with the space behind the seats on both sides choc-a-bloc with standing men, and the space between the track and the raised seats on the 27th Street side filled three rows deep. The inside of the track was almost full as well.

The famous figure of Edward Hanlon was causing quite a stir amongst the crowd and everywhere he went, he was followed by the intrigued. *"He was the lion of the evening, receiving quite as much observation as the greatest favourite amongst the pedestrians."* The champion oarsman of the world had visited the Garden the day before after enjoying a ride behind a fast pair of trotters with manager Peter Duryea. Hanlan appeared rosy and robust. He saw Rowell about to start a run around the track and shouted, "Wait until I get my sweater on, Charlie, and I'll give you a race." Hanlan came out dressed in flannels and the pair of them started to trot around. After competing just seven laps of an intended seven miles, the rower retired *"puffing and perspiring."*

Mr. Busby appeared on the course followed by Hazael and the rest of the "peds." Hart however, was the only one who got a real rousing cheer from the crowd, that is until the people's favourite Charlie Rowell walked up to the scorers' stand with a look of determination on his face.

Patrick J. Fitzgerald: From County Longford, Ireland. He was 35 years old, 5 feet 11 inches tall and weighed 165 pounds. He wore blue drawers, white shirt and blue trunks. **Frank Hart:** From Haiti, West Indies. He was 25 years old, 5 feet 7½ inches tall and weighed 147 lbs. He wore a white shirt, red drawers and grey trunks. **George Hazael:** From London, England. He was 37 years old, 5 feet 6½ inches tall and weighed 141 lbs. He wore buff drawers, blue trunks and a blue hat trimmed with gold. **Daniel J. Herty:** From Boston, Massachusetts. He was 23 years old, 5 feet 8 inches tall and weighed 147 lbs. He wore a purple shirt and white drawers. **John Hughes:** From Tipperary, Ireland, was 42 years old, 5 feet 9 inches tall and weighed 158 lbs. He wore a grey shirt trimmed with blue. **George D. Noremac:** From Edinburgh, Scotland, was 28 years old, 5 feet 3½ inches tall and weighed 150 lbs. He wore grey striped drawers, blue trunks and a red and blue cap. **Peter J. Panchot:** From Buffalo, New York, was 40 years old, 5 feet 4½ inches tall and weighed 128 lbs. He wore red drawers, white shirt and blue trunks. **Charles Rowell:** From Chesterton, Cambridgeshire, England, was 29 years old, 5 feet 6 inches tall and weighed 138 lbs. He wore a red and blue shirt and trunks. **Robert Vint:** From County Down, Ireland, was 36 years old, 5 feet 2 inches in height, and weighed 127 lbs. He wore a blue shirt trimmed with white, blue trunks and white drawers.

"Pop" Whitaker stood on a reporter's bench and theatrically instructed the crowd to clear the track. The competitors were arranged in three lines with Hart, Fitzgerald and Hazael in the first, Rowell and Hughes the second, and Panchot, Vint, Noremac and Herty the third. At five minutes past midnight, Hanlan shouted "Go!" The band played "Yankee Doodle," and Hart, to the most tremendous roar from the crowd, shot into the lead. Hughes passed him almost straight away and led for a lap. Hart then retook the initiative to make the first mile in a time of 6m.16s. He led at the end of the second mile too in 12m.50s, the third in 19m.29s, and the fourth in 26m.15s. Hazael took control on the seventh lap of the fifth mile making the sixth in 40m.14s, the seventh in 47m.35s and the eighth in a time of 8m.55s. At 01:00, and with the place still crowded, there was just a mile and a half between the leader and Panchot who was the back-marker.

As the morning dwindled, the crowd slowly disappeared, but there was still a healthy congregation of people watching the men run around the course. And run they did, with the only walking being done when any of them wanted a short rest. The boys went well, especially Hazael as he *"skimmed nimbly along."* Hart also went into the notebooks as he moved effortlessly. Even the normally ungainly "Lepper" impressed with his gliding gait. Rowell moved nicely too, and it was noticeable that he wasn't forcing the pace like some of the others. Instead he allowed them to run past him without batting an eyelid. Spell "Cameron" backwards and you have "Noremac." —George put in some nice spurts for the admiring punters and looked in great shape, but his team had told him to take it easy and he took their advice and settled into some steady work. Fitzgerald went around in a steady trot, occasionally altering his gait with a sprint which sometimes his fellow competitors joined in.

As daylight entered the building and the dampness mixed with the lingering tobacco smoke created earlier by thousands of cigars, the men breathing the filth had an occasional race against each other. The dull and gloomy appearance of the Garden didn't seem to dampen the spirits of the pedestrians whose only interest was to watch the blackboard. The scorer, who neglected to tally properly, was sharply reminded of his duty by the man whose score he was keeping. At nine o'clock, the men were running round in Indian file. Just after ten o'clock, there were already rumours circulating the place that Rowell had *"broken down,"* having been off the track for 1h.7m. However, when the *"little un"* returned wearing a grey shirt and drawers and dark blue trunks, and appearing only slightly flushed, all the punters who had backed him breathed a sigh of relief.

King of the Peds

The scores for the morning session:

TIME	HR	Hughes	Hazael	Noremac	Rowell	Hart	Fitz	Panchot	Herty	Vint
01:00	1	8.6	8.6	8.2	8.2	8.6	8.2	7.1	8.3	8.3
02:00	2	16	17	16	16	16	16	14	16	16
03:00	3	24.2	24.5	23.2	23.2	22.1	23.3	20.4	23.4	22
04:00	4	31.1	32	29.3	30.2	27.7	28.7	25.6	28.6	25
05:00	5	38.2	38.2	34.7	37.3	33.4	33.4	31.3	32.7	30
06:00	6	45.4	44.4	40.1	44.1	39.5	38.1	37.1	38.2	35.6
07:00	7	52.1	50.5	46.4	50.4	45	44.1	43.1	44.1	40.1
08:00	8	58.4	58	51.4	56.2	50.4	49.5	49.6	49.2	44.7
09:00	9	65	64.2	57.7	62.6	56.2	54.7	54.4	54.1	49.7
10:00	10	72	71	63	69	62.2	61.1	60	59.3	51
11:00	11	78.6	78	69.7	70.4	68.2	67.1	65.3	64.6	51.1
12:00	12	85.3	83	75.2	74	72.5	72.4	70	69.6	61

Rowell joined the likes of Hart, who, now wearing a red hose and yellowish olive coloured shirt went along well. Hughes had also changed and was plodding around in bright green trunks, a white shirt and dark blue drawers, whilst Hazael had attired himself in a flamingo red shirt and drawers, blue trunks and similar coloured jockey cap. Noremac wore a suit of light brown.

The meagre few watching appreciated the peds efforts and many noticed that Vint was beginning to tire. He took numerous visits to his cabin, and when he emerged he appeared "*listless and careworn. He walked with an uneven step when on the track and disappeared so often that it was impossible to keep track of him.*" Hughes however, went along splendidly and he arrived at the 100-mile mark at 13:57. Thirteen minutes later, Hazael made the same score, and like the Irishman before him, was roundly cheered by the fans for his achievement. The others knocked up their centuries one after the other, apart from Noremac and Vint, who at 18:00, were 2 miles and 15 miles off that target respectively.

As the evening wore on, the band began to entertain the crowd to an ever increasing assemblage. Many of those watching wondered whether Hughes would be able to break Rowell's 24-hour record of 150 miles and 220 yards. At 20:00, he was just 18 miles behind it and going great guns.

Fitzgerald appeared stiff when he re-emerged at 21:50, and when he did, the lights in the building suddenly went out causing problems for the scorers and the astonished men on the track. But with the little light that there was, the men carried on until at 10 o'clock when they suddenly went back on and all was well again. The band celebrated with a lively air, and the crowd applauded the fact that they could see what they had paid for. Hughes thereafter continued with his pursuit of the record, and with some of the others resting in their houses, he hit the 149 marker at 23:00. A great yell went up, which he and the others pounding the ellipse, responded to by running with more enthusiasm. Indeed, in a race between Fitzgerald and Noremac, the Irishman made a mile in exactly seven minutes, which was remarkable for someone who had barely rested in 23 hours. Then at 23:11, Hughes made his 150th mile and was promptly hauled to his cabin by his attendants who either had no idea that there was a record to be broken, or just thought their man had done enough for the day. Whatever, the "Lepper" was soon in the land of nod along with Hazael, and Rowell, the still current record holder, who was totally oblivious to what had just happened. Hart went into second place at 23:40 and was now ahead of the slumbering Brits. Vint made his 100 at 23:53 and he got a good reception for the effort.

The rest of the first day's scores:

TIME	HR	Hughes	Hart	Rowell	Hazael	Noremac	Panchot	Fitz	Herty	Vint
13:00	13	93	78.1	81.3	90.6	80.2	73	78.1	74.3	65.3
14:00	14	100.2	84	86.7	98.3	84.7	79	82.3	79.4	70
15:00	15	104.4	90.3	93.1	100.6	89	84.5	88.1	85.3	74.1
16:00	16	110.6	96.3	99.1	106.5	91.3	89.5	93	90.4	79.7
17:00	17	114.4	101.4	102.4	113.1	93.7	94.7	98.2	96.4	82.6
18:00	18	120.6	106.7	108.4	118.1	99.7	100.8	101.1	100	85
19:00	19	126.5	111.7	114.5	124.5	105	106	105.3	104	85
20:00	20	132.1	117.1	120.5	125.8	109.1	111	109.3	109.6	85
21:00	21	138.1	123.1	126.7	131.2	114.5	114.5	109.3	113.7	86.7
22:00	22	143.5	126.2	133.2	135	119	120.1	110.3	116	91
23:00	23	148.6	131.4	135.1	135	123.4	120.1	114.4	116	95.5
24:00	24	150	136.1	135.1	135	126	120.1	118.1	116	100

The second day was dreary for the weary. The men on the track stuck to their job of circling the circle, but it was hard with so few people encouraging them on; and the only thing the small gathering had to celebrate was when Hughes scored his 200th mile at 11:42.

Below is a summary of the morning's scores:

TIME	HR	Hughes	Hazael	Rowell	Hart	Fitz	Noremac	Herty	Panchot	Vint
01:00	25	150	137	133.1	139.1	122.3	126	120	120.1	101
02:00	26	153.4	138.1	139.3	141.7	129.5	126	123.6	121.6	101
03:00	27	157.4	141.2	144.7	141.7	132	127.1	128.3	123.1	103
04:00	28	160	144.1	150.2	142.3	136.6	131.6	131	127.6	105.2
05:00	29	164.7	149.3	154.6	148	141	136	131	132.3	110.2
06:00	30	170.3	153.7	159.2	153	146.1	140.7	136.1	134.3	112
07:00	31	175	158.6	164.7	158.2	151.1	144.7	141.7	138.6	117
08:00	32	181.3	164.6	167.1	164.2	156.4	151.1	147.2	142.6	121.2
09:00	33	187	171	171.1	168.4	160.4	155.1	152.4	146.7	126.1
10:00	34	191.7	175	175.7	173.2	165.4	160.4	158	151.1	129.4
11:00	35	196.3	180.4	180.3	178.5	170.1	168	162.7	154.2	134.6
12:00	36	201	186	185.7	182.1	175.6	168.1	168	159.2	140

Hazael was the next man to get a second century at 14:06; and when the Seventh Regiment Band arrived at 15:00 and played their first tune, the "peds," as was the norm, responded positively and upped their pace. However, there was trouble for the walkers brewing in the entertainment department as Judge Barrett, sitting in the Supreme Court Chambers, issued a temporary injunction restraining the managers from playing music in the building until further orders from the court. The injunction was issued on behalf of "The Society for the Reformation of Juvenile Delinquents" under an act prohibiting amusements without the payment of a licence fee. With an understanding that the problem would be investigated later, the band was allowed to play on.

Frank Hart *(Illustration no: 93)* celebrated his "double" at 16:17 by gnawing on his toothpick with even greater relish than usual. It was 17:10 when Fitzgerald saw the number "200" put up against his name, and Noremac followed his example 25 minutes later. The air was fresher in the house and Hart's lungs appreciated its benefits as he waltzed around. As Panchot struggled, Hughes maintained his lead, but Rowell had him in his sights having reduced the deficit from 16 miles at 10:00 to 10 miles at 18:00.

Two hundred members of the fairer sex were amongst the estimated 3,000 who watched the proceedings in the evening. That figure expanded to 4,000 when the theatres closed and their audiences went along afterwards to watch some alternative entertainment. At 20:07, having scored 239 miles,

Hughes was brought into his tent by his trainer where his rubbers gave him a thorough going over. The Irishman returned 55 minutes later, with his team insisting he was physically well apart from having a small blister.

News emerging from the bookmaking firms was that they were offering the following odds: **Rowell, 7/10; Hazael, 6/4; Hart and Fitzgerald, 4/1; Hughes, 5/1; Noremac, 8/1; Herty, Panchot and Vint, 15/1:**

Panchot made his 200 and went for a rest. A few minutes later at 22:00 "Black Dan" got the audience going by putting on an exhibition of heel-and-toe walking which Noremac, although copying, couldn't keep up with. The two of them then went for a run and the Scotsman eventually beat Frank round the track. Rowell, now resting, was now only 5 miles or so behind Hughes. That got the Irishman glancing at the leader board and he looked worried. By the time the race favourite had left the track at 10 o'clock, he was 4 miles in front of Hazael, and his plan was to follow his fellow countryman when he reappeared. However, as Hazael resumed his labours at 23:30, Rowell continued to sleep. At midnight, when he was two and a half miles behind him, Rowell was woken up and told to get back on the track which he did, and from thereon dogged his pursuer.

The rest of the second day's scores:

TIME	HR	Hughes	Rowell	Hazael	Hart	Noremac	Fitz	Herty	Panchot	Vint
13:00	37	204.7	191.6	192.7	183	174.3	180.2	172.7	161.7	144.2
14:00	38	209.3	196.7	199.1	188.2	180.2	184.7	177.8	165.2	149.1
15:00	39	211.7	200.1	200	194.3	186.2	190.4	182.4	169.1	150.5
16:00	40	216.7	205.3	202.6	198.6	191.6	194.7	186.4	174.1	156
17:00	41	221.6	211.1	208.5	203.6	197	199.2	190	178.1	160.2
18:00	42	227.3	216.7	214.2	207.2	200	202.1	193	182.3	164
19:00	43	233	222.4	220	212.6	205	207.5	199.7	187.1	169
20:00	44	238.3	227.7	224.5	218	210.6	212.4	204	190.7	172.4
21:00	45	240	233.4	230.2	224.4	216.2	218	208.5	195.4	177.1
22:00	46	244.4	239.2	235.1	229.4	221	221.1	213.1	200	179.5
23:00	47	249.4	240.1	235.1	232.2	221.2	222.1	218	200	184
24:00	48	250	240.1	238.5	232.2	224.2	222.1	219.3	200	190

Hazael, who had done some spirited work on the track during the early hours, drew level with Hughes just before eight o'clock in the morning. The alarm bells clanged loudly inside the "Lepper's" camp, and he was summoned on to the track by his aides who told him to redress the situation. He spent the next hour in a private spurting duel with the Londoner and came off best, leading the race by a mile.

The band played its heart out when it began its matinee performance, due to the fact that the managers had paid the entertainment licence— which had cost them $225 for the next three months.

Hazael passed Hughes on his 315th mile at 15:40. At 17:19, and after completing his 250th mile, Panchot sent word to the referee that he had quit the race. Only minutes earlier he had remarked, "Its all up with me, I'm on my last legs." Poor old Panchot had entered the race late, foolishly doing so with a strained tendon in his right groin. He had worn a rubber stocking during the race which was too tight and this had rubbed on the limb he was wearing it on. Every step he took was painful thus he reluctantly had to pull out. He hadn't a clue how he was going to get back home as he stated he was penniless, and in desperation was trying to sell the O'Leary belt he had previously won, for $150.

There was a rumour floating around that the famous Lily Langtry, who was in New York at the time, might be visiting the Garden. The story brought in a few extra visitors, but they were to be disappointed that she decided to stay away. *"The spectacle of eight haggard wretched looking men torturing themselves into a dangerous physical condition for the sake of making a little money for themselves and their managers, trainers and bottle holders is scarcely one which a refined woman would enjoy."*

Hughes retook the lead at 18:40 and stayed on the track for a full hour. After completing his 332nd mile he remarked to someone why he was going back to his tent, "To get a wink o'sleep you know." While he snored on, at 20:35, Rowell moved into second position with 333. The unconscious Irishman was demoted to third place when Hazael again became the race leader on a score of 337 miles. In front of nearly 5,000, he scored another three and went for a rest.

Hughes then came back on to the loop while Hazael put his feet up, but his incredible efforts were catching up with him and he looked ready to fall. Rowell however, looked well; after making a total 341, and now the new leader, he too made for his cabin. Hughes walked around till 23:47, and after he had made 342 miles to reclaim his former position, hobbled to his house. By the end of the day Fitzgerald had moved into fourth position after making 109 miles in the 24 hours, his effort being the most mileage made among the men. He was now just 10 miles and 3 laps behind the leader, Hughes.

Those third day's scores:

TIME	HR	Hughes	Hazael	Rowell	Fitz	Noremac	Hart	Herty	Vint	Panchot
03:00	51	259	251	252	237	236	239	225	190	205
04:00	52	264	257	252	243	240	245	230	196	208
05:00	53	268	261	256	247	243	250	234	201	208
06:00	54	273	267	262	253	248	255	239	205	208
07:00	55	274	274	267	258	255	260	245	210	208
08:00	56	279	279	273	263	259	264	250	213	212
09:00	57	285	283	278	267	262	269	255	219	216
10:00	58	290	288	282	272	267	274	260	223	218
11:00	59	296	293	288	277	272	279	265	228	221
12:00	60	301	300	292	283	277	280	270	233	224
13:00	61	302	300	298	285.6	282.1	280	275.1	235.4	229.6
14:00	62	306	305	300	290	287	284	278	240	234
15:00	63	311	311	305	296	292	287	283	245	239
19:00	67	328.4	328.3	324.5	315	308	307	300	260	Withdr
21:00	69	332	338	335	325	317	315	305	270	
22:00	70	332	340	340.3	329	322	320	309	273	
24:00	72	342	341.1	341	331.5	330	325	309.7	282.6	

Between midnight and 08:00, Fitzgerald took only 17 minutes rest and ate up the miles at an average of five an hour. He was the only one on the track at 01:00. Hazael, who joined him thereafter, stumbled and fell from sheer exhaustion at 02:00 thus forcing him to go back to his booth. It came as no surprise to his careful and judicious trainers when "Fitz" started to move up the leader board to pass Hazael at 03:50, then Rowell, who he had been in a running skirmish with between 6 and 7 o'clock, and finally Hughes between 8 and 9 o'clock. During the next hour Hughes retook the lead, but 30 minutes later, again became third man as Hazael, although suffering from a painful swollen knee which had never completely healed from his last race, took second "pozzy" at 10:07.

After midday Rowell, who was now in fifth place on a score of 377, left the building to indulge in a Turkish bath. He was now behind Noremac who had elevated himself to fourth spot, having been as much as 11 miles ahead of him at the start of the day. Hazael, who continued to suffer with his knee, was the subject of much concern by his trainers. They had practically given up on him winning the race, but his physician Dr. Naylor said he could overcome his difficulties.

Hughes, now stimulated by a large dose of quinine, dogged Hazael in his challenge to retrieve the second spot. His trainers raised their worried eyebrows when he began running along instead of the expected walk. The race leader however, produced a round of applause at 14:34 when he made his 400th mile. Even though his long ungainly figure swayed unsteadily along the track, he still made a good impression. Meanwhile, the *"infernally lazy"* Frank Hart, although looking in better shape than his opponents, was satisfied to propel himself forward at a steady rate of 3 mph. His team made the usual excuses for him announcing that he was saving himself for the last two days. Rowell arrived back at headquarters at 15:00. He went back on the track, walked for 6 miles or so, and then went back to his tent. Herty walked and ran well; whilst Vint, who appeared pale and sickly, made sound progress.

King of the Peds

As the hour hand struck four in the afternoon, the house began to fill up and those entering the Garden saw the men going round in Indian file, some quickening or slowing the pace in response to the tempo of music on offer by the band. Fitzgerald maintained his advantage, and while his record showed 406 miles, Noremac had his eye on taking the third prize away from Hughes. Hazael made the four century mark at 16:07 and Hughes copied him 30 minutes later. Both left the sawdust immediately satisfied with their accomplishment. Noremac watched Hughes close the door of his house and then went on to bag his 400 at 16:41.

The half-full Garden listened intently at 19:55 as Mr. Busby made the announcement that Rowell had permanently retired from the race "suffering to such an extent from nervous prostration as to render his further continuance in the race useless." Five minutes after that, his name was taken off the bulletin board. The Englishman had last been seen leaving track at 17:23 on a score of 384.3. As he lay on his bed in his racing costume with his feet up, and expressing confidence in his ability to win, he begged his trainers to let him continue. His doctor however, said it was inappropriate for him to do so as his heartbeat was spasmodic and weak. Rowell said, "I am not weak, nor are my feet blistered, but I am nervous. When I go onto the track and try to run, dizziness seizes me and I grow confused and oblivious to my surroundings. I cannot account for my failure. It is probably one of those things which no one can account for, which occur in every contest of this kind." He did sadly add that he would never race again, and it sadly seemed at that point in his career that his days as a professional ped were over.

As Rowell contemplated his future, on the track, Hart and Herty put on a good show of running together. Later more gloom and doom was to follow for the management as Mr. Busby, the referee, made another announcement at 22:19 to the effect that Rowell's fellow Brit, Hazael had also hung up his shoes; he having made 413 miles.

Whilst Rowell was resting in the Ashland House, his hut was being dismantled at the track. Meanwhile, as Hazael laid down in his, he remarked of his failure saying, "I am alright, except my swollen knees. It is pretty tough after having the race well in hand to meet with such an accident as this."

Most of the 4th day's scores follow:

TIME	HR	Fitz	Hughes	Noremac	Hart	Herty	Vint	Hazael	Rowell
03:00	75	344	353	339	330	313	285	349	349
04:00	76	350	357	344	333	318	288	350	354
05:00	77	355	362	348	335	322	292	356	356
06:00	78	360	367	352	337	326	297	359	358
07:00	79	366	371	357	340	328	304	363	360
08:00	80	370	371	362	344	332	304	365	363
09:00	81	374	373	369	348	337	309	370	367
10:00	82	378	377	374	353	342	315	377	368
11:00	83	383	380	378	357	347	319	382	370
12:00	84	387	384	381	361	351	323	383	375
13:00	85	392	387	385	365	355	328	387	377
14:00	86	397	390	388	369	358	331	390	377
15:00	87	403	393	391	372	363	336	393	377
16:00	88	406	399	396	376	367	340	399	382
17:00	89	410	400	401	381	373	340	402	383
18:00	90	412	402	404	385	377	346	404	383
21:00	93	423	405	416	397	391	360	413	Withdr
23:00	95	431	417	418	406	400	366	Withdr	
24:00	96	431	419	418	408	402	370		

With the loss of the two Englishmen, the stuffing had been taken out of the race, and the Garden was the turkey that no one wanted to consume. As a consequence, few bothered to turn up the next morning to enjoy what was left of the feast.

The only person who was *really pleased* about England's failures was Hughes, who was known to hate anybody who lived east of the Irish Sea. The demise of his sworn enemies was like music to his ears, and he took great pride in his part in "knocking out them Britishers!" He told a reporter that he could live without his entrance fee and didn't see the point of working too hard. Hart too didn't appear interested on the job in hand and spent far too much time in his house. Vint though, did show some enthusiasm. He chalked up his 400th mile at 09:21, but must have found it dispiriting to hear the little bit of clapping which acknowledged his feat.

Meanwhile, it was Scotland versus Ireland on the track as George Noremac looked to make up the 14 miles deficit between himself and Fitzgerald. *"The appearance of Fitzgerald, Noremac and Hughes was wretched in the extreme. Fitzgerald with a bad stoop limped around the track as if he were treading on live coals. Noremac's face was wasted and he walked round with his body bent as if he had pains in his stomach."* The leader wore the colours he began the race in, and having taken a while to *"limber up,"* moved a little easier.

Dan Herty, wearing a handsome new silk jockey cap, red flannel suit and black trunks, was now the fourth placed man. He in turn led the *"lazy darky"* who had only added six miles to his total in the six hours between 06:00 and 12:00. Now wearing bandages on both legs, Hughes was doing no better. He managed a meagre 11 miles in the same time and the pale faced Irishman was described as a *"pitiable wreck."* By 13:00, Herty had credited himself with 450 miles, and as the afternoon wore on, he continued to make a good score for himself. Meanwhile Hughes told the press he was about to retire. What he said was one thing but what he did was another as it transpired that he would remain on the track, following information that it would be in his interests to continue!

The race returns from 03:00 till 15:00 on the 5th day:

	HR	Fitz	Noremac	Herty	Hughes	Hart	Vint
03:00	99	439	432	408	424	413	375
04:00	100	444	435	412	428	417	376
05:00	101	449	440	416	430	421	380
06:00	102	454	445	420	434	425	385
07:00	103	458	447	425	436	425	390
08:00	104	462	448	430	438	425	394
09:00	105	466	452	434	439	427	398
10:00	106	471	456	439	442	429	400
11:00	107	472	458	441	445	429	402
12:00	108	476	461	445	450	431	406
13:00	109	481	465	450	450	434	410
14:00	110	485	468	454	450	435	413
15:00	111	489	472	458	453	439	415

Vint retired after he completed 425 miles at 16:24. Ten minutes later he would have heard the applause as Fitzgerald made his 500th mile.

The race was proving to be a financial disaster for the management. The withdrawal of Rowell had taken so much interest out of the event that on the last day few people were bothering to part with their hard earned cash and go along to watch the tired athletes.

Information was given to the press that Rowell was to receive 5% of the net receipts after expenses were paid. It was said that when Rowell realised that his five percent would be dramatically less than what he expected, he used his diagnosis as an excuse to permanently withdraw. Indeed he was seen on the day after his retirement sitting in a box at the Garden looking cheerful and relaxed, his appearance adding to the speculation as to why he left the race when he did. Rowell's excuse for his failure was the lack of rest since his last race which may have been one cause for his breakdown. There again Fitzgerald, Hughes and Hart had as little rest as Rowell, but they had gone on much longer than he did. There were also questions raised about the withdrawal of Hazael. Much money had been wagered on him too, so why did he retire when he did? Did he fall or was he pushed?

King of the Peds

The despondency of the management permeated down to the men providing the entertainment, and they went about their business with little or no enthusiasm. There was little point in putting a lot of effort in for such little reward, that is, if there was to be a reward. There would be little or no gate money for the pedestrians and that meant reliance on the sweepstakes which amounted to a pot of $4,500 which had to be divided amongst the finishers.

Of the race itself, very little happened between midnight and noon on the last day. Herty scored the much sought after 500 at 04:55, and the "couldn't care less" Hart left the race permanently at 08:00, his trainer advising the referee formally at 10:00 that he was going home. Hughes, who disliked "Black Dan," and who often referred to him as that "nagur," would have gained satisfaction at that fact as he passed the post to complete his 500th mile. Hart had left the building at 14:36 with 482.2. There were people in the press who speculated that his retirement was due to in some way to bets placed on him behind the scenes on his getting a place. However, there were many cynics who hated the six-day events and would write anything to influence them to end forever.

In front of enough of a crowd to make an atmosphere, Herty and Noremac put on a show for the visitors after 19:00, and there was a stir when Rowell walked down the track after eight o'clock. As he neared the scoring stand, the official that counted his laps shouted out, "Time on Rowell!" and the little man laughed in response as he sat down and examined his score sheets. The ill looking, and somewhat unpleasant, Hughes, wearing a new silk shirt, eyeballed the Englishman and laughed at him as he passed him on the path.

A few mischievous boys had gate-crashed the building and began fighting amongst themselves on the track. They were eventually caught by the police and evicted from the premises.

As the race was just about to finish, the band played "Rory O'Moore" in a lively fashion. The leader, wearing new white flannel tights ran the last few laps along with Noremac who wore a white suit, blue silk cap and breech cloth. Herty meanwhile, wowed the girls in a purple number. Hughes tried to keep up with them, but his legs buckled underneath him. Someone in the crowd shouted out, "Take him off the track!" and a woman shouted in response, "Why, the idea. Let him go on!"

The race finally finished and everybody was put out of their misery. Fitzgerald bore the new crown, having scored 577.2. He was just under ten miles ahead of Noremac who scored 567.4. Herty made a splendid 541.1 and Hughes stayed on well to score 525.

The management had steadfastly refused to release any figures about the financial state of the event, but the following figures were given to the press. The income from the race was $26,373. Mr. Duryea, the manager's slice was 15% which would equate to $3,955. The rental of the Garden came to $10,000. The amounts of the other expenses were never divulged, but let's assume that they were the same as the previous race there in March of that year, $20,000. That would leave about $2,500 to share amongst the successful "peds." Of that, the winner got 50% or $1,250, 2nd, 25% or $625, 3rd, 15% or $375 and 4th 10% or $250. Fitzgerald received 70% of the stake money, or $3,150, which meant he made a nice little profit of $2,650 on that alone. Noremac earned 20%, or $900, thus making $400. Herty would lose $50, as he got 10% of the stake money totalling $450, but with his estimated share of the gate receipts, and from his profit of $325, he would have had to pay his training expenses and the like. Hughes, who got nothing from the sweepstakes, would of course have used the $250 he earned to pay his expenses, which would have left him with a loss of $300 to $400.

The last scores recorded were:

Time	HR	Fitzgerald	Noremac	Herty	Hughes	Hart
03:00	123	527	508	496	474	482
04:00	124	528	510	498	475	482
05:00	125	530	513	501	477	482
06:00	126	532	515	504	481	482
07:00	127	534	516	505	485	482
08:00	128	536	518	508	490	482
09:00	129	542	524	513	493	482
10:00	130	547	529	518	496	482
11:00	131	550	532	520	500	482
12:00	132	554	536	523	500	482
13:00	133	557	540	526	504	With
14:00	134	561	541	528	506	
15:00	135	565	547	528	511	
16:00	136	569	551	530	515	
17:00	137	572	555	534	516	
18:00	138	572	555	534	518	
19:00	139	574	558	535	521	
20:00	140	575	558	535	521	
21:00	141	576	564	539	525	
22:00	142	577.2	567.4	541.1	525	

CHAPTER 40

3rd Astley Challenge Belt

Out of 22 original entrants, there would be 20 starters for the *third* contest for the Sir J. D. Astley "Champion Challenge Belt" worth £100 and prize money of £100 (as described in Chapter 37) for a six-day (12 hours per day) go-as-you-please competition.

The men who would take part in the race between Monday and Saturday, the 25th and 29th of December 1882, were:

1	**T. Ashbourne**	Nottingham	11	**Pat McCarty**	Leeds
2	**George Cartwright**	Walsall	12	**C. McKenna**	Lambeth
3	**William Clarkson**	Leeds	13	**James McLeavy**	Alexandria
4	**William Corbett**	Aberdeen	14	**George Mason**	Ratcliffe
5	**"Corkey"**	London	15	**H. Mundin**	Arbroath
6	**Peter Crossland**	Sheffield	16	**P. Noonan**	Felling-upon-Tyne
7	**Sam Day**	Birmingham	17	**Albert Pierce**	New York, U.S.A
8	**Franklin**	Birmingham	18	**J. S. Robson**	Liverpool
9	**Stephen Jones**	Sheffield	19	**H. Vandepeer**	Sittingbourne
10	**George Littlewood**	Sheffield	20	**H. Winterburn**	Acomb

Mr. Begley of London had constructed the track which was 14 laps to the mile, and the contest was once again under the management of the *Sporting Life*. Because the race started on Christmas Day, the start of the contest was to be at 14:00 instead of the normal time of noon. The crowds waiting to be admitted to the Drill Hall, Clough Road, Sheffield, were enormous, so much so that there was quite a crush when the doors were opened to allow most of them in. Many would-be patrons were therefore not inside the building to view the prompt start of the race, and indeed, there were said to be hundreds who had to be turned away.

Noonan the "Geordie" was briskly away when the referee, Mr. Atkinson, shouted "Go!" Before the first lap had been completed the men were spread out on the track like the *"tail of a peacock."* Noonan continued to lead affairs scoring 9.10 in the first hour. At that point, he led the likes of Cartwright with 9.9, Littlewood with 9, and Mundin and Mason in that order. Franklin, who wasn't around for the start, and who began racing five minutes after the rest, was the first one to retire with 5 miles and 13 laps, followed by McLeavy, who surprisingly, called it a day having made 14.6. Winterburn was the next man to decide enough was enough, and he left the path on 19.

"The old man," of the race, J. S. Robson, the Liverpudlian, must have amused the reporter for the *Sheffield Independent* who wrote of him: Although no one knew his real age, he was thought to be around fifty years of age and is a familiar figure at these gatherings. He wore a sealskin cap, flesh coloured Guernsey and pants, a dilapidated pair of shoes, and a collar and plaid neckerchief. He came in for plenty of banter, but he was in a merry mood throughout, and although his rate of progress was by no means rapid, still he jogged along, heedless of almost everything but the record board. He provoked much amusement at one time during the afternoon by playing on a tin whistle as he journeyed around the hall, and the laughter was greatest when he struck up the notes of, "Home, sweet home."

By 16:00, and with the initial race leader Noonan from Felling falling further and further behind, Littlewood had taken the lead, and in his wake was followed by Mason and Cartwright. The excitement of the crowd was intense for the next four hours and the scoreboard at 20:00 showed: **Littlewood, 42.8; Mason, 41.12; Cartwright, 40.12; Vandepeer, 40.7; Jones, 39.6; Day, 38.7:**

With Ashbourne now out of the race having made 40.6, there was quite a race developing between the four leaders. In front of an estimated 5,000 crowd at 20:35, and on the third lap of the 46th mile, Mason, now walking in *"fine form,"* gave the Sheffielder the *"go by"* and went on to make the first half-century of the match at 21:10, at which time Littlewood was half a mile behind his great rival. The score at 22:00 was: **Mason, 55.6; Littlewood, 54.5; Vandepeer, 51.13; Cartwright, 51; Jones, 50.10; Day, 49:**

The last couple of hours of Christmas Day saw some sterling work being done by Littlewood who retook the lead at 23:37:45. The spectators gawped in amazement as he turned a disadvantage of just under a mile to an advantage of just under a half a mile, as the record for midnight shows when hoisted on the bulletin board: **Littlewood, 66.1; Mason, 65.6; Vandepeer, 62.10; Cartwright, 60.7; Jones, 60.4; Day, 58.5:**

George Mason however, had other ideas as to who should be the race leader, and just before "Time!" was called to end the first 12 hours at 02:00, he caught Littlewood up, passed him, and went three laps in advance of his old foe, as the following record indicates:

Pos		Miles	Laps	Pos		Miles	Laps
1	Mason	75	7	9	Corkey	61	8
2	Littlewood	75	4	10	Clarkson	60	1
3	Vandepeer	73	8	11	Robson	53	1
4	Jones	71	4	12	Pierce	52	3
5	Corbett	68	4	13	Noonan	51	3
6	Day	66	6	14	McCarty	50	5
7	Cartwright	66	1	15	Crossland	50	0
8	Mundin	62	1	16	McKenna	50	0

Noonan and McKenna were the two non starters on Boxing Day when proceedings got under way at midday. Littlewood must have been feeling a little uneasy for he had twice been overtaken by Mason during the first day of the race. As he looked around he would have noticed that compared to the day before, the building in which he was competing was nowhere near as full. McKenna at last made an appearance, but quickly sought a seat after competing only a mile. However, he returned later and gave an impressive exhibition of upright fair-heel-and–toe walking which brought *"approving remarks from onlookers."*

Mason pushing himself forward, and trotting in grand style, was soon creating quite a gap between himself and his hated rival Littlewood, who stuck to a tactic of alternating between walking and sprinting. Meanwhile, behind him, Henry Vandepeer complained of feeling unwell and offered his resignation, having traversed 78.10. That put the Gleadless contender Jones in third spot, but he couldn't hold on to it, soon relinquishing it to Cartwright who forged ahead of him. After going through a rough period, the plucky Sheffielder rallied, and making ground on the "Flying Collier," pushed himself vigorously forward to get within a lap of him.

Mason was the first man to accomplish 100 miles at 15:31, and the appreciative Yorkshire crowd, although disappointed at not seeing one of their sons in that position, offered the Londoner a generous round of applause. The labouring figure of Littlewood, now three miles back in second, had to wait till 16:05 before he received applause for achieving the same distance. Cartwright was next in line for the cheers as he hit his 100 at 17:21, and a minute or so later, the Sheffield youth Jones must have received an even bigger ovation when he made the same score. A few minutes after that at 17:30 the telegraph board showed the following: **Mason, 111.12; Littlewood, 107.12; Cartwright and Jones, 100.8; Corbett, 99.2; Day, 92.4; Corkey, 90.11; Clarkson, 84.2; Mundin, 81.5; Pierce, 82.3; McCarty, 76.7; Robson, 74.8; Crossland, 60 (retired); McKenna, 57.6:**

The race leaders at this time all appeared a little fatigued, and it was noted that they offered those observing the struggle little entertainment in the speed stakes. As the evening wore on, the brass band hired to entertain piped up, and Mason, who positively loved to hear music while he worked, dashed about the place as though he were impersonating a cheetah. One man who found the pace too hot was Cartwright, who by then had slowed right down after his previous exertions. Whilst he ambled lethargically around the path, the Scot, Corbett, took his 4th position at 19:30, after which the "black countryman" left the path to sit down and contemplate his next move.

King of the Peds

Of the others who were going reasonably well at the time were Corkey, Corbett and Day; whilst the squarely built American, Pierce, attracted attention as he plodded along wearing a bright yellow jockey cap.

Cartwright returned to the track after a short break, but on his return moved slowly along; and when Jones sat down to take a breather, his third position was taken by Corbett at 20:16. Meanwhile, the top man in the race moved along effortlessly as he continued to add more distance between himself and the rest.

Littlewood, who hadn't been going very well earlier, and who had been indulging in frequent short rests, began to be constantly cheered by his supporters who urged him to close the gap. He responded to their encouragement by walking along at a brisk pace as Jones and Day both ran in their quest to catch Corbett who trotted. The 10 p.m. scores: **Mason, 138.13; Littlewood, 131.9; Corbett, 124.8; Jones, 120.13; Cartwright, 118.8; Day, 116.7; Corkey, 111.12; Pierce, 101.9; McCarty, 98; Clarkson, 89; Robson, 87.13; Mundin, 85.1:**

Johnny Dobler's 24-hour record of 150 miles and 800 yards made in Buffalo, New York State on August the 10th 1880 was up for grabs, but could Mason summon up enough strength to pass it? Thoughts of cracking it must have been passed through his mind, but he seemed more preoccupied with how much more distance he could put between himself and Littlewood by the end of the night. Noticing that his adversary was flagging, and urged on by the impartial crowd who cheered him on his way, Mason pulled out all the stops to ensure that when "Time!" was called at midnight, he would be leaving the hall with a huge smile on his face. And that is exactly what he did!

Pos		Miles	Laps	Pos		Miles	Laps
1	Mason	149	11	7	Corkey	121	0
2	Littlewood	140	11	8	Pierce	107	3
3	Corbett	135	3	9	McCarty	107	2
4	Jones	130	1	10	Robson	92	7
5	Cartwright	126	10	11	Clarkson	89	0
6	Day	126	4	12	Mundin	85	1

Before the start of the next day's racing, there had been a rumour that Littlewood had *"broken down."* As a result there was some concern that he might not turn up to respond to the starter. Those rumours were evidently wrong, for when the word "Go!" was shouted, he recommenced business along with Cartwright, Corbett, Day, Jones, McCarty, Mason, Pierce and Robson. Watched by a very large crowd, the local lad, then nine miles behind Mason, set off with the idea in mind that he must conjure up something really special if he had any chance of winning the contest. George began running, and within the first hour, had gained 13 laps on the race leader, who at 13:00 topped the leader board with a score of 156.13. Ten minutes later Day cruised passed Cartwright into fifth position. At half past one, Littlewood settled into a walk, having made 13.3 since the start. At this stage, he was less than 8 miles behind Mason.

Corbett's day however, had started poorly, and he soon went a further three miles behind Littlewood. Jones meanwhile was roundly applauded by the partisan crowd as he made 2 miles on Cartwright, who, unusually for him, walked around the track. Despite his woes, Corbett tramped on to make his 150th mile at 14:22, but, try as he might, he was unable to shake off the attentions of Jones, who trotted along splendidly, much to the delight of his supporters.

Later on, Littlewood lost some of the ground he had made on his rival, who retrieved some of it back when the Yorkshireman fell into a walk. At one stage, as the walking Mason's effort dimmed, and that of the running Littlewood's shone, the 2nd placed man got within seven miles of the leader. Then at five o'clock, Corbett at last got his act together and recovered the mile he had lost to Jones earlier in the afternoon. Day managed what a lot thought he couldn't, by taking the fifth spot with a mixture of "wobble" and walk to get him a mile and three quarters ahead of Cartwright. Mason meanwhile, having left to change his costume, returned and proceeded to run around the path uncharacteristically. The leader board at 17:30 showed the following score: **Mason, 183.1; Littlewood, 178.2; Corbett, 166.13; Jones, 163.11; Day, 155: Cartwright, 153.4; Pierce, 133.12; McCarty, 130.6:**

After 6 p.m., and to the relief of many of his friends, Mason got his act together at last and resumed his normal running gait thereafter.

Whilst the race continued, the Londoners, Jack Hibberd and W. Franks had been engaged by the management to offer some alternative entertainment to the crowd in the guise of a four-mile walking handicap race, with Hibberd receiving a lap and a half advantage at the start. Jack eventually won the money by 20 yards, but Franks had shown what a good performer he was by making the distance in 31m.17s, which was quite good considering he had to overtake others on a 14 lap to the mile track. Following this, there was a three-hour go-as-you-please handicap for local pedestrians which started at 8 p.m.

Back in the "big match," Mason scored his 200 at 20:10, and a minute before Littlewood scored his second century at 21:49, Corbett had been passed by Jones. Littlewood then made another 5 laps before leaving both the track and the building, with apparently every intention that he would return later. However, the scores recording the last three hours of the days competition below show that after he had been *"moving along in a very stilted manner, the action of his right leg being anything but assuring to his friends,"* he remained absent. Whilst he was away, the complexion of the race changed profoundly. Predictably Mason pulled right away from him, and by the end of the day, was nearly 20 miles ahead of the now second placed Jones. The teenager must have felt ecstatic having found himself the runner-up in such a prestigious event *and* leading Littlewood!

	22:00				23:00				Midnight		
Pos		M	L	Pos		M	L	Pos		M	L
1	Mason	209	13	1	Mason	215	0	1	Mason	220	8
2	Littlewood	200	2	2	Littlewood	200	5	2	Jones	202	1
3	Jones	190	3	3	Jones	195	12	3	Littlewood	200	5
4	Corbett	190	1	4	Corbett	195	0	4	Corbett	200	4
5	Cartwright	173	5	5	Cartwright	176	10	5	Day	180	2
6	Day	171	12	6	Day	175	10	6	Cartwright	178	0
7	Pierce	148	5					7	McCarty	161	0
8	Robson	129	10					8	Pierce	152	3

There was a small crowd to witness the start of the next day's proceedings, which was sadly missing the veteran Robson, he having retired the previous day with a score of 130. The rumour mill regarding Littlewood's participation in the race had been as strong earlier in the morning as it had been on the previous day. The mere idea that the immensely popular local ped wouldn't be in the line-up was seen as calamitous for the "City of Steel." Alas, the tales of woe were unfounded, for when the fourth day's racing got under way, not only did George appear to have new purpose in his step, he was soon seen lapping his arch-enemy Mason after the race got under way.

The second placed Jones, now feeling the effects of his previous day's exertions, moved slowly along and was readily passed by the much lither Corbett who moved into third place. Mason indulged in a spot of lively racing with Littlewood, but wisely let the Sheffield man go on, such was the enormous distance between them. Jones, realising he wasn't going well, took a rest at two o'clock in the afternoon, thus leaving Corbett to do his stuff on the track and reinforce his third position. McCarty put a little more effort into his performance which had been woefully inadequate up-to-date, as the *"darkie,"* Pierce, plodded along as he always had done.

The cheers went up as the match between Mason and Littlewood resulted in some entertaining and speedy spurting. Indeed, the latter mentioned was seen to be frequently lapping the leader. Meanwhile, young Jones reappeared on the scene fresher for his rest and commenced the task of eating into Corbett's lead, which he did in style. As the young "Tyke" impressed, the diminutive figure of Sam Day progressed further away from his local rival Cartwright. Between five and six o'clock, Littlewood made more advances into Mason's score as the leader faltered in front. The belt holder had put in a score of 40.9 at half-time as opposed to Mason's 38 and 2. Jones had to go off track again after not feeling too well, and as a result, handed more miles to the much fitter Scotchman, Corbett. The score at 18:00: **Mason, 258.10; Littlewood, 241.1; Corbett, 231.10; Jones, 227.7; Day, 208.9; McCarty, 191; Cartwright and Pierce, 177:**

Mason regained his 20-mile advantage after six o'clock due to the title holder moving along slower than earlier. Jones retired for the night at 21:34 with 239 miles, and Pierce excited the crowd with a fine display of running as he lapped the rest of the field continuously for a short time. Mason went along soundly and was already being touted as the winner. Day alternated his gait from a fast walk to a slow jog, and slowly but surely, advanced on the

King of the Peds

tired Jones. Cartwright left the path before nine o'clock; no matter how he tried in the last hour, Littlewood made absolutely no impression on Mason's lead, as Pierce passed the 200 mark at 23:28.

	22:00				23:00				Midnight		
Pos		M	L	Pos		M	L	Pos		M	L
1	Mason	283	3	1	Mason	288	11	1	Mason	294	6
2	Littlewood	263	6	2	Littlewood	268	3	2	Littlewood	273	7
3	Corbett	251	8	3	Corbett	255	10	3	Corbett	261	1
4	Jones	239	1	4	Jones	239	1	4	Jones	239	1
5	Day	228	6	5	Day	233	0	5	Day	236	10
6	McCarty	209	7	6	McCarty	214	8	6	McCarty	219	5
7	Cartwright	203	0	7	Cartwright	205	0	7	Cartwright	205	0
								8	Pierce	201	8

Cartwright *"cried a "Go!"* the next day and that left seven starters for the penultimate day of the race. Mason had his opponent Littlewood's fifth day record of 355 miles and 1,110 yards made in Birmingham only 3 months previous in mind. He needed to make 60 miles that day to beat it as the two leaders set off at a walk. Some in the crowd knew that there was a very good chance that the record might be broken as the race leader appeared to be in top form and going well. When the news was released that he was going to have a go at beating it, there was much anticipation in the crowd of a favourable outcome. After two o'clock, Mason set to work, and running at quite a clip, continually lapped the walking Littlewood.

Jogging along as he had done from the start, Day had passed Jones (who had earlier left the track at 1 p.m., having added just five miles to his score) at 13:29, thus enabling him to move into fourth place. However, the plucky teenager returned just before three o'clock and began to run in an attempt to get back his former position. He went along so well that Day had to move up into a higher gear and trot along faster to repel his challenge. Corbett saw his chance to take on Littlewood and pushed himself relentlessly in his pursuit of securing the £20 second prize money, at one stage reducing the deficit between them from an overnight eight, to six miles.

At teatime, the two leaders indulged in a few laps of fast walking. Littlewood came out on top in that contest, but it didn't last long, because the Londoner reverted to his more favoured mode of travel and ran along, to the dismay of the Sheffield crowd who barracked him. The booing and hooting didn't last long as the crowd, now realising there was real possibility that Mason would accomplish his target, heartily urged him on. When half-time arrived at 18:00, Mason glanced at the scoreboard and knew he was just 27 miles and 4 laps from glory and a new record: **Mason, 328.6; Littlewood, 304.12; Corbett, 288; Day, 263.12; Jones, 258.9; McCarty, 243.1; Pierce, 226.11:**

As the leader stuck to his task and made excellent progress, Jones performed poorly, having to take frequent breaks, which meant that by 22:30, Day had managed put nearly ten miles between the pair. As there was *"no racing"* on the track between 22:30 and 23:00, Mason easily made the new record, amid appreciative applause, at 23:15:30.

The scores to midnight were as follows.

	22:00				23:00				Midnight		
Pos		M	L	Pos		M	L	Pos		M	L
1	Mason	349	2	1	Mason	354	4	1	Mason	359	3
2	Littlewood	323	12	2	Littlewood	327	5	2	Littlewood	330	0
3	Corbett	304	0	3	Corbett	306	10	3	Corbett	311	1
4	Day	281	11	4	Day	285	12	4	Day	289	4
5	Jones	272	3	5	Jones	274	12	5	Jones	275	0
6	McCarty	260	9	6	McCarty	265	9	6	McCarty	270	10
7	Pierce	242	9	7	Pierce	247	0	7	Pierce	250	3

It was soon evident after an hour into the start on the final Saturday, that because of the distance existing between the two leaders, there would be no "racing" as such between them except maybe the odd exhibition of spurting. More interest was therefore directed in the fortunes of the other contestants on show, notably the struggle between Day and Jones. However, at the recommencement of business, the Sheffield lad was a full 14 miles behind Day, and though he tried hard to close the gap, and succeeded quite a lot in his ambition to do so, it would have taken something like Day's breakdown to provide him with fourth place. The brave boy made his third century at 16:54:57 with McCarty accomplishing the same distance an hour later.

The Sheffield public had been hugely disappointed with Littlewood's performance especially after their lad had performed with so much promise in Birmingham. An estimated 5,000 had turned up on Christmas Day but that figure had dropped to a consistent 2,000, which was just enough to keep the managers happy. As it was, Mason received the belt and the ovation of the crowd as the band played, "See the Conquering Hero comes!" For his efforts, the Londoner received £72 which was £50 prize money and the combined entrance fee of the 22 original contestants, all of whom had put up £1. Littlewood got the £20 second prize. Corbett made £10 for finishing third and Day took £6 back to Birmingham for his fourth place. The other Sheffielder, Jones, must have thought he'd won a fortune when he received £4 for his efforts in finishing fifth. Only McCarty would receive a £2 consolation prize which would cover the cost of his entrance fee, help with his fare back to Leeds, and provide him with a few luxuries in life. The same couldn't be said for the unfortunate Pierce who failed in his quest to score 300 miles.

Day by day and final scores of the first six past the post:

	Mon		Tue		Wed		Thur		Fri		Sat		Total	
	M	L	M	L	M	L	M	L	M	L	M	L	M	L
Mason	75	7	74	4	70	11	73	12	64	11	39	0	**398**	**3**
Littlewood	75	4	65	7	59	8	73	2	56	7	40	2	**370**	**2**
Corbett	68	4	66	13	65	1	60	11	50	0	29	3	**340**	**4**
Day	66	6	59	12	53	12	56	8	52	8	34	1	**323**	**5**
Jones	71	4	58	11	72	0	37	0	35	13	39	0	**314**	**0**
McCarty	50	5	56	11	54	0	58	4	50	8	30	0	**300**	**0**

GEORGE MASON was born at Limehouse, London, on September the 4th 1851. After gaining a large number of minor prizes, he won the £30 first prize in a 50-mile handicap at the Agricultural Hall, Islington, on June the 23rd 1878. George then took on James Bailey of Sittingbourne for the "Fifty miles Running Championship Challenge Belt" on Tuesday, the 30th March 1880 at Lillie Bridge for stakes amounting to £50. The first 25 miles was finished by Bailey in 2h.42m and by Mason a couple of minutes later, Bailey going on to win the argument at the finish. He then collected £20 which was the reward for being the winner of a six-hour go-as-you-please contest at the Alexandra Grounds in Cardiff on May the 1st 1880. Then, between September the 6th and the 11th at the Agricultural Hall in Islington, he won £10 for coming in 3rd position behind Littlewood and Simpson with a score of 350.4 (See Chapter 26). After that he travelled to Bristol, where, between the 11th and 16th of October at the Rifle Drill Hall, he finished in 5th spot with a score of 305 miles behind George Noremac. In the fifth contest for the "Astley Fifty Miles Running Championship Challenge Belt" at Lillie Bridge Grounds, London, on Monday, the 14th of March 1881, Mason of "Shadwell" made 25 miles in a time of 2h.36m.34s. Bailey of Sittingbourne eventually ran on to win the race covering 48½ miles in 5h.48m.35s after the other two competitors, which included Mason, retired prematurely. Bailey, who had won the belt a couple of times previous, was now the outright owner. He also won £75 for winning. George Noremac of "Glasgow," retired on a score of 42.3 whilst Mason who had initially led the trio made 47 before he threw in the towel. George followed that up with another third place and £10 in prize money in the "1st Astley Challenge Belt" between April 24th and the 29th 1882 which was won by Sam Day at the Sheffield Drill Hall when he made 335.10 (See Chapter 37). Then between Monday, the 29th of May and Saturday, June the 3rd 1882, in a six-day go-as-you-please race of six hours duration at the Sheaf House Grounds in Sheffield, Mason, with a score of 237.6, won £12 by coming second to George Cartwright (See Chapter 41). After that he went to Birmingham for the "2nd Astley Challenge Belt'" between September 25th and 30th but was unplaced with a score of 155 miles and 610 yards (See Chapter 38).

CHAPTER 41

What Else Happened in 1882

About 1,000 spectators were present at Madison Square Garden on the night of January 7th 1882 for a testimonial benefit for Fred Krohne *"the Prussian grenadier,"* to witness a series of walking, running and boxing contests.

The first contest was a five-mile running match between Jerry Hourihan, Peter Golden and W. Hegelman; which was won by Hourihan in 27m.58s. Dooney Harris and Pat Jordan then sparred three rounds in *"good style."* The next contest was a one mile walk between Frank Edwards and "Ed" Wigzell which the latter won in 9m.3s.

Rowell, Price and McLeavy then ran five miles, the distance being covered by Rowell first in 28m.41s, after which Noremac, Herty, Vint and Fitzgerald set out on a two-mile race. Noremac won, beating Herty in a time of 11m.27s.

The evening closed with a two-mile walk between Krohne, Harriman and Edward Scott which was won by the latter in 17m.58, the other two dead heating for second place.

A couple of interesting long distance six-day races of six hours duration attracted huge crowds to the Sheaf House Grounds in Sheffield, England, between Monday, the 29th of May and Saturday, June the 3rd 1882. Both competitions, one a walking race and the other a go-as-you-please event, were for prize money of £75. The heel-and-toe race, which always started first on each of the six days, attracted the likes of Clarkson, Crossland, Hibberd, Ide, McCarty, Parry and Robson, was eventually won by Jack Hibberd, who took the £50 first prize with 205.4. McCarty finished runner-up taking £12 with 200.3. Hartley of Sheffield, who finished in 3rd spot and won a "fiver," would have been well pleased with himself because he beat his fellow townsman Crossland (£4) into 4th position, their scores being 194.6 and 190 respectively.

The other event was won by George Cartwright, who made £50 for scoring 242 miles when he beat George Mason (£12), by just over 4½ miles, the Londoner scoring 237.6. David Ferguson with 226.6 finished third (£5), and Harry Carless on 202.4 (£4), came in 4th in a race that also had Mundin competing in it.

Seven pedestrians began a six-day go-as-you-please contest for the "Police Gazette Diamond Championship Belt" on a five laps to the mile track at the Casino in Boston, USA, just after midnight on Sunday, the 31st of July 1882 in the presence of 7,000 people. The race, which was for a sweepstakes of $100 each and 50 per cent of the gate receipts, attracted the likes of Campana, Dufrane, Gallagher, Harriman, Hart, Hughes and Noremac.

All the men kept together making the first mile in 6m.10s. Campana had fallen one lap behind at the end of the second mile. Hughes left the race after scoring 50 miles at 11:30. At the end of the first day, Hart was the race leader with 124 miles and Noremac, on 108, was in second position. Harriman at the time was third, five miles behind, with Gallagher 4th on 96, and Campana some way adrift on 91. Hart maintained his lead throughout the match and in the end won quite easily with a score of 527. Noremac finished runner-up with 505. Harriman with 500 did just enough to secure part of the gate money. Campana made 360. Due to the attendance being *"slim,"* apart from Thursday and the last night, and generally cheap admission prices, the successful pedestrians received little in financial reward.

The start of the race at the Casino in Boston

The National Police Gazette   (Illustration no: 94)

A six-day *walking* match commenced at the Norfolk Drill Hall in Sheffield, on Monday, the 13th of November 1882, but it didn't involve George Littlewood. He was to turn up on the Thursday evening, the 16th, to contest a six-hour go-as-you-please match, 2 hours per night starting at 8 o'clock in the evening for a prize of £10 against the 50-mile champion, Arthur Hancock. At the start, the *"world champion"* took the lead with a fast run of 20 minutes. Arthur followed him, and when George settled down to a walk, so did his pursuer. When the leader recommenced his run however, the second man continued to walk in splendid style. At the end of the two hours, Littlewood led Hancock with the scoreboard showing 14.12 to 13.8.

On the second night of the match, Littlewood immediately set off running, but after 15 minutes he walked. The scores for the second night's work showed Littlewood winning with a score of 28.2 to 26.1. The third night proved to be financially lucrative for the Sheffield ace as he beat Arthur easily in the end and earned the tenner. The final score was Littlewood, 40.5, Hancock, 36.12.

In the walking match, Jack Hibberd won £50 and a silver cup for scoring 350.12. He beat Harry Carless by 13 miles and 5 laps, the latter collecting £25 for his efforts. Third place went to Crossland who covered 332 miles. Crossland won £5 more than Clarkson, who, with a score of 315.4, took the fourth prize of £10. The rest of the finishers who went home with nothing were in order of result: **Williams, 291.1; Corbett, 282.11; Higgins, 280; Parry, 269; Robson, 260; Hope, 253; Fitzpatrick, 244.7:**

On the 28th of September 1882, the *Waukesha Freeman* of Wisconsin, USA, reported that: "**O'Leary, the pedestrian, has gone to Europe. He is a wreck physically and financially and his visit to foreign lands is said to be an idle whim.**" Later, on December the 5th, it was stated by the *Fort Wayne Daily Sentinel,* that whilst still in London, O'Leary was trying to organise a six-day walking match in Paris. After that it was reported that he went to France, presumably in the same month and gave an exhibition of walking before the French President and the Chamber of Deputies; for which he received a large sum of money.

CHAPTER 42

Murder and Suicide!

George Cameron, the former lithographic printer of Edinburgh, Scotland, better known as "Noremac," had married the 18-year-old Elizabeth Edwards, a native of Woodside, Aberdeen, in 1874. After their marriage, his wife ran a small confectionery shop in Edinburgh, and the couple set about raising a family. Sadly four of them died, but the two who survived, Alexander, then aged 3 and Jessie, aged 1, accompanied their mother to join their father arriving in New York on the 12th of October 1881 on the steamship *Circassia* from Glasgow. Noremac had previously arrived in the USA accompanied by his trainer George Beattie, whom he had met whilst pursuing a career as a professional pedestrian and athlete.

According to the ship's papers, George Beattie was 41 when he arrived in New York and it is understood he was born in Edinburgh. He had served 22 years in the British Army in the Rifle Corps and other regiments. Twelve of those years were spent in India, and he fought in the Afghanistan war. For his bravery on the field, he was promoted to a Sergeant. When he was discharged in the early part of 1880, he was granted a pension which he received quarterly.

After settling down to life in his adopted country, Noremac opened a liquor store called *"The Walker's Rest,"* at Prince and Mulberry Streets in New York, employing his friend Beattie as the bar-keeper. Whilst working there, Beattie, who lived with them, was treated as one of the family. Although having a penchant for alcohol, he nevertheless kept off the booze, despite being surrounded by the stuff. However, after a couple of years of temperance, Beattie began drinking again, and on occasions after having had "a few too many," he started to become a nuisance, his resulting behaviour causing the Camerons distress. During these bouts of drunkenness, he began telling Noremac that Elizabeth was not only going out, but staying out late as well; the insinuation being that she was up to no good and was possibly being unfaithful. The effect of the slurs was that husband and wife were becoming unhappy with each other, and whereas Mrs. Cameron had previously liked Beattie, she now began to hate him.

At the beginning of August 1883, Noremac sold the Walker's Rest and began negotiating the purchase of a public house at No. 466, Eighth Avenue, which, when he opened it on Saturday, the 18th of August, he would call the "Midlothian Arms." It was during these negotiations that Beattie was said to be annoyed with Noremac because he didn't involve him with his plans, evidently giving him a lot of grief over the matter.

Beattie asked Noremac to be made head bar-keeper at the new pub, but this request was refused by the new owner due to the slip-shod way Beattie had behaved in that role at the Walker's Rest. Instead, Noremac offered him the position of taking charge of the pool-room. This apparently greatly offended Beattie who told Noremac that he would only accept his old position, or he wouldn't work for him. As a consequence a terrible atmosphere between the pair ensued, and their relationship thereafter suffered.

George, Elizabeth and the children, lived on the third floor of the premises; the second and fourth floors being occupied by other families. On the floor they lived in, the front room was used as a parlour. This is where Beattie slept on a sofa, and adjoining that, there was a bedroom where the children slept. There were two other *"dark bedrooms"* which had a corridor between them. One of these bedrooms was rented to two individuals called Peter Campbell, who was a young sailor and a distant relative of the family, and James Barclay, a boarder. The corridor led into the back room which the family dually used as a living and dining room; this is where George and his wife slept, on a folding bed. The rear hall bedroom was used as a kitchen and this had a door between it and the dining room.

The proud new owner took his wife to a picnic which was held by the Midlothian Society at Jones's Wood, on Friday the 17th, leaving his new bar-keeper and a friend called Joseph Miller to finish off arranging the new bar-room ready for opening the day after. Whilst they busied themselves, Beattie entered the bar and said, "What are you fellows doing here, don't you know I'm in charge?"

Miller told Beattie to leave as he had nothing do with the new establishment. The advice fell on deaf ears as Beattie, choosing to remain, began annoying the men by demanding beer. As time wore on Beattie, now supplied with a pitcher full of ale, and becoming more and more inebriated, made a nuisance of himself by turning the gas off and arguing with the two men.

When the Camerons returned to the premises at 2 a.m. on Saturday morning, and after Miller had informed them of what had been happening, Noremac became very angry calling Beattie an "old loafer" and insisting that he went to bed. Beattie responded to the insult by attacking Noremac, who in turn gave him a couple of black eyes, a bent nose and a swollen lip.

When all the fuss had died down, according to one of Noremac's friends, as the Camerons slept, Beattie attempted to steal $60 from the pedestrian's trouser pocket. However, he was caught by Noremac who, after taking the money back off him, kicked him out of the room.

With no reports of any incident happening on Sunday, Beattie made it his intention of making the journey to Canada on Monday, the 20th to collect an instalment of his pension. However, Mrs. Cameron dissuaded him, advising him to remain in the house a few days longer until his wounds healed. Heeding that advice, he did stay there and waited for his face to look something like it used to.

At about 9 o'clock on the morning of Wednesday the 22nd, having prepared breakfast for her husband, the children, and herself, Mrs. Cameron began quarrelling with her husband about a domestic matter. As the atmosphere became more strained between the pair, and after a certain amount of bad feeling was displayed, Noremac, bad-temperedly left the table without eating his breakfast and went downstairs to the bar-room. As he left his wife remarked, "I know what's the matter George, this man (referring to Beattie) has been talking about me again."

What happened next is a mystery, despite the fact that the eldest child, Alexander was still in the room. He was reported later to have been too frightened to give an *"intelligent account"* of what he saw. However, what was thought to have happened was that Mrs. Cameron berated Beattie for saying terrible things about her husband.

Beattie responded to her tongue bashing by taking out his revolver and pointing it at her. Faced with awful prospect of being shot, she attempted to escape from the room, and as she turned to face her assailant on reaching the door, he shot her in the head.

The National Police Gazette **portrays Beattie shooting Mrs. Cameron.** *(Illustration no: 95)*

King of the Peds

The murderer then went to a corner of the room, stood in front of a mirror which sat on top of a bureau, and using his left hand, shot himself in the left side of his head. As he fell, his head struck the window sill leaving a blood stain on the bureau.

On hearing the shots Barclay and Campbell went rushing downstairs to the bar and told Noremac that they had been woken by the sound of gunfire, and whilst hurriedly getting dressed to investigate the cause, heard another shot being fired.

Noremac, who had only been in the bar for about five minutes, ran upstairs and on opening the door leading from the hall into the dining room, found his wife lying in a pool of blood on her back with one hand on her left breast next to the door leading from the kitchen to the dining room.

In the opposite corner of the room, Beattie was also lying on his back on the floor in a pool of blood, his still warm revolver next to his left hand. Noremac swiftly picked up his very scared son and ran downstairs raising the alarm.

The scene of the crime was quickly investigated by patrolman Hughes of the Twentieth Precinct, and ex-Police Surgeon Felter who was summoned to the scene. There were no signs of a struggle and the furniture in the room appeared not to have been disturbed.

After a brief examination it was confirmed that both Beattie and Mrs. Cameron were dead. It was noted at the time that the bullet had entered her mouth, broke her two front teeth and then headed in an upward direction, before making its exit through the crown of her head. The nickel plated, pearl handled, 38 calibre weapon that had killed the pair, had one of its five chambers still loaded while empty shells filled two more.

Coroner Martin gave instructions that Beattie's body should be taken to the morgue, whilst allowing that of Mrs. Cameron to be placed in an ice chest in the parlour, where it would remain until the day after until interment in the Evergreen Cemetery the next day. The inquest was said to be heard in the next few days.

CHAPTER 43

4th Astley Challenge Belt

The start for the *fourth* 12-hour contest for the "Astley Challenge Belt" (which had been on show at Mr. T. Blair's, Toutine Hotel, Haymarket, Sheffield), and £100 in prize money, took place at two o'clock on the afternoon of Christmas Eve, 1883. The venue was again the Norfolk Drill Hall at Sheffield, and once again, this contest would take place under the auspices of the *Sporting Life*. The race would start at the same time on Christmas Day, but on Boxing Day it would commence at 11:00.

Interestingly, and according to the *Sheffield and Rotherham Independent,* this race should have taken place at Newcastle-Upon-Tyne in late May/early June of the same year, but was postponed. That meant that George Mason, the then current belt holder was able to take on Cartwright, Fitzpatrick, Hope and Littlewood in a six hours per day, six-day event at the Sheaf House Grounds in Sheffield between Monday and Saturday, the 14th and 19th of May. This race, which followed a similarly timed walking race, and which had total prize money of £65, was won by **Littlewood (£45)** who beat Mason (£10), Cartwright (£5), Hope (£3), and Fitzpatrick (£2) in that order, the scores being: **243 miles 954 yards; 226 miles, 1,625 yards; 215 miles, 1,486 yards; 210 miles, 536 yards; 202 miles, 1,385 yards:** (Incidentally, J. W. Raby of Huddersfield, with a score of 203 miles and 1,043 yards was the victor in the heel-and-toe affair winning £45.)

"The arrangements for the accommodation of the competitors and spectators were perfected under the supervision of Mr. G. Bayley and were similar to those of previous contests decided at this hall. A fair track composed of black loam, intermixed with sawdust had been laid down, fourteen laps of which **measured 28 yards and 1 foot over a mile**.*"* Mr. Atkinson was once again the referee and Mr. J. H. Gillett relied upon a *"decimal chronograph by Kendal and Dent of Cheapside"* to help him with his job as official timekeeper.

Littlewood had trained hard for this one and was determined to win. The then present holder of the belt, George Mason had apparently been in the city for ten days where *"the air and the water suit him exactly."* It was reported, that in training he had been making distances of 45 miles per day. Harry Carless had also made the trip up from London the week previous. Jones, from Gleadless, a suburb of the *"cutlery capital,"* had also been preparing assiduously, and he was quietly confident of success. He was 5/1 to win the big prize and had even taken those odds himself only the night before. Littlewood and Mason though were the big guns in the race and their ante-post prices in the betting market reflected their chances of success: **Littlewood, 6/4; Mason, 2/1; Day, 6/1; Simpson, 8/1; Bar these, 100/8:**

King of the Peds

The 25 competitors taking part were:

1	**Charles Brooks**	New Swindon	12	**J. Knapton**	Sheffield
2	**John Brown**	Sheffield	13	**George Littlewood**	Sheffield
3	**Henry Carless**	Millwall	14	**Pat McCarty**	Leeds
4	**George Cartwright**	Walsall	18	**George Mason**	Ratcliffe
5	**George Connor**	Hackney	19	**H. Mundin**	Arbroath
6	**William Corbett**	Aberdeen	20	**Fred Newsome**	Sheffield
7	**Sam Day**	Birmingham	21	**Albert Pierce**	New York, U.S.A
8	**Thomas Fitzpatrick**	Sheffield	22	**Johnny Simpson**	Cambridge
9	**Sam Green**	Sheffield	23	**Tom Smith**	Sheffield
10	**Thomas Hoyle**	Sheffield	24	**Walter Whale**	Clerkenwell
11	**Stephen Jones**	Sheffield	25	**George Wilkinson**	Sheffield

The men were marshalled on to the track near the scoreboard, and in front of less than a thousand spectators, the referee, Mr. Atkinson of the *Sporting Life,* got them on their way. Mason, who immediately took the lead ahead of Littlewood, Jones and Cartwright, relinquished it to Littlewood who made the first mile in 6m.10s. Cartwright as was his character, had a little sniff up front, but Littlewood, then took over matters and completed 9 miles and 6 laps in the first hour, leading the chasers Mason, Jones and Cartwright by between one and two laps.

By the end of the 4th hour, Mason was a mile and four laps behind Littlewood who had by then made 29.6. However, and as the leader appeared *"to flag"* somewhat, he managed to reduce this distance. Littlewood though went on to reassert his superiority, and by the end of the fifth hour at 19:00, he went further ahead of the then current belt holder by 2 miles and 10 laps. Mason thereafter began to experience some difficulty on the track, his misery being compounded when the veteran Fitzpatrick overtook him at 19:47. While the Ratcliffe man walked, the older man continued running, thus causing the distance between the new runner-up and third man to increase. One man who was going particularly well was Sam Day. In the first hour he had been in 13th "pozzy," but now with some improved work, he had manage to push himself up to fourth spot.

The races first casualties were Newsome with less than 20 miles to his credit, Knapton with 25 and 7, and Jones (who had sprained his back whilst going well) with 30. This injury caused a great deal of disappointment for his connections. Brooks followed him back to the dressing rooms having scored 35.1, Smith doing the same with 44.13.

At half-time, or six hours after the start, Littlewood had made 44.12, Fitzpatrick 41.9 and Mason 41.7. Cartwright was on a score of 40.10 which was a lap in front of Day who led Corbett by 1.1. Littlewood maintained his lead and completed the races first 50 miles in 6h.48m.45s. The Irishman, Fitzpatrick, remained in second place 2 miles and 3 laps behind.

Between eight and nine o'clock, Day, who had been creeping up on the leaders, firstly passed Cartwright and then Mason at 21:15 when both men were on a score of 48 miles. This move seemed to wake the Ratcliffe man up, and whilst Fitzpatrick celebrated his 50th mile ten minutes later, he (Mason) put on a fast exhibition of walking which prompted Day to follow suit, the pair passing the rest to register 3rd and 4th spots with the Northamptonian having a couple of seconds advantage over his rival. The punters loved it and while it was all going on, the shouts of "Go it George!" and "Bravo Sammy!" rang out to urge the men on.

The scores at 10 o'clock with Cartwright and Corbett registering 50-mile honours at 21:49 and 21:53 respectively were: **Littlewood, 57.8; Fitzpatrick, 54.1; Mason, 52.3; Day, 52.2; Corbett, 50.8; Cartwright, 50.1; Green, 49.12; Carless, 49.3; Hoyle, 49; Connor, 48; Pierce, 46.11; Mundin, 46.3; McCarty, 45.5; Wilkinson, 44.1; Brown, 42.12; Whale, 42.5:**

An hour later, and with Littlewood in some apparent difficulty, the green light was given to those following him to make a move and take advantage. The *Sheffield Telegraph* took up what happened next, and referring to Mason, wrote: He was however too susceptible to conviviality and on some liquor being gratuitously being offered by a spectator, he imbibed to such an extent to greatly prejudice his chances and for a time travelled queerly and Day seeing his chance commenced to put on a pace and at one o'clock he had assumed second position.

It was now an hour into Christmas Day and the reporter from the London based *Sporting Life* was busily writing down what he had observed in his notebook: **Throughout the evening, and at a time when matters were approaching a state of quietude, a raised platform in the centre of the hall was occupied by a number of gentlemen who, with brass instruments, played a well assorted selection of music in excellent style, and whose efforts were of such an entrancing nature, that the entire floor was quickly occupied by lovers of the mazy waltz, and the intricate though graceful movements required in perfectly mastering the Prince Imperial and Caledonian quadrilles. Meanwhile the competitors, invigorated by the music, gaily trotted round, attired in gorgeous costumes which scarcely harmonised with the appearance they presented on making their debut in the ranks.**

By end of play, and two hours into Christmas Day, the score was:

Pos		Miles	Laps	Pos		Miles	Laps
1	Littlewood	79	4	10	Simpson	65	2
2	Day	75	4	11	Connor	65	0
3	Corbett	73	1	12	Pierce	63	1
4	Mason	71	12	13	McCarty	61	0
5	Fitzpatrick	71	0	14	Brown	60	12
6	Cartwright	70	0	15	Wilkinson	58	0
7	Hoyle	69	4	16	Mundin	55	0
8	Green	68	1	17	Whale	55	0
9	Carless	67	13				

Of the original 25 starters, 17 reported for duty again at 2 p.m. on the afternoon of Christmas Day. As the race developed, Cartwright rolled off the laps in his own indomitable style passing everybody who got in his way during the first hour. Littlewood watched him quietly along with one of his old rivals, "Sammy" Day. They kept each other company for the next 2h.37m but the Sheffielder proved too speedy for the "Brummie" who had to resort to slow trotting and walking. The belt holder, Mason, meanwhile, was having major problems with one of his legs. He made frequent stops and was passed by both Cartwright and Fitzpatrick. At 16:45, and on a score of 87.5, he left the track, a sight that must have registered a wry smile on Littlewood's lips. Thirteen minutes later at precisely 16:58:50, that smile would have been replaced by a grin as the race leader notched up the first 100 of the match. The effort was vociferously applauded by the partisan crowd of several thousand onlookers. Day registered his century at 17:47:02, Corbett making the same score 50 minutes later. Cartwright went on to celebrate his at 19:03:09, and Fitzpatrick did the same at 19:24.

With so many people crammed into the place, some spectators climbed the buildings girders where they watched the "big match" *"with a most comfortable and self satisfied air of monarchical supremacy."* Those with the bird's eye view must have enjoyed the sight of the 18-year-old Connor making his hundredth mile at 20:25, for which he received quite an ovation.

It was now odds on that George Mason would lose his belt. The holder was observed to be spending far too much time in his quarters, reportedly suffering from a sprained tendon. Whilst Corbett plodded, McCarty jocosely entertained the crowd as the two leaders, led by the pacemaker Mundin, kept the scorers busy.

Much of the crowd had gone home to spend the night in front of the fire and celebrate was left of Christmas. Day by the time the 10 o'clock score was hoisted up. It showed: **Littlewood, 129; Day, 123; Corbett, 117.3; Cartwright, 112.9; Fitzpatrick, 110.12; Connor, 105.7; McCarty, 103.6; 100.2; Simpson, 94.11; Whale, 94.7; Mundin, 85.3:**

When Boxing Day began, the reporter covering the race for the *Sporting Life* wrote: **During the small hours the men continued their peripatetic ramble around the track, the monotony being occasionally relieved by the witticisms of the spectators, which became so infectious, that the competitors also at times indulged in pleasant repartee.** Littlewood wasn't having a laugh though when he expressed his intention to beat Dobler's two-day record of 150 miles and 800 yards made in Buffalo on the 10th of August 1880. Keeping any jokes he wanted to utter to himself till later, he put his head down and broke the record at 01:22 after altering his pace from a fast walk to the occasional trot. After that, the Leeds based McCarty passed young Connor at 01:30 to go into sixth position.

King of the Peds

The score at 2 a.m:

Pos		Miles	Laps	Pos		Miles	Laps
1	Littlewood	*150	5	9	Whale	110	0
2	Day	143	9	10	Mundin	100	1
3	Corbett	137	8	11	Simpson	100	0
4	Cartwright	128	0	12	Carless	93	2
5	Fitzpatrick	127	0	13	Mason	87	4
6	McCarty	123	6	14	Hoyle	88	0
7	Connor	122	4	15	Green	77	0
8	Pierce	113	12	16	Wilkinson	75	8

*Although this was the distance as recorded by tallying the distance at 14 laps to the mile, it has to be remembered that 28 yards and a foot had to be added to each mile; so in fact Littlewood's 2-day distance was 152 miles and 1,100 yards.

At the start of proceedings on the third day at 11:00, Brown, Carless, Green, Hoyle, Mason, Simpson and Wilkinson had already decided that they wanted to spend their Boxing Day doing something different. All were missing as the men set off from the post, and so was George Littlewood! Sam Day thought his Christmas Day had started all over again, but as he completed his third lap, he saw the race leader enter the arena, late, due to a slight misunderstanding as to the actual starting time. The Yorkshireman quickly had him in his sights and passed him with ease in no time. Third placed Cartwright went along badly and Fitzpatrick passed him at 11:32, thus moving up a position into fourth place. That move must have been the nail in the coffin for the suffering Cartwright then advised the referee that he could no longer continue; he probably went on to join the rest of the retirees for a festive drink in a nearby pub. By 12:30 the in form, and very fit leader, went 4 more laps in front of Day.

George Mason must have made a remarkable recovery from the previous day's injury because he returned to the hall and re-entered the race at 14:27. Littlewood and Day walked most of the time, except of course when the brass band played!

As the afternoon light slowly faded away, the encroaching darkness in the evening brought with it thick fog. The conditions were so bad that apparently many people got lost in it as they made their way to the venue. Those that did make it safely were treated to the sight of their fellow Sheffielder making the first 200 miles in the event at 19:22. Some of the 5,000 in the hall then entertained themselves by dancing *"to the strains of an excellent quadrille band."*

The men on the track would be joined at 8 p.m. by some *"fresh arrivals"* in the form of a group of ten athletes who would be performing in the first heat of a two-hour go-as-you-please event. The inconvenience certainly didn't bother Corbett, who, although passed repeatedly by the quicker group, ran with a lot of determination to improve his position markedly. The end of the day totals were:

Pos		Miles	Laps	Pos		Miles	Laps
1	Littlewood	214	11	6	Pierce	167	6
2	Day	202	8	7	Connor	163	4
3	Corbett	196	0	8	Mason	138	4
4	Fitzpatrick	192	5	9	Whale	127	0
5	McCarty	176	13	10	Mundin	119	0

There were nine competitors who attended for the start of the fourth day in a contest which still held a lot interest for the public of Sheffield. Whale was the absentee.

The reporters of the day concentrated on the state of the remaining men and informed their readers that Littlewood had a sore toe, which wasn't causing him much inconvenience. They observed that none of his rivals were able to match him on the path when he gave his all, and they expected him to win. Of Sam Day; he was reported to be sticking to his work with *"unflinching determination,"* even though he walked with difficulty and glanced anxiously at the scoreboard. The black American Pierce was described as wearing a *"killing costume"* who *"perambulates around with a self satisfied air."* "Mac," an affectionate name for McCarty of Leeds was making strenuous efforts to catch *"Fitz"* and was making relentless progress in that goal. They noted that the latter named recent admirable efforts were beginning to take their toll. They did comment about his age and that he had showed wonderful form despite it. Their prognosis for his chances however, weren't good, and they predicted ultimately that he would slow down considerably over the last two days. Not too much was mentioned about the tall Scot Corbett, apart from the fact that he was trying hard for third place. They did however mention Connor, expecting him to try and make 300 miles and therefore take some pocket money back to London with him. They also predicted that if he did make that score, he would retire.

Fitzpatrick was the first of the men to receive the first heart-felt cheer of the day when, after an indifferent first couple of hours, he made his second century *"in good style"* at 13:08. Having accomplished that feat, he set his sights on Corbett with a goal of overhauling him and taking third position.

All the men at work appeared in good spirits, particularly McCarty who went on his way *"without the assistance of any artificial stimulants."* With Mason leading along at a good rate of knots, Fitzpatrick started to make good progress towards his objective of wrestling the third medal place from Corbett. However, the effort used pulling it off later told on the veteran, and realising he had cracked "Fitz," Corbett moved up a gear to finally win the argument, and as a consequence, pulled six miles ahead by 18:00. The cost to both men though had caused real strain on their bodies, Corbett, his *"body very much bent,"* whilst the Irishman *"limped listlessly."* After seven o'clock, the four race leaders led by Littlewood, began pulling further away from the rest of the field; by eight o'clock when the 2nd heat of the 2-hour go-as-you-please started, the same men, minus Fitzgerald, but plus McCarty, ran around the track in good form.

At 20:53, the young lad Connor was cheered by the crowd as he bagged his double century. Would he get that money? With "Mac" hot on "Fitz's" toes there was an intriguing 5th day ahead. The tired but magnificent seven leaving the track at eleven o'clock that night took one last look at the bulletin board and observed the score to be:

Pos		Miles	Laps	Pos		Miles	Laps
1	Littlewood	271	11	5	McCarty	241	11
2	Day	258	9	6	Pierce	218	5
3	Corbett	252	3	7	Connor	200	0
4	Fitzpatrick	241	12				

The next day, Connor was the only contestant to refuse to get out of bed; and McCarty must have slept well in his previous night, for when he hit the track on Friday, the 28th of December he took no time in overtaking Fitzpatrick. It had been noted that his previous day's efforts had rewarded him with a score of 64.12 against Littlewood's 57, and he was easily the best man on the track. He had it in his mind to have a go for Corbett's third place, but the latter, sensing the danger, kept to his work despite circumnavigating the path with great difficulty, but closely stalking his pursuer. The other factor was that Corbett had *"tee total principles"* and wouldn't take stimulants, which would have helped him alleviate his apparent fatigue.

Meanwhile, miles "up front," the two race leaders Littlewood (who was described as appearing as though he had had enough) and Day, took their time in front of an average afternoon crowd. At 15:30, they were the only two occupying the path, the others presumably having what materialised to be a two-hour tea break together? The rest must have helped Corbett, Fitzpatrick and McCarty as they all returned to the track with a sense of purpose; but Pierce kept away having adding another 20 miles or so to his total.

The audience which had swollen considerably in the evening would also watch two heats for a minor two-hour contest which ran alongside the main race. Apparently they enjoyed the entertainment on offer and offered the other athletes lots of encouragement and applause. The scores at the end of the day were:

Pos		Miles	Laps	Pos		Miles	Laps
1	Littlewood	321	13	4	McCarty	272	3
2	Day	302	5	5	Fitzpatrick	280	1
3	Corbett	290	10	6	Pierce	238	8

King of the Peds

The final day saw a predictably listless performance from the remaining men on the track. The two leaders walked along all through the day, and it wasn't till the evening that they hurried things up a bit, putting on some speedy running for the spectators. At the conclusion of the race shortly before ten o'clock, with the remaining men on the track all walking slowly round, the belt was handed to the winner, Littlewood.

The Final Score!

Pos		Miles	Yards	Prize
1	**Littlewood**	**366**	**1,291**	**£50**
2	Day	342	230	£20
3	Corbett	325	1,664	£10
4	McCarty	319	97	£6
5	Fitzpatrick	305	1,351	£4
6	Pierce	271	653	£3

There were originally 28 entries, and although nothing was mentioned in the press about entry fees, it can safely be assumed that each paid £1 as was the case in previous contests. The winner would have therefore pocketed £28 along with the £50 prize money and of course the belt worth £100.

CHAPTER 44

What Else Happened in 1883

Between Monday, the 12th and Saturday, the 17th of March 1883, William Edwards, the champion walker of Australia, took on the Irish American, Daniel O'Leary, in a six-day walking contest at the Exhibition Building in Prince Alfred Park, Sydney, Australia.

About 4,000 people watched the start of the race, which was originally planned to take place in Melbourne, at five minutes past midnight. On Tuesday, the track, which was measured by the City Surveyor, was found it to be 10 inches under the alleged distance, requiring it to be corrected, with the scores having to be subsequently adjusted. During it, O'Leary believed his water was interfered with by *"treacherous attendants,"* causing him to become sick. As a result, the enforced and unwanted breaks caused him to lose the contest by 23 miles, with his opponent winning with a final score of 373½ miles.

On the 9th of April 1883, the *Reno Evening Gazette* made reference to a feat which had been performed by Charles Harriman between Friday, the 6th and Sunday, the 8th of the same month. A certain Colonel Irons, had apparently been negotiating with the famous pedestrian a couple of weeks earlier, with a view to have him make the longest continuous walk ever made in the *"quiet mountain town of Truckee,"* where Harriman had previously ran 10 miles on the evening of Saturday, the 17th of March, in a time of 1h.15m. The newspaper wrote: **The 'all-absorbing' topic for the past week in Truckee has been the Harriman walk, which terminated about midnight Saturday. He commenced his walk on Friday evening at 7 o'clock and stopped, at 12:40 Sunday morning, making 121 miles and 7 laps in little less than 29 hours without stopping for anything whatever. The attendance from the start was large, and standing room only was the order. A large number of ladies were present, and the excitement toward the last was great. The fastest mile was the 42nd, which was made in 9 minutes. The last half mile was made in 5 minutes and 36 seconds. This is the longest walk ever made by anyone *without rest.**

NB: Readers may remember the previous record when Peter Crossland made 120 miles and 1,560 yards on September the 12th 1876 without rest at Manchester, England. His effort however, was made in 24 hours.

A six-day go-as-you-please race for the "Fox Diamond Belt" took place between Monday, the 28th of May, and Saturday, the 2nd of June 1883. It was held at Kernan's Garden, Baltimore, USA, and finished at about 10 o'clock when Hughes and Panchot left the track an hour after Noremac and three hours after Hart had succumbed. Hart was unable to make the 500 miles which would have entitled him to his entrance fee. The score at the conclusion was: **Hughes, 553; Noremac, 516; Panchot, 504; Hart, 400:** The attendance had been large during the week, and the gate money was estimated to amount to $12,000, of which Hughes received $6,000, Noremac $4,000 and Panchot $2,000. Hughes had hoped to make 600 miles, but was so lame all day that he could only continue his walk with great difficulty. Noremac was apparently in the best condition at the close of the match.

The other competitors in the match had been, Albert, Bennett, Burns, Gould, Graham, Sweeney, and Ward. The match was noted for Hughes and Hart coming to blows on the track on Thursday night, the Irishman accusing Hart of colluding with Noremac to run him off the track.

King of the Peds

On the 5th of July 1883, the *Manitoba Daily Free Press* reported that: Daniel O'Leary has suffered a second defeat in Australia. In the six-day walk with William Edwards, at Sydney, O'Leary was beaten by seven miles, the score standing at 466 to 459. This was the second time that William beat the champion, but as the attendance at both contests was large, the loser doubtless obtained a good sum of money.

Whilst O'Leary was in Australia, where he was reported to have won six important matches, he was given a banquet in Sydney by Sir Joseph Banks and received a parchment testimonial from the citizens.

In another six-day go-as-you-please match again held at Kernan's Monumental Theatre, Baltimore, for the "Richard K. Fox Diamond Belt" worth $2,000 and the gate receipts, between Monday, the 10th and Saturday, the 15th of September in the same year, none of the contestants made 500 miles, which was the distance required to claim a prize. The score at the close of the match stood: **Hart, 417; Panchot, 406; Elson, 401:** George Noremac, William O'Leary, George Hazael and Robert Vint (who had a $500 side-bet with each other) had also starred in the race.

At the Pavilion, San Francisco, on an 8 laps to the mile track, between Monday, the 19th and Saturday, the 24th of November 1883, Frank Hart and Daniel O'Leary won the honours in a 142 consecutive hour, *"combination walking match,"* Hart scoring 500 miles and his team-mate 475. Harriman and McIntyre, who were the other team in the race, scored 481 miles each. The match was said to have been contested for $4,000 a side and the gate money.

During the match on the penultimate night, Hanlan the sculler was reported to have walked round the track with O'Leary to rapturous applause.

Edward Payson Weston set off on his infamous 5,000 miles in 100 days walk shortly after midnight on Wednesday, the 21st of November 1883. The feat was to be performed under the auspices of the Church of England Temperance Society, and it was outside their headquarters opposite the Houses of Parliament in London where he took his first steps on his long journey. A route had been prepared by the Ordnance Survey Department; he was to be accompanied on his long hike by members of the branches of the society and a press reporter. After each 50-mile day, excluding Sundays, Weston would offer his listening audience advice on the *"merits of alcohol abstinence from an athletic point of view."*

Heading down Birdcage Walk, he ventured on to Green Park, Hyde Park Corner, Hammersmith, Barnes, Putney, Wimbledon, Kingston, Ewell, Epsom, Leatherhead, Dorking, Reigate, Bletchingley, Mertham and Croydon, where he ended his first 50 miles by lecturing at the towns skating rink at 7 p.m.

Jack Hibberd of London won the *"ten hours per diem"* six-day walking tournament, which concluded at the Cardiff Skating Rink in Wales on Saturday night the 29th of December 1883, in front of about 1,000 spectators. The £25 first prize was given to him for making a score of 294 miles and 9 laps in the time allowed. Second man was the Sussex champion, Thomas of Eastbourne with 291.11, and he just beat an array of local contenders who finished in the following order. A. Thomas of Cardiff won the third prize of £7 with 290.13. He wasn't far in front of the Welsh champion of the same city, James Sexton who made exactly 289 miles. He received 30 shillings along with numerous others who made the necessary 200 miles.

CHAPTER 45

$1,400 Go-As-You-Please Sweepstakes

George Hazael arrived in New York on the 24th of October 1883 on the steamship *Wyoming*. Earlier that year, he, his wife, and 10-year-old son Alf, arrived in the same city on the 20th of April on the steamship *Abyssinia*. It is supposed that the Hazaels were starting a new life in America, where the professional pedestrian could make a more lucrative living than in his homeland. Following him a week later, Rowell arrived in New York on the steamship *Alaska* on the morning of Monday, the 29th of October with his manager and backer, Peter Duryea.

"Handsome Charley" was said to look in better condition than at any other time when he had visited the USA, and told reporters at the Ashland House Hotel that as he felt so well, he would like to indulge in a little racing again. "I inserted a challenge in the London Sporting Life, inviting Alderman Fitzgerald of Long Island City, to contest a six days walk with me, and I see that he has accepted and deposited $1,000 in the *Turf, Field and Farm* office. I shall go down there in a day or two and cover his money, and I hope he will consent the race open to the world. This is my idea though of course; if he insists on walking with me alone, I shall have to give in, as I challenged him first. I want to tell you why I broke down in the last race. When I got home, I had myself examined by Sir William Gull, physician to the Queen, and he told me that I had enlargement of the spleen caused by malaria. You see, I trained in New Jersey, near to where they were building a railroad and the freshly broken ground gave me the malaria. I shall do better this time, and I don't believe I shall break down through enlargement of the spleen. I have not walked in any race since I went home. I have been resting all the time."

Peter Duryea in a later interview would comment further on what happened to Rowell, saying, "Dr. Gull found that he was suffering from an enlargement of the spleen, due to a neglected attack of malaria, which pressed upon the heart, and thus brought palpitations or intermittent action. After preparing some proper treatment, which relieved the difficulty, Rowell was recommended to take a voyage of three months duration. Upon his return he was thoroughly examined by Sir William, who pronounced him "sound as a ball," and one of the strongest men, constitutionally and physically, that he had ever come across.

"Rowell was not quite satisfied at this, but a short time ago consulted Dr. Hood, who was Sir William Gull's assistant, who confirmed the latter's opinion. He told Rowell to run eighty miles which he did, and then returned to be examined. Dr. Hood pronounced him sound in every way, and said he ought to make the best race of his life this time.

"Still somewhat in doubt, Rowell went to Dr. Hall, physician in Cambridge University just before he sailed for this country. That gentleman after a most intensive examination said that he was sound in every respect – without a trace of any heart or other trouble.

"Dr. Robert W. Taylor had examined Rowell too since his arrival and confirmed the opinion given by his English brethren in the profession."

On arriving at New York, Duryea received a dispatch from Boston, offering him the use of the Agricultural Hall in that city for the proposed race. "I am thinking very much of accepting the offer. I am not going to pay $10,000 a week for Madison Square Garden again, that's sure. Paying such a price takes off all the profits from the walkers, and they growl at me for running up all the expenses. I think Boston would patronise the race as well as New York, and if Fitzgerald is willing, I think we will make the race there."

King of the Peds

The two leading contenders to take part in the six-day go-as-you-please, "Champion of Champions" race, signed an agreement on the 7th of November, and also deposited $500 with the editor of the *Turf, Field and Farm*. Originally the contest had been arranged to take place in either February or March of 1884 in Boston, Chicago, Philadelphia or New York, but just before Christmas it emerged that the dates the contest would be between Monday, the 25th of February and Saturday, the 1st of March 1884, and that the venue would be Madison Square Garden.

Of the forthcoming race, the *Brooklyn Daily Eagle* commented: Rowell, who retains the Astley Belt, went home to England a physical wreck. He placed himself under the care of one of the most eminent of the Court physicians and a complete restoration of his physical and staying powers was the result. His great ambition was to retrieve his lost laurels, and when he received the assurances that he was in trim to undertake a six day's run he came back to New York and challenged Fitzgerald, who promptly took up the gauntlet. Mr. Vanderbilt was waited upon and he consented to let them have the use of the Garden for $5,000, on condition that they would adhere to their proposition to charge only fifty cents for admission. Theretofore the rent of the Garden was $10,000 and the admission fee $1. The terms of the match were that that they put up $500 each, and that any man who desires can enter the race by putting up a like sum on or before the 4th of February. The winner gets the sweepstake and fifty per cent of the gate money after all expenses shall have been paid. The remaining fifty per cent shall be divided up amongst the men covering 525 miles, and the man who fails to perform the feat receives nothing.

On the 22nd December, the London based *Penny Illustrated*, reported that: CHARLES ROWELL, the long-distance pedestrian, was one of the hounds in the first annual chase of the West Side Athletic Club, which was held at Fort Lee, N.J., on Thanksgiving Day. Nine and a half miles were run, and Rowell finished second to M. Garwood in one hour and five minutes. Seventeen athletes participated.

On the 10th of February 1884, it was reported that Rowell and Fitzgerald had gone into training around the sixteen lap track at the covered Woods Athletic Grounds, Williamsburg, on Second and North Nine Streets. Others training alongside them were George Hazael, George Noremac, Robert Vint, Winston H. Burrell and Ernest Smith who had at that time, every intention of taking part too. The track, within the *"handsome grounds,"* which was a sixteenth of a mile in circumference, was said to be covered in sawdust and *"suitable for practice."*

Fitzgerald, under the auspices of "Happy Jack" Smith, had been in training since the previous summer. Of late however, he had started to be more serious in his commitment, and during the last month, had been observed putting in double the amount of work than that of Rowell, who had only been in serious training at the same venue for a month. Fitzgerald was observed to walk from his home in Astoria and arrive at the facility to meet his trainer who, on occasions, walked there with him. He would then train both in the morning and afternoon, whereas Rowell, who was trained by Charlie Barnsley, only exercised in the morning. One man who had trained there for a few days less, and was said not to be as punctual in his exercise, was George Hazael. Another, who had been in training for three weeks, and was reported to arrive about ten o'clock every morning, was the tiny Robert Vint. Noremac had only started his exercise regime a couple of weeks earlier. He was reported to do his own thing but rarely missed a day to train.

All the men would change into their walking costumes in a small apartment which was heated by a large stove adjacent to the track. Observers would marvel at the men's routines and comment on how different their running and walking styles were. Whilst training, the men would wear their running costumes atop heavy woollen underclothing. On the day the reporter went along for his story, Rowell wore a soiled and unattractive white shirt, Fitzgerald a blue flannel shirt with green trunks around his loins, and Vint, who was described as the neatest dresser, red, white and blue stockings and dark velvet tights.

On commencement of training they would all run at a brisk pace, their coaches not allowing them to stop until they got through their session. Rowell, Fitzgerald and Hazael were apparently encouraged to run between 14 and 16 miles whilst Vint and Noremac were seen to be covering 12. Fitzgerald and Hazael, who were said to be alike in build and style of running, were said to have *"lumbering awkward gaits."* Both were said to stride along with *"their shoulders stooped, heads thrust forward and chin elevated as if winded and gasping for as much air as possible."* Rowell, who was described as being *"strongly built,"* and *"small in stature, moved along with a steady determined but laboured trot,"* whilst Vint and Noremac, who were both small in stature too, *"skipped or hopped"* lightly over the sawdust.

The following conversations with some of the athletes took place at Wood's.

The conversation with Rowell:

Rowell: "I have never felt better in my life, and the very fact of my being in the race is proof that I believe I will win."

Reporter: "Are you not afraid that the machinery will break down, the same as your last race?"

Rowell: "I have the assurances of Sir William Gull, my physician, who is also physician to the Queen, that I am in excellent condition and able to undertake the run without any danger of breaking down."

Reporter: "Was the rumour which prevailed after your breakdown in New York, to the effect that you had the heart disease true?"

Rowell: "No, Sir William Gull said that my heart was alright; that I was only temporarily affected with palpitations which produced my weakness. I was under his direct care three months and was at the seaside five weeks after going to England that time."

Reporter: "What do you think was the cause of your sickness during the race of champions?"

Rowell: "I contracted malaria while training in New Jersey for the race."

Reporter: "And are you fully recovered?"

Rowell: "Yes, I never felt in better condition."

Reporter: "Why do you want to run again?"

A friend of Rowell: "He don't want to labour under defeat, that's the short and the long of it."

Rowell: "I suppose that's so. This race will be my last one, win or lose. I brought some horses with me and I intend buying a farm somewhere in the west and settling down. I am very fond of farming. I will make my home here and live the quiet life of a farmer. I have made 150 miles in 22 hours, the best on record, and in three days, I have covered over 350 miles, the best on record also."

The conversation with Fitzgerald and "Happy Jack" Smith:

Smith: "The machinery in Fitzgerald is in first class order, and there is not the remotest chance of its breaking down. We are working the hardest of any of the men, and we can stand it. I believe in hard training. We are working twice a day now, forenoon and afternoon, and we will likely work three times a day. I think this will be the greatest race that we ever had, and that we will be able to solve the problem of whether 600 miles cannot be covered by a man. It was only covered once."

Reporter: "Have you done much in the training line, Mr Smith?"

Smith: "I have been at it nearly all my life. You see I trained Hart, the negro, when he won $18,000. I trained him well. I was only paid $750 for my services, and do you know that the fellow, when he got his $18,000 never made me a present of a cent, although a well known sporting man counted me out $5,000 to me on my little table in the tent at Madison Square Garden, if I would throw the race. I told him that the building full of money could not induce me to do it."

Fitzgerald: "I ran in three six-day matches inside of nine months; so you can understand that I must have pretty good endurance. In the race in which Hazael made the 600 miles I came second, making 577 ½ miles. I made 583 miles in the American Institute. I finished a six-day run on New Years Eve, 1881, ran again in the following February, and seven months later ran in a third six-day race."

Smith: "As I said before, this will be the best race that we ever had and Fitz is the coming man. In the last race that Fitz won he did the most work in 84 hours on record."

When he was approached about his chances in the race, Hazael, who owned a saloon on Grand Street, and was rumoured to have a *"nice little bank account,"* said, "I'm in fine trim now and expect to win the match. The race is going to be a fine one, for we are all in good condition. Charlie is looking good, and I understand feels better than ever he did. Fitzgerald looks fine, and Vint and Noremac are in good condition."

Robert Vint, who owned a saloon on Fulton Street, Brooklyn and a farm on Long Island, said, "I am not over confident about winning the race, but I don't think I will be the last in it. My ambition is, anyway, to have Brooklyn represented. I will give a good account of myself.

All the above were considered financially comfortable. It was well known that Rowell was rich. He stayed at the Ashland House Hotel and had brought a fine blooded stallion and a mare with him. Fitzgerald had built himself a comfortable home in Astoria from his winnings. George Noremac owned a sporting saloon on Eighth Avenue, New York, and the business was said to be doing well.

The contest had to be cancelled because only Rowell and Fitzgerald had lodged their $500 stakes with the *Turf, Field and Farm* before the 4th of that same month. Of the collapse of the race, the *New York Times* wrote: **Rowell is especially anxious to meet Hughes and Hazael in this his last contest, in order to show that now, in restored health, he can win back from them, the laurels they won from him. This being his wish, the match has been declared off, and the stakes for a new match, to take place in April, are to be fixed at $300 each.**

The entry fee thereafter was further reduced to $100 and this lower figure later influenced quite a number of recognised pedestrians to make their deposits apart from Rowell and Fitzgerald. The articles of agreement had been be drafted and ready for signature at 3 p.m. on Monday, the 25th of February with entries for the race to be received no later than April the 1st at the *Turf, Field and Farm*.

By the 3rd of April, the other nine men entered were: Peter Napoleon Campana, Frank H. Hart, William Wallace Lounsbury, George D. Noremac, Daniel J. Herty, George Rains, Charles Thompson, Robert Vint, and Nit-Aw-E-Go-Bow who would be arriving in the city the week after. For some unknown reason, George Hazael was not one of them. The contestants represented three different races and five nationalities.

The Moseley Harriers, of Birmingham, England, had entered their trainer Sam Day, who at the time was quoted as being the "champion twelve hours a day pedestrian of England," into the race. On Saturday, the 5th of April he duly arrived in New York on the White Star steamship *Baltic*. Sam, who was born in Kingston-on-Thames in September of 1852, was described as being *"a stoutly built, florid complexioned Englishman, 5 feet 3 inches high, and weighs when in condition 128 pounds."* On his arrival he told reporters that he would go into training the day after on the track of the Manhattan Athletic Club. Up to arriving for the race, he had participated in 38 walking and go-as-you-please contests, in which he had won eight, been runner-up thirteen times, came third on seven occasions, and had been unplaced eight times.

By the 20th of April, the contestants in the race had been reduced to 14 due to the withdrawal of J. B. Russell, the *"half-breed Indian,"* who had given up the contest to attend to Nit-Aw-E-Go-Bow (two translations of his name were: "The-man-that-stands-where-the-land-meets," and "Man-Who-Has-Struck-a-Hard-Trail") who, *"last summer walked 350 miles in three days, without sleep, for a prize of six ponies."* The Chippewa Indian was a celebrated long-distance runner among his own people. He would now be trained by Mr. Finlay. Although he was said to have already been taking practice runs at Woods Athletic Grounds, he nevertheless complained of feeling somewhat stiff from *"his long confinement in the cars on his journey from Dakota."* He was confident that no white man could beat him, and his connections were further confident that he would cover 600 miles in the six days.

P. S. Marshall

(Illustration no: 96)

A reporter for the *New York Sun* wrote of what he witnessed at Wood's: **Nit-Aw-E-Go-Bow**, the Dakota delegate in the six day's race, is always ambitious, while running with the other men in training, to keep at the head of the line. Yesterday morning when Fitzgerald, winner of the last long distance race started in with the other racers he felt like having a brush with the Indian. Darting to the head of the procession he set a pace which soon left the old stagers in the rear. The Indian accelerated his gait and his good natured bronze face almost rested on the ex-alderman's right shoulder. This gave Fitzgerald the inside of the track; of which he has trained so much during the past few years that he can go around the sixty four turns to the mile at top speed blindfolded. He believed that he could shake the Indian off within five miles, but the red man of the forest stuck to him like a burr to a buffalo's mane, mile after mile, until twelve had been reeled off. Then Paddy, as the boys familiarly call the ex-alderman of Long Island City had enough of it. He dropped to the rear of the procession, and soon afterward disappeared in the dressing room. Rowell ran twenty miles without distress. Vint skimmed over eighteen. Noremac shows remarkable improvement; He ran sixteen miles as light footed as a greyhound and was to repeat the performance in the afternoon. He is becoming a favorite among the sporting fraternity for first honors in the race. The grounds were packed again yesterday thousands coming and going while the pedestrians were running. When exciting brushes occurred, shouts from the spectators could be heard blocks away.

Robert Vint and Charles Thompson were being trained respectively by James Smith and George Wilson. Thompson appeared overworked, but it was stated that the reason for this was *"a peculiarity of his physique."* The other two Englishmen in the race, Sam Day and Alf Elson, were promising to be in the front rank towards the end of the race. Harry Hill. Jr., was attending to the latter's preparations in Flushing. John Sullivan, of Saratoga, Campana, George, the short-distance runner, Lounsbury and Hart were also reported to be *"actively preparing for the struggle."*

That being the case, there was a smashing match in prospect when it was confirmed on the 13th of April that the event was booked to start on Monday, the 28th of April and end on the following Saturday, the 3rd of May, between the champions of pedestrian matches held in the past six years. The winner would receive the sweepstakes plus fifty per cent of the gate money after expenses had been paid. The other fifty per cent would be divided amongst the finishers who would have to complete 525 miles. The second placed man would get 20%, third, 12%, fourth, 8%, fifth, 6%, sixth 4%, and seventh, 2%.

During the afternoon of Friday the 25th, the competitors met in the ballroom adjacent to the building in order to draw lots for the huts they would be occupying during the race. The huts would be situated on the Fourth Avenue side of the Garden. Hut number one began at the Twenty Seventh Street side and the hut number would be displayed on the chests of the athletes. The result was: 1, **Hart**; 2, **Sullivan**; 3, **Noremac**; 4, **Vint**; 5, **Rowell**; 6, **Thompson**; 7, **Nit-Aw-E-Go-Bow**; 8, **Elson**; 9, **Panchot**; 10, **Lounsbury**; 11, **Herty**; 12, **Fitzgerald**; 13, **Campana**; 14, **Harnes** (did not start); 15, **Day**:

The day before the start, after the workmen had finished their respective jobs, the residing judges declared the track the best in the country. It had been carefully measured by City Surveyor, George C. Holleritch, who found it to be seven-eighths of an inch over an eighth of a mile.

King of the Peds

Because of previous complaints, and in order to prevent the contestants from being interfered with, like having to endure tobacco smoke being blown into their faces by spectators whilst they ran past, the track was railed off by a picket fence. There would be a smoking ban on the Twenty Seventh Street side of the amphitheatre which would be reserved for ladies and families, and where *"no gentlemen will be admitted there unless accompanied by ladies or children. Instrumental concerts will be the rule every afternoon and evening."* Indeed the entertainment starting on the Sunday night at 9 p.m. would be provided by a 40-piece band under the directorship of Mr. Ned Innes, a trombone soloist who was hired to conduct the Brighton Beach Orchestra for the summer months.

Inevitably the *New York Times* described some of the scenes the paying spectator would encounter on admission to the building: In the semi-circle of the arch over the east end of the Garden is hung the bulletin upon which the records of the walkers are to be displayed to the admiring spectators. Entrance is obtained to the inner space within the ring by a broad flight of stairs at the west end of the Garden which lead up over the track and deposit the spectator upon the main floor; or, if he be religiously inclined, he may turn up the path to his right and he will find himself within the precincts of the restaurant whose refreshing bar extends the entire length or the southern side or the building and is relieved at regular intervals by handsome bar-tenders with big diamonds and welcoming smiles. In the centre of the Garden, bordering on the northern side of the track, a big wooden cage has been built for the scorers and reporters, and on the opposite side of the sawdust, facing the seats, is the starting-point and the bulletins upon which each pedestrians record is kept. A handsome clock six feet high with a mahogany case swings its great brass pendulum before the bulletins, and a telephone hangs on the opposite pillar, by which the records are transmitted by each mans scorer to the recording angel at the big bulletin in the east end of the Garden.

On the day of the race, the following advertisement appeared in the *Brooklyn Daily Eagle*:

MADISON SQUARE GARDEN.
TO-NIGHT
THIS SUNDAY, April 27th
GRAND SACRED CONCERT!

Commencing at 9 o'clock, preceding

THE START OF THE RACE
COMMENCING MONDAY. April 28, at 12:05 A. M., or
FIVE MINUTES AFTER MIDNIGHT THIS SUNDAY
NIGHT
THE RACE OF CHAMPIONS
SIX DAYS GO-AS-YOU-PLEASE

The Great Trombone Soloist, late of

GILMORE'S BAND

FRED N. INNES, and his new

GRAND MILITARY BAND OF ONE HUNDRED.
ADMISSION TO CONCERT AND RACE, 50 CENTS,

Seats reserved for ladies. No extra charge.

THE GREATEST RACE AND MOST EXCITING
START THE WORLD HAS EVER KNOWN.
CHARLES ROWELL, THE ENGLISH CHAMPION
NIT-AW-E-GO-BOW, INDIAN RUNNER.

The entries contain a stronger array of pedestrians than any former event.

PATRICK FITZGERALD, ROBERT VINT,
GEORGE D. NOREMAC, FRANK H. HART,
DANIEL J. HERTY, PETER N. CAMPANA,
WM. W. LOUNSBURY, SAMUEL DAY,
JOHN SULLIVAN, ALFRED ELSON,
PETER J. PANCHOT

ADMISSION TO GARDEN, 50 CENTS

On the morning of the race, the *New York Times* prepared its readers for the forthcoming event: **Preparations were completed yesterday for the six-day's go-as-you-please match, which begins at 12 o'clock to-night. The tanbark, loam, and sawdust track was put in condition for the final touches today. The men who looked at it yesterday afternoon for the last time prior to their entrance tonight, said that it could not well be improved. "If it's as good as Rowell's condition," said an Englishman, who has his money wagered on the race, "it's all right."**

Rowell is said to be in excellent form. He ate a hearty supper last evening at the Ashland House, and at an early hour went to bed for his last night's uninterrupted rest. To make free with the flowing English of one of his bankers, "Ees goin' in to win you know," His food will be prepared in the kitchen of the Ashland House under the special supervision of his trainers, when will be given the freedom of the whole place.

Nit-Aw-E-Go-Bow, the Indian, ate a very able bodied supper at the Putnam House and retired early in the evening. He is said to be in almost perfect condition. In speaking with a friend after supper he said that he fully appreciated the work before him, but that he wanted to go in and do his best. He expects to suffer much from an unruly stomach, which has already shown symptoms of a dislike for tobacco smoke and impure air. He does not go into the race with the confidence that he still win first prize. He will simply do his level best. A well-known sporting man who has staked his money on the Indian, said late last evening that the managers of the race looked upon Nit-Aw-E-Go-Bow as the principal advertising card, and that the effort would, no doubt, be made to keep him running during the first two or three days of the race, in order that he may get far in advance of the others, and so attract a large crowd to the Garden. Campana, Herty, and Sullivan were sleeping peacefully at the Putnam House, opposite Madison-Square Garden, at midnight. The other pedestrians were scattered about the city.

The champion Rowell was the even money favourite to win the race. He had recently been running and walking up to 50 miles a day and had spent a lot of time training at the American Institute Building in Manhattan. He appeared very well, in excellent condition, and was said to be "really looking forward to the race." He was asked whether the 575-mile mark would be made. With a smile on his face he said, "Well, I can say this, and see if I don't speak the truth, the man who wins the race has got to be a good man, and he will have to make at least six hundred and twenty-five miles, because there are plenty of good men entered, who can easily make five hundred and seventy-five miles; and this will be my last race."

Fitzgerald priced at 3/1, was said to be in good condition. Like Rowell, he had been totting up the same amount of mileage during training, and had based himself at Wood's Gymnasium in Brooklyn. He stated he would need to cover 600 miles if necessary to win. He was, however, 38 years old, and there was some doubt that he could regain his form of old. This angered Fitzgerald and he was determined to prove everybody wrong in their negative assumptions of him. Peter Panchot, the Buffalo postman, stated he was going to run the race of his life. He appeared very well and in excellent condition too. Sullivan was said to have improved recently. Noremac at 3/1 was one of the bookies' favourites, especially for those frequenting the pool rooms of the city. An old veteran of the game said to a reporter, "Look at the Scotchman will you. He moves like a locomotive. There is no jar or jerk to him. I'll wager that he will win the race, for he's plucky, and will hold out to the last." The dark horse of the race was said to be Charles Thompson, whose only claim to fame was making 420 miles in an 84-hour contest at the Chatham Square Museum several years earlier.

One of the greatest attractions of the race however, was Nit-Aw-E-Go-Bow. *"He is a beautiful specimen of copper-colored manhood, only 19 years old with the figure of an Apollo. He has been educated and speaks English without a trace of the Indian accent."* Claiming to have made a record of 342 miles in three days over the plains, he stated that he was *"the only real*

King of the Peds

American in the race," and considered *"that no white man has the ghost of a show against him."* Richard Macnamara would assist Russell in the charge of the *"headstrong young aborigine."* The Indian scout who was visited by a *"great medicine man from the west,"* prior to competing in the big race, was reportedly also to be visited by a band of Indians, who would give him a grand salute of war whoops before the off. He was 8/1 to win the race, as was Sam Day.

The judges' and scorers' stand was in the centre of the north side of the building facing the track. The scorers' blackboard was at the east end of the track, and a telephone was installed to facilitate instant communication amongst all concerned. The judges were Messrs. Leslie Bruce and L. E. Myers. Colonel Hamilton Busby had been selected as referee and the scorers were: Harry Fredericks, J. L. Lambrecht, M. Johnson, F. S. Peixotte and A. Camachs, all of the Manhattan Athletic Club; Frank P. Murray and Charles Todd of the Williamsburg Athletic Club; J. Fennersey, John Rayner, Arthur Hazenfort, R. Bauer and T. Reporteruinn of the Pastime Athletic Club, and finally, S. F. Gursay, F.A. Coulter, C. L. Clusher, A. S. Young, C. R. Young and G. W. Young of the Jersey City Athletic Club.

A committee of medical experts would observe the competitors in the race from start to finish, and would examine each man whenever he left the track.

Hart, who had arrived in New York the previous night, stated he intended to win the race but sent word at the last moment that he couldn't take part as he had joined the coloured baseball team in Chicago. William Burrell, another black athlete who had been training for the race for the past couple of months took his place in the line-up as his substitute; so whether Hart had paid Burrell's entry fee is a mystery.

Each contestant was given 10 tickets for the match. A genuine ticket had been created, and many counterfeits were reproduced. However, all tickets bought outside of the building would prove useless for admission, their owners being refused and turned away at the gate.

The pedestrians' accommodations consisted of a set of small huts, all of which had one room, which had been erected at the east end of the building. During the afternoon some of the competing pedestrians went along to the track to inspect it, with some indulging in a more practical test of its condition by taking a little run over its surface. Whilst they studied its qualities, their attendants and trainers were administering the final touches to their men's accommodation by carrying in all the objects they would need to care for their respective competitors, including mattresses, pillows, sheets, gas stoves and crockery, along with medical preparations and other items.

The relaxed and *"rather handsome"* figure of the 26-year-old Dan Herty spent most of the afternoon in the Garden. His room was said to have been furnished with, *"a luxury carpet, a big bath tub, ice box, oil stoves, a trunk of sponges, towels and brushes, and a lot of provisions."* George Noremac's business partner, A. L. Balmer, meanwhile, ensured that the Scotsman would have *"the most attractive façade in pedestrian row,"* by securing a gorgeous floral "N" to the outside of his dwelling.

The 50-year-old *"Clown of the walking matches,"* Campana, had sat fidgeting upon the narrow cot provided for him within his tiny house. Upon the door he had nailed a horseshoe and over this were inscribed the words, "Clinton Engine. Old 41 Stag." The *"tall, elastic figure,"* with *"wrinkled bronzed features,"* said, "I'm entered by the city of Bridgeport, and I'm going to do that city honour, if I am a New Yorker born and bred. I tell you just where I've got the best of the rest of these fellers. They've got to sleep, and I'm going to keep on the track all the week with the exception of six hours. I've given myself just one hour each day for rest, and so I shall be on the track a hundred and thirty-six hours out of the hundred and forty-two, which is the only way I can win. The rest of 'em are faster than I am, but I'm the toughest. I got trainers that I can depend on, too. I never allow a trainer to dictate to me; all they will have to do will be to take care of me when I come off the track and wake me up after my hour of sleep each day."

"Come back here!"

The National Police Gazette (Illustration no: 97)

As early as seven o'clock that evening, the braver boys in a gang which had collected outside the building were already making their ascents up the walls towards the roof, where they hoped to view the race below.

When the gates were finally opened at eight, there was a sufficient throng of *"gaily dressed women and swell young men"* to fill the reserved boxes to wait patiently for the fun to begin four hours later. At 21:30, the band began the entertainment with, "The Skids are out today," which so enlivened the crowd that, *"the dudes pounded with their canes, the women clapped their hands, and the unwashed stamped in unison."*

All the pedestrians arrived early and lost no time in taking possession of their several huts, where they donned their racing gear in which they reclined until told to get ready.

The colours which the men would don that first night would be: **1. Burrell:** Blue and white. **2. Sullivan:** Flesh-coloured tights, red trunks. **3. Noremac:** (120lbs) the "plaid of the Camerons." **4. Vint:** Black tights and trunks. **5. Rowell:** (140lbs) *"Guards colours."* **6. Thompson:** White pants, blue trunks and cap. **7. Nit-Aw-E-Go-Bow:** Blue tights, white belt and cap, and a blue shirt. **8. Elson:** White and black velvet trunks. **9. Panchot:** (128lbs) Red drawers, brown and blue trunks. **10. Lounsbury:** Dark blue and white shirt. **11. Herty:** (150lbs) All red with black trunks. **12. Fitzgerald:** (165lbs) Green cap, blue trunks, red drawers. **13. Campana:** Flesh coloured shirt, blue tights, white cap. **15. Day:** Moseley Harrier's colours consisting of a white jersey, with a black gate upon the breast, black cap.

As the time approached, and an hour from the start, the Garden was entertaining about 8,000 people, many of whom were forcing tobacco smoke into its atmosphere from their lungs, thus creating a *"nebulous gloom above the community,"* the catalyst of which was provided by hundreds upon hundreds of lit cigars.

As the minutes ticked away and the beer flowed in the bar-rooms, Rowell made his way on to the track accompanied by the pugilist Charlie Mitchell. The sight caused quite a commotion with the excitable crowd, and this was further exacerbated when Campana came out to give an exhibition walk after the band had whetted the appetites of the crowd with "Yankee Doodle" and "Irish Patrol." Nit-Aw-E-Go-Bow, dressed in full Indian costume, then made his appearance and caused a real sensation, particularly amongst the small boys in the crowd who howled their approval. A group of his fellow tribesmen sat in a box overlooking the track, and the rumour was that they had come along, *"armed to the teeth and determined to see fair play for their compatriot."*

The start was made at 12:05 a.m. Campana started off with the lead, which he soon relinquished to Noremac who made the first mile in 6m.40s. Rowell was a yard away in second, then Fitzgerald, with Herty close up. The second mile was made in the same order. There was no change in the third mile. The Indian was going along at a fine loping trot which kept him close up, and in the fourth mile he was in sixth place with Noremac still in the lead. At 01:00, the score stood: **Day, Elson, Fitzgerald, Herty, Noremac, Rowell and Sullivan, 8; Vint, 7.7; Thompson, 7.5; Campana and Lounsbury, 7.3; Nit-Aw-E-Go-Bow, 7.2; Panchot, 7:**

It was estimated the attendance between eight o'clock in the evening and two o'clock in the morning to be in the region of 13,000. Sullivan up to that point had been in his hut for half an hour, but the others had taken scant opportunities to rest. Noremac, who had been in front up to the 27th mile, then left the track. His lead was taken over by Herty who was followed by Rowell. Noremac returned at 03:29 but was already six laps behind the leaders.

King of the Peds

Ten minutes later Herty departed giving the signal to Rowell to turn up the heat on the rest and he became the new leader at 28 miles. At 04:30, many of the 1,000 or so spectators watched intently as the contestants, who were now taking things more easily on the track after the frenzied opening hours when the pace was more frantic, were now walking.

When the city was fully awake, there was only one subject that New Yorkers were discussing, and that was the race at the Garden. Meanwhile, on the track at 08:13, Day spurted and left the rest 5 laps behind. The injection of pace didn't last long and Rowell took the advantage at 08:30 when he went three laps in front of the chasing pack. At 10:00, Noremac started to really quicken for about six laps and his fans urged him to take the lead, but he contented himself to a slower trot thereafter.

Nit-Aw-E-Go-Bow, the *"Bona Fide American,"* who was brought into the contest as a side attraction, and who was running in paint and feathers, was struggling. He appeared off-colour and was having trouble with his right leg. Some said he wouldn't last the day. Others said he would get a second wind. Whatever, he was popular with the crowd; his bright appearance and fancy costumes making him attractive with the *"fairer sex"* who urged him forward. *"He is a handsome lithe young fellow, and keeps on with his work utterly oblivious of applause and admiration."* He seemed to enjoy the tunes played by the band, and when the cornetist played, "See that my Grave's Kept Green," he dashed away and kept going at a fast pace for three miles.

Herty went well in the morning putting in some lively spurting. Sam Day, the trainer of the Moseley Harriers carrying his club's emblem of a swing gate on his back, trotted continually. Rowell, who was said to look remarkably like Day, and who could have been mistaken for his brother, followed the blonde "Brummie" around. He looked straight ahead with his eyes on Day in front. Sam's eyes however, wandered around the place as he continually surveyed and chatted to the both the spectators and scorers.

The morning scores on the first day:

AM	3		4		5		6		7		8		9		10		11	
	M	L	M	L	M	L	M	L	M	L	M	L	M	L	M	L	M	L
Rowell	23	3	30	2	37	1	43	3	49	4	56	1	62	7	68	5	74	2
Day	23	2	30	3	37	4	43	2	49	2	56	0	62	7	68	1	74	0
Noremac	23	3	29	0	35	7	42	3	48	2	54	4	60	5	65	1	70	5
Fitzgerald	22	5	29	3	34	7	41	3	47	3	53	4	59	0	64	6	70	4
Elson	23	3	29	1	34	3	39	7	44	1	49	5	53	5	59	1	64	7
Herty	23	3	29	6	34	2	39	8	43	7	49	0	55	4	58	5	63	5
Vint	22	3	26	6	31	7	37	4	42	0	46	4	52	5	56	7	60	6
Panchot	21	0	27	0	30	0	34	2	39	5	46	2	47	7	53	3	59	3
Thompson	20	6	24	4	27	3	31	4	33	5	39	2	44	0	48	1	48	5
Ebow	20	0	24	0	28	8	33	3	36	5	40	4	44	1	46	7	48	3
Burrell	19	3	23	3	25	1	28	1	32	2	35	2	39	2	42	7	47	4
Campana	17	5	20	1	22	6	27	4	31	6	35	7	39	0	42	3	46	6
Sullivan	17	4	20	7	26	0	29	2	31	2	36	1	38	1	43	0	46	5
Lounsbury	17	3	21	6	25	6	28	5	32	6	37	1	41	0	45	3	46	4

At 12:07, Rowell stepped into his booth having achieved 81 miles. There he stayed till 12:40 and by 13:00 he was three miles behind his fellow countryman who was the first one in the race to knock up the century at 15:29, after which the band celebrated by playing, "He is an Englishman." The *New York Times* described the race leader thus: Day is a well built fellow, about 5 feet 3 inches in height, with the chest, arms, and legs of an athlete and an enduring pair of lungs. He is not by any means such an easy, graceful walker as Rowell. He swings his arms vigorously and appears to work very hard, but his trainer's declare that he doesn't. It is a prevalent belief, though, that he is going altogether too fast to hold out. Rowell achieved the same feat at 15:57; and when Fitzgerald made his ton, he *"grinned and whooped."*

As the sun disappeared and the Garden became cold, the contestants put extra garments on to keep themselves warm. Lounsbury, the Chicagoan, was the first to hang up his running costume having scored 48 miles. Apparently, *"he lay groaning on his bed with pain all the afternoon, "throwin' up," as his trainer expressed it. At 6:35 he threw up the sponge."* As the poorly lad suffered in his small and poorly ventilated room, the air inside would have been *"thick with the fumes of liniments, washes and hot stimulants,"* smells which were far more welcoming than the awful tobacco smoke that William's mother had blamed for her son's plight and his early demise from the race.

On the track, the men went about their business in a cordial manner. *"They were perfectly friendly and as playful as kittens."* Already the leading men in the race were being given floral gifts by their many female admirers. Day made his way round the place sporting a red rose pinned to his chest, and Rowell carried a bunch of violets for a few furlongs. Whilst Elson shone under the bright electric lights in a new orange costume, Fitzgerald was observed to be the sorest man on the track. The Irishman, who appeared uneasy when walking, had to revert to a type of trot in order to keep going. Campana, always one to bring a smile to people's faces, wore a waistcoat that was far too big for him. He enjoyed the reaction he got and grinned and shook his fist at the crowd when they mocked him. He was strangely quiet, and although insisting he would be there until the end of the race, he actually semi-retired from it when his score was 71 miles, where in the comfort of his cabin he, *"would grunt, and writhed in the agonies of colic."*

Day, who was getting a little leg weary by half past ten, still persevered in his attempt to regain second place from the sleeping Fitzgerald who had gone to bed at 22:15. Panchot found the going easier than the rest, bowling along in his own trot-like gait doing what he normally did and chewing at a toothpick. Elson meanwhile, conveyed himself along like *"clock-work."* Rowell moved along employing his relentless but effective dog-trot, usually on the heels of another competitor. He later indulged in little races with the colourful little Indian, despite having very little rest during the first day. The leader was 9 miles ahead of Fitzgerald when he went to bed at 23:50, whilst Herty proved what a plucky young chap he was by making 120 miles without a break.

Some more scores during the afternoon, early and late evening and midnight:

PM	12		13		14		18		21		24	
	M	L	M	L	M	L	M	L	M	L	M	L
Rowell	80	2	82	6	88	4	107	5	120	4	135	0
Fitzgerald	75	1	79	5	85	4	107	2	119	5	126	0
Day	80	5	86	0	91	4	106	3	116	1	125	0
Noremac	74	2	80	2	83	4	95	3	110	0	120	7
Panchot	64	5	70	1	74	0	92	0	109	2	123	5
Herty	68	3	74	1	79	1	100	0	114	2	120	0
Vint	66	5	70	0	74	6	94	0	105	3	116	1
Elson	69	4	73	5	78	0	94	0	104	2	113	7
Burrell	50	0	52	5	57	3	71	0	84	3	96	3
Thompson	54	1	58	5	60	4	78	0	86	0	95	0
Lounsbury	46	4	46	4	46	4	46	4	Ret			
Nit-Aw-E-Go-Bow	52	4	55	4	59	0	73	0	83	0	94	5
Sullivan	51	0	53	2	57	0	70	0	78	0	78	0
Campana	50	5	53	2	57	4	69	0	71	1	71	1

Fitzgerald returned from a 2h.50m period of slumber which meant he had notched up a grand total of 5h.10m of rest time since the start of the race. Vint had slept from 23:23 till 02:17, and Rowell continued on his journey just before 03:00 having spent 3h.8m on his back. Employing his familiar dog-trot to eat up the laps, he was soon accompanied by Fitzgerald, Noremac and Herty who went round the ring with him in Indian file, whilst Panchot and Burrell (who rested for 3h.13m during the night and was never seen to say a word to any of his foes on the track), preferred to keep their own company on the path.

The "Bona Fide American" made his re-appearance at 04:20, and although being given lots of encouragement to make his mark on the race, soon sought the comfort of his hut after covering a paltry two miles. Another athlete in the doldrums was Day who initially, and on his return to the fray, had appeared the freshest man on the track.

King of the Peds

However, at 04:30 he came to a halt before the scorers' stand and said to the sitting officials, "Boys, I am afraid I cawn't run any more. I've 'urted my knee, y'know, and it's a hawfully bad thing." Despite his plight, the Brit made his way round for a few more laps; but giving the idea up of carrying on any further, opened up the door of his wooden hut and went inside. At 05:15, Sullivan announced to the scorers, "You can put me on the retired list." He was the second man in the contest to give it up, owing to stomach problems, having made just 78 miles.

The early morning scores till 10 a.m:

AM	3		4		5		6		7		8		9		10	
	M	L	M	L	M	L	M	L	M	L	M	L	M	L	M	L
Rowell	137	0	142	2	147	1	152	2	157	7	163	4	169	3	174	7
Fitzgerald	133	2	137	3	141	4	146	0	149	6	155	2	160	6	165	3
Noremac	130	0	135	1	138	6	143	7	149	4	152	1	157	4	160	0
Herty	129	7	134	0	138	6	143	0	148	2	152	4	158	1	162	0
Panchot	125	0	125	3	129	6	133	6	137	7	143	0	148	4	152	4
Vint	119	0	123	0	126	0	131	0	136	0	139	0	144	5	150	1
Elson	114	6	120	3	125	4	129	2	134	7	139	5	143	0	147	6
Day	131	1	131	6	132	4	132	6	132	6	136	0	138	0	138	3
Thompson	100	9	104	2	105	0	105	0	106	6	110	0	112	6	113	6
Burrell	100	0	102	7	107	5	110	6	115	5	118	0	121	3	124	7
Nitaw	100	0	100	0	102	3	102	3	102	3	102	3	102	3	102	3
Campana	71	1	71	1	71	1	71	1	71	1	71	1	71	1	71	1

Nit-Aw-E-Go-Bow, who slept for a long time during the night, was, as a consequence well down the field on his return to the ring later in the morning. On recommencing his tramp, he looked well but wasn't seen to be running quickly or "spurting," instead concentrating on steadily trotting around the track. *"It was current talk that the management paid him a little something to keep jogging around as a side attraction. His bright appearance and fancy costumes kept him popular with the women, but he was as stoical and indifferent to their attentions as any wooden representative of his race in a Broadway cigar store."*

Alfie Elson, whose backer in the race was the well known sporting man Harry Hill, plodded along saying nothing leaving his trainers to state his performance later in the week would do the talking for him. He had rested for three hours before noon was up.

Noremac, who earlier had took about six laps to warm up, and who at seven o'clock had been just a couple of laps away from taking second place in the race, was in fourth position at noon. *"He is not by any means a handsome fellow, but beauty doesn't count in a contest like this. He is light and strong, and moves along with a springy step which augurs well for a good position at the close."* Herty meanwhile, though not a graceful runner or walker, raced along in third, his style and pace being the same as when he started.

The *New York Times* compared the various styles of some of the men in the race starting off with Rowell: **He keeps his shoulders and head well back as he runs, so as to get the fullest amount of breathing room. Fitzgerald, on the contrary, with his extremely bad stoop and contracted stomach, hardly gives his lungs fair play. Day has the biggest calves of any man on the track, and is more fully developed above the waist. But he handles his feet and arms very clumsily. Herty's square heel-and-toe stride reminds one of O'Leary. He walks with the whole centre of his body, from the waist to his knees, bent forward, and keeps his shoulders well back. Panchot springs along lively enough on the ball of his foot, but he has a thinness of flank and sunken appearance at the waist which does not indicate endurance. The Indian is a well formed fellow, but the present strain on his stomach is proving too much for him.**

Rowell was the first man to break the 200-mile barrier at 14:44; whilst Campana, who insisted that his name stay up on the telegraph board, sat on a chair in his hut complaining of the pain in his right leg. Meanwhile, between the hours of one and three o'clock, Sam Day had added very little to his score owing to a strained tendon in his leg. His trainer though, rather than allow his man to retire, said he would try to "bolster him up to last the week" and try to make the coveted 525. As Day was sent back in to struggle round, the as ever impressive Rowell, who was in a different class to the rest of the field, continued to show just why he was considered to be the best at his chosen profession as he traversed the track at 6 mph. He was a good natured fellow and he showed this side of his personality as he stopped to receive a horseshoe made up flowers from a pretty little blonde haired girl, who he made blush as he threatened to kiss her, but only if he was allowed to climb over the fence adjacent to the track!

The resting times since the start of the race up until 18:00 on the second day were: **Rowell,** 6h.57m.30; **Fitzgerald,** 5h.17m.42s; **Noremac,** 4h.30m; **Panchot,** 7h.44m.30s; **Vint,** 9h.16m.15s; **Herty,** 5h.17m; **Day,** 9h.40m.50s:

The scores from 11 a.m. till 6 p.m:

AM/PM	11		12		13		14		15		18	
	M	L	M	L	M	L	M	L	M	L	M	L
Rowell	179	7	186	5	189	7	195	1	201	3	217	6
Fitzgerald	170	0	175	3	181	0	185	4	191	2	203	1
Herty	166	5	169	0	171	7	176	5	182	4	197	0
Noremac	165	2	170	7	174	7	178	5	183	7	198	0
Panchot	155	4	161	0	163	3	167	6	169	7	186	1
Vint	154	7	159	2	163	2	167	5	170	7	184	3
Elson	151	7	155	6	160	4	165	2	169	7	181	0
Day	140	1	142	7	144	2	144	2	147	2	154	0
Burrell	128	3	132	3	135	1	140	0	143	7	150	0
Thompson	117	1	117	2	123	0	126	6	130	6	144	1
Nitaw	106	3	109	3	110	0	110	0	110	0	110	0
Campana	71	1	71	1	71	1	71	1	71	3	71	1

The turnstiles clicked away merrily after six o'clock giving entrance to the many who had been working all day. As they entered the arena they would have seen Herty trying hard to gain third position in the race. His efforts to do so were made easier due to Noremac's enforced absence from the track due to a dodgy right knee. As the Scotsman rested, the American's praises were sung by the howling mob as he passed the scorers' stand to register his second hundred at 18:35.

Mr. Vanderbilt, owner of the Garden, watches proceedings with his friends.

The National Police Gazette (Illustration no: 98)

A few minutes after 19:00, Campana, now dressed in his civvies, stopped to have a chat with a bunch of reporters telling them, "I've been so disgusted and disheartened by the jibing of this 'ere crowd that I'm not going any further. As an old New York boy, I should have been treated with more consideration. I intended to make at least five hundred seventy-five miles when I started out, but now the d*** old show can bust up. I shan't help it any more."

Noremac re-entered the ring soon after Campana's name was taken off the board and took back his former position within half an hour of doing so. Thompson battled on, and Day carried on with the task of making sure that the ailing Burrell wouldn't make a laughing stock of him by demoting him to tail-ender. As all this was happening,

King of the Peds

Nitaw entertained his fans by running in reverse around the place before apparently breaking off to smoke a cigar in his cabin. Rowell went on to make 240.1 before calling it a day having made 105.1 since he left the comfort of his house in the morning. Whilst the rest snoozed, Burrell was the only man plodding round the track at midnight.

The midnight scores: **Rowell, 240.1; Fitzgerald, 226; Herty, 217.1; Noremac, 216.5; Panchot, 212.4; Vint, 211; Elson, 200; Day, 172.6; Burrell, 165.7; Thompson, 156.7; Nitaw, 125:**

Fitzgerald re-appeared on the track at 01:12 having slept for three hours. Initially he appeared wobbly, but soon worked off the stiffness in his legs. He then jogged along reducing the distance between himself and Rowell by three miles by the time the leader re-entered the arena at 01:43 having rested for 3h.33m. Rowell thereafter followed the Irishman around, but when he rested for the briefest of moments in his hut, "Fitz" started to run. Rowell then made up the lost ground after about six laps. As soon as Fitzgerald walked, Rowell followed suit, and thus for the first time in the contest, was seen to be employing his infamous stalking tactics always travelling about four feet behind his opponent. It was noted at the time that Rowell appeared the best in spirit and style and this was reinforced by comments from friends who stated he was in prime condition from his stomach to his feet, as his eyes were bright and face full.

Meanwhile, Day, who had taken 2h.43m rest between midnight and noon, appeared perkier on his return, engaging in banter with his scorer. Noremac had rested for 4h.43m after midnight. On his return he kept up the same jogging pace he said he would maintain till the end of the contest. Panchot slept for 2h.37m. On his reappearance he wasn't looking as good as he had been, but kept on with the task in hand. Herty's stride remained the same, and he appeared as well as could be expected. The Indian was finding the pace too hot and he was seldom seen on the track; his performance disappointing many.

As Elson plodded along, the weary Thompson retired at 07:25 having made 161.4, claiming he was suffering from a bad stomach. His withdrawal left nine of the original fourteen on the track, and that number was further reduced to eight an hour later when Burrell retired at 08:30. Apparently young Winston pleaded to be left alone after his four hours of sleep, and with his wish respected by his trainer, he later left the Garden stating, that for the last six miles he had competed, every step he took produced a stinging pain in his feet. After completing the 2nd lap of his 180th mile at seven o'clock, he complained that he couldn't walk without eating, and due to the fact that his backer abandoned him, and because his trainer had no money to buy his food, it was a pointless exercise. He told reporters, "Cheap hash and a few trimmin's and three glasses of beer a day won't do for a man in such race as this is."

The scores up until 10 a.m:

AM	3		4		5		6		7		8		9		10	
	M	L	M	L	M	L	M	L	M	L	M	L	M	L	M	L
Rowell	246	4	251	4	256	4	261	1	266	5	271	7	277	4	282	3
Fitzgerald	235	1	240	1	245	0	250	0	255	2	260	4	265	6	270	5
Herty	222	7	227	4	232	0	236	5	242	0	246	0	251	3	255	7
Noremac	225	2	229	2	234	0	236	5	241	0	245	4	250	0	254	4
Vint	215	1	220	0	225	1	229	5	234	1	239	0	243	0	247	6
Panchot	214	6	218	0	221	6	226	1	230	6	235	3	238	6	243	5
Elson	204	0	209	5	214	1	217	0	222	5	227	3	232	2	237	3
Day	182	6	187	1	191	0	191	0	195	2	199	6	204	0	208	3
Thompson	156	7	156	7	156	7	156	7	156	7	161	4	Ret			
Ebow	125	0	125	0	125	0	125	0	125	0	125	0	127	0	128	0
Burrell	170	0	170	6	175	4	180	0	180	2	Ret	0				

The weather got hotter during the day. The sun shining through the glass roof had a marked effect on the performing peds causing them to sweat profusely which necessitated frequent changes of clothing. At 13:24, Rowell made his 300th mile, and from thereon copied every mode of travel Fitzgerald indulged in including rest breaks. The strategy of course was quite simple. Rowell was 12 miles ahead; by employing these tactics to the end of the race, he couldn't lose could he?

At 15:39, Fitzgerald had the number "300" posted up next to his name, but the numbers next to Rowell's "312" reminded him that he had an awful lot of work to get through if he wanted replace the Englishman at the top of the blackboard. He started his task by offering Rowell the challenge of a run and Rowell took it up. The two then hit top gear for a few laps with Rowell inevitably winning the spurt due to his superior speed. The leader then went in for another rest at 16:05 which gave Fitzgerald a chance to reduce the arrears. Within 20 minutes of Rowell's departure he had gained 2 miles. His trainer shouted to him, "Better come in Pat and not try to do much." Patrick replied, "Let me alone. I'm alright." His trainer then told a reporter, "Talk about endurance! That man's tougher than hickory. His early training ain't gone for nothin'. If this was a good track, he'd be 50 miles better off by this time. There's too much sawdust on it." He then informed the press that he would make Rowell cover 600 miles and also gave some information about what they were feeding Pat during the event, stating that his diet was made up of beef tea, thin oatmeal, well beaten eggs and the occasional cupful of mustard and soda.

Nitaw went back on to the track at 16:25, and when the band saw him set off, they welcomed his renewed participation with "Sweet By and By." The *New York Times* commented about the participating pedestrian's favourite tunes: The resources of the band-master are tasked to their utmost. He has played every tune within the capacity of wind instruments over and over again, but he hasn't found one yet which suited the Indian. Rowell's favorite is "The British Brigade," Fitzgerald brightens up with "The Wearing of the Green," Noremac likes "The Campbell's are Coming," Panchot wants, "Marching through Georgia," while Day thinks he never heard a prettier tune than "The Star Spangled Banner." The Indian is only happy when the musicians are taking a rest. The trombone man played a solo yesterday, and he fled in dismay to his hut.

Rowell came back into the race at 16:45 and predictably stalked his rival. Referring to Rowell's tactics, Fitzgerald said to his trainers, "I'll make him follow me closer than that before the week is out." Whilst most of the men frequently wore eye catching nationalistic themed costumes, Fitzgerald was happy to trudge along in non-descript ones. For instance whilst Rowell liked to wear a Union Jack emblazoned shirt, and Noremac was partial to donning Scotch plaid knickerbockers and Vint exhibited the American flag on his cap, "Fitz," was happy not to wear a trace of green.

The scores from 11 a.m. till 6 p.m:

AM/PM	11		12		13		14		15		18	
	M	L	M	L	M	L	M	L	M	L	M	L
Rowell	287	6	292	2	297	5	303	3	308	7	321	0
Fitzgerald	275	7	280	3	285	5	291	0	296	3	313	3
Noremac	259	4	262	0	267	4	273	3	277	7	288	0
Vint	252	7	257	0	260	0	265	1	270	3	282	5
Herty	260	0	261	7	267	1	272	3	275	3	290	0
Panchot	247	6	251	0	255	1	260	6	264	3	278	2
Elson	241	4	244	7	249	1	252	7	256	7	268	0
Day	213	0	217	3	221	3	224	0	228	1	235	6
Ebow	128	0	128	0	128	0	128	0	128	0	130	0

With 7,000 people looking on, Herty made his 295th mile in a time of 8m.15s, but that would be easily be beaten by Noremac, who at 20:30, made his 300th in a fast time of 6m.40s whilst the band played "Bonnie Doon." The crowd were in their element and they squealed with pleasure at the sight of the *"flying Scotsman."* Vint followed that effort ten minutes later with his 3rd century as Noremac was admiring a handsome basket of flowers which had been given to him by a group of people from the Midlothian Society. Another man to get the floral treatment was Ebow who received a bunch from an unknown person. The greeting read, "To Sitting Bull," with the clever message referring to the amount of time that player sat on his backside. Whilst Fitzgerald enjoyed a rest to drink a bottle of *"labeled water"* and accept a bouquet at 22:10, Rowell leant up against a fence and waited for him to recommence his tramp.

It was learned from Day's trainers at 23:00 that their man, who had been off the track since 18:18, would no longer be continuing; the reason for his failure being a *"disordered stomach and swollen limbs."* On waking from a deep sleep,

King of the Peds

he suffered symptoms of severe colic and cramps. *"His defeat leaves him without a dollar to pay incurred expenses, to say nothing of getting home. His backer said that the fault was in his training. He never considered it necessary to practice more than 25 miles a day."*

At 23:05, Fitzgerald sought the comfort of his tent. He had been out for 22 hours during which time he had made 110 miles, a new record for the third day in a six-day event. Rowell had covered an impressive 106 and Vint had scored 99, even with a sore knee.

The midnight scores: **Rowell, 346; Fitzgerald, 336; Noremac, 312.1; Vint, 310;Herty, 306.4; Panchot, 302; Elson, 286.2; Day, 237; Nitaw, 136.3:**

And the latest odds at that time: **Rowell, 1/2; Fitzgerald, 8/5; Noremac, 5/1; Vint, 10/1, Panchot, 20/1; Elson, 100/1; Ebow, 200/1:**

Fitzgerald had had been off the track from 22:10 to 01:54, and on returning, proceeded to trot along. The Limey's trainers woke up their man immediately. Rowell, who had rested for 2h.36m, quickly got himself dressed, threw a drink down his neck and resumed his "dogging" tactics for about 6 laps; after which time "Fitz" turned the heat up on him by sprinting away. Rowell managed to keep up with him for one lap and one lap only, and unable to keep up with his pace, gradually fell back. Fitzgerald kept on running, but Rowell, apparently dispirited by his failure, could only walk. *"His eyes were sunken and it was evident he was in poor condition."* From there on, the ex-Alderman closed the gap between them both with his relentless pace.

At 03:20, Rowell, having made 355 miles, returned to his hut where he stayed for 59m.55s. His rival on the track however spun round it at a rate of 6 mph, and by 04:00 was just 2 miles behind the race leader. The Chesterton man went on to make a further 8 miles before leaving the track on a score of 362.7 for 1h.38m at 06:00 with his pursuer now just a few laps behind. While Rowell slept, his trainers were visibly upset because unbeknown to the slumbering Brit, Fitzgerald had overtook him and was 4 miles in the lead when he woke up. That there was to be a significant change in the fortunes of the two leading players at this stage of the race would have been beyond comprehension just 12 hours earlier. The small number of spectators watching went wild when the new race leaders name went to the top of the scoreboard, and it was said that they made more din than ten times their number.

The early morning records from 3 a.m. till 10 a.m:

AM/PM	3		4		5		6		7		8		9		10	
	M	L	M	L	M	L	M	L	M	L	M	L	M	L	M	L
Fitzgerald	349	6	350	2	354	6	360	5	366	0	370	7	377	1	381	6
Rowell	353	1	355	4	357	6	362	7	362	7	365	5	371	7	376	5
Noremac	325	4	329	4	333	1	337	2	341	5	344	4	347	4	352	2
Vint	312	6	317	5	320	7	326	2	330	5	336	0	341	0	345	1
Herty	319	5	322	5	325	0	328	5	332	3	336	6	340	4	344	1
Elson	291	5	295	7	299	6	302	7	308	0	313	2	317	2	322	1
Panchot	305	2	308	0	313	1	316	7	320	0	324	3	329	3	332	3
Ebow	136	3	136	3	136	3	126	3	136	3	136	3	136	3	136	3

Ed Plummer, the official time scorer, ran on the track just after 10:40 and informed Fitzgerald that he had 16 minutes to make a mile and a lap, to beat the old record of 386 miles and 1,540 yards. Pat responded with a smile and proceeded to spurt for several laps and was thus able to accomplish beating the highest score for the 83rd hour made by Rowell in 1882 by making 387 miles at 10:58. Continuing on his way at a staggering 8 mph, he improved his score before taking a two-minute rest at 11:20. By midday, he was 5 miles ahead of the ailing Rowell. Noremac continued to trot along in third place and had achieved 360 miles at noon. Vint followed him on a mark of 353.7, and Herty, who was 2½ miles in his rear, was trying hard to gain his position. Interestingly Rowell had made the fewest miles in the 10-hour period before noon amongst any of the competitors, apart from Herty and Panchot; at 12:45, he took himself out of the game again, but this time to change into lighter clothing.

On his return Rowell had no answers to the machine-like action of his rival, who with a dazed stare that looked straight ahead, continually lapped him with precise regularity. *"His shoulders twitched at every step, and the veins on his brawny arms stood out like whip chords."* After every mile Fitzgerald would dunk his head into a pail of water placed next to the track and refused to waste energy by picking up the towel to dry himself off, instead choosing to continue with the water dripping over his bent shoulders.

News of the change of events at the Garden spread around the big city, and many thousands arrived to see for themselves the unfolding story. The managers were rubbing their hands together as they watched the ticket collectors rake in the cash. With so many in the building, it was decided to treat the customers with fresh air, and this rare luxury was facilitated by opening up the port hole windows and the sky lights in the glass roof. This gave the green light to the hundreds of mischievous boys milling around outside to concoct plans on how they should make their assaults on the now vulnerable building and gain admission to watch the famous Englishman, Rowell, getting well and truly annihilated inside by his adversary, "Fitz."

The *New York Times* was always on hand to tell its readers snippets of information about the past performing pedestrians, performing pedestrians, and those who looked after them: Of the men who started out in the race, but failed to keep up, Day, Thompson and Campana were around the building during the day. Thompson looked badly worn out. Day was in tolerably fair condition. "Me stomach is steadier, y'know but me legs is weak," he said. "Old Sport" and his trainer were reported to be waiting for means to get home with. A drunken sailor wandered into the Garden during the early morning hours and two sharpers got him into the bar-room. They were appropriating his watch and money when Campana came to the rescue. The sailor generously handed him $3. The trainer heard of it and started to look for his "man." He found him after a long search, and "Old Sport" generously handed out one-half of what was left. A little breeze disturbed the peaceful and perfunctory operations of the trainers. Rowell's trainer, Barnsley, told another trainer, who immediately communicated it to a third that "Happy Jack Smith," Fitzgerald's trainer, had stood in front of his door and used insulting language. Simmered down to bare facts, it seems that when the ex-Alderman put his name at the head of the list his trainer indulged in an exultant yell as he passed Rowell's quarters. Rowell's English trainers, in their flannel coats and jockey caps are rather inclined to look down on their shabbier, but well-meaning, co-laborers, as the journeyman barber loftily snubs the apprentice. The trainers are hardly more sociable than the pedestrians themselves, and that's saying a great deal. It was reported that Elson never uttered a word for seven hours. "Cheer up, old boy," said a friend who called on him with a bag of oranges. "I'm all right," was the answer; "but I'm walking, not talking."

Vint would eventually pass his closest rival in the race, Noremac, at 13:45, whilst Panchot ran along holding a wet sponge. The ex-postman's trainers, although not expecting him to win, nevertheless thought he could make somewhere in the region of 575 miles by the end of the match. The problem with his current performance, as was the case in other like contests, was his inability to keep down any food, and that ultimately was his downfall. That said, during the present race he had sustained himself on gruel and beef tea. One of the other Englishmen in the race, Elson, ran along in his stocking feet due to swollen insteps.

Fitzgerald made his 400th mile at 13:52. Rowell was now 5½ miles behind him. The Englishman looked a little better at this stage and was seen to take frequent swigs of *"Apollinaris"* water which was the in-vogue drink at the time. Rowell had to wait till just after three o'clock till he scored his 400 after which went back to his room for 35 minutes. During his rest, Ebow, who came back out to play in a new costume, stayed on the path for a short time, and went back to change. *The Indian lays on his couch like a nabob, and smokes chick-weed, while a devoted half-breed cools him with a bamboo fan and reads him the newspapers. When he gets tired of loafing he comes out and runs a mile or two.* On his reappearance he had a flower tossed at him by a cross-eyed girl but because he viewed the situation superstitiously, refused to pick it up. By 16:30 the leader, who was now a full eight miles ahead of his rival, decided to carry around a flower festooned horse shoe whilst the band played, "Little Widow Dunn."

King of the Peds

The scores from 11 a.m. till 6 p.m:

AM/PM	11		12		13		14		15		18	
	M	L	M	L	M	L	M	L	M	L	M	L
Fitzgerald	387	0	391	2	396	0	400	0	405	5	420	4
Rowell	381	1	386	1	390	1	394	7	399	7	412	4
Vint	350	0	353	7	358	6	363	6	368	7	381	3
Herty	346	4	351	5	356	1	360	1	362	6	374	6
Panchot	337	1	341	1	344	4	349	0	352	3	365	7
Noremac	355	6	360	2	363	0	363	0	366	0	380	0
Elson	326	2	330	0	333	4	338	0	343	2	350	0
Ebow	136	3	136	3	136	3	136	3	136	3	142	0

Noremac decided it was time for a rest at 6 p.m. so off he toddled to his shack to indulge in one. While he was out for the count, Vint stamped his mark on the 3rd place by extending the gap between him and the sleeping Scotchman by 10 miles. Meanwhile, the two leaders fought tooth-and-nail for superiority, each circumnavigating the ring at a steady 5 mph. Refusing to rest, Fitzgerald told his trainer, "Make me plenty of good strong beef tea, and I'll get over the ground." And get over the ground he did, but this time in the wake of Rowell who now was the one to be dogged. The Englishman though didn't appear too concerned that the roles had been reversed. On he plodded, occasionally having to crank up a gear, as his rival upped his pace by breaking into a long swinging stride in his pursuit of glory.

Before 9 o'clock thousands of people were standing four rows deep behind the railing surrounding the course. Many women were present and they waved their handkerchiefs, and fans threw *"nosegays"* at the feet of the busy pedestrians on the eight feet wide track.

The arrangements for upholding the rule for law and order that night was described by the *New York Times*: **Capt. Williams took up a squad of 80 policemen and stationed them about 20 feet apart along the edge of the sawdust race course. The wearied pedestrians passed and re-passed rows of glittering brass buttons and mischievous looking clubs. A guardian of the peace was perched on the wooden railing surrounding the army of musicians. A hundred more wandered around at will.**

And of the crowd inside: The down-town side of the building was packed close with a shouting crowd of men and boys. The up-town side was mostly filled with hundreds of excited gesticulating women and the men who were fortunate enough to accompany them. No man was admitted to the red leather cushioned chairs unless he was with a woman. Thousands of those present took no apparent interest in the race. They simply paid for the privilege of going in with the crowd and listening to the music.

The long ellipse-shaped promenade in the centre of the building was swarming with the same crowd of men who had been present all through the contest, the majority of them gambling on the strength of the men's legs and the quality of their grit. At the east end of the building, where the trainers' quarters are located, men were placed to keep an eye on the doors of the houses and report anything in the conduct of the walkers that might influence the betting. Not a movement of the men or their trainers escaped them. If a weary walker went in for a drink of beef tea or ginger ale, the bookmakers knew it. Odds of one hundred to twenty on Fitzgerald were offered, five to one against Rowell, and fifteen to one against Noremac and Vint.

The exhausted competitors kept trotting around the track, followed by shouts and cheers from thousands of throats. No attention was paid to what they said, but noisier men insisted on crying out, "Go it. Pat," "Keep close to him, Charlie," "Don't fake, Pete," and like encouraging or discouraging remarks, at the tops of their voices. Half-drunken enthusiasts pushed their way to the railing and tried to touch the pedestrians as they went by.

The little Scot, having rested and bathed, returned to the track at 21:09 and immediately set to work in trying to retrieve some of the 11 miles Vint had robbed him of. Ebow condescended to leave his abode to make a couple of miles, and Elson's feet were once again covering the ground with shoes on them. Panchot made a good showing between ten and eleven o'clock, and Vint made his fourth hundred at 22:50. As Fitzgerald was drinking a bottle of ginger beer, Rowell began to hurtle around the place at 8 mph. The leader dropped his drink and chased after him. Pat had travelled a quarter of a mile short of 112 on the fourth day, which was another record as well as being 14 miles ahead of the old one. He left the track at 23:30, Rowell doing likewise 20 minutes later, still trailing by nearly eight miles.

The midnight scores: **Fitzgerald, 447.6; Rowell, 440; Vint, 404.2; Herty, 395; Panchot, 392.3; Noremac, 392.3; Elson, 372.2; Nitaw, 150:**

Fitzgerald had been off the track between 23:51 and 02:30 the next morning. He appeared refreshed by his sleep, and when passing the scorers' stand he shouted out, "How do I stand?" When informed he was fully eight miles in the positive, he replied, "Good, he'll never catch me at this rate."

Rowell, for his part had left the Garden to indulge in a Turkish bath after which, he slept at Ashland House. He had been out of the ring for 3h.37m when he arrived back in the building to recommence his journey at 03:27, a full 13 miles in rear of his enemy. A rumour had been circulating around the Garden that Rowell had been carried there after vomiting blood, but it was only that, *a rumour*.

Vint had left the track seven times since midnight, the longest period for 1h.28m. Noremac followed the same tactics, his longest time out being 2 hours. Panchot had excused himself at 23:26 and 02:01. The ex-mail deliverer's gait was described *"as beautiful,"* his step being short, but light and elastic. His efforts had enabled him to catch Herty and go into fifth place, the capable Bostonian having rested for 2½ hours. A close fight was developing on the track between Vint, Noremac, Herty and Panchot with Noremac, who had been relegated down to sixth position during the latter part of the previous evening, gradually prevailing and re-taking the third position he had held earlier.

Many of the spectators who had witnessed the racing in the big crowd the night before stayed until four o'clock the next morning. As they left, others on their way to work at 5 a.m., including a group of labourers, decided to pop in and shout encouragement at Fitzgerald. The race leader would thereafter be dogged by his rival till 06:27 after which Rowell again rested for breakfast and a bath; the time taken, 1h.13m.

The leader saw his chance to go further ahead and whilst the English cat was away, boy, did the Irish mouse play, adding another six miles plus to the distance between them!

At 09:00, Fitzgerald headed towards his room to take a break. Watching him leave the track was Rowell who upped his tempo believing the Irishman would take a long nap. He was wrong. The leader came out after just five minutes, his trainer "Happy Jack," telling the reporter for the *New York Times* that his man was in fine condition and was quite able to do his work even with the minimal amount of sleep he was getting. He said that "Fitz" was always easy to wake. Smith was asked how *he* found time to sleep. With a resigned smile said, "I don't. I had less than three quarters of an hour yesterday afternoon, and that is all I have had since Sunday. It is difficult to remain awake so long and keep a clear head too, but it has to be done, and that's all there is to it. When there is excitement in the place it is all right." Of Rowell, Smith stated, "he is good for second place."

"What do we do to him?" said Smith, repeating the reporter's question. "Well, come inside and I'll show you."

He led the way into a badly ventilated room about 6 by 12 feet, lighted with an oil lamp. A camp bed covered with thick blankets stood in the centre, with a bath tub directly at the foot. A gallon can of beef tea steamed over a gas stove in one corner, while a dozen bottles of imported ginger ale were packed in a bucket of pulverized ice in the other. Bottles, tin tea-pots, sponges, and a variety of kitchen utensils littered the shelves and tables. Directly over the gas stove shirts, trunks, towels, stockings and handkerchiefs were found drying on a clothes line.

Smith continued, "When he comes in we strip him and tumble him into the bath tub, which is filled with water as hot as he can bear it. He lays flat on his back with his feet up on that shelf. A man gets on each side of him and rubs in a preparation to take the soreness out of his limbs."

"What is that preparation?" asked the *Times* correspondent.

"Oh, come now; it has taken me twenty-five years to find that out. After five minutes steeping we lift our man on the bed and wrap him up in hot cloths. An hour's sleep, a drink of beef tea or ginger ale, and away he goes again as fresh as a daisy. See? It's very simple."

King of the Peds

Meanwhile, his man was pounding the track, *"thin faced holding sunken eyes,"* a sure sign of the strain he was under. Rowell's trainers were hoping that Fitzgerald would weaken considerably owing to the miniscule amount of rest he was getting, and that their man would ultimately prevail. One of them was asked, "Do you think Rowell will be able to overtake him?"

"No, it doesn't look like it. Rowell is tired and needs sleep. There's no man in the world that can beat Fitzgerald. His endurance is simply wonderful."

"Was Rowell in his usual good trim when he began this race — that is, was he in as good condition as when he made his big record in England or when he made his first appearance in this city?"

"No, he was not."

The early morning returns from 3 a.m. till 10 a.m:

AM	3		4		5		6		7		8		9		10	
	M	L	M	L	M	L	M	L	M	L	M	L	M	L	M	L
Fitzgerald	450	0	455	6	460	2	465	3	470	5	474	5	479	5	483	6
Rowell	440	0	442	6	447	0	452	3	454	1	455	4	460	4	465	2
Vint	411	1	416	0	420	0	425	2	430	7	433	5	437	7	442	5
Noremac	406	4	411	1	414	6	420	1	424	1	429	0	433	6	438	4
Panchot	397	1	402	2	407	0	412	1	417	7	421	1	426	3	431	0
Herty	396	3	400	7	405	0	410	2	415	0	419	0	423	6	428	3
Elson	374	6	379	0	384	0	388	7	392	3	397	2	400	1	403	5
Ebow	150	0	150	0	150	0	150	0	150	0	150	0	150	0	150	0

The *Olean Democrat* described an incident involving the two leaders in its edition of the 3rd of May: Fitzgerald and Rowell, the leading figures in the pedestrian contest at the Madison Square Garden, had a lively brush this morning. It occurred about 10:30 o'clock. The Long Island City alderman was dreamily plodding along at a five mile an hour gait. He was on his 488th mile. Rowell had been in his hut for a few moments, and emerging from it started on a run to reduce Fitzgerald's lead of nineteen miles. The latter was, not aware of the little Briton's presence on the track until the cheers and applause of the thousand or more spectators notified him. Glancing up the track he beheld the little Englishman briskly speeding ahead of him. Setting his teeth he sailed in on a lumbering run to overhaul Rowell. For three laps the little Englishman led his pursuer and then succumbed. The ex-alderman smiled sardonically and assumed a no-you-don't expression when he dropped into a walk at his doughty opponent's heels. The failure to gain an inch upon the leader seemed to worry Rowell, and the hard lines in his face grew deeper and more marked.

At 12:30, "Fitz" was 5 miles ahead of the record and 19 ahead of Rowell. Noremac yet again regained the 3rd spot he had lost during the morning, and Vint's leg was bothering him so much that he left the track. Herty and Panchot competed with each other at a lively rate with Noremac following in their footsteps; and there was some commotion in the crowd when, after having a fit, a man fell in the north east corner of the building.

Fitzgerald completed his 500th mile at 13:20 and was now 6 miles ahead of the best record and 23 ahead of Rowell who had drifted out to 20/1 in the betting. At this point, the leader went to his house to rest for a period of 90 minutes. When he came back he continued on his quest to become "champion of the world." The fact that he had been doing so well in the race ensured that he was the recipient of a steady stream of gifts. One of those gifts was a basket of fresh eggs and another, a silver handled cane dressed in colourful ribbons, which was waved around in the air as he showed it off in front of the hysterical plaudits in the crowd.

Tom Davies, Fitzgerald's other trainer, in replying to a question as to how it was that his protégée stayed so long on the track and went so fast when he was there, said, "The winner will get more out of this race than anyone has done since Rowell first won the Astley Belt. That is the reason that Fitzgerald is making such a record. Besides this, he started out with the intention of beating George Hazael's record of six hundred miles in a hundred and forty-two hours. So you see it is a case of wealth and ambition."

Of the others, Panchot was looking *"tolerably bright,"* having managed to keep down the solid food that he had eaten earlier. Whilst Vint sweated in the heat of the day, Elson, wearing a new blue shirt, shyly struggled round. Alf kept himself to himself, and as always said nothing to no one as he plodded around. He became so embarrassed that someone had taken the trouble to present him with a basket of flowers that he hurried away with them and deposited them in his room. The reclusive chap was very rarely seen going as he pleased with any of the other competitors on the track, preferring instead to traverse the course half a furlong or so behind the rest. The old stager had a penchant for alcohol and was notorious for indulging in a tipple whilst competing. However, during this race, he indulged in only a little of the hard stuff, apparently only limiting himself to a drop of port the day before.

What the scoreboard said from 11 a.m. till 6 p.m.

AM/PM	11		12		13		14		15		18	
	M	L	M	L	M	L	M	L	M	L	M	L
Fitzgerald	489	2	493	7	498	2	500	1	505	4	510	2
Rowell	470	1	474	6	476	6	479	0	484	4	498	2
Noremac	443	1	448	5	453	1	458	3	463	5	476	5
Panchot	434	2	440	2	446	1	451	3	456	6	470	7
Herty	430	3	436	3	442	2	447	4	452	6	468	3
Vint	445	6	450	4	451	5	455	7	460	0	470	7
Elson	407	4	411	2	413	1	418	2	421	6	433	3
Ebow	150	0	150	0	150	0	150	0	150	0	155	0

By teatime that day, all were doing the business on the track apart from the predictably absent Dakotan. Nitaw was attracting the attention of the bookmakers who offered even money that the lazy Indian wouldn't make 200 miles. He was said to be sulking in his room at the time due to the fact that he hadn't got a new suit to change into. As Nitaw fretted in his chambers, Rowell looked to be making his way ever so nicely on the track, and his promising efforts soon rewarded him with the envious score of 500 miles at 18:45. That said the "Cambridge Wonder" was still 20 miles behind the Long Islander. Herty, who had left the track at 18:17 to eat his tea, returned to overtake Vint at a quarter to seven. He went back in at 19:30 giving specific instructions that, if the little shoemaker from Brooklyn reappeared, he was to be woken up. That didn't happen till 21:20, when sure enough, and true to his word, young Daniel was woken from his slumbers and followed Bobby on to the path.

At 20:00, there was hardly any room to manoeuvre in the building. Thirty policemen had to stand themselves 20 feet apart around the inside of track to stop the crowd spilling on to it, and with the attendance estimated at 9,000 at 9 p.m., Sam Day's trainer, Harry Vaughan, the English walker, appeared alongside his 12-year-old son on the track dressed in a *"neat blouse trimmed with British colors."* Vaughan must have been hired by the management to give an exhibition of heel-and-toe, and this he set off to do, the target being 6 miles in the preceding hour.

By 22:00 Fitzgerald's previous efforts were having a detrimental affect on his performance, and Rowell, who was now going very well, was only 15 miles behind him and closing rapidly having gained six miles on his rival in four hours. The position for the leader deteriorated, and despite being plied with *"stimulants,"* he lost further ground, and by 11 p.m., had lost a further three miles, the score being 535 to 523 prompting one of Rowell's trainers to comment. "Chawley's more like 'imself to-night, an 'e'll make it warm for the big un afore 'e gets through wiv' 'im."

As the leader wilted and his pursuer continued to improve, the Irish contingent in the crowd got behind their man. "Run, Patsy, run!" "Go on Pat, don't let him bate ye," and, "Warrum his heels me bhoy!" Pat couldn't respond though, and his dispirited figure was frequently seen going back into his hut, where he was being given instructions as to what to do next by his trainers, as the bookmakers' spies watched and listened intently outside. Their observations were relayed back to the betting ring, which became a frenzy of activity as the information their employers gleaned was acted upon and odds changed accordingly.

King of the Peds

The *New York Times* described the mood of the place at the time: **The crowd showed no signs of going home. Some tired women dropped asleep with their heads on their husband's or some other man's shoulders. The atmosphere was hot and smoky. Waiters in white jackets sold thousands of glasses of beer to the thirsty throng. The Indian came out and bought one. The betting, bargaining, swearing, jeering, smoking, and shouting went on under the full glare of 20 electric lights. The band played "Good Night, Ladies," and went home. Capt. Williams dismissed half of his policemen. The trainers made up the beds in the huts.**

At 23:17, Fitzgerald went to bed leaving Rowell to tramp on for another 10 minutes before taking his leave to do the same. These events signalled a mass exodus from the building. Before leaving the ring, Elson looked up at his score and reminded himself that he had just 60 miles to make to make some money out of the race, and if he did, he might be able to afford a bottle of champagne to celebrate. Now that would be worth the effort!

The midnight scores on the fifth day: **Fitzgerald, 536.5; Rowell, 525; Panchot, 496; Noremac, 494; Herty, 483.5; Vint, 480; Elson, 455; Nitaw, 157.5:**

The Doctors' Box during the night!

The National Police Gazette   *(Illustration no: 99)*

On the final day, Saturday, May the 3rd, one of the managers of the event was emphatic when he said, "Any talk about collusion is entirely wrong. There is no collusion in any way, and each man wants his own to win on his merits. You have no idea of the rivalry there is between the two parties, the Duryea party, who back Rowell, and the Davies party, who back Fitzgerald. They are watching their every movement and are urging them forward. If the men don't do any more than they are doing it is simply because it is not in them. Davies has not left Fitzgerald's room since midnight and has done all he can to urge Fitzgerald on.

"This is a race between a bulldog and a man who has no heart. If Fitzgerald knew when he was beaten he would stop now. He has hardly strength to stagger across the street; but see him keep up to Rowell mile after mile. He would drop dead on the track sooner than give up. He has been taking one hour of sleep and rest while the other has been taking three, and that's why he don't go faster. Anybody who sees what he is doing will agree that the race is as square as it can be. Now, as to Rowell, he hasn't any heart. His friends are now urging him and begging him to keep on, but they have all they can do. A physician who examined him this morning pronounced him physically in perfect condition. Yet he wants to give up the race to a wreck like Fitzgerald. Instead of pushing on he lets Fitzgerald set the pace, and he wants to go into his tent every time Fitzgerald enters his."

The manager was then asked if Rowell had shown any lack of spirit in previous races.

"He was always sleepy and a trifle lazy, and then he was never pushed as hard as he has been in this. There are no records like it. Now he is getting a trifle stupid. His own trainers are abusing him for not going on. Charlie Mitchell, the prize-fighter, told him to his face that he could never be a prize-fighter, because he hasn't heart enough. The other man tumbled down this morning from fatigue, and yet Rowell, in the splendid condition he is, wants to give up to that man because he hasn't heart for the race."

The intention was to allow Fitzgerald four hours in his cot when Smith called him in earlier. The hardy Irishman however, had other ideas and insisted on continuing on his tramp. The *New York Herald* described what happened next: At twenty minutes past one the door opened in the wall of flowers which the front of Fitzgerald's cabin has become, and between the fresh roses and lilies appeared a pale, yellow face, with dull, glazed eyes, staring at the track, but not seeing it. The under jaw was drooping. The big, bent body trembled at each movement, and the long muscular limbs gave way under him. Fitzgerald made a few uncertain steps, paused and tottered on in the direction of the yellow track. Once in the well trodden path he moved at a snail's pace, staggering along a crooked course. With dogged determination he reeled around the course, although a child could have beaten him at the time. After that be was able to walk straight, but his frame was bent and his steps uncertain. Few had seen before a sight like that presented by his sallow face, made darker by a week's growth of beard; his low knit brow, dull staring eyes and drooping jaw, which shook as he walked. He was greeted by a roar from his expectant fans who shouted, "Ceade mille failthe!" ("A thousand welcomes!") to which Pat replied, "Faugh-a-ballaghh!" ("Clear the way!")

Rowell arrived back on the track at 02:10 having rested for 2h.43m *"looking bright and strong and running with ease."* Fitzgerald went after him, but after keeping up with him for just a few yards, began to fall behind and soon dropped into a walk. When Rowell passed him, he made another effort to keep up with the effervescent Englishman, but again failed miserably. After that he plodded on wearily and slowly, while Rowell ran around him gaining lap after lap.

As Fitzgerald struggled, Noremac thrilled the audience by spinning around the place at a rate of knots that brought the audience to their feet. The lively Scotsman made the four miles preceding his 500th in a staggering 24m.20s during which time one of his laps was recorded in 36½ seconds.

After completing his 550th mile at 03:58, the clearly exhausted Fitzgerald appeared an absolute wreck. When he inadvertently tried to enter Rowell's tent, Smith ran up to him and pointed him in the right direction. As the leader reached the turn near his cabin he suddenly stumbled, staggered forward and crashed into the railing which held him up. His attendants came rushing over to him and took him to his own tent at 03:59 where he fell asleep.

He was abruptly woken up by Smith after he observed the closely shaven head of Rowell bob back on to the track at 04:10, and after speaking some encouraging words to his man, sent him back into action. As he fought on a physician was summoned to examine him every few laps. His trainers told reporters that his condition was due to lack of sleep and not to any ailment.

At 04:35, Fitzgerald, still looking quite ill, took a further 12 minutes rest. He then went back on the track again where he later got himself in a running race with Rowell and Panchot at 05:00. After the sawdust had been flying through the air for 30 minutes, Jack Smith sent word to his man that he should stop running straight away and this advice was taken after the leader had charged round for another lap. He was summoned inside at 05:33 where no doubt Smith gave him an ear bashing before allowing him a rest of 1h.8m, during which time he was given more stimulants, and a plaster was applied to the back of his neck in attempt to cool him down by drawing the heat from his head.

"Wake up! Wake up!"

The National Police Gazette (Illustration no: 100)

King of the Peds

Whilst Rowell ran on jauntily holding a sponge to his neck, Vint could but only walk round the path due to his poorly knee. Herty looked the best of the others who had spent a lot of time being prepared for the final stages of the contest by their trainers. Whilst the rubbers got to work on tired limbs, the blisters on the men's feet were being removed by syringes for the water variety and scalpels for the blood type.

The scores till 7 a.m:

AM	1		3		4		5		6		7	
	M	L	M	L	M	L	M	L	M	L	M	L
Fitzgerald	536	5	545	7	550	0	552	7	554	7	556	5
Rowell	525	0	529	3	530	6	534	3	540	1	546	0
Panchot	497	0	506	5	511	6	516	3	521	7	526	1
Noremac	494	0	504	5	510	0	514	1	515	7	519	7
Herty	485	0	489	5	493	0	495	2	498	7	502	3
Vint	482	0	483	0	489	3	490	0	491	7	495	5
Elson	455	0	457	5	462	2	466	4	470	4	474	2

By 07:00, the nimble Rowell had reduced the 20-mile gap by half and at 07:53 Fitzgerald had a break of 7 minutes. He then took further breaks of 8m at 09:37, 26m at 10:07 and 16m at 10:52. He appeared very tired and his head and shoulders hung forward, his movements described as laboured, and he appeared anxious. Worst of all, he was only 8 miles ahead of the revolutionised Rowell who looked in a different class. Rowell now moved elegantly compared to Fitzgerald who had earlier commented that he would, "make that fellow work today." The leader though had other ideas saying, "I'll die but that I'll keep ahead."

The crowd was very large for the morning session. At 11 o'clock, it was estimated to be 3,000 in number. On admission many were asking, "Is Rowell ahead?" The general belief was that the leader was going to pieces and that Rowell was ultimately about to replace him as front runner. *"Young swells and men about town"* thought they would pop in to see what all the fuss was about, and *"gaily dressed women with fresh flowers on their bosoms drifted into the boxes,"* where they waited for the chance to cheer their heroes on.

Once again, the *New York Times* described the scenes inside: **The liveliest place in the Garden at this hour was the refreshment-room, where trainers, hangers-on, and all-night spectators were making inroads upon the celluloid sandwiches, the India rubber pig's-feet, the highly tempered beer, and the pink whisky. The bar-room was crowded with Bowery waiters, pool-room sluggers, free-and-easy sparrers, Houston-street "statues" and bouncers, and "beer-jerkers" from the downtown dives. Half-drunken sports who had been up all night and looked weary and worn were trying to make bets upon the favorites, and thieves, pickpockets, and crooks crowded around the men as they nourished their money. High words and blows followed the discussion of the respective merits of the two leaders in the match, and Mr. Andy Kelly, one of Mr. William McGlory's late henchmen, appointed himself a committee to preserve order, and achieved his object with great success on the principle inaugurated by Mr. Buck Fanshaw, who invariably quelled a riot before it began by sending the prospective combatants home on a shutter. The north side of the long bar-room resembled West Brighton in its palmy days, for there were health-lifts, rifle-galleries, doll-targets, and peanut stands in lively operation, and scores of inebriated and disheveled merrymakers were amusing themselves with the rifles and the balls.**

Herty, who had taken eight small naps earlier, alternated his gait between a walk and a run. Lame but game, he was only too aware that if he relaxed his attitude to preserving fourth place, Bobby Vint would be the man to take his valued position away from him. Vint himself appeared pale and thin, but went on his way with courage despite having major problems with his left leg which made him limp along. *"He walked erect and solemn, like an Alderman in a St. Patrick's day procession."*

Elson, with a red spot on the end of his nose persisted in his attempt to save his entrance fee. Needing just 37 miles to achieve his goal, he trekked on with the utmost concentration and, as always, he did it without saying a word.

Just after 11 o'clock, Fitzgerald went in to sleep and, in the ten minutes that he was allowed to do so, Rowell had gained another mile and a half on him. Rudely awakened from his slumber, the leader was bundled back on to the track by his handlers and told to get to work. Patrick, appearing at his worst during the match, could hardly move, and as he laboured, Rowell made even more inroads into his faltering score. The mob yelled, "Go it Fitz, he will never catch you!" "Hurry up Rowell or you'll be left!" "You ain't no better than are the Indian and Elson!" and, "You've broke his heart Rowell!"

Rowell then went off for 2 minutes at 11:24, and then at 11:26, when within just 4 miles of the leader, he was carried to his tent, undressed, given a hot bath and fell asleep as his aching legs were rubbed down. During his 22-minute absence he lost a mile to his rival. On his return he walked round the circle and so did Fitzgerald who followed him.

Rowell gets a bath!

The National Police Gazette (Illustration no: 101)

Noremac at that time wasn't going very well, despite having been the best man on the track for the last two days. After resting for 1h.34m from 10:20, and wearing bandages on his right leg, he returned limping. At this stage, he was 11 miles behind Panchot, and as a consequence, gave up the chase for third spot.

Panchot had just over an hours rest between 00:15 and 01:21, and despite having other short rests, stuck to the task in hand and moved ahead of Noremac. Wearing red trunks atop blue tights, he looked the best on the track at the time, walking in a determined fashion and ever so eager to cling on to the 3rd position that he had worked so hard for during the night. He appeared quite happy as he strolled along always having time to smile at those who supported him and winking at the scorers as he passed them. His friends told reporters that he had had a "dickey tummy" for the past four days, and that he couldn't keep anything down, sustaining himself entirely on ice during that time. His trainer was said to be astonished by his grit, and that if he hadn't had any physical problems to hold him back, he would have surely gone 650 miles. Incredibly the day before he had made 104 miles!

In the half hour before noon, both leaders appeared pitiful as they struggled to keep going, the Irishman sticking closely to the Englishman's heels. This frustrated Rowell so much that he attempted to pull away from the shadow of Fitzgerald, who was following Smith's instructions. As much as he tried to conjure up the speed to create the necessary distance in order to make a further impact on decreasing the score, the "little un" couldn't shake off the "big un" who stuck to him as a limpet would to a rock in the sea.

The appearance of the two leaders was picked up by the *Brooklyn Daily Eagle* who wrote: **Fitzgerald's face - unshaven, uncouth, distorted and ungainly, withered by the tremendous strain and lined like a cobweb, was a more repulsive sight than anything in the *Eden Musee. His eyes were sluggish, bloodshot and heavy and encompassed by huge purple circles. His cheeks had so sunk in that the contour of the teeth could almost have been seen through them and every movement was an illustration of acute agony. He swung his arms painfully, his head dropped on his chest, his shoulder blades stuck out sharply from his attenuated body, his legs dragged lamely, one after the other, and the muscles of his neck twitched nervously with every step. He dragged himself steadfastly ahead, never turning his eyes to the right or the left until he came to the scorer's stand, when he painfully and laboriously turned his head towards the figures, to see that they were correctly given.**

The change in Charlie Rowell is even more pronounced and if possible a bit more pitiable. At the start he was a handsome, chunky, well fed and athletic specimen of a man as one could declare to see. He was trained down

perfectly. His eyes were bright, his color good and his muscles superbly developed. He moved gracefully and quickly and looked like a winner from the start. As the race progressed, the color faded from his cheeks, his eyes grew heavy and brow wrinkled until it shrivelled. His shoulders drooped and his cheeks fell away until he was almost unrecognisable. The terrible strain drew his face almost out of proportion and made it repulsive to look upon.

*Wax effigies of the two pedestrians were being exhibited here at the time.

Panchot, who had been resting for 1h.30m from 10:51, returned to the race wearing his coat which he soon removed and dogged Rowell, the pair passing Fitzgerald every third lap. The old postman must have warned up pretty quickly for it was written that, *"Panchot ran easily, with a fan in his hand, and fanned Noremac as he went by. His brown face seemed free from care and his striped shirt looked as if he had worn it through the race."*

Some more last day scores from 08:00 till midday:

AM/PM	8		9		10		11		12	
	M	L	M	L	M	L	M	L	M	L
Fitzgerald	561	0	566	3	571	1	572	7	577	3
Rowell	552	2	557	1	562	5	568	4	573	6
Panchot	530	4	534	3	538	6	543	0	543	0
Noremac	523	4	526	0	529	7	530	4	530	5
Herty	503	1	508	1	512	5	516	0	518	5
Vint	496	7	498	1	500	5	504	0	506	2
Elson	477	2	482	0	485	4	489	0	493	1

At 12:30, Fitzgerald blinked wearily at the scoreboard and shouted for a cup of beef tea. Having received it from Mr. Smith, he gulped it down and made a spurt. As his fellow countryman in the crowd urged him forward, the bar-rooms rapidly emptied as the whole place reacted to what was happening on the path. *"The entire throng inside the track tore madly around close to the fence, some of them shouting wildly towards Fitzgerald, and the others endeavoring to urge Rowell into a run."* Rowell tried to go with him, but failed miserably to maintain his challenge, instead almost falling, and finally, whilst mopping his brow with a handkerchief, resigned himself to a slow walk on the path of despondency. Just before one o'clock, the leader, who had resorted to walking again, bravely began another run, and as he went passed Rowell, the mob shrieked, "Somebody else's heart is broke now, eh Fitz?!"

Early in the afternoon, the attendance exceeded anything seen since the opening nights in the races for the Astley Belt. Hundreds had to wait patiently for their turn to reach the box offices, while inside the Garden every seat was occupied. The main floor filled up rapidly and three feet deep lines of spectators peered over the railings around the track. The estimated 4,000 crowd was very supportive of every man on the circuit and cheered loudly whenever a significant move was made. At 1 p.m., Fitzgerald, now with a score of 581.6, as opposed to Rowell's 577 and 3, was "even money" to win the race. Rowell was now being offered at 2/1 by the bookies who were shouting, "Give us your bets gentlemen," at the stands. Considering the closeness of the race, the management decided to raise the price of a ticket, which doubled to a dollar.

At three o'clock, Fitzgerald, who was now on a score of 589, led Rowell by 5 miles. At the same stage in 1882, Fitzgerald had made 565, but Rowell had already retired on that occasion, and Noremac in second place had scored 548.

There were rumours flying around that "Happy Jack" had sold the race, causing Fitzgerald to confront him on the issue in his tent. Upon entering it, he said, "Jack, somebody's been trying to fix me. I understand Duryea's given you $2,000 to lay me out. Give me my Hibernian sash." Effectively the hysterical pedestrian was accusing his coach of trying to poison his food, but the old pro's response was to placate his man, soothe him to a sound sleep for thirty minutes, wake him up, tell him he'd been out for four hours and send him back to work.

Fitzgerald maintained his lead in the afternoon, but was noted to be quite groggy at four o'clock after an astonishing ding–dong battle which saw the two principals in the race passing each other on the track. This spectacle caused pandemonium in the crowd who were beside themselves with excitement. Pat left the track to Charlie who made three quick laps in his absence. Charlie Mitchell, the English pugilist who was at the track-side was observed giving his fellow countryman moral support by patting him on the back and whispering words of encouragement to him.

The exhausted Fitzgerald was seen leaving the track on numerous occasions to lie down and recuperate. Now in such a pitiful state, and hardly able to stand, he was whisked away back to his hut to be sorted out once and for all. Old Jack had one last trick up his sleeve, but would it work? He called upon his man's medical advisor, Dr. Taylor, to attend to him. The patient was sat on a chair and a "scarificator" was produced from the quack's bag. The bronze rectangular instrument which bore 16 retractable semi-circular razor sharp blades was placed on his left thigh. The blades were plunged into his flesh at a depth of an eighth of an inch in three areas, the process being repeated on the other limb in the same place. The intention was to reduce inflammation and the soreness he was suffering from. He was then sent back out on to the track with a mouthful of ice and told to get stuck in! He did just that and then turned the tables on Rowell, dogging him for a change. At this stage, Rowell was three miles behind and no matter how he tried he just couldn't shake the leader off.

Meanwhile, Alfie Elson was protesting at the scorers' table that the officials there hadn't credited him with a lap. Vint came along and offered his knee as a seat. Ashamed with his behaviour, Elson carried on with his struggles whilst the crowd laughed at him. The rest of the athletes all took advantage of rest periods between 9 minutes and nearly 3 hours. Herty was one of the men who opted for the latter, having already made the requisite 525 miles and some welcome place money. Noremac's right leg was handicapping his progress so much that he had to spend many a minute under his roof as well. Vint's leg was also troubling him, causing him to walk laboriously around the path.

One of the Irish spectators, who was ignorant of the performing contestants, was heard shouting for Rowell until embarrassingly put right by his fellow countrymen. Two women spectators nearly got into a fight with each other; the incident though seen by many in the crowd, was unnoticed by the travelling peds who were oblivious to the screaming felines.

The 5 o'clock hour saw the leading pair running competitively against each other. When Rowell made another spurt, Fitzgerald went after him, sticking to him like a leech for an astonishing 4 laps causing the 5,000 plus crowd to go wild. At the time, Pat was 4 miles and 3 laps ahead of Rowell, and as he neared his 600th mile, the Garden fell into an eerie silence. Rowell, startled by the change in atmosphere, looked around mystified by its cause. He had forgotten how close his opponent was to the coveted score, but soon realised what was happening at 17:48:10 when the magic number was hauled up! Yells, howls, and screams from the hysterical crowd were accompanied by hats being flung into the air, and handkerchiefs being waved.

Listening to the uproar and unable to comprehend what the commotion was about, Fitzgerald asked, "What's that for?" He was told by many who heard him that he had just made 600 miles. "Is that so?" he replied, "Why, I thought I had another lap to go yet." He then told the scorers that he would, "make one more lap and crawl in." However, he mustered another mile from his aching limbs and staggered to his den. As he lay down on his bed, he was just beginning to enjoy his new place in the record books, when Rowell re-appeared on the track. That move gave him the signal to get back out, and after only six minutes of rest!

Both were roundly cheered on their reappearance. The ensuing commotion attracted Noremac and Vint back in the ring, and both men began the task of trying to protect their respective positions. Fitzgerald was then presented with a silver goblet lined with gold which he carried along and tried to show Rowell, but the little fellow ignored him and carried on with his work.

"Shortly before seven o'clock Fitzgerald was again seized with a crazy fit. Noticing Charles Mitchell, the pugilist, standing in front of his hut, he stepped up to that young man and accused him of trying to destroy his chances in the race. He was eager to engage in a contest of fisticuffs with Mitchell. As before, he was laughed at and induced to resume his weary way."

Rowell went on to complete his 600th mile at 18:53. He was only the third man ever to cover that distance within 142 hours, and after he covered another mile, he went to his hut at 19:13. Peter Duryea, his backer, attributed his man's "*defeat*" to a badly sprained left ankle which Charlie had been suffering from for two days. Indeed,

King of the Peds

the affected limb was described as, *"being double its size and black and blue."* As he lay in his hut nursing it, Rowell immediately issued a challenge to Fitzgerald for a race of $5,000 a side.

Some further scores from 1 p.m. till 7 p.m:

PM	13		14		15		16		17		18		19	
	M	L	M	L	M	L	M	L	M	L	M	L	M	L
Fitzgerald	581	6	585	4	589	0	594	3	599	1	601	6	605	2
Rowell	577	3	579	6	584	0	589	3	594	0	596	6	600	2
Panchot	546	3	550	2	553	0	557	2	557	2	559	6	560	7
Noremac	535	0	538	4	541	0	542	7	542	7	542	7	544	7
Herty	523	1	525	3	526	0	527	0	530	2	534	3	536	0
Vint	510	3	512	1	515	0	518	7	522	7	525	0	526	3
Elson	497	3	501	0	506	0	509	7	513	0	516	6	521	1

After Elson finished his 525th mile at 19:54, he was given some generous applause as the band played, "The Babies on Our Block."

An estimated 12,000 people descended on the Garden on the last night of the race. It was probably unsafe for that amount to be in such a building and the over-crowding was noted with unease at the time. There was lot of Irish in the throng, and they had been making themselves heard! Likewise, and unusually, the English supporters threw away their natural reserve and were observed to be noisily egging on Rowell too. The Scots in the audience were somewhat muted as George Noremac wasn't doing as well as they had wished. The neutrals in the crowd leant on the side of Fitzgerald and they cheered him on because of his guts and determination.

After carrying round an Irish flag, and being presented with a huge floral piece in the shape of a barrel of India ale (which had been his favourite tipple during the contest), which had been presented to him by a brewery, Fitzgerald went to his hut at eight o'clock. It was here that he put on a new suit of a red shirt and trunks, green breech cloth and a green jockey cap embroidered with red, white and blue stars. As he entered the arena at 12 minutes past the hour, many hats were lost when they were flung high into the air amid the electric atmosphere. People hooted and shouted themselves silly as the plucky Irishman painfully went on his way. Panchot, Noremac, and little Vint, also made regular appearances to add to the interest.

Just before the finish, the two leaders ran around the ellipse at a rapid pace. The winner gave the runner-up an Irish flag which Rowell courteously accepted. Fitzgerald picked up an American flag and the pair completed another lap before stopping in front of the scorers' stand. "Let's stop," said Fitzgerald. Mr. Busby turned to Rowell and said, "What do you say?" As Rowell was within 2 laps of completing his 602nd mile, the Englishman replied, "Let me make two more laps and I'll do it." On seeing the Briton walking past the big clock, many in the crowd baited him by childishly yelling in his direction, "Rowell, Rowell, bully boy, Rowell!" The derisive chant soon built up momentum and followed the same path of its more positive predecessor only seconds earlier, in favour of the winner, by echoing round the building. The theme carried on outside and was repeated by the ecstatic throngs outside, "Rowell, Rowell, bully boy, Rowell!"

The distance was made and the crowd cried, "Fitzgerald, hurrah for Fitzgerald!" *"The shout traveled down the big building like a wave at sea, turned the corner by the entrances and came racing up the other end like a cyclone. In an instant it had made the circuit of the Garden, like an electric current, and the excitable men in the centre of the ellipse caught up the sound and swelled the cry into a roar: "Hurrah for Fitzgerald!"*

At 39 minutes past eight, Patrick Fitzgerald made a new world record of 610 miles and 220 yards in a time of 140 hours and 39 minutes.

At 20:40, the two men stood on the same line from which they had started the contest. Fitzgerald then received three hearty cheers. They were followed by three even heartier ones for the runner-up. The cry then went up from the crowd for them to shake hands. For what seemed to be an eternity, the pair stood before each other as though each one was waiting for the other to draw their pistols; then bang! Rowell offered his hand to Fitzgerald, who, after hesitating a second, grudgingly put out his fingers and allowed them to rest momentarily in the Englishman's palm. Their faces had changed dramatically over the week. From having fresh vibrant complexions when they started, their skin was now a dull yellow colour and their eyes were surrounded by dark tinges. The packed hoards of standing men and the pretty women sitting with their cool drinks who sat in the tobacco poisoned atmosphere of the Garden had no comprehension of what the men had just put themselves through.

At 20:45, the race was over and the exhausted finishers, helped by the police, were given a clear path back to their tents. The winner had just covered an amazing 610 miles in 6 days.

Fitzgerald was whisked off to the Putnam House Hotel where "Happy Jack" had prepared a hot bath with the added "mysterious solution" for him to soak in. He was then allowed to sleep for three hours after which he was woken up and rubbed down. His trainer felt that if he was allowed to sleep uninterruptedly, he would be ill.

After sunrise, he was pulled from his bed, dressed, and taken for a walk. As he breathed the fresh morning air, the new world champion said, "Lord, how good that seems!" He limped up Fourth Avenue to 42nd Street and back, and as he did so, he was watched by a large contingent of people who had gathered to see him. He then ate a wholesome breakfast after which he was whisked back off to the Garden where he sorrowfully witnessed a different scene to what he had been accustomed to during the race. The track had already disappeared, and the 5,000 chairs which had been sat on by the spectators, were all haphazardly stacked up around the place.

He then went back to his hotel and slept for a while. Later, and now clean shaven, he sat in an armchair in his room and enjoyed a glass of wine as he told reporters, "I feel all right. I rested well and was up early. I was out of my head at the last, but I have got all over that now. I never touched a drop of liquor all last week until Saturday afternoon when I was given some champagne and seltzer. If I had not been sick on Saturday morning, I could have easily covered 660 miles. There was not a day that I felt able to do just a little more, but my men wouldn't let me unless I was pushed to it. I am feeling very well, and am not so badly broken up as your papers want to make me out."

"He is alright," said Tom Davies. "I calculated that he would make six hundred and twenty miles, and I think he could have gone to six hundred and eighteen if there had been any need of it. I had no doubt at any time that he would win. I was sure of it."

"I can't say anything about further races," said Fitzgerald. "I want to get through with this one before I make any arrangements as to a race with Rowell. As to Hughes, I don't want to be in any race with him."

Jack Smith, who was with him said, "Pat apologised to me this morning for saying that his food had been poisoned and that we had sold out to the Englishman. He says he was dazed by the bad air, the noise and the crowd and did not know what he was doing. Someone at the foot of the track said, "They've fixed you Pat, sure," and the man rushed into his quarters with his brain afire. He didn't remember saying it this morning till we told him."

At the conclusion of the match, Rowell was taken to the Ashland House and put to bed. Because he was suffering so much from his swollen ankle, and therefore unable to sleep, he was given a dose of bromide of potassium. He awoke at a late hour on Sunday, but was so stiff in his limbs that he had to remain in his room due to his badly injured foot which was bandaged. "I am feeling well. I sprained my ankle on Tuesday, but I was too proud to go lame," he said showing the reporter his swollen, blistered foot. "You would never have guessed what I suffered from seeing me run around the track would you? Sometimes I groaned aloud with pain. Of course it wouldn't do for me to let those other fellows know anything about it, though. I am surprised I was able to keep up as long as I did. For the last four days, it was pound, pound, pound with that every time I put my foot down. I could not think of anything else. I feel all right every other way. That last five-mile run called for all the grit I could summon." He said he expected to leave very shortly for England, expecting to return to the United States to prepare for his proposed contest with Fitzgerald in the following autumn. He also mentioned that he thought that *"walking matches"* were more appreciated in America than in England.

King of the Peds

PAT'K FITZGERALD,
610 MILES 146 DAYS

(Illustration no: 102)

Below is a summary of the final positions, distances made, time made in, and final prize money for each pedestrian. Included in the following amounts is 70%, or $980.00 to Fitzgerald for winning the sweepstakes, 20%, or $280 for Rowell for coming in second, and 10%, or $140 was given to Panchot for third place.

Name	Pos	Miles	Laps	Hrs	Mins	Prize Money
Fitzgerald	**1st**	**610**	**1**	**140**	**39**	**$9,418.15**
Rowell	2nd	602	0	140	39	$3,655.27
Panchot	3rd	566	4	140	36	$1,996.39
Noremac	4th	545	5	140	37	$1,181.35
Herty	5th	539	3	140	0	$843.81
Vint	6th	530	0	140	14	$675.06
Elson	7th	525	3	140	4	$506.28

The daily records of all the finishers were:

Day	Fitzgerald	Rowell	Panchot	Noremac	Herty	Vint	Elson
1	**126**	135.1	123.4	120.7	120	116	113.7
2	**100**	105	89	95.6	97.1	94.7	86.1
3	**110**	105.7	89.4	95.4	89.3	99	86.2
4	**111.6**	94	90.3	80.2	88.4	94.2	86
5	**88.7**	85	103.5	101.6	88.5	75.6	82.6
6	**73.4**	77	70.4	51.3	55.6	50	70
Tot	**610.1**	**602**	**566.4**	**545.4**	**539.3**	**530**	**525**

The cumulative totals of the finishers were:

Day	Fitzgerald	Rowell	Panchot	Noremac	Herty	Vint	Elson
1	126	135.1	123.4	120.7	120	116	113.7
2	226	240.1	212.4	216.5	217.1	211	200
3	336	346	302	312.1	306.4	310	286.2
4	447.6	440	392.3	392.3	395	404	372.2
5	536.5	525	496	494.1	483.5	480	455
6	610.1	602	566.4	545.4	539.3	530	525

The table below shows the amount of rest each finishing competitor took during the race.

	H	M	S	POS
Rowell	26	55	55	2nd
Herty	27	15	31	5th
Fitzgerald	28	41	12	1st
Elson	30	20	27	7th
Panchot	35	19	41	3rd
Vint	39	3	40	6th
Noremac	45	32	35	4th

The day after the race, the *New York Times* wrote about the interest the race had created amongst the city's citizens: Rowell's success in closing upon Fitzgerald, together with the prospects of the great record about to be made, drew greater attention yesterday to the match than had before been paid to it, and deepened the interest all over the city. Hourly bulletins were posted in front of most of the newspaper offices in Park-row, and crowds lined the sidewalks and overflowed into the roadways. Drivers stopped their horses to read the scores, but were made to move on. Businessmen tried to force their way along the sidewalks, but often had to give it up and turn out into the road. Newsboys and bootblacks wagered small going on the result, and now and then a bank bill came out. Many of the saloons received the scores every hour and posted them in their windows. A few clothing stores did the same. At the head of most of the bulletins were the words, "beware of pickpockets." A German saloon-keeper in the bowery put up a sign of "Pickpockets beware." The "tickers" carried the news to the hotels. Around the Garden the interest in the race was intense. Madison Avenue was packed with people last night, so that it was difficult for visitors to the race to make their way to the door, and almost impossible for a vehicle to go through the street without running over some one. In Twenty Sixth Street there was a motley mob of men and boys, most of them clad in garments of antique mold and subdued value. Many stood closely pressed together gazing up at the circular windows, when occasionally some kind friend would shout out the score. "Sure. Fuz has bruk the heart av Rowell intirely," remarked one gentleman. "Wall, eully, yer can jest betcher sweet boots on dat," was the reply of a small boy beside him. Occasionally the half-dozen stalwart policemen in the street would attempt to drive the crowd away. The crowd always went and always came back. In Fourth-avenue the crowd early in the evening composed of small boys, who did gymnastic feats and poured forth their opinions in the vernacular of the slums. After the race was over, hundreds of men rushed to that side of the Garden to see the departure of the walkers When Fitzgerald entered a carriage and was driven outward through Twenty-sixth-street the crowd rushed after the vehicle and shouted madly. A large number followed it down to Lexington Avenue, and then returned to witness the going of the next. Every departure was cheered madly. Horse ears and lumbering mail vans had to make frequent stops to avoid running over the enthusiastic admirers of the pedestrians. The crowd was good natured, and jests of a poor quality hurled about by the small boys, who had learned them for a quarter in some bowery show house, aroused storms of laughter. It was a rather excited crowd. Most of the men had been in the Garden, and were full of excitement. Dazed, tired and thirsty, they had only one aim, to see as many heroes as they could, to yell as much as they were able, and to occupy their spare moments in quaffing beer. Great crowds watched the bulletin boards in Printing House Square until the end of the race was announced. On some boards the score was posted half hourly, and on others hourly, and the people waited patiently in the street for the figures to be put up. When one set was posted they would discuss them until the next appeared. Fitzgerald's steady gain on Rowell during the evening excited the wildest enthusiasm, and his score was invariably greeted with cheers. There were women in the crowds, and they took as much interest seemingly as the men. Finally, when the end same, some one yelled:

King of the Peds

"Hooray: we don't expect first money."

Beyond the cheering there was no disorder. The saloons in the vicinity had not done such a thriving business since the opening of the bridge. After the last figures were received crowds remained discussing the result for some time.

On the same day, Panchot was located hobbling around the Putnam House with the aid of a stick. "I don't feel any more tired than if I had not been in the race," he said. "My feet are not a bit sore, and I have been walking about all day. I was sick for a time after I had made twenty miles, but I was alright at the last, and if there had been ten more hours to run I would have come in ahead. I could have made more miles, as it was, but there was no object in it." Of Rowell's lame leg, he claimed that if he had known about it, he would have taken second place. "I never supposed he was in such a fix or I'd have run him down," he said. His trainer chipped in, "To think of that man Rowell having all he could do to keep up with a broken ankle and our man doing nothing but simply trying to hold third place. Why, he was good for twenty-five miles or more on Saturday. See the way he pulled up on Noremac and Vint. Why, the man never ate a mouthful of food for the first two days. Oh, my, to think what an opportunity lost." Panchot stated that he wished there was another six-day race to begin immediately so that he might enter it. He also said that 600 miles was nothing to him, and only sickness had prevented him from scoring 625. He mentioned that he would like to enter the Rowell-Fitzgerald race, but $5,000 was a great deal of money for him to raise.

Meanwhile, upstairs on the fifth floor, Nit-Aw-E-Go-Bow was laid on his bed reading the papers. "Of course," he said, "I will get paid for what I did and my expenses. I made no arrangements about coming here. It was all fixed with my chief. He sent me. I had no idea what such a race was like. I thought the men ran so many hours at a time and all ran at once. I did not think they starved themselves and went without sleep. Then the bad air made me sick." The *Fulton Times* was later to write of the Dakotan: **Nit-Aw-E-Go-Bow was, as an Indian walker, a dismal failure, but as a go-as-you-please eater and smoker he was ahead of his pale faced rivals. Dakota will soon gather her son to her bosom, and sporting circles will know him no more. He was a great card, however, but he thoroughly demonstrated that although "he could run down a deer in the forest" he could not hold his own on a saw dust track amid a dense volume of tobacco smoke. Verily, the Indian does degenerate.**

Elson was another man who limped about, but he was staying at the Warwick House on Sixth Avenue. He said, "When I came down here untrained and poor, Hazael and other sporting men laughed at me. They didn't believe I could go three hundred miles. I ought to get six hundred or seven hundred dollars at least, and I'll put myself in trim to show them something next time."

Noremac stayed at home nursing his sore knee and claimed it prevented him from advancing up the scoreboard. Of his feet he said, "They feel a little sore, but I am all right otherwise. I was down to my shop today. I overdid myself by racing too much, because I had fallen behind my schedule." Vint, also with sore feet, stayed indoors at his house in Brooklyn and was looked after by his wife. Herty, who was suffering from swollen limbs said, "I was not well and my foot had a bad strain, which kept me back. Besides, it was different with me than with men who went through a long training with this race in view. A number of the sporting men of New York have offered to back me for another race, but I will do nothing without the consent of my Boston friends." Sam Day, who promised so much earlier in the race, visited all the sufferers.

Whilst resting in his hotel room, the victor wrote the following letter:

PUTNAM HOUSE, May 5, 1884

MESSRS. LEAVY & BRITTON BREWING Co.

Jay and Front Streets. Brooklyn.

GENTLEMEN – I take great pleasure in acknowledging the fact that I trained exclusively on your ales, and I attribute my staying power and success in no small degree to the merits of your goods.

Yours respectfully

PATRICK J. FITZGERALD.

In an article entitled, **THE WALKERS AT REST**, the *Brooklyn Daily Eagle* on the 6th of May wrote: One by one the walkers who are entitled to a share of the gate money in the recent contest at Madison-Square Garden dropped into the building yesterday in search of the gentlemen who have charge of the proceeds. They were unable to gain any information. All of them, however, were satisfied that the money was in responsible hands, and said that they had no cause for alarm. Hamilton Busby, the referee, to whose account the money is placed in the Second National Bank, was out of town all day Sunday. He began the work of auditing the bills yesterday, and he is of the opinion that the money will not be distributed until to-day or perhaps tomorrow. Peter Duryea, Rowell's backer, said that the total would not fall much short of $35,000. The rest of the Garden was fully covered by the sale of the privileges. The bar, refreshment stand, shooting gallery and other rights sold for $5,410, which is just $410 in excess of the rent of the building. The manager's of the walk will have to pay for the laying of the track the building of the tents, the gas and electric light, the scorers, judges, and, in fact, every expense incurred during the week, as they agreed to pay $5,000 for simply the use of the Garden during the six days.

The successful pedestrians were in a happy mood yesterday. Fitzgerald sat in a cozy room in the Putnam House, surrounded by his friends, trainer, and backer, and told funny stories of incidents that occurred during his long walk. He took a good night's rest on Sunday and awoke yesterday feeling much better than he has after any of his contests.

"What are you going to do with your money?" he was asked.

"What would any ex-Alderman do but stay right here and enjoy it."

"There is a report that you intend starting for your native country. Is there any truth in it?"

"No sir. Sure, if I went to Ireland they would put me in jail for a Fenian."

Rowell was very sore yesterday. He took a walk, and it was very evident, that he was in great pain. His feet were incased in a pair of kid shoes that were destitute of heels. He ate his lunch early, and took a nap in the afternoon to try and get some relief from the pain that his sore ankle caused him. Panchot was in first-class shape, and took a trip to Brooklyn to visit a friend. Noremac was nursing sore limbs at his home in this city, and Vint was similarly employed in Brooklyn. Herty started for his home in Boston. Elson was about town as usual, and Netaw-eg-Ebow was still in bed.

On the same day the men who had made 525 miles in the race met at the Ashland House to receive the fruits of their efforts. They were paid in cheques on the Second National Bank. All of the men thought that they would receive more than they actually did but were satisfied that the accounts were in order. The total receipts for the event were $36,446 of which $19,569.69 were expenses.

On the night of May the 8th at 19:30, Fitzgerald accompanied by Tom Davies, William Kenny and Peter Panchot emerged from the side entrance of the Putnam House. They were engulfed by a huge crowd of well wishers who cheered them as they stepped into an open barouche. Rowell wasn't with them. Although invited along for the ride, he was too sick to do so. They were followed along by two more carriages and headed towards the 34th Street ferry. When on board, his admirers stared at him as though he was from a different planet, and when they reached the landing at Long Island City, fireworks were set off to greet him. The air was filled with rockets and noise as the ex-Alderman was ushered through the gates by an army of policemen whilst sat in his carriage.

He was driven a short distance up Ferry Street where the party of vehicles came to a halt. The excited encircling crowd moved in to listen to the speech of ex-Corporation Counsel Noble. Patrick stood up, took off his brown derby hat and listened.

"I welcome you on behalf of the people of Long Island City to the home of your adoption. Some men achieve greatness and some have greatness thrust upon them. Your record shows that in this go-as-you-please country you cannot be beaten in running for anything, office included. Occurrences like these are bright spots in the chequered history of a young city like this. They foster the spirit and local pride of our young men and excite a worthy ambition in all. They make us reflect on the past and gather encouragement for the future. If our city had walls we would as in olden times, make a breach for you to enter. If we had poets and sculptors and painters, we would make the canvas blush, the statue speak and talking words that breathe and burn. Enough! You are home again. God bless you and yours."

King of the Peds

The victor bowed, sat down, and was once again conveyed on his way between the crowds up Jackson Avenue, followed by several truck and hose companies in the Fire Department of Long Island City. They, in turn, were followed by the carriages containing the dignitaries, then two trucks decorated with flags and red and green lights and a barrel presented by Leavy & Britton, brewers of ale, surrounded in flowers. Behind them marched people carrying torches which were interspersed with bands which moved noisily along. From there he was whisked along followed by the cheerful throng to his cottage where the band played, "Lo, the conquering hero comes."

On May 31st, it was reported that Rowell would begin his journey back to England that day on the steamer *Arizona*. He was said to have completely recovered from the effects of the race and was *"getting fat."* The expectation at the time was that he would remain in England until he went back into training for his race with Fitzgerald in the autumn.

CHAPTER 46

<u>Man v Horse</u>

Sometime in mid July 1884, George Littlewood's father, Fred, hired a five-year-old bay horse of fifteen and a half hands in height called Charlie which belonged to Mr. "Aby" Bower to convey him to his son's birthplace, the village of Rawmarsh, near Rotherham in Yorkshire. He wasn't very happy with the horse's performance and quipped that "Our George would beat it." A couple of days later he discovered that one of his son's backers had deposited a sum of £5 to bind a match between man and horse. George duly went into training under the watchful eye of Mr. J. Dickenson, and the match was looked forward to by the sporting fraternity of Sheffield. The amount they were running for was said to be £50.

Articles of agreement were drawn up, and one of the clauses was that the horse should be driven personally by Mr. Bower in as light a trap as possible, but not in a trotting sulky. A start time for the match would be as early as possible to satisfy police worries about problems caused by interest en route.

On the Friday, the 19th of September 1884, the test of stamina and speed between them took place from the third milestone on the Bawtry Road to Tinsley Bridge, which was three miles from Sheffield, a distance of about 18 miles. The route would take them principally on the Bawtry to Doncaster and Doncaster to Sheffield roads, the route of which was familiar to Littlewood. He knew there was a level stretch of road to Doncaster of about three miles, then hillier terrain would have to be encountered after Hooton Roberts, on steeply up through Conisborough.

Journalists from the *Sheffield Telegraph* and *Sheffield and Rotherham Independent* were invited by "Old Fred" to stay in Rawmarsh the night before the event. They were warmly entertained on the eve of the race where they stayed. Charlie was put up in an adjacent stable.

In the morning they were driven to the Shakespeare Inn at Doncaster for the start. The race began at 06:28 when the referee, Mr. A. Darwent of Sheffield, after receiving an affirmative to the question, "Are you both ready?" said, "Go!" The competitors went on their way accompanied by three other traps, one containing the referee and official timekeeper, the second George's trainer and *"bottler,"* and the third *"Old Fred"* and the reporters.

George took an early lead, but relinquished the same to Charlie after three quarters of a mile. The horse by then had warmed up and was reported to be going along nicely, and by the time the two competitors had made it to the outskirts of Doncaster, Charlie was in front of his two legged opponent by 50 yards. Running into Doncaster's main road, George made some inroads into Charlie's lead, but Mr. Bower was getting a better than expected performance from his "nag" and there were some surprised spectators. Heavy bets at "even money" had been placed on either party the day before, and the punters who had backed the professional pedestrian were getting anxious. The hill into Conisborough was supposed to cause problems for the horse as it tried to negotiate it, but contrary to expectations, it handled it well, and this meant George would fall further back than he already was. When the horse trotted up to the Star Inn it was a full two minutes ahead and Mr. Bower pulled the horse up for a drink of water to quench its thirst. This took a minute and helped to reduce the gap between man and horse of about 200 yards.

As the race progressed through Thrybergh and Dalton Brook, there were large numbers of spectators lining the roads cheering the participants on. The crowds were so big, that there were fears that the race would have to be stopped at Rotherham, but that never happened. As the contestants approached Rotherham, the roads were crowded with vehicles resembling the evening of the return from the St. Leger race meeting. Crowds cheered

King of the Peds

Littlewood as he passed through the town. Charlie moved on towards the finish with George chasing him determinedly, but alas, he was unable to get near.

When George was three quarters of a mile from the finish, he learned that he had been beaten, and with that, he stopped in his tracks, jumped into a trap and was driven to meet his foe and admit defeat. The time of the winner was 1h.39m.38s.

George Littlewood

By permission of Sheffield City Libraries. (Illustration no: 103)

CHAPTER 47

5th Astley Challenge Belt

On Monday, the November 24th 1884, a 72-hour go-as-you-please *"International Six day's Competition,"* began at 11 o'clock at the *London Aquarium for the *"Six Days Champion Belt"* and **£300 in prizes. This race, which was described at the time as, *"the most promising event witnessed within the shores of the Britain,"* was the *fifth* contest for the "Astley Challenge Belt" which was then held by George Littlewood. It would be his to keep outright if he could only win it this time around, having done so on two previous occasions as described in Chapters 38 and 43.

*The belt worth £100, first prize of £100, and although there was no information about how the other £100 would be distributed, it is estimated that these would be double what was awarded in similar contests as described before: £40 for the second, £20 for third, £12 for fourth, £8 for fifth, and £6 for sixth, etc.

**Costing nearly £200,000, the 600 feet long, red-brick building, which sported a glass roof, was opened by the Duke of Edinburgh on Saturday, the 22nd of January 1876.

The *"Westminster"* Aquarium would be visited by Sir John Astley during the course of the first day along with many other notable sportsmen of the time, and the race would be timed officially throughout by Messrs. W. E. Fuller and C. H. O'Dowd using a chronometer by Kendal and Dent. A lot of effort had been put in to construct an elevated 174 yards to the lap, 10 laps to the mile track, which measured 10 feet in height and 8 feet wide. Of the fifty entries that were sent in, only 19 were selected to race with 12 men eventually lining up at the post.

Two of those competitors, Rowell and Littlewood, both looked fit, and were confident of making new records during the race. The Americans who had entered for it hadn't arrived, and several others who had been expected to compete had dropped out. Littlewood, who had been trained for the race near Brigg in Lincolnshire, was the favourite and was said to be confident of success. He would be cared for by his father and Fred Bromley. Rowell on the other hand *"is splendidly trained, and has been practicing for weeks on a track at his noble patron's country seat."* Indeed this race would be Rowell's first crack at a *"limited"* six-day event. Littlewood on the other hand was used to this sort of contest, and should he win this one, he would carry off the championship prize for good. The others taking part were:

J. BERGIN of Brighton: No details available for this pedestrian.

GEORGE CARTWRIGHT of Walsall, otherwise known as the "Flying Collier," was born in Bilsford, Staffordshire. He was 35 years of age, weighed 10st.2lbs and was 5ft.5½in in height. George won first prize in a six-day contest at the Exhibition Building, Nottingham, on February 14th 1880, when he beat Littlewood into 4th place. After that he again took the first prize of £20, in a 6 days, 8 hours per day, go-as-you-please contest at the Agricultural Hall, Wolverhampton, on March 30th. Then on October the 2nd, and for scoring 371 miles, he took the second prize of £15 in a 12 hours per day, six-day contest at Birmingham won by Noremac. A first prize of £50 beckoned him to compete in a six hours per day, six-day running contest at Sheaf House Grounds, Sheffield, on June the 3rd 1882, which he won with a score of 244 miles. The horses for courses mentality must have attracted him to try again at the same venue on May 19th 1883 in a similar event where he came in third to Littlewood and Mason. He also ran the greatest distance on the first (82 miles 390 yards), and second day (74 miles 1,712 yards), in 12 hours each day at Birmingham on September the 25th 1882. "Brummy" Meadows would look after him during the match.

GEORGE CONNOR of Bow was only 21 years old. He weighed 7st.8lbs, and stood 5ft.2in, when he took on the much older and more experienced athletes in this race. George had taken third place in a 125-yard handicap at Balham Grounds on April 1st 1882. He followed that effort up with fourth place in a 3-hour go-as-you-please at Bow Grounds on May the 29th in the same year, then beat a chap called Vincent in a 30-minute race for £20 at Jackson's Gymnasium at Camden Town on September the 12th 1882. The young Irishman's interests would be looked after by Walter Whale and his brother F. Connor during the race.

King of the Peds

H. HUNT of Acton: No details available for this pedestrian.

GEORGE MASON at the time of the race was the fifty miles champion and ex-72-hour champion. He weighed 9st.8lb and was 5ft.6in tall. See Chapter 40 for the story of the race when he beat Littlewood, thus winning the "4th Astley Belt Challenge Trophy and Sweepstakes" between the 25th and 30th December 1882 at the Sheffield Drill Hall. After that Littlewood beat him when he came second, winning a prize of £10 in the May contest of 1883 at the Sheaf House Grounds at Sheffield (See Chapter 43) where George Cartwright came third. After that he won £35 and a gold medal in the 50-mile championship at the Prince of Wales Ground, Bow, London, on June the 4th 1883 where his times from 21 miles to 33 miles were still the best on record up the time of this race. He would be attended by Dick Harding and T. Yardley during the race.

PAT McCARTY was living in Leeds at the time of the race. He was born in Roscommon, Ireland, in 1844. He tipped the scales at 10st.2lbs and stood 5ft.6½in tall. Pats earlier career can be read about in Chapter 9 when he took part in the 1st International Astley Belt contest in which he finished 8th with a score of 264.2. He then took the second prize of £50 losing out to Harry Vaughan by 22 miles in a six-day, 14 hours per day contest at the "Aggie" which finished on July the 5th 1879 during which he scored 377 miles. He also claimed that place, and a reward of £20, in a similar event at Bingley Hall, Birmingham, which concluded on October the 11th 1879. Three further runner-up prizes were then added to his resume. The first one of £15 was earned at Dundee in a 12-hour, six-day event finishing on the 14th of February 1880. The second one was won in a similar contest at the Sheffield Drill Hall ending April the 29th 1882, and the third was in a six "dayer" at the Sheaf House Grounds in Sheffield which finished on June the 3rd of the same year. Pat's attendants would be his brother and C. Chillingworth.

GEORGE PETTITT, then based in London, was born in Sittingbourne in 1851. He weighed in at 9st.10lbs and was 5ft.6in in height. George made a "score" when he claimed third position in a six-day, 14 hours a day event in Islington on July the 5th 1879. He capped that effort by taking the top prize in a six hours per night, six-day contest at Newport in Monmouthshire which climaxed on the 14th of August 1880. He then won £40 at the same town in a six-day go-as-you-please event which finished on the 2nd of December 1882. The capable contender also won a six-day go-as-you-please at Bristol as well as a number of minor prizes at *"all distances."* George would be helped in the race by F. Howarth.

WILLIAM FRANK SAVAGE, better known as **W. Franks** of Marylebone, London, was born in Charles Street, Hampstead, on August the 14th 1851. He weighed 9 stones and was 5ft.6in tall. *"Franks"* began his career in 1872, winning a lot of walking matches. On the 21st of November 1881 at Lillie Bridge, he won £30 by walking 8 miles in 59m.36s. Then on March 13th 1882, he beat H. Thatcher in a 12-mile walking contest winning £20. In the same year on August the 28th, he won the 30-mile walking championship for residents of Marylebone, again at Lillie Bridge, where he broke all records in the race from 23 to 29 miles. On December the 3rd 1883, he came second to J. W. Raby in the three-hour walking championship, and in 1884, on September the 17th, won the one hour go-as-you-please handicap at West Harp, London, where he made 9½ miles and 300 yards. His last two races had involved him beating W. Griffiths over a distance of 5 miles on October the 13th 1884 again at Lillie Bridge. Finally, he took third prize in the four-hour walking championship at the Clay Hall Grounds on November the 17th. For this race, he would be attended to by W. A. Sinclair and B. Skinner.

HENRY VANDERPEER of Sittingbourne: No details available for this pedestrian.

JAMES WREN, otherwise known as "Harlequin" was born in Paddington, London, in 1846. He weighed 9st.6lbs and was 5ft.9½in tall. Wren won £40 for beating R. Winston in a 20-mile match at Lillie Bridge on November the 14th 1881. He then made £30 for beating H. Head over a similar distance on the same track on October the 20th 1882. He had just lost his title as the *"Cabmen's Champion."* He would be attended to by his brother while he stayed in the race.

CONDITIONS TO BE OBSERVED BY THE CONTESTANTS

1. The contestants will be started in rows of three, each man opposite his own scorer, and with left hand to the inside of the track.

2. Contestants will be allowed to reverse in front of their scorer but must notify him one lap in advance.

3. Contestants travelling with their left hands to the inside will have right of way and those going the opposite direction must pass outside of all whom they meet.

4. Contestants must not travel abreast of each other, as such practice hinders those who are going faster and wish to pass.

5. One contestant will be allowed to pass another on the outside only, and must not step in front of another until he has a lead of at least six feet.

6. Except when passing another, each contestant must travel close to the inside of the track, so as to allow others to pass him without hindrance.

7. When a contestant wishes to stop for any reason, either for a long or short time, he must step off the track.

8. Great care must be taken to avoid accidental fouls or annoyances; and if the judge on duty reports to the referee that any contestant has wilfully and intentionally fouled, hindered, or annoyed another, the offender will be disqualified.

9. No contestant will be allowed to stop in front of the scorer's stand as such practice annoys the scorers, and is apt to cause errors.

10. When any contestant has any complaint to make he should not waste his own time, but should explain the matter to his trainer, and have him attend to it.

11. Only male attendants will be allowed, and they must remain in the places assigned to them, and not accompany their men around the track.

12. The contestants in this race will have no time to respond in receiving visitors and will not be allowed to annoy their opponents. No one will be allowed in the enclosure containing the quarters of the pedestrians, except their attendants and the reporters on duty.

13. Each contestant while on the track must wear neat and clean clothing, treat his opponents with fairness and courtesy, and travel as far as he possibly can in the seventy two hours.

14. The Sporting Life will appoint the referee, whose decision in any and every case shall be final, and subject to no appeal in any court of law.

15. Any man not covering fifty miles on the first day forfeits his right to further competition, and in order to give the likely men a chance of making a record, the track will be cleared at the referees decision, of such competitors as have not made sufficiently good scores to give reasonable expectation of their earning the talent money.

On a bitterly cold morning in London, in front of a large contingent of Littlewood's supporters (estimated at between 300 and 400) who had made the journey down from Sheffield, Lieutenant General Goodlake sent the men on their way at 11:04. Littlewood, the 5/4 "jolly," who was in the rearmost division with the 6/4 second favourite Rowell, soon made his way to the front, and then settled in a line of three with Mason and Cartwright. The latter named showed the way thereafter, and at the end of the first mile, and for the first two hours, kept on in the lead with Littlewood and Rowell keeping him close company. Cartwright returned 9 miles 7 laps for his first hour's work and was two laps ahead of the rest headed by Littlewood, and Mason who was a close third. This state of affairs continued when the scores were hoisted at 13:00, with the "Brummie" leading the "Tyke" by a further lap on 18.8.

During the third hour, Littlewood, who had been snapping at the Walsall man's heels, took the lead. Rowell meanwhile, advanced into fifth position, a move which apparently caused the crowd to become quite *"excited."* By the end of the hour the northern candidate had thrilled the ever increasing crowd by extending his lead to seven laps over his midland rival who was next best man in the race with 26.5. Mason remained in third with 25.8. Franks was three laps behind him with Rowell a lap behind him and Vandepeer, sixth, on a score of 24.3.

At the end of the fourth hour, the positions had altered somewhat. Rowell had moved himself up to third after quickening up his pace significantly to lop three laps off the distance between himself and the leader. The Cambridge man was now only a mile and a half behind the Sheffielder, and gaining with every stride. This quickly diminishing lead was further eroded when Littlewood had to significantly slow down due to an attack of rheumatism in his left leg. This meant that by the end of the fifth hour, Rowell had reduced the gap to just four laps on a score of 40.8. Furthermore, he was now in second position. The fifth hour scores: **Littlewood, 41.2; Rowell, 40.8; Cartwright, 40.4; Franks, 39.3; Mason, 39; Vandepeer, 37:**

King of the Peds

With Franks the *"dough puncher,"* as he was affectionately named by one of his admirers, doing surprisingly well, the teatime scores at 17:00 were: **Littlewood, 49; Rowell, 48.4; Franks, 45.9; Cartwright, 45.4; Mason, 44.4; Vandepeer, 44.3; Connor, 39.6; Hunt, 39.3; McCarty, 37.3; Bergin, 33.5; Wren, 31.1; Pettitt, 30.2:**

The record for the fastest 50 miles created by George Hazael at the Agricultural Hall on 21st April 1879 of 6h.14m.47s was beaten firstly by Littlewood when he covered the same distance in 6h.8m, and later by his nearest adversary, Rowell, in 6h.11m.30s. Rowell soon had a short rest, and Littlewood taking advantage of it, went on to put three laps between himself and his great rival. After that they both went on to break the old 60-mile record, again made by Hazael, but this time in New York on May the 23rd 1881, which he achieved it in a time of 7h.47m. The old record was broken firstly by Littlewood in a time of 7h.33m.10s, and then by Rowell in 7h.39s.

Whilst the racing was taking part, there were other attractions on offer within the building. One was a circus, and the other was a billiard match between Cook and Peall. Both attractions however, failed to win over the many spectators who were far more interested in the *"doings"* on the track where the band and the peds were far more entertaining. The competitor who responded to the musicians' urgings most was the *"Black-countryman,"* Cartwright who, according to the tempo of the music, made spurt after spurt. Wren also ran well and *"little Hunt"* reminded some observers of Peter Crossland with the way he carried himself around the ring.

The eight o'clock scores: **Littlewood, 69.6; Rowell, 69; Cartwright, 64.8; Franks, 63.6; Mason, 60.8; Vandepeer, 56.5; Hunt, 53.8; Connor, 53.3; McCarty, 50.3; Wren, 45.3; Bergin, 45.1; Pettitt, 40.7:**

Another of Hazael's records was to be broken by the race leaders. This time it was the 70 miles that the ex-142-hour champion had made in a time 9h.12m.45s (It must be remembered that Hazael was competing over 142 hours and not in six 12-hour sessions as in the present race). This was beaten in a time of 9h.3m.15s by Littlewood and 9h.4m.12s by Rowell. Of the crowd's reaction to the new records, the *Sporting Life* wrote: **In America every man amongst the thousands of lookers on would have been in a ferment of excitement as the previous best performance were eclipsed, but only people not affected to enthusiasm by that sort of thing. Besides, they had not altogether a good opportunity of what was being done, unless they kept themselves to themselves. So it was not a cheer that was made when Littlewood smothered the 70 miles record.**

Later, there was some talk of one of the leaders making 90 miles by the end of the night, and the possibility of the feat being achieved might have had a marked affect on the ever increasing attendance. There were many bookmakers in the crowd, but there was no betting as such, as gambling had been banned by the management within the building. That doesn't mean that some private bets hadn't been made outside, that the score would be made. Those that had wagered for that total to be achieved would have their "fingers burnt," for as the record shows below, when "Time!" was called at 23:04, the scores stood at:

	Miles	Laps		Miles	Laps
Littlewood	89	5	**McCarty**	65	1
Rowell	88	9	**Connor**	65	0
Cartwright	80	0	**Hunt**	60	0
Franks	78	8	**Wren**	57	9
Mason	75	6	**Bergin**	55	3
Vandepeer	68	0	**Pettitt**	51	1

On that first day of the race Littlewood created the following records: 56 miles 552 yards in 7 hours; 65 miles 1,584 yards in 8 hours; 69 miles 1,056 yards in 9 hours; 76 miles 880 yards in 10 hours; 82 miles 1,584 yards in 11 hours (beating Cartwright's best first day effort of 82 miles and 320 yards which he passed in a time of 10h.53m.10s) and 89 miles 1,510 yards in 12 hours, and *also*.....

Miles	Hours	Minutes	Seconds	Miles	Hours	Minutes	Seconds
62	7	50	40	74	9	39	10
63	8	0	40	75	9	48	30
64	8	9	50	76	9	57	50
65	8	19	0	77	10	7	0
66	8	28	10	78	10	15	30
67	8	37	10	79	10	24	40
68	8	46	0	80	10	33	56
69	8	54	40	81	10	42	10
70	9	3	15	82	10	51	10
71	9	11	40	83	11	0	30
72	9	20	50	84	11	9	50
73	9	30	0				

On the second day of competition, the building was said to be very cold. Only nine of the original twelve started. Hunt, Vandepeer and Burgin were the absentees when the lads went on their way at 11:02.

As the day wore on, and with an ever swelling audience, there was no change in the positions. Littlewood kept the freezing temperature at bay by maintaining a consistent three quarter of a mile advantage between himself and Rowell, the two hardly resting in comparison with the rest of the field. The race leader went on to add another two laps in distance, owing to Rowell taking a short respite from the fast and furious pace.

It was rumoured at the time that Rowell's plan was to follow Littlewood closely till Thursday afternoon, pass him, and then build a sizable lead thereafter. It was further reported that whilst Rowell took little refreshment, Littlewood drank the occasional bottle of ale.

The best record for 15 hours was 107 miles and 1,210 yards, made by Rowell in New York on the 27th of February 1882. Both leaders had clearly demolished it when the scores at 14:00 were announced as: **Littlewood, 111.5; Rowell, 110.8; Cartwright, 99.4; Franks, 96.3; Mason, 95.6; Connor, 83.3; McCarty, 82.9; Wren, 75.3; Pettitt, 63.2:**

Soon after, Mason passed Franks to take fourth position. The band then made an appearance which enlivened the atmosphere somewhat, and there were occasional spurts witnessed by the spectators. Apart from the two leaders, only Mason kept up good work, the rest reduced to walking through fatigue. The 5 p.m. scores: **Littlewood, 130.2; Rowell, 129.7; Cartwright, 114.6; Mason, 112.3; Franks, 105.8; McCarty, 96.2; Connor, 92.8; Wren, 82.5; Pettitt, 74.4:**

Little happened thereafter apart from McCarty, *"the low, low comedian"* making the crowd chuckle with his clowning, and Cartwright bringing about some cheering with his spectacular sprinting. Only Mason was making some real headway in the race. Lap by lap he made relentless progress, until at 8 p.m., when the following returns were released, he found himself only 7 laps adrift of his flamboyant opponent Cartwright: **Littlewood, 146.9; Rowell, 146.2; Cartwright, 129.7; Mason, 129; Franks, 116.9; McCarty, 110.2; Connor, 105; Wren, 93.2; Pettitt, 85.4:**

By taking a break of 20 minutes Mason lost all the gains he had made in the previous hour. Later, and in a time of 21h.51m.30s, Littlewood made 150 miles and 1,408 yards, which beat his own best performance made on Christmas Day of the previous year by 40 yards *and* with 2h.8m to spare! The 9 p.m. scores: **Littlewood, 151.4; Rowell, 150.7; Cartwright, 134.3; Mason, 132.4; Franks, 120; McCarty, 114.2; Connor, 109.8; Wren, 96.5; Pettitt, 90.1:** After that at 21:58 he made the best ever distance made in 24 hours.

The building was choc-a-bloc when McCarty, who had been determined to occupy Franks's position, succeeded in his mission after ten o'clock. Mason continued to duel with Cartwright, but it was the former who left the track with the advantage. Rowell was content to follow in the northerner's footsteps and he got plenty of support from his fellow townsmen who supported him in his work. As was always the case, all the men improved their speed in the last few minutes; the excitement created giving many people watching sore throats to take to work with them the following day. At the end of the 24 hours, the two leaders were almost 10 miles ahead of the record for a 12 hours a day event which had been 152 miles and 1,100 yards, made at Sheffield by Littlewood the previous December:

Pos		Miles	Laps	Pos		Miles	Laps
1	Littlewood	162	4	6	Franks	121	0
2	Rowell	161	7	7	Connor	118	8
3	Cartwright	146	2	8	Wren	104	7
4	Mason	143	4	9	Pettitt	95	0
5	McCarty	124	7				

After being set on their way punctually at 11:00 by Mr. Atkinson on the third day, Littlewood continued to maintain both his good form, and the relatively short distance of eight laps he had created between himself and the pursuing Rowell. The leaders both added seven miles and eight laps in the first hour during which Wren arrived on the track 35 minutes late due to missing a train because of the fog.

The two o'clock scores: **Littlewood, 181.9; Rowell, 181.1; Cartwright, 161.8; Mason, 161.1; McCarty, 139.7; Franks, 134.4; Connor, 131.7; Wren, 115.6; Pettitt, 107.8:**

After three and a half hours, Mason re-caught and passed Cartwright, after which the pair jogged along together. Whilst Connor made good progress, Littlewood maintained his seven-lap advantage over Rowell. However, as the day wore on, with the two leaders varying their gait between running and walking, the northern based candidate slowly added valuable distance between himself and his southern rival, due to some fast work, which brought roars of approval from his supporters. Cartwright and Mason also went well in his rear. Meanwhile, Connor continued to improve and moved up to sixth position.

The "half-time" scores at 17:00: **Littlewood, 198.6; Rowell, 197.7; Mason, 177.6; Cartwright, 175.3; McCarty, 153.5; Connor, 147; Franks, 141.4; Wren, 128; Pettitt, 118.6:**

Littlewood arrived at the 200-mile mark in 30h.13m.30s and was a mile to the good of his ever attentive rival. Indeed, when Rowell accomplished the same feat soon after, Littlewood responded by going into a different gear and added another lap to the distance between them. With some judicious running, the race leader managed to add a couple more laps to the gap at seven o'clock, and when the next hour's scores were hoisted, yet another lap was added as can be seen: **Littlewood, 214.3; Rowell, 213; Mason, 190.4; Cartwright, 189.7; McCarty, 167; Connor, 161; Franks, 148.6; Wren, 136.1; Pettitt, 127.5:**

In the *"other race,"* third placed Mason was soon passed by fourth placed Cartwright. Wren seemed to struggle when walking, but when he upped his pace to a run, he seemed to go along just tickety-boo. Pettitt, who was *"queer on his pins,"* struggled on gamely despite looking all used up at the beginning of the day, whilst the sturdy McCarty jogged on quietly.

By 20:22 the race leader managed to put a mile and a half between himself and Rowell, and at 21:34, he had succeeded in passing the previous best record which he had made in Birmingham in September of 1882, which stood at 222 miles and 960 yards. Again, that fact, when hoisted, wasn't recognised by the masses that had congregated and pushed themselves together like sardines in a tin, all apparently struck by the phenomenon called the *"wobbling fever!"*

George Mason was the third man in the contingent to make 200 miles, which he accomplished in a time of 34h.53m. He was slowly pulling away from Cartwright when the 10 o'clock scores were announced as: **Littlewood, 224.6; Rowell, 223; Mason, 200.5; Cartwright, 198; McCarty, 175.8; Connor, 168; Franks, 154.3; Wren, 143.6; Pettitt, 133.9:**

With the "flyer" from the Midlands making his "double" in 35h.27m, and little Connor impressing everyone by keeping up with the *"swells,"* the crowd was entertained to the mandatory frenzied pace by many of the contestants in the last twenty minutes.

At close of play for the third day, the score was:

Pos		Miles	Laps	Pos		Miles	Laps
1	Littlewood	229	8	6	Connor	173	5
2	Rowell	228	3	7	Franks	157	0
3	Mason	205	8	8	Wren	147	9
4	Cartwright	200	0	9	Pettitt	139	1
5	McCarty	180	7				

Just before Mr. Atkinson gave the word at the start of day four, neither Franks nor Cartwright were at the start. Of those who turned up, Littlewood appeared *"fatigued,"* Rowell looked *"ill,"* Mason was *"all right,"* and Pettitt, the back-marker in the race, appeared *"the freshest of the lot."*

After being dispatched on their journey, the men were joined by the previously missing Cartwright. While he un-stiffened his legs, Littlewood led the way, followed by Rowell who was clearly in a lot of trouble. Charlie had a pained expression on his face which was devoid of its usual colour, but, to give him credit, he put up with whatever troubled him for nearly four and a half miles before seeking the sanctuary of his tent. Under normal circumstances, Littlewood would have increased his speed to take full advantage of his rival's absence, but the race leader plodded on at the same speed possibly with the knowledge something was clearly amiss with his rival. It was already known that Rowell was suffering with a blister but what sort of blister ailed him? The *Sporting Life* tried to explain to its readers that: **A blister may mean merely the detachment of a tiny layer of the outside skin, and forming a sac which breaks with very slight pressure or friction. The same homely word also is used to describe an injury involving bruising of everything, membrane, flesh, muscle, tendon, sheaths, &c., between the bone and the outside covering, with a collection of watery or serous matter, virtually forming a wedge to cut into the most acutely suffering part of the flesh. These and all intermediate grades are all blisters.**

The curtains to Rowell's tent remained closed, and as Littlewood went by it lap after lap, the distance between the pair increased by the minute. No news was good news for the supporters of the "Yorkie" who, by noon, had gained 32 laps on Rowell since the start, Littlewood's score at the time being 237.4. That meant he was 25 miles and a lap to the good of Mason who was back in third place on 212.3.

It wasn't until 13:43 that the doors of Rowell's tent were opened. Out came his trainers one by one, headed by Asplen, then Barnsley, then Simpson. A cheer went up in expectation that Rowell would follow, but when he didn't, there was a deafening silence apart from the thud, thud, thud, of the passing pedestrians' feet. All eyes in the building were now fixed waiting for something to happen. Rowell then appeared… dressed in a thick coat… and looking very ill. A groan went up as the unfortunate, but plucky "crack," hobbled his way out of the staff exit, the cheers of the sympathetic multitude ringing in his ears behind him.

The 2 p.m. scores: **Littlewood, 248.7; Rowell, 232.7 (retired); Mason, 223.4; Cartwright, 213.6; McCarty, 197.4; Connor, 188.2; Franks, 170.6; Wren, 162; Pettitt, 154.2:**

Rowell's premature departure didn't stop Littlewood from keeping up to his work. After completing his 250th mile in 39h.13m, he joined in the excitement as Mason and Cartwright electrified the atmosphere with some gritty racing. Mason later equalled Rowell's final score of 232.7 at 15:37, and Cartwright accomplished the same feat at 17:25. McCarty jogged on relentlessly behind as the rest went along wearily.

The six o'clock returns: **Littlewood, 269.2; Mason, 243.7; Cartwright, 234.6; McCarty, 217.7; Connor, 206.6; Franks, 186.8; Wren, 176.7; Pettitt, 168.1:**

By seven o'clock, Littlewood needed to make 21 miles and 3 laps to beat the longest distance achieved in a 12-hour event at the end of the fourth day. That record which belonged to him, equated to 296 miles and 320 yards. With the turnstiles continually click, click, clicking away, the building was now filling up nicely. Mason and Littlewood, although not the greatest of friends, nevertheless condescended to keep each other company around the track. Meanwhile, the improving little Irish lad, Connor, chose Wren as his trotting partner, whilst Franks and Pettitt, who were both now walking fast, chose to march round together. As time went on, Littlewood, who had been walking stiffly for a while, suddenly picked up his heels and began running at a fast pace. This gave the signal for the quicker Cartwright to raise his game just when the place was getting full to the brim; and with Connor also contributing positively to the speed stakes for a while, there could be only one winner; the *"Walsall Flyer!"*

The scorer's returns at 9 p.m: **Littlewood, 285; Mason, 259.3; Cartwright, 249.8; McCarty, 231.9; Connor, 220.9; Franks, 200.6; Wren, 187; Pettitt, 179.7:**

Many gifts of bouquets of flowers and potted plants had been given to the leading athletes during the last two hours. The management decided that that the public needed to know that Littlewood was going for a new record, so they put up a notice board informing them of his attempt. Needing six miles to accomplish his goal, he was pulled along by Mason, McCarty and Connor, who, roused by the band, put their best effort in to help him secure the distance before the bell rang. Along with the roars of the crowd and the contribution of the fast pace that ensued, eventually brought a successful conclusion for Littlewood, who beat his old record by 410 yards. The score therefore, at the end of the fourth day was thus:

Pos		Miles	Laps	Pos		Miles	Laps
1	Littlewood	296	6	5	Franks	230	0
2	Mason	271	0	6	Connor	210	0
3	Cartwright	257	0	7	Wren	194	8
4	McCarty	241	3	8	Pettitt	187	0

Rowell's departure from the contest made a tremendous difference to the attendance at the Aquarium on the fifth day of the race, especially during the earlier hours. When it became known however that there was a close race going on between some of the other pedestrians, visitors began to flock in, but alas the attendance was poor compared with the previous days.

Considering the work done by the eight remaining men, they all turned out wonderfully fresh in the morning and broke away at a strong run when started by the officials. Littlewood made his 300th mile in 48h.33m.20s, and after that Connor and McCarty went the fastest during the first two hours, the race leader being content to follow in the footsteps of Mason.

The three o'clock account: **Littlewood, 315.4; Mason, 289.7; Cartwright, 276.8; McCarty, 262; Connor, 249.2; Franks, 229.2; Wren, 211.5; Pettitt, 195:**

Throughout the day the proceedings were very tame and uninteresting as the men appeared satisfied with their respective positions. As his long lead was sufficient to give him no cause for alarm, Littlewood took little notice of the faster pace covered by his opponents, and contented himself by going along at a walking pace as the others ran. He wasn't in the least daunted by Mason or McCarty's splendid performances, but it has to be said, matters might have been different had Rowell stayed well.

The 6 o'clock totals: **Littlewood, 330.2; Mason, 305.3; Cartwright, 290.3; McCarty, 276.1; Connor, 261.7; Franks, 242.3; Wren, 222.1; Pettitt, 205.1:**

When the music arrived, it had the effect of perking up both on-lookers and competitors. Several of the pedestrians maintained a steady run while the band played, but relapsed back into a walk when it ceased. Some brisk walking was indulged in during the evening by Littlewood, Mason and McCarty, with the leader initiating the style. Wren put in a lot of running to enable him to seriously think about making 300 miles, whilst Pettitt hurried himself forward with heel-and-toe. There was some hope that Littlewood might go through the six days beating every record for each day, and at 7 p.m., there was an expectation that he might attempt to beat Mason's five-day record (59 miles and 378 yards). That meant however, that he would need to make 24 miles in the remaining four hours – a tall order.

By the ninth hour when the scores at 20:00 were: **Littlewood, 340.6; Mason, 315.5; Cartwright, 299.8; McCarty, 285.6; Connor, 270.6; Franks, 251.4; Wren, 229.4; Pettitt, 212.9;** he had made 5½ miles so there was still some hope, but by the end of the 10th hour it was clear that he wouldn't be able to score the necessary miles required, due to him making just 4.3.

Because the word had gone out that he would try, it meant another whopping attendance would make their way to the building for the evening's performance. Along with the average Joe Bloggs, many famous athletes and celebrities also went along to see the sport. Due to the leader falling behind the previous best record, there was an absence of the excitement that had been witnessed the previous evening; at least until the last hour, when the building was close to bursting point. Littlewood finished his 350 miles at ten o'clock, and as the minutes ticked by, good work was done by all.

At end of the day, the scores read:

Pos		Miles	Laps	Pos		Miles	Laps
1	Littlewood	354	8	5	Connor	284	0
2	Mason	330	5	6	Franks	264	8
3	Cartwright	313	6	7	Wren	241	8
4	McCarty	300	8	8	Pettitt	223	0

The final day of the contest saw Littlewood contenting himself with *"easy work"* all day in front of an ever increasing crowd which, in the final session, had been forced to pay double the normal admission price of a shilling to watch the race. As was normally the case at the end of such a contest, the men on the track would make a real effort to entertain the crowd, by exhibiting their sprinting skills as well as finding other ways to please the audience. *"Plenty of amusement was provided after the gas was lit, several of the competitors going in for antic display when they found their tedious journey almost over."* For their efforts many of pedestrians were rewarded with the usual gifts of flowers and other presents.

A couple of interesting events occurred just after seven o'clock when George Chapman Littlewood, aged one year old, and son of the famous pedestrian, made his first appearance on the track. As his dad was otherwise engaged, the task of carrying him round was given to Pat McCarty. Not to be outdone by the Irishman, George Cartwright introduced an *"aged irascible monkey"* to the crowd, and to much amusement, the pair walked round the path together. Charlie Rowell then turned up at the track accompanied by his trainer Charlie Asplen and it was obvious from the way he struggled to walk that he was still in a great deal of pain.

Littlewood was so far ahead of the rest that he unofficially retired from the race well before the end at 20:30 when he went off the track for nearly half an hour to change his suit. With a real effort during the day, he could have easily beaten his best previous record of 415 miles 960 yards. The winner, wearing a bright white costume, was presented with the belt by Captain Hobson at the conclusion of the event in front of thousands of people who stretched their necks to watch the presentation in front of the scorers' stand. After a speech was made by Hobson, the victor walked a lap wearing the belt which was the same one that had originally been won by Corkey and "Blower" Brown in the former six days and nights contests at the Agricultural Hall. It was now his to keep having won it three times in succession. He was later presented with the £100 prize money.

The Final Score!

Pos		Miles	Laps	Pos		Miles	Laps
1	**Littlewood**	**405**	**4**	5	O'Connor	331	0
2	Mason	384	3	6	Franks	305	2
3	Cartwright	357	4	7	Wren	277	7
4	McCarty	348	0	8	Pettitt	260	6

King of the Peds

The Distances Covered Each Day:

	MON		TUE		WED		THUR		FRI		SAT		TOTAL	
	M	L	M	L	M	L	M	L	M	L	M	L	M	L
Littlewood	89	5	72	9	67	4	66	8	58	2	50	6	405	4
Mason	75	6	67	8	62	4	65	2	59	5	53	8	384	3
Cartwright	80	0	66	2	53	8	57	6	56	6	43	8	357	4
McCarty	65	1	59	6	56	0	60	6	59	5	47	2	348	0
Connor	65	0	53	8	54	7	56	5	54	0	47	0	331	0
Franks	78	8	42	2	36	0	53	2	54	6	40	4	305	2
Wren	57	9	46	8	43	2	46	9	47	0	36	9	277	7
Pettitt	51	1	43	9	44	1	47	9	36	0	37	6	260	6
Rowell	88	9	72	8	66	6	4	4					232	7

The *Sheffield Telegraph*, on Tuesday, the 2nd of December 1884, wrote of **LITTLEWOOD'S RECEPTION AT SHEFFIELD:** Judging from the unusual scene at of bustle and excitement the ordinary bystander in the Victoria Station road yesterday afternoon would have imagined that a terrible railway accident would have occurred. Thousands of spectators lined the sidewalks and blocked the main roads, their presence being occasioned by the return home of George Littlewood, the champion six day's go-as-you-please pedestrian, who proved successful in the competition at the London Aquarium last week. Thousands assembled to give the champion a welcome, and after he had been carried out of the station the horses were un-harnessed from the carriage in waiting, and the vehicle drawn by the populace, while the brass band played "See the conquering hero comes." The first house visited was that of the champion's father, the Old Harrow, Broad Street, Park, and thence a round was made to various sporting houses. The utmost enthusiasm prevailed, and a most cordial greeting was extended to Littlewood, who has now proved his superiority over the best exponents of long distance pedestrianism.

The progress of the Astley "Long Distance Challenge Belt" is shown below. The races in **bold type** denote that the race was a 72-hour event:

VENUE	FROM	TO	WINNER	Miles	Yrds/Laps
Agricultural Hall, London	28-10-1878	02-11-1878	Corkey	520	503
Agricultural Hall, London	21-04-1879	26-04-1879	Brown	542	440
Agricultural Hall, London	16-02-1880	21-02-1880	Brown	553	165
Drill Hall, Sheffield	**24-04-1882**	**29-04-1882**	**Day**	**373**	**5**
Bingley Hall, Birmingham	**25-09-1882**	**30-09-1882**	**Littlewood**	**415**	**960**
Drill Hall, Sheffield	**25-12-1882**	**30-12-1882**	**Mason**	**398**	**3**
Drill Hall, Sheffield	**24-12-1883**	**29-12-1883**	**Littlewood**	**366**	**1,291**
London Aquarium, London	**24-11-1884**	**29-11-1884**	**Littlewood**	**405**	**4**

CHAPTER 48

What Else Happened in 1884

"Blower Brown" died on the evening of Sunday, March the 9th in London.

Weston successfully completed his feat at 21:35 on Saturday night, the 15th of March 1884, having *"scrupulously fulfilled the conditions were laid down for the walk."* He had walked 2,000 of his miles in buildings and the rest on the high roads of England, and during the last week of the walk, performed at the Victoria Coffee Hall, Waterloo Road, London.

 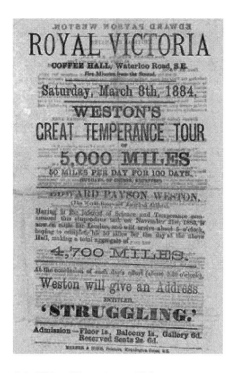

Reproduced with kind permission from John Weiss (Illustration no: 104)

On Wednesday, the 4th of June 1884, the *Atlanta Constitution* in reply to J. M. T., of Macon, Georgia, who wrote in with the question; **"Please give me some facts and figures concerning great walkers and runners:"** Four miles an hour is the ordinary standard pace for a good, brisk country walk; what shall we say, then, to eight miles in an hour, fair heel and toe? Yet this has been done by W. Perkins, J. Raby, Griffin and other professors of the art. Perkins, indeed, has walked one mile in 6 minutes and 23 seconds – a rate of progression nearly approaching 9 ½, miles an hour. On the same occasion he walked two miles in 13 minutes 20 seconds, and

King of the Peds

three in 20 minutes 47 seconds, both unequalled records. The greatest distance ever walked without taking a rest is 120 miles 1,560 yards by Peter Crossland, of Sheffield. The greatest distance ever run in one hour is 11 miles 970 yards, by Deerfoot, at Old Brompton in 1863; Deerfoot's real name being L. Bennett. The fastest time in which one mile has ever been run on level ground is 4 minutes 16 1/5 seconds, by W. Cummings, of Paisley, in 1881, at Preston: but in 1863, W. Lang ran a mile over a course which was partly down hill in 4 minutes and 2 seconds. The swiftest runner hitherto seen is a man named Hutchens, formerly a newsboy at Putney station. In a Sheffield handicap he has covered 131 ½ yards in 12 ½ seconds, a performance which shows him many yards better than "even time" at one hundred yards, and even time is the unattained ambition of the great array of amateurs. (A hundred yards in "even time" means one hundred yards in ten seconds, or a rate averaging ten yards per second.) And he has performed the prodigious feat of covering 300 yards in 30 seconds, dead, the most wonderful piece of running on record. In 1873, R. Buttery, of Sheffield, ran a quarter of a mile in 48 ¼ seconds, which remains unbeaten to this day. George Hazael has run 50 miles in three seconds less than six hours and a quarter, and he has also performed the prodigious feat, only recently outdone in New York, of covering 600 miles in six days, "go-as-you-please," a pedestrian journey in which the competitors may run or walk as they prefer.

On the 4th of May 1884, it was reported that Kate Harriman, wife of Charles Harriman, had begun a suit of divorce against her husband in Truckee, California, alleging *"desertion and failure to provide."*

A six-day heel-and-toe walking-match between William Edwards, champion of Australia, and Frank Hart of Boston, for $1,000, was concluded at the rink in Denver, Colorado, at midnight on Saturday, May the 25th 1884, Edwards winning by 9 miles and 5 laps. The score at the close stood: **Edwards, 428.6; Hart, 416.10:** After the match it was announced that the proprietors of the rink, Belmont & Hanson, would back Edwards against any pedestrian in the state of Illinois from $100 to $1,000 in a similar contest, to take place in Chicago, and that they had already deposited a $100 forfeit with the editor of the *Chicago News*.

After hearing about Weston's 5,000-mile feat which had been performed in England, Capt. Paul Boyton, the swimmer, made a bet that George Noremac, who had stated that he could beat it, could walk 5,100 miles in 100 days. Mr. Herbert Carpenter, the proprietor of the St. Omer Hotel, said he couldn't, and both wagered $1,000 on the outcome.

The rules of the walk stated that Noremac should cover 51 miles per day for 100 days between 9 a.m. and midnight on a small, narrow 44 laps to the mile sawdust track at the 70 feet long by 28 feet wide Midlothian Hall which was situated at No. 466 Eighth Avenue, New York. To accomplish the feat Noremac would have to cover 2,244 laps daily. A hundred people could squeeze themselves into the tiny hall where a piano and a violin were provided to spur the walker on; and to entertainment the crowd, Norman Taylor, the "pie eater" was employed as one of the lap scorers.

Noremac started his task on November the 3rd 1884 at 10 a.m.

CHAPTER 49

International Pedestrian Tournament

The following advertisement appeared in the *Sporting Life* on the morning of the 27th of April 1885. One of the "hot" favourites for 1st place honours was Charlie Rowell who left for the metropolis on the five o'clock train from Cambridge the day before and spent that night with his trio of trainers Asplen, Barnsley and Longford at the Westminster Hotel. Many of the other competing pedestrians had been observed *"walking about the precincts of Westminster Abbey with hair cropped short and light ash sticks in their hands, accompanied by their trainers."*

ROYAL AQUARIUM WESTMINSTER.

Open at 10.30 a.m; close at 11.30 p.m.

THIS DAY (MONDAY APRIL 27) to SATURDAY, MAY 2 1885.

11 a.m. to 11 p.m. each day.

SIX DAYS' INTERNATIONAL PEDESTRIAN

TOURNAMENT

(Twelve Hours per Diem) for the

GO-AS-YOU-PLEASE

CHAMPIONSHIP OF THE WORLD (open to all).

First prize, Gold Championship Medal) and £100; second £25; third, £20; fourth, £7 and £5 to all men not getting a prize who travel 300 miles.

SELECTED COMPETITORS

GEORGE LITTLEWOOD, Sheffield (seventy two hours go-as-you-please champion of the world).

CHARLES ROWELL, Chesterton (ex-long distance champion of the world).

L'EcLAIRE ACHILLE, (long distance champion of France).

W. CORKEY, Bethnall Green (ex-long distance champion of England).

GEORGE MASON, Ratcliffe (ex-seventy two hour champion).

PETER CROSSLAND, (ex-long distance champion walker of the world).

A. W. SINCLAIR, (ex-amateur long distance champion walker of the world).

GEORGE CARTWRIGHT, (the flying collier) of Walsall.

H. CARLESS, Millwall (winner of several provincial tournaments.

GEORGE CONNOR, Bow (a young and promising long-distance runner.

E. WARNER, Poplar (undoubtedly a flyer, and if a stayer, will about win).

King of the Peds

*H. VANDERPEER Sittingbourne (long distance champion of Kent.

PAT McCarty, Leeds (an old stager and place getter).

ALF DAY, Fulham (a promising novice).

A. STEVENS, Camberwell (a plodder that will beat 300 miles).

GEORGE J. DAY, Islington (a novice with an iron constitution).

W. SLATER, Winchmore Hill (has covered fifty miles inside seven hours).

J. WADE, London, (Brummy Meadows novice).

C. SMITH, Hackney (a good all round ped).

ALF PERRY, Old Brompton (the Regent Pet's novice).

*Doubtful starter.

Racing hours, 11 a.m. till 11 p.m. each day. Competitors to attend not later than ten o'clock on Monday morning next.

Prizes and prize money amounting to £250 would be awarded to those competing certain distances during the week, *"whilst the referee has the power to stop any runner who did not show a fair prospect of putting in a decent record."* One of the main attractions in the race would be the champion of *"La Belle France, L'Eclair Achille, the most illustrious pedestrian on the Continent."* The Frenchman was reported to have made 600 kilometres on the roads of his home country in six days, and had reportedly done so with ease. He was described as a *"nimble little Zouave-like figure, with short black hair and moustache and olive complexion."*

For anybody wishing to make their way to the track by train, the *Sporting Life* published the following information on how to get there: -

RAILWAY ARRANGEMENTS, &c

LONDON, BRIGHTON, AND SOUTH COAST RAILWAY. – Trains from all stations to Victoria. Visitors to Epsom Races can journey direct from Epsom Downs Station only to Victoria.

LONDON AND SOUTH-WESTERN RAILWAY. – Trains from all stations to Waterloo. Visitors to Epsom Races can journey direct from Epsom Town Station to Waterloo.

Victoria and Waterloo Stations are within a few minutes walk of the Royal Aquarium.

The Metropolitan and Metropolitan District (outer and inner circle) trains run to St. Jame's Park and Westminster Stations (close to the Aquarium).

Omnibuses from all parts of the metropolis pass the Aquarium.

And for anybody who wanted to experience the food on offer in the building: -

REFRESHMENTS can be obtained in the dining galleries, where Messrs,. Bertram and Roberts supply hot or cold luncheons, chops and steaks from the silver grill, dinners *a la carte* , at fixed prices, at any hour, also the Club Dinner daily from 5:30 till 9:30 (3s.6d per head).

The arrangements for the track which was *"a substantial wooden stage raised upon trestles,"* was exactly the same as in the last competition held in the same building the year before with the *"pad"* being made up of *"cocoanut fibre refuse, faced with loam."*

The betting at the start: **Littlewood, 5/4; Rowell, 2/1; Cartwright, 10/1; Warner, 12/1;** *"Bar four,"* **20/1:**

With Sheffield's Crossland, and Sittingbourne's Vandepeer, failing to turn up, the 18 competitors who took part got on their way at 11:04 following the command by Mr. Atkinson. Smith took an immediate lead, but it was

Archie Sinclair who led after a mile in a time of 6m.11s. The same man led them round at the two and four-mile marks in times of 12m.40s, and 25m.53s, respectively. As expected, Cartwright took control after 4½ miles with the two top contenders for first prize, Rowell and Littlewood, happy to tag along behind, the Sheffielder appearing somewhat relaxed as he ran.

As the clock struck midday, Cartwright, who was described as *"a beautiful runner with a bounding stride like an antelope,"* and with a *"good tempered grin, which is very taking with the multitude,"* was joined in the lead by Mason. With both men registering the same distance of 9.2 on the leader board, they were hotly pursued by Sinclair, Littlewood, Warner, Connor and Wade. During that first hour Rowell, who refused to join in the mandatory fast paced run, jogged along at his own familiar pace, inspiring a comment from one of the "knowing ones" in the crowd who quipped, "He's clocking it."

1st hour scores: **Cartwright, 9.3; Mason, 9.2; Littlewood, Sinclair and Warner, 9.1; Connor and Wade, 9; Smith, 8.6; Stevens, 8.4; Achille and A. Day, 8.3; Slater, 8.2; Carless, Corkey and Rowell, 8; J. Day and McCarty, 7.6; Perry, 7.1:**

The warm climate inside the building made it necessary for the competitors to be administered with the obligatory cold sponge on a regular basis.

2nd hour scores: **Cartwright and Warner, 17.5; Mason and Sinclair, 17.3; Connor and Littlewood, 17.2; Wade, 17; A. Day and Smith, 15.9; Slater and Achille, 15.7; Corkey and Rowell, 15.4; Carless, 15.1; J. Day, 14.7; Stevens, 14.2; McCarty, 12.9; Perry, 12.4:**

Warner continued to make good progress. By the end of the third hour, and as the record below shows, he just nipped in front of Mason to lead the race. Rowell was still happy to watch the leaders scrap it out for supremacy, his early race companion, Corkey, unable to match his jog-trot. The ex-champion preferred to walk along with the Frenchman who *"looked out of his element."* **Warner and Mason, 25; Cartwright and Sinclair, 24.8; Littlewood, 24.5; Connor, 23.6; A. Day and Rowell, 22.6; Corkey, 21.6; Achille, 20.3; Carless, 20.2:**

The "Cambridge Wonder," the proven athlete that he was, relied upon his many years of experience to take opportunities to advance in his races when they came. He was quite happy to bide his time and wait in mid-division knowing full well that his proven method of conveyance was his personal insurance policy for achieving good results. Thus "Ansome Charlie" plodded along as the fleet footed "Flying Collier" once again took hold of the reins "up front." Warner couldn't match his speed and the Poplar man quickly fell back to fourth "pozzy" by the end of the fourth hour having been overturned by him and Mason on the 26th mile. Meanwhile, the "Tyke" now nestled himself behind the leader as the record below illustrates: **Cartwright, 32.3; Littlewood, 31.7; Mason, 31.4; Warner, 31; Sinclair, 30.3; Rowell, 29.8; Connor, 28.6; Smith, 28.4; A. Day and Wade, 27.4; Corkey, 27.1:**

The turnstiles had been clicking away merrily since midday. True, there was the big attraction of watching a score or so of colourfully costumed men endlessly circling a dirt track, but there was also plenty of other entertainment on offer to the general public. Such attractions were the subject of another advertisement on the day of the race, again, placed in the *Sporting Life*.

The monster entertainment consisting of Miss. Nelly Reid and her wonderful Australian Jumping Horses, Barnum's Flying Woman, Maggie Claire, Pierce and Monaghan (negro delineators), Schmidt Michel (feats of strength), Ouzalo (high trapeze), Bobee Brothers, Professor Sawyer, Miss Kate Sullivan (the charming Ballad singer), &c., &d., will be continued during the week. Band of 100 performers. Admission. 1s.

During the week the Beckwith Family, in the Annexe, will give their swimming entertainment, and in the billiard gallery, John Roberts, jun. (champion) and William Cook (ex-champion) will play each afternoon and evening their match of 12,000 up (Cook receiving 2,000 start), for £100.

A few of the above performers had managed to attract some of race-goers to part with an extra "bob" and watch their acts. For those who chose to keep their silver in their pockets, the accompanying band which came with the price of admission, provided an alternative and cheaper attraction not only to the punters but to the peds as well. The music which was provided was certainly well received by the competitors who appreciated every note above

King of the Peds

the din from the crowd. It also served as an inspirational medium to spur the more jaded on. One of those was Sinclair and he soon found the going too tough to keep up with the big boys at the front. Falling back through the pack, he was passed by the likes of Rowell, who as the score shows below, now went into fifth place at 4 o'clock: **Cartwright, 39.5; Littlewood, 38.8; Warner, 38.1; Mason, 37.7; Rowell, 36.8; Sinclair, 34.8; Connor, 34.1; Smith, 34; A. Day and Wade, 33.3:**

With six hours completed, Rowell was observed to be showing better form, whilst Littlewood was described as appearing *"decidedly queer."* Whatever the reporter meant really didn't matter to the gritty Yorkshireman, for during the hour he managed a sterling effort of 6.9 miles. This was one lap less than Rowell, who much to the pleasure of his fan club, now moved smoothly into fourth position, Mason dropping back to accommodate the Chesterton's mans former place. Thus the *"half time"* scores at 5 o'clock were: **Cartwright, 46.5; Littlewood, 45.7; Warner, 43.9; Rowell, 43.8; Mason, 43.2; Sinclair, 40.3; Smith, 40.3; Connor, 39.4; A. Day, 39.2; Wade, 38.6; Slater, 37.2; Corkey, 36.5; J. Day, 35.7; Carless, 34.6; Stevens, 33.8; Achille, 32.8; McCarty, 31.8; Perry, 29.2:**

The next hour saw the *"ladies' pet"* George Cartwright going all out to repel the challenges of the other top three contenders in the race which really enlivened the *"doings"* on the track.

The 7th hour scores (6 p.m.): **Cartwright, 53; Littlewood, 52; Warner, 50.9; Rowell, 50.1; Mason, 48.1; Sinclair, 45.3; Smith, 45.2; Connor, 45.1; Wade, 43.8; A. Day, 43; Corkey, 42; Carless, 40.6; J. Day, 40:**

Rowell was the star of the show during the next hour. Taking advantage of Littlewood being off the "pad" for several minutes to "sup some tea," he managed to reduce the distance between himself and the Sheffielder who, when he returned, wasn't going along as well as he normally did. Thus, Rowell not only managed to gain eight valuable laps on Littlewood, but he also overtook Warner to go into third place: The scores at 19:00 with Littlewood and Rowell the **55/40** and **60/40** 1st and 2nd favourites: **Cartwright, 59.4; Littlewood, 58.1; Rowell, 57; Warner, 56.4; Mason, 54.4; Sinclair, 50.9; Connor, 50.4; Wade, 50.2; Smith, 50; A. Day, 49; Carless, 44.8; J. Day, 44.7:**

As the above scores were hoisted at seven o'clock, the bookmakers licked their chalks and scribbled the new odds of winning on their blackboards. "Eleven to eight Littlewood!" they shouted, "Six to four Rowell!" The "jolly," then pulling himself together, held off the persistent challenges of "the little un," who, in league with "Gorgeous George" Mason, really began to turn the screw. The pressure worked on Rowell's 59th mile when the pair finally prized themselves away from the champion with Mason, then getting the better of the "Fen-man." Another of the lads on the track who was impressive was the diminutive Georgie Connor, as little by little, he made progress towards the front.

What the scoreboard said at 8 o'clock: **Cartwright, 65.4; Littlewood, 64.5; Rowell, 63.5; Warner, 61.9; Mason, 60.3; Sinclair, 55.4; Connor, 55.1; Smith, 55; Wade, 54.6; A. Day, 53.1; Carless, 49.9; J. Day, 49.2:**

Mason took the longest break of the day of any of the men at the head of affairs, which ended up being seven minutes. Egged on by the now performing band, Littlewood swept passed Cartwright at 20:41 on the eighth lap of his 68th mile to take the lead. After 10 hours from the start he showed three laps in front of the Walsall man, with Rowell back in third planning his next move: **Littlewood, 70.6; Cartwright, 70.3; Rowell, 69.5; Warner, 67.2; Mason, 65.1; Connor, 60.1; Smith, 59.9; Sinclair, 59.6; Wade, 58.9:**

Sir John Astley accompanied by Edward Payson Weston and General Goodlake V.C. now entered the building and watched the race with keen interest from the stands. When Littlewood left the track for half a minute, the ever improving Rowell saw his chance to nick a few yards off the race leader, and this he jolly well did as the 10 o'clock scores showed: **Littlewood, 76.5; Cartwright, 76.4; Rowell, 75.5; Warner, 73.3:**

In front of an *"enormous crowd"* there was to be some *"hot"* racing before the end of the day between Rowell, Littlewood and Cartwright. Rowell was in really sparkling form and lapped the two front runners constantly in his determined effort to reach pole position before "Time" was called. At 22:41, and in his 78th mile, he managed to wrest second place from the tiring midlander. The target now was the top "pozzy" and to get that he had to conquer his old foe. The relentless Rowell kept on biting away at Littlewood's heels until at last, at 22:45, the announcement was made: "Eighty miles, five laps all!" George wasn't up for the fight as much as Charlie, and amid the appreciative applause, it was the "little un" who went on to secure the lead at the end of the first day.

Pos		Miles	Laps	Pos		Miles	Laps
1	Rowell	82	1	10	Corkey	66	2
2	Littlewood	82	0	11	Carless	64	3
3	Cartwright	80	5	12	A. Day	64	2
4	Warner	78	6	13	J. Day	61	0
5	Mason	77	7	14	Achille	60	5
6	Sinclair	72	2	15	McCarty	58	5
7	Connor	69	2	16	Slater	56	0
8	Smith	68	1	17	Perry	51	8
9	Wade	66	5	18	Stevens	43	6

In front of a fair sprinkling of spectators, the second day of the match started at the prescribed time with three of the original 18 starters missing. Stevens had effectively barred himself from continuing as he hadn't amassed the requisite 50 miles, and Alf Day quite rightly decided that 300 miles in six days was beyond his capability. Perry however, although absent, was expected to rejoin the race later.

Of the men who *"toed the line"* that morning Rowell looked in the best shape. Littlewood however, didn't look right, and as the race progressed started to lose ground. With Perry now back in the race, Rowell was the first man to make 100 miles in 14h.36m followed by Cartwright, who had earlier robbed Littlewood of his second spot, in 14h.44m. The Sheffield man later made the same score in 14h.48m. These centuries were made at a time when the men made their way around the course at walking pace.

The 2 o'clock scores: **Rowell, 102.5; Cartwright, 101.6; Littlewood, 101.2; Warner, 96.3; Mason, 94.4; Connor, 86.5; Corkey, 83.6; Sinclair, 83.5; Wade, 81.8; Smith, 80.7; Carless, 79.6; Achille, 76.6; Day, 72.9; McCarty, 71; Slater, 66.3:**

As soon as the band arrived, and the building began to fill up, the enlivened atmosphere facilitated a speedier gait from the performing pedestrians. All good things come to an end, and as was usual in these sorts of contests, the men after being unable to keep the quicker pace up, were soon moving round the track a little less enthusiastically. Mason made ground on Warner who began to flag and Cartwright relaxed his grip of second place after five o'clock allowing Littlewood, not only to reclaim that position, but to gradually pull away. That happened after Cartwright had found the challenge of taking on the Frenchman irresistible. Goading him to spurt, Cartwright fell into the his Gallic trap, and playing to the audience, sped away, later paying the price for his naivety by having to drop into a walk which didn't suit him one iota. Of the others, the irrepressible William Gentleman crept into the equation after making 100 miles in 18h.25m.24s. "Bravo Corkey!" and "Go on old man!" the crowd roared and off the veteran went to make another lap. Sinclair also produced some acclaim when he made his century five minutes after Rowell had claimed his 125th mile in a time of 18h.35m.22s.

The six o'clock scores: **Rowell, 127; Littlewood, 125.4; Cartwright, 123.8; Mason, 116.3; Warner, 115.1; Connor, 104.5; Corkey, 102.7; Sinclair, 100; Smith, 97.9; Wade, 96.3; Achille, 96; Carless, 95.2; Day, 87.3; McCarty, 82.3; Slater, 76.8; Perry, 56.4:**

After his earlier exertions and subsequent rest from them, Cartwright resumed "business" by flying around the track at the pace he liked best. Carless, who had been plodding away relentlessly all day, finally delivered the goods when he secured his one hundred at 19:01, thus joining Wade who had accomplished the same score a few minutes earlier. Achille was the next man to make the ton four minutes later celebrating with a frisky run which lapped his British opponents. Warner, who had gone so well the day before, eventually retired altogether due to a tendon giving way in his left leg on a score of 128.7 at 20:45. While Corkey and Sinclair hurried themselves along splendidly, Achille began to falter.

King of the Peds

The 9 p.m. scores: **Rowell, 146.7; Littlewood, 145; Cartwright, 138.8; Mason, 135; Connor, 118.5; Corkey, 117.4; Sinclair, 111.7; Smith, 110.6; Carless, 109.2; Wade, 108.8; Achille, 108.5; Day, 99; McCarty, 92.3; Slater, 90.5:**

Mason then led the two race leaders round for the next few miles, and whilst Slater also did some good work, Achille amused the huge crowd by waltzing and whistling around the path. Rowell went on to make 150 miles in 22h.56m.31s. As he made that score, Littlewood was a mile and seven laps in rear with Cartwright 8.7 behind him. The then improving *"Yorkshire idol"* went on to record his ton and a half, in a time of 23h.14m. The last few minutes of the proceedings created quite a stir in the crowd when the 100-piece band played the *"Newcastle National Anthem"* - "The Keel Row," and as the men left the track, they were *"cheered to the echo."* The distances between the leaders remained the same when the state of play at the end of the second day showed:

Pos		Miles	Laps	Pos		Miles	Laps
1	Rowell	156	6	8	Smith	119	3
2	Littlewood	154	9	9	Achille	118	5
3	Cartwright	147	4	10	Wade	117	0
4	Mason	143	9	11	Carless	116	6
5	Connor	126	5	12	J. Day	106	0
6	Corkey	126	2	13	McCarty	100	5
7	Sinclair	119	9	14	Slater	97	7

The next morning many people crowded around the door that led into the dressing rooms waiting to catch a glimpse of the arriving "peds." Such was the pull of these men that they were treated like actors arriving at the stage door. A similar crowd had gathered the night before waiting patiently to catch a glimpse of their idols before they toddled off to their respective hotels. How the men behaved, how they appeared, and what they said, was all interpreted by the perceiver, either in positive or negative terms. Any information would then be used constructively or destructively by "interested parties" like bookmakers for example.

As the hour to start drew close, with many of the men changing into their battle dress inside the vast building, Miss Nellie Reid, *"the fair equestrienne"* was being watched by the gathered crowd, schooling one of her horses over some low lying hurdles.

As the time arrived for the start, all eyes were diverted to the door that led from the changing rooms on to the track. Fourteen men, dressed in an array of gaudy coloured clothing that would put an equivalent number of jockeys to shame appeared, like gladiators entering a Roman arena. Of all the contestants, the little Frenchman stood out as he bowed to the crowd and then to his fellow competitors, before Mr. Atkinson asked them all for their attention before shouting "Go!"

With much interest in the race being maintained on the third day, the ever increasing crowd witnessed the two main principals in the affair continuing to battle it out for "top dog". As the morning progressed, the Frenchman was noted to be putting in a much better performance by keeping up in *"easy style"* with the leaders. The first couple of hours saw Mason, Carless and McCarty indulging in frequent rests, whilst Wade was noted to be moving impressively through the pack thus bettering his position with every step made. With Cartwright indulging in some spurting, Corkey displayed a nice steady trot to keep him up there with the leaders. Whilst Rowell went along in his own indomitable style, there were a few concerns that Littlewood wasn't quite himself, and that his previous days' efforts on the track were having a detrimental effect on his overall performance. His indifferent display meant that as the day progressed, "Chesterton Charlie" was able to put even more distance between him and his rival, in his quest for supremacy. Indeed Littlewood offered very little resistance when the leader drew up beside him and spurted away every time.

The two o'clock scores: **Rowell, 176.6; Littlewood, 173.7; Cartwright, 165.8; Mason, 157.8; Corkey, 143.4; Connor, 140.3; Achille, 136.2; Wade, 135.6; Sinclair, 133.6; Smith and Carless, 131.5; Day, 118.2; McCarty, 111.8; Slater, 103.3:**

Cartwright and Sinclair then started to offer some promise, the former running with gusto at times, and the latter showing good speed whilst walking, despite suffering from the swollen knee that had been troubling him for the past couple of days. As Sinclair was resting on 138 miles, and Achille was taking a bath on 143, the ever improving Wade passed them both. After his soak, the Frenchman tried another tactic which he thought might help him go along in a more positive way – reversing. That didn't work for him either when he soon realised that he was losing too much ground, having to dodge out of his competitors' way as they came towards him, thus losing valuable distance especially on the turns. Giving up on that he threw cold water all over himself, and when that wasn't of too much benefit to him, he tramped around slowly.

The scores at 5 o'clock: **Rowell, 194.5; Littlewood, 191.1; Cartwright, 180.2; Mason, 172.4; Corkey, 157.8; Connor, 153.4; Wade, 149.2; Achille, 146.8; Sinclair, 145.8; Carless, 144.1; Smith, 143.7; Day, 129.1; McCarty, 122.3; Slater, 110.4:**

Achille, despite his best efforts and some concern that he might have to permanently retire from the event, left the track just after six o'clock, having made 150 miles.

Rowell continued to make easy work of his task thereafter. Whenever an opportunity arose to tack himself on to the back of somebody who was willing to make a spurt, he took it. Using Slater then Wade as a pacemaker, he continued to increase the gap between himself and the second placed man. When he became the first to register 200 in 31h.5m.12s, he was 3.7 ahead of the faltering Littlewood who later made the same distance in 31h.46m.47s. Continually urged on by others, the race leader carried on increasing the gap, lap by lap, until he had accomplished a margin of five miles at 19:30.

After eight o'clock, with the band in full swing, Cartwright put on quite a show for the excited throng. It was a well known fact that George loved his music, and his performance at that time eclipsed any other that he had shown previous. Littlewood meantime was clearly in a lot of trouble, his right leg causing such considerable pain that he had no option but to settle himself into a slow walk. Just before 9 o'clock when the scores below were recorded, the Sheffielder must have thought his chances of even coming third were dismal, as he watched Cartwright celebrate his 200th mile in a time of 33h.56m.54s from the start: **Rowell, 216.6; Littlewood, 209.6; Cartwright, 200.1; Mason, 187.3; Corkey, 176.4; Connor, 171.3; Wade, 166.3; Sinclair and Smith, 161.9; Carless, 161.5; Achille, 150; Day, 143.8; McCarty, 138.1; Slater, 125.6:**

During the last couple of hours, Rowell continued to add more space between himself and the ailing Littlewood who was reported to be suffering from *"weakness in the knees."* The end of the day three scores:

Pos		Miles	Laps	Pos		Miles	Laps
1	Rowell	227	7	8	Smith	171	2
2	Littlewood	217	5	9	Sinclair	170	5
3	Cartwright	212	2	10	Carless	168	5
4	Mason	198	1	11	Achille	150	0
5	Corkey	185	3	12	J. Day	150	0
6	Connor	181	0	13	McCarty	147	6
7	Wade	174	4	14	Slater	135	8

Littlewood could barely walk to the starting point on the track at the beginning of the fourth day. But start he did, though it was to no one's surprise that he retired 56 minutes later after making 3 miles and 6 laps due to his knees and feet giving out; his final score being 221.1. After getting himself dressed and shaking the hands of his friends, he left the building. *"With Littlewood out of the way, Rowell had nothing to fear, Cartwright being too far behind to cause him any anxiety."* It was reported that the contest had lost all interest owing to the Sheffield ace's retirement, but that didn't stop the spectators from flocking to the building to watch the other peds battling it out for the other prizes. As forecast, Achille didn't bother turning up for that fourth day.

With the interest in the race fizzling out, the big question was, would Rowell last out till the end? The experienced and clever athlete knew he needed to just stick with the task and not overexert himself to be sure of success. The

King of the Peds

only possible danger was Cartwright, who, at that stage, was about 16 miles adrift. Expectations were that he would take things easily during the course of the day, hoping that the minimum effort would reward him with a nice prize of £25. Mason, in third position, was looking at earning the third prize of a "tenner." He had been having problems with several blisters on his right foot the night before and was evidently still suffering with them. Connor, Sinclair, and the ever popular Corkey, who notched his second century at 13:38, were the only ones of the others who looked as though they might make their presence felt later.

The three o'clock scores: **Rowell, 251.6; Cartwright, 234.4; Mason, 217.5; Corkey, 205.7; Connor, 199.8; Wade, 197.3; Sinclair, 187.5; Smith, 187.3; Carless, 185.6; Day, 165.1; McCarty, 160.2; Slater, 147:**

With little progress being made on the track especially by the tail-enders, it was a godsend that other attractions in the building kept the paying public occupied. The band did their best to enliven the proceedings, but with the withdrawal of Littlewood and Achille, the stuffing had effectively been knocked out of the contest. There was some excitement adjacent to the track when the Frenchman mounted the ladder leading to the Press Stand after five o'clock, where, holding his hat in his hand and bowing respectfully, he handed a formal letter to the referee advising that he would no longer be taking part. On the outside it was addressed to the **"Gentlemen of the Jury for the Pedestrian Contest, Royal Aquarium, Westminster."** Inside it read:

Gentlemen, - I beg you to kindly excuse me for not continuing to take part in the six days' pedestrian contest after my indisposition of yesterday. I find I have lost too much time, and it would be useless for me to try to continue in the same time. I beg you to accept my sincere thanks for the kind reception I have received from you.

Truly yours, Achille.

Meanwhile, on the track, the men were happy to walk for their living, that is, until some pace was injected into the race when Rowell, Slater, and Cartwright decided to hurry things up a bit. After a mile or so, after stretching his legs in the process, it was inevitable that that "Mr. Speedy" would open up the throttle and bring some life into the depressing procession. So that's what George Cartwright did for 20 minutes before settling down to a slower pace along with the rest. Then at 17:57, after he had made his 250th mile, he put on another show of fast running to celebrate the occasion.

The scores at six o'clock: **Rowell, 267.3; Cartwright, 250.3; Mason, 229; Corkey, 219.4; Connor, 213.7; Wade, 207.7; Smith, 198.4; Sinclair, 197.6; Carless, 196.6; Day, 175.9; McCarty, 169.3; Slater, 156.4:**

Corkey made his 220th mile soon after the above scores were registered. Later on in the hour, there was an interesting race between Carless and Sinclair as to who would reach 200 first; the honour eventually falling to Sinclair who beat his opponent to that mark in 43h.29m. Having accomplished that, the ex-amateur went for a wash and brush-up leaving his fellow Londoner to make the same score five minutes later.

The bands' arrival produced the usual reaction on the track, and as was always the case, the man they inspired most, the *"ladies' ped"* responded with predictability. Round and round he went lapping the leader, too many times to count, until at the end of the hour he had increased his score to 267.2. Interestingly Cartwright made 7 miles and 4 laps during the hour and that compared much more favourably to Rowell's 6.1:

The 9 p.m. returns: **Rowell, 284.3; Cartwright, 267.2; Mason, 245.8; Corkey, 233; Connor, 227.7; Wade, 218.6; Carless, 210.2; Smith, 209.9; Sinclair, 208.8; Day, 185.9; McCarty, 180.8; Slater, 167.2:**

The best record for the end of the fourth day, which was 296 miles and 6 laps, was made by Littlewood in the previous contest at the same venue in November of 1884. The possibility that Rowell might attempt to beat that record was one of the talking points amongst the spectators that night. The band didn't help matters by stopping playing, and when that happened, the result was usually a negative display on the track. That is exactly what occurred with the men settling down to a walk. However, after the musicians' tea-break was over, they all piped up again to reinvigorate the performers, and by the start of the penultimate hour, Rowell was seven laps adrift of his target for that hour. Slater was the first of the men to respond to the music and Sinclair and McCarty put on a show of fast heel-and-toe. The race however was now devoid of Smith, who took himself off to the hospital to have his swollen ankles checked out.

As it was, despite the best efforts of the band to rouse him with *"a grand old Irish quadrille embracing "The Shangraun," "Reep o' Day Boys," "Pat Molloy," and other favourite airs,"* Rowell was unable to deliver what might have been and left the track at the end of the day with the scores showing:

Pos		Miles	Laps	Pos		Miles	Laps
1	Rowell	295	4	7	Sinclair	217	7
2	Cartwright	278	6	8	Carless	217	0
3	Mason	256	0	9	Smith	212	1
4	Corkey	241	8	10	J. Day	192	0
5	Connor	237	1	11	McCarty	191	4
6	Wade	225	0	12	Slater	175	5

The fifth day was noted for the return to the track of Achille who somehow managed to influence the judges in allowing him to take a second crack in the race, albeit as a demonstration of his skills for the benefit of some of his fellow countrymen who were in the building. His involvement however, seemed to perk up the rest of the contenders and it was said his presence renewed the spectators' interest in the event. Rowell made his 300th mile in a time of 48h.42m.57s, just before midday, and Connor the youth of *"slight proportions,"* who was considered the champion of the future, made 250 miles in 51h.13m.26s.

The 3 p.m. scores: **Rowell, 318.8; Cartwright, 299.5; Mason, 277.8; Corkey, 261.8; Connor, 252; Wade, 241.6; Carless, 233.5; Sinclair, 232.9; Smith, 228.6; McCarty, 209.2; Day, 206.4; Slater, 191.9:**

Just after the above score was announced, Cartwright made his 300th mile in 52h.2m.23s. As the day progressed, Rowell continued to add further daylight between himself and the rest of the field (4.5 by 17:00 on Cartwright alone, while curiously the Walsall man showed immaturity by indulging in bouts of spurting followed by slow walks). Achille impressed the crowd when he made seven miles in an hour *"in a joyous and light hearted manner,"* but, unable to maintain the pace, quickly slowed and went to his tent.

The six o'clock scores: **Rowell, 336.4; Cartwright, 314.5; Mason, 295.8; Corkey, 275.7; Connor, 265.2; Wade, 253.8; Carless, 245.8; Sinclair, 245; Smith, 239.6; McCarty, 223.8; Day, 216.8; Slater, 203.8:**

Rowell left the race for a short time thereafter, and on his return, walked with the rest. Drama was to follow at half past the hour when Pat McCarty left the track briefly to punch a spectator in the face who had been insulting him. That settled, he rejoined the men on the track to an ovation from the crowd, some of whom apparently tossed presents at his feet! Sinclair made 250 miles in 55h.3m and Mason was next in line for the 300 which he accomplished at 19:20. For going 50 miles further than that at 43 minutes past eight, Rowell received a standing ovation by the vast crowd.

The record for 9 o'clock showed: **Rowell, 351.6; Cartwright, 329.2; Mason, 308.3; Corkey, 289.2; Connor, 279.8; Wade, 263.7; Sinclair, 257.2; Carless, 256.2; Smith, 250.6; McCarty, 235.2; Day, 228.2; Slater, 215.3:**

Cartwright continued to amuse the crowd with his style of stop-start running for the rest of the evening, and the steadily trotting Rowell managed to beat the best record for 60 hours—which belonged to George Mason when he made 359 miles and 377 yards the Sheffield Drill Hall on December the 29th 1882. At the end of the night, after the men had *"run like greyhounds"* during the last few laps, Sir John Astley stepped on to the track to reward Cartwright, Connor, Corkey, McCarty and Sinclair for their efforts with monetary gifts in the form of *"a golden coin of the realm."* At the end of the night, the band once again played "The Keel Row," and when the departing peds took one last look at it before heading off for the dressing rooms, the scoreboard showed:

Pos		Miles	Laps	Pos		Miles	Laps
1	Rowell	362	3	8	Carless	264	4
2	Cartwright	339	1	9	Smith	258	3
3	Mason	314	6	10	McCarty	246	4
4	Corkey	298	0	11	J. Day	236	0
5	Connor	289	2	12	Slater	225	9
6	Wade	271	3	13	Achille	170	9
7	Sinclair	265	9				

On the last day, and as was now the normal practice, the admission price was doubled from a shilling to a "florin." Achille made another appearance, but his interest in the race didn't last long, and he left after performing for an hour. Corkey managed to turn up late, but when he did hit the track, made eye-catching progress. The two leaders propelled themselves forward differently, Rowell adopting the style that had brought him so much success in his career and Cartwright happy to walk in order to achieve his objective of second place. There was another reason for his slower gait. He wanted to save all his energy to show off his speed in front of the packed galleries later on in the day–another of his idiosyncrasies. Little Connor appeared fresh as he pushed himself forward and he was rewarded with scoring his third century in a time of 62h.32m.30s.

The three o'clock score: **Rowell, 384.3; Cartwright, 352.6; Mason, 331.3; Corkey, 314.9; Connor, 303.5; Wade, 285.2; Sinclair, 282; Carless, 279.8; Smith, 273.2; McCarty, 266.1; Day, 250.2; Slater, 236.4:**

Rowell went on to complete his 400th mile at 17:52. There was plenty of time to beat Littlewood's record of 415 miles and 960 yards made in the second Astley Belt contest on September the 30th 1882. There was also the question as to whether he could beat the best sixth day distance, in a similar event made by Peter Panchot in New York on the 1st of May 1880, when that man made 64 miles and 1,120 yards. With Rowell now settling down to a regular five-mile an hour gait, things were looking promising for the *"Little wonder."*

What the scoreboard revealed at 6 o'clock: **Rowell, 401.3; Cartwright, 361.6; Mason, 342.2; Corkey, 327.3; Connor, 314; Wade, 295.3; Sinclair, 294.4; Carless, 291; Smith, 283.8; McCarty, 279.1; Day, 261.8; Slater, 246.1:**

Pat McCarty was determined to earn one of the "five quid" prizes. His work rate during the day was quite beyond what he had been exhibiting during the week, and if he kept it up there was an excellent chance he would be receiving the money later. Meanwhile, the pace-making duties to get Rowell past the old record initially fell on Wade's shoulders; but when he could cope no more, "Gorgeous George" took over the job.

The record at 8 p.m: **Rowell, 412.6; Cartwright, 370; Mason, 353.1; Corkey, 334.9; Connor, 321.5; Sinclair and Wade, 300.1; Carless, 299.3; Smith, 291.1; McCarty, 288.4; Day, 269.6; Slater, 252.6:**

As the evening progressed, the audience grew and grew to watch the conclusion of the race. Many in the now swelling audience had been to Sandown Park racecourse where they had been shouting four-legged animals home. The *Sporting Life* described the scene in the Aquarium: Soon after eight o'clock, notwithstanding the advance in prices of admission, the vast building was crowded to excess - in fact, so densely packed that an expert gymnast could have walked on the heads of the spectators from end to end without the slightest inconvenience. As regards good humour and appreciation, there was no lack. And as the spectators were always on the point of expectation, it required but the slightest spurt on the part of the competitor to create the most intense excitement. Long before the welcome hour arrived the contestants appeared, after a brief retirement, clad in the most tastefully arranged costumes, and as each received a large bouquet the applause became deafening. After eight o'clock the scene almost baffles description, and even when the men simply walked round in Indian file, the sea of upturned faces betrayed the most wonderful interest in each competitor, until a perfect roar proclaimed that one of them had raced away with a spurt, which culminated in the entire contingent following suit with a result that can be better imagined than described.

It was inevitable with the way that the race leader was going that he would beat the old record, and that is precisely what he did at 20:29. History made, he now had 2h.33m.45s to make the best possible score ever in a 12-hour event. Having gone on to accomplish the feat of beating Panchot's sixth day record, he then set out determinedly to make 430 miles before the end of the day. He managed to achieve this objective in great style covering his last mile in 6m.20s which was only 9 seconds slower than the first mile of the contest made by Sinclair. The feat was accomplished with just 4 seconds to spare amid the usual racket with Cartwright playing his part by being the pacemaker, and the band doing their bit by again playing the lively air "The Keel Row."

There was immense cheering when the contest finished at 23:03. Rowell received much praise from the crowd, as he and the rest of the successful men were awarded their prizes from Lord Algernon Lennox in front of the scoreboard. To the strains of "See the Conquering Hero Comes," Rowell and company left the building where a large crowd outside gave them one final cheer.

The Final Score!

Pos		Miles	Laps	Prize	Pos		Miles	Laps	Prize
1	**Rowell**	**430**	**0**	**£100**	8	McCarty	301	8	£5
2	Cartwright	382	9	£25	9	Smith	300	3	£5
3	Mason	370	2	£10	10	Carless	300	2	£5
4	Corkey	343	2	£7	11	Day	281	0	
5	Connor	336	6	£5	12	Slater	264	0	
6	Sinclair	310	7	£5	13	Achille	199	0	
7	Wade	303	3	£5					

Scores by Days:

	Mon	Tue	Wed	Thur	Fri	Sat	TOTAL
Rowell	**82.1**	**74.5**	**71.1**	**67.7**	**66.9**	**67.7**	**430**
Cartwright	80.5	66.9	64.8	66.4	60.5	43.8	**382.9**
Mason	77.7	66.2	54.2	57.9	58.6	55.6	**370.2**
Corkey	66.2	60	59.1	56.5	56.2	45.2	**343.2**
Connor	69.2	57.3	54.5	56.1	52.1	47.4	**336.6**
Sinclair	70.2	49.7	50.6	47.2	48.2	44.8	**310.7**
Wade	66.5	50.5	57.4	50.6	46.3	32	**303.3**
McCarty	58.5	42	47.1	43.8	55	55.4	**301.8**
Smith	68.1	51.3	51.8	40.9	46	42.2	**300.3**
Carless	64.3	52.3	52	48.5	47.4	35.7	**300.2**
J. Day	61	45	44	42	44	45	**281**
Slater	56	41.7	38.1	39.7	50.4	38.1	**264**
Littlewood	82	72.9	62.6	3.6			**221.1**
Achille	60.5	58	31.5	0	20.9	22.1	**199**

CHAPTER 50

What Else Happened in 1885

Daniel O'Leary was interviewed by the press in the early part of 1885. This is what he had to say.

O'Leary: "I do not think pedestrianism is on the wane, although for a year or two past not as much interest as formerly has been manifested in sports of this character."

Reporter: "What effect does these long distance matches have on the human system?"

O'Leary: "Great endurance and physical power is required, as well as intelligent appreciation of the feat to be accomplished and thorough acquaintance with the best methods of caring for yourself. You become exhausted, your feet swell and become sore and your mind is dazed. After the contest absolute rest and as much sleep as your exhausted condition requires is needed. Perhaps for a day or two after the close of a race, with your mental faculties still clouded, you'll start suddenly from your sleep under the impression you must make the track. I am accustomed to use but little alcoholic stimulants during my races. Food nourishment is better, but if the contestant is accustomed to the use of intoxicating liquor, it is preferable he should he allowed them." And with reference to George Littlewood's distance of 531 ½ miles which beat his own best record by 11 ½ miles, in a six days' contest, "I am sure that 550 miles will yet be made in a six day's square heel-and-toe walk."

.... O'Leary would be in a state of shock to know that up till the year 2008, Littlewood's record hasn't been broken!

Reporter: "Are you in good condition; that is, do you feel any evil results from the severe races you have had?"

O'Leary: "I am in good condition and can walk as fast as I ever could. I feel as well as I ever did, and do not think that the matches I have been in have injured me a particle. I expect to visit Australia again in the fall."

On Monday, the 23rd of February 1885, a six-day go-as-you-please race commenced on a 20-lap to the mile *"sifted cinder and sawdust"* track in a large marquis somewhere in Dunedin, New Zealand. There were just four competitors at the start, these being R. Crofts, A. Fosse, J. Rayner and C. Swan. The match was for a sweepstakes of £10 with the winner receiving the total of the combined stakes, and 30% of the gate money, the remainder being divided *"pro rata amongst those covering 300 miles."* In a closely contested event, only three of the men would complete the race on Saturday, the 28th, with Rayner beating Swan and Crofts with scores of 365.14, 362.9 and 359.8 respectively.

Many, many days into George Noremac's attempt to walk 5,100 miles in 100 days, a reporter for the *Mail and Express* asked him how he felt after scoring 4,908 miles?

"Oh, pretty well, so and so. I started in weighing a hundred thirty-eight pounds, and in a few weeks dropped down to a hundred and two. But of late I am gaining in flesh. I shall be glad when I have finished this walk. It has been a long and tedious undertaking. Sick or well, I have to walk every day. A week after I got on the track I began to have pains in my stomach and cramps in my limbs. It was fearful, but I hung on and walked them away. One day in January, I became so sick I had to lay off three hours and then I had to run hard to catch up. I never sleep any during the time of the walk. My appetite is splendid and I eat five and six times a day, with a desire to increase the meals to eight and ten. This is harder than rushing around Madison Square Garden day and night. Here it is spiritless, and the excitement is wanting; hence the task is monotonous and dreary. Why, when I would catch sight of Fitzgerald and Rowell dashing by me it seemed to give me wings, and, for a moment, the pain and cramps would leave me. The public may think this is merely a hippodrome, but it is not. The men who have put up this wager are honest in their intentions, and I have covered every day the distance allotted."

"He's game to the button," said Peter Hegelman, his trainer. "If any other fellow had been struck with cramps like he was along in November, they would have given this walk up. But he is going to win it and I'd stake all I've got on it." The spectators then cheered when Norman Taylor shouted from the scorers' stand, "I'll eat ten thousand pies in that many minutes if he don't win."

Noremac eventually succeeded in accomplishing his task finished at 23:10 on February the 26th 1885. His best mile was made in a time of 6 minutes 39½ seconds in January.

George D. Noremac

5,100 miles in 100 days! *(Illustration no: 105)*

A 50-mile walking match for £50 and the championship of *"the Colony"* took place at Christchurch, New Zealand, on Saturday, the 16th of May 1885, which was won by Arthur Hancock by about 230 yards. John Rayner, the Australian champion, was second and F. Moorhead of Christchurch, third. G. Mublieson of Christchurch also competed, but retired after doing 14 miles. The time of the winner was 8h.10m.4s, and the race finished at 22:20.

The six-day go-as-you-please pedestrian contest on a 14 laps to the mile track at the Monumental Gardens in Baltimore, Maryland, USA, which began on Monday, June the 8th 1885, *"was not a success."* The match was for half the gate receipts and was governed by the Astley rules. *"The garden was packed almost to suffocation"* when the nine starters, which were Elson, Ford, Hart, Hegelman, Panchot, Mackey, Noremac, Sweeney and Vint, set off at five minutes past twelve. Only Panchot finished covering 505 miles in the 142 hours. The others dropped out when they were satisfied that the exhibition would not pay. Panchot received about $200 for his trouble.

The Event of the Season.
Grand pedestrian Contest

75-hours go-as-you-please for a

PURSE OF $500.00!

DIVIDED AS FOLLOWS:

First prize, $250; Second prize, $150; Third Prize $75; Fourth prize, $25.

300 miles must be covered to entitle contestants to a prize. The contest will take place at the

PRINCESS RINK!

Commencing Wednesday, Nov, 18 at 8 P. M., and ending Saturday, Nov. 21, at 11:46 P. M.

LIST OF ENTRIES:

Chas. A. Harriman, of Havre, Mass., champion heel and toe walker of America. Daniel Burns, of Elmira; record 578 miles in six days, horse V. man. Frank L. Hart, of Boston, Mass., ex-champion of the world, record 565 miles. Gus Guerrero, champion of California and winner of the Diamond Belt; John Hanley, of Binghamton; William Day, of England; Calvin Cole, of Binghamton; W. A. Hoagland, of Auburn; Anthony Strokel; champion of Michigan; Michael Tierney, of Wilkesbarre; John George, of Auburn; John Chisnell, of Providence; Benny Jones, of Scranton; Peter Panchot, of Buffalo; Geo. Noremac, of Scotland; Daniel J. Herty of Boston, Mass.

Music by Dabinette's Band.
ADMISSION 20 CENTS.

No extra charge for reserved seats for ladies: Extra attractions each afternoon and evening: The contest will be conducted with strict regard to the rules of propriety, and good order will be positively enforced.

For information call on B. K. Gannon or I. N. Davis, Managers; J. W. Straight, Business Manager, at Gaylord House. Entrance fees $10. Entries close Wednesday, Nov. 18tb. Contestants will hold a meeting at Genesee rink on Tuesday evening, Nov. 17th, at 8 o'clock.

Under electric lighting, nearly 1,500 spectators gathered within the walls of the Princess Rink, Auburn, Massachusetts, to watch the start of the race. Around the outside edge of the skating surface, a sawdust track seven feet wide and an eleventh of a mile in length was laid. Within that, many were seated as they waited the arrival of the pedestrians as the orchestra *"discoursed music more or less entertaining and enjoyable."*

In front of the mile board at 20:30, the local athlete, W. A. Hoagland, introduced the eight starters to the crowd. They were: Dan Burns, Calvin Cole, Gus Guerrero, Frank Hart, John Hanley, Charles Harriman, Dan Herty and Simon Townsend. The men were asked to stand on the track in rows of three where they were read the articles governing the race before being sent on their way at 20:35.

At midday, the day after, Harriman led the race with 89 miles, Hart was in second position with 84 and Herty was a mile back in third. Townsend had only ever raced once on a sawdust track and that was at a fair ground. He trained himself for one week before the race and surprised everybody when he defeated Herty in a heel-and-toe spurt during the early stages of the contest. The 45-year-old went on to complete his century in little less than 26 hours.

Just after 3 p.m. on Friday the 20th, Harriman continued to lead the rest by about ten miles, with the other two leading positions remaining the same.

The close of the match was witnessed by nearly two thousand people on Saturday evening at 22:30, or 74 hours after the start. The contestants retired one by one after eight o'clock, with Harriman and Townsend being the last to go. The official score was: **Harriman, 304.3; Burns, 291.6; Herty, 287.8; Hart, 276.3; Guerrero, 255.4; Hanley, 250; Cole, 171.10; Townsend, 162.4:** The prizes of $250, $150, $75 and $25 were awarded to the first four men in the order named.

On the 14th of November 1885, it was reported that the old rivals, Weston and O'Leary, had met at the office of the *Turf, Field and Farm* in New York, where they signed articles of agreement to challenge each other in a heel-and-toe walking race of 2,500 miles for a purse of $3,000 offered by a New York advocate of temperance, and the net gate receipts.

Both men proposed to walk in skating rinks and covered enclosures throughout the country. Walking 12 consecutive hours a day, between 10:30 a.m. and 10:30 p.m., omitting Sundays, until the entire distance had been made, they agreed not to walk in places where intoxicating liquors were sold. An official scorer had been appointed to follow the contestants, and it was estimated that the long journey would be completed in 48 to 50 days. The winner would take $2,000 of the purse and two-thirds of the net gate receipts, with the loser getting the remainder.

Ten days after the above announcement was made, it was learned that the race would begin at the Metropolitan Rink, Newark, New Jersey, on Monday, December the 7th. The plan thereafter was to walk a week in New Brunswick, a week in Jersey City, then Brooklyn, New York, Syracuse, and finally Chicago.

After Mayor Haynes said the word "Go," and, "may the best man win," O'Leary, wearing a close-buttoned winter sack coat, white tights and light laced shoes, traversed the 13-lap to the mile track at 5 mph *"like a piece of machinery."* As Dan walked with determination, his opponent trailed in his wake finding time to talk to the players in the band and the newspaper reporters. "I haven't walked since March eighteen eighty-four in England and then I covered five thousand miles," said Weston. "O'Leary has always beaten me and he says he can again on a long trip. Now I don't think so. I propose to give his boast a practical test."

O'Leary finished his first five miles in 58m; his opponent finishing the first hour having scored four miles and one lap. Whilst the men went about their business on foot, many women and children wearing skates aped their actions on the ice which the track surrounded and had a lot of fun as they glided around the place keeping in time to the music played by the band. The score at 22:00, a half an hour before the end of the first day's work was: **O'Leary, 52.2; Weston, 50.4:**

On the second day, in front of a larger evening audience, and with both men reported to be in excellent condition, the score at 22:30 was: **O'Leary, 106; Weston, 101:** On the third day, the rink was visited by a large number of city and county officials. They would have been entertained by Weston playing his cornet as he walked round the track. The score at 22:30 with Weston having gained on the leader who had stopped for an hour on his 126th mile due to sore feet was: **O'Leary, 150; Weston, 147:** An extra prize of $300 was offered to the man who led the race after a week and this gave an added incentive for Weston to make significant inroads on his old foe's score. At the end of the fourth day, and despite "Ned" leading Dan earlier in the evening, both men went home with the same score of 193 miles. During Friday the 11th, Weston lost six miles to his opponent, and when both men retired for the night at 22:30, the score stood: **O'Leary, 240; Weston, 234:** O'Leary bagged the extra money by being the leader in the race on Saturday night when the score stood: **O'Leary, 284; Weston, 280:**

After a day of rest to observe the Sabbath, both men began their second weeks walk at New Brunswick, New Jersey, both men finishing their efforts the day after at 22:20 having made 378 and 371 miles, O'Leary still in command. The pair went on to entertain the citizens of Plainfield, New Jersey, the next day, Wednesday. Weston

King of the Peds

was reported to be labouring when he started his work in the morning, but the stiffness in his legs seemed to wear off as he warmed to his work. The score at the end of the day was: **O'Leary, 426; Weston, 417:** On Thursday the score at 10:30 p.m. was: **O'Leary, 473; Weston, 464:**

The returns at eleven o'clock at night on Monday, the 21st of December on the third week which began at the Cosmopolitan Skating Rink in New York, on a 14 laps to the mile track, was: **O'Leary, 606; Weston, 605:** The next day's record at 14:00 was 615 to 613, and at the end of the session, those scores had been increased to: **O'Leary, 658.7; Weston, 657:** By Wednesday at 2 p.m., O'Leary was maintaining his narrow advantage by a couple of miles, the record showing, 666 to 664.

The attendance on Christmas Eve was much larger than on any previous day, and by midnight, O'Leary, who was going along very nicely had added 49.10 to his aggregate of 754.4. Weston's blistering feet, which had troubled him during the day, had nevertheless carried him 47.6, thus making his overall score 752.7.

On Christmas Day, O'Leary increased his lead by half a mile in front of a small crowd. In an attempt to cheer them all up, Weston, *"sang snatches of songs in a cracked and uncertain tone of voice."*

"Shut up, you jumping-jack!" shouted O'Leary across the rink in the evening, when Weston was at his musical exercise.

I'll take my oath," retorted Weston, *"that man has no ear for Eye-talian opera!"*

O'Leary was thereafter said to be in a *"demonstrative mood and kept up a one-sided argument directed at Weston and the spectators for several hours, and at the close of the day's walk, made desultory and amusing speeches to a crowd of boys."*

By the end of the day, O'Leary had walked 51.4, his total score being 805.8. Weston was still close up, having made 50.7, his score showing as 803 miles.

Boxing Day would attract a huge crowd to the rink especially in the late evening where they would watch Weston limping painfully around. This however didn't seem to bother him too much, and at times he appeared quite indifferent to his plight as he indulged in the odd spurt which delighted his supporters. O'Leary though covered his ground with the grace and style he always showed, but as the day came to its conclusion, he, like Weston, appeared glad to hear the call of "Time!" when the scoreboard showed that he was six miles ahead with the tally being: **O'Leary, 854; Weston, 848:**

Both men reached Syracuse, New York, from Cohoes at an early hour on the morning of Thursday, December the 31st where they restarted their tramp at 11 o'clock at the Alhambra Rink. At the close of the night, the score was: **O'Leary, 1,026.5; Weston, 1,020.1:**

On Saturday, January the 2nd 1886, both competitors finished their travels in Syracuse and headed off to Rochester where they would continue their journey on Monday the 4th. O'Leary's Saturday total saw him make 39.1 whilst his opponent tramped 38.13 thus making the aggregates: **1,107.9 to 1,100.4:**

In Rochester on January the 4th, the score in the match was: **O'Leary, 1,158.1; Weston, 1,142:** On January the 6th, Weston made 42.2, and O'Leary 47.9, making a day's end score of: **O'Leary, 1,247.13; Weston, 1,228.14:** The next day, Weston was seized with an attack of vertigo and had to rest for a couple of hours, the closing score on the day being: **O'Leary, 1,292.9; Weston, 1,260.5:**

For whatever reason, the walk would resume in Lockport the day after. The last record of the match as it progressed there was established on Saturday the 9th when, at 2 o'clock in the afternoon, O'Leary was leading Weston by 1,356 miles and 12 laps to 1,311 and 14 laps. Weston evidently had been suffering from a sore foot.

On Monday, the 11th of January, both men had trekked to Buffalo where in front of a small crowd, O'Leary left the 9 laps to the mile track at 22:10 on a mark of 1,418.2. Weston continued walking until time was up having made a total of 1,386.

Still in Buffalo on Friday January the 15th, and with both men described as being in good condition, the score at the end of the day's walk stood at: **O'Leary, 1,603.7; Weston, 1,578.3:** The day was a good one for Weston as it showed a gain for him of 1 mile and 8 laps.

The week's walk which was poorly attended, concluded the next day, and when O'Leary left the track at 9 o'clock, he had scored 1,650 miles. When Weston left an hour and a half later, his score was 1,627.7. The two men then left for a two-day walk in Erie, after which they were destined to travel on to Cleveland.

On Wednesday, January the 20th, whilst they battled for supremacy in Erie, O'Leary was said to have become *"terribly abusive"* towards his opponent; finally pushing Weston off the track twice after Weston had asked for police protection. The audience was reported to have cheered the American and hissed the Irishman. Weston, who had apparently made a speech begging the crowd to excuse O'Leary, was said to have been working hard to make up the miles he had lost on account of sickness and, being in prime condition, was confident of ultimate victory. When the bell was rung at the end of time, Weston had gained a mile and a half on O'Leary, and the score at that stage of the contest was: **O'Leary, 1,744.4; Weston, 1,723.4:** From there, the pedestrians would then compete for two days on the road to Cleveland with the expectation then being that they would finish their walk in sixteen days.

Very little was reported about the match (which ended in Chicago on the 6th of February), except that they had competed in Cincinnati and that the 42nd day score showed that Weston had reduced O'Leary's winning margin to nine miles, the record showing: **O'Leary, 1,932.7; Weston, 1,923.7:**

Then on the 44th day of their match, both men were observed to have covered 42 miles on the road at which time the score stood: **O'Leary, 2,067; Weston, 2,058:** This last report on the 28th of January concluded with the fact that both men left at 6:45 p.m. that evening for Chicago, where they would recommence their struggle during the evening the day after.

On Thursday, the 4th of February, it was learned that the contest had been conceded to Weston who, by 17:00, had registered 2,376 miles for himself, as O'Leary had *"not put in an appearance."*

The final report from Chicago on Saturday, the 6th of February indicated that Weston, who had been walking 54 days and averaging about 46¼ miles per day, had not only finished his walk of 2,500 miles, but that he had been in sufficiently good condition an hour after the race's conclusion to take the train for New York. The story goes that O'Leary having scored 2,292 miles, didn't appear after collapsing on the track on Tuesday the 2nd due to *"too free use of stimulants,"* meaning he was as probably as drunk as a lord at the time.

"Two thirds of the amount and a share of the gate receipts will be awarded Weston, who, as a life long teetotaler, was pitted for endurance against O'Leary, a habitual partaker of liquid stimulants."

CHAPTER 51

What Else Happened in 1886

William Perkins died of Bright's disease in Guys Hospital, London, in February of 1886.

At the Princess Rink in Auburn, New York, on February the 20th, W. A. Hoagland of that city, who traversed the track employing a square heel-and-toe walking gait, defeated the bicycle riding Miss Elsa Van Blumen in a 51-hour contest in the presence of a large crowd at eleven o'clock that evening. The score was: **Van Blumen, 324.5; Hoagland, 165:** With Miss Van Blumen having failed to cover twice the number of miles made by her rival, the race was given to Hoagland.

She may have lost the race when she came into collision with a man who crossed the track near the close of the contest, causing her to sustain quite severe injuries as a result of her fall.

A six-day heel-and-toe walk between O'Leary and Harriman ended on Saturday night, March the 28th at the Casino Rink in Oskosh, Wisconsin, the result of which was a win for Harriman by three miles and a few laps. O'Leary, who was apparently under the influence of alcohol toward the end of the race, was said to stagger and fall on the track. There was lot of indignation about O'Leary's drunken escapades by punters who had placed their money on him. Harriman, who was said to be full of himself after the match, also came in for a lot of criticism after he had been boasting about his success.

On April 15th 1886, *The Daily Era*, serving Bradford, McKean County, Pennsylvania, reported that eight pedestrians started a 75-hour race on a 22 laps to the mile sawdust track at the city's Parlor Rink at 8:30 p.m. the previous evening.

The men engaged in the contest who all wore trunks and tights of *"variegated patterns,"* were: Daniel Burns of Elmira, Peter Golden, the *"swarthy Mexican"* Gus Guerrero, the closely cropped haired Frank Hart, Dan Herty, someone called Keefe, *"a boy of whom no one knows much about,"* a 15-year-old boy called La Pointe, and the 56-year-old Norman Taylor who was wearing his *"traditional costume"* of linen pantaloons, suspenders and white shirt.

The report on the start of the race stated: **Col. Adams, as judge, briefly addressed the men. Instead of giving the advertised purse of $400 it had been decided to distribute fifty per cent, of the gate receipts among the four winners in amounts of 40, 30, 20, and 10 per cent. No man who did not cover 300 miles could receive a portion of the purse.**

"Then I won't walk," exclaimed the Mexican, Guerrero, as he stalked off the track.

This caused a hitch in proceeding, during which the large crowd stood around and discussed the situation with off hand freedom. Finally the good offices of Manager Ring prevailed and the men went back. The 300 mile stipulation in order to keep the interest keen spectators until the close, otherwise the peds might be disposed to shirk and travel no more than was absolutely necessary.

After the first hour Guerrero created a mild sensation by leaving the track. He said he took second money in a match with the same party at Scranton last week.

At the beginning of the match, Guerrero began to hurl insults at Frank Hart, the reasons for which, nor the language, nobody understood. The recipient of the abuse after trading a few remarks himself, soon got on with the task in hand, and as the Mexican calmed down, the spectators' attention became focused on the race, where the oldest competitor in it started to take control. Taylor was still in front 24 hours later with a score of 127.6, having made his century in 20 hours. He was followed by Hart, who had 123.4; Burns, on 118.1, Golden with 116, La Pointe on 114, Herty with 112.20 and Keefe, the back-marker having scored 111.

Taylor held on to his place till about 8:30 the next morning when he had to leave the race due to intense pains in his stomach. Rumours were rife that his coffee had been drugged, while his opponents suggested that he was suffering because of the *"free use of cider the day before."* There were more incidents later when La Point threw sawdust into one of the spectator's eyes; and later, when Keefe was attacked by someone in the crowd who hit him over the head.

Hart, who took over the lead from Taylor, maintained it till the end of the race which he won with 265 miles. The rest of the scores were: **Golden, 262.19; Burns, 260.8; Herty, 259.11; Keefe, 212.1: La Point, 190.12; Taylor, 180.8:**

On Friday, the 23rd of July 1886, Stephen Brodie, the ex-Brooklyn pedestrian, jumped from the centre span of the Brooklyn Bridge, escaping without injury and winning $100 on a bet in the process. He was arrested for attempted suicide and held on $1,000 bail.

At the Princess Rink, Auburn, New York, on Saturday, the 20th of November, a 75-hour go-as-you-please race was won by Harriman, who covered 304 miles. Burns finished second with 291. Herty was third with 287; Hart, fourth with 276; Guerrero, fifth with 255; Hanley, sixth with 250; Cole, seventh with 171 and Townsend, eighth with 162.

At the same venue as above, and just six days later, Harriman took on Hoagland in a 24-hour, eleven laps to the mile, heel-and-toe walking match, starting on Friday, the 26th of November. Hoagland won, covering 128 miles and 10 laps to Harriman's 123.7.

In a closely contested 300-mile heel-and-toe walking match for a purse of $500 which started at 8 p.m. on Wednesday, the 8th December 1886 in Utica, O'Leary defeated Hoagland by just three laps when the contest finished at 23:15 the following Saturday.

A six-day, 12 hours per day, 72-hour match, which began on Monday morning at 11 o'clock on the 20th of December 1886 at the Elite Rink, in Philadelphia, closed on Christmas night. The twelve laps to the mile track had been pronounced the finest ever put down. *"There are and no sharp turns, which will aid the men in making fast time. The entries are large and comprise all of the prominent walkers of the country."*

Of the fourteen starters which included Albert, Burns, Cox, Guerrero, Howarth, Noremac and Taylor, only six remained in the race at the close. Strokel, with 386.3 won the main prize of $600. Hegelman with 372.1 made $300, Vint, with 359.9 laps got $200 and Hughes took $100 for a score of 356.11. Elson, with 345.8 and Golden with 315.2 missed out on the money.

King of the Peds

Another 300-mile heel-and-toe walking match between Hoagland and O'Leary was concluded at the Alhambra Rink in Syracuse at 10:30 p.m. on Christmas night. This time the Auburn man was the first of the pair to reach the 300-mile mark, thus taking the $1,000 sweepstakes, and two thirds of the gate money. The Chicagoan managed only 291.5 in the same time with the contest said to excite little interest. The original contest, set to take place at the rink in Binghamton in the early part of December, had to be cancelled due to the roof falling in, and Hoagland chose Syracuse as the venue when he won the toss of a coin, O'Leary preferring Buffalo.

CHAPTER 52

International Pedestrian Go-As-You-Please Tournament

It would be the third time that the Royal Aquarium, Westminster, would be used for a six-day, *"twelve hours per diem, international go-as-you-please contest."* The conditions of the race which were to be observed by the contestants were exactly the same as those as described in the competition for the "5th Long Distance Astley Belt" held at the same venue in November of 1884.

The now *"naturalized"* American, George Hazael, crossed the Atlantic to contend for the race, whereas the notable absence of Rowell meant that the Littlewood would be the people's choice to win; the reward for doing so, £100. The man coming in second would receive £25, third £10, fourth £7, and as in the previous race of two years earlier, any person making 300 miles would get £5.

The only professional not to make the start on Monday, the 21st of February 1887, was Frank Gleeson of Warren County, Pennsylvania, USA; so the men who "toed the line" at the start were: **H. Baker**, Dover; **George Cartwright**, Walsall; **Joe Chadwick**, Manchester; **James Cliff**, Cardiff; **George Connor**, Bow; **William Corbett**, Aberdeen; **Nicholas Cox**, Bristol; **James Dick**, Forfar; **W. Franks**, Chelsea; **William Griffin**, Chelsea; **George Hazael**, New York, USA; **Hullet**, Hoxton; **Charles Keeble**, Suffolk; **Tom Kirby (The "Flying Milkman")** Kentish Town; **George Littlewood**, Sheffield; **George Mason**, Ratcliffe; **Arthur Norris**, Brentwood; **J. Saull**, Northampton; **A. W. Sinclair**, Chelsea; **G. Smitten**, Faversham; **J. Spicer**, Folkestone; **E. Thomas**, Eastbourne; **W. Toey**, Brixton; **Henry Vandepeer**, Sittingbourne; **E. Warner**, Nottingham:

The cocoanut fibre track, *"which created no dust,"* and which stretched from the organ gallery to the fountain at the swimming bath end, was eleven laps to the mile. It was raised a foot from the floor as opposed to being built up eight feet around the galleries as in previous contests. This made the viewing of the race a little more difficult for the spectators.

Of his observations of what the competitors wore on the morning of the start, the *Sporting Life's "Special Connoisseur"* wrote: Littlewood, disdaining adornment, appeared - as to his upper and lower self - in simple white with sky blue trunks, and a waistline of chocolate braid. Hazael also affected simplicity - grey flannel was his principal wear. Mason was "bodied" in "warm grey, and trunked in sky blue scarlet, and wore a striped neckerchief." Cartwright wore to begin with a sky blue cap with trunks of the same, and a corset, or a corslet - that quite warranted the probably defective joke about his going well in "stays". Then without further particularisation, we had a runner in cinnamon brown, one in grey and mustard coloured breeches, another whose thigh-pieces were the hue of a ripe plum, and yet another – in yellow and black so far as the extreme back view of him were concerned – that gave one the idea of a sort of athletic Mephistopheles 'I dwell not upon the "grey and black" the "white and navy blue," "the black, white, and indigo," or even the "all grey."

In the presence of gallery packed with spectators, who also were found in abundance in the centre of the track and round the kiosks, the race finally started fifteen minutes later than the advertised time of 11 a.m. by Mr. Atkinson of the *Sporting Life*. The delay had been due to problems with some of the runners not having their numbers fixed on properly; but when it did get underway, Sinclair, Kirby, Warner, Littlewood, Cartwright, Cox and Connor, in that order, raced to the front of the pack with Keeble being the only man content to project himself forward with a straight forward heel-and-toe method of conveyance. They were later joined by Saul, Spicer and Corbett. With Cox leading the men at the mile stage, Littlewood led the "American" Hazael by a yard as the Yorkshireman crossed the five-mile post in a time of 30m.18s; the pair being chased along by Cartwright, Norris and Warner.

The end of the first hour saw five of the leaders covering nine miles and nine laps. These were, in alphabetical order: Cartwright, Hazael, Littlewood, Norris and Warner. During the next hour, Littlewood stuck like glue to the shadow of the "American" who moved himself along in his *"deceptive elastic "dot and go" style."* Whilst Sinclair sweated in mid-division, Chadwick's *"good natured"* face was noticed to be rather crimson in colour as he tried to keep up with the pace. Then, during the 13th mile, Norris decided he'd like to go much faster, so upping the tempo to a spurt, he forged ahead. Cartwright and Warner followed in his wake, and for the next three miles, they proceeded to sprint against each other with the Nottingham man coming out the winner when it was finished. At the end of the first two hours, during which time several changes of leader had occurred, a similar distance to the first hour was covered, the leaders being: **Norris and Warner, 19.3; Cartwright, 19.2; Hazael and Littlewood, 19.1; Kirby, 18.5:**

Connor, followed by Corbett, was the first of them men to leave the track, but only for a couple of minutes. Activity in the pit stops was now seen to be quite frenzied as the teams began to make their preparations to welcome in their stars to be either, sponged and/or rubbed down, watered, fed, toileted, and even bathed. The sturdy, good looking Cartwright took the lead, passing Norris who had taken the opportunity to snaffle away at a chicken leg whilst walking. Littlewood, who was observed to be *"sporting a Palmerstonian straw in his mouth,"* also adorned the top of the leader board at that stage, the scores of which at 2 p.m. were: **Cartwright and Littlewood, 27.5; Hazael, 27.4; Norris and Spicer, 27.1; Warner, 26.5:**

Spicer, the *"light-framed, well-knit runner"* that he was, after introducing himself and making his presence felt in the top division, went along very nicely, as did some of the other *"feathers"* in the contest, Saull, Mason and Connor. The *"light brigade"* weren't bothering the *"flying collier"* or the *"Sheffield blonde"* in the least, and that pair dictated matters from the front, Cartwright pulling a mile ahead of his rival later. With Warner urging himself past Spicer and Norris, the 4th hour record showed: **Cartwright, 35.6; Littlewood, 34.7; Hazael, 34.4; Spicer and Warner, 34; Norris, 33.4:**

Away from the track, there were some at work trying to divert the attention of the large crowd that had assembled to watch the racing. Shouts of, "this way for the billiards!" rang down from upstairs in the gallery. Then there was the other entertainment on offer which principally would take place on the variety theatre stage where attractions like the *"feats of the web-footed Beckwith family were on view to enchant the beholder."* The reporter for the *Sporting Life* gave us an idea of what was happening elsewhere in the building: Upstairs, the merry click of the billiard cues formed a not inept accompaniment to the pretty music of the ballet. The stage was brilliant with colour, and the gyrations of the quaintly-dressed background "Champagners" seemed quite in keeping with the constantly shifting kaleidoscope jerseys that flitted past the orchestra. All was life, light, and animation. The holders of season tickets had helped to increase the muster, and both on ground floor and gallery the fair sex were deprived of their usual promenade, and formed a fair percentage of the company.

On the track meanwhile, the brightly costumed "peds," responding to the faster pace of the music, which had initially been supplied by the loft organ, and now replaced by the more industrious band, trotted whence they once jogged. Cartwright, who had lost a little bit of distance to Littlewood, went on to recover it by adopting the tactics of settling in behind his rival, then passing him at lightening speed, then catching him up again when a lap to the good. With Franks now starting to make his presence felt in the race, and Connor, and the stocking clad Smitten showing up well, the scores of the leading half dozen at the end of the fifth hour were: **Cartwright, 43.2; Littlewood, 41.8; Warner, 40.3; Spicer, 40.1; Hazael, 39.1; Norris, 38.9.**

The field was reduced by one owing to the defection of Chadwick on a score of 21.10, his ankle being the culprit. Whilst Cartwright ate jelly, Littlewood reduced the deficit to 12 laps, but after it had been consumed, the "black-countryman" kept up with the "tyke." George Mason, *"his bloom contrasting with the worn expression some of the competitors had,"* now started to make his presence felt on the scene by making a move into the front line.

Meanwhile, on a score of 47.7, the race leader decided to have a pop at the 50-mile record of 6h.8m which belonged to Littlewood, which was made in the same building on the 24th of November 1884. Having 28 minutes in hand in which to deliver the goods, he began *"running with a beautiful springy stride."* Accompanied by Saull for part of the way, and egged on by the crowd, he went like the clappers for a few laps, during which time he passed and re-passed some of the "cracks" in the race. Cartwright went on to produced the desired distance in 5h.55m.4½s, after which he was *"warmly cheered"* for his fine effort. Hazael meanwhile, had spent some time off the path and had dropped back. Warner, due to a strained right knee joined Chadwick in the pedestrian's infirmary. Then 5h.55m into the contest, and 5 minutes after he left, the sixth hour scores when they were hoisted showed: **Cartwright, 50.7; Littlewood, 48.10; Mason, 45.4; Saull, 45.1; Spicer, 44.6; Hazael, 44.2; Norris, 43.9.**

The electric and gas lights in the well attended building were now doing their job and some in the crowd sought better views of the race by climbing the fountains. Whilst aloft, they would have got a good view of the "American" retaking the position that Saull had robbed him of, together with the sight of Cartwright "dogging" Littlewood. They would have also seen the *"greyhound-like representative of the Granite City,"* Corbett now beginning to get into the mix. The seventh hour scores: **Cartwright, 57.2; Littlewood, 55.10; Mason, 51.4; Hazael, 51.3; Saull, 50.3; Spicer, 50.2; Corbett, 50.1:**

The times that the first 50 miles were achieved in were: **Cartwright, 5h.55m.4½s; Littlewood, 6h.9m.27½s; Mason, 6h.46m.9½s; Saull, 6h.46m.52s; Hazael, 6h.47m.4s; Spicer, 6h.58m.50s; Norris, 7h.47s; Franks, 7h.3m.28½s; Connor and Smitten, 7h.3m.51s:**

When on a score of 57 and 5, the leader, who had made it known he was hungry, ate his take-away on the hoof, but at a much slower pace than what he was used to. That gave the signal for Littlewood, whose blood sugar was in order, to take some distance out of his rival's lead. Of the others, Norris and Kirby made some ground, whilst Toey and Griffin worked hard at improving their positions. The last man, Keeble, meanwhile, wore a wide belt as he struggled round. Mason, who had been passed by the "Yank" on the 53rd mile, took his revenge in the 55th, but Hazael gained 4 laps on Saull and Spicer whilst Corbett looked dangerous as he, and the *"beautifully"* walking Franks, crept closer. At the end of the 8th hour, with the organist playing the *"ever popular "Mikado,""* the score was: **Cartwright, 62.10; Littlewood, 62.5; Mason, 58.1; Hazael, 57.6; Saull, 56.2; Corbett, 55.9; Franks, 55.7; Connor, 55.6; Spicer, 55.4; Norris, 55.1:**

Little Georgie Connor's enthusiasm to improve his position inspired his namesakes Cartwright and Mason to do the same, and both went about their business with renewed vigour. By seven o'clock, most of the men were walking, but this didn't last long as the spectators were treated to an exhibition of alternating spurts by the two leaders along with Corbett, Norris, Baker and Spicer. As Cartwright sprinted along on his 67th mile, Vandepeer, Mason and Cliff walked; and while Franks made things lively for Thomas, Hazael put in some good work. What the scoreboard revealed at the end of the ninth hour: **Cartwright, 69.2; Littlewood, 68.2; Hazael, and Mason, 63.4; Connor, 62.3; Saull, 62; Corbett and Franks, 61.6; Spicer, 61.4:**

Saull appeared as *"fresh as paint"* after his 66th mile, and he and Norris caught the eye as they powered themselves around the track giving everyone else the *"go-by."* At the conclusion of the 10th hour, Cartwright was 18 laps in front of Littlewood as the scores below indicate: **Cartwright, 75.1; Littlewood, 73.5; Hazael, 69.6; Mason, 67.7; Saull, 66.10; Corbett and Spicer, 66.5:**

As the three leaders slowed down, Mason caught them up, and the four kept each other company till he led the quartet after exhibiting a fine burst of speed. With the diminutive Dick having scored 66, and Keeble eventually making his half century, the score at 10 o'clock was: **Cartwright, 81.2; Littlewood, 79.3; Hazael, 75; Mason, 73.5; Saull, 73.2; Franks, 71.10; Spicer, 71.8; Corbett, 71:**

Norris was the first man in the dressing rooms at 22:35 with a straight 70, while Saull and Connor evidently made their ways around the path like *"cats on hot bricks."* Saull would recover later in the hour though, changing his gait to a more positive pace as he ended the night impressively with a run; the effort waking up Hazael as he followed suit.

King of the Peds

After 12 hours and at the end of the day, the leading scores were:

Pos		Miles	Laps	Pos		Miles	Laps
1	Cartwright	87	1	13	Smitten	69	8
2	Littlewood	85	3	14	Toey	69	6
3	Hazael	80	8	15	Baker	67	6
4	Mason	79	6	16	Vandepeer	66	3
5	Saull	78	2	17	Cliff	64	0
6	Franks	77	3	18	Sinclair	63	4
7	Corbett	76	7	19	Hallett	61	7
8	Spicer	76	3	20	Kirby	58	6
9	Connor	75	5	21	Cox	51	0
10	Griffin	72	5	22	Thomas	51	0
11	Dick	71	6	23	Keeble	50	3
12	Norris	70	0				

It was a bright, beautiful and cheerful spring morning outside the imposing Victorian building on the next day of the competition. Inside there was a marked reduction in the number of people watching the *"foot-race."* The match correspondent for the *Sporting Life* wrote: A saunter round the track proved that the "'ammer, 'ammer, 'ammer" of flying feet had so much consolidated the fibre as to have created quite a footpath close to the inside edging - an improvement, if any were wanted in the going. But the figures destined to occupy it during the day were soon as evidence. Worn-looking, clean-shaven specimens of humanity muffled in great coats and attended by taciturn gentlemen, for the most part carrying bags, began to pass behind the curtain of the dressing room while others who betrayed a glimpse of colour and an absence of the conventional trousers under the mufflers needed not the cut of their wide shoes to stamp their individuality.

Chadwick, Warner and Kirby were the only ones not to present themselves to the officials for the start, the latter sending a note to the press explaining that his absence was due to a strained left knee and enlarged varicose veins. At the start, the race leader looked resplendent dressed in sky blue which included his jockey cap.

At 11 o'clock, Mr. Atkinson shouted, "Are you ready?..........GO!" and the men bounded away enthusiastically, headed by Littlewood. Smitten was the first man to head for the dressing room, having managed 73 miles. He was followed off by Hullet, Thomas, and Norris, who had made a good show the day before. Norris made 7.7 before packing his bag. He told reporters he had been running in a horrible nightmare race during his sleep "to tones produced by organs, musical shows, frying pans, plates, runners, fiddles and all kinds of music." After apparently breaking down on a score of 89.4 Hazael got himself dressed and joined Charlie Rowell in the bar, after announcing his retirement from the contest at 11:47.

The energetic efforts of Cartwright, who had increased his lead, didn't appear to trouble Littlewood, who was obviously biding his time and pacing himself for the long haul. Cartwright completed the ton in 13h.56m.4s, which was nowhere near Rowell's best record of 13h.26m.30s. Littlewood went on to make his 100 at 13:04, Mason his at 14:03, and Franks his at 14:58. That takes us nicely up to 15:00 when the scores of the leading contenders were: **Cartwright, 114; Littlewood, 110.10; Mason, 105.10; Franks, 100.1; Spicer, 98.7; Connor; 97.7; Corbett, 96.7:**

Saull, who had moved well the previous day, now returned after attending the Westminster Hospital having been off track for 4 hours due to *"inflammation of the shin bone."* At 16:35, after having had a short rest of four minutes to change his shoes, Cartwright made six more laps and left the track again on a score of 124.9. It was rumoured that he had *"broken down."* He was still *"resting"* by the time the score was hoisted at 5 p.m., and that showed that Littlewood was now just 5 laps behind the leader: **Cartwright, 124.9; Littlewood, 124.4; Mason, 118.4; Franks, 110; Spicer, 109.8; Connor; 108.3; Corbett, 104.6; Griffin, 102.2:**

Littlewood passed Cartwright's score at six minutes past the hour. While the new leader was being chased along by Mason, the unsubstantiated stories emanating from the then second placed man's tent, that his ankle had given way, proved to be true, when at half past five, Cartwright was seen in his civvies. At six o'clock, when the electric lights were switched on, the Yorkshireman was well over six miles in the lead in a race now comprising of just fourteen men; Henry Vandepeer and Nick Cox being further casualties.

With the places of the men remaining relatively unaltered by eight o'clock, the *Sporting Life* informed its readers: The fun of the fair was now in full swing. In addition to the bright principal burners, the glow warm like festoons round the galleries, and alternate red and green diamonds adorning their front, lent a soft, moonlight-like effect to the scene. One of the charms of the orchestra is the "chic" and go which distinguishes its selections, and as the airs were singularly appropriate to the occasion, they helped to cheer the somewhat weary way of the peds.

Littlewood was certainly *"weary"* when he registered his 150th mile in 22h.58m.54s, but he was still well ahead of "Gorgeous George" at 22:00, the Ratcliffe man's distance being recorded as 143.3. As the two foes walked quickly together, the rest went along indifferently until the band struck up the *"Champagne Ballet"* which inspired Connor to kick up his heels, the move having a domino affect amongst those on the track at the time. With the diminutive figure of Connor showing improved form, Saull, despite his poorly "pin," demonstrating true grit, the fleet footed Corbett *"improving like a good wine with time,"* and the persevering Dick, brave Baker and Toey sticking to their missions, the scores at the end of the second day were:

Pos		Miles	Laps	Pos		Miles	Laps
1	Littlewood	154	6	8	Cartwright	124	9
2	Mason	147	9	9	Dick	117	7
3	Spicer	143	0	10	Baker	110	0
4	Connor	139	2	11	Cliff	106	2
5	Franks	135	8	12	Sinclair	103	0
6	Corbett	135	4	13	Saull	100	1
7	Griffin	129	5	14	Toey	100	1

The times that the first 100 miles were achieved in were: **Cartwright, 13h.56m.4½s; Littlewood, 14h.4m.6s; Mason, 15h.3m.39s; Franks,15h.58m.30s; Connor, 16h.21m.46s; Corbett, 16h.34m.40s; Griffin, 17h.31m.3s; Cliff, 18h.17m.15s; Dick, 18h.53m 53s; Saull, 22h.14m; Sinclair, 22h.36m.44s; Toey, 23h.50m.16s:**

At the start of the third day's proceedings, Saull wasn't present as thirteen men turned up to hear the starter's gun. As they waited for the big bang to get them going, Littlewood's trainers, comprising of his dad and Fred Bromley, sat him down on a chair beside the track. As he waited, the other dozen strolled out. Franks, trained by W. Pennys, turned up wearing a heavy sweater over his drab costume. The Walter Whale-trained George Connor arrived wearing a white jersey and trunks and sky blue drawers, whereas Dick thought he might do better donning red drawers with his white top. Baker chose a purple and black quartered top, but he was outshone by Spicer in *"waspish"* yellow and black, Cliff in blue black and red, Toey in lavender and white stripes, and Keeble, who was described as wearing a *"Zingari"* vest and a green satin *"hip piece."*

As the men set off it was clear that George Mason, who had been going so well the previous day, was already in a degree of trouble, and he predictably began sending out distress signals. After completing just two miles and two laps, despite the valiant efforts of his trainers, F. Sheppard and J. Bones to get him up and running again, the situation proved hopeless. Mason later had to relinquish the contest after seeking treatment in hospital, the doctors prescribing *"perfect rest"* after applying iodine to *"the big inside leader behind the left knee."* Others evidently suffering were Sinclair (blister), Griffin (instep), and Dick (swollen knee).

With Mason now out of the contest, the chase was on for the next three in the race, Connor, the Harry Carless-trained Corbett, and Spicer, to fight it out for the second prize money, should Littlewood stay the course. As can be seen by the scores at 4 p.m. the scores of the last two mentioned were neck-and-neck: **Littlewood, 185; Connor; 171.2; Corbett and Spicer, 167.1; Franks, 160.5; Griffin, 149.6;** and as can be deduced by the tally an hour later, Corbett had pulled away from Spicer: **Littlewood, 191.2; Connor and Corbett, 173.3; Spicer, 171.6; Franks, 165.10; Griffin, 153.8:**

At 18:30:28, the race leader had scored his second century and barring him breaking down, he looked assured to collect the first prize. Meanwhile, and as the race progressed, Connor began putting on an impressive display,

King of the Peds

eventually making his second century at 20:47. Between the hours of 11 o'clock in the morning and 9 o'clock at night, he had made up two and a half miles on Littlewood who appeared to be content with his long lead. The now well established third placed Corbett also scored 200 at 21:16. After that not much happened to thrill the *"densely packed house,"* apart that is, from Sinclair indulging in a spurt with the eccentrically attired Keeble, the sight apparently producing much laughter among the crowd.

The scores at the end of the third day were:

Pos		Miles	Laps	Pos		Miles	Laps
1	Littlewood	225	5	6	Griffin	180	0
2	Connor	212	5	7	Dick	171	4
3	Corbett	210	8	8	Baker	151	3
4	Spicer	199	1	9	Keeble	131	0
5	Franks	187	0	10	Cliff	115	4

Only seven men lined up for the start of the fourth day, and the only real absentee was Toey. Griffin rejoined the race after seven minutes, Spicer after nine, and Keeble after twenty. Not surprisingly, many of the men had changed their colours for the day's work with the race leader, who went along at a brisk trot, looking particularly well adorned in white, sky blue drawers and his trademark red necktie. Connor too, stood out; his brown eyes providing a twinkle for those who cared to look hard enough. Corbett though appeared a little jaded, and it was said he had had trouble with his stomach during the night. That ailment certainly took its toll in the first hour with the two leaders seen to be steadily pulling away from him. Spicer jogged on his way to his 200th mile in 36h.21m, but the effort told, and he slowed down to a walk after the usual celebrations.

The midday scores: **Littlewood, 232.3; Connor; 219.1; Corbett, 217.4; Spicer, 202.8; Franks, 191.9; Griffin, 185.8; Dick; 175.10, Baker, 156.2; Sinclair, 154.9; Keeble, 133.7:**

As the top three slowed, Baker quickened, and Griffin gave himself the hurry up to leave Franks behind in his wake. Meanwhile, Connor decided to take advantage of Corbett's woes, and by 1 p.m. had made seven laps on his rival. What was more significant was that Littlewood had made 8 laps on him as the following scores suggest: **Littlewood, 238.2; Connor; 224.4; Corbett, 222; Spicer, 205.8; Franks, 196.8; Griffin, 191.9; Dick; 179.5; Baker, 160.2:**

At 13:12, the trotting Littlewood and Corbett, who were joined by Griffin, later dropped into a walk. All three were passed by the sprinting Baker whose move inspired Connor to run. Littlewood thought he'd better do the same, and Franks decided to catch the bug too as Corbett kept his walking shoes on. Not being able to do much however, the Scot left the track for an 18-minute break as the two front men sprinted along at a ten-mile an hour gait. While Corbett was out of the ring, Franks made his second ton in a time of 38h.39m, and for that he was given a well deserved round of applause. All the exertion had made little Connor hungry, and to appease his appetite, his trainer handed him a big plateful of custard pudding, which he chucked down his throat as the organist played the "Scott's March."

The 39th hour scores at 2 p.m: **Littlewood, 243.7; Connor; 229.6; Corbett, 225.2; Spicer, 208.9; Franks, 201.9; Griffin, 197.8; Dick; 182.9; Baker, 164.8; Sinclair, 160.9; Keeble, 140.7:**

During the next hour, when Griffin had joined the 200 club, many of the peds took rests of varying lengths. Even Littlewood decided he deserved a break, going off to eat some jelly, whilst Sinclair left to change into a *"gorgeous suit"* made up of white with a purple cap. As he showed it off to the crowd at 15:00, the scores were: **Littlewood, 248.7; Connor; 234.2; Corbett, 229.10; Spicer, 211.5; Franks and Griffin, 203; Dick; 186.4; Baker, 166.4; Sinclair, 164.5; Keeble, 140.10:**

As expected, the enterprisingly running Griffin passed Franks just after three o'clock and the event was celebrated by the string band who played a lively tune. The noise they produced enthused Sinclair to run for a mile, after which he went to his tent. Franks donned a sweater while Baker took on Littlewood, the pair passing Corbett and Connor who took exception to the move by running with them. However, the leader lapped him and while Baker spurted, Dick trotted round for three laps. After that it was off to their respective tents for a few of the men, where they doubtless had their legs rubbed, their stomachs replenished, and words of advice given as to how they should improve their positions. When the clock struck four, and as Griffin, Connor, and Littlewood caused the crowd to go wild with excitement as they pushed themselves to the limit, the scoreboard showed: **Littlewood, 254.3; Connor; 239.8; Corbett, 234.7; Spicer, 216.8; Griffin, 208.3; Franks, 207.3; Dick; 189.9; Baker, 170.10; Sinclair, 165.3; Keeble, 144.3:**

As the men sped round, there was other entertainment on offer in the Aquarium. Many in the crowd headed for the seats in front of the stage to watch, knowing full well that all the scores would be displayed on a board at its side at 15-minute intervals. As Franks followed the quick walking Sheffielder, Griffin *"wobbled"* behind him, and Connor and Corbett chose the trot as their method of movement. However, it was the latter who was the shiniest of all the stars on the track during the hour, as he made up lots of ground on the two leaders as the 5 o'clock score attests to: **Littlewood, 260.3; Connor, 245.7; Corbett, 241.9; Spicer, 221.5; Griffin, 213; Franks, 210; Dick; 193.5; Baker, 173.1; Sinclair, 168.1; Keeble, 148.6:**

With the gas lit, and the electric lights now switched on and with the ballet on the stage having finished at 17:20, Keeble was seen tucking into jelly, and Neapolitan ice cream, provided for him by his trainer H. Wyatt as a reward for making 150 miles. Connor's trainer wasn't so generous. He tossed his man a lemon to suck at, presumably to try and remind him of his bitter performance. Indeed at 17:45 the man from Bow was just 2 miles ahead of the Scottish *"greyhound"* who was now beginning to look very dangerous as the six o'clock scores show: **Littlewood, 266; Connor, 250.1; Corbett, 248.6; Spicer, 225.10; Griffin, 217.7; Franks, 213.5; Dick; 196.10; Baker, 176.8; Sinclair, 172; Keeble, 151.6:**

The continuously running Corbett, who finished his 250th mile in 43h.12m.18s, finally took second place from Connor at 18:46 due to the latter named being "off track." By 19:00, and as the scores below prove, the man from north of the border went on to add further daylight between himself and the Londoner who came back in the ring at 18:52: **Littlewood, 272.1; Corbett, 255.4; Connor, 254.5; Spicer, 229.4; Griffin, 222.3; Franks, 216; Dick; 200.2; Baker, 180.5; Sinclair, 176; Keeble, 155.9:**

Oysters were all the rage in the next hour with Spicer, Griffin, and Dick all partaking of the slimy delicacy. Little else happened on the track, apart from Littlewood indulging in some heel-and-toe, and Corbett opening up more of a gap between himself and the faltering Connor, as the telegraph board showed at 20:00: **Littlewood, 277.9; Corbett, 263.3; Connor, 258.3; Spicer, 232.6; Griffin, 227.6; Franks, 220.10; Dick; 203; Baker, 184.5; Sinclair, 176.2; Keeble, 158.5:**

"Brave Connor" was *"the lion of the hour."* After being given a significant rest by his trainer "Brummy" Meadows, he came back on the track as though he had been rejuvenated in some way. Invigorated by the band, he thrilled the enormous crowd which had been geed up by the orchestra, as he traversed the path in devastating form. Both Franks and Sinclair rejoined the battle after an hour with their feet up; the latter rejoining the race wearing a pair of red and purple drawers. At 15 minutes to the hour, all the men were on the course moving around it as they pleased and at 9 p.m. the records showed: **Littlewood, 283.6; Corbett, 267; Connor, 263.9; Spicer, 236.10; Griffin, 232.6; Franks, 222.10; Dick; 206.7; Baker, 188.1; Sinclair, 179.1; Keeble, 163.2:**

The huge crowd was causing a problem for the participating athletes. The heat from their bodies was making the building quite warm, and the men on the track responded by asking for the "magic sponge." Such nominal dousing wasn't good enough for Sinclair, who took himself off to the toilets for a *"rough shampoo."* Apart from the "pit stops," little else happened.

The score at 10 p.m: **Littlewood, 288.10; Corbett, 272.2; Connor, 267.5; Spicer, 239.6; Griffin, 236.5; Franks, 224.3:**

Baker, wearing a purple jacket and crimson drawers, although putting in a commendable performance towards the end of the day, failed to make the 200 that would have helped him sleep better. He was one of eight of the men who finished off the day with a grand spurt before time was called; the man winning it - the one and only George Littlewood!

King of the Peds

The scoreboard at the end of the fourth day displayed the following score:

Pos		Miles	Laps	Pos		Miles	Laps
1	Littlewood	294	3	6	Franks	227	8
2	Corbett	277	6	7	Dick	214	1
3	Connor	271	5	8	Baker	197	6
4	Spicer	243	6	9	Sinclair	186	5
5	Griffin	236	5	10	Keeble	167	8

The attendance for the next day's sport was reported to be good. At the start, the race leader looked slightly *"drawn,"* but compared with the rest, he looked positively well. Sinclair was described as *"as miserable as a man on his wedding morning!"* The gang started proceedings at a sedentary pace, each one waiting for someone else to make the running, but after a short while it was business as usual. Littlewood's left leg was playing him up, but he was in much better condition than Corbett, whose trainer Carless was observed to be *"as attentive as a hen with one chick."* With Littlewood keeping up well with the pace, he made his 300th mile at 11:52.

A quick glance at the distances the men made in the first hour gives us an indication of how fast they were travelling: **Spicer, 6.8; Corbett, 6.7; Littlewood, 6.6; Griffin, 6.4; Baker, 4.8; Franks and Sinclair, 4.3; Keeble, 4; Connor, 3.3; Dick, 3.1:**

Corbett was next of the best to make a third century, which was timed at 52h.28m.36s from the start. The others went well, but their previous days' exertions were having an effect on them. However, Griffin and Spicer did make some major inroads into Connor's score, and at 17:00 the bulletin board showed the following records: **Littlewood, 324.6; Corbett, 305.10; Connor, 294.9; Spicer, 272.6; Griffin, 268.2; Franks, 250.1; Dick, 236.4; Baker, 220.8; Sinclair, 210.9; Keeble, 185:**

At 20:02, Sinclair made his intentions clear that he would try to walk a mile in 8m.30s. He failed miserably however, making it in 40 seconds longer than he desired. Following that, there was very little running offered, apart from Spicer who moved around at jogging pace.

The 9 p.m. scores: **Littlewood, 343.2; Corbett, 323.6; Connor, 311.6; Spicer, 293.4; Griffin, 283.5; Franks, 262.4; Dick, 250.8; Baker, 233.7; Sinclair, 221.2; Keeble, 195.7:**

At 22:15, Littlewood made 350 miles at which time, accompanied and enlivened by the music, he began dogging Corbett around the path, in front of an ever increasing crowd of people shouting encouragement. Forty four minutes later, as the athletes left the track yearning for their beds and the last night's sleep, the score was:

Pos		Miles	Laps	Pos		Miles	Laps
1	Littlewood	353	7	6	Franks	267	1
2	Corbett	333	6	7	Dick	258	0
3	Connor	318	0	8	Baker	238	1
4	Spicer	303	2	9	Sinclair	227	1
5	Griffin	283	5	10	Keeble	201	4

Barring a disaster, Littlewood was booked for the winner's podium. It was mooted that he would try and beat Rowell's 60-mile last day record, but as it was he took things easy, and imagined how useful that £100 first prize would be to him. Apart from appearing a bit thin in the face, he was reported to appear fit and good enough to go on for another week.

Nothing much happened during the day apart from Dick passing Franks and many of the men taking long rest breaks. The price of admission to the match was doubled after 18:00, but that didn't stop many, many, people from filling the auditorium for the final evening's performance. A special 10-mile match had been arranged starting at 21:30 that night, between Cartwright and Hazael; the result of which was a win of 25 yards by Cartwright. However, it was significant that at the start of that race, Littlewood sat on the bench for 43 minutes to rest before returning to the track to complete his 400th mile at 22:19, amidst the appreciative cheers of the crowd. The fact was that he could have hung his running shoes up some three hours earlier and still have won the race quite comfortably. He refused himself that luxury and continued to entertain the crowd until the end or at least till the peds linked arms as the band played the mandatory "See the Conquering Hero Comes!" To frenzied cheering, the musicians then played "Auld Lang Syne," after which everyone went home, leaving the carpenters alone in the building.

The Final Score!

Pos		Miles	Laps	Prize	Pos		Miles	Laps	Prize
1	**Littlewood**	403	5	£100	6	Dick	307	2	£7
2	Corbett	380	8	£25	7	Franks	302	5	£7
3	Connor	360	5	£12	8	Baker	279	6	£5
4	Spicer	340	8	£8	9	Sinclair	261	7	£5
5	Griffin	312	7	£7	10	Keeble	217	8	£5

A summary of the day to day scores made by all the finishers is below:

	Mon	Tue	Wed	Thur	Fri	Sat	TOTAL
Littlewood	85.3	69.3	70.10	68.9	59.4	49.9	**403.5**
Corbett	76.7	58.8	75.4	66.9	56	47.2	**380.8**
Connor	75.5	63.8	73.3	59	46.6	42.5	**360.5**
Spicer	76.3	66.8	56.1	44.5	59.7	37.6	**340.8**
Griffin	72.5	57	50.6	56.5	47	29.2	**312.7**
Dick	71.5	46.2	53.8	42.8	43.10	49.2	**307.2**
Franks	77.3	58.5	51.3	40.8	39.4	35.4	**302.5**
Baker	67.6	42.5	41.3	46.3	40.6	41.5	**279.6**
Sinclair	63.4	39.7	48.5	35	40.7	34.6	**261.7**
Keeble	50.3	35.6	45.2	36.8	33.7	16.4	**217.8**

CHAPTER 53

"Championship of the World" Sweepstakes

On August the 20th 1887 it was being reported that George Littlewood and Jimmy Albert had arranged a $100 *"open to all"* six-day go-as-you-please sweepstakes race for the "Championship of the World" at Philadelphia, USA, between Monday, November the 21st and Saturday, November the 26th, which was "Thanksgiving week."

Littlewood arrived in the "Quaker City" on the 15th of October and began training at the University of Pennsylvania Athletic Grounds, where, up to the 13th of November, he brought his weight down from 170 to 154 pounds. He was reported to be running 3 miles before breakfast, 15 miles after resting, and then making another 22 to make his total to 40 for the day. His plan thereafter was to increase that distance by a further 20 miles, to make 60 miles a day in all.

The following advert then appeared in the *Philadelphia Inquirer* on Saturday, November the 19th 1887.

An International Sporting Event!
FOR THE WORLD'S CHAMPIONSHIP!

Six Days Go-As-You-Please
Race!

**THE RINK, TWENTY THIRD AND CHESTNUT STREETS.
BEGINS 15 MINUTES AFTER MIDNIGHT SUNDAY NIGHT.**

The first hour's running will doubtless be the best exhibition of this kind ever seen on this Continent. The newspapers of this city unanimously declare this GREAT GO-AS-YOU-PLEASE RACE to be a sporting event of the first importance. These Champions of the Tan bark have paid their $100 entrance fee and will positively start.

George Littlewood, champion of England: James Albert of Philadelphia: Peter Panchot, champion of America: Frank Hart, the colored champion: George Noremac, champion of Scotland: Anton Strokel, the tireless Austrian: Dan Burns of New York State: E. C. Moore of Philadelphia:

Jerry Cronin of Elmira, N. Y.: Frank Le Grand, champion of the United States: Hamilton's Un-known, believed to be Bobby Vint, the "Little Shoemaker."

LITTLEWOOD, THE ENGLISH CHAMPION

Came to America for this race, and challenges ALL AMERICA to beat him.

James Watson, sporting editor of the "Press," referee; H. H. Diddlebock, sporting editor of the "Times," assistant referee.

W. VOLTZ, Manager.

The men who entered for the championship struggle at that time were regarded as the best in the world, and the contest created a huge amount of interest in the United States before it began. Each man who entered made a deposit in accordance with the articles of agreement, and the money would be divided into the prizes for first, second and third. It was arranged that the contestants should have 50 per cent of the gate receipts which would be divided between those who made 500 miles or more.

The 13 competitors contesting the event would have to make their way 12 laps around the nine feet wide track, which was made up of sawdust and tan bark, and measured 440 feet in circumference. No bookmaking or public betting would be allowed inside the Rink during the race.

George Littlewood, who was the favourite to win, and who had been covering 40 miles a day in training for the event, had just recovered from a *"painful boil on his leg."* There were rumours that some of his opponents had been conspiring in a *"scheme,"* which they hoped to beat him with. Of the plan George said, "Everything is fair of that kind. If the men think they can beat me in that way, they have a perfect right to try it. I am sure none of them will interfere with me, but they will give me a clear course. If I can't win with that, I don't ask any more." Then, referring to the hospitality he had received from the people of the city he was to compete in, he went on, "I want to make a big record in this race, and a combination to force me along is just what I should like to have. I may never get so well again as I am now and I am only speaking the truth when I say that no people have ever treated me so kindly as those of Philadelphia. I would like to make some little return for the kindness shown me, and I don't know of anything that would please my new friends better than to beat the record. I have set my mind on doing that if I can; so you see, instead of being put out about any combination, I shall be very glad of any help in that way."

Joe Miller, the trainer of George Noremac who had been exhibiting some good work in his build up to the race, said of his man, "There is only one who George can't outrun in practice and that is the Englishman, but when it comes to the race on the track I think the Scotchman will show to the front." Noremac, speaking of the coming contest said of Littlewood, "We will have to make much better time than we did last winter or the Englishman will run away with us."

With all the pre-race build-up, the match caught the public's eye; consequently there was a lot of interest which brought many through the turnstiles on that first night. Mayor Fitler had told his blue coated guards who stood on the gate not to sell any tickets till after midnight. As a consequence, anybody who hadn't purchased a ticket in advance before that time wouldn't be admitted. This ruling ensured that the ticket touts outside made a killing on over-inflated prices for their cherished pieces of paper. When the doors were opened at 8 p.m. the crowd *"began pouring into the building,"* and by 10 o'clock 500 were inside.

Anton Strokel was the first of the peds to be seen walking around the track before the start of the race. He was cheered by the waiting crowd as he took a stroll with a couple of ladies. Littlewood was given an ovation by some university students who were said to be his *"devoted admirers"* when he arrived. He would later be seen to be wearing their *"colors"* at the start. Vint, his wife, and their three sons, were next seen inspecting the track along with the accommodation that had been built for them. This consisted of huts which had been sparsely furnished with the usual basic requirements. Some of the roofs had been lined with felt, for reasons unknown.

Two men not mentioned in the advertisement would also line up at the start, these being Alfred Elson and Tom Cox. When the word "Go!" was finally given by Frank Richter the sporting editor of the *Ledger* at the agreed time, there were fully 4,000 people present. Cronin led them on the first lap, but thereafter it was a race between Littlewood and Hart to see which would make the first mile. As it was, they both passed the post together in a time of 6m.30s. The Englishman led the pack on the hour with a score of 6.7, "Black Dan" being three laps behind at the time.

Despite every attempt to keep up with Littlewood during the early stages of the race, not one of the competitors could match his pace. Hart's attempt to stay with him proved futile. Cox, Moore and Panchot also gave their all in an attempt to keep abreast, but alas, to no avail. Hart and Strokel were later reported to be suffering from stomach troubles, whilst Vint was said to have been inconvenienced by a sprained ankle. Jimmy Albert maintained a steady gait throughout the morning, but as the scores of the top half-dozen at 13:00 suggest, he was nowhere near the Littlewood at the time: **Littlewood, 88.6; Albert, 79.9; Moore, 77.9; Noremac, 76.7; Cox, 74.7; Elson, 74.5:**

The leader went on to make the first hundred of the race in 15h.5m, and that effort was recognised by the band which played "God Save the Queen" and "Rule Britannia" in celebration.

King of the Peds

The attendance for the first day had far exceeded the expectations of the managers, and the crowd, estimated at 4,000 in the evening, had been described as *"very large."* When Littlewood, who had been off the track for only a few minutes during the day, went off for a rest at 10:28 p.m., he had made an excellent score of 140 miles in a time of 22h.13m. With that wonderful performance in mind, the press was asking the question; "Will the record be broken?"

The scores at midnight: **Littlewood, 140; Albert, 136.2; Panchot, 117.5; Elson, 117; Cox, 112.11; Moore, 110.1; Noremac, 106; Cronin, 103; Burns, 100; Hart, 98.9; Vint, 87; Strokel, 86.2; Le Grand, 62.8:**

By the end of the second day, four of the competitors had dropped out. These were Vint, Moore, Cronin and Le Grand. All the remaining nine competitors were going well, with the exception of Strokel, who was having significant problems with his stomach. Littlewood stalked Albert around persistently and kept up the long distance he had created between himself and his rival for first place. The rest of the men went well, apart from Elson, who was slowing up somewhat, his age beginning to tell.

The score at 23:00 was as follows: **Littlewood, 245; Albert, 220; Panchot, 210; Noremac, 200.3; Elson, 197.1; Cox, 186.3; Burns, 186.2; Hart, 183.2; Strokel, 164.9:**

During the early hours of the next morning Strokel succumbed to stomach problems on a score of 180.2 at 04:36, and Burns, whose legs had *"given out,"* followed suit and hung up his costume at 07:07 having mustered 197.2. Another man who went for an early bath was Frank Hart at 08:23 after scoring 208.7, his excuse being that he was suffering from a bad cold.

The 10:00 score: **Littlewood, 283; Albert, 252; Panchot, 249; Noremac, 238; Elson, 232; Cox, 196:**

Tom Cox, who had been walking round the course for five hours *"on one leg"* finally succumbed at 11:30 with a score of 202 miles, and with Littlewood passing Fitzgerald's best time at noon, when the latter mentioned made his record of 610 miles, the score on the telegraph board at 13:00 showed: **Littlewood, 300; Albert, 268; Panchot, 264; Noremac, 250; Elson, 242:**

All the remaining five contestants were said to be moving along well as the evening approached and the crowd at the rink swelled to similar volumes as the preceding evening. Albert was presented with a cheque for $100 by some of his friends from Atlantic City, and there were also some other items presented to the tramps by their admirers in the form of bouquets and the like.

Littlewood's supporters were said to be very confident that their man would win the race. Indeed an announcement was made that the leader would try and break the world record. Odds of 1/2 were being offered that the Yorkshireman would prevail and huge amounts of money were being wagered at that price. At 10 p.m., the leader, who had taken very little rest during the day, was taken off the track and given a hot bath after which his head was allowed to hit his pillow for a short sleep. At 23:00, not only was he within six miles of Rowell's world record time, but he was also four miles ahead of Fitzgerald's best distance for 71 hours.

At midnight, the scores showed: **Littlewood, 342.6; Albert, 315.1; Panchot, 310; Noremac, 283.7; Elson, 282.5:**

On the next day, Thanksgiving Day, the management doubled the admission price to take advantage of the holiday, and were duly rewarded with their decision to so, as there was another large attendance at the venue.

During the morning the thought in everybody's minds was that the record would be broken, as Littlewood had passed Rowell's best 82-hour distance created on May the 9th 1881, at a few minutes past nine o'clock. From thereon, making good progress, he went on to steadily increase his lead, till at 19:16, and at the end of the 91st hour, he was 2 miles and 73 yards ahead of Fitzgerald's record, at the same juncture he made on May the 2nd 1884. Taking things a little more sedately thereafter, and allowing the others on the track to pass him at will, Littlewood went for his nightly rest at 22:00 just 1,166 yards ahead of the old record.

Jimmy Albert, the second man in the event, was being given some favourable reports by the press. *"Of all the men on the track Albert is in the best condition. His step is elastic and springy, almost as it was on the first day, while his face is noticeable for the absence of the hard, drawn lines that mark the faces of the others."* He enjoyed the exuberant acclaim he was receiving from his fellow Philadelphians who continually gave him lots of encouragement. Whilst Littlewood slumbered, Jimmy went on to claim one hundred miles for the day at 22:40. This amount was actually better than the leader's 97.5, which in turn, was nowhere near Fitzgerald's fourth day 111 miles and 6 laps of three years previous.

Of the rest, Peter Panchot, in third place, went along with his familiar swinging gait, his method of travel not changing in the least from day one. George Noremac, on the other hand, appeared tired. There was much disappointment that he could only muster a score of 88 miles during the day, having spent much of his evening alternating between track and tent. Alfie Elson, the last man, was putting in some good work and it was fully expected that he would make the necessary 500 to give him a share of the gate.

The management announced that the sum of $500 would be offered as an added incentive to the record being broken. The news that such a reward was on offer was on the lips of the spectators as they watched Noremac and Elson, the only two men on the track, trying to better their respective scores, which at midnight amongst the others, were: **Littlewood, 439.11; Albert, 417; Panchot, 400; Noremac, 378.4; Elson, 359.11:**

On Friday morning at 01:30 Littlewood made his way from his hut on to the track. Later it emerged that Albert had made an announcement that he was going to take the lead. He started at an 8 mph gait and Littlewood kept at his heels. Albert responded by increasing his speed to 9 mph and kept up the same pace for two hours or more. Littlewood dogged him incessantly, and when he saw Jimmy tiring, said, "Albert, you're not keeping me warm," as he went past him and increased his speed to 10 mph!

The 10 a.m. score: **Littlewood, 476; Albert, 440; Panchot, 416; Noremac, 396; Elson, 386:**

During the day, and watched by a packed Rink, the men on the track received many *"tokens of appreciation,"* with Littlewood receiving a $20 gold piece, the giver or givers of such a present, not mentioned. Noremac received some flowers, wine, and a new silk cap; whilst Elson was observed to be more than happy with the *"handsome gold headed cane"* that had been presented to him, his face beaming with appreciative delight.

When Littlewood left the track at 21:28 for his quarters in front of the largest crowd of the week, he had covered 524 miles. That left him 87 miles to make in the remaining 25 hours or so of the race to succeed in his objective of beating Fitzgerald's old record. Since starting early that day, and with few rest breaks, he had made a respectable 84 miles. When interviewed by the press, his trainer Frank Dole told reporters that he intended to wake up his lad at half past one, and then go for the record. During the day Littlewood had been issued with a couple of challenges, firstly from John Hughes for a sweepstakes of $5,000 a side to contest any race from 72 hours to six days in duration. The other had been from Bill Hoagland (who had a record up to that time of 480 miles to Littlewood's 531) to make a $3,000 square "heel and toer" over 142 hours.

All the other men in the race were expected to score 500 miles. When the scores at midnight were being scribbled down in the reporters' notebooks, the only pedestrians circling were Noremac and Panchot: **Littlewood, 524; Albert, 481; Panchot, 467; Noremac, 446; Elson, 443:**

On Saturday, November 26th, the 142-hour go-as-you-please race ended shortly before 10 o'clock in the evening, with Littlewood, in first place, nearly 40 miles ahead of his nearest competitor. It was early in the morning that he abandoned his expressed intention of trying to beat the world's record of 610 miles, and jogged along easily throughout the day. A good crowd was in attendance up to the close of the race, although there was no likelihood of any change of position of the five pedestrians. The only feature of interest on the last night was Elson's successful effort to reach 500 miles. His last few hours on the track however were rather a distressing sight. The old man was a physical wreck, and, but for the kindly help of the other men, latterly Albert, who remained on the track and walked around with him, it is believed he would have given it up before he reached the desired goal. He was later accompanied by *"Miss Myrtle Peek, the pretty equestrienne,"* who walked round with him on the last three laps. He finally completed 500 miles at 21:30 and then hobbled around an extra lap.

Final Scores!

1st: Littlewood, 569.1;

2nd: Albert, 530; 3rd: Panchot, 511.9; 4th: Noremac, 501.6; 5th: Elson, 500.1:

There was some disappointment that the winner didn't beat the record, but there would always be another day to try again. During the race the English raider, who had made new records from the 82nd till the 94th hour, rested for 27h.19m during the week of competition.

That night, after his victory, the winner could afford the luxury of walking back to his apartments at No. 3408 Sansome Street. After all he had only made 45 miles during the day, so the distance would have been no effort for him. Fred Bromley, his other trainer, accompanied him, and after undergoing a thorough rubbing down, George went to bed and was soundly asleep by 11 p.m. The next morning he went out for a five-mile stroll, ate a hearty breakfast, and then spent the rest of the day in bed, during which time he received the *"congratulations of his friends."* The other "peds," apart from Elson, who was so *"fagged out"* that he had to remain in bed all day, spent the day walking about.

The total amount of the gate receipts which was divided amongst the five prize winners was $2,908.12. Littlewood received $1,200.25, Albert, $667.03, Panchot, $400.22, Noremac, $266.81, and Elson $133.41. In addition to this, the entrance fees of $1,300 (each of the thirteen having paid in $100), was divided among the first three winners. Of this amount Littlewood received $780, Albert $390, and Panchot $130. The pedestrians, who were unhappy with their share of gate receipts which they had been assured would far exceed $10,000, apparently accepted the money given them reluctantly.

Elson, who succeeded in making the 500 miles, allowing him to receive a portion of the gate money, left *"penniless, footsore and broken-hearted."* His backer, who paid his entrance fee of $100, took every penny of the $133 allotted to him for making 500 miles; ignoring the old man's protests.

Littlewood, accompanied by trainer Fred Bromley left New York on December the 10th on the Cunard steamship *Etruria*. It arrived at the port of Queenstown in Ireland at 04:10 on December the 17th, the passage being a very quick one. He was amongst 975 passengers (this number being the most carried by any steamer on an eastern voyage) on the ship which had been anchored outside the port all the previous night.

He was cheered loudly after the late arrival of his train in Sheffield by the large crowd waiting outside on the most miserable of nights. He looked the picture of health, and after acknowledging the compliments of his numerous acquaintances, he left in the company of his father and other friends. His visit to America had been exceedingly profitable as he had received altogether about £700.

At the time, his intentions were to spend Christmas in Sheffield, and return to America to compete in another great race early the year after.

CHAPTER 54

Riot!

Earlier that year, on the evening of Monday, the 19th of September 1887, many people gathered at Lillie Bridge Grounds in London to watch a 120-yard race for £200, or £100 a side, and the championship, between Harry Hutchens of Putney and Harry Gent of Darlington.

For some years, Hutchens, who had been regarded as the finest amateur and professional short distance runner in the world, and held the short distance championship for several years, was at the time of the race, the record holder for the three great handicaps which were held periodically in Sheffield: 140 yards, 300 yards, and 350 yards. Indeed Hutchens had just arrived from Australia, *"where he had shown splendid speed on two occasions."* Gent had also won two Sheffield £100 handicaps. On one occasion at Easter, he had done so in such time that it was thought he would be an appropriate opponent for the Londoner to do battle with. Both competitors, who appeared fit and well, had indulged in careful preparation for the event, Gent in Yorkshire, and Hutchens in Leicester. With both men being *"touted like Derby favourites for the day,"* an *"exciting combat"* was anticipated in the fine weather that surrounded the venue.

"The utmost good order prevailed" amongst the 5,000 to 6,000 spectators who were present at the venue; many of whom had made long journeys from various parts of the country to witness the action, especially Sheffield, where these types of races were very popular. Three quarters of them were situated in the lower priced enclosure, whilst the remainder stood in front of the veranda-fronted range of buildings which were used as dressing rooms and bars.

Initially odds of around 2/5 and 1/2 were being advertised by the bookies on the northern raider Gent, who, being much the younger man, was greatly fancied to be victorious. However, as the time to start the race at five o'clock drew ever closer, the punters were taking the longer odds on Hutchens retaining his title, and within minutes, Gent, *"was no better fancied than his rival, whilst a little later on odds were offered on the latter, which quickly expanded to two, four, five, six and even ten to one. The betting veered round to such an extent that the public began to suspect something was wrong. The effect of this thorough reversal created great consternation, and was the subject of much unfavourable comment amongst the spectators, who began to call on the men to come out."*

Shortly after the advertised time for the race to start at five o'clock, Hutchens, who appeared in fine fettle, came out of the pavilion and walked round the ground with his trainer and two other men. Gent followed shortly afterwards; and after both had inspected the track, tossed a coin for *"choice of station."* Gent won, and both men appeared to retire back to their dressing rooms, their reappearance being eagerly awaited by the public who, waiting patiently, were only too aware that such events were held back as late as the light would permit.

Both men were now thought to be donning their racing costumes in the dressing room. In fact, what was actually happening was that Gent's handlers had informed Hutchen's party that because Gent had ran badly in a recent trial, they considered him to have no chance of winning the race. They had, therefore, decided to withdraw him, and although losing the stake money, they wouldn't lose their bets on the result as they would do if Gent did run and was defeated. This state of affairs apparently really upset the Hutchen's team and *"a free fight between the two factions was narrowly averted."*

Meanwhile, patience amongst the some of the crowd was wearing thin as the night was beginning to close in, and many in the ground were shouting, "Bring out the men!" That was followed by some *"rather ominous hooting."*

King of the Peds

A rumour then began to surface suggesting that both Hutchens and Gent had changed back into their civilian clothes and had left the Grandstand by the back doors, and furthermore, that there wouldn't be a race. Initially the rumour was generally dismissed by the public, but after half an hour had passed, and after waiting for some time for an official announcement on the subject, many of the crowd made their way to the pay office with the objective of getting their admission money back. That meant the management now had a couple of real problems on their hands. Firstly, all the entrance money from the pay boxes had been taken away for safety, and secondly, they knew that many more than those who had paid were sure to try and demand reimbursement. One report even suggested that the "money-taker" was *"spirited away"* with the takings.

Then, when some in the crowd began shouting that they had been *"duped,"* the inevitable and predictable trouble began, *"as having no one to wreak their vengeance on, the mob started wrecking the place."* The first thing that *"the rougher division in the cheap reserve"* decided to attack was the high partition near the gymnasium, thereafter focusing their attention on the palings around the track which were situated in front of the pavilion. This initial onslaught was repulsed due to the heroic efforts of several constables; but soon the wooden rails, which offered feeble resistance to the intentions of *"the wreckers,"* gave way, and an *"ugly rush"* ensued for the middle of the track, where *"a well dressed young man, possessed himself of the flag"* from the mast in the middle of the enclosure who *"proposed burning it."* After the flagpole that it flew from was pulled over, and the telegraph board was quickly smashed into pieces, much of the lighter woodwork which had been pulled away from the front of the buildings, along with about 300 yards of the wooden paling enclosing the running track, and about a hundred yards of the board fencing around the ground itself, were set alight. The actions of the few were soon to give an example to others and hundreds of others followed suit. *"It was at once seen that a regular riot was imminent."*

Whilst mayhem ensued within the ground, outside of it some of the bookmakers were running a gauntlet of hate as they tried to make their escape. *"They jumped into their cabs, and the angry crowd held on so to the cabs as to lift the horses off their feet."*

The *Times* wrote: **It is said that that the people who began the riot were decently dressed people from the North, such as are to be seen in the Pomona Gardens at Manchester and in the sporting places of Sheffield, with a wonderful amount of time and money to devote to pedestrian and horse racing.**

The three or four policemen defending the refreshment and dressing rooms stood their ground, and for a while were left alone as another *"organised attack"* was made on the *"long shed"* running down the whole Seagrave Road side of the course. This was demolished *"with the recklessness of savages,"* relieving it of its corrugated iron roofing.

Soon after the riot began, a mounted constable who was on duty near the grounds was informed by a messenger that his inspector *"was being kicked to death in the grounds."* He immediately made his way to the Seagrave Road entrance, where, after forcing his way in and being subsequently knocked off his horse, he was immediately attacked by the crowd who pelted him *"with brickbats; sticks and broken bottles."* Seeing that he had no chance, he wisely decided to beat a hasty retreat, and *"striking out right and left with his truncheon,"* he made his way to the railway embankment and thereafter ran for his life. After finding refuge in the adjacent railway station, his severely cut hands, arms, and face, were dressed by Mr. E. R. Goodwin of the General Post Office, a recent volunteer at the American Exhibition for the St. John's Ambulance Association.

There were thousands in the crowd though that had no intention whatsoever of disturbing the peace. When they couldn't make their escape out of the usual exists where the pay boxes were being smashed, they instead headed towards the fence at the railway bank. Whilst some of the more able bodied were able to climb over, the less fortunate, in their desperation to escape, resorted to tearing apart the high railing adjoining the railway which ran parallel with one side of the ground, and thereafter swarmed over the lines. Their actions were seen in a dim light by the railway officials, who were reported to have resented the presence of the intruders on the grounds used by them *as "kitchen gardens."* As a consequence, an attempt was made to keep them from trespassing further, which resulted in some heated arguments between those seeking to flee the chaos nearby.

One of those objecting to their presence was Mr. William Coombes, aged 50, a railway inspector of the West London Extension Railway at Addison Road. While he was engaged in keeping people clear of the lines, he suddenly staggered down the bank, and died from what turned out to be *"syncope from heart disease accelerated by intense excitement,"* the diagnosis being made known at the subsequent enquiry on the 22nd of September at Brompton Road Station.

The mob, now in full flow, began demolishing seats, chairs, and tables, indeed anything that was of a combustible nature from the buildings, which was used as kindling. In no time at all, they had succeeded in warming the neighbourhood with three giant bonfires, the flames from which rose 40 feet in the air. Whilst this was burning, hundreds of men and youths were actively engaged in destroying the woodwork which they then fed the flames with.

Meanwhile, *"the rabble"* continued with their previous assault on the pavilion and side buildings by driving back the small contingent of police. They hurled sticks, stones, and other missiles at them until they had succeeded in getting into the refreshment room which they ransacked and torched. *"Mrs. King, of the Nell Gwynne Tavern, Fulham, the refreshment contractor for the meeting, had her entire stock of liquids and solids stolen or destroyed."* The police initially succeeded in subduing the fire, but their efforts were in vain as the blaze took hold; flames also started to appear at a corner of the Drill Hall.

During the hour after the fires had been started, whilst the police were waiting for reinforcements to arrive, the place was left practically to the mercy of the mob, which did as they pleased. They bombarded both the pavilion, which was *"burning furiously,"* and the Seagrave Road shed, which was by this time alight in three places. They even destroyed about a dozen bicycles and tricycles belonging to some amateurs who habitually practiced at the grounds, much to the consternation of many in the crowd.

The rioting at Lillie Bridge where a fireman can be clearly seen in the middle of the mob.

© *The British Library. All Rights reserved. The Penny Illustrated. (Illustration no: 106)*

After some time a fire engine arrived. The men accompanying it tried to put some of the flames out, but as they did so, they were set upon by the rioters who pelted them with more stones and other missiles in the most *"cowardly manner."* The firemen responded by pointing their hoses at the *"maddened crowd,"* but found the water pressure too weak to be effective. The rioters interrupted the efforts of the firemen to cope with the flames three times, and

King of the Peds

"one of the firemen who was struck by a piece of wood left his hose and stepping forward challenged anyone to "come on like a man." A faint cheer greeted this action, but as the stone throwing continued, the fireman was compelled to seek shelter with his companions."

Responding to telegraphic summonses which had stated that a riot was in progress, Superintendent Fisher of Hammersmith, Inspector Cox of Chiswick, Inspector Brown of Fulham, Chief Inspector Giles of the "F" Division, and Sergeant Hambling of the "B" Division, dispatched and accompanied the police reinforcements who forced their way in by the members' entrance adjoining West Brompton Station and Seagrave Road. About half a dozen fires were ablaze when they got in. As they made their way forwards, they were pelted with missiles, before forcing the mob to retreat, which meant that the firemen were able to extinguish the blazes by 19:30.

According to a report in the *Sioux Valley News*, of Correctionville, Iowa, USA, on Thursday, the 22nd of September, the rioters later *"looted the liquor saloons in the neighborhood."*

During the disgraceful scenes, Inspector Moss, a sergeant, and some constables, were also injured. Constable Thompson (*"60 T"*), who was cut about the face with a bottle, also suffered a black eye, whilst Constable Marwood (*"38 TR"*), was the recipient of many injuries after being trampled upon and kicked. Other members of the force that were licking their wounds were Constable (*"23 TR,"*) who had his mouth severely cut, Sergeant Edwards, who had the misfortune of having his front teeth knocked out, and Sergeant Wisby was badly cut by a broken bottle.

The aftermath! The burnt down stands.

© The British Library. All Rights reserved. The Penny Illustrated. (Illustration no: 107)

In its edition of the 20th of September, *The Times* described the damage: **Nearly every building in the grounds had been either wholly or partially destroyed by fire or otherwise. The building containing the dressing rooms was standing, and its exterior bore few marks of violence. Inside, however, there was ample evidence that the place had not escaped the notice of the rioters. All the private lockers belonging to members were broken open and ransacked. Padlocks had been wrenched bodily from their fastenings and, everything at all valuable and portable carried off. The mob apparently expected to find the "gate money" in the place, and being disappointed smashed even the mantelpiece and fireplace in pure wantonness.**

"We have no doubt the scoundrels who perpetrated these outrages will be soundly punished. The public would not be not be sorry were the lash applied to their backs."

It later transpired that there was another version of events that led to the non-appearance of the participants, and once again *The Times* on September the 21st takes up the story: **One of the competitors came upon the ground yesterday and stated that the dressing rooms where the men were preparing for the race were broken into** and threats of violence were used towards both if they dared to appear. An endeavour had been made, so it is alleged, on behalf of those who gull the betting public to cause the race to go one way. Failing success in this endeavour, a gang of roughs, stated to have been engaged by a bookmaker, broke into the dressing place of the men who were to run and resorted to intimidation in order to prevent the race. Certain it is that before the competitors, Hutchens and Gent disappeared, bookmakers offered to bet "100 to 10 the race does not come off at all." This was heard by the occupiers of the ground, and they made preparations to secure the gate money, which, considering that between some 6,000 and 7,000 people had paid a shilling a head, and some four of five shillings in addition for reserved seats, must have been considerable in amount.

It was later ascertained that most of the rioters were men living in the vicinity of Chelsea, Wandsworth, Battersea, Kensington, Putney and Hammersmith. One of them was a man called Richard Wilson. He was charged at the Hammersmith Police Court the day after with *"violently assaulting Police Constable Acheson 141 T by cutting his head open with a ginger-beer bottle."*

PC 39T giving evidence for the prosecution, said, "I saw the rush into the refreshment bar, and a number of bottles brought out and thrown at the police. I distinctly saw the prisoner throw one at the constable."

Mr. Bennett, the magistrate, then questioned Dr. F. Egan, the police divisional surgeon of Fulham who had examined Constable Acheson at Walham Green Station.

Mr. Bennett. – "Is he unfit for duty?"

Dr. Egan. – "Yes, Sir; he will be unfit for a fortnight."

Wilson, who denied the charge, was remanded by Mr. Bennett, who denied him bail.

Of the others in court that day was William Wasley, a bootcloser, who was charged with stealing a silver plated ice pail from the refreshment bar belonging to Mrs. King. Detective Humphrey told the court, "I followed the prisoner, who was armed with a broken piece of chair, breaking everything he saw. The prisoner went behind the bar and took the ice pail. I took him into custody when he conducted himself in a violent manner, and there was great difficulty getting him out of the grounds. He was followed by a disorderly mob who threw missiles in all directions."

Harry Farmiloe, a labourer, who was charged with stealing bottles of ginger beer and lemonade from the bar, was also remanded in custody as he had been observed breaking the fence and therefore would also be considered for the offence of rioting.

On the 26th of September, Samuel James Rabbatts, a butcher and Samuel Godwin, a blacksmith, who had both been arrested on Saturday, the 24th of September, went up before Mr. Bennett at Hammersmith, the pair being accused of being involved with the riot. Apparently, the police had ejected Rabbatts for drinking and creating a disturbance after which he returned, to be seen by them, pulling down the fences. After the officers arrested Godwin, and whilst being transported to the station, the prisoner, after earlier admitting having been in the ground said, "It would have been a good thing for me if I had not gone. I had a run down and paid my bob, and not seeing the race, I was annoyed." Godwin was apparently seen breaking up chairs, and after loosening the flagstaff, carrying it away. Both were remanded in custody.

The day after Wilson was fined £5 or one-month imprisonment.

Mrs. King, who was in charge of the refreshment bars, estimated the damage commited by Wasley to be eight shillings and by Farmiloe one shilling and sixpence. Both were fined 40 shillings or two weeks "inside."

CHAPTER 55

What Else Happened in 1887

A six-day go-as-you-please race for the "Championship of the World" and the diamond belt promoted by Richard K. Fox of the *Police Gazette*, opened at the Elite Rink in Philadelphia, sixteen minutes into Monday morning, February the 21st in the presence of about 6,000 people.

Among the 40 starters were Jimmy Albert, Thomas Cox, Sam Day, Lawrence Donovan (the Brooklyn bridge jumper), Alfred Elson, Christian Faber, Peter Golden, Carlisle D. Graham (*"the Niagara Falls barrel man"*), Frank Hart, Peter Hegelman, Dan Herty, Fred Krohne, George Noremac, Peter Panchot, Anton Strokel, George Tilly and Bobby Vint. John Hughes, who had entered, didn't start. Frank Hart was the first to score a mile, his time being a little less than six minutes.

Some of the competitors!

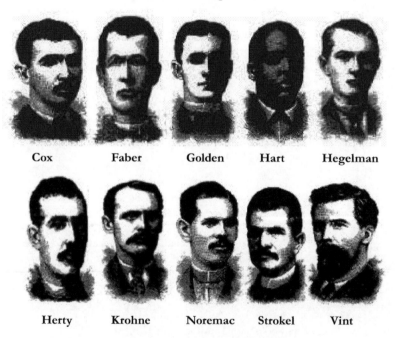

The National Police Gazette   (Illustration no: 108)

During the week 32 men dropped out of the race; the winner, when the contest finished on Saturday, the 26th was Vint. The Brooklyn man, with a final score of 530 miles, won the belt and $3,500, which came from half of the gate receipts of $14,000, the rest being shared out by those who had covered more than 500 miles. Hart claimed the runner-up prize with a score of 518.8. Panchot was third with 511 miles, Dave Bennett, fourth with 506.3, and Noremac, fifth with 500 miles. The other finishers were Elson, with 362, Tilly with 352.2 and Newhart with 291.8.

As the referee was announcing the result, the floor gave way under the reporters' stand; and in the ensuing panic, many were hurt as a rush was made for the exits.

A fifteen mile walking match for $2,000 between Frank Hart, of Fell River, Massachusetts, and Bill Hoagland of Auburn, New York, took place at the Assembly Hall, Jackson, Michigan, on Saturday night, the 2nd of April, before a huge crowd. Hart was given a half mile start.

With just over seven miles being walked in the first hour, Hart won the race by four laps in a time of 2h.34m. In the ninth mile Hoagland's right leg became badly swollen and he was unable to keep up his pace but nevertheless remained in the race until the finish.

Hart, who was reported to have fainted at the end of the race, had to be carried to his room.

There was a large attendance to see the conclusion of a 72-hour contest which closed on Saturday night the 16th of April, at the rink at Lawrence, Massachusetts, where the final score was: **Hegelman, 401; Golden, 390; Herty, 382; Coburn, 324; Day, 280; Cunningham, 274; Sullivan, 265:** The *"whole affair,"* was said to have been very successful.

A large crowd assembled to witness the start of a novel four hours per night, six days, go-as-you-please race at the Stockton Street Rink in Trenton, New Jersey, which began at 7:30 p.m. on Monday, the 11th of April on a 16 laps to the mile track.

The starters were: Adams of Millham, J. Adams of Bristol, J. Albert of Atlantic City, D. Bennett of Canada, D. Burns of Elmira, J. La Point of Elmira, J. McTague of Trenton, G. Noremac, A. Strokel, of Saginaw, Michigan, and Brooklyn's R. Vint.

La Point made the first mile; but by the end of time on the first night, the *"collar and elbow man,"* Strokel led the field with 29 miles, Albert being the second man with 28.

The Austrian would faint on the track on the second night, due to stomach problems, during which Albert would add 30 miles to his overnight score to lead the race, Vint being his nearest rival with 51 miles.

The athlete's diet was again being scrutinised by the press which, was once again, reporting on what individual competitors were consuming during their tramp. Of Strokel, *"who walks like a crab and swings him arms over the head of little Vint, and scratches his head with his shoulders,"* they wrote that he attributed his previous night's fainting episode to unwisely eating beef-steak. They went on to comment on his previous race in Philadelphia; *"Strokel's only solid food was light sponge cake, apples, peanuts, and chicken broth which he took from a bottle."* Vint's eating habits were also being observed. He *"never eats on the track but in his rests drops into his tent and partakes of food as solid as can be laid before him and plenty of it,"* whereas *"Noremac in his recent travel of five thousand miles in a hundred days, appeased his appetite on chicken and the most substantial kinds of food, aided by wines."*

During that evening Vint was seen to be arguing with the referee Christian Huber, claiming that his score wasn't correct. After assurances that everything was in order, the Brooklynite bet Albert, the race leader, $100 that he would win the race, and the two of them thereafter duelled it out for the rest of the night. Noremac was now however, the danger having moved up from sixth to second place by the close of proceedings, when the score showed Albert leading him by eight miles, the record at 23:30 being: **Albert, 86; Noremac, 78; Vint, 76:**

With Winkler's Band influencing them with its inspiring music, Noremac and Strokel were being looked upon as the eventual race winners and both were leading the betting market. Strokel, now only four laps behind Noremac, *"says he will wake them all up,"* whilst Vint, *"glides over the surface as if he were on wheels, and for a man forty years of age to travel at the rate of eight miles an hour day after day and keep it up is, to say the least very remarkable."*

King of the Peds

By the penultimate night, *"excitement was at fever heat"* as interest in the contest had intensified with a good race in prospect for first place. Strokel continued to challenge Noremac for second place, but Vint's efforts to gain some money out of the match were now looking forlorn as he suffered from a badly swollen ankle. Albert completed his 129th mile in 6m.10s and ran his 130th mile in seven minutes even. Noremac's trainer Joe Miller however, was confident that his man would still the win race despite being 5 miles or so behind him at the end of the evening when the score showed: **Albert, 150; Noremac, 145; Strokel, 134; Vint, 125:**

Miller's confidence in the Scotchman's ability to close the gap proved wrong; during the last four hours of competition his man failed miserably to make any impression on Albert's lead. So it was Jimmy Albert who took the spoils, by winning the race with 177 miles, taking 40% of half the gross receipts of $1,620 which amounted to $324. Noremac, who eventually made 168 miles, won $243, and Strokel who finished third, made $162 for his effort of 158. Vint, who scraped home in front of Leadom by a mile and a half to take fourth place, earned $81 for scoring 143 miles.

Out of 48 entries, there were 41 starters at the beginning of a six-day go-as-you-please contest which commenced at midnight on May the 2nd at the Elite Skating Rink, on the corner of Twenty Third and Chestnut Streets, Philadelphia. Cash prizes totalling $5,000 were offered and there was an additional prize of $1,000 which would be given to the man who broke the six-day record.

The match ended on Saturday, May the 7th. Anton Strokel claimed first prize with 515 miles. Albert was the runner-up with 505 miles. Noremac, who made 492 miles, beat Hart who was seven miles behind him in fourth place with 485 miles. Vint, Hughes, Day, Cox and Elson were others that took part.

In the opinion of Referee, L. J. Shyne who declared "all bets off," Guerrero's *"ugliness had spoiled the race,"* and he *"ought never to be allowed on a track again,"* after the spectators had become thoroughly disgusted with his performance as he *"loafed around the track."*

The 72-hour race in which he was competing ended at 10 o'clock on Saturday night, May the 21st at Lawrence, Massachusetts, when the referee stepped on to the platform and announced Guerrero had left the track. The Californian was reported to have said that there was no money in the result and therefore he wouldn't be putting any more effort into the race. His decision meant that his fellow competitors also took it easy, and that attitude was reflected in the final result of: **Herty, 116.12; Meagher, 113.5, Driscoll, 102.8:**

After the race, the Mexican was reported to have narrowly escaped a mobbing, after the crowd had expressed a rather negative opinion of him.

Betting had been reported to be heavy in Kansas City before the big six-day walking match which took place at the skating rink between Monday, the 24th and Saturday, the 29th of October. Punters in the city were said to have bet liberally on John S. Dobler, *"the gamest boy who ever wore a shoe,"* the letter carrier from Chicago, to prevail. Bill Hoagland, *"tall, beautifully built, with almost uncanny powers of endurance,"* had also attracted a lot of interest among the gamblers of the city. The Auburn man, who had trained hard in Aurora, Missouri, where he had been living, and who went to Kansas City in the *"pink of condition,"* was backed into 3/1 joint favourite from 9/1.

For three days Bill and John had fought for the lead (48-hour score: **Hoagland, 200.11; Dobler, 198.9; O'Leary, 175.10; Messier, 162.9; Hoffman, 143.1; Smith, 142.1; Zang, 123.12; Hawley, 116.5**), and acting under his trainer Daniel O'Leary's instructions on the fourth day, Dobler, *"tried to walk Hoagland off his feet."*

For 17¼ hours the two men walked without once stopping. At the end of that time, Dobler left the track, and rushing over to O'Leary, shouted, "Dan, where has the crowd gone? The hall is empty. That is no way to treat a man."

O'Leary, trying to calm him down, pointed out that the audience watching the contest was the same as ever, but it was to no avail. Dobler didn't believe him, and he was taken to his dressing room, where O'Leary emerged an hour later to confront Hoagland on the track saying to him, "Bill, it is all off with Johnny. You will win."

In the end Hoagland beat Dobler by exactly seven miles with a score of 480 miles and a lap. Messier was third with 465 miles, Hoffman fourth with 417 miles, and Smith fifth with 365.5, in a race where there was said to be about 30 starters.

In an interview with the *Kansas City Star*, Hoagland told a reporter from the newspaper: "Walking is a science. It is strange how few people know how to walk. I can walk 100 miles without stopping to rest, and yet the average man seems tired after a two miles spin. A mistake most people make when they attempt to walk fast is in turning out their toes, throwing back their bodies and trying to walk with their knees. The joints of the toes run back at an angle from the main bone of the foot, so that when the foot is thrown out and points in a different direction from that in which you are moving, the entire strain is put upon the center of the angle, and the foot soon becomes tired. When the foot is placed so that all the toes point forward, the strain is evenly divided and the exertion is much less tiresome. The body should rest easily on the hips, and if the arms are swung in time with the motion of the legs, they will lift the entire weight of the body from the hips. In a long race it is necessary to walk with both arms and legs. The principal strain in a heel and toe contest is on the calf of the leg, although of course every muscle in the body is brought into play. In running, the great strain is on the hip muscles. Of course a six days walking match will lay a man up, for during a whole week he is practically without sleep, can take but very little food and undergoes constant exertions. But the great strain has no lasting effect. All the long distance walkers keep on the track for years, entering race after race. There is Taylor, who is still walking, though he is over 60 years old. Walking is exercise natural to a man, and does not hurt him in the least."

Hoagland won a handsome gold watch, chain, and charm with diamond setting valued at $300 as part of the spoils of his victory.

Any contestant that covered 400 miles would be able to claim a share of the gate receipts in a square heel-and-toe walking match which took place at Kansas City during Christmas week of 1887.

Twelve men appeared on the opening night which began unusually at 9 o'clock on Monday, December the 26th. Willard. A. Hoagland went on to break the 100-mile record, making that distance in 16h.55m.

Only six pedestrians remained at the close on Sunday night, the 1st of January 1888, with Hoagland keeping on to win with a score of 439 miles. Hart, with 429.5 finished a close second, and Henry O. Messier was third, having made 425. The other finishers were Oddy with 410 and Townsend with 406.2. Last man was Hoffman on 400.10.

After the race, the *Kansas City Times* wrote: Hoagland is today beyond a question, the champion heel and toe walker of the world, a great pedestrian and a perfect gentleman making friends wherever he goes. His style when walking is the embodiment of ease and grace and his appeal is simply phenomenal. If the great three cornered race for the championship of the world and $1,000 a side between Littlewood, champion of England, Scott, champion of Australia and Hoagland should be arranged, the winner will have to eclipse all previous records to beat Hoagland.

CHAPTER 56

Hall's Tournament

George Littlewood wasn't able to attend the *"International Go-As-You-Please"* contest which had been arranged between February the 6th and 11th 1888 at Madison Square Garden. However, by mid January, four of his fellow countrymen had arrived in the city on the steamship *Umbria,* seeking fame and glory in a six-day match which was to begin three weeks later. They were George Cartwright, Richard Hales, Archie Sinclair, and William Griffin, all residents of London.

It was Cartwright's first visit to the United States and he was eager to make predictions on how he would fair. "I don't care how far your walkers on this side have gone," he said, "Records don't frighten me. Anybody who beats me in this race will have to beat 625 miles." Indeed, Cartwright's record was most impressive: He held the best records in the world from 41 to 61 miles and he had recently scored 61 miles in 7h.40m. Since his race at the London Aquarium in November of 1884 (See Chapter 47) when he had come third with 357.4, he had come second to Rowell (See Chapter 49) at the same venue with 383 miles on May the 2nd 1885. A week later on Saturday, the 9th of May, he won the "Fifty-Mile Running Championship" at the same venue in a time of 6h.19m.20s. Sometime in 1886, he was reported to have made 42 miles in 5 hours at Birmingham in a race where he beat Bond and Connor easily. On February the 21st 1887, he had run 50 miles in 5h.55m.4½s in the race won by Littlewood (See Chapter 52), in a time which had beaten Littlewood's 1884 record by 13m.4½s. He then won a six-hour race at Kendal, England, beating T. C. Herbert, W. Smith and others, after which he won a 50-mile handicap by four miles from the *"virtual scratch"* at the Agricultural Hall in London on Saturday, the 19th of November 1887 in a time of 5h.46m.12s. After that he went on to win a 20-mile handicap from the scratch at the Olympian, London, where he beat Arthur Norris. A 26-hour race in South Wales followed that effort which he won, beating Sam Day. In addition to the above, he was reported to have won 13 races in St. Petersburg and Moscow, *"beating all the noted winners."* It was also reported that he had won a 7-day, three hours per day race at Aberdeen. What is really interesting about George's career is that the *Boston Globe* on March the 5th 1888 claims that in a six-day, 142-hour race at a place called Sharonen, he, and I quote, made *"570 miles, completing 157 miles in the first 24 hours!"*

Sinclair was the celebrated long distance amateur champion heel-and-toe walker of England having made 120 miles in 23h.53m on Saturday, the 27th of August 1881 at Lillie Bridge. During the feat he had also managed to beat all previous best records from 51 to 120 miles inclusive. Hale and Griffin were both seen in a similar vein to Rowell, with all three being reliant on stamina. Joe Scott the Australian champion was also expected in the big city to take part.

On the 31st of January, it was reported that Cartwright, Gus Guerrero, Peter Hegelman, H. L. Lurkey and Peter Panchot were stopping at Skinner's Iron Pier Hotel at West Brighton, where they were said to be covering distances of up to 60 miles per day on the beach and at Baur's Casino.

The race attracted a total of 72 competitors who stumped up $25 to even be considered to take part. Of those who were originally declared (many of whom had never been heard of), about 55 would eventually appear at the starting post. Any man not completing 100 miles in the first 24 hours would be asked to leave the race. The prize for the winner was half the net gate receipts; and should that winner break the record of 610 miles, a princely sum of $1,000.

All the competitors were allocated a small wooden hut to operate from. A previous lottery held earlier on the Saturday before the race had decided which competitor should occupy which hut. There had been a bit of a fracas earlier when the athletes' attendants hadn't been given entry badges so that they could be distinguished from *"the mob."* They were promised however that they would get them on the Monday, and this calmed them down.

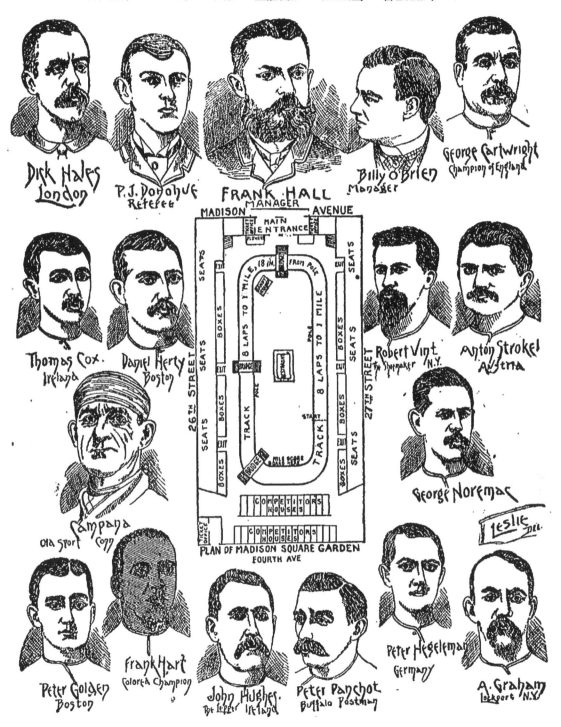

The Boston Globe (Illustration no: 109)

King of the Peds

The scoreboard, which was found at the eastern end of the building and built half way between the floor and the roof, would accommodate the names and scores of the first twelve in the race. There were 150 scorers employed, half working during the day and half on the night shift. They were safely fenced off away from the public and out of sight of people who might like to offer them inducements to make the *"odd mistake."* Opposite the scoreboard was an array of 72 small clock dials which contained the figures 1 to 8 for the lap count, and where a *"white knobbed peg"* slotted into the holes of each of the eight numerals as it passed around the dial. In the centre of each was a space for the total miles scored. All official scores would of course be recorded on paper as well.

There was very little activity during the day before the start of the race. A few youngsters hung around outside hoping to sneak in, but the door keepers only waved in respectably dressed people and *"Gentlemen wearing pilot coats."* The place began to fill up as soon as the gates were opened at 7 o'clock on the evening of the 5th of February, the price of admission being 50 cents. For that amount, the ticket holder could stand and watch the fun and walk within the confines of the picket fence surrounding the track. A reserved seat would cost an extra 25 cents and a box would be double that amount. About 2,000 people had gathered around the doors, and as they piled into the building, they were supervised by about 130 policemen. The "candy butchers" and peanut vendors started to sell their wares and the cake and pie stand began serving its first customers, along with the oyster stalls. Beer and whiskey was being sold in the basement along with sandwiches; and if anyone wanted to test their strength, there were machines on hand to help them. There were also shooting galleries, strength testing machines and the chance to win between 2 and 5 cigars in the baseball-throwing alleys, where the targets, amongst other things, were brightly coloured dolls.

Some of the leading contenders! *(Illustration no: 110)*

Connor   **Hegelman**   **Herty**   **Hughes**   **Moore**

While the thirty piece Bauland's Band played something called *"sacred music"* to entertain the waiting crowd estimated to be around 4,500 at 10 p.m., the bookmakers went quietly about their business in the area provided inside the track. The favourite was Cartwright and he was followed in the betting market by, Connor, Sinclair, Hart and Hughes with Ranhoffer of New York, the ex-champion walker also being "fancied."

At 23:45, the management and police had agreed to close the buildings doors for safety reasons as there were already 9,000 spectators inside. That decision meant that some in the huge crowd outside were desperately offering box office employees $2 for a ticket.

Most of the contestants had spent the evening sleeping at their homes or in nearby hotels, and didn't arrive in the building until just before the official start at midnight. Hart, who was the first of the big stars to arrive, was readily applauded when he walked towards his allocated quarters. Then, with just five minutes till the "off," Campana was given a tumultuous reception, when, wearing a bandana, he emerged from his dwelling followed by Cartwright.

Another mighty roar greeted the arrivals of the "Lepper," the tiny 7½ stone figure of the 22-year-old George Connor, and Dan Herty who was followed by other well known "peds."

The *Boston Globe* takes up what happened next: The men swarmed down from their huts at the end of the building like a pack of wild Indians, nor were they much unlike the children of the plains in their appearance. Anything more grotesque than the costumes in which these champions for pedestrian honors were apparelled cannot be imagined. Green skullcaps were pulled down over the heads of thin-legged comical looking little fellows, whose bodies encased in yellow undershirts, and whose legs were adorned with faded brown velvet trunks and red stockings. Some were hatless, some were in slippers, others wore high-laced boots. Many of them had fanciful sashes of bright colored ribbons thrown over their shoulders. One venerable contestant wore a slouch gray felt hat and spectacles.

There were no rules as to the amount of clothing which any could wear. Some were in sleeveless gauze shirts and knee breeches; others black trousers of regulation length and were in waistcoats of shirts sleeves. Each man carried pinned, or sewed to the back of his body garments, a large number painted on a square of white cambric, but as these numbers did not correspond with the numbers appended on to the list of entries as published in the official programme, they were of little use in the identification of the runners.

Although an ample number of efficient scorers had been provided, their penned-in quarters, which they shared in common with the afflicted newspaper reporters were invaded, just as the start was made by a mob of people who broke down a corner of the fence and swarmed through the opening like flies into an open molass jug.

All walked to the judges' stand where they were ticketed before taking their places in the line-up in front of the race officials. Then, Referee Pete Donahue, shouted the word "Go," so loudly at 12:05 a.m. that it could be heard all over the building!

The start!

The National Police Gazette (Illustration no: 111)

According to at least two newspaper reports which give us some idea of who was in the race, first off the mark was; *"**Field** followed by **Cox, Hughes, Cartwright, Albert, Panchot, Herty, Guerrero, Hart, Sinclair, Elson, Hales, Hegelman, Strokel, Curran, Dillon, Campana, Tilly, Callaghan, Ranhoffer, McLaughlin, Selin, Paul, Dufrane, Keeshon, Call, Horan, Hoag, Johnson, Hoagland, Newhart, Day, Burrell, Petello, Delrica, Lurkey, Schwenk, Richards, Taylor, Munson, Shopla, Thomas, Stout, Vint, Sullivan, Bird** and **Connor**."*

King of the Peds

Interestingly, **Attwood, Dempsey, Golden, Gutterman, Moore, Noremac, Schriver** and **Winters** were not mentioned in the above report, but nevertheless *were* in the race, whereas ***Bird, Delrica, Ranhoffer, Richards,*** and ***Thomas's*** names were never mentioned again…?

The crowd screamed themselves silly for at least 15 minutes as normally composed people transformed themselves into something alien to their true nature and, as the race progressed, they all calmed down - but only by a bit. The pedestrians sped around the tanbark as though their lives depended on it. Now and again, one of the men would spurt with another, and this delighted the fans who shrieked their pleasure and screamed at the competitors, "Go on!" and "Beat him!" Guerrero made the first mile, in 6m.20s with Herty immediately behind him.

At 1 o'clock, the score of the leading contenders *officially* stood: **Cartwright, Golden and Guerrero, 8.6; Albert and Hegelman, 8.5; Strokel and Hart, 8.3; Connor and Herty, 8: Vint, 7.7; Sinclair, 7.5; Panchot, 7.1; Hughes and Elson, 6.7; Field and Sullivan, 6.6; Munson and Schwenk, 6.2; Hales, 5.2:** There was some cynicism as to the validity of this "early" score because it was reported that *"the mob"* had invaded the scorers' quarters causing havoc. At 02:00, the leading men in the race were: **Cartwright, 16.4; Albert and Guerrero, 16.3; Golden and Hegelman, 16.2; Panchot, 15.4; Hart and Strokel, 15.2; Connor, 15.1; Sinclair, 14; Dufrane, 13.6; Hughes, 12:**

With the exception of Gutterman, who left at 3 o'clock, Winters, who left at 4 o'clock, Hoag, who went out at 5 o'clock, and Shopla who left ten minutes later, all the competitors worked hard during the night with many in the race only leaving the track to get the occasional rub down. Call, a *"rosy cheeked boy of 13 years old,"* who made his way along with what was described as a *"springy action,"* was already way behind the race leaders, one of whom of course was Cartwright who at 06:00 had notched up a score of 42.2. Both he and the *"smooth faced youth,"* Hegelman, had led by several miles throughout the early morning hours; by 07:17, when they passed the scoring point side by side, both had made their half centuries.

At 7:30, while Vint and Dempsey (*"Kenny's Unknown"*) were trotting along on the south side of the track, they got into an altercation. After both men stopped and exchanged a few words, Dempsey punched Vint in the mouth causing him to stagger. Vint returned the blow with two punches, but before Dempsey could have another pop at Vint, they were separated. Both men appeared angry when they went to their huts and the ex-cobbler's lip was cut and very swollen. Dempsey meanwhile, who was in a real old lather about the incident, claimed that after he had caught Vint's foot, the Brooklyn man swung round, said a few choice words and then hit him. Vint, who was much calmer than the fiery Dempsey, claimed his attacker had been fouling him at every opportunity and *"applying vile epithets to him whenever within speaking distance."*

E. C. Moore, otherwise known as *"Manhattan Moore,"* who was said to be an *"elevated railroad employee,"* was keeping up with the leaders, running along stylishly. In the following references to Hoagland's performance, the *New York Evening World* wrote: **As the plodders went on in their journey under the eyes of the thousand, the dog persevering way in which the long legged heal and toe man, Hoagland, pushed one foot ahead of the other, the gunshot speed and the "business-is business" air of the "Shoestrings" roused the interest and admiration of the spectators and he was applauded at every turn. He walked. Every one else ran or trotted, yet at 8 o'clock he was only six miles behind the Greaser, who was still leader of the pack.**

At 08:00, and whilst there were about 400 spectators inside the Garden, Hegelman had increased his score to 54.6. The *Boston Globe* which described the German contender as a *"tow-headed man,"* wrote of him: **His hair is closely cropped, showing a large head set on a short, bull neck on broad shoulders. While either walking or running he carries his arms extended at full length, and for the most part, his eyes are fixed on the ground.**

The small number in the crowd cheered vociferously at every spurt made by the runners. Cartwright wasn't going too well, and the distance between him and Hegelman was slowly increasing in the latter's favour, possibly due to the leader's better condition, as a result of the constant training which he had indulged in for several weeks before the race.

The 9 a.m. scores: **Hegelman, 62.4; Cartwright, 60.2; Albert, 57.1; Guerrero, 56.1; Hart, 54.2; Moore, 53.4; Golden and Herty, 52.6:**

There was a lot of dissatisfaction and discontent with the management of the race. The contestants too were becoming uneasy with the way that the scores were being recorded; and there were shouts of "Hippodrome!" and "It's a sell!" from the crowd. Hughes, Hart, Burrell and indeed many of the contestants stopped at the scorers' stand and protested strongly. The big bulletin board was giving a so-called record of the distances covered, but only twenty-six of the runners names appeared on it. For example, Hughes's score on the board was 45 miles. On the dials it was 46 and on the score sheets 47. The "Lepper" kicked up a big fuss about the anomalies but couldn't get the management to agree with him.

The midday scores: **Hegelman, 77.7; Cartwright, 73.7; Albert, 73.5; Guerrero, 73.2; Hart, 72; Moore, 68.7; Panchot, 68.1; Strokel, 67.2; Day and Herty, 66.6; Golden, 65.7; Dillon, 63.1; Horan, 61; Campana, 60.7; Connor, 59.7; Sinclair, 59.6; Dufrane, 57.7; Elson, 57.4; Sullivan, 56.5; Cox and Vint, 56.4; Lurkey, 56.3; Curran, 56.2; Petello, 56; Noremac, 55; Keeshon, 54.5; Tilly, 54.2; Johnson, 53.4; Stout, 50.4; Hughes, 49.6; Newhart, 48.1; Munson, 48; Call, 47; Selin, 46; Field, 45; Burrell, 44.6; Paul, 43.5; McLaughlin, 43; Hoagland, 40.3:**

A somewhat pitiful sight was the plucky little Saratogan, John Sullivan, who had covered 60 miles. He had remained on the track from the start and was observed to run with his mouth constantly wide open, appearing as though every lap would be his last.

The score at 14:00: **Hegelman, 86.4; Albert and Cartwright, 84.4; Guerrero, 84; Hart, 81; Panchot, 78.4; Moore, 78.3; Herty, 77.5; Day, 77.2; Horan, 76.6; Golden, 76.5; Strokel, 74.6; Connor, 70.2:**

Guerrero went into the lead at 16:00. Five minutes later, Emil Paul, who was famous for eating quails, threw in the towel on a score of 53. Some punters had put lots of cash on him scoring 100 in 34 hours, but he left the course *"fagged out!"* Twenty minutes later, and amid a roar from the 2,000 throng, the *"Greaser,"* as Guerrero was known, was the first of the 37 who remained on the racecourse, to score the first century. However, his achievement was nothing compared with Rowell who, in a previous race had gone 14½ miles further, 25 minutes earlier!

By 18:00, other starters that had, or were just about to officially announce their retirement from the race, were: Callaghan, Hales, McLaughlin, Munson, Schwenk, Schriver, Selin and Hoagland. The scores of the men who did remain in the race were: **Guerrero, 104.6; Albert, 104.4; Hegelman, 102.6; Hart, 102.1; Cartwright and Panchot, 100; Golden, 98.2; Moore, 97.6; Herty, 97.4; Day, 96.4; Horan, 88.5; Strokel, 88; Cox, 86.1; Connor, 85.6; Noremac, 85.5; Sinclair, 82.4; Sullivan, 82.1; Taylor, 81.1; Lurkey, 79.3; Dufrane, 79; Elson, 76.1; Tilly, 76; Stout, 74.4; Johnson, 74.1; Vint, 73.3; Campana, 73; Curran, 72.1; Call, 70.1; Newhart, 68.3; Hughes, 64.4; Burrell, 63.6; Attwood; 62.2:**

Cartwright, having earlier at 7:30 p.m., *"kicked up his heels as though he had been stabbed in the back with a pin,"* left the track at 21:00. His team said he had a cold, but later, at 23:35 a story doing the rounds stated that he had been taken to the Putnam House in a *"critical condition,"* due to bleeding from the lungs.

One of the rules of the race was that anyone not completing 100 miles in the first 24 hours would have to leave the race. At midnight, the following notice was served on the backers of the men who had failed to reach that score:

"As your man has failed to cover 100 miles in the first twenty four hours, he is hereby notified to discontinue walking, as he will not be scored in the future."

Consequently the following were barred from taking further participation in the contest: **Attwood; 98; Elson, 93; Curran, 92; Dufrane, 89; Newhart, 84; Burrell, 82; Hughes, 81; Call, 78; Campana, 70.** Hughes, however was the exception, and by *"special arrangement"* with Mr. Hall the manager, he was supposed to be allowed to stay in. However, when Referee Donohue got wind of the scheme, he put his foot down, stating, "Under no circumstances should the "Lepper" be allowed to continue unless he fulfilled all the necessary requirements!" So it was bye-bye John….or was it…because as the 24 hours were up, and according to the reporter of the *Boston Globe*: **Poor old Hughes at this time was "lepping" around in a most insane and imbecile manner. He seemed utterly regardless of the cruel limitations of time and space.**

King of the Peds

With Collins's score being unknown, the following were the top scores at midnight, the end of the first 24 hours: **Hart, 130.3; Albert, 130.1; Guerrero, 129; Golden, 126; Panchot, 125.1; Herty, 122; Day, 118.1; Moore, 115.2; Hegelman, 112.1; Cox, 110.1; Cartwright, 105.4; Horan, 105.2; Dillon, 104.2; Connor and Strokel, 102.2; Tilly, 101.7; Sullivan, 101.2; Noremac and Vint, 100.3; Sinclair, Stout and Taylor, 100.2; Johnson and Lurkey, 100:**

It was finally announced that Cartwright had permanently retired from the event due to *"inflammation of the lungs"* at 01:00. The English "ace" told reporters that he had caught a cold whilst training on the Coney Island beach. He was apparently inconsolable when he knew he had to retire. Later, he would have been unaware that a fight took place outside his hut at 03:10 amongst several of the trainers who were smashing sticks and chairs over each others' heads. No explanation was given for the trouble. Later, as daylight peeped through the soiled windows of the building, and as 500 spectators watched the monotonous tramping, more fighting broke out amongst some of the spectators. This time the weapons of choice were beer glasses, which were said to sail through the air at a lively rate. No one was seriously injured; again, no explanation was given except that the crowd was probably bored, because the pace resembled that of a funeral cortège.

Another possible explanation for the discontent was the fact that there was no music being played because the management had dispensed with the band—much to the consternation of the peds, who relied on their offerings to motivate them on the track. The reason that the race organisers had adopted this policy was because they had been given a choice by the powers that be to either sell liquor without music, or play music without selling liquor. In their wisdom they chose the former option because at least they made money that way. Thus the men on the path plodded on, despite it being abundantly clear that they were losing interest in their tasks. A music free atmosphere meant little stimulation for the contestants, thus resulting in below par on-track performances, which inevitably caused poor attendances. Still, from a management point of view that could be seen in a positive light because at least none of the pedestrians would make the requisite 525 miles which would ensure a share of the gate money.

The 6 a.m. scores: **Albert, 153.3; Guerrero, 144; Panchot, 142; Hart, 141; Day, Herty and Moore, 136:**

After Horan had to leave the race in a rather pitiable condition due to a poorly performing leg, Sullivan created a few smiles at 08:40, in an otherwise miserable atmosphere, by sitting on a chair in front of the scorers' stand where he began to read the morning papers saying, "Wait until I read an account of the race and I'll run some more." Needless to say, his attendants were not impressed with his behaviour and ushered the *"ghost,"* as he was fondly known, back on the track as a matter of urgency. At 9 o'clock, Albert was in the lead with 170, whilst Panchot and Guerrero stuck closely together behind. As the leader plodded round dreaming of making a new world record, the holder of the existing one, Patrick Fitzgerald, appearing rather fat and sporting a paunch, turned up to watch the fun at 11 o'clock. He was asked if he was sorry not to be competing. Shaking his head, he replied, "No, not for me." Asked which of the men he fancied to take off the first prize, he answered, "Herty I think is about the best of them."

Hegelman had earlier left the track at 08:00 looking unwell due to a dodgy stomach. Apparently, "Happy Jack" Smith, his trainer, had given instructions that his German star be driven to have a Russian bath. So Peter was *"hustled into a coupe"* and sent away, but alas, when he returned to the race at 11:20, his stomach continued to protest, and sadly, the one time race leader was forced to give his dream of winning up.

At 14:00, the score showed: **Albert, 194.6; Guerrero, 184.5; Panchot, 184.4; Hart, 176; Golden, 173; Herty, 171.3; Moore, 168.5; Day, 167.2; Strokel, 167; Noremac, 152.3; Cox, 149.3; Connor, 148.6; Dillon, 139; Sullivan and Sinclair, 134.5; Vint, 133.1; Taylor, 127.3; Collins, 125; Lurkey, 118.3; Stout, 114:**

During the first day, the race leader had refused to eat. The atmosphere of the place sickened him. He was used to training in the open air and the tobacco smoke-filled building had made him feel really ill since the start. By all accounts he had had every intention of breaking Rowell's first day record of 150 miles, but claimed he had felt weak owing to the fact that he had not been able to nourish himself. Despite the problems he had with his diet, he had managed to finish with 130 miles in the 24 hours. Jimmy's wife would take care of his meals as he was very particular about what he ate and drank; for the rest of the race her intention was to feed him soups and calves foot jelly as well as only give him milk and seltzer to drink. Albert was the first man to score 200 miles in the race at 14:56. He was ten miles ahead of Panchot when he made the same score and postman Pete was followed by Guerrero 30 minutes later. After the "Greaser" celebrated his, the *"dark skinned dude,"* Hart made the same.

Sammy Day was described as the jolliest man on the track. He would laugh continuously, sing, "Oh! Mary," shout at his rivals to, "Cheer up!" and tell the scorers, "No need to hurry, this is a day's race!" Someone later presented him with a new running suit, which he found to be extremely funny.

Between eight and nine o'clock in the evening, Panchot gained a mile and a half on the leader, and by 23:00, was 3 miles in front of Guerrero. At the end of the first 48 hours of the match Albert led with a score of 238 miles, which was 20 behind the world record made by Rowell in 1882. Thus the full score at midnight with Horan, Johnson and Lurkey missing, was: **Albert, 238; Panchot, 234.7; Guerrero, 232.6; Hart, 226.6; Herty, 221.7.; Golden, 212.2; Strokel, 207.3; Moore, 205.3; Day, 201; Cox, 193.3; Noremac, 187; Connor, 175.1; Dillon, 163.3; Sullivan, 162.5; Taylor and Sinclair, 160; Collins, 145.6; Tilly, 139; Stout, 114:**

Scarcely more than 200 sleepy spectators were at the Garden in the morning watching as the walkers continued on their weary way. Sullivan, who fainted on the track early in the morning, was constantly on and off it. Panchot, who had been performing since before midnight, and who was reported to have said he was determined to do or die, was seen to be rushing around the ring, whilst Guerrero, who had appeared weary during the morning, was travelling slowly. This was probably due to the fact that Steve Brodie, his trainer, was asleep. Herty had not been off the track since before midnight. He was going well, and a lot of people thought he would be the dark horse in the race should anything happen to Albert who was woken up by his wife at 02:00 to continue his trek.

Vint, who rested from 00:05 to 03:18, and from 07:48 to 08:32, was plodding along as was his customary gait and then running for two to three laps, and when he passed the second century mark, he was roundly applauded. He was ahead of his 1884 record and was expected to do well. Meanwhile, it was predicted that Archie Sinclair, who was another eye-catcher, would make a fair distance during the forthcoming twelve hours as he rested from 21:41 the previous evening till 02:35 and then took another hour out from 06:00. Hart, having slept from 00:03 to 02:40, went around the track part of the time with his eyes closed. He stated that the man who beat him would have to be a good one. He also said that he intended raising his personal record to some considerable extent. Connor took only three or four minutes rest during the morning till shortly after 9 o'clock when he retired, *"faint hearted"* to his hut. It was said officially an hour later that he had decided to declare himself out. Neither he nor his trainer would make further comment, apart from that a cold had *"settled in his joints."* Tilly and *"the Arabian,"* Stout, were observed taking lots of rest. Both were disliked by the crowd. Anton Strokel, the Austrian, employing his unusual combination of *"double shuffle, and high kicking step,"* kept working well. At the time he was considered a favourite for gate money. His wife watched him constantly, and it was only when passing her at his hut, that he was seen to *"turn his squint eyes from the inspection of the base of his brain."* Tommy Cox was falling behind because he had been spending too much time away from the path, having been in his hut from midnight till 04:11 and 05:22 till 09:25.

Meanwhile, off the track, there was trouble brewing. The walkers and their representatives were in a right old flummox with the management, because they said they were entitled to a percentage of sales from reserved seats. Also, Pete Golden's backer and trainer alleged that he had seen those running the show selling complimentary tickets at 25 cents apiece on Sunday and Monday night. The peds were ready to walk out and they were also threatening to take the matter to court after the race. In the twenty-four hour period from noon to noon, the gate receipts amounted to $2,077 of which the lads on the track would receive $1,038.50. When the total receipts were counted from the opening day, they were found to be $7,697.50; the pedestrians' share being $3,818.75.

Albert, who was slowly but surely increasing his lead, was the most cheerful man pounding the sawdust, with the exception of the *"Joker,"* Day. The race leader, who had been full of hope that he would make a 100 miles that day, had a pleasant word for anyone he recognised on his way around the track. His *"cheerful buxom wife"* Sue said she was very confident that her husband would be victorious and take away first prize money. "Any other result would be a bitter disappointment." His 60th hour score of 288.4 was still nearly 20 miles behind Rowell's record at the same stage. At this time, all the peds were competing, apart from Noremac, Dillon, Taylor and Collins. All were going at a lively rate and making a splendid race for the spectators. Nearly all the contestants, with the exception of Albert, Panchot and Guerrero, were beginning to complain of sore feet. Both Panchot, who glided along easily, and Guerrero who also impressed, were both starting to gain on the race leader: **Albert, 288.4; Panchot,**

281.2; Guerrero, 278.1; Herty, 273.2; Hart, 268.4; Moore, 250.6; Golden, 249.4; Strokel, 239.2; Day, 234.1; Noremac, 227.2; Cox, 207; Dillon, 205; Vint, 203; Sinclair, 192; Taylor, 190; Sullivan, 188; Collins, 176; Tilly, 160; Stout, 144:

The backers of the many contestants who had fallen by the wayside were trying to hedge their losses by betting heavily on the more promising competitors who remained. Interest was again reviving, and the attendance was good.

The score at 2 p.m: **Albert, 298.4; Panchot, 292.4; Guerrero, 285.6; Herty, 284.2; Hart, 274.2; Moore, 259.3; Golden, 257.6; Strokel, 248.2; Day, 238.3; Noremac, 236.6; Dillon, 213.1; Vint, 210.4; Cox, 208; Sinclair, 200.2; Sullivan 197.5; Taylor, 190; Collins, 182.4; Tilly, 162.5; Stout, 145.4:**

Albert continued to increase his lead, and there were many who expected him to break the record, having completed 300 miles just after 3 o'clock. He went easily, varying the pace of his rapid walk, but never running. Panchot pursued him and looked booked for the runner-up position. Hart and Guerrero ran for long distances and lessened the gap between themselves and the leader. However, the effort was too much for Hart's stomach and he went to his shed at 18:00. He returned a fresher man and led the men around the course in front of an ever burgeoning crowd later, having, it is said, consumed a few lagers! Another of the athletes seemingly enjoying himself was Dan Herty, who, wearing a costume where all the colours of the rainbow blended together, traversed the course smoking a cigar. Now that must have been a sight for sore eyes!

Cox (12:04), and Sinclair (19:10), had by now waved goodbye to their supporters and left the race for good, whilst Stout, the *"Thompson street Arab"* reminded all watching him of a tortoise as he barely moved around the track. Word was that he was under contract from the management to keep walking for the week for which his remuneration would be $25. A visiting physician said that all the poor chap was fit for was a stint in the local lunatic asylum!

Earlier that day, after Guerrero had been involved in a hot race with Noremac around 9 a.m., which the Mexican had won, Gus had called Referee Donohue onto the track and said to him, "Please put this in the papers that I will run any man in the world from one to one hundred miles two days after this race has ended." Later on in the evening, George Cartwright approached Donohue in the presence of Al. Smith and said, "I will run Guerrero any distance for any amount. I will run any man in the world twenty-four hours. I have a record of one hundred and fifty-six miles in twenty-four hours, and I can go further than that."

The score at midnight at the end of day three, and with Albert failing in his quest to beat Rowell's three-day record (353.1), was: **Albert, 348; Panchot, 342.7; Herty, 332; Guerrero, 330.2; Hart, 313; Golden, 300; Strokel, 290.5; Moore, 290; Noremac, 277.6; Dillon, 252; Vint, 249; Day, 239; Sullivan, 224.3; Taylor, 222; Collins, 218.1; Tilly, 192.6; Stout, 156.6:**

There weren't any incidents of interest during the early morning hours, at least until after 01:30, when the manager of the tournament, Frank Hall, was struck in the nose by *"that unusually good natured sport,"* Louis Waldron of the *Illustrated Sporting Times*. Hall was hated by everybody, and there was a general feeling that he was running the *"farce"* at the Garden for his own personal benefit. A reporter wrote, *"Hall's meanness had become a matter of history about the Garden, and even those who were disposed to be friendly to him have turned against him. Waldron, who has done much in the way to make the walk a success, asked Hall for some tickets. Hall curtly refused and Waldron punched him on the nose. Hall says he struck at him, but many doubt this. Waldron was arrested."*

Albert tied the best record made by Rowell in March of 1882 at 06:56:56, and at 07:00 was ahead of it by 350 yards. A weak cheer greeted the effort due to the fact that there were less than one hundred customers in the building at the time, the majority of which had been there since Sunday night and who were poor, down and outs. *"The Garden is a Fifth Avenue Hotel to them, and all that troubled them was the daily struggle for Coney Island buns, beer and sausages."*

There were seventeen names still on the score sheet at 8 o'clock. Day had been off the track since 18:00 the previous night. Tilly retired for rest at 02:00 and had not reappeared. Others taking long rests were Collins, Stout and Sullivan. Norman Taylor slept from 23:00 till 06:00. Vint rested between 5 and 6 o'clock. Hart, the *"dandy colored fellow,"* hadn't been seen between 3 and 4 o'clock, and Noremac had slept the three hours between 02:00 and 05:00.

At 9 o'clock, Albert was 425 yards ahead of the best record as made by Rowell, and at 10:00, the 82nd hour, he was four miles and 640 yards ahead of Littlewood's 393 miles and 1,320 yards made in Philadelphia in the previous November. He left the track for ten minutes between 10 and 11 o'clock during which time he apparently had a shave, had his hair dressed, and slept. He was said to reappear on the track looking better than he did when he went to work on Sunday night.

There had been very few spectators in the Garden when morning dawned, but as the day wore on the attendance increased, with an estimated 1,000 people watching the proceedings at midday. There were still only seventeen of the pedestrians remaining on the track, and of those, seven were virtually out. They had absolutely no chance of winning, or even taking a share in part of the gate receipts. Why some of them trudged on despite the fact that they were hopelessly behind was a conundrum that only they themselves could answer. One of them, Sullivan, who was one of the back-markers, had deteriorated from a *"first class pedestrian,"* which he stated he was at the beginning of the race, to a *"sandwich man,"* as he made his way around the track carrying an advertisement for a firm which sold sports goods, for which he would paid $10 at the end of the week. Noremac, his head bent down, trotted around with a look of dogged determination on his face; whilst on occasions, Albert, Moore and Panchot chatted with each other as they walked. Stout meanwhile ambled around with *"a mincing step"* that looked like he was *"tramping on hot coals."*

The following was the score at noon: **Albert, 397; Panchot, 385; Herty, 377; Guerrero, 369; Hart, 346; Golden and Moore, 335; Strokel, 317; Noremac, 313; Dillon, 300; Vint, 264; Sullivan, 250; Taylor, 242; Day, 238; Collins, 223; Cox, 208; Tilly, 211; Stout, 158:**

At 12:30, the first hearty burst of applause of the day greeted the walkers when Albert was collectively challenged to a spurt around the track. As the group, which included Panchot, Vint, Sullivan, and even Stout, sprinted around the track with the Philadelphian in the lead and Dillon at his heels, Hart, showing his white teeth, grinned as he joined in the fun. Because they were both going so well at the time it was felt that both Albert and Panchot would beat Fitzgerald's 610-mile record. Accordingly, bets were being offered that the leader would make at least 625 miles, due to the fact that he had been making an average of 6 mph.

When the Philadelphian made 400 miles, his manager Hall looked worried as he came out of his office, believing that the din which was being made at the time was the mob breaking into the building.

The 2 o'clock score, after Day and Collins had made it known they would be permanently retiring from the race: **Albert, 405.4; Panchot, 393.6; Herty, 384.6; Guerrero, 379.4; Hart, 355.6; Golden, 344.3; Moore, 341.7; Strokel, 326.6; Noremac, 321.5; Dillon, 308.6; Vint, 269.5; Sullivan, 255.5; Taylor, 242; Tilly, 215.2; Stout, 160.6:**

Guerrero had another severe nose bleed in the afternoon and was thought to have been in a bad way. He said he saw "three tracks in front of me continually," and was puzzled "which one to take." The rest of the leaders in the contest however were generally in fair shape, indeed Albert expressed himself as "never feeling better." He kept a good lead, and seemed determined to keep the ten-mile gap between himself and Panchot, who, in turn, was confident of passing the then race leader in the end. Both declared they could make 640 miles, and both were confident of carrying off the top prize even though at the time, third placed Herty was looked upon as the race's most dangerous man. At 23:29, Albert had completed 450 miles, and was 2 miles and 660 yards ahead of the world record which was held by Fitzgerald. He then went to bed for a well earned rest.

At midnight, at the end of day four, the score was: **Albert, 450.1; Panchot, 437; Herty, 427.3; Guerrero, 420; Hart, 393.2; Golden, 389.3; Moore, 377; Strokel, 356; Noremac, 348; Dillon, 340.5; Vint and Taylor, 278.1; Sullivan, 277.7; Collins, 223.1; Tilly, 240.7; Stout, 171.2:**

Again there were less than 100 drowsy spectators standing around the track in the early morning of the 11th of February watching the steady thump, thump, thump on the sawdust. There was more enthusiasm displayed by the participants than the sleepy heads on the benches, some of whom weakly cheered the spurts made by the tramps.

Later on there was a big surprise for the people who had just ventured through the gates. The big blackboard at the Fourth Avenue end showed that Panchot had dropped from second place, which he had held for about 36 hours, to fourth. Many thought that he would be unable to last throughout the day. He certainly looked in a bad way and, judging from the expression he carried around the track, he felt it. He obviously couldn't bear any weight on his right foot. While he slept between 23:47 and 03:16, his trainers set to work trying to reduce the inflammation in his leg. His disappearance was noted by Herty who had returned to the track at 03:10 after a good sleep. Despite showing slight signs of lameness himself, he set out to overtake the ailing Buffalonian, and during the following four hours made 19 miles. Although the prognosis wasn't good for Panchot, his team managed to get him back in the ring where he lasted exactly 1h.26m. However, a reoccurrence of the problem forced him back indoors.

Of the others, and despite suffering from numerous nose bleeds and other problems, Guerrero went as well as when he did at the start. He rested from 00:50 to 03:25, and reports suggested that he expected to stay on the track until midnight. Moore, *"the amateur"* who was competing in his longest race to date, appeared quite fresh, whilst Sullivan, although displaying the most eccentric antics in the match, kept up his entertaining methods of locomotion. Vint meanwhile, was considered to be irretrievably lazy; everyone was said to becoming disgusted with him and his performance. He looked and moved well enough to warrant the frequently expressed conviction that he would have been better placed if only he would have made more of an effort.

At 06:00, the race leader was just over 2 miles short of Fitzgerald's record for that stage of the event, and at 08:00, he was 6 laps adrift. He lifted his feet well and trotted around focusing on trying to make at least 100 miles for the day. Flowers, which were given to him by his *"admirers,"* were passed to his wife who didn't appear in the least jealous as she decorated the outside of his hut with them.

Panchot by now was hopelessly out of the race and striving only to make 525 miles. It was stated that his failure to stay among the leaders was due to the *"disability of his left hip,"* which *"gave out"* after he returned to the race earlier in the morning, but which fact he concealed from his trainer for four hours. It was said to be in bad condition, being out of socket and *"devoid of oil."* He was *"game"* though, and *"will stay at all costs until he makes the seventy three miles additional to give him a share in the gate money."* Despite his brave attempt to continue, his situation was hopeless and he withdrew from the race on a score of 445 miles at 2 p.m. The newspapers reported that Panchot, from Hastings, Minneapolis, where he lived with his wife and six small children, was devastated by his premature retirement, because *"his failure left himself and family destitute."*

In 1884, Fitzgerald had travelled 505 miles in 111 hours. At the rate of speed that Albert was going, he would at the end of the same hour be five miles ahead of the record; and as he was travelling at 5 miles or more an hour, it was considered he would far outstrip it. Fitzgerald's record for the 114th hour was 519 miles and 440 yards and for the 117th hour, 530 miles and 220 yards. The 120th hour record, which was 540 miles and 170 yards, was held by Hazael.

The following shows how the leaders fared till mid afternoon:

	08:00	09:00	10:00	11:00	12:00	13:00	14:00	15:00
Albert	472.2	476.7	482.1	486.5	491	496.2	501.4	505.2
Herty	452	456	459	463	467	471	475	481
Guerrero	448	450	454	458	462	465	469	474
Panchot	441	441	443	443	443	444	445	Ret
Hart	420	424	428	432	435	437	442	444
Golden	409	413	417	419	423	425	429	434
Moore	405	408	412	416	417	421	426	430
Strokel	386	392	397	400	400	405	410	415
Dillon	374	376	379	386	388	391	395	399
Noremac	373	373	376	383	384	388	393	397
Sullivan	281	288	290	292	294	299	301	303
Vint	287	291	293	296	296	296	296	296

Sullivan was to be the unfortunate recipient of a practical joke. Flowers from his hut were given to a pretty girl who was told to present them to him as he plodded slowly around. The gesture was said to uplift his spirit so much that he responded by quickening his pace. When the exercise was repeated, and repeated again, and when he saw his hut devoid of blooms, the penny dropped and he realised he was being made a fool of.

At 16:00 (the 112th hour), Albert drew alongside Fitzgerald's record with a score of 510 miles and stated he was saving himself to make one big effort to pass it in the evening. He relaxed by playing on his banjo, before skipping along the path.

During the evening, the building was a positive hive of activity with swarms of people invading its interior and heading over the bridge at the Madison Avenue end into the enclosures. At 19:00 it held almost as many spectators as at any time the previous night.

Albert had received an anonymous letter intimating that he would be badly beaten up if he beat the record. The threats were taken seriously and assistant manager O'Brien had half a dozen policemen stood around his hut. It was thought that the letter had been written by some bookmakers who had even approached Albert's trainer about the matter. It was said the bookmakers were prepared to do almost anything to save themselves on heavy bets that the record would not be broken. Manager Hall also said that he had been offered $6,000 not to allow the record to be passed. At 21:00, Albert was observed running gracefully around the track carrying a light cane. "Break the record Jimmy!" they shouted from the seats. At 22:00 (118th hour), Guerrero was over 10 miles behind Herty who was stalking him. Albert, now 5 miles in advance of Fitzgerald's record, was on a score of: **536.5; Herty, 515; Guerrero, 505.1; Hart, 475; Golden, 462; Moore, 455.1; Strokel, 442.3; Dillon, 432; Noremac, 420.1; Sullivan, 328.7; Taylor, 319.2; Vint, 301.6; Tilly, 272; Stout, 185.4:**

Cartwright and Hegelman, although out of the contest, came on the track and ran round with the remainder. Their presence seemed to inspire the fatigued participants, and they all responded by breaking into a trot for half an hour. The Canadian, George Tilly, affectionately known as "Parson Tilly" amused the crowd by *"paddling"* round, the motion of his arms akin to the action of oars. Sullivan and Vint joined in the fun with the crowd appropriately entertained. The Parson had been interviewed earlier in the race and it was gleaned from him that he was using the experience gained in the race to prepare a lecture on *"pedestrianism from a physical and moral standpoint."* Indeed, his influence on the race produced the following poem which was written by one of Mr. Plummer's scorers, who was thankfully off duty when he composed it:

Ode to Parson Tilly

Walk, walk, walk

On the sawdust track Til-lee;

And I would that my tongue could utter

The thoughts that arise in thee

O well for the Philadelf boy

That he shouts as he runs on his way

O well for the Buffalo lad

As he smiles at the frequent bokay!

And these stately legs go on

To their haven after the race;

But oh for the touch of a mothers hand

That would quicken thy funeral pace,

Walk, walk, walk

On the sawdust track Til-lee;

But the coppered ace of a well run race

Will now be played by thee

King of the Peds

With Albert having been tucked up in bed by his pretty wife at 23:43, the midnight score at the end of day five was: **Albert, 545; Herty, 521.1; Guerrero, 512.3; Hart, 483.6; Golden, 470.4; Moore, 464.4; Strokel, 445.7; Dillon, 432; Noremac, 430.6; Sullivan, 335; Taylor, 325.3; Vint, 306.5; Tilly, 278.4; Stout, 187.5:**

As the sixth day and last day of the contest began, the cold air within the building was thick with smoke. The rain outside danced on its roof, underneath which many of the occupants had been drinking all night. A few however had been indulging in more questionable activities. A bag of cash containing $353 went missing from the reserve seat box office. A nickel weighing machine was somehow pried open in the bar where 200 patrons had been enjoying a tipple. Patent selling machines were also successfully attacked, and a clubman wearing a diamond ring had it skilfully removed from his finger while he dozed off.

As the drunk got drunker, some took themselves to the track side where, along with some bookmakers, they threw money at the walkers. John Dillon, the New Yorker, made a $100 picking up small bills and change off the floor. Albert also made a small fortune and so did Herty. The lazy Stout however, who was not liked by the crowd, had little or nothing offered him.

Albert had appeared back on the track at 04:12 after taking his longest rest of the race. On a score of 545 miles, he was extremely confident of breaking the record and moved himself along at a rate of 4 mph. Herty, although obviously very tired, kept plugging on in his desire to keep second place out of the clutches of Guerrero. Behind him a fresh looking Hart bounded along in front of the next two on the leader board, the sorry looking pair of Golden and Moore.

Whilst the ever caring Mrs. Albert busied herself attending to her husband's interests, in and around his quarters, there were very few people watching the weary at six o'clock that morning. She had met her husband at a go-as-you-please match several years before, when as a spectator; she couldn't take her eyes off the good looking pedestrian. When their eyes met it was said to be love at first sight and the rest was history. She told reporters she had hardly slept while looking after her dear Jimmy. She was however aware that a group of gamblers had pooled $10,000 between them, and through their representative, told her they would give it to him if he scored less than 610 miles. She also was the person who received other threats that had been made against him. The culprits however, could not be found.

Dillon made his 469th mile in 8 minutes at 9 o'clock, and an hour later all the men who had any chance in the race were weighed. Albert had lost just one pound, whereas Herty had gained one, Guerrero three and Moore, four. The first six on the scoreboard at noon showed the following totals: **Albert, 577.5; Herty, 552; Guerrero, 539; Hart, 516; Golden, 504; Moore, 498:**

Crowds of people gathered outside the Garden attempting to gain entry, and it was discovered that counterfeit reserved seat tickets were being sold. Posters were put up warning that holders of such would be refused entry.

Meanwhile, back inside, the antics of some of the competitors were causing many in the audience to have a right good old laugh at them, principally Tilly who wandered around with the brilliantly illuminated letters S.S.S. in blue and silver on his back. Moore drew on a cigarette while walking around. Golden ate broiled chicken, and the sad Stout was apparently just "sad."

Whilst the main band took a rest, a group of *"colored minstrels"* made a small fortune for themselves in loose change as they amused the crowd by singing along to the accompaniment of their musical instruments. The management took a dim view of their act and told them to stop.

Madison Square Garden was packed *"from wall-to-wall and door-to-door with a crowd of all classes"* for the last night of the contest. Many in the shivering crowd which stood outside on the slippery pavements in streets covered in snow found it almost impossible to gain admission into the building at any price, and for those who were lucky enough to get in, that bad man Mr. Hall had raised admission to $1! News from inside the building consequently was greatly appreciated by those locked out.

There was a heavy force of police under the command of Inspector Steers. The reserves of the Thirteenth street Station under Captain Reilly were stationed in parties among the audience, and a platoon under Sergeant Sheldon at the huts of the contestants. Soon after, a disturbance took place in box 39, but it was quickly brought under control. John Murphy, of 645 Tenth Avenue, a ticket speculator, was detected early in the evening selling counterfeit tickets at the Madison Avenue entrance. He was arrested and locked up in the Nineteenth precinct. Mingling with the crowd were a host of pickpockets, but all managed to keep out of the clutches of the law.

It was a foregone conclusion that Albert would beat Fitzgerald's record, but everyone wanted to see him do it. As he promptly completed his 600th mile at 16:44, the band played, "Tramp, tramp, tramp, the boys are marching," and he was applauded for a full five minutes.

Of Dillon's two trainers who had been arguing on Friday morning, the elder of them had been given his marching orders by the other one. However, unbeknown to his younger English trainer, the older one had been giving Dillon frequent drinks of whisky behind his back. Of the incident, the *Brooklyn Daily Eagle* wrote: **The doses proved too much for the walker who had 501 miles and a good chance with steady work, to come in for a share of the gate receipts and he insisted on keeping going around the track, instead of being rubbed down, as the young Englishman, who pushed him so well during the last twenty four hours, desired. The old trainer interfered and the two came to blows. A policeman easily proved to them he was able to go it alone on clubs and the matter was left to the management to arbitrate. He gave Dillon into the custody of the Englishman, who spent 27 minutes in getting rid of the whiskey from the system of his man by some art only known to trainers. Then Dillon returned to the track and was enthusiastically cheered as he set to work in earnest to put twenty four miles behind him. The old trainer was bounced.**

Before he reached his 610th mile Albert got himself changed, and wearing a tight fitting white shirt and pants *"with a blue trunk,"* came out looking immaculate. He twirled his little cane and progressed into a trot as the band played "Yankee Doodle." At 7 o'clock, all the men left on the track were making good time, and the 8,000 spectators, despite the tobacco smoke which *"hung like a thick curtain,"* were enjoying themselves.

Albert (whose real name was James Albert Cathcart) tied the record at 19:23:58 running the 610th mile *"like a deer, stepping high and without apparent effort."* Jimmy, who made that mile in 11m.58s, enjoyed the moment as the Garden erupted in response as an ecstatic surging crowd followed his progress along the rails. *"Every lap of the saw dust track which the bright faced and handsome little athlete made was a triumphal march. All the other athletes were apparently forgotten."* During the next mile, both Herty and Guerrero chased the new champion at top speed, but the Philadelphian kept well ahead of them both. When he got two miles ahead of the old record, he celebrated by running between Guerrero and Noremac for two laps. His face showed how happy he was, and even the ex-Arabian Stout, when he heard the cheers, ran a lap. The race leader then slowed down to a walk, but when he recognized an old plantation ditty being played on a banjo, he ran another two laps without stopping.

To a tremendous reception and shortly before 9 o'clock, Albert came out of his hut with a big flag in each hand and ran a lap at speed. When the new champion had completed the lap, he handed the flags over to Herty, who also ran a lap with them. Then Guerrero took them around the tanbark, then Hart and finally Stout who skipped around with the colourful emblems. Then Guerrero, who was a great favourite with the crowd, having been presented many presents including a gold watch and a beaver overcoat, retired from the track at 20:53. He was driven in a cab by his trainer to Brodie's Saloon at 114 Bowery Street. Herty was another who had been given gifts. Earlier on at 8 o'clock, he was the recipient of an elegant suit of clothes.

There were 150 policemen in the place trying to keep order. A man hit a woman in one of the boxes and a brewing company attempted to serve Albert with an attachment for $125 whilst he was on the track. Manager Hall had to sort the problem out as the men who serving it were insistent on taking him away, but he eventually persuaded them to let him remain.

Along with Herty on a score of 582, Strokel left the track at 9 p.m. having made his 525th mile at 20:28. His departure from the race was copied at regular intervals by Hart, Taylor, Tilly, Golden, Moore at 21:40, and Stout 10 minutes later. Although having ceased racing, Tilly stayed with the new champion. After attempting to have a go at carrying the flags round and failing to successfully complete a handspring in front of the scorers' stand, he was warned by Referee Donohue to desist from any further gymnastics. After being hissed by the crowd he left the circuit, and 5 minutes later he too went home.

King of the Peds

Before 10 o'clock arrived Albert continued to delight the spectators by sprinting around the course in an attempt to finish his 622nd mile by the end of the 142nd hour, but, though encouraged by yells from the crowd, he was two laps short when *"Scorer Plummer"* instructed him that the 142 hours were up. After running round the track yet again carrying flags with his trainer "Frozen Bill" Carney, Albert went into his hut accompanied by his wife who had her arms around his neck. The winner was then taken to the scorers' stand by his trainer, who said that he had just received telegrams of congratulations from Rowell, Littlewood, and other prominent pedestrians. He then asked Albert to make a speech. As his proud wife stood next to him gazing adoringly at him with tears in her eyes, the new world record holder said:

"Ladies and Gentlemen, I have done so much running during the past week that I have no wind with to make a speech. It was a very good race and everything went smoothly and to my complete satisfaction. The number of entries was larger than any other race I have entered. There was no trouble and I have no fault to find with the scorers or management. I am 36 years old and will retire on my laurels. It is my last race. I thank you for the demonstration and will say good night."

Someone yelled, "Give us one more lap." Albert shook his head and said, "No, I wish to state publicly now that I am getting old and this is my last race." He retired with three cheers for him, three for "Frozen Bill" and three more from his wife. As soon they could, he, his trainer Joe Miller, and the rest of his party, left the building and were taken to the Ashland House chased by a mob of screaming fans.

The following affidavit was given to the press during the evening:

"We the undersigned, hereby certify that we have scored on James Albert's tally sheets, and they are correct in every detail and sworn to before me, E. Chamberlain, Jr., notary public. Thomas H. Sell, P.H. Buckley. R. J. Campsie, J. C. Thornton, Arthur B. Ellain, Samuel Whitehead, assistants; Ed. Plummer, chief."

It was dubbed the *"Greatest contest in pedestrianism ever seen on earth."* A reporter went on to say, *"The record was knocked sky high by the easiest and most graceful runner ever seen in a six days contest. Albert, the handsome and youthful Philadelphian who went to the track weighing 135 pounds lost only six pounds in the 142 hours of work and had plenty of fire and energy left. The world has a new champion, and human bipeds have stronger reason than ever before to feel proud of the means of locomotion with which nature has provided them."*

The new World Champion!

Jimmy Albert; 621 ¾ miles *(Illustration no: 112)*

The table shows the finishers' distance, time, rests and prize money:

	DISTANCE		TIME		RESTED			WINNINGS	BONUS
	Miles	Yards	Hours	Mins	Hours	Mins	Secs		
Albert	621	1,320	142	00	19	21	50	$4,313.70	$1,000
Herty	582	600	141	00	17	16		$2,696.06	
Guerrero	564		140	53	13	42		$1,294.11	
Hart	546	660	141	2	29	47		$ 862.74	
Golden	538	880	141	29	15	52		$ 647.65	
Moore	531	1,320	141	30	20	10		$ 431.77	
Strokel	526	880	141	00	16	40		$ 327.53	
Noremac	525	440	140	55	17	30		$ 213.69	
Dillon	504	1,820	139	00	16	40			
Tilly	320	1,320	141	27					
Taylor	361		141	23					
Sullivan	383	110	140	50					
Stout	209	880	141	40					

After his exertions the winner was reported to have eaten porterhouse steak, smoked two cigars, and after a short rest, it was claimed he beat both his trainers up two flights of stairs!

Below is a summary of the final hours of the race.

	15:00	16:00	17:00	18:00	19:00	20:00	21:00	22:00
Albert	591	596	601	603	608	612	617	**621**
Herty	563	567	570	573	576	578	582	**582**
Guerrero	548	551	554	557	560	562	564	**564**
Hart	526	530	534	536	539	542	546	**546**
Golden	516	520	524	525	529	532	537	**538**
Moore	510	512	517	520	524	527	531	**531**
Strokel	503	506	510	515	520	523	526	**526**
Noremac	500	503	508	512	517	520	525	**525**
Dillon	494	499	501	501	OFF			
Sullivan	367	372	374	378	380	382	383	**383**
Taylor	339	345	349	350	350	354	357	**358**
Tilley	302	306	310	313	313	314	319	**320**
Stout	199	199	202	202	204	206	207	**207**

Apparently the day after, according to those who pursued him, Albert was as *"fresh as any man in the Ashland House."* He went to bed at half past eleven and woke up at eight o'clock. After taking a short walk he had breakfast, and later in the day walked with his wife from Twenty Fourth Street to Central Park and back. He stated that he would continue taking moderate exercise instead of lapsing into idleness. One of his trainers Mr. Miller stated that Jimmy would never enter another pedestrian contest, although he might participate in exhibitions, stating the new champion would return to Philadelphia either the same day or the day after.

Of the other pedestrians, many of whom were staying at the Putnam House, Hart, who was in bed suffering with sore feet and lame joints, said that he had ran his last six-day race. He attributed his poor showing to the fact that he had been involved in too many races of late. He also complained about the poor management of the contest, and was angered that Mr. Hall had allegedly kept the money from the sale of the reserved seats.

The Boston Globe (Illustration no: 113)

Herty was feeling well and talked of starring in a race in April, which he expected to win. Guerrero had slept well until 05:00. He said he had taken several short walks and naps during the day. Moore was troubled with sore and blistered feet, whilst Noremac felt terrible but expected a full recovery within days. Sullivan said he felt better on the last day than any other; while Dillon remarked he felt alright, Tilly, when asked why he had entered the race simply replied, "To win it!"

The total prize money awarded to the pedestrians was $10,787.25. According to the arrangement with the management, this amount was 50% of the gate receipts which came to $21,574.50. The amounts awarded to the men each day were: Monday, $1,679.75; Tuesday $1,130.5; Wednesday, $1,038.50; Thursday, $1,441; Friday, $1,379.75; Saturday, $4117.75:

All the men were waiting to be whisked off to the *New York Clipper* office to receive their proportion of the gate receipts from Mr. Hall later that afternoon. Meanwhile, the unpopular manager of the race was being pursued by the press. They caught up with him at the Ashland House describing him as "unkempt" in appearance. When approached by reporters, he yelled at them, "You fellows have jumped on me all through, and now the race is over the only thing left for you to do is kill me altogether. Every newspaper in this city braced me for money on condition that they should boom the race, giving me to understand that if the boodle was not forthcoming, they would jump on me. They didn't get the boodle and they did jump on me." He was later asked if he could substantiate the charges against the press that he was making and he said he could and was prepared to bet $10,000 on it. When he was asked to identify the reporters he was making the allegations about, he reduced his bet to a miserly $100. There were to be more problems for Hall later in the day when he was served an attachment on behalf of William P. Corney, William O'Brien and James C. Kennedy, who were his assistants in the management of the race. This was for salaries they claimed that Hall owed them.

At the *Clipper* office, everyone, except Jimmy Albert in the *"tired disgruntled"* group of competitors, were showing some ill effects of their long haul. Their main complaint though was the distribution of the prize money and in particular the 4th and 5th placed men, Frank Hart and Peter Golden, were up in arms about the management of the affair. Golden told a reporter, "I am not one of those who are kicking about the amount of money received. I am satisfied with that and if there was any peddling of complimentary tickets by Hall or any one else I was too busy counting my miles to know it. But I object to Noremac's money, about two hundred and sixteen dollars being taken out of the lump that was to go to Hart and myself, instead of being taken proportionally from each man who came within the five hundred and twenty-five limit. The division of the money for seven men was to be as follows: First man forty per cent; second, twenty-five per cent; third, fifteen per cent; fourth, eight per cent; fifth, six per cent; sixth, four per cent, and seventh, two per cent. Then they propose to pay Noremac from our money. We shall not allow this and will make trouble if the managers insist on attempting it."

When Vint was interviewed about the race, he said, "I stood no chance of doing anything after the trouble I had on Monday when I was struck by one of the alleged walkers who had run against me on the track. My hip was cut open by the blow and the shock and time I lost from this affair put me out or the race. After Wednesday when I saw I was no good, I kept walking simply in order to keep my muscles in good condition. It does not do to stop after two or three days and I thought the garden as good a place to walk in as elsewhere. About the receipts and attendance, there is a good of grumbling but there always is. When a man enters for one of these long walks he is buried to the world, and even to what is going on about him. I know nothing as to the truth of the reports that a complaint was made about selling tickets. My men took no more interest in the race after they saw I was out of it, so that I had no one watching out for me. The most pitiful thing about the contest was the breaking down of Panchot. He is still suffering and is likely to be in agony for some time. He was forced to a gait for which he was not gauged, and ran constantly on the sloping surface near the rail thus overtaxing the limit. His hip joint gave out finally, and he was forced, while in sight of his money, to step down and out."

On February the 15th there was a report from Omaha, Nebraska, that a local sporting man named Charles Bibbins offered to bet $2,000 at 5/2, that Albert didn't make the 621 miles plus in the recent race and that he couldn't make 550 miles in six days. It was understood that if the bet was accepted, Mr. Bibbins would have to prove that the 621 miles was accomplished by Albert, *and an identical twin brother* who looked precisely like him, competing alternately.

King of the Peds

Following is an excellent article found in the *Marion Weekly Star* of Marion, Ohio, from their edition of the 10th of March 1888.

'HOW TO GET REAL TIRED.'

'THE WAY IT WAS DONE AT THE RECENT WALKING MATCH'

Walking matches are made up principally of tanbark and tension. The management furnishes the tanbark and the peds furnish the tension. The other things that go to make up a great walking match are fakirs and flowers - fakirs for the spectators and flowers for the tired ones - pretty girls and peanuts, sporting men and curious ones. This is what our special commissioner, who saw the recent walking match at the Madison Square Garden in New York, writes us. He says further: I went up the walking match at the Madison Square the other day while it was in full heat. The first thought a man has when he looks down on the weary wights pegging away for dear life is that of pity. Then he laughs.

Why? Because, it's funny.

Just as soon as a man sets out to do one thing, to the exclusion of everything else, he loses control of himself in everything else. Every man has so much will power, and he is obliged to concentrate it on the object in view. The consequence is all his little peculiarities crop out, and they are sure to make the spectators laugh. Parson Tilly was the funniest of the lot. He has a crook in his back like an Alpine stick, and he tries to counteract this by holding his head high up. His arms stuck out on each side of him like a pair of awning rods, and his feet went ahead of him at a great rate, but they came back nearly as far. Perhaps that's why he didn't "get there."

"Well. I never," said an old lady from the country. "I thought this 'ere was a walking match, but I declare to goodness if they ain't running."

That is one of the privileges of a walking match. You can run. You can even start in at 12 o'clock Sunday night and run all the week as hard as you want to.

That is if you can stand it.

But they don't all do it. Sometimes they run and sometimes they walk. Then they will vary the monotony by snatching up something to eat. A cup in one hand and a spoon in the other, joggety jog, joggety jog, around the track they go, through the long, weary hours.

Do they get tired?

Well, rather.

There is no more utterly woebegone specimen of humanity than a pedestrian who has just finished a six-day contest.

And yet when they get through they are willing to do it over again. One would think that one such trial would be enough. But it isn't. Future matches are often made on the last day of a race.

How do they go into it? What are their methods of training, etc?

Well, they go into it to make money. Rowell the great English pedestrian has made a good thing out of walking matches; so has Fitzgerald who wound up 610 miles at the Madison Square in May 1884 and cleared over $5,000. Albert has made money since he began walking, and he will probably make more before he gets through. The training depends on the man. Rowell used to get up early in the morning and spend most of the day walking over boulders and crags in a hilly country. He ate what ever he wanted. Dieting isn't practiced so much as it used to be. It is getting to be a pretty well established fact now that whatever the man wants is good for him.

Generally each man who goes into a walking match has a booth built alongside of the track, where he can eat and sleep while the contest is in progress. Here his trainer hangs out, and here is where he dives in to catch a catnap occasionally. Some of them have great trouble in sleeping, while others get to sleep before their clothes can be taken off. Some of them sleep while thy walk. Strokel the Austrian, who, by the way is another funny walker, went to sleep on the track during the match and was run into by another ped. Strokel made things lively for a few minutes after this.

But, to return to the booths. Some of them are models of neatness, while others are extremely untidy. When they are neat there is usually a woman in the case. There is as much difference in trainers as can be. When a man comes off the track, his trainer will strip him and run him down with a hard towel, and then to bed. After he has slept an hour or so he is waked up, and here is where the trouble begins.

Those who have difficulty in getting down to breakfast at the proper time every morning will appreciate the feelings of a man who has walked several hundred miles, more or less, and who is pulled out of bed just when he is in full swing. Here the trainer comes to the front, he humors, he cajoles, he scolds, he fights his man. He pulls out his legs and starts him off. Tom Cox, the young Irishman, is one of the hardest men to start after a nap. He will fight like a tiger.

When he is asleep he looks like a dead man. During one of my visits to the recent match his friends were holding a bogus wake over him. Fitzgerald, who is another Irishman, is like a big baby in the hands of his trainer. The want of sleep is what tells in these walking contests. Each man has to cover 525 miles in order to get back his entrance fee, and in order to do even this he would have to average over three and a half miles an hour. Fitzgerald, in his famous walk in 1884, averaged 4 miles an hour, and during the whole six days, he got but twenty eight hours sleep. Albert in his recent walk in Philadelphia averaged three hours of sleep in the twenty four during the six days.

It is a terrible strain, and when a man gets through he looks more dead than alive.

Naturally, during a contest like this, unlike the period of training, what a man eats has a good deal to do with the matter, and only the most nourishing foods are taken. Albert don't believe in stimulants, and never takes anything stronger than coffee. Rowell on the contrary, when he was in this country, declared that no man could live through a six day's walk without the use of stimulants.

But what do you think of cold cabbage?

Strokel is an Austrian, and this is what he likes. He jogged around the track with a plate of "cold slaw" in his left hand and ate it with fingers on the right. Strokel, next to Tilly, the Canadian parson, was the funniest walker. They called him "The Crab." He has big hands, and he wags them incessantly. One would think to look at him that this ceaseless motion alone would tire him out, but it doesn't seem to.

Another curious character is Sullivan. He is a young fellow, and had to be carried out of the great race of 1884 before it was over. He was nicknamed the Ghost, and he looked it every inch. He carried the specter of a sickly smile along with him, and if he had been going to his own funeral he couldn't have presented a more woebegone appearance. The most graceful man on the track was Hart, the negro. He stood up as straight as a string and his carriage was beautiful. Next to him in poise came Albert. Albert carried a little sponge under his nose most of the time, slightly tinctured with ammonia to keep him a wake. In his left hand he carried a black cane which he says he wouldn't part with for anything. He has had it for years, and when he was wrecked in the steamer Narragansett, in Long Island sound, some years ago, his little black cane went to the bottom; but it was rescued and he has kept it ever since.

There are many interesting and curious things to be seen at a walking match, but when a man goes a way he thinks to himself, "What fools these mortals be."

CHAPTER 57

O'Brien's Tournament

When George Littlewood landed in New York, having sailed over on the steamship *Etruria* on Sunday, the 11th of March 1888 from Liverpool, he was considered the finest pedestrian in the world. It was stated in the press that he had made the journey to compete with George Cartwright in a $1,000 a side 72-hour contest and that "*he would post a forfeit to bind the match in a few days.*"

Littlewood went straight into training in Philadelphia for the forthcoming six-day go-as-you-please race at Madison Square Garden, which was to take place between the 7th and 12th of May. He was anxious to prove that he could cover more than the 621 miles that Albert had made earlier in the year. He had tried to make a bet with the American in April whilst in training in the city in the grounds of the University of Pennsylvania under the watchful eye of his trainer Mr. Dole. "I don't see how Albert can ignore my proposition," he said. "He claims to be the champion of the world and is credited with the best record. Now, as a matter of fact, Albert has never beaten me, while I have whipped him with comparative ease. Last December in Philadelphia, we met in a race and I beat him easily. In doing so I was only compelled to cover five hundred and sixty-nine miles. If I had been pushed I could easily have gone six hundred and forty miles. During the last two days of the race I did little or no work on account of the lead I had secured in the early part of the contest. Now, if my proposition is not a fair one, I will make another. I will bet that I can cover more miles in one day than, two days, three days, four days, five days or six days than any other man in the race. This will give Cartwright and Hughes, who are regarded as flyers for twenty-four hours, a chance to show their speed."

The *National Police Gazette* wrote: **George Littlewood the famous English pedestrian was in the city on April 10. His coming from the training grounds near Philadelphia created quite a stir among the ambitious athletes who are getting ready for the six-day race. Littlewood looks like a man of the most wonderful endurance. His limbs are all that the most critical could desire, the legs, chest and powerful loins showing that he is a natural racer. Littlewood spoke of defeating Rowell in their last race with becoming modesty, but added that he was especially anxious to meet him in this contest and that he would be greatly pleased to have a chance to show a clean pair of heels to Albert. Preparation for the match goes on rapidly. Manager O'Brien smiled cheerfully when asked if the race would be a success. "When these men get on the track," he said, "and commence to tear down records, the big garden will not hold the crowd. We have now all the best men in the country, and I am sure the contest for first place will be exciting up to the finish." Entries are coming in from all over the country.**

One of his rivals, George Cartwright, was considered to be a match for his fellow Englishman over a 24-hour period, but not over six days. He had been hard at work training in England and had recently written that he intended on retrieving his lost laurels by making a grand record. He had arrived in New York on the steamship *Servia* on the 16th of April, on which he would run three times a day around the deck. An 8-lap track was measured off and he was said to cover as much as 45 miles a day whilst on board. His training was watched with interest by other passengers. He claimed he was sick in the last race but was confident that he would be able to give a good account of himself in this one. "I would give a thousand pounds," he said "to beat George Littlewood. Since Rowell's retirement he claims the championship of England, while in reality I am the champion. This race however will settle the question." When he arrived in New York he immediately went into training in Staten Island.

Of his other rivals, Dan Herty had the best general average of the athletes on show. He had competed in six contests and had never taken less than 3rd prize. Dan was born in Ireland and was 31 years of age. Along with his parents he emigrated to America at the age of 5 and where the family settled in Revere, four miles from Boston. His first race was at Revere Beach in the spring of 1877 where he beat ten others in a five-mile heel-and-toe race. In the same year he took second prize in a 27-hour go-as-you-please race at Haverhill, Massachusetts, under the management of Charles

Harriman where he made 130 miles in 26 hours. In his last race, he had come second to Albert in the race at Madison Square Garden in February, when he scored 582 miles and 600 yards.

Gus Guerrero, another dangerous contender, was born on a ranch which it was said his father owned in Western California where, as the story goes, he spent his boyhood chasing deer across the mountains. He went to San Francisco in 1879 where he covered 430 miles in a six-day race without any training. His last big six-day event resulted in a score of 564 and his best in that type of race was 590. Another hopeful for the competition was dealt with in the *Atlanta Constitution* dated the 19th of April 1888:

PEDESTRIAN PRATER. Preparing To Win the Championship of the World. The Great Walking Match in New York – An Atlanta Man to Compete for the Great Prize – Can He Win?'

The greatest walking match on record will begin at Madison Square Garden, New York, May the 6th and will last six days. The most famous professional walkers of the world will be competitors in this trial of agility and endurance. Among others, Albert, the present champion, the two Harts, Vint, Noremac, and Cox will engage in the contest. Three of the swiftest walkers from England will contend for the prize, and other foreign countries will send representatives. The match will be open to the world. A prize of $2,000 will be given to the man who beats the record of 621 miles in six days.

Atlanta will figure in that great contest.

Alf Prater, the "mountain wonder" will be there. And it is believed that the same speed, pluck and endurance which enabled him to win so many matches in the south will make him a formidable competitor for the first prize.

He is backed by Mr. Bidwell and other Atlanta gentlemen, who have implicit confidence in his powers. They believe he can win the first prize and expect him to do it. Their expectations are based upon Prater's past achievements. They remember his having made 98 miles in the first twelve hours; 92 miles the second 12 hours, and 93 miles the third twelve hours. In every match he has done splendid work, his deer like fleetness, his steady gait, and his marvelous staying qualities have excited the envy of his rivals and the admiration of his spectators. They who are familiar with his powers declare that he is equal to Albert or any other pedestrian in the United States.

(Illustration no: 114)

Prater is a man of strong points. He has subjugated his appetites and practices abstemiousness worthy of stoic. He has never drunk ardent spirits, and has never used tobacco in any shape. Neither does he use any other stimulant. He is a moderate eater. He never goes into any excesses of any sort. His frame is closely knit, and his legs are seamed with muscles as hard as whale bone. His feet are as firm as rock, and he can shell chestnuts with them. For several weeks he has been in active training. He runs his fifty miles a day and thinks nothing of it accomplishing the distance in five hours.

"I don't want to live unless I win that race," said Alf yesterday afternoon. "I am going in with the grim determination to win that prize. I am preparing to do the greatest work of my life. I was never in so good a condition, and I shall be in still better form by the first of May when I and my backers will leave Atlanta for New York. Lack of sleep and crippling are the two things which will break up the best walkers. Crippling comes from chafing of the feet. I do not fear either. My feet are beyond chafing. They are as tough as lightwood knots. And I don't fear loss of sleep, because I've trained myself to do without sleep. I can easily go a week and sleep only two and a half hours out of every twenty four. I have tested my ability to do this and have never failed yet. I ran every day fifty miles barefooted and soon will double the distance."

"What is your plan? How do you expect to win?"

"My program will be to make 125 miles the first day, 120 miles the second, and never less than 100 miles any day. I am satisfied I can do it."

"Then you expect to win?"

"Expect to win!" exclaimed the 'mountain wonder,' "I am certain to win. You need not be afraid of my crippling. If you'll go with me to New York, I'll die on the track before I'll get beaten. I won't cripple; I'll just die."

As this great match in New York will be open to the world, the man that wins the first prize will be entitled to the world's championship. If Alf Prater wins the match, he will were the belt. Who can tell? And then Atlanta will come into greater prominence than before. Less probable things have happened...............

Alf then pops up again in a report in the same newspaper on May the 2nd 1888. The headline was **'CONFIDIDENT OF SUCCESS,'** Alf Prater **and His Backers on Their Way to New York.** Alf makes the most amazing claim by telling the interviewing reporter.................. "I will win that match or be brought back to Atlanta in my coffin," said Alf Prater, the "Mountain Wonder," last night as he boarded the passenger train of the East Tennessee, Virginia and Georgia railroad.

He was accompanied by Mr. C. Treadwell, his backer, who remarked. "Yes, I and Alf are confident of success. We are going to New York to win the prize. I will see that Alf is taken care of. One of the best trainers in New York has been engaged to look after him, from the time be reaches New York till the close of the walking match."

"Is Prater in good condition?" was asked by the reporter.

"Yes; he never was in such good condition, and when he steps into the arena, next Sunday night at twelve o'clock, he will be in as prime trim as the best of them."

"How will you manage him during the match?"

"I will have the assistance of some of the most experienced pedestrians in New York. They know exactly how to treat a man in a walking match. They understand just how much food to give him and how much sleep to allow him. As much depends upon good handling as upon speed and endurance in the ring. We will be very careful to buy the best food and to keep it beyond the reach of outsiders. Many a good one has come out behind in walking matches because his victuals were tampered with. Then it is very important to know when to take rest and when to sleep. I am backing Prater, and you may be certain that I'll look after all these essentials."

Prater here spoke: "I feel it is in my bones that I will bring back to Atlanta the first prize and the championship belt of the world. You know that whoever wins this match will be the champion of the world. I expect to win by hard work. They can't tire me out, and I can get along with less sleep than any of them. My feet are so hard and tough that I do not fear crippling. Yesterday I ran nearly a hundred miles, and when I quit was not much fatigued I could have gone another fifty without taking any rest."

Early yesterday morning Mr. Treadwell telegraphed enough money to the manager of the match to cover the entrance fee.

The match will start precisely at midnight Sunday next, and will last six days. It is predicted by the New York newspapers that this will be the greatest walking match ever contested, and that the record will be beaten. The people of Atlanta will watch closely the scores, and will watch with keen interest the daily achievements of the "Mountain Wonder."

William O'Brien

The National Police Gazette (Illustration no: 115)

"Billy" O'Brien was the man who was organising the event. He had earlier invited Charlie Rowell to take part, but without success. Another man he would have dearly loved to join in was Jimmy Albert, the world champion. Albert was determined to prove to the public that he could beat Littlewood. "Another reason," Albert said, "that would lead me to start is that I want to prove that my record of six hundred and twenty-one miles is correct. If in good condition I can not only repeat that performance but eclipse it."

The race was reported at the time to be the last at the Garden and the arrangements for it were said to be more satisfactory than in previous contests. The 220-yard track made up of tanbark, loam and sawdust, had been carefully measured, and eight laps made a mile and 9 inches. It cost $400 to construct and measured 18 inches from the inside rail. On May Day, many of the stars of the track took their first footsteps on it including Herty, Cartwright, Connor, Guerrero, "Old Sport," Golden and Hughes. The track was described as solid, yet springy. Its curves had canvas filled with sawdust placed on the inside of them to protect the runners should they fall. This was yet another safety measure introduced by the management, one of many such improvements made. Even the big blackboard at the Fourth Avenue end of the building had been upgraded. The size of the letters and numbers had been increased and now the first ten in the race could be identified.

Ninety-six men had originally entered the six-day pedestrian contest that would begin at one minute after midnight on Monday, the 7th of May. This number had been whittled down 44 who had each paid $50 for the privilege of *"toeing the line."*

1	**J. C. Adams**	Bristol, Penn	23	**John Hughes**	Ireland
2	**E. Albert**	Toronto	24	**Augustus Kline**	Germany
3	**Dan Burns**	Elmira	25	**Sgt. Kramer**	New York
4	**"Old Sport" Campana**	Connecticut	26	**George Littlewood**	England
5	**George Cartwright**	England	27	**James McEvoy**	Brooklyn
6	**George Connor**	England	28	**E. C. Moore**	Philadelphia
7	**Coughlin M.**		29	**William Morlanger**	Sweden
8	**Thomas Cox**	Bradford, Penn	30	**Alf Newhart**	Easton
9	**Sam Day**	England	31	**William Nolan**	Denver
10	**Dan Dillon**	Ireland/N Y	32	**George Noremac**	Scotland
11	**C. Drake**		33	**Peter Panchot**	Buffalo
12	**J. Dully**		34	**Robert Peach**	New York
13	**Alfred Elson**	Meridien	35	**Alf Prater**	Atlanta
14	**H. Esterline**	Reading, Penn	36	**Charles Russell**	New York
15	**Peter Golden**	Boston	37	**James Saunders**	Brooklyn
16	**C. B. Graves**	New York	38	**Emil Schroeder**	New York
17	**Gus Guerrero**	Mexico/Calif	39	**Augustus Stein**	New York
18	**Frank Hart**	Boston	40	**John Sullivan**	Saratoga
19	**Peter Hegelman**	Germany/N Y	41	**Norman Taylor**	Vermont
20	**James Henry**	New York	42	**George Tilly**	Philadelphia
21	**Daniel Herty**	Boston	43	**Robert Vint**	Brooklyn
22	**George Howard**	Atlantic City	44	**H. Williams**	

The rules were that to stay in the race each competitor must make 100 miles in the first 24 hours. As an inducement to take part, in addition to the percentage of the gate money, the management had offered to give $2,000 in special prizes. They would award the winner of the race who broke Albert's record $1,000 and $500 to the second place contestant who did the same. The third person to beat it would get $250. An extra $250 would be given to any man who could beat Rowell's record of 150 miles and 395 yards in 24 hours, as made by that man on February the 28th 1882.

The contestants' quarters were described as *"palatial"* compared with the huts allotted the men in the last event. They were situated in a semi-circle at the Fourth Avenue end of the building and were described as being small wooden structures with a sloping roof of striped cotton. During the early part of the evening, the huts were surrounded by a very large gathering of men, reckoned to be in the region of 100. They wore tight trousers and

King of the Peds

very tight short jackets and were all enthusiastically talking about the forthcoming race. All were connected in some way to the sport. Amongst them were some of the contestants, trainers and attendants.

All of the huts had the names of the contestants on small tin signs on their front. George Cartwright's home had "Champion of England" emblazoned on it. The "Flying Collier" appeared rather perky, and messed about by jumping about on the edge of the path he inevitably would be running around later. Some said he looked quite old and many thought he didn't have much of a chance of winning. When somebody shouted in his direction, "You won't be able to do that next Saturday night," Cartwright replied that he would be satisfied just to be alive by then. His answer was acknowledged by the cigar smoking Edward C. Moore, another competitor, who nodded in agreement. Kelly & Bliss the bookmakers, were laying 50/1 that Cartwright wouldn't pass Albert's record. Meanwhile the even money favourite, Littlewood, stayed in his hotel and took it easy.

The beautiful weather drew thousands of spectators and the scenes within the Garden were something unprecedented in the history of go-as-you-please matches in the city. Long before the hour of opening the building to the public, the crowds had collected around the entrances and the neighbouring streets were lined with people anxiously waiting to get in. At 8 o'clock in the evening they got their wish and there was a real old rush into the place. A police captain was present with a detail of one hundred men to assist him. In the first half hour, 3,000 people entered the building, and at ten o'clock, a further 500 were milling about inside. A concert by the Sixty Ninth Regiment band preceded the starting of the race. One of the numbers they played was "Paddy Lafferty's leather breeches." There were a large number of ladies in the boxes and reserved seats; at 23:30 the place was jammed by an eager jostling crowd, whilst outside there were hundreds still struggling for admission.

The Garden was described as being *"very trim and cheerful."* The oblong picket fence was in its usual spot and looked spick and span. The scorers' stand was also in its usual place, but this time it was built on an incline so that the officials who occupied the back seats could see the track like their front seat counterparts. The race reporters occupied the same stand and they worked opposite the area where the little tin blackboards which recorded the laps and miles were located. One of them working for the *Boston Globe* wrote: **The circles of colored gas jets once more made feeble effort to outshine the electric lights, and naturally failed. The sawdust and loam track was rolled smooth before the start, and looked much like a muddy ditch, separating the opposing forces of the aristocrats in the galleries, from the democratic crowd on the main floor.**

The first competitor to appear on the track was Cartwright, who made a lap at 23:40. He passed before the spectators almost unnoticed. Before midnight, Campana, attired in a red and white striped shirt and cloth cap arrived on the track and his appearance was greeted with wild applause. He was followed by Herty and ex-champion John Hughes, and at 12:03 all the pedestrians joined them around the scorers' stand. Every single spectator stood and stretched their necks to witness the large contingent of *"tramps"* start their gruelling task.

The announcement that John L. Sullivan would start the contestants was a real draw for the crowd, but alas he didn't arrive due to being apparently sick in Boston. However, Jack Dempsey was asked to start the race and he glided through the crowd, accompanied by a phalanx of admirers. Vaulting over the railing into the track, he was introduced by Billy O'Brien, who said, "John L Sullivan promised me faithfully that he would be here tonight to start the race. It is not my fault that he is not here, and I regret the disappointment very much, for I never promise anything unless I intend to do it. As Mr. Sullivan is not here, I have asked Mr. Jack Dempsey to start the race."

Referee Kennedy then said, "They are all ready Jack." Dempsey bowed and immediately shouted, **"Go!"** and there was uproar in the place as the men darted forward. The band cranked itself into performing another number as the two Dans - Dillon and Burns, shot to the front of the pack, with Guerrero in third. The winner of the first lap was the giant sized Henry, and he headed a string of runners which went half way around the path. The first mile was covered by Dillon in a frantic pace of five minutes. He was hotly pursued by Littlewood, Cartwright and Hughes. Guerrero was also in the shake-up with Campana also up with the leaders.

The score at 01:00 was: **Cartwright, Guerrero and Littlewood, 9; Connor, Cox, Golden, Hart, Hegelman, Herty, Hughes, Panchot and Vint, 8; Dillon, Newhart and Noremac, 7:**

Many of the spectators who remained in the Garden until day light peeped through the windows the next morning. Just after 04:00, Panchot began limping painfully but kept on the track until 04:40 when he retired permanently from the contest due to the same old trouble with his hip. *"He was broken hearted with his failure and left the track with the despairing exclamation, "I ain't got the stuff in me I used to have!""* Littlewood meanwhile ran 50 miles in just over 6 hours. The *Boston Globe* wrote of him: Sunrise found him trotting nimbly around the big circle as fresh as when he came on the big track. His mind was fixed upon his work, and he neither looked to the right nor the left. He recognized no one but his trainer, and the word of the latter was law with him.

All of the competitors were obliged to wear their numbers on their front and back whilst on the course. Here is an idea of how *some* of the men fared during the early hours that first day in race card order: **No 1: Dan Herty:** A dangerous customer! He was tall and well built with square shoulders and strong good looking legs. He was described as being a strong walker that ran fairly well. He had won one six-day race and was booked for a leading place. **No 2: John Hughes:** Went along like a cart horse! His gait was described as "throwing himself forward with his prize-fighter like shoulders. Stuck to his work, glares at Littlewood and is friendly with Cartwright." **No 3: George Littlewood:** He was described as being *"above average height, with a bullet shaped head underneath reddish blonde hair and a similar colored moustache."* Many people's first impression of him was that he was too heavy to be a professional pedestrian, but closer examination made them realise that most of the weight he carried was in his legs, and his thighs were described as being *"tremendous."* He was perceived as not being the most graceful of runners but had a fast gait when either running or walking. He ate lots of roast chicken, his favourite dish, which he was known to have a weakness for and wore a small band of red flannel around his neck. **No 4: George Cartwright:** Was shorter than Littlewood and when he moved himself along at 10 mph, he was described as being graceful whilst running. He held his elbows against his sides with his hands in front with an inward bend. His head and body was thrown slightly forward and his feet just cleared the ground. He had penchant for ginger beer and wore a blue and grey shirt and drawers. He also sported a pair of black trunks. Unlike the bare headed leader Littlewood, he wore a cap. **No 5: Frank Hart:** Trailed along behind. **No 6: Gus Guerrero:** *"Was graceful and well formed."* He was expected to make some place money. **No 9: Dan Burns:** Was a cleanly built man who walked most of the time. **No 10: Peter Golden**: Was the ex-champion amateur 5-miler. He was described as being a very stocky individual and his chances of staying for a week were handicapped by that fact. **No 11: Edward C. Moore:** A tall well built chap who covered 531 miles in his last race. **No 12: Sam Day:** Was observed to have a paunch, and with that hindrance around his midriff, was scribbled out of the equation. **No 14: Dan Dillon:** Was tall and straight and described as a fast walker and a thorough stayer. He made a good account of himself in the last race without assistance. **No 15: Napoleon Campana:** Was vilified as being a mere spectacle! He should never have been in the race in the first place! **No 16: George Connor:** Too short in his stride to be fast. **No 17: Peter Hegelman:** Was described as being a natural walker with a long, easy stride. **No 19: James Saunders:** Was described as the nattiest looking man on the track who looked for applause and had a host of friends. He wore a blue worsted shirt and blue satin knee breeches. **No 20: Tom Cox:** Was a coal miner and had been walking for money for a few years. **No 21: Robert Vint:** The little shoemaker was well out of his depth in this company who were much too fast for him. **No 26: Alfred Newhart:** Was described as a short distance style walker without a chance. **No 30: Alf Prater:** The "Mountain Wonder" *was not a wonder at all.* **No 38: Augustus Kline:** All the ladies were said to have fallen in love with this young man. *"So young and so innocent for such a place,"* they said. *"He is the handsomest man on the track."* **No 44: George Howard:** Was the other black competitor in the race. He was described as a no hoper as he was *"neither a walker, nor a runner, nor a stayer."* He is *"short and chunky, but he spreads his feet about half a yard and a half every time he walks. He has a mouth like a half moon and his nickname is "Tutti Frutti.""* **C. B. Graves:** Who the crowd named "Death," was about *seven feet tall,* very thin and with a sunken face and hollow eyes. He was said to be a telephone operator seeking fame and fortune, and attracted a lot of attention as he moved his gangly frame around the course.

At 10:00, the score was: **Littlewood, 68.7; Cartwright, 65.5; Hughes, 61.6; Moore, 60.3; Herty, 60.2; Golden, 59.5; Day, 59; Hegelman, 58.5; Noremac, 58.4; Connor, 56.7; Burns and Saunders, 55:**

It was quite obvious that a few of the men at least were trying very hard to beat the record. Littlewood was the obvious one, and he went about his work in a determined and methodical way. The perception that his adversary Cartwright was going to push him to his limits did not materialise, and it was the "Lepper" who was giving the doughty Englishman a serious cause for concern. He dogged him at a rate of about 55 seconds a lap all morning, gaining ten seconds every time he went round. The Yorkshireman, seeming indifferent to his attention was content to walk at a fast rate, except when the band played up. He would then push himself around the place at running speed along with the likes of Herty, Moore and Golden.

King of the Peds

At 11 o'clock, and on a score of 44.3, George Howard, a devout Methodist, limped to his room to pray. He told a reporter "De Good Lord is a punishin' me for jiuin any such unholy bizness." Then in prayer he muttered, "O, Lor', you done know dis Mister Howard. Forgive him an' only let 'im git back home agin and he swars nebber to tempt de God of Fortune again."

At midday the score was: **Littlewood, 74.3; Cartwright, 70.2; Hughes, 69.1; Herty and Moore, 65.4; Golden, 65; Day, 64.5; Hegelman, 64; Noremac, 62.4; Connor, 61; Burns and Saunders, 59.7:**

At 14:00, the score, without Graves and Taylor who had both dropped out, was: **Littlewood, 91.6; Hughes, 87.5; Cartwright, 86.5; Herty, 80.5; Day, 80.4; Golden, 80.1; Moore, 80; Hegelman, 78.5; Noremac, 76.4; Hart, 73.1; Saunders, 71.5; Burns, 71.4; Connor, 69; Dillon, 59.7:**

At 3 p.m., Littlewood was 9 miles off the record and showed no signs of tiredness. All the while Hughes maintained his relentless chase. Cartwright would dash by them both every other lap and looked impressive, but those who knew him also knew his weakness; although the fastest man on the track, he didn't possess the stamina factor that was so important in races of this kind.

Littlewood finished the first 100 miles at 15:29 by which time he was still the even money favourite to win the title. Meanwhile, the "Mountain Wonder" wasn't going too well and he eventually retired for good at 17:30 with a score of 72.1.

When Littlewood left the track at 22:42 and headed for his hut having made 137.1 he had been off the track for only 11 minutes during the day. The 23:00 scores: **Littlewood, 137.1; Hughes, 128; Cartwright, 125; Herty, 122.3; Golden, 121.3; Noremac, 115.1; Saunders, 111.2; Day, 110.7; Hart, 110.1; Hegelman, 105:**

At midnight, those who had have covered the requisite 100 miles in twenty-four hours were: ***Littlewood, 137.1; Hughes, 131; Cartwright, 125; Golden, 124.5; Herty, 123.4; Noremac, 118.1; Saunders, 115; Day and Hart, 114; Cox and Hegelman, 105; Vint, 103; Campana, 101; Dillon, Guerrero and Moore, 100:** And those who hadn't covered the required amount were: Adams, 64.2; Albert, 57.1; Burns, 95.7; Connor, 80.6; Coughlin, 60.5; Drake, 45.3; Dully, 33.7; Elson, 78.1; Esterline, 78.2; Graves, 25.7; Henry, 57.7; Howard, 57.6; Kramer, 49.3; McEvoy, 61.6; Morlanger, 26.2; Newhart, 96.1; Nolan, 73; Panchot, 55.5; Peach, 71.6; Prater, 72.1; Russell, 58.2; Schroeder, 85.1; Stein, 53.6; Sullivan, 86.1; Taylor, 38.4; Tilly, 85; Williams, 70:

*Littlewood failed, as will be seen by the above record to make good his promise to beat Rowell's record of 150 miles in the first 24 hours.

The competitors above who had failed to reach 100 miles had been shown the door by the referee. Many had shown little inclination to move towards the century mark and their behaviour had been described as *"infantile."* Many plunged their heads and arms into the barrel of water near the scorers' stand on a regular basis. The leaders were far too busy in their objective to consider doing the same. Incredibly many had indulged in more questionable activities, much to the amusement of the crowd, and that included drinking beer and even smoking cigarettes! Needless to say, there was much consternation amongst the officials about the non-tryers, and there had been a scene in the scorers' stand as they argued.

Since the start of the race, Littlewood had been off the track for only 2h.28m when he returned to it again after indulging in his longest break at 01:15. His nearest rival, Hughes, who had had 3h.19m rest since the start, and with reference to his two principal English rivals said, "Oill' bate them or doy' on the track."

The following was the score of the leaders at 02:00: **Littlewood, 140.7; Hughes, 131.7; Cartwright, 129.2; Golden, 127.5; Noremac, 127.4; Herty, 124.4; Hart, 120; Saunders, 115.3; Day, 114; Hegelman, 111; Cox and Vint, 105; Dillon, 103; Guerrero, 102; Campana and Moore, 101:**

Williams didn't make the required 100 miles by 12 o'clock on the first night. Although informed that he wasn't in the race, he kept on the track just the same. Cox eventually gave up having made 109.7, and Day permanently retired at 02:30. Moore also retired at 3 o'clock having covered 102.4. Hart was another of the big fish that named himself as a permanent withdrawal at 05:35 with a score of 122.1. Earlier at 5 a.m., Herty passed the faltering Cartwright to take third place. The Englishman was already being criticised for being lazy, as he had up to that point, spent

4h.51m.30s resting, during which time he had *"appeared free from any ailment."* While *"chunky and cheery,"* Pete Golden reversed his course to break the monotony of the long tramp during the small hours, Peter Hegelman, although sticking to his task, appeared worn out, and soon retired to the comfort of his quarters having managed to make 125.6, his return a matter of conjecture.

The air was chilly and raw, and the scene rather dismal when Cartwright left the track for 26 minutes after 8 o'clock. During that time Herty closed the gap between the pair, and whilst the self proclaimed "Champion of England" rested, the Bostonian made considerable progress by the time he made his reappearance at 08:50.

At 9 a.m., the score, with scarcely over a hundred people watching, including scorers and trainers was: **Littlewood, 171; Hughes, 162; Cartwright, 155; Golden and Herty, 153; Noremac, 149; Guerrero, 135; Dillon, 129; Campana, 128; Vint, 127; Hegelman, 125; Saunders, 124:**

Later, the "Lepper" assumed the familiar method of progression that gave him his nickname. He plodded steadily along with his eyes fixed on Littlewood who appeared to be fearful of the Irishman overtaking him. For his part, Littlewood's right foot appeared to trouble him, and caused him to take frequent short breaks, after which he appeared to return to the track a little stiffer. Meanwhile, Herty, despite his appearance of being *"broken up,"* travelled well alongside Cartwright. As the former fought with the Briton to keep his third place, Cartwright at the time appeared to be in good condition and going well.

The 11 a.m. score: **Littlewood, 175; Hughes, 172; Herty, 164; Cartwright, 163; Golden, 162; Noremac, 157; Guerrero, 142; Campana and Dillon, 136; Vint, 135; Saunders, 132; Hegelman, 125:**

There was a fair bit of banter amongst the Irish and the English who were obviously very vocal in supporting their toiling countrymen on the path to glory; or were they? The Irish contingent initially took little notice of the "Lepper" as he struggled on in his customary ungraceful manner. Littlewood held the lead up until noon when Hughes, hearing that the leader was probably disabled, rolled off lap after lap in his desire to catch him. The Irish spectators, now alerted to the fact that their man was catching up, cheered and urged him on with shouts of encouragement. Slowly he gained on Littlewood, until at 12:16 on his 180th mile he passed him amid the enthusiastic shouts amongst the thousand or so watching, and as the band played "St. Patrick's Day in the Morning" and "Erin Go Bragh," Hughes smiled for once. It was well known that he hated the English and it must have given him great satisfaction to pass the race favourite.

The new leader's fellow countrymen in the crowd then had a dig at Littlewood for having promised that he would stay in front. Ignoring their taunts, the brave former steel worker stuck with the task and kept close to Hughes, even though he looked ungainly in his movements due to a bothersome hip which slowed him down. Every step he took was said to produce a stabbing pain in his pelvis. His physician, Dr. Prendergast gave him the once over and could find nothing wrong with him, saying of his plucky patient that he had both wonderful lung power, and in his opinion, didn't need to retire.

Hegelman inevitably gave notice of his permanent retirement from the track at 14:00. Hughes continued to move swiftly around the ellipse in his traditional cumbersome manner, and by 16:30, had made his second century. At this stage of the race, he was an hour and a half behind Albert's record in the last race. He was presented with a bouquet by a fervent fan which he sniffed as though it contained a bomb!

Cartwright left the contest intending to rest for a while, but returned sooner than anticipated, and then went on to do some impressive mileage. Earlier in the afternoon, the white suited Englishman had challenged the maroon costumed Guerrero to a sprint, much to the delight of the gathered. The Californian based Mexican had only just raced with Dan Dillon, but nevertheless, politely accepted. Cartwright set off at a pace of 11 mph, and as the two flew around, some spectators dashed from side-to-side so as not to miss the spectacle. The pair raced like this for a mile with Cartwright forging ahead by half a lap, only to be overhauled by Guerrero, whose stamina took him way past his rival. The crowd were beside themselves at the scene before them, and as a consequence, went *"mad with excitement."*

Meanwhile, Golden was surprising many with his performance, but even he was getting a bit dizzy heading in one direction. To counteract this, he occasionally raced in reverse around the track. Dillon also went well and looked as though he had just started the match, going round at the same speed and never altering his gait. Noremac, looking as miserable as he always did, said nothing and just got on with the job of securing the miles. "Old Sport" busied himself with amusing the crowd, and ate strawberry cheesecake as he progressed, that was of course if anybody would buy him some! Whilst Vint kept glancing at the scoreboard, Saunders crept around as *"though walking on eggs."*

As the day wore on, Hughes continued to increase the gap between himself and the rest of the field. By midnight, he had turned the earlier (09:00) nine-mile deficit between himself and Littlewood, to a seven-mile advantage over the same competitor. Below are some other scores given at three-hour intervals up until the end of the second day.

	15	18	21	Midn		15	18	21	Midn
Hughes	192	207	221	232.7	**Cartwright**	174	187	192	204.7
Littlewood	187	203	217	225.4	**Dillon**	155	169	178	190
Herty	184	198	211	225.1	**Campana**	153	166	166	186.1
Golden	179	194	205	218.6	**Vint**	147	155	168	184.5
Guerrero	164	179	195	210.6	**Saunders**	147	154	154	154.7

After making two laps after midnight, Littlewood returned to his tent complaining about his hip. His trainer said he was in a bad way. It was thought by many at the time that if this were true, Herty, who was said to be the best man on the track, would be the eventual winner. However, after wobbling around the place for a few laps, Littlewood started to look his old self and moved reasonably well thereafter.

The race leader had gone to bed with the mistaken notion that his lead would enable him to get a decent rest, but while he slept Littlewood made serious inroads into it. Hughes was summoned by his trainer to repair the damage. He made a poor mile and had to go in for another rest of 23 minutes. After emerging again, and making another three miles, he went off again after which Littlewood passed him at 04:26 amid the tumultuous cheers of his supporters and the neutrals in the crowd. Whereas Hughes had been ahead of him for fifteen hours, he led the Irishman an hour later by two miles, which he later increased to four and a half. Behind him, about the same distance, was Herty who appeared in first class condition. He was followed by Golden, the *"flying Scotchman,"* Noremac, and the *"nimble footed"* Guerrero.

Earlier, Cartwright had dropped out at 04:22 having *"again failed, and purely from lack of heart. He was in perfect condition when he stopped, and there was no earthly reason, so say his trainers why he should not have won the race. He had 210 miles and four laps to his credit."* Indeed Cartwright was seen as a bit of a flop. His Monday performance was deemed only satisfactory, and on Tuesday, he was denounced as *"No good."*

As Dillon, the longshoreman, went along slowly, Campana created much amusement in the morning, when, with his knees *"swathed in huge bandages, he stopped opposite the scorers' stand, unrolled yards of rag and disclosed a large porous blister. Tenderly lifting up one end, he gently scratched his knee which brought a smile of satisfaction and relief over his face. The crowd responded by laughing. He grew very indignant with a lady who was slightly under the weather and who persisted in shouting after him, "Ah, there you Connecticut chestnut."*

Saunders, who had made 158.2 dropped out of the race at 08:00.

Gus Guerrero *(Illustration no: 116)* was making a very good impression on everybody at the Garden. He dressed well, always appeared clean and tidy, and was thoroughly pleasant to all he encountered. He possessed a sense of humour too, and was seen now and then to shout out at the scorers' table, "Guerrero, a mile!" when in fact he hadn't scored one. He would sometimes play a mouth organ whilst walking along so as to introduce some music when the band was silent. However, it was his inspiring performance where it mattered on the track which impressed the punters. He possessed an amazing turn of foot and was able to run consecutive miles in six and seven minutes at a time. During the afternoon he was able to get within four miles of Herty with his persistent running. The second man, realising the danger that the advancing Mexican posed, increased his speed and kept him at bay and was therefore able to maintain the gap between them both. Herty was considered a very dangerous man. He always appeared dog tired, and the perception was he could give up at any time, but when serious questions were asked of him, he answered them very, very well indeed. As the two men battled for second spot and put in shows of spurting for their enthralled audience, the 50-year-old Campana joined them, during which time he was tossed money from his army of fans. Guerrero would eventually leave the track after completing his 264th mile with the deafening applause of the appreciative crowd ringing in his ears.

At midday, and at the end of the 60th hour of competition, Littlewood was still six miles and 2 laps behind Albert's record at the same stage, which was 288 miles and 1,320 yards. The man whose record he was chasing was watching the afternoon's proceedings with interest from the stands. It was said that he secretly wanted his record to be broken so that he could then challenge the winner to a sweepstakes, but he knew in his mind that it probably wouldn't happen. As he toyed with facts and figures, he would have remembered that on the third day at 6 o'clock in the evening in his record breaking race, he was 5 miles ahead of Littlewood in this one, Jimmy's score at the time being 318 miles and 440 yards (Rowell at the same stage had mustered 336.5). Although the Englishman was good, was he that good? Only time would tell.

Hughes, the long term leader in the race, was now a lost cause. His old enemy, rheumatism, had covered its ugly tentacles around his legs and he virtually had to crawl around the path. At 22:00, he was in fourth position and was in danger of losing more places due to his horrendously slow progress. Golden and Noremac gradually crept up on the struggler and by midnight both were nearly ready to reel him in.

The scores up to midnight and the first three hours of the next day were:

	13:00	15:00	18:00	Midn	01:00	02:00	03:00
Littlewood	287	298	313.1	326.2	327.5	331	335
Guerrero	274	274	291	316.2	318.2	324	328.1
Herty	271	281	295.2	315.7	320.5	323	324.2
Golden	257	265	279.5	302.7	304.3	304	306
Hughes	275	281	288.4	300	300	300	302.2
Noremac	259	260	273.6	287.7	290.3	290	298.1
Dillon	235	243	254.3	279	280	280	281.4
Campana	223	225	233.1	250.1	250.1	250.1	252.5
Vint	215	220	230	251	251.4	251	251.4

On Thursday it was reported that most of the participating athletes appeared to be in first-class condition. Observers were particularly impressed with the extraordinary work of Guerrero commenting that he was, *"the feature of the night, and still traveling along in his peculiar gliding stride, apparently without exertion. Today he appears as fresh as when he started on his tramp."*

Noremac took a rest of almost an hour between eight and nine o'clock, but when he went back on the track he limped painfully. Guerrero went well in second place, and it looked as if there would be a hard fight between him and Littlewood for winning honours. Herty kept up the same gait and seemed determined to cover a certain number of miles. The opinion in the betting was that it was anybody's race, with not many willing to back Littlewood to win because of the dangerous proximity of Guerrero.

The nine o'clock score: **Littlewood, 361; Guerrero, 355; Herty, 349; Hughes, 330; Golden, 320; Noremac, 310; Dillon, 307; Campana, 260.7; Vint, 251.4:**

Vint eventually retired full time from the race at 10:00, at which time Littlewood was 21 miles behind Albert's February record of 388.2. Whilst Guerrero was away from the fray, the men in first and third positions quickened their speed, the leader attempting to increase his overall lead whilst Herty tried to close the gap between himself and the slumbering Mexican.

At 10:50, the notoriously argumentative Hughes, approached the scorers' stand and began to complain that the officials had cheated him out of 5 laps stating that his score should have been recorded as 339 miles. Ed Plummer, the referee, refusing to comply with his wishes, offered him a personal scorer but it is not known whether the

King of the Peds

garrulous Irishman accepted it. Campana pulled out of the race at 11:50 with a score of 260.7 having not been seen on the track since 05:11. His withdrawal left only seven men now remaining in the tournament.

The noon score: **Littlewood, 378.1; Guerrero, 365; Herty, 362.3; Golden, 341.3; Hughes, 341; Noremac, 325; Dillon, 319.4:**

The 2 p.m. score: **Littlewood, 388.5; Guerrero, 374.7; Herty, 367.1; Hughes, 349; Golden, 347.3; Noremac, 335.1; Dillon, 327.5:**

Guerrero caused a stir in the building when he fainted in front of his tent during the afternoon. He was carried inside by his handlers but soon recovered, and much to the relief of everybody, continued on his journey.

Both Littlewood and the "Greaser" indulged in a bit of fun for the benefit of the crowd when they gave each other a shampoo using a sponge and the water from the barrel at the side of the track. The escapade went down well with the crowd. "Old Sport," who was reported to be out of the contest at that time, stayed on the track to satisfy a bet that he made with a man that he wouldn't cover 400 miles.

The record at 15:00: **Littlewood, 393; Guerrero, 379; Herty, 371; Golden and Hughes, 351; Noremac, 339; Dillon, 330:**

Hughes was relegated into fifth position at nine o'clock. He was passed by Golden who employed a short striding jog when the band played, and a slow careless walk when they were silent as well as stopping once in every mile to plunge his head into *"the big barrel."*

The odds of success in the race being offered by the bookmaking firms were on these lines: **Littlewood, 1/1; Guerrero, 2/1; Herty, 6/1; Golden, 20/1; Dillon, 100/1:**

Littlewood removed himself from the track at 22:00; Guerrero seeing his chance, went about cutting into his lead. Whilst on show, his fans continually sent him flowers which he would carry for a lap and then have them stuck up with the rest on his hut. Herty now walked with a bit of a hunch, and apart from occasionally looking up to watch Guerrero pass him, he always kept his eyes on the track. Whilst Herty called in for a rest at 22:30, Campana was seen to wait for the crowd to throw dollar bills in his direction, which he picked up and waved in the air.

As the midnight hour arrived to bring to the close the end of the fourth day, Littlewood was 22 miles behind the best record ever made in a six-day event. During the last big race at that time, Albert's score was 450 miles, which was a record for 96 hours. Albert then slept for 4 hours. Littlewood's plan however was to sleep for less than that in his desire to make 105 miles on the fifth day and about 100 miles on the last. His objective was a whopping 640 and with Guerrero hopefully keeping him up to his work, that score just might be achievable.

The score at midnight was: **Littlewood, 427.2; Guerrero, 422; Herty, 406.6; Golden, 387.6; Hughes, 371; Noremac, 368.4; Dillon, 356; Campana, 280:**

The audience cheered and shouted when, after an absence of two hours, Littlewood appeared on the track at 00:10 followed by Herty five minutes later. As the three leaders went around, a smile was brought to the Sheffielder's face as someone in the crowd yelled, "Go it John Bull!"

The 1 a.m. returns: **Littlewood, 431; Guerrero, 423; Herty, 411.2; Golden, 389.1; Hughes, 371.3; Noremac, 370; Dillon, 359.1; Campana, 280:**

As the Mexican did what he loved most dearly, sleeping, Littlewood took advantage and increased his lead from 5 to 12 miles at 03:00, to sixteen at 04:00 and at 07:00 he was 18 miles ahead.

The *Brooklyn Daily Eagle* wrote of the race at that time: Guerrero still continues to excite wonder at Madison Square Garden, New York. He is an enigma to pedestrians, trainers, and spectators. How is it possible for a man to run almost continuously, as he has done for four days, and then get up from a sound sleep of three hours and start right off into a brisk run, almost a sprint, is something that no one can make out, and why he does not get over more ground is a puzzle.

Trainers and walkers are worried over a dark horse which has appeared in the shape of the "Flying Scotchman," George Noremac. No one has noticed him, but he has been going like clockwork. He is pretty far behind, but that is nothing, say his friends. There is some truth in that too, for Noremac is famed for his work on the last two days, and is said is good for at least 225 miles. John Hughes it is probable will get the last piece of the pie. He is all broken up and his struggles to get into something like his old trot are pitiable to behold. "Old Sport" Campana now runs in the day and sleeps at night. Some one had sent him a package through the mail. He wouldn't open it, but gave it to Special Officer Harry Nugent, who bravely undertook to see what was in it. It contained a toy pistol, with the name Daisy on it. Around the popgun was a piece of paper, on which was written by some very bad poetry.

The incidents of the night were not many. The brutal conduct of one of Captain Reilly's policeman, however, might be recorded. He was engaged in waking up sleepers. He came across a respectable colored man who was sleeping in one of the boxes. He shook him without avail. Finally he took him bodily and threw him to the floor. The man was naturally indignant and endeavored to remonstrate against such treatment, but the policeman banged him over the back of the legs with the club and then put him out. The few spectators gave vent to their feelings by hissing the cowardly patrolman. An individual in one of the boxes, whose snore reminded one of the whistle of an ocean steamer in distress, created a deal of innocent amusement. Around his neck hung a square card with the words "Natural Gas" printed upon it. A youth, who is bound to get into trouble some day, went around through the sleepers with a bottle of strong ammonia, a sniff of which would wake the dead.

The 06:00 score: **Littlewood, 456.2; Guerrero, 438.2; Herty, 423.2; Golden, 401.6; Noremac, 393; Hughes, 386.6; Dillon, 376.4; Campana, 280:** Littlewood was 9 miles and 1 lap behind Fitzgerald's 1884 record of 465.3.

At 09:00 although Guerrero was running in his usual fast style, Littlewood still continued to maintain his long lead. General opinion at the time was that there was no way that the Mexican would catch him, barring something going badly wrong.

At noon, the score was: **Littlewood, 487.6; Guerrero, 465.2; Herty, 450.7; Golden, 426.7; Noremac, 424.7; Hughes, 404.5; Dillon, 395.7; Campana, 303:** Littlewood was now just 4 miles and a lap behind Albert's record, and 6 miles and 1 lap behind Fitzgerald's 1884 record of 493.7. His trainers planned for him to make 534 miles by 21:00 and if he achieved that objective, they would tuck him up in bed and give him sufficient rest to enable him to make his effort for the world record the next day. At the time the bookmakers made him 1/10 favourite to win the contest.

Dillon had taken only three hours rest during the last twenty-four. There was a bit of a scene when he headed for his tent at 12:50 demanding that he be allowed to sleep. Burns, his trainer, told him to keep on the track, but as Dillon argued his case Burns relented and finally allowed him to go to bed.

During the day, news had emerged that George Cartwright had issued the following challenge:

"I hereby challenge Littlewood to run me 50 or 100 miles for $1,000 a side. Time and place to be settled by him. I will meet him at the *World* office on Monday, and post $200 forfeit. I am also willing, if he likes, to leave the match open for a sweepstake barring no one."

Guerrero saw the enormous task ahead of him and decided that if he had any chance of victory, he needed to act quickly and reduce the distance that the leader had created between them. After running mile after mile, he started to make an impression on Littlewood's score which, along with the rest at 3 p.m., showed: **Littlewood, 500; Guerrero, 482; Herty, 468; Golden, 435; Noremac, 427; Hughes, 417; Dillon, 398:Campana; 314:**

When the race returns at 18:00 were released they showed the race leader not only fighting back, but also 5 miles and 1 lap behind Fitzgerald's 1884 record of 519.2: **Littlewood, 514.1; Guerrero, 494.4; Herty, 479.4; Noremac, 452; Golden, 448.2; Hughes, 425; Dillon, 398; Campana; 325.3:**

At 19:23, Guerrero was 15 miles behind Littlewood, who had gone to his house with the intention of resting for two hours, and it was at this stage of the race where things started to get rather interesting. While Littlewood's head graced his pillow, Guerrero ran like a deer. The spectators clapped and stamped their feet and their eyes were transfixed on two objects before them that fascinated their attentions, *that Mexican* and the scoreboard! As he ran he was showered with roses by the hundreds, whilst the rest of the athletes could only watch in disbelief. As the scorecard for 21:00 suggests, the 22-mile lead between the pair had quickly disintegrated to 10 miles: **Littlewood, 519; Guerrero, 509; Herty, 492; Noremac, 465; Golden, 461; Hughes, 437; Campana, 336:**

Then at 21:45 the English gladiator entered the arena. His supporters shouted themselves hoarse in an effort to cajole him into producing an enormous effort to thwart Guerrero's challenge. By then he had a mere 4½ mile advantage, and as he accepted a bunch of flowers from a well wisher with a grateful smile, he knew the task ahead was going to be difficult. Pulling his frame on to the track he continued the fight. He went along stiffly at first and many in the crowd were ready to back him to lose, but the ones who knew him knew also that this phenomenal athlete had the *"heart of a lion."* As he limbered up, and only too aware of the close proximity of his closest rival, he glanced nervously towards the scoreboard. At 23:10 it informed him he had an advantage of three and a half miles. A few laps later his mind told him that the now even further reduced gap of two and a half miles needed to be extended. However, his exhausted body said, stick to the same pace and wait for the Mexican to tire himself out. Evaluating the situation quickly, George erred on the side of logic and responded by running FAST! With Guerrero following him at a similar pace, many in the crowd stood on chairs and waved hats and handkerchiefs as they tried to comprehend the scene before them.

The original intention was to let Guerrero have a well deserved break before midnight but "Happy Jack" Smith his trainer had other ideas. With him being so close to catching Littlewood up, the wily old trainer kept him to his work, but not wanting to be too harsh on him, did allow him the luxury of a rub down. When he returned looking as immaculately attired as ever wearing *"gorgeous tights of purple and bright green trunks,"* he continued to reel off the laps at an astonishing rate.

There was a silly rumour being touted about the place that he was on a champagne diet! On hearing of this, Smith stopped his man at the reporters' stand and presenting him to the press said, "Does he look like a drunken man?" Although his eyes were sunk deep into their sockets, and the skin on his face looked tightly drawn, he appeared fine, and certainly not inebriated! Indeed as if to reinforce the point, the lap after the incident, Guerrero shouted out in broken English, "No drunk!" much to the amusement of the reporters.

Of the other performers that night, Herty, who had made his 500th mile at 22:55, was unaware that a deputy sheriff was waiting to serve two attachments on him for unpaid bills, one of which for $84 was to the gas company.

The midnight score: **Littlewood, 528; Guerrero, 524.2; Herty, 504.6; Noremac, 477.1; Golden, 471; Hughes, 445.6; Campana, 341.1:**

The leader's score at midnight was 17 miles less than what Albert had recorded at the end of the fifth day in the last "big match." That left Littlewood needing just over 93 miles to beat the world record before 10 o'clock that night. He could achieve his goal by going at a rate of 4½ mph, but could he actually do it?

The crowd at the Garden after midnight was one of the largest since the week began, and it was estimated that about 10,000 spectators were present. At 00:05, Guerrero was observed staggering around the track *"like a drunken man"* eventually falling at the Madison Square entrance causing dozens of voices in the crowd to cry, "He's been drugged." His trainers denied anything of the kind saying he was simply tired and consequently light headed. He walked along in a vague, wandering way, and continually rubbed his head. With the distress signals at full blast, he tried to enter his hut but his trainers mercilessly ushered him back on the track where he again staggered along until, once again, he fell to the ground twice in succession. After that the door of his room was left open for him to enter at 00:12.

Frank Dale, Littlewood's backer, was said to be disheartened by the fact that Guerrero was getting so close to leading the race and was about to catch the early morning train from Philadelphia when he was sent a telegram by Bromley, Littlewood's trainer, to tell him that George had recovered and had increased his lead. Indeed, when the scores were released at 01:00, they showed: **Littlewood, 533; Guerrero, 525.6; Herty, 507.3; Noremac, 477.1; Golden, 471; Hughes, 450; Campana, 341.1:**

At 2 a.m., Littlewood, who had covered 537 miles, and was 11 miles ahead of the Mexican, later increased his lead during the night. As Guerrero rested, the leader of the pack went 18 miles up on him at 06:00.

At 08:15, Guerrero, now said to be a *"trifle more lazy"* in his work, climbed over the reporters' table and took a *"high hat"* off the head of one of the journalists, after which he made a lap of the track with it hanging down over his shoulders. About 45 minutes later, he jumped over the fence that surrounded the track and sat down on a weighing machine. Registering 142 pounds on the scales, he announced he had gained a pound since Monday. Meanwhile the other comedian in the race, Campana, entertained the crowd by parading about the place *"in all manner of costumes."*

The score at 09:00: **Littlewood, 568; Guerrero, 552; Herty, 531; Noremac, 500; Golden, 489; Hughes, 474; Campana, 342:**

At 09:35, Littlewood had beaten Albert's record of 571 miles with 25 minutes to spare. He was then only a mile and four laps behind the best ever record and had twenty minutes to accomplish that distance. At 10:01, he promptly delivered the goods when he finished his 572nd mile in 130h.49m.30s which was 2m.35s better than Hazael's 1882 feat. At 11 o'clock, Littlewood was one mile ahead of Albert's best distance, and it was established that if he could pace himself at 4½ mph until the finish, he would beat his world record. At that time, there were an estimated 10,000 people watching the sport. *"They cheer and yell, running from side to side, like wild men. Enthusiasm is rampant. Guerrero and Littlewood run and kick around the track and are on the very best of terms. "The Colored Skin," as Guerrero is called, makes no effort to overtake the subject of the Queen."* At 11:30, Guerrero and Herty told journalists that they would enter against any other team in the world in a six-day race for, *"$500 a corner, $2,000 in the pool."*

At noon, and with the leader 4 miles ahead of Albert's total at the same stage, the score stood: **Littlewood, 581; Guerrero, 561; Herty, 541; Noremac, 505; Golden, 496; Hughes, 485; Campana, 354:**

Golden made 500 miles at 12:50 and was cheered enthusiastically by the crowd. Guerrero left the track for about 30 minutes at 1 o'clock to take a rest. Herty was said to be smiling whilst Hughes, *"wears his usual frown and plods wearily around the ellipse in his endeavor to get to the mark which entitles him to gate money."* At 2 o'clock, Golden, *"received the handsomest basket of flowers that has been seen on the track since the walk began."*

The 15:00 score: **Littlewood, 593; Guerrero, 568.7; Herty, 551; Noremac, 514.3; Golden, 505.6; Hughes, 495; Campana, 363.6:**

At 15:15, George Cartwright, dressed in a sky blue suit with black velvet trunks, went on to the track and ran for about a mile. At this time, there were about 4,000 spectators who had paid 50 cents at the turnstiles; 500 of them had paid $1 for the privilege of a seat. At 15:30, Littlewood was one and a quarter miles ahead of the best record running easily in his attempt to make the desired 625 miles. He said he was unhappy that his trainers didn't start him earlier in the day so that he would have had more time to make the distance.

Herty and Guerrero went around the track hand in hand laughing and joking, and it was quite evident that Noremac and Golden were only trying to get in the frame to win some gate money. Hughes's trainer said that he would come on again and go five miles, thus gaining the 500 he needed for prize money. The Irishman had been off the track since 20:40 the previous night.

For the very first time in his career, Littlewood completed 600 miles at 16:59 and was awarded a $20 gold piece for his wonderful achievement. George would be only the fifth person to accomplish such a feat having been preceded by Hazael, Fitzgerald, Rowell and Albert. To celebrate, he went around the track, followed by Campana carrying a broom and Guerrero, an American flag. Shortly after 5 o'clock "Old Sport" re-emerged wearing a flannel red shirt and, wearing his fire helmet with the number "41" on the shield, he ran for a couple of laps as the spectators went wild with enthusiasm.

An immense crowd of people went along to the Garden in the early evening fully expecting to see the old world record beaten. After all, Littlewood's trainers had been confidently proclaiming that he would deliver the goods and positive statements of the kind were the perfect excuse to go along and watch history being made. However, they were to be greatly disappointed, because what many of them witnessed on arrival was the leader hobbling around the track putting his right foot down gingerly and gazing wistfully at both the scoreboard and clock. As he trudged along slowly, it was quite evident that he was in bad shape as he painfully limped along.

King of the Peds

At 18:30 and after Littlewood's trainer announced that his man would not beat the record because of a split toe, there was little interest in the struggles. Bromley said, "No, we don't intend him to beat the record. He has been beaten three times in the week; rallied every time. He would never quit though till he fell dead on the track. We don't think there is any necessity for his beating the record, so he will take it easy until nine o'clock and then retire." Asked if Littlewood would compete in a race with other well known pedestrians, Bromley replied that he would. He also made reference to the fact his man had only done a week's training and weighed 25 lbs too much and would never had made so good a showing but for his grit and patience. When asked what was troubling his star, Fred said that for the last three days, George had been suffering with a split toe, which had become so bad that the bare bone struck the bottom of his shoe every time he stepped on it.

Captain Reilly stationed 150 policemen about the Garden, but their presence seemed hardly necessary, as the crowd was not disorderly. The order maintained throughout the week has been admirable.

At 7 o'clock, all the peds retired to their huts to freshen up a bit for the benefit of the crowd. "Parson" Tilly, who had retired early in the contest, appeared on the track several times during the evening, and amused the crowd with a number of antics.

At 19:30. Littlewood went back to his tent so stiffly that he fairly wobbled. Thereafter he left the track on a number of occasions, but at every appearance, was heartily cheered while the band played *"enlivening airs."*

At 8 o'clock, and carrying a large bottle of beer, Tilly playfully poured some over Noremac's shoulder, much to the Scotchman's disgust. "This is to see you win!" he said to George before being hustled off the track a moment later by a big policeman. Soon after that, Herty and Golden had the track to themselves and they were soon joined by Guerrero, who, together with Herty, thrilled the crowd with an exhibition of heel-and-toe. Guerrero was then presented with a wooden Chinese baby by an enthusiastic lady admirer who was reported to have *"stuck it up over his score."*

As the sun went down, the crowd which was estimated to be about 4,000, started to increase by the minute. Workmen went around lighting the many gas jets with long tapers and the building *"assumed a bright appearance."* The weary competitors continued on their journey and were urged on by the crowd who were noticeably quieter than the previous evening owing to the fact that by now, they knew the record would not be broken. Littlewood continued to walk slowly around the track, but nevertheless was reported to be, *"cheerful and happy."* Some said he *"was reserving himself for the last hour. They did not know, though, that the cheerful expression concealed the real feelings of the heroic pedestrian. His foot was in a terrible condition. Underneath the big toe the flesh was seamed and cracked clear through to the bone, leaving it almost bare. This was the result of the opening which appeared from time to time."*

At 19:45, Guerrero received an elegant cane from Mrs. John B. Mason of the Boston Museum Company. It was made of Malacca and had a silver head which was described as being *"elegantly chased."* She also presented him with a solitaire diamond ring which was too small for him, but would be made larger at her expense. Earlier in the afternoon, the Mexican had been given a solid silver ring in the shape of a serpent with two tiny rubies for eyes by Emil Paul, the "Champion Quail Eater." Mrs. C. B. Reid of California, an old friend, also presented him with a bouquet of roses. He was also to receive several cash presents totalling $43 before 9 o'clock.

Golden completed his 529th mile at 20:03, at which time Hughes came back on having been out of the ring for nearly five hours. He wore a green silk jockey cap and wore a small American flag around his neck. He was very stiff, and walked slowly around the ring and was truly a pitiful sight being hardly able to move. The crowd cheered him as he took five minutes to complete his first lap. Some indignation was expressed at his being allowed to continue and he then left the race for good.

An artist from a newspaper asked Campana to stand in front of the reporters' stand at 20:20 to draw him. "Sport," stood posing with his head thrown to one side, with the money that he received tied on his shirt front. When the artist had finished, he quipped, "That picture will never go through the press without breaking it."

Littlewood surprised everybody shortly before 9 o'clock by breaking into a run, keeping up the pace for a lap before giving up for which he was loudly cheered. When Campana came on the track in street costume at 21:33, it was realised that he had permanently retired from the race on a score of 380¼ miles. The audience yelled itself hoarse as the men marched around on a final lap before leaving it collectively a minute later. Littlewood made another appearance at 21:40, but was too shattered to continue, and Guerrero empathising with his predicament, rushed over to the ailing pedestrian, linked arms with him and helped him around the track.

The winner was then presented with a floral horseshoe, which Jimmy Albert helped carry around the track as he walked by his side to the accompaniment of the band playing, *"For he's a jolly good fellow."* Guerrero then ran around the track at full speed carrying an American flag in his hand. Herty joined him as he bore an Irish flag which he dropped when it became too heavy for him to hold. Noremac trod in his footsteps as he struggled with an abundance of emblems, and Golden brought up the rear. Littlewood then left the track for good, but it was Noremac, who, after bowing graciously to the crowd, was the last man to leave at one minute to ten. As the band serenaded the departing crowd with "Home Sweet Home," the building slowly began to empty, and within a few minutes the Garden was *"as quiet as a church."*

The following table shows the work of the pedestrians during the closing hours:

	17:00		18:00		19:00		20:00		21:00		22:00	
	Miles	L	Miles	L	Miles	L	Miles	L	Miles	L	Miles	L
Littlewood	600	1	602	4	605	1	607	5	611	0	**611**	2
Guerrero	576	4	578	4	581	1	583	3	586	6	**590**	0
Herty	559	0	559	0	561	5	565	5	569	5	**572**	3
Noremac	520	6	523	2	525	3	527	7	530	0	**533**	0
Golden	513	1	516	1	521	3	524	2	526	7	**530**	1
Hughes	495	2	495	2	495	2	495	2	495	2	**495**	4
Campana	368	6	371	4	372	7	375	7	379	0	**380**	2

The first three home were all driven to Everard's Russian baths in Twenty Eighth Street, where they were followed on their journey by hundreds of people eager to get a closer look at them all. The rest of the competitors went to the Putnam House where they later enjoyed the desperately desired sleep they yearned for.

The scores made by the men who remained on the track for the whole of the six-day period is as follows with the race leader highlighted in bold for each day:

	Monday	Tuesday	Wednesday	Thursday	Friday	Saturday
Littlewood	**137.1**	225.4	**326.2**	**427.2**	**528**	**611.2**
Guerrero	100.4	210.6	316.2	422	524.2	590
Herty	123.4	225.1	315.7	406.6	504.6	572.5
Noremac	118.1	206.1	287.7	368.4	477.1	533
Golden	124.5	218.6	302.7	387.6	471	530.1
Hughes	131	**232.7**	300	371	445.6	495.4
Campana	101	186.1	250.1	280	341.1	380.2

The scores of each man on and off the track are as follows:

	Miles	Laps	IN Hours	Minutes	RESTING Hours	Minutes	Seconds
Littlewood	611	2	141	44	22	7	47
Guerrero	590	0	141	49	24	25	
Herty	572	5	141	49	21	11	
Noremac	533	0	141	58	25	44	
Golden	529	1	141	43	21	11	
Hughes	495	4	140	9	30		
Campana	380	2					

Manager O'Brien was asked, "Is there any truth in the talk that Littlewood refrained purposely from beating the record?" to which he replied, "No truth whatsoever. We are one thousand dollars in pocket by Littlewood not breaking it, and he is that much money out. He would have got one hundred dollars a mile for those last ten miles, but he could not do it. Go look at him and you will see."

At the Ashland House, Littlewood limped into the office with his right foot turned inward, surrounded by a crowd of admirers. Asked by the press how he was, he replied, "Oh, I'm alright, I could have kept on if I wanted to, but my foot got sore on Monday from the track. The track was too hard, for they had sand instead of the tanbark on top and that's what hurt my foot." He admitted to the press that he kept the condition of his feet a secret because had he made it known, his rivals would have run him ragged and he would have broken down. He also mentioned that his lameness during the last three days was caused by the trouble with his feet and not his hip. The reporter added that his face was pinched and drawn and his cheeks and eyes hollow and sunken.

The condition of Littlewood's foot at the end of the contest was described by the *Brooklyn Daily Eagle* as: **shocking to see. Taking off his shoe, Littlewood exhibited his lame foot. It was in a horrible condition, the flesh between the two smaller toes having been literally worn away and the bone of the little toe uncovered of its flesh coating. Nothing but shear pluck and Spartan disregard of pain could a man on his feet in such condition of physical suffering.** On the same subject, the *New York Times* wrote: It became known yesterday that it was pluck alone that enabled Littlewood, the Englishman, to win the six-day go-as-you-please contest in Madison Square Garden which ended Saturday night. Littlewood's feet are in a terrible condition. On the second day of the race a huge blister appeared under the ball of his right foot. On the following day another blister appeared on his left foot. On Wednesday, his little toes began to swell, and on Friday they gathered and burst, laying open the flesh so that the bones were visible. His running on Friday and Saturday chafed the broken flesh apart so that it hung in flaps from both of his little toes. In the meantime the skin on the blisters had been worked off, and the man ran for two days on raw flesh. He must have been in excruciating pain during the greater part of the contest. On the third day his hip became swollen and inflamed through rheumatism. At four different times during the race it was thought by his trainers that that he would have to abandon the contest, but the plucky fellow determined to go on as long as he could hold the lead.

A reporter asked Littlewood, "Why didn't you try and break the record?" to which he answered, "I ain't breaking records. I'm going to keep ahead of the man that's behind me. I had three chances in England to break records, but I don't care for that. I want to get in first and get the money." He went on to say that he would run any man in the world in the autumn for between $1,000 and $10,000 a side. After the race he had a long soak and slept till nine o'clock in the morning.

All the men who covered more than 525 miles gathered at the office of the *Sporting Times* on the 14th of May, to receive their share of the gate receipts, which day by day added up as follows: To 12 noon Monday, $2,361: From 12 noon Monday to 12 noon Tuesday, $1,781: From 12 noon Tuesday to 12 noon Wednesday, $1,761: From 12 noon Wednesday to 12 noon Thursday, $2,035.50: From 12 noon Thursday to 12 noon Friday, $2,413.50: From 12 noon Friday to 12 noon Saturday, $2,630.50: From 12 noon Saturday to 10 o'clock Saturday night, $2,914: The total receipts were $15,896.50. Half or $7,948.25 less $514 for expenses went to the pedestrians. Littlewood would get 50% or $3,717.13, Guerrero got 20% or $1,486.84, Herty received 15% or $1,155.14, Noremac, 10% or $743.43 and Golden 5% or $371.71.

Hughes was given $100 as a reward for his gutsy performance earlier in the race, for which he thanked the management, going on to say, "But if it hadn't rained during the week I would have won first money. Rain and rheumatism don't agree in a six-day walk."

On the Tuesday night after the race, and at the invitation of Mr. J. W. Rosenquest of the Fourteenth Street Theater, all of the winning walkers would witness the play of "The Still Alarm." Each pedestrian would occupy a box, which would be appropriately draped with his national colours, which his name and record was emblazoned on the front of.

The story of Alf Prater re-emerged in an amusing article found in the *Atlanta Constitution* dated the 15th of May:
THE MOUNTAIN WONDER: Believed to Be In the City, But Diligent Search Fails to Find Him.

Wild rumors filled the air last night that Alfred Prater, the mountain wonder, had returned to the city. A reporter took the town and made diligent search for the great walkist. All the haunts which it was Mr. Prater's want to frequent before he left for the metropolis were visited, people about the depot were closely questioned, the police were interviewed - and even the hackmen were interrogated - but the mountain wonder was not found.

Intimate friends of Mr. Prater stated that they had heard of his return to the city, had heard also of his giving as a reason for not winning the race that he grew very sick at the stomach early in the action, and was compelled to abandon the sawdust arena. Other intimate friends made bold to say that if the great pedestrian was really in the city he was hiding out from the newspaper men, as an interview under all the circumstances would prove quite painful to Mr. Prater, however interesting a talk with him in the prints might be to the public.

As Mr. Prater remarked with a flourish of triumph that he would win the race or be brought back to Atlanta a dead man, it was thought that his remains, stowed away in a neat pine coffin, might have come in on a late train. Inquiry was made at the various undertaker shops, but no such corpse had materialized.

Railroad attaches around the depot were confident that no stiff of a departed pedestrian had shown up during the day. It may be that the corpse was put off at Oakland and buried "darkly at dead of night with the lanterns dimly burning," but it was too late to take a turn in the graveyard when the search was being made.

But, after all, the best opinion would seem to be that the mountain wonder is in the city, that he is not only alive but kicking himself in some sequestered nook of the corporation, where the weary tread of the policeman never treads or the eagle glance of a reporter never glances.

Or, it may possibly be that Prater has "gone fishing." Some slight ground for this belief may be gleaned from the fact that one of his intimate friends, in answer to a question cutely observed "Prater hain't here, I don't think, but if he is here he's out on there Chattyhoochy river a-fishin."

Then on the 19th in the same newspaper, the saga of Alf Prater continued...**PRATER'S BACKER BACK: Mr. Charles Treadwell Tells the Story of Prater's Walk.**

Mr. Charles Treadwell, Prater's backer in the walking match at New York, returned to the city yesterday at twelve o'clock from the metropolis. Mr. Treadwell is in splendid health and spirits and gave a CONSTITUTION man a cordial welcome at his furniture house in Marriatta Street yesterday afternoon.

"Glad to see you back."

"And I am glad to get back."

"Had a good time, I suppose?"

"Oh, splendid, splendid!"

"How about Prater's walk? What was the matter?"

"Well I'll give you the whole truth about it. But first let me say that I was very much surprised that THE CONSTITUTION did not receive my special telegram of nine pages which, I sent the night of the 7th. It contained a full statement of Prater's walk. I handed it in at the telegraph office in New York and thought that it would certainly be forwarded."

"It was not received."

"No, I guess they didn't send it to you. I am at a loss to know why because that telegram set Prater right. You see the trip was something entirely new to Prater. He had never been north before, and what he saw naturally excited him. On the way up he was constantly exclaiming at what he saw and heard, and when we crossed the bay at Baltimore with the full train of cars on the boat, Prater could contain himself no longer, but, with, his eyes wide open with wonder, exclaimed "WELL THIS DO SETTLE IT!"

Every thing seemed to excite him and by the time we got to New York, his nervous system was almost unstrung. The excitement together with the cold weather coming upon him so short a time before be entered the race, worked directly against him."

"The weather was cold?"

"Very. It was as cold as it is in Atlanta in midwinter and Prater was not used to walking in any such weather. I had thought that the weather would be pleasant at this time of the year, but the same cold snap which visited Atlanta about the time the match opened in New York with great intensity, Prater was not acclimated. The truth is that he should have gone to New York six weeks before the race to have equal advantages with the other walkers."

"About the walk?"

"Well, Prater went on, and for the first three hours be made the very best walk on the track, despite all the disadvantages which I have mentioned."

"Who handled Prater?"

"Thomas F. Delaney, a professional trainer and runner, Mr. G. B. Beadwell and my self took care of him and we went in to win, but the severity of the weather was against him. The scene, too, was very much against him. There he was at Madison Square garden with myriads of arched lights overhead, so dazzling that you could not distinguish a man across the garden - the place packed with people and almost every man smoking. Of course Prater was not accustomed to this and he got sick – but still he kept bravely on, and as I said before, for three hours made the best run on the track, never once making a break in his dog-trot. About 5 o'clock in the afternoon he became terribly cramped in the stomach, but he was full of grit, and would have DIED ON THE TRACK if we had not concluded to take him off. There was no give up in Prater. He acted on the dead square and did his level best. But under all the circumstances we thought it better to withdraw him from the race and did so. I can safely say that Prater made the best race on the track considering his exhaustion, his long journey, which was enough to undo him in itself, to say nothing of the cold weather which made so much against him."

Those words had hardly fallen from Mr. Treadwell's lips when a shadow fell athwart the doorway and a small man in a light suit gave a yell of joy and bounded into the store.

It was Alf Prater. He was so overwhelmed with delight at once more seeing his backer that he stood before him for FULLY TEN SECONDS without speaking a word, his eyes dilating, his whole face beaming with unutterable pleasure. He then, caught Mr. Treadwell around the neck with both arms and drawing him closely to his breast, kissed him on the cheek as rapturously as a maiden ever kissed her lover. Then he hugged him so vigorously that it looked as if he never intended to go to into any other business.

Prater was certainly the happiest man in the world. He looked it and he was sincere. When he recovered his power of speech he turned to the smiling crowd and said.

"That man," pointing to Mr. Treadwell, "has been more than a father to me. No use in talking, he's my daddy, and I'd die for him a heap quicker than I'd die for myself," and then he sat down by his backer and hugged, him again in a transport of joy, "I just love this man," said Alf; "you don't know how good he's been to me,"

"That's all right," said Mr. Treadwell, laughing, "You are a good boy, Alf, and certainly deserved all that was done for you. It wasn't your fault that you did not get there. You did the best that could be done under the circumstances and the people will know it."

"How did you like your trip from New York to Savannah on the boat?"

"Bully! Bully but, I tell you, I was sick oh, so sick. I wasn't used to the sea, you see and got so sick that I haven't got over it yet," and as Mr. Prater uttered these words his face suddenly changed expression, and for fully half a minute he looked like the sickest man, that ever staggered to the side of a ship."

On the 20th of May, the victor sailed for England from New York on the Inman liner, the *City of Chester*. On the 29th of May it was reported that the ship arrived at Queenstown the day before, and it was expected that Littlewood would arrive in Sheffield early in the afternoon, probably about two o'clock. Many of his friends assembled at the city's Victoria Station to give him a welcome. On the same date, the *Sheffield Telegraph* reported: He claims that he could have beaten the record had not his became swollen and inflamed with rheumatism. He will probably meet Scott, the Australian champion, in England, and return to the States in the autumn to run any man in the world.

Accompanied by his trainer Fred Bromley, the man himself duly arrived in Liverpool at 09:30 after the ten-day voyage. The early part of the trip home saw rough weather but the passage became smoother as the ship neared the British Isles. Having been met at Liverpool by their wives and George's mother, sister and Mrs. T. Dickinson, the party boarded the Liverpool to Sheffield *"fast express train"* at two o'clock and reached Victoria station at ten minutes to four. *"By four o'clock there was no computing the crowd in attendance and a strong body of police, under the charge of Inspector Bridgman, were dispatched to keep order."* They were all met on arrival on the platform by his father Fred Littlewood, his brother in law, Mr. T. Dickenson and Mr. Joe Dixon of the George Inn, Saville Street East, who was one of his principal supporters in Sheffield. Other sporting personalities and some of the privileged few were also allowed on the platform to shake hands with the champion. The great man himself appeared in excellent condition and was bronzed from his trip over the *"herring pond."*

As the party walked over the bridge towards the station exit, they were greeted with an incredible din as the famous ped left the station. The cheering crowds had gathered in and around the square in front of the station and had lined the footpaths along the approach road stretching as far as the wholesale markets. When the cheers eventually subsided, the Druids brass band struck up a "See the Conquering Hero Comes," and headed a procession in front of two open wagonettes, upon the first of which a man carried a Union Jack. A third wagon, laden with enthusiastic admirers joined in the fun, followed by a coal wagon decorated with a banner and numerous other horse drawn vehicles; lumbering wheel drays tagged on behind. All made their way out of the station surrounded by the excited crowds of well wishers.

The route home took the procession by Exchange Street, Castle Street, Snig Hill and West Bar to the Red Lion public house in Gibraltar Street. All the way the crowds lined footpaths and cheered the returning athlete. The traffic in West Bar stopped, and at the narrower parts of the route, the police had difficulty in regulating it. After a short stay at the pub, the procession continued to the George Inn on Saville Street where there was a *"gay display of flags."* Here Littlewood went upstairs, and as he waved to the cheering crowd from an upper window, he thanked them for their welcome. After an hour he left for the Bridge Inn on Newhall Road, Brightside Lane, for many years kept by his father-in-law Mr. C. Chapman, and this is where he stayed for the night.

In a subsequent interview, Littlewood complained of the hardness of the track in New York, describing it as the worst ever he had run on. It appears that the loam was above the tan bark instead of under it and for a few days after the contest his feet duly suffered from the battering they had received. Indeed he mentioned that they were still causing him trouble, going on to describe a *"slight"* strain in his hip during the race. He went on to say that he might go back to the United States in September or October to try and make the 650 miles he always knew he could accomplish. However, he stated that he and his backer were willing to enter a sweepstake of between £1,000 and £10,000 a side to run any man in the world, and that if this happened, he would not revisit America.

He was asked if he would be involved in any competitions at home before then and replied no; with reference to a match with the Australasian champion, he said that Joe Scott should have accepted his challenge when issued. He did say he was treated very well abroad and mentioned about the Union Jack being twined over the box he occupied in the New York theatre he was invited to attend after his win.

The winner with 611 miles in six days!

George Littlewood

(Illustration no: 117)

CHAPTER 58

Joe Scott

Joe Scott, the son of John and Hannah Scott, who was born in Lettermacaward, County Donegal, Ireland, possibly in January of 1862, moved to Dunedin, New Zealand, when he was a young boy after his family had initially emigrated to the state of Victoria, Australia. He would later become a boot maker at the age of 13 in Dunedin, but it was before this that Alfred Austin, a sports handicapper in the field of athletics, got to know him and began to train him with the aim that one day, he would become a professional walker.

He made his first public appearance in a two-mile handicap walk at the Caledonian Sports gathering of 1874 in Dunedin. Although he was disqualified for breaking into a run, the performance of the *"plucky little fellow,"* who was apparently just three feet six inches tall, and who weighed under four stones, was said to be *"astonishing."* He was presented to the governor, Sir James Fergusson, who said to him, "Bravo little man. Well walked indeed. Some day you will be champion of the world." Of the young wonder, the *Otago Witness* on January the 10th 1874 wrote:
A little fellow named Scott, aged 12½ years, was entered for all the matches, and even contested with such a veteran as McGregor. His speed and powers of endurance were marvellous, and in the Handicap Walking Race of two miles, he came in first, beating McGregor, Campbell and J. Spence. Of course, he had a considerable start–220 yards from scratch–but on even terms almost he would have beaten his opponents. Unfortunately, a protest was entered against him in this race, on the ground of breaking when passing McGregor, so that it is doubtful whether he will get the prize. The spectators cheered the plucky little fellow most enthusiastically, and after each race he was carried shoulder high. At the conclusion of the sports, he was brought on the grandstand and exhibited for a few minutes to all who were present, and was loudly cheered.

1875

On Tuesday, the 6th of July 1875, the *"13 years and seven months old,"* 4st.8lbs Scott walked 25 miles around the Queens Theatre in Dunedin on a track measuring 56 yards, 2 feet and 3 inches, or 31 laps to the mile, the course being around the stalls and greater part of the pit in a time of 4h.47m. The next day he made 18 miles at the same venue in 3h.26m. After the trial, he was observed to appear *"quite fresh."* Arrangements were already being made for the young lad to attempt to beat William Edward's time of walking 100 miles in 23h.55m, which the Australian pedestrian had made at the Drill Shed in Dunedin during the previous month between Friday, the 18th and Saturday, the 19th of June (See Chapter 3).

Later that week, after his trainer Austin announced that the boy Scott would walk 100 miles around the Queens Theatre, arrangements were made to facilitate the attempt by Joe to tackle the task of beating Edward's time between Friday, the 9th and Saturday, the 10th. Scott could have used the same venue that Edwards had accomplished his feat which had been on a level surface and 25 laps to the mile, but instead, chose the Queens Theatre because that facility was warmer than the Drill Shed. The course at the theatre had five corners, four of them were very sharp with a rise of about 2 feet *"walking up about 30 feet on one side, and a similar fall in coming down on the other. The opinion of those who walked with Scott by turns while he was accomplishing his task, was that the sharp corners, and the rise and fall in level were as bad as ten miles added to the journey."*

At 17:00 on Friday afternoon, the wee laddie set off on his journey into the unknown. Could the young boy really accomplish the task that he, or perhaps his astute trainer, had set for him?

The first five miles were made in 58 minutes, 10 miles in 1h.57m, 15 miles in 2h.57m, 20 miles in 3h.58m, and 40 miles in 4h.59m. The boy then had a rest of 25 minutes during which time he was given a warm bath *"which brought him round."* A further rest of half an hour was taken when fifty miles were made in 10h.52m. Thereafter, everything went smoothly in front of the large attending crowd until the 92nd mile when he was attacked with cramp in the legs. Shaking this off, he continued on his way. Although tripping over the carpet and falling down during his 97th mile, he finally accomplished his task at 16:42:30 completing his journey in two and a half minutes under Edward's time, his last mile being made in 10m.54s. After time was called, he was carried shoulder high around the place. Joe Scott was indeed the boy wonder! *"A handsome silver cup"* was later bought for him to display on the sideboard at home.

Finally on Tuesday, the 7th of September, a seven-mile match for £50 a side took place at the Dunedin Drill Shed between Edwards, who had been training under the direction of trainer Reece at Mosgiel, and Scott who had been preparing locally. Due to the track not being big enough to accommodate the two men, Edwards was the first man to occupy the course setting off just after eight o'clock in the evening and eventually making the distance in 61m.11s.

Satisfied with his time, Edwards was confident that he could not be beaten, and this view was supported by many watching the proceedings. Scott, who set off some minutes after nine o'clock, went about his work with determination and wasn't the least put off when to groans from the crowd, Edwards appeared at the trackside, complaining to the judges that the boy was running and not walking. "Objection overruled!" was the judge's decision.

Scott went on to win the money, which was paid over the following night at the Empire Hotel for a time of 60m.26½s. He was carried home, accompanied by a fife and drum band, whilst Edwards continued to protest to the judges, stating that Scott's *"action"* wouldn't be allowed in London; the officials dismissing his appeal with utter disdain.

1879

A 24-hour *"walking match"* for the "Championship of the Colonies," commenced on a 22 laps to the mile track at Garrison Hall, Dunedin, on Friday, the 28th of November 1879. There were 500 people in the building to give the nine competitors a cheer after a word from Alfred Austin about their conduct on the track. Mr. J. McGregor, the starter, then got the lads who wore easily recognisable coloured costumes, on their way. Brooks, who led the contestants after a mile, maintained his lead until he had covered 76 miles at 12:30 when he was disqualified for unfair walking by the judge after being repeatedly warned about his gait. Henderson, with a score of 79 led the ever diminishing field at 14:00 with a mile lead over Drummond, who in turn, led Scott by a mile. Three hours later, Scott took the lead, and due to the retirement of the rest of the field, finished the course at 22:00 with a remarkable score of 106 miles. Joe's performance was quite incredible considering the fact that during the afternoon he had to leave the race for a couple of hours due to suffering from diorreah, and despite that ailment, was still able to put in a 12-minute mile to finish off the day. Joe actually completed his century at 21:31, but given the incentive of earning a silver cup to carry on, did so, and made the six miles in 29 minutes. Henderson, who came in second with 91, finished five miles in front of Drummond. Brooks registered the next best score with 76 and he was followed by Malcolm with 60. Delaney, West, Allen and Hegarty were the other competitors, and their scores were 52, 47, 23, and 22 respectively.

A journalist later wrote of the winner: *"Scott is, without doubt, one of the most extraordinary pedestrians this or any other country has produced. He is only sixteen, and presents an exceedingly juvenile appearance, no hair being apparent on his face, and his full muscular development being not nearly attained. He stands about 5ft 6in in height, and weighs, as nearly as possible, 7st.10lb. Unlike the general run of men who submit themselves to the severest tests of endurance Scott carries no worn or haggard look; but, on the contrary, is fresh complexioned and rather jaunty than otherwise."*

1880

Scott was described as being about 7st.6lbs, and a little over 16 years old when he commenced his attempt to walk 112 miles in 24 hours at the skating rink in Christchurch at 10 p.m. on Friday night, the 17th of January. To help him achieve his objective, a couple of other *"well known peds,"* O'Connor of Timaru, and Swan of Christchurch, had been hired to take it in turns to accompany him for the first couple of hours on the asphalt flooring; this being a bit of a worry for his trainer, as Joe had never performed on that type of surface before.

A nine-minute break at 03:02 was followed by an unfortunate accident at 06:47 when, after leaving the track for a short time, the boy tripped over as he re-entered the ring causing an unexpected delay of eight minutes as his trainer attended to him. He was thereafter taken over to the Commercial Hotel for a 40-minute break where a bath had been prepared for him. It was there that two large blisters were found, one on each foot, and these had apparently been caused from the constant pounding on the hard surface, despite the *"precaution of placing India rubber on his heels by his trainer."*

Scott's half-time score was 55 miles, and during the start of his 87th mile around 17:20, he had to leave the track for a period of 1h.10m which put to rest all chance of completing the feat on time. When the finish was called at 10 p.m. his score for the 24 hours was 103 miles and 800 yards. A total of 1,560 people had paid to see him perform during the two days.

Three weeks later, the *Wellington Evening Post* was advertising Scott's second attempt to make 112 miles in a day.

ARCADE! ARCADE!

FRIDAY NIGHT NEXT, 6TH FEB.

Y O U N G   S C O T T,

YOUNG SCOTT,

Holder of the Champ Belt of New Zealand and cups value £200, in his Great Feat,

112 MILES IN 24 HOURS!

Young Scott will start at 10 p.m. Friday, and finish, 10 p.m. Saturday.

Previous to his starting, a SEVEN MILE HANDICAP, open to all amateurs, for Silver Cup, value £5, will start at 8 o'clock. Entrances close on Wednesday. Cup in Kohn's, jeweller, window, with certificate of value.

Before the start, the 1,500 people who were in the building were being entertained by a band which had been employed to *"enliven the proceedings."* Mr. N. Marchant, C. E., who measured the track, issued a certificate authenticating his findings, and Messrs. Kohn and Co. of Lambton Quay lent the clock which would be used to *"mark the time."*

Scott made his appearance a few minutes before ten o'clock accompanied by Austin, and commenced his walk at the advertised time on a 23 laps to the mile track at the venue in Manners Street, Wellington. Going along at a brisk 5½ mph pace, *"His style is well calculated to impress one with the idea of staying, as he carries his body in a good position, neither too far forward nor too far back, accompanies the movements of his legs by an easy counterpoising swing of the arms, and betraying none of the jerky action of the hips which disfigures the going of so many heel and toe performers, gets over the ground very fast in a graceful and effective manner."*

King of the Peds

Scott covered 10 miles at 11:47, 20 miles at 01:45, took a rest of 8 minutes at 03:00, made 30 miles at 03:45, 40 miles at 05:58, 50 miles at 07:57, and stopped 20 minutes for breakfast at 08:30. He had scored 53 miles by 9 o'clock, and at "half-time," had made 58 miles and 90 yards. At 11:00, he had walked 62 miles and 160 yards, and then went on to make 70 miles at 12:42. *"The lad is a total abstainer, and his diet, although scrupulously plain, is a most generous one. When at work, the lad invariably has an excellent appetite, and a prominent feature in his performances is that he finishes a long distance walk with the same freedom of stride and erect carriage as he shows at the commencement."*

By 7 o'clock, when he had finished 95 miles, it was pretty clear that he wouldn't be able to accomplish the 112 within the time stipulated. However, there was still a chance that he would beat Edward's record of 108 miles which he managed at 21:55, winding up with a splendid spurt of a quarter of a mile. During those last few miles, *"Young Joe"* walked his 100th mile in a shade over nine minutes, which turned out to be his fastest mile. About 1,000 people witnessed the conclusion of the exhibition, and it was estimated that 3,000 had paid the admission price during the two evenings. Immediately after his retirement, he was examined by Dr. Gillon, who dispatched the following report to the press:

Wellington Hospital, 7th February, 1880.

"I examined Scott immediately on the cessation of his 108 miles walk, and found him to be apparently not much distressed. His face was pale, his eyes very much dilated, and his sense of vision good. The temperature of his body, taken at the axilla registered 98.4 Fahrenheit with a pulse of 92, and 25 respirations to the minute. The heart's action was quite regular, the sounds being rather indistinct. The sensibility of his skin was unaffected, but the muscles of the legs were slow in responding to stimulus. He was able to converse quite well. His skin was in a moderate perspiration." — G. GORE GILLON.

A total of 2,834 people paid to watch Scott accomplish his objective of walking 112 miles in 34 hours between Friday and Saturday, the 26th and 27th of June. In fact, young Joe went one mile better, walking his 113th and last mile alone, having been accompanied by a host of local pedestrians during the attempt. The timing of the feat which took place at the Garrison Hall in Dunedin was administered by the Caledonian Society who appointed all the timekeepers. His penultimate mile was made in 9m.45s and his final mile was scored in 10m.11s, with the whole distance being completed in 23h.55m.41s. Joe's 24-hour performance is summarised below.

Hour	Miles	Laps	Hour	Miles	Laps
23:00	5	15	11:00	63	18
00:00	11	7	12:00	68	11
01:00	16	20	13:00	73	0
02:00	22	3	14:00	77	0
03:00	27	3	15:00	81	17
04:00	31	19	16:00	86	4
05:00	37	2	17:00	90	14
06:00	41	12	18:00	94	17
07:00	46	0	19:00	100	3
08:00	51	0	20:00	104	5
09:00	54	19	21:00	108	13
10:00	59	10	22:00	113	0

1881

Joe married Isabella Rachel Jarvis at Dunedin on the 8th of December 1881.

1883

At 10 p.m., on the evening of Friday, the 5th of October, after the Rev. C. A. Byng had addressed the crowd which consisted of about 500 spectators, Scott of Dunedin, and Edwards of New South Wales, began their long awaited 24-hour walking competition on the 22 laps to the mile track at the Garrison Hall, Dunedin.

After initially leading the race till 04:00, the tables were turned on the Australian as the younger Scott asserted his superiority and began to slowly increase the distance between them until 10:00, when he had four miles to the advantage. Scott, who was clearly in much better shape than his opponent, was brought off the track for a 1h.45m rest in the afternoon by his trainer, thus allowing Edwards to get as close as three miles from him. When Scott completed his 100 miles at 19:40, Edwards was on a score of 93 miles and the match finished on time with the leader rushing round the path to complete his victory with a score of 111 miles to 104.6.

A young Joe Scott stood in front of his trophies.
Photograph with permission of the NZ Sports Hall of Fame (Illustration no: 118)

At the presentation at the Princess Theatre on the following Monday night, Edwards told the gathered audience, " Ladies and gentlemen, it is a long time since I had the mortification of coming before the public a beaten man, and I do not like it at all, I can assure you. Nevertheless I have been beaten on this occasion, horribly beaten, on my merits, and I am man enough to own it. But I should like to say a word as to the circumstances of my defeat. In the first place, during the early part of the match I was suffering from slight indisposition, but besides this I held Scott altogether too cheap. I do not wish to detract for a moment from the grand performance he is capable of doing. I do not believe, in fact, that there is a man south of the line that could beat Scott for twenty-four hours; but still I may be allowed to say that I held him much too cheap. Nevertheless I hope you will look over my defeat and in the next contest this week I may hope to reverse matters. I wish to say that I always walk, and always throughout my career have walked, to win; and when I am beaten, I am beaten on my merits."

On the evening of the following Thursday, the 11th of October, a large number of people gathered at the same venue to witness the start of the 48-hour walking match—again between the pair. The conditions of the contest were understood to be the same as on the previous occasion; Scott's trainer, Mr. Austin offered Edwards £100 to defeat his man with a percentage of the gate money being offered to Edwards for expenses. This would be Scott's first ever 48-hour race, and based on Edward's experience in longer distances, the latter was the favourite to win.

Both men matched each others pace until Scott began suffering from a touch of dysentery at about 10 a.m. This caused him to go much slower, but after pluckily fighting against his ailment, he was able to make up the lost distance three hours later, and as the Australian rested, the Kiwi went ahead by a mile. The men continued to be on close terms thereafter during the rest of the day, and when Edwards went to his bed at 23:12, he had scored 115 miles. Scott however, stayed on the track, finishing his 25 hours and 35 minutes work two miles ahead of his rival.

The younger man, wearing a thick jumper and heavy overcoat due to the bitingly cold conditions, was back in the ring at 03:30 on the last day of the contest. He was followed by his rival a few minutes later. The second placed man, despite his best efforts, wasn't able to gather in the miles lost to his opponent the previous evening. Edwards had assumed that Scott would stay in bed longer, and that by making an earlier start than the New Zealander, he would retrieve the lost distance. However, as he made his way round, he must have realised that his opponent would make it very difficult for him to get back on terms; this proved to be the case as there was always a two to three-mile gap between the pair during the day. At 20:00, the score stood: **Scott, 183.20; Edwards, 182.2:** Half an hour later it was: **Scott, 186.5; Edwards, 184.15:**

Near the northern end of the building under the platform, a number of boys were standing applauding the contestants when Edwards suddenly stopped and bashed John Miles, a 14-year-old boy, in the face cutting his cheek and blackening his right eye. Miles stated that he offered no provocation for the assault, saying that he had shouted, "Go it Joe," towards Scott, "He's beaten you," at Edwards. *"The crowd, fortunately, did not rush the track and prevent the match being concluded upon its merits, but it is not surprising that Edwards was loudly hooted for several subsequent laps."* What was of some concern though, was that at about the same stage in the previous contest the week before, Edwards had stopped in his tracks and walloped another spectator in the face, this time with a wet handkerchief.

Scott in the end held on to his slender lead, winning the race with a score of 192.16 to Edwards 191 miles. The Australian's score was almost ten miles better than he had accomplished before with his best previous distance, being 181 miles and 1,360 yards. After the conclusion of the race, it was made known that a number of gentlemen were seeing to it that Scott would be presented with a belt for winning the two events.

The advertisement below was being displayed in the Christchurch *Star* a day or so before the match between the pair started in that city at 10 p.m. on Thursday, the 25th of October 1883.

NEW PUBLIC HALL, TUAM STREET,

THURSDAY, FRIDAY & SATURDAY NEXT.

AUSTRALIA V. NEW ZEALAND.

The Great Forty Eight Hour Walk.

EDWARDS

v.

SCOTT,

FOR £100

Previous to the start of Edwards and Scott (by request of the local Pedestrians), there will be a Half-hour's "Go-as-you-please," in place of Boxing; this race will start at 8 o'clock. Edwards and Scott will start at 10.

Admission 1s.

An 80 yards circular track which was covered with matting had been *"marked off"* in preparation for the race on the floor of the hall, and a temporary bar presided over by Mr. G. S. Marshall, of the Terminus Hotel, had been erected in the centre of the room. The City Guards Band had been hired and positioned in the gallery to play to the crowd at intervals during the evening, and notices prohibiting smoking had been posted in various parts of the hall.

The race started as advertised in front of 300 people. After the first hour, Edwards, with 5 miles and 5 laps, was 2 laps ahead of Scott.

On the next day, Friday at 15:00, the score was: **Scott, 81.16; Edwards, 81.5:** Up to that point, the leader had been off the track for 69½ minutes as opposed to Edwards who had rested for a minute and a half more. The local man was the first of the pair to complete the big 100, which he made at 19:34. Edwards followed suit ten minutes later.

Later that day at 23:00, Scott maintained his slim advantage over the visitor with a score of 117.2 to 116.8, and eight minutes after those scores were recorded, the Australian went to bed, having made 117 miles. His opponent waited till three minutes after midnight until he retired for the night and at that time he was exactly five miles ahead.

Edwards was first man back on the path at 02:58, and he was joined by his opponent 52 minutes later. As the morning progressed, Edwards was able to make up the deficit, and both men were all square at 12:30. By 13:15, he led Scott by 157 to 156.14.

During the evening, and in front of a crowd of 3,000 people, *"The two men who had been pacing the strip of matting laid round the hall for two days and nights, with less than nine hours' intermission were still walking at a brisk pace, with scarcely any perceptible sign of exertion though some persons thought Scott's eyes were rather bloodshot, and the Australian champion passed his hand across his brow and pushed up his moustache more frequently than he had done before."*

The excitement increased as the finish approached, with Edwards occasionally spurting and passing Scott, who, maintained his stereotypical steady pace. Towards the end of the last hour Scott gamely responded to his opponent's challenge, thwarting all efforts to pass him. Scott was definitely the crowd's favourite, and although they cheered Edwards as he gradually increased his lead, they were far more vociferous in their applause when the little fellow took any form of advantage.

With Edwards managing to maintain the mile advantage he had secured for himself an hour before the finish, the Australian eventually won the contest with a score of 192.16, to Scott's 191.15. At the conclusion of the match, there were loud calls for both competitors to make an appearance, but neither responded. Mr. Seymour said the competitors were too tired and thanked the public for their attendance, adding that the stakes would be handed over on Monday night at Richardson's Hotel.

1885

The 24-hour walking contest arranged between Arthur Hancock (the 50-mile champion of England) and Joe Scott which was to have taken place at the Garrison Hall, Dunedin, between Friday and Saturday, the 16th and 17th of January, had to be postponed till Friday the 23rd of the same month, owing to the Englishman having met with a slight accident which caused him to give up training. Whilst he rested, his future opponent was readying himself for the encounter on the main road between Dunedin and Palmerston, the effort in doing so bringing the local lad down to a racing weight of about 8st.2lb.

The conditions of the match were that if Hancock should be victorious, he would receive £100 and 15% of the gate money, but if he lost, *"the takings would go to Scott."*

Joe started the match with a considerable disadvantage, having learned earlier in the day that his father had died; the dreadful news coming within days of his mother also passing away.

After shaking hands, the men were sent on their journey by Mr. Wilson. Hancock, *"of pleasing appearance, of stouter build than Scott, and weighing about 10st.,"* started the match with his arm wrapped up in a bandage. *"He seemed to walk with much greater exertion than Scott, and very quickly got into a state of perspiration. This was probably the result of the greater pace he kept up at the start, and the great amount of arm and hip action which he maintains. His stride is considerably shorter than Scott's, and the excessive hip action which he indulges in gives his walk a kind of waddling appearance."*

Hancock went off into the lead after a few laps attempting to increase his advantage during the third mile. The effort proved fruitless however, as Scott responded to the pressure, and there was much excitement in the building as the two men entertained the crowd by passing and re-passing each other. *"Scott was evidently just having a quiet bit of fun with his opponent, and during the lap of the third mile he dropped in the rear with a good humoured smile on his face, and began plodding along at his ordinary pace."* Thereafter Arthur began to pull away from Joe, but after six hours of competition, the Kiwi passed him. Hancock kept up well for the next six hours, but when the pair had done about 68 miles, and with Hancock three quarters of a mile behind, he began to lose touch with the leader.

The match eventually resulted in an easy win for Scott who made 114 miles *"comfortably"* in the time allocated, the English raider giving up as he trailed his opponent by 7.2 after making his century. At the time, he wasn't in good health, evidently walking along in a state of distress all of Saturday afternoon, due to a couple of swellings under his arm and groin.

Scott, by his performance, had equalled his best previous record and was in no way pushed or distressed. An announcement was made after the end of the race that the men would probably meet again in three weeks time in a 12-hour walk for £100 a side.

Before the second match took place between them, a *"pedestrian exhibition, arranged as a benefit"* for Scott took place at the Garrison Hall between Friday, the 31st of January, and Saturday, the 1st of February. The two days featured races between local pedestrians who competed against each other at varying distances. One of the races, which was a 24-hour walking match between Brooks, Crofts, Johnson (the Tasmanian) and Swan was won by the latter, who covered a similar distance to Scott in his last race, but in ten minutes less time. Joe gave an exhibition of his powers during the evening.

King of the Peds

The promised 12-hour walking match began at 11:00 on Saturday, February the 21st on a 22 laps to the mile track. A good deal of money changed hands before the event with Hancock being the favourite to get the money. Messrs. J. Wain, J. Macgregor and T. Cornish acted as judges, and Mr. G. Dowse was the referee. Hancock weighed 10st.7lb as against Scott's 7st.13½lb.

For the first two hours Hancock walked at the rate of 7 mph, *"hoping to burst Scott up,"* but he never got more than three quarters of a mile ahead. After four hours, Hancock, who was *"beginning to fag,"* was joined by his adversary at 16:00, but after an hour or two, went a few laps ahead again after the Kiwi appeared distressed. However, at eight o'clock, Scott rallied and later took a lead of half a mile just before 21:00. Thereafter, and realising the futility of the exercise, Hancock left the track altogether on a score of 59.14. Scott continued to walk on amid a good deal of enthusiasm and covered 68.14.

On March the 28th 1885, the *Otago Witness* produced the following article: In reference to J. Scott's challenge to walk anyone in the world from twelve to twenty four hours, the Melbourne Sportsman says: - Here, then, is a show for some of our Colonial long distance pedestrians. Should there be no response from the Colonies, someone will surely reply from England or America. A match of this kind would be interesting as affording some information as to the correctness of the distances of the long distance walkers are credited with. O'Leary, for instance while in the Colonies failed to get any way near the distances be is alleged to have covered.

The first in a series of races, a 50-mile walking match for £100, and the *"championship of the world,"* between Hancock and Scott, began at 15:00 on Monday, the 27th of July 1885 at the Garrison Hall in Dunedin. Both men were said to be in *"the pink of condition,"* with Hancock weighing in at 10st.4lb and his diminutive opponent tipping the scales at 8st.5lb.

During the first mile, Hancock secured a lead of one lap which he maintained throughout the race, except for when Scott got within half a lap of him on the 22-lap to the mile course. Hancock won the money in a time of 8h.8m.

A 12-hour contest between the pair then took place at the same venue a couple of weeks later on Monday, the 11th of August. In front of about 100 spectators, Mr. Gourley, the starter, referring to the shabby treatment that Hancock had received at the hands of the public in the previous contest, asked for the winner of this race not to be treated in a similar manner before sending them on their way at 11:00.

The competitors, who were going round together at an average speed of 6 mph, clocked up 25 miles at 14:50, and slowing down later, 50 miles at 19:06. The two men battled for the lead with Scott gaining the upper hand at 22:10 when he went a quarter of a lap in front. Pluckily though, Hancock caught him back up and stuck with him until, with just five minutes to go, Scott pulled away again. However, there was drama to follow because as the seconds approached for the end of the race, Mr. Dowse's pistol misfired and that meant the peds carried on walking. "Time!" was called from the stands, and on that signal, the track was occupied by the crowd which in the process, knocked the Englishman down. After a great deal of confusion, and much discussion by the judges, Scott was called the winner, despite protests in the audience that Hancock had been the victim of *"unfair play."* Both men, who had stuck together like glue during the race, scored 72 miles and 8 laps.

Arthur Hancock never turned up for his 3rd match, a 24-hour event against Scott in Dunedin, which was scheduled to take place on Friday, the 27th of August, *"having decided not to go in consequence of the rough treatment he received during the last match."* With, or without Hancock accompanying him on the track, Scott was determined to break the *24-hour walking record of 127 miles and 1,210 yards created by Billy Howes. He was already £50 richer following the Englishman's withdrawal and had nothing to lose, but plenty to gain.

*This record was probably broken in the 26-hour "Champion of England" race at the Agricultural Hall, Islington, between Friday and Saturday, February the 22nd and 23rd 1878, when Howes walked 129 miles in 24h.20m (See Chapter 13).

Scott set off in front of a well patronised hall and with all guns blazing, managed to set a new 100-mile world *walking* record when he covered that distance in 17h.59m, his time being almost 8 minutes better than Howes's at the same juncture (18h.7m.57s). Due to the fast pace made in achieving the record, Scott then suffered from one of his familiar ailments during the effort, nausea, (the other two being vomiting and diorreah) causing him to make just one mile in the next hour due to an enforced rest. Had he been alright, he would have beaten the record easily, as in the end, he made 125 miles.

Below is Scott's scoring record:

Hour	Miles	Laps	Hour	Miles	Laps
Midnight	6	14	12:00	75	10
01:00	13	6	13:00	81	0
02:00	19	11	14:00	85	6
03:00	25	11	15:00	89	5
04:00	30	1	16:00	94	14
05:00	36	0	17:00	100	0
06:00	42	11	18:00	101	0
07:00	45	0	19:00	108	0
08:00	53	15	20:00	111	0
09:00	58	12	21:00	115	1
10:00	63	14	22:00	120	0
11:00	68	16	23:00	125	

Joe's spectacular failure was quite remarkable insomuch that Howes had achieved his record on an eight laps to the mile track, whereas the Kiwi had had to contend with one of 22 laps. The other factor that played against the "little fella," was that he had had to compete on his own. These observations were relayed to the crowd in a speech by Mr. F. G. Wheetman, Scott's stakeholder, during which he presented the brave lad with a gold watch and his prize money as he paid tribute to his tenacity and guts.

The advertisement below, again featuring in the Christchurch *Star*, invited the public to attend the next race between the pair on Monday, the 20th of October. With a lot of money to play for, the two men (Scott being the slight favourite to take the spoils) set off at the advertised time. Both went along admirably until Hancock had the misfortune to *"break down"* due to his right foot giving way in his 57th mile after walking 10½ hours. Up until then, Arthur had stuck close to his adversary, both men's performances enthralling the large crowd. Scott, who walked on until he had completed 59 miles at 21:25, left the track with the cheers of the audience ringing in his ears. A local journalist, in awe of what he had witnessed wrote, *"His performance was, without exception, the finest exhibition of pedestrianism we have ever had here."*

Tuam Street Hall,

MONDAY NEXT, OCT. 20.

THE GREAT INTERNATIONAL 12 HOURS' WALK.

HANCOCK		SCOTT
HANCOCK		SCOTT
HANCOCK	V.	SCOTT
HANCOCK		SCOTT
HANCOCK		SCOTT

FOR £500 AND THE 12 HOURS' CHAMPIONSHIP

STAKEHOLDER
C. Hood Williams, Esq.

JUDGES:

A. M. Oliver, Esq. T. R. Jacobson, Esq.

J. Campbell, Esq. J. S. Monck, Esq.

The start will take place at 11 a.m.

Admission – Gallery, 2s 6d; Stage, 5s; reserve on Stage, seats numbered, 10s. These tickets can be obtained from Mr. A. Dunbar, Rotherfield Hotel, until 10 a.m. on Monday, and no tickets are transferable. The public will not be admitted to the Body of the Hall.

1886

Pegasus of *The News of the World* wrote that he had been authorised by Charles Rowell to issue a challenge for both a 12 and 24-hour "go-as-you-please" match against Scott for any sum the latter pleases: If Scott desires it, Rowell is willing to go over to New Zealand and compete with him there accepting reasonable expenses Rowell's great opponent, Littlewood, offers an unconditional acceptance of Scott's challenge. Littlewood is considered our best man, but judging by the reports which have reached us of the New Zealander's prowess; it is thought doubtful whether he will be able to beat Scott.

On Saturday, the 9th of January 1886, Scott failed in his attempt to walk 50 miles in eight hours at the Garrison Hall in Invercargill. He was sent on his way by the judge, Mr. H. Feldwick punctually at 2 p.m. and finished the first hour with a score of seven miles, the ten miles being made in 85m.15s. When time was called however, Joe's final score was 160 yards short of 49 miles. It was announced at the event that Scott was desirous of taking on D. Libeau, the pedestrian from Akaroa for £150 a side. This fact was reiterated in the January 23rd edition of the *Otago Witness*, which added that the 50-mile match would be held at the Caledonian Grounds on the 21st of February, which was oddly enough a Sunday. The stakes had been reduced to £100 in this report. There is no evidence that this match ever took place.

The next that is heard of young Joe was on the 13th of March when he was reported to be in Melbourne, Australia, where he had arranged a six-day match with William Edwards for £200 a side and the *"Championship of Australia."* Thus, between Monday, the 12th and Saturday, the 17th of April, Scott competed against Edwards at the Exhibition Building in Melbourne on a track which was 12 laps to the mile.

On Monday at 22:00 the scores were: **Scott, 93; Edwards, 89:** At the same time on Tuesday, Scott led by: **185 to 182;** and on Wednesday, at midnight, he had increased his lead to eight miles, the leader board showing: **230 to 222.** By Friday Scott had increased his lead even further when he got 16 miles ahead of his opponent.

A large section of the 6,000 strong crowd rushed onto the track to congratulate both men after Scott had beaten his opponent by **424.8 to 406.4.** *"Scott's backers wagered that he could cover six miles in the last hour, which was accomplished with half a mile to spare."*

The two athletes appeared on the stage to rapturous applause from the crowd. The organiser of the contest, Mr. Spofforth, congratulated Scott, but said he would have liked to have seen him pushed further so the public might have a better idea of his speed and quality.

A report on July the 23rd said that Scott had challenged the Victorian pedestrian M. Cann, to walk a 50-mile match for £100 a side.

Exactly a month later, the American, Walter Harriman of Boston, turned up to race against Scott in a six-day *"International Walking Match"* at the Pavilion in Launceston, Tasmania, on Monday, the 23rd of August. Before starting the men on their way at nine minutes past midnight, Professor Miller explained to the attending crowd that Launceston had been selected for the contest because a suitable hall couldn't be found elsewhere.

The 8st.5lb New Zealander immediately went in the lead, and quickly gained a lap on his opponent. Harriman, weighing 13 stones, and who never changed his pace, walked along at a steady 4 mph. Following a yard or two behind him, was the slight figure of Scott who would dog him for a mile or so, then, putting on a spurt, pass him, gain a lap on him during the next four laps, and then slow down for another mile only to repeat the process again. By this strategy, the little Kiwi gained two miles on his giant American opponent in the first 12 hours.

At midnight on Tuesday, the scores were: **Scott, 188; Harriman, 185.22:**

At midday on Wednesday, the scores were: **Scott, 225.4; Harriman, 223:** Later that day at 18:00, the score read: **Scott, 243.16; Harriman, 241.9:** During the last two hours of that third day, Harriman, who was walking at the rate of 5 mph, was desperately trying to reduce Scott's lead, and in the process initiated several spurts during which there was *"considerable excitement."* When the scores were recorded at 23:30, or within half an hour of three days, Scott continued to lead by: **262.16 to 260.2:**

From 9 o'clock on the last morning of the race, both men kept up a 5 mph pace, and by midday, Harriman, who was by then was just under three miles ahead **(Harriman, 410; Scott, 407.6)** of the stiffly walking Scott showed *"no greater signs of fatigue than he did on the second day."*

There were many in the crowd who expected to see Scott make up the distance by employing some of his notorious *"sensational spurts,"* and as the race drew to its finale, he didn't disappoint them, managing to reduce the gap between himself and his opponent, who plodding along at his usual speed, didn't appear unduly worried by the little chap's progress. Scott was loudly cheered by his supporters in the packed building as he gained on the American, who at one stage, walked alongside Scott at a rate of 7 mph for a couple of laps as the band played "Yankee Doodle."

At 11 o'clock, Professor Miller fired a pistol to end the contest amid a good deal of cheering among the 2,000 people who had filled the place. Harriman in the end had held on, securing victory by just one mile, having covered 448.10 laps in the six days.

After the crowd had calmed down, Professor Miller said, "I have much pleasure in announcing Harriman as the winner. The contest was a close one, and I am sure everybody has admired Scott's pluck and the way he has stuck to the track under considerable disadvantages, especially that of having a bad knee." The referee, Mr. Bradshaw, then confirmed the score and paid the highest compliment to Scott for his determined effort. Professor Miller, speaking on behalf of Scott, said that he was prepared to compete in a 50-mile match against Harriman or any man in Australia and furthermore give his opponent a mile start. He also said Scott would race against any man in the world for 50 miles, or for 12 or 24 hours for £100 to £500 a side. He was also willing to indulge in a contest to walk any two men in Launceston for 24 hours, *"one man to start at the expiration of half the time,"* and also to compete against Harriman over 24 hours, 48 hours, three days or a six-day walking match. After three cheers were given for both men who briefly replied, the crowd went home.

On the Tuesday, the 15th of October 1886, it was reported by the *Otago Witness* that: **Joe Scott accomplished the task at walking 125 miles in 26 hours in Latrobe, Tasmania. He intended to try and break the world's record of 130 miles in just 24 hours at Hobart on the 8th inst. He then proceeds to Melbourne to meet Harriman again in a six days' contest.** A week later, on the 22nd of October a further clipping from the *same journal* stated: **Joe Scott finished his self imposed task at Hobart of doing 127 miles in 26 hours in 6 minutes under the time, doing the last mile under 8 minutes. The Hobart Mercury states that Mr. Alfred Lord handed Scott a monetary gift which had been subscribed, and Mr. Webster presented him with a handsome gold medal suitably inscribed from the people of Hobart. Altogether Scott has impressed the Hobart people.**

The six-day walking match at Melbourne referred to above between Scott and Harriman was reduced to 75 hours, and in the end, took place at the Hobart Exhibition Building between Wednesday, the 27th and Saturday, the 30th of October.

King of the Peds

From 8 o'clock until the close, the two pedestrians stuck pluckily to the track, and towards the finish Harriman made the pace *"rather warm."* Scott however, was equal to the occasion, and made several brilliant spurts which placed three additional laps to his record over that of his opponent. *"The building towards the close of the contest was literally packed, and the finish was watched with the utmost enthusiasm."*

The contest was brought to a close by the two competitors leaving the track and ascending the platform, where Mr. Alfred Lord, the referee, announced the result that Scott had won with a final score of 266.5 laps beating Harriman by a mile and 4 laps. After the announcement and *"amid much enthusiasm,"* he then complimented both men on the exhibition of fair heel-and-toe walking they had entertained the spectators with. Calls were made for Scott to make a speech, but he said he wasn't a man of words. Mr. Lord subsequently thanked the crowd for their attendance on his behalf. When Harriman spoke however, he told the large audience that he had been beaten on his merits, to which some wag in the hall shouted, "Never mind, old man, you will beat him next time!"

The 100 sovereigns stakes, inside a silk purse, were paid over to Scott in a presentation ceremony at the Theatre Royal on the following Monday by Mr. W. Webster. Mr. Frank Gerald, on behalf of Messrs. MacMahon and Leitch, then presented Scott with a gold medal, manufactured at Mr. Goulding's establishment. Scott thanked him for the handsome trophy they had presented him. *"Hearing that Harriman was not satisfied with the result of the match, he said he was prepared to walk him again and stake £100 to £70, or give him three miles and walk him for £100 a side. This plucky announcement was received with cheers."*

A 75-hour walking match for £50 a side between Scott and Harriman finished at Hobart on the 27th of November 1886, Scott winning by 271 miles 16 laps as opposed to the American's 269.11. After the race Scott was presented with a handsome wreath of flowers, and J. McGrath announced that he was ready to back Scott against Harriman in a six-day match for £200 a side, with Harriman expressing a desire to accept the offer, providing that the race didn't take place in Hobart.

1887

Then a 24-hour walking match between *Captain Cotton, who would be handled by Austin, Scott's old trainer, and Scott, commenced at 22:00 on Saturday night the 3rd of June 1887 at the Tuam Street Hall in Christchurch. The Captain was given a 10-mile start. Joe, who was being cared for by his new trainer, McGrath, *"was dressed in the usual pedestrian costume, with "Austin's" walking shoes, has filled out a good deal since his last appearance in Christchurch, and if a little less wiry looking, certainly shows more muscle. Captain Cotton, clad in rowing costume, and with ordinary shooting boots, looked wonderfully muscular and well.*

* **"The plucky amateur,"** who had previously walked 100 miles and 380 yards in 23h.5m between Wednesday, the 8th and Thursday, the 9th of September in the previous year, at the Tuam Street Hall, Christchurch, on a track measuring 74 yards, 1 foot and 6½ inches.

At the end of the contest, and in front of between two and three thousand onlookers, the amateur beat the professional with a score of 119.1 (effectively 109.1), to 117.6. The Captain donated his 75% of the gate money to the Little Volunteer Corps, of which he was in command.

The following letter then appeared in the *Otago Witness* on Friday, July the 29th 1887:

Christchurch, July 25th 1887

Kindly allow through the medium of your columns, to accept the repeated challenges of Scott to walk against him for 24 hours in the Garrison Hall, at Dunedin, on Monday and Tuesday, the 15th and 16th of August. Allow me also to say that when I first met him I had not the slightest intention of ever walking again. Circumstances, however, alter cases. But once and for all I distinctly assert that, whether I win or lose, I will not be induced to walk again. The conditions of this match are as follows, viz. That he gives me 10 miles start, and that the winner takes every farthing that may be taken at the gate. If I win, I shall not appropriate any of the gate money, but shall, after deducting expenses, give it to some institution that I consider deserving; if I lose, I shall not take anything for expenses.—I am, &c,

FREDERICK COTTON.

The return match, which was due to take place at the Garrison Hall in Dunedin at 22:00 on Friday, the 26th of June 1887 sensationally *"collapsed in a most remarkable manner."* At the hour that the match should have started, Mr. McGrath, Scott's trainer, standing both next to the costume attired athlete and Mr. Baxter on the platform, addressed the audience and said that about 8 o'clock that evening, Austin, Cotton's trainer, asked him to let his man win the race. McGrath replied that he wouldn't, and that if he wanted to beat Scott he must beat him on his merits. Austin allegedly replied that if McGrath and Scott wouldn't allow Cotton to win, he would get a doctor's certificate. Mr. Baxter then read out a certificate signed by Dr. Ferguson which stated:

"I hereby certify that Captain Cotton is at present suffering from severe indisposition, and in my opinion it would be extremely injudicious for him to attempt to walk any distance until he had recovered."

After Scott had entertained the crowd with an hour's walk, during which he made a half a lap less than seven miles, Austin reacted to the earlier events by issuing the following statement, which was later corroborated by a Mr. D. Keys who was present at the interview.

"The facts regarding my interview with Mr. McGrath this afternoon: Owing to the fact of Captain Cotton becoming unwell to and showing signs of getting so much worse as to be quite unable to attempt the performance of the match, I deemed it advisable to seek a meeting with Mr. McGrath. In the course of conversation, I pointed out that it would be advisable to postpone the match for three or four days until Captain Cotton recovered. Mr. McGrath refused to entertain the idea. I then communicated the conversation to Captain Cotton, and hold him that the match must take place, as the other side objected to a postponement. The physician after careful consideration put a veto on anything of the sort, and supplied a certificate, which was read at the Garrison Hall at 10 P. M."

The match was then re-arranged for the following Tuesday, the 30th, and started promptly after the Captain gave his version of events, informing the attentive crowd that although he was willing to compete, he was unfit to do so and therefore sent his apologies thereafter.

The match was eventually won by Scott, who, in great style, was able to whittle away Cotton's lead until, at last, at 21:00 on Wednesday night he got within half a dozen laps of him. Within 20 minutes when both men were on the 20th lap of the 109th mile, Scott, to rapturous applause from the 1,000 spectators, took the lead and won the match when the Englishman left the race *"dead beat"* with a score of 109.7, the New Zealander then being 4 laps in advance.

Cotton then climbed the platform where he delivered a speech which went something like this. "Ladies and gentlemen, if you wish it, I will go on, but I am beaten. You are all aware of the unfortunate circumstances which decided that I was utterly unfit to walk a few days earlier, and that I was determined not to leave Dunedin without giving you satisfaction. If there was anything perceived to be crooked about the match, I certainly had nothing to do with it." (Applause.) "Both McGrath and Scott would bear me out in that." (A voice from the crowd: "You *are* a plucky man!") "I was fortunate enough to beat Scott in Christchurch when I was fit, and I would admit that I would not be a man to give ten miles to if I was in proper form. However, I was entirely unfit on this occasion, and have been suffering greatly all day. This is my last walk. I am bidding farewell to the sawdust, and if I appear on it again, it would have to be as a clown in a circus. I would like to thank you all most heartily for the kind treatment I have received throughout the match. I have never walked against any professional except Scott, and I must say I could not have had a more fair and gentlemanly opponent to meet. Three cheers for Joe Scott!"

That was Joe's last race that year, for on Saturday, the 15th of October, he left New Zealand along with Austin, to sail to England on the *S.S. Ionic,* courtesy of a public subscription. On arrival in England on the 1st of December, he would be met and looked after by Mr. W. Jarvis, who would arrange matches for him against the best pedestrians in the "mother country." Before leaving, Joe told reporters that he only intended to walk in races from 50 to 100 miles or 12 to 24 hours *"for any part of £500."*

1888

His first contest in the British Isles was against his old foe, and the recognised champion for that distance, the 36-year-old Arthur Hancock, who was then working as a licensed victualler. On the 11th of February, a 12-hour walking championship match for a prize of £100 at the London Aquarium was arranged between the pair. Reports in the press suggested that young Joe had arrived in England with a *"good racing reputation,"* and that Hancock *"stood just about as much chance as a carthorse would against a thoroughbred"* of winning. Arthur had been training at the Tower Hamlets Drill Room in Whitechapel Road. His backer, Mr. Hearn, told the press, "He weighs ten stone eight pounds, and although not so well as we should like him to be, still he is alright." Joe meanwhile, who had based himself at the Roebuck Hotel in Buckhirst Hill, Essex, had been training within the Aquarium, and also indulging in 18 and 20 mile walks in the surrounding countryside.

Interestingly, George Littlewood was reported to be one of a *"select company"* in the building before the start of the race, which the *Sporting Life* commented on when it described how the two men were dressed and how they initially conveyed themselves around the track: **The Australian was attired in true orthodox athletic costume. He was bareheaded and habited in a crimson leotard minus the sleeves, the removal of which exposed the entire arm and a portion of the shoulders. His black pants reached nearly to the knees, and he wore laced boots perforated, brown socks, and carried a pair of corks firmly attached to each hand by means of a string. Hancock was very differently dressed and wore a cap, white jersey, long pants reaching to the feet, and a pair of blue (Oxford) running drawers. He preferred low shoes to boots, wore brown socks, a handkerchief around his neck, and carried corks. Beyond his face and arms from the elbow, every portion of his frame was well protected.**

Unquestionably there was a marked difference in the mode of progression. In Hancock, there is more incessant vigour and activity. As he struck the ground the concussion perceptibly shook the extremities, and his arms and shoulders were perpetually on the strain. This was absent in Scott, whose stride was particularly short, averaging scarcely more than half a yard. But he is very erect and firm on his legs, with a light elastic tread, his arms being well at ease, and his body nicely balanced and unfettered by any undue action during the race.

The two men walked in close proximity for the first 8 miles, after which Hancock pulled away from his old rival to create a gap of 26 seconds. Joe's response was to exhibit *"a remarkable turn of speed"* which he employed to good advantage by catching Arthur up. The Londoner tried the trick again on the ninth mile, and this time he was able to open up a gap of 46 seconds which he maintained till the 13th mile, when again, Scott drew up alongside his opponent. Matters were even till the 23rd mile, there being just a couple of yards in it, and then Joe sped to the front creating a gap of 50 yards between the two of them.

That lead was effectively stolen from him due to *"an objection"* by some of the directors of the race who were upset with his racing costume. Notice of this must have been given to Scott's trainer before Joe was compelled to leave the track to change, as apparently, he had purchased an *"ill-fitting jersey"* at a local hosier's for his man to wear. The change meant Scott was off track for 3m.50s and that gave his opponent the advantage. Joe made after him!

Whilst all this was going on the track, there was a huge programme of other activities to attract the spectator on offer in the centre of the course, including *"the artistic and clever movements of La Petite Amoros on the single bar,"* and latterly the *"Beckwith aquatic entertainment."* Due the monotony of the proceedings on the path, many in the crowd had watched the fun elsewhere, but when that was over, they returned to see what story was unfolding on the track. To their dismay, Hancock was struggling around it evidently lame. Then, when on a score of 42 miles, Scott left the track to change his costume. His absence meant that his opponent was able to gain a mile advantage on him at the 6h.50m mark. After that, it all went seriously wrong for the Londoner, for after he had made 43 miles and 5 laps, he had to be carried from the track to his room. A note was subsequently sent to the nearby Westminster Hospital and Mr. E. Cox the house surgeon arrived to examine him.

Of the accident the *Sporting Life* wrote: **The sufferer was examined, and the accident proved to be far more serious than was at first supposed. Hancock, however, was determined if possible to get on to the track, and requested Mr. Cox to bandage the part, so that he might give it a trial. This was done, but as soon as Hancock made an effort to cross the room he almost shrieked with pain, and the idea was abandoned. To inquiries made, the doctor feared that the large tendon had snapped, and strongly advised Hancock's removal either to the hospital or his home. He prescribed cold water bandages and absolute rest. It would, he said, be quite ten days before he could use the leg, and certainly two months before he would be able to enter into competition. If, as he feared, the tendon was ruptured, it would be necessary to undergo an operation, so as to bring about a re-union of the parts. The following certificate was handed in.**

February 11

I hereby certify that A. Hancock has ruptured the tendo achillis of his right leg.

E. OWEN COX, L.R.C.P. Ed., &c.

House Surgeon, Westminster Hospital.

Scott insisted on walking till the end though, and eventually made 64 miles in a time of 11h.52m.27s making his last mile in 9m.43s.

There were some questions being asked about Joe's ability to perform as well on tracks that he wasn't accustomed to using. So on the same day of the race, Mr. Austin was asked, "Is there any truth in the statement that you positively decline to walk on any track other than a boarded one?" to which he replied, "No truth whatsoever, and further, I am very much surprised to find that we have been so unfairly represented. In order to prove my assertion, we are prepared to fall back upon the old style of walking over main roads. Scott can be backed to walk any man in England on a country road in athletic or everyday costume, and if the money already at the *Sporting Life* office is covered, a match can be relied upon. Again, we are ready to walk upon a properly prepared track in an enclosed building, insisting, of course that we are made acquainted with the materials of which said track is composed. It has been argued that a boarded track is unfair, but I contend that it is a more natural one, insomuch as it is not specially prepared, as it is the case with those manufactured in England or elsewhere. Again statements have gone forth that we are accomplishing our performances in an enclosed building, but whilst pointing to the fact that nearly every latter day record has been accomplished under precisely the same conditions, we are, as I said before, both anxious and very willing to waive all such objections and take the road for it on the good old fashioned style. Please let the public know our meaning on this question, so first no person will be able to say when we have left for home that we shirked any of the conditions set forth by our rivals in England."

Joe's next race *"for £100"* would be against Jack Hibberd of Bethnal Green, who held the record for distances between 51 and 70 miles, and had spent a total of five weeks preparing for the match. The 24-hour *"walking match"* would take place at the same venue between Friday, the 17th and Saturday, the 18th of February. The start was made at 11:02. Scott wore a silk salmon coloured jersey, black university pants with red stripes down the sides, brown socks and laced up perforated boots, whereas his opponent was happy to wear a Guernsey, a silk handkerchief around the neck, *"drawers to the feet"* and shoes. Both men carried corks in their hands.

Hibberd's first mile was made in 7m.35s, Scott's in 8m.10s. By the seventh mile, Hibberd led by five laps, and as Scott followed the Londoner round, he quipped, "I'm like the cow's tail, all behind!" At the end of two hours, the scores read 13.6 to Hibberd and 12.8 to Scott, and when the leader took his first refreshment of the match just before the end of three hours, he consumed *"bitter beer which he imbibed from a bottle."* Later at 18:02, when Scott was already ahead, the Londoner went on to take a 34-minute rest which effectively gave the visitor a commanding lead as illustrated when the scores were hoisted at the 12-hour stage: 88.1 to 57.9:

Scott went on to easily outpace his opponent to win the contest by a stunning 28 miles and 8 laps, the final score being 122.4 to 92.6. His century was made in 18h.46m.33s. Hibberd meanwhile took lots of rests, but did finish off with a flourish, his last two miles being made in 8m.25s and 8m.35s respectively.

Joe then went into six-day, twelve hours a day, walking contest against William Howes, again for a prize of £100, and again at the Aquarium between Monday, the 27th of February, and Saturday, the 3rd of March. Howes, who initially led the race up until the 30th mile, allowed Scott to overtake him to lead the race by nearly two miles, and at the end of the first day of play, the scores were 62.6 to 60.8. Scott, who kept the momentum going throughout the rest of the match, easily won the race with a score of 307 miles and 5 laps. Howes meanwhile, was over 50 miles in his rear at the finish with a mark of 253.2 next to his name.

There would be a change of scene for Scott's next reported encounter, this time being at the Agricultural Hall in the less salubrious surroundings of Islington. The following advertisement appeared in the *Sporting Life* leading up to the race:

LONG DISTANCE WALKING.

NOTICE TO CHAMPIONS. – Mr. R. Lewis, of the Maid and the Magpie, 239, Oxtord-street, Stepney, London, will give £145 to be walked for, twelve hours per day, for six days' at the Agricultural Hall, London on May 14 and five following days, First prize, £100; second, £25; third, £15; fourth, £5, and £3 will be given to each competitor

not gaining a prize providing they walk 300 miles in the seventy two hours. A champion silver belt will ha added to the first prize, to become the winner's own property first time of winning.

J. Ray, Plymouth	Joe Scott, Australia
*A. Oldis, Lillie Bridge	W. E. Green, Soho, London
*W. H. Thomas, Sunderland	G. Day, Islington
J. Lowdell (champion of Kent)	W. Bevins, Kingsland
H. Carless, Poplar (late Mile End)	W. Griffin, Marylebone
*W. Ellmer, Sussex	*W. Slater, Bethnal Green
*H. King, Rotherhithe	*Patsy Walsh, Borough, London
J. Hibberd, Bethnall Green	J. Wade, Tottenham
W. Howes, Haggerston	W. Oliver (Champion of Lincolnshire)
W. Franks, Chelsea	G. Blair, Newcastle
G. Ide, Woolwich	H. Reeve, Hoxton
G. Farron, Hoxton	W. Hyde, Birmingham
D. Greig, Sunderland	F. Gregory, Hoxton
*H. Savage, Kilburn	T. Gown, Covent Garden, London
E. Luck, Hoxton	W. Clarkson, Bakewell
W. Williams, South Wales	*W. Hopwood, Leeds
*Ambrose Smith, Northampton	H. Munroe, Tottenham
J. W. Raby, Elland	T. Hook, Brixton
B. Thomas, Tottenham	Tom. Jagot, Hackney

The above is a list of accepted competitors.

RULES GOVERNING THIS CONTEST.

An efficient number of trustworthy persons, mostly members of the Press, will be appointed to check against the lap-takers, and any lap-taker making any mistake by taking one lap or one mile more than what his man is entitled to will be pegged back double the distance he may have taken wrongly, and expelled from the score-board by the police for the second offence, if requested by the referee.

The promoter wishes to say why he has introduced the new mode of each man finding his own lap taker. First, in past competitions I have engaged a number of men that have no interest but their own in the competition. They did not care for the man who they were scoring for, and sometimes did not know him. The competitor had to look out for himself that his number went up, and frequently had to call out to his man to see it.

By the present arrangement, every lap-taker will know his man personally as well as by his number, and there should be no mistake. Each competitor will have to engage his own lap-taker, but to meet this expense I will give every man not gaining a prize of £3, provided he walks 300 miles.

If there are any in the above list cannot accomplish that distance, they had better stay at home. Every man must walk in clean and becoming costume. All will walk one way, with left hand to near edge of track. No attendant will be allowed to go more than thirty yards, on the outside edge of track, with his man. Any competitor walking unfairly will be cautioned but twice during the week, and be disqualified the third time. Each man must wear a light blue sash over his right shoulder with his number printed on his breast. This will be provided for by the promoter. The track will be a fair one, composed of tan, mould and sawdust, well rolled, and seven laps to the mile.

A separate compartment, with a hasp and staple on each door, will be provided for each competitor, but he must find padlock and key. A small box, with lock, will be found very useful.

The prize money has been deposited in the hands of the *Sporting Life*, who will act as referee. The times will be taken daily with one of Kendal and Dent's (of 106 Cheapside) chronographs, where the champion silver belt will be on view next week.

A splendid band will enliven the proceedings at twelve daily.

Contractor for track and fittings, Mr. Cann, of the Agricultural Hall. Lap scoring under Mr. Meadows.

The whole of the management will be under the hands of Mr. Charles Hill, of Agricultural Hall.

P. S. Any man who has no intention of competing will please communicate with the prompter to the above address. It will be taken as a great favour. - R. LEWIS.

LONG DISTANCE WALKING.
IMPORTANT NOTICE.

All intending competitors must be at Barford-street entrance to the hall from nine till half-past ten, when they and their attendant - and lap taker will be admitted.

The race, promoted by Mr. R. H. Lewis, would again be a twelve-hour six-day walking contest with the 29 competitors making their way around the course at 11:20 on Monday, the 14th of May. One of *eight absentees from the above list was Ambrose Smith who sent in the following certificate:

Northampton, May 13, 1888

This is to certify that Ambrose Smith is weak and out of condition, owing to an attack of piles, and is unfit to compete in a six days' walking competition.

Mr. H. B. Stringer, surgeon, Northampton.

Hibberd, who had led Munroe from the second lap, made the first mile in 7m.55s, the first five miles in 44m.16s, and 6½ miles in the first hour. With Munroe hard at his heels, this state of affairs continued till the end of the second hour with Scott content to plod on in about 12th "pozzy," getting used to the track *"somewhat indifferently."* The leader went on to make ten miles in 1h.30m.43s, but it was Munroe who passed him to lead the van at the 15th mile post in a time of 2h.14m.10s. Franks was now in third, a full six minutes behind the leading pair. However, it wasn't until the sixth lap of the 23rd mile that Hibberd really turned up the heat on his nearest rival, firstly pulling away from Munroe, then lapping him after six more circuits of the track and repeating the same a mile further down the road.

By the 25th mile, the Bethnall Green man, now hungry for success, was 4m.4s further on and looking good. Old Jack was determined to make a record for himself on the day. He knew little "Billy" Howes had made the fastest 50 miles ten years earlier at the "Aggie" on March the 30th 1878 in a time of 7h.57m.44s (Won £70 by beating A. Hancock who received £15 and who made the same distance in a couple of minutes less). So that was his target and the old pro delivered the goods going on to beat that time by 3m.28s. As the new record was announced he was congratulated by the band with a rendition of the "Conquering Hero," *"and the spectators cheered the plucky peds to the echo."* Joe Scott could only look on in envy as he pushed himself on in eleventh. Were the critics correct? Was he really any good on anything but a boarded surface? There was still plenty of time to answer them, and this he did by moving steadily through the field claiming eighth position by the end of the eighth hour.

By the time the *"gasmen"* had finished lighting all the lamps in the building at 8 p.m. the place was awash with people, estimated to be in the region of five to six thousand. Hibberd, who had been continually breaking records from 50 miles upwards, was the recipient of continuous applause by the ever increasing crowd and at the end of 11h.40m of competition, when "Time" was called at 23:00 he led the field on a score of 70.1. Munroe was second with 68 miles, and Wade was third on 62.2. Scott, who had been seventh by the end of the tenth hour, had improved that position by one in the penultimate hour, and by a further two by the end of the day, finishing his work with a respectable score of 60.4 in a contest where Gown, Hook and Oliver were the only retirees.

The full scores at the end of the day were: **Hibberd, 70.1; Munroe, 68; Wade, 62.2; Scott, 60.4; Raby and Williams, 60.1; Franks, 60; Ide and Griffin, 59.6; Luck, 59.1; Hyde and Ray, 58; Howes, 57.5; Jagot; 57.2; Lowdell, 56; Reeve, 55.6; Carless and Gregory, 55.3; Clarkson, 55.1; Bevins, 55; G. Day, 52.6; Blair, 52; Thomas; 50.1; Farron, 49.5; Green, 47.5; Greig, 43:**

The second day, which started at 11:00, saw 16 of the original 29 step up to the mark. The other nine followed at intervals up to 47 minutes after the "off." Considering the records set the day before by Hibberd, many people were ready to stump up the admission fee to see if he could do any better. Because the previous day's racing had been over a period of 11h.40m, Hibberd had a full 20 minutes to make the 426 yards needed to beat his personal best in a 12-hour event. However, his old record made in Sheffield on November the 13th 1882 still stood because of the break in the racing. Still, the 72.1 made by the end of that twelfth hour must have pleased him greatly.

Scott, who had been creeping closer to Wade then shook off Raby *"who was going dickey, the right pin being troublesome."* Munroe, sporting the *"Professional Pedestrians' Association"* Maltese Cross, robbed a lap off Hibberd whilst on a score of 52.5. Thomas was the first man on the day to announce his retirement.

Whilst proceedings on the track were hotting up, a Scotchman who had been denied the chance to take part in the event was *"heel-and-toeing"* it around the gallery in a pair of hob-nailed boots, employing a young boy to count the laps. The sight proved very popular with the crowd and many were amused by the man's antics. When an enquiry was made as to how far he had gone after being at it for 1h.20m, the answer before he was "turfed" out of the building by the police was a commendable, but questionable, 11½ miles!

Scott later had a good race with Wade; by the end of the 14th hour, and through a mixture of guts and determination, he was able to gain a mile and 753 yards on him to draw level and thereafter, pull away. By the end of the sixteenth hour, due to Wade resting for 20 minutes, Scott, then on a score of 84.1, had been able to pull 2 miles further away from him. The race leader meantime was almost 8 miles ahead on a score of 93.6. By the termination of the next hour, although Hibberd went further ahead, the New Zealander glided into the runner-up position eliminating Wade to third spot. Munroe was now resting in fourth, Griffin was in fifth and Franks in sixth. The leader went on to make his century in 17h.11m.2s whilst many of the leading men were resting, including Williams who had *"left the tan and sought nature's sweet restorer, converting a couple of chairs into a couch."*

The half-time scores at 17:00: **Hibberd, 104.1; Scott, 94.3; Griffin, 91.5; Munroe, 90.2; Franks, 90.1; Luck, 89.3:**

Scott the *"Cornstalker"* was the next man to make his 100 in 19h.5m.11s. Franks followed his example just before the end of the same hour. By the end of the night when the walkers were called off the track, Franks, after a tough battle with Griffin, who had maintained his 3rd position till the 22nd hour, managed to pass him to end the second day just under 4 miles behind Scott. The permanent retirees for the day, who were Green (51.2), Thomas (52.3), Jagot (58.6), Reeve (60), Raby (61.2), Ide (66.4), Hyde (70), Williams (83), and Wade (89), meant that the remaining scores in the contest were: **Hibberd, 130.6; Scott, 121.3; Franks, 117.4; Griffin, 116; Munroe, 111.2; Luck, 111.1; Clarkson, 109.9; Ray, 108.6; Howes, 108.3; Day, 105.2; Carless, 103.6; Bevins, 101.1; Farrow, 100; Blair, 83; Greig, 77.2:**

Several hundred people watched the start of the third day of the contest which began without Munroe. Bevins was the next to permanently quit with a score of 104.1; and when the band played the "Bonlanger March" during the 27th hour, all the "peds," including Greig, responded with a collective spurt. By the 28th hour, Scott had managed to reduce the gap between him and the slower walking leader by 7 miles and 1,506 yards, and by the end of the day, had reduced it even further to 5 miles and 6 laps as the following scores show: **Hibberd, 190.3; Scott, 184.4; Franks, 173.6; Ray, 162.3; Carless, 159.1; Day, 157.2; Clarkson, 155.1; Farrow, 149.6; Howes, 147.1; Griffin, 142.6; Blair, 125; Greig, 96 (Luck retired with 132.6):**

Greig was the only one of the previous day's competitors who didn't don *"the war paint"* for the start of the fourth day. As events materialised, the *"Australian"* had made such significant headway by 16:30, that he was only 3 miles and 4 laps behind Hibberd. A couple of hours later he had further reduced that distance by 2 miles and 502 yards, and by 20:20, and in front of 3,000 noisy spectators, found himself just 280 yards in arrears. Then, 45h.3m.45s from the start, and amid an *"Australian war whoop,"* many a hat was flung into the air to celebrate what had seemed impossible only a couple of days earlier. Scott not only took the lead, but soon after, he gradually pulled away from the rest of the field, so that by the end of the fourth day the records showed: **Scott, 246; Hibberd, 244.4; Franks, 226.6; Ray, 216.5; Carless, 209.2; Day, 206; Farrow, 197.6; Clarkson, 181.2; Howes, 163.3; Blair, 163.1(Griffin retired with 156.3):**

On Friday, the 18th of May, the following notice was placed in the *Sporting Life*:

"The backer of Scott (who is at the present moment competing for Mr. R. Lewis's Champion Belt and £200, at the Agricultural Hall) wishes it publicly known that he is willing to wager £500 that his representative beats the six days'(twelve hours a day record). If any gentleman is desirous of accepting the offer, Mr. Alfred Austin (Scott's trainer) will be prepared any time today (Friday) to deposit £500 or £100 with the referee."

It wasn't till 9 o'clock that evening that Scott *"consented"* to go for the previous best record of 363 miles, which was made by Christian Faber on July the 3rd 1880 at Pittsburgh, USA. Up till that point, the New Zealander had been described as *"simply a triton amongst minnows, being in splendid fettle."* Joe had really pressed the button during the day to open up a lead of 8 miles and 1 lap between himself and Hibberd, who although going at it *"hammer and tongs,"* seemed content to settle for the £25 second prize.

The scores at the end of fifth day: **Scott, 303.4; Hibberd, 295.3; Franks, 276.4; Ray, 269; Carless, 258.1; G. Day, 251.3; Farrow, 235.6; Blair, 204.6; Howes, 197; Clarkson, 196:**

Having scored 350 miles in 69h.14m, and having been presented with a *"magnificent bouquet consisting of the choicest scarlet and white exotics,"* Joe went to work to make the necessary 13 miles and 6 laps, which he did with the enthusiastic support of the crowd. It was a foregone conclusion that Joe would win the race, and this he did in tremendous style, grabbing a new world record of 363.6 in a time of 71h.51m.23s, for which he was rewarded with £100 in cash and the *"magnificent"* silver world championship belt manufactured by Kendal and Dent. What isn't known is whether someone actually took up his backer's offer of that £500 bet; because if they did, they would have had a very sorry looking face when the race finished at 11 o'clock that night.

The Final Scores!

Pos		Miles	Laps	Prize	Pos		Miles	Laps
1	**Scott**	**363**	**6**	**£100**	6	Carless	300	1
2	Hibberd	337	0	£25	7	Farrow	274	3
3	Franks	318	6	£15	8	Blair	244	0
4	Ray	315	2	£5	9	Clarkson	229	0
5	Day	301	0		10	Howes	223	2

The last match that he competed in before touring around England, racing in various matches and giving walking displays, was on a 12 laps to the mile track at the Bingley Hall in Birmingham between the 4th and 9th of June. This was a 12 hours a day walking contest which was promoted by *Sport and Play*, 151 Edmund Street, Birmingham. The prizes on offer were £75 for the winner, £20 for second, £10 for third and £5 for fourth. In addition, £3 would be awarded to any man completing 300 miles in the allotted time of 72 hours.

The contest which started at 11:15 in front of a small audience, apart from Joe, attracted the following competitors: **C. Chates** (Birmingham), **W. Clarkson** (London), **W. Corbett** (Aberdeen), **J. Crowley** (Birmingham), **G. Downing** (North Ormesby), **W. Franks** (Chelsea), **H. Head** (Brighton), **H. Loder** (London), **E. Owers** (Surrey), **J. S. Robson** (Everton), **J. Sexton** (Cardiff), **A. Shipley** (Birmingham), **R. H. Smith** (London), **W. Smith** (Worcester), **W. Sutcliffe** (Lower Bridge), **A. Tomlan** (Birmingham), and **E. Wallani (London).** Mr. E. Russell of the *Sporting Life* acted as referee and time keeper.

R. H. Smith took the lead and maintained it till the 20th mile when Scott overtook him *"and was applauded as he passed man after man. His style differs almost entirely to that of any of the other contestants, and is greatly admired. Treading most firmly on his heel he maintains a very upright posture, and does but little "work" with his arms as compared with some famous pedestrians."* By 21:00, the Kiwi led the field by almost 3 miles, his score showing 54.2. Head of Brighton was in second position with 51.5, with Franks 3 laps behind him.

The contest was not well reported on in the newspapers, but what has been gleaned was that at the beginning of the second day the track was in such a *"wretched condition"* that it was with great difficulty that some of the participants could be persuaded to start at all. At the end of that day's competition, Scott led the way with 125 miles, scoring his century in a time of 18h.43m.30s. The second man in the race was Owers, who was ten miles behind, having secured his ton in a time of 20h.40m.20s. The third placed man, Clarkson, who was four miles adrift of the Surrey man, had made his hundred in 21h.25m.40s.

Apparently on the evening of the third day, a large attendance had gathered to watch the sport on offer. Scott continued to be in a class of his own and finished that day with 184.1 with Owers having made 172.11, Clarkson 168.3 and Corbett 165.2.

On the fifth day, at the end of 60 hours, Joe had scored 294 miles. On the last day, he went on to make 300 miles the next morning in 61h.5m.10s. The next man to make the same distance was Owers, who succeeded it in 64h.18m.10s.

Scott went on to win with 345 miles. Owers having scored 326 took second booty, whilst Clarkson and Corbett with 315 and 270 miles respectively, took minor honours. A report later suggested that the winner had issued a challenge to George Littlewood, *"the Sheffield flyer,"* with the expectation being that the New Zealander would *"make his next appearance in the Yorkshire cutlery town."*

1889

Joe arrived back in New Zealand on the steamship *Ruapehu* and was later given a hero's welcome at the Caledonian Sports meeting. The *Otago Witness* in their weekly edition on the 4th of January takes up the story: **A gratifying portion of the day's proceedings was the hearty reception accorded to Joe Scott, our Dunedin-born champion of the world. Scott and his trainer, Alfred Austin, who returned here on Sunday last after a triumphant tour of Great Britain, entered the ring during the afternoon, and were there met by the leading office-bearers of the society. The president (Mr. J. Barron) greeted Scott in a few appropriate words, congratulating him on his successes at home, and adding that by his unparalleled deeds he had done honour not only to himself but also to the colony at large. Scott who was in pedestrian costume, and wore the silver champion belt won by him in England, having acknowledged the compliment paid to him, the band struck up "See, the conquering hero Comes!" A procession was then formed, with Scott and Austin at its head, followed by a detachment of the band, and a circuit of the ring was made amidst a continual peal of applause from the spectators. The belt referred to is valued at £75, and is a very handsome piece of silversmith's work. It bears the following inscription: – "72-hours' Champion Belt of the World. This champion silver mounted belt, with £200 was presented by Mr. R. H. Lewis as a prize in a walking competition, commencing May 14 and finishing May 19, 1888. First prize won by Joe Scott, of Otago, N.Z., at the Royal Agricultural Hall, London, May 14 to 19, beating 20 competitors and all previous records, Distance walked 363 miles l,5l0yds. Trained by Alfred Austin; backed, Walter Jarvis, Esq,"**

It is said Joe's family only survived while he was in England by selling his cups and medals.

CHAPTER 59

What Else Happened in 1888

George Cartwright thought he had a new 72-hour record when he scored 396 miles in 69h.10m, but to his despair, he learned that the track at the Mechanics Hall at Boston was one mile short in every 26. *"Discounting this, the American record for five days was broken by a few yards."* The race, which was started by the then 142-hour record holder, Jimmy Albert, and which finished at 11 o'clock on the night of Saturday, the 10th of March, was said to be a big financial success, with about $2,000 divided among the competitors, of which Cartwright got about $700. Burns, Herty, Hughes and Noremac also started in this one.

The following was the final score: **Cartwright, 396; Guerrero, 375; Hegelman, 356; Sammy Day, 350; Taylor, 331; Dan Collins, 293; J. C. Sullivan, 275; C. Cunningham, 261; George Connor, 225; William Edwards, (New South Wales, Australia) 211; W. E. Cotter, 156:**

On the last day at 1 p.m., the *Boston Globe* reported that John Sullivan was: Espied running around the track with a mammoth watering pot well filled and his next feat was trundling a 54-inch bicycle for a lap at a smart run. Then, not satisfied with that, he left the course two or three times during the next hour, and danced clogs and horn pipes for the diversion of the spectators.

Of the winner Cartwright, who after he had been watching the bulletin board intently at one stage in the afternoon, apparently remonstrated with his scorer over the young man's recording of his laps. *"That's bloody 'umbug,"* he cried, leaving the track to expostulate. *"I've been watching you 'alf an hour, and I've been sure I saw you doing it. You're cheating me on the lap. You took one off instead of giving me one."* Ironically, the judges found that he had been scored one lap too much and docked him one!

Daniel Burns won a six-day go-as-you-please race with a score of 485 miles at the Chestnut Street Rink in Philadelphia. The match, which is believed to have commenced on Monday, the 14th of May 1888, was contested by fifteen men.

In the *Fresno Weekly Republican* of Fresno, California, on Friday, the 28th September 1888, in two articles on the same page, there is a reference to a rather dubious race: Between 5 and 6 o'clock this evening there will be a foot race, five miles, on the race track between George Littlewood and J. J. Morgan, for a private purse of $200.

Then, in the second article, entitled **That Foot Race:** "Oh, if it were only cooler," was the cry of about 4,000 people as they made their way in vehicles of all sorts, sizes and kinds to the fair grounds yesterday. The dust was so thick that a vehicle ten feet ahead of you was completely obscured and everybody and the horses were coughing and sneezing, and we were going to say swearing, but the ladies managed to express their disgust in some other manner. Once at the fair grounds however, all the discomfort vanished and there was not one of the 4,000 or 5,000 people that were on the grounds yesterday but enjoyed themselves, even the fellows that bought the wrong horse in the pool. This closed the racing proper and the track was then given up to a foot race between Morgan and *Littlewood, both professional foot racers, who started to run fifteen miles for a purse of $200. Littlewood won the first mile in 6:15. He ceased running at the end of the second mile, but Morgan continued. About this time the judges received information that the race was not a fair one, and that the race and all bets were declared off.

*George Littlewood was according to all the evidence, in England at the time of this race. The reader can therefore draw their own conclusions.

CHAPTER 60

Fox's Tournament

Richard K. Fox

The National Police Gazette (Illustration no: 119)

In mid October of 1888, it was reported that Rowell would be going to the United States to compete in a six-day contest at Madison Square Garden. The go-as-you-please contest, which was promoted by Richard K. Fox for his *diamond belt, would start on Monday, the 26th of November and last till Saturday, the 1st of December. Other professional pedestrians, including the arch rivals Littlewood and Mason, had also been secured to race, along with the great Rowell, by William O'Brien of the *Sporting Times*, who was to manage the match, and who had been in England for a month engaging professional pedestrians to take part in it.

The Fox Belt

The National Police Gazette (Illustration no: 120)

*The belt was described as being *"composed of eight silver clasps, each four inches wide and a shield shaped centre piece 6 inches wide. The centre piece is gold plated and surmounted with an American eagle rampant, whilst the central portion is adorned with a foxes head in solid gold with diamond eyes, this being surrounded by a horseshoe embedded with eight large diamonds. The large shield shaped centre piece bears the following description: - "The Championship Belt, typical of the Six Day's Go-as-you-please Championship of the world. Presented by Mr. Richard K. Fox, Editor and Proprietor of the Police Gazette, of New York."*

On October the 28th, O'Brien arrived back in New York on the steam ship the *City of Berlin*. Referring to Albert's record, and the fact that most of those he had engaged to race wanted to beat it, he said, "In regard to that record, the English pedestrians do not believe that it was ever made. In a conversation with me, Rowell said that he thought Herty, Hughes or Hart might break the record, but he did not believe that Albert was capable of doing it. On his arrival here, Rowell will at once challenge Albert to meet him on the tanbark. Rowell has amassed a large sum of money, and he told me that he would wager from one thousand to five thousand dollars or more, that he can defeat Albert, if the latter meets him in the coming race. This will be Rowell's last attempt in a walking match, and he will make a strong effort to surpass all previous performances. He is training every day with Charlie Mitchell, the pugilist, and he is in the pink of condition. Mitchell and Kilrain will train him here. Littlewood, too, wants to meet Albert. So confident am I that he can beat Albert, that I will wager any sum from one thousand dollars upward on the result. George Hazael, who was the first man to cover six hundred miles, thinks he can eclipse that performance."

The National Police Gazette (Illustration no: 121)

A few days before the start of the great race, **Dan Herty** arrived in New York from his training quarters at Revere Beach, Massachusetts. He was said to be in excellent form and was expected to do *"big work."* Having heard that Gus Guerrero had stated that he would win the race, he issued a challenge and offered to bet $1,000, or any part of it, that he would cover more miles than the Mexican. Guerrero, when spoken to on the subject, said that he did not know whether to accept the offer or not. Indeed, Guerrero had been causing a few problems for the managers of the race. Apparently he wanted to be paid a stated sum to run, but that request was not acceded to by the management who had already given the competing Englishmen a *"guarantee"* because they had all come such a long way to take part in the race. However, they objected to paying men anything when they were already on the ground - or nearby, as was Guerrero's case.

Meanwhile, George Littlewood who was covering in the region of 40 miles on a daily basis, in and around the Polo Grounds, told a reporter, "I am fine as a fiddle and I will do a grand performance." He could be seen there morning, noon and night training on the three-lap cinder path rattling off mile after mile. His trainer, "Happy Jack" Smith, said of the man in his care, "He does twice as much work as any other pedestrian while preparing for a race. Last week he covered nearly two hundred miles on the Polo Grounds, besides spins morning and night through Central Park and up the road." Indeed he was observed by Manager Mutrie of the New York Club running round the track wearing a big overcoat while the rain came down in torrents. "You couldn't induce a ball player to do that if you promised him a Cabinet position."

There would be some welcome news for Littlewood. His father Fred had arrived in New York on the *Etruria on the 19th of November, which was the same ship George Mason had travelled in from Liverpool. He was accompanied by the 38-year-old Archie Sinclair, the *"champion English walker"* from Scotland, and an *"unknown".* When the pair arrived, they called on manager O'Brien who they had discussions with for some time. Mason said that he didn't fear any man in the race and had come to take the champion diamond belt back to England.

*The voyage was reported on in the American press due to the severity of the weather that the ship had to contend with. One of the newspapers to report about it was the *Newark Daily Advocate* on the 19th of November: On Tuesday afternoon a huge wave than any yet encountered was seen approaching. The seamen uttered cries of warning

King of the Peds

and attempted to seek places of safety, but when the mountain of water fell with a crash upon the vessel the men were swept in a heap against one of the deckhouses. When the water receded it was found that George Wornald, an able seaman, of Liverpool, was fatally crushed and bruised. He died soon afterwards.

On the 20th, George Mason took himself down to the Garden for a 25-mile *"spin"* on the track. Whilst running impressively around it, he was closely watched along with several other contestants by Herty, Hughes, Hegelman, Dillon, Littlewood and "Happy Jack" Smith. Herty said of his performance, "He runs more like Rowell than any man I ever saw. My impression is that Mason will give us all a hard race. He has beaten Rowell and Littlewood, and any man capable of doing that is a good one." He went on to say that he would win the race or force the winner to go way beyond the record. Herty, who had never before had the benefit of a professional trainer would be looked after by George McDonald, the man who trained John L. Sullivan in England.

Littlewood was very angry when he found out that Mason was considering betting $500 that he wouldn't win the forthcoming six-day race. Even though there was much jealousy *"and bad blood"* between the pair, Littlewood, watching quietly from the seats, couldn't help admiring his antagonist as he flew around the track. Before the impressive Londoner had completed his workout, the Yorkshireman left and headed back to his training quarters where he ran harder than ever knowing full well that the contest he was about to enter would be the most difficult of his career.

"After taking his exercise Mason was about town as lively and 'chipper' as though nothing had occurred. The little Englishman is quite a swell, and will undoubtedly be the favourite of the feminine portion of the crowd who will throng the Garden next week. His features are decidedly prepossessing, and besides, he is a clever fellow and a bright conversationalist." "I have just turned thirty," he said, "but never before have I felt so fit for a race. As for Littlewood, I shall do no boasting, but it is no harm to say I believe myself capable of defeating him."

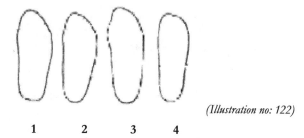

(Illustration no: 122)

1   2   3   4

The soles of the feet of four of the pedestrians who to take part in the race were outlined, sketched and printed in many newspapers of the time, such was the interest in the sport. 1. George Littlewood: 2. Dan Herty: 3. Edward C. Moore: 4. George Mason:

Among the forty men who it was reported would make the start was the *"Belfast Spider,"* Ike Weir, the *"champion light weight pugilist, amateur jockey and song and dance man."* Weir had a notion that he had the necessary staying powers to enable him to win the race. The betting fraternity generally believed he would be one of many who would fail to cover 100 miles in the first 24 hours, and as a consequence, he would be thrown out of the contest.

On the 24th of November, the carpenters at the Garden were working fast to prepare the venue for the forthcoming race. The newly constructed track of tanbark and sawdust was as per the norm, an eighth of a mile around, according to the official measurement made on the day of the Amateur Athletic Union games when it was laid out. The pedestrians had tried it and found it to their liking in every way. As at previous similar events, the arrangement of the track, the private boxes, and the seats for the spectators were the same as usual. The quarters for the contestants were located at the eastern end of the Garden, 15 of them facing the track, and the rest opening into the barn-like end of the structure. The 40 huts consisted of little oblong rooms furnished with a hard cot, two or three chairs, a rough table and a gas jet.

Charlie Mitchell and Jake Kilrain, the pugilists, had been engaged to act as judges, and the Marquis of Queensbury (John Sholto Douglas), a recent arrival in New York, would start the race. It was expected by the management that this trio would draw in the crowds as much as the contestants.

The arrangement between the management and the pedestrians was that the gate receipts would be divided equally between the two so that half of the gate receipts would be divided pro-rata among the finishers. It was agreed that every contestant must cover at least 100 miles in the first 24 hours or else be declared out. Apart from the belt which was worth $2,500, any competitor who beat Albert's record of 621¾ miles would get an extra $1,000. Littlewood and Mason were the favourites to take home the first prize, the former heading the market at even money. Both had been rivals for years, and both had been training assiduously for the contest which was to determine the superior. Both had run 40 miles the day before the race and on the morning of it both took a final run of 20 miles before retiring for a long sleep in preparation for their forthcoming struggle.

The scoring would be carried out by a number of members of athletic clubs under the direction of "Ed" Plummer, who had officiated in a similar capacity in many six-day races. Referee James W. Kennedy of the *Sporting Times*, and Manager Billy O'Brien had stated that it had been a *"difficult task"* to select the following list of starters from the 172 applications received.

	Name	Where From		Name	Where From
1	**Henry Brown**	Hartford	21	**C. P. Lewis**	Lowell, MA
2	**Campana "Old Sport"**	Connecticut	22	**George Littlewood**	England
3	**George Cartwright**	England	23	**James Mahoney**	New York
4	**George Connor**	England	24	**George Mason**	England
5	**John Craig**	Ireland	25	**John Moloney**	Centerville
6	**Tim Curley**	England	26	**Edward C. Moore**	Philadelphia
7	**Sam Day**	Philadelphia	27	**Myerley**	
8	**Frank Desmond**	Pennsylvania	28	**Henry Myers**	Germany
9	**Dan Dillon**	Ireland	29	**William Nolan**	Denver
10	**Electric's "Unkn"**	New York	30	**George Noremac**	Scotland
11	**Alfred Elson**	Connecticut	31	**Robert Peach**	New York
12	**Peter Golden**	New York	32	**Rafferty's "Unkn"**	Yonkers N.Y.R.K
13	**Joseph Gretzna**	Australia	33	**Charlie Smith**	England
14	**Frank Hart**	Boston	34	**W. Smith**	
15	**Peter Hegelman**	Germany	35	**Mathew Smyllie**	Scotland
16	**Daniel Herty**	Boston	36	**Norman Taylor**	Vermont
17	**George E. Hoffman**	Nebraska	37	**George Tilly**	Philadelphia
18	**Thomas Howarth**	Atlantic City	38	**Peter Van Ness**	New York
19	**John Hughes**	Ireland	39	**Robert Vint**	Brooklyn
20	**Sergeant Kramer**	New York			

Madison Square Garden, the *"Mecca"* of people who *"worship the shrine of athletics,"* ordinarily was a cold and dispiriting sort of place, but on the night of the start of "The Championship of the World," it had been transformed by the management. Within the building's confines had been placed a *"plenteous profusion of highly decorative colorful flags,"* which were representative of most of the world's nations. Banners and bunting were also put up to make the place more pleasing to the eye.

The enclosure in the centre of the big building was occupied by people operating all sorts of money-making contraptions like chest developers, shooting galleries, weighing machines, lung testers, grip expanders, hoopla, and knife throwers. There was also the *"omnipresent African who puts his head through a hole in a blanket and waited whilst amateur baseball players paid to use him as a target."* Apart from the fun of the fair, a vast array of food stalls were selling chewing gum, peanuts, sausages, doughnuts, pies and *"Weiss beer,"* which could be drunk whilst listening to the likes of "Johnny Get Your Gun" played by Bayne's Sixty Ninth Regiment Band. The match would bring together people from all walks of life that inhabited the big city, which would include the *"Fifth Avenue "dude" to the Bowery "tough" and the staid business man to the "flashy gambler.""*

The race would be started by the Marquis of Queensbury, who would occupy a box which had his name in large letters on the outside. Leaning on a silver handled cane, he wore a beaver overcoat trimmed with bearskin, and as he nonchalantly whistled to himself, he responded to those who caught his eye appropriately. He had held an informal reception before the start where he had been cordially welcomed by Captain Reilly, Mike Kelly, Jimmy Alberta and "Mike" Hartigan of the Fifty Seventh Street Court. When Mr. O'Brien presented Mr. Kennedy, the referee, to the Marquis, he was greeted with a round of applause, but when Mr. O'Brien introduced Charlie Mitchell as "the champion boxer of the world" to the nobleman, the announcement was greeted with cheers and hisses. Somebody in the crowd proposed three cheers for John L. Sullivan and as the shouts went up, *"Kilrain's ruddy face took on a brighter hue."*

There was a large crowd in attendance, many of whom had been in the building since the doors opened at 19:00, estimated at midnight to be nearly 10,000. The numbers reminded many of the days when Rowell was champion, and the enthusiasm that was endemic whenever he raced.

Some of the other contestants moving towards the start included: **Sam Day** who was described as the most *"eccentric"* of all pedestrians. **Alf Elson** was called the *"wooden nutmeg tramp."* **Peter Golden** was an athlete *"who never knew when he was beaten."* **Peter Hegelman** was called the *"German New-Yorker."* **Norman Taylor** was known as the *"Vermont pie eater."* **Parson Tilly**; who was anything but a parson, was noted for *"divinity and pie eating."* **Tim Curley** and **Charlie Smith** arrived from England only the day before. They were supposed to have come over as *"steerage passengers,"* but the suggestion was that Smith, the 19-year-old *"cabinet maker,"* was said to have *"stowed away"* on the steamship *Celtic*. Both were without a cent and that meant that they had to carry their trunks from Castle garden to the track. Smith, who looked more like a 14-year-old, told reporters he had walked 55 miles in 12 hours in 14 consecutive days back in England. He also told them that he would be happy to win a $50 prize. **Campana,** who was the first man on the track headed towards the scoreboards to inspect the set up there.

THEY'RE OFF!

Promptly at 12 o'clock, the Marquis of Queensbury shouted "Go!" After the contestants bounded away, it was Campana who won $5 for winning the first lap. He led Noremac, Littlewood, Herty and Cartwright, but it was the even money "jolly" favourite who went on to complete the first mile in 5m.2s. Herty was next man over the line, with Hughes a close third. The Yorkshireman kept up his steady pace, and although constantly followed by Herty, Cartwright, Hughes, Mason and Noremac, he had slight advantage over them at the end of five miles, which he completed in 30m.10s. The race leader was presented with a floral horseshoe, a gift from the two boxers, Mitchell and Kilrain, on the last lap of that fifth mile.

The score after one hour's competition was: **Littlewood, 9.5; Cartwright, 9.4; Herty, 9.2; Connor and Hegelman, 9; Howarth, 8.6; Mason, 8.5; Golden, 8.3; Dillon and Hughes, 8.1; Elson and Moloney, 8; Curley, Nolan and W. Smith, 7.7; Day, Myerley and Smyllie, 7.5; Rafferty's "Unknown," 7.4; Desmond, 7.3; Taylor and the Electrics Club "Unknown", 7.2; Campana, 7.1; Tilly, 7; Lewis, Hoffman and Van Ness, 6.5; Gretzna and Peach, 6.4; C. Smith, 6; Brown, 5.6; Myers, 5.5: (No scores available for Craig, Hart, Kramer, Moore, Noremac and Vint.)**

The departure of the Marquis of Queensbury at 01:00 gave the signal for many in the crowd to leave the building too. Before he left, he remarked of one of the *"feathers"* in the race, Charlie Smith, who he appeared to be greatly impressed with commenting, "I wouldn't be in the least surprised to see the little un carry off some of the honours." The diminutive figure of Smith, who before the race, had turned the scales at six and a half stones, and who was a popular figure with the crowd, was tossed a handful of silver at his feet by one female admirer sitting in one of the boxes. As well as that, a fellow countryman also handed him a $5 note, which he held in his hands for many a lap before secreting it within his shoe.

At 2 a.m., the records with George Tilly, *"the lantern jawed ecclesiastic from Quakerville"* being one of the first retirees having covered just 10.1, showed: **Littlewood, 17.6; Connor and Hart, 16.5; Cartwright and Moore, 16.4:**

When a *"young tough smiled audibly"* at him from the stands at 04:00, Campana, taking offence, threw a bottle he was carrying at the offender and tried to climb over the fence to give him a good hiding; but the police probably saved him the energy when they threw his tormentor out of the building. Meanwhile, one of the competitors who hadn't been causing trouble, Gretzna, *"the Australian kangaroo,"* was one of the first fallers in the race on a score of 26.2.

The band, which had stopped entertaining the 1,000 strong assemblage at three o'clock, resumed its efforts at 05:30 when it played "St Patrick's Day in the Morning."

The work done during the first six hours was about average. Littlewood led his closest competitor Moore by a half mile. Cartwright was a good third, and Hart, Mason and Connor were also in the equation. Shortly before daylight Littlewood complained of nausea, and it was reported that he had been suffering from a *"bilious attack."* Despite that ailment, he kept doggedly on his way. Golden's stomach also suffered, his symptoms necessitating a swift journey back to his tent. Myers was the next man to leave the race at 7 o'clock with 24 miles. Another man suffering was Noremac who was observed to have *"vomited all over the track."* As Moore (alias Cuthbertson) completed his 50th mile, Campana got the tongues wagging again at 07:30 when he created something of a sensation by running a couple of laps at an *"extraordinary gait."* He was described as being, *"badly in need of a shave and looks rather more cadaverous than usual. He is high in spirits, however; he wears an American flag around his waist, an old pair of white zouave gaiters and a boutonnière of greasy silver certificates."*

The score at 08:00: **Littlewood, 54; Moore, 53; Cartwright, 51.4; Mason, 51.1; Hart, 50.1; Connor, 50; Hegelman, 48.5; Herty, 48.2; Elson, 48; Golden, 47; Craig, 46; Day, 45.3; Noremac, 43.5; Smyllie, 42.5; Curley, 41.2; Vint, 41.1; Hughes, 41; Campana, 40.4; Taylor, 39.7; Moloney, 38.3; Van Ness, 37; Nolan, 36.6; Desmond, 36.1; Brown, 36; Dillon, 33.5; Rafferty's "Unknown," 33.5; W. Smith, 33.2; Hoffman, 32; Peach, 30.5; Kramer, 30.4; C. Smith, 30; Myerley, 22.5; Lewis, 21:**

Littlewood went really well in first position and appeared as though he was enjoying himself. He was closely pressed by Moore and Herty who both took the eye with polished performances. The tipsters were booking the Bostonian for a spot on the podium and large amounts of money were being placed on him to finish in the first two positions. He stuck gallantly to his work, didn't overexert himself, and seemed to be saving his strength till the end of the week.

A telegram had been received from John L. Sullivan *"and his seventy-five pound bull dog"* early in the morning, saying that they would be arriving on Wednesday to look out for his interests.

The score at noon, with the race leader 12 miles and 66 yards behind Rowell's 1882 record, was: **Littlewood, 77; Moore, 75; Cartwright, 73; Connor, 72; Howarth, 71; Hegelman and Herty, 70; Golden, 69; Mason and Day, 67; Hart, 65; Elson, 64; Craig, 63; Noremac, 62; Taylor, 61; Campana and Vint, 59; Hughes, 58; Nolan and Smyllie, 57; Moloney and Van Ness, 53; C. Smith, 52; Brown, 51; Desmond and W. Smith, 50; Curley, 49; Dillon and Rafferty's "Unknown," 48; Hoffman, 47; Peach, and Kramer, 45:**

In spite of the weather, and before an average attendance of 2,000 throughout the afternoon, the peds more or less occupied the same positions. Although Littlewood still led, he was closely pressed by a half a dozen others.

The 3 p.m. score, with the leader keeping the two-mile gap between him and his nearest rival: **Littlewood, 94; Moore, 92; Cartwright, 91; Connor, Golden and Howarth, 88; Hegelman, 85; Herty, 84; Day, 83; Golden and Mason, 82; Elson and Hart, 75; Vint, 73; Campana, 72; Hughes, 71; Noremac, 70; Craig and Smyllie, 69; Taylor, 68; Rafferty's "Unknown" and Van Ness, 65; Moloney, 64; Brown, Dillon, Kramer and W. Smith, 62; Hoffman, 59; Peach, 54; Curley, 52; C. Smith, 48:**

Littlewood was the first of the athletes to secure the first century at 16:04, before receiving the usual adulation from the crowd. After he had been given a floral horseshoe which he took back to his tent, he opened and drank a bottle of "Bass ale" to celebrate his achievement. The others who had covered the same distance by 19:00 when Littlewood, on a score of 122 abruptly left the track for what appeared to be a rest, were Moore and Cartwright (16:24), Connor (17:19), Herty and Howarth (17:49), Mason (18:14), Golden (18:16), and later Hegelman.

The increased crowd of between 3,000 and 4,000 which brought with them a general spirit of liveliness into the Garden during the evening, seemed to inject new life into the men. The Marquis of Queensbury, who had once again graced the event with his presence, occupied his box opposite the scorers' stand surrounded by a host of famous sporting personalities. The world record-holder, sitting with his wife, applauded the hard working peds from a nearby box. Frank Hart, as usual, was a big favourite with the crowd and as such, had been presented with an abundance of flowers. At 20:00, he was observed scampering around the track holding a large horseshoe made up of roses. At 20:30, Littlewood, Moore and Cartwright were tying on a score of 122 miles. Behind them, Herty and Connor were each on 114, with Day and Golden 2 miles away.

(Illustration no: 123)

Edward C. Moore *(drawing from National Police Gazette)* now led the race. Littlewood had now been off the track for 1h.30m. Many in the crowd who had backed him were starting to get a little edgy as he remained behind the closed canvas doors. Little did they know that the celebratory bottle of beer which he had drunk earlier had caused him such severe stomach pains later that he had but no choice to leave the track, despite his protestations. While the suffering athlete slept, his father bathed his head in vinegar, and while Fred tried to heal his son, Campana, *"whose homely figure and good natured smile had been seen on every sawdust track for many a year,"* received hearty applause after scoring his one hundred.

The scores at 10 p.m: **Moore, 128; Cartwright, 127; Littlewood, 122; Herty, 120; Connor, 119; Golden, 117; Mason, 116; Day, 114; Howarth, 110; Hart and Hegelman, 108; Campana, 102; Elson, 97; Noremac, 94; Hughes, 93; Vint, 91; W. Smith, 88; Taylor, 83; Hoffman and Smyllie, 82; Moloney, 80; Dillon, 78; Brown, 73; Peach, 72; Desmond, 67; C. Smith, 57:**

It was nearly midnight when the crowd eventually began to head home. Most of the pedestrians had now been on the track for nearly 24 hours without rest, and many were already showing the symptoms of their hard work. For some of them, their efforts had been successful. Well over a dozen had guaranteed their place in the next stage of the race by making the necessary 100 miles, which also meant that they had saved their entrance fee. Only Moore and Cartwright had managed to pass the 130-mile mark which Albert had covered when he beat the record, and no one had got any way near Rowell's 24-hour record of 150 miles. For some though, the race was definitely over. Apart from the earlier "fallers," Tilly, Gretzna, Mahoney, Myers and the Electric Clubs "Unknown," Lewis had dropped out at 09:00, having tramped 23 miles, and an hour later Myerly also departed on 22. They were later joined by the likes of Nolan, Craig, Van Ness and the *"stowaway,"* Tim Curley.

It wasn't until the start of the second day that Littlewood came back out of his tent to re-engage in a race many thought he had given up. As a consequence of his six hours of sleep, and having dropped from first to fifth place, George had taken a considerable walk in the betting market with odds of 10/1 being offered on his winning. Apparently refreshed, he rejoined the fray when the scores were: **Moore, 135.1; Cartwright, 135; Connor, 125.5; Golden, 125; Herty, 123; Littlewood, 122.2; Day, 117.6; Mason, 116.3; Howarth, 115; Hart, 114; Hegelman, 111; Campana, 110.2; Smyllie, 101.2; Elson, Noremac and Hughes, 100; Vint, 97.4; W. Smith, 89.7; Taylor, 83; Dillon, 82.3; Hoffman, 82; Moloney, 81; Peach, 75.2; Brown, 73.4; Desmond, 67.7; C. Smith, 58:**

The 27th of November brought nice weather with it to New York. Many used the conditions as the perfect excuse to go and see the action at the Garden. The next of the men to leave the race were Hegelman, who had succumbed to tiredness, sore feet and a *"faint heart"* on a score of 117, and Hughes. The "Lepper" had gone into the race in good condition and was determined to do well. Alas, the damp weather had unfortunately played havoc with the rheumatism he classically suffered with, and as a consequence, he was forced to withdraw at 9 o'clock in the morning with only 101 miles on his scorecard. Interestingly, in relation to the "100-mile rule," whilst Brown, Desmond, Dillon, Hoffman and Moloney had failed to reach that total, and were therefore barred from continuing, the others like Peach, C. Smith, W. Smith, Taylor and Vint, despite also failing to secure that amount, were still, for some reason, allowed to plod on.

The 13:00 scores: **Cartwright, 163; Herty, 162; Moore, 161; Littlewood, 156; Day, 156; Howarth, 153; Connor, 152; Golden, 148; Mason, 147; Hart, 143; Campana, 141; Noremac, 130; Elson, 129; Vint, 120; Smyllie, 118; W. Smith, 115; Taylor, 111:**

Passing the scorers……Cartwright leading the way.

The National Police Gazette (Illustration no: 124)

The afternoon crowds were as large as on Monday as they watched the *"tramps"* go-as-they-pleased around the track. With the exception of Campana and Peach, the men appeared a little more fatigued than they had 24 hours previous and they were reported to be sticking very closely to the track, taking little rest and making good scores. At 18:00, the returns were: **Moore, 214.3; Herty, 205.1; Cartwright, 202.6; Littlewood, 198.5; Howarth, 191.7; Day, 190.5; Golden, 189.4; Connor, 186.2; Mason, 185; Hart, 184.6:**

"Although the band played lively airs of the Scottish proclivities and the jingling discord of the "Pearl of Pekin Wedding March," there were but a thousand people in the Garden at 8 p.m." Then, and to the relief of all the participants on the course, the turnstiles began to click just that little bit quicker as the public started to arrive in their droves. The fact that *"Manhattan Moore"* was the leader was enough to persuade people through the entrance doors; and at that time, there was some expectation that the record would ultimately be broken. One of those who decided to turn up that night was Paddy Fitzgerald, who paid a visit to the pedestrians' huts. After carefully scrutinising the remaining contestants he said, "In my opinion, Herty will win the race." His "fancy" for the "gold medal" position later received a magnificent horseshoe from John L. Sullivan. On receipt of the gift, the crowd *"cheered lustily and the hundreds of pretty women who were on hand to see the heroes of the track and hear their footfalls music waived their delicately scented handkerchiefs."* Herty was then seen tugging the big gift around for several laps, after which his trainer McDonald took it away from him.

The Marquis of Queensberry arrived shortly before 10 o'clock. He and his friends amused themselves for the next hour or so by throwing dollar bills in the direction of Campana and *"Pretty Smith"* who, although was said to be out of the race at the time, was still apparently entertaining the crowd with *"exhibition spins."*

Moore left the track at 23:00 with a graceful trot. He looked much fresher than any other man on the path, apart from Herty, who didn't appear to be under the slightest strain. The leader had earlier received a generous round of applause when he finished the 238th mile that beat Albert's two-day record in February.

Of the 43 original entries only 19 remained when the midnight score was hoisted: **Moore, 240.1; Cartwright, 225.2; Herty, 225.1; Littlewood, 217.7; Golden, 216.6; Day, 215.1; Howarth, 212.6; Mason, 205.2; Hart, 204.6; Connor, 202; Campana, 190; Elson, 186.3; Noremac, 183.1; Vint, 178.7; Taylor, 170.4; W. Smith, 160; Smyllie, 151.1; Peach, 120.1; C. Smith, 80:**

King of the Peds

The crowd didn't thin out until after midnight. Those that stayed watched Howarth putting in the most impressive performance of the men out on the path. Cartwright was observed to be shirking and Golden indulged in a long rest in the early part of the morning. When Day reappeared apparently refreshed, Campana, who followed him, was described as *"frisky as a kitten."*

Dawn brought with it a bright and clear day for the remaining 19 men who were said to astonish the early visitors with their splendid appearance. The audience was comparatively small during the morning, but as they ringed the ring, the peds were helped along with some rather *"lugubrious"* music played by the band. By this time Littlewood's stomach was now behaving itself, and "Happy Jack" said his lad was alright. Moore bounded along with a spring in his step and many were already speaking of him as the winner. The thing that impressed the observers was the fact that although the leaders were in such close proximity in relation to their scores they had all nevertheless made long distances.

The score of the first nine on the leader board at 12:30 was: **Moore, 289; Herty, 281; Littlewood, 272; Howarth, 267; Cartwright, 263; Day, 260; Golden, 254; Mason, 246; Connor, 240:**

Early in the afternoon, Moore began to send out distress signals, so much so that the famous trainer John Fraser was sent for. He tended the suffering race leader and did his best to alleviate his man's suffering during the frequent rest periods he was forced to take. As can be seen by the 6 p.m. score, his lead had been whittled down to a couple of miles: **Moore, 309; Herty, 307; Littlewood, 298; Cartwright, 288; Howarth, 285:** Herty meanwhile, seeing his chance, piled on the pressure. He had taken just two small rests of 10 minutes duration since nine o'clock in the morning, but this didn't stop him passing the race leader at 20:37 whilst Moore was once again being attended to.

Campana, along with Charlie Smith continued to amuse the audience. They were both rewarded by some in the crowd who appreciated their clowning by giving them money. At 9 o'clock, Littlewood was observed going along at a fair clip in third place. By 22:00, as the score shows at the time, he was 6 miles or so behind the new race leader: **Herty, 323; Moore, 320; Littlewood, 317; Cartwright, 306; Day, 290; Golden and Howarth, 288; Mason, 287; Noremac, 282; Hart, 280; Connor, 278; Campana, 257:**

By 22:30 Littlewood had reduced Herty's lead to just 3 miles and was at that stage even money favourite to bag the contest. As his fellow countryman Cartwright, moved along smoothly in fourth place, Herty, who had sought his shelter at 21:30, came out for another crack of the whip at 22:50, much to the delight of the crowd who clapped him back on the track. As can be seen by the midnight score, Dan managed to repel Littlewood's encroachment into his lead by pulling 7 miles and 2 laps ahead of him whilst still in a comfortable lead over second place Moore: **Herty, 328; Moore, 325.1; Littlewood, 320.6; Cartwright, 315; Day, 299.6; Golden, 296.7; Howarth, 296.5; Mason, 294; Noremac, 283.6; Hart, 283.6; Connor, 278.1; Campana, 263; Vint, 261; Elson, 254; Taylor, 248.1; W. Smith, 207.6; Smyllie, 180; Peach, 161; C. Smith, 107.3:**

Sixteen men were now left in the race. Sam Day, who was one of them, started the morning for his fourth day's work lying down in his hut suffering from inflammation of the bowels. At 04:30, with a score of 309.4, he finally gave up and left the track for good. Half an hour later W. Smith (of Paisley?) and Smyllie also withdrew, having covered 207 and 180 miles respectively. The other news was that *"little Smith's"* foot was now so well healed that he decided to try and make 100 miles in the next 24 hours.

Herty was encouraged in his objective of overall victory during the afternoon when a contingent of his friends arrived at the Garden from Boston. They constantly shouted, "Who's all right?" and answered in chorus, "Why, Herty! He's alright! You bet!" To the amusement of the crowd, they cleverly imitated the music of Barnum's *"steam piano,"* and were particularly boisterous when their man completed his 400th mile at 15:31, a fact which resulted in the liveliest kind of din all over the enclosure. Herty had travelled 72 miles in 15½ hours, or at the rate of nearly 5 mph, and was said to be *"going like a steam engine."* Having conquered the milestone, he immediately sought the sanctuary of his hut for a well deserved 15-minute break. On his return, he doggedly pegged away, evidently determined to beat Albert's world record. Hart by this time had made 350 miles which he had achieved by employing a fast walk during the day.

When Littlewood returned his 400 at 16:32, he was seen to be snapping at Herty's heels.

Cartwright, meanwhile, had tired out anyone who had dared to keep up with him, and as he played "catch me if you can," Littlewood continued to try and get nearer to the race leader. At this time, the English raider was 5 miles behind Herty, 15 ahead of Moore, and 23 ahead of Cartwright. At the time, he remarked that he was certain to win the race due to the faith he had in his ability to eventually tire the Bostonian out. Despite Herty's advantage, Littlewood was still the favourite in the betting at even money and the bookies were now advertising Herty at 3/1. Many of the Yorkshireman's friends who had backed him at odds of 8/1, when he had been as much as 17 miles adrift of the race leader at the time, were now keeping their fingers crossed that their shrewd bets might just come off.

The Garden was reported to be overcrowded during the evening. That fact made the pedestrians very happy as they knew there would be larger gate receipts due to the management refusing to give away any complimentary tickets. At 20:45, Moore, who was traversing the path impressively, also secured 400 miles but was nearly 25 miles behind Herty at 21:00.

The real sufferer on the track seemed to be Campana, whose gait seemed to indicate that he had hurt his back. Despite his plight, he persevered and picked up the odd coins and notes that were thrown on the path before him. The veteran Elson circled the track in a dazed sort of way, and it was observed that he actually walked several laps whilst *"fast asleep,"* apparently waking only when he collided with one of the other walkers. Smith copied Campana and went along the tanbark collecting money, turkeys, chickens, grapes and flowers. Indeed, "Ed" Plummer had over $100 of the money he had been given, in his possession. Peach, the grey haired veteran, was the oddest figure in the ring. Although he knew he hadn't any chance of earning any gate money, he stated he didn't want or didn't need any of it, and was in the race "to kill the rheumatism." Having apparently paid his $50 entrance fee willingly, as he did his training expenses, he added, "because the exercise keeps me free from rheumatic pains for several months following each race, and this method of cure is cheaper and better than any doctors have ever given me."

At 22:20, having covered 430.4, Herty left the track to rest. Littlewood took advantage of his absence to cut down his lead. By 23:00, he had managed to get within half a mile of the sleeping leader who, six minutes later, was totally unaware that the gutsy "Tyke" had once more taken top spot in the race on a score of 430.5. The announcement that Littlewood had covered 431 miles on the bulletin board brought a round of applause from the crowd at 23:10. He then called it a day for the time being and went to his quarters for a bit of a rest and some necessary grooming.

At the same time, most of the boys had retired for their night's rest with only Noremac, Golden, Hart, Mason, Elson and Campana on the track at 23:30, the latter becoming quite *"animated"* as he received several dollar notes whilst the band played a *"lively jig."* The crowd then began to thin out very rapidly until there were about 3,000 people watching proceedings at midnight, the 96th hour, when (with Albert's February score at the same stage shown in brackets) the returns showed: *(Albert, 450.1);* **Littlewood, 431; Herty, 430; Moore, 410; Cartwright, 400; Noremac, 391; Howarth, 389; Golden, 380; Hart, 376; Mason, 373; Connor, 365; Campana, 330; Elson, 328; Taylor, 322; Vint, 297:**

Littlewood's lead however, was short lived, for Herty, who now appeared refreshed after his nap, and who had resumed his work at 23:50, was soon back in the lead with 432 miles. Indeed at 1 o'clock, he went four miles ahead of the prostrate Littlewood. When the Brit left his quarters to return at 01:10, he had two goals in mind, re-taking the lead and becoming the world record-holder. After being barely able to move due to the stiffness in his limbs, he slowly built up his pace until his joints allowed him to start running. Herty tried to follow, but had to give up the chase following advice from his trainer.

Just before 4 a.m. Littlewood made a determined effort to reduce the relatively small gap between himself and Herty. When the Bostonian left the track half an hour later, the lithe and fleet footed Sheffielder soon had the score level at 454 apiece before going back into the lead. At 07:00, he led the Irish-American by four miles and began to increase his advantage with every step taken. As can be seen by the 11:00 score (107th hour), not only had he managed to create a handsome margin of ten miles between the pair, he had more or less matched Albert's February score: *(Albert, 486.5);* **Littlewood, 486; Herty, 476; Moore, 453; Cartwright, 437; Noremac, 430; Howarth, 427; Connor, 412; Mason, 407; Golden, 404:**

King of the Peds

When Littlewood completed his 500th mile at 14:02, not only was he a mile and a half behind Albert's 110th hour record, but he found himself 121¾ miles behind that man's world record which he had 32 hours to break. "Happy Jack" was so confident that he would accomplish his objective that he had built up a schedule for his man to follow in his bid for glory. For his part, Herty went on to score his the 500 at 17:10.

The *"Sheffield Blonde"* took up his familiar trot and set to work on "mission impossible." Appearing very well, he moved along easily as he looped the loop with predictable repetition. A third of the 5,000 crowd there to watch him were women, and they watched him with fascination as he took his afternoon tea on the move. When he had finished eating three chops, which were swilled down with beef tea followed by ice cream and coffee at 18:00, he wiped his mouth and looked up, to compare the scores on the big board. They showed: *(Albert, 519.2);* **Littlewood, 516; Herty, 503; Moore, 472; Cartwright, 463; Noremac, 454; Hart, 447; Howarth, 445; Connor, 442; Mason, 435; Golden, 431; Campana, 378; Taylor, 366; Elson, 359; Peach, 219:**

Having covered 107 miles for the day, Littlewood went to bed at 22:57 at which time he was about 2½ miles behind Albert's record. Herty, who had made 90 miles in the previous 24-hour period, followed the leader off the track and while their heads were on their pillows, the score at midnight showed: *(Albert, 545);* **Littlewood, 538.5; Herty, 525; Moore, 493.4; Cartwright, 484.5; Noremac, 472.2; Hart, 467.1; Howarth, 458.4; Connor, 460; Golden, 456.7; Mason, 455.3; Campana, 400; Taylor, 394.2; Elson, 381; C. Smith, 168.1:**

"Happy Jack's" plan was to wake his man at 01:00 and motivate him to trudge the last 84 miles to break the record which now looked "on". When *"he found him in a dazed condition and apparently oblivious of his actions and whereabouts, he bathed his head in ice water for about five minutes; after a rubbing and a short nap he returned to the track looking much refreshed."*

At 07:00, and with Herty 18.3 behind him, the leader had beaten Hazael's record of 563½ miles in 127 hours. At that juncture, all the men were on the track and going well. Littlewood was in excellent condition and covered the miles rapidly. He showed little or no evidence of his long hike and went along easily. All the experts were unanimous in the opinion that the present race had been the most hotly contested on record, particularly between the two leaders. Both still exhibited a great determination, dogging each other incessantly. At 10 o'clock, Littlewood found himself 11 miles ahead of Albert's record for that hour. 60 minutes later the big bulletin board showed: **Littlewood, 584;** *(Albert, 572.6);* **Herty, 560; Moore, 528; Cartwright, 511; Noremac, 508; Hart, 502; Connor, 500; Howarth, 498; Golden, 492; Mason, 491:**

At 13:00, or the end of the 133rd hour, when Littlewood was exactly eight miles ahead of his own previous record of 585 miles, he went off the track to be rubbed down. At 14:00, the *"pride of Sheffield town of cutlery renown,"* was 6 miles 6 laps ahead of Albert's old record of 587.2 and an hour later, the score stood at: **Littlewood, 600;** *(Albert, 591.6);* **Herty, 567; Moore, 539; Cartwright, 525; Noremac, 520; Hart, 516; Connor, 508; Mason, 501:**

THE FINAL PUSH!

There was a massive gathering of people to witness the closing scenes at Madison Square Garden that night. As the evening advanced and the building began to fill up, the *Brooklyn Daily Eagle* wrote of the prevailing atmosphere: **Happy as Little Nock clams in their shells, 7,000 men jostled each other in Madison Square Garden, New York, and they all smoked. Pounding the tan bark with their feet were fifteen men, and they were all weary. Behind big brass instruments were twenty men trying to make music, and they were all windless. Taking liquid refreshment at the bar were 1,000 men, and oh! what a thirst they had! There were some of them from Brooklyn, too, and in every respect they kept up the reputation of the town as to its sporting proclivities. Occasionally there were little spurts amongst the men that called forth cheering enough to drown the noise of the tired musicians and an occasional row in the galleries helped along the interest. The little officious and pugnacious Ed. Plummer was willing to start a fight, but he wasn't allowed to and the way he was sat upon made him mad. In high collar, double watch chain and boutonnière the only Mike Kelly was on hand many were those who sought the attention of Boston's "ten thousand dollar beauty."**

The swift pace at which Cartwright reeled off lap after lap under the enlivening music of the band was especially commented on and provoked round after round of applause. The pundits unanimously declared that, but for lack of heart, the "Flying Collier" would be pushing the "Sheffield Flyer" for first place.

Spurt! Cartwright goes for it!

The National Police Gazette   (Illustration no: 125)

Littlewood was ten miles ahead of Albert's record. Although he was going round gamely, it was evident that one of his feet was sore as he limped in rather a painful way. Jack Smith however, declared that he was in good form and that the trouble with his foot was of no consequence. Littlewood's intention when he started was to cover *"675 miles,"* and although his sickness precluded this, he was determined to break the record. At 19:30, he made his 619th mile as the crowd cheered and yelled until they fairly shook the rafters.

The excitement grew more intense as Littlewood drew nearer and nearer to the record, the holder of which was sat with his wife watching in the seats. At 19:37, he completed the 620th mile which was a signal for more cheering, and as he started his 621st mile, he was greeted with cries of "Go it George!" As he finished it at 19:52 and started out to pass Albert's record, pandemonium in the building reigned. *"Albert, with a smile of apparent contentment on his face, here jumped on the track and shook hands with Littlewood. Ned Plummer then handed the champion and ex-champion, the boy Smith and Campana, small American flags attached to brooms, and forming a group they thus went round the ellipse twice, amid the deafening applause of 10,000 spectators."* Shortly after starting out on the 622nd mile it was stated that he would, on completing it, retire for good.

Whilst Littlewood went round, the crowd was fairly beside itself with excitement. Every lap brought forth more cheers, howls, yells and shouts. Umbrellas and canes pounded on the floor and hundreds of handkerchiefs were waived by ecstatic women.

"Then the thunder of applause which greeted the champion as he went around the track would have put a good size earthquake to shame." As the band played "Rule Britannia," a triumphal procession which included the other pedestrians who carried the Stars and Stripes around, riveted the crowd to their seats. Having completed a furlong in this fashion, the race leader left the path at 20:07 having completed his 622nd mile.

Gus Guerrero then presented the winner with a handsome wreath, which was a present from the jockey, "Snapper" Garrison, while the band played "Hail to the Chief" followed by "Yankee Doodle."

"Another explosion occurred" when Herty, who had remained on the track, finished his 600th mile at 20:30. It was announced that he was determined to beat Rowell's best record of 602 miles and 185 yards which he achieved at 21:04.

All the contestants later returned to the golden path between 9 and 10 o'clock and gave the crowd an exhibition of sprinting. Whilst they performed for the enthralled crowd, many of them were given presents of flowers, Miss Daisy Sheldon being one of the more liberal contributors of such. Another floral piece in the shape of a shield, amongst other gifts, was presented by a young English lady called Miss Collier; which bore the legend, "Champion of the World" in purple immortelles. The band then struck up, "See the Conquering Hero Comes," the music continuing as Littlewood marched to his tent.

King of the Peds

At 21:26, and limping badly, the new world record holder, escorted by Manager O'Brien, went round the track amid tumultuous cheers, as Herty got hold of Smith and ran around the track with him. As they did so, many bank notes were given to the "little un."

After making a couple of laps Littlewood and Herty were stopped by Mike "Ball Tosser" Kelly of the Boston Baseball Club and presented with wreaths of laurels. After Littlewood had scored 623 miles at 21:40, he went on to make another three quarters of a mile before he was stopped in front of the scorers' stand at 21:57:30, again by Mike Kelly, who presented him with the diamond championship belt and proclaimed him as "the best pedestrian in the world."

Above all the din, Kelly shouted, "Although Americans bowed to your superiority now, I hope that within a year from now an American will be found that will gain possession of it and the title of champion of the world." After fastening it around Littlewood's waist, Littlewood made the following speech:

"Ladies and Gentlemen; I have won the belt once, and I suppose I must win it twice more to hold it. It is a nice belt, and I am proud to hold it."

His words were greeted with cheers. When silence was restored, the ex-champion stepped forward and challenged him to another race for the championship of the world, the conditions being that each man entering the race would contribute $1,000 each to a sweepstakes to be divided amongst those taking part in addition to the gate receipts.

Dan Herty was the last man off the track. He stayed on to the very last minute to score 605 miles. He would be the last man ever to make a distance of 600 miles in such contests. When he left the track at 10 p.m., the final score was:

		Miles	Yards			Miles	Yards
1st	Littlewood	623	1,320	8th	Golden	534	440
2nd	Herty	605		9th	Mason	528	665
3rd	Moore	553	700	10th	Taylor	439	880
4th	Cartwright	546		11th	Campana	450	220
5th	Noremac	542	410	12th	Elson	421	1,540
6th	Hart	539	1,160	13th	Peach	252	880
7th	Howarth	535	410	14th	C. Smith	201	1,510
8th	Connor	535					

THE WINNER AND THE NEW WORLD RECORD HOLDER

On his return to England they called him "Littlewood the Lionheart"

Photograph kindly donated by Sue Crowther (Illustration no: 126)

King of the Peds

*Author's note: It was generally felt that if George really wanted to, he could have covered the 650 miles easily. It was probably in his own interests, and those of the promoters, that he didn't want to make it too hard for the record to be broken again. There was probably a lot of pressure put on him not to go for the kill as this would have dampened the enthusiasm of future crowds for such contests, and crowds meant big money for those individuals who organised them. Indeed, and as Littlewood later stated in an interview with the press, he was urged to cool things down during the race by the race manager, Billy O'Brien. It must also be remembered that Littlewood had to indulge in an enforced rest due to illness of several hours on the first day. The mind boggles as to what he could have achieved if he hadn't?

Below is an hourly summary of Littlewood's final scores:

HOURS	Miles	Yards	HOURS	Miles	Yards
129	573	1,000	136	604	700
130	579	700	137	608	1,540
131	585		138	613	400
132	590		139	617	600
133	593		140	621	1,380
134	595	600	141	622	250
135	600		142	623	1,320

Some of Littlewood's times towards the end of the race:

Miles	H	M	S	Miles	H	M	S
561	126	10	0	580	130	7	0
562	126	32	0	590	132	0	0
563	126	45	0	600	135	0	0
564	126	58	0	610	137	16	0
565	127	10	0	620	139	37	0
566	127	22	0	623	141	40	30
567	127	35	0	623.6	141	57	30
568	127	48	0				

During the race, Littlewood rested for 16 hours and 26 minutes. Herty's rests added up to 15 hours and 19 minutes. Incredible!

Of his victory, the *Chicago Tribune* wrote: **Littlewood has not only won the belt and a respectable nucleus to a comfortable little fortune but has proven iconoclast in various ways. He has broken the record, has broken down several of his adversaries, and has broken the old proverb that says the race is not always to the swift, nor victory to the strong, for it was owing to these two qualities that he won. When he retired after his last lap tonight to have balm applied to his wounded feet and recalcitrant joints, the knowledge that his six day's work had netted him about $6,000 and a $2,000 belt flowed up in both mind and body as a balm of Gilead.**

After the race Littlewood went to the Ashland House, where, as he *"had a good pull of Bass's ale,"* he told a reporter, "The Americans are a decidedly fair people. No American could receive such fair treatment in England I am sorry to say."

The day after, Elson and Taylor had apparently gone back to the Garden early in the morning before breakfast and ran around the track to *"work up an appetite."* Littlewood awoke at 7 o'clock and was reportedly *"bright, cheery and good natured."* Indeed, he stated that he never felt better! He said that he planned to sail for England on the 15th of December as he was anxious to spend Christmas at home with his family, thereafter going on to complain about the condition of his feet which he said were quite sore.

Both first and second placed men later relaxed amongst their numerous friends. Albert went to see Littlewood at his hotel during the day where Littlewood told him, "I could have easily gone ten to fifteen miles more had I desired, but I thought six hundred and twenty-three miles, beating your mark by two miles brought as much glory as any number of miles could." Both claimed they could beat each other, and Littlewood talked of organising a

$3,000 a side race between the pair. Albert however, although keen to compete, was willing to risk a sweepstakes of $1,000 plus half the gate receipts.

After consulting with Mr. O'Brien who would manage the event it was agreed that race should take place on March the 1st or at least around that time. It was also suggested that Guerrero, Herty and Rowell would also enter. For anybody else interested in participating who couldn't afford $1,000, it was suggested that a *"second class entry"* could be organised, whereby for an entrance fee of $200, any winner of the race from that class would be entitled to all of the entrance money of his own class *plus* $200 from each of the competitors in the *"first class."* The other suggestion was that remainder of the sum total of entrance fees for the first class would be given to that competitor of the first class who had covered the greatest number of miles in the time specified for the race. Also, if any competitor in the first class won, then he would be entitled to claim the entire stakes of *both* classes. Another suggestion was that the contest should take place in England, but both men were against the idea, Albert's excuse being that he enjoyed competing on home soil. Littlewood too gave the notion little credence, saying that Londoners were against him because he had beaten Rowell who was a great favourite with them, and because they "didn't 'ave the brass, anyway."

Later on in the afternoon, Littlewood went to Braun's Bathhouse on East Sixty Fifth Street. Whilst the new champion relaxed there, Dan Herty, who was observed to be *"well rested and placid,"* went back to the Garden where he said he was ready to leave at once for his home in Revere. Of the others, Moore, who was said to have really suffered more than any of the others during the race, was said to be returning to Philadelphia to convalesce. Cartwright made it known that he would accompany Connor to Coney Island; whilst Noremac, Vint, and Hart were in the process of making their way to Philadelphia. Howarth planned to return to Bristol, Pennsylvania; the disappointing George Mason said he would remain in New York. Campana said he would go home to Bridgeport.

The pedestrians were said to be satisfied with the management of the event and the 10 men who covered 525 miles assembled in the afternoon on Tuesday, the 4th of December to receive their financial rewards at the office of Richard K. Fox. George Littlewood was officially presented with the world championship diamond belt which he was told by Mr. Fox that he must win one more time to keep it permanently. Manager O'Brien also presented him with a gold watch, which was manufactured by the American Watch Company. Inside, it was engraved with the following inscription:

G. Littlewood. World's Champion. From Billy O'Brien. N.Y. 1888. 623 miles.

The gross receipts from the match amounted to $19,306.50 of which $9,260.75 was to be distributed among the ten winning contestants. Littlewood's share was 40%, or $3,704.30, plus $1,000 for beating the record. Herty received $1,666.93 or 18%; Moore, 12% or $1,111.29; Cartwright, 9% or $833.46; Noremac, 6% or $555.64; Hart, 5% or $463.03; Howarth, 4% or $370.43; Connor, 3% or $277.52; Golden, 2% or $185.21; Mason, 1% or $92.60. In addition to scooping the above amounts, the winner had backed himself liberally at 8/1 when the race was going against him and was estimated to have won $3,000!

On the 7th of December the *Massillon Independent* of Massillon, Ohio, also reported: **In addition to the above amount named, Littlewood wins five hundred dollars on a wager with Mason, the latter betting that the winner would have to cover over six hundred and twenty five miles.**

George and his father decided to sail for England the next morning on the Inman liner, *City of Berlin*. Before he left he reiterated that he expected to return to America in February to defend his title to the championship.

The ship which ferried them from New York was delayed into Liverpool owing to a faulty cylinder which was actually mended by the crew of the *Umbria*, that ship having left three days after the *City of Berlin*. The Littlewood's arrived in Liverpool on Saturday night, the 15th. Although the impression was that the champ would arrive the day after on the later 18:03 from Liverpool where George had been met by his wife and mother, the party actually arrived back in Sheffield's Victoria station on the earlier 10:50 train. The news had leaked out that he was arriving early and there was a considerable crowd numbering at least a thousand people gathered in the station yard waiting to greet him. The station-master, Mr. Hodkinson, had arranged that only his immediate friends would be admitted to the platform, and as a consequence, half a dozen or so headed by John Bee greeted the champion as he left

King of the Peds

the train. When he emerged from the station, there was an immense cheer from the crowd, which, along with thousands of other Sheffielders had been enthralled with his performance overseas.

Safely in the carriage, he was first driven to his friend Bee's house and then on to see his brother-in-law, Tom Dickinson of the "Red Lion" on Shalesmoor. It was here that he exhibited his prize for winning the contest. Although not the owner of the belt, he was allowed to bring it with him to England after he had deposited the sum of one penny as security with the promoters. Apparently that concession had been made due to the grittiness of his performance and the way he had conducted himself during the match

It was here that he discussed his future racing plans with reporters from the local press and where he informed them of his meeting with Albert before leaving New York. "I am going to see Charlie Rowell, and see if we can arrange the money here; but if not, I shall go back to America. The race will be open to everybody, the more, the merrier." He also told of how his father followed him to New York shortly after he arrived. He spoke highly of the American trainers, "Happy Jack" Smith and Jake Hyams who looked after him so well during the contest. Littlewood was later interviewed about the race by a reporter:

Reporter: When did you leave England?

Littlewood: I sailed on the Servia October 20th and arrived in New York on October 28th.

Reporter: Where did you locate yourself for training operations?

Littlewood: I stayed at Mr. Brown's, 65th Street, East River and trained at the Pastime Athletic Club Grounds.

Reporter: What was your weight when you commenced training?

Littlewood: I scaled 13 stones 5 pounds but when the contest started, I weighed 11 stone 13 pounds or 20 pounds less than when I started training.

Reporter: I suppose you were in good condition?

Littlewood: I never felt better in my life and I was confident of doing a great performance if necessary.

Reporter: Did you hold the lead at the end of the first day?

Littlewood: No, I was about 17 miles behind.

Reporter: How was that?

Littlewood: Well about 4 o'clock on Monday, I drank a bottle of beer which had gone slightly sour and this disagreed with my stomach and the consequence was that I was obliged to take a rest.

Reporter: What means did you employ to bring about your recovery?

Littlewood: None in particular. After I had a rest, I set to work again, and had no more beer for a time, and my stomach recovered its natural tone, and I became alright.

Reporter: When did you get near the leaders?

Littlewood: Moore held the lead up to Wednesday night, 68 hours from the start, when Herty passed Moore, and I on Thursday night I passed Herty; but on Friday morning when I was resting, Herty again passed me, and it was not until Friday evening that I was able to catch him.

Reporter: Had you a hard task to beat Herty?

Littlewood: No; I was going so strong and well that I thought it was no use distressing myself. In fact, I considered the race was mine, and that I could easily pass Herty whenever I wanted.

Reporter: When did you pass the record?

Littlewood: At 5:32 on Saturday morning, I had beaten the 129 hours record of 562 miles, and at ten o'clock in the morning when I had still 13 hours to travel, I was ten miles in front of the record.

Reporter: You were then travelling well?

Littlewood: Rather. Why on Saturday morning I ran 23 miles without taking a break and never felt as though I had been running; I don't know how far I should have ran without stopping had not Billy O'Brien come to me and asked me to stop and not to beat the record too much.

Reporter: How far do you think you would have travelled?

Littlewood: I feel confident I could have covered 650 miles had it been necessary. Why, I never ran a yard from 11 o'clock on Saturday forenoon until 8 o'clock in the evening, and during that time I was off the track for two hours.

Reporter: When did you pass Albert's record of 621 miles?

Littlewood: At ten minutes to eight on Saturday night, and at 8:10 I had covered 622 miles. After that I only covered 1,320 yards, so you see I had plenty of time to beat the record still further if I wanted to.

Reporter: I suppose there was a lot of excitement on Saturday evening?

Littlewood: I guess there was. Why, I had a bouquet presented to me that was so large that I had to get two men to carry it round the track with me.

Reporter: Then the affair was a financial success for the promoters?

Littlewood: Oh yes; when the public found out that that I was likely to break the record they came in thousands and Billy O'Brien made a lot of money out of the race.

Reporter: Do you feel any effects of your last years work?

Littlewood: On the contrary, I never felt better in my life. Remember this is the third six days race I have won within twelve months, and I think that's what makes my performance all the more remarkable.

Reporter: Where were the three contests decided that you won inside twelve months?

Littlewood: All in America. I won at Philadelphia last November, at Madison Square Gardens last May, and the last contest makes the third.

Reporter: Who attended to you during the contest?

Littlewood: My father and Happy Jack Smith, of New York, who is considered the prince of American trainers.

Reporter: Did you lose much weight during the race?

Littlewood: Only a pound and a half: I weighed 11 stone 13 pounds when I started and 11 stone 11 and a half at the finish.

Reporter: Were you well treated in America?

Littlewood: I was never treated better and I should like to return tomorrow. I was exceptionally well treated at Mr. Brown's where I trained, also by Mr. O'Brien, Mr. Kennedy, the referee, Jacob Hyams, who is now matched to fight Jack McAuliffe for the lightweight championship of America, Doctor McDonald and Doctor Wetherley.

Reporter: What are your intentions respecting a sweepstakes race with Albert of America, and Rowell of England?

Littlewood: Well, I hardly know whether Albert or Rowell will enter in a sweepstakes. Albert came to the Ashland House in New York and told me he would enter in a sweepstake of from £20 to £100, but I want it for £1,000.

Reporter: When will the race take place?

Littlewood: If the sweepstake race is made I cannot say exactly when it will take place but there is sure to be another race either in England or America during the months of April or May next year.

Reporter: Do you think you will win?

Littlewood: The one who beats me will have to cover over 650 miles.

On the 16th of December, a cable dispatch was received from George W. Atkinson, editor of the *Sporting Life*, which contained a challenge from Rowell (who said he wouldn't go to America) to Albert to run six days for $2,500 a side, either at the Agricultural Hall or the London Aquarium. Rowell also offered to make a match on similar terms with Littlewood, or to enter a sweepstakes race for £100 or £500 each for the "Police Gazette Diamond Belt" against Littlewood, Albert and Herty; the contest to take place in England. The dispatch added that it was expected Littlewood would accept Rowell's challenge, and that a race would be arranged for a sweepstakes of £100 each, open to all, for the long distance championship of the world.

The match never took place.

THE OLD RECORD BEATEN AFTER 96 YEARS!

Yiannis Kouros, a 28-year-old Greek runner didn't think George Littlewood's 1888 record was "humanly possible" when he set off in the New York "Six-Day Run" on the all-weather track at Downing Stadium, Randall's Island, on Monday, July the 2nd 1984. Yiannis "did the impossible" when he covered 635 miles and 1,023 yards *with two hours remaining* to win a total of $7,500. Fred Lebow, president of the New York Road Runners, showed Yiannis the documentary evidence of George's daily performance. "That convinced him," stated Lebow. "Little by little he chopped away at the record and finally achieved it. I think it's going to take another century before somebody breaks this one."

"I am very, very tired," said Yiannis, "I am really surprised that I broke the record. I didn't think it was humanly possible, and I doubt that the man ran that many miles such a long time ago."

SUMMING UP

Before we look at the credentials of the contenders for the title of **King of the Peds**, I have provided a table illustrating how the long distance world record progressed from 1874 till 1888. The original 500-mile world record changed on 16 separate occasions. The last record made in the 19th century was not beaten until 1984, a period of 96 years. An individual account of each record breaking race can be found in the chapter indicated on the left of the table below.

CH	Competitor	From	To	Miles	Yards	Venue
2	E. P. Weston	14-12-1874	19-12-1874	500	0	TR, Newark, USA
4	D. O'Leary	15-11-1875	20-11-1875	503	586	EB, Chicago, USA
7	D. O'Leary	02-04-1877	07-04-1877	519	1,585	AH, London, England
9	D. O'Leary	18-03-1878	23-03-1878	520	440	AH, London, England
11	W. Gentleman	28-10-1878	02-11-1878	521	503	AH, London, England
18	H. Brown	21-04-1879	26-04-1879	542	440	AH, London, England
19	E. P. Weston	15-06-1879	21-06-1879	550	110	AH, London, England
24	H. Brown	16-02-1880	21-02-1880	553	165	AH, London, England
25	F. Hart	05-04-1880	10-04-1880	565	0	MSG, New York, USA
27	C. Rowell	01-11-1880	06-11-1880	566	165	AH, London, England
29	J. Hughes	24-01-1881	29-01-1881	568	825	AIB, New York, USA
31	R. Vint	23-05-1881	28-05-1881	578	440	MSG, New York, USA
33	P. Fitzgerald	26-12-1881	31-12-1881	582	55	AIB, New York, USA
35	G. Hazael	27-02-1882	04-03-1882	600	0	MSG, New York, USA
45	P. Fitzgerald	28-04-1884	03-05-1884	610	220	MSG, New York, USA
56	J. Albert	06-02-1888	11-02-1888	621	1,320	MSG, New York, USA
60	G. Littlewood	27-11-1888	02-12-1888	623	1,320	MSG, New York, USA

AIB = American Institute Building: AH = Agricultural Hall: MSG = Madison Square Garden: TR = the Rink:

Some other important races which didn't produce records are indicated below:

Chap	Winner	From	Till	Miles	Yards	Venue
10	D. O'Leary	30-09-1878	05-10-1879	403	0	MSG
15	C. Rowell	10-03-1879	15-03-1879	500	180	MSG
20	C. Rowell	22-09-1879	27-09-1879	*524	7	MSG
21	N. Murphy	06-10-1879	11-10-1879	505	220	MSG
22	F. Hart	22-12-1879	27-12-1879	540	220	MSG
39	P. Fitzgerald	23-10-1882	28-10-1882	577	440	MSG

*530 miles originally, but reduced because of shorter measurement of track.

Now lets us look at all the arguments as to who might be worthy of the title **King of the Peds.** However, before we do, we must remind ourselves about what pedestrianism is. Do you remember the definition at the front of the book? Well, to remind you, it is:

"The act, art, or practice of a pedestrian; walking or running; travelling or racing on foot."

As we have dealt with *competitors* in this book, a race can either be against "time," against another, or against others. Set distances in races can vary from say 50 yards upwards. A race against "time" and others can be under varying conditions. The weather has to be taken into consideration, the types of surface walked or run on, or, as in the case of the races at the time, a mixture of either. The other equations to be taken into consideration in a race would be whether the terrain competed on is flat, hilly, or undulating; whether the going is wet, muddy, sandy, or slushy; whether the temperature is hot or cold or whether it is sunny, raining, frosty, snowing or windy.

You the reader must remember that pedestrianism covers the art of getting from point A to point B in whatever conditions dictate. Thus, when choosing the candidate to be the "best," all areas that influence that progression must be considered.

Many of you who have read the preceding pages will have decided who you think deserves the title, the **King of the Peds.** Some of you may need reminding of a few facts before making your choice.

In my opinion, and in alphabetical order, the following peds are worthy of being prime candidates for the title: **James Albert, "Blower" Brown, Patrick Fitzgerald, Frank Hart, George Hazael, George Littlewood, Daniel O'Leary, Charles Rowell** and **Edward Payson Weston,** so it is these that I will be arguing the merits for.

NB: Little **Joe Scott** might also have come into the reckoning had he been involved in 142-hour go-as you-please races.

The Argument for James Albert:

Jimmy's first win of note was in a six-day walk at Philadelphia in April of 1879 where he made 460 miles. In February 1880, by making 136 miles, he then won a 27-hour race at Dover, New Hampshire. He followed that up in March of 1880 by being victorious in a 75-hour event at Brockton, Massachusetts, with 435 miles. After that, and with a really commendable performance, he then took the 72-hour go-as-you-please world record of 412 miles in April and May of 1880 at Philadelphia. A win in Boston in June followed, when, in a 72-hour event, he made 360 miles.

He then put in a really scintillating effort to finish ten miles behind the "Lepper" who scored a world record of 568 miles in the 142-hour 1st O'Leary International Belt competition in February of 1881. Following that, he was matched against Rowell in the "Four-Cornered" event, but due to injury had to pull out early.

Very little was heard about him until 1887 when in Philadelphia in the "Championship of the World" sweepstakes in November, he came in second position on a score of 530 miles which was 39 behind the winner, Littlewood.

His last race was his greatest. This was when he beat the old 142-hour world record of 610 miles made by Patrick Fitzgerald four years earlier. Making a stunning 621¾ miles at Madison Square Garden in February of the following year, he beat the chasing pack with ease, the second placed man being 39 miles behind.

The Argument for Henry Brown:

As well as being an accomplished short distance runner in his early career, "Blower" went on to distinguish himself in the field of ultra long distance go-as you-please racing.

An encouraging start of 477 miles which gained him 3rd prize money in the 1st International Astley Belt at the "Aggie" in March of 1878, was followed when he came in the runner-up position to Corkey in the 1st "Long Distance Champion of England" belt competition held in the same building in the following November.

King of the Peds

After securing the 142-world hour record in April of 1879 with 542 miles, he then went over to the USA where he failed miserably in two races to get in the frame. However, on his return to England, in February of 1880, he returned to his winning ways when securing a new world record of 553 miles.

The Argument for Patrick Fitzgerald:

"Paddy" Fitzgerald won five big races in his remarkable career. Before he embarked in his long distance go-as-you-please career, he was the champion 10-mile runner. In his first crack at the big time, he led the 1st O'Leary Belt race in October of 1879 for about 50 miles before retiring hurt.

Remarkably, and a week later, Pat won the O'Leary sponsored 14 hours a day, six-day go-as-you-please match at Madison Square Garden with a score of 377 miles.

He then came in a creditable 5th of 65 starters when he scored 520 miles in the Rose Belt contest held in New York in December.

On April the 26th 1880, he started a 72-hour competition at Buffalo a couple of days later. Incredibly, he took the bronze medal position with 386 miles!

He wasn't seen on the racecourse again until the 1st O'Leary International Belt contest began in January of 1881. Having made a promising start, he gave it up after scoring 113.7. Then in the 2nd O'Leary International Belt in May, he ended up in 4th with a very respectable 536 miles, Vint being the victor.

It wasn't until December of that year that, once again, his name graced the leader board at the end of the match. However, this one would be really special. The "Grand World Championship Six-Day Go-As-You-Please Tournament" was held at the American Institute Building in New York and provided the perfect setting for Pat to overcome the existing world record held by Hughes. Bettering it by 4 miles, his final tally was 582 miles and 55 yards. His score had crushed his previous best by 46 miles!

He made 5 miles less than that when losing out to Hazael, who broke his record by going 18 miles further in October of 1882.

Finally, between the 28th of April and the 3rd of May 1884, *"Plucky Paddy"* went 10 miles further than Hazael had done 2 years previously when he scored 610 miles and 220 yards. Again, and in comparison with Littlewood's total rests, Pat was off track for 28 or 12 hours more. Without those extra hours he too could have made somewhere in the region of 650 miles upwards!

The Argument for Frank Hart:

When Frank started off his career, the world was a much different place. He is the only contender for the title of **King of the Peds** who is black, and that fact alone makes it remarkable that he achieved what he did. He would have certainly been up against it in a society predominantly made up of white people, but despite that, it was they who took him to their hearts and made him the success story that he was.

Hart was taken on by O'Leary after showing much promise by winning some noteworthy events in 1879. His first win was a 30-hour event in April when he scored 119 miles. After making the frame in some decent races thereafter, he then went on to beat 29 others at Providence, Rhode Island, in a 75-hour event in September with a score of 362 miles. It was after this that Hart was hired as O'Leary's protégé and fondly became known as "Black Dan."

He then went up in class and made a very promising 4th place in the 5th Astley Belt in New York in late September, that race being won by Rowell. Now under O'Leary's mentorship, he followed that effort up by winning the Rose Belt with a score of 540 miles in December. O'Leary's faith in him was eventually rewarded with a wonderful win and a brand new world record of 565 miles in the 2nd O'Leary Belt in April of 1880.

Frank then went on to star in many a race thereafter which he won and came placed. For his efforts, he earned a hell of a lot of money, and he must have been a real inspiration for thousands of other young *"colored"* lads in America at the time.

The Argument for George Hazael:

George Hazael wasn't pretty, but boy, could he run! Before he went for prizes over long distances, George had made quite a name for himself in his chosen profession over shorter distances starting from 10 miles upwards. He did very well to beat Peter Crossland in Manchester in early 1878, but let himself down, when, after harassing O'Leary during the 1st International Astley Belt in March, he scored just 50 miles.

He then went on to win the 50-mile Astley "Champion Challenge Belt" in July at Lillie Bridge before trouncing the rest of the field in a race for *"second class men"* at the Agricultural Hall with a mediocre 403 miles in November. That performance though brought him sufficient recognition to be able to compete against the likes of Brown, Corkey, and Weston in the 2nd Long Distance Astley Belt in April of 1879 in which he took the 2nd prize, scoring 492 miles as against the 542 and new world record made by the winner, "Blower" Brown.

The Londoner then took a trip over to America, where, for finishing in 3rd place with a score of 500 miles, he made the staggering sum of $ 4,192.50. Now an established name in the sport, George went back home where in February of 1880 he took on Brown and Day, but was only able to muster a score of 480 miles, which was 73 behind "Blower's" winning total.

In May of 1881, and now back over the pond, George starred in the 2nd O'Leary International Belt where he finished in 8th position having made exactly 5 centuries, Vint winning the money with a world record score of 578 miles.

After a failed attempt to take part in the 7th International Astley Belt, George prepared himself to take on the best in the world in the $1,000 sweepstakes race in March of 1882. Not only did he win by 23 miles, but he was also the first man ever to have travelled 600 miles in six days! What was even more incredible was that he rested for 35h.21m.35s. If we compare that with Littlewood's 16h.26m of rest for his world record score of 623¾ miles, in reality, if Hazael had indulged in the same amount, in theory he could have made something over 50 miles extra!

After that, George did a little more racing, but after a couple of disappointing efforts in another sweepstakes, and a 12-hour affair back in London in 1887, nothing more was heard of him.

The Argument for George Littlewood:

Below are Littlewood's career details covering the period from 1879 till 1888:

START	VENUE	FINISH	POS	M	L	TYPE
10-11-1879	Wolverhampton, England	15-11-1879	4th	275	0	72 hr G-A-Y-P
09-02-1880	Nottingham, England	15-02-1880	5th	252	0	42 hr G-A-Y-P
29-03-1880	**Leeds, England**	**03-04-1880**	**1st**	**374**	**6**	**72 hr G-A-Y-P**
06-09-1880	**London, England**	**11-09-1880**	**1st**	**406**	**6**	**72 hr G-A-Y-P**
01-11-1880	London, England	07-11-1880	2nd	470	0	142 hr G-A-Y-P
23-05-1881	New York, USA	28-05-1881	10th	480	3	142 hr G-A-Y-P
06-03-1882	**Sheffield, England**	**11-03-1882**	**1st**	**531**	**5**	**142 hr Walking**
24-04-1882	Sheffield, England	29-04-1882	Rtd	122		72 hr G-A-Y-P
25-09-1882	**Birmingham, England**	**30-09-1882**	**1st**	**415**	**9**	**72 hr G-A-Y-P**
16-11-1882	**Sheffield, England**	**18-11-1882**	**1st**	**40**	**6**	**v A. Hancock**
25-12-1882	Sheffield, England	30-12-1882	2nd	370	2	72 hr G-A-Y-P
14-05-1883	**Sheffield, England**	**19-05-1883**	**1st**	**243**	**5**	**36 hr G-A-Y-P**
24-12-1883	**Sheffield, England**	**29-12-1883**	**1st**	**366**	**0**	**72 hr G-A-Y-P**
24-11-1884	**London, England**	**29-11-1884**	**1st**	**405**	**4**	**72 hr G-A-Y-P**
27-04-1885	London, England	03-05-1885	Rtd	221	1	72 hr G-A-Y-P
21-02-1887	**London, England**	**26-02-1887**	**1st**	**403**	**6**	**72 hr G-A-Y-P**
21-11-1887	**Philadelphia, USA**	**26-11-1887**	**1st**	**569**	**1**	**142 hr G-A-Y-P**
07-05-1888	**New York, USA**	**12-05-1888**	**1st**	**611**		**142 hr G-A-Y-P**
27-11-1888	**New York, USA**	**02-12-1888**	**1st**	**623**	**6**	**142 hr G-A-Y-P**

George was just 21 years old when he won his first professional and *"greatest race"* at Leeds, England, ending on April the 3rd of 1880, when, on a *dizzying* 38 laps to the mile track, he scored 374 miles and 277 yards in 72 hours. He followed that up with an eye-catching performance when beating 28 fellow competitors in the "Aggie" in London in September of the same year. .

His first crack at a 142-hour race brought him up against a most formidable opponent, one Charlie Rowell! Despite the reputation of the "Cambridge Wonder," George stuck to his task, and besides managing to beat some of the top "pros," namely Johnny Dobler of Chicago and the famous "Blower" Brown (who had held the world record earlier in the year), he scored 470 miles to finish second in the 6th International Astley Belt contest.

A trip over the pond to feature in the "2nd International O'Leary Belt" six months later proved fruitless. Despite making a commendable 480 miles, he had to retire prematurely from the race won by Vint.

With lessons learned in the New World, he headed back to Sheffield, where, in March of 1882 he made over 531 miles in a heel-and-toe walking match. This record still stands today and will be a tough nut to crack if anyone should *dare* try!

After mysteriously retiring prematurely from his next 72-hour event (1st Astley Challenge Belt) before his disappointed supporters on home turf in April of 1882, he travelled south to Birmingham, where he beat John Dobler's world record in the 2nd race of the series later in the year. Many were expecting him to beat the field in the 3rd version of the race 3 months later, but he could only manage 2nd place to George Mason who he took his revenge on when beating him conclusively in a 36-hour event 5 months later again on home soil. Littlewood then asserted his superiority in the 72-hour scene in Britain by winning both the 4th and 5th Astley Belt races. Indeed, his victory in the London race of November 1884 in which Rowell retired, secured the belt for good.

After retiring early in another 72-hour event in 1885, he bounced back to take a similar event in early 1887. He then concentrated his efforts on the 142-hour racing scene where he took on the world's best peds. Travelling to Philadelphia in November of the same year, he won his race with ease; then in New York in May of the following year, became only the fourth man to score over 600 miles in a race when he made 611. That set him up for his final race when he made the world record of 623¾ miles in December of 1888; a record that wasn't beaten for 96 years.

Below are Littlewood's "form" figures from 1879 till 1888:

Year	1879	1880	1881	1882	1883	1884	1885	1887	1888
Pos	4	5112	0	10112	11	1	0	11	11

The Argument for Daniel O'Leary:

If he had set his mind to it, the *"Plucky Pedestrian"* could have really gone places in his chosen profession, as his early career as a walker was really promising. Some people may argue that O'Leary did very well using his favoured heel-and toe method of conveyance, but there again, it never got him further than the 520-mile mark. Nevertheless, he was still an exceptional athlete, more so because he went against the rules in that he didn't seem to train for his contests. If he had and set his mind to running in his races, he may have gone so much further. His other problem of course was his penchant for alcohol, which was his undoing in the defence of his world champion title in 1879.

O'Leary's golden years were between 1875 and 1878, which is comparatively short compared with many other of the contenders for the title.

But what a gutsy performer Dan was! Looking back on his career, one has to admire his dedication to duty. From humble beginnings, the brave fellow set the world of pedestrianism alight with his remarkable achievements on the track. Always trying to prove that he was good enough to take on and beat Weston, he eventually got a crack at him, and from thereon, beat him easily every time. "Westy" always thought he could come from behind and pass the Irishman at the wire, but alas, the Chicagoan proved he was living in cloud cuckoo land time and time again.

Like Weston, he liked the idea of battling against time and many of the *"Plucky Pedestrian's"* feats were performed on his own against the ticking of the clock. Dan also liked to compete against others and in this fashion managed some remarkable results.

Another good thing going for O'Leary was his easy going personality and he certainly wasn't the showman that Weston was. Whereas "Ned" played to the crowd, Dan would put his head down and concentrate on the task in hand. Whereas the American wore his eccentric attire, the Irishman competed conservatively clad.

It is quite possible that after the disaster of the 3rd Astley Belt, he knew his limits and thereafter went into promoting. What is quite obvious was his passion for his chosen profession. He was as keen as Weston in educating the masses about the benefits of walking and he was also a willing tutor– as the then young Frank Hart found out. Indeed, Hart was to copy O'Leary's style of walking, and look how *he* developed when he became his protégé!

Still, he had a remarkable record, and to highlight some of these we must go back to his very first trial against time in July of 1874, when, and with a pair of ill fitting shoes, the *"amateur pedestrian"* lost 5 toe nails when he walked 100 miles in 23h.15m. A month later, setting a bigger target of 105 miles, he made the required distance in 23h.17m.

A trip to St. Louis to walk 200 miles in 40 hours in September was successful before taking on an opponent in the form of Wilson Reid who he beat in a 20-mile race in New York, winning $500 in the process. He then won a similar amount against John DeWitt in the same city after giving that man a 10-mile start in a 100-mile contest.

Things really started to hot up for O'Leary then, for he went on to beat Weston's old 115-mile record of 23h.59m by an hour in April of 1875. After being turned down by Weston who wanted him to prove himself before condescending to do battle with him, Dan managed to make 500 miles in 153½ hours. That performance set Chicago alight, and its citizens were ecstatic at their man's success. He then beat John Ennis in a world record time of 18h.53m before he was given the chance to have a match with Weston. He went on to beat him conclusively over six days, the final score being 503 to 461 in a time of 143h.13m.

King of the Peds

Not satisfied with that, O'Leary went over to California and made 500 miles in 139h.32m at San Francisco in May of 1876.

Drawn by the urge to have another crack at Weston, Dan set off for England where the American was touring in September of the same year. He immediately made an impression by beating the 500½ miles the "Wily Wobbler" had made shortly after his arrival at Liverpool.

He then took on the formidable Peter Crossland who first he beat then lost to in the space of 4 months, before beating Weston again at a packed Agricultural Hall, with a new world record of 519 miles and 1,585 yards.

Having gone back home, he returned back to England in March of 1878 to compete against Britain's best athletes in the 1st International Astley Belt contest, which he won with yet another world record of 520 miles and 440 yards. The runner-up, Henry Vaughan, who was considered the best in the country at the time, was 20 miles away.

O'Leary returned home and indulged in a farce of a race with Campana, which he won before taking on John Hughes in the 2nd International Astley Belt. Again he won, but his opponent wasn't in the same league as him. After that, in March of 1879, it all went badly wrong for the champ when Charlie Rowell robbed him of his beloved belt, and that sadly was the end of O'Leary.

The Argument for Charles Rowell:

From humble beginnings, Rowell impressed enough to be offered to take on Weston at the "Aggie" in February of 1876. He subsequently made his mark on the on the track when he came a creditable third in the match won by Corkey in the "1st Long Distance Championship of England" race between October and November 1878 when he scored a respectable 470 miles. Although he finished 51 miles behind the winner and 36 behind "Blower," it must be remembered that this was his first 142-hour race.

Astley then threw Charlie in at the deep end when he sent him over to America to compete for the "3rd International Astley Belt in March of 1879." He won this easily, and with 25 miles to spare over the runner-up, took a bumper harvest of $18,398.31 back to the motherland with him. Unable to compete in the 4th contest he nevertheless re-crossed the pond to take the belt in the 5th contest with an improved score of 525 miles which earned him another $26,000!

Rowell was then at the top of his profession and 14 months later reinforced his position with a smooth success, and a new world record, over the up-and-coming George Littlewood in London. After winning the Astley belt outright in June of 1881 (which wasn't a sufficient test of his capabilities), his next test ended in disaster when he failed to finish in the race won by Hazael in February and March of 1882. It was in this race that he made 100 miles in 13h.26m.30s (not bettered till 1953 when Wally Hayward made the same distance in 12h.46m.34s), and 150 miles in a time of 22h.30m (not beaten for 49 years when Arthur Newton ran 152 miles and 540 yards at Hamilton, Canada, in 1931).

Worse was to follow later in the year when he had to retire prematurely from another big race. After a period of convalescence Charlie became only the third person to cover 600 miles in the given time, but still found one too good for him in Fitzgerald in the April/May race of 1884.

Trying his luck over the shorter 12 hours a day 72-hour race, he yet again had to retire early after initially putting up a good show against Littlewood who went on to score 405 miles in the allocated time. The pair would meet just one more time when Charlie beat Littlewood's old record 72-hour record of 415 miles with a stunning effort of 430! That was his last race.

Details of Rowell's career covering the period from 1878 till 1885 are found below:

START	VENUE	FINISH	POS	M	L	TYPE
28-10-1878	London, England	02-11-1878	3rd	470	1	142 hr G-A-Y-P
10-03-1879	**New York, USA**	**15-03-1879**	**1st**	**500**	**1**	**142 hr G-A-Y-P**
22-09-1879	**New York, USA**	**27-09-1879**	**1st**	**524**	**7**	**142 hr G-A-Y-P**
01-11-1880	**London, England**	**06-11-1880**	**1st**	**566**	**1**	**142 hr G-A-Y-P**
07-03-1881	**New York, USA**	**12-03-1881**	**1st**	**272**	**0**	**142 hr G-A-Y-P**
20-06-1881	**London, England**	**23-06-1881**	**1st**	**280**	**0**	**142 hr G-A-Y-P**
27-02-1882	New York, USA	03-03-1882	Rtd	415	3	142 hr G-A-Y-P
23-10-1882	New York, USA	28-10-1882	Rtd	384	3	142 hr G-A-Y-P
28-04-1884	New York, USA	03-05-1884	2nd	602	0	142 hr G-A-Y-P
24-11-1884	London, England	29-11-1884	Rtd	232	7	72 hr G-A-Y-P
27-04-1885	London, England	03-05-1885	1st	430	0	72 hr G-A-Y-P

Rowell's "form" figures:

Year	1878	1879	1880	1881	1882	1884	1885
Pos	3	11	1	11	00	20	1

The Argument for Edward Payson Weston:

"E. P." was to the pedestrian era what Mohammed Ali was to the boxing scene of the 1960's and 70's. His personality was his best asset and boy did he use it to his advantage! Although excelling at ultra long distance walking during his career, he did manage to win the 4th International Astley Belt in London, and at the age of 40, made a new world record of 550 miles for good measure. That was his best performance against other competitors on the track, but it was when he competed on his own and, "against time" when he really showed his credentials for being one of the best in his chosen profession.

The planned 478-mile journey from Boston to Washington in 10 days in 1861 didn't turn out as expected, but what he did apparently achieve was an estimated journey, *"including deviations,"* of 510 miles in 10d.4h.12m. Still that didn't win him his bet!

Despite failing to walk 100 miles in a day, which was part of the agreement he had entered into, he nevertheless succeeded in walking from Portland to Chicago in 1867 in 26 days, a distance of 1,226 miles, and what a reception he received! The crowd loved him and he knew how to play to them. That was part of his success and he used his enigmatic personality to woo them along to watch him perform.

In January of 1869, after many ups and downs at various attempts to make certain distances in certain times in the previous year, he failed in his ambition to make 5,000 miles in 100 days giving up the attempt on the 36th day. Later on, between the height of summer and the end of autumn, he would spend time attempting to walk 50 miles in 10½ hours on 30 separate occasions, with the added bonus of a ½ mile being walked backwards.

In 1870 he managed to walk 100 miles in less than 22 hours, but later on in the year failed to make 400 miles in 5 days. The year after he succeeded in scoring 200 miles in 41 hours at St. Louis, and then accomplished the feat of walking 400 miles in 120 hours in New York as well as securing 112 of them in the first 24 hours.

Weston however, wanted to walk 500 miles in 6 days and he eventually accomplished his objective in December of 1874 at Newark, New Jersey. After being unsuccessful in a race against O'Leary in Chicago in November of 1875, he went to England.

The *"Wily Wobbler"* took the country by storm. After just a few weeks of stepping onto British soil, his name was on everybody's lips. Almost a quarter of a million people paid to see him perform by the end of March of 1876 as he took on the likes of Crossland, Ide, Parry, Perkins, Rowell, Smalley and Vaughan. He then toured both England and Scotland performing at various locations "against time" before preparing himself for his second unsuccessful encounter with O'Leary at the Agricultural Hall in March of 1877, which he lost with a commendable score of 510 miles.

He then managed to make 400 miles in 5 days at Hull and Newcastle-Upon-Tyne before accomplishing the feat of walking 1,000 miles in 400 hours again at Newcastle.

This was followed by his infamous attempt to walk 2,000 miles in 1,000 hours around the shires of England. As we know, he failed, but he did manage to make 1,977½ miles in the allocated time despite all the problems he encountered on the way. That was a reasonable effort considering the time of the year and the type of going he had to put up with — mud, slush, and the like.

His next "track" race for the "2nd Long Distance Champion of England" belt was against the likes of "Blower" Brown, Corkey and Hazael in London in April of 1879 when he came last of the quartet, a distant 92 miles behind the winner and new world record holder, Henry Brown.

Undeterred by his humiliation in that one, he went on to surprise everybody by taking the international version of the Astley Belt back to the United States in June of the same year, *and* with a new world record of 550 miles! With more effort he could have gone further, but what was refreshing about the way he competed was that he ran in this one, and ran effectively at that! The then 40-year-old had now proved himself not only as a gritty long distance walker, but as a competent runner against some of the best peds in the world.

The new world champion followed that with an indifferent performance in the 5th Astley Belt competition in New York in September of 1879 finishing 75 miles behind the winner, Rowell, in 6th place.

Then, in March of 1880, he took on his old adversary O'Leary in San Francisco for $5,000 and lost the lot, with a finishing tally of 490 miles against the victor's 516. That was followed by an attempt to re-take the Astley Belt in June of 1881 in a two-man race against the in-form, and much younger Rowell which ended prematurely due to illness.

Weston then went on to make 5,000 miles in 100 days between November of 1883 and March of 1884. Two thousand of those miles were performed in buildings, but the rest were made on the roads of England. This was an excellent performance considering the time of the year and the type of terrain and going he must have encountered on his formidable journey.

His final escapade was another challenge against O'Leary in 1885 over 2,500 miles in the USA when he had the last laugh by winning. True, Weston was nowhere near as good as the old enemy in a "six-dayer," but when it came to the ultimate challenge, "E. P." beat him hands down.

Well ladies and gentlemen, I would like to thank you all for your attention.

You are now free to close the final page of this book and consider your verdict as to who you think is the......

King of the Peds

PEDESTRIAN INDEX

00 are chapter numbers where a listed pedestrian can be found. **00 numbers mean that a history of that pedestrian's performances can be found in that chapter:** <u>00 are numbers where a pedestrian is mentioned in a chapter:</u>

Achille L'EcLaire: *France:* 49

Adams: *Millham:* 55

Adams J. C: *Bristol: USA:* 55 57

Alana E: *London:* 58

Albert E: *Toronto:* 57

Albert James: *Philadelphia:* 23 28 29 30 44 51 53 54 55 56 <u>57</u> <u>59</u> <u>60</u>

Alcock Thomas: 4

Alderton: <u>37</u>

Allen: 58

Allen Joe: *Renfrew, Mass:* **21** 25 30

Allen Paxton: *Auburn Me:* <u>15</u>

Armstrong Charles: *New York:* 17

Armstrong Harry: 23

Armstrong Lewis: *Huddersfield:* 37

Ashbourne T: *Nottingham:* 26 37 40

Attwood: 56

Bailey James: *Sittingbourne:* **9** 13 <u>24</u> <u>26</u> <u>40</u>

Bailey John: <u>9</u>

Baker: 34

Baker H: *Dover:* 37 52

Banks John: *Chicago:* 23 <u>27</u> 28

Barber George: *Jersey City:* 17 23 29 33

Barker E: *Rotherham:* 26

Barker Sam: <u>5</u>

Barnett William: *Leeds:* <u>9</u> **11** 26

Barnhart C: 1

Barrow: 27 28

Behrman John Henry: *Jersey City:* **21**

Bargozzi Achille: *Forli:* <u>9</u>

Bateman T: *Birmingham:* 26

Baxter N: *Sheffield:* 37

Beaven T: *Islington:* <u>18</u>

Belden Edward: 23

Bell: 23

Bendigo W: *Boston:* 30

Bennett Dave: *Canada:* 44 55

Benton Frank: 23

Berdan C: *Philadelphia:* 22

Bergin J: *Brighton:* 37 47

Bevers: 28

Bevins W: *Kingsland:* 58

Biggs: 4

Bird: 56

Bissett W: 23

Blair G: *Newcastle:* 58

Blake Allen: *Chicago:* 28

Bluett: 28

Bolstridge W: *New York:* 28 30

Bolton Mr: <u>9</u>

Bowman: 23

Booker A: 28

Boyle Charles: *Montreal:* **21**

Bracknell: <u>9</u>

Bradley David: *New York:* 17

Brand E: *Asbury Park, N. J:* **21**

Brandes Fred: *New York:* 22

Brandsetter George: *Chicago:* 23 28

Brighton J: *Moston:* 26

Brinkman Corporal: 5

Briody J: *Greenpoin L. I:* 21

Briody Thomas: *Brooklyn:* 22

Britain Clement: *New York:* 17

Brodie Stephen: *New York:* 17 22 51

Brondgeest John Albert: *Toronto:* **21**

Brookes: *Christchurch:* 28 58

Brooks Charles: *New Swindon:* 43

Brown Henry: *Hartford:* 60

Brown Henry "Blower": *Fulham:* **9 11** <u>12</u> <u>15</u> 18 19 <u>20</u> 21 23 24 <u>25</u> <u>26</u> 27 <u>28</u> <u>32</u> 35

Brown H. F: 31

Brown J. F: *New York:* 25

Brown John: *Sheffield:* 43

Bruce J: *Arbroath:* 23

Bruchs J: *Burlington. Iowa:* 29

Burdett Sam: *Derby:* 26

Burke T: *Brooklyn:* 29

Burns Daniel: *Elmira: N. Y:* 28 29 30 33 44 50 51 53 55 57 59

Burns Guy: 23

Burrell William: 45 56

Bush John H: <u>21</u>

Butler E: *Lambeth:* <u>18</u>

Buttery R: *Sheffield:* <u>48</u>

Byrne M. J: *Buffalo:* 17 28

Cahill: 23

Call: 56

Callaghan: <u>35</u>

Callaghan Thomas: *New York:* 17 56

Campbell: 34

Campbell: <u>58</u>

Campana Peter Napoleon: *Bridgeport:* **12** <u>15</u> <u>17</u> <u>20</u> <u>21</u> 22 23 28 29 30 <u>35</u> 41 45 56 57 60

Carless Henry: *Millwall:* 26 27 28 36 37 38 41 43 49 58

Cartwright George: *Walsall;* 26 27 28 37 38 40 41 43 **47** 49 52 **56** 57 59 60

Casey John: 1

Cassidy Matt: <u>12</u>

Cattle F: *Holloway:* 37

Cattle W: *Holloway:* 37

Caustin Charles H: *St. Charles, Illinois:* 28

Chadwick Joe: *Manchester:* 52

Charlesworth G: *Brightside:* <u>26</u>

Chates C: *Birmingham:* 58

Chillman W: *Brixton:* 26

Chisnell John: *Providence:* 50

Clark Alexander: *Hackney:* 5 6 <u>9</u>

Clarkson William: *Hull:* **11** 14 23 <u>24</u> 26 28 40 41 58

Clasper Harry: <u>5</u>

Clayton: <u>9</u>

Cliff James: *Cardiff:* 26 52

Clifford: *York:* <u>11</u>

Clow Ephraim: *P. E. Island:* 22 28 31 33

Coburn: 55

Colbert Robert: 23

Cole: 23 51

Cole Calvin: *Binghampton:* 50

Cole J: <u>9</u>

Collins: *Methven:* 28

Collins Dan: 58 59

Connor George: *Hackney:* 43 **47** 49 52 56 57 59

Colston John P: <u>20</u> 23 28 <u>30</u> <u>35</u>

Cooper: *Northampton:* 6 37

Corbett William: *Aberdeen:* 27 37 38 40 41 43 52 58

Cornforth C: <u>5</u>

Costello Micheal M: *Fishkill-on-the-Hudson:* **21**

Costello Thomas T: **21**

Cotter W. E: 59

Cotton Captain: 34

Coughlin M: *Erving:* <u>20</u> 57

Coughlin J. E: *Orange. Mass:* 29

710

Courtney Arthur: *Barnet:* 6 **11** 13

Cox John: *Petrolia. Pa:* 29 31 33

Cox Nicholas: *Bristol:* 52

Cox Tom: *Bradford, Penn:* 51 53 55 56

Coyle George B: 2

Craig John: *Ireland:* 60

Crawford M: *Salamanen: N. Y:* 22 28

Crawley C: 26

Crawley H: *Grantham:* 26

Croft Arthur: *Little Falls: N. Y:* <u>20</u> 22

Croft William: *Hull:* **11**

Crofts R: 50 58

Cromwell Richard: *San Francisco:* **21** 22

Cronin Jerry: *Elmira: N. Y:* 53

Crossland Peter: *Sheffield:* 4 5 6 <u>7</u> 8 <u>9</u> **11** 13 <u>20</u> 21 23 <u>27</u> 28 36 37 38 40 41 44 <u>47</u> <u>48</u> 49

Crowley J: *Birmingham:* 58

Crowley William: *Freeport, Illinois:* 28

Cummings W: <u>9</u> <u>48</u>

Cunningham C: 55 59

Curley Tim: *England:* 60

Curran Ben: *New York:* **21** 23 29 30 31 33 56

Curtis A. P: 33

Curtis C. H: *Cleveland. Ohio:* 28

Dalton P: 31

Dalziel J: 28

Dammers John P: 23

Dana A. M: 23

Daniels C. P: <u>15</u>

Daniels G. R: 23

Davies W. H: *New York:* 17 22

Davis Edward: *Kerry, Ireland:* 21

Davis: 28

Davis Richard: 22

Dawson Sanfield: *Canada:* 28

Day Alf: *Fulham:* 49

Day George J: *Islington:* 49 58

Day James: *New York:* 17

Day Sam: *Northampton:* **11** 13 23 **24** 26 27 <u>28</u> 37 38 <u>39</u> 40 43 45 50 55 <u>56</u> 57 59 60

Dean J: *Winchmore Hill:* 26

"Deerfoot" (L. Bennett): <u>9</u> <u>48</u>

DeForrest: <u>20</u>

Delaney: 58

Delrica: 56

Dempsey: 56

Desmond Frank: *Pennsylvania:* 60

DeWitt John: *Auburn:* 4 <u>21</u>

Dick James: *Forfar:* 52

Dickenson A: *Edenbridge:* <u>18</u>

Dickenson John: *Philadelphia:* **21**

Dickie P: 23

Dillon Dan: *Ireland:* 60

Dillon John: *New York:* 21 29 56 57

Dobler John: *Chicago:* <u>20</u> 23 25 <u>26</u> **27** <u>30</u> 35 <u>38</u> <u>40</u> 43 55

Dodge R. H: 23

Donovan: 31

Donovan Lawrence: 55

Dootson George: 6

Downing: *North Ormsby:* 58

Drake: 57

Driscoll: 28 55

Drummond: 58

Dufrane George: *New York:* 22 23 28 29 31 41 56

Dufrane Philip: 28

Dully: 57

Dunning G. A: 34

Dushane J. P: *Newcastle, Pa:* **21**

Dutcher William: *Lee, Mass:* 17 20

Easthall Thomas: *Brighton:* <u>9</u>

Eaton: 35

Eckersall Walter: *Chicago:* 21

Edwards Frank L: *New York:* **21** 23 41

Edwards P: 33

Edwards William: *Australia:* 3 23 34 44 48 58 59

Elder Sam: *Chicago:* 28

Electric's Unknown: *New York:* 60

Elmer W: *Sussex:* 58

Elson Alfred: *West Meriden, Conn:* 20 **21** 23 29 33 44 45 50 51 53 55 56 57 60

Ennis John: *Chicago:* 4 7 **11 15** 19 20 21 25 26 30 33

Estrline H: 57

Faber Christian: *Buffalo:* **21** 22 23 25 28 30 55 58

Farron G; *Hoxton:* 58

Federmeyer Leon P: *France:* **20**

Feeney O: *Haverstraw. N.Y:* 29

Fenlon Peter: *New York:* 17

Ferguson David: *Pollockshaws:* 23 27 **28** 37 41

Ferguson E: 5

Field: 56

Fitzgerald: Garrett: 35

Fitzgerald Patrick: *Long Island:* 10 21 22 23 28 29 31 **33** 39 41 45 50 53 56 60

Fitzpatrick Dan: *New York:* 22

Fitzpatrick J: *Manchester:* 13 26 41

Fitzpatrick Thomas: *Manchester:* 37 43

Flandon Michael: *Niagara Falls:* 28

Flaunty A: *Woolwich:* 18 24 26

Fleet J: *Manchester:* 9

Flitchcroft Peter: *New York:* 17

Fosse A: 50

Ford: 50

Forth B: *Dewsbury:* 26

Fox Charles: *Austin, Ill:* 21

Fox M: *Dundee:* 26

France: 13 18

Franklin: *Birmingham:* 40

Franks W (William Frank Savage): *Marylebone:* 26 28 38 40 **47** 52 58

Freeman: 23 28

Gale William: *Cardiff:* 6 **8** 34

Gallagher: 41

Garnham W: *Bulwell:* 26

Gebring: *Rahway. N. J:* 22

Geldert E: *Worcester. Mass:* 22 28 33

Gent Harry: 54

Gentleman William: "Corkey": *Bethnall Green:* **9 11** 12 15 18 19 20 27 40 49

Geraghty John J: 23

George John: *Auburn:* 50

Gibb W: *Aberdeen:* 23

Gettings P: 33

Gilbert W. G: 14

Gilbert W. H: *Freeport, Illinois:* 28

Gilloon I: *New York:* 22

Gilmore T. A: 1

Goodman H. L: 23

Goodwin John W: *New York:* 17

Golden Peter: *Boston:* 51 56 57 60

Gorman T. N. *Peoria. Ill:* 22

Cotton Federick Captain: 58

Gould: 44

Goulden E: *Canterbury:* 9

Goulding Thomas: *New York:* 30

Gown T: Covent Garden: 58

Graham: 44

Graham Carlisle D: 55

Grant: *Islington:* 26

Graves C. B: *New York:* 57

Green Sam: *Sheffield:* 43

Green W. E: *Clerkenwell:* 18 58

Gregory F: *Hoxton;* 58

Gregory W: *Hoxton:* **9** 18

Greig D: *Sunderland:* 58

Gretzna Joseph: *Australia:* 60

Griffin William: 48 52 56 58

Groves Joseph: *Oswestry:* **9**

Guerrero Gus: *California:* 50 51 55 56 57 59

Gutterman: 56

Guyon George: *Chicago:* 11 12 15 **20** 23 27 28 29 30 31 35

Hales Richard: 56

Hall John: *Brooklyn:* 17

Hamilton T: *Homerton:* 18

Hamilton's Unknown: 53

Hancock Arthur: 8 11 13 28 34 41 50 58

Hancock Owen: *Shadwell:* **11** 13 28

Hanlon: 23

Hanley John: *Binghampton:* 50

Hanwaker George: *New York:* 22 25 30

Harding Richard: *Blackwall:* 19 26

Harding William E: 7 **11** 28

Hardie F: *London:* 26

Harmer: 23

Harnes: 45

Harriman Charles A: *Haverhill:* 10 11 12 **15** 16 20 21 23 28 29 30 31 32 33 34 35 36 41 44 48 50 51

Harriman Walter: 10 58

Harriman's "Unknown": *Boston:* 28

Harry Capt: *Chicago:* 23 28

Hart Frank (Fred Hichborn): *Boston:* **20** 21 22 23 25 27 28 29 30 31 32 33 34 35 39 41 44 45 48 50 51 53 55 56 57 60

Hartley C: *Sheffield:* 6 41

Hatchjin William: *Buffalo:* 28

Hayden William: 4

Hawley: 55

Hayward Joseph: *Billingsgate:* **11**

Hazael George: *London:* **9** 13 18 19 20 24 25 27 31 32 33 35 39 44 45 47 48 52 60

Head H: *Brighton:* 58

Hefferman John: *Chicago:* 28 50

Hegarty: 58

Hegelman Peter: *New York:* 41 51 55 56 57 59 60

Henry James: *New York:* 57

Henderson: 58

Herbert T. C: 56

Herty Daniel: *Boston:* 28 30 33 *35* 39 41 45 50 51 55 56 60

Hewett F: *Millwall:* 26

Hibberd Jack: *Bethnall Green:* **11** 13 23 24 26 28 36 37 40 41 44 58

Higgins John: *Hornsey:* **11** 23 28 41

Hill H: *Swansea:* 26

Hilton G: *Derby:* 26

Hilton George T: *Brooklyn:* 22 23

Hindle R: 9

Hoagland Willard A: *Auburn:* 50 51 53 55 56

Hoffman George T: *Nebraska:* 60

Hoffman William H: 17 23 28 55

Holmes John J: *Nottingham:* **11**

Holske Edward: *New York:* 18 23

Hook T: *Brixton:* 58

Hooker: 28

Hope John: *Richmond:* 9 26 37 41 43

Hopwood W: *Leeds:* 58

Horan: 56

Hornby: 26

Horton W: *Croydon:* 26

Houghton A: *Islington:* 18

Houran William: *Chicago:* 28

Hourihan Jerry: *Boston:* 28 35 41

Howard Clarence G: *Huntingdon. USA:* 22

Howard George: *Atlantic City:* 57

Howard Harry: *Glen Cove. L. I:* 17 **21** 22 23 25 27 29 30 31 33

Howarth Thomas: *Atlantic City:* 51 60

Howes William: *Haggerston:* 4 <u>5</u> 6 <u>7</u> 8 <u>9</u> **11** 13 23 28 <u>35</u> 58

Hoyle Thomas: *Sheffield:* 43

Hughes: 14

Hughes F: *Birmingham:* 26 28

Hughes John "Lepper": *New York:* **10** <u>11</u> <u>12</u> 17 22 23 28 **29** 30 31 33 35 39 41 44 <u>45</u> 51 <u>53</u> <u>55</u> 56 57 60

Hullett: *Hoxton:* 52

Hunt H: *Acton:* 47

Hunter William: 8

Hurst: *Sittingbourne:* 26

Hutchens Harry: <u>48</u> 54

Hutchins: *Cambridge:* <u>5</u>

Hyde W: *Birmingham:* 38 58

Ide George: *Woowlich:* 5 6 **9 11** 13 14 23 31 41 58

"Indian Smith": <u>12</u>

"Iowa George": 23

Ireland Daniel: 35

Isaacs H: *Tottenham:* 38

Ives: *St. Lukes:* 26

Jackson Hiram: *New Bedford:* 20

Jackson W (the "American Deer"): <u>9</u>

Jagot Tom: *Hackney:* 58

Jaybee Mr: *New York:* 25 31

Johnson: *Tasmania:* 58

Johnson: 56

Johnson Frank: *New York:* 22

Johnson George: *Barrow-in-Furness:* **9** 13

Johnson S: R: *Wrexham:* **9**

Jones Benny: *Scranton:* 50

Jones Stephen: *Sheffield:* 37 40 43

Judd Professor: 2

Keeble C: *Suffolk:* **11** 52

Keefe: 51

Keeshon: 56

Kelly: *Pittsburgh:* 28

Kemmerer Martin: *Lock Haven:* **21**

Kennaven Edward: *New York:* 17

Kerwin W. H: *Tarrytown. N. Y:* 25

King H: *Rotherhite:* 26 37 <u>58</u>

Kirby Tom: *Kentish Town:* 52

Kline Augustus: *Germany:* 57

Knapton J: *Sheffield:* 43

Koeble: 28

Kraft: 28

Kramer Sergeant: *New York:* 57 60

Krohne Frederick: *New York:* 17 20 <u>21</u> 22 23 25 28 29 30 33 34 41 55

Kunz: *New York:* 28

Kyleburg Ludwig M: 17

Lacouse Richard: *Boston:* <u>20</u> 22 28 29 30 33

La Pointe J: *Elmira:* 51 55

Landin: 28

Lang: <u>48</u>

Laycock: 2

Layton Arthur: *Shenectady:* 28

Le Grand Frank: 53

Le Petit: 34

Leifield A. S: 28

Leith J: Aberdeen: 23 <u>24</u>

Leonardson Frank E: *New York:* 17 23

Levery: *Providence:* <u>20</u>

Lewis C. P: *Lowell. Mass:* 29 <u>35</u> 60

Lewis Walter: *Islington:* 8: **9** <u>11</u> 13 23 28

Libeau D: *Akaroa:* 58

Lion B: *Chepstow:* 38

Littlewood George: *Sheffield:* <u>5</u> **26** 27 <u>28</u> <u>30</u> 31 <u>32</u> 36 37 38 <u>39</u> 40 41 43 46 47 <u>50</u> 52 53 <u>55</u> 56 58 <u>59</u> 60

Loadsby David: <u>5</u>

Lockton W: *Stratford:* 26

Loder H: London: 58

Lounsbury William: 45

Lowery John: *New York:* 22

Lowdell J: *Kent:* 58

Luck E: *Hoxton:* 58

Lurkey H. L: 56

Lynbrook: <u>12</u>

Mackey: 50

Madden Ben: *New York:* 22

Madden P: *Marlborough: Mass:* 22

Mahoney James: *New York:* **21** 22 60

Malcolm: 28 58

Marshall P: 28 31

Mahoney James: *New York:* 60

Mahoney Micheal: *Norwich. Conn:* 17

Mann: <u>6</u>

Manning John F: *Brighton, USA:* <u>20</u>

Manks R: <u>9</u>

Martin G: *Camden:* **5** <u>18</u>

Martin James: <u>10</u>

Martyn C. C. Mr: *Yatton:* <u>9</u>

Mason George: *Ratcliffe:* 26 28 37 40 41 43 **47** 49 52 60

Mathews: *Haverstraw:* 22

McAndrews James: 23

McCann James: *New York:* 28

McCarty J: *Manayunk. Pa:* 30

McCarty Patrick: *York/Leeds:* **9** 13 14 <u>18</u> 23 26 27 28 37 38 40 41 43 **47** 49

McClean W. H: *Philadelphia:* 21

McCormick J: *Bolton:* 26

McCormick Joe: *New York:* 22

McCoy Ira D: *Cleveland. Ohio:* 29

McDonald's entry: *Chicago:* 28

McElvey T: <u>5</u>

McEvoy James: *Brooklyn:* 17 28 57

McGregor: <u>58</u>

McIntyre P: *California:* 23 25 44

McInernay Peter: <u>20</u>

McKee David: *Boston:* 21 22

McKenna C: *Lambeth:* 40

McKellan Peter: *Edinburgh:* 6 13 23 <u>24</u> 28

McKewan: 28

McLaughlin: 56

McLeavy James: *Bonhill. Scotland:* **9** 21 28 40 41

McLellan J: *New York* **(***A. M. C. N.Y):* 22

McManus: *Dundee:* 28

McTague: *Trenton:* 55

Meadows "Brummy": *London:* 26

Meagher: 55

Merritt Sam: *Bridgeport:* <u>12</u> <u>15</u> 17 20 <u>21</u> 22 25 <u>28</u>

Merryweather J: *Grantham:* 26

Messier Henry O: 55

Meyer Gustav: *New York:* 17

Mignault Philip: *Boston:* 22 28 29 33

Miles James: *Brixton:* <u>4</u> 6 <u>18</u>

Miles S: *Cardiff:* <u>18</u>

Mills J: <u>9</u>

Mills W: <u>9</u>

Moloney John: *Centerville:* 60

Molineaux Paul: *Boston:* 22

Moore Edward C: *Manhattan:* 53 56 57 60

Moore J: *New York:* 29

Moore Richard: *New York:* 29

Moorhead F: 50

Morgan J. J: <u>59</u>

Morlanger William: *Sweden:* 57

Mublieson G: 50

Mulgrew John C: *New York:* 30

Mullen Edward: 2 4

Mundin H: *Hull:* 26 28 37 38 40 41 43

Munroe H; *Tottenham:* 58

Munson Harry: <u>10</u> 56

Murphy Charles: *New York:* 22 23

Murphy J: *Stamford. Conn:* 22 25

Murphy Nicholas: *Haverstraw:* **21** 22 <u>23</u>

Murray J. B: *New York:* 17

Myerley: 60

Myers: 60

Nash Frederick W: *Brooklyn:* 17

Nelson: *Camden Town:* 6

Neville W: *York:* 26

Newhart Alf: *Easton:* 55 56 57

Newman W: *Camden Town:* **5** 6 13

Newsome Fred: *Sheffield:* 43

Newton T: *Holbeck:* 26

Nichols E: *Rotherhite:* <u>18</u>

Nill G: <u>26</u>

Nitaw-eg-Ebow: *Dakota:* 45

Noden Thomas: *Brooklyn:* 17 23

Nolan William: *Denver:* 57 60

Noonan P: *Felling-upon-Tyne:* 40

Noremac G. D: *Edinburgh:* 26 27 **28** 33 35 39 40 41 42 44 45 <u>47</u> 48 50 51 53 55 56 57 60

Norman H: *Holloway:* <u>18</u>

Norris Arthur: *Brentwood:* 52 <u>56</u>

O'Brien P: *Covington. Ky:* 22

O'Brien William S: *New York:* 11 <u>15</u> 17 <u>31</u>

O'Burke Timothy: *New York:* 17

O'Connor: *Timaru:* 58

O'Donnell Bartholomew: *Brooklyn:* 23

O'Leary Daniel: *Chicago:* 2 **4** <u>6</u> 7 9 10 <u>11</u> 12 15 <u>18</u> <u>19</u> <u>20</u> <u>21</u> <u>22</u> <u>23</u> <u>25</u> <u>26</u> <u>27</u> 28 <u>29</u> 30 <u>31</u> <u>32</u> <u>33</u> <u>34</u> <u>35</u> 41 44 <u>45</u> <u>50</u> 51 <u>55</u> 58

O'Leary P: *South Amboy. N. Y:* 29

O'Leary Thomas: *New York:* 28

O'Leary William: *Bridgeport, Conn:* <u>27</u> 44 55

O'Toole: 28 <u>33</u>

Oddy: 55

Oldis A: Lillie Bridge: <u>58</u>

Oliver W: 58

Olmstead Gus: *Chicago:* <u>27</u> 28 <u>31</u>

Otto: 28

Owers E: *Surrey:* 58

Padley W: *Nottingham:* 26

Palfreyman H: *Leeds:* 26

Palmer: 34

Palmer J. H: *Plymouth:* <u>24</u> 26

Panchot A: *Minnesota:* 22

Panchot H: *Minnesota:* 22

Panchot Peter: *Buffalo:* <u>15</u> **17** <u>19</u> 20 21 22 23 27 30 <u>31</u> <u>33</u> 35 39 44 45 <u>49</u> 50 53 55 56 57

Panchot's entry: *Chicago:* 28

Paris August: *New Jersey:* 22

Parry George: *Manchester:* 4 5 <u>6</u> <u>9</u> 13 14 <u>18</u> 23 <u>24</u> 26 <u>27</u> 28 34 41

Patterson: 28

Paul: 56

Payn Cornelius N: 2

Peach Robert: *New York:* 57 60

Pegram William: *Boston, Mass:* 22 25 27 <u>28</u> 29 <u>31</u> <u>33</u>

Perkins John: *Brooklyn:* **21**

Perkins William: *Camberwell:* <u>4</u> 5 6 13 <u>48</u> 51

Perrin: 23

Perry Alf: *Old Brompton:* 49

Perry E. G: *Birmingham:* 26

Pettello: 56

Pettitt George: *Sittingbourne:* **11** 23 26 28 **47**

Pettitt H: *Walsall:* 38

Phillips E: *Boston:* 29

Pierce Albert: *New York:* **21** 38 40 43

Pinder: *Sheffield:* <u>37</u>

Prater *Alf; Atlanta:* 57

Potter Lyman: <u>20</u>

Preuss Charles A: 23

Price: 41

Price Charles: 13

Raines John G: *New York:* 17 45

Ranhoffer: 56

Rankin David M: *New York:* 17

Rattigan: 28

Ray J: *Plymouth*: 58

Ray Toddy: <u>9</u>

Rayner John: 34 50

Raby J. W: *Huddersfield:* 37 43 <u>48</u> 58

Rae J. M: *Canada:* 22 23

Rafferty's Unknown: *New York:* 60

Redding: 23 28

Reed David: *New York:* 22

Reeves Edgar H: *Brooklyn:* 17

Reeve H: *Hoxton:* 58

Reid: <u>35</u>

Reid Wilson: *New York:* 4 <u>21</u>

Rier Charles: <u>27</u>

Richards: 56

Richards W: <u>9</u>

Richardson J ("Treacle"): *Whitworth:* <u>9</u>

Richardson W. H: *USA:* **11** 13 23 26

Ridley J. S: <u>9</u>

Riley's Unknown: 28

Ring: 23

Robinson W: *Bow. London:* 26 28

Robson J. S: *Liverpool:* 6 <u>18</u> 23 <u>24</u> 26 27 28 38 40 41 58

Roe Harry: 4

Roebuck T: *Sheffield:* 37

Roller: 28

Ross R. D: 28

Rowe Joe: <u>9</u>

Rowell Charles: *Cambridge:* **5** <u>6</u> **11** 14 15 <u>19</u> 20 <u>21</u> <u>22</u> <u>24</u> <u>25</u> <u>26</u> 27 <u>28</u> <u>29</u> 30 <u>31</u> <u>32</u> <u>33</u> 35 39 41 47 49 <u>50</u> <u>53</u> <u>56</u> <u>57</u> <u>58</u> <u>60</u>

Russell Charles: *New York:* 57

Russell Samuel P: *Chicago:* **11 21** 22

Ryan Pierce: *New York:* 30

Ryan William: *New York:* 22

Sabin Charles: *London:* 38

Salisbury J: *Aberdeen:* 23

Salman Otto: *Chicago:* 23 28

Sanders W: <u>5</u>

Sanderson James: <u>9</u>

Saul G: *Northampton:* 52

Saunders Amos: *Brooklyn:* <u>12</u>

Saunders James: *Brooklyn:* 57

Savage H: *Kilburn:* <u>58</u>

Say G: *Haggerston:* 28

Scanlon David M: *Brooklyn:* 17 23 31

Schmehl Henry: 4 <u>12</u> 34

Schock Albert: 23

Schring P: *Rahway. N.J:*

Schriver: 56

Schroeder Emille: *New York:* 57

Schwenk: 56

Scott Edward: 41

Scott Joe: *Dunedin. NZ:* <u>28</u> <u>55</u> <u>56</u> 58

Scott William H: *California:* 35

Selin: 56

Sexton James: *Cardiff:* <u>18</u> 44 58

Shannon Thomas: *New York:* 22

Shewan A: *Aberdeen:* 23

Sherry John: *Waukegan:* <u>27</u> 28

Shipley A: *Birmingham:* 58

Shipley T: *Birmingham:* 26

Shopla: 56

Shrubsole W: <u>5</u> 13

Simmonds: *Nottingham:* 6

Simpson J. G: *Cambridge:* <u>18</u> <u>24</u> 26 43

Sinclair A W: *Chelsea:* 49 52 56

Slater W: *Winchmore Hill:* 49 <u>58</u>

Smalley Henry: *Birmingham:* 5 6

Smith A: *Brompton:* <u>18</u>

Smith Ambrose: *Northampton:* <u>58</u>

Smith: 28

Smith C: *Hackney:* 26 49

Smith Charlie: *England:* 60

Smith J: *Hackney:*

Smith J: *York:* **9** 13 26

Smith James: 2 <u>20</u>

Smith Jim: <u>10</u>

Smith R. H: *London:* 58

Smith Tom: *Sheffield:* 43

Smith W: 60

Smith W: *Worcester:* 58

Smith William: *Paisley:* **9** 13 <u>18</u> 23 26 28 <u>56</u>

Smitten G: *Faversham:* 52

Smythe: 4

Smyth R. J: *Islington:* 26

Smythe W. H: *Dublin:* **9 11**

Spear W. H: *New York:* 17

Speed P: *Chesterton:* 11

Spellacy Timothy: *Millerstown, Pa:* **21**

Spelling Tim: 28

Spence J: <u>58</u>

Spencer Joseph: 5 <u>9</u>

Spicer J: *Retford:* 26 52

Sprague A. B: *New York:* 17

Sprague J. R: 4

Sprague William: *Chicago:* 22

Stanley G. L: *New York:* 17

Stearns J: 4

Steel James: *New York:* 22

"Steeprock": <u>9</u>

Stein Augustus: *New York:* 57

Stephenson G: *Battersea:* <u>9</u>

Stevens A: *Camberwell:* 49

Stevens R. H: *Paddington:* 26

Strokel Antoine: 34 50 51 53 55 56

Stout: 56

Sullivan Cornelius: *New York:* 17

Sullivan John C: *Saratoga:* 28 **30** 31 33 35 45 55 56 57 59

Sutcliffe W: *Lower Bridge:* 58

Swan C: *Christchurch. NZ:* 28 34 50 58

Sweeney: 44 50

Swemling Frederick: *New York:* 29

Tait William: *New York:* **21**

Taylor Alfred: **5**

Taylor Norman: *Vermont:* 15 20 <u>21</u> 51 56 57 59 60

Tell William: <u>12</u>

Thatcher Alfred: *Canning Town:* **11**

Thomas: 56

Thomas (the "Northern Deer"): 5

Thomas A: 44

Thomas B: *Tottenham:* 58

Thomas C: *Kilburn:* 26 31 37

Thomas E: *Eastbourne:* 44 52

Thomas E: *Wolverhampton:* 26 28

Thomas W. H: *Sunderland:* <u>58</u>

Thompkins A: *Armonck. N. Y:* 22

Thompson Charles: 45

Thorold: 13

Tierney Micheal: *Wilkesbarre:* 50

Tiers Samuel: *Paterson. N. J:* 17

Tilly George: 55 56 57 60

Toey W: *Brixton:* 52

Tomlan A: *Birmingham:* 58

Toomey Patrick: *New York:* 22

Topley George: 2

Townsend Simon: 50 55

Tracey Edward: *Cincinnati:* 34

Tynan Michael: *New York:* 30

Van Castella P: 23

Van Ness Peter: 7 <u>15</u> 23 60

Vannett W: *Arbroath:*

Vandepeer Henry: *Sittingbourne:* <u>11</u> <u>18</u> <u>24</u> 26 27 28 40 47 52

Vaughan Henry: *Chester:* <u>4</u> 5 6 <u>7</u> 8 **9** **11** <u>12</u> 13 14 <u>15</u> 23 <u>24</u> 28 30 <u>35</u> 39 <u>45</u> <u>47</u>

Vincent R: *Richmond:* <u>9</u>

Vint Robert: *Brooklyn:* <u>20</u> 22 23 28 29 <u>30</u> **31** <u>33</u> 35 39 41 44 45 50 51 53 55 56 57 60

Virtue W: <u>9</u>

Wade J: *London:* 49 58

Waldo W: 33

Walker Cyrenius: *Buffalo:* <u>17</u> **21** 22 23 28

Walpole's Unknown: *Austria:* 28

Walsh Michael: *Chicago:* 28

Walsh Patsy: *Borough, London:* <u>58</u>

Walty: 28

Ward: 44

Warner E: *Nottingham:* 49 52

Washington Professor: *Baltimore:* <u>21</u>

Waters: 23

Weaver D: *Stroudburg. Pa:* 22

Webster Isaac: *Wallacebury. Canada:* 22

Weekman Henry: *Newark:* 33

West: 58

Weston Edward P: *Litchfield. Conn:* 1 2 4 5 6 7 <u>9</u> 11 <u>12</u> 13 14 <u>15</u> 18 19 20 <u>21</u> <u>26</u> <u>27</u> 28 <u>30</u> 32 <u>35</u> 44 48 <u>49</u> 50

Westhall Charlie: <u>5</u> <u>8</u>

Whale Walter: *St Lukes:* 38 43

Wheeler W. E: *Boston:* 22

White Eagle: *Warm Springs:* 28

White F: *Wolverhampton:* 26

Whitley: *Hyde:* <u>18</u>

Wigzel "Ed": 41

Wilkinson George: *Sheffield:* 43

Wilmot: <u>33</u>

Williams: 34

Williams E: 25

Williams Edward: *New York:* 22

Williams H: *Gloucester:* 28 36 41 57?

Williams J. C: 23

Williams W: *South Wales:* 58

Williamson: <u>26</u>

Willis B: *Maidenhead:* 26

Willis H. L: *New Milford, Conn:* 17

Wiltshire: 6

Winn Ted: *Swindon:* 26

Winterburn H: *Acomb:* 40

Winters: 56

Woodhead W: 13

Wood James: <u>9</u>

Woodhead W: *Oughtibridge:* <u>26</u>

Woods J: *Jersey City:* 23 25

Woolfe J: *Chichester:* 23 28

Wren W: *Paddington:* **47**

Zang: 55

NAMES INDEX

Symbols

125th Street 142

18th Street 63

1st Astley Challenge Belt 483, 511, 704

1st Avenue 150

1st International Astley Belt 562, 701, 703, 706

1st O'Leary Belt viii, 253, 305, 312, 328, 343, 702

1st O'Leary International Contest 404, 701, 702

22nd Street 28

24th Regiment 88

27th Street 496

2nd Astley Challenge Belt 489, 511

2nd International Astley Belt 143, 706

2nd O'Leary Belt 351, 377, 415, 702

2nd O'Leary International Belt 426, 451, 702, 703

34th Street ferry 557

3rd Astley Challenge Belt 506

3rd International Astley Belt 192, 223, 706

3rd O'Leary Belt 412

4th Astley Belt Challenge Trophy and Sweepstakes 562

4th Astley Challenge Belt 517

4th International Astley Belt 238, 364, 707

5th International Astley Belt 249

5th Long Distance Astley Belt 593

65th Street 696

78th Street Band 496

7th International Astley Belt 434, 703

7th Regiment 215

A

A.A.C 78

Aberdeen 345, 348, 366, 388, 389, 399, 483, 489, 506, 514, 518, 593, 616, 677

Aberdeen Recreation Grounds 389

Aboriginees 27

Abyssinia 412, 525

Academy of Music 343

Adam's School 1

Adams 306, 414, 590, 613, 639, 642

Adams, Massachusetts 306, 414

Ada Street 57

Addison County 38

Addison Road 608

Admiral Street 76

Adonis xi, 282, 295, 323, 325

African 300, 325, 355, 358, 683

Agricultural Hall vii, viii, xii, 82, 84, 85, 92, 95, 97, 99, 101, 102, 106, 107, 113, 122, 125, 127, 136, 151, 153, 164, 174, 175, 181, 233, 236, 238, 245, 246, 247, 249, 268, 272, 335, 343, 347, 363, 369, 375, 376, 384, 387, 511, 525, 561, 564, 569, 570, 616, 666, 673, 675, 677, 678, 698, 700, 703, 706, 708

Albany 14, 16, 36, 39

Albany turnpike 14

Albert Gate 378

Albion Society 298, 304

Alburgh, New York. 38

Ald. Charlick 142

Aldan 18

Alderman and Citizen's Association 63

Aldershot 123

Alexandra 186, 246, 511

Alexandra Grounds 511

Alexandra Palace 246

Alexandria: 129

Alexandria Hall 246

Alhambra Rink 588, 592

Allegheny City 308

Allen Street 16

Alloa 399

Allyn House Hotel 14

All Comers Walking Competition 105

Amateur Athletic Union 682

America iv, vii, xi, 8, 24, 30, 31, 32, 33, 43, 49, 56, 69, 70, 75, 82, 88, 96, 113, 115, 119, 125, 136, 138, 140, 150, 163, 189, 191, 193, 221, 226, 233, 238, 241, 243, 245, 247, 248, 252, 253, 254, 261, 301, 303, 305, 306, 334, 347, 348, 376, 377, 385, 391, 397, 404, 412, 423, 426, 434, 439, 450, 472, 489, 492, 525, 553, 564, 586, 602, 606, 636, 655, 666, 695, 696, 697, 698, 703, 706

American xii, 5, 6, 7, 14, 31, 32, 33, 36, 42, 46, 60, 68, 72, 74, 75, 76, 77, 78, 80, 82, 84, 85, 86, 88, 90, 91, 92, 93, 94, 97, 99, 100, 101, 107, 108, 110, 113, 114, 116, 117, 122, 123, 126, 127, 128, 132, 135, 137, 138, 143, 149, 152, 155, 172, 178, 179, 181, 182, 183, 184, 185, 188, 190, 191, 193, 200, 204, 208, 209, 212, 214, 217, 218, 221, 222, 223, 226, 230, 235, 239, 240, 241, 242, 243, 244, 246, 247, 250, 251, 254, 255, 257, 259, 261, 274, 280, 281, 282, 283, 285, 287, 292, 294, 298, 301, 305, 306, 323, 328, 329, 332, 340, 342, 359, 372, 373, 375, 376, 377, 378, 379, 380, 381, 382, 390, 391, 397, 399, 401, 404, 406, 408, 410, 412, 413, 414, 415, 416, 423, 424, 426, 429, 436, 438, 439, 440, 442, 446, 447, 449, 451, 479, 492, 494, 508, 520, 523, 527, 531, 532, 534, 535, 537, 539, 552, 589, 593, 594, 595, 608, 636, 649, 650, 651, 669, 670, 679, 680, 681, 685, 689, 691, 692, 694, 695, 696, 697, 700, 702, 705, 706

American Consul 97

American Exhibition 608

American Hotel 7

American House Hotel 14

American Institute 46, 60, 72, 74, 75, 114, 193, 261, 404, 410, 412, 416, 438, 439, 442, 447, 449, 451, 527, 531, 700, 702

American Institute Building 72, 193, 261, 404, 416, 438, 447, 451, 531, 700, 702

American Institute Hall 75, 442

American International Championship Belt 328

American International Champion of the World 328

American Revolution 6

American Tract Society 32

American Watch Company 695

Amherst 39

Amsterdam 14

Anchor Line 253

Andover 13, 14

Andover, Connecticut 13

Anglo Saxon 300

Annapolis 9

Antique House Hotel 6

Arabian 242, 623, 629

Arbroath 345, 371, 483, 489, 493, 506, 518

Arcade Garden 422

Archibold 24

Argyll Street 122

Armonck, New York 329

Armory 72, 336, 397

Army Hospital Corps 100

Arundel 177, 179, 479

Asbury Park 306

Ashby De-La-Zouch 187

Ashel 412

Ashford and Devey 363

Ashland House Hotel 250, 253, 412, 525, 528

Ashtabula 19, 23, 39

Assembly Hall 613

Assembly Rooms 179, 188

Astley 50-Mile Championship Belt 366

Astley Belt vii, viii, ix, 123, 124, 125, 136, 138, 141, 143, 150, 153, 192, 220, 223, 227, 230, 232, 233, 236, 238, 244, 249, 250, 253, 254, 256, 262, 264, 300, 303, 304, 305, 317, 324, 330, 334, 347, 359, 364, 375, 377, 391, 413, 414, 424, 434, 436, 438, 439, 447, 483, 526, 544, 550, 562, 582, 593, 701, 702, 703, 704, 705, 706, 707, 708

Astley Champion Belt 163

Astley Fifty Miles Running Championship Challenge Belt 511

Astley Ten Mile Championship Belt 363

Astoria 464, 526, 528

Astor House Hotel 470, 473

Atcham Church 182

Athletic Club 59, 77, 144, 170, 182, 194, 226, 260, 434, 435, 496, 526, 528, 532, 696

Atlanta ix, 46, 246, 254, 258, 261, 571, 637, 638, 639, 652, 653, 654

Atlantic City 604, 613, 639, 683

Attercliffe 186, 362, 366, 368, 377

Auburn, Massachusetts 586

Augusta 254

Aurora, Missouri 614

Austin 44, 88, 233, 307, 342, 657, 658, 659, 663, 670, 671, 673, 677, 678

Australia xi, 105, 163, 252, 343, 445, 523, 524, 572, 584, 607, 615, 657, 668, 669, 674, 679, 683

Australian 55, 325, 345, 575, 585, 616, 654, 657, 661, 663, 664, 665, 672, 676, 677, 685

Austrian 394, 395, 602, 613, 623, 634, 635

Avon 14

Axminster 179

Aylesbury 152

Aylstone Park Grounds 443

Ayrshire 130

B

"B" Division 610

"Bethnall Green Wonder" 157

"Black Dan" 330, 354, 359, 500, 603

Bacchus 201, 202

Back Bay 262

Back Lane 86

Balaclava 88

Baldwin House 433

Balham Grounds 561

Baltic Street 337

Baltimore, Maryland 343, 585

Bangor, Maine, 35

Bank of England 101

Bank of London 112

Bank Street 18

Barford Street 378, 385

Barmby Bar 185

Barnes 87, 524

Barnet 103, 128, 151, 174, 368

Barnsley 177, 186, 250, 251, 304, 373, 377, 449, 494, 526, 541, 567, 573

Barnstable 177

Barnum's "Roman" Hippodrome 49

Barnum's Flying Woman 575

Barnum's Hippodrome 59

Barnum's Museum 197, 310

Barrhead 389

Barrow-in-Furness 129, 174

Bartlett 224

Barton and Rice 398

Base Ball Grounds 11, 32

Bass ale 65, 685

Batavia 16, 17, 18

Bates 205

Bath viii, xii, 5, 72, 84, 87, 121, 135, 207, 219, 237, 259, 276, 291, 299, 323, 383, 384, 385, 407, 409, 418, 501, 532, 543, 549, 553, 579, 593, 604, 622, 657, 659

Bath Road 116

Battersea 127, 611

Battle Creek 43

Battle of Alma 123

Bauland's Band 618

Baur's Casino 616

Bawtry 559

Bawtry Road 559

Bayne's Sixty Ninth Regiment Band 683

Beacon Street 4

Bean & Clayton 4

Beckwith and Taylor 364, 388

Beckwith Family 575

Bedford 151, 177, 189, 263, 371

Bedfordbury 128

Belair 8

Belfast 38, 682

Belfast Spider 682

Belleview Hospital 205

Bellevue 23

Bellows Falls, Vermont 38

Belmont & Hanson 572

Belvedere 178

Belvoir Inn 367

Benson's chronograph 235

Berea 23

Berkeley 180

Berkshire 105

Berlin 39, 247, 680, 695

Bertram and Roberts 574

Berwick 10, 12, 180, 345

Berwick Arms Inn 180

Bethnall Green 127, 131, 152, 153, 157, 233, 343, 364, 388, 475, 477, 488, 573, 674, 675

Betram 246

Beverly 12

Bexley Heath 178

Billesdon 187

Billingsgate 152

Bilsford 561

Bilston 181

Bilston Road 181

Bilston Street 181

Binfield 190

Binghamton 586, 592

Bingley Hall 181, 348, 474, 489, 562, 570, 677

Bingley Hall Tavern 181

Birdcage Walk 524

Birmingham ix, 93, 101, 104, 155, 177, 181, 348, 362, 363, 364, 365, 366, 403, 474, 483, 489, 491, 492, 493, 494, 506, 510, 511, 518, 528, 561, 562, 566, 570, 616, 674, 677, 704

Birtley 184

Blackburn 183

Blackwall 238, 239, 364, 371

Blackwater 180

Blackwell Heath 99

Black Lion 184, 185

Black Lion Hotel 185

Black Rock 398

Black Swamp 23

Bleeding Heart 222

Bletchingley 524

Blower Kearney 325

Blythburg 187

Board of Managers 257, 258, 302

Bobee Brothers 575

Bodmin 177, 180

Bohemian 139

Bolton 129, 177, 183, 364

Bonhill 129, 308

Bonney's 18

Boothroyd and Milner's Sprint Handicap Race 362

Boroughbridge road 184

Boston viii, ix, 1, 3, 4, 5, 7, 9, 13, 14, 15, 35, 126, 143, 146, 150, 163, 193, 224, 225, 250, 261, 262, 266, 288, 300, 323, 328, 329, 352, 359, 375, 377, 378, 388, 389, 394, 397, 400, 404, 414, 422, 426, 427, 430, 431, 434, 438, 441, 442, 467, 495, 497, 512, 513, 525, 526, 556, 557, 572, 586, 616, 617, 619, 620, 621, 632, 636, 639, 640, 641, 650, 679, 683, 688, 690, 692, 701, 707

Boston Baseball Club 692

Boston Museum Company 650

Boston Music Hall 261

Bothnia 250

Bow 16, 113, 148, 171, 207, 468

Bowery 297, 445, 548, 629, 683

Bowery Street 629

Bowmansville Road 18

Bow Grounds 127, 561

Boylston Bank 224

Bradford 118, 177, 185, 393, 404, 407, 434, 590, 639

Bradford, Pennsylvania 393, 404, 407, 434

Bradford rink 118

Bradley 181, 227, 228, 229

Brampton 183

Brandywine River 8

Bricklayers Arms 363

Bridgeport 6, 160, 161, 162, 164, 165, 167, 168, 170, 171, 172, 173, 227, 229, 263, 299, 303, 328, 352, 376, 377, 404, 414, 532, 695

Bridgewater 177

Bridge Inn 655

Bridlington 177, 185

Bridport 177, 179

Briggs House Hotel 15

Brighton 85, 87, 88, 93, 95, 104, 120, 126, 129, 177, 179, 233, 261, 336, 364, 371, 435, 483, 530, 548, 561, 616, 677, 678

Brighton Beach Orchestra 530

Brightside 362, 655

Brightside Lane 655

Brimfield 25

Bristol 7, 43, 84, 114, 115, 129, 133, 177, 180, 181, 403, 511, 562, 593, 613, 639, 695

Bristol, Pennsylvania 695

Bristol Brass Band 7

Bristol House Tavern 43

Bristol Road 181

Britain xi, 82, 92, 191, 227, 245, 303, 404, 450, 561, 678, 704, 706

British Army 514

British Columbia 307

British Isles 126, 426, 654, 671

British Provident Association 304

British Vice Consul 211

Brixton 71, 102, 104, 233, 593, 674

Broadway 3, 4, 7, 125, 147, 191, 222, 448, 449, 536

Broad Street 52, 570

Brockton, Massachusetts 389, 411, 422, 701

Brocton, NY 10

Brodie's Saloon 629

Brompton 77, 120, 126, 127, 233, 572, 574, 609, 610

Brompton Road Station 609

Bromsgrove 177, 181

Brooklyn ix, xi, 7, 50, 53, 147, 152, 161, 168, 193, 195, 201, 204, 208, 210, 215, 222, 226, 227, 242, 246, 259, 268, 271, 279, 285, 293, 295, 300, 301, 303, 307, 308, 313, 317, 325, 327, 328, 329, 334, 335, 336, 337, 344, 345, 351, 358, 359, 390, 400, 404, 407, 410, 420, 421, 422, 428, 432, 434, 438, 447, 451, 457, 467, 468, 496, 526, 528, 530, 531, 545, 549, 556, 557, 587, 591, 612, 613, 620, 629, 639, 646, 652, 683, 690

Brooklyn Bridge 591

Brooklyn Cobbler xi

Brooklyn Electric Lamp factory 327

Brooklyn Furniture Company 410

Brook House 185

Brownhelm 39

Brown and Jahr 419

Brunswick Hotel 260

Bryan 6, 10, 23, 24, 125, 323, 410, 413

Buckhirst Hill 672

Buckingham 177, 189

Buckinghamshire 86, 152

Buffalo, New York 261, 497, 508, 519

Buffalo Opera House 16

Bullwell 366

Bull Hotel 188

Burke's Hotel 64, 341

Burlington, Iowa 404

Burnley 128

Burton 177, 183, 187

Burton on Trent 187

Bury St. Edmunds 188

Busby Stokes 184

Bush Hotel 183

Butler 24, 233, 309, 421

Butlerville 6

Butler Street 421

Byron Centre Hotel 17

C

"Cambridge Wonder" 436, 545

"Cast-Iron George" 438

C. Connelly 371

C. Crossley 371

C. Ellison 151

Calais 130

Caledonian Road Joinery Works 151

Caledonian Society 660

Caledonian Sports 657, 678

California ix, 1, 142, 253, 307, 328, 352, 353, 572, 586, 637, 650, 679, 706

Californian 307, 314, 354, 451, 454, 614, 643

Californian Scout 307

California Diamond Belt 307

Calumet, IN 10

Calumet Avenue 63

Camberwell 102, 104, 152, 233, 574

Camborne 180

Cambridge ix, xi, 78, 86, 87, 90, 92, 153, 177, 188, 191, 222, 233, 249, 261, 304, 348, 371, 373, 382, 435, 436, 518, 525, 545, 563, 573, 575, 704

Cambridgeshire 86, 260, 371, 377, 497

Cambridge Heath 78

Cambridge Road 86

Cambridge University 86, 525

Camden Town 88, 102, 103, 233, 561

Canada 1, 2, 230, 261, 306, 329, 387, 400, 401, 442, 515, 613, 706

Canal Street 125

Canning Town 153

Cannock 370

Canterbury 126, 127, 128, 178

Canterbury Rural Fete 126, 127

Canton Hotel Grounds 120

Capitol 3, 8

Cardiff 101, 102, 120, 121, 141, 233, 364, 511, 524, 593, 677

Cardiff Giant 141

Cardiff Skating Rink 524

Carley House Hotel 14

Carlisle 25, 26, 32, 177, 183, 306, 352, 612

Carnforth 183

Castle garden 684

Castle Hotel 190

Castle Street ix, 655

Catholic 113, 148

Cattaraugus Bridge 40

Caxton 189

Celt 57, 300

Celtic 313, 684

Centerville 683

Central City Park 46

Central Park 141, 142, 223, 251, 495, 631, 681

Central Park Garden 142

Cerno Mr. 57

Chadd's Ford 8

Chalk Farm Grounds 127

Challenge Belt 151, 233, 347, 483, 484, 487, 489, 506, 511, 517, 561, 570, 703, 704

Chamberlain E. 630

Chamber of Deputies 513

championship belt of the world 338, 638

Championship Challenge Belt 487, 511

championship of America 697

Championship of Australia 668

championship of England challenge belt 483

Championship of the Colonies 658

championship of the world viii, 75, 164, 192, 377, 468, 666, 692, 698

Championship Pedestrian Belt of the United States 226, 308

Championship Pedestrian Medal 57

champion belt of America 391

Champion Belt of Scotland 345

champion boxer of the world 684

Champion Cup of America 376

Champion Cup of the Midland 337

Champion Gold Medal 370

Champion Long Distance Pedestrian of England 84

Champion medal of Louisiana 377

Champion of Canada 401

Champion of Champions 526

champion of England 310, 573, 602, 615, 665

champion pedestrian of the world 58, 75

Champion Quail Eater 650

Champion Walker of America 75

Champion Walker of Scotland 104

Champion Walker of the World 69, 472

Channel Island 152

Chapel Street 222

Charing Cross 79

Charlestown 13

Charles Street 562

Charmouth 179

Charter House Hotel 8

Chase 26, 370

Chasetown 489

Chataqua County 19

Chatham 10, 14, 178, 531

Chatham Square Museum 531

Cheapside 517, 675

Chelsea 13, 343, 593, 611, 674, 677

Chelsea, Massachusetts 343

Cheltenham 234

Chepstow 489

Cheshire 120

Chester-le-Street 184

Chesterton 86, 87, 153, 191, 200, 222, 249, 260, 375, 377, 382, 435, 494, 497, 540, 573, 576, 578

Chester County 8

Chester Moor Colliery 184

Chestnut Street Rink 60, 679

Chicago ix, xii, 9, 10, 11, 15, 16, 17, 19, 21, 22, 23, 25, 26, 27, 28, 29, 30, 31, 32, 33, 37, 53, 56, 57, 58, 60, 61, 62, 63, 65, 66, 67, 68, 69, 70, 71, 79, 108, 109, 110, 113, 115, 126, 130, 138, 141, 143, 144, 147, 150, 152, 163, 164, 172, 201, 202, 204, 238, 248, 261, 262, 270, 303, 305, 307, 308, 310, 312, 316, 319, 329, 337, 338, 339, 340, 341, 342, 352, 354, 363, 375, 376, 377, 390, 391, 394, 397, 404, 426, 427, 434, 439, 443, 446, 449, 453, 476, 526, 532, 572, 587, 589, 614, 694, 700, 704, 705, 707

Chicago, Illinois 9, 30, 32, 150, 152, 262, 305, 352, 376

Chicago Ward 12 56

Chichester 128, 153, 179, 343, 388

Chippewa Indian 528

Chiswick 127, 233, 610

Chit Chat 117

Christmas Day 3, 167, 168, 331, 506, 507, 511, 517, 519, 520, 565, 588

Church of England Temperance 524

Church Street 362

Cincinnati, Ohio 2, 308

Cincinnati blackleg 286

Cinque Port Hotel 178

Circus Royal 380

City Driving Park 43

City Grounds 128

City Hotel 7, 13

City of Berlin 247, 680, 695

City of Chester 654

City of Richmond 412, 426

City of Steel 362, 509

City Road, 128

Civil Service Athletic Club 77

Clapham Junction 435

Clapham Road 435

Clapham Road Athletic Club Grounds 435

Clarksville 7

Clark Street 29

Claverick Street 13

Clerkenwell 233, 370, 518

Clevedon 129

Cleveland, Ohio 404

Cleveland Road 181

Clifton House Hotel 25

Clinton County 38

Clonakilty 56

Clough Road 474, 506

Clyde 23, 390

Coach and Horses Hotel, 181

Coakley Hall Walking Rink 335

Cockney 276

Coddenham Road 188

Cohoes 588

Colchester 177

Coliseum 325, 326, 327

Collingwood Street 184

Colnbrook 77

Columbia County 14

Columbus 37, 261

Commercial Hotel 659

Commissioner of Police 125

Common Council 15, 299

Company No. 29 161

Compton 86

Concert Hall 222, 435

Coney Island 263, 300, 450, 622, 624, 695

Congress Hall 16

Conisborough 559

Conneaut 20, 21, 22, 23, 39

Connecticut 1, 3, 4, 6, 13, 14, 16, 19, 160, 169, 170, 227, 230, 253, 258, 263, 285, 303, 307, 316, 328, 343, 352, 353, 377, 414, 639, 644, 683

Connecticut Hotel 6

Continental Hotel 8

Cook 33, 255, 363

Cooke's Circus 345

Cooke's Royal Circus 388

Cookridge Street 368

Cook and Peall 564

Cool White 7

Copenhagen champion belt 127

Corbridge 184

Corby hill 183

Corfu 18

Cornstalker 676

Cornwall Bridge, CT 10

Corn Exchange 183, 188, 189, 399

Correctionville, Iowa 610

Corry 391

Corthinian Hall 35

Corunna 25

Cosmopolitan Skating Rink 588

Cottage Grove Avenue 28

County Cavan 131, 153

County Cork 56

County Donegal 657

County Longford 152, 442, 497

County Tipperary 141

Court House 289

Coxhoe 184

Cranborne 179

Cranston 13

Cranswick 185

Crawley Athletic Sports 128

Cremorne Gardens 93

Crimea 123

Crooklands 183

Crosby's Opera House 29

Crosby House Hotel 25

Croton water 267

Crowcatcher 131, 377

Crown Street 6

Croydon 86, 366, 524

Cunard 222, 606

Cuthbertson 685

D

D. A. Curtis 46

D. Edwards 151

D. F. Draper 4

Dabinette's Band 586

Dalton Brook 559

Danbury 160

Danby, Vermont 38

Darien 6

Darlington 177, 184, 607

Darnall 363

Dartford 152, 178

Davenport, Iowa 43

Deaf and Dumb Institution 99

Dearborn Seminary 63

Dearhorn Street 29

Dedham 13

Deering 150

Defiance 202

Delaware River 7

Delta 24

Denistoun 118

Denver, Colorado 572

Deptford 347, 475

Derby 130, 177, 187, 256, 298, 366, 367, 370, 424, 495, 607

Derbyshire 307

Detroit, Michigan 42

Devon 86

Devonshire 179, 181

Devonshire Park Estate 179

Dewsbury; 364

Dexter Park 28, 29, 72

Dinton 152

District line 77

Division Avenue 299

Dodworth's band 253

Dodworth & Co 250

Dog and Gun Inn 185

Doncaster 362, 363, 559

Donegal 306, 657

Donet 130

Dorchester 177, 179

Dorking 524

Dough puncher 564

Douglas Hotel 184

Dover 178, 422, 483, 593, 701

Dover, New Hampshire 422, 701

Downing Stadium 699

Dr. Craig 147

Dr. Dunn 61

Dr. Frankish 55

Drill Hall viii, 186, 390, 403, 474, 477, 479, 483, 506, 511, 513, 517, 562, 570, 581, 609

Drill Shed 55, 657, 658

Driving Park 42, 43

Droitwich 177, 180, 181

Druids brass band 655

Dublin vii, 131, 139, 143, 153, 174, 280, 335

Dubuque Driving Park 42

Dunbartonshire 129

Dundee 129, 345, 348, 363, 368, 370, 388, 399, 562

Dundee Sporting Club 345, 348, 368

Dunedin 55, 399, 584, 657, 658, 660, 661, 665, 666, 670, 671, 678

Dunkswell 86

Dunstan Corner's 12

Durham 27, 177, 184

Duryea and Co 419

Dwight House Hotel 26

Dymchurch 178

E

E. Clackett 371

Eagle Hotel 18, 24

Eagle House Hotel 224

Eagle Street 18

Earl's Court Road 122

Earl of Arundel and Surrey Hotel 479

Eastbourne 177, 179, 524, 593

Eastern walkist 58

Eastertide 79

Eastrea 188

East Avenue 16

East Bridgeport 161

East Brookfield 5

East Chatham 14

East Dereham 187, 188

East Greenwich 178

East Hartford 10, 14

East Lee 14

East Main Street 161

East Retford 153

East River 303, 696

East Sixty Fifth Street 695

East Temple Chambers 187

East Tennessee 638

East Twenty Ninth Street 360

Eben's band 300

Edding's Corners 25

Edenbridge 233

Edgbaston 487

Edgerton 24

Edinburgh 95

Edmund Street 677

Edwards 55, 105, 151, 211, 301, 307, 312, 313, 314, 343, 345, 440, 445, 512, 514, 523, 524, 572, 610, 657, 658, 661, 663, 664, 665, 668, 679

Elite Rink 591, 612

Elizabethtown 7

Elkan and company 492

Elkhart 25, 26

Elkhart Brass Band 25

Ellenborough, New York 38

Elliott 12, 306, 423

Elmira 328, 400, 404, 414, 438, 586, 590, 602, 613, 639

Elmore 23

Elsham Hall 117

Elyrin 39

Emerald Isle 76, 432

Emerald Snow Shoe Club 306

Emerson 301

Emmanuel road 188

Empire City Rink 44

Empire Hotel 658

Empire Skating Rink 43

Empire State 1

England viii, ix, xii, 13, 16, 29, 31, 43, 64, 71, 75, 77, 82, 84, 85, 91, 92, 94, 95, 101, 102, 113, 114, 115, 119, 122, 124, 125, 129, 130, 137, 138, 143, 150, 151, 153, 157, 161, 163, 172, 174, 178, 180, 188, 189, 191, 193, 196, 199, 219, 220, 221, 226, 227, 233, 238, 241, 244, 245, 247, 248, 249, 250, 251, 252, 254, 260, 261, 267, 281, 282, 300, 301, 304, 306, 307, 309, 310, 319, 325, 334, 337, 338, 339, 340, 342, 346, 347, 352, 360, 362, 364, 375, 376, 377, 378, 388, 390, 391, 394, 403, 412, 421, 423, 434, 435, 438, 439, 443, 448, 449, 450, 462, 468, 472, 474, 483, 484, 489, 494, 497, 503, 512, 523, 524, 526, 527, 528, 544, 553, 558, 571, 572, 573, 586, 587, 602, 615, 616, 636, 637, 639, 640, 643, 652, 654, 665, 666, 671, 672, 673, 677, 678, 679, 680, 681, 682, 683, 684, 693, 694, 695, 696, 698, 700, 701, 702, 704, 706, 707, 708

Englehardt Gold Medal 261

English 14, 32, 35, 69, 70, 75, 76, 78, 79, 96, 97, 99, 101, 105, 107, 113, 115, 129, 130, 148, 196, 201, 208, 212, 221, 223, 238, 244, 247, 250, 253, 254, 255, 256, 283, 285, 287, 300, 301, 307, 334, 343, 385, 399, 410, 412, 415, 426, 427, 429, 434, 446, 450, 458, 462, 465,

467, 494, 495, 525, 531, 541, 543, 545, 551, 552, 606, 622, 629, 634, 636, 642, 643, 648, 665, 681, 689, 691

English Channel 107

English Opera Troupe 250

Ennis International Belt 438

Epping Road 371

Epsom 127, 524, 574

Epsom Races 574

Epsom Town Station 574

Erie, Pennsylvania 18, 35, 39

Erie county 19

Escanaba 339

Essex 12, 672

Essex House Hotel 12

Ethrington and Co 187

Etruria 606, 636, 681

Euclid 39

Europe 28, 44, 56, 247, 282, 513

Eutaw House Hotel 8

Everard's Russian baths 651

Exchange 23, 178, 181, 183, 186, 188, 189, 190, 222, 399, 655

Exchange Hotel 23

Exchange Street 655

Exeter 177, 179

Exhibition building 345

Exhibition Palace 174

Exposition Building 54, 64, 66, 68, 115, 152, 261, 337, 340, 376, 443, 446

F

"F" Division 610

Fairfield 6

Fairport 16

Falcon Hotel 188

Falkirk 130

Fall River, Massachusetts 263

Falmouth 177, 180

Falstaffian 123

Fareham 93

Farwell's 63

Farwell Hall 34

Fashion race-track 142

Fashion trotting course 142

Faversham 178, 593

Federal Street 12

Fell River, Massachusetts 613

Felthorpe 153

Fenian 557

Fenton G. 151

Ferguson Dr. 671

Fernleigh 181

Ferry Street 557

Field & Leter's 63

Fifield 71

Fifth Regiment Armory 336

Fifty miles Running Championship Challenge Belt 511

Fifty Seventh Street Court 684

Finlay Mr. 528

Fire Department 161, 558

Fishergate 183

Fishkill-on-the-Hudson 307

Flaunty A. 233, 348, 366, 371

Fleet Street 187

Fletcher Rev. J. C. 1

Flushing 529

Flying Collier xi, 489, 507, 561, 575, 640, 690

Flying Irishman 218

flying Paddy 402

flying Scotsman 539

Folkestone 126, 177, 178, 593

Fonda 14

Fond du Lac 43

Forest City Park 35

Forlì 128

Fort Hamilton 283

Fort Tompkins 161

Fort Wayne, Indiana 42

Fountainbridge 104

Fourteenth Street Theater 652

Fox Mr. 14, 695

Framingham 5

Framwellgate Moor 184

France 64, 125, 128, 140, 161, 174, 175, 233, 234, 261, 263, 306, 513, 573, 574

Franklin House Hotel 14

Fredonia 41, 42

French 64, 399, 435, 513

French President 513

Frodsham 182

Frontier Police 17

Fulham 126, 127, 138, 151, 153, 236, 239, 240, 241, 306, 347, 376, 574, 609, 610, 611

Fulham Pet 236, 239

Fuller W. E. 561

full Military Band 44

Fulton Market Boys 161

Fulton Street 308, 432, 528

G

G. Freeman 153

Galena 339

Gallic 577

Gardner House Hotel 67

Garrison Hall 399, 658, 660, 661, 665, 666, 668, 670, 671

Garstang 177, 183

Gateshead 129, 151, 184, 378

Gateshead Clipper 378

General Post Office 608

Genesee Street 18

Geneva, OH 10

Geordie 506

George Dickenson 491

George H. Bailey 441

George Hotel 179

George Inn 655

Georgia 46, 214, 254, 261, 285, 539, 571, 638

Georgia State Fair 46

German 71, 228, 259, 263, 276, 312, 322, 331, 339, 358, 392, 394, 398, 418, 424, 460, 472, 555, 620, 622, 684

Gibraltar Street 655

Gibson's Station 28

Gilmore's band 448, 455, 466, 468

Gilmore's Garden 143, 145, 163, 164, 192, 193, 197, 199, 204, 211, 213, 246, 247, 261, 262, 307, 308, 327, 337

Gilsey Building 448

Gilsey House 163, 257, 468

Gilsey House Hotel 257, 468

Ginnet's Circus 179

Girard 19, 20, 22, 40

Glasgow 118, 129, 130, 388, 390, 511, 514

Gleadless 507, 517

Glengary 253

Glenham House Hotel 254

Glen Cove ix, 227, 307, 308, 328, 334, 352, 404, 414, 416

Globe Hotel 15, 180

Glossop 307

Guards colours 533

H

"Happy" Jack Smith 316, 357, 392

"Hippodroming" 254, 413

"Honest John" 196, 218, 438, 439

J

J. Donovan 448

J. Gibbons 370

L

Lady Lane 185

Lagrange 23, 261

Lake Front 377

Lake Michigan 33

Lake Shore road 39

Lake Street 29, 65, 340

Lambeth 233, 347, 348, 388, 506

Lambeth Baths 347, 348, 388

Lambe Mrs. 6

Lambrecht J. L. 532

Lancashire 101, 120, 182, 307, 377

Lancaster 177, 183

Landman J. T. 42

Landsworth 412

Laporte, Indiana 25

Laporte County 27

Lathrop Mr. 209

Latrobe 669

Laudanum 204

Launceston 177, 669

Lawrence, Massachusetts 613, 614

Laws 362

League Hall 182

Leander L. 57

Leatherhead 524

Leavy & Britton Brewing Co 556

Leconsfield 185

Lecture Hall 188

Lee, Massachusetts 227

Leeds 113, 126, 129, 151, 177, 185, 343, 363, 364, 368, 371, 388, 389, 403, 483, 489, 506, 511, 518, 519, 520, 562, 574, 674, 704

Lee G. 151

Leicester 5, 177, 187, 443, 607

Lent's Hotel 25

Lettermacaward 657

Levy's cornet 427

Lewes 177, 179

Lewis vii, 78, 94, 102, 119, 129, 131, 132, 133, 134, 135, 136, 152, 153, 174, 175, 205, 234, 335, 336, 396, 404, 405, 448, 483, 673, 675, 677, 678, 683, 684, 685, 686

Lewiston 193

Lewis Mr. 78, 94, 335

Lexington Avenue 555

Liebig's extract 96

Lillie Arms 127

Lillie Bridge Grounds, 70, 87, 127, 128, 511

Lincoln 3, 5, 6, 8, 9, 63, 151, 152, 177, 186, 187, 193, 465

Lincoln House Hotel 5

Lincoln Mrs. 8

Lincoln Park 63

Lion Hotel 182, 185

Liskeard 177, 180

Litchfield 1

Little Falls 14, 262, 328

Little Freddie 6

Little Shoemaker 545, 641

Little Volunteer Corps 670

Liverpool ix, 75, 76, 78, 79, 80, 90, 97, 104, 120, 130, 131, 143, 152, 177, 182, 191, 233, 250, 251, 343, 348, 368, 376, 378, 388, 395, 403, 412, 426, 472, 489, 506, 636, 654, 681, 682, 695, 706

Liverpool Road 90, 378

Livingstone Hall 184

Lloyds Minstrels, 7

Lockhart's Cocoa Rooms 184

Lock Haven 308

Logan 86

London vii, xii, 1, 42, 69, 70, 71, 75, 77, 78, 82, 84, 88, 95, 97, 102, 104, 106, 107, 108, 110, 112, 113, 114, 119, 120, 122, 125, 126, 127, 128, 129, 137, 140, 141, 142, 143, 144, 146, 150, 151, 152, 153, 155, 160, 163, 164, 172, 174, 175, 177, 178, 179, 188, 190, 191, 192, 193, 196, 201, 213, 221, 222, 226, 234, 235, 238, 241, 242, 244, 245, 247, 248, 249, 251, 252, 253, 254, 257, 261, 262, 270, 272, 278, 280, 283, 289, 291, 296, 302, 304, 307, 310, 317, 335, 343, 345, 347, 348, 363, 364, 366, 368, 369, 370, 373, 375, 376, 378, 380, 382, 385, 388, 408, 417, 422, 423, 429, 434, 435, 438, 443, 445, 450, 453, 468, 472, 474, 483, 484, 489, 494, 497, 506, 511, 513, 517, 519, 521, 524, 525, 526, 561, 562, 563, 570, 571, 574, 590, 607, 608, 616, 658, 671, 673, 674, 677, 678, 698, 700, 703, 704, 706, 707, 708

London, Brighton, and South Coast Railway 574

London, Ontario 345

London Aquarium 561, 570, 616, 671, 698

London Bridge 178

London Champion Belt 174, 175, 335

London Irish Volunteers 88

Longfellow 301

Longshoreman 307

Long Distance Challenge Belt 570

Long Distance Championship of England 151, 233, 238, 706

long distance championship of the world 192, 698

Long Distance Champion Belt 143

long distance champion of the world 573

long distance champion walker of England 85

Long Island 227, 306, 328, 331, 352, 404, 414, 494, 525, 528, 529, 544, 557, 558, 635

Long Island City 525, 529, 544, 557, 558

Long Newton 184

Lord Balfour 191

Lord Hill Column 182

Lorraine 263

Los Angeles 250

Louisville 143

Lowell, Massachusetts 262, 390, 397, 404, 442

Lowestoft 177, 187, 188

Lowndes Square 112

Lucas H. 151

Ludberge 184

Lutchford W. 153

Lyceum Hall 263

Lynn 1, 13, 161, 186, 188

Lyons 15

Lytchett 179

M

Macedon 16

Macgregor J. 666

Mackay Mr. 183

MacMahon and Leitch 670

Macon 46, 571

Macon, Georgia 46, 571

Madison viii, xii, 29, 39, 62, 63, 144, 191, 194, 197, 204, 215, 216, 226, 249, 257, 258, 268, 278, 284, 295, 305, 311, 328, 343, 351, 375, 411,

412, 413, 414, 415, 421, 426, 432, 433, 434, 442, 443, 445, 446, 450, 451, 471, 472, 495, 496, 512, 525, 526, 527, 531, 544, 555, 557, 585, 616, 627, 628, 629, 634, 636, 637, 646, 648, 652, 654, 680, 683, 690, 697, 700, 701, 702

Madison Avenue viii, 144, 194, 197, 204, 215, 216, 249, 268, 284, 445, 450, 495, 496, 555, 627, 629

Madison Square Garden viii, xii, 257, 258, 278, 305, 311, 328, 343, 351, 411, 412, 413, 414, 421, 426, 432, 433, 434, 442, 446, 450, 451, 471, 472, 495, 512, 525, 526, 527, 544, 585, 616, 628, 634, 636, 637, 646, 652, 680, 683, 690, 700, 701, 702

Madison street 443

Madison street bridge 443

Maidenhead 86, 190, 191, 364

Maidenhead road 190

Maidstone 88

Maid and the Magpie 673

Main Street 18, 161

Malacca 14, 650

Maltese Cross 676

Manager Mutrie 681

Manayunk, Pennsylvania 414

Manchester 38, 77, 93, 94, 101, 105, 120, 126, 128, 143, 152, 174, 177, 180, 182, 183, 233, 335, 337, 339, 348, 364, 368, 375, 388, 443, 476, 483, 523, 593, 608, 703

Manhattan Athletic Club 496, 528, 532

Manhattan Grounds 307

Manners Street 659

Manning A. 371

Manor Tavern 127, 233

Mansion House Hotel 15, 18, 52

Marble Rink 435

March vii, xii, 1, 7, 8, 10, 35, 36, 39, 46, 52, 56, 59, 70, 81, 87, 90, 92, 100, 118, 120, 124, 125, 127, 128, 129, 131, 136, 138, 151, 152, 153, 157, 186, 188, 192, 199, 201, 206, 210, 211, 214, 218, 221, 222, 231, 233, 238, 244, 247, 259, 263, 307, 308, 324, 336, 337, 347, 362, 368, 388, 389, 411, 412, 420, 421, 422, 434, 446, 463, 470, 472, 474, 480, 490, 504, 511, 523, 526, 561, 562, 571, 587, 590, 598, 616, 624, 634, 636, 666, 668, 673, 675, 676, 679, 687, 695, 701, 703, 704, 706, 707, 708

Market Deeping 187, 188

Market hill 189

Market Street 8

Market Street Bridge 8

Market Weighton 177, 185

Markham 187

Marlborough, Massachusetts 328

Marlborough Street Police Court 435

Marquis of Queensbury 384, 682, 683, 684, 685

Marriatta Street 653

Marshall G. S. 664

Martin Dr. 162

Maryland 8, 9, 343, 585

Marylebone 370, 491, 562, 674

Mason W. 151

Massachusetts 1, 3, 7, 9, 12, 14, 193, 224, 227, 261, 262, 263, 269, 302, 306, 328, 343, 352, 375, 376, 377, 388, 389, 390, 397, 404, 411, 414, 422, 438, 442, 497, 586, 613, 614, 636, 681, 701

Massicot 328

Mather Mr. 90

Maxwell Mr. 322

Mayor Flagg 14

McAndrews J. W. 65

McAuliffe 74, 75, 697

McComb's dam 142

McCormick Hall 377, 394, 446

McEwen J. 73

McFarlane 152

McGlinchey Ed. 285, 296

McKean County 590

McOscar Dr. 122

McVicker's 62

McWhacktery and O'Shaughnessy 269

Meagher 150, 614

Mecca 305, 683

Mechanics Hall 185, 187, 679

Mechanics Pavilion 70

Melbourne ix, 105, 523, 666, 668, 669

Mellish W. 151

Member of Parliament 100, 111, 123

Memphis, Tennessee 445

Mendota 339

Mephistopheles 460, 593

Mercantile Library 34

Mercer W. 129

Mercury ix, 244, 439, 669

Meriden 6, 307, 316, 343

Mertham 524

Messenger J. 370

Messrs. Elliman 134

Metcalfe's brass band 181

Metropolitan 7, 38, 163, 171, 203, 360, 410, 411, 574, 587

Metropolitan District 574

Metropolitan Hotel 7, 38, 163, 171, 203, 360, 410

Mexican 250, 590, 591, 614, 624, 643, 644, 645, 646, 647, 648, 650, 681

Mexican Indian 250

Michigan 33, 37, 38, 42, 43, 62, 339, 393, 586, 613

Michigan Central Railroad 33

Middlesborough 377

Middlesex Court of Sessions 435

Midlothian Arms 514

Midlothian Hall 572

Midlothian Society 515, 539

Milford 6, 230

Miller's Station, Indiana, 28

Millerstown 308

Miller Mr. 631

Miller Street 152

Millgrove 18

Millham 613

Mills W. 127, 233

Millwall 362, 370, 388, 474, 476, 483, 489, 492, 518, 573

Mill dam 4

Milton County 261

Milwaukee 43, 163, 336

Minnesota 35, 37, 45, 329, 414

Minstrels 628

Mishawaka, IN 10

Mississippi 37, 56, 464

Miss Ada Wallace, 467

Mitchell Mr. 286

Mitchell T. 128

Modbury 180

Moderation Society 465

Mohawk Minstrels 244

Monck J. S. 668

Monmore Green 181

Monmore Lane 181

Monmouthshire 475, 562

Monroe Street 28, 29

Montana 256, 257, 307

Montclair 376, 377

Montclair Hunting Club 376

Montgomery County 14

Montreal 306

Monumental Gardens 585

Mooers 38

Moore viii, 26, 27, 57, 162, 233, 322, 404, 405, 504, 602, 603, 604, 618, 620, 621, 622, 623, 624, 625, 626, 627, 628, 629, 631, 633, 639, 640, 641, 642, 682, 683, 684, 685, 686, 687, 688, 689, 690, 692, 695, 696

Morey Mr. 38

Morgan J. J. 679

Morpeth Castle 233

Morris W. 152

Moscow 616

Moseley 371, 528, 533, 534

Moseley Harriers 528, 534

Moses Gate 183

Mosgiel 658

Mott Dr. 287

Mountain Wonder 637, 638, 653

Mozart Garden 193, 335

Mr. and Mrs. Martin 205

Mr. Conlin 8

Mr. Crosby 29

Mr. Curtis 59, 168, 171, 194, 309, 310, 311, 319, 330, 352, 408, 409, 410, 420, 467

Mr. Dalton 26

Mr. Davis 286, 289, 434, 435

Mr. Dole 636

Mr. Edwards 105, 211

Mr. Ellinson 190

Mr. Fairbrothers 7

Mr. Foster 3

Mr. Frazer 212

Mrs. Corkey 158

Mrs. Ennis 208

Munson F. 28

Murray 142, 143, 150, 227, 228, 229, 532

Music Hall 143, 193, 261, 262, 388, 442

Myers E. L. 496

Myers L. E. 532

Mystic Hotel 223

Mystic Park 35

N

N. Y. P. O 229

Nag's Head 152

Narragansett 422, 635

Nassau Street 3, 144

Natick 5, 13

National Circus Building 161

National Fire Insurance Company 28

National steamer 251

Naylor Dr. 299, 313, 462, 501

Needham 177, 187, 188

Needham Market 188

Nell Gwynne Tavern 609

Nelson & McClean 419

Nelson Street 118

Nevada 211, 242, 251, 252, 337, 387

Newark, New Jersey 143, 307, 345, 352, 400, 587, 707

Newburyport, Massachusetts, 12

Newcastle-upon-Tyne 114

Newhall Grounds 94, 101, 104

Newhall Road 655

Newman Dr. 253

Newmarket 119, 177, 188, 370

Newmarket road 188

Newport 177, 189, 475, 562

Newport Pagnell 177, 189

Newsome's Circus 348, 368, 388

Newton 4, 179, 180, 184, 262, 368, 706

Newton Abbott 179, 180

Newton Street 262

New Bedford 263

New Berwick 12

New Boston, Massachusetts 14

New Brigate 185

New Brompton 77

New Brunswick, New Jersey 587

New Carlisle 25, 26, 32

New Castle, Pennsylvania 307

New Durham 27

New England 13, 16, 161, 193

New England House Hotel 16

New Grainger Street 184

New Hampshire 12, 39, 422, 701

New Haven, Connecticut 3

New Haven Center 38

New Inn 189

New Jersey 143, 227, 306, 307, 328, 329, 345, 352, 377, 400, 451, 525, 527, 587, 613, 707

New London 307

New Millford 227

New Orleans 142, 377, 471

New Rochelle 6

New Romney 178

New South Wales 661, 679

New Street 492

New Swindon 518

New York ix, xii, 1, 2, 3, 4, 6, 9, 10, 14, 16, 30, 33, 35, 36, 37, 38, 42, 43, 44, 45, 46, 47, 49, 50, 51, 52, 53, 56, 58, 59, 60, 66, 72, 74, 75, 81, 88, 106, 107, 109, 113, 114, 124, 125, 137, 140, 141, 142, 143, 144, 145, 148, 150, 160, 161, 162, 163, 164, 165, 167, 169, 170, 171, 172, 173, 190, 191, 193, 194, 197, 201, 203, 204, 209, 215, 222, 223, 224, 225, 226, 227, 229, 233, 236, 237, 238, 240, 243, 244, 246, 247, 248, 249, 250, 251, 252, 253, 254, 257, 258, 260, 261, 262, 263, 266, 270, 272, 274, 278, 284, 286, 287, 294, 299, 302, 303, 304, 305, 306, 307, 308, 310, 311, 313, 314, 321, 328, 329, 330, 334, 336, 337, 339, 343, 345, 351, 352, 354, 360, 375, 376, 377, 384, 385, 390, 391, 392, 393, 394, 397, 398, 400, 402, 404, 406, 412, 413, 414, 415, 420, 421, 423, 425, 426, 430, 434, 435, 436, 438, 439, 440, 441, 442, 445, 448, 449, 451, 453, 464, 467, 471, 472, 494, 495, 497, 500, 506, 514, 518, 525, 526, 527, 528, 529, 530, 531, 532, 534, 536, 537, 539, 541, 542, 543, 546, 548, 555, 556, 564, 565, 572, 582, 587, 588, 589, 590, 591, 593, 602, 606, 613, 618, 620, 633, 634, 636, 637, 638, 639, 646, 652, 653, 654, 655, 680, 681, 682, 683, 686, 690, 695, 696, 697, 698, 699, 700, 702, 704, 705, 707, 708

New York Athletic Club 59, 194, 226, 260

New York Central Railroad 307

New York Club 681

New York Fire Department 161

New York Furniture Company 425

New York Post Office 229

Niagara Falls 8, 400, 612

Nicholls Mr. 370

Nichols W. G. 6

Niles 43

Nineteenth precinct 629

Norfolk 188, 483, 513, 517

Norfolk Drill Hall 483, 513, 517

Normansell Mr. 493

Northallerton 184, 185

Northampton 103, 152, 174, 175, 307, 343, 348, 368, 593, 674, 675

Northern Deer 93

Northern Indiana Hotel 27

Northumberland Cricket Club 114

Northumberland Street 116

North America xi

North American Indian 127, 226

North Anderson Street 377

North East, Pennsylvania 19

North Georgia Stock Association 261

North Lincolnshire 100, 117, 123

North Road 184

North Side 83, 107, 203, 405, 450, 532, 548

North Woolwich vii, 127, 128, 153

North Woolwich Gardens 127

Norwalk 6, 23

Norwich 153, 177, 187, 188, 227, 307

Norwich, Connecticut 227

Nottingham 78, 94, 104, 153, 177, 186, 187, 337, 365, 366, 368, 483, 506, 561, 593, 594, 704

Nottinghamshire 187

Nugent brothers 73

O

O. Dowd 151

O'Brien viii, 74, 152, 193, 227, 228, 229, 230, 329, 330, 331, 332, 333, 433, 443, 444, 627, 633, 636, 638, 639, 640, 652, 680, 681, 683, 684, 692, 694, 695, 697

O'Connell 288

O'Leary 72 Hour Pedestrian Contest 397

O'Leary Belt viii, 250, 253, 305, 306, 312, 323, 328, 343, 344, 351, 359, 377, 378, 397, 411, 412, 413, 414, 415, 421, 426, 427, 451, 702, 704

O'Leary Champion Belt of the World 400, 404, 411

O'Leary Diamond Belt 394

O'Leary International Belt Championship of the World" 404

Oaken Gates 182

Oak Hill 12

Oddfellows Hall 55

Ohio ix, 2, 18, 24, 37, 40, 211, 308, 385, 404, 634, 695

Ohio Street 40

Oldham 128

old Bowery Garden 445

Old Brompton 126, 127, 572, 574

Old Cricket Ground 120

Old Elvet 184

Old Ford 128

Old Harrow 570

Old Kent Road 178

Old Miles 370

Old West London Running Grounds 128

Oliver A. M. 668

Olive House Hotel 23

Olmsted 39

Oncco 13

Oneida 15

Opera House 16, 28, 29, 30, 185, 389, 414

Orawarhum Hotel 36

Ordnance Survey Department 524

Ordway Hall 1

Ormskirk 177, 182, 183

Oskosh, Wisconsin 590

Oswego, New York 38

Oswestry 128

Otterington 184

Oughtibridge 362

Oulton 151, 368

Ouzalo 575

Oxford 90, 102, 123, 133, 177, 190, 233, 672

Oxford and Cambridge diet 90

P

Pacific 325, 335, 388, 451

Pacific Street 335

Painsville 23

Paisley vii, 130, 131, 175, 233, 345, 363, 364, 365, 371, 388, 389, 572, 688

Palmer 5, 6, 38, 162, 348, 364, 371, 372, 373, 374, 445

Palmerston 665

Palmer Mr. 38

Palmyra 10, 15

Palmyra House Hotel 15

Palsca Band 93

Pangbourne 190

Park 28, 29, 33, 35, 36, 42, 43, 46, 63, 72, 75, 76, 80, 97, 102, 141, 142, 153, 179, 185, 193, 223, 251, 254, 263, 306, 337, 343, 345, 362, 363, 371, 432, 443, 494, 495, 523, 524, 555, 570, 574, 582, 631, 681

Park-row 555

Parker House Hotel 13

Park Garden 142, 254, 343, 432

Park Lane 185

Park Skating Rink 75, 76, 80

Parliament 83, 100, 111, 113, 123, 135, 138, 524

Parlor Rink 590

Parolo 242

Pastime Athletic Club 532, 696

Pastime Athletic Club Grounds 696

Paterson 227

Pavy Dr. 88, 91, 92

Pawtucket, Rhode Island 13

Payne A. G. 107, 178, 186

Pearl Street Skating Rink 152

Pearson A. 371

Pedestrian xi, xii, xiii, 1, 4, 6, 7, 8, 9, 13, 14, 15, 18, 19, 20, 22, 23, 24, 25, 26, 27, 28, 29, 30, 31, 32, 33, 35, 37, 38, 39, 43, 45, 46, 47, 50, 51, 52, 53, 55, 56, 57, 58, 59, 60, 61, 62, 63, 64, 65, 66, 71, 72, 74, 75, 76, 84, 85, 86, 88, 94, 96, 97, 101, 102, 105, 110, 114, 117, 119, 120, 121, 122, 124, 125, 128, 130, 132, 133, 136, 138, 139, 141, 150, 151, 152, 153, 160, 161, 162, 163, 164, 167, 170, 174, 179, 181, 183, 184, 185, 188, 189, 193, 198, 199, 201, 203, 204, 211, 214, 215, 221, 222, 223, 224, 225, 235, 236, 239, 242, 244, 245, 246, 247, 249, 250, 251, 253, 254, 258, 260, 262, 269, 277, 283, 286, 287, 288, 290, 297, 300, 301, 304, 306, 307, 309, 312, 313, 314, 316, 323, 325, 326, 335, 337, 338, 341, 343, 344, 345, 352, 356, 358, 359, 363, 373, 375, 376, 377, 385, 388, 390, 391, 395, 399, 401, 405, 410, 412, 414, 421, 422, 430, 434, 438, 439, 443, 444, 445, 446, 451, 467, 470, 472, 483, 484, 487, 494, 513, 514, 515, 523, 525, 526, 528, 529, 532, 539, 544, 550, 554, 559, 561, 562, 569, 570, 572, 574, 580, 585, 586, 591, 595, 608, 615, 619, 625, 628, 631, 634, 636, 637, 639, 641, 650, 651, 652, 653, 657, 665, 668, 670, 678, 681, 692, 700, 705, 707

Pedestrianism 30, 31, 32, 37, 53, 62, 63, 64, 72, 75, 76, 95, 104, 108, 123, 126, 180, 186, 204, 212, 244, 246, 247, 248, 253, 262, 357, 363, 374, 377, 385, 391, 443, 467, 570, 584, 627, 630, 667, 700, 701, 705

Pedestrian Congress 254

Pedestrian of the World 58, 75, 338

Peixotte F. S. 532

Pembroke Grove 161

Pendleton 22, 183

Pennsylvania 7, 18, 19, 35, 39, 307, 308, 329, 391, 393, 400, 404, 407, 414, 434, 494, 590, 593, 602, 636, 683, 695

Pennys W. 597

Penrith 177, 183

Penzance 177, 180

Percy Street 380, 382

Perkins W. 69, 70, 151, 571

Perry N. 151

Perth 388, 389, 390

Peterborough 177, 187, 188

Petrolia 308, 400

Pevensey 179

Philadelphia ix, 7, 8, 9, 37, 49, 53, 56, 60, 61, 114, 143, 161, 163, 222, 223, 224, 307, 308, 328,

343, 393, 400, 404, 411, 421, 422, 434, 526, 591, 602, 603, 612, 613, 614, 625, 631, 635, 636, 639, 648, 679, 683, 695, 697, 701, 704

Phillips S. 370

Phoenix House Hotel 13

Pickering 177, 185

Pierce and Monaghan 575

Piershill 100

Pie Eater 193, 271, 273, 276, 294, 572, 684

Pimlico Gold Medal 343

Pine Street 58

Pinhook 27

Piper Heidsick 472

Pittsburgh 37, 161, 394, 397, 400, 460, 677

Pittsford 16

Pitt Club 189

Pitville Gardens 234

Pity Me 184

Plainfield, New Jersey 587

Plymouth 177, 180, 348, 364, 371, 674

Plympton 180

Pocklington Riverhead 185

Podokis 120

Police Gazette Diamond Belt 698

Police Gazette Diamond Championship Belt 512

Pollockshaws 130, 345, 389, 399, 483

Polo Grounds 495, 681

Pomona Large Agricultural Hall 335

Poplar 151, 573, 575, 674

Portland ix, 9, 10, 11, 12, 13, 15, 16, 17, 21, 24, 29, 30, 31, 32, 33, 35, 56, 222, 707

Portland, Maine, 9, 11, 30, 32, 33

Portland Arms 222

Portobello 104

Portsmouth, 12

Portsmouth, New Hampshire 12

Port Byron 15

Port Chester 6

Port Deposit, Maryland 8

Post Road 9

Potter Mr. 304

Potter W. 376

Poughkeepsie 307

Powderhall Grounds 119, 390

Powell 366

Powlton Fair Grounds 161

Prebble House 11

Precinct No. 1 18

Prendergast Dr. 643

Prescot 182

Prescott 36, 37

Prescott & Gage 36

President 5, 8, 9, 28, 144, 257, 288, 513

Preston 120, 177, 182, 183, 572

Preston Gubbals 182

Price H. 151

Princess Rink, 586, 591

Princess Street 114

Princess Theatre 663

Princes Theatre 179

Prince Alfred Park 345, 523

Prince Edward Island 328, 401

Prince of Wales Grounds 119, 127, 128

Prince of Wales Tavern 233

Printing House Square 555

Printing Square 267

Prior's Lee 182

Priory Tap 188

Professional xi, 47, 56, 57, 63, 119, 142, 143, 152, 160, 164, 193, 201, 246, 257, 262, 302, 359, 363, 374, 385, 389, 429, 444, 447, 467, 487, 496, 502, 514, 525, 559, 593, 607, 637, 641, 654, 657, 670, 671, 679, 680, 682, 704

Professor of Gymnastics 212

Prospect Park 263

Providence, Rhode Island 1, 262, 307, 343, 377, 390, 414, 422, 451, 702

Prussia 261

Public Hall 186, 189

Public Rooms 185

Putnam House Hotel 553

Putney 524, 572, 607, 611

Putney station 572

Q

Quakerville 684

Quaker City 602

Quarry Hill 185

Quebec 1

Queenstown 191, 606, 654

Queens County Hunt 308

Queens Railway Hotel 182

Queens Theatre 657

Queen Victoria 86, 282

R

R. Gentleman 233

R. J. Cross 46

Racine 377

Rahway 7, 328

Rahway, New Jersey 328

Railroad House Hotel 7

Railway Hotel 182, 184

Ram's Head Hotel 472

Rampant Horse Hotel 188

Randall's Island 699

Randall E. K. 16

Ratcliffe 371, 372, 373, 483, 489, 506, 518, 573, 593, 597

Rawmarsh 362, 559

Reading 177, 190, 639

Read J. 151

Recorder of Deeds 224

Redruth 177, 180

Red Leary's Hotel 283

Red Lion 655, 696

Regents Park 371

Regent Street Pet 127, 233

Rehm Mr. 30, 32

Reich Dr. 146

Reigate 524

Reina Victoria 271

Relay House Hotel 8

Relief of Lucknow 88

Renfrew 306

Rensselaer Park 36

Reporteruinn T. 532

Reservoir Grounds 487

Rewsham 184

Rhode Island 1, 3, 8, 13, 261, 262, 307, 343, 377, 390, 414, 422, 451, 702

Richardson's Hotel 665

Richardson F. 151

Richardson S. 151

Richmond 13, 126, 127, 152, 223, 224, 364, 366, 368, 371, 412, 426

Richmond Harbour 152

Ridgeville 39

Ridley Street 116

Rifle Barracks 115

Rifle Corps 514

Rifle Drill Hall 403, 511

Rimmel's Vinegar 105

Rip Van Winkle 263, 272

Riverside Park 35

River Thames 86

Robert's Grounds 128

Roberts 182, 246, 464, 559, 574, 575

Roberts Mrs. 182

Robey Street 61

Robinson 8, 151, 170, 212, 371, 372, 391, 392, 397, 398, 399

Rochester ix, 16, 17, 18, 19, 178, 261, 588

Rochester road 18

Rockport 39

Rockwell 328

Roebuck Hotel 672

Rogers Mr. 8

Rolling Prarie 25

Rome, Indiana 23

Rome City 25

Rome Station 25

Roscommon 129, 562

Roscommon County 129

Roscrea 141

Rose Belt 328, 377, 411, 433, 442, 702

Rossmore Hotel 252, 253, 260

Rossmore House 299

Roswell 43, 390

Rotherfield Hotel 668

Rotherham ix, 362, 363, 366, 475, 478, 517, 559

Rotherhite 233, 371, 483

Roundsman Kelly 213

Rowe N. Dr. 340

Royal Exchange 178, 190

Royal Free Hospital 121

Royal Gymnasium 99, 104, 389, 390

Royal Gymnasium Grounds 96

Royal Horse Artillery 188

Royal Pomona Gardens 77

Royal Victoria Hotel 186

Rubber Clothing Co 4

Ruffin C. 288

Ruscoe W. 128

Russian 117, 214, 407, 456, 622, 651

Ryder Sports 128

Rye 36, 178, 241

Rye Station 36

S

"Sharp Sheffield Blade" 154

"Sheffield Blonde" 378, 690

"Snapper" Garrison 691

Saco 12

Sadler D. & J. 56

Saginaw, Michigan 613

Saint Charles, 395

Salaman 328

Salamanca, New York 393

Salcoats 130

Salem 12, 302

Salford 153

Salisbury 101, 177, 179, 182, 345

Salisbury Hotel 101

Salmon Mr. 38

Samuells A. R. 226

Sam Smith 233

Sandgate 178

Sandhutton 184

Sandown Park 582

Sandusky 39

Sand Lake 14

Sand Lake, New York 14

Sansome Street 606

San Francisco 70, 71, 72, 143, 163, 263, 307, 325, 343, 388, 451, 524, 637, 706, 708

Saratoga 49, 390, 414, 428, 438, 451, 529, 639

Saratoga Springs 414, 451

Savannah 654

Saville Street 655

Saville Street East 655

Saxilby 187

Saxmundham 187, 188

Sayers 201

Scales Hotel 222

Scarborough 177, 185

Schenectady 10, 14, 400

Schuyler County 263

Scole 188

Scots Fusilier Guards 123

Scots Guards 104

Scottish 212, 366, 388, 451, 599, 687

Scottish-American Grounds 451

Scottish American Club 212

Scott and Earle's Hotel 299

Scott D. 493

Seabrook 12

Seagrave Road 608, 609, 610

Searle's boathouse 86

Searle W. 151

Sebastopol 88, 123

Second and North Nine Streets 526

Second Army Corps 312

Second International Tournament for the O'Leary Belt 426

Second National Bank 557

Second Regiment Armory 72

Sedgefield 184

Sedoff J. 370

Seneca 40

Servia 636, 696

Seventh Regiment Band 499

Seventieth Street 3

Seven Stars Hotel 183

Seward R. 370

Seymour Mr. 665

Shakespeare Inn 559

Shalesmoor 696

Shang 325

Shaw-Lucas H. 151

Shawfield Grounds 390

Shaw E. B. 6

Shaw Mr. 6

Shaw T. F. 66

Sheaf House Grounds 511, 512, 517, 561, 562

Sheerness Royal Hotel Gardens 371

Sheffield viii, ix, xi, 77, 94, 99, 101, 103, 104, 111, 126, 152, 154, 174, 177, 185, 186, 307, 337, 338, 339, 362, 363, 364, 365, 366, 371, 373, 376, 377, 378, 379, 381, 412, 474, 475, 478, 479, 483, 484, 489, 490, 491, 492, 506, 507, 509, 510, 511, 512, 513, 517, 518, 520, 559, 560, 561, 562, 563, 566, 570, 572, 573, 574, 577, 579, 581, 593, 594, 606, 607, 608, 654, 655, 676, 678, 690, 695, 704

Sheffield Drill Hall 511, 562, 581

Shefford 261

Shepard F. M. 4

Sheppard F. 597

Sheppard T. 151

Sheridan House Hotel 14

Sheriff's Jury 304

Sherman 29, 446

Sherman House Hotel 29

Sherman Street 29

Shifnal 177, 182

Shincliffe 184

Shirland Lane 362

Shook and Palmer 162

Shrewsbury 182

Shyne L. J. 614

Sibery's Hotel 6

Sillack & Co 419

Silver Bean Pot 262

Sinclair A. W. 573

Sing Sing 142, 336

Sittingbourne 126, 153, 175, 178, 233, 343, 348, 364, 366, 371, 506, 511, 562, 574, 593

Sitting Bull 539

Sixth Police Precinct 60

Sixth Ward 125

Sixty Ninth Regiment band 640

Six Day's Pedestrian Championship of the World 150

Six Day Run 527

Skating Rink 314, 524, 614, 659

Skelmersdale 183

Skinner's Iron Pier Hotel 616

Slyne 183

Smith, Payne & Smiths 70

Smithfield Club 78

Smith C. 131, 153, 371, 372, 373, 374, 684, 685, 686, 687, 688, 690, 692

Smith J. 127, 130, 132, 133, 134, 135, 136, 151, 364, 371, 372, 373, 374, 382

Smith V. W. 144

Snedeker H. 419

Snowdon Mr. 448

Snow Hill 182

Society for the Prevention of Cruelty to Children 430

Society for the Reformation of Juvenile Delinquents 499

Southampton 177, 179

Southern Rebellion 9

Southwell 186

South Amboy, New York 404

South Bend 26

South Berwick 12

South Brook 335

South Brookfield 5

South Brunswick 7

South Clarke 341

South Park Hotel 337

South Providence 11

South Side 62

South Wales 128, 233, 616, 661, 674, 679

Spain 64, 140

Spalding & Rogers Circus 1

Spalding A. 151

Spanish 64

Special Connoisseur 593

Spofforth Mr. 668

Sprague Mr. 299

Springfield 10, 20, 23

St. Albans 38

St. Austell 180

St. Bartholomew's Hospital 86

St. Cecille 261

St. Clair Mr. 342

St. Clement Danes 82

St. Denis Hotel 250

St. Georges Hall 185

St. Germans 180

St. Helena Gardens 371

St. Helens 80, 101

St. Jacob's Oil 472

St. James Hall 35, 79

St. James Hotel 191, 192, 193, 218, 222, 223, 224

St. John's Ambulance Association 608

St. Johnsville, NY 10

St. Johns Hall 188

St. Leger 559

St. Louis ix, 34, 37, 45, 57, 58, 143, 705, 707

St. Neots 177, 189

St. Omer Hotel 296, 300, 572

St. Patrick's day 548

St. Paul, Minnesota 35

St. Paul's Street 185

St. Petersburg 616

Staffordshire 561

Stafford W. H. 59

Stamford 6, 177, 187, 188, 253, 328, 370, 414

Stamford, Connecticut 253, 328, 414

Stamford Hotel 6

Stanford H. 419

Stanley Arms Hotel 183

Stanley Grounds 104

Stars and Stripes 214, 230, 298, 359, 691

Star Grounds 127, 151

Star Inn 559

State House 3, 4

State Street 16, 62

Station F 229

Steadman H. 126

Stead C. H. 151

Steamboat xi, 197, 208, 209, 218, 223, 344

Stephens D. S. 6

Sterling Hill 13

Sterling House Hotel 6

Steubenville 37

Steuben House Hotel 304

Stewart R. 151

Stockbridge 14, 179

Stockton 177, 184, 613

Stockton road 184

Stoney Stratford 189

Stowmarket 177, 188

Stratford 152, 189

Strathbungo 390

Streatham 370

Stretten Mr. 189

Strood 178

Stryker 23, 24

Suffenham 188

Suffolk Street 181

Sullivan 59, 227, 228, 229, 256, 257, 281, 286, 289, 299, 306, 308, 348, 390, 414, 415, 416, 417, 418, 419, 420, 427, 428, 429, 430, 431, 432, 433, 438, 449, 451, 452, 453, 454, 455, 456, 457, 458, 459, 460, 462, 463, 464, 465, 466, 467, 468, 469, 470, 471, 475, 529, 531, 533, 534, 535, 536, 575, 613, 619, 620, 621, 622, 623, 624, 625, 626, 627, 628, 631, 633, 635, 639, 640, 642, 679, 682, 684, 685, 687

Sullivan Street 308

Sunderand 122

Supreme Court 225, 499

Supreme Court Chambers 499

Surrey 153, 336, 479, 677, 678

Susquehanna River 8, 9

Sussex 88, 104, 128, 179, 233, 524, 674

Sussex County Cricket Ground 88, 104, 233

Sutton Bank 185

Sutton Glassworks 101

Swaffham 177, 186, 188

Swallow Circus 184

Swann H. 493

Swansea 371

Swanton Falls 38

Swan Hotel 185, 188

Swede 337

Swedish 445

Sweeny's Hotel 256

Swindon 364, 518

Syracuse, New York 397, 588

T

"The Time Table" 12

T. A. Gilmore 25

T. Cornish 666

T. J. Englehardt 52

Tadcaster 185

Talcott Mountain 14

Tammany Hall 141, 453

Taplow 86

Tarrytown 352

Tasmania 669

Taunton 177

Tawd Bridge 183

Taylor Dr. 48, 51, 461, 551

Taylor M. H. 40

Teagarden House Hotel 26

Teddington 86, 239

Temperance Hall 185, 187

Terminus Hotel 664

Terre Coupe 26

Terro Haute 37

Tewkesbury 177, 180

Thanksgiving Day 26, 31, 526, 604

Theatre Royal 186, 670

Theodore 140, 224

The Fox Belt viii, 680

The Great 300 Miles Anglo-American Walking Match 77

The Quadrant 492

The Still Alarm 652

Thirsk 177, 184, 185

Thirteenth street Station 628

Thomas 61, 74, 75, 82, 90, 91, 93, 97, 120, 126, 129, 140, 150, 153, 227, 254, 307, 328, 329, 345, 364, 371, 372, 399, 400, 414, 448, 470, 475, 483, 484, 518, 524, 593, 595, 596, 612, 619, 620, 630, 639, 654, 674, 676, 683

Thomas H. 153, 674

Thompson Dr. 86

Thornton J. C. 630

Thrybergh 559

Thurds W. H. 66

Tiffany's 303

Tiffany & Co 75, 337

Tift farm 19

Timaru 659

Tinsley Bridge 559

Tipton 339

Titusville, Pennsylvania 35

Tiverton 177

Toledo 23, 24, 30

Tontine Hotel 3

Toronto 306, 400, 401, 639

Toronto Walking Tournament 401

Totnes 177, 180

Totten Mr. 38

Toutine Hotel 517

Tower Hamlets Drill Room 672

Toxteth Park 97

Trafalgar Square 270

Traveler's Home 18

Tremont House Hotel 4, 20, 143

Trenton, New Jersey 613

Trent Bridge Cricket Ground 94

Tresillion 180

Troy 14, 36, 328

Truckee 523, 572

Truro 177, 180

Tuam Street Hall 670

Tuckerman R. 371

Turf Club 78

Turf Exchange 222

Turnham Green 233, 238, 435

Tutti Frutti 641

Twentieth Precinct 516

Tynan Mrs. 421

Tyne and Wear 122

Tyngsboro, Massachusetts 1

U

Ulster 111, 218, 298, 329

Union Club 47

Union Hotel 14

Union Jack 157, 214, 298, 539, 655

United Brethren Meeting House 25

United Kingdom 124

United States iv, 9, 44, 46, 56, 58, 60, 163, 226, 227, 230, 244, 255, 305, 308, 319, 342, 354, 395, 472, 553, 602, 616, 637, 655, 680, 708

University Ground 153

University of Pennsylvania 602, 636

University of Pennsylvania Athletic Grounds, 602

Upholland 183

Upperhead How 185

Upper Quarantine 252

Upper Street 378

Uppingham 187, 188

Utica 14, 15, 16, 18, 261, 591

V

Vale of Clyde Grounds 390

Vancouver Island 307

Vandpoel A. J. 46

Van Cott Avenue 257

Van Duyne 345

vermillion 460

Vermont 38, 193, 263, 639, 683, 684

Vernon 14, 367

Victoria, Australia 657

Victorian 596, 668

Victoria Cross 88

Victoria Hall 179, 183, 188

Victoria Hotel 182, 186

Victoria Rooms 179

Victoria Skating Rink and Athletic Grounds 78

Victoria Station 183, 570, 654

Violette House Hotel 25

Virginia 223, 638

Vittles 27

Voltz W. 602

Volunteer Fire Department 161

W

"Walk and Talk" 35

"Weary wobbler" 180, 436

"What I know about walking" 178, 186

W. Collins 126

W. Crossland 129

W. H. Davis 227, 288

Wabash Avenue 28, 29, 56

Wade Mr. 227

Wain J. 666

Wakefield 177, 186

Walham Green Station 611

Walkeeha 64

Walkegau 64

Walker's Dictionary 64

Walker's Rest 514

Walker E. 371

Walking Sweepstakes 474

Walkonda 64

Wallacebury 329

Wallingford 3, 6, 190

Walnut Creek 39

Walpole 13, 394, 395

Walsall 363, 364, 366, 370, 403, 483, 485, 489, 506, 518, 561, 563, 568, 573, 576, 581, 593

Walsall Flyer 366, 568

Walsall Street 363

Walton Mr. 193, 222, 224

Wandle & Co 419

Wandsworth 126, 611

Wankegan 64

Warren Bridge, 13

Warren County, Pennsylvania 593

Warrington 177, 182

Warwick bridge 183

Washington band 254

Washington County 451

Washington Hotel 8

Washington Junction 8

Washington Riding Academy 49

Waterbury 160, 307

Waterford 129

Waterloo 24, 25, 105, 113, 184, 571, 574

Waterloo Bridge 113

Waterloo Hotel 105, 184

Waterloo Road 571

Watson J. 107

Watson Mr. 109, 346

Watton 185

Waukegan 339, 394

Waukesha ix, 43, 513

Wauseon 24

Waverley House Hotel 16

Waverley Railway Station 96

Wawaconnuck Hotel 5

Webb's Hotel 180

Webster 151, 301, 329, 330, 331, 669, 670

Wedder Dr. 114

Wednesbury 181

Weedsport, NY 10

Weighton 177, 185

Weiss beer 683

Welch F. G. 57

Wellington ix, 105, 177, 182, 659, 660

Wellington Hospital 660

Wellingtown Baths 151

Welsh 120, 524

Welshman 127

Wem 182

Wenham 12

Wenlock Sports 128

Westborough 5

Westchester County 36

Western California 637

Western Islands 1

Westfield 19

Westgate Road 114

Westhall C. 151

Westminster Abbey 573

Westminster Hospital 596, 672, 673

Westminster Palace Hotel 113

Weston's Retreat 127

Weston Mrs. 49, 246, 254

Westport 6

West Bar 655

West Brighton 548, 616

West Brompton 120, 610

West Brompton Station 610

West Bromwich 181

West Brookfield 5

West Cliff Hotel 178

West Harp 562

West Lake Street 65

West London Cricket Ground 126, 127

West London Extension Railway 608

West Madison Street 62

West Meriden 307, 343

West Side Athletic Club 526

West Side Rink 57, 58, 62, 66

West Stockbridge, Massachusetts 14

West Warren 5, 6

West Wittering 128, 153

Wetherley, Dr. 697

Weymouth 177, 179

Whale W. 371

Wheatsheaf Hotel 182

Wheeling 37

Whitchurch 177, 182

Whitechapel Road 672

Whitefield 193

Whitehall, New York 414

White Cross Colliery Works 183

White J. 151

White Plains 36, 42, 261

White Star 528

White Swan Hotel 185

White W. 151

Whittlesey 14, 188

Whittlesey Mr. 14

Whitworth 128

Whyland 16

Wickham 177, 187

Wigan 177, 182, 183

Wilbraham 6

Wilcox T. F. 9, 10

Willenhall Brass Band 364

Williams's Hotel 7

Williamsburg 289, 344, 434, 438, 495, 526, 532

Williamsburg Athletic Club 434, 532

Williamsport 308

Williams A. 151

Williams County 24

Williams T. 336

Williams W. 129, 674

William Fletcher 252

Willimantic 13

Willoughby 23, 39

Will County Fairgrounds 43

Wilmington 179

Wilson A. 371

Wilson Mr. 59, 90, 665

Wily Wobbler xi, 1, 151, 245, 706

Wimbledon 524

Wimborne 179, 180

Wimborne Minster 179

Winchelsea 177, 179

Winchester 177, 179

Winchmore Hill 370, 574

Windsor 134, 177, 190

Winkler's Band 613

Winsted 14

Winterbourne 179

Wisbech 177, 186, 188

Wisconsin 25, 43, 113, 336, 376, 377, 395, 494, 513, 590

Wisden S. 151

Wolverhampton viii, 181, 348, 363, 364, 366, 389, 399, 561, 704

Women's Temperance Union 63

Wood's Athletic Grounds 438, 495

Wood's Gymnasium 447, 531

Woodbridge 187, 188

Woods H. 151

Wood and Turner 366

Woolpit 188

Woolwich vii, 104, 127, 128, 153, 178, 233, 366, 371, 674

Woonsocket 307

Worcester 3, 5, 7, 177, 180, 181, 328, 438, 677

Worcester, Massachusetts 3, 7, 328, 438

Worksop 177, 186, 187

Wrentham 13

Wrexham 129

Wright's Hall 307

Wrights restaurant 29

Wyatt H. 599

Wyoming 412, 525

Y

Yalesville 6

Yambridge-gate 180

Yardley T. 562

Yarmouth 177, 187, 188

Yatton 129

Yealmpton 180

Yeaton C. C. 4

York ix, xii, 1, 2, 3, 4, 6, 9, 10, 14, 16, 30, 33, 35, 36, 37, 38, 42, 43, 44, 45, 46, 47, 49, 50, 51, 52, 53, 56, 58, 59, 60, 66, 72, 74, 75, 81, 88, 106, 107, 109, 113, 114, 124, 125, 129, 130, 137, 140, 141, 142, 143, 144, 145, 148, 150, 152, 160, 161, 162, 163, 164, 165, 167, 169, 170, 171, 172, 173, 174, 177, 185, 190, 191, 193, 194, 197, 201, 203, 204, 209, 215, 222, 223, 224, 225, 226, 227, 229, 233, 236, 237, 238, 240, 243, 244, 246, 247, 248, 249, 250, 251, 252, 253, 254, 257, 258, 260, 261, 262, 263, 266, 270, 272, 274, 278, 284, 286, 287, 294, 299, 302, 303, 304, 305, 306, 307, 308, 310, 311, 313, 314, 321, 328, 329, 330, 334, 336, 337, 339, 343, 345, 351, 352, 354, 360, 368, 375, 376, 377, 384, 385, 390, 391, 392, 393, 394, 397, 398, 400, 402, 404, 406, 412, 413, 414, 415, 420, 421, 423, 425, 426, 430, 434, 435, 436, 438, 439, 440, 441, 442, 445, 448, 449, 451, 453, 464, 467, 471, 472, 489, 494, 495, 497, 500, 506, 508, 514, 518, 519, 525, 526, 527, 528, 529, 530, 531, 532, 534, 536, 537, 539, 541, 542, 543, 546, 548, 555, 556, 564, 565, 572, 582, 587, 588, 589, 590, 591, 593, 602, 606, 613, 618, 620, 633, 634, 636, 637, 638, 639, 646, 652, 653, 654, 655, 680, 681, 682, 683, 686, 690, 695, 696, 697, 698, 699, 700, 702, 704, 705, 707, 708

Yorkshire 77, 113, 185, 337, 362, 364, 368, 377, 474, 485, 507, 559, 578, 607, 678

York Skating Rink 129

Yosefellows 63

Young A. S. 532

Young C. R. 532

Young G. 153

Young G. W. 532

Young Men's Christian Association 63

Yuma 250

Z

Zulu 354